Wissenschaftliche Untersuchungen
zum Neuen Testament · 2. Reihe

Herausgegeben von
Martin Hengel und Otfried Hofius

120

Saeed Hamid-Khani

Revelation and Concealment of Christ

A Theological Inquiry into the Elusive Language of the Fourth Gospel

WIPF & STOCK · Eugene, Oregon

Wipf and Stock Publishers
199 W 8th Ave, Suite 3
Eugene, OR 97401

Revelation and Concealment of Christ
A Theological Inquiry into the Elusive Language of the Fourth Gospel
By Hamid-Khani, Saeed
Copyright © 2000 Mohr Siebeck All rights reserved.
Softcover ISBN-13: 978-1-7252-9157-7
Publication date 11/5/2020
Previously published by Mohr Siebeck, 2000

Preface

The present book is a revised version of my doctoral dissertation submitted to the University of Cambridge in January, 1997. In this revision, I have enlarged the chapters and included the relevant publications since 1997. I have also endeavoured to make this work useful not only to specialists, but also to a wider audience of informed students of Scripture. I wish I could have made the work even more user-friendly and developed areas which I have had to leave for the future, but I have been intensely pressed for time by other responsibilities. The footnotes, which may appear to some as cumbersome and 'overkill', are intended for those who wish to follow further the various topics I have discussed.

Words fail me even to begin to thank those who have held such high aspirations for my life and have made significant contributions to my intellectual and spiritual nurture to reach the present point. The limited space given to this preface does not allow me to make note of them by name. I shall acknowledge them fully in an appropriate context, even as I do often before the throne of Grace. I thank my God upon every remembrance of you! I hope the fruit of my life proves worthy of your aspirations for me.

Within the confines of the present monograph, I should thank Professor Dr. Martin Hengel and Professor Dr. Otfried Hofius, editors of the *Wissenschaftliche Untersuchungen zum Neuen Testament*, who read and accepted this work for publication in the series. I thank Herr Dr. Georg Siebeck and the staff of Mohr Siebeck Publishers of Tübingen, Germany, who kindly accepted this work for publication and have patiently awaited its preparation for the press. I thank Dr. Leslie McFall and Mr. Jonathan Ryder for their assistance in preparing the work for publication. I thank especially Dr. Daniel Bailey for his careful editorial work and typesetting of the book for camera-ready production.

I am most deeply grateful to Rev. Professor C. K. Barrett and Rev. Professor William Horbury, who were my doctoral examiners. Their critique of my work, helpful observations, encouragement and approval were invaluable.

My heartfelt gratitude belongs to my tutor, the Rev. John Philip M.

Sweet, DD, for his unwavering commitment to my training and development during my years in Cambridge and his unceasing interest in me and assistance in so many ways even after my graduation. This book would have not reached publication without his encouragment and sacrificial giving of his time to see it to the end. I was his last doctoral student before his retirement, and he has always gone far beyond the call of duty. The shortcomings in the present work are indicative of my failure to give heed to his persistent, yet gentle and gracious, advice. Many thanks also to Mrs. Mary Sweet for her friendship which my family and I have come to treasure.

I wish to extend my gratitude to the following academic members of the University of Cambridge who at various stages of my studies either taught me, interacted with me intellectually, offered helpful suggestions on my work, or encouraged me when I could not see my way clear. These are: Professor Morna D. Hooker, the late Dr. Ernst Bammel, the late Professor Sir Harold Bailey, Professor Sir John Lyons, Professor John Emerton, Professor Robert Gordon, Professor William Horbury, and Dr. Eamon Duffy. I should also thank deeply Professor Sebastian Brock, my Oxford tutor, for his encouragement and support when I was in the midst of preparing this work for publication while at the same time carrying on with my studies in Oxford. I extend my profound appreciation to the Faculty of Divinity in Cambridge, the Board of Graduate Studies of the University of Cambridge, and the tutors, the governing body and staff of Magdalene College, Cambridge, and Christ Church, Oxford.

I am certain that I have expressed opinions and conclusions with which my teachers and examiners may disagree. All blame, criticism and shortcomings lie squarely at my own feet.

I am indebted to the late Professor Raymond Brown, and Professors Martin Hengel, Bruce Metzger, C. F. D. Moule, Herbert Leroy, Brevard Childs, Wayne Meeks, Don Carson, and Rudolf Schnackenburg for their input and suggestions whenever I wrote or called with questions. My gratitude also goes to my teachers at my theological alma-mater, Dallas Seminary. They laid the biblical and exegetical foundation upon which I have tried to build. They gave me an appreciation for the study of the sacred Scriptures in the original languages. I especially thank my teachers, Professors Stanley Toussaint and Dwight Pentecost who never ceased to emphasise the importance of tempering the pursuit of scholarship with the discipline of godliness. From professors S. Lewis Johnson and Bruce Waltke I learned that theological scholarship ought to be a reverent scholarship. And there were many others who made significant contributions to my spiritual life and learning.

One of the main difficulties encountered by any one who wishes to write about the Fourth Gospel is the vastness of secondary literature in most European languages. Here I benefited greatly from the assistance I received from the Librarians of the Divinity Faculty, the Oriental Studies Faculty, and the University Library, Cambridge, as well as the Theology Faculty Library and the Bodleian Library, Oxford. I should also thank my friends at the Tyndale House Research Library. I made much use of the library and was happy to know them.

I am deeply grateful to the Committee of Vice-Chancellors and Principals of the Universities of the United Kingdom for the three-years award of an Overseas Research Students scholarship (ORS) and to the governors of the Cambridge Overseas Trust for the award of a Bursary. I am profoundly thankful to the directors of the Crosse Studentship for a two-year studentship award, and to the directors of the Hort Memorial Fund of the Divinity Faculty.

I can not even begin to thank my wife, Rebecca Ann Walter, for the countless hours spent into the early hours of the morning in reading and correcting the drafts of this work. I thank her and our sons, Benjamin Arya, Cyrus Matthew Christopher, and Josiah Kyan Bahram for their patience for such a very long time.

For all of you, I thank the Lord God who has looked upon me with unmerited favour, His matchless grace! It is to Him that this book is given as an unworthy token of my love.

Oxford, January, 2000   Saeed Hamid-Khani

Table of Contents

Preface V
Abbreviations XIV

Chapter 1
INTRODUCTION 1
  1.1. Background: John Wrote a 'Spiritual Gospel' 1
  1.2. The Problem: Enigmatic Language of Jesus and John 4
      1.2.1. A Brief History of Research 5
      1.2.2. Justification for the Present Study 17
  1.3. Thesis and Aims 19
  1.4. The Question of Method 20
  1.5. Plan, Scope, and Limitations 28

Chapter 2
THE STRUCTURE OF JOHN'S ENIGMATIC LANGUAGE 33
  2.1. Defining Ambiguity in the Fourth Gospel 33
      2.1.1. The General Problem of Ambiguity in Literature 33
      2.1.2. General Definition of Ambiguity 34
            2.1.2.1. The Linguistic Definition 36
            2.1.2.2. The Literary Definition 38
      2.1.3. The Role of Context in Ambiguity 39
  2.2. The Compositional Fabric of Ambiguity in the Fourth Gospel 41
      2.2.1. The Linguistic Fabric of Johannine Ambiguity 43
            2.2.1.1. Grammatical and Syntactical Ambiguity 43
            2.2.1.2. Lexical Amphibologia (Double Meaning) 46
            2.2.1.3. Conceptual Amphibologia (Double Reference) 52

2.2.1.4. Use of Cluster Concepts	60
2.2.2. The Literary Fabric of Johannine Ambiguity	62
2.2.2.1. Johannine Symbolism and Metaphor	65
2.2.2.2. Johannine Irony	75
2.3. Figurative versus Plain Speech	85
2.4. Johannine Allusions to the Old Testament	91
2.5. Conclusion: The Compound Structure of John's Language	121

Chapter 3
THE CONCEPTUAL MILIEU OF THE FOURTH GOSPEL ... 123

3.1. The Context of Thought out of Which the Gospel Emerged	123
3.2. Various Proposals for the Johannine Conceptual Setting	125
3.2.1. Gnosticism	126
3.2.2. Qumran	130
3.2.3. Judaism and the Jewish Scriptures	132
3.2.4. The Centrality of the Scriptures in Judaism	136
3.3. The Fourth Gospel in Its Old Testament Literary Setting	137
3.3.1. The Semitic Style of the Fourth Gospel	140
3.3.2. Comparative Stylistic Analysis	144

Chapter 4
THE PURPOSE OF THE FOURTH GOSPEL ... 157

4.1. The Intentions of John	157
4.1.1. Clarification of Two Assumptions	160
4.1.2. The Purpose of the Gospel as Viewed in the Early Church	161
4.2. John's Stated Purpose	162
4.3. A Record for Posterity	164
4.3.1. The Jewish Readership	165
4.3.2. The Gentile Readership	168
4.3.3. The Universal Appeal of the Fourth Gospel	172

4.4. Pastoral Focus But Not Sectarian Perspective	174
4.4.1. The Alleged Sectarianism of the Fourth Gospel	175
4.4.2. Analysis and Criticism of Martyn, Leroy, and Meeks	181
4.4.2.1. Martyn's Reconstruction	181
4.4.2.2. Leroy's Form-Critical Analysis	190
4.4.2.3. Meeks's Sociological Application	193
4.4.3. Further Criticism of the Sectarian Model	197
4.4.4. The Non-Sectarian Emphasis of the Gospel	208
4.5. The Centrality of the Messianic Identity of Jesus in the Purpose of the Gospel	220

Chapter 5
ISRAEL'S SCRIPTURES AND THE LANGUAGE OF JOHN'S GOSPEL 230

5.1. The Primary Key to the Function of John's Perplexing Language	230
5.2. Addressees of the Johannine Polemic: The Identity of 'the Jews'	232
5.2.1. Who Then Are the Johannine Jews?	238
5.2.2. 'The Jews' at the Level of Johannine Theology	247
5.3. John's Appeal to Israel's Scriptures and Its Implications for His Language	251
5.3.1. The Distinctions in Johannine Citations of Scripture	253
5.3.2. The Significance of Direct Citations in Determining the Function of the Indirect Allusions	257
5.3.3. Johannine Allusions to Consummation of Jewish Religious Institutions in Christ	258
5.3.3.1. Jesus as Fulfilment of the Law	259
5.3.3.2. Jesus as the Completion of the Sacrificial System	270
5.3.3.3. Jesus as the Locus of God's Presence – The True Temple	280

5.4. The Witness of the Scriptures to Jesus and the Johannine Hermeneutic 285

5.5. The Prophecy of Isaiah and an Explanation of the Opponents' Incomprehension 296

    5.5.1. Incomprehension and Spiritual Blindness 296

    5.5.2. Isaiah's Message and Rejection of Revelation in John 306

    5.5.3. Revelation of the Arm of YHWH and Rejection of His Servant 307

    5.5.4. Incomprehension and the Question of Divine Determination 312

5.6. The Witness of the Scriptures to Jesus and the Prophetic 'Lawsuit' 324

5.7. Implications of the Witness of the Scriptures for the Johannine Audience 326

Chapter 6
SPIRITUAL PERCEPTION AND THE LANGUAGE OF JOHN'S GOSPEL 331

6.1. The Language of John as a Theological Language 331

6.2. The Resurrection and Its Implication for John's Language 333

6.3. The Work of the Spirit of Truth in Illuminating the Truth 337

    6.3.1. The Nature of Truth in the Fourth Gospel 341

    6.3.2. Revelation of Truth in the Person and Work of Jesus Christ 345

    6.3.3. The Witness of the Written Word to the Living Word 357

    6.3.4. Illumination of the Revelation of Truth by the Holy Spirit 358

6.4. Spiritual Birth as a Necessary Condition for Comprehending the Truth 361

    6.4.1. Spiritual Perception 366

    6.4.2. Circumcised Ears 369

6.5. Comprehension of Truth and the Johannine Conception of Faith 372

    6.5.1. Spurious Faith Does Not Lead to Life and Illumination 374

    6.5.2. Abiding Faith 381

6.6. The Polarising Effect of Light Shining in Darkness 384

    6.6.1. Divisiveness of the Revelation of God in Christ 385

    6.6.2. The Johannine 'World' and the Function of the Believing Community within It 395

    6.6.3. Unbelief and 'Evil Works' 398

6.7. Concealment of the Word 400

Chapter 7
CONCLUSION: THE ENIGMATIC LANGUAGE OF THE 'SPIRITUAL GOSPEL' 407

Bibliography 411
Index of References 511
Index of Authors 548
Index of Subjects 567
Index of Greek Words 573

Abbreviations

Abbreviations have been taken in the first instance from the "Instructions for Contributors" in *JBL* 117 (1998) 567–579 or from the longer list in Patrick H. Alexander et al., eds., *The SBL Handbook of Style for Ancient Near Eastern, Biblical, and Early Christian Studies* (Peabody, Mass.: Hendrickson, 1999), 121–152. Additional abbreviations have been derived from S. M. Schwertner, ed., *Theologische Realenzyklopädie Abkürzungsverzeichnis*, 2nd edn (Berlin: de Gruyter, 1994) and from Edward Malatesta, *St. John's Gospel, 1920–1965: A Cumulative and Classified Bibliography of Books and Periodical Literature on the Fourth Gospel*, AnBib 32 (Rome: Pontifical Biblical Institute, 1967).

AB	Anchor Bible
ABRL	Anchor Bible Reference Library
AGJU	Arbeiten zur Geschichte des antiken Judentums und des Urchristentums
AJBI	*Annual of the Japanese Biblical Institute*
AJSL	*American Journal of Semitic Languages and Literature*
AJT	*The American Journal of Theology*
AnBib	Analecta Biblica
ANRW	*Aufstieg und Niedergang der römischen Welt: Geschichte und Kultur Roms im Spiegel der neueren Forschung*, II: *Prinzipat*. Edited by A. Temporini and W. Haase. Berlin, 1972–
AnSTar	Analecta Sacra Tarraconensia
AOAT	Alter Orient und Altes Testament
APOT	*The Apocrypha and Pseudepigrapha of the Old Testament*. Edited by R. H. Charles. 2 vols. Oxford, 1913
ATANT	Abhandlungen zur Theologie des Alten und Neuen Testaments
ATR	*Anglican Theological Review*
ATRSS	*Anglican Theological Review Supplementary Series*
AusBR	*Australian Biblical Review*
BA	*Biblical Archaeologist*
BAGD	W. Bauer, W. F. Arndt, F. W. Gingrich, and F. W. Danker. *A*

Abbreviations

	Greek-English Lexicon of the New Testament and Other Early Christian Literature. 2nd edn. Chicago, 1979
BAR	*Biblical Archaeologist Reader*
BBB	Bonner biblische Beiträge
BBET	Beiträge zur biblischen Exegese und Theologie
BBR	*Bulletin for Biblical Research*
BDB	F. Brown, S. R. Driver, and C. A. Briggs. *A Hebrew and English Lexicon of the Old Testament.* Oxford, 1906
BDF	F. Blass, A. Debrunner, and R. W. Funk. *A Greek Grammar of the New Testament and Other Early Christian Literature.* Chicago, 1961
BeO	*Bibbia e orienta*
BETL	Bibliotheca ephemeridum theologicarum lovaniensium
BETS	*Bulletin of the Evangelical Theological Society*
BFCT	Beiträge zur Förderung christlicher Theologie
Bib	*Biblica*
BibLeb	*Bibel und Leben*
BibSac	*Bibliotheca Sacra*
BJRL	*Bulletin of the John Rylands Library*
BJS	Brown Judaic Studies
BK	*Bibel und Kirche*
BO	*Bibliotheca orientalis*
BR	*Biblical Research*
BT	*The Bible Translator*
BTB	*Biblical Theology Bulletin*
BTSt	Biblisch-theologische Studien
BWANT	Beiträge zur Wissenschaft vom Alten und Neuen Testament
BZ	*Biblische Zeitschrift*
BZAW	Beihefte zur Zeitschrift für die alttestamentliche Wissenschaft
BZNW	Beihefte zur Zeitschrift für die neutestamentliche Wissenschaft
CB	*Cultura bíblica*
CBQ	*Catholic Biblical Quarterly*
CBQMS	Catholic Biblical Quarterly Monograph Series
ConBNT	Coniectanea biblica, New Testament
ConNT	Coniectanea neotestamentica
CRINT	Compendia rerum iudaicarum ad Novum Testamentum
CTAP	*Cahiers théologiques de l'actualité protestante*

CUP	Cambridge University Press
DRev	*Downside Review*
Ebib	Études bibliques
EHS	Europäische Hochschulschriften
EKKNT	Evangelisch-katholischer Kommentar zum Neuen Testament
EPRO	Etudes préliminaires aux religions orientales dans l'empire Romain
EstBib	*Estudios bíblicos*
ET	English translation
ETL	*Ephemerides theologicae lovanienses*
ETR	*Études théologiques et religieuses*
EvQ	*The Evangelical Quarterly*
EvT	*Evangelische Theologie*
Exp	*The Expositor*
ExpTim	*The Expository Times*
FRLANT	Forschungen zur Religion und Literatur des Alten und Neuen Testaments
FS	Festschrift
FTS	Frankfurter theologische Studien
GBS	Guides to Biblical Scholarship
GCS	Die griechischen christlichen Schriftsteller der ersten drei Jahrhunderte
HAW	Handbuch der Altertumswissenschaft
HBT	*Horizons in Biblical Theology*
HeyJ	*Heythrop Journal*
HNT	Handbuch zum Neuen Testament
HPR	*Homiletic and Pastoral Review*
HTKNT	Herders theologischer Kommentar zum Neuen Testament
HTR	*Harvard Theological Review*
HTS	Harvard Theological Studies
HUCA	*Hebrew Union College Annual*
ICC	International Critical Commentary
IDB	*The Interpreter's Dictionary of the Bible.* Edited by G. A. Buttrick. 4 vols. Nashville, 1962
IDBSup	*Interpreter's Dictionary of the Bible: Supplementary Volume.* Edited by K. Crim. Nashville, 1976
Int	*Interpretation*

ITQ	*Irish Theological Quarterly*
JAC	Jahrbuch für Antike und Christentum
JBL	*Journal of Biblical Literature*
JBTh	*Jahrbuch für Biblische Theologie*
JES	*Journal of Ecumenical Studies*
JETS	*Journal of the Evangelical Theological Society*
JJS	*Journal of Jewish Studies*
JQR	*Jewish Quarterly Review*
JR	*Journal of Religion*
JRH	*Journal of Religious History*
JRT	*Journal of Religious Thought*
JSJ	*Journal for the Study of Judaism in the Persian, Hellenistic and Roman Periods*
JSNT	*Journal for the Study of the New Testament*
JSNTSup	Journal for the Study of the New Testament Supplement Series
JSOT	*Journal for the Study of the Old Testament*
JSOTSup	Journal for the Study of the Old Testament Supplement Series
JSPSup	Journal for the Study of the Pseudepigrapha Supplement Series
JSS	*Journal for Semitic Studies*
JTS	*Journal of Theological Studies*
JTSA	*Journal of Theology for Southern Africa*
KEK	Kritisch-exegetischer Kommentar über das Neue Testament
KJV	King James Version
KuD	*Kerygma und Dogma*
LCL	Loeb Classical Library
LS	*Louvain Studies*
LSJ	H. G. Liddell, R. Scott, H. S. Jones, and R. Mackenzie. *A Greek-English Lexicon*. 9th edn. Oxford, 1940
LXX	Septuagint
MLN	*Modern Language Notes*
MNTC	Moffatt New Testament Commentary
MT	Masoretic Text
n.s.	new series
NCB	New Century Bible
Neot	*Neotestamentica*
NHC	Nag Hammadi Codices

NHS	Nag Hammadi Studies
NICNT	New International Commentary on the New Testament
NIDNTT	*New International Dictionary of New Testament Theology.* Edited by C. Brown. 4 vols. Grand Rapids, 1975–1985
NIV	The New International Version
NKZ	*Neue kirchliche Zeitschrift*
NovT	*Novum Testamentum*
NovTSup	Novum Testamentum Supplements
NRSV	New Revised Standard Version
NRT	*La nouvelle revue théologique*
NTD	Das Neue Testament Deutsch
NTOA	Novum Testamentum et Orbis Antiquus
NTS	*New Testament Studies*
NZSTh	*Neue Zeitschrift für systematische Theologie*
OG	Old Greek
OPTAT	*Occasional Papers in Translation and Text Linguistics*
OTP	*The Old Testament Pseudepigrapha.* Edited by J. H. Charlesworth. 2 vols. New York, 1983
OUP	Oxford University Press
PEQ	*Palestine Exploration Quarterly*
PMLA	*Proceedings of the Modern Language Association of America*
QD	Quaestiones disputatae
RB	*Revue biblique*
RelSRev	*Religious Studies Review*
ResQ	*Restoration Quarterly*
RevEcl	*Revista eclesiástica*
RevExp	*Review and Expositor*
RevQ	*Revue de Qumran*
RevSR	*Revue des sciences religieuses*
RHPR	*Revue d'histoire et de philosophie religieuses*
RivB	*Rivista biblica italiana*
RSR	*Recherches de science religieuse*
RThom	*Revue thomiste*
RTL	*Revue théologique de Louvain*
SANT	Studien zum Alten und Neuen Testament
SBL	Society of Biblical Literature

SBLDS	SBL Dissertation Series
SBLMS	SBL Monograph Series
SBLSBS	SBL Sources for Biblical Study
SBLSCS	SBL Septuagint and Cognate Studies
SBLSP	*SBL Seminar Papers*
SBLTT	SBL Texts and Translations
SBS	Stuttgarter Bibelstudien
SBT	Studies in Biblical Theology
SCHNT	Studia ad corpus hellenisticum novi testamenti
SE	*Studia evangelica I, II, III* (= TU 73 [1959], 87 [1964], 88 [1964], etc.)
SEÅ	*Svensk exegetisk årsbok*
SJLA	Studies in Judaism in Late Antiquity
SJT	*Scottish Journal of Theology*
SNT	Studien zum Neuen Testament
SNTSMS	Society for New Testament Studies Monograph Series
SNTU	Studien zum Neuen Testament und seiner Umwelt
ST	*Studia Theologica*
Str-B	H. L. Strack and P. Billerbeck. *Kommentar zum Neuen Testament aus Talmud und Midrasch.* 6 vols. Munich, 1922–1961
STRT	Studia Theologica Rheno-Traiectina
StudBib	Studia Biblica
SUNT	Studien zur Umwelt des Neuen Testaments
TBT	*The Bible Today*
TDiss	Theologische Dissertationen
TDNT	*Theological Dictionary of the New Testament.* Edited by G. Kittel and G. Friedrich. Translated by G. W. Bromiley. 10 vols. Grand Rapids, 1964–1976
TE	*Theologia Evangelica*
TGl	*Theologie und Glaube*
THAT	*Theologisches Handwörterbuch zum Alten Testament.* Edited by E. Jenni, with assistance from C. Westermann. 2 vols. Stuttgart, 1971–1976
ThD	*Theology Digest*
TLZ	*Theologische Literaturzeitung*
TQ	*Theologische Quartalschrift*
TRE	*Theologische Realenzyklopädie.* Edited by G. Krause and G. Müller.

	Berlin, 1977–
TRu	Theologische Rundschau
TS	Theological Studies
TSAJ	Texte und Studien zum antiken Judentum
TSJTSA	Texts and Studies of the Jewish Theological Seminary of America
TSK	Theologische Studien und Kritiken
TT	Theology Today
TTZ	Trierer theologische Zeitschrift
TU	Texte und Untersuchungen
TWAT	*Theologisches Wörterbuch zum Alten Testament* Edited by G. J. Botterweck and H. Ringgren. Stuttgart, 1970–
TWNT	*Theologisches Wörterbuch zum Neuen Testament.* Edited by G. Kittel and G. Friedrich. Stuttgart, 1932–1979
TynBul	Tyndale Bulletin
TZ	Theologische Zeitschrift
UNT	Untersuchungen zum Neuen Testament
VE	Vox Evangelica
Vox Theol	Vox Theologica
VT	Vetus Testamentum
VTSup	Vetus Testamentum Supplements
WBC	Word Biblical Commentary
WMANT	Wissenschaftliche Monographien zum Alten und Neuen Testament
WTJ	Westminster Theological Journal
WUNT	Wissenschaftliche Untersuchungen zum Neuen Testament
YJS	Yale Judaica Series
ZAW	Zeitschrift für die alttestamentliche Wissenschaft
ZKT	Zeitschrift für katholische Theologie
ZNW	Zeitschrift für die neutestamentliche Wissenschaft
ZRGG	Zeitschrift für Religions- und Geistesgeschichte
ZTK	Zeitschrift für Theologie und Kirche

Chapter 1

Introduction

1.1. Background: John Wrote a 'Spiritual Gospel'

The enigmatic quality of the language of the Fourth Gospel has intrigued students of the sacred Scriptures throughout history. The Gospel seems to be so simple to grasp, and yet it unremittingly points beyond itself to profound truths which inattentive readings miss and which are not apparent to undiscerning eyes.

As early as AD 200, Clement of Alexandria is reported by Eusebius of Caesarea as having said that since the knowledge of the 'physical' data about the Lord was already contained in the Synoptics, John wrote a 'spiritual gospel'.[1] Earlier still, the Valentinian gnostic Heracleon gave a highly symbolic interpretation of John, treating it very much as a 'spiritual' document.[2] Origen, one of the earliest interpreters of John, systematically gave it a deeper spiritual sense and may even have derived his hermeneutical principles from his impressions and intense study of it.[3]

In modern times, especially since the 1920s, this enigmatic character

---

[1] Eusebius, *Historia ecclesiastica* 6.14.7: τὸν μέντοι Ἰωάννην ἔσχατον, συνιδόντα ὅτι τὰ σωματικὰ ἐν τοῖς εὐαγγελίοις δεδήλωται, ...πνεύματι θεοφορηθέντα πνευματικὸν ποιῆσαι εὐαγγέλιον.

[2] Elaine H. Pagels, *The Johannine Gospel in Gnostic Exegesis: Heracleon's Commentary on John*, SBLMS 17 (Nashville: Abingdon, 1973).

[3] A. Skevington Wood, *The Principles of Biblical Interpretation as Enunciated by Irenaeus, Origen, Augustine, Luther and Calvin* (Grand Rapids: Zondervan, 1967); Joseph W. Trigg, *Origen: The Bible and Philosophy in the Third-Century Church* (London: SCM, 1985); A. E. Brooke, *The Commentary of Origen on St. John's Gospel*, 2 vols (Cambridge: CUP, 1896); Cécile Blanc, ed. and trans., *Origène, Commentaire au Saint Jean*, 5 vols (Paris: Éditions du Cerf, 1970); Henry Chadwick, *Early Christian Thought and the Classical Tradition: Studies in Justin, Clement and Origen* (Oxford: OUP, 1966); Eugene V. Gallagher, *Divine Man or Magician? Celsus and Origen on Jesus*, SBLDS 64 (Chico, CA: Scholars Press, 1982); Origen, *Commentary on the Gospel According to John*, Books 13–32, trans. by Ronald Heine (Washington, D.C.: Catholic University Press of America, 1993); Erwin Preuschen, *Origenes Werke: Der Johanneskommentar* (Leipzig: Hinrichs, 1903).

of John's language has been noted in various ways.[4] Many students of John have described his Gospel as a mystical work whose language is too

---

[4] E.g., W. M. Milligan, 'Double Pictures in the Fourth Gospel and the Apocalypse', *Exp*, 2nd Series 4 (1882), 264–78, 430–47; H. C. Vedder, *The Johannine Writings and the Johannine Problem: An Aid to the Critical Study of the Bible as Literature* (Philadelphia: Griffith and Rowland Press, 1917), H. A. A. Kennedy, *Philo's Contribution to Religion* (London: Hodder and Stoughton, 1919), 47–8; P. Rudel, 'Das Missverständnis im Johannesevangelium', *NKZ* 3 (1921), 351–61; H. J. Flowers, 'Interpolations in the Fourth Gospel', *JBL* 40 (1921), 146–58; W. Drum, 'Calmes and the Allegorical Interpretation of John', *HPR* 22 (1921–22), 18–24; idem, 'The Symbolism of the Fourth Gospel', *HPR* 22 (1921–22), 162–9; idem, 'A Résumé of Johannine Symbolism and Allegory', *HPR* 22 (1921–22), 257–63; idem, 'Johannine Thought-forms in the Discourses of Jesus', *HPR* 21 (1920–21), 722–32; idem, 'The Words of Jesus and the Meditation of John', *HPR* 21 (1920–121), 813–21; E. von Dobschütz, 'Zum Charakter des 4. Evangeliums', *ZNW* 28 (1929), 161–77; L. Cerfaux, 'Le thème littéraire parabolique dans l'Évangile de S. Jean', *ConNT* 11 (1947), 15–25; F. Verhelst, 'Sur quelques caractères distinctifs du IV Évangile', *Collectanea Mechliniensia* n.s. 2 (1928), 189–95; R. J. Drummond, 'The Johannine Writings: An Old Man's Speculations', *EvQ* 21 (1949), 219–23; W. F. Howard, 'Symbolism and Allegory', in idem, ed., *The Fourth Gospel in Recent Criticism and Interpretation*, rev. C. K. Barrett (London: Epworth, 1955 [orig. 1931]), 185–6; C. F. Burney, *The Poetry of Our Lord: An Examination of the Formal Elements of Hebrew Poetry in the Discourses of Jesus Christ* (Oxford: Clarendon, 1925); W. Wrede, *Charakter und Tendenz des Johannesevangeliums*, Sammlung gemeinverständlicher Vorträge und Schriften aus dem Gebiet der Theologie und Religionsgeschichte 37 (Tübingen: Mohr-Siebeck, 1903, repr. 1933); A. von Harnack, *Das Wir in den Johanneischen Schriften*, Sitzungsberichte der Preussischen Akademie der Wissenschaften (Berlin: Verlag der Akademie der Wiss., 1923), 96–113; M. Ayala, 'El Evangelio de San Juan: su forma literaria', *RevEcl* 24 (1920, 2), 288–91; 331–5; Edwin A. Abbott, *Johannine Vocabulary* (London: Adam and Charles Black, 1905); idem, *Johannine Grammar* (London: Adam and Charles Black, 1906). See also M. Blumenthal, 'Die Eigenart des johann. Erzählungsstiles', *TSK* 106 (1934–1935), 204–12; W. von Loewenich, *Johanneisches Denken. Ein Beitrag zur Kenntnis der Johanneischen Eigenart* (Leipzig: Hinrichs, 1936); James Muilenburg, 'Literary Form in the Fourth Gospel', *JBL* 51 (1932), 40–53; J. Trepat, 'L'evangelista Sant Joan: Idees característiques', *AnSTar* 3 (1927), 405–22; H. Preisker, 'Zum Charakter des Johannesevangeliums', in *Luther, Kant, Schleiermacher in ihrer Bedeutung für den Protestantismus: Forschungen und Abhandlungen George Wobbermin zum 70. Geburtstag*, ed. by F. W. Schmidt, et al. (Berlin: Collignon, 1939), 379–93; E. Hirsch, 'Stilkritik und Literaturanalyse im vierten Evangelium', *ZNW* 43 (1950–51), 128–43; S. Virgulin, 'Caratteristiche del quarto Evangelo', *Bibbia e oriente* 2 (1960), 152–6; D. W. Wead, *The Literary Devices in John's Gospel*, Theologische Dissertationen 4 (Basel: Friedrich Reinhart Kommissionsverlag, 1970); H. Thyen, 'Die Einheit der johanneischen Sprache als methodologisches Problem', *TRu* 39 (1974), 48–52; F. M. Braun, 'La réduction du Pluriel au Singulier dans l'Evangile et la Première Lettre de Jean', *NTS* 24 (1977), 40–67; George MacRae, 'Theology and Irony in the Fourth Gospel', in *The Word in the World*, ed. by R. J. Clifford and G. W. MacRae (Cambridge: Weston, 1973), 83–96; R. E. Brown, 'The Language, Text, and Format of the Gospel – and some considerations on style', in idem, *The Gospel According to John*, AB, 2 vols (Garden City: Doubleday, 1966–70), 1:cxxix–cxxxvii; R. Schnackenburg, 'Sprache, Stil, Gedankenbewegung', in idem, *Das Johannesevangelium*, HTKNT 4/1–4, 4 vols (Freiburg: Herder, 1965–84), 1:88–101; F. Kermode, 'John', in *The Literary Guide to the Bible*, ed. by Robert Alter (Cambridge, MA: Belknap Press of Harvard University Press; London: Collins, 1987), 440–66; W. S. Vorster, 'The Gospel of St. John as Language', *Neot* 6 (1972), 19–27; L. Hartman, 'Aspects of Johannine Literature', *Literature and Theology* 1 (1987), 184–90; Mark W. G. Stibbe, *John as Storyteller: Narrative Criticism and the Fourth Gospel*, SNTSMS 73 (Cambridge: CUP, 1992); Norman Petersen, *The Gospel of John and the Sociology of Light: Language and Characterization in the Fourth Gospel* (Valley Forge, PA: Trinity Press, 1993).

elusive for human grasp.⁵ Martin Hengel, for example, has characterised this Gospel as 'the most mysterious writing of the New Testament.'⁶

In fact a whole range of descriptions have been used to indicate the same phenomenon. John's language has been described as a 'closed system of metaphors', a 'private language', 'parabolic language', 'anti-language', 'mystical', 'mysterious', 'strange', 'unfamiliar', 'beyond reach', 'incomprehensible', 'evasive', 'elusive', 'perplexing', 'allegorical', 'enchanted', 'esoteric', 'enigmatic', 'deep', 'profound', 'coded', 'cryptic', 'spiritual', or in similar terms,⁷ all highlighting its elusive character.

---

⁵ J. Ernst, 'Das Johannesevangelium – ein Frühes Beispiel Christlicher Mystik', *TGl* 81 (1991), 323–38; R. Kieffer, 'Det gåtfulla Johannesevangeliet', *STK* 67 (1991), 109–12; Jey J. Kanagaraj, *Mysticism in the Gospel of John: An Inquiry into Its Background*, JSNTSup 158 (Sheffield: Sheffield Academic Press, 1998); J. McPolin, 'Johannine Mysticism', *The Way* 18 (1978), 25; W. J. Fulco, *Maranatha: Reflections on the Mystical Theology of John the Evangelist* (New York: Paulist Press, 1971); D. L. Mealand, 'The Language of Mystical Union in the Johannine Writings', *DRev* 95 (1977), 19–34; E. R. Goodenough, *By Light, Light: The Mystical Gospel of Hellenistic Judaism* (New Haven: Yale University Press, 1935), 7–8; X. Léon-Dufour, 'Ouvertures johanniques sur la mystique', *Christus* 162 (1994), 180–8; E. Underhill, *Mystic Way* (London: J. M. Dent and Sons, repr., 1914), 217, 226, 254–5; B. Maggioni, 'La Mystica Di Giovanni Evangelista', in *La Mistica: Fenemenologia e Riflessione Teologica*, ed. by E. Ancilli and M. Paparozzi, vol. 1 (Rome: Citta Nuova, 1984), 223–4, 248–9; Jakob Jónsson, *Humour and Irony in the New Testament* (Leiden: Brill, 1985), 200; C. Hélou, *Sumbole et langage dans les écrits johanniques. Lumière – ténèbres* (Paris: Mame, 1980).

⁶ Martin Hengel, 'The Old Testament in the Fourth Gospel', in *The Gospels and the Scriptures of Israel*, ed. by Craig A. Evans and W. Richard Stegner, JSNTSup 104 (Sheffield: Sheffield Academic Press, 1994), 384; idem, *The Johannine Question*, trans. by John Bowden (London: SCM; Philadelphia: Trinity Press, 1989), 13.

⁷ For these and similar descriptions see W. Meeks, 'The Man From Heaven in Johannine Sectarianism', *JBL* (1972), 44–72; H. Leroy, *Rätsel und Missverständnis. Ein Beitrag zur Formgeschichte des Johannesevangeliums* (Bonn: Hanstein, 1968); Underhill, *Mystic Way*, 217, 226, 254–5; B. Maggioni, 'La Mystica Di Giovanni Evangelista', 223–4, 248–9; Cerfaux, 'Le thème littéraire parabolique'; Ian T. Ramsey, *Religious Language* (London: SCM, 1993 [1957]), 124–5; M. F. Wiles, *The Spiritual Gospel: The Interpretation of the Fourth Gospel in the Early Church* (Cambridge: CUP, 1960), 1ff.; I. De La Potterie, 'L'emploi du verbe "demeurer" dans la mystique johannique', *NRT* 117 (1995), 843–59; Léon-Dufour, 'Ouvertures johanniques sur la mystique'; B. F. von Hügel, 'John, Gospel of St.', *Encyclopaedia Britannica*, 11th edn (Cambridge: CUP, 1911), 15:455; Goodenough, *By Light*, 7–8; J. H. Neyrey, *An Ideology of Revolt: John's Christology in Social Scientific Perspective* (Philadelphia: Fortress, 1988), 137; Hélou, *Sumbole et langage dans les écrits johanniques*; Kieffer, 'Det gåtfulla Johannesevangeliet', 109–12; Drum, 'Calmes and the Allegorical Interpretation', 18–24; idem, 'Symbolism of the Fourth Gospel', 162–9; idem, 'Résumé of Johannine Symbolism', 257–63; Verhelst, 'Sur quelques caractères distinctifs du IV Évangile', 189–95; Thyen, 'Die Einheit der johanneischen Sprache als methodologisches Problem'; Kermode, 'John', 440–6; Stibbe, *John as Storyteller*; B. Malina, 'The Gospel of John in Sociolinguistic Perspective', in *Protocol of the 48th Colloquy of the Center for Hermeneutical Studies in Hellenistic and Modern Culture*, ed. by H. C. Waetjen (Berkeley: Graduate Theological Union and Univ. of California-Berkeley, 1985), 1–23; Rensberger, *Overcoming the World: Politics and Community in the Gospel of John* (London: SPCK, 1989), 137; J. Colson, *L'Énigme du disciple que Jésus aimait*, Théologie historique 10 (Paris: Beauchesne, 1968).

Chapter 1: Introduction

In comparison with Matthew, Mark, and Luke, John is said to present a theologically reflective side of the New Testament interpretation of Jesus.[8] This is not surprising for an author who insists that the spirit is what gives life, while the flesh is of no avail, and that the words of Jesus are spirit and life (John 6:63; cf. 4:24). Consequently, the Fourth Gospel is often regarded as both the best introduction to the Christian faith and the most sublime meditation on what Christians believe about the person at the centre of their faith.

1.2. The Problem: Enigmatic Language of Jesus and John

It is frequently observed that Jesus in the Synoptic Gospels speaks in a double-edged and ambiguous manner. When we come to the Fourth Gospel, this feature of language not only is greatly accentuated, but is further transformed into a special literary style which characterises the entire document. In John, ambiguity moves beyond the words of Jesus or anything comparable in the Synoptics (i.e., parables). Not only are the reported expressions of Jesus ambiguous, but also the language of the Fourth Evangelist himself is highly enigmatic.[9] D. A. Carson traces this quality of speech back to Jesus and writes, 'It is altogether plausible that Jesus sometimes spoke in nothing less than what we think of as "Johannine" style, and that John's style was to some degree influenced by Jesus himself.'[10] Both in the past and present, those who have seriously studied John's Gospel have had to wrestle with what the Fourth Evangelist seems to say denotatively and with the significance of his statements connotatively. The profound expressions in this Gospel often seem to be in one's grasp moments before they once again slip away. It is this quality which sets apart the Fourth Gospel from the other three canonical Gospels and results in its being characterised as a supplement to them, as 'spiritual' or 'theological'.

From the very first verse of the first chapter, the difficulty of relating conceptually to the writing becomes apparent.[11] John's language speaks

---

[8] Rensberger, *Overcoming the World*, 17.

[9] Ramsey, *Religious Language*, 124–5.

[10] D. A. Carson, *The Gospel According to John* (Grand Rapids: Eerdmans, 1991), 48.

[11] In everyday language, words do not 'become flesh', neither do they possess the property of 'glory'. In the Fourth Gospel, being 'born' takes on a new spiritual dimension when John talks about 'becoming children of God', of which he only tells what becoming children of God is not. This problem is, in part, linguistically created through the utilisation of words as synonyms when

about a world that is incompatible with our world in a language which we find difficult to penetrate. In this, John imitates the language of the one who claims to be not of this world but from the world above (8:23). Therefore, the author insists that in order to understand the language of the world of Jesus and to perceive its reality, one must be born anew spiritually from above (3:3, cf. 3:6, 12–13; 15:19; 16:28; 17:14, 16, 18; 18:36, 37) – that is, born 'not of blood, nor of the will of the flesh, nor of the will of man, but of God' (Jn. 1:13). And this is also the central thesis of the present work.

1.2.1. A Brief History of Research

To give a comprehensive account of what has been written on various aspects of the language of John's Gospel in general[12] and this feature in particular is beyond the scope of the present study. The following survey is a selection of some of the more prominent works in this area of Johannine scholarship.

One may begin with H. A. Kennedy's comparative study of John and Philo in 1919, where he devoted considerable attention to the 'symbolic element in the Fourth Gospel' in contrast to the Alexandrian's allegorical method of interpretation. He observed in the Fourth Gospel 'mysterious sayings' that yield divergent explanations and are often capable of expressing twofold meaning. Kennedy also pointed to the elusiveness of various

---

such words are not synonyms in everyday use of language. Cf. Petersen, *Gospel of John*, 10. Synonymy in everyday language is a matter of 'sameness of meaning'. The linguistic categories such as synonymy, reference, denotation, connotation, etc. are defined in chapter two of the study.

[12] Franz Mussner, *The Historical Jesus in the Gospel of St. John*, trans. by W. J. O'Hara (New York: Herder, 1967); E. D. Freed, 'Variations in the Language and Thought of John', *ZNW* 55 (1964), 167–97; Hirsch, 'Stilkritik und Literaturanalyse', 128–43; F. M. Melús López, 'Características del Evangelio de San Juan', *Cultura Bíblica* 12 (1955), 288–95; S. Virgulin, 'Caratteristiche del quarto Evangelo', *Bibbia e Oriente* 2 (1960), 152–6; T. T. Rowe, 'Science, Statistics and Style', *London Quarterly and Holborn Review* 33 (1964), 231–5; G. D. Fee, 'The Use of the Definite Article with Personal Names in the Gospel of John', *NTS* 17 (1970–71), 168–83; Wead, *Literary Devices*; Thyen, 'Die Einheit der johanneischen Sprache', 48–52; V. S. Poythress, 'Testing for Johannine Authorship by Examining the Use of Conjunctions', *WTJ* 46 (1984), 350–69; Brown, *John*, 1:cxxix–cxxxvii; E. Haenchen, 'Die Sprache des JE', *Das Johannesevangelium* (1980), 57–74; J. H. van Halsema, 'Het raadsel als literaire vorm in Marcus en Johannes', *Gereformeerd theologisch tijdschrift* 83 (1983), 1–17; Johannes Beutler, 'Literarische Gattungen im Johannesevangelium. Ein Forschungsbericht 1919–1980', *ANRW* II.25.3, 2506–68; J. H. Moulton, *A Grammar of New Testament Greek*, vol. 4: *Style*, by N. Turner (Edinburgh: Clark, 1976), 64–79; Lindars, 'The Language of John', in *The Gospel of John* (London: Marshall, Morgan and Scott, 1972), 44–6; E. Ruckstuhl, 'Johannine Language and Style: The Question of Their Unity', in *L'Évangile de Jean: Sources, rédaction, theologie*, ed. by M. de Jonge, BETL 44 (Leuven: Leuven University Press, 1977), 125–47; Schnackenburg, 'Sprache, Stil, Gedankenbewegung', *Das Johannesevangelium*, 1:88–101 (ET, 1:105–118); Vorster, 'The Gospel of St. John as Language', 19–27.

passages such as the Samaritan scene of 4:15-26. These elements, Kennedy concluded, were the hallmark of the author's symbolism whereby a particular term or expression 'stands for something more general than itself.'[13]

In 1921, Rudel in his article 'Das Missverständnis im Johannesevangelium'[14] gave exclusive attention to the problem of misunderstanding in the Gospel. During the same period W. Drum published several articles in which he highlighted the symbolic nature of John's language. This symbolic element, he believed, led to the allegorical interpretation of the document.[15]

A series of studies between 1921 and 1948 further accentuated the multiple layers in the language of John.[16] Charles C. Torrey captured the sentiment shared by a not a few readers of the Gospel when he observed how John uses simple, everyday language to express ideas which are easily understood by a child and yet puzzling to a wise man.[17] Ten years after Kennedy's work, W. F. Howard incorporated his observations in a chapter entitled 'Symbolism and Allegory', in *The Fourth Gospel in Recent Criticism and Interpretation*.[18] In 1929, J. H. Bernard in his commentary took note of the phenomenon by focusing again upon episodes of misunderstanding. Bernard isolated six instances of misunderstanding in chapters 3, 4, and 6 which, he concluded, followed a common pattern: a saying of Jesus, misunderstanding, repetition, expansion, and an explanation.[19] Almost twenty years later, F. W. Gingrich in a brief article listed a number of words which he observed simultaneously carried two distinct meanings,

---

[13] *Philo's Contribution to Religion* (London: Hodder and Stoughton, 1919), 47-8.

[14] *NKZ* 3 (1921), 351-61.

[15] His articles are noted above in footnote 4.

[16] These include A. E. Baker, 'The Parables and the Johannine Problem', *Exp* 8th series 24 (1922), 305-15; Julius von Grill, *Untersuchungen über die Entstehung des 4. Evangeliums*, 2 vols (Tübingen: Mohr, 1902, 1923), Vol. 2: *Das Mysterienevangelium des hellenisierten kleinasiatischen Christentums*, 10ff.; Blumenthal, 'Die Eigenart des johann'; P. Doncoeur, 'Des silences de l'Évangile de Saint Jean', *RSR* 24 (1934), 606-9; Johannes Jeremias, 'Die vier Stimmen im vierten Evangelium', printed in *Theologisches Literaturblatt* 56 (1934), 81-7 and in *Nieuwe Theologische Studien* 17 (1934), 37-46; idem, *Die vier Stimmen im 4. Evangelium in den ursprünglichen Stilformen verdeutscht* (Herrnhut: Gustav Winter, 1934); von Dobschütz, 'Zum Charakter'; W. von Loewenich, *Johanneisches Denken. Ein Beitrag zur Kenntnis der Johanneischen Eigenart* (Leipzig: Hinrichs, 1936); C. Lavergne, *Les silences de S. Jean* (Paris: Desclée, 1940).

[17] 'When I Am Lifted Up From the Earth', *JBL* (1932), 320.

[18] Revised by C. K. Barrett (London: Epworth, 1955 [orig. 1931]), 185-6.

[19] *A Critical and Exegetical Commentary on the Gospel According to St. John*, ed. by A. H. McNeile, 2 vols (New York: Scribner's, 1929), 1:cxi-cxii.

neither of which seemed to be contradictory. This, he believed, was deliberate on the part of the author.[20]

In 1941, with the publication of Rudolph Bultmann's influential commentary on the Fourth Gospel,[21] this feature of John's language was further brought into prominence. Bultmann noticed many expressions with symbolic significance. He also noted words of double meaning, but denied that both meanings could have been intended.[22] Later in 1948, in the second volume of his *New Testament Theology*, Bultmann focused exclusively on the theology of the Fourth Gospel. This volume also contains scattered comments about John's language.[23] Also in 1948 O. Cullmann, in an article entitled 'Der johanneische Gebrauch doppeldeutiger Ausdrücke als Schlüssel zum Verständnis des vierten Evangeliums',[24] set out to show for the first time in a clear and precise manner that there was an intentional use of *double entendre* in the Fourth Gospel. Indeed as the title of his article indicates, he believed that this stylistic feature is the 'key' to understanding the symbolic and mystical character of the Fourth Gospel.

During the years 1929–59, H. Clavier devoted considerable research to irony and related dramatic techniques in the Gospel.[25] However, it was C. K. Barrett's important commentary of 1955 which had the farthest-reaching influence in this area, since he consistently pointed out ambiguous expressions with multiple meanings throughout the Fourth Gospel.[26]

---

[20] 'Ambiguity of Word Meaning in John's Gospel', *Classical Weekly* 37 (1943), 77.

[21] *The Gospel of John: A Commentary*, trans. by G. R. Beasley-Murray, et al. (Philadelphia: Westminster, 1971).

[22] One has to sift through Bultmann's whole commentary to gather up his scattered comments and observations. What is important in this commentary is Bultmann's painstaking attention to the details of John's language.

[23] *Theology of the New Testament*, vol. 2, trans. by K. Grobel (New York: Scribner's, 1955), which appeared in its original German edition between 1948 and 1953.

[24] 'Der johanneische Gebrauch doppeldeutiger Ausdrücke als Schlüssel zum Verständnis des vierten Evangeliums' [The Johannine use of expressions with double meanings as key to the understanding of the Fourth Gospel], *TZ* 4 (1948), 360–72 = *Vorträge und Aufsätze 1925–1962*, ed. by K. Fröhlich (Tübingen: Mohr, 1966), 176–86.

[25] Clavier, 'La méthode ironique dans l'enseignement de Jésus', *ETR* 4 (1929), 224–41, 323–44; also *ETR* 5 (1930), 58–99. See further Clavier, 'Autour de Jean 5:17', *RHPR* 34 (1944), 82–90; 'Le problème du rite et du mythe dans le quatrième évangile', *RHPR* 31 (1951), 275–92; 'La structure du quatrième évangile', *RHPR* 35 (1955), 174–95; 'L'ironie dans l'enseignement de Jésus', *NovT* 1 (1956), 3–20; 'Les sens multiples dans le nouveau testament', *NovT* 2 (1957), 185–98; and 'L'ironie dans le quatrième évangile', *SE* 1 = TU 73 (1959), 261–76.

[26] *The Gospel According to St. John* (London: SPCK, 1955; future references will be to the second edition; London: SPCK, 1976; Philadelphia: Westminster, 1978).

E. C. Hoskyns[27] and C. H. Dodd,[28] whom Barrett acknowledged as his teachers,[29] had earlier noted the same phenomenon.

If Cullmann laid the foundation, and Barrett made the first clear systematic articulation of the problem of ambiguity in John, then Herbert Leroy's thesis *Rätsel und Missverständnis* (1968) provided the single most focused work to date. Leroy approached the subject from the form-critical angle and focused his attention upon eleven instances of Johannine misunderstanding within John 2–8. He proposed that each of these can best be understood as a form of 'riddle' *(Rätsel)* cast within a dialogue.[30]

Since the 1960s, Johannine research has advanced essentially on three fronts: traditional exegetical and historical-critical studies; literary criticism; and sociology. Within the confines of the traditional approach,[31] J. C. Fenton's concise and informative commentary provides in a brief introduc-

---

[27] *The Fourth Gospel*, ed. by F. N. Davey (London: Faber and Faber, 1947).

[28] *The Interpretation of the Fourth Gospel* (Cambridge: CUP, 1953).

[29] See prefaces to both editions of his commentary.

[30] In chapter four I have interacted with his proposal.

[31] Within the confines of the 'classical critical' approach, one may distinguish several varying emphases. For example, a diachronic source and redactional-critical approach, or the traditions and religionsgeschichtlich approach. The first one focuses upon the history of the language, or the 'evolution' of the text to reach its final state. The term 'diachronic' owes its conception to Ferdinand de Saussure in *Cours de linguistique génerade* (Paris: Payot, 1916, trans. by W. Baskin, London: Fontana, 1974), 117–40, and refers to linguistic theories which are preoccupied with the history of language. The second approach focuses upon the intellectual milieu or the context of thought out of which the text emerged. See R. Kysar, *The Fourth Evangelist and His Gospel* (Minneapolis: Augsburg, 1975), 102–46. There are two components within the diachronic source and redactional-critical approach: a literary component and a historical one. The literary element became the focus of Bultmann in his commentary where he proposed to restore the Fourth Gospel to its 'original order'. He further proposed three sources behind the Gospel, a 'passion narrative', a 'signs-source', and a 'discourse source'. The 'sign-source' is now widely accepted. R. T. Fortna has combined Bultmann's 'signs-source' with passion narrative to form a pre-existing 'Signs-Gospel'. R. T. Fortna, *The Gospel of Signs: A Reconstruction of the Narrative Source Underlying the Fourth Gospel*, SNTSMS 11 (Cambridge: CUP, 1970); also U. von Wahlde, *The Earliest Version of John's Gospel* (Wilmington: Michael Glazier, 1989). See especially the exhaustive survey of Gilbert van Belle, *The Sign Source in the Fourth Gospel: Historical Survey and Critical Evaluation of the Semeia Hypothesis* (Leuven: Leuven University Press, 1994). But see Barrett's response, *The Gospel According to St. John*, 2nd edn (London: SPCK, 1978), 19; Martin Hengel, 'The Interpretation of the Wine Miracle at Cana: John 2:1–11', in *The Glory of Christ in the New Testament*, ed. by in L. D. Hurst and N. T. Wright (Oxford: OUP, 1987), 90 n. 95; F. Vouga, 'The Johannine School: a Gnostic Tradition in Primitive Christianity?', *Bib* 69 (1988), 381. Also see Robert Alter, *The Art of Biblical Narrative* (London: George Allen and Unwin Pubs., 1981), 19–20. The historical component of the diachronic source and redactional-critical method did not receive adequate attention from Bultmann. It was J. L. Martyn's *History and Theology in the Fourth Gospel* in 1968, revised and enlarged in 1979, and his subsequent articles which focused on the historical element. The three main articles are collected in his *The Gospel of John in Christian History: Essays for Interpreters* (New York: Paulist Press, 1978).

tion a summary of misunderstanding and irony, furnishing a list of terms and metaphors that are believed to be of a polysemantic nature.[32] Raymond Brown, on the other hand, in his extensive two-volume commentary devotes only two brief paragraphs to John's use of 'twofold or double meaning' words and 'misunderstanding'.[33] But he does discuss some of the unique features of John's language in the main body of his commentary. Barnabas Lindars in his commentary devotes two pages to a very general observation of John's language but makes no reference to the problem of ambiguity.[34] Similarly Rudolf Schnackenburg in his multi-volume commentary bypasses any detailed treatment of John's language.[35] The excursus in Ernst Haenchen's commentary covers many details of the vocabulary and grammar of koine Greek, but likewise fails to address Johannine ambiguity.[36]

Most commentaries on the Fourth Gospel discuss its language simply as part of the exegetical analyses. Johannine language rarely has received the treatment which it deserves, even though by all accounts it is of fundamental importance in the interpretation of the Gospel's message and in the accurate formulation of its theology. Among the critical commentaries published since the 1960s, in my assessment, there has been no significant breakthrough or additional insight beyond the works of the past (e.g., Bultmann, Hoskyns, Brown, Barrett) in the treatment of the Gospel of John and its language.

Among the articles and essays, the brief discussion by R. Shedd, entitled 'Multiple Meanings in the Gospel of John',[37] deserves to be noted. Shedd focuses on the multiple meanings embedded in 'the Johannine signs'. George MacRae's 1973 essay, entitled 'Theology and Irony in the Fourth Gospel',[38] looked at Johannine irony in the context of the Evangelist's theology.

J. D. Derrett has made a significant contribution to this topic by his

---

[32] J. C. Fenton, *The Gospel According to John* (Oxford: Clarendon, 1970), 19–22.

[33] Brown, *John*, 1:cxxix–cxxxvi.

[34] Lindars, 'The Language of John', in *The Gospel of John*, 44–6.

[35] R. Schnackenburg, *The Gospel According to St. John*, ET, vol. 1 (New York: Herder and Herder, 1968).

[36] E. Haenchen, 'Die Sprache des JE', *Das Johannesevangelium* (1980), 57–74; ET: 'The Language of the Gospel of John', *A Commentary on the Gospel of John*, trans. and ed. by R. W. Funk, with U. Busse, 2 vols (Philadelphia: Fortress, 1984), 1:52–66.

[37] In *Current Issues in Biblical Interpretation*, ed. by G. F. Hawthorne (Grand Rapids: Eerdmans, 1975), 247–58.

[38] In *The Word in the World*, ed. by R. J. Clifford and G. W. MacRae (Cambridge: Weston, 1973), 83–96.

studious observations of rabbinic and scriptural allusions in John. In a series of articles he has examined potential Old Testament and rabbinic undercurrents in several of the Johannine accounts. Derrett's contributions include 'Fig Trees in the New Testament';[39] 'Fresh Light on the Lost Sheep and the Lost Coin (Jn. 2:13–17)';[40] 'Why and How Jesus Walked on the Sea';[41] 'The Samaritan Woman's Pitcher';[42] 'The Samaritan Woman's Purity';[43] 'Peter's Sword and Biblical Methodology';[44] 'The Bronze Serpent';[45] 'Τί ἐργάζῃ (John 6:30): an Unrecognized Allusion to Isa. 45:9';[46] and 'John 9:6 Read with Isaiah 6:10; 20:9'.[47]

Paul Trudinger is another contributor who in several essays has pointed out the Johannine tendency to say far more than is evident at first sight. Among his contributions are 'Subtle Word-Plays in the Gospel of John and the Problem of Chapter 21';[48] 'The Seven Days of New Creation in St. John's Gospel: Some Further Reflections';[49] and 'An Israelite in Whom There Is No Guile: An Interpretative Note on Jn. 1:45–51'.[50] Similar subtleties have been pointed out in such engaging studies as Bruce H. Grigsby, 'Washing in the Pool of Siloam: Thematic Anticipation of the Johannine Cross (John 9:7)';[51] H. Hollis, 'The Root of a Johannine Pun';[52] Craig R. Koester, 'Messianic Exegesis and the Call of Nathanael (John 1:45–51)';[53] idem, 'The Saviour of the World: Jn. 4:42';[54] Edwin D. Freed, 'Ego Eimi in John 8:24 in Light of Its Context and Jewish Messianic Belief';[55] A. J. Hultgren, 'The Johannine Foot Washing (Jn. 13:1–11) as a

---

[39] *HeyJ* 14 (1973), 249–65.
[40] *NTS* 26 (1979–80), 36–60.
[41] *NovT* 23 (1981), 330–48.
[42] *DRev* 102 (1984), 252–61.
[43] *EvQ* 60 (1988), 291–8.
[44] *BO* 32 (1990), 180–92.
[45] *EstBib* 49 (1991), 311–29.
[46] *ZNW* 84 (1993), 142–4.
[47] *EvQ* 66 (1994), 251–4.
[48] *JRT* 23 (1971), 27–31.
[49] *EvQ* 44 (1972), 154–8.
[50] *EvQ* 54 (1982), 117–20.
[51] *NovT* 27 (1985), 227–35.
[52] *NTS* 35 (1989), 475–8.
[53] *JSNT* 39 (1990), 23-34.
[54] *JBL* 109 (1990), 665–80.
[55] *JTS* n.s. 33 (1982), 163–7.

Symbol of Eschatological Hospitality';[56] and C. H. Cosgrove, 'The Place Where Jesus Is: Allusions to Baptism and the Eucharist in the Fourth Gospel'.[57]

In three important articles, J. H. van Halsema (1983),[58] Earl Richard (1985),[59] and F. Manns (1988)[60] once again documented John's tendency to use double-meaning words and allusive expressions in his Gospel account; they also argued that the topic merits far more attention than it has received. As Richard observes,

Throughout the history of Johannine studies, the fact has been noted repeatedly that John employs numerous ambiguous expressions or terms of double meaning. Nonetheless, this topic has attracted surprisingly little attention, while the function these expressions serve within the Gospel has gone virtually unexplored.[61]

Since the early 1960s with the increased application of literary criticism in biblical studies,[62] literary critics have had a field day in John's

---

[56] *NTS* 28 (1982), 539-46.

[57] *NTS* 35 (1989), 522-39.

[58] 'Het raadsel als litteraire vorm in Marcus en Johannes', *Gereformeerd theologisch tijdschrift* 83 (1983), 1-17.

[59] 'Expressions of Double Meaning and their Function in the Gospel of John', *NTS* 31 (1985), 96-112.

[60] 'Les mots à double entente. Antécédents et fonction hermeneutique d'un procédé johannique', *Studii Biblici Franciscani Liber Annuus* 38 (1988), 39-57.

[61] Richard, 'Expressions of Double Meaning', 96.

[62] A vast body of literature has been generated in this area since early 1970s, so much so that there are now indexes just on the literature produced in this field. See for example David Norton, *A History of the Bible as Literature*, 2 vols (Cambridge: CUP, 1993); Mark Minor, *Literary-Critical Approaches to the Bible: An Annotated Bibliography* (West Cornwall, CT: Locust Hill Press, 1992); Duane F. Watson and Alan J. Hauser, *Rhetorical Criticism of the Bible: A Comprehensive Bibliography with Notes on History and Method* (Leiden: Brill, 1993). See also Ernest Findlay Scott, *The Literature of the New Testament* (Norman, OK: University of Oklahoma Press, 1972); Thomas Rice Henn, *The Bible as Literature* (London: Lutterworth, 1970); J. Muilenburg, 'Form Criticism and Beyond', *JBL* 88 (1969), 1-18; Stephen A. Geller, 'Through Windows and Mirrors into the Bible: History, Literature, and Language in the Study of the Text', in *A Sense of Text: The Art of Language in the Study of Biblical Literature* (Winona Lake, IN: Eisenbrauns, 1983), 3-40. Some have seen this as the most significant shift of direction in biblical studies. Edgar Krentz, *The Historical-Critical Method*, GBS (Philadelphia: Fortress, 1975); Mark Allan Powell, *What Is Narrative Criticism?* (Minneapolis: Fortress, 1990); Frank Kermode, 'St. John as Poet', *JSNT* 28 (1986), 4. See John Ashton's evaluations in *Understanding the Fourth Gospel* (Oxford: Clarendon, 1991), 114; idem, *The Interpretation of John* (Philadelphia: Fortress, 1986), 14-16. The contemporary New Testament scholarly interest in literary criticism may be traced to Amos Niven Wilder and his book, *Early Christian Rhetoric: The Language of the Gospel* (Cambridge, MA: Harvard University Press, 1964); William A. Beardslee, *Literary Criticism of the New Testament*, GBS (Philadelphia: Fortress, 1969); cf. William E. McDonald, 'The Literary Criticism of Amos Wilder', *Soundings* 52 (1969), 99; M. Weiss, *The Bible from Within: The Method of Total Interpretation* (Jerusalem: Magnes, 1984), 1-46; William A. Beardslee, 'Amos Niven Wilder: Poet and Scholar', *Semeia* 12 (1978), 8-9. The literary interest in the Bible is evident even

Gospel.[63] This approach is seen by some biblical scholars as the 'cutting edge' in Johannine research.[64] Research into the fabric of John's language and various elements of its literary composition has produced hundreds of essays, articles, and books, including works such as R. Allan Culpepper's *Anatomy of the Fourth Gospel*.[65] Culpepper is often credited with the first in-depth literary criticism of John, when in fact it was D. W. Wead who paved the way almost twenty years earlier in his doctoral thesis supervised by Oscar Cullmann, *The Literary Devices in John's Gospel*.[66]

One result of such intense interest in the literary criticism of this Gospel has been a greater awareness of the intricacies of its language in such features as the author's use of irony,[67] symbolism and metaphor,[68]

---

further back in history. See Richard G. Moulton, *The Literary Study of the Bible*, rev. edn (Boston: D. C. Heath, 1899); Lyman Abbott, et al., eds, *The Bible as Literature* (New York: Thomas Y. Crowell, 1896).

[63] E.g., R. Alan Culpepper, *Anatomy of the Fourth Gospel: A Study in Literary Design* (Philadelphia: Fortress, 1983); Kermode, 'John', 440–66; S. Van Tilborg, 'The Gospel of John: Communicative Processes in a Narrative Text', *Neot* 23 (1989), 19–43; Amos Wilder, *Early Christian Rhetoric: The Language of the Gospel* (New London: SCM, 1964), 32–3; Charles H. Giblin, 'The Tripartite Narrative Structure of John's Gospel', *Bib* 71 (1990), 449–68; Jeffrey L. Staley, *Reading with a Passion: Rhetoric, Autobiography and the American West in the Gospel of John* (New York: Continuum, 1995); J. Edgar Bruns, *The Art and Thought of John* (New York: Herder and Herder, 1969); and George Mlakuzhyil, *The Christocentric Literary Structure of the Fourth Gospel* (Rome: Editrice Pontificio Instituto Biblico, 1987); M. J. J. Menken, *Numerical Literary Techniques in John* (Leiden: Brill, 1985); G. R. O'Day, 'Toward a Narrative-Critical Study of John', *Int* 49 (1995), 341–6; J. A. Du Rand, 'Repetitions and variations: experiencing the power of the Gospel of John as literary symphony', *Neot* 30 (1997), 59–70.

[64] Ashton, *Understanding*, 113–14; Carson, *Gospel According to John*, 38. Cf. J. D. Crossan, '"Ruth Amid the Alien Corn": Perspectives and Methods in Contemporary Biblical Criticism', in *Biblical Mosaic*, ed. by R. Polzin and E. Rothman (Philadelphia: Fortress, 1982), 199.

[65] (Philadelphia: Fortress, 1983). Mark W. G. Stibbe, *John as Storyteller*, SNTSMS 73 (Cambridge: CUP, 1992), is a further development of Culpepper's *Anatomy of the Fourth Gospel*.

[66] Basel: Friedreich Rinehardt, 1970; cf. also Wead, 'The Johannine Double Meaning', *RQ* 13 (1970), 106–20.

[67] Some representative studies in this area are H. Clavier, 'L'ironie dans le quatrième Evangile', *SE* 1 = TU 73 (1959), 261–76; David W. Wead, 'Johannine Irony as a Key to the Author-Audience Relationship in John's Gospel', in *Biblical Literature, 1974 Proceedings: Preprinted Papers for the Section on Biblical Literature, American Academy of Religion, Annual Meeting, 1974*, ed. by the American Academy of Religion, compiled by Fred O. Francis (Missoula, MT: Scholars Press; Tallahassee: The Academy, 1974), 33–50; Paul D. Duke, *Irony in the Fourth Gospel* (Atlanta: John Knox Press, 1985); Severino Pancaro, 'People of God in St. John's Gospel', *NTS* 16 (1969), 114–29; J. E. Botha, 'The Case of Johannine Irony Reopened: I and II', *Neot* 25 (1991–92), 209–20, 221–32; D. Myers, 'Irony and Humor in the Gospel of John', *OPTAT* 2 (1988), 1–13; O'Day, *Revelation in the Fourth Gospel* (Philadelphia: Fortress, 1986); George Johnston, 'Ecce Homo! Irony in the Christology of the Fourth Evangelist', in *The Glory of Christ in the New Testament*, ed. by L. D. Hurst and N. T. Wright (Oxford: Clarendon, 1987), 125–38.

poetry,[69] dramatic style,[70] dualistic expressions,[71] characterisation,[72] and many other literary features.[73] While these studies have brought about a

---

[68] F. F. Ramos, 'Simbolismo del Templo en el Cuarto Evangelio', *Studium Legionense* 4 (1963), 11–99; idem, 'Simbolismo en el Cuarto Evangelio' *Studium Legionense* 3 (1962), 41–114 and 5 (1964), 77–144 (extracts of his dissertation at Pont. Univ. Ecclesiastica Salamanca); Sandra M. Schneiders, 'Symbolism and the Sacramental Principle in the Fourth Gospel', in *Segrie Sacramenti nel Vangelo di Giovanni*, Studia Anselmiana 66, ed. by Pius-Ramon Tragan (Rome: Editrice Anselmiana, 1977), 221–35; idem, 'History and Symbolism in the Fourth Gospel', in *L'Évangile de Jean*, ed. by M. de Jonge (1977), 371–76; W. Drum, 'Dr. Calmes and the Allegorical Interpretation of John', *HPR* 22 (1921–22), 18–24; idem, 'The Symbolism of the Fourth Gospel', *HPR* 22 (1921–22), 162–9; Xavier Leon-DuFour, 'Towards a Symbolic Reading of the Fourth Gospel', *NTS* 27 (1981), 439–56; Paul Diel, Symbolism in the Gospel of John, trans. by Nelly Marans (San Francisco: Harper and Row, 1988); J. Bryan Born, 'Literary Features in the Gospel of John', *Direction* 17 (1988), 3–17; Thomas Soeding, 'Wiedergeburt aus Wasser und Geist: Anmerkungen zur Symbolsprache des Johannesevangeliums am Beispiel des Nikodemusgesprächs (John 3:1–21)', in *Metaphorik und Mythos im Neuen Testament*, ed. by Karl Kertelge, QD 126 (Freiburg: Herder, 1990), 168–219.

[69] Frank Kermode, 'John'; idem, 'The Uses of Error', *Theology* 89 (1986), 425–31; H. Vedder, *Johannine Writings*, 67. See further James Drummond, *Johannine Thoughts* (London: Lindsey Press, 1909); W. Schmidt, *Der strophische Aufbau des Gesamttextes der vier Evangelien* (Sonderabdruck aus: Anzeiger d. phil.-hist. Kl. d. Ak. d. Wiss. in Wien 1921, Nr. IX); Stanley Fish, 'How to Recognize a Poem When You See One', in idem, *Is There a Text in This Class? The Authority of Interpretative Communities* (Cambridge, MA: Harvard University Press, 1980).

[70] A. Jülicher, *An Introduction to the New Testament* (New York: Putnam's Sons, 1904), 389; R. H. Strachan, *The Fourth Evangelist* (New York: Doran, 1925), 14–31; Clayton R. Bowen 'The Fourth Gospel as Dramatic Material', *JBL* 49 (1930), 292–305; J. Muilenburg, 'Literary Form in the Fourth Gospel', *JBL* 51(1932), 40–42; C. M. Connick, 'The Dramatic Character of the Fourth Gospel', *JBL* 67 (1948), 159–69; F. R. M. Hitchcock, 'The Dramatic Development of the Fourth Gospel', *Exp* 7th series 4 (1907), 266–79; idem, 'Is the Fourth Gospel a Drama?', *Theology* 7 (1923), 307–17; E. L. Pierce, 'The Fourth Gospel as Drama', *Religion in Life* 29 (1960), 453–55; C. H. Talbert, 'Artists and Theology: An Analysis of the Architecture of Jn 1.19–5.47', *CBQ* 32 (1970), 341–66; N. Flanagan, 'The Gospel of John as Drama', *BT* 19 (1981), 264–70; W. R. Domeris, 'The Johannine Drama', *Journal of Theology for Southern Africa* 42 (1983), 29–35.

[71] The literature on Johannine dualism is considerable. Among these see, for example, O. Böcher, *Der johanneische Dualismus im Zusammenhang des nachbiblischen Judentums* (Gütersloh: Mohn, 1965, diss., Mainz); Otto Schwankl, 'Die Metaphorik von Licht und Finsternis im johanneischen Schrifttum', in *Metaphorik und Mythos im Neuen Testament*, ed. by Karl Kertelge, QD 126 (Freiburg: Herder, 1990), 135–67; J. Becker, 'Beobachtungen zum Dualismus im Johannesevangelium', *ZNW* 65 (1974), 71–87; C. K. Barrett, 'Paradox and Dualism', in *Essays on John* (London: SPCK, 1982), 98–115; Kysar, 'The Johannine Dualism', in *The Fourth Evangelist*, 215–21.

[72] Culpepper, *Anatomy*, 101–48; Ashton, *Understanding*, 194; 470–76; George W. Buchanan, *Typology and the Gospel* (Lanham, MD: Univ. Press of America, 1987); William H. Marty, 'The New Moses' (Th.D. diss., Dallas Seminary, 1984), 142–43; W. Meeks, *The Prophet-King: Moses Traditions and the Johannine Christology*, SNT 14 (Leiden: Brill, 1967), 29–31; Raymond F. Collins, 'Representative Figures of the Fourth Gospel', *DRev* 94 (1976), 26–46, 118–32; idem, *These Things Have Been Written: Studies on the Fourth Gospel* (Grand Rapids: Eerdmans, 1990), 8–45; J. S. Billings, 'Judas Iscariot in the Fourth Gospel', *ExpTim* 51 (1939), 40; Trudinger, 'An Israelite in Whom There is No Guile', 117–20.

[73] Jeffrey Lloyd Staley, *The Print's First Kiss: A Rhetorical Investigation of the Implied Reader in the Fourth Gospel*, SBLDS 82 (Atlanta, GA: Scholars Press, 1988); S. C. Chang, 'Repetitions

greater appreciation of the literary intricacies of the language of the Fourth Gospel, they have stopped short of taking the needed step of connecting John's language to its theological message.[74] Perhaps the most significant contribution of literary critics to the Scriptures in general and to the Fourth Gospel in particular has been to revive the focus upon the text as a text on its own terms before it is treated as evidence for something else.[75]

Nevertheless, amid this enthusiasm, there have been significant scholarly reservations.[76] A purely literary approach to the Bible is seen as a regression into the pre-critical era.[77] Extreme spin-offs of literary studies,

---

and Variations in the Gospel of John' (Ph.D. diss., Strasbourg, 1975); John O'Rourke, 'Asides in the Gospel of John', *NovT* 21 (1979), 210–19; U. C. von Wahlde, 'A Redactional Technique in the Fourth Gospel', *CBQ* 38 (1976), 520–33; D. W. Deakle, 'A Study of Literary Pairs in the Fourth Gospel' (Ph.D. diss., New Orleans Baptist Theological Seminary, 1985); Peter Cahill, 'The Johannine Logos as Center', *CBQ* 38 (1976), 54–72; Hendrikus Boers, 'Discourse Structure and Macro-Structure in the Interpretation of Texts: Jn. 4:1–42 as an Example', in *Society of Biblical Literature 1980 Seminar Papers*, ed. by Paul J. Achtemeier (Chico, CA: Scholars Press, 1980), 159–82.

[74] This has been an important concern for James Barr. See Barr, 'The Bible as Literature', in idem, *The Bible in the Modern World* (London: SCM; New York: Harper and Row, 1973), 53–74; idem, 'Reading the Bible as Literature', *BJRL* 56 (1973), 10–33. See also E. D. Hirsch, *Validity in Interpretation* (New Haven, CT: Yale University Press, 1967), 112–3; René Wellek and Austin Warren, *Theory of Literature*, 3rd edn (New York: Penguin, 1980 [1st edn, 1948]); C. H. Talbert, 'Artistry and Theology: An Analysis of the Architecture of John 1:19–5:47', *CBQ* 32 (1970), 341–66; Stephen A. Geller, 'Through Windows and Mirrors into the Bible: History, Literature, and Language in the Study of the Text', in *A Sense of Text: The Art of Language in the Study of Biblical Literature* (Winona Lake, IN: Eisenbrauns, 1983), 3–40.

[75] See Culpepper, *Anatomy*, 5; Northrop Frye, *The Great Code: The Bible and Literature* (New York: Harcourt, Jovanovich, 1982), xiii; Hans W. Frei, *The Eclipse of Biblical Narrative: A study in eighteenth and nineteenth century hermeneutics* (New Haven: Yale University Press 1974); Mark Allan Powell, 'The Bible and Modern Literary Criticism', in *Summary of Proceedings: Annual Conference – American Theological Library Association* 43 (1989), 78–84; idem, *What is Narrative Criticism?*, 2; Arthur Quinn, 'Rhetoric and the Integrity of Scripture', *Communio* 13 (1986), 326–41; Norman Petersen, *Literary Criticism for New Testament Critics* (Philadelphia: Fortress, 1978), 20.

[76] See John Ashton's assessment of it in his book, *Studying John: Approaches to the Fourth Gospel* (Oxford: Clarendon, 1994), 141–65.

[77] K. Stendahl, 'The Bible as a Classic and the Bible as Holy Scripture', *JBL* 103 (1984), 6; C. S. Lewis, *Reflections on the Psalms* (Glasgow: Collins, 1961), 10; J. G. Herder, quoted in F. Kermode, *The Genesis of Secrecy* (Cambridge, MA: Harvard University Press, 1979), 120; T. S. Eliot, *Essays, Ancient and Modern* (London, n. pub., 1936), 95; Geller, 'Through Windows and Mirrors', 3–40; Barr, 'Reading the Bible as Literature' and 'The Bible as Literature'; Harold Bloom, 'Literature as the Bible', *New York Reviews of Books* 35 (1988), 23–5; Walter Reed, 'A Poetics of the Bible: Problems and Possibilities', *Literature and Theology* 1 (1987), 154–66; Mieke Bal, 'The Bible as Literature: A Critical Escape', *Diacritics* 16 (1976), 71–9; Stanley E. Porter, 'Can Traditional Exegesis Enlighten Literary Analysis of The Fourth Gospel? An Examination of the Old Testament Fulfilment Motif and the Passover Theme', in *The Gospels and the Scriptures of Israel*, ed. by Craig A. Evans and W. Richard Stegner, JSNTSup 104 (Sheffield:

such as deconstruction and reader-response criticism,[78] have only reinforced this scepticism.

The feverish fascination of literary critics with the Fourth Gospel has caught the attention of the sociologists, who since the early 1970s have also found in John's Gospel an ideal testing ground for their theories.[79] These studies have focused not so much on the text as on speculations concerning the function of the text in its social setting.

The study most often cited is Wayne Meeks's celebrated article 'The

---

Sheffield Academic Press, 1994), 421-27; Tremper Longman III, 'The Literary Approach to the Study of the Old Testament: Pitfalls and Promise', *JETS* 28 (1985), 385-98.

[78] Exemplified by those such as Jacques Derrida, 'Living On/Border Lines', in *Deconstruction and Criticism*, ed. by H. Bloom, et al. (New York: Seabury, 1979), 75–176; idem, *Dissemination*, trans. by B. Johnson (Chicago: University of Chicago, 1981 [Fr. 1972]); Wolfgang Iser, 'The Reading Process: A Phenomenological Approach', in *Reader Response Criticism*, ed. by J. Tompkins (Baltimore: John Hopkins Univ. Press, 1980); idem, *The Act of Reading: A Theory of Aesthetic Response* (Baltimore: John Hopkins Univ. Press, 1978); J. Kristeva, *Desire in Language*; Danna Nolan Fewell, 'Glossary', in idem, ed., *Reading Between Texts: Intertextuality and the Hebrew Bible* (Louisville, KY: Westminster/John Knox Press, 1992), 22–4; Elizabeth Freund, *The Return of the Reader: Reader-Response Criticism* (New York: Methuen, 1987); Edgar McKnight, *Postmodern Use of the Bible: The Emergence of Reader-Oriented Criticism* (Nashville: Abingdon, 1988); Jane Tomkins, ed., *Reader-Response Criticism: From Formalism to Post-Structuralism* (Baltimore: John Hopkins University Press, 1980); Thaïs E. Morgan, 'Is There an Intertext in This Text? Literary and Interdisciplinary Approaches to Intertextuality', *American Journal of Semiotics* 34 (1985), 1–40.

[79] A small sample of such sociological interest in New Testament studies in general and the Fourth Gospel in particular may include J. Louis Martyn's *History and Theology in the Fourth Gospel* (Nashville: Abingdon, 1968; rev. and enl. 1979), idem, *The Gospel of John in Christian History: Essays for Interpreters* (New York: Paulist Press, 1978); Oscar Cullmann, *The Johannine Circle*, trans. by John Bowden (Philadelphia: Westminster Press, 1976); Raymond E. Brown, *The Community of the Beloved Disciple: The Life, Loves, and Hates of an Individual Church in New Testament Times* (New York: Paulist, 1979); D. Moody Smith, *Johannine Christianity: Essays on its Setting, Sources, and Theology* (Columbia, SC: University of South Carolina Press, 1984); Howard Clark Kee, *Christian Origins in Sociological Perspective* (Philadelphia: Westminster Press, 1980); B. Wilson, *Religion in Sociological Perspective* (Oxford: OUP, 1982); Kenelm O. L. Burridge, *New Heaven, New Earth: A Study of Millenarian Activities* (Oxford: OUP, 1969); John G. Gager, *Kingdom and Community: The Social World of Early Christianity* (Englewood Cliffs, NJ: Prentice Hall, 1975); John H. Elliott, *A Home for the Homeless* (Philadelphia: Fortress, 1975); idem, 'Social-Scientific Criticism of the New Testament: More on Methods and Models', *Semeia* 35 (1986), 1–33; Bengt Holmberg, *Paul and Power: The Structure of Authority in the Primitive Church as Reflected in the Pauline Epistles* (Philadelphia: Fortress, 1980); Edwin A. Judge, *Rank and Status in the World of the Caesars and St. Paul*, University of Canterbury Publication 29 (Canterbury: University of Canterbury, 1984); idem, *The Social Pattern of the Christian Groups in the First Century* (London: Tyndale Press, 1960); Ronald F. Hock, *The Social Context of Paul's Ministry: Tent-Making and Apostleship* (Philadelphia: Fortress, 1980); Christopher Rowland, 'Reading the New Testament Sociologically: An Introduction', *Theology* 88 (1985), 358–64; Thomas F. Best, 'The Sociological Study of New Testament: Promise and Peril of a New Discipline', *SJT* 36 (1983), 181–94; J. H. Neyrey, 'The Trials (Forensic) and Tribulations (Honor Challenges) of Jesus: John 7 in Social Science Perspective', *BTB* 26 (1996), 107-24.

Man From Heaven in Johannine Sectarianism' (1972). He is credited as the first scholar consciously to seek to apply insights from sociology to the study of the Fourth Gospel. Building upon the work of J. Louis Martyn and the sociologists Peter Berger and Thomas Luckmann, Meeks explored the role which the 'ascent-descent' language of John might have played for a community experiencing alienation and hostility. He concluded that the language of the Fourth Gospel reflected the sectarian tendencies in the Johannine community.

However, Herbert Leroy had already reached the same conclusion as Meeks in his thesis *Rätsel und Missverständnis* (1968), and indeed Meeks acknowledges his agreement with Leroy. Leroy, too, had argued that John's language had a social function, tending to reinforce the distinction between 'insiders' and 'outsiders'. Whereas in the past the distinction was usually made only between different levels of meaning in John's language, such as literal and spiritual, Leroy and Meeks placed the question of meaning in a social context in order to interpret opposing linguistic usage.

Others who have built on Leroy and Meeks's sociological hypotheses have reinforced this sectarian interpretation of the setting of the Gospel. Bruce Malina, for example, goes so far as to characterise John's language as 'anti-language'.[80] In his somewhat limited study, Malina introduces the categories of anti-languages and anti-societies developed by the socio-linguist M. A. K. Halliday[81] and relates them to the work of anthropologist Mary Douglas.[82] Norman Petersen follows the same line of reasoning. His brief book *The Gospel of John and the Sociology of Light: Language and Characterization in the Fourth Gospel* (1993) describes John's language as a 'private language'.

Jerome Neyrey in *An Ideology of Revolt: John's Christology in Social Scientific Perspective* (1988) moves from the category of anti-language to that of socio-linguistics. He uses concepts such as confession, dualism, and dichotomy to analyse his linguistic observations. Other important contributions to the sociological study of John's Gospel include Bruce D. Woll, *Johannine Christianity in Conflict: Authority, Rank, and Succession in the First Farewell Discourse*;[83] Takashi Onuki, *Gemeinde und Welt im Johannesevangelium: Ein Beitrag zur Frage nach der theologischen und*

---

[80] 'Gospel of John in Sociolinguistic Perspective', 1–23.

[81] *Language as Social Semiotic: The Social Interpretation of Language and Meaning* (London: Edward Arnold, 1978).

[82] *Natural Symbols: Explorations in Cosmology* (New York: Vintage, 1973).

[83] SBLDS 60 (Chico, CA: Scholars Press, 1989).

pragmatischen Funktion des johanneischen 'Dualismus';[84] David Rensberger, *Overcoming the World: Politics and Community in the Gospel of John*;[85] and Walter Rebell, *Gemeinde als Gegenwelt: Zur soziologischen und didaktischen Funktion des Johannesevangeliums*.[86] All these studies are united in the conclusion that the enigmatic language of the Fourth Gospel reflects the reaction of a sectarian community experiencing alienation and hostility within its social context. Such studies are discussed in greater detail in chapter four.

1.2.2. Justification for the Present Study

In spite of such varied and intense interest in the Fourth Gospel and its perplexing language, when one surveys the massive corpus of secondary literature generated around this Gospel[87] one is hard pressed to find either a satisfactory explanation for the enigmatic quality of its language, or even an examination which takes into account all the varied aspects of this unique language feature. Birger Olsson's lament is as fitting today as it was twenty-five years ago:

---

[84] WMANT 56 (Neukirchen-Vluyn: Neukirchener Verlag, 1984).

[85] (London: SPCK, 1989).

[86] BBET 20 (Frankfurt: Lang, 1987).

[87] The following indexes and surveys are good indications of the size of the secondary literature generated around the Fourth Gospel: W. E. Mills, *The Gospel of John*, Bibliographies for Biblical Research, New Testament Series 4 (Lewiston, NY; Lampeter, UK: Mellen Biblical Press, 1995); W. Nicole, 'The History of Johannine Research During the Past Century', *Neot* 8 (1972), 7–16; J. Zumstein, 'Chronique Johannique, *ETR* 59 (1984), 547–56; J. Becker, 'Aus der Literatur zum Johannesevangelium (1978-1980)', *TRu* 47 (1982), 279–301, 305–47; E. Malatesta, *St. John's Gospel 1920–65* (Rome: Pontifical Biblical Institute, 1967); Gilbert van Belle, *Johannine Bibliography 1966–1985* (Leuven: Leuven University Press, 1988); E. Haenchen, 'Aus der Literatur zum johannesevangelium 1929-56', *TRu* 23 (1955), 295–335; R. Kysar, 'Community and Gospel: Vectors in Fourth Gospel Criticism', *Int* 31 (1977), 355–66; idem, 'The Gospel of John in Current Research', *RelSRev* 9 (1983), 314–23; idem, 'The Fourth Gospel: A Report on Recent Research', *ANRW* II.25.3 (1985), 2389–480; idem, *Fourth Evangelist*; B. Vawter, 'Some Recent Developments in Johannine Theology', *BTB* 1 (1971), 30–58; B. M. Metzger, *Index to the Periodical Literature on Christ and the Gospels* (Leiden: Brill, 1966); H. Thyen, 'Aus der Literatur zum Johannesevangelium', *TRu* 39 (1975), 22–52, 269–330; idem, 'Aus der Literatur zum Johannesevangelium', *TRu* 42 (1977), 211–70; 'Aus der Literatur zum Johannesevangelium', *TRu* 43 (1978), 325–59; 'Aus der Literatur zum Johannesevangelium', *TRu* 44 (1979), 97–134; S. S. Smalley, 'Keeping up with Recent Studies: St. John's Gospel', *ExpTim* 97 (1986), 4, 102–8; C. H. H. Scobie, 'New Directions in the Study of the Fourth Gospel', *Studies in Religion* 6 (1977), 185–93; R. Schnackenburg, 'Zur johanneischen Forschung', *BZ* 18 (1974), 272–78; idem, 'Entwicklung und Stand der johanneischen Forschung Seit 1955', in *L'Évangile de Jean*, ed. by M. de Jonge (1977), 19–44. The above list is not comprehensive, but the limited space does not permit me to cite other collections.

Chapter 1: Introduction

The linguistic problems occupy little space in modern Johannine research which is dominated by source criticism and *Religionsgeschichte*. The perspective is almost invariably comparative and historico-genetic. To arrive at analyses of Johannine language and style one must, if one ignores the commentaries, go back to works published at the turn of the century and decades immediately thereafter.[88]

Those investigations (including the commentaries) that have undertaken to study John's language have often overlooked its intricate, web-like compositional structure. They isolate one element or another, such as irony, metaphor, or double-meaning words, without recognising the relationship among these features, which form a compound literary structure and which therefore work together to produce the phenomenon of ambiguity in John. Inquiries into the function of enigmatic expressions in the Fourth Gospel have often been confined to the problem of 'misunderstandings'. And yet the problem is more complex and far more extensive than incidents of misunderstanding. Some scholars have attributed this stylistic feature to the 'symbolic world' of John without any clear articulation of what such a symbolic world represents. Others have thought that behind John's enigmatic expressions may lie the hypothetical original Aramaic words of Jesus. However, this proposal has never achieved consensus and remains inconclusive. John's language lies far beyond such explanations.

Over the past thirty years, as noted above, sociological studies focusing on the Fourth Gospel have explained its ambiguity in terms of an assumed social setting in which a hypothetical (i.e., Johannine) community experienced rejection and isolation. These studies see the peculiar enigmatic language of the Gospel as a reflection of a coded language of a sectarian community experiencing alienation and hostility within its social context. However, in this study, I question the accuracy of these reconstructions and characterisations. I argue that the language of the Fourth Gospel does not reflect the language of a sect; the Johannine community, if such a community ever existed as a discreet social entity, was no more sectarian than any other segment of the early church. I find the sociological solutions to be very much divorced from the reality we encounter in the Gospel and out of harmony with its theology. It is in the context of this theology that I propose to set forth an explanation for John's perplexing language.

---

[88] Birger Olsson, *Structure and Meaning in the Fourth Gospel*, trans. by Jean Gray (Lund, Sweden: CWK Gleerup, 1974), 3.

1.3. Thesis and Aims

This study examines the phenomenon of ambiguity in the language of the Fourth Gospel and endeavours to explain this feature in the context of John's theology. The language of the Fourth Gospel is a theological language. Its function is a theological function and its significance is a theological significance. Indeed, I hope by the end of this study to have shown that Johannine theology cannot be fully appreciated apart from proper attention to the intricacies of its language.[89] Therefore the central concern of this study is to understand John's language in the context of its theology and vice versa. I shall argue that the primary purpose and function of John's language and its peculiar enigmatic character is directly linked to the Evangelist's theology, a theology which is firmly grounded in Israel's Scriptures.

In order to accomplish these aims, the first segment of the book (chapters 2–3) defines ambiguity in John's language and delineates its complex literary fabric. The enigmatic quality of John's language at a compositional level relates to the author's deliberate use of linguistic and literary features which often consciously echo and allude to the Scriptures of Israel in whose pages the Evangelist sees the revelation of Jesus as the Messiah of the Jews, the Saviour of the World. These features are woven together in a literary fabric which is the Gospel text; and this text communicates at several levels which in turn gives the document its enigmatic and allusive quality. To understand the dynamics of John's language better, it is necessary to establish the probable literary and conceptual context out of which the text emerged. I suggest that this was an environment in which the Hebrew Scriptures and the traditions surrounding them were the dominant ideological forces in the lives of both the Jews and the Christians.

In the second and more important segment of the thesis, comprising chapters four through six, the objective is to set forth an alternative hypothesis for the function and significance of John's language. Here the theological assumptions behind John's language will be discussed. Many of the examples which are provided to explain John's theological thinking will themselves constitute further examples of the phenomenon I have called 'ambiguity' or the 'enigmatic' character of John's language, even though neither of these rubrics really captures the real essence of what the

---

[89] Cf. H. A. Lombard, 'Prolegomena to a Johannine Theology: Sources, Method and Status of a Narratological Model', *Neot* 29 (1995), 253–72; Gail O'Day, *Revelation in the Fourth Gospel* (Philadelphia: Fortress, 1986), 47.

reader encounters in the Fourth Gospel. In place of the various sociological hypotheses, I try to explain this phenomenon within the context of the Evangelist's reasons for writing the Gospel and to show that this feature is related to his belief that the Scriptures are fulfilled in the life and work(s) of Jesus. I propose that the essential function of John's language is wedded to his purpose: a steadfast focus upon setting forth that Jesus is the Christ according to the witness of Israel's Scriptures. For the author of the Fourth Gospel, above all else, Jesus is the Christ because the Scriptures anticipate him, speak of him, witness to him, and find their supreme realisation in him. It is here, in these conscious echoes and thematic allusions to the Old Testament, that we find the answer to the function of John's elusive language: Jesus is the Christ, the embodiment of the self-revelation of God. However, for John, this truth lies beyond the capacity of unaided men and women to comprehend. This is not to say that the Johannine Jesus or the Evangelist intends to conceal the revelation by this elusive language. Rather, the significance of this feature is to accentuate that ultimately the perception of the revelation of God in Jesus Christ and the recognition of the fulfilment of the Scriptures in him is open only to those who are born 'not of blood nor of the will of the flesh nor of the will of man, but of God.' In Christianity according to John, as elsewhere in the New Testament, spiritual perception ultimately rests on spiritual regeneration, leading to an abiding faith through the work of the Holy Spirit.

1.4. The Question of Method

The question of method has played a very significant role in Johannine studies, especially in so far as the language of the Gospel is concerned. The Fourth Gospel in many respects has been a testing ground for methods.[90] In my own study, I express doubt about some of these methods (see chapter four). I examine the topic under consideration by means of a more

---

[90] Jürgen Becker, 'Das Johannesevangelium im Streit der Methoden 1980–1984', *TRu* 51 (1986), 1–78, reviewing the literature on the Fourth Gospel published between 1980 and 1984, employed the now often quoted phrase 'Streit der Methoden' to summarise the period, and proceeded to delineate no fewer than twelve 'Ansätze' in Johannine studies, many of which were distinguishable at the point of method. These 'Ansätze' are not mutually exclusive. Insights drawn from several of these may be employed in the course of a single study. Cf. S. Schulz, *Untersuchungen zur Menschensohn-Christologie im Johannesevangelium. Zugleich ein Beitrag zur Methodengeschichte der Auslegung des 4. Evangeliums* (Göttingen: Vandenhoeck & Ruprecht, 1957); S. Motyer, 'Method in Fourth Gospel Studies: A Way Out of the Impasse?', *JSNT* 66 (1997), 27–44.

traditional approach to the study of the Scriptures. I characterise this approach as the exegetical and theological method so nobly set forth by Sir Edwyn Hoskyns in his commentary *The Fourth Gospel* (1947). My method is exegetical in so far as my concern is the text of the Gospel and the explanation of its meaning in the context of my inquiry. My focus is theological in so far as the parameters of the study are defined theologically. This is not to say that I find other approaches to the study of John's Gospel to be without merit. However, it seems to me that much of the Bible was written (and here I have in view the Fourth Gospel in particular) out of deep spiritual and theological concerns, both for the Church in the case of the New Testament writings, and for the ancient people of God (Israel) in the case of the Old Testament. These texts were written to say something about God, something about humans and their relation to their creator and, with these in the background, something about the way humans ought to relate to each other. The fundamental moving dynamic and impetus behind these writings were theological, spiritual, and moral concerns. The Fourth Evangelist is clear about his reasons: 'these have been written that you may believe that Jesus is the Christ, the Son of God, and that believing you may have life in his name' (Jn. 20:31). It is in the light of this theological conviction that the document was originally penned, and it is in the light of this same theological conviction that the Fourth Gospel in general and its unique language in particular needs to be understood. I am profoundly doubtful that any model which loses sight of these spiritual and theological dynamics within the sacred Scriptures can do justice to these texts or avoid arriving at erroneous conclusions.

Several presuppositions undergird my thinking and my approach to the Fourth Gospel. These include first the need to locate John's Gospel properly within the *history of ideas*.[91] I believe the Fourth Gospel belongs to a context of thought deeply entrenched in the Old Testament world of ideas. This 'world' was dominated conceptually by the Hebrew Scripture and the traditions built around its interpretation. I shall endeavour to validate this claim throughout the study.

My second assumption is this: the Fourth Gospel is unique in relation to the Synoptics in that it is independent of them in its language.[92] To

---

[91] See the discussion in Kysar, *Fourth Evangelist*, 102–46.

[92] Through the first half of the twentieth century, it was generally assumed that John had used Mark and perhaps even Luke as source material for his work. See Howard, *The Fourth Gospel in Recent Criticism*, rev. by Barrett (1955), 130–31. In 1938 Percy Gardner-Smith in his study, *Saint John and the Synoptic Gospels* (Cambridge: CUP, 1938), challenged that consensus and argued that the Fourth Evangelist wrote completely independently of the Synoptic Gospels. Thirty

arrive at its meaning, as Bultmann correctly argued, there is little point in adducing a Synoptic or Pauline analogue for this or that expression. John's language should be reckoned with on its own terms as a unified and individual whole; and it is within this whole that each individual word finds its meaning.[93] This does not mean that the Synoptic accounts or Pauline epistles are irrelevant to John. On the contrary, they share much in common in their theological perspective. However, the Gospel of John in its theological formulation, articulation, and vocabulary must be examined on its own terms.

Thirdly, whatever the sources and the alleged layers of redaction, the Fourth Gospel as we have it in the canon is the work of one hand. This

---

years later, C. H. Dodd in *Historical Tradition in the Fourth Gospel* (Cambridge: CUP, 1963), affirmed that view and argued that the material in John belonged to its own tradition and was not dependent on the Synoptics. But, once again in recent years, some scholars have resurrected this topic and have argued that John is dependent on Mark and the Synoptic tradition even though their evidence and their arguments remain unpersuasive. In support of such alleged dependence see, for example, F. Neirynck, 'De Semeia-bron in het vierde evangelie: Kritiek van een hypothese', ET: 'The Signs Source in the Fourth Gospel: A Critique of the Hypothesis', *Evangelica* 2 (1991), 651–79, who rejects sign source in the interest of defending John's dependence upon the Synoptics. Other influential studies in support of John's dependence upon the Synoptics include F. Neirynck, 'John and the Synoptics', in *L'Évangile de Jean*, ed. by M. de Jonge (1977), 73–106; M. de Solages, *Jean et les synoptiques* (Leiden: Brill, 1979). Cf. the essays on John in vol. 3 of *The Four Gospels 1992: Festschrift Frans Neirynck*, ed. by F. van Segbroeck, C. M. Tuckett, et al., BETL 100, 3 vols (Leuven: Leuven University Press, 1992). Essays in this collection include D. M. Smith, 'John and the Synoptics: And the Question of Gospel Genre', 1783–97; U. Schnelle, 'Johannes und die Synoptiker', 1798–814; P. Borgen, 'The Independence of the Gospel of John: Some Observations', 1815–33. On the alleged relation between John and Synoptics, see L. R. Kittlaus, 'The Fourth Gospel and Mark: John's use of Markan Redaction and Composition' (Ph.D. diss., University of Chicago, 1978); D. G. Boyd, 'The Sources Used by John and Their Relation to the Synoptic Gospels' (Ph.D. diss., McGill University, Canada, 1972); R. M. A. McDonnell, 'The Interdependence of Luke-Acts and the Fourth Gospel Considered against the Background of a Common School' (Ph.D. diss., Boston University, 1977); D. L. Dungan, 'John and the Synoptics: The Empty Tomb Stories', *NTS* 30 (1984), 161–87; Barrett, *St. John*, 42–54; idem, 'John and the Synoptic Gospels', *ExpTim* 85 (1973–74), 228–33; T. Onuki, 'Die johanneischen Abschiedsreden und die synoptische Tradition', *AJBI* 3 (1977), 226ff; David Catchpole, 'The Beloved Disciple and Nathanael', in *Understanding, Studying, Reading: New Testament Essays in Honour of John Ashton*, ed. by Christoper Rowland, et al. (Sheffield: Sheffield Academic Press, 1988), 69–92; M. E. Glasswell, 'The Relationship Between John and Mark', *JSNT* 23 (1985), 99–115; Richard Bauckham, 'John for Readers of Mark', in *The Gospels for All Christians: Rethinking the Gospel Audiences*, ed. by Richard Bauckham (Grand Rapids, MI: Eerdmans, 1998), 147–71; D. Moody Smith, *John Among the Gospels: The Relationship in Twentieth-Century Research* (Minneapolis: Fortress, 1992); idem, 'John and Synoptics: Some Dimensions of the Problem', *NTS* 26 (1979–80), 425–44. However, if there is such a relation between John and the Synoptics, then it is at least possible that dependence may be reversed – i.e., the Synoptics were influenced by the Johannine tradition.

[93] R. Bultmann, 'Johanneische Schriften und Gnosis', *Orientalische Literaturzeitung* 43 (1940), 150–75; also C. H. Dodd, *The Interpretation of the Fourth Gospel* (Cambridge: CUP, 1953), 3.

'one hand' throughout my study is referred to as 'John', 'the Evangelist', or 'the author'. Much has already been said by other scholars about the authorship of the Fourth Gospel.[94] There is no need for further discussion. Suffice it to say that I find the traditional view which attributes the Gospel to the Beloved Disciple, John the apostle of our Lord, to be more believable[95] than some of the modern, fantastic proposals, such as a community authorship.[96] In the early stages of my research, it became clear that the various elements which contribute to the elusive texture of John's language permeate the entire fabric of the Gospel. These stylistic 'finger prints' are not confined to one segment of the Gospel, a proposed source or a particular text-type (e.g., Alexandrian, Western). Rather, the Fourth Gospel possesses a remarkable stylistic unity and thematic coherence[97] in

---

[94] Most standard commentaries on the Fourth Gospel have detailed discussions on its authorship. C. K. Barrett, *St. John*, 100–34 provides a balanced view. In terms of monograph length discussion, see J. J. Colson, *L'Énigme du disciple que Jésus aimait*, Théologie historique 10 (Paris: Beauchesne et ses fils, 1968); Kevin Quast, *Peter and the Beloved Disciple: Figures for a Community in Crisis*, JSNTSup 32 (Sheffield: Sheffield Academic Press, 1989); Lutz Simon, *Petrus und Der Lieblingsjünger im Johannesevangelium: Amt und Autorität* (New York: Peter Lang, 1994); A. Grassi, *The Secret Identity of the Beloved Disciple* (New York: Paulist Press, 1992); F. W. Baltz, *Lazarus and the Fourth Gospel Community*, Mellen Biblical Press Series 37 (Lewiston, NY; Lampeter, UK: Mellen, 1996); M. Rese, 'Das Selbstzeugnis des Johannesevangeliums über seinen Verfasser', *ETL* 72 (1996), 75–111; James H. Charlesworth, *The Beloved Disciple: Whose Witness Validates the Gospel of John?* (Valley Forge, PA: Trinity Press, 1995).

[95] Eusebius, *Historia ecclesiastica* (H.E.), 6.14.7; 3.36–39; 5.20.5–6; B. F. Westcott, *The Gospel According to St. John: The Greek Text with Introduction and Notes*, 2 vols (n. p.: John Murray, 1908), 1:ix–lxvii; A. H. N. Green-Armytage, *John Who Saw: A Layman's Essay on the Authorship of the Fourth Gospel* (London: Faber and Faber, 1952); Theodor Zahn, *Introduction to the New Testament*, 3 vols (ET, Grand Rapids: Kregel, 1953 [from 3rd German edn, 1909]), 1:3; J. A. T. Robinson, *The Priority of John* (London: SCM, 1985), 93ff.; idem, *Redating the New Testament* (London: SCM, 1976), 254ff.; L. Morris, *Studies in the Fourth Gospel* (Exeter: Paternoster, 1969), 139–92; Carson, *Gospel According to John*, 68–81.

[96] Meeks, in 'Son of Man in Johannine Sectarianism', 145, argues, 'Nevertheless, it has become abundantly clear that the Johannine literature is the product not of a lone genius but of a community or group of communities that evidently persisted with some consistent identity over a considerable span of time.' In contrast see Martin Hengel's conclusion in *The Johannine Question*, 104: 'Here, then, was a towering creative teacher who ventured with reference to the activity of the Spirit Paraclete to paint a quite different picture of the activity and proclamation of Jesus from that which we can see in the Synoptic tradition.'

[97] Stylisitc unity of the Gospel has been demonstrated by such scholars as E. Schweizer, *Ego Eimi. Die religionsgeschichtliche Herkunft und theologische Bedeutung der Johanneischen Bildreden, zugleich ein Beitrag zur Quellenfrage des vierten Evangeliums* (Göttingen: Vandenhoeck & Ruprecht, 1939), 82–7; E. Ruckstuhl, *Die Literarische Einheit des Johannesevangeliums: Der Gegenwärtige Stand der Einschlägigen Forschung* (Freiburg: Paulus, 1951), 1–19; idem, 'Johannine Language and Style: The Question of Their Unity', in *L'Évangile de Jean* ed. by M. de Jonge (1977), 125–47; J. Gerhard, 'The Literary Unity and the Compositional Methods of the Gospel of John' (unpublished dissertation, Washington: The Catholic University of America, 1975); V. S. Poythress, 'Testing for Johannine Authorship by

which central themes are interlocked like the warp and woof of a tapestry. It was this thematic coherence that led David Friedrich Strauss to draw his often quoted analogy by which he compared the Gospel to 'jener ungenähte Leibrock'. He wrote: 'might not this very Gospel itself be said to be that seamless robe of which it tells us, about which one may draw lots but which one may not divide?'[98] But as Martin Hengel points out, 'Nowadays even a conservative theologian would no longer dare to say anything like that. "Christ's seamless robe" has long become a patchwork coat of many colours.'[99]

Examining the Use of Conjunctions', *WTJ* 46 (1984), 350–69; J. E. Botha, *Jesus and the Samaritan Woman: A Speech-Act Reading of John 4:1–42* (Leiden: Brill, 1991); H. N. Ridderbos, 'The Structure and Scope of the Prologue to the Gospel of John', *NovT* 8 (1966), 188–201; Mlakuzhyil, *Christocentric Literary Structure*; Fee, 'Use of the Definite Article'; G. van Belle, *De semeia-bron in het vierde evangilie: Ontstaan en groei van een hypothese* (Leuven: Leuven University Press, 1975); André Feuillet, 'Les christophanies pascales du quatrième évangile sont-elles des signes?', *NRT* 97 (1975), 577–92, W. Nicol, *The Semeia in the Fourth Gospel: Tradition and Redaction* (Leiden: Brill, 1972). Recent commentaries such as Thomas L. Brodie, *The Gospel According to John: A Literary and Theological Commentary* (New York and Oxford: OUP, 1993), have further demonstrated the compositional unity of the Gospel.

[98] Preface to the conversations of Ulrich von Hutten, *Gesammelte Schriften VII* (Leipzig, 1860, xliv; 2nd edn, 1877), 556, reprinted in W. F. Howard, *The Fourth Gospel in Recent Criticism*, 258.

[99] Hengel, *Johannine Question*, 136. An example of this 'patchwork' is Bultmann's proposa (e.g., John, 10f). Bultmann argues a redactor had radically disturbed the 'original order' of the Gospel and also contributed several new sections to it. In the course of 'reconstructing' the Gospel to its original order Bultmann divides chapter 8:12–59 into no fewer than ten fragments and disperses them among the material in chapters 5–12. Consistent with this approach, Bultmann also proposes three sources behind the Gospel, a passion narrative, a signs-source, and a discourse source (John 6–7). Though discourse source failed to win general agreement, the 'sign-source' did win wide acceptance. R. T. Fortna has further developed this aspect of Bultmann's work. Fortna amalgamates Bultmann's 'sign-source' with passion narrative to form a pre-existing 'signs-Gospel'. Fortna, *The Gospel of Signs: A Reconstruction of Narrative Source Underlying the Fourth Gospel* (Cambridge: CUP, 1970); idem, *The Fourth Gospel and its Predecessor: From Narrative Source to Present Gospel* (Edinburgh: Clark, 1988); also U. von Wahlde, *The Earliest Version of John's Gospel* (Wilmington: Michael Glazier, 1989). See E. Ruckstuhl's devastating criticism of Fortna in *Johannine Language and Style*, 125–47; and C. K. Barrett's 'Review of Fortna, Gospel of Signs', *JTS* n.s. 72 (1971), 571–4. In his redactional hypothesis Bultmann left a gap because of his inattention to the historical setting of the Gospel's pre-history. Ashton, *Understanding The Fourth Gospel*, 101f., suggests that the reason for this oversight was Bultmann's theological existentialism, 'the situation in which the message was first proclaimed had...no importance for Bultmann.' This gap was bridged by M. Boismard and A. Lamouille, *Synopse des Quatre Évangiles en francais III: L'Évangile de Jean* (Paris: Éditions du Cerf, 1977) in one of the most comprehensive, if individual hypothesis in Johannine studies. Boismard and Lamouille proposed four redactional stages in the composition of the Gospel: (1) a Document C, a pre-Johannine source, written in Aramaic in Palestine at about AD 50 by the Beloved disciple; (2) the first redaction of the Gospel by the Evangelist (John II-A), also written in Palestine (ca. AD 60–65); (3) the second redaction by the same Evangelist (John II-B), written in Ephesus (ca. AD 90); and (4) the final redaction by a Jewish Christian of the Johannine school, also in Ephesus in the early second century AD. Boismard and Lamouille's theory is similar to that of Lindars, *Behind*

Nevertheless, increasingly scholars are going back to the traditional view. D. A. Carson argues,

> Regardless of who wrote the Fourth Gospel, however, the presumption that the Evangelist used written sources is quite different from the assumption that we can retrieve them. One of the features of John's Gospel on which all sides agree is that stylistically it is cut from one cloth. The very feature that raises a difficulty should also serve as a warning to those who think they can distinguish separate sources buried in the text.[100]

Gilbert van Belle at the end of his exhaustive survey of *The Signs Source in the Fourth Gospel: Historical Survey and Critical Evaluation of the Semeia Hypothesis* concludes: 'I am inclined to refuse the semeia hypothesis as a valid working hypothesis in the study of the Fourth Gospel.'[101] Indeed, in view of the diversity of opinions and the varied source and redactional proposals set forth in this century, one is hard pressed to give much credence to the Johannine source and redaction theses.[102] Ruckstuhl has appropriately characterised the whole enterprise as

---

the Fourth Gospel (London: SPCK, 1971), 59–60, who suggested that the Gospel was developed by the Evangelist in four successive stages between the '80s and '90s: (1) traditional material, mainly story items and sayings from the Jesus-tradition, was developed by the Evangelist (2) first as homilies and then (3) in written form as a gospel at the request of his hearers; finally it was (4) subsequently revised and expanded in a second edition. It is also suggested that some of the Gospel material could have existed independently before being incorporated into the present Gospel, for example, 'a collection of miracle stories' (the SQ or Document C) (Bultmann, Fortna, Nicol and Boismard-Lamouille), a 'Reisebericht' of Jesus from Galilee through Samaria to Jerusalem (Wellhausen, Schwartz, Wilkens), 'homilies' (Lindars, Schnackenburg, Braun, Barrett, Sanders) and 'catechetical instructions' (Riesenfeld, Lindars). Some Johannine passages are also regarded as dominical sayings (3:3; 4:34) or as proverbs (4:35, 37). A technical description of the pre-Gospel forms of the Gospel material can be found in Martin Dibelius, *Die Formgeschichte des Evangeliums* (Tübingen: Mohr, 1919, 1933); Bultmann, *History of the Synoptic Tradition* (Oxford: Blackwell, 1968); see in particular his index references to John (p. 641).

[100] Carson, *Gospel According to John*, 41. Apart from Carson, many scholars in recent years have begun to adapt the compositional integrity of the Gospel as a working hypothesis. Among them see, for example, Hengel, *Johannine Question*, 89–92; Marinus de Jonge, *Jesus – Stranger from Heaven and Son of God: Jesus Christ and the Christians in Johannine Perspective*, ed. and trans. by John E. Steely (Missoula, MT: Scholars Press, 1977), 98; G. C. Nicholson, *Death as Departure: Johannine Descent-Ascent Schema* (Chico, CA: Scholars Press, 1983), 14–17; R. Whitacre, *Johannine Polemic: The Role of Tradition and Theology*, SBLDS 67 (Chico, CA: Scholars Press, 1982), 3–4. A vocal proponent of interpreting John 1:1–21:25 as a coherent literary unity in its present form is Hartwig Thyen. He is sceptical of the attempts to distinguish sources behind the Gospel and proposes instead a consistently redactional-critical approach that takes all elements within the Gospel as integral parts of it. See the appreciative but critical comments of Klaus Wengst, *Bedrängte Gemeinde und verherrlichter Christus: Der historishe Ort des Johannesevangeliums als schlüssel zur seiner Interpretation* (Neukirchen-Vluyn: Neukirchene Verlag, 1981), 19–20.

[101] (Leuven: Leuven University Press, 1994), 376.

[102] R. Nicol, *Semeia in the Fourth Gospel*, 4, writes that source criticism, for example, 'often

a flight of fancy and a 'mere rational exercise'.[103] This diversity of opinion[104] on one hand and a 'remarkable stylistic unity and thematic coherence'[105] of the Gospel on the other should be sufficient to militate against any arbitrary, speculative fracture of the document.[106]

Whatever legitimate meaning the different contents of the Gospel material may have had in their previous contexts,[107] their meaning deserves special attention in the context of this present Gospel, put together by the

---

becomes so hypothetical that no one but the critic himself believes in it.' See also H. Teeple, 'Methodology in Source Criticism of the Fourth Gospel', *JBL* 81 (1962), 279–86; Kysar, *Fourth Evangelist*, 279; D. A. Carson's criticism in 'Current Source-Criticism of the Fourth Gospel: Some Methodological Questions', *JBL* 97 (1978), 411–29; idem, *Gospel According to John*, 39; H. P. Heekerens, *Die Zeichen-Quelle der johanneischen Redaktion. Ein Beitrag zur Entstehungsgeschichte des vierten Evangeliums* (Stuttgart: Katholisches Bibelwerk, 1984), 23–4, 34–9.

[103] Ruckstuhl, *Johannine Language and Style*, 147. See also Howard Clark Kee, *Miracle in the Early Christian World: A Study in Sociohistorical Method* (New Haven: Yale University Press, 1983), 226; F. F. Bruce, *The Gospel of John: Introduction, Exposition and Notes* (Grand Rapids: Eerdmans, 1983), 5.

[104] Apart from van Belle's study, *The Signs Source*, see the surveys of conflicting opinions by H. Teeple, *The Literary Origin of the Gospel of John* (Evanston: Religion and Ethics Institute, 1974), whose research covers the period from 1796 to the 1970s. Further Lindars, *Behind the Fourth Gospel*, 11–60; Kysar, *Fourth Evangelist*, 9–78; Thyen, 'Aus der Literatur', 39, 289–326; S. D. Moore, *Literary Criticism and the Gospels* (New Haven: Yale University Press, 1989), xv–xix; W. Nicol, *The Semeia in the Fourth Gospel: Tradition and Redaction* (Leiden: Brill, 1972), 4–15; Carson, 'Current Source-Criticism', 411–29; Heekerens, *Die Zeichen-Quelle der johanneischen Redaktion*, 23–4, 34–9; J. Louis Martyn, 'Source Criticism and Religionsgeschichte in the Fourth Gospel', in *Jesus and Man's Hope*, ed. by David G. Buttrick (Pittsburgh: Pittsburgh Theological Seminary, 1970), 1:247–73; D. Moody Smith, 'The Milieu of the Johannine Miracle Source'; idem, 'The Setting and Shape of a Johannine Narrative Source', in idem, *Johannine Christianity: Essays on Its Setting, Sources, and Theology* (Columbia, SC: University of South Carolina Press, 1984), 62–79, 80–93; originally in *Jews, Greeks, and Christians*, ed. by Robert Hamerton-Kelly and Robin Scroggs (Leiden: Brill, 1976); George Richter, 'Präsentische und futurische Eschatologie im 4. Evangelium', in *Studien zum Johannesevangelium*, ed. by George Richter, Biblische Untersuchungen 13 (Regensburg: Pustet, 1977), 346–82; Hartwig Thyen, 'Entwicklungen innerhalb der johanneischen Theologie und Kirche im Spiegel von Joh. 21 und der Lieblingsjüngertexte des Evangeliums', in *L'Évangile de Jean*, ed. by M. de Jonge (1977), 259–99.

[105] So W. Meeks, 'Man from Heaven', 144, and one concedes his point also for the weak transitions between episodes.

[106] So Dodd, *Interpretation of the Fourth Gospel*, 289f. Cf. Alter, *Art of Biblical Narrative*, 19–20; Powell, *What is Narrative Criticism?*, 2, idem, 'Bible and Modern Literary Criticism', 78–84; Petersen, *Literary Criticism*, 20; Culpepper, *Anatomy of the Fourth Gospel*, 4–5; Krentz, *Historical-Critical Method*; Quinn, 'Rhetoric and the Integrity of Scripture'.

[107] For example, Brown's proposal, *John*, 1:xxxiv–xxxix; or Lindars, *John*, 46–54; idem, *Behind the Fourth Gospel*, 38–60, 62–63, 73–77; Boismard and Lamouille, *L'Évangile de Jean*; Fortna, *Gospel of Signs*; idem, *Fourth Gospel and its Predecessor*. However, one may acknowledge a literary history behind the present document, but nevertheless insist that John 1–21 should be interpreted as a unit. See M. de Jonge, *Jesus – Stranger from Heaven*, vii–viii.

Evangelist and addressed to his audience, the church,[108] in a new life situation.[109] Whatever conclusions one may come to on the issues of authorship, composition, source, tradition and redaction, failure to interpret the Fourth Gospel holistically is to fracture a theological unity which depends upon every part of the whole for its full vitality. It is surprising how few studies of John's Gospel take this matter seriously and attempt to see the relationships among its ideas as they now meet the reader.[110] Yet it is precisely in its present form that this document as a whole has its power. In its present form, it has impressed its readers since its conception as the 'Spiritual Gospel'. Failure to pursue this must stand as one of the modern critical movement's most serious defects.[111]

It is not necessary to say that one author wrote every word of this text in precisely the present order to explain its force. But the suggestion that scholars should first posit a group of unknown persons[112] who made addi-

---

[108] See my relevant discussion in chapter four.

[109] Cf. de Jonge, *Jesus – Stranger from Heaven;* viii; Frye, *The Great Code;* xiii; Frei, *Eclipse of Biblical Narrative*; Meir Weiss, 'Die Methode der "Total-Interpretation": Von der Notwendigkeit der Struktur-Analyse für das Verständnis der biblischen Dichtung', in *Congress Volume: Uppsala, 1971*, ed. by G. W. Anderson, et al., VTSup 22 (Leiden: Brill, 1972), 93–5 (88–112); James A. Sanders, *Torah and Canon* (Philadelphia: Fortress, 1972); idem, 'Text and Canon: Concepts and Method', *JBL* 98 (1979), 5–29; Brevard Childs, *Introduction to the Old Testament as Scripture* (Philadelphia: Fortress, 1979); idem, 'The Exegetical Significance of Canon for the Study of the Old Testament', in Congress Volume: Göttingen, 1977, ed. by J. A. Emerton, VTSup 29 (Leiden: Brill, 1978), 66–80; Michael Fishbane, *Biblical Interpretation in Ancient Israel* (Oxford: Clarendon, 1985); idem, *Garments of Torah: Essays in Biblical Hermeneutics* (Bloomington, IN: Indiana State University, 1989).

[110] Several scholars vehemently have vehemently attacked such a synchronic approach to the Gospel. Ashton in his *Studying John*, 90 n. 2, characterises this movement as 'a conspiracy of the like-minded' and later the scholars within this 'conspiracy' are described as 'a handful of like-minded enthusiasts', 144, see 91–165. Cf. Becker, 'Das Johannesevangelium im Streit der Methoden', 15–16, see particularly the section 'Der Ansatz beim Text als literarischer Einheit'.

[111] It is remarkable that despite the seriousness with which this issue has been discussed for decades, those preoccupied with Johannine source and redaction have not reached a universal consensus. In fact they are far from it. This is in part due to the arbitrary and subjective criteria used to isolate different sources and stages and levels of redactions. But more significantly, the phenomenon of the variations often attributed to redactional levels need not be explained in redactional terms. There are many other possible explanations beside assimilation of multiple sources and the editorial work of multiple hands. For example, the variations may be explained by the dialectic dimension of the Evangelist's own style. This does not dismiss the past historical reconstructions of the Gospel, rather it pinpoints that these reconstructions were conjectural attempts to explain abrupt breaks and disjunctions in the text.

[112] Richard A. Burridge, 'About People, by People, for People: Gospel Genre and Audiences', in *The Gospels for All Christians: Rethinking the Gospel Audiences,* ed. by Richard Bauckham (Grand Rapids, MI: Eerdmans, 1998), 116, characterises this inconspicuous authorship committee as 'merely stenographers at the end of the oral tunnel, stringing together the pearls of wisdom composed by various early preachers. This is thus authorship by committee, with notes from a secretary. Finally, the subject of the Gospel is not Jesus, but the kerygma, the preaching of the

tions to a central idea from time to time[113] and should then try to decide what was contributed by each person seems to me quite unpersuasive.[114]

1.5. Plan, Scope, and Limitations

A series of steps will accomplish the stated aims of the book. Chapter two elucidates what is meant by 'enigmatic' or 'ambiguous' language of the Gospel and sets forth the various components and contributing factors to this feature. In the third chapter, I argue that the probable context of thought out of which the Fourth Gospel emerged was an environment in which the Hebrew Scripture and the traditions surrounding it were the dominant conceptual and literary forces. In the fourth chapter, the purpose of the Evangelist in writing his Gospel is articulated; and then in chapter five, the function of John's language is ascertained in the light of this purpose and in view of the author's allusions to the Old Testament. In the sixth chapter, the language of John is set in the context of its theology in order to understand its significance and implications. A brief, concluding remark constitutes the seventh chapter.

As I have brought this study to a conclusion, many questions remain, at least in my own mind, in need of discussion and examination, each of which could have become an additional chapter or a separate study on its own. The potential hermeneutical implications of John's language for matters such as 'intentionality', 'single meaning', and the 'sensus plenior'

---

early faith of the church. Thus our three questions about the Gospels of author, subject, and audience can be answered as "by committees, for communities, about the faith."'

[113] See Alexander Schweizer, *Das Evangelium Johannes nach seinem innern Werthe und seiner Bedeutung für das Leben Jesu kritisch untersucht* (Leipzig: Hinrichs, 1841); D. M. Smith, 'The Sources of the Gospel of John: An Assessment of the Present State of the Problem', *NTS* 10 (1963–4), 336–51; idem, *The Composition and Order of the Fourth Gospel: Bultmann's Literary Theory* (New Haven: Yale University, 1965); Brown, *John*, xxviii–xxxii; Ashton, *Understanding the Fourth Gospel*, 114 n.1; and *Studying John*, 90–113, 141–65.

[114] Tzvetan Todorov, a brilliant literary critic, has gone even further and has challenged the whole notion of 'primitive narrative' as a kind of mental mirage engendered by modern parochialism. Todorov argues that it is only by imposing a naive and unexamined set of standards based on modern expectations that modern scholars are able to declare so confidently that certain parts of the ancient text could not belong with others. The primitive text is judged by such standards as the law of stylistic unity, of noncontradiction, of nondigression, and of nonrepetition. Then by these dim, but purportedly universal lights, the text is declared to be composite, deficient, or incoherent. Todorov points out that if just these four laws were applied respectively to *Ulysses*, *The Sound and the Fury*, *Tristram Shandy*, and *Jealousy*, each of these novels would have to be 'relegated to the dustbin of shoddily "redacted" literary scraps.' Tzvetan Todorov, *The Poetics of Prose*, trans. by Richard Howard (Ithaca, NY: Cornell University Press; Oxford: Blackwell, 1977), 53–65.

is one such topic which I have been unable to address. For some exegetes trained to see exegetical options in an 'either/or' fashion, the notion of multiple meanings in the biblical text may be quite disconcerting.[115] There are also those scholars for whom *sensus literalis* is the cardinal hermeneutical principle and the best safeguard against subjectivity in interpretation. But Meeks defends a subjective approach to the Fourth Gospel on the premise that an appeal to the reader's subjective experience 'is grounded in the stylistic structure of the whole document'.[116] It is precisely this unique stylistic feature which caused F. F. Bruce to warn scholars that the Gospel of John is of such a nature that may easily 'lend itself to allegorical exegesis'.[117] 'If commentators are not content to confine themselves to literal and surface meaning, their symbolic interpretations are likely to reflect their own mode of thinking rather than the evangelist's intention.'[118] By contrast, C. H. Dodd maintained that

to a writer with the philosophical presuppositions of the Evangelist, there is no reason why a narrative should not be at the same time factually true and symbolic of a deeper truth, since things and events in this world derive what reality they possess from the eternal ideas they embody.[119]

Cullmann, addressing the same interpretive issues in the Fourth Gospel, contended that

the search for a meaning going beyond the once-for-all event would have to be rejected as "allegorical" error if it was a case of a document which was obviously concerned to present only a historical fact. We have seen, however, that the Gospel of John indicates in so many places the necessity of a double meaning, that enquiry into the deeper unexpressed sense is to be raised, in this Gospel, to the status of a principle of interpretation. The deeper understanding, of which we speak, refers to the connection between the historical life of Jesus and the entire history of salvation.[120]

Nevertheless, I am acutely aware of the concerns of those linguists and commentators who resist any suggestion that there may be levels of

---

[115] V. Mennicke, 'Bible Interpretation', in *The Abiding Word*, ed. T. Laetsch, 2 vols (St. Louis, MO: Concordia, 1947), 2:54. Cf. Moises Silva, *Biblical Words and Their Meaning: An Introduction to Lexical Semantics* (Grand Rapids: Zondervan, 1983), 153; Martin Joos, 'Semantic Axiom Number One', *Language* 48 (1972), 257–65.

[116] 'Man From Heaven', 69.

[117] 'History of New Testament Studies', in *New Testament Interpretation*, ed. by I. Howard Marshall (Grand Rapids: Eerdmans, 1977), 23.

[118] Ibid.

[119] *Interpretation of the Fourth Gospel*, 142.

[120] *Early Christian Worship*, 56–57.

meaning in the Scriptural texts.[121] Their justified reservation has to do with the worry that conceding the possibility of multiple meaning opens the door to uncontrolled fanciful interpretations which, as Bruce noted, reflect one's own mode of thinking rather than the Evangelist's intention. These scholars prefer to view the exegetical task as a scientific process rather than an art. In this respect, exegesis must be governed by the same principles of 'verifiability' or 'falsifiability' which govern the sciences.

This need for verifiable interpretation has been heightened in recent decades by the advent and the onslaught of deconstructionists, post-modernists, and the socio-political activist-readers of literature, including the sacred Scriptures. Often, these reading circles or schools either have denied the possibility of an objective meaning in a text or they have undermined it by imposing their own preconceived social, historical, and political models upon biblical writings and have read the text through their own particular grids in order to reach their interpretive objectives. At the opposite extreme are those who strongly advocate hermeneutical literalism. But as Robert Funk has correctly warned,

modern literal-mindedness has collapsed description and convention into one on a scale perhaps never before attained in the West. And the confluence of the two has produced a modern version of idolatry: the conviction that descriptive language corresponds in so far as it is accurate, precisely to reality, to the really real.[122]

The potential harm to the text in this instance is as grave as that inflicted by the socio-political activist-readers in so far as both groups mishandle the text in pursuit of their own interpretive agendas. Both disallow the text to speak for itself, one by perverting its meaning, the other by limiting it.

---

[121] The following studies are useful in the clarification of some the questions in this area: Raymond Brown, 'The Sensus Plenior of Sacred Scripture' (Ph. D. diss., Baltimore: St. Mary's University, 1955); H. J. B. Combrink, 'Multiple Meaning and/or Multiple Interpretation of a Text', *Neot* 18 (1984), 26–37; J. R. Riggs, 'The Fuller Meaning of Scripture', *Grace Theological Journal* 7 (1986), 213–227; David Newton-DeMolina, ed., *On Literary Intention* (Edinburgh: University Press, 1976); J. P. Louw, 'Primary and Secondary Reading of a Text', *Neot* 18 (1984), 18–25; idem, 'How Do Words Mean – If They Do?', *Filología Neot* 4 (1991), 125–42; B. S. Childs, 'Critical Reflections on James Barr's Understanding of the Literal and the Allegorical', *JSOT* 46 (1990), 3–9; Walter C. Kaiser, Jr., *Toward An Exegetical Theology* (Grand Rapids: Baker Book House, 1981); E. E. Johnson, 'What I Mean by Historical-Grammatical Interpretation and How that Differs from Spiritual Interpretation', *Grace Theological Journal* 11 (1990), 157–69; idem, 'Why I Am Not a Literalist', *Grace Theological Journal* 11 (1990), 137–49; Hirsch, *Validity in Interpretation*; Faju D. Kunjumnen, 'The Single Intent of Scripture: Critical Examination of a Theological Construction', *Grace Theological Journal* 7 (1986), 81–110; Susan Wittings, 'A Theory of Multiple Meanings', *Semeia* 9 (1977), 75-103; Leonard L. Thompson, *Introducing Biblical Literature: A More Fantastic Country* (Englewood Cliffs, NJ: Prentice-Hall, 1978), 29.

[122] Robert Funk, *Parables and Presence* (Philadelphia: Fortress, 1982), 118.

Plan, Scope, and Limitations

In this study, I have had to wrestle with a perplexing language problem. In response I have endeavoured to allow the text to speak for itself and the meaning to emerge from the text. In particular, I have maintained a distinction between *sense* and *significance* in relation to meaning.[123] However, since my focus has been steadfastly fixed upon John's Gospel, my conclusions in this area should not be applied indiscriminately to other biblical texts. By all accounts, the Fourth Gospel is a unique piece of sacred writing within the canonical Christian Scriptures, and each biblical writing must be understood within its own context.

I have tried to demonstrate, in so far as the Fourth Gospel is concerned, that if one simply focuses upon the surface sense of the language, one may actually misinterpret the intended meaning. Nevertheless, Scripture is an ancient collection of highly diverse texts and genres written centuries apart from each other. In this collection, which we call the Bible, there are also numerous lexical, textual, grammatical, and syntactical uncertainties combined with the use of highly complex ancient rhetorical features, stylistic variations, and figures of speech. A monolithic approach to 'meaning' in such varied texts is destined for failure.

Past generations of Christian scholars spoke of the 'inexhaustible riches' hidden in the Scriptures. If this inexhaustibility is to be realised today among those who continue to see these texts as 'revelation' and to speak of them with reverence as 'the word of God', then care must be taken not to impose preconceived models upon the text which do not emerge from the document itself, nor to read the writing through a particular socio-political agenda, nor to limit the riches of the text by imposing upon it various hermeneutical strait-jackets. The meaning must emerge from the text itself, even if that meaning negates one's own particular social or theological agenda. A document must be allowed to speak for itself and determine its own parameters.

On another front, the seemingly universal vilifying designation of Jesus' opponents as 'the Jews' has caused no end of problems for students of the Fourth Gospel. One of the most Jewish of all New Testament writings is wrongly viewed by some readers as anti-Semitic. These characterisations are wholly unjustified. There is as much reason to characterise John's Gospel as anti-Semitic as there is to accuse Isaiah of promoting anti-Semitism. In chapter five of the present study, I have endeavoured to show that the seemingly indiscriminate and negative

---

[123] See Louis Berkhof, *Principles of Biblical Interpretation* (Grand Rapids: Baker Book House, 1950), 59; Geoffrey Leech, *Semantics* (Baltimore: Penguin, 1974), 78–9.

Johannine reference to 'the Jews' has a very specific group within the Jewish nation in view. However, between the present chapter and chapter five there is a considerable distance, and in between there are numerous references to the Johannine 'Jews' in the Johannine sense. Lest these references be misunderstood, Jewish readers of my work are invited to read first the beginning segment of chapter five and then come back and read the rest of the book. In that segment, I have tried to clarify that the Evangelist has in view the Pharisees and the Pharisaic party in the Sanhedrin when he refers negatively to 'the Jews'. John's Gospel is not anti-Jewish at all. It is rather a very Jewish Gospel by a very Jewish author.

In this study I also faced a descriptive difficulty: how best to characterise the peculiar nature of John's language. I have failed to find an adequately precise English word that captures what the reader encounters in John's language. Therefore I have used such descriptions as 'elusive', 'ambiguous', 'enigmatic', 'remote', and similar qualifiers. They all refer to the same phenomenon which I have discussed in chapter two under the lacklustre rubric of 'ambiguity'.

While I have tried to approach the topic thoroughly in view of the limited scope of studies of this nature, the citation of all noted instances of Johannine enigmatic expressions has proved impossible. Even those examples which I have chosen could have extended this monograph into multiple volumes, had I attempted detailed exegesis. Of course, I could have chosen only a handful of examples, as in many of the works of the past, then provided an extensive exegetical analysis for each, and finally drawn general conclusions based on those few examples. However, I did not find this approach to be useful in achieving my aims. My objective has been to show that enigmatic words and expressions permeate the entire composition of the Gospel. Therefore I have chosen to give ample illustrations but to keep the exegetical treatments simple and brief.

However, I have also provided extensive references in the notes. I therefore trust that my premises and conclusions may be more easily verified and that those who may wish to use my study as a launching pad for further studies of their own will be able to do so.

Chapter 2

The Structure of John's Enigmatic Language

2.1. Defining Ambiguity in the Fourth Gospel

In this chapter I analyse the phenomenon which I have qualified quite broadly under the rubric of 'ambiguity' in the Fourth Gospel. The various factors contributing to linguistic ambiguity are here analysed together, since the overall function and significance of ambiguous language cannot be assessed until its complexities have been understood. In particular I shall seek to establish that such ambiguity is not accidental, but is in most cases planned.

2.1.1. The General Problem of Ambiguity in Literature

Ambiguity is a major problem for writers and their interpreters.[1] As early as the second century AD, the Stoic Chrysippus observed that 'ambiguity is a pervasive feature of language.'[2] Ambiguities in Scripture pose a significant difficulty for the modern interpreter who is removed from the original setting by a substantial distance in time and culture. However, even those in closer proximity might have found the words of the biblical writers at times difficult to decipher. Philo speaks of Scripture as full of obscurities and 'enigmas' (*Leg. all.* 3.226) and argues that one must use the allegorical method to interpret them (*Leg. all.* 3.231).[3] Ambiguity is prevalent in litera-

---

[1] C. Schaar, 'Old Texts and Ambiguity', *English Studies* 46 (1965), 157–65; R. Norrman, *Techniques of Ambiguity in the Fiction of Henry James* (Abo, Finland: Acta Academiae Aboensis, 1977), 66.

[2] Quoted by R. B. Edlow, 'The Stoics on Ambiguity', *Journal of the History of Philosophy* 13 (1975), 423–35.

[3] Dreams too contain enigmas (Philo, *Somn.* 2.3, 4) and must be interpreted the same way. An 'enigmatic' word contains symbols (Philo, *Spec. leg.* 1.200). Cornutus speaks of the ancients as 'philosophizing through symbols and enigmas' (76.4, 5, Lang). This was also the practice of the poets. Those who transmitted myths spoke enigmatically (28.1; 32.14; 62.11). This was a common view: Plutarch (*Pyth.* 407 b), Celsus (Origen, *C.Cels.* 6.42), Maximus of Tyre (*Diss.* 4.5a, Hobein). Porphyry (*De Styge* ap. Stob. *Ecl.* 2.1.19) states that enigma is characteristic of ancient poets and oracles: Trypho, the grammarian, says enigma 'is a form of expression arranged

ture for several reasons, including the individual style of an author, time lapse between the writing and the reading, bad grammar, bad composition leading to opacity, vagueness consisting of generalisation, indeterminacy, excessive verbal economy, and lexical polysemy (i.e., words with several meanings).[4] S. Rimmon makes a correct distinction between what Stanford calls 'inescapable ambiguity', which is the function of what the reader brings into the verbal structure of a text, and 'ambiguity proper', in which the ambiguity is located in the verbal structure itself.[5] Rimmon considers Stanford's 'inescapable ambiguity' to be really a matter of the multiplicity of subjective interpretations, rather than a real case of ambiguity.[6] G. B. Caird breaks down 'ambiguity proper' or intentional intransparency into five general subcategories: oracular, ironic, parabolic, exploratory, and associative.[7] In many of the Johannine lexical ambiguities, the cause is often intransparency within the verbal structure itself.[8]

2.1.2. General Definition of Ambiguity

There are many different kinds of ambiguity. William Empson distinguishes seven types in literature (see below),[9] while Caird specifies four

---

with the wrongful purpose of concealing the meaning in unclarity, or setting forth something impossible or impracticable'. He explains that while allegory is obscured in either expression or thought, enigma is obscure in both (*Rhet. graeci* III 193.14, Spengel). Quotations in R. M. Grant, *The Letter and the Spirit* (London: SPCK, 1957), 120.

[4] Cf. Anthony C. Thiselton, 'Semantics and New Testament Interpretation', in *New Testament Interpretation*, ed. by I. Howard Marshall (Grand Rapids: Eerdmans, 1977), 75–104; N. Frye, *Anatomy of Criticism: Four Essays* (New Jersey: Princeton University Press, 1957), 72; Stephen Ullmann, *Semantics: An Introduction to the Science of Meaning* (Oxford: Blackwell; New York: Barnes and Noble, 1962), 54; D. A. Cruse, *A Lexical Semantics* (Cambridge: CUP, 1986); G. B. Caird, *The Language and the Imagery of the Bible* (Philadelphia: Westminster, 1980), 96; P. Ricoeur, *Interpretation Theory, Discourse and the Surplus of Meaning* (Fort Worth, TX: Christian University Press, 1976), 77.

[5] S. Rimmon, *The Concept of Ambiguity: The Example of James* (Chicago: University of Chicago Press, 1977), 17–18.

[6] Ibid., 12. Since the advent of post-modern reader-response criticism, a given text can be read and interpreted in more than one way. In other words, the autosemantic and intrinsic interpretation of the text has been undermined. See J. V. Harari, ed., *Textual Strategies: Perspectives in Post-Structuralist Criticism* (London: Methuen, 1979), 30; Ricoeur, *Interpretation Theory*, 77.

[7] Caird, *Language and Imagery*, 103–8.

[8] Moises Silva, *Biblical Words and Their Meaning: An Introduction to Lexical Semantics* (Grand Rapids: Zondervan, 1983), 149–56 calls attention to the difference between what he calls 'deliberate' and 'unintended' ambiguity. S. Levinson, *Pragmatics* (Cambridge: CUP, 1983), 101–2, sees unintentional ambiguity as a violation of the basic 'cooperative principle' of communication.

[9] W. Empson, *Seven Types of Ambiguity: A Study of Effects in English Verse* (New York: Meridian, 1955).

areas of ambiguity in language: phonetic, lexical, grammatical, and functional.[10] Caird further attributes ambiguity to three causes: accidental, historical, and deliberate.[11] There are many other similar analyses depending upon the context and the discipline within which ambiguity is studied. The topic has been extensively examined in the fields of linguistics and literary criticism. However, for reasons that hopefully will become self-evident as this study progresses, I do not wish to make a sharp distinction between these two disciplines.[12]

---

[10] Caird, *Language and Imagery*, 95-102.

[11] Ibid., 102ff.

[12] The assumption that linguistics and literary criticism should be seen as a unified field, rather than two separate disciplines, is by no means orignal to my study. Scholars both in Europe and the United States have endeavoured to unify these disciplines in so far as they directly focus on the study of language. One of the earliest such scholars was the linguist (philologist) Leo Spitzer who aimed to unify linguistics and literary history through the use of stylistics. On Spitzer, see René Wellek, *Discriminations: Further Concepts of Criticism* (New Haven: Yale University Press, 1970), 187-224. See also Leo Spitzer, *A Method of Interpreting Literature* (North Hampton, MA: Smith College, 1949), 64; idem, *Linguistics and Literary History: Essays in Stylistics* (Princeton: Princeton University Press, 1948), 24, 38 n.17. In the United States, Archibald Hill, Samuel Levin, and Richard Ohmann were among the scholars who sought to combine the studies of language and literature. See especially Archibald Hill, 'An Analysis of the Windhover: An Experiment in Structural Method,' *Publications of the Modern Language Association* 70 (1955), 968-78. See further Curtis W. Hayes, 'Linguistics and Literature: Prose and Poetry', in *Linguistics Today*, ed. by Archibald A. Hill (New York: Basic Books, 1969), 173; Julie Ann Carson, 'The Linguist and Literature: A Critical Examination of Contemporary Theories of Stylistics in America' (Ph.D. diss., Indiana University, 1972), 3-16, 213-14. Nils Erik Enkvist, 'On Defining Style: An Essay in Applied Linguistics', in *Linguistics and Style*, ed. by John Spencer (London, 1964), 3 writes, 'It is symptomatic of our age, and most regrettable, that literary scholars and professional linguists often find themselves on different sides of a mountain-like barrier, with philologists struggling for a precarious foothold on one slope or the other.' See also Geoffrey Leech, *A Linguistic Guide to English Poetry* (London: Longman, 1969) and his foreword. The linguist may consider the literary critic too vague, imprecise, and subjective. See for example Werner Winter, 'Styles as Dialects', in *Proceedings of the Ninth International Congress of Linguists, Cambridge, MA, August 27-31, 1962*, ed. by Horace G. Lunt, Janua Linguarum Series Marior XII (The Hague: Mouton, 1964), 1139. On the other hand, the literary critic considers that strict linguistic analysis destroys or impairs a text's beauty. What is needed is aesthetic value judgments which lead to proper judgment. E.g., Ivor A. Richards, *Principles of Literary Criticism* (London: Routledge and Kegan Paul, 1926 [repr. 1952]), 35. There is now a further combination of the disciplines in that linguistics and literary studies are merged with stylistics. For a brief overview of this merging of discipline in Russia, Germany, and Spain, see René Wellek, *Concepts of Criticism*, ed. by Stephen G. Nichols, Jr. (New Haven: Yale University Press, 1962), 349-51. Cf. Helmut Hatzfeld, 'Methods of Stylistic Investigation', in *Literature and Science: Proceedings of the Sixth Triennial Congress, Oxford 1954*, International Federation for Modern Languages and Literatures (Oxford: Blackwell, 1955), 44-51. But see John Spencer, Nils Erik Enkvist, and Michael Gregory, *Linguistics and Style: Language and Language Learning* (London: OUP, 1964), 48 n. 1. Stephen Ullmann, *Semantics*, 9, suggests that 'every major problem of semantics has stylistic implications', and in some cases, as for example in the study of emotive overtones, the two approaches are inextricably intertwined. Nevertheless, he treats stylistics, the science concerned with 'the expressive and evocative values of language' as a

2.1.2.1. The Linguistic Definition

In linguistics, ambiguity is studied at the levels of phonology, lexis, and surface and deep structures.[13] In other words, linguists analyse ambiguity in three main forms: phonetic, lexical, and grammatical. By far the most prominent form of ambiguity in literature is lexical polysemy, i.e., a case where a word can have more than one meaning or definition.[14] Generally this involves individual terms (nouns, verbs, adjectives, adverbs, prepositions, or pronouns) which have more than one meaning or reference.[15] Yet polysemy may also occur in grammatical forms or in syntactical construc-

---

different approach from semantics. Cf. René Wellek and Austin Warren, *Theory of Literature* (New York: Harcourt, Brace, 1949), 180; Richard A. Lanham, *Style: An Anti-Textbook* (New Haven: Yale University Press, 1974). R. Hagenbuchle, 'The Concept of Ambiguity in Linguistics and Literary Criticism', in *Modes of Interpretation: Essays Presented to Ernst Leisi*, ed. by R. Watts, et al. (Tübingen: Gunter Narr Verlag, 1984), 213–21.

[13] As in D. G. Mackay, 'To End Ambiguous Sentences', *Perception and Psychophysics* 1 (1966), 426–36; Geoffrey Leech, *Linguistic Guide to English Poetry* (London: Longman, 1969), 205–14. Ferdinand de Saussure is considered to be the 'father' of modern linguistics. His lectures on the subject were published posthumously in 1915–16 as *Cours de linguistique générale*, trans. Wade Baskin, ed. by Charles Bally, A. Sechehaye and A. Reidlinger (London: Peter Owen, 1974). See John Lyons, *Introduction to Theoretical Linguistics* (Cambridge: CUP, 1968), 38; and Gustav Herdan, *Quantitative Linguistics* (Washington: Butterworths, 1964), 3. Several decades later, Leonard Bloomfield and Noam Chomsky caused an increased interest in applied, practical linguistics by developing and elaborating upon the description and analysis of language. Modern structural linguistics is generally dated as beginning in 1933 with the publication of Bloomfield's *Language* (London: George Allen and Unwin, 1935). Transformation-generative linguistics may be dated from 1957, when N. Chomsky's *Syntactic Structures* (The Hague: Mouton, 1966) was published.

[14] Indeed, as early as Aristotle (and the Stoics), the importance of considering lexical ambiguity as a class by itself was understood. In *De Sophisticis Elenchis* (165ff), Aristotle lists six types of ambiguity, one of which is lexical ambiguity. He clearly differentiates between ambiguity located in words and ambiguity found in sentences. See Kooij, *Ambiguity in Natural Language*, 2–3; Edlow, 'Stoics on Ambiguity', 427. J. J. Katz and J. A. Fodor, 'The Structure of Semantic Theory', in *The Structure of Language: Readings in the Philosophy of Language*, ed. by J. A. Fodor and J. J. Katz (New Jersey: Prentice-Hall, 1964), 497, point out that 'a necessary condition of the semantic ambiguity of a sentence is that it contains an ambiguous lexical item'. See also R. M. Kempson, 'Ambiguity and Word Meaning', in *Studies in English Linguistics for Randolph Quirk*, ed. by S. Greenbaum, G. Leech and J. Svartvik (London: Longman, 1979), 7–16.

[15] The *lexical* system is non-systematic in some aspects as compared to the phonological or grammatical systems. For instance, there is a finite number of phonemes or grammatical rules, but the lexical code is relatively open so that it is possible for new entities to be added, hence word-coinages, and changes in, or additions to, the meanings of established words. This feature of openness renders the vocabulary 'an unstable structure in which individual words can acquire and lose meanings with the utmost ease' (Ullmann, *Semantics*, 195; cf. 56). Although Ullmann may be overstating the case, nevertheless it is true that such instability makes the lexical level an especially fertile area for causes of ambiguity. Soon Peng Su, *Lexical Ambiguity in Poetry* (London: Longman, 1994), 26–32; R. Kempson, *Semantic Theory* (Cambridge: CUP, 1977), 103, 195; idem, 'Ambiguity and Word Meaning', 7–16.

tions.[16] According to Ullmann, this 'polyvalency' of words, as it is sometimes called, may take two different forms: the same word may have two or more different meanings,[17] or two or more different words may be identical in sound (i.e. *homonyms*) but have different meanings.[18] In the context of biblical literature, *homonymy* appears to be much more prevalent in Hebrew and Semitic than in Greek and the Romance languages.[19]

In John's Gospel, linguistic ambiguity applies to words and verbal structures with two or more references, senses, denotations, or connotations, each of which may be equally relevant.[20] To say that an expression has a 'double meaning' or 'multiple meanings'[21] may therefore imply ambiguity at the level of the denotative or the connotative.[22]

---

[16] E.g., hendiadys, tense, mood. J. Beekman and J. Callow, *Translating the Word of God* (Grand Rapids: Zondervan, 1974), 212ff.

[17] Ullmann, *Semantics*, 59–75, 158–9. *Polysemy* (*poly* = many + *semeion* = sign). The sources of polysemy, according to Ullmann, are: (1) shifts in application, (2) specialisation in a social milieu, (3) figurative language, (4) homonyms reinterpreted, and (5) foreign influence. See further A. Lehrer, 'Homonymy and Polysemy: Measuring Similarity of Meaning', *Language Sciences* 3 (1974), 33–9.

[18] Ullmann, *Semantics*, 176.

[19] *Homonymy* is more complex than polysemy, and its effect can be just as serious and even more dramatic. There are only three ways in which it can arise, and the third of these is of subsidiary importance: (1) *Phonetic convergence*. The commonest cause of homonymy is converging sound-development. This form of homonymy is commonest in languages with many monosyllabic terms. Thus it is more frequent in English and French and less widespread in German or Italian. (2) *Semantic divergence*. That is, diverging sense-development. See Ullmann, *Semantics*, 177-8. (3) *Foreign influence*. See Ullmann, *Semantics*, 180–1. For a more thorough discussion, see Arne Rudskoger, *'Fair, Foul, Nice, Proper': A Contribution to the Study of Polysemy*, Gothenburg Studies in English, I (Stockholm: 1952); M. M. Mahood, *Shakespeare's Wordplay* (London: n. pub., 1957). On polysemy and homonymy, see Lehrer, 'Homonymy and Polysemy'.

[20] M. H. Abrams, *A Glossary of Literary Terms*, 3rd edn (New York: Holt, Rinehart, and Winston, 1970), 9 prefers to speak of multiple meanings and plurisignation, since they have the advantage of avoiding the pejorative aspect of the word 'ambiguity'. Cf. W. F. Thrall, A. Hibbard, and C. Hugh Holman, *A Handbook to Literature* (New York: Odyssey Press, 1936; revised by H. Holman, 1960), 295.

[21] On 'meaning' see R. A. Waldron, *Sense and Sense Development* (London: André Deutsch, 1967), 68; John Lyons, *Semantics*, 2 vols (Cambridge: CUP, 1977), 551; C. K. Ogden and I. A. Richards, *The Meaning of Meaning* (London: Routledge and Kegan Paul, 1923), 186–7 who provide more than twenty definitions. See also Leech, *Linguistic Guide*, 40, idem, 'Being Precise about Lexical Vagueness', *York Papers in Linguistics* 6 (1976), 149–65.

[22] The *denotative* meaning of words is that typically described by means of componential analysis in which a lexical item is decomposed into sense components or features which may be thought of as universal atomic concepts. Some or all of these components are shared by different lexemes in the lexicon. Cf. Katz and Fodor, 'The Structure of a Semantic Theory', *Language* 39 (1963), 479–518. Their version of componential analysis is to break a word into several categories, e.g., man = human, male, etc. Leech, *Semantics*, 12 defines *connotation* as 'the communicative value an expression has by virtue of what it *refers to*, over and above its purely

Several different levels of linguistic ambiguity and their distinctions need to be kept in mind. According to John Lyons, *sense* is a relationship which obtains 'between the words or expressions of a single language independently of the relationship, if any, which holds between those words or expressions and their referents or denotata'—i.e., the things denoted by the words.[23] *Denotation* differs from *sense* because to *denote* something is to point to classes of 'persons, places, properties, processes and activities external to the language-system.'[24] For example, the word 'cow' has a sense that is different from that of the word 'horse', while both words denote classes of animals that exist in the real world independently of the language system. *Reference*, however, is not a property of words, but a function of their use in individual utterances or expressions to 'refer' to things, be they concrete, abstract, or fictional. Individual words and expressions have both sense and denotation, but only expressions have reference in so far as they identify 'whatever we are talking about when we make a statement about something.'[25]

2.1.2.2. The Literary Definition

Ambiguity in a text at a literary level is often linked to its linguistic components, although it is possible to have conceptual ambiguity where ambivalence revolves around an idea rather than individual words. This is not uncommon in the Fourth Gospel. Empson's book *Seven Types of Ambiguity* has been a standard reference for different types of ambiguity in literature since its publication in the 1930s.[26] Empson defines ambiguity as 'any verbal nuance, however slight, which gives room for alternative reaction to the same piece of language.'[27] However, since almost any expression could be declared ambiguous based on this explanation,

---

conceptual content.' What goes beyond the conceptual content may include the attributes that are additional to the critical attributes found in the denotation of a word, or may include the emotive or affective component frequently associated with the word. Cf. Lyons, *Semantics*, 176; U. Eco, *A Theory of Semiotics* (Bloomington, IN: Indiana University Press, 1976), 86; Ogden and Richards, *Meaning of Meaning*, 186–7; Waldron, *Sense and Sense Development*, 68; Norrman, *Techniques of Ambiguity*, 6; R. Page, *Ambiguity and the Presence of God* (London: SCM, 1985), 13.

[23] Lyons, *Semantics*, 1:206.

[24] Lyons, *Semantics*, 1:207.

[25] Lyons, *Semantics*, 1:23; cf. 206. For a briefer account see F. R. Palmer, *Semantics*, 2nd edn (Cambridge: CUP, 1981), 1–43. See also Roger Fowler, *Linguistic Criticism* (Oxford: OUP, 1986).

[26] But further back see Aristotle in *De Sophisticis Elenchis* (165ff); Edlow, 'Stoics on Ambiguity', 427.

[27] W. Empson, *Seven Types of Ambiguity*, 3rd edn (Middlesex: Penguin, 1961), 19.

Empson further narrows his definition to seven categories or *types* of ambiguity in literature. These may be summarised as follows. Ambiguity arises when (1) a detail is effective in several ways at once, for example, in comparisons with several points of likeness, antitheses with several points of difference, comparative adjectives, subdued metaphors, and extra meanings suggested by rhythm; (2) two or more alternative meanings are fully resolved into one;[28] (3) two apparently unconnected meanings are given simultaneously; (4) alternate meanings combine to make clear a complicated state of mind in the author; (5) there is a fortunate confusion, as when the author is discovering an idea in the act of writing, or not holding it all in mind at once;[29] (6) what is said is contradictory or irrelevant and the reader is forced to invent an interpretation; (7) there is full contradiction, marking a division in the author's mind.[30]

Empson's analysis, strictly speaking, is within the confines of literary criticism and not linguistics. He has been criticised for allowing the reader 'an unbridled liberty to project ambiguity onto any word or part of a text', giving rise to overreading.[31] Since Empson, there have been other attempts to define, analyse, and classify various forms of ambiguity in literature,[32] but his is still the standard.

2.1.3. The Role of Context in Ambiguity

James Barr in his influential study *The Semantics of Biblical Language*[33] has demonstrated that in determining the meaning of a word, the context is of indispensable importance. Accordingly, those studies which rely on etymological analysis alone and disregard the contextual usage of words

---

[28] P. Wheelwright, 'On the Semantics of Poetry', in *Essays on the Language of Literature*, ed. by S. Chatman and S. R. Levin (Boston: Houghton Mifflin, 1967), 266, calls this 'plurisignation', i.e. multiple meaning or complexity.

[29] A potential problem in this category is that it appears to rely upon the reader to determine what goes on in the mind of the author and seeks to establish ambiguity in the author's mind.

[30] Empson, *Seven Types of Ambiguity*. See the introduction.

[31] James Jensen, 'The Construction of Seven Types of Ambiguity', *Modern Language Quarterly* 27 (1966), 248; R. Fowler, ed., *A Dictionary of Modern Critical Terms* (London and New York: Routledge and Kegan Paul, rev. ed, 1987), 8; D. M. Miller, *The Net of Hephaestus: A Study of Modern Criticism and Metaphysical Metaphor* (The Hague: Mouton, 1974), 55.

[32] E.g., A. Kaplan and E. Kris, 'Aesthetic Ambiguity', *Philosophical and Phenomenological Research* (1948), 415–35. Rimmon, *Concept of Ambiguity*, has provided highly precise definitions of ambiguity but has been criticised for over-rigid schematization. See J. H. Miller, 'The Figure in the Carpet', *Poetics Today* 1 (1980), 112.

[33] (Oxford: OUP, 1961). See also L. M. Vassilyev, 'The Theory of Semantic Field: A Survey', *Linguistics* 137 (1974), 79–93; W. L. Chafe, *Meaning and the Structure of Language* (Chicago: University of Chicago Press, 1970).

are in danger of false conclusions in their exegesis. 'Context' here refers to all the relevant factors which give an utterance meaning or influence interpretation. E. D. Hirsch in *Validity in Interpretation* defines these relevant factors as a very complex and undifferentiated set of issues, beginning with

> the words that surround the crux and expanding to the entire physical, psychological, social and historical milieu in which the utterance occurs. We mean the traditions and the conventions that the speaker relies on, his attitudes, purposes, kind of vocabulary, relation to his audience, and we may mean a great many other things besides.[34]

There is an integral relation between *meaning* and *context* because every utterance conveys information about the kind of situation in which it occurs, and that situation significantly influences the meaning.[35] Context need not be any larger than necessary in order to arrive at an interpretation.[36] Therefore context is important in determining the nature of an ambiguity in a given verbal environment.

Traditional linguistic studies seem to bypass context, particularly in relation to linguistic ambiguity.[37] In linguistics, context refers to the verbal surrounding of a given word, phrase, or sentence, i.e., the grammatical and semantic relations it contracts with other elements of the text. The most immediate contextual environment is the sentence in which the potentially ambiguous word is located. To interpret the word within this context, one must be aware of its semantic range and also of the syntactical relationships within the sentence. In literary analysis, this verbal surrounding is expanded to include the immediate paragraphs, chapters, and the work in its entirety. This circle may be expanded even further to include other writings of the same author and the historical and social setting of his or her work(s). J. R. Firth refers to this as the 'context of situation'.[38] This

---

[34] (New Haven and London: Yale University Press, 1967), 86–7. According to Lyons, *Semantics*, 572, 'context' is a communicative situation which consists of factors that 'by virtue of their influence upon the participants in the language-event, systematically determine the form, the appropriateness or the meaning of the utterances'. See further D. Sperber and D. Wilson, *Relevance: Communication and Cognition* (Oxford: Blackwell, 1986), 15; E. Hill, *The Concept of Meaning* (London: George Allen and Unwin, 1974), 61.

[35] Leech, *Linguistic Guide*, 183; W. Nowottny, *The Language Poets Use* (London: Athlone Press, 1962), 15.

[36] See G. Brown and G. Yule, *Discourse Analysis* (Cambridge: CUP, 1983), 59.

[37] J. G. Kooij, *Ambiguity in Natural Language* (Amsterdam: North-Holland, 1971), 5–6, excludes context from his study of ambiguity because he believes there are too many variables in situations of utterance. See Katz and Fodor, 'Structure of Semantic Theory', 484; Lyons, *Introduction to Theoretical Linguistics*, 410.

[38] *Papers in Linguistics* (London: OUP, 1957), 182, 226. Firth regards meaning as an essentially social phenomenon. Cf. Palmer, *Semantics*, 53; Lyons, *Structural Semantics: An*

external social context, however, may actually skew interpretation if the interpreter reads into the text an external social and cultural setting without adequate textual information to support it. This is indeed precisely one of the problems we encounter in some of the sociological readings of the Fourth Gospel.[39] The same problem is detectable in some of the Greco-Roman background studies of the New Testament, where predetermined social and historical settings are read back into a text whose milieu may have been completely non-Hellenistic and Semitic in origin.[40]

Against this background we may now offer the following general definition for ambiguity. An expression is ambiguous when two conditions exist. First, semantically, a word may be ambiguous due to polysemy. Polysemy or multiple meaning results when an expression bears more than one *referent* or when an expression in a given context has a stated and an unstated sense, a *denotatum* and a *designatum*. The tension between *denotatum* and a *designatum* becomes the source of ambiguity. Secondly, an item may be considered ambiguous when these different meanings, the stated or *denotative* and the unstated or *connotative*, are both tenable in a given context.[41]

2.2. The Compositional Fabric of Ambiguity in the Fourth Gospel

Years ago, Sir Edwyn Hoskyns wrote that the student of John 'will not be true to the book he is studying if, at the end, the gospel does not remain strange, restless, and unfamiliar.'[42] Much of this strangeness or unfamiliarity results from the enigmatic language of the Fourth Gospel – a stylistic feature which scholars have noticed for centuries.

Generally speaking, ambiguity in John's Gospel is not the result of coincidental vagueness or lack of clarity due to awkward composition. In comparison to the Pauline epistles or Luke-Acts, John's composition is

---

Analysis of Part of the Vocabulary of Plato (Oxford: Blackwell, 1963), 83; Brown and Yule, *Discourse Analysis*, 37; and P. Werth, *Focus, Coherence and Emphasis* (London: Croom Helm, 1984), 37–8.

[39] See chapter four in the present study.

[40] See chapter three of the present work.

[41] H. J. B. Combrink, 'Multiple Meaning and/or Multiple Interpretation of a Text', *Neot* 18 (1984), 26–37; Su, *Lexical Ambiguity in Poetry*, 59.

[42] *The Fourth Gospel*, ed. by Francis Noel Davey, 2nd edn (London: Faber and Faber, 1947), 20.

relatively simple both lexically and syntactically. The style is quite different from that of the Synoptics, and apart from its close resemblance to the three Johannine epistles,[43] the document stands alone in the New Testament.[44] The sentences in John are short and the vocabulary limited, repetitive, and simple. Some of John's most frequently used words occur comparatively rarely in the Synoptics. On the other hand, there are common Synoptic expressions which are rare or absent in the Fourth Gospel.[45] Yet careful study of John's simple expressions, statements, and ideas reveals an admirable literary complexity and sophistication. Beneath many apparently innocent references lie undercurrents with manifold theological implications.

Linguistically, ambiguity in the Fourth Gospel essentially consists of numerous lexical and conceptual expressions which have more than one meaningful reference in context. What contributes to the enigmatic, aloof, or unreachable quality of John's language is the tension between a surface, literal meaning and a deeper, significant meaning or meanings in which the figurative meaning is suggested by the literal. The two are not necessarily mutually exclusive, for had they been exclusive, the literal would have been incapable of suggesting the figurative.[46]

In the following treatment, a few examples have been extracted like threads from John's literary fabric. The recognition that these thread-like examples are taken out of a tightly knitted fabric is crucial. Here they are presented in isolation as part of the analysis of the Johannine phenomenon. But within the compositional fabric of the Gospel, they contribute to the overall design upon the face of the tapestry, the design which presents, as I shall reiterate in this study, Jesus as the Messiah according to the witness of Israel's Scriptures.

It is crucial to recognise the interrelatedness of these various linguistic-literary elements. Every thread in this tapestry-like language is tied to another thread. Collectively, they produce the enigmatic, elusive character of the Fourth Gospel. In John, a double meaning may be related to a

---

[43] Ambiguity seems to be a shared feature of Johannine literature. See Ernst R. Wendland, 'What is Truth? Semantic Density and the Language of the Johannine Epistles with Special Reference to 2 John', *Notes on Translation* 5 (1992), 21–59.

[44] Barrett, *St. John*, 5.

[45] M. Goguel, *Introduction au Nouveau Testament, II: Le Quatrième Évangile* (n.p., 1924), 244f.

[46] Cf. Rimmons, *Concept of Ambiguity*, 23; R. Page, *Ambiguity and the Presence of God* (London: SCM, 1985), 13; W. M. Urban, *Language and Reality* (1939), 112 quoted in Ullmann, *Semantics*, 163.

metaphor, and the metaphor itself may occur in the context of irony, and the irony in conjunction with an allusion to the Old Testament (e.g., 1:5; 2:19; 3:5, 14–21; 6:33; 11:49-52). The Old Testament Scriptures provide the substance for John's compositional fabric, the design of his christology, and the source from which he has gathered his ideological threads. It would be a mistake to dismiss this feature as coincidental, because its existence can be verified contextually within the Gospel. By locking into the recurring patterns throughout the text, one is alerted to the undercurrent. Furthermore, John's elusive language should not be simply explained away as a matter of style or literary artistry. Both of these factors are only secondary to the primary theological argument of the Gospel.

Since there are many overlaps between the various categories I have used to analyse John's composition, the categories are not meant to be taken too definitively. Yet such overlapping forms of analysis may themselves highlight the tapestry-like structure of John's language.

2.2.1. The Linguistic Fabric of Johannine Ambiguity

Linguistic ambiguity in John is mostly lexical-semantic. However, since the Gospel also contains many grammatical and syntactical ambiguities, we may begin here.

2.2.1.1. Grammatical and Syntactical Ambiguity

Grammatical uncertainties are not unique to the Fourth Gospel. They are found in written Greek, both inside and outside the New Testament. However, in John grammatical and syntactical ambiguities combine with other forms of ambiguity to create a unique cumulative effect.

Many instances of ambiguity are caused by the formal identity of the second person plural indicative and imperative—a recurrent problem for translators. Such forms in John include ἐραυνᾶτε, 'you search' or 'search!' (5:39); ποιεῖτε, 'you do' or 'do!' (8:38); πιστεύετε, 'you believe' or 'believe!' (14:1), and γινώσκετε, 'you know' or 'know!' (15:18). Is Jesus in John 8:38, 41 telling his opponents to *do* (ποιεῖτε) the work of their father if they really are the children of God? Or is he telling them that they already *are doing* the work of their father and that their father is identified by this work? John 8:39 lays emphasis on the first, 8:41–44 on the second. Again, John 14:1 could be translated, 'You believe in God (naturally, since you are Jews, therefore) believe also in me.' Or it could be rendered, 'Believe (truly) in God (as I reveal Him, and you will) believe also in me.'

Other examples of grammatical ambiguity with verbs are closely analogous to the problem of the indicative and imperative.[47] The verb ἀπόλλυμι is a characteristic Johannine term.[48] It is used transitively in the active, with a corresponding intransitive use supplied by the middle. In 6:39 the active ἀπολέσω may mean 'I shall not lose' or 'I shall not bring about [his] ruin or eternal destruction'. The intransitive use is two-fold: 'to be lost' (6:12), or 'to perish', 'to suffer destruction' (3:16; 6:27; 10:28; 11:50). The same ambiguity applies to the cognate noun ἀπώλεια (17:12 only). Destruction is the inevitable fate of all those separated from God (cf. 12:25), since life exists only in God. There is no neutral ground between 'destruction, perish' and 'eternal life'.

The unusual use of the particle ἐάν plus the *indicative* (θέλω) in the Lord's exchange with Peter about the fate of the Beloved Disciple in 21:22 (ἐὰν αὐτὸν θέλω μένειν ἕως ἔρχομαι) creates ambiguity because in the Koine it could be read as a condition of fact, using ἐάν in the normal sense of εἰ (as possible in classical Greek)—as if to say that Lord does indeed intend the disciple to remain (alive) until he comes.[49] But the next verse (21:23) denies that the disciple would live to see the Lord's return, leaving the Lord's prediction ambiguous.[50]

In John 1:9 the participle ἐρχόμενον, 'coming', may be either neuter nominative, agreeing with τὸ φῶς, 'the light', or masculine accusative, agreeing with πάντα ἄνθρωπον, 'every person'. The first option refers to the incarnation when the light, namely *Jesus*, came into the world; the second option refers to the true light as enlightening *every other person* who comes into the world. Since the latter would in any event depend upon the former, this may be a case of 'both/and' rather than 'either/or'.

The apparent redundant particle γάρ, 'for', in John 4:44 seems to contribute to the double meaning and irony inherent in 4:43–45. Though γάρ usually expresses a causal relation, it can also mean 'certainly,' 'by all means' or 'but'.[51]

In John 6:66 ἐκ τούτου can be rendered either 'for this reason' or

---

[47] Edwin Abbott, in his pioneering work, *Johannine Grammar* (London: Adam and Charles Black, 1906), cited a number of such ambiguities. See also R. Mörchen, '"Weggehen": Beobachtungen zu John 12:36b', *BZ* 28 (1984), 240–2; Barrett, *St. John*, 456.

[48] The accumulation of such words in this passage shows its importance; John is summarising his message.

[49] Cf. BDF §373 (1); and §372 (1a) for other examles of ἐάν plus the indicative.

[50] Barnabas Lindars, *The Gospel of John*, NCB (London: Marshall, Morgan and Scott, 1972), 639.

[51] A. Stimpfle, 'Das "sinnlose γάρ" in Joh 4, 44. Beobachtungen zur Doppeldeutigkeit im Johannesevangelium', *BN* 65 (1992), 86–96.

'from this time'. There is a similar ambiguity at 19:12. Perhaps both senses can be retained: 'for this reason and from this time'. Ambiguity in the reference of a demonstrative also appears in 21:15, where Jesus asks Peter: ἀγαπᾷς με πλέον τούτων, 'Do you love me more than these?' This may mean 'do you prefer me to these things (i.e., the fisherman's way of life)?' Or it may mean 'do you love me more than these other disciples do?' Lindars believes that the use of πλέον with genitive for *more than these* is decisive for the second. However, this conclusion is based upon his assumption that if John had meant the first one (i.e., more than the fisherman's lifestyle), he 'would probably have used μᾶλλον ἤ as in 3.19; 12.43.'[52] The grammatical anomaly in itself may not be sufficient to rule out the possibility of a deliberate ambiguity on the part of the author.

Another illustration of grammatical ambiguity is the Gospel's purpose statement in John 20:31, where the manuscripts support either the present subjunctive πιστεύητε or the aorist subjunctive πιστεύσητε. While the initial problem is text-critical, solving it does not answer the exegetical question.[53] The primary question is whether John is trying to deepen faith in those who already have it, or engender faith in those who do not.[54]

A final example of a grammatical ambiguity includes the transitivity or intransitivity of the verb καθίζειν in 19:13. In its transitive sense, the verb means 'cause to sit down',[55] but in its intransitive sense, it means 'to sit down'.[56] Did Pilate himself sit down on the judgment seat in the intransitive sense? Or did he put Jesus on the judgment seat, thereby ironically acknowledging his authority?[57] Some scholars have argued that the

---

[52] Lindars, *John*, 635 (Greek font added).

[53] For further discussions about the grammatical and textual issues see Brown, *John*, 2:1056–61; Barrett, *St. John*, 478–9; Lindars, *John*, 617; R. Schnackenburg, *The Gospel According to St. John*, trans. by Kevin Smyth (New York: Herder and Herder, 1968), 3:337–39; Rudolf Bultmann, *The Gospel of John: A Commentary*, trans. by G. R. Beasley-Murray (Philadelphia: Westminster, 1971), 698.

[54] T. C. De Kruijf, '"Hold the Faith" or "Come to Belief"? A Note on John 20:31', *Bijdragen* 36 (1975), 439–49; also my discussion on this text and topic in chapter four.

[55] BAGD, 389.

[56] BAGD, 90.

[57] Cf. Ignace de la Potterie, 'Jesus: King and Judge According to John 19:13', *Scripture* 13 (1961), 97–111; R. Robert, 'Pilate a-t-il fait de Jésus un juge? ἐκάθισεν ἐπὶ βήματος (Jean, xix, 13)', *RThom* 83 (1983), 275–87; A. Kurfess, 'ἐκάθισεν ἐπὶ βήματος (Jo 19,13)', *Bib* 34 (1953), 271; A. E. Harvey, *Jesus on Trial: A Study of the Fourth Gospel* (London: SPCK, 1976), 15; Wayne Meeks, *The Prophet-King: Moses Traditions and the Johannine Christology* (Leiden: Brill, 1967), 73–8; John Ashton, *Understanding the Fourth Gospel* (Oxford: Clarendon, 1991), 228 n. 41. Among the commentaries see Schnackenburg, *St. John*, 3:263–4; J. H. Bernard, *A Critical and Exegetical Commentary on the Gospel According to St. John*, ICC, 2 vols (Edinburgh: Clark, 1928), 2:662-23; B. F. Westcott, *The Gospel According to St. John* (Grand Rapids:

intransitive sense of this verb is well-attested in judicial language and that the historical character of John's text as well as the seriousness of the Roman law militates against the gesture indicated by the transitive sense.[58] Thus a grammatical double meaning, one historical (intransitive) and one theological (transitive), is ruled out. On the other hand, the irony is both structural and theological, and although the primary sense is intransitive, nevertheless the transitive sense lies below the surface when viewed in the light of Johannine irony.[59]

We have just surveyed a few examples of grammatical and syntactical ambiguity in John. But the primary source of apparent vagueness is lexical polysemy. The following Johannine wordplays could be categorised in different ways. I have supplied my own analysis, using distinctions that are not intended to be absolute. There are many possible overlaps in analysis.[60]

2.2.1.2. Lexical Amphibologia (Double Meaning)

The play on words is an ancient rhetorical device. It was extensively used in the classical[61] as well as biblical and post-biblical periods. It is prevalent in the prophetic section of the Hebrew Bible.[62] However, it is not pervasive in the New Testament except in the Fourth Gospel and, in a different form, in the book of Revelation.

In John there are two primary manifestations of this: a regular and a conceptual *amphibologia*[63] or double-meaning.[64] Some linguists refer to

---

Eerdmans, 1954), 272; Hoskyns, *Fourth Gospel*, 524; Bultmann, *John*, 664; Barrett, *St. John*, 453; Ernst Haenchen, *John: A Commentary on the Gospel of John*, Hermeneia Series, translated by Robert W. Funk and edited with Ulrich Busse (Philadelphia: Fortress, 1984), 2:183; R. H. Lightfoot, *St. John's Gospel: A Commentary*, ed. by C. F. Evans (Oxford: Clarendon, 1956), 325–6; Carson, *Gospel According to John*, 603, 607–8.

[58] Brown, *John*, 880–1; Bultmann, *John*, 664 n.2.

[59] The reader can proceed through the trial narrative without being aware of the second meaning. Herbert Leroy, *Rätsel und Missverständnis. Ein Beitrag zur Formgeschichte des Johannesevangeliums* (Bonn: Hanstein, 1968), 21–5, 45–47, sees this in terms of initiation into the Johannine language and perspective where he believes there exists in John evidence for a *Sondersprache* which is only intelligible to the initiated.

[60] The variations in categories are also evident in Ullmann, *Semantics*; Lyons, *Semantics*; Wilfred Watson, *Classical Hebrew Poetry: A Guide* (Sheffield: JSOT Press, 1984); Shimon Bar-Efrat, *Narrative Art in the Bible* (Sheffield: Almond Press, 1989); Leech, *Linguistic Guide*.

[61] E. S. McCartney, 'Puns and Plays on Proper Names', *Classical Journal* 14 (1919), 343–58, and a rejoinder fourteen years later by C. J. Fordyce, 'Puns on Names in Greek', *Classical Journal* 28 (1932–33), 44–6.

[62] Watson, *Classical Hebrew Poetry*, 237–50; Bar-Efrat, *Narrative Art*, 197–213.

[63] From Greek *amphi*, 'on both sides', *bolos*, 'a throw', and *logos*, 'word'; hence a word or phrase susceptible to two interpretations. So E. W. Bullinger, *Figures of Speech Used in the Bible* (Grand Rapids: Baker Book House, 1898, reprint, 1968), 804; cf. J. P. Louw and E. A. Nida,

the phenomenon as polysemantic pun instead of double meaning since it involves a word, a phrase, or a sentence which can have two or more meanings.[65] A word is *amphibological* when it simultaneously carries two denotations, neither of which is necessarily contradictory to the other, and both of which fit the context where the word occurs. Amphibologia may be used in a context where the author wishes to express a deeper additional meaning, a 'fuller meaning' which cannot be expressed simply by adding a synonym. The amphibological figure encapsulates two dimensions of the same thought in a situation where the author does not wish to force an either/or choice.[66]

This linguistic form abounds in John's Gospel.[67] Most commentaries note its presence, but some scholars[68] deny its existence and invariably opt for one of the two possible dimensions of meaning. Bultmann, for example, believes that misunderstandings in John come as a result of concepts and statements which at first sight refer to earthly matters, but properly refer to divine matters.[69] In principle, the observation is correct in most cases (e.g., 'living water' or 'bread from heaven'), but not correct in all cases. There are instances in the Gospel where a fuller meaning is not grasped until

Greek-English Lexicon of the New Testament Based on Semantic Domains, 2 vols (New York: United Bible Society, 1988), 1: xv–xx.

[64] F. Manns, 'Les mots à double entente. Antécédents et fonction herméneutique d'un procédé johannique', *Studii Biblici Franciscani Liber Annuus* 38 (1988), 39–57; E. Richard, 'Expressions of Double Meaning and Their Function in the Gospel of John', *NTS* 31 (1985), 96–112.

[65] E.g., Watson, *Classical Hebrew Poetry*, 241. For further discussion, see Anthony Thiselton, *The Two Horizons* (Exeter: Paternoster, 1980), 407ff. J. D. Apresjan, 'Regular Polysemy', *Linguistics* 142 (1974), 5–32; L. M. Vassilyev, 'The Theory of Semantic Field: A Survey', *Linguistics* 137 (1974), 79–93; Louw and Nida, *Greek-English Lexicon*, vi–xx.

[66] Empson's fourth category noted earlier. See also Harry Shaw, *Dictionary of Literary Terms* (New York: McGraw-Hill, 1972), 122, s.v. 'double entente'; C. O. Sylvester Mawson, *Dictionary of Foreign Terms*, 2nd edn (New York: revised by Charles Thomas and Crowell, 1934, 1975), 115, s.v. 'double entente'; *Oxford English Dictionary* (Oxford: Clarendon, 1933), 3, s.v. 'double entente'; R. W. Burchfield, ed., *A Supplement to the Oxford English Dictionary* (Oxford: Clarendon, 1972), 1:850, s.v. 'double entente'; C. Hugh Holman and William Harmon, based on the original ed. by William Flint Thrall and Addison Hibbard, *A Handbook to Literature*, 5th edn (New York: Macmillan Publishing, 1986), 154, s.v. 'double entente'; Richard A. Lanham, *A Handlist of Rhetorical Terms: A Guide for Students of English Literature* (Berkeley: University of California Press, 1968), 59; David W. Wead, 'The Johannine Double Meaning', *ResQ* 13 (1970), 106; Caird, *Language and Imagery*, 96–7.

[67] Leroy, *Rätsel*, and an abstract of his thesis, 'Das Johanneische Missverständnis als Literarische Form', *BibLeb* 9 (1968), 196–207; Cullmann, 'Der johanneische Gebrauch doppeldeutiger Ausdrücke als Schlüssel zum Verständnis des vierten Evangeliums', *TZ* 4 (1948), 360–72; H. Conzelmann, *Grundriss der Theologie des Neuen Testaments* (Munich: Kaiser, 1967); Manns, 'Les mots à double entente', 39–57.

[68] E.g., Bultmann, *John*, 135 n.1; Schnackenburg, *St. John*, 368.

[69] Bultmann, *John*, 135 n.1.

both meanings are apprehended. For example, one can make the case that ἄνωθεν in the dialogue with Nicodemus in 3:3–8 should be rendered 'from above', as Jesus meant it (cf. 3:31; 19:11), even though Nicodemus understands ἄνωθεν in terms of physical birth 'again'. Yet according to the Evangelist, Jesus also means a real second birth spiritually (3:7; 1:13). The failure of Nicodemus is not due to selecting the earthly meaning 'again', but rather failure to see the spiritual dimension of the expression, namely, 'born again from above'.[70] Here John is able to synthesise two fundamental truths of the Christian experience: people must be born *again* from *above*. For one to enter the kingdom of God, the new birth or 'regeneration' is needed, the source of which is 'from above', referring to the divine origin and the supernatural character of the event (cf. 1:12–13). In fact, this principle is of fundamental importance in the Johannine theological formulation for understanding the deeper meanings and references of Scriptures which speak of Jesus. Illumination, for John, ultimately rests on regeneration.

When in John 1:29 the Baptist cries out: 'Behold the Lamb of God who takes away (ὁ αἴρων) the sin of the world', the word αἴρω is capable of meaning 'to take upon oneself' as well as 'to take away, remove'.[71] Hence John Calvin commenting on this word concludes:

The verb (to take away) may be explained in two ways; either that Christ *took* upon himself the load which weighed us down, as it is said that he carried our sins on the tree (1 Pet. 2:24) and Isaiah says that *the chastisement of our peace was laid on him* (Isa.

---

[70] Cullmann, 'Johanneische Gebrauch', 364–5; idem, *Early Christian Worship* (Philadelphia: Westminster Press, 1953), 51, argues that characteristic of Johannine style, the Evangelist has not set before us an alternative, rather, both are meant. He goes on to explain that Nicodemus' misunderstanding of ἄνωθεν as if it was a question of physical birth ἐκ τῆς κοιλίας τῆς μητρός (from his mother's womb) concerns only the verb γεννηθῆναι (to be born), not the interpretation of the ἄνωθεν in the sense of δεύτερον, since according to the Evangelist, Jesus also means a real second birth (v. 7). There can be no doubt, however, that here, as in 3:31 and 19:11, it means also, and at the same time, 'from above', and Nicodemus has failed to recognise it. Cf. BAGD, 77; F. W. Gingrich, 'Ambiguity of Word Meanings in John's Gospel', *Classical Weekly* 37 (1943–44), 77; Gail O'Day, *The Word Disclosed* (St. Louis: CBP Press, 1987), 21–3; Barrett, *St. John*, 205–6; R. V. G. Tasker, *The Gospel According to St. John*, TynNTC (Grand Rapids: Eerdmans, 1960, reprinted, 1988), 70; Brown, *John*, 130. Cf. M. de Jonge, 'Nicodemus and Jesus: Some Observations on Misunderstanding and Understanding in the Fourth Gospel', *BJRL* 53 (1970–71), 337–59; Lindars, *John*, 150, who believes, 'These words replace Matthew's "turn and become like children." In the Matthean context, the attitude of the heart is in view. In John, regeneration is the point.' See further C. H. Dodd, *The Interpretation of the Fourth Gospel* (Cambridge: CUP, 1953), 303; Wayne A. Meeks, 'The Man from Heaven in Johannine Sectarianism', *JBL* 91 (1972), 52–3; J. C. Fenton, *The Gospel According to John* (Oxford: Clarendon, 1970), 53; D. A. Carson, *The Gospel According to John* (Grand Rapids: InterVarsity Press, 1991), 188–90; Hoskyns, *Fourth Gospel*, 212–14.

[71] BAGD, 24; J. Jeremias in *TDNT* 1 (1964), 185–6.

53:5) or that he *blotted out* sins. But the latter statement depends on the former. I gladly embrace both; namely, that Christ, by bearing our sins, takes them away.[72]

For John, the 'lamb of God' has 'taken away the sin' by taking it 'upon himself' (cf. 2 Cor. 5:21).

Another instance where it is unlikely that an 'either/or' was intended is in John 1:5. The word καταλαμβάνω in the statement καὶ ἡ σκοτία αὐτὸ οὐ κατέλαβεν (1:5) is capable of several nuances. On the one hand it means to 'seize, win, attain'.[73] On the other hand it means 'to seize with hostile intent, overtake'.[74] It also entails the idea of 'grasp, find, understand',[75] which well fits the context: The darkness was able neither to understand the light nor to overcome the light.[76]

In John 4:36 near the end of the Samaritan discourse, the expression μισθός (Heb. פעלה), means both 'wages for work' and 'reward'.[77] In this context, the harvesting work set before the disciples itself is seen as 'receiving' (λαμβάνειν) wages as well as its own reward, but not as reward for one's own sowing. Here μισθὸν λαμβάνει and συνάγειν καρπόν are almost synonymous terms: 'fruit-gathering' describes the content proper of the harvester's work, but this work is also its own reward (μισθὸν λαμβάνειν).[78] A similar double meaning is implied in the word κοπιᾶν (4:6, 38) which refers to the 'tedious nature of the work itself' (4:38) and the 'resulting tiredness by the one engaged in the work' (4:6).[79] Theologically, John views salvation offered to humanity as the gift of God (3:16; 4:10a), but he also sees the very mission of each of the agents such as John the Baptist (3:27-30) or Jesus himself (5:36; 17:4) and the Holy Spirit (16:13-15) as a gift. In view of this, and in a similar way, the work or mission of the disciples in 4:36 also is seen as a gift and its own reward.

The word κρίνειν occurs about nineteen times in John, as opposed to no occurrences in Mark and six each in Matthew and Luke. John commonly uses the word in reference to 'judgment' (e.g., 3:16-19; 5:22,

---

[72] *Gospel According to John*, vol. 1, trans. by Rev. William Pringle (Grand Rapids: Eerdmans, 1956), 65. See further Str-B, in loc. 1:29 and vol. 2; Carson, *Gospel According to John*, 150; Hoskyns, *Fourth Gospel*, 176; Lightfoot, *St. John's Gospel*, 96-8.

[73] Both in the active and passive moods. Cf. 1 Cor. 9:24, Phil. 3:12a. Cf. BAGD, 412.

[74] John 12:35, 6:17; 1 Thess. 5:4. Cf. BAGD, 413.

[75] Acts 25:25; Eph. 3:18. BAGD, 413; G. Delling in *TDNT* 4 (1967), 9-10.

[76] Cf. Hoskyns, *Fourth Gospel*, 139; contrast Lindars, *John*, 87.

[77] BAGD, 523.

[78] This interpretation is made possible on both grammatical and theological grounds. For the etymological study of the word itself, see H. Preisker in *TDNT* 4 (1967), 695-728.

[79] Cf. BAGD, 443; F. Hauck, *TDNT* 3 (1965), 827-30.

27, 30; 9:39). It is a prominent Johannine theological term with multiple meanings. The verb has the following nuances: (1) separate, distinguish, select; (2) judge, consider; (3) reach a decision, decide; and (4) condemn.[80] Most translations fail to capture all these distinct nuances.[81] The idea emerges at the climactic points in the narrative of John to accentuate the decisive dilemma humanity faces when confronted by the light (i.e., 3:16–19; 7:51; 9:39–41; cf. 15:22). In John 9:39, the crisis of 'spiritual illumination' versus 'blindness' becomes tragically evident when Jesus declares to the Jewish religious leaders: εἰς κρίμα ἐγὼ εἰς τὸν κόσμον τοῦτον ἦλθον, ἵνα οἱ μὴ βλέποντες βλέπωσιν καὶ οἱ βλέποντες τυφλοὶ γένωνται, 'For judgment I came into this world, that those who do not see may see, and that those who see may become blind' (9:39).[82]

The verb ἐλέγξαι in John 3:20 carries two distinct nuances, 'expose, bring to light' (cf. Eph. 5:11, 13), as well as 'convict, reprove' (cf. Jn. 8:46; 16:8; Lk. 3:19).[83] Later in Jesus' pronouncement in 3:36, ὁ δὲ ἀπειθῶν τῷ υἱῷ οὐκ ὄψεται ζωήν ('the one who does not obey the Son shall not see life'), the word ἀπειθέω, which generally is translated 'disobey', could also be rendered 'refuse to believe', particularly in view of its contrast with πιστεύω (cf. v. 18). Walter Bauer correctly notes that 'since, in the view of the early Christians, the supreme disobedience was a refusal to believe their gospel, ἀπειθέω may be restricted in some passages to the meaning *disbelieve, be an unbeliever.*'[84]

The word παρρησία is a characteristically Johannine word, occurring nine times in the Gospel. It is used in two senses: first, 'plainly', without the

---

[80] The noun κρίμα has the same range of meaning. See BAGD, 450–1 and Büchsel, *TDNT* 3 (1965), 921–41.

[81] Ashton, *Understanding*, 220–26.

[82] Hoskyns, *Fourth Gospel*, 324–6; Lightfoot, *St. John's Gospel*, 203; Westcott, *St. John*, 55–6; Lindars, *John*, 159–60; Dodd, *Interpretation of the Fourth Gospel*, 208–12; George R. Beasley-Murray, *John*, WBC 36 (Waco, TX: Word Books, 1987), 51, 160; Ashton, *Understanding*, 221; Schnackenburg, *St. John*, 1:398–407, 2:255; Barrett, *St. John*, 181–2, 308.

[83] BAGD, 249; F. Büchsel in *TDNT* 2 (1964), 473–475; cf. John 8:46; 16:8; Lk. 3:19. Zane C. Hodges, 'Problem Passages in the Gospel of John, Part 4: Coming to the Light – John 3:20–21', *BibSac* 135 (1978), 314–22; Schnackenburg, *St. John*, 1:406; Bernard, *St. John*, 1:122; Beasley-Murray, *John*, 51; Hoskyns, *Fourth Gospel*, 220; Barrett, *St. John*, 227; Brown, *John*, 1:135; Westcott, *St. John*, 57; R. C. H. Lenski, *The Interpretation of St. John's Gospel* (Minneapolis: Augsburg Pub. House, 1961), 276; Lindars, *John*, 161; Carson, *Gospel According to John*, 207–8; Leon Morris, *The Gospel According to John* (Grand Rapids: Eerdmans, 1989), 234; Frederick Louis Godet, *Commentary on John's Gospel* (Grand Rapids: Kregel Publications, 1978, reprinted, 1980), 399.

[84] BAGD, 82. Cf. J. Wilson, 'The Integrity of John, 3:32–36', *JSNT* 10 (1981), 34–41; F. F. Bruce, *The Gospel of John* (London: Pickering Paperbooks, 1983), 97–8; Bultmann, *John*, 166; Westcott, *St. John*, 62; Barrett, *St. John*, 227; Lindars, *John*, 171; Morris, *John*, 248–9.

obscurity of parabolic utterance, and secondly, 'publicly', 'openly'.[85] Although the word occurs elsewhere in the New Testament, its double meaning is brought out most clearly in John's Gospel. Either meaning makes sense in the context of John, and this causes ambiguity.

In John 8:37 the word χωρεῖν means both 'to find no place in' and 'to make no progress or headway'. If this latter sense is adopted, those who seek to kill Jesus (8:37) may have taken an initial step of faith, but they have not remained in the word (e.g., Judas). However, if the former sense 'to find no place in' is adopted, the Gospel has a greater deterministic sense.

In John 12:6 both verbs in the phrase τά βαλλόμενα ἐβάσταζεν (said of Judas) have secondary meanings. Βάλλειν, originally 'to throw', is often weakened in Hellenistic Greek to mean 'to put', while βαστάζειν, originally meaning 'to carry or bear' a physical burden or object, can also mean 'to take surreptitiously, pilfer, steal'.[86] Here the double meaning of βαστάζω is deliberate sarcasm against Judas. The reference, of course, suits the character of Judas, who is depicted as dishonest, disloyal, and a thief. The *double entendre* is underscored by κλέπτης ἦν, 'he was a thief'.[87]

In the extended metaphor of the vine and the branches in John 15:1–12, there are several amphibological terms. A notable example is the expression καθαίρω in 15:2, which means 'pruning' in a horticultural sense, but also 'cleansing and purifying' figuratively.[88]

Other examples of amphibological words may include δίδωμι, 'send' or 'hand over' (e.g., 3:16),[89] or the complex wording of 3:8 in which there are three terms of double meaning: πνεῦμα (Spirit/wind),[90] πνέω (breathe/blow),[91] and φωνή (voice/sound). The use of πνέω in this context is a case

---

[85] BAGD, 630. See also John 7:13, 26; 10:24; 11:14, 54; 16:25, 29; 18:20.

[86] BAGD, 137; Büchsel, *TDNT* 1 (1964), 596.

[87] David Wead, *The Literary Devices in John's Gospel* (Basel: Friedreich Rinehardt, 1970), 32; John Calvin, *Commentary on the Gospel According to John*, trans. by Rev. William Pringle, 2 vols (Grand Rapids: Eerdmans, 1956), 2:12; Bultmann, *John*, 415; Lindars, *John*, 417–18; Hoskyns, *Fourth Gospel*, 414–16; Bruce, *John*, 57; Carson, *Gospel According to John*, 429; Brown, *John*, 452–3; Bernard, *St. John*, 2:420; Tasker, *St. John*, 146; Barrett, *St. John*, 344; Westcott, *St. John*, 177.

[88] BAGD, 386–7.

[89] Cullmann, 'Johanneische Gebrauch', 366; A. Jaubert, *Approches de l'Evangile selon saint Jean*, Cahiers Évangile 17 (Paris: Cerf, 1976), 79.

[90] BAGD, 674–8, also the extensive etymological study of the use of the term 'spirit' in the Scriptures by Marie E. Isaacs, *The Concept of Spirit: A Study of Pneuma in Hellenistic Judaism and Its Bearing on the New Testament*, Heythrop Monographs 1 (Huddersfield, England: H. Charlesworth, 1976).

[91] BAGD, 679; G. Schwarz, '"Der Wind weht, wo er will"?', *BN* 63 (1992), 47–8.

of planned ambiguity, since the author could have employed ἐμφυσάω (breathe upon), as he does in 20:22.[92]

There are many similar words of double meaning throughout the Gospel. In these examples, far from needing to read into the text, one can easily verify the double meaning contextually and exegetically. The recurring pattern eliminates the possibility that these words are coincidental and unintentional. This raises the obvious question, Why would John choose to communicate in this unusual way? There appear to be various reasons and factors for this method of communication. Suffice it to say at this point that the immediate and overall contexts in which an enigmatic expression occurs are of decisive importance. In some instances, John uses words of double meaning for their precision and efficiency. They encapsulate a range of meanings which otherwise would require an explanation through the use of several words or sentences. At other times, the expressions are related to Johannine irony and theology. In still other examples, the double meanings may aim to show the gap between an earthly and a spiritual understanding of the encounter with the same reality, as Bultmann has argued. Moreover, the Evangelist may have wished to draw his audience deeper into the Scriptures to see their fulfilment in the person and work of Jesus Christ. The answer to the above question is not simple; but I hope that the enigma of why John communicates in this fashion becomes more clear by the conclusion of this book.

2.2.1.3. Conceptual Amphibologia (Double Reference)

There is a second and very important category of ambiguity in the Fourth Gospel: conceptual double references. Here the ambiguity is not usually inherent in the word itself.[93] Rather, it has to do with the usage in a context where both an immediate and a less immediate reference may be in view. There can also be a tension between a surface, literal meaning and an extended or figurative meaning which it suggests.[94] The two are not

---

[92] See E. Schweizer, *TDNT* 6 (1968), 332–451; Cullmann, 'Johanneische Gebrauch', 364. Cf. Beasley-Murray, *John*, 49; Brown, *John*, 131, 135–48; Bultmann, *John*, 142; Barrett, *St. John*, 210–11; Hoskyns, *Fourth Gospel*, 202–5; Fenton, *John*, 54; Morris, *John*, 220; Carson, *Gospel According to John*, 197–8.

[93] Madeleina Boucher, *The Mysterious Parable: A Literary Study*, CBQMS 6 (Washington, DC: Catholic Biblical Association of America, 1977), 17–18 talks of certain figures of speech which involve little or no change in the meaning of words 'since all the words are used literally.'

[94] W. M. Urban, *Language and Reality*, 112, observes: 'The fact that a sign can intend one thing without ceasing to intend another, that, indeed, the very condition of its being an *expression* sign for the second is that it is also a sign for the first, is precisely what makes language an instrument of knowing. This "accumulated intention" of words is the fruitful source of ambiguity,

mutually exclusive. Acknowledging the deeper implication is as important as understanding the literal sense.

The use in John 1:11 of the neuter expression τὰ ἴδια, 'his own (sc. *property* or *home*)' and of the masculine expression οἱ ἴδιοι, 'his own (sc. *people*)' may be an example where the basic denotations of the expressions are not ambiguous, but the references are. The expression 'his own (sc. people)' is not ambiguous until we ask how wide the reference is. Here 'his own' could be ethnic Israel or all humanity. Bultmann believes that οἱ ἴδιοι refers to all people as part of creation and that τὰ ἴδια refers similarly to 'the world of men', but not to Jesus' own 'home'.[95] Schnackenburg similarly reasons that εἰς τὰ ἴδια ἦλθεν cannot mean the Word's entrance into own home, 'since the true homeland of the Logos is with God (cf. v. 1b).'[96] On the other hand, Hoskyns uses the Old Testament to argue that the expression τὰ ἴδια designates Jesus' *home* to be 'the house of Israel' as the special property of God.[97] Fenton believes that each of the two Greek expressions refers both to humanity in general and to Israel in particular, since both live in the darkness of sin and hence are inclined to reject the true Light.[98] Although one can use different statements in the Gospel to support either of these references, it is more likely that in the light of Johannine theology, which is both particular and universal, we should allow for both readings. Both 'the house of Israel' and 'the world' in their bondage to sin have rejected their Creator-Redeemer.

Although there are many referentially unclear expressions in John, the author has provided an explanatory 'footnote' in only a few of these instances.[99] These occasional authorial asides take many different forms. Among their various functions, they provide an important clue that there is deliberate ambiguity in the document.

---

but it is also the source of that analogous predication, through which alone the symbolic power of language comes into being' (quoted in Ullmann, *Semantics*, 163).

[95] Bultmann, *John*, 56 with n. 1.

[96] Schnackenburg, *St. John*, 1:259.

[97] Hoskyns, *Fourth Gospel*, 146.

[98] Fenton, *John*, 36. Cf. Shedd, 'Multiple Meanings', 253; Carson, *Gospel According to John*, 125.

[99] See G. Van Belle, *Les parenthèses dans l'évangile de Jean. Aperçu historique et classification. Texte grec de Jean*, Studiorum Novi Testamenti Auxilia 11 (Leuven: Leuven University Press, 1985); idem, 'Les parenthèses johanniques', in *The Four Gospels: Festschrift F. Neirynck*, ed. by F. Van Segbroeck, C. M. Tuckett, G. Van Belle, and J. Verheyden, BETL 100 (Leuven: Leuven University Press, 1992), 3:1901-33; M. C. Tenney, 'The Footnotes of John's Gospel', *BibSac* 117 (1960), 350; John J. O'Rourke, 'Asides in the Gospel of John', *NovT* 21 (1979), 210-19.

The word ναός (temple), which occurs three times in John 2:19–22 (v. 19: λύσατε τὸν ναὸν τοῦτον καὶ ἐν τρισὶν ἡμέραις ἐγερῶ αὐτόν, etc.), is a case in point. The expression takes on added significance in conjunction with the 'glory' motif in 1:14 and the reference to Jacob's ladder in 1:51, together with its Old Testament background in Jacob's dream at Bethel (Gen. 28:10–19). The Evangelist does not explicitly say in his explanation (v. 21: ἐκεῖνος δὲ ἔλεγεν περὶ τοῦ ναοῦ τοῦ σώματος αὐτοῦ; cf. v. 22) that there is an undercurrent in his account. Nevertheless, by supplying the explanation of one dimension that contains a deeper meaning, he draws attention to other deeper levels.

Jesus' remark about the temple would have confused even the post-resurrection Johannine audience, let alone Jesus' original hearers,[100] were it not for John's explanation. But with John's explanation we are keyed in to the deeper meaning of Jesus' words and also alerted to the Evangelist's own language pattern. In his polemic-apologetic engagement with the Jewish religious authorities, for whom the temple stood as the meeting place of heaven and earth, John asserts that 'the place' where heaven and earth now meet is in Jesus Christ.[101] In the statement of 2:19 about the destruction of the temple, John also may have been implying that Jesus was warning 'the Jews' that the Jerusalem temple would be destroyed. But this tragic event was connected to the emergence of a new temple, in his own person and his body, the church. Hence the implication may have been among others: 'If you destroy this temple (my body), you will bring about the destruction of this temple (the one in which we are standing)'. From his post-Easter perspective, the Evangelist seems to have understood the coming of Jesus as the cessation of the function of the physical temple.

This conclusion is confirmed in two subsequent passages. Jesus' teaching in John 4:21–3 and his reference to the time when worshippers will worship the Father neither at the Samaritan mountain nor in Jerusalem is actually a statement about the Jerusalem temple, not the city of Jerusalem. The contrast is between the Samaritan temple on Mount Gerizim and the Jewish temple on Mount Zion. Jesus predicts that soon

---

[100] The ambiguity of John 2:19–22 would have been compounded for Jesus' immediate audience by his use of the verb λύσατε, 'destroy, tear down', and the verb ἐγερῶ, 'lift up, raise up, erect'. Compare this with 'be lifted up' (i.e., 3:14; 8:28; 12:32, 34).

[101] W. H. Cadman, *The Open Heaven: The Revelation of God in the Johannine Sayings of Jesus*, ed. by G. B. Caird (Oxford: Blackwell; New York: Herder and Herder, 1969), 26–32; Aileen Guilding, *The Fourth Gospel and Jewish Worship* (Oxford: Clarendon, 1960), 171; W. D. Davies, 'The Johannine "Sign" of Jesus', in *A Companion to John*, ed. by Michael J. Taylor (New York: Alba House, 1977), 91–115. See also chapter five in the present book.

these locations will become irrelevant. Given that the Samaritan temple had already been destroyed 150 years earlier, his words 'neither in Jerusalem' contain a harsh prediction that soon the Jerusalem temple will suffer the same fate as its Samaritan counterpart. That this will come about because of the incarnation, the resurrection, and the sending of the Holy Spirit is then made clear in the otherwise repetitive verse 4:23.

With Jesus' high-priestly prayer of chapter 17, the temple theme once again resurfaces: glory (vv. 1, 4, 5, 10, 22, 24), holiness and consecration (vv. 11, 19, 25), the revelation of God's name (vv. 6, 11, 26), and divine indwelling (vv. 21-3). There is also an implicit contrast with the Jerusalem temple in one important respect: whereas that temple had excluded Gentiles, now Jesus prays that all those who believe will be 'one even as we are one' (vv. 20-23). From this the conclusion can be drawn that, in the Johannine theological thinking, the temple in Jerusalem had lost its essential function with the coming of Jesus. In calling it his 'Father's house' Jesus indeed affirmed its previous status, but now he fulfils its essential meaning. Jesus is a new tabernacle (1:14), a new temple (2:19), the one in whom the temple rituals and festivals have found their true significance. Moreover, his disciples can share in something of that status through the indwelling of the Holy Spirit.

In John 11:9 the *sensus literalis* of 'the light of this world' is *the sun*. But the readers of the Gospel can recall 8:12 and understand Jesus' symbolic reference to himself as 'the light of the world'. There is only a limited time left until this Light will be withdrawn ('Are there not twelve hours in a day?'). The one who walks in the darkness of the night will stumble and fall (compare the departure of Judas by night in 13:30).

In John 13:1 εἰς τέλος is an adverbial phrase which in Hellenistic Greek means 'completely', 'utterly'.[102] This yields a satisfactory sense here. Jesus' love for his own was capable of any act of service or suffering: εἰς τέλος ἠγάπησεν αὐτούς. But it is probable that here, as well as in Mark 13:13 and parallels (cf. also 1 Thess. 2:16), τέλος yields its primary significance of 'end' as well. Jesus loved his own up to the last moment of his life. Moreover, τέλος recalls an earlier eschatological expression, the 'hour' of Jesus. The hour of his suffering was an anticipation of the last events. 'It would be characteristic of John to see a double meaning in εἰς τέλος'.[103]

Later in the same chapter in John 13:33 (cf. 7:33), the verb ὑπάγω no

---

[102] See Moulton and Milligan, *The Vocabulary of the Greek Testament*, s.v. τέλος.
[103] Barrett, *St. John*, 438.

doubt is intended to cover both the departure of Jesus in death and his ascent to the glory of the Father. The word is much more common in the last discourse than in the rest of the Gospel (in chapter 17 it naturally gives place to ἔρχεσθαι). The use of the word arises out of John's characteristic thinking about the death of Jesus; it is rarely used elsewhere with the connotation of 'dying' (though cf. Mt. 26:24; Mk. 14:21).

Earlier in John 7:8 there is a similar conceptual double meaning in the conversation of Jesus with his half-brothers and the word ἀναβαίνω. The verb ἀναβαίνω carries the twofold meaning of going up to a physical location, in this case, Jerusalem, and going up in ascension by way of the cross.[104]

When viewed purely from the standpoint of the night in which Jesus was betrayed, the reference of the expression τὰ ἐρχόμενα, 'the coming things' in John 16:13 must be to the events of passion as they are about to unfold, including perhaps both the crucifixion and resurrection. But from the standpoint of the beloved disciple, τὰ ἐρχόμενα must be events still future, that is, eschatological events in the proper sense of the word.[105]

Similarly, in the Samaritan discourse in John 4:35b and Jesus' exhortation to the disciples to see and perceive, each of the following expressions seems to operate at two levels: ἰδού, 'behold'; ἐπάρατε, 'lift up (your eyes)'; χώρας 'fields', and θερισμόν, 'harvest'. There is a surface level and a deeper symbolic level.[106]

Many of the Johannine ironies revolve around such conceptual double references. The fourfold use of ἀκολουθέω, 'follow' in 1:37, 38, 40, and 43 is not ironic in the strictest sense, though it anticipates such irony in that eventually Jesus' disciples are required to follow him in far more particular senses (cf. Jn. 15:19–20; 16:2; cf. Mt. 10:38). That the disciples should physically follow Jesus who was described as 'walking by' in 1:37 is natural; but the Johannine audience probably knew that these men would soon 'follow' Jesus in the sense of becoming disciples. 'Following' may further imply that some of the disciples would follow Jesus in giving up their lives (Jn. 13:36; 21:20–22).[107] In effect, the author progressively leads up to the climactic statement of 1:43: 'Follow me', where the concept of discipleship

---

[104] BAGD, 50; Brown, *John*, 1:308–9; Lightfoot, *St. John's Gospel*, 175–6; Barrett, *St. John*, 312.

[105] So Barrett, *St. John*, 502.

[106] See Teresa Okure's excellent exposition of this passage in *The Johannine Approach to Mission: A Contextual Study of John 4:1–42* (Tübingen: Mohr-Siebeck, 1988), 147ff.

[107] Cullmann, 'Johanneische Gebrauch', 367; Bultmann, *John*, 99; Barrett, *St. John*, 180; 586–7; Lindars, *John*, 113; Brown, *John*, 2:117–20.

is unmistakable. The use of 'follow' in 13:36 in relation to the double-meaning verb ὑπάγω, 'depart' should also be noted, since in this case it means 'to follow' Jesus not to the Father, but to martyrdom.

Similar conceptual undercurrents are suggested in association with εὐχαριστεῖν (give thanks) in the episode of the multiplication of the loaves (6:11, 23; cf. Mark 8:6).[108] Yet another example with a deeper connotation is found in the verb ἀνίστημι, 'rise' in 11:23. It looks to the immediate raising of Lazarus while also giving the assurance of rising to eternal life in the eschatological sense.[109]

The pericope of the blind man in chapter nine hinges upon the conceptual double meaning of τυφλός, 'blind', which seems to indicate both physical and spiritual blindness. Throughout the Gospel, the tragedy of 'seeing' and 'not being able to perceive' constitutes a well-developed theme, calling to mind the lamentable spiritual condition of the Jewish nation in Isaiah 6:9–10. Indeed, in many respects John stands firmly in the Isaianic tradition and once again reminds the religious leaders of Israel of their indifference and blindness to the revelation. They have eyes, but cannot see beyond appearances. Whenever they are introduced into the narrative, the author purposefully shows that they can stare at the truth and not see it. But there are others such as Pilate (e.g., 18:37–38) who cannot see either. All those who are not born of God, in the Johannine formulation, are plagued by the same blindness (3:3, 5, 6, 12).

In John 9:16, 33 the expression παρὰ θεοῦ εἶναι operates at two levels which correspond to the two senses given to the σημεῖα by the Jews. In 9:16 the expression is used by the Pharisees, and in verse 33 by the blind man healed by Jesus. In both instances the claim is opposed to ἁμαρτωλὸς εἶναι (Jn. 19:6, 31). The Pharisees wonder, 'Is this man from God?' – in other words, 'Is this man a prophet of God?' Jesus here is considered a prophet in the general sense (cf. 4:19, 44): a 'man of God', and not a 'sinner', as the Pharisees charge.[110] But at the deeper level, as S. Pancaro has said,

---

[108] Schnackenburg, *St. John*, 2:16–17, especially 17 n. 31, lists Strachan, Temple, Bultmann, Johnston, and Heising as denying a reference to the Eucharist, but Barrett and Brown as presenting the alternative view. Schnackenburg remains uncommitted, leaving open the possibility. On the sacramental undercurrent in John, see Kysar, *Fourth Evangelist*, 249–59; Barrett, *St. John*, 82–5; idem, 'The Dialectical Theology of St John', in *New Testament Essays* (London: SPCK, 1972), 67–8; Brown, *John*, cxi–cxiv.

[109] Cullmann, 'Johanneische Gebrauch', 369–70; Schnackenburg, *St. John*, 2:330; Barrett, *St. John*, 395.

[110] Severino Pancaro, *The Law in the Fourth Gospel: The Torah and the Gospel, Moses and Jesus, Judaism and Christianity According to John*, NovTSup 42 (Leiden: Brill, 1975), 23–24.

The question is not, 'Can Jesus be a man of God and notwithstanding that still work on the Sabbath?' but, 'As the Son of God *must* Jesus not work also on the Sabbath?' The answer to this last question is affirmative (Jn 5,17) and it shows that, although the Sabbath is abolished, the law is fulfilled, not violated.[111]

The origin of Jesus is one of the central subjects in chapters 7–9. John's audience has already been told that the origin of Jesus is from God (cf. 1:1–14; 3:2, 13, 19, 31; 6:33–58). Both in chapter 5 and later in chapter 9, the Evangelist shows that Jesus is from God. It is in this light that he is the one who fulfils rather than violates the law.[112]

In John 19:28, there is a subtle thematic play on the idea of 'thirst', specifically as it relates to the word of the crucified Lord upon the cross when he said, διψῶ, 'I thirst' (19:28). Was the cry of thirst an innocent request for water because of dehydration? Was it to fulfil the Scriptures, as the author says?[113] Or did it have an even greater theological significance for the Evangelist? Pancaro believes the link to Psalm 69:21 (MT v. 22) is strong since in the Psalm 'thirst' is seen as one of the sufferings of the righteous sufferer. In addition, the interpretation of the death of Christ as that of the righteous sufferer has a long history in the church.[114] In the Johannine theological formulation Jesus, the Lamb of God, by taking upon himself the sin of the world (1:29), experienced the same spiritual separation and 'thirst' common to those for whom he came to provide the living water. He, having 'nothing to draw with', gave Israel 'living water' (Exod. 17:1–7; Num. 20:1–18), when 'water came forth abundantly, and the congregation drank and their cattle' (Num. 20:11). An implied condition of those who thirst in this Gospel (e.g., the Samaritan woman in chapter 4; the multitudes in chapter 7) is spiritual separation from God (cf. Jn. 1:13; 3:3; 5:40; 8:23, 24, 42, 47; 14:6).

According to the Synoptic account of the crucifixion, Jesus was crucified about 9:00 a.m. A supernatural darkness covered the land from about noon until 3:00 p.m. The Synoptics record that at that time (3:00 p.m.), Jesus cried: ηλι ηλι λεμα σαβαχθανι; τοῦτ' ἔστιν· θεέ μου θεέ μου, ἱνατί με ἐγκατέλιπες, 'My God, my God, why have you forsaken me?' (Mt. 27:46; cf. Mk. 15:34; Lk. 23:46). In response to this, someone ran and

---

[111] Pancaro, *Law*, 29–30.

[112] Ibid., 23–30.

[113] In the entire Gospel, only here in 19:28 does the Evangelist speak of a τελειοῦν of the Scriptures: ἵνα τελειωθῇ ἡ γραφή. This is an intensification of John's previous formula involving πληροῦν (ἵνα ἡ γραφὴ πληρωθῇ: Jn. 13:18; 17:12; 19:24; also later in 19:36), which expresses the 'ultimate fulfilment' of the Scriptures.

[114] Ibid., 353.

filled a sponge with vinegar (Mk. 15:36; Mt. 27:48). However, in John's account of the cross, where Jesus is presented as the exalted King, the Evangelist does not record the Lord's cry of forsakenness. Rather, he writes Jesus' words, 'I thirst', which in Johannine theology amounts to the same cry of spiritual separation and forsakenness from God. Jesus, by taking upon himself the sin of humanity, becomes the sacrificial lamb bearing upon himself (αἴρω, 1:29) the sin of the world, just as the Paschal lamb foreshadowed this reality in the Old Testament for Israel.

The pronouncement of the Lord upon the cross, τετέλεσται (τελέω) in 19:30 (see also 19:28),[115] is noted for its probable theological deeper meaning by most commentators.[116] The verb τελέω signifies bringing to completion a task. In addition, it carries the idea of fulfilment in a religious sense (cf. Lk. 12:50).[117] The verb has both chronological and theological implications in this context.[118] The work of creation and salvation which began in Genesis 1:1 and John 1:1 is now finished on the evening of the sixth day.

There are many other potential cases of conceptual ambiguity in the Fourth Gospel. They include ἠκολούθησαν, 'they followed' (1:7); θεὸν οὐδεὶς ἑώρακεν πώποτε, 'no one has ever seen God' (1:18); Τί ζητεῖτε, 'what do you seek?' (1:38); Ἔρχεσθε καὶ ὄψεσθε, 'come and you will see' (1:39); Ἔρχου καὶ ἴδε, 'come and see' (1:46); Ἰησοῦς οὐκ ἐπίστευεν αὐτὸν αὐτοῖς, 'Jesus did not commit himself to them' (2:24); αὐτὸς γὰρ ἐγίνωσκεν τί ἦν ἐν τῷ ἀνθρώπῳ, 'for he knew what was in man' (2:25); ποιῶν τὴν ἀλήθειαν, 'doing the truth' (3:21); ἔρχεται πρὸς τὸ φῶς, 'coming to the light' (3:21); ἵνα φανερωθῇ αὐτοῦ τὰ ἔργα ὅτι ἐν θεῷ ἐστιν εἰργασμένα, 'that it may be manifested that his deeds have been wrought in God' (3:21); Οὐ δύναται ἄνθρωπος λαμβάνειν οὐδὲ ἓν ἐὰν μὴ

---

[115] Cf. τελειόω, 4:34; 5:36; 17:4; εἰς τέλος, 13:1.

[116] E.g., Brown, *John*, 2:930–1, 954–6; Hoskyns, *Fourth Gospel*, 531; Schnackenburg, *St. John*, 3:284–5; Alf Corell, *Consummatum Est: Eschatology and Church in the Gospel of St. John* (New York: Macmillan, 1958), 105–12; Haenchen, *John*, 194; Beasley-Murray, *John*, 352–3; Lindars, *John*, 582; Barrett, *St. John*, 553–4; Bernard, *St. John*, 2:638–9; Bultmann, *John*, 675; Tasker, *St. John*, 211; William Loader, *The Christology of the Fourth Gospel: Structure and Issues* (Frankfurt am Main: Verlag Peter Lang, 1989), 101; Westcott, *St. John*, 277.

[117] BAGD, 810–11; G. Delling, *TDNT* 8 (1972), 57–62. There are nineteen occurrences of the term τελέω (verb) or τέλος (noun) 'finish' in its various grammatical forms in the Fourth Gospel (cf. two occurrences in the Synoptics).

[118] The verb is in a perfect passive construction. Grammatically, it is generally rendered as an intensive perfect, thus emphasising the present result of a past action. Cf. Loader, *Christology of the Fourth Gospel*, 101; Beasley-Murray, *John*, 352–53; Westcott, *St. John*, 277; J. N. Sanders, *A Commentary on the Gospel According to St. John*, ed. by B. A. Mastin (New York: Harper and Row, 1968), 410; Morris, *John*, 815.

ᾗ δεδομένον αὐτῷ ἐκ τοῦ οὐρανοῦ, 'no one can receive anything except what is given him from heaven' (3:27); ἐκεῖνον δεῖ αὐξάνειν, ἐμὲ δὲ ἐλαττοῦσθαι, 'He must increase, but I must decrease' (3:30); Ὁ ἄνωθεν ἐρχόμενος ἐπάνω πάντων ἐστίν· ὁ ὢν ἐκ τῆς γῆς ἐκ τῆς γῆς ἐστιν καὶ ἐκ τῆς γῆς λαλεῖ. ὁ ἐκ τοῦ οὐρανοῦ ἐρχόμενος ἐπάνω πάντων ἐστίν, 'He who comes from above is above all; he who is of the earth belongs to the earth, and of the earth he speaks; he who comes from heaven is above all' (3:31); ἔδει δὲ αὐτὸν διέρχεσθαι διὰ τῆς Σαμαρείας, 'and it was necessary for him to pass through Samaria' (4:4); Κύριε, δός μοι τοῦτο τὸ ὕδωρ, 'Sir, give me this water' (4:15); Ὁ ποιήσας με ὑγιῆ, 'the one who made me whole' (5:11, 14); οἱ νεκροὶ ἀκούσουσιν τῆς φωνῆς τοῦ υἱοῦ τοῦ θεοῦ, 'the dead will hear the voice of the son of God', and οἱ ἀκούσαντες ζήσουσιν, 'the ones who hear will live' (5:25, 28); περιπατεῖν, 'to walk' (cf. 7:1; 11:54); τὰς ἐπιθυμίας, 'the desires' (8:44); ἵνα τὰ τέκνα τοῦ θεοῦ τὰ διεσκορπισμένα συναγάγῃ εἰς ἕν, 'to gather into one the dispersed children of God' (11:52); and ἀπελθὼν ἐκρύβη ἀπ' αὐτῶν, 'he departed and was hidden from them' (12:36). Similar examples permeate the fabric of the Gospel.

2.2.1.4. Use of Cluster Concepts

Within the fabric of Johannine language are woven several theologically pregnant words. I have called these 'cluster concepts' since as used in this Gospel, each one covers a spectrum of abstract meanings. A simple dictionary definition does not adequately capture these meanings, since the context within which the words occur plays a very important part in the determination of their meanings. This context, which in the Fourth Gospel is emphatically theological, is of utmost importance in our understanding of the full meanings of these concepts. The Fourth Evangelist has tailored these terms to his own purpose in explicating the meaning of the saving revelation of God in the incarnation, cross, and resurrection of our Lord for Israel and the world in salvation history. Each term represents a cluster of associations and makes a collective impact on the mind. Though many of these terms are not unique to John, yet their frequency and use in the Gospel make them a pool of special enriched Johannine vocabulary.

To understand the *sense* and *reference* of such terms, one must first come to grips with other theological assumptions in the Fourth Gospel, and then ascertain the meaning of the terms in each context. Words such as 'truth',[119] 'life',[120] and 'light'[121] depict the Johannine Jesus as the revelation of God's essence and character (Jn. 1:4, 5, 8, 9; 3:19–21; 8:12; 9:5; 12:35, 36, 46). Indeed, as Bultmann has said,

> The concepts light, truth, life, and freedom explain each other: so do the concepts darkness, falsehood, death, and bondage.... They all derive their meaning from the search for human existence – for 'life' as 'life eternal' – and denote the double possibility of human existence: to exist either from God or from man himself.[122]

Other distinctly Johannine expressions which may be characterised as clusters include (1) 'darkness'; (2) 'know'; (3) 'glory'; (4) 'hour'; (5) 'work'; (6) 'sign'; (7) 'birth'; (8) 'remain'; (9) 'seek'; (10) 'belief'; (11) 'love'; (12) 'world'; (13) 'see'; (14) 'hear'; (15) 'walk'; (16) 'follow'; (17) 'witness'; and (18) 'above versus below'.[123]

---

[119] The words ἀλήθεια, ἀληθής, ἀληθινός occur forty-six times in John as opposed to twice in Matthew, four times in Mark and four in Luke. 'Truth' is one of the most distinct words in John's specialised vocabulary. Like many other Johannine concepts, truth is deeply Hebraic and bears various polysemantic nuances (e.g., reliable, faithful, trustworthy, lawful). It is also a fundamental notion in the Johannine dualism. See Schnackenburg, *St. John*, 2:225–37, BAGD, 35–7; S. Aalen, 'Truth: A Key Word in St. John's Gospel', in *SE* 2 = TU 87, ed. by F. L. Cross (Berlin: Akademie-Verlag, 1964), 3–24; Dodd, *Interpretation of the Fourth Gospel*, 170–8; W. Reiser, 'Truth and Life', *The Way* 19 (1979), 251–60; J. R. Barlow, '"Truth" in John's Gospel' (unpublished thesis, Dallas Seminary, 1971); Ignace de la Potterie, 'The Truth in Saint John', in *The Interpretation of John*, ed. by John Ashton (London: SPCK, 1986), 53–66; idem, 'I Am the Way, the Truth, and the Life', *Theology Digest* 16 (1968), 59–64; R. H. Strachan, *The Fourth Gospel: Its Significance and Environment*, 3rd edn (London: SCM, 1943), 141–4.

[120] The word ζωή occurs thirty-five times in John as opposed to seven times in Mattew, four times in Mark and five times in Luke. In John, it is used seventeen times with αἰώνιος, 'eternal'; and in the remaining occurrences outside the Prologue, it is clear from the context that 'eternal' life is meant (the two usages in 1:4 may be the only exception). See further C. F. D. Moule, 'The Meaning of "Life" in the Gospel and Epistles of St. John', *Theology* 78 (1975), 114–125; J. C. Davis, 'The Johannine Concept of Eternal Life as a Present Possession', *ResQ* 27 (1984), 161–9.

[121] The word φῶς occurs twenty-three times in John as opposed to seven times in Matthew, once in Mark, and seven (six) times in Luke. For further discussion, see E. L. Miller, *Salvation-History in the Prologue of John* (Leiden: Brill, 1989), 55–89; J. P. Weisengoff, 'Light and Its Relation to Life in St. John', *CBQ* 8 (1946), 448–51; Gerald A. Laursen, 'A Study of Johannine Terminology Relative to the Holiness of God' (Th. D. diss., Dallas Seminary, 1976), 192; Corell, *Consummatum Est*, 93; Lindars, *John*, 86–7; R. J. Raja, 'Notion of Light in St. John', *Bible Bhashyam* 1 (1975), 126–34; Tenney, 'The Imagery of John', 13–21.

[122] Bultmann, *Theology of the New Testament*, 2:20 (§42).

[123] Literature and statistics on selected numbered themes above include the following:

(1) See the play upon words associated with light and darkness in John 9:4, 5 and also in 11:9, 10. Cf. Jn. 1:9; 3:19; 8:12; 9:5; 11:9; 12:45. 'Darkness' is personified in 1:5 and points beyond mere spiritual or physical darkness. Behind John's use of darkness lies the force of evil (cf. John 8:44). In fact, at the climactic moment when 'darkness' seems to have overtaken 'the light' on the cross, darkness is defeated in the resurrection and exaltation of the Light (cf. 1:5). See John Navone, 'A Theology of Darkness, Terror, and Dread', *Theology* 80 (1977), 348–53; D. O. Via, Jr., 'Darkness, Christ, and the Church in the Fourth Gospel', *SJT* 14 (1961), 172–93.

Chapter 2: The Structure of John's Enigmatic Language

To illustrate the point, the Johannine concept of 'truth' signifies among its various nuances that which 'corresponds to the facts' (Jn. 4:18; 10:24); that which is 'reliable, trustworthy, faithful', in line with Old Testament

---

(2) 'Know' is another key concept in John's Gospel. The verb γινώσκω (BAGD, 160–61) in its various grammatical forms occurs approximately 56 times, and the term εἰδέναι (BAGD, 220–21) in its different grammatical forms occurs some 85 times in the Fourth Gospel. The Evangelist rarely uses the noun form for 'knowledge'. For various distinctions between γινώσκω and εἰδέναι, see R. Bultmann, *TDNT* 1 (1964), 711–13 and G. Kittel, *TDNT* 2 (1964), 373-5.

(3) 'Glory' is used forty-four times in John as opposed to thirty-eight times in the Synoptics. Cf. G. B. Caird, 'The Glory of God in the Fourth Gospel: An Exercise in Biblical Semantics', *NTS* 15 (1968–69), 265–77; M. Pamment, 'The Meaning of Doxa in the Fourth Gospel', *ZNW* 74 (1973), 12–16; D. Hill, 'The Request of Zebedee's Sons and the Johannine δόξα-Theme', *NTS* 13 (1966-67), 281–5.

(4) On the 'hour' see G. Ferraro, *L' "ora" di Cristo nel Quarto Vangelo* (Roma: Herder, 1974).

(5) The words ἐργάζεσθαι and ἔργον occur thirty-five times in John as opposed to nine times in Matthew, three times in Mark and three times in Luke.[124] The term ἔργον is used in its various grammatical forms in John twenty-seven times as opposed to nine times in the Synoptics. See Peter W. Ensor's helpful discussion in *Jesus and His Works: The Johannine Sayings in Historical Perspective*, WUNT 85 (Tübingen: Mohr-Siebeck, 1996).

(6) On the signs see G. Miller, 'The Nature and Purpose of the Signs in the Fourth Gospel' (Ph.D. diss., Duke University, 1968); F. E. Rainey, 'Semeion in the Gospel of John: A Clue to the Interpretation of the Gospel' (Ph.D. diss., Ft. Worth, TX: Southwestern Baptist Theological Seminary, 1968).

(8) The verb μένω is a favourite Johannine expression. It is used forty times in the Gospel and twenty-seven times in the Epistles (sixty-seven times together) against one hundred eighteen times total in the New Testament. The general significance of μένω for John is to express the permanence of relationship between the Father and the Son, and the Son and the believer.

(9) The verb ζητεῖν, 'to seek' is used thirty-four times in the Gospel, that is, one quarter of the usage of this verb in the entire New Testament. In many of the instances of its usage in John, the word bears a deeper significance.

(10) The word 'believe', with its various nuances and appearances in verb form no less than ninety-eight times, may indicate the active nature of the Johannine understanding of its use as a 'cluster-word'.

(11) Cf. C. R. Bowen, 'Love in the Fourth Gospel', *JR* 13 (1933), 39–49; J. A. Scott, 'The Words for "Love" in Jn. 21:15–17', *Classical Weekly* 39 (1945–46), 71–2; T. Barrosse, 'The Relationship of Love to Faith in St. John', *TS* 18 (1957), 538–9; P. S. Naumann, 'The Presence of Love in John's Gospel', *Worship* 39 (1965), 363–71; F. C. Fensham, 'Love in the Writings of Qumran and John', *Neot* 6 (1972), 67–77; S. van Tilborg, *Imaginative Love in John* (Leiden: Brill, 1993).

(12) The word κόσμος occurs seventy-eight times in John as opposed to eight times in Matthew, two times in Mark and three times in Luke. The 'world' in John may represent the whole of humanity (3:16), the whole created order (1:9–10a), and also all that has fallen under the dominion of the evil one (1:10b; 7:7; 8:23). Cf. BAGD, 445–47; W. G. Henderson, 'The Ethical Idea of the World in John's Gospel' (Ph.D. diss., Louisville: Southern Baptist Theological Seminary, 1945).

(13) On the narrative level, the verb 'to see' (1:38) obviously refers to physical sight. Yet on the symbolic level, 'to see' suggests recognition of God in Jesus Christ. The various Greek terms for 'seeing' are used in John interchangeably for both the physical perception and the faith perception. The various words that John utilises meaning 'to see' are found in 1:14, 50–51; 3:11, 32; 5:19;

usage (Jn. 1:14; 2 Jn. 3); that which is 'genuine as opposed to being false or counterfeit' (Jn. 4:23-24; 6:55, 15:1); that which has been 'testified or attested to' (Jn. 5:31-32; 14:6); and that which is 'revealed in contrast to hidden' (Jn. 8:32, 14:17; 1 Jn. 4:6).[124] Above all else, 'truth' is that which Jesus reveals about the Father (1:18).

2.2.2. The Literary Fabric of Johannine Ambiguity

Linguistic ambiguities are the micro-components of a highly complex literary tapestry;[125] they make up John's enigmatic language at the macro-compositional level. John's ambiguity consists of a small pool of vocabulary to which he has given special meaning contextually by way of echoes of and allusions to the Old Testament.

6:40; 9:39; 14:7, 9; 17:24; 19:35-37; 20:8, 25, 29. Cf. Rene Kieffer, 'Different Levels in Johannine Imagery', in *Aspects on the Johannine Literature*, ed. by Lars Hartman and Birger Olsson, ConBNT 18 (Uppsala: Almqvist and Wiksell, 1986), 74-84; C. F. D. Moule, 'The Individualism of the Fourth Gospel', *NovT* 5 (1962), 171-90, esp. 174-75; idem, 'The Influence of Circumstances on the Use of Christological Terms', *JTS* n.s. 10 (1959), 258; Brown, *John*, 2:955.

(14) To hear is both a sensory act as well as the inner discernment of truth in John. See the various connotations associated with 'hearing' in 3:32; 5:24-26, 30, 37; 6:45, 60; 8:26, 40-43, 45-47; 10:3, 18, 26-27; 12:45-47; 15:15; and 18:37.

(17) The words μαρτυρεῖν, μαρτυρία, and μαρτύριον, occur forty-seven times in John as opposed to four times in Matthew, six times in Mark and five times in Luke. The verb μαρτυρέω occurs thirty times (cf. once in Mt., once in Lk., and none in Mk.) and the noun μαρτυρία fourteen times (cf. none in Mt., once in Lk., three in Mk.).

(18) On 'above and below' see O. Böcher, *Der Johanneischen Dualismus im Zusammenhang des nachbibliischen Judentums* (Gütersloh: Mohn, 1965); J. Becker, 'Beobachtungen zum Dualismus im Johannesevangelium', *ZNW* 65 (1974), 71-87; Barrett, *Essays on John* (London: SPCK, 1982), 98-115.

[124] Louw and Nida, *Greek-English Lexicon*, 2:673; cf. 1:9-10; BAGD, 35-36; W. Detzler, *New Testament Words in Today's Language* (Wheaton: Victor Books, 1986), 380-81; Ernst R. Wendland, 'What Is Truth? Semantic Density and the Language of the Johannine Epistles with Special Reference to 2 John', *Notes on Translation* 5 (1991), 36.

[125] This complex literary tapestry may also shed some light on the so-called various redactional layers in the Gospel. Many Johannine problems attributed to the different levels of composition and redaction may yet receive new solutions when they are viewed in the context of John's rhetorical method: the formal rhetorical traits in John's Gospel and the ever-recurrent and cumulative presence of these traits in passage after passage. For example, the rhetorical frame of the passages in chapters 5-10 revolves around the concepts of witness, advocate, accuser, and judge. Not only are individual passages affected, but the entire Gospel seems to possess a markedly rhetorical structure. These traits would seem to accentuate the importance of these rhetorical features in the Gospel and to the Evangelist's persuasive thrust (20:30-31). As early as J. Weiss, 'Beiträge zur paulinischen Rhetorik' (Göttingen: Vandenhoek und Ruprecht, 1897), if not earlier, there has been a general recognition of the importance of rhetorical considerations in the exegetical process, in Johannine as well as other New Testament studies. See, for example, the

Chapter 2: The Structure of John's Enigmatic Language

The language of the Fourth Gospel has in some respects the quality of prose-poetry. It is characteristic of such language to be infused with metaphor, irony, symbolism, and thematic plays on words or ideas of historical import. The ambiguity associated with such language may have troubled the Evangelist's own immediate historical audience. But it is even more of a problem for modern readers, separated from the original setting by a considerable span of time. Present-day readers have to wade through the ambiguity without fully sharing the linguistic medium of John. Recognising *double entendre* and irony in one's own native language tends to create uncertainty. The question therefore arises: Did the author really intend to exploit, for example, the double-meaning words noted earlier? Or is it the case that some scholars are reading into the text more than is actually there? While one must remain aware of the dangers of over-reading, it is far more likely that our lack of familiarity with the wider connotations of words and phrases in their historical setting will result in under-reading. This tendency is evident from the persistence with which scholars either amend away or otherwise eliminate the intentional ambiguity in relatively clear cases of this literary feature.

The aim of the present chapter is to examine the various literary components which give John's language its particular elusive property. The important point to keep in view is that the author employs these devices as a compound literary device in conjunction with other literary features which communicate at two levels.[126]

---

massive undertaking by H. Strack and P. Billerbeck (Str-B), *Kommentar zum Neuen Testament aus Talmud und Midrasch*, 4 vols (Munich: Oscar Beck, 1922-1928), as well as Bultmann's *Der Stil der paulinischen Predigt und die kynisch-stoische Diatribe* (Göttingen: Vandenhoek und Ruprecht, 1910); also Daube who popularised this area both in his lectures and in his works, in particular, 'The New Testament and Rabbinic Judaism: Rabbinic Methods of Interpretation and Hellenistic Rhetoric', *HUCA* 22 (1949), 237-64. By this observation, on the other hand, I do not mean that the rhetorical studies should or could substitute for the traditional historical, exegetical models for interpreting the Gospel. Neither do I believe that literary and rhetorical methods can ever, in and of themselves, adequately do justice exegetically to a text. Rather, they should become one further step in the exegetical process and integrated as part of the tradional analysis and study of the text.

[126] I have yet to locate a work which sees the interdependence of these literary features (e.g., irony, ambiguity, polysemy, etc.) in the Fourth Gospel, even in such excellent treatments as J. Bryan Born, 'The Literary Features in the Gospel of John', *Direction* 17 (1988), 3-17; Louw, 'On Johannine Style', 5-12; and Alan Culpepper, *Anatomy of the Fourth Gospel: A Study in Literary Design*, 2nd edn (Philadelphia: Fortress, 1987 [1983]).

2.2.2.1. Johannine Symbolism and Metaphor

Johannine symbolism and metaphoric language has caught the imagination of generations of specialists and non-specialists alike.[127] One cannot speak of the elusiveness of John's language without immediately thinking of Johannine symbolism and metaphor. Both are important elements in the 'spiritual', 'mysterious' aura of the Gospel's language. While there are many interpretive perils in reading too much symbolism into John's Gospel and many exegetical errors have resulted from such over-reading, one must still be sensitive to the presence of figurative undercurrents in its language. The understanding of the Gospel is not possible without an appreciation of the role of *symbolism* in John's composition.[128]

Symbolism in its most basic sense involves representation. A symbol has more than one legitimate reference, so that its full meaning involves a tension between two or more directions of semantic stress. Though symbolism is present in John's language, yet metaphor appears to be the dominant category.[129] Metaphor is pervasive in the language of the

---

[127] On the importance of metaphor in language and its contribution to the creation of a double-layer disposition in language see M. S. Kjargaard, *Metaphor and Parable* (Leiden: Brill, 1986); Sallie McFague, *Metaphorical Theology: Models of God in Religious Language* (Philadelphia: Fortress, 1982); Ullmann, *Semantics*, 212; George Lakoff and Mark Johnson, *Metaphors We Live By* (Chicago: University of Chicago Press, 1980); Jonathan Culler, *The Pursuit of Signs: Semiotics, Literature, Deconstruction* (London and Melbourne: Routledge and Kegan Paul, 1981), 188 Donald Davidson, 'What Metaphors Mean', in *On Metaphors*, ed. by Sheldon Sacks (Chicago: University of Chicago Press, 1979); Christine Brooke-Rose, *A Grammar of Metaphor* (London: Secker and Warburg, 1958); R. Samuel Levin, *The Semantics of Metaphor* (Baltimore: John Hopkins University Press, 1977); P. Henle, 'Metaphor', in *Language, Thought, and Culture* (Ann Arbor, MI: University of Michigan Press, 1965), ch. 7; L. G. Knights and B. Cottle, eds, *Metaphor and Symbol*, Colston Research Society, Colston Papers 12 (London, 1947).

[128] G. H. C. MacGregor, *Gospel of John*, MNTC (London: Hodder and Stoughton, 1928), xxv; Xavier Léon-Dufour, 'Towards a Symbolic Reading of the Fourth Gospel', *NTS* 27 (1981), 439–56; *Der Glaubende und die feindliche Welt: Beobachtungen zum gnostischen Dualismus und seiner Bedeutung für Paulus und das Johannesevangelium*, WMANT 37 (Neukirchen-Vluyn: Neukirchener Verlag, 1970); P. Diel and J. Solotareff, *Symbolism in the Gospel of John*, trans. by Nelly Marans (San Francisco: Harper and Row, 1988); C. Geertz, 'Ethos, Worldview and the Analysis of Sacred Symbols', in *The Interpretation of Cultures* (New York: Basic Books, 1973), 126–41; Warren Carter, 'The Prologue and John's Gospel: Function, Symbol and the Definitive Word', *JSNT* 39 (1990), 35–58; C. F. Dumermuth, 'Number Symbolism in the Gospel of John', *Asia Journal of Theology* 4 (1990), 108–19; J. D. M. Derrett, 'John 9:6 Read with Isaiah 6:10; 20:9', *EvQ* 66 (1994), 251–4. Cf. Dodd, *Interpretation of the Fourth Gospel*, 133–43; Sandra M. Schneiders, 'History and Symbolism in the Fourth Gospel', in *L'Évangile de Jean*, ed. by M. de Jonge (1977), 371–6; Meeks, 'Man From Heaven', 44–72; idem, 'Galilee and Judea in the Fourth Gospel', *JBL* 85 (1966), 159–69.

[129] R. Kysar, 'Johannine Metaphor – Meaning and Function: A Literary Case Study of John 10:1–18', *Semeia* 53 (1991), 81–112; Jaubert, *Approches de l'évangile de Jean*, 54–86; M. Pamment, 'Path and Residence Metaphors in the Fourth Gospel', *Theology* 88 (1985), 118–24.

Scriptures,[130] and the Johannine metaphors number among some of the best-known in the Bible. They are also a significant contributing factor to the enigmatic quality of the Gospel's language. Meeks characterises John's language as a 'closed system of metaphors'.[131] Metaphor is a feature by which the Evangelist captures spiritual reality in earthly language; he depicts the Son's relationship to the Father and the implication of his life, death and resurrection for both the world and his disciples. Many Johannine metaphors and symbols are rooted in Old Testament ideas and images which John believes have found their realisation in Jesus' life.

If defining 'metaphor' in literature is problematic, it is even more so in the Fourth Gospel, whose metaphors are characterised by Meeks as a 'closed system'. Janet Soskice, wrestling with the problem writes, 'Any one who has grappled with the problem of defining a metaphor will appreciate the pragmatism of those who proceed to discuss it without giving any definition of it at all.'[132] There are numerous definitions for metaphor, e.g., implied comparison, analogy, substitution, and interaction.[133]

---

[130] Peter W. Macky, *The Centrality of Metaphors to Biblical Thought* (Lewiston, NY: Edwin Mellen Press, 1990).

[131] Meeks, 'Man from Heaven', 68.

[132] Soskice, *Metaphor and Religious Language*, 15.

[133] Lakoff and Johnson, *Metaphors We Live By*, 5; Stephen Ullmann, *Semantics*, 213, sees the basic structure of metaphor as always having two terms present: 'the thing we are talking about and that to which we are comparing it.' On the other hand, Max Black, 'More About Metaphor', in *Metaphor and Thought*, ed. by Andrew Ortony (Cambridge: CUP, 1979), 28, denies the comparative nature of metaphor; cf. his *Models and Metaphors* (Ithaca: Cornell University Press, 1962). See also I. A. Richards, *The Philosophy of Rhetoric* (New York: OUP, 1936), 93; Caird, *Language and Imagery*, 17; Edwin M. Good, 'Ezekiel's Ship: Some Extended Metaphors in the Old Testament', *Semitics* 1 (1970), 70–80; W. B. Stanford, *Greek Metaphor: Studies in Theory and Practice* (Oxford, 1936), quoted in W. K. Wimsatt, *The Verbal Icon: Studies in the Meaning of Poetry* (New York, 1966 [paperback reprint of 1954 edn]), 128. Aristotle believed, 'Metaphor consists in applying to a thing a word that belongs to something else; the transference being either from genus to species or from species to genus or from species to species or on grounds of analogy', quoted in W. Nowottny, *Language Poets Use*, 49. Nowottny himself (*Language Poets Use*, 175), using Friedman's definition, speaks of metaphor as one thing (tenor) spoken in terms which are appropriate to another (vehicle), with the vehicle serving as the source of traits to be transferred to the tenor. However, in symbol, we have the vehicle itself (cf. Friedman, *Form and Meaning*, 289). See further definitions and discussions by Monroe Beardsley, *Aesthetics: Problems in the Philosophy of Criticism* (New York: Harcourt, Brace, 1958); idem, 'The Metaphorical Twist', *Philosophy and Phenomenological Research* 22 (1962), 294; James Edie, 'Ideality and Metaphor: A Phenomenological Theory of Polysemy', *Journal of the British Society for Phenomenology* 6 (1975), 32–41; Philip Wheelwright, *The Burning Foundation*, rev. edn (Bloomington: Indiana University Press, 1968), 102, idem, *Metaphor and Reality* (Bloomington: Indiana University Press, 1962), 45–69; Ogden and Richards, *Meaning of Meaning*, 23; Sheldon Sacks, ed., *On Metaphor* (Chicago: University of Chicago Press, 1979); Israel Scheffler, *Beyond the Letter: A Philosophical Inquiry into Ambiguity, Vagueness and Metaphor in Language* (London: Routledge and Kegan Paul, 1979); C. S. Lewis, *Miracles: A Preliminary Study* (New

Metaphor may be explained in terms of an analogical association or working together of two distinct semantic entities with distinct references in order to create a single new perception. A characteristic of a metaphor is the absurdity between the object described and the description if taken literally. In the sentence, 'I am the door', the literal interpretation of 'I am' and 'the door' may be blocked semantically through logical absurdity, or pragmatically through factual impossibility or implausibility.[134] In order to resolve this clash so as to make sense of a metaphor, a shift takes place from the literal to the figurative meaning. The figurative meaning is fundamental to understanding metaphors. Moreover in metaphoric analogy, there is a correspondence between semantic distance and effectiveness. The more unlike the literal meanings of the two terms in a metaphor, the more striking the metaphor.[135]

Herein lies the reason for the effectiveness of Johannine metaphors. Among the various categories of metaphor in biblical literature, three major groups may be singled out in the Fourth Gospel: (1) anthropomorphic metaphors,[136] e.g., the arm of the Lord, the voice of God; (2) agricultural, architectural, or nature metaphors, e.g., the Lamb of God, the Vine and the branches, the temple of his body, the good shepherd, living water;[137] and (3) concrete to abstract metaphors, e.g., the bread of life.

Often symbolism and metaphor are confused because of overlaps.[138]

York: Macmillan, 1947); Earl R. MacCormac, *Metaphor and Myth in Science and Religion* (Durham: Duke University Press, 1976); Margaret Davies, *Rhetoric and Reference in the Fourth Gospel*, JSNTSup 69 (Sheffield: Sheffield Academic Press, 1992), 117; Soueif, 'A Linguistic Analysis of Metaphor with Reference to its Historical Development in English Poetry from 1500 to 1950' (Ph.D. thesis, University of Lancaster, 1977), 21-3; Alston, *Philosophy of Language* (a succinct and valuable treatment of metaphors); Elizabeth Harris, *Prologue and Gospel: The Theology of the Fourth Evangelist* (Sheffield: Sheffield Academic Press, 1994), 140; T. Hawkes, *Metaphor* (London: Methuen, 1972), 1. One of the most detailed treatises ever published on metaphor is C. F. P. Stutterheim's *Het Begrip Metaphoor: Een taalkundig en wijsgering onderzoek* (Amsterdam, 1941).

[134] Richards, *Philosophy of Rhetoric*, 96.

[135] If the two terms are very close to each other, for example, if one flower is likened to another, then the metaphor will be appropriate but without any expressive quality. However, the more remote the two terms are from one another in character, the greater is the tension. See further Sayce, *Style in French Prose: A Method of Analysis* (Oxford: 1953), 62f.; Eva F. Kittay, *Metaphor: Its Cognitive Force and Linguistic Structure* (Oxford: Clarendon, 1987); M. S. Kjargaard, *Metaphor and Parable* (Leiden: Brill, 1986).

[136] The most comprehensive study on anthropomorphic metaphors is J. J. De Witte, *De Betekeniswereld van het lichaam* (Nijmegen, 1948).

[137] Ullmann, *Semantics*, 215.

[138] The confusion is evident in the following definitions of allegory. Leech, *Linguistic Guide*, 163 describes allegory as closely related to symbol, a 'multiple symbol'. Harris, *Prologue and Gospel*, 140, on the other hand, explains allegory as a story made up of a series of connected

Like metaphor, symbolism also depends on the distinctions between literal and figurative meanings.[139] But while symbolism involves representation, metaphor has to do with analogy. The symbolic representation may have become universally recognised, e.g., the cross; the dove. Or it may not be universal, but quite exclusive, as in the case of the bread and the cup bearing a sacramental or symbolic representation for Christians only.[140]

In metaphoric language, the author often speaks of X in terms of Y, where Y refers to X. In other words, the parameters of the analogy are narrowly defined. With symbolism this analogical correspondence is not explicitly defined, either because it is already known, or it is deliberately left vague. An object X may be mentioned without necessarily naming a further object to which X is analogous.[141] Here the reader sees X not only as X, but also as something more than itself. In symbolism, the discernment of the deeper meaning is left to the reader.

Apart from the distinction between symbolism and metaphor, there is a necessary distinction between metaphor and simile. Simile as a form is not as prominent a figure of speech in John's Gospel as it is in the Synoptic Gospels and in various portions of the Hebrew Bible. The difference between simile and metaphor lies outside the area of pure form. A simile is an explicit comparison using such terms as 'like' or 'as', while a metaphor is an implied comparison. Or again, a simile is an overt comparison, while the metaphor is a covert comparison.[142] A simile is basically illustrative in

---

metaphors. Paul Ricoeur, *The Rule of Metaphor: Multi-Disciplinary Studies of the Creation of Meaning in Language*, trans. R. Czerny (Toronto: University of Toronto Press, 1977), 53–55 sees a close affinity between metaphor and symbol in that a metaphor consists of speaking of one thing in terms of another that resembles it; that 'another' he calls 'the symbol'. Macky, *Centrality of Metaphors*, 54, claims, 'Every metaphor refers to a "symbol" as we are using the term here.'

[139] It is described as an 'optional extension, as it were, of the meaning from literal to figurative'. See Leech, *Linguistic Guide*, 162.

[140] For example, the 'symbol' of the 'cross' has become a permanent representation of Christianity. However, in the metaphor, 'I am the door of the sheep' (John 10:7), neither does the 'door' depict a permanent picture of Christ, nor the 'sheep' comprise a permanent picture of his followers.

[141] Wheelwright, in *Metaphor and Reality*, 99–110, suggests four categories from which the meanings of symbols may be derived: (1) Archetypal symbols. These derive their meaning from contexts which are virtually universal, such as the basic opposition of light and darkness. (2) Symbols of ancestral vitality. These derive their meaning from earlier sources. In our Gospels, these include images drawn from the Old Testament, i.e., the wilderness as a place of testing, the number twelve as suggestive of Israel, and so on. (3) Symbols created by the implied author. These can be understood only within the context of the particular narrative. The reader of Mark's Gospel, for example, may be led to identify the withered fig tree (11:12–24) as a symbol of Israel's obsolete temple cult. (4) Symbol of cultural range. These derive their meaning from the social and historical context of the real author and his or her community.

[142] Leech, *Linguistic Guide*, 156.

nature, whereas a metaphor is a bearer of that very reality to which it refers. The metaphor is not a comparison but a union of terms. The declaration of John the Baptist in 1:32, 'I beheld the Spirit descending as a dove out of heaven' or the statement in 3:14, 'As Moses lifted up the serpent in the wilderness, even so must the Son of man be lifted up' are examples of Johannine simile.

In the Gospel of John, symbolism has been attributed for example to wine (2:1–10), birth (3:3), water (4:14), bread (6:33), food (6:27ff.), sleep (11:23 ff.), washing (13:5–10), way (14:6), light versus darkness (1:5; 3:19; 8:12; 9:1–4); death (11:1–44), and references to time (e.g., 3:2; 4:6; 13:30)[143] and to geography (e.g., Cana, Jerusalem).[144] The purification of the temple is seen by some scholars as a symbolic fulfilment of Psalm 69:10 and the coming Kingdom of God.[145] The reference to 'the temple of his body' in John 2:19–22,[146] Jesus' remark about the 'fig tree' in his response to Nathanael's question in 1:48,[147] the allusion to being 'born of water and Spirit' in John 3:5,[148] or the episode of the washing of the feet of the

---

[143] See especially G. Stemberger, 'Untersuchungen zur johanneischen Symbolik von Gut und Böse' (diss., Innsbruck, 1967); idem, *La simbolica del bene e del male in S. Giovanni*. Traduzione di A. Candelaresi e G. Adani (Milano: Edizione Paoline, 1970); Léon-Dufour, 'Towards a Symbolic Reading', 439–56; Barrett, 'Symbolism', in *Essays on John*, 65–79.

[144] Meeks, 'Galilee and Judea', 159–69; Francis J. Moloney, 'From Cana to Cana (Jn. 2:1–4:54) and the Fourth Evangelist's Concept of Correct (and incorrect) Faith', *Salesianum* 40 (1978), 817–43.

[145] Cf. Richard Hiers, 'Purification of the Temple: Preparation for the Kingdom of God', *JBL* 90 (1971), 82–90; R. Bultmann, *Jesus and the Word* (New York: Scribners, 1958), 29; idem, *John*, 122–9; Bertil Gärtner, *The Temple and the Community in Qumran and the New Testament* (Cambridge: CUP, 1965), 105–22; J. C. O'Neill, 'The Silence of Jesus', *NTS* 15 (1968), 164; Schnackenburg, *St. John*, 343–56; Niel Q. Hamilton, 'Temple Cleansing and Temple Bank', *JBL* 83 (1964), 372; Barrett, *St. John*, 162–8; Lindars, *John*, 135–45; Bruce, *John*, 73–7; and Hoskyns, *Fourth Gospel*, 192–9. The disapproving challenge of 2:18 seems to imply that the Jewish audience may have been cognisant of the Messianic connotation behind Jesus' action. See R. M. Grant, 'The Coming of the Kingdom', *JBL* 67 (1948), 298; J. Blenkinsopp, 'The Oracle of Judah and the Messianic Entry', *JBL* 80 (1961), 58; Millar Burrows, 'Thy Kingdom Come', *JBL* 74 (1955), 1–8.

[146] Leon-Dufour, 'For a Symbolic Reading', 447; Guilding, *Fourth Gospel and Jewish Worship*, 171–9; Davies, 'Johannine "Sign" of Jesus', 91–115; Cadman, *Open Heaven*, 26–32.

[147] Some have denied it any significance: B. Newman and E. Nida, *A Translator's Handbook on the Gospel of John* (London: United Bible Societies, 1980), 49. Others acknowledge the potential symbolism: J. D. M. Derrett, 'Fig Trees in the New Testament', *HeyJ* 14 (1973), 249–65; J. R. Michaels, 'Nathanael Under the Fig Tree', *ExpTim* 78 (1966–67), 182–3.

[148] X. Léon-Dufour, 'Et là, Jésus baptisait (Jn 3:22)', in *Mélanges Eugène Tisserant*, tome 1 (Rome, 1964), 295–309; I. de la Potterie, '"Naître de l'eau et naître de l'esprit": Le texte baptismal de Jn 3:5', *Sciences ecclésiastiques* 14 (1962), 417–43; H. Köster, 'Geschichte und Kultus im Johannesevangelium und bei Ignatius von Antiochien', *ZTK* 54 (1957), 63–4; M. Barth, *Die Taufe, ein Sakrament? Ein exegetischer Beitrag zum Gespräch über die kirchliche Taufe* (Zürich: Theologischer Verlag, 1951), 443–53.

disciples[149] have all been viewed by many scholars as having symbolic connotations.

The symbolic element of the Johannine 'signs' is implied by John's placing the term σημεῖα (2:18) into the mouth of 'the Jews' after the temple cleansing and by John's own clarification of Jesus' statement about 'destroying this temple' (2:19) in 2:21–22. In the account of the wedding in Cana of Galilee, where Christ performed his first sign of turning the water into wine, the 'wine' and the 'wedding' are seen as symbolic allusions to the Messianic age.[150] The argument has also been propounded that the account of 'water and blood' issuing forth from the side of Jesus in John 19:34 symbolises the sacraments of baptism and the Eucharist.[151]

The symbolic undercurrent in Jesus' dipping the bread and offering it to Judas in John 13:26 is unmistakable. Jesus' offering of the bread in this episode can, in the light of chapter 6, be seen as the offering of himself as the bread of life to the one who is about to betray him. Satan enters Judas and Jesus tells him, 'Do quickly what you need to do'. No one at the table knows what Judas is going to do. Some think Jesus is telling him to buy what is needed for the Feast of Passover or that he is to give something to the poor. In an ironic sense, in both cases, the disciples are right. Judas leaves and facilitates the greatest provision for the festival – Jesus, the Passover Lamb – and the result of that provision is life in all its fullness offered to humanity in need of such life.

Some see symbolism even in Johannine characterisations.[152]

---

[149] A. J. Hultgren, 'The Johannine Foot Washing (13:1–11) as Symbol of Eschatological Hospitality', *NTS* 28 (1982), 539–46; B. W. Bacon, 'The Sacrament of Foot Washing', *ExpTim* 43 (1931–32), 218–21; K. Hein, 'Judas Iscariot: Key to the Last Supper Narratives?', *NTS* 17 (1970–71), 227–32; E. Lohmeyer, 'Die Fusswaschung', *ZNW* 38 (1939), 74–94; J. D. G. Dunn, 'The Washing of the Disciples' Feet in John 13:1–20', *ZNW* 61 (1970), 247–52; H. Weiss, 'Foot Washing in the Johannine Community', *NovT* 21 (1979), 298–325; F. F. Segovia, 'John 13:1–20, The Foot Washing in the Johannine Tradition', *ZNW* 73 (1982), 31–51; G. Richter, 'The Washing of Feet in John 13:1–20', *Theology Digest* 14 (1966), 200–5; S. M. Schneiders, 'The Foot Washing (John 13:1–20): An Experiment in Hermeneutics', *CBQ* 43 (1981), 76–92; G. G. Nicol, 'Jesus' Washing the Feet of the Disciples: A Model for Johannine Christology?', *ExpTim* 91 (1979), 20–1.

[150] In two passages in Isaiah, the imagery of 'wedding' is used to describe the Messianic age (Isa. 61:10; 62:5). See also Amos 9:13; Hos. 2:24; Joel 4:18; Isa. 25:6; 29:17; and Jer. 31:5. Cf. William H. Marty, 'The New Moses' (Th.D. diss., Dallas Seminary, 1984), 142–3; Collins, *These Things*, 118–9; A. T. Hanson, *The Prophetic Gospel: A Study of John and the Old Testament* (Edinburgh: Clark, 1991), 42ff.

[151] Teresa Okure, *Johannine Approach to Mission* (Tübingen: Mohr, 1988), xix.

[152] See D. R. Beck, *The Discipleship Paradigm: Readers and Anonymous Characters in the Fourth Gospel* (Leiden: Brill, 1997); J. Rena, 'Women in the Gospel of John', *Eglise et Théologie* 17 (1986), 131–47; Raymond F. Collins, 'Representative Figures of the Fourth Gospel'.

Sacramental symbolism in association with the discourse on the bread of life (John 6) is as old as the Gospel itself.[153] Warren Carter argues that the whole of the prologue in the Fourth Gospel involves a 'cluster of sacred symbols'.[154] Scholars have proposed various readings of ἰχθύς in 21:1–14 and have seen symbolic significance in the catch of 153 fish.[155] In this account, the Evangelist also tells his audience that the net was not torn, οὐκ ἐσχίσθη (21:11). Some have seen the net as a symbol for the church and its unbrokenness despite the tremendous weight it carried, which may reflect the Evangelist's concern for unity and oneness in the church. Schisms and divisions may arise as believers encounter the unbelieving world (cf. σχίσμα in 7:43; 9:16; 10:19). But such schisms are not to mark out the believing community itself.

In commenting on John 19:25–27, where Jesus instructs his mother Mary to make her new home with the beloved disciple, Bernabé claims that Mary represents the daughter of Zion (i.e., the church) and that John signifies all the disciples of Jesus. The fulfilment of Jesus' testament is Mary, who is endowed to the highest degree with grace, truth, and the Holy Spirit.[156]

There may also be some Johannine subtlety in the account of the empty tomb in John 20:11–12. Here, in contrast to the Synoptics' report of an empty tomb, it is reported that two angels sit where the head and the feet of the body of Jesus had been. The position of the two angels symbolically corresponds to the cherubim at the two ends of the mercy seat on the

---

[153] X. Léon-Dufour, 'Le mystère du pain de vie (Jean VI)', *RSR* 46 (1958), 481–523; Sandra M. Schneiders, 'Symbolism and the Sacramental Principle in the Fourth Gospel', in *Segnie Sacramenti nel Vangelo di Giovanni*, Studia Anselmiana 66, ed. by Pius-Ramon Tragan (Rome: Editrice Anselmiana, 1977), 221–35.

[154] Carter, 'Prologue and John's Gospel: Function, Symbol and the Definitive Word', *JSNT* 39 (1990), 35–58, p. 35. Cf. Geertz, 'Ethos, Worldview and the Analysis of Sacred Symbols', 126–41.

[155] For the various proposals as to the possible significance see R. M. Grant, 'One Hundred and Fifty-three Large Fish (Jn. 21, 11)', *HTR* 42 (1949), 273–5; J. A. Emerton, 'The Hundred and Fifty-three Fishes in John XXI, 11', *JTS* n.s. 9 (1958), 86–9; P. R. Ackroyd, 'The 153 Fishes in Jn 21, 11 – A Further Note', *JTS* n.s. 10 (1959), 94; B. Grigsby, 'Gematria and John 21, 11: Another Look at Ezekiel 47, 10', *ExpTim* 95 (1983–84), 177–8; J. A. Romeo, 'Gematria and John 21:11 – The Children of God', *JBL* 97 (1978), 263–4; N. J. McEleney, '153 Great Fishes (John 21:11): Gematriacal Atbash', *Bib* 58 (1977), 411–17; K. Cardwell, 'The Fish on the Fire: Jn. 21:9', *ExpTim* 102 (1990), 12–14; P. Trudinger, 'The 153 Fishes: A Response and a Further Suggestion', *ExpTim* 102 (1990), 11–12; A. Pitta, 'Ichthys ed opsarion in Gv 21, 1–14: semplice variazione lessicale o differenza con valore simbolico?', *Bib* 71 (1990), 348–364; M. Rissi, 'Voll grosser Fische, hundertdreiundfünfzig, Joh 21, 1–14', *TZ* 35 (1979), 73–89; Lindars, *John*, 629–31; Barrett, *St. John*, 581.

[156] C. Bernabé, 'Transfondo derásico de Jn 20', *EstBib* 49 (1991), 209–28.

ark of the covenant (Exod. 25:10, 17–22). Thus, the tomb where Jesus' body was laid now symbolises the new ark of the covenant.

However, caution is required to detect symbolism when it is present but to avoid overgeneralisation, where every element in the document becomes symbolic for something else. It is, in part, this kind of eisegetical approach which has caused some scholars to overreact and completely dismiss even legitimate symbolic elements in the Fourth Gospel. The important point in the present study is that symbolism in the Gospel is one of the contributing factors in the enigmatic nature of John's language.

Among the Johannine metaphors, perhaps the most prominent are those associated with the 'I am' passages. The expression ἐγώ εἰμι occurs about thirty times in John's Gospel, twenty-seven times in the mouth of Jesus. Taken together, these form one of the most intriguing theological statements in the whole of the New Testament.[157] They are an important component of Johannine christology and a further contributing factor to John's enigmatic language. The Evangelist has fused together in these statements a whole range of literary features to capture the saving revelation of God in the incarnate Word.

The 'I am' sayings may convey a simple, straight-forward self-disclosure. But they also frequently communicate Jesus' mission as the revealer of the Father and mediator of salvation (e.g., John 6:35, 41, 48; 8:12; 10:7, 9, etc.).[158] They convey the unity between the Father and the Son (10:30; 17:11, 22) and Jesus' self-identity with the deity encountered by Israel in Exodus 3:14 (cf. John 8:58–59; 13:19; 18:8).[159] The self-disclosure

---

[157] Cf. George MacRae, 'Theology and Irony in the Fourth Gospel', in *The Word in the World*, ed. by Richard J. Clifford and George W. MacRae, 83–96 (Cambridge, MA: Weston College Press, 1973), 94, George Johnston, 'Ecce Homo! Irony in the Christology of the Fourth Evangelist', in *The Glory of Christ in the New Testament: Studies in Christology*, ed. by L. D. Hurst and N. T. Wright (Oxford: Clarendon, 1987), 130; Philip Harner, *The 'I AM' of the Fourth Gospel: Study in Johannine Usage and Thought* (Philadelphia: Fortress, 1970), 5; Oscar Cullmann, *Vorträge und Aufsätze 1925–1962*, ed. by K. Fröhlich (Tübingen: Mohr, 1966), 176–86; Kysar, *John, the Maverick Gospel*, 40–4, Leon Morris, *Jesus is the Christ: Studies in the Theology of John* (Grand Rapids: Eerdmans, 1989), 107–25.

[158] Werner George Kümmel, *The Theology of the New Testament* (New York: Abingdon, 1973), 283–8; Raymond E. Brown, 'The Ego Eimi (I AM) Passages in the Fourth Gospel', in *A Companion to John*, ed. by Michael J. Taylor (New York: Alba House, 1977), 117–26; John Painter, *John: Witness and Theologian* (London: SPCK, 1975), 38–49, Leonard Goppelt, *Theology of the New Testament*, ed. by Jürgen Roloff and trans. by John E. Alsup, 2 vols (Grand Rapids: Eerdmans, 1982), 1:293–6.

[159] Also Deut. 32:39; Isa 41:4; 43:10; 46:4. Karl Kundsin, *Charakter und Ursprung der Johanneischen Reden*, Acta Universitatis Latviensis, Theologisjas Fakultates Series 1 (Riga: n. p., 1939), 267–8; Henrich Zimmermann, 'Das absolute Ego Eimi als die neutestamentliche offenbarungsformel', *BZ* 4 (1960), 54–69; A. M. Hunter, *The Gospel According to John*, The

of God or theophany is a central theme of the book of Exodus. God makes himself known to the Hebrew nation, not only in supernatural signs, but also by his name. Yet he can never be fully known. This paradox both of the veiled mystery and of the knowledge revealed to God's people is captured well in Deut. 29:29 ('the secret things' versus 'the revealed things'). This paradox is also significant for our understanding of the Johannine 'I am' statements and crucial to the idea of revelation in the Fourth Gospel.[160] The 'I am' statements encapsulate the character, nature, and mission of Jesus. They, too, are part of the vast web of allusions to the Old Testament supporting the Evangelist's claim that Jesus is the mediator of salvation for Israel and the world according to Israel's Scriptures.

Among other noteworthy Johannine metaphors associated with the 'I am' sayings are 'light',[161] 'water', and 'bread', all of which, in John's case, are drawn from corresponding ideas in the Old Testament. For example, the imagery of 'living water', ὕδωρ ζῶν (מַיִם חַיִּים) (Jn. 4:10; 7:39) may echo such passages as Genesis 26:19, Leviticus 14:5, and Jeremiah 2:13. In Leviticus 14:5, for example, the 'living water' simply means fresh running water as opposed to stagnant water. This seems to be how the Samaritan woman understands Jesus' reference in John 4:11. But later in Jeremiah 2:13, the 'living water' has taken an additional figurative nuance with an eschatological salvific connotation. This seems to be what Jesus has in mind in the Samaritan discourse. Some have argued for an additional nuance in the metaphor whereby 'living water' signifies the Holy Spirit. Others see it as a reference to the revelation of truth in Christ.[162]

The extended metaphor of the vine and the branches in John 15:1–12

Cambridge Bible Commentary on the New English Bible (Cambridge: CUP, 1965), 89; Dodd, *Interpretation of the Fourth Gospel*, 93–6.

160 T. W. Manson, 'Ego Eimi of the Messianic Presence in the New Testament', *JTS* 48 (1947), 137–45; Andre Feuillet, *Johannine Studies* (New York: Alba House, 1965), 83–91; D. Daube, 'The "I am" of the Messianic Presence', in *The New Testament and Rabbinic Judaism* (London: Athlone, 1956), 325–9; Paul C. Rogers, 'Manna as a Motif' (thesis, Dallas Seminary, 1983), 51–7.

161 Otto Schwankl, 'Die Metaphorik von Licht und Finsternis im johanneischen Schrifttum', in *Metaphorik und Mythos im Neuen Testament*, ed. by Karl Kertelge, QD 126 (Freiburg: Herder, 1990), 135–67.

162 J. Blenkinsopp, 'John 7:37–39: Another Note on a Notorious Crux', *NTS* 6 (1959), 95–9; Beasley-Murray, *John*, 60; Brown, *John*, 178–9; Calvin, *Gospel according to John*, 1:149–50; Okure, *Johannine Approach to Mission*, 88; P. W. van der Horst, 'A Word Play in John 4:12?' *ZNW* 63 (1972), 280–2; Jeffrey L. Staley, *The Print's First Kiss: A Rhetorical Investigation of the Implied Reader in the Fourth Gospel* (Atlanta, Ga.: Scholars Press, 1988), 101–2; Robert Alter, *The Art of Biblical Narrative* (New York: Basic Books, 1981), 52–62; Bultmann, *John*, 180–1; Schnackenburg, *St. John*, 425–8; Lindars, *John*, 182–4; Hoskyns, *Fourth Gospel*, 241–2; Haenchen, *John*, 1:220; Morris, *John*, 253–61; and Fenton, *John*, 60.

is another well-known example of ambiguity in the 'I am' sayings. The ambiguity is bound up with double-meaning word καθαίρειν in 15:2 which means 'to prune' in a horticultural sense and 'to cleanse or purify' figuratively.[163] The word is used of cleansing grain by winnowing[164] and of cleansing weeds from the ground before sowing.[165] Καθαίρειν can be used of religious ceremony[166] and in a moral sense.[167] Philo uses the agricultural sense in a moral allegory.[168] In the Old Testament imagery, Israel is the vine.[169] In the Johannine post-resurrection interpretation, Jesus is the genuine vine.[170] There seems also to be a paronomastic word play between the two verbs αἴρει and καθαίρει, which suggests an original Greek composition rather than the translation of a Semitic original of the Gospel.

Moving on from the 'I am' sayings, the language of 'descent' and 'ascent' is viewed by some as a metaphor of allegiance.[171] The expression 'lamb of God' is another well-known Johannine metaphor (cf. John 1:29, 36). It has long been recognised and interpreted by the Christian church as a graphic presentation of Jesus as the Paschal lamb who, in his sacrifice, has atoned for sin.[172] The conceptual correspondence between the Baptist's declaration in its soterio-christological significance in John 1:29, 36 and the suffering Servant of Isaiah 53:6–7 has been set forth by several Johannine scholars (cf. Acts 8:32; 1 Pet. 1:9; 1 Cor. 5:7).[173]

---

[163] Both of these elements are entwined so that the care of the fruitbearing branches as well as their purification seems to be in view in John. See Barrett, *St. John*, 395; Calvin, *Gospel According to John*, 2:108; Bernard, *St. John*, 2:479; Hoskyns, *Fourth Gospel*, 474–5; Lindars, *John*, 488; Schnackenburg, *St. John*, 3:95, 97–8; Bultmann, *John*, 532–3; Morris, *John*, 669–70; Westcott, *St. John*, 217.

[164] Xenophon, *Oeconomicus*, xviii, 6.

[165] Xenophon, *Oeconomicus*, xx, 11.

[166] Iliad, xvi, 228, purifying a cup for a libation.

[167] Plato, *Phaedo*, 114c.

[168] Philo, *Som.*, II, 64. On this topic, see also Dodd, *Interpretation of the Fourth Gospel*, 136; and Barrett, *St. John*, 473.

[169] Cf. Ps. 80:8–19; Isa. 5:1–7; Jer. 2:21; Ezk. 15:1–8; 17:5–10; 19:10–14.

[170] The Old Testament background of the metaphor is widely accepted. Barrett, *St. John*, 392–4; Beasley-Murray, *John*, 271–2; Hoskyns, *Fourth Gospel*, 474–5; M. C. Tenney, *John: The Gospel of Belief* (Grand Rapids: Eerdmans, 1948), 226; J. N. Sanders, *St. John*, 336–7; Bruce, *John*, 308; and Tasker, *St. John*, 173–4; Brown, *John*, 2:660; Lightfoot, *St. John's Gospel*, 291.

[171] Margaret Davies, *Rhetoric and Reference*, 117.

[172] Cf. Barrett, *St. John*, 147; idem, 'The Lamb of God', *NTS* 9 (1962–63), 193–207; idem, 'The Old Testament in the Fourth Gospel', *JTS* 48 (1947), 155–69; Dodd, *Interpretation of the Fourth Gospel*, 236–38; Merrill Tenney, 'The Old Testament and the Fourth Gospel', *BibSac* 120 (1963), 302, 307.

[173] Brown, *John*, 60–61; Ray Summers, *Behold the Lamb* (Nashville: Broadman Press, 1979); Cullmann, *Early Christian Worship*, 55–56; T. F. Glasson, *Moses in the Fourth Gospel* (London:

What is important in the context of the present study is that both symbolism and metaphor are effective 'literary tools' (to use the modern nomenclature) in the hand of the Fourth Evangelist to accentuate two levels of meaning, between an image and the deeper reference, or between what is denoted and connoted. There is a finely-honed balance between the earthly appearance and the deeper heavenly reality which John sees hidden in Israel's Scriptures but revealed since the resurrection and the coming of the Holy Spirit to those who have believed. This adds further to the ambiguity of the Gospel's language.

2.2.2.2. Johannine Irony

Irony is a common literary feature in both the Old and New Testaments.[174] In the New Testament, it is most often noticed in the Fourth Gospel (cf. 2:9-10; 4:12; 7:27, 33-34, 42, 52; 8:21-22; 11:16, 36; 12:19; 13:37; 18:31; 19:5, 14, 19ff.).[175] And yet the connection between irony and ambiguity is

---

SCM, 1963), 96. Wead, *Literary Devices*, 38-9; Carson, *Gospel According to John*, 148-51; Bultmann, *John*, 94-6. Lindars, *John*, 108-9, writes, 'we conclude that the title is based on Isaiah 53 interpreted in the light of the Passover sacrifice'. On the other hand, some scholars have argued that the term refers to the 'conquering Lamb' of the Apocalypse who will deliver, lead, and rule the flock of God in the kingdom of God. See Dodd, *Interpretation of the Fourth Gospel*, 230-8; Carson, *Gospel According to John*, 150; Beasley-Murray, *John*, 24, Barrett, *St. John*, ad. loc.; idem, 'The Lamb of God', 210; S. R. Infante, 'L'Agnello nel Quarto Vangelo', *RivistB* 43 (1995), 331-61; J. Nortjé, 'Lamb of God (John 1:29): an explanation from ancient Christian art', *Neot* 30 (1996), 141-50; J. H. Roberts, 'The Lamb of God', *Neot* 2 (1968), 41-56; Douglas Moo, *The Old Testament in the Gospel Passion Narratives* (Sheffield: Almond Press, 1983), 312-14.

[174] Edwin Good, *Irony in the Old Testament* (London: SPKC, 1965); W. L. Halladay, 'Style, Irony and Authenticity in Jeremiah', *JBL* 81 (1962), 44-54; James G. Williams, '"You Have Not Spoken Truth of Me": Mystery and Irony in Job', *ZAW* 83 (1971), 231-55; James G. Williams, 'Irony and Lament: Clues to Prophetic Consciousness', *Semeia* 8 (1977), 51-75; Menakhem Perry and Meier Sternberg, 'The King Through Ironic Eyes' (Hebrew), *HA-Sifrut* 81 (1968), 263-92; Alter, *Art of Biblical Narrative*, 18-20. For irony in Jesus, see Henri Clavier, 'L'Ironie dans l'Enseignement de Jésus', *NovT* 2 (1956), 3-20; idem, 'Les sens multiples dans le Nouveau Testament', *NovT* 2 (1958), 185-90; Elton Trueblood, *The Humour of Christ* (NY: Harper and Row, 1964), 53-67; W. Harnisch, 'Die Ironie als Stilmittel in Gleichnissen Jesu', *EvT* 32 (1972), 421-36; Jerry Gill, 'Jesus, Irony and the "New Quest"', *Int* 41 (1980), 139-51. To study irony in Luke, see James Dawsey, 'The Lucan Voice: Confusion and Irony', in *The Gospel of Luke* (Macon, GA: Mercer University Press, 1986). For irony in Paul, see Aida Besancon Spencer, 'The Wise Fool and the Foolish Wise: A Study of Irony in Paul', *NovT* 23 (1981), 349-60; W. L. Halladay, 'Style, Irony and Authenticity in Jeremiah', *JBL* 81 (1962), 44-54; Jakob Jónsson, *Humour and Irony in the New Testament: Illuminated by Parallels in Talmud and Midrash* (Leiden: Brill, 1985), 201.

[175] Irony as a literary phenomenon in John's Gospel has been studied since the 1800s and the work of George Salmon, *A Historical Introduction to the Study of the Books of the New Testament* (London: John Murray, 1885), 346-9. But see especially Wead, 'Johannine Irony as a Key to the Author, Audience Relationship in John's Gospel', *Biblical Literature* (1974), 33-44;

often overlooked. Irony the Fourth Gospel depends upon a variety of double meanings and ambiguous expressions.[176] Moreover, a distinction needs to be maintained between the irony of John and the irony of Jesus. The irony of the Gospel originates in Jesus himself, who is the master ironist. This irony exposes the blindness of Israel's teachers to their own Scriptures and the inability of unaided humans to see the truth even when it stares them in the face (hence John's emphasis upon new birth and abiding faith). John's use of irony therefore expresses tragedy rather than humour. It reveals the supremacy of the divine will as it encounters the naive human will seeking to challenge it.[177]

Irony, like metaphor, is difficult to define.[178] D. C. Muecke begins his work *The Compass of Irony* with the warning: 'Getting to grips with irony seems to have something in common with gathering the mist; there is plenty to take hold of, if only one could.'[179] And in a later work Muecke notes that 'The principle obstacle in the way of simple definition of irony is that irony is not a simple phenomenon.'[180] In its most basic sense irony expresses dissimulation between what is asserted on the surface and what is actually meant at a deeper level.[181] It is saying one thing and meaning

---

idem, *Literary Devices*, 47–68; MacRae, 'Theology and Irony', 83–96; Culpepper, *Anatomy*, 165–80; Paul D. Duke, *Irony in the Fourth Gospel* (Atlanta, GA: John Knox Press, 1984); H. Clavier, *Études Théologiques et Réligieuses* (Montpellier: 1929 and 1930); idem, 'La méthode ironique dans l'enseignement de Jésus'; idem, 'L 'ironie dans le quatrième évangile', *SE* 1 = TU 73 (1959), 261–76; J. E. Botha, 'The Case of Johannine Irony Reopened: I and II," *Neot* 25 (1991–92), 209–32; Myers, "Irony and Humor in the Gospel of John', 1–13; G. Johnston, 'Ecce Homo!', 125–38; O'Day, *Revelation in the Fourth Gospel;* and P. P. A. Kotze, 'John and Reader's Response', *Neot* 19 (1987), 50–63.

[176] Lists of passages are given by Clavier, 'La structure du quatrième évangile', *RHPR* 35 (1955), 178–92; idem, 'Ironie dans le quatrième évangile', 268–75; MacRae, 'Theology and Irony', 84–9; Lindars, *John*, 53–4. Fenton in *John*, 20–1, lists such sections as: 2:9f; 4:12; 7:27, 33f., 42, 52; 8:21f.; 11:16, 36; 12:19; 13:37; 18:31; 19:5, 14, 19ff.

[177] Cf. Jónsson, *Humour and Irony in the New Testament*, 201.

[178] Good, *Irony in the Old Testament*, 13, admits: 'Irony, like love, is more readily recognised than defined.'

[179] D. C. Muecke, *The Compass of Irony* (London: Methuen, 1969), 3

[180] Muecke, *Irony: The Critical Idiom* (London: Methuen, 1970), 7. See also Wead, *Literary Devices*, 47–68; Myers, 'Irony and Humor', 1–13; Wayne Booth, 'The Pleasures and Pitfalls of Irony: Or, Why Can't You Say What You Mean?', in *Rhetoric, Philosophy,. and Literature: An Exploration*, ed. by Don M. Burks (West Lafayette, IN: Purdue University Press, 1978). Cf. G. G. Sedgewick, *Of Irony, Especially in Drama* (Toronto: Univ. of Toronto Press, 1948) and M. J. Niedenthal, 'The Irony and the Grammar of the Gospel', *PSB* 64 (1971), 22–9.

[181] Abrams, *Glossary of Literary Terms*, 80. For an examination of the history of the term, see especially J. A. K. Thomson, *Irony: An Historical Introduction* (Cambridge: Harvard University Press, 1927). For a more narrowly focused survey, see Norman Knox, *The Word Irony and Its Context, 1500–1799* (Durham, NC: Duke University Press, 1961), vii.. See also Muecke, *Compass of Irony*, 7–9, 12–13, 46–52; Robert Scholes and Robert Kellogg, *The Nature of*

another. James Miller speaks of these two levels as 'text' and 'subtext'.[182] Madeleina Boucher classifies irony under the wider category of the 'trope' along with metaphor, synecdoche, metonymy, and allegory. She offers the following general definition of the trope:

A trope, as its name implies, is a turn or change which occurs when an unexpected word is placed in a syntactic structure and is thereby given another meaning in addition to its literal one.... *In every trope, then, the word has two levels of meaning, the direct and literal and the indirect and tropical.* Between the two levels of meaning there is both similarity and dissimilarity.[183]

Irony, together with parables and other forms expressing two layers of meaning, entails a comparison between two dimensions of reality; one is implied in the other. The deeper meaning requires the insight of the audience in order for it to be recognised. Irony often entails a conflict of values in which the audience is required to make a moral or social judgment.[184]

Thus irony always involves two levels of communication.[185] There is a perceived, apparent, surface (usually also 'literal') level and a deeper, assumed (usually also 'figurative') level.[186] The tension between these levels leads to ambiguity and misunderstanding. The literal meaning of an

---

Narrative (New York: OUP, 1966), 240; Bar-Efrat, *Narrative Art*, 125–8; Bullinger, *Figures of Speech*, 807; Boris Uspensky, *A Poetics of Composition: The Structure of the Artistic Text and Typology of a Compositional Form* (Berkeley and Los Angeles: University of California Press, 1973); Joseph T. Shipley, *Dictionary of World Literature, Criticism, Forms, Technique* (New York: Philosophical Library, 1943), 331; J. A. Cuddon, *A Dictionary of Literary Terms*, rev. ed. (New York: Penguin Books, Doubleday, 1980), 338; Haakon Chevalier, *The Ironic Temper: Anatole France and His Time* (New York: OUP, 1932), 42.

[182] Miller, *Word, Self, and Reality* (New York: Dodd, Mead, 1972), 46f.

[183] Boucher, *Mysterious Parable*, 17–25, here 18.

[184] M. D. de Wolff, 'Irony and Lexical Meaning', in *Linguistics in the Netherlands*, ed. by H. Bennis and F. Benkema (Dordrecht: Foris, 1985), 230 observes, 'The traditional accounts of irony indicate, albeit in a rough and very implicit way, the fact that ironical language involves a relational comparison between systems of values.... The important thing is that the outcome of this comparison does not turn out to the advantage of the object in question.' Cf. Jerry Camery-Hoggatt, *Irony in Mark's Gospel*, SNTSMS 72 (Cambridge: CUP, 1992), 13–4, who believes that 'Irony is a function of interfacing and conflicting points of view: the points of view of the story's readers set against those of the story's characters. Its explication requires systematic attention to both the point of view of the characters and the point of view of the reader. But these two points of view are differently informed and differently framed. The point of view of the characters is rightly contained within the narrative – a literary concern. The point of view of the reader is informed by the "language-world" of the community for which the text was intended – a sociological concern.'

[185] Duke, *Irony in the Fourth Gospel*, 14.

[186] Watson, *Classical Hebrew Poetry*, 306. Watson warns that 'It is not enough to determine the literal meaning of a sentence or phrase since the overt sense is not always what is intended. In fact, in an ironical statement, the literal significance is precisely the opposite of what must be understood.'

overt linguistic construction conceals its intended opposite meaning. This often expresses some form of discrepancy of understanding,[187] based upon a conflicting perception of what constitutes 'truth' and 'reality'. The ironist expects his audience or readers to recognise the irony from their own background knowledge[188] and to reject the surface meaning because of its incongruity with the *implied* or *real* meaning.[189] It is characteristic of irony to contain an element of concealment. Naturally, what is concealed is meant to be discovered.[190]

Irony also involves what the poet John Frederick Nims has called binocular vision. The Fourth Evangelist brings about such binocular vision by presenting two versions of each episode. First there is what the story's participants at the time saw, did, and said, and then what the Evangelist himself can see from his post-resurrection perspective. John uses irony to express the discrepancy between who 'the Jews' determined Jesus to be and who the disciples came to believe he was from their post-Easter vantage point under the guidance of the Holy Spirit (cf. 14:25 and 2:22).

Irony in John is both verbal and situational.[191] In verbal irony, the author intentionally says one thing but means another (e.g., deliberate ambiguity, sarcasm, hyperbole, and meiosis or understatement). Situational or dramatic irony, on the other hand, contains an element of 'unawareness'[192] where people are unwitting victims, unaware of being

---

[187] A major property of irony is lack of understanding, either real or pretended. See Duke, *Irony in the Fourth Gospel*, 16. Bullinger, in *Figures of Speech*, 807, proposes that a speaker may not intend to conceal his real meaning, except 'for the purpose of adding greater force to it'.

[188] This awareness is often arrived at by means of conventional or cultural knowledge which brings about the recognition of the incongruity of ideas, propositions and events found in the text. Since irony is dependent on contextual clues from the text and or real-world knowlege, the double meaning is not inherent in linguistic expressions, but only words in context. Thus as in the case of metaphor, the irony may focus on a word. In irony, this word takes on a negative surface value and a positive deeper value which replaces, but does not eradicate, the literal sense. According to Muecke, *Compass of Irony*, 29, since the surface meaning is not eradicated, there is a possibility for what he describes as a 'double exposure...on one plate', involving 'two co-existing but irreconcilable, irrelatable realities', to occur.

[189] Muecke, *Compass of Irony*, 23, views this as simple irony 'in which an apparently or ostensibly true statement, serious question, valid assumption, or legitimate expectation is corrected, invalidated, or frustrated by the ironist's real meaning, by the true state of affairs, or by what actually happens'. Muecke sums up the definition of irony as consisting of 'the duality, the opposition of the terms of the duality, and the real or pretended 'innocence' (p.49).

[190] Leech, *Linguistic Guide*, 171.

[191] Wayne Booth, *A Rhetoric of Irony* (Chicago: University of Chicago Press, 1974), 5–6, defines irony in terms of 'stable' and 'unstable' irony, 'covert' and 'overt' irony. One important issue in the whole discussion is whether irony must neccessarily involve opposition. See Duke, *Irony in the Fourth Gospel*, 7–27.

[192] Muecke, *Compass of Irony*, 19–20. Dramatic irony seems to be the dominant form of irony

ironic. Verbal irony is more overt while situational irony is more covert.[193] Dramatic irony generally postulates a double audience,[194] but verbal irony presupposes not so much a double audience as a double response from the same audience.[195] The prophetic section of the Hebrew Bible is dominated by the use of verbal irony. The prophets used irony to criticise[196] the unfaithfulness of the people of God and to accentuate their spiritual dullness. They also used it to critique the status quo;[197] to taunt, gibe, scoff, and mock the wicked by means of ironic wordplays; and to deride, scorn, and ridicule the enemies of the righteous.[198]

A classic instance of situational irony in John occurs in 11:49–52 when Caiaphas the High Priest declares that Jesus will die 'for the people'. Those who hear or read the Gospel recognise this as an inadvertent admission to the triumphant and saving effect of Jesus' death. Caiaphas never intended his words to be interpreted in this way, nor was he aware that they might be. The high priest, who should have known better, is devoid of any theological discernment. His remark can be called an 'unconscious prophecy', since Caiaphas was essentially summing up the Gospel of John 3:16. Although Caiaphas accuses the rest of the council of knowing nothing at all (11:49), they seem to know this, as the post-70 AD hearers and readers of the Gospel will certainly have known.

---

in the Fourth Gospel. See MacRae, 'Theology and Irony', 87; C. M. Connick, 'The Dramatic Character of the Fourth Gospel', *JBL* 67 (1948), 159–69.

[193] Bar-Efrat, *Narrative Art*, 125.

[194] H. W. Fowler, *A Dictionary of Modern English Usage* (Oxford: OUP, 1926; reprint, 1944), 295–6.

[195] Leech, *Linguistic Guide*, 171.

[196] Robert C. Elliott, *The Power of Satire: Magic, Ritual, Art* (Princeton: Princeton University, 1966), 66–78, esp. 67–68.

[197] Thomas Jemielity, *Satire and the Hebrew Prophets* (Louisville, KY: Westminster, John Knox Press, 1992), 85.

[198] For example, 2 Kings recounts King Ahaziah's mission to a false god. The text states that the king 'sent messengers to inquire of Baal-Zebub of Ekron whether he would recover from his illness' (2 King 1:2, NEB). The god's name, meaning 'lord of the flies', is, according to the New English Bible, 'a distorted, contemptuous alteration of Baal-Zebul, "Baal the Prince"'. In Genesis, humanity is covertly reminded of its humble origin with the play on the word 'ground'. The repeated wordplay between 'man' (adam) and 'ground' (adamah) in Genesis 2:6, 7, 19; 3:17, 19; and 4:11 emphasises this relationship. Terms like 'dust', 'form', and 'living creature' (nepesh hayah) belong to the same complexity of thought. The alienation of man from the ground is expressed by the term 'curse' (in Gen. 3:14, 17; 4:11). Hosea speaks ironically of divinity being appealed to by a chief priest for advice: 'He makes inquiry of his wood, and his staff reports to him' (Hos. 4:12, AB). Many times indistinguishable from the prophetic message itself, irony serves as a major weapon in the arsenal of the Hebrew prophets, whose careers and writings strongly buttress the Psalmist's confidence: 'He that dwelleth in heaven shall laugh them to scorn; the LORD shall hold them in derision' (Ps. 2:4).

There is a similar combination of tragic irony and hope in John 4:21, where true worshippers are said to worship 'neither on this mountain nor in Jerusalem'. When this text was read in a post-70 AD setting, the fate that had earlier befallen the schismatic Samaritan temple at the hands of John Hyrcanus[199] had also befallen Jerusalem at the hands of the Romans. 'You shall not worship on that mountain' had been the Jewish charge against the Samaritans for centuries. Jesus here quotes this charge and amends it with a tragic complement – 'nor in Jerusalem.' He then transforms it into a statement of hope about the purpose of God and what he seeks (4:23).

In chapter 11, Caiaphas speaks in terms of political expediency. John sees beneath the surface of Caiaphas's words to a far deeper, theological significance. He sees an unwitting prophecy of redemption, in which Jesus brings a peace more vital than that which the appeasement of the Romans could have brought, namely, peace between the creator and the creature. Nevertheless, John's idea of regathering the nation from exile in 11:52 may imply the restoration of the temple or rather of 'the place' (ὁ τόπος) after its destruction, which is alluded to in John 11:48. The term ἔθνος of v. 48 is picked up in v. 51, while the idea of a 'place' may be implied in the expression ἵνα τὰ τέκνα τοῦ θεοῦ...συναγάγῃ εἰς ἕν in v. 52. The background is the Old Testament prophetic expectation of the gathering of the nation εἰς ἕν, which suggests the restoration of the 'place' where they gather.[200] Here the irony is clarified by the author's explanation.

Elsewhere there are ironic undertones in such subtle statements as 'Are you greater than our father Jacob?' (John 4:12),[201] and 'Are you greater than our father Abraham?' (8:53). In each case, the Evangelist's unstated response is, 'greater indeed!'

In 7:50–52 John's ironic scorn once again is directed towards the whole of the Sanhedrin. Nicodemus is identified by the author as 'one of

---

[199] Josephus, *Ant.* 13.9.1 §§254–258.

[200] On this passage see W. Wolbert, '"Besser, dass ein Mensch für das Volk stirbt, als dass das ganze Volk zugrunde geht" (Joh 11, 50): Überlegungen zur Devise des Kajaphas', *TGl* 80 (1990), 478–494; J. Kennedy, 'The Abuse of Power', *ExpTim*, 85 (1973–74), 172–3; C. H. Dodd, 'The Prophecy of Caiaphas: John 11:47–53', in *More New Testament Studies*, ed. by C. H. Dodd (Grand Rapids: Eerdmans, 1968), 58–68; Carson, *Gospel According to John*, 421–2; Bruce, *John*, 250; Lindars, *John*, 406–7; Schnackenburg, *St. John*, 2:348–9; Morris, *John*, 566; Beasley-Murray, *John*, 196–8; Peter F. Ellis, *The Genius of John* (Collegeville, MN: The Liturgical Press, 1984), 188; Calvin, *Gospel According to John*, 452–5; Brown, *John*, 440–4; Bultmann, *John*, 410–12; Barrett, *St. John*, 338–40; Haenchen, *John*, 2:75; Hoskyns, *Fourth Gospel*, 408–12.

[201] Jerome H. Neyrey, 'Jacob Traditions and the Interpretation of John 4:10–26', *CBQ* 41 (1979), 419–37.

them' (v. 50). He asks the other chief priests and Pharisees in v. 51, 'Does our law judge a man without first giving him a hearing and learning what he does?' The audience of John knows the answer to Nicodemus' rhetorical question. The implication is clear: the teachers of Israel are not only blind to the truth but also stand in violation of the Mosaic law.[202] Of course, the real answer to Nicodemus' question will be given later during the trial where the law of Moses is entirely disregarded. Also of significance is v. 52b: 'Search and you will see that no prophet is to rise from Galilee.' Here the author once again emphasises the ignorance motif regarding Jesus' origin, a recurring theme in the Gospel.[203] By employing the technical term for resurrection, ἐγείρω (which had acquired the meaning 'to rise from the dead'),[204] John imposes a second level of meaning upon the episode ('arise out of Galilee') and further heightens his polemical assault.

Some Johannine ironies are even more covert, since the author does not provide an explanatory note (as he does in John 11:51-52) and depends upon his audience to detect the irony. I have already dealt with the potential transitive and intransitive uses of καθίζειν in John 19:13 as a case of grammatical ambiguity (above §2.2.1.1), which raises the possibility that Pilate may have seated Jesus on the judgment seat (the transitive sense). If this sense is in the background, it is highly ironic. Probably such irony is intended, in the light of the dominance of irony elsewhere in this passage (e.g., note the play on the title ὁ βασιλεὺς throughout this account, cf. 18:28-19:15).[205] The Evangelist wishes his audience to be aware of both levels,[206] and in deliberate irony he implies that any judgment upon Jesus is a judgment upon the one passing judgment.[207] Indeed in the trilingual

---

[202] See the discussion of the technique of unanswered questions by Clavier, 'Ironie dans l'enseignement de Jésus', 4-6; and Wead, *Literary Devices*, 59f.

[203] Schnackenburg, *St. John*, 2:160-2; Lindars, *John*, 304-5; Barrett, *St. John*, 333.

[204] A. Oepke, *TDNT* 2:335.

[205] Meeks, *Prophet-King*, 82-99; Richard, 'Expressions of Double Meaning', 99.

[206] Sometimes the author may simply desire that the reader be aware of both levels of meaning regardless of whether they will be complementary or contradictory. Instances of amphibology differ from most forms of irony in that the two levels of meaning are not opposed and the reader is not asked to decide which one of the two references the narrator wishes to present to the exclusion of the other. Rather, the reader is asked to recognise both levels of meaning intended by the author. This sharing of understanding between narrator and reader assumes an awareness of the multiple meanings by the author which would correspond to Wayne Booth's definition of 'stable irony'. Booth, *Rhetoric of Irony*, 5-6. Cf. Ullmann, *Semantics*, 157-91; Caird, *Language and Imagery*, 95-108.

[207] Ashton, *Understanding*, 228 n. 41. Cf. A. E. Harvey, *Jesus on Trial: A Study of the Fourth Gospel* (London: SPCK, 1976), 15; Kysar, *John*, 282; Schnackenburg, *St. John*, 3:263-4; Lightfoot, *St. John's Gospel*, 325-6; Barrett, *St. John*, 453.

inscription written in Hebrew, Latin, and Greek, 'JESUS THE NAZARENE, KING OF THE JEWS' (Jn. 19:20), there is the irony of 'the universal condemnation of those who thus condemned Jesus, and the universal offer of salvation to the universally condemned.'[208]

Earlier in 18:3, Judas comes with a band of soldiers and their feeble lights (lanterns and lamps) to extinguish the one who stood in relation to them as 'the light of world'. The author ironically stresses the darkness of the night in which the light of the world was for the moment quenched.

In John 18:28, the Jews stay outside the Praetorium because the dwelling places of Gentiles are considered unclean.[209] On the day before the Passover therefore the Jews remained outside, 'in order that they might not be defiled, but might eat the Passover.' The irony is characteristically Johannine: 'those who plot the murder of the Son of God mind to the last detail their formal religious punctilio.'[210] Elsewhere, the irony of Pilate's question, 'What is truth?' (18:38) in the presence of the one who embodies the truth (14:6; 1:9) is left to the reader or hearer of the Gospel to detect, just as is the chief priests' obsession to maintain their ritual purity at the very moment they are engaged in an obscene murder.[211] John's irony functions as a critical appraisal of the religious leaders who doggedly claim to know the identity of Jesus when in reality they do not. They claim to see while they are completely blind (9:39–41).

Irony inherently is a two-level communication. It is used John's Gospel together with other literary features possessing a similar stated and implied level of communication. Duke and Culpepper have argued that the value of irony lies with the reader response. Duke sees the irony of the Fourth Gospel as a 'lure'.[212] Culpepper speaks of irony in terms of a 'net' used to draw readers to the Evangelist's theology.[213] Both Duke and

---

[208] Barrett, *St. John*, 548.

[209] Technically unclean. See J. Bonsirven, *Le Judaïsme Palestinien au temps de Jésus-Christ*, Bibliothèque de théologie historique (Paris: G. Beauchesne, 1934-35), 2:262.

[210] Barrett, *St. John*, 532. Whether the implication of John's statement that the uncleanness acquired was of a major degree, lasting seven days, or it was of a minor degree, lasting only till the end of the day when it could be removed by a bath in the evening (the beginning of the next day), is unclear. See J. B. Segal, *The Hebrew Passover* (n.p., n.pub., 1963), 36 n. 2. Cf. Mt. 27:11f.; Mk. 15:2f.; Lk. 23:1f. The controlling biblical passage according to Barrett is Numbers 9:7–10 (pp. 232–33).

[211] See Myers, 'Irony and Humor', 10; Suggit, 'John 19:5 – "Behold the Man"', *ExpTim* 94 (1982–83), 333–4; also Timothy Cargel, 'His Blood Be Upon Us and Upon Our Children: A Matthean Double-Entendre?', *NTS* 37 (1991), 101–12.

[212] Duke, *Irony in the Fourth Gospel*, 151, 153.

[213] Culpepper, *Anatomy*, 180.

Culpepper use images of intimate or secretive communication such as the wink or the smile to describe the relationship between the Evangelist and his readers.[214] However, John communicates by his irony something far more serious than is traditionally communicated by a wink.[215]

At one level, John uses irony as a critical polemic against the Jewish religious hierarchy whom he addresses as 'the Jews'.[216] They expect a spectacular visible manifestation of God, but in their preoccupation with the spectacular, they miss the presence of God in their midst in the unassuming, seemingly vulnerable earthly person of a Galilean (cf. 1 Kings 19:12). Beneath this polemic against 'the Jews', there is also a critical commentary on the world of humanity, of whom 'the Jews' are but a representative. Humanity, by spurning the truth and loving darkness, has rejected its creator. People reject the light because they prefer darkness and wish to hide their evil deeds (Jn. 3:19–20). Yet in so doing, they remain in darkness, blinded to the revelation that is their only source of healing (Jn. 5:40; 12:40).

At a different level, Johannine irony is also an integral part of John's theological perspective. Jesus, son of Mary, son of Joseph, is the Jewish Messiah. He is God enclothed in flesh, born and yet existing eternally.[217] Here irony is essential to the dynamics of revelation in John.[218] Implicit in this irony is the scriptural idea that God's purposes are achieved regardless of human efforts to oppose them. Those who seek to thwart God's work become victims of a twist of 'fate' (cf. Gen. 50:20).[219] In John's Gospel, the Jewish authorities who have set themselves in opposition to Jesus are instruments of bringing about the intended divine result. This is for the Son of Man to be lifted up, to draw all men to himself (John 12:32), and thus to draw them to God (14:6). Caiaphas, the high priest, may think he is in charge, but his very words serve to fulfil the purposes of God (11:49–52). The same goes for Pilate (18:5). Both are unwitting agents of God's will.

---

[214] Duke, *Irony in the Fourth Gospel*, 156: 'John punctuates his witness to Jesus with an occasional wink or grin or tear'; Culpepper, *Anatomy*, 179: 'a wink or a smile creates a bond of secret communication.'

[215] Cf. Gail O'Day, 'Narrative Mode and Theological Claim: A Study in the Fourth Gospel', *JBL* 105 (1986), 664..

[216] Such polemic would have been acutely felt by those such as Nicodemus who came to Jesus under the cover of darkness (3:20). See chapter five in the study.

[217] Cf. Johnston, ''Ecce Homo!'', 125–38; MacRae, 'Theology and Irony', 83–96, 99.

[218] Bultmann, *John*, 63; Herbert Schneider, 'The Word Was Made Flesh: An Analysis of the Theology of Revelation in the Fourth Gospel', *CBQ* 31 (1969), 344–56; René Voeltzel, *Le Rire de Seigneur* (Strassburg: Oberlin, 1955), 103; O'Day, 'Narrative Mode', 663–8.

[219] Bar-Efrat, *Narrative Art*, 128.

Both the Jewish and Roman authorities unconsciously declare Jesus to be the one he claimed to be. So in John, as in Isaiah, we encounter a sovereign God who is absolute master and everything else is *sub specie aeternitatis*.[220]

Another ironic twist is the Johannine theology of the cross captured in the 'lifted up' statements in the Gospel, where the cross is seen as a victory rather than a defeat (3:14; 8:28; 12:32). At the heart of these statements is an amphibological expression, ὑψωθῆναι, meaning both 'to be lifted up' in a literal sense into space, but also figuratively 'to be lifted up' in a sense of enhancement in honour.[221] The expression speaks of Christ's manner of death, but this death itself is seen as exaltation and glorification from the author's post-resurrection perspective, in keeping with New Testament usage (Acts 2:33; 5:30; Phil. 2:9). Each of the three Johannine passages where ὑψόω occurs keeps in view both the cross and the glory of the resurrection and ascension (cf. Jn. 3:14; 8:28; 12:32).[222] The third instance, regarding Jesus' being lifted up and drawing all people to himself, prompts the Evangelist to add a footnote: 'He said this to show by what death he was to die' (12:33). The expression is identical to the one used in 18:32 to refer to the crucifixion (σημαίνων ποίῳ θανάτῳ ἤμελλεν ἀποθνῄσκειν). The Johannine 'lifted up' formula, however, does not simply denote death or exaltation. It shows how these are kept in paradoxical tension in John's theology, which is distinct from that of the Synoptics. Jesus, in the Passion narrative of the Fourth Gospel, does not appear as one humiliated,

---

[220] Clavier, 'L'Ironie dans l'Enseignement de Jésus', 273ff; Voeltzel, *Le Rire de Seigneur*, 103.

[221] See BAGD, 850–1; G. Bertram in *TDNT* 8 (1969), 606–13. The word ὑψόω is used fifteen times in the New Testament outside of the Gospel of John.

[222] Some have placed this expression against the background of Genesis 40:13, 19, and the play on the word 'lift up' נשׂא where in Genesis 40:13, 'enhancement in honour' seems to be intended while in Genesis 40:19, the reference is to execution and physical death. Also it may be that John has synthesised the imagery of 'death' and 'exaltation' into one word in light of the opening sentence of the last servant's song in Isaiah 52:13. In this passage, both the 'lifting up' (ὑψωθήσεται) and 'glorification' (δοξασθήσεται) are in view. Cf. Wheelwright, *Burning Foundation*, 96–100; Alfred N. Whitehead, *Symbolism: Its Meaning and Effects* (Cambridge: CUP, 1928). See further C. Torrey, 'When I AM Lifted Up from the Earth', *JBL* 51 (1932), 320–2; H. Hollis, 'The Root of the Johannine Pun', *NTS* 35 (1989), 475–8; Lightfoot, *St. John's Gospel*, 132; Bernard, *St. John*, 112–4; Brown, *John*, 133–46; Jaubert, *Approches de l'Évangile de Jean*, 56; Cullmann, 'Johanneische Gebrauch', 365–6; Barrett, *St. John*, 72–3, 214; Westcott, *St. John*, 53; Beasley-Murray, *John*, 50; J. Louis Martyn, *History and Theology in the Fourth Gospel*, 2nd edn (Nashville: Abingdon, 1979 [1st edn, New York: Harper and Row, 1968]), 129–43.; Cullmann, 'Johanneische Gebrauch', 365–6; Cullen Story, 'The Bearing of Old Testament Terminology on the Johannine Chronology of the Final Passover of Jesus', *NovT* 31 (1989), 316–24.

distraught, and in emotional agony. Instead he emerges as a deliberate exalted King who 'behaves as the sovereign and Lord of the proceedings'.[223] From the Johannine theological point of view, the Passion is the procession of the King on his way to his coronation where his true identity is revealed for οἱ ἴδιοι to behold.

Irony in John is more than a dramatic device by a literary artist. It has a polemical and theological function. And in conjunction with other multi-layered literary features such as symbolism, metaphor, and words of double meaning, it contributes to the perception of elusiveness and remoteness in John's language.

2.3. Figurative versus Plain Speech

In addition to John's explanatory remarks, clues to the undercurrents in his language may be provided when Jesus speaks 'in figures of speech', ἐν παροιμίαις (Jn. 16:25; singular, 10:6; 16:29) rather than 'plainly' or 'literally', παρρησίᾳ (a word occurring nine times in John's Gospel). Yet speaking παρρησίᾳ or ἐν παρρησίᾳ can itself have two distinct meanings. It can mean to speak or move about 'publicly' or 'openly' rather than 'privately' or 'secretly' (with λαλέω, 7:13, 26; 18:20; with εἶναι, 7:4; with περιπατέω, 11:54). Or it can mean to speak 'plainly' rather than 'figuratively' (with λέγω, λαλέω, or ἀπαγγέλω). The latter sense occurs especially when speaking (ἐν) παρρησίᾳ is contrasted with speech by means of a παροιμία in the space of a single verse, as in 16:25 and 29; yet παρρησίᾳ can also occur in the sense of 'plainly' all on its own, as in 10:24 and 11:14. Therefore when Jesus speaks 'figuratively', he is speaking a special language.

At the end of the discourse with his disciples about his return to the Father in John 16:4b–15, Jesus says, 'A little while, and you will see me no more; again a little while, and you will see me' (16:16).[224] In reaction to this, the disciples inquire among themselves about what Jesus is saying to

---

[223] Robert Kysar, *John, the Maverick Gospel* (Atlanta, GA: John Knox Press, 1976), 37. See also Loader, *Christology of the Fourth Gospel*, 107–35; F. J. Moloney, 'The Fourth Gospel's Presentation of Jesus as the Christ and J. A. T. Robinson's Redating', *DRev* 95 (1977), 239–53; D. M. Smith, 'The Presentation of Jesus in the Fourth Gospel', *Int* 31 (1977), 367–78; Nicholson, *Death as Departure*, 75–144; Rita J. Burns, 'Jesus and the Bronze Serpent', *The Bible Today* 18 (1990), 84–9; J. A. du Rand, 'The Characterization of Jesus as Depicted in the Narrative of the Fourth Gospel', *Neot* 19 (1985), 18–36; G. Fackre, 'Narrative Theology: An Overview', *Int* 37 (1983), 340–52.

[224] Cf. 7:32–35; 8:21–22; 13:33, 36–37; 14:18–20, 28; 16:5.

them (16:17-18). They do not know what he 'means' because they do not understand that to which he refers.

The disciples in chapter 16 are in fact little better off than the others who for example have misunderstood Jesus' 'going away' (ὑπάγω) in 7:33 and 8:21 as a reference to his going off to teach the Greeks (7:35) or perhaps even to his killing himself (8:22). It is the same with Peter. Jesus speaks about his going to a place where his disciples cannot go (again ὑπάγω, 13:33), and Peter asks 'where' Jesus is going and cannot understand why he cannot follow him there now (13:36-37). Later in chapter 14, Thomas tells Jesus that the disciples do not even know where he is going and therefore can hardly know the way (14:5: οὐκ οἴδαμεν ποῦ ὑπάγεις, etc.). In all these instances, the interlocutors of Jesus know the denotation or basic meaning of his terms, in this case ὑπάγω, in everyday language. But they fail to grasp the precise reference that arises when Jesus uses the term in a figurative sense.

Returning to John 16, Jesus responds to the disciples' questioning. After a not very lucid explanation about labour pains and subsequent rejoicing (16:19-24), he tells them that he has spoken to them ἐν παροιμίαις, 'in figures', but he will soon speak to them 'plainly' (παρρησίᾳ) about the Father (16:25). After a few more words, he concludes, 'I came from the Father and have come into the world; again, I am leaving the world and going to the Father' (16:28). Upon hearing this, his disciples respond, 'Ah, now you are speaking plainly, not in any figure' (16:29), and they proceed to profess that now they 'understand' that he is omniscient and for this reason 'believe that he has come from God' (16:30).

A factor in this figurative versus plain speech is what appears to be a deliberate vagueness on the part of Jesus. An *equivoque* is a play on words by means of an evasive answer that can be interpreted in more than one way. If an equivoque is deliberately misleading, it becomes equivocation.[225] In the Fourth Gospel, several times the response of Jesus seems to be deliberately vague, lacking specifics. An obvious example is John 2:19-22 and the reference to 'temple'. But the conversation with Nicodemus, the Samaritan discourse, and the discourse on the bread of life in chapter 6 also contain cryptic remarks. A prime example of this occurs in John 19:11 in which Pilate, in his conversation with Jesus in the Praetorium, tells Jesus that he has the authority to set him free. Jesus replies, 'You would have no authority over me, unless it had been given you from above; for this reason

---

[225] Shaw, *Dictionary of Literary Terms*, 140, s.v. See also Thrall, et al., *Handbook to Literature*, 182.

the one who delivered me (ὁ παραδούς με) to you has the greater sin.' Ultimately the political authorities that allowed Jesus to be handed over to death are part of God's dominion (cf. Rom. 13:1-2).[226] But an identification of the Father himself as ὁ παραδούς would be tantamount to blasphemy and inconceivable from the lips of Jesus (cf. 10:17-18). The referent behind ὁ παραδούς has been seen as the high priest Caiaphas,[227] 'the Jews' (i.e., Jewish leaders), the Jewish nation as a whole (cf. 18:35-36), the world,[228] or Judas as the tool of the devil (Jn. 6:70; 13:2, 27; 18:35-36).[229] In the light of 8:44, the devil himself may ultimately have been Jesus' intended reference.

In the discourse with the disciples in John 14:4-10, the problem of evasive speech once again becomes an issue. The cause of misunderstanding is the verb ὑπάγω, 'to depart or go away', coupled with the noun ὁδός, 'way', already considered briefly above. Since in vv. 1-3 it is clearly indicated that Jesus will depart to the Father, the lack of comprehension on the part of Thomas seems strange; there appears no need to seek a hidden key to the meaning. Instead, John employs a simple, rather superficial play on words – Jesus mentions the 'way' and teaches: 'I am the way' (v. 6). Here the literary technique may be simple, but the goal is not. The sequence is well-defined: ambiguity is introduced, misunderstanding (or lack of comprehension) occurs, and clarification is required. This sequence generally seems to revolve around the disciples, for the clarification of misunderstanding usually does not characterise Jesus' interaction with his opponents, who are often left in the dark. What is puzzling in John 14:4 is the use of an ambiguous word in a context where an unambiguous expression could have been used. The verb ὑπάγω is often employed in contexts that allow more than one meaning. When used with the verb ζητέω ('seek') it can introduce misunderstanding.[230]

In the story about Lazarus in John 11, two instances of Jesus' speech are a problem for his audience. First, he tells his disciples that the deceased

---

[226] Barrett, *St. John*, 543.
[227] Brown, *John*, 2:893; Morris, *John*, 705.
[228] Bultmann, *John*, 511.
[229] Barrett, *St. John*, 542-3.
[230] See John 8:21-22 ('I am going away...will he kill himself?') and 13:33 (without the misunderstanding). See also the misunderstanding associated with the combination of ζητέω and πορεύομαι in 7:34-35 ('You will search for me, but you will not find me.... Does he intend to go to the Dispersion among the Greeks and teach the Greeks?'). See further Richard, 'Expressions of Double Meaning', 100; Hoskyns, *Fourth Gospel*, 319-20; J. Marsh, *The Gospel of St John* (Baltimore: Penguin, 1968), 358; Fenton, *John*, 20-1; Barrett, *St. John*, 325, 341; Clavier, 'L'ironie dans le quatrième Evangile', 272; Leroy, *Rätsel*, 59-67; Meeks, 'Man from Heaven', 64; Lindars, *John*, 296, 319; Schnackenburg, *St. John*, 2:150, 197-8.

Lazarus has 'fallen asleep' and that he is going to 'awaken' him (11:11). Like Nicodemus, the disciples take his words literally and suggest that if Lazarus is only asleep or resting, there is no need to go to him because σωθήσεται, i.e., he will 'recover' or 'be all right' (11:12; cf. NASB; NRSV). At this point, the narrator intervenes to tell us that Jesus had spoken of Lazarus' death, but that the disciples had thought that Jesus meant only that Lazarus was asleep (11:13). The Evangelist then proceeds to explain that Jesus told them 'plainly' (παρρησίᾳ) that Lazarus was dead. The word plays are well reflected in the NJB:

> He said that and then added, 'Our friend Lazarus is at rest; I am going to wake him.' The disciples said to him, 'Lord, if he is at rest he will be saved (σωθήσεται).' Jesus was speaking of the death of Lazarus, but they thought that by 'rest' he meant 'sleep'; so Jesus put it plainly, 'Lazarus is dead....' (John 11:11-14)

The problem here is lexical polysemy and misunderstanding of the denotation. The disciples use a verb for 'awakening' which can also mean to be 'saved' or 'healed'. This is therefore another instance of Johannine double meaning in the context of dramatic irony: the disciples are right, but do not realise it. The possibility of such irony is reinforced when Jesus subsequently says that he is 'the resurrection and the life' and that whoever believes in him will live, even if he has died (11:25-26). When Lazarus comes back to life, he is by implication 'saved' from death.

In John 10, Jesus is speaking to the Pharisees (cf. 9:40) and he employs an analogy about sheep, a shepherd, and robbers (10:1-5), following which the author explains, 'This figure (ταύτην τὴν παροιμίαν) Jesus used with them, but they did not understand what he was saying to them' (10:6). Jesus' explanation makes it clear that the failure to understand his analogy derives from his audience's ignorance of the referents of his metaphors. A new episode appears in 10:22-30, but the author links it to 10:1-21 by picking up the theme of the sheep and the shepherd, and by having Jesus tell his audience ('the Jews') that they do not believe him because they do not belong to his sheep (10:26). Jesus draws this conclusion after 'the Jews' complained that he was keeping them in suspense: 'If you are the Christ tell us plainly' (παρρησίᾳ, 10:24), picking up the narrator's comments in 10:6. Implicitly, the audience has been befuddled by what they construe as figurative speech and, like Jesus' disciples in John 16, they demand plain speech. Jesus says that he has told them, but that they do not believe, implying that he has told them in plain speech.

In the conclusion of his discourse with Nicodemus, Jesus explains to him that because he does not believe the 'earthly things' of which Jesus

Figurative versus Plain Speech 89

has spoken, he cannot believe the 'heavenly things' either (3:12). Another version of this is seen in 1:50–51 in the story about Nathanael. In both 1:51 and 3:13, Jesus speaks about 'ascent' and 'descent' (ἀναβαίνω, καταβαίνω) in connection with 'the Son of Man', though only in 1:51 is the Son seen as the ladder between heaven and earth. John 1:18 says that 'No one has ever seen God; the only Son [or *God*], who is in the bosom of the Father, he has made him known' (1:18).[231] Several parallels between 1:18 and 3:12–15 need to be observed. Clearly there is a relationship between 'no one has ever seen God' and 'no one has ascended to heaven'. On the one hand, it is said that no one has done either of these, and this looks like a rejection of the claim that someone has. The narrator never identifies the one to whom such a claim might apply, but some Jewish traditions maintained that Moses had done both, and this would make sense of John's denial that he had.[232] On the other hand, the narrator positively states that Jesus comes from 'heaven' or 'above' (3:31). Therefore the contrast is not only between Moses and Jesus, but also between 'ascending' and 'descending'. Humans go up to heaven and come down, but heavenly beings come down and go back up.

This pattern of Jesus speaking figuratively (ἐν παροιμίαις) rather than 'plainly' or 'literally' (παρρησίᾳ) may constitute the Johannine counterpart to the Synoptic parables: there Jesus speaks in parables, here Jesus speaks 'figuratively' rather than 'plainly'. However, it is not only Jesus who speaks figuratively. In John 3:30–34 it seems that John the Baptist is also speaking figuratively. But in the Johannine discourses, it is usually Jesus who speaks in unusual language. Yet this oddity is not always figurative. For example, in chapter 5, Jesus speaks about the time when the dead will hear his voice and those who have heard will live, ἀμὴν ἀμὴν λέγω ὑμῖν ὅτι ἔρχεται ὥρα καὶ νῦν ἐστιν ὅτε οἱ νεκροὶ ἀκούσουσιν τῆς φωνῆς τοῦ υἱοῦ τοῦ θεοῦ καὶ οἱ ἀκούσαντες ζήσουσιν, 'Truly, truly, I say to you, the hour is coming, and now is, when the dead will hear the voice of the Son of God, and those who hear will live' (5:25). Later in v. 28, Jesus tells his audience not to marvel at his words (knowing that they do), but then rather than explaining his preceding words, he goes on to speak in the same unfamiliar language:

μὴ θαυμάζετε τοῦτο, ὅτι ἔρχεται ὥρα ἐν ᾗ πάντες οἱ ἐν τοῖς μνημείοις ἀκούσουσιν τῆς φωνῆς αὐτοῦ καὶ ἐκπορεύσονται, οἱ τὰ ἀγαθὰ ποιήσαντες εἰς

---

[231] Cf. O. Hofius, 'Der in des Vaters Schoss ist: Joh 1:18', *ZNW* 80 (1989), 163–71.

[232] Meeks, *Prophet-King*, 297–301; idem, 'Man from Heaven'. Meeks locates the 'seeing' of God in the context of traditions dealing with both ascent and descent and vice versa.

ἀνάστασιν ζωῆς, οἱ δὲ τὰ φαῦλα πράξαντες εἰς ἀνάστασιν κρίσεως. Οὐ δύναμαι ἐγὼ ποιεῖν ἀπ' ἐμαυτοῦ οὐδέν· καθὼς ἀκούω κρίνω, καὶ ἡ κρίσις ἡ ἐμὴ δικαία ἐστίν, ὅτι οὐ ζητῶ τὸ θέλημα τὸ ἐμὸν ἀλλὰ τὸ θέλημα τοῦ πέμψαντός με.

Do not marvel at this; for the hour is coming when all who are in the tombs will hear his voice and come forth, those who have done good, to the resurrection of life, and those who have done evil, to the resurrection of judgment. I can do nothing on my own authority; as I hear, I judge; and my judgment is just, because I seek not my own will but the will of him who sent me. (John 5:28-30)

In chapter 6 the language that dominates Jesus' discourse about 'eating his flesh and drinking his blood' (6:51-58) is once again figurative. The incomprehension of his audience is here described as 'murmuring' (γογγύζω) rather than 'wondering' or being 'astonished' (θαυμάζω). Many of those present upon hearing his claims reject Jesus' words as 'hard sayings', Σκληρός ἐστιν ὁ λόγος οὗτος (6:60) and cease to follow him (6:66). Similar figurative speech by Jesus is seen throughout the Gospel (e.g., 8:35; 12:24-25; 16:21-22).

As in the Synoptics, so in the Fourth Gospel, the aim of this pattern of speech seems to be the same: 'to you has been given the secret of the kingdom of God, but for those outside everything is in parables' (Mk. 4:10, cf. Mt. 13:10-12). In John, Jesus says to those who do not understand his language, ὁ ὢν ἐκ τοῦ θεοῦ τὰ ῥήματα τοῦ θεοῦ ἀκούει, 'the one who is from God hears God's words' (8:47). Earlier he explains to the bewildered Nicodemus that in order to comprehend his speech (i.e., Jesus' revelation of heavenly truths), he, Nicodemus, must be born anew from above (Jn. 3:3-12). Later in chapter 6 of the present study, I shall argue that in Johannine theology, the 'new birth' is the necessary prerequisite to comprehending this language, whether it is the language of Jesus or the language of the Evangelist himself. The Gospel's language can be explained by the author's emphasis upon the resurrection, the coming of the Holy Spirit, and the new birth. These events condition the way in which the Evangelist and his audience understand Jesus' discourses before the resurrection, and they are necessary for understanding John's own language after the resurrection. John's emphasis upon the figurative versus the plain speech of Jesus is one more indication that Johannine ambiguity is deliberate, a further cue to the complex nature of the language of the Fourth Gospel.

2.4. Johannine Allusions to the Old Testament

Some of the most significant contributions to the enigmatic quality of John's language can be found the Evangelist's subtle allusions to the Old Testament.[233] There are obvious allusions, such as the Baptist's claim to be 'the voice of one crying in the wilderness, "Make straight the way of the Lord"' (Jn. 1:23), and less obvious ones, such as his admission that 'among you stands one...whose sandal I am not worthy to untie' (Jn. 1:26), together with his eschatological proverb, 'He who has the bride is the bridegroom; the friend of the bridegroom, who stands and hears him, rejoices greatly at the bridegroom's voice' (3:29).

Throughout John's Gospel, one emphasis appears again and again: Jesus is the one 'about whom Moses in the law and also the prophets wrote' (1:45). For the Fourth Evangelist, Jesus is the embodiment of the reality spoken of in 'shadows' in Israel's Scriptures. He is the fulfilment of the aspirations of the prophets and the realisation of the hope embedded in salvation history. Johannine allusions to and echoes of the Old Testament Scriptures are the Evangelist's means of supporting this assertion.

By allusions and echoes I do not mean 'intertextuality',[234] at least not

---

[233] According to Watson, *Classical Hebrew Poetry*, 299-300, 'Allusion is the reference (usually not explicit) within one body of literature to the culture and letters of another body.' Watson, quoting the *Princeton Encyclopedia of Poetry and Poetics*, further writes, 'The technique of allusion assumes: 1) an established literary tradition as a source of value; 2) an audience sharing the tradition with the poet; 3) an echo of sufficiently familiar yet distinctive elements; 4) a fusion of the echo with the elements in the new context. It usually requires a close poet-audience relationship, a social emphasis in literature, a community of knowledge, and a prizing of literary tradition.' There are two classes of allusions: inner-biblical allusion and extra-biblical allusion. The majority of Johannine allusions appear to be inner-biblical allusions in so far as they refer to various particulars in the Hebrew Bible. Allusion differs from motif. Alter, *Art of Biblical Narrative*, 95, defines motif as when a 'concrete image, sensory quality, action, or object recurs through a particular narrative. It has no meaning in itself without the defining context of the narrative; it may be incidentally symbolic or instead, primarily a means of giving formal coherence to a narrative.' For further study in this area, see Ziva Ben-Porat, 'The Poetics of Allusion' (Ph.D. diss., Berkeley: University of California, 1973); idem, 'The Poetics of Literary Allusion', *PTL: A Journal for Descriptive Poetics and Theory of Literature* 1 (1976), 105–28; William Freedman, 'The Literary Motif: A Definition and Evaluation', *Novel* 4 (1971), 123–31; Abrams, *Glossary of Literary Terms*, 101-2. In a broader context, see Jonathan Culler, 'Presupposition and Intertextuality', *MLN* 91 (1976), 1380–96; Sipke Draisma, ed., *Intertextuality in Biblical Writings: Essays in Honor of Bas van Iersel* (Kampen: J. H. Hok, 1989); Lyle M. Eslinger, 'Inner-biblical Exegesis and Inner-biblical Allusions: The Question of Category', *VT* 42 (1992), 47–58; J. Udo Hebel, *Intertextuality, Allusion, and Quotation: An International Bibliography of Critical Studies* (New York: Greenwood, 1989); J. Carter Swain, *Unlocking the Treasures in Biblical Imagery* (New York: Association Press, 1966); Allan Palvio, *Mental Representations: A Dual Coding Approach* (New York: OUP, 1986).

[234] The term 'intertextuality' seems to have been coined by Julia Kristeva, *Desire in Language:*

Chapter 2: The Structure of John's Enigmatic Language

as it is articulated by post-modernists, deconstructionists, and reader-response advocates.[235] Neither do I refer to unconscious literary borrowing or poetic influence.[236] Intertextuality has been a significant topic of discussion in linguistic and literary studies since the late 1970s. It has particularly appealed to the post-modernists who have questioned any profitable discussion about an 'objective meaning'.[237] In this post-modern

---

A Semiotic Approach to Literature and Art, ed. by L. S. Roudiez, trans. by T. Gora, A. Jarine, and L. S. Roudiez (New York: Columbia University Press, 1980 [Fr.1969]); idem, *Revolution in Poetic Language*, trans. by M. Waller (New York: Columbia University, 1984), 60, 65; idem, 'Semiotics: A Critical Science and/or a Critique of Science', in *Kristeva Reader*, ed. by T. Moi (New York: Columbia University, 1986), 74–88.

[235] See, for example, *The Postmodern Bible:* Collection of Essays, no editor; part of The Bible and Culture Collection (New Haven: Yale University Press, 1995); Linda Hutcheon, 'Postmodern Paratextuality and History', *Texte* 5/6 (1986/7), 301–12; J. Culler, *On Deconstruction: Theory and Criticism after Structuralism* (London: Routledge and Kegan Paul, 1983); Danna Nolan Fewell, ed., *Reading Between Texts: Intertextuality and the Hebrew Bible* (Louisville, KY: Westminster/John Knox Press, 1992), 22; V. B. Leitch, *Deconstructive Criticism: An Advanced Introduction* (New York: Columbia University Press, 1983); D. Tracy, *Plurality and Ambiguity* (San Francisco: Harper and Row, 1987); Owen Miller, 'Intertextual Identity', in *Identity of the Literary Text*, ed. by M. J. Valdes and O. Miller (Toronto: University of Toronto, 1985); Fredric Jameson, *The Political Unconscious: Narrative as a Socially Symbolic Act* (Ithaca: Cornell University Press, 1981); Lynn Poland, 'The Bible and Rhetorical Sublime', in *The Bible as Rhetoric: Studies in Biblical Persuasion and Credibility*, ed. by M. Warner (London: Routledge, 1990), 29–50; Michael Riffaterre, 'Intertextual Representation: On Mimesis as Interpretive Discourse', *CI* 11 (1984), 141–62; Louis A. Renza, 'Influence', in *Critical Terms for Literary Study*, ed. by F. Lentricchia and T. McLaughlin (Chicago: University of Chicago Press, 1990), 186–202; and Elaine Rusinko, 'Intertextuality: The Soviet Approach to Subtext', *Dispositio* 4 (1979), 213–35.

[236] Cf. T. S. Eliot, 'Tradition and the Individual Talent', in *Selected Essays, 1917–1932* (New York: Harcourt, Brace, Jovanovich, 1964 [orig. 1919]), 3–11; Harold Bloom, *The Anxiety of Influence: A Theory of Poetry* (New York: OUP, 1973); idem, '"Before Moses was, I Am": The Original and Belated Testaments', in *Notebooks in Cultural Analysis: An Annual Review* 1 (1984), 3–14.

[237] For example, Jacques Derrida, 'Living On Border Lines', in *Deconstruction and Criticism*, ed. by H. Bloom, et al. (New York: Seabury, 1979); *Dissemination*, trans. by B. Johnson (Chicago: University of Chicago, 1981 [Fr. 1972]); David C. Hoy, 'Must We Say What We Mean? The Grammatological Critique of Hermeneutics', in *Hermeneutics and Modern Philosophy*, ed. by B. R. Watchterhauser (New York: SUNY, 1986), 397–415; Roland Barthes, 'The Death of the Author', in *Image, Music, Text*, trans. by S. Heath (New York: Hill and Wang, 1977), 142–8; idem, 'Theory of the Text', in *Untying the Text: A Post-Structuralist Reader*, ed. by R. Young (Boston: Routledge and Kegan Paul, 1981); Kristeva, *Desire in Language;* Elizabeth Freund, *The Return of the Reader: Reader-Response Criticism* (New York: Methuen, 1987); Edgar Mcknight, *Postmodern Use of the Bible: The Emergence of Reader-Oriented Criticism* (Nashville: Abingdon, 1988); A. Thiselton, *The Two Horizons: New Testament Hermeneutics and Philosophical Description* (Grand Rapids: Eerdmans, 1980); Jane Tomkins, ed., *Reader-Response Criticism: From Formalism to Post-Structuralism* (Baltimore: John Hopkins University Press, 1980); Wolfgang Iser, 'The Reading Process: A Phenomenological Approach', in *Reader Response Criticsm*, ed. by J. Tompkins (Baltimore: Johns Hopkins University Press, 1980); Thaïs E. Morgan, 'Is There an Intertext in This Text?: Literary and Interdisciplinary Approaches to Intertextuality', *American Journal of Semiotics* 34 (1985), 1–40; idem, 'The Space of

hermeneutical programme, one can no longer speak of 'what this text means'. Instead one can only ask 'what does this text mean to me or to you?' However, the proposition is self-defeating since it assumes for its own validation what it denies.[238] In this present study, by intertextuality I do not mean what the post-modernists mean.

Within the field of biblical studies, the concept of 'intertextuality' has captured the attention of Pauline scholarship since the publication of Richard B. Hays's book *Echoes of Scripture in the Letters of Paul.*[239] Hays tries to demonstrate that echoes of Scripture resonate within the Pauline epistles as part of Paul's theological presentation and discourse. Central to Hays's project is the rhetorical technique of *metalepsis*[240] or transumption. This he describes as 'a device that requires the reader to interpret a citation or allusion by recalling aspects of the original context that are not explicitly quoted.'[241] Elsewhere Hays gives a fuller definition of metalepsis:

When a literary echo links the text in which it occurs to an earlier text, the figurative effect of the echo can lie in the unstated or suppressed (transumed) points of the resonance between the two texts.... [This technique] functions to suggest to the reader that text B should be understood in light of a broad interplay with text A, encompassing aspects of A beyond those explicitly echoed. This sort of metaleptic figuration...places the reader within a field of whispered or unstated correspondences.[242]

What Hays wishes to show (in Paul's letters) is that uncited scriptural echoes resonate in tones of meaning which, although not explicitly, play a part in the unspoken undercurrents of Paul's theological formulations,

---

Intertextuality', in *Intertextuality and Contemporary American Fiction*, ed. by P. O'Donnell and R. Con Davis (Baltimore: John Hopkins, 1989), 259-79.

[238] See John Ashton's remarks in *Studying John: Approaches to the Fourth Gospel* (Oxford: Clarendon, 1994), 196-204. Much earlier still in the late '60s and '70s, when these new approaches to the text were beginning to take shape, E. D. Hirsch, quite persuasively exposed some of their basic flaws. See his influential works, *Validity in Interpretation* (New Haven, CT: Yale University Press, 1967) and *The Aims of Interpretation* (Chicago: University of Chicago Press, 1976). See also Stephen E. Fowl, 'The Ethics of Interpretation, or What's Left After the Elimination of Meaning?', in *The Bible in Three Dimensions*, ed. by D. J. A. Clines, et al. (Sheffield, England: JSOT Press, 1990), 379-98; Howard Felperin, *Beyond Deconstruction: The Uses and Abuses of Literary Theory* (Oxford: Clarendon, 1985). Cf. R. M. Fowler, 'Who Is "the Reader" in Reader Response Criticism', *Semeia* 31 (1985), 5-23; George A. Lindbeck, *The Nature of Doctrine: Religion and Theology in a Postliberal Age* (Philadelphia: Westminster, 1984).

[239] (New Haven: Yale University Press, 1989).

[240] So called by J. Hollander, *The Figure of Echo: A Mode of Allusion in Milton and After* (Berkeley: University of California, 1981).

[241] R. B. Hays, 'Echoes of Scripture in the Letters of Paul: Abstract', in *Paul and the Scriptures of Israel*, ed. by C. A. Evans and J. A. Sanders, JSNTSUP 83 (Sheffield: JSOT, 1993), 42 (42-46).

[242] Hays, 'Echoes of Scripture', 20.

thereby supporting his explicit argument. Certainly the same can be said of John as well. The primary assumption in intertextuality is that both writers and readers are readers of other texts. They consciously or subconsciously interject their past readings into the present one. Writers may consciously or subconsciously allude to, echo, or reflect in their writings what they have read. Therefore texts often 'spill over into other texts'.[243]

In the case of the Fourth Gospel, if one chooses to describe Johannine allusions to the Old Testament as intertextuality, such 'intertextual echoes' are conscious and systematic. In the present study, by Johannine allusion, I mean the conscious, systematic, extensive, exegetically-planned, subtle, yet specific references to Old Testament images and ideas.[244] These are part of the Evangelist's conscious Messianic exegesis to demonstrate his central proposition as stated in John 20:30–31. John's use of implicit references to the Old Testament is so thoroughly pervasive[245] yet so consistently allusive that it may be considered the dominant factor in the elusive quality of John's language, unfailingly pointing the reader beyond what appears on the surface of the text. Nestle and Aland in their 26th–27th edition of the Greek New Testament cite some two hundred allusions and parallels to the Old Testament in the Fourth Gospel. Günter Reim in his *Studien zum alttestamentlichen Hintergrund des Johannesevangeliums* gives his own extensive list.[246] Similar citations are found in hundreds of articles, essays, and monographs which point out additional parallels and allusions.[247]

---

[243] Fewell, ed., *Reading Between Texts*, 23; Peter D. Miscall, 'Isaiah: New Heavens, New Earth, New Book', in *Reading Between Texts*, ed. Fewell (1992), 41–56.

[244] Ullmann, *Language and Style*, 193–201, postulates that there are six frequent ways imagery functions in a work. An image may function as a symbol (to express one of the main themes of a work and recur repeatedly in a work), to furnish the implicit motivation of an action, to convey value judgments, to express the philosophical ideas or personal aspirations of a writer, to express experiences which cannot be conceived of otherwise, and to portray or caricature a person. Some of these are evident in the Johannine purpose.

[245] Cf. A. Loisy, *Le Quatrième Evangile* (Paris: Picard, 1903), 80, M. Hengel, 'The Old Testament in the Fourth Gospel', *HBT* 12 (1990), 31–2; Brown, *John*, lix–lxii.

[246] (Cambridge: CUP, 1974), 97–109.

[247] For example, A. T. Hanson's, *The Prophetic Gospel: A Study of John and the Old Testament* (Edinburgh: Clark, 1991); E. D. Freed, *Old Testament Quotations in the Gospel of John* (Leiden: Brill, 1965) T. Francis Glasson, 'Exodus Typology in the Fourth Gospel', *JBL* 81 (1962), 329–42; James Drummond, 'Genesis 1 and John 1:1–14', *ExpTim* 49 (1937–38), 568; Pancaro, *The Law in the Fourth Gospel;* J. V. Dahms, 'Isaiah 55:11 and the Gospel of John', *EvQ* 53 (1981), 78–88. T. L. Brodie, 'Jesus as the New Elisha: Cracking the Code', *ExpTim* 93 (1981–82), 39–42; E. Dahood, 'Genesis and John', *Christian Century* 98 (1981), 418–21; J. D. M. Derrett, 'John 9:6 Read with Isaiah 6:10; 20:9', *EvQ* 66 (1994), 251–4; idem, 'Impurity and Idolatry: John 13:11; Ezekiel 36:25', *BO* 34 (1992), 87–92; W. F. Hambly, 'Creation and Gospel: A Brief Comparison of Genesis 1:1–2, 4 and John 1:1–2, 12', *SE* 5 = TU 103 (1968), 69–74; Henry Mowvley, 'John 1:14–18 in the Light of Exodus 33:7–34:35', *ExpTim* 95 (1983–84), 135–

Earlier in this chapter, I used the analogy of a literary 'fabric' to describe the structure that makes John's language enigmatic. Old Testament Scriptures provide the 'substance' of this language. To illustrate the significance of Old Testament allusions to Johannine language and its elusive quality, a few examples have been selected and briefly discussed here, with further examples in the fifth and the sixth chapters of this book. In the succeeding analysis, John's tapestry-like structure should become apparent. All the literary and linguistic phenomena noted earlier, such as amphibological words, conceptual multiple meanings, and metaphors, must be used to evaluate Old Testament allusions. Johannine ambiguity is the collective product of such features.

The very first words of the prologue, ἐν ἀρχῇ in John 1:1, echo Genesis 1:1–2:2. The allusion is to the Word of God who made heaven and earth (cf. Ps. 33:9; 148:4–5; Isa. 40:26; 55:10).[248] Genesis begins with the creation of light in darkness. John begins with the eternal Word, as light shinning in the darkness. The climax of the Genesis account is when humanity is made in the image of God. The Johannine account of the new creation begins with God 'being made' in the image of humanity when the Word became flesh. John introduces the readers to Christ by showing that a new act of creation as great as the creation of the world has occurred when 'the Word became flesh' (1:14). God is recreating humanity through the Word made flesh, the same Word that created humanity in the first place.

The term σκηνόω in John 1:14a (καὶ ὁ λόγος σὰρξ ἐγένετο καὶ ἐσκήνωσεν ἐν ἡμῖν) is rooted in Old Testament history. The verb means 'to live, dwell', but it is also reminiscent of a 'pitched tent, tabernacle', recalling the tabernacle or σκηνή of Israel's wilderness wandering.[249] This

---

7. Many citations of possible and potential Old Testament allusions in John may also be found in most standard commentaries on the Gospel, some of which have been referred to in the preceding footnotes in this chapter. Also consult the bibliography.

[248] Cf. Goppelt, *Theology of the New Testament*, 2:296–300; Loader, *Christology of the Fourth Gospel*, 55–89; Paul Lamarche, 'The Prologue of John', in *The Interpretation of John*, ed. by John Ashton (London: SPCK, 1986), 36–52; Millar Burrows, 'The Johannine Prologue as Aramaic Verse', *JBL* 45 (1926), 57–69; R. G. Hamerton-Kelly, *Pre-Existence, Wisdom, and the Son of Man* (Cambridge: CUP, 1973), 200; Edwin D. Freed, 'Some Old Testament Influences on the Prologue of John', in *A Light Unto My Path: Old Testament Studies*, ed. by Howard Bream and Ralph D. Heim (Philadelphia: Temple University Press, 1974), 145–6; Dodd, *Interpretation of the Fourth Gospel*, 263–85; A. B. du Toit, 'On Incarnate Word: A Study of John 1:14', *Neot* 2 (1968), 9–21; Basil Pinto, 'Word and Wisdom in St. John', *Scripture* 19 (1967), 19–27, 107–25.

[249] See BAGD, 755; C. R. Koester, *The Dwelling of God: The Tabernacle in the Old Testament, Intertestamental Jewish Literature and the New Testament*, CBQMS 22 (Washington: Catholic Biblical Association, 1989), 100–15; Brown, *John*, 32–4; Reim, *Studien zum*

is particularly important in the context of what John tells us in 1:14b: ἐθεασάμεθα τὴν δόξαν αὐτοῦ, δόξαν ὡς μονογενοῦς παρὰ πατρός, 'we beheld his glory, glory as of the only begotten from the Father'.[250] The collocation of σκηνόω with δόξα (= כָּבוֹד) works together with a possible wordplay between σκηνή and שְׁכִינָה ('shekinah') or σκηνόω and שָׁכַן (the Greek and Hebrew terms share the same consonants in each case)[251] to recall the presence of God dwelling in the innermost sanctum of the tabernacle.[252] Jesus embodies the divine presence once again in Israel; he is the very locus of God's self-revelation (cf. 1:18). This conception of Jesus as the locus of revelation is fundamental to Johannine thought. Therefore, the word choice in 1:14 seems to have been intended as a thematic play on

---

alttestamentlichen Hintergrund, 105f., 140–3; 223f.; Bruce, *John*, 39–40; Carson, *Gospel According to John*, 127; Collins, *These Things Have Been Written*, 199–206; Kent, *Light in the Darkness*, 34.

[250] This statement may literally be the recollection of John upon the experience of the transfiguration described in Matthew 17:1-13, Mark 9:1-13, and Luke 9:28-36. In addition, in a deeper sense, 'the manifestation of His glory' may also be an allusion to 'the Messianic signs' (e.g., John 2:1-11, 4:36-54, 5:2-16, etc.), or his being 'lifted up' in exaltation when the true identity of the Son of Man is revealed. See Painter, *John: Witness and Theologian*, 51, where he argues for a relationship between the verb 'to glorify' and 'to lift up' or 'exalt' (cf. 12:23, 31; 3:14; 8:28; 12:34 in light of Exod. 15:2; Isa. 33:10; 52:13, etc.). Tenney, 'Old Testament and the Fourth Gospel', 302, notes, 'The "glory" mentioned in Isaiah 6 is ascribed to the Jehovah of Hosts; according to John, it is attributed to Jesus. The allusion to Isaiah 66:14 in John 16:22 contains a parallelism in the words, "Your heart shall rejoice", but the resemblance is not strong enough to possess interpretive value.' According to Dodd, *Interpretation of the Fourth Gospel*, 206, the concept of 'glory' means 'the manifestation of God's being, nature and presence, in a manner accessible to human experience, and the manifestation was conceived in the form of radiance, splendor, or dazzling light. It is, therefore, not surprising that δόξα and φῶς are found in parallelism referring to the manifestation of the power of God for the salvation of His people.' See further Caird, 'The Glory of God in the Fourth Gospel'; W. R. Cook, 'The "Glory" Motif in the Johannine Corpus', *JETS* 27 (1984), 291–7; M. Pamment, 'The Meaning of Doxa in the Fourth Gospel', *ZNW* 74 (1973), 12–6; Reim, *Studien zum alttestamentlichen Hintergrund*, 140f., 277; Anthony Hanson, 'John 1:14–18 and Exodus 34', *NTS* 23 (1976), 90.

[251] שְׁכִינָה itself is a post-biblical word which can represent the *divine presence*, functioning almost as a substitute for the divine name; see Marcus Jastrow, *A Dictionary of the Targumim, The Talmud Babli and Yerushalmi, and the Midrashic Literature*, 2 vols. in 1 (New York and Berlin: Verlag Choreb; London: Shapiro, Valentine, 1926), 1573 s.v. On the possible wordplay σκηνή – shekinah see Beasley-Murray, *John*, 14, though with cautions by Schnackenburg, *St. John*, 269–70. On the root שָׁכַן see M. Görg in *TWAT* 7 (1993), 1337–48. See further Cadman, *Open Heaven*, 59–62; Braine, 'Inner Jewishness', 115–6; Brown, *John*, 1:503–4; D. H. Read, 'Inside John's Gospel: Introducing Jesus', *ExpTim* 88 (1976), 46–7; Loader, *Christology of the Fourth Gospel*, 107; and especially Bernd Janowski, '"Ich will in eurer Mitte wohnen". Struktur und Genese der exilischen *Schekina*-Theologie', *JBTh* 2 (1987), 191–93 (165–93) on John 1:14, with further literature; reprinted in Janowski, *Gottes Gegenwart in Israel. Beiträge zur Theologie des Alten Testaments* (Neukirchen-Vluyn: Neukirchener Verlag, 1993), 119-47.

[252] On God or his glory dwelling among his people (especially in the sanctuary) see Exod. 25:8; 29:49; 33:7-11; 40:34-38; Num. 9:15, 16; Zech. 2:14.

the idea of the tabernacle in the Old Testament as the locus of God's self-revelation.

The tabernacle (and subsequently the temple) was the focal place where oracles of God were given and his word heard. The Evangelist seems to imply in 1:14 that the Word, as the 'tabernacled' presence of God, also embodies the revelatory word of God.[253] Jesus himself is now the locus of divine revelation; he is the tent of meeting as well as the tent of testimony. He is the true tabernacle, the real temple. This takes on a special significance in light of the prophetic challenge of Jesus in John 2:19: λύσατε τὸν ναὸν τοῦτον, καὶ ἐν τρισὶν ἡμέραις ἐγερῶ αὐτόν, 'Destroy this temple, and in three days I will raise it up.' The Evangelist in 2:21, in one of his asides, quickly clarifies that the temple of which Jesus spoke was his own body. Thus the Johannine allusion in 1:14, in anticipation of 2:21, seems to have in view the establishment of the new temple, first in the bodily temple of the Son of God and later in the church, the body of Christ, where the triune God dwells and continues to manifest his light throughout the world.

Closely connected with this theme in which Jesus is presented as the true temple of God, the Evangelist ties in another significant thematic allusion to the Old Testament: Jesus is the ultimate Passover sacrifice.[254] John refers to the Passover more than any other New Testament writer. The idea is keynoted in the Baptist's exclamation in 1:29, restated briefly in 1:36, and then developed in the rest of the document. Finally it climaxes in chapter 19 when the Evangelist singles out the time of the crucifixion of Jesus in the context of the time of the Passover sacrifice as the two coincide. John 19:36 ('Not one bone of his will be broken') is probably an allusion to the Passover regulations in Exod. 12:10, 46 and Num. 9:12 (cf. Ps. 34 [LXX 33]: 21). The image is that of all Israel gathered around the Passover lambs. Jesus is depicted as the paschal lamb which all in the congregation of Israel are intended to consume to maintain their covenant position before God. The Evangelist expects such a correlation to take place in the mind of his readers through echoes of Scripture which, although unstated, carry a weight of meaning that surpasses the limitations of the explicit citation itself.

In this way, John has tapped into the Pentateuchal story of the paschal

---

[253] John C. Meagher, 'John 1:14 and the New Temple', *JBL* 88 (1969), 57–68; Reim, *Studien zum alttestamentlichen Hintergrund*, 10–11.

[254] John refers to the Passover ten times whereas Luke mentions it seven times and Matthew and Mark four times each. This development of Jesus as the true Passover is highly significant to the thrust of author's theological argument. See my discussion in chapter five.

lamb, allowing it to resonate within his own narrative in order to address a particular situation. Included in the Evangelist's citation at John 19:36 are scriptural echoes which resonate from the deep resources of the Jewish Passover ritual. We cannot know whether or not these echoes were heard by anyone within the Evangelist's original sphere of influence. We have only an indication of the Evangelist's own supposition that echoes of Scripture might be heard in 19:36.[255] In the recorded incident of the stabbing of the side of the Lord by the Roman soldier and the subsequent flow of water and blood (19:34), there may be a further allusion to Exodus 17:6, 'Strike the rock, and water will come out of it for the people to drink.' The frequency of exodus motifs in the Fourth Gospel (paschal lamb, bronze serpent, manna from heaven) leads quite naturally to the supposition that the Evangelist is here drawing on the account of Moses' striking the rock in the wilderness to bring forth water (Num. 20:8ff).[256] That such imagery was readily identified with Jesus in the early church is demonstrated by Paul's understanding of the event in 1 Cor. 10:4. Jesus is the rock from which the living water – the Spirit – will flow.

Apart from the Passover allusions, which are central to Johannine theology, there are many other examples of thematic undercurrents in the language of the Fourth Gospel. In the discourse with Nathanael, for example, there is a subtle contrast between Jacob and Nathanael. Jacob was the first to bear the name 'Israel' (Gen. 32:28). Nathanael is also a Jew of the stock of 'Israel', but of a different type. According to John 1:47 he is judged to have no 'deceit' in him, as Jacob did (cf. Gen. 27:35), perhaps because he very quickly recognises Jesus as the Messiah. Nathanael exemplifies a true Israelite by his immediate acceptance of Jesus as the Christ and by his perception of truth in the face of scepticism.[257] In this episode, there is a subtle contrast between 'true' and 'false' children of Abraham. Nathanael as a 'true Jew' is a man of faith. Abraham was a man of faith. John repeatedly accuses the opponents of Jesus of unbelief, and in fact Jesus, on this very ground, rejects their claim of having Abraham as

---

[255] Bruce Longenecker, 'The Unbroken Messiah: A Johannine Feature and its Social Functions', *NTS* 41 (1995), 428–41.

[256] The Johannine exodus associations are intentional and are part of the theme of the revelation and redemption offered in Christ as fulfilling the hope of a second exodus. In fact, the six main institutions (the festival of Passover, the festival of Unleavened Bread, the offering of firstlings, theophany, covenant, and law) set forth in narrative form in the book of Exodus are also present in the narrative account of John in association with Jesus as their fulfilment. See my discussion in chapter five.

[257] M. de Goedt, 'Un schème de révélation dans le quatrième évangile', *NTS* 8 (1961–62), 142–50; Meeks, *Prophet-King*, 82.

their father (Jn. 8:33–47). Like Nathanael, Abraham was a man without guile. He was characterised by a steadfast faith in God. Thus he was given a vision of Jesus' day and rejoiced in its anticipation (Jn. 8:53–56; cf. Genesis 15). John 1:47–51 may be considered in the light of Isaiah 44:1–5. Nathanael is called 'Israel' because he is faithful to God and does not serve false gods as do the accusers of Jesus who claim to have Caesar as their king (19:15) when, in fact, as the chosen community, they should have God as their king.

Jesus' reference to the fig tree in his encounter with Nathanael in John 1:48 is deemed important by most Johannine scholars, though a few have denied its significance.[258] However, in John's Gospel, such details are rarely coincidental or inconsequential. The astonishment provoked by Jesus' remark cannot be explained unless some symbolism is contained in the affirmation. But opinions vary on the nature of the symbolism. The reference may be to the piety of Nathanael or an allusion to his study of Scripture and its Messianic prophecies.[259] The rabbinic writings compared the law to a fig tree, and rabbis sometimes studied and taught under a fig tree.[260] In this incident, perhaps Nathanael was given the insight to see in the law the one of whom the law spoke (cf. Jn. 5:46–47). In confessing Christ, he recognised Jesus as the fulfilment of the law. If this is the background, then the references further emphasise John's assertion that the Scriptures speak of Jesus and that those who are able to see can perceive that they point forward to him.

Another suggestion, put forward by J. R. Michaels, is that Jesus in John 1:48 may have been alluding to Hosea 9:10, 'When I found Israel, it was like finding grapes in the desert; when I saw your fathers, it was like seeing the early fruit on the fig tree.'[261] J. Jeremias sees the reference to the fig tree as alluding to confession of sin and Jesus' assurance of forgiveness against the background of Psalm 32 (LXX 31): 2, μακάριος ἀνήρ οὗ οὐ μὴ λογίσηται κύριος ἁμαρτίαν, οὐδέ ἔστιν ἐν τῷ στόματι αὐτοῦ δόλος (compare δόλος in John 1:47).[262] There may also be an echo of scriptural allusions to Israel's life in the eschatological kingdom (1 Kgs. 4:25; Mic. 4:4; Zech. 3:10; cf. 1 Macc. 14:12) and an association with the coming of a

---

[258] Newman and Nida, *Translator's Handbook*, 49. Cf. Kysar, *John, the Maverick Gospel*, 41; Bernard, *St. John*, 1:63.

[259] Qoh. R. 5:11; Str-B, 1:857–8 and 2:371.

[260] Str-B, II, 371.

[261] J. R. Michaels, 'Nathanael Under the Fig Tree', *ExpTim* 78 (1966–67), 182–3. The quotation is from the New International Version (NIV).

[262] J. Jeremias, 'Die Berufng des Nathanel', *Angelos* 3 (1928), 2–5.

100   *Chapter 2: The Structure of John's Enigmatic Language*

Messianic figure called the 'Branch' in Zechariah 3:18–10.[263] And yet others see in Jesus' reference to the fig tree a further indication of his omniscience.[264]

John 1:48, like many Johannine allusions, does not quote the Scriptures directly. The original sense of the Hebrew texts (i.e., Mic. 4:4; 1 Kings 4:25; Zech. 3:8–10) in which a man calls or invites another under a fig tree at the advent of the Messianic 'branch' (צמח, Zech. 3:8) is not

---

[263] John alludes to Zechariah a number of times. These instances show that the Evangelist would have been very familiar with Zechariah. In this context, the author connects the imagery of the fig tree in Zech. 3:10 with the messianic reference in 3:8 and he seems to relate passages from Zechariah to similar Old Testament texts, conflate the passages, and recast these texts to fit the new context. Cf. John's formal citation of Zech. 12:15 as fulfilment of Zech. 9:9 which may be conflated with Isa. 35:4; 40:9. The reference is preceded by a paraphrase of Ps. 118:25-26 coupled with Zech. 3:15 and the kingship theme in Jn. 12:13. Also John quotes Zechariah 19:37. Nathanael's recognition of Jesus as the 'Son of God' and 'king of Israel' further explicates the recognition of his kingship. Once Jesus is understood to be the Branch foretold by Zech. 3:8, he could be acclaimed as 'the Son of God' and 'king of Israel' because these titles singled out the Davidic Messiah. Evidence from the Qumran scrolls seems to verify that Jewish exegetes of the New Testament period had identified the Branch foretold by Zechariah and Jeremiah as Messiah, Son of God, and King of Israel. The scrolls also understood the Davidic Messiah to be the fulfillment of the law and the prophets (Jn. 1:45). The three significant texts are 4QFlorilegium, 4QPBless, and 4QpIsa 8–10. 4QFlorilegium is a midrash which draws on disparate Old Testament texts to elucidate a paraphrase of 2 Sam. 7:10–14. The text is significant because it assumes that the Davidic Branch was a well-known Messianic designation which could be applied to the 'Son' of God mentioned in 2 Samuel 7. 4QPBless is a midrash on Gen. 49:10. This text is significant because it identifies the Davidic Branch as 'Messiah of Righteousness' and the 'King of Israel'. It also shows that the interpreter assumed that the Davidic Messiah was foretold in the law as well as the prophets. 4QpIsa 8–10 is a text which includes an interpretation of Isa. 11:1 identifying the Branch with the Isaianic 'shoot'. See for further details J. M. Allegro, 'Further Messianic References in the Qumran Literature', *JBL* 75 (1956), 174–87; J. Painter, 'Christ and the Church in John 1:45–51', in *L'Évangile de Jean*, ed. by M. de Jonge (1977), 359–62; Cadman, *The Open Heaven*, 28; D. Juel, *Messianic Exegesis: Christological Interpretation of the Old Testament in Early Christianity* (Philadelphia: Fortress, 1988), 31–57; John J. Collins, 'The Son of God Text From Qumran', in *From Jesus to John: Essays on Jesus and New Testament Christology in Honour of Marinus de Jonge*, ed. by M. C. de Boer (Sheffield: JSOT Press, 1993), 65–82.

[264] For various interpretive nuances, see O. Betz, '"Kann denn aus Nazareth etwas Gutes kommen?" (Zur Verwendung von Jesaja Kap. 11 in Johannes Kap. 1)', in *Wort und Geschichte: Festschrift für Karl Elliger zum 70. Geburtstag*, ed. by H. Gese and H. P. Rüger; AOAT 18 (Kever: Butzon und Bercker/Neukirchen-Vluyn: Neukirchner, 1973), 14; F. Hahn, 'Die Jüngerberufung Joh. 1:35–51', *Neues Testament und Kirche: Für Rudolf Schnackenburg*, ed. by J. Gnilka (Freiburg: Herder, 1974), 187–9; Michaels, 'Nathanael Under the Fig Tree', 182–3; Craig R. Koester, 'Messianic Exegesis and the Call of Nathanael', *JSNT* 39 (1990), 23–34; J. D. M. Derrett, 'Fig Trees in the New Testament', *HeyJ* 14 (1973), 249–65; Paul Trudinger, 'An Israelite in Whom There is No Guile', *EvQ* 54 (1982), 117–20; Bultmann, *John*, 104; Bruce, *John*, 61; Lindars, *John*, 118; Carson, *Gospel According to John*, 161; Hoskyns, *Fourth Gospel*, 182; Bernard, *St. John*, 1:63–4; Brown, *John*, 1:83; Barrett, *St. John*, 185; M. J. Lagrange, *Evangile selon saint Jean*, EBib; 5th edn (Paris: Gabalda, 1936), 51; C. F. D. Moule, 'A Note on "Under the Fig Tree" in John 1:48, 50', *JTS* n.s. 5 (1954), 210–11; Dodd, *Historical Tradition in the Fourth Gospel* (Cambridge: CUP, 1963), 310. Cf. W. R. Telford, *The Barren Temple and the Withered Tree*, JSNTSup 1 (Sheffield: JSOT Press, 1980).

identical to the Johannine sense. However, such modifications and conflations of Old Testament texts are characteristic of Johannine allusions as he interprets the Scriptures from his post-resurrection insight and point of view; a number of possible passages may have been blended (see above and further Jer. 23:5, 33:15; Isa. 11:1; 1 Kings 5:5 [MT]).

Philip calls Nathanael, who was already under the fig tree (1:48), to confirm the advent of the Messianic 'branch' (Zech. 3:8) and the Messianic age. The resulting faith of Nathanael is entirely in keeping with the Evangelist's purpose (Jn. 20:31). Nathanael seems to have understood Jesus' response in terms of the Jewish Messianic expectations, already having in mind Philip's statement, 'We have found him of whom Moses in the law and also the prophets wrote' (1:45) and echoing Andrew's statement, 'We have found the Messiah' (1:41). Nathanael's recognition of Jesus as the Messiah, the Son of God (cf. Jn. 20:31), is grounded in his understanding of Old Testament passages which use the terms מָשַׁח or מָשִׁיחַ (though 2 Samuel 7 does not) and which in any case designate the king of Israel in 'messianic' fashion as God's 'son' or 'firstborn' (e.g. Psalm 2:2, 7; 89:20, 26–27 [MT vv. 21, 27–28]; 2 Sam. 7:14). Nathanael's recognition combined with Jesus' reference to him as a 'true Israelite' captures a subtle but consistent emphasis in the Gospel: true Israelites see in Jesus the Messiah of Israel's Scriptures and see the Scriptures fulfilled in this Messiah.

The mysterious pronouncement of Jesus in 1:51 is a thematic allusion to Jacob's vision at Bethel (Gen. 12:8; 13:3–4).[265] It was at Bethel that Israel consulted the LORD (Jud. 20:18, 26; 21:2–5; 1 Sam. 10:3). Bethel stood as the 'locus of ancient theophany and divine revelation'. For the Evangelist, Jesus epitomises the supreme 'Bethel' (i.e., the real house of God). In him, in the truest sense, is the place for people to see God (Jn. 14:9) and to behold the divine glory (1:14, 18; 2:11; 5:41). The functions which had primitively accrued to Bethel are now fulfilled in Jesus. Not only has Jesus replaced the tabernacle (Jn. 1:14), he has also superseded Israel's most ancient sanctuary. He is the authentic dwelling place of God and the true Word, the divine wisdom who reveals the mind of God.[266]

The entire Samaritan discourse is infused with imageries and thematic

---

[265] W. Michaelis, 'Joh. 1:51 – Gen. 28:12 und das Menschensohn-problem', *TLZ* 86 (1960), 561ff; R. H. Strachan, *The Fourth Gospel: Its Significance and Environment*, 3d edn (London: SCM, 1943), 120–2; Reim, *Studien zum alttestamentlichen Hintergrund*, 100–4; Barrett, *St. John*, 155–6; J. H. Neyrey, 'The Jacob Allusions in John 1:51', *CBQ* 44 (1982), 586–605.

[266] For an excellent article on the topic see O. Hofius, 'Der in des Vaters Schoss ist: Joh 1:18', *ZNW* 80 (1989), 163–171; Strachan, *The Fourth Gospel*, 8–9.

allusions to the Old Testament. For example, the encounter between Jesus and the Samaritan woman by the well echoes the encounter stories of the Patriarchs by various wells (e.g., Abraham's servant and Rebekah, Gen. 24:10–19; Jacob and Rachel, Gen. 29:1–14; Moses and Zipporah, Exod. 2:15–21).[267] Furthermore in Jesus' remark, 'salvation is of the Jews', Otto Betz detects an allusion to Genesis 49:10, 'The sceptre shall not depart from Judah, nor the ruler's staff from between his feet, until he comes to whom it belongs; and to him shall be the obedience of the peoples.'[268] Betz believes Genesis 49:10c here is interpreted Messianically. When the Samaritan woman says, 'I know that the Messiah is coming', she is indicating her recognition and awareness in Jesus' reference to the Genesis 49:10 tradition that he is speaking of salvation coming from the Jews. There is even an implied pun on Jesus' own name when in 4:42 she describes Jesus as ὁ σωτὴρ τοῦ κόσμου, 'the Saviour of the world.'[269] The entire discourse in 4:35–38 about the readiness of the harvest abounds with Old Testament overtones in such eschatological images as 'harvest' (Isa. 62:8–9; 65:21–23; Amos 4:7, 9:14b; Hos. 6:11; 9:3, 18:5, Joel 1:11, 3:13), 'reapers' (Hos. 8:7; Mic. 6:15), and 'sowers' (Ps. 126:5; Isa. 28:24; Jer. 31:27; Mic. 6:15; Hag. 1:6). As the water promised to the Samaritan woman earlier was of a wholly different nature, so here is the eschatological 'harvest'. Both have their own unique, non-natural modes of operation.

The association between John 8:12 and 9:5 and Isaiah 9:2 (MT 9:1: 'The people who walk in darkness will see a great light', etc.) is conceded by most commentators.[270] The idea of the dawning of light dominates John's prologue (1:4–5, 9). Jesus as the one coming from the Father and sent into the world is the one who can illuminate humanity with the knowledge of God. The circumstances of the Samaritan woman, the invalid man and the blind man vividly capture the vision behind Isaiah's prophetic utterance. Race, rank, and learning are irrelevant in this eschatological era. Only those who are aware of their blindness will see the light. In this dispensation, God seeks those who worship him in Spirit and in truth

---

[267] The imagery of Christ as the bridegroom and the church as his bride is familiar in Johannine literature (Jn. 3:39; Rev. 21:2, 9; 22:17). See further J. M. Poffet, *Jésus et la Samaritaine (Jean 4, 1–42)*, Suppléments aux Cahiers Evangile (Paris: Cerf, 1995); Normand R. Bonneau, 'The Woman at the Well: John 4 and Gen. 24', *The Bible Today* 67 (1973), 1252–59; Okure, *Johannine Approach to Mission*, 88; Van der Horst, 'A Word Play in John 4:12?' 280–82; Staley, *Print's First Kiss*, 101–2; Alter, *Art of Biblical Narrative*, 52–62.

[268] O. Betz, '"To Worship God in Spirit and in Truth": Reflections on John 4:20–6', in *Standing Before God*, ed. by A. Finkel and R. Frizzel, ET (New York: 1981), 53–72.

[269] Ibid., 67.

[270] Cf. John 3:17–21, 7:27ff., Lindars, *John*, 315–16.

(4:23-24). The prime example of this eschatological fact is the Johannine contrast between Nicodemus and the Samaritan woman. Nicodemus is a male Jew, a Pharisee, a teacher of Israel, a member of the Jewish ruling aristocracy who comes to Jesus under the cover of night and departs from him still oblivious to the truth. By contrast, this woman, a person with a questionable lifestyle, a female by gender and a Samaritan by birth, encounters the light of the world in broad daylight. Incidentally while Nicodemus comes to Jesus, it is Jesus who had to go through Samaria (Jn. 4:4) and meet the woman who will become a witness for him, calling the people of her village to him and announcing, 'Is not this the Christ?' (4:29, cf. 4:39-42; 1:45-49). Both the Samaritan woman and Nicodemus are presented as historical figures who, according to John, had an encounter with the Jesus of history.

A similar unstated contrast is between the Pharisees and the blind man in chapters 8 and 9. Chapter 8 opens with Jesus' revelatory statement: Ἐγώ εἰμι τὸ φῶς τοῦ κόσμου (8:12, cf. v. 58), and the episode closes in chapter 9 with another revelatory statement: καὶ εἶπεν ὁ Ἰησοῦς, Εἰς κρίμα ἐγὼ εἰς τὸν κόσμον τοῦτον ἦλθον, ἵνα οἱ μὴ βλέποντες βλέπωσιν καὶ οἱ βλέποντες τυφλοὶ γένωνται (9:39). The implications are clear. While teachers of Israel are blind to the truth,[271] a cast-away Jew, walking in darkness, 'born altogether in sin' (9:1, 34), has seen the light of the world and possesses greater sensitivity to the light of truth than the rulers of Israel. And to the revelation that 'before Abraham was, I am' (8:58), the response of the religious leaders is rejection. In stark contrast is the response of the blind man who, when asked by Jesus, 'Do you believe in the Son of Man?' affirms, 'Lord, I believe.... And he worshipped him' (9:35, 38).

A similar contrast of characters occurs throughout the Gospel.[272] In these contrasts, John does not simply report. He also interprets and singles out details which he deems significant to his message or useful for heightening its central point. He expects an astute reader or hearer to discern the

---

[271] Cf. J. L. Staley, 'Stumbling in the Dark, Reaching for the Light: Reading Character in John 5 and 9', *Semeia* 53 (1991), 55-80. John is not alone in giving 'sight' a symbolic significance (cf. 2 Kings 6:15-17). For a different use of the image in Greek, see J. Gregory, 'Some Aspects of Seeing in Euripides' Bacchae', *Greece and Rome* 32 (1985), 23-31. More immediate to John is the way Mark follows his story of the disciples' failure to see or hear because of their hardness of heart (8:14-21). The parabolic significance is made plain by the disciples' confession of faith at Caesarea Philippi which follows. The use of spittle in that miracle, as well as in John 9:6, may point back to the same event.

[272] E.g., between Nathanael and Jacob; Beloved Disciple vs. Judas, Beloved Disciple vs. Peter after Jesus' arrest.

unstated. In Jesus Christ, all the traditional categories are done away. In the sight of the creator, a promiscuous Samaritan woman and a blind beggar stand in greater stature than the teachers of Israel. The castaways know their dismal condition. Their response to the revelation of the Son of Man is unequivocal and immediate – faith, worship and obedience. But the Evangelist drives home his prophetic criticism – these social castaways have more sense and sensibility when confronted by the light of the world than the spiritual teachers of Israel who are utterly blind to the revelation.

In the narrative of the call of the first disciples, there is an echo of Isaiah 55:6, 'Seek the Lord while he may be found'. The second theme is in Hosea 5:6, 'They shall go to seek the Lord, but they shall not find him.' And wisdom declares: 'Those who seek me find me' (Prov. 8:17), or in the negative: '(The wicked) seek me but find me not' (Prov. 1:26). Jesus in John asserts, 'Whoever serves me must follow me, and where I am, there also will my servant be' (John 12:26; cf. 14:3; 17:24).[273] These two themes are united, but in the negative, in John 7:34, in regard to 'the Jews' who will not believe. Jesus says to them: 'You will look for me but not find me, and where I am you cannot come' (7:34; cf. 8:21). But in the story of the call of the first disciples the theme is described in a positive way. Jesus asks them: 'What do you seek?' (1:38). And the disciples themselves answer a little later, 'We have *found* the Messiah' (1:41), and we have found 'the one about whom Moses wrote in the law and also the prophets' (1:45).

In the healing of the invalid man in John 5, among the potential Old Testament echoes in this account, there is a reference to the circumstantial detail of the man's disability – thirty-eight years. Apart from 1 Kings 16:29 and 2 Kings 15:8, thirty-eight years only occurs in Deuteronomy 2:14 as the duration of the wandering of the children of Israel. Lindars does not believe there is any intended association between this number and that number. His conclusion is clear, 'another flight of fancy presents itself to those who think that numbers must always have meanings'.[274] Of course, numbers do not always have meanings unless the context within which they occur solicits them. Yet in the Fourth Gospel, such details do not appear to be fortuitous. The number here is significant or it would not have been recorded. It is unlikely that it simply represents a precise yet trivial recollection of an eye-witness. In several instances, John draws attention to numbers. For example, he singles out the specific number of fish caught in

---

[273] R. J. Tournay, *Word of God, Song of Love: A Commentary on the Song of Songs* (New York: Paulist, 1988), 72–3.

[274] Lindars, *John*, 214.

21:1–14 (one hundred and fifty-three); the specific number of barley loaves and fish in 6:9 (five loaves and two fish), or the number of baskets of leftover fragments of bread in 6:13 (twelve baskets), and the six stone water jars in 2:6 (cf. 21:11). Barrett, commenting on this last passage, points out that it is possible that the number six has some symbolic significance.

> Six, being less by one than seven, the number of completeness and perfection, would indicate that the Jewish dispensation, typified by its ceremonial water, was partial and imperfect. Perhaps it should be noted that the event took place on the sixth day (see on 2:1); on the other hand, no numerical interpretation of the miracle can be entirely satisfactory since Jesus does not create a seventh vessel.[275]

Whatever the possible significance of such numerical details may be, the Evangelist, by singling out such details, may have intended to trigger shared associations in the minds of his hearers and readers. If the modern reader can detect such possible connotations, surely the original audience, for whom the Old Testament was 'Scripture', would have been particularly sensitive to such details and more than able to detect similar overtones. To choose a non-numerical example, in the extended metaphor of the vine and the branches in chapter 15, John capitalises on the Old Testament picture of Israel as the vine (cf. Ps. 80:8–19, Jer. 2:21; Ezk. 15:1–8; 19:10–14) to present Jesus as the true Israel, the genuine vine and the fulfilment of that of which the old vine was but a shadow.[276]

In each of the Johannine signs recorded in the Gospel, there is an associative allusion to the actions of YHWH, and what he alone can do, thus authenticating Jesus' claim to be one with the Father or to be the 'I Am'. For example, in the episode of Jesus walking on the sea (Jn. 6:19–21), there is an echo of Job 9:8b where YHWH alone is the one who treads upon the crests of the sea. Such implicit associations between the actions of Jesus and those of the supreme deity in the Old Testament reoccur in many of Johannine allusions to the Scriptures. Here it is significant, particularly in view of Exodus 3:14, Isaiah 41 and 43 where 'I Am' is a formula of divine self-revelation, that Jesus declares, 'It is I' (6:20). This association is then developed elaborately in conjunction with Johannine metaphors and the 'I Am' formulas.

In this sign of Jesus walking on the sea, John records that Jesus was doing what the Scripture says God alone can do, thus identifying Jesus

---

[275] Barrett, *St. John*, 190. Cf. Dodd, *Historical Tradition*, 299.
[276] Cf. Hoskyns, *Fourth Gospel*, 474–5; Brown, *John*, 2:660; Lightfoot, *St. John's Gospel*, 291; Barrett, *St. John*, 392–4; Beasley-Murray, *John*, 271–2; Hunter, *Gospel According to John*, 148; Tenney, *John*, 226; Sanders, *St. John*, 336–7; Bruce, *John*, 308; Tasker, *St. John*, 173–4.

with YHWH.²⁷⁷ Earlier in turning water into wine, Jesus demonstrates his creative power, thus identifying himself with the creator who alone can change matter (2:1–11; cf. 10:30). Glasson connects this first miracle with the first sign of Moses: 'The changing of water to wine should remind the reader of the first of the plagues in Egypt, the changing of water to blood.'²⁷⁸ However, it is more likely that Jesus' sign signified the arrival of the blessings of the Messianic age (Jer. 31:12; Hos. 14:7; Amos 9:13). If this is right, then it seems quite appropriate for Jesus to perform his first sign at a wedding, which itself was a picture of the Messianic age (Isa. 61:10; 62:5). Both 'wine' and 'wedding' are images associated with the Messianic era (Amos 9:13; Hos. 2:24; Joel 4:18; Isa. 25:6; 29:17; Jer. 31:5). With the coming of the Son of Man, the kingdom of God has been inaugurated, though not yet consummated. In the New Testament, this kingdom is often portrayed in terms of a banquet, especially a wedding feast (Mt. 8:11; 22:1–14; Lk. 13:29; 14:15–24; Rev. 19:7–9). This gives significance to the temporary lack of wine. The old wine had run out, yet the Messiah was here to bring the new.²⁷⁹

In John 6 there may be a play on the motif of the reversal of the effects of eating the forbidden fruit from the tree of the knowledge of good and evil. Genesis 3:3 gives the command of God, 'You shall not eat from it...lest you die.' Yet the man eats, and he is driven out of the garden 'lest he stretch out his hand, and take also from the tree of life, and eat, and live forever' (Gen. 3:22). Jesus in John 6:58 invites men and women to eat the

---

²⁷⁷ Cf. A. Probst, 'Jésus et Yahvé', *Revue Réformée* 41 (1990), 44–5; J. Duncan Derrett, 'Why and How Jesus Walked on the Sea', *NovT* 28 (1981), 330–48; C. H. Giblin, 'The Miraculous Crossing of the Sea (Jn. 6:16–21)', *NTS* 29 (1983), 96–103; G. Krodel, 'John 6:63', *Int* 37 (1983), 283–8; Suriano, 'Who Then Is This?' 449–56; A. M. Denis, 'Jesus' Walking on the Waters: A Contribution to the History of the Pericope in the Gospel Tradition', *LS* 1 (1967), 284–97; J. Heil, *Jesus Walking on the Sea*, AnBib 87 (Rome: Biblical Institute Press, 1981).

²⁷⁸ *Moses in the Fourth Gospel*, 26.

²⁷⁹ For various suggestions about the significance of this first sign of Jesus, see Raymond F. Collins, 'Cana (Jn. 2:1–12) – The First of His Signs or the Key to His Signs?', *ITQ* 47 (1980), 79–95; Marty, 'The New Moses', 142-3; Lightfoot, *St. John's Gospel*, 336; Schnackenburg, *St. John*, 1:515–28; M. C. Tenney, 'Topics in the Fourth Gospel: Part II. The Meaning of Signs', *BibSac* 132 (1975), 145–60; M. Inch, 'Apologetic Use of "Sign" in the Fourth Gospel', *EvQ* 42 (1970), 35–43; F. E. Rainey, Jr., 'Semeion in the Gospel of John: A Clue to the Interpretation of the Gospel' (Ph.D. diss., Fort Worth, TX: Southwestern Baptist Theological Seminary, 1968); Kysar, *John, the Maverick Gospel*, 67–73; S. D. Toussaint, 'The Significance of the First Sign in John's Gospel', *BibSac* 134 (1977), 50; Hoeferkamp, 'The Relationship Between *Semeia* and Believing in the Fourth Gospel', 43; Olsson, *Structure and Meaning*, 18–114; Richard Trench, *Notes on the Miracles of Our Lord* (Grand Rapids: Baker Book House, 1949), 74; Christian P. Ceroke, 'The Problem of Ambiguity in John 2:4', *CBQ* 21 (July 1959), 316–40; Tasker, *St. John*, 55–6; Reim, *Studien zum alttestamentlichen Hintergrund*, 195f. and 264f.; Bultmann, *John*, 118–19; Staley, *Print's First Kiss*, 83–90; Corell, *Consummatum Est*, 58.

bread of life so that they will live forever. In Genesis 3:24, God drove the man out of the garden of Eden; Jesus draws people to himself with the invitation that 'the one who comes to me, I will certainly not cast out' (Jn. 6:37).

John 6 reverberates with echoes, allusions, and thematic plays upon Old Testament images and ideas which give the language of the Gospel its unique quality. Among them is one of the most prominent, yet subtle contrasts in the Fourth Gospel – the comparison between Moses and Jesus, which by implication is a comparison between the old dispensation and the new, or law versus grace. In the history of Israel, there were at least three eschatological personalities whom the Jewish people believed might appear at any moment: the Messiah, Elijah, and the prophet like Moses. All three appear within the first chapter of the Fourth Gospel.[280]

In the New Testament Jesus is presented as one who occupies three offices – the office of a prophet, priest, and king. As a prophet, Jesus represents God to the human race.[281] He speaks for God, the words of God are upon his lips, he is the Word of God. As a priest, Jesus' function is opposite of that of a prophet. Here he represents people before God.[282] He bears blood, his own, into the presence of God to make atonement for sin. As a priest, he also prays for his disciples and intercedes on their behalf (John 17). As the Messiah, Jesus occupies the office of a king (Jn. 1:49). As a king, he represents God's people before the world.[283] He rules over them,

---

[280] J. A. T. Robinson, 'Elijah, John and Jesus', *NTS* 4 (1958), 277; A. Mayer, 'Elijah and Elisha in John's Sign Sources', *ExpTim* 99 (1988), 171–3; Georg Richter, '"Bist du Elias?" (Joh. 1,21)', *BZ*, N.F. 6 (1962), 79–92, 238–56; and 7 (1963), 63–80; idem, 'Die Logosliede im Prolog des vierten Evangeliums', *TZ* 31 (1975), 321–36; Harald Sahlin, *Zur Typologie des Johannesevangeliums*, Uppsala universitetsskrift, Bd. 1950/4 (Uppsala: Lundequistska Bokhandeln, 1950); Dieter Zeller, 'Elijah und Elischa im Frühjudentum', *BK* 41 (1986), 154–60.

[281] This prophetic perspective can be traced back to Jesus himself. In the Book of Acts, Luke has Peter (3:22) and Stephen (7:37) appeal to Deuteronomy 18:15 to show that Jesus was a prophet like unto Moses, as though the early church has been using this passage with reference to Jesus' prophetic dignity. See Paul E. Davies, 'Jesus and the Role of the Prophet', *JBL* 64 (1945), 241; Adele Reinhartz, 'Jesus as Prophet: Predictive Prolepses in the Fourth Gospel', *JSNT* 36 (1989), 3–16.

[282] The two extensive works in this area belong to B. Giles, 'Jesus the High Priest in the Epistle to the Hebrews and the Fourth Gospel' (Ph.D. diss., Manchester, dir.: F. F. Bruce, 1974) and M. W. Henderson, 'The Priestly Ministry of Jesus in the Gospel of John and the Epistle to the Hebrews' (Ph.D. diss., Louisville, KY: Southern Baptist Seminary, 1966). See also Cullmann, *Christology*, 83ff.; T. W. Manson, *Ministry and Priesthood: Christ's and Ours* (London, 1959). See also my discussion in chapter five under the title 'Jesus as the Passover sacrifice'.

[283] Cf. 2 Sam. 7:14; Ps. 2:7; 1 Enoch 105:2; 4 Ezra 7:28f.; 13:52; 14:9; Mk. 1:11; Rom. 1:3f. The term *basileus*, 'king' occurs twice as often in John's account of the trial of Jesus as in the corresponding section of any of the Synoptics. On the kingship of Jesus, see Barrett, *St. John*, 186, 549; Dodd, *Historical Tradition*, 112; Ernst Haenchen, 'Jesus vor Pilatus (Joh. 18, 28–29,

defends them, and leads them forth into a holy war. He occupies all three of these offices as 'the anointed of the Lord'. All three offices with varying emphases are either explicitly or implicitly alluded to in the Fourth Gospel. Needless to say from the Johannine perspective, Jesus is not simply a latter-day priest, prophet, and king. He is priest, prophet, and king *par excellence*.

W. Meeks in his 1967 monograph *Prophet-King* argued convincingly that within the Jewish setting out of which John's Gospel emerged, Moses was regarded as a king as well as a prophet, and that 'the depiction of Jesus as prophet and king in the Fourth Gospel owes much to traditions which the church inherited from Moses piety'.[284] Moses stood as a monumental figure in later Judaism. In view of this, John, in his presentation of Jesus, continuously points to the fact that Jesus is the promised prophet-king: a prophet like unto Moses (cf. Deut. 18:15). The reference in John 6:15 to 'the prophet' (cf. 1:21) means the prophet like Moses.[285] The Fourth Evangelist repeats the tradition about a prophet not without honour (4:44). The Baptist in the Fourth Gospel denies that he is the Christ, Elijah, or the prophet, as though these terms naturally went together in the Christian mind. Twice the outsiders call Jesus a 'prophet' on the basis of signs or miracles (6:14; 9:17). John 7:52b, 'Search and you will see that no prophet is to arise from Galilee', has the ring of some early challenge to Christian claims for Jesus as a prophet.[286] In John's Gospel, Jesus is 'the prophet' whom 'the Jews' have awaited based upon Deuteronomy 18:15. These Johannine citations are more impressive when they are viewed in the light of the christology of this Gospel.

Centuries earlier Moses, after having led the children of Israel out of Egypt to Sinai, was nearing the end of his life. And the people of Israel were wondering who would speak to them from God. Moses warned the people not to go to astrologers, wizards or necromancers. He said that God would instead raise up in their midst another prophet like himself (Deut.

---

15)', in *Gott und Mensch*, ed. by Ernst Haenchen (1965), 149, 152; Meeks, *Prophet-King*, 64, 76, 81; Heinrich Schlier, 'Jesus und Pilatus nach dem Johannesevangelium', in *Die Zeit der Kirche*, ed. by Heinrich Schlier, 4th edn (Freiburg: Herder and Herder, 1966), 56–74; idem, 'The State According to the New Testament', in *The Relevance of the New Testament*, by Heinrich Schlier (Freiburg and New York: Herder and Herder, 1968), 215–25.

[284] Meeks, *Prophet-King*, 318–19. See also M. de Jonge, 'Jesus as Prophet and King in the Fourth Gospel', *ETL* 49 (1973), 160–77; R. E. Brown, 'Jesus and Elisha', *Perspective* 12 (1971), 85–104; S. E. Johnson, 'Notes on the Prophet-King in John', *ATR* 51 (1969), 35–7.

[285] Lindars, *John*, 244; Barrett, *St. John*, 330.

[286] The use of the definite article in 1:21; 6:14; 7:40 is noteworthy for the Synoptics do not use the expression and Jesus appears there as one of the older prophets returned.

18:15). But how shall Israel recognise a prophet sent from God? One of the worst problems plaguing Israel throughout its history was false prophecy. How does one distinguish the true prophet from the false? In Deut. 18:15-22 (cf. Deut. 13:1-3), Moses lays down three criteria by which the congregation of Israel may determine whether a man is a prophet sent from God:

1. He must be an Israelite, a Jew (Deut. 18:15). It is a historical fact that the Gospels present Jesus as a Jew (e.g., Mt. 1:1). John assumes that fact (although see 4:9; 6:42; 19:19).

2. He must foretell the future accurately (Deut. 18:22). In the Gospels, including the Fourth Gospel, the evangelists give detailed accounts to demonstrate this. The supreme example of this in the Fourth Gospel is Jesus' foreknowledge of the resurrection.

3. He must be like Moses (Deut. 18:15). To a certain extent, all Israel's prophets were like Moses in so far as they all spoke for God. And yet in another sense none apart from Jesus was like Moses. In Deut. 34:10, we read these startling words: 'And there arose not a prophet since in Israel like unto Moses whom the Lord knew face to face.' It would appear that whoever wrote the last chapter of the book of Deuteronomy was one who had seen all the prophets of Israel and was able to make this assessment. In the Johannine account, the last criterion is emphatically underlined: 'No one has ever seen God; the only Son who is in the bosom of the Father, he has made him known' (Jn. 1:18; cf. 3:13).

The major point of the Johannine comparison between Jesus and Moses seems to be theological rather than historical. Nevertheless, in the broader combined Gospel accounts, most major historical events in the life of Moses seem to have their counterpart in the life of Jesus. For example, both Moses and Jesus are born when the nation is in bondage. Moses is born when the children of Israel are in bondage in Egypt. Jesus is born when people are in bondage to Rome. Both Moses and Jesus are born under the sentence of death. At the time of Moses' birth, Pharaoh gives the edict to the midwives to kill all the male children when they are born (Exod. 1:15). Likewise Jesus is born under the sentence of death. Herod had given the edict that all the male children in the city of Bethlehem two years of age and under were to be put to death, which is fully consonant with his character (Mt. 2:16). Both Moses and Jesus are miraculously delivered in the land of Egypt. Both of them grew up to be heirs to a throne. Moses as the son of Pharaoh's daughter is heir to the throne of Egypt; Jesus as the son of David is heir to the throne of Israel. But both are rejected and are refused that throne for spiritual reasons. Both are rejected by their people at their first coming. The Israelites said to Moses, 'Who made you to be judge over us?' (Exod. 2:14). And their descendants said to Pilate and to Jesus, 'We have no king but Caesar' (Jn. 19:15). During the period of their rejection, both choose a Gentile bride. Moses flees to the land of Midian, and marries Zipporah, the daughter of Jethro, a Gentile. Likewise, Jesus spiritually today has in effect chosen a 'Gentile bride', since the church is composed mostly of Gentiles. Nevertheless, both Moses and Jesus are received at their second coming. When Moses comes the second time, he comes with mighty signs and wonders and the people believe in him. Likewise when Jesus finally comes a second time to 'his own' (cf. Jn. 1:11), he will come with similar signs and wonders and the people will believe in him (Revelation 16). During his time in the wilderness, Moses fasts forty days and forty nights; Jesus also fasts forty days and forty nights. Moses goes to the top of the mountain and he returns shining with the glory of God; Jesus, too, is on top of the Mount of Transfiguration and his glory shows forth (though the Synoptic account is of course not repeated in John).

In John's account, the 'gifts' of Moses become the activities of the 'new Moses'. As the first redeemer delivered the people of God from slavery to Pharaoh, so the last Redeemer will liberate men from slavery to the 'father of lies'. Moses was heralded as a great 'shepherd/leader of the Hebrew nation. The Johannine Jesus is the 'good shepherd' (10:11ff). Just as the Israelites murmured against Moses (Exod. 16:2, Psalm 106:25 [LXX 105]), John also records the murmuring of 'the Jews' (γογγυσμός) against Jesus since he claims to be the bread coming down from heaven (6:41).[287] As the first redeemer provided bread and water for the people of God in the wilderness, likewise the last Redeemer satisfies the thirst of his flock and feeds them the true manna (cf. Isa. 49:10), provides for them the bread of life, and satisfies their thirst with the living water.[288] Moses instituted the Passover. In John, Jesus is the Passover. Moses was the mediator of a divine covenant. Jesus is the mediator of a new and everlasting covenant in His blood.[289] The first Moses gave the people of God the law which they

---

[287] Glasson, *Moses in the Fourth Gospel*, 101, sees a link between John 6:51 and Exodus 16. E. D. Freed, *Old Testament Quotations in the Gospel of John* (Leiden: Brill 1965), 19, believes the allusion is to Psalm 106:25. See also R. Beauvery, 'Le Fils de Joseph! Manne Descendue du Ciel?' *Assemblés du Seigneur* 50 (1974), 43–9.

[288] See G. Geiger, 'Aufruf an Rückkehrende: Zum Sinn des Zitats von Ps. 78, 24b in Joh 6, 31', *Bib* 65 (1984), 449–64, who traces verbal and theological echoes of Psalm 78 in Jn. 6:1–71; Meeks, *Prophet-King*, 29–31; Bas van Iersel and Anton Weiler, eds, *Exodus: A Lasting Paradigm* (Edinburgh: Clark, 1987).

[289] Glasson, *Moses in the Fourth Gospel*, 10, goes a step further and argues that the Messianic

could not keep; the last Moses gives grace. Indeed 'at the very time the Law was given through Moses, Israel stood in need of grace' (cf. Exod. 32-34; Jn. 1:14–18).[290] As YHWH's agent, Moses receives his credentials (How will they believe in me?) in the power to work signs (Exod. 4:1–9). In a similar fashion, the signs of Jesus authenticate his claim to be the Messiah (Jn. 20:31).

The most significant point of comparison between Jesus and Moses in the Johannine account is the manner in which they gave their revelation. The writer of Deuteronomy presents Moses as having spoken face to face with God. Moses does not receive his revelation in a vision, a trance, or a dream. He is said to have spoken directly with God and was given the revelation. No other canonical prophet records such a direct claim to revelation. However, John from the start presents Jesus as one who was from the beginning 'with God', πρὸς τὸν θεόν (Jn 1.1; cf. 1:18). He speaks directly for God with all the authority of God. John presents Jesus as the realisation of the expectation of the 'prophet *like* Moses' – not simply a 'second Moses', but one greater than Moses.[291]

Similar thematic undercurrents echo throughout this Gospel. The pericope of the blind man in chapter 9 hinges upon a conceptual double meaning of τυφλοί which predicates both physical and spiritual blindness. Throughout the Johannine Gospel, the tragedy of 'seeing' and 'not being able to perceive' comprises a well-developed motif, calling to mind the lamentable curse uttered in Isaiah 6:9–10. Jesus' claim at the outset of the story to be the 'light of the world' (9:5) signals the re-emergence of another central theme which began in the prologue (1:5).

In John 9:7 'sight' is connected with another conceptual double meaning associated with the word νίπτω, 'wash'. The expression here not only entails a physical act but also may imply a deeper significance. The allusion to Siloam's waters as part of the Johannine thematic development of 'living water' introduced in John 4 is noteworthy. The Hebrew name שִׁלֹחַ (Shiloah) is derived from the verb שָׁלַח, meaning to send. John's gloss on this word in 9:7 (ὃ ἑρμηνεύεται ἀπεσταλμένος) shows that he considers the pool of Siloam to be the pool of 'The one who is sent', and sending is of course a frequent Messianic motif applied to Jesus (cf. Jn. 3:17; 4:34; 5:24, 30, 37; 6:29, 38, etc.).

---

hope of the new exodus and the Messiah as the new Moses is one of the keys to understanding the Fourth Gospel.

[290] Zane Hodges, 'Grace after Grace – John 1:16', *BibSac* 135 (1978), 41.

[291] Meeks, *Prophet-King*, 313ff.

Furthermore, it is interesting that in the Targumic paraphrase of Song of Solomon 4:15, the 'waters of Shiloah' (מיא רשׁי לוח) are seen as a 'fountain of living water' (באר מיין חיים).²⁹² Therefore, the more astute among John's audience may have seen Jesus' command to 'wash in the Pool of Siloam' as almost synonymous with 'wash in my pool' or even 'wash in my fountain'. The blind man's *washing* is almost synonymous with the Samaritan woman's *drinking* from the same fountain of living water. From the post-Easter perspective of the Evangelist, the command could then have been understood in a deeper sense as alluding to washing in Calvary's cleansing fountain.²⁹³ 'This eschatological fountain, like Siloam, will gurgle forth from a rock as the crucified Christ of the Johannine passion narrative fulfils the rabbinically embellished peripatetic rock in the Moses water-miracle.'²⁹⁴

If true to John's intention, this interpretation may go hand-in-hand with his 'inaugurated' eschatology. The day when streams of living water will gush forth from the new temple (Ezk. 47:1–12; cf. 1:14, 18; 2:19–21; 7:37–38) has, according to John, now arrived. This also corresponds with the developing theme of 'living water' – a motif which culminates in the effluence of water of life from the crucified Christ. For an original audience who heard the expression 'waters of Shiloah' as a symbolic representation of the 'fountain of living water' (באר מיין חיים) and who moreover deemed the Pool of Siloam highly significant in a cultic sense, Jesus' words in John 9:7 might furthermore have recalled the Feast of Tabernacles with its 'waters of expiation' (מי חטאת). The 'water' theme is in any case consistent with John's argument for Jesus as the 'new temple' (Jn. 2:21; 4:21–23). For from the temple come forth both the 'glory of the LORD' (cf. Exod. 40:34; Ezk. 8:4) and the fountain of 'living water'. John's language of the temple and of living water is reminiscent of passages such as Jer. 2:13; 17:13; Ezekiel 47; and Zech. 14:8.²⁹⁵

In the incident of cleansing the temple, John may have intended to trigger in the mind of his audience an association with Psalm 69:10. Or the

---

²⁹² Tg. Hag. SSol. 4:15, Sperber edition cited by Bruce Grigsby, 'Washing in the Pool of Siloam', *NovT* 27 (1985), 227–35.

²⁹³ Grigsby, 'Washing', 234.

²⁹⁴ Ibid. 234, 227 respectively.

²⁹⁵ Cf. Guilding, *Fourth Gospel and Jewish Worship*, 121–9, 216–20; Painter, 'John 9 and the Interpretation', 31–61; Schnackenburg, *St. John*, 2:238–58; Bultmann, *John*, 329–42; Brown, *John*, 1:369–82; John Bligh, 'Four Studies in St. John: I, the Man Born Blind', *HeyJ* 7 (1966), 129–44; Calvin L. Porter, 'John 9:38, 39a: A Liturgical Addition to the Text', *NTS* 13 (1966–67), 387–94.

Evangelist may have viewed Jesus' act as an indication of the coming kingdom of God.[296] The disapproving challenge of 2:18 seems to imply that 'the Jews' were aware of the Messianic connotation behind Jesus' action and that he was being challenged on that account.

On the negative side, later Christians did not hesitate to interpret the subsequent destruction of the temple as a judgment upon the Jews for their rejection of their Messiah.[297] W. D. Davies argues that Jesus' departure from the temple in John 8:59 is a deliberate act of judgment, a final rejection of the Holy Place:

For John, 'I am' has departed from the Temple, that 'holy space' is no longer the abode of the Divine Presence. The Shekinah is no longer there, but is now found wherever Christ is, because later (10:36 makes this probable, if not unmistakably clear) Christ himself is the Sanctified One, the altar and Temple, the locus of the Shekinah.[298]

The fact that Jesus replaces the temple and is now 'the locus of the Shekinah' for John is indicated by more than John 10:36. It may be that some readers would hear overtones of Ezekiel's vision of the departure of the *merkabah* from Jerusalem (cf. Jn. 12:36), which heralded the destruction of the city in 587 BC (cf. Ezekiel 10), especially since an equivalent departure before the final destruction in AD 70 had become a popular legend, even finding its way into Roman history with Tacitus.[299] There were widespread legends about the portents that preceded and warned of the coming judgment: *b. Yoma* 39b records the tradition that Yohanan b. Zakkai saw the doors of the temple opening by themselves and took this as a sign of coming destruction.[300]

The title ὁ υἱὸς τοῦ ἀνθπώπου, 'Son of Man', is the title Jesus uses most often of himself in the Fourth Gospel (e.g., 1:51; 3:14; 5:27; 6:27, 53,

---

[296] For various proposals as to the implication of the Lord's action in the temple, see Hiers, 'Purification of the Temple', 82–90; Hoskyns, *Fourth Gospel*, 192–9; Grant, 'Coming of the Kingdom', 298; Blenkinsopp, 'The Oracle of Judah and the Messianic Entry', 58; Burrows, 'Thy Kingdom Come', 1–8; Bultmann, *Jesus and the Word*, 29; idem, *John*, 162–8; Hamilton, 'Temple Cleansing and Temple Bank', 372; Gärtner, *The Temple and the Community in Qumran*, 105–22; O'Neill, 'The Silence of Jesus', 164; Schnackenburg, *St. John*, 343–56; Lindars, *John*, 135–45; Bruce, *John*, 73–7.

[297] E.g., Justin, *Dial.* 108:1–3 or 16:2–3. The Christian editing of T. Levi 16:3–5 makes this point also and must be early because it antedates the whole extant MS tradition.

[298] W. D. Davies, *The Gospel and the Land: Early Christianity and Jewish Territorial Doctrine* (Berkeley: University of California Press, 1974), 295; O. Cullmann, 'L'Evangile Johannique at L'Histoire du Saltut', *NTS* 11 (1965), 111–22.

[299] *Histories* 5:13; Josephus, *War* 6:297–300. Cf. 2 *Apoc. Bar.* 8:1–5; Josephus, *War* 5:412.

[300] Neusner, *A Life of Rabban Yohanan ben Zakkai Ca. 1–80 C.E.*, 2nd edn (Leiden: Brill, 1970 [1962]), 64f. See also Josephus, *War* 6:288ff.

62; 8:28; 9:35–39; 12:34). The Old Testament origin of this title is well established.[301] In John there are additional titles ascribed to Jesus with Messianic associations and rooted in the Old Testament. These christological titles are primarily intended to allude to his Messianic office (prophet, priest, king).[302] The most obvious Messianic title of all is μεσσίας, 'the Anointed One'. Other titles include ὁ προφήτης, 'the prophet', ὁ ἐρχόμενος, 'the coming one' (12:13),[303] and ὁ ἅγιος τοῦ θεοῦ, 'the Holy One of God' (6:69).[304] There may also be an implicit title in John 1:18,

---

[301] V. Hampel, *Menschensohn und historischer Jesus: Ein Rätselwort als Schlüssel zum messianischen Selbstverständnis Jesu* (Neukirchen-Vluyn: Neukirchener, 1990), believes the title 'Son of Man' provides the key to the Messianic self-consciousness of Jesus. He further argues that the Son of Man tradition shows a clear continuity between the preaching of the historical Jesus and the kerygma of the early church. See also William Horbury, 'The Messianic Associations of "the Son of Man"', *JTS* n.s. 34 (1985), 34–55; John Bowman, *The Fourth Gospel and the Jews* (Pittsburg, PA: Pickwick Press, 1975), 210; Bruce Vawter, 'Ezekiel and John', *CBQ* 26 (1964), 450–8. Francis J. Moloney, 'The Johannine Son of Man', *Bibliotech di Scienze Religiose* 14 (1976), 219, sees the title 'Son of Man' as a continuation of a dynamic, growing interpretation of Daniel 7:13. Cf. T. W. Manson, 'The Son of Man in Daniel, Enoch and the Gospels', *BJRL* 32 (1950), 171–93; Margaret Pamment, 'The Son of Man in the Fourth Gospel', *JTS* n.s. 36 (1985), 56–66; Merrill Tenney, 'The Imagery of John', *BibSac* 121 (1964), 20; Oscar Cullmann, *The Christology of the New Testament*, trans. by S. C. Guthrie and C. A. M. Hall (Philadelphia: Westminster Press, 1959), 137; Mogens Müller, 'Have You Faith in the Son of Man?', *NTS* 37 (1991), 292; Robert Rhea, *The Johannine Son of Man*, ATANT, Band 76 (Zürich: Theologischer Verlag, 1990), 9; E. D. Freed, 'The Son of Man in the Fourth Gospel', *JBL* 86 (1967), 402–9; Barnabas Lindars, 'The Son of Man in the Johannine Christology', in *Christ and Spirit in the New Testament*, ed. by B. Lindars and S. S. Smalley (Cambridge: CUP, 1973); idem, *Jesus, Son of Man* (London: SPCK, 1983); Stephen S. Smalley, 'The Johannine Son of Man Sayings', *NTS* 15 (1968), 278–301; C. F. D. Moule, *Essays in New Testament Interpretation* (Cambridge: CUP, 1982), 75–90; idem, 'Individualism of the Fourth Gospel', 82 n. 3; Dodd, *Interpretation of the Fourth Gospel*, 249; David Dorman, 'The Son of Man in John: A Fresh Approach Through Chapter 6', *Studia Biblica et Theologica* 13 (1983), 121–42; J. P. Brown, 'The Son of Man: "This Fellow"', *Bib* 58 (1977), 361–87; R. Maddox, *The Function of the Son of Man in the Gospel of John: Reconciliation and Hope* (Exeter: Paternoster Press, 1974); I. H. Marshall, 'The Synoptic Son of Man Sayings in Recent Discussion', *NTS* 12 (1965–66), 327–51; W. O. Walker, Jr., 'The Origin of the Son of Man Concept as Applied to Jesus', *JBL* 91 (1972), 482–90; Bruns, *Art and Thought*, 78–85; Goppelt, *Theology of the New Testament*, 178–205.

[302] Warren E. Bathke, 'The Titles of Christ in the Gospel of John' (Thesis, Dallas Seminary, 1957); Moule, *Essays in New Testament Interpretation*, 165–83, and his discussion in chapter 12, 'The Influence of Circumstances on the Use of Christological Terms'; Goppelt, *Theology of the New Testament*, 159–205; Richard, 'Expressions of Double Meaning', 102.

[303] See Barrett, *St. John*, 418, 549. He has argued that ὁ βασιλεύς in the context of John 12 is the interpretation of the *Coming One*; thus the two titles, 'the Coming One' and 'king' are co-ordinating and are synonymous. The claim to be the king meant to be the Messiah.

[304] W. R. Domeris, 'The Holy One of God as a Title for Jesus', *NTS* 19 (1985), 9–17; idem, 'The Confession of Peter according to John 6:69', *TynBul* 44 (1993), 155–67; Gunter Reim, 'Jesus as God in the Fourth Gospel: The Old Testament Background', *NTS* 30 (1984), 158–60; H. L. N. Joubert, 'The Holy One of God', *Neot* 2 (1968), 57–69.

where Jesus is said to be the one who has revealed God (ἐξηγήσατο).³⁰⁵ This title sums up Jesus' life as 'the revealer of God'.³⁰⁶

In the majority of these associations, John does not view Jesus' relationship to the Old Testament merely in terms of fulfilment but as both fulfilment and transcendence. Thus while the Evangelist uses Old Testament concepts and ideas of God's messengers to emphasise the Messianic identity of Jesus and underline his mission as the anointed of the Lord, yet he makes it equally clear that these figures serve merely as witnesses to Jesus (5:39, 46). Jesus' uniqueness as God's agent lies in the fact that he is both Son and God (1:1, 18; 5:18; 10:33, 36; 19:7). Since all contemporary Jewish ideas concerning the Messiah or other divine messengers were derived from the Scriptures, the judgment in 5:39 would apply with biting force.³⁰⁷

The sheep and the shepherd in John 10 are also very familiar Old Testament images. The allusion may go back to the vision of Ezekiel (chapter 34; cf. Numbers 27:17), which describes Israel as sheep and their leaders (either Joshua in Numbers, or the kings and elders of Israel in Ezekiel) as shepherds. In Ezekiel, just as in the Fourth Gospel, a bitter criticism is levelled against the elders of Israel. But as is characteristic of many Johannine allusions, there may be a blending of several strands into one idea. Therefore Psalm 23, in which the Lord is the true and faithful shepherd, may also be in view. The Lord is the faithful shepherd in contrast to the present regime which is compared to a band of thieves and robbers (Jn. 10:8). In Ezekiel the prophet, having criticised Israel's shepherds (34:2-10), registers the promise that YHWH himself will become Israel's shepherd (34:15). YHWH as shepherd will judge between sheep and sheep, rams and goats (34:17); this role is analogous to the implicit division of sheep in John

---

³⁰⁵ Cf. BAGD, 275–76; J. P. Louw, 'Narrator of the Father', *Neot* 2 (1968), 32–40; I. de la Potterie, '"C'est lui qui a ouvert la voie." La finale du prologue johannique', *Bib* 69 (1988), 340–70.

³⁰⁶ Cf. Westcott, *St. John*, 15–6; Barrett, *St. John*, 141; Carson, *Gospel According to John*, 134–5; Beasley-Murray, *John*, 16; R. Robert, 'Le mot final du prologue Johannique: A propos d'un article récent', *RevThom* 89 (1989), 279–88; idem, 'Un Précédent platonicien à l' équivoque de Jean 1:18', *RevThom* 90 (1990), 634–9.

³⁰⁷ One would be hard pressed to find any Jewish Messianic idea which did not take its departure point from God's promises to Israel in the law and the prophets or was not a function of these promises. Indeed, the first level at which the New Testament Christians themselves understood the identity and mission of Jesus was in terms of his fulfilling these Old Testament promises (e.g., Jn. 1:41; Lk. 4:16–30, 24:27; Acts 2:14–36, 13:13–41). The knowledge of Jesus' divine ontological sonship does not seem to have fully dawned on the disciples until later, which is not to deny that this knowledge could have been received in some form or other from the historical Jesus himself.

10:3, between the shepherd's 'own' sheep and all the others. The image reappears in 1 Enoch 89:12–90:41 as well, wherein the entire history of Israel is recounted, with sheep representing the Israelites and the shepherds representing their leaders, whether good or bad. The Septuagint version of Psalm 2:9 designates the Messianic king as 'shepherd'. Early in his ministry, this image is associated with Jesus and his disciples. The quotation of Zechariah 13:7 by another New Testament author, Mark (14:27), 'I will strike the shepherd and the sheep will be scattered', also supports the association. In this allusion, John triggers the thematic associations without having to spell them out.[308]

The anointing of Jesus at Bethany resonates with several Messianic echoes from the Old Testament. In the context of John 12:1–8, the term משחת (MT Isa. 52:14) is ambiguous and may mean 'anoint' or 'marry'.[309] The Targum presents Isaiah 52:13–53:12 in an overtly Messianic manner (cf. 52:13, 'Behold, my Servant, the Messiah'; cf. 53:10), although how early this interpretation can be assigned is problematic.[310] If such an anointing tradition was known to the Evangelist, then he may have had in mind such a correspondence between the Servant's anointing and the anointing of Jesus at Bethany (12:1–8). Mary's anointing of Jesus' feet echoes also Isaiah 52:7, 'How beautiful upon the mountains are the feet of him who brings good tidings, who publishes peace, who brings tidings of good, who publishes salvation, who says to Zion, "Your God reigns"'. The verb

---

[308] The association of Jesus and his disciples with the pictures of sheep and shepherd is a familiar, early Christian theme (cf. 1 Pet. 2:25, 5:4 and Heb. 13:20). The parable about the shepherd who loses one sheep and goes to look for the missing one is the picture in the Synoptics. There the shepherd is God, and varying interpretations and emphases are given to the story each time it appears. Cf. Mt. 18:12–14; Luke 15:3–7; *Gospel of Thomas*, 107; and *Gospel of Truth*, NHC 1.31:35–32:30. See also the *Shepherd of Hermas*, Vis. V.I.3ff., where the one to whom Hermas has been entrusted and the giver of commandments and teachings is a shepherd. However, according to Bultmann, *John*, 367, John's blending in chapter 10 marks a radical change from any of these antecedents. These new elements in John's use of the shepherd/sheep image were identified by Bultmann and later by Karl-Martin Fischer, 'Der johanneische Christus und der gnostische Erlöser', in *Gnosis und Neues Testament: Studien aus Religionswissenschaft und Theologie*, ed. by K. Tröger (Berlin: Evangelische Verlagsanstalt, 1973), 245–66. The most striking feature of the Johannine blending, according to Bultmann, is the reciprocal relationship (referred to by γινώσκειν) between the shepherd and the sheep, which is described in terms of the shepherd's calling and the sheep hearing his voice.

[309] W. H. Brownlee, *The Meaning of the Qumran Scrolls for the Bible, with Special Attention to the Book of Isaiah* (New York: OUP, 1964), 204–15.

[310] B. D. Chilton, *The Glory of Israel: The Theology and Provenience of the Isaiah Targum*, JSOTSup 2 (Sheffield: JSOT Press, 1993), 91–6. Chilton concludes that the portrait of the Servant as a victorious Messiah arose prior to Bar Kohkba (132–135 CE); also S. H. Levey, *The Messiah: An Aramaic Interpretation: The Messianic Exegesis of the Targum*, Monographs of the Hebrew Union College 2 (Cincinnati: Hebrew Union College, 1974), 67–70.

εὐαγγελίσασθαι is found in the eschatologically-understood Isaiah 61:1 passage: 'The Spirit of the Lord is upon me, because the Lord has anointed me to bring good tidings' (v. 1).

Among the (Messianic) blessings mentioned in this passage from Isaiah is the giving of the 'oil of gladness' to 'those who mourn in Zion' (61:3). Anointing was an aspect of grooming and beauty. In Matthew 6:16-18, a gloomy face and a neglected appearance stand in sharp contrast to an anointed head and washed face. In Ruth 3:3, Naomi, Ruth's mother-in-law, tells her to wash, anoint herself, and put on her best clothing in a bid to capture the heart of Boaz.[311] In the Fourth Gospel, the anointing of Jesus' feet may anticipate the inauguration of the Messianic age. Subsequently, the account of the crowd which went out (ἐξῆλθον) of Jerusalem to greet Jesus (12:12-13) may have been seen by the Evangelist as the fulfilment of the exhortation in Isaiah 52:11 to go out (ἐξέλθατε) of Jerusalem. This same verse in Isaiah 52 also instructs its readers to 'touch nothing unclean' but to 'purify' themselves, an idea which is in harmony with the Johannine Passover context, since on such an occasion there would have been a concern for ritual purity (see 18:28).

The jubilant shouting of 'Hosanna' by the people in John 12:13 echoes Isaiah 52:8-9. The reference in John 12:12 to the return of Jesus to Jerusalem, which he has previously visited, is reminiscent of the return of the Lord to Zion, as described in Isaiah 52. When the people see Jesus, they see the Lord (cf. Jn. 12:45, 'the one who sees me sees the one [i.e., the Lord] who sent me'). The use of Psalm 118:25-26 to express this is no doubt traditional, and the Isaianic background enriches it. Hailing the approaching Jesus as 'king' (see Jn. 12:13, where 'king of Israel' is added to the Ps. 118 citation; cf. the quotation of Zech. 9:9 in Jn. 12:14) correlates with Isaiah 52:7 which announces to Zion: 'Your God is king!' (MT reads מלך 'is king' or 'reigns'). The LXX uses the future, βασιλεύσει ('He will be king,' or 'He will reign'), which lends the passage more readily to the idea of fulfilment. Moreover, when the Greeks (perhaps a reference to foreign Jews, Ἕλληνες) come to worship at the feast and request to see Jesus (Jn. 12:20-21), there may be an echo of Isaiah 52:10: 'The Lord has bared his holy arm in the sight of all nations; that all the ends of the earth may see [LXX: 'will see'] the salvation of our God.' With reference to the final line of Isaiah 52:10, we should recall that Jesus' very name, in its full Hebrew form, means 'YHWH saves'. Thus, it is possible that the Fourth Evangelist

---

311 Psalm 45, interpreted messianically in early Jewish and Christian tradition, describes the king as beautiful (vv 2-3, 8, 11, 12b-14). Heb. 1:18-9 applies vv. 6-7 to Jesus.

would have us understand the Greeks' desire to see Jesus as the fulfilment of the promise that all people would one day see God's salvation.

In John 19:1, the Evangelist's wording may constitute an allusion to Isaiah 50:6, 'I gave my back to those who scourge me.' John's emphasis upon the time of Jesus' crucifixion underlines yet another Old Testament association. It is by no means coincidental that Jesus in the Johannine record is crucified at the time when the Passover lambs were slain in the temple. For the Evangelist, the time of Jesus' crucifixion signals a prophetic fulfilment, recalling his earlier account of John the Baptist's words, 'Behold the Lamb of God who takes away the sin of the world' (1:29). Consequently that concept is developed in John 18–19. For example, as I noted earlier, Pilate's pronouncement of the verdict against Jesus 'about the sixth hour' (i.e., 12 noon, John 19:14) coincides with the time when the Passover lambs were brought to the temple for the offering. The implication is clear: the Jewish religious order is superseded through its fulfilment in Jesus.[312] For the Fourth Evangelist, the sacrificial offering of Jesus on the cross not only recapitulates the highest expression of immolation; but also, it has forever rendered the Jewish sacrificial system obsolete.

John 19:17 bears overtones of Genesis 22:6 and the offering of Isaac. In the Markan account of the Passion (Mk. 15:21), Simon of Cyrene is compelled to carry the cross; by contrast, in the Fourth Gospel, Jesus carries his own cross. The Markan and Johannine narratives may be harmonised by supposing that Jesus began to carry the cross himself, fainted under the burden, and was relieved by the forced assistance of Simon.[313] In the Johannine account, the church Fathers saw a typological significance.[314] They saw in Isaac, who carried the materials for the sacrifice of himself (Gen. 22:6), a picture of Jesus. Philo comments on this incident (*Abr.*, 171), and it does not seem impossible that John also may have seen such typological association. This connection is perhaps reinforced by the comment on Genesis 22:6 in *Genesis Rabbah* 56:4: 'as one bears the cross (צלוב) on his shoulders'. Barnabas 7:3, however, already takes Isaac to be a type of Christ.[315]

In John 19:28, there is a subtle thematic play on the idea of 'thirst',

---

[312] David E. Garland, 'John 18–19: Life through Jesus' Death', *RevExp* 85 (1988), 494 (485–99).

[313] Barrett, *St. John*, 548.

[314] E.g., Chrysostom, *In Joh. Hom.*, LXXXV, 1.

[315] On the significance of the 'binding of Isaac' in Judaism, see G. Vermes, *Scripture and Tradition in Judaism* (Leiden: Brill, 1961), 193–227.

specifically as it relates to the word of the crucified Christ upon the cross when he said, διψῶ, 'I thirst' (19:28).³¹⁶ Was the cry of thirst simply a request for water because of physical dehydration, or to fulfil the Scriptures, or did it once more implicitly accentuate the Johannine idea of substitution in the making of atonement? This same idea is expressed by Paul explicitly in his soteriological formula, 'He made him who knew no sin to be sin on our behalf, that we might become the righteousness of God in him' (2 Cor. 5:21). In the Johannine theological programme, as I have already stated earlier in this chapter, Jesus, the Lamb of God, by taking upon himself the sin of the world (cf. 1:29), experienced the same spiritual separation and thirst common to those for whom he came to provide the living water.³¹⁷

Just as in John's ἐν ἀρχῇ there were echoes of Genesis and the beginning of the creation account, so in the pronouncement of the Lord upon the cross in John 19:30, τετέλεσται! (19:28; 4:34; 13:1), there are echoes of the conclusion of the new creation. In the entire Gospel, here alone does the Evangelist speak of a τελειοῦν of the Scriptures, an increase over the previous formula πληροῦν, which expresses the 'ultimate fulfilment' of the Scriptures. As noted above, the work of creation and salvation which began in Genesis 1:1 and John 1:1 is now finished on the evening of the sixth day. The Gospel began ἐν ἀρχῇ, at the very beginning, before the six days of creation or the new creation, and God's work of salvation is finished on the evening of the sixth day of the week. John seems consciously to place his ἵνα τελειωθῇ ἡ γραφή between the twice occurring τετέλεσται, to underline Jesus' knowledge that the end had come (19:28, 30).

At the beginning of the Lord's prayer for the disciples in chapter 17, John records him as having said: 'I glorified you on earth, having finished (τελειώσας) the work (τὸ ἔργον) that you gave me to do' (17:4). In these

---

³¹⁶ In the account of John 19:30, there may also be an allusion to Psalm 69:22, 'and for my thirst they gave me vinegar to drink'.

³¹⁷ A common characteristic of all those who thirst in this Gospel (i.e., the Samaritan woman in chapter 4, the multitudes in chapter 7, etc.) is spiritual separation from God. According to the Synoptic account of the crucifixion, Christ was crucified about 9:00 a.m. A supernatural darkness covered the land from about noon until 3:00 p.m. The Synoptics record that at that time, namely, the ninth hour (3:00 p.m.), Jesus cried, 'My God, my God, why have you forsaken me?' (Mk. 15:34; Mt. 27:46; cf. Lk. 23:46: 'cried with a loud voice'). In response to which, someone ran and filled a sponge with vinegar (Mk. 15:36; Mt. 27:48). However, in the Johannine presentation of Jesus as the exalted King who is master of the proceeding, John does not record our Lord's cry of forsakenness. He only writes Jesus' words, 'I thirst', which in the context of this Gospel amounts to the same spiritual cry of separation.

words of Jesus, an echo of Genesis 2:2 is unmistakable, 'and on the sixth day God finished his works (ἔργα) which he had done (ἐποίησεν).' According to a widespread Jewish haggada, the first human couple were created on the sixth day, and then at the tenth hour – about the time of Jesus' death – they sinned. This means that Christ 'finished' the work of God's creation, disrupted by the introduction of sin into the creative order.[318] Jesus' exaltation (ὑψωθῆναι) and glorification (δοξασθῆναι), foretold in Isaiah 53:12, paradoxically occur in the deepest humiliation. In light of the Johannine theology of the cross and in view of the resurrection, the death of Jesus upon a Roman cross is not tantamount to defeat, but is itself the death of death.

The possible overtones of Genesis 2 and the paradise motif in John 20:15 reveal the touch of a literary master. When Mary confronts Jesus in her state of grief and thinks that he is the gardener, she responds to his question, 'Woman, why are you weeping? Whom do you seek?' with the entreaty, 'Sir, if you carried him away (εἰ σὺ ἐβάστασας αὐτόν), tell me where you put him' (20:15). Curiously, her suspicion 'if you carried him away' calls to mind an ironic truth, for Jesus himself says in John 10:18 (though by means of different verbs) that no one can take his life away from him (οὐδεὶς αἴρει αὐτὴν ἀπ' ἐμοῦ) and that he has authority take up his life again (ἐξουσίαν ἔχω πάλιν λαβεῖν αὐτήν). Old Testament garden imagery or the paradise motif (as in Genesis 2) may furthermore be in view in the statement, 'Now in the place where he was crucified there was a garden' (Jn. 19:41). Among the canonical evangelists, only John remarks that the crucifixion and burial took place in a garden. For Christians, the cross was often identified as the tree of life. In Genesis 2:9, in the midst of the garden of Eden is a tree whose fruit brings death to humanity. In John 19:41, in the midst of another garden there is a 'tree' (i.e. the cross) which becomes a tree of life to all those who partake of its fruit.[319]

---

[318] See Martin Hengel, 'The Old Testament in the Fourth Gospel', *HBT* 12 (1990), 32–4; Calum M. Carmichael, *The Story of Creation: Its Origin and its Interpretation in Philo and the Fourth Gospel* (London: Ithaca, 1996); Brown, *John*, 2:930–31; Hoskyns, *Fourth Gospel*, 531; Schnackenburg, *St. John*, 3:284–85; Tenney, *John*, 267–68; Corell, *Consummatum Est*, 105–12; Beasley-Murray, *John*, 352–3; Ellis, *Genius of John*, 273; Bultmann, *John*, 675; Calvin, *Gospel According to John*, 2:235–37; Hambly, 'Creation and Gospel'.

[319] Barrett, *St. John*, 560, is doubtful about the association and argues that if John had intended an allusion to the Garden of Eden, he would have used the παράδεισος of the LXX. Nicolas Wyatt, '"Supposing Him to Be the Gardener" (John 20:15): A Study of the Paradise Motif in John', *ZNW* 81 (1990), 21–38, 37, criticises Barrett's conclusion as prosaic. He argues that the Johannine intent is to hint, to suggest, to lead the mind of his audience to make the association without spelling it out. Therefore the reader must be sensitive to all the possible overtones in the text. Thus when we read in 19:41 that in the place where Christ was crucified, there was a garden,

2.5. Conclusion: The Compound Structure of John's Language

Several conclusions may be drawn from the preceding analysis. First, the foregoing examples, presented under many different categories, should illustrate the complexity of John's language and the various linguistic and literary components which contribute to its elusive, enigmatic quality. The ambiguous character of the Johannine Gospel is not precipitated by a single factor but by a multitude of factors. These diverse elements contribute to a sense of remoteness and mystery in John's language.

Secondly, while there are many distinctions among these linguistic-literary strands, they share one common fundamental feature – the creation of two primary levels of perception in the text, or two impressions of reality, one on the surface, the other beneath the surface; one explicit, the other implied.[320] However, while in a metaphoric expression, for example, the two levels are identified, in irony, there is a contrast between appearance and reality. The 'lifted up' saying of Jesus in John 3:14, for example, consists of a metaphor, a conceptual double-meaning word, and irony in the context of an allusion to the Old Testament Scriptures. That which is implied at the deeper level in the Fourth Gospel is as important as what seems to be asserted on the surface. Often it seems as though the true meaning of John lies beneath the surface.

Thirdly, the 'mysterious' character of John's language revolves around the ever-present images, conflated references, associations, and echoes of the Old Testament which the Fourth Evangelist sees fulfilled in Jesus of Nazareth. The author does not utilise these allusions to impress the reader with his versatile grasp of the Scriptures, nor does he choose this style to show his literary sophistication. Rather, his objective is to impress upon his audience the truth of John 5:39 (cf. Lk. 24:27, 44–46): 'You search the Scriptures because you think that in them you have eternal life; and it is they that bear witness to me (i.e., Jesus himself).' John's thematic echoes

---

'We should not dismiss it as a mere geographical aside of the Evangelist, a snippet of information which the Synoptics did not know. The ecclesiastical interpretation of the Johannine scene as paradise was surely built on more than pious fancy in the early church.' Also see Wyatt, 'When Adam Devolved: The Meaning of Genesis 3:23', *VT* 38 (1988), 119; E. C. Hoskyns, 'Genesis 1–3 and St. John's Gospel', *JTS* 21 (1920), 210–18; Brown, *John*, 2:990; Bernard, *St. John*, 2:666; J. D. M. Derrett, 'Peter's Sword and Biblical Methodology', *BO* 32 (1990), 180–92; M. R. D'Angelo, 'A Critical Note: John 20:17 and Apocalypse of Moses 31', *JTS* n.s. 41 (1990), 529–36.

[320] Clavier, 'La structure du Quatrième Evangile', 175, uses a musical analogy; the 'lower' line (the surface level) is earthly, temporal, human–the 'higher' (the deeper level) is celestial, eternal, divine, which is incarnated into the earthly surroundings without losing its own character.

and associations are composed so that people 'may believe that Jesus is the Messiah, the Son of God, and that through believing [they] may have life in his name' (20:31). In these allusions, as I shall argue in the fourth chapter, the author has also painstakingly put together a lasting record of the grounds upon which Christians base their claim that Jesus of Nazareth is the Jewish Messiah (1:41, 45), Saviour of the world (4:42), whose birth, death, and resurrection is in fulfilment of the Scriptures (20:31).

Presumably John could have engaged in a kind of philosophical treatise somewhat akin to Paul's epistles and explained his views in a 'straightforward' propositional manner, explicitly stating important echoes and associations (though of course even Paul often leaves these implicit). But the enchantment of John lies in his allusive language pattern. It is also crucial to recognise that in the Fourth Gospel, the medium – the style of language – is linked to the message.[321] It is one thing to make the claim that the Scriptures speak of Jesus, it is another actually to show *how* the Scriptures speak of Jesus and are fulfilled at specific points in his life. It is through these intricately assembled details in John's echoes and allusions to the Old Testament that the Evangelist invites his audience to search the Scriptures and discover their testimony to Jesus and their fulfilment in his life and works (cf. 5:39; 20:31).

In his complex and subtle language, John emphasises a final important theological point. The deeper meaning of the Scriptures and their fulfilment in Jesus are not open to the natural eyes of a spiritually unregenerate person, let alone to the unbelieving eyes of those who have rejected and continue to reject Jesus. To see and perceive, one must be born of God (1:12–13). Only those who believe and are led by the Spirit of God may recognise that Jesus is the Christ according to the witness of Israel's Scriptures. The profound truth revealed in the incarnation, cross and resurrection lies beyond the boundaries of natural perception apart from the guiding and indwelling Spirit of God.

---

[321] H. A. Lombard, 'Prolegomena to a Johannine Theology: Sources, method and status of a narratological model', *Neot* 29 (1995), 253–72.

Chapter 3

The Conceptual Milieu of the Fourth Gospel

3.1. The Context of Thought out of Which the Gospel Emerged

To understand the language of the Fourth Gospel, it is important to establish the probable *context of thought* from which the text emerged.[1] However, defining the context of thought for Johannine literature has been a significant bone of contention for a long time. In the earlier part of the twentieth century, Adolf von Harnack concluded, 'The origin of the Johannine Gospel is...the greatest riddle presented to us by the earliest history of Christianity.'[2] The same sentiment is still expressed in New Testament studies (though now to a lesser degree) because of the complexities of issues and the many interactive factors.[3]

---

[1] R. Kysar, *The Fourth Evangelist and His Gospel* (Minneapolis: Augsburg, 1975), 102–46.

[2] *Lehrbuch der Dogmengeschichte* (Freiburg: Herder, 1931), 1:108. Cf. W.C. van Unnik, 'The Purpose of St. John's Gospel' (1959), reprinted in *The Gospels Reconsidered: Selected papers read at the International Congress on The Four Gospels in 1957* (Oxford: Blackwell, 1960), 167–96, especially 168.

[3] E.g., interaction between several cultures, languages, religions, and literatures. These complexities are brought out in such studies as Saul Lieberman, *Hellenism in Jewish Palestine: Studies in the Literary Transmission, Beliefs, and Manners of Palestine in the I Century BCE–V Century CE*, TSJTSA 18, 2nd edn (New York: The Jewish Theological Seminary of America, 1962); Emil Schürer, *The History of the Jewish People in the Age of Jesus Christ (175 BC–AD 135)*, rev. and ed. by Geza Vermes, Fergus Millar, and Matthew Black, vols 1–2 (Edinburgh: Clark, 1973–79); Helmut Koester, *History, Culture, and Religion of the Hellenistic Age* (Philadelphia: Fortress, 1982); and *History and Literature of Early Christianity* (Philadelphia: Fortress, 1982); S. A. Cook, F. E. Adcock, and M. P. Charlesworth, eds., *The Cambridge Ancient History*, vol. 8: *Rome and the Mediterranean 218–133 BC*; vol. 10: *The Augustan Empire 44 BC–AD 70* (Cambridge: CUP; New York: Macmillan, 1930, 1934); P. R. Ackroyd and C. F. Evans, eds, *The Cambridge History of the Bible*, vol. 1: *From the Beginnings to Jerome* (Cambridge: CUP, 1970); David R. Cartlidge and David L. Dungan, eds, *Documents for the Study of the Gospels* (Cleveland: Collins, 1980); Howard Clark Kee, *The Origins of Christianity: Sources and Documents* (Englewood Cliffs, NJ: Prentice Hall, 1973); Martin P. Nilsson, *Geschichte der griechischen Religion*, vol. 2: *Die hellenistische und römische Zeit*, HAW 5.2.2, 3rd edn (Munich: Beck, 1974); Arthur Darby Nock, *Essays on Religion and the Ancient World*, 2 vols (Cambridge, MA: Harvard University, 1972); F. E. Peters, *The Harvest of Hellenism: A History of the Near East from Alexander the Great to the Triumph of Christianity* (New York:

Certainly John's Gospel did not originate in a literary or intellectual vacuum. There is sufficient evidence to justify the conclusion that the Johannine literary and conceptual context is Palestinian and Jewish, even though there is very little agreement which particular brand of Judaism provided the background. Yet there also remains a continuing reluctance among some Johannine scholars to abandon theories about non-Jewish influences.

The present study holds that the Fourth Gospel emerged from an environment in which the Hebrew Scriptures were the dominant conceptual and literary force. John's world of ideas never departs from its Old Testament, Jewish orbit. The Hebrew Scriptures left the most profound and enduring impression upon the Jewish people's social, political, religious, and intellectual-literary life. A cursory glance through the New Testament will readily show the extent to which these documents reflect and share the Old Testament's historical, theological and ideological perspective.[4] The fundamental, all-embracing New Testament hermeneutic seems to be the belief that Jesus fulfilled the law and the prophets (Jn. 1:45; 5:39, 46; cf. Luke 24:27). I therefore proceed in this chapter from the assumption that John's literary milieu, style, imagery and theology can all best be explained in the context of the Hebrew Scriptures.

Simon and Schuster, 1970); J. A. Fitzmyer, 'Did Jesus Speak Greek?', *BAR* 18 (1992), 58–63, 76–77; J. W. Voelz, 'The Linguistic Milieu of the Early Church', *Concordia Theological Quarterly* 56 (1992), 81–97; R. Buth, 'Language Use in the First Century: Spoken Hebrew in a Trilingual Society in the Time of Jesus', *Journal of Translation and Textlinguistics* 5 (1992), 298–312; S. Safrai, 'Spoken Languages in the Time of Jesus', *Jerusalem Perspective* 3 (1991), 3–8; C. Tresmontant, *The Hebrew Christ. Language in the Age of the Gospels*, trans. by K. D. Whitehead (Chicago: Franciscan Herald Press, 1989); Raymond A. Martin, *Syntactical Evidence of Semitic Sources in Greek Documents*, SBLSCS 3 (Missoula, MT: Scholars Press, 1979); Matthew Black and William Smalley, eds, *On Language, Culture and Religion: in honor of Eugene A. Nida* (The Hague, Paris: Mouton, 1974); Franz Cumont, *The Oriental Religions in Roman Paganism* (New York: Dover, 1956); W. O. E. Oesterley, *The Jews and Judaism During the Greek Period: The Background of Christianity* (London: SPCK, and New York: Macmillan, 1941); William R. Farmer, *Maccabees, Zealots, and Josephus: An Inquiry into Jewish Nationalism in the Greco-Roman Period* (New York: Columbia University, 1956); Peter R. Ackroyd, *Israel under Babylon and Persia* (London: OUP, 1970); J. F. Drinkard, et al., eds, *Benchmarks in Time and Culture* (Atlanta, GA: Scholars Press, 1988); Charles Osgood and Oliver C. S. Tzeng, eds, *Language, Meaning, and Culture: The selected papers of C. E. Osgood* (New York: Praeger, 1990); Francis N. Lee, *The Central Significance of Culture* (Philadelphia: Presbyterian and Reformed Publishing Co., 1976).

[4] Cf. Helmut Koester, *An Introduction to the New Testament*, vol. 1: *History, Culture, and Religion of the Hellenistic Age* (Philadelphia: Fortress Press, 1982), 111–12; D. Moody Smith, *The Theology of the Gospel of John* (Cambridge: CUP, 1995), 56.

3.2. Various Proposals for the Johannine Conceptual Setting

Many possible settings and influences have been proposed for John's Gospel. Because of John's mysticism, some have argued that Greek philosophy in general[5] or the highly Hellenised Jewish philosophy of Philo in particular provides a logical starting point, and this appeal to Hellenism has never been completely abandoned.[6] By drawing parallels between John and Hellenistic literary features, literary critics have often inadvertently given further credence to the assumption that the Fourth Gospel belongs to a Hellenistic literary setting.[7] Early in the twentieth century the mystical elements in John's Gospel were traced to Hellenistic mystery

---

[5] L. Hurtado, *One God, One Lord: Early Christian Devotion and Ancient Jewish Monotheism* (Philadelphia: Fortress, 1988), 44–50; T. H. Tobin, 'The Prologue of John and Hellenistic Jewish Speculation', *CBQ* 52 (1990), 252–69; Brown, *John*, 1:33, 521–3; Francois-Marie Braun, *Jean le théologien*, vol. 2, *Les grandes traditions d'Israel et l'accord des Écritures, selon le Quatrième Évangile. Études bibliques* (Paris: Gabalda, 1967), 137; A. F. Segal, *Two Powers in Heaven: Early Rabbinic Reports about Christianity and Gnosticism*, SJLA 25 (Leiden: Brill, 1977), 159–81; C. H. Dodd, *The Interpretation of the Fourth Gospel* (Cambridge: CUP, 1953), 54–73; Andre Feuillet, *Le prologue du quatrième évangile* (Paris: Brouwer, 1968), 224–5, 239–42; H. R. Moeller, 'Wisdom Motifs and John's Gospel', *BETS* 6 (1963), 93–8; Basil de Pinto, 'Word and Wisdom in St. John', *Scripture* 19 (1967), 19–27; Ceslaus Spicq, 'Le Siracide et la structure littéraire du Prologue de saint Jean', in *Memorial Lagrange: Cinquantenaire de l'école biblique et archéologique française de Jérusalem* (Paris: Gabalda, 15 Novembre 1890–15 Novembre 1940), 183–95; Dodd, *Interpretation of the Fourth Gospel*, 274–7; Rudolf Bultmann, 'Der Religionsgeschichtliche Hintergrund des Prologs zum Johannesevangelium', in *Exegetica: Aufsätze zur Erforschung des Neuen Testaments*, hg. Erich Dinkler (Tübingen: Mohr-Siebeck, 1967), 1035; Barrett, *St. John*, 153, 165–66; Rudolf Schnackenburg, *The Gospel According to St. John*, trans. by Kevin Smyth, vol. 1 (New York: Herder and Herder, 1968), 124, 231, 269; John Painter, 'Christology and the Fourth Gospel: A Study of the Prologue', *AusBR* 31 (1983), 45–62; idem, 'Christology and the History of the Johannine Community in the Prologue of the Fourth Gosepl', *NTS* 30 (1984), 460–74; J. Ashton, 'The Transformation of Wisdom: A Study of the Prologue of John's Gospel', *NTS* 32 (1986), 161–86; Walter Grundmann, *Der Zeuge der Weisheit: Grundzüge der Christologie des Johannesevangeliums*, Mit einer Einführung heraugegben von W. Wiefel (Berlin: Evangelische Verlagsanstalt, 1985), 16–29; Michael E. Willett, 'Wisdom Christology in the Fourth Gospel' (Ph.D. diss., Southern Baptist Theological Seminary, 1985), 63–113; Benjamin Wisner Bacon, *The Gospel of the Hellenists* (New York: Holt, 1933).

[6] R. Wilson, 'The Fourth Gospel and Hellenistic Thought', *NovT* 1 (1956), 225–7; J. Sell, 'A Note on a Striking Johannine Motif Found at C[optic] G[nostic] VI, 6,19', *NovT* 20 (1978), 232–40; H. Noetzel, *Christus und Dionysos. Bemerkungen zum religionsgeschichtlichen Hintergrund von Johannes 2, 1–11* (Stuttgart: Calwer Verlag, 1959).

[7] Paul Duke, *Irony in the Fourth Gospel* (Atlanta, GA: John Knox Press, 1985), 141; W. H. Domeris, 'The Johannine Dram', *Journal of Theology for Southern Africa* 42 (1983), 29–35; N. Frye, *Anatomy of Criticism* (Princeton: University Press, 1971), 36, 207; R. Alan Culpepper, *Anatomy of the Fourth Gospel* (Philadelphia: Fortress, 1983), *passim;* idem, *The Johannine School: An Evaluation of the Johannine-School Hypothesis Based on an Investigation of the Nature of Ancient Schools*, SBLDS 26 (Missoula, MT: Scholars Press, 1975); Mark W. G. Stibbe, *John as Storyteller: Narrative Criticism and the Fourth Gospel* (Cambridge: CUP, 1992), 121–47.

religions.[8] Bultmann brought gnosticism into focus as the conceptual and intellectual background. With the discovery of the Dead Sea Scrolls, the attention shifted to Palestine. The Essene community at Qumran is thought to have shared a world view with the Fourth Evangelist. However, in recent years, a few have looked to rabbinic Judaism for answers.[9]

3.2.1. Gnosticism

The question of the relationship between the Gospel of John and gnosticism goes back to the second century AD, where it appears that the Valentinian gnostics took special interest in the Fourth Gospel and indeed were the first interpreters of it. Irenaeus, Origen, and others were therefore forced to defend its 'orthodoxy'.[10] Thus it is natural that among the various conceptual backgrounds offered for the Gospel, gnosticism has occupied a major position.[11] This proposition stems mainly from the similarity of ideas

---

[8] E. Russell, 'Possible Influence of the Mysteries on the Form and Interrelation of the Johannine Writings', *JBL* 51 (1932), 336–51; H. Becker, *Der Kosmische Rhythmus der Sternenschrift im Markus-Ev. u. im Johannes-Ev.* (Basel: Geering, 1930); and *Der Kosmische Rhythmus,* vol. 2, *Das Sternengeheimnis und das Erdengeheimnis im Johannes-Evangelium* (Basel: Geering, 1930); R. Bultmann, 'Johann: Schriften u. Gnosis', *OLZ* 43 (1940), 150–75; Wilson, 'Fourth Gospel and Hellenistic Thought'; Noetzel, *Christus und Dionysos;* M. E. Lyman, 'Hermetic Religion and the Religion of the Fourth Gospel', *JBL* 49 (1930), 265–76; Sell, 'Striking Johannine Motif', 232–40.

[9] Some have even proposed a Samaritan setting for the Fourth Gospel. George W. Buchanan, 'The Samaritan Origin of the Gospel of John', in *Religions in Antiquity: Essays in Memory of E. R. Goodenough,* ed. by Jacob Neusner (Leiden: Brill, 1968), 149–75; Wayne Meeks, *The Prophet-King: Moses Traditions and the Johannine Christology,* NovTSup 14 (Leiden: Brill, 1967), 216–57; E. D. Freed, 'Samaritan Influence in the Gospel of John', *CBQ* 30 (1968), 580–7; John Bowan, 'The Fourth Gospel and the Samaritans', *BJRL* 40 (1958), 298–315.

[10] Irenaeus, *Adv. Her.* 1.8.5; Epiphanius, *Adv. Her.* 33.3.6. The earliest known commentary on the Gospel of John was written by Heracleon, a Valentinian gnostic, fl. mid-second century AD. His work survives only in fragments quoted by his great opponent Origen, in the latter's own *Commentary on John,* written in AD 230. For an introduction to these two commentaries, see M. F. Wiles, *The Spiritual Gospel: The Interpretation of the Fourth Gospel in the Early Church* (Cambridge: CUP, 1960), and Elaine Pagels, *The Johannine Gospel in Gnostic Exegesis.*

[11] T. P. Letis, 'The Gnostic Influences on the Text of the Fourth Gospel', *BIRBS* 1 (1989), 4–7; M. Lidzbarski, *Das Johannesbuch der Mandäer,* 2 vols (repr.; Giessen: Töpelmann, 1966 [1905–15]), ET of portions in G. Meade, *The Gnostic John the Baptizer* (London: Watkins, 1924); and *Mandäische Liturgien* (Berlin: Weidmann, repr.; 1962 [1920]); E. Haenchen, 'Gab es eine vorchristliche Gnosis?', *ZTK* 49 (1952), 316–49; A. D. Nock and A. J. Festugière, *Corpus Hermeticum,* 4 vols (Paris: Les Belles Letters, 1945–54); W. C. Grese, *Corpus Hermeticum XIII and Early Christian Literature,* SCHNT 5 (Leiden: Brill, 1979); U. Schnelle, *Antidocetic Christology in the Gospel of John* (Minneapolis: Fortress, 1992); E. Schweizer, 'Jesus der Zeuge Gottes: Zum Problem des Doketismus im Johannesevangelium', in *Studies in John,* ed. by A. S. Geyser, et al., NovTSup 24 (Leiden: Brill, 1970), 161–8; J. M. Sevrin, 'Le quatrième évangile et le gnosticisme: questions de méthode', in *La communauté johannique et son histoire: La trajectoire de l'évangile de Jean aux deux premiers siècles,* ed. by J. D. Kaestli, et al. (Geneva: Labor and

between the Fourth Gospel and what is known of the gnostic system of belief.[12] Bultmann was persuaded that gnosticism was a pre-Christian movement and a significant influence upon Johannine thinking.

While Bultmann pointed to Mandaean gnostic texts, as represented by the Coptic tractates from Nag Hammadi, as offering clues to understanding John,[13] others of the same persuasion pointed to the Hermetic literature.[14]

Fides, 1990), 251–68; Wolfgang Langbrandtner, *Weltferner Gott oder Gott der Liebe: Der Ketzerstreit in der johanneischen Kirche. Eine exegetisch-religionsgeschichtliche Untersuchung mit Berücksichtigung der koptisch-gnostischen Texte aus Nag-Hammadi*, BBET 6 (Frankfurt/M-Bern, 1977, diss. Heidelerg, 1975; dir. H. Thyen); A. H. B. Logan, 'John and the Gnostics: The Significance of Apocryphon of John for the Debate about the Origins of the Johannine Literature', *JSNT* 43 (1991), 41–69; H. Koester, 'The History-of-Religions School, Gnosis, and the Gospel of John', *Studia Theologica* 40 (1986), 115–36; P. Perkins, 'John's Gospel and Gnostic Christologies', *Anglican Theological Review Suppl.* 11 (1990), 68–76; I. S. Gilltus, 'The Tree of Life and the Tree of Death: A Study of Gnostic Symbols', *Religion* 17 (1987), 337–53; S. Brown, 'Religious Imagination – Then and Now', *Bible Today* 29 (1991), 237–41; E. Käsemann, *Jesu letzter Wille nach Johannes 17* (Tübingen: Mohr, 1966); M. McGuire, 'Conversion and Gnosis in the Gospel of Truth', *NovT* 28 (1986), 338–55; L. Schottroff, *Der Glaubende und die feindliche Welt: Beobachtungen zum gnostischen Dualismus und seiner Bedeutung für Paulus und das Johannesevangelium*, WMANT 37 (Neukirchen-Vluyn: Neukirchener Verlag, 1970); G. Richter, 'Die Fleischwerdung des Logos im Johannes-Evangelium', *NovT* 13 (1971), 81–126, 14 (1972), 257–76.

[12] On gnosticism, its origin and its ideas, see Hans Jonas, *The Gnostic Religion*, 2nd rev. edn (Boston: Beacon, 1963); idem, *Gnosis und spätantiker Geist*, vol. 1: *Die mythologische Gnosis*, FRLANT 51, 3rd edn (Göttingen: Vandenhoeck & Ruprecht, 1964 [orig. 1934]); vol. 2: *Von der Mythologie zur mystischen Philosophie*, FRLANT 63, 2nd edn (Göttingen: Vandenhoeck & Ruprecht, 1966 [orig. 1954]); Barbara Aland, ed., *Gnosis: Festschrift für Hans Jonas* (Göttingen: Vandenhoeck & Ruprecht, 1978); Layton, *Rediscovery of Gnosticism*, 2 vols; Karl-Wolfgang Tröger, ed., *Altes Testament – Frühjudentum – Gnosis: Neue Studien zu Gnosis und Bibel* (Berlin: Evangelische Verlagsanstalt, 1980); Gershom Scholem, *Jewish Gnosticism, Merkabah Mysticism, and Talmudic Tradition*, 2nd edn (New York: Jewish Theological Seminary of America, 1965); Kurt Rudolf, *Die Gnosis: Wesen und Geschichte einer spätantiken Religion* (Göttingen: Vandenhoeck & Ruprecht, 1978). See also the collection of essays in *A Green Leaf: Papers in Honour of Professor Jes P. Asmussen*, ed. by W. Sundermann, et al., Acta Iranica 28, vol. 12 (Leiden: Brill, 1988). These essays include Jacques Deuchesne-Guillemin, 'On the Origin of Gnosticism', 349–69; Ugo Bianchi, 'Sur la Question Des Deux Âmes de l'Homme Dans le Manichéisme', 311–16; Alexander Böhlig, 'Zum Selbstverständnis des Manichäismus', 317–38; Hans-Joachim Klimkeit, 'Das Tor Als Symbol im Manichäismus', 365–81; Samuel N. C. Lieu, 'Sources on the Diffusion of Manichaeism in the Roman Empire', 384–99.

[13] Bultmann, 'Der religionsgeschichtliche Hintergrund des Prologs zum Johannesevangelium', in *EYXAPIΣTHPION: Studien zur Religion und Literatur des Alten und Neuen Testaments*, ed. by H. Schmidt, 2 vols (Göttingen: Vandenhoeck & Ruprecht, 1923), 2:3–26; idem, 'Die Bedeutung der neuerschlossenen mandäischen und manichäischen Quellen für das Verständnis des Johannesevangeliums', *ZTK* 24 (1925), 100–46; idem, *Primitive Christianity in Its Contemporary Setting* (London: Thames and Hudson; New York: Meridian, 1955), 162. Bultmann seems to have been influenced by M. Lidzbarski, *Das Johannesbuch der Mandäer*; idem, *Mandäische Liturgien* (Berlin: Weidmann, 1920, repr. 1962); idem, *Ginza: Der Schatz oder das grosse Buch der Mandäer* (Göttingen: Vandenhoeck & Ruprecht; Leipzig: Hinrichs, 1925). See also E. Haenchen, 'Gab es eine vorchristliche Gnosis?'; W. Bauer, *Das Johannesevangelium*, HNT 6, 3rd edn (Tübingen: Mohr-Siebeck, 1933); J. Robinson, *The Nag Hammadi Library in English*, rev. edn

128 Chapter 3: The Conceptual Milieu of the Fourth Gospel

Among the gnostic texts often cited to explain John are *The Apocryphon of John*, *The Gospel of Truth*, *The Gospel of Thomas*, *The Thunder, Perfect Mind*, and *Trimorphic Protennoia*.¹⁵ For many years, *The Odes of Solomon* was thought to be a gnostic writing,¹⁶ and it was used to draw comparisons with John because of the apparent literary affinities between the two works.¹⁷ But that idea is now abandoned. In fact, *Odes* is believed to have been an early Christian hymn book. It is also believed that its author probably had knowledge of the Johannine tradition and many other important Christian writings or ideas.¹⁸ However, in terms of illuminating

---

(San Francisco: Harper and Row, 1988 [orig. Leiden: Brill, 1977]); G. MacRae, 'Nag Hammadi', *IDBSup* (1976), 613–9; idem, 'Nag Hammadi and New Testament', in *Gnosis: Festschrift für Hans Jonas*, ed. by Barbara Aland (Göttingen: Vandenhoeck & Ruprecht, 1978); David M. Scholer, *Nag Hammadi Bibliography, 1948–1969*, NHS 1 (Leiden: Brill, 1971) who cited 2500 items; continued as *Nag Hammadi Bibliography, 1970–1994* (Leiden: Brill, 1997); John Dart, *The Laughing Savior: The Discovery and Significance of the Nag Hammadi Gnostic Library* (New York: Harper, 1976); C. M. Tuckett, *Nag Hammadi and the Gospel Tradition*, SNTW (Edinburgh: Clark, 1986); J. P. Meier, *A Marginal Jew: Rethinking the Historical Jesus*, Anchor Bible Reference Library (Garden City, NY: Doubleday, 1991), 123–39, 159–62.

¹⁴ The collection *Corpus Hermeticum* is mostly preserved in Greek. It is an attempt to reconcile gnosticism and philosophy. See Nock and Festugière, *Corpus Hermeticum*; A. J. Festugière, *La révélation d'Hermès Trismégiste*, 4 vols (Paris: Gabalda, 1950–54); G. van Moorsel, *The Mysteries of Hermes Trismegistus*, STRT 1 (Utrecht: Kemink en zoon, 1955); Richard Reitzenstein, *Poimandres: Studien zur griechisch-ägyptischen und frühchristlichen Literatur* (Leipzig: Teubner, 1904; reprint; Darmstadt: Wissenschaftliche Buchgesellschaft, 1966); idem, *Das iranische Erlösungsmysterium* (Bonn: Marcus und Weber, 1921); cf. Richard Reitzenstein and H. H. Schaeder, *Studien zum antiken Synkretismus aus Iran und Griechenland* (Darmstadt: Wissenschaftliche Buchgesellschaft, reprint, 1965 [1926]); Karl-Wolfgang Tröger, *Mysterienglaube und Gnosis in Corpus Hermeticum XIII*, TU 110 (Berlin: Akademie-Verlag, 1971); Grese, *Corpus Hereticum XIII*; Andrew K. Helmbold, *The Nag Hammadi Gnostic Texts and the Bible* (Grand Rapids: Baker Books, 1967).

¹⁵ *The Gospel of Thomas* is a collection of 114 sayings attributed to Jesus. None of these documents actually corresponds to the New Testament Gospel genre. *The Thunder, Perfect Mind*, and *Trimorphic Protennoia* come under the heading of *revelational discourses* where the revealer is a female and speaks in first person.

¹⁶ H. Gunkel, 'Die Oden Salomos', *ZNW* 11 (1910), 291–328; idem, 'Die Oden Salomos', *Deutsche Rundschau* 154 (1913), 25–47; H. M. Schenke, 'Die zweite Schrift des Codex Jung und die Oden Salomos', in *Die Herkunft des sogenannten Evangelium Veritatis* (Göttingen: Vandenhoeck & Ruprecht, 1959), 26–9. Cf. James H. Charlesworth 'The Odes of Solomon – Not Gnostic', in *Papyrus Bodmer VII–IX*, ed. by M. Testuz (Cologne and Geneva: Bibliothèque Bodmer, 1959), 357–69.

¹⁷ Both Charlesworth and Culpepper have collected many alleged parallels between the Fourth Gospel and *Odes of Solomon*. Parallels such as 'Word', 'living water', the heightened relationship between the Father and Son, the connection between abiding and the vine, the use of such terms as 'love', 'truth', and 'know', the identification of crucifixion and exaltation, and the emphasis on the present experience of eternal life by those who are united with the Lord. J. H. Charlesworth and R. A. Culpepper, 'Odes of Solomon', in *John and the Dead Sea Scrolls*, ed. by James H. Charlesworth (New York: Crossroads, 1990), 298–322.

¹⁸ The original language of the author of *Odes* is a form of early Syriac. The author seemes to

our knowledge about the conceptual setting of the Gospel, *Odes* adds very little.

The thesis concerning the gnostic influences upon the Fourth Gospel has never gained dominance,[19] first, because of the lateness of the gnostic sources in relation to the Fourth Gospel,[20] and secondly, because of persistent questions about method.[21] In fact, some scholars have argued

---

have been influenced by both Jewish and Christian traditions. He may have been a Jew before his conversion to Christianity, and it is assumed that he composed the hymn around AD 100 in or near Antioch. See the following series of articles and monographs by J. H. Charlesworth: 'Qumran, John, and the Odes of Solomon', in *John and Qumran*, ed. by Charlesworth (London: Geoffrey Chapman, 1972), 107–36; idem, *John and the Dead Sea Scrolls;* idem, *The Odes of Solomon*, SBLTT, Pseudepigrapha Series 7 (Missoula, MT: Scholars Press, 1978); idem, 'Paronomasia and Assonance in the Syriac Text of the Odes of Solomon', *Semitics* 1 (1970), 12–26. See also J. Carmignac, 'Les affinités Qumrâniennes de la onzième Ode de Salomon', *RevQ* 3 (1961), 71–102; idem, 'Un Qumrânien converti au Christianisme: l'auteur des Odes de Salomon', in *Qumran-Probleme*, ed. by H. Bardtke (Berlin: Akademie Verlag, 1963), 75–108; J. A. Emerton, 'Notes on Some Passages in the Odes of Solomon', *JTS* n.s. 28 (1977), 507–19.

[19] E. M. Yamauchi, 'Some Alleged Evidences for Pre-Christian Gnosticism', in *New Dimensions in New Testament Study*, ed. by Richard N. Longenecker and Merrill C. Tenney (Grand Rapids: Zondervan, 1974); H. Koester, 'GNOMAI DIAPHOROI: The Origin and Nature of Diversification in the History of Early Christianity', in *Trajectories through Early Christianity* (Philadelphia: Fortress, 1971), 130; C. A. Evans, 'Current Issues in Coptic Gnosticism for New Testament Study', *Studia Biblica et Theologica* 9 (1979), 97; William W. Combs, 'Nag Hammadi, Gnosticism, and the New Testament Interpretation', *Grace Theological Journal* 8 (1987), 195–212.

[20] It has never been succesfully demonstrated that the Mandaean sources, for example, are earlier than John. This is the crux of the problem. All that these sources show is the similarities between the Johannine-like themes and the gnostic documents. But it is yet to be demonstrated that these cited Mandaean motifs were either earlier than John or were independent of Johannine traditions. In fact, some of the most promising parallels between the Fourth Gospel and gnostic writings are not even close enough to establish a definitive relationship or to significantly clarify Johannine christology. See H. Lietzmann, 'Ein Beitrag zur Mandäerfrage', *Sitzungsberichte der Preussischen Akademie der Wissenschaften: Phil. Hist. Klasse* 17 (1930), 595–608, who identified the presence of Syrian Christian liturgy in the Mandaean texts. See also F. C. Burkitt, *Church and Gnosis* (Cambridge: CUP, 1932); R. M. Grant, *Gnosticism: A Sourcebook of Heretical Writings from the Early Christian Period* (New York: Harper and Brothers, 1961), 14; E. C. Hoskyns, *The Fourth Gospel*, ed. by Francis Noel Davey (London: Faber and Faber, 1947), 140–1; Dodd, *Interpretation of the Fourth Gospel*, 130.

[21] Sevrin, 'Le quatrième évangile et le gnosticisme', 251–68; Henry A. Green, 'Gnosis and Gnosticism: A Study in Methodology', *Numen* 24 (1977), 95–134; Grant, *Gnosticism: A Sourcebook*, 14; Dodd, *Interpretation of the Fourth Gospel*, 128–30; C. Colpe, *Die religionsgeschichtliche Schule: Darstellung und Kritik ihres Bildes vom gnostischen Erlösermythus*, FRLANT 60 (Göttingen: Vandenhoeck & Ruprecht, 1961), 10–57; idem, 'New Testament and Gnostic Christology', in *Religions in Antiquity*, ed. by J. Neusner, NovTSup 14 (Leiden: Brill, 1968), 227–43; R. P. Casey, 'Gnosis, Gnosticism and the New Testament', in *The Background of the New Testament and its Eschatology*, ed. by W. D. Davies and D. Daube (Cambridge: CUP, 1956), 52–80; R. N. Frye, 'Reitzenstein and Qumran Revisited by an Iranian', *HTR* 55 (1962), 261–8; T. K. Rudolph, *Die Mandäer*, 2 vols, FRLANT 56, 57 (Göttingen: Vandenhoeck & Ruprecht, 1960–61), 1:9 n. 3, 65–80; Fredrick Wisse, 'The Sethians and the Nag Hammadi Library', in *SBL 1972 Proceedings*, ed. by Lane C. McGaughy (n.p.: Society of

that dependency may be the reverse – i.e., these gnostic texts, including Mandaean, writings were influenced by John and even borrowed directly from the Fourth Gospel.[22] Finally, in spite of the alleged conceptual similarities between John and gnosticism,[23] the tradition and ideological foundations of gnosticism are fundamentally different from those which sustain the New Testament in general and Johannine christological formulations in particular.[24]

3.2.2. Qumran

With the discovery of the Dead Sea Scrolls, the attention shifted to a Palestinian setting and the community at Qumran.[25] Once again, because of apparent parallels in language and thought, particularly those that expressed or presupposed dualism, some jumped to the conclusion that John must have shared similar ideologies with Qumran, and therefore Qumran provided the ideological context for the Fourth Gospel.[26] Indeed

---

Biblical Literature, 1972), 2:601–7; C. H. Talbert, 'The Myth of a Descending-Ascending Redeemer in Mediterranean Antiquity', *NTS* 22 (1976), 418–40.

[22] E. M. Yamauchi, *Pre-Christian Gnosticism: A Survey of the Proposed Evidences*, 2nd edn (Grand Rapids: Baker Books, 1983), 117–42; idem, 'Jewish Gnosticism? The Prologue of John, Mandaean Parallels, and the Trimorphic Protennoia', in *Studies in Gnosticism and Hellenistic Religions*, ed. by R. van den Broek and M. J. Vermaseren, EPRO 91 (Leiden: Brill, 1981), 467–97; idem, *Gnostic Ethics and Mandaean Origins*, HTS 24 (Cambridge, MA: Harvard University Press, 1970); Pheme Perkins, 'Gnostic Christologies and New Testament', *CBQ* 43 (1981), 590–606; idem, 'New Testament Christologies in Gnostic Transformation', in *The Future of Early Christianity*, ed. by B. A. Pearson (Minneapolis: Fortress, 1991), 433–41; Carsten Colpe, 'Heidnische, jüdische und christliche Überlieferung in den Schriften aus Nag Hammadi, III', *JAC* 17 (1974), 109–25. Tuckett, *Nag Hammadi and the Gospel Tradition*, in the case of the Synoptics and Nag Hammadi parrallels, has argued for the movement from the Synoptics to Nag Hammadi.

[23] Many of such alleged similarities from the Nag Hammadi texts are collected by Karl Martin Fischer, 'Der johanneische Christus und der gnostische Erlöser', in *Gnosis und Neues Testament: Studien aus Religionswissenschaft und Theologie*, ed. by K. Tröger (Berlin: Evangelische Verlagsanstalt, 1973).

[24] Perkins, 'Gnostic Christologies'; idem, 'New Testament Christologies', 433–41; Colpe, 'Heidnische, jüdische und christliche Überlieferung'; idem, *Die religionsgeschichtliche Schule*.

[25] The discovery of the Qumran Scrolls also weakened the assumed gnostic influences on John's Gospel. See Martin Hengel, 'The Old Testament in the Fourth Gospel', in *The Gospels and the Scriptures of Israel*, ed. by Craig A. Evans and W. Richard Stegner, JSNTSup 104 (Sheffield: Sheffield Academic Press, 1994), 384.

[26] Among the scrolls, 1QS 3:13–4:26 is the primary text for the dualistic comparisons: for example, light and darkness, truth and falsehood, 'Spirit of truth' (1QS 3:18–19; 4:21, 23; cf. Jn. 14:17; 15:26; 16:13; 1 Jn. 4:6); 'sons of light' (1QS 3:13, 24, 25); 'the light of life' (1QS 3:7; cf. Jn. 8:12); 'walk in darkness' (1QS 3:21; 4:11; cf. Jn. 8:12; 12:35); 'full of grace' (1QS 4:4, 5; cf. Jn. 1:14). See also, in 1QS 8:6, the phrase 'witness of the truth' (cf. Jn. 5:33; 18:37), and in CD 19:33–34, 'living water' (Jn. 4:14); or in 4QMyst 6, 'darkness overcome by light' (cf. Jn. 1:5; 1 Jn. 2:8). Otto Betz in his monograph, *Der Paraklet: Fürsprecher im häretischen Spätjudentum, im*

some scholars in recent years have postulated that the Fourth Evangelist originally may have been an Essene.[27] Whether or not these proposals are accepted, the discovery of the Dead Sea Scrolls substantially undermined the hypothesis for the non-Palestinian origin of the Gospel.[28] Conclusions long regarded as certain were now open to question. Qumran discoveries showed a Hebrew and Aramaic-speaking Jewish sect in first-century Palestine which expressed itself in similar dualistic terminology as John. Assuming that Qumran provided the conceptual context of the Fourth Gospel, this link, however, did not necessitate the composition of John in Palestine.[29] While with discovery of the Dead Sea scrolls some scholars

---

Johannesevangelium und in neu gefundenen gnostischen Schriften, AGJU 2 (Leiden: Brill, 1963), showed similarities between the Johannine Paraclete and Qumran's 'Spirit of Holiness' (1QS 4:21) which, as in the Fourth Gospel, seemed also to be called the 'Spirit of truth' (1QS 3:18; 4:21, 23). See further A. R. C. Leaney, 'The Johannine Paraclete and the Qumran Scrolls', in *John and the Dead Sea Scrolls*, ed. by J. H. Charlesworth (1990), 38–61; idem, 'A Critical Comparison of the Dualism in 1QS 3:13–4:26 and the "Dualism" Contained in the Gospel of John', *NTS* 15 (1969), 389–418; R. E. Brown, 'The Qumran Scrolls and the Johannine Gospel and Epistles', *CBQ* 17 (1955), 403–19, 559–74; K. Stendahl, ed., *The Scrolls and the New Testament* (New York: Harper and Row, 1957; London: SCM, 1958); W. S. LaSor, *The Dead Sea Scrolls and the New Testament* (Grand Rapids: Eerdmans, 1972); J. A. T. Robinson, 'The New Look on the Fourth Gospel', in *Twelve New Testament Studies* (London: SCM, 1962), 94–106; W. F. Albright, 'Recent Discoveries in Palestine and the Gospel of St. John', in *The Background of the New Testament and its Eschatology*, ed. by W. D. Davies and D. Daube (Cambridge: CUP, 1956), 153–71; S. T. Neill, *The Interpretation of the New Testament 1861–1961* (London: OUP, 1966), 308ff.; O. Böcher, *Der johanneische Dualismus im Zusammenhang des nachbiblischen Judentums* (Gütersloh: Gerd Mohn, 1965); J. Becker, 'Beobachtungen zum Dualismus im Johannesevangelium', *ZNW* 65 (1974), 71–87.

[27] See John Ashton, *Understanding the Fourth Gospel* (Oxford: Clarendon, 1991), 232–37.

[28] H. Braun, *Qumran und das Neue Testament*, 2 vols (Tübingen: Mohr-Siebeck, 1966), 1:98, 2:118–144; idem, 'Où en est l'étude du quatrième Evangile?', *ETL* 32 (1956), 535–46; K. Schubert, *Die Gemeinde vom Toten Meer: Ihre Entstehung und ihre Lehren* (Munich: Reinhardt, 1958), 131–3, 152; both of whom concluded that the Qumran research conclusively had proven the Jewish origin of the Gospel of John. See also Howard M. Teeple, 'Qumran and the Origin of the Fourth Gospel', *NovT* 4 (1960), 6–25.

[29] The translation of such words as 'rabbi', 'Messiah', and similar expressions (1:38, 41, 42; 4:25; 5:2; 9:7; 19:13, 17; 20:16) may indicate that among John's audience were those who did not know Hebrew and Aramaic and were not familiar with Palestine and the city of Jerusalem. However, the knowledge of Jerusalem and various aspects of Jewish history and religious practices (2:20; 3:22–23; 4:5–6, 9, 20–24; 8:48; 11:18) seems to indicate the Palestinian origin of the author himself. He seems to know, for example, of the feast of Hanukkah or 'feast of dedication' and knows that it is celebrated in winter (10:22–23). He is also aware of the last day of Sukkot ('feast of Tabernacles') where water is poured out in front of the altar (7:2, 14, 37–38). W. H. Brownlee, 'Whence the Gospel According to John?', in *John and the Dead Sea Scrolls*, ed. by J. H. Charlesworth (1990), 166–94; O. Betz, '"To Worship God in Spirit and in Truth": Reflections on John 4:20–26', in idem, *Jesus, der Messias Israels: Aufsätze zur biblischen Theologie*, WUNT 42 (Tübingen: Mohr-Siebeck, 1987), 420–38; M. Hengel, *Johannine Question* (London: SCM; Philadelphia: Trinity Press, 1989), 111; C. H. Dodd, *Historical Tradition in the Fourth Gospel* (Cambridge: CUP, 1963), 423.

immediately recognised the potential Iranian influences upon both Qumran and John,[30] others, such as Robinson, who was unwilling to abandon the alleged Hellenistic influences, argued that Qumran writings themselves revealed a theological synthesis of Hellenistic and Jewish concepts.[31] Over the course of the past forty years while some scholars with much confidence have asserted that in Qumran lies the answer to the riddle of the Johannine milieu, others with equal confidence have denied such a link.[32]

3.2.3. Judaism and the Jewish Scriptures

Judaism has increasingly come into focus for understanding the New Testament writings, including John's Gospel.[33] Yet there are disagreements about which particular form of Judaism provides the Gospel's intellectual milieu. Much emphasis has been placed on locating this or that New Testament writing or idea within the context of rabbinic literature.[34] Needless to say, this venture is just as prone to misconstrued conclusions as those which insist on finding the conceptual correspondences between John and Hellenistic writings. Philip Alexander, in a studious, yet mostly

---

[30] K. G. Kuhn, 'Die Sektenschrift und die iranische Religion', *ZTK* 49 (1952), 312; D. Winston, 'The Iranian Component in the Bible, Apocrypha, and Qumran: A Review of the Evidence', *History of Religions* 5 (1966), 200–1; Albright, 'Recent Discoveries in Palestine', 153–71; Lucetta Mowry, 'The Dead Sea Scrolls and the Background for the Gospel of John', *BA* 17 (1954), 78–97; John Breck, *Spirit of Truth: The Holy Spirit in Johannine Tradition*, Vol. 1: *The Origin of Johannine Pneumatology* (Crestwood, NY: St. Vladimir's Seminary Press, 1991), 3, 53–87, 157–8.

[31] This Jewish, Hellenistic conceptual fusion is believed by Robinson to characterise John as well. J. A. T. Robinson, 'New Look on the Fourth Gospel', 98–102, idem, 'The Baptism of John and the Qumran Community', 11–27 (loc. cit.). On the other hand, see G. W. MacRae, 'The Jewish Background of the Gnostic Sophia Myth', *NovT* 12 (1970), 86–101; Charlesworth, *John and the Dead Sea Scrolls;* Norman Petersen, *The Gospel of John in the Sociology of Light* (Valley Forge, PA: Trinity Press, 1994), 80–132.

[32] Cf. H. H. Rowley, 'The Baptism of John and Qumran Sect', in *New Testament Essays*, ed. by A. J. B. Higgins (Manchester: University Press, 1959), 218–29; Teeple, 'Qumran and the Origin of the Fourth Gospel'; Meeks, *The Prophet-King*, 11–12.

[33] C. K. Barrett, *Das Johannesevangelium und das Judentum*, Franz Delitzsch-Vorlesungen 1967 (Stuttgart, Berlin: W. Kohlhammer, 1970), trans. by D. M. Smith, *The Gospel of John and Judaism: The Franz Delitzsch Lectures, University of Münster, 1967* (London: SPCK, 1975); C. J. A. Hickling, 'Attitudes to Judaism in the Fourth Gospel', in *L'Évangile de Jean*, ed. by M. de Jonge (1977), 347–54; Jack P. Lewis, 'The Semitic Background of the Gospel of John', in *Johannine Studies: Essays in Honor of Frank Pack*, 97–110, ed. by James E. Priest (Malibu, CA: Pepperdine University Press, 1989); Lynn A. Losie, 'The Cleansing of the Temple: A History of a Gospel Tradition in Light of Its Background in the Old Testament and in Early Judaism' (Ph.D. diss., Fuller Theological Seminary, 1984).

[34] J. C. Thomas, 'The Fourth Gospel and Rabbinic Judaism', *ZNW* 82 (1991), 159–82; F. Manns, 'Exégèse rabbinique et exégèse johannique', *RB* (1985), 525–38; S. Sandmel, *Judaism and Christian Beginnings* (New York: OUP, 1978), 370–92.

disregarded, article, pointed out that there is little in the New Testament that does not 'parallel' something that one rabbi or another may have said at one time or another in the course of the first six centuries of the Christian era. He charged, 'Many New Testament scholars are still guilty of massive and sustained anachronism in their use of Rabbinic sources.'[35] This censure was in view of Samuel Sandmel's criticism of a similar misuse some twenty years earlier in his inaugural address to the Society of Biblical Literature under the title 'Parallelomania'.[36] Few have given heed to these cautions. It is important to recognise that most of the wisdom and rabbinic parallels also may be traced back ultimately to a single literary source, the Hebrew Scriptures, from which rabbis drew many of their diverse concepts and upon which they spent their interpretive energies.[37]

It seems to me whether we speak of the community at Qumran, rabbinic writings or John and his Gospel, the most plausible natural conceptual context is Judaism.[38] Judaism which, in spite of its diversities, was united around 'the law and the prophets' – Israel's Scriptures, the common pool out which the Jews drew their contrasting ideas. Amidst the varying proposals for the conceptual setting and ideological influences upon the Fourth Gospel, whether Qumran or rabbinic sources, the most obvious place to begin is with the document sacred to all of them, whether they lived in Palestine or the Diaspora, and the most influential upon their thinking: their sacred Scriptures, our Old Testament. For example, in the

---

[35] Philip S. Alexander, 'Rabbinic Judaism and the New Testament', *ZNW* 74 (1983), 237–246, here 246.

[36] *JBL* 81 (1962), 1–13.

[37] In the Old Testament wisdom tradition, conceptual parallels have been drawn between *Sirach* (particularly 24, 46, 48) and John, especially in terms of christology. However, on closer examination, it is clear that in spite of these apparent parallels, the christology of John is rooted in Old Testament language, imagery and concepts. Cf. further Delbert Burkett, *The Son of Man in the Gospel of John*, JSNTSup 56 (Sheffield: JSOT Press, 1991); J. D. Dunn, *Christology in the Making: A New Testament Inquiry into the Origins of the Doctrine of the Incarnation* (London: SCM, 1980), 163–212; J. R. Harris, *The Origin of the Prologue of John's Gospel* (Cambridge: CUP, 1917); E. D. Freed, 'Theological Prelude to the Prologue of John's Gospel', *SJT* 32 (1979), 257–69; J. Jeremias, *The Central Message of the New Testament* (London: SCM, Philadelphia: Fortress, 1965), 71–90; L. J. Kuyper, 'Grace and Truth: An Old Testament Description of God and its Use in the Johannine Gospel', *Int* 18 (1964), 3–19; B. Lindars, 'Traditions Behind the Fourth Gospel', in *L'Évangile de Jean*, ed. by M. de Jonge (1977), 107–24; T. E. Pollard, *Johannine Christology and the Early Church*, SNTSMS, 13 (Cambridge: CUP, 1970), 9–15; G. Schimanowski, *Weisheit und Messias: Die jüdischen Voraussetzung der urchristlichen Präexistenzchristologie*, WUNT 2.17 (Tübingen: Mohr-Siebeck, 1985).

[38] Already in 1929, Hugo Odeberg had begun to draw on Jewish mystical texts in interpreting John. See his work, *The Fourth Gospel Interpreted in Its Relation to Contemporaneous Religious Currents in Palestine and the Hellenistic-Oriental World* (Chicago: Argonaut, 1968, repr. from Amsterdam: Grüner; 1929).

case of Qumran, the Jewish Scripture was at the very heart of this community. The daily life of this group of separatist Essenes revolved around the study of Scriptures.[39] The often discussed apocalyptic experiences in Qumran, which also have been traced to Hellenism, seem to have been primarily of a literary character rooted in the tradition that arose from the Old Testament.[40] Among its various claims, one that is of particular interest to my study is the community's claim to have been given the correct insight into the Scriptures. Some of their writings were eschatological commentaries on the Old Testament Scriptures, wherein they believed they had uncovered the exclusive inner meaning of the biblical texts.[41] This conceptual dependence upon the Hebrew Bible is also evident in John from its prologue to its epilogue. In John's record, when Philip calls Nathanael, he alerts him to the fact that 'we have found him of whom Moses in the law and also the prophets wrote' (Jn. 1:45). When Jesus is accused by his opponents of violation of the Mosaic law, he confronts the religious leaders with their Scriptures, 'You search the Scriptures, because you think that in them you have eternal life; and it is they that bear witness to me...if you believed Moses, you would believe me, for he wrote of me' (Jn. 5:39, 46).

This conclusion neither denies nor disregards that Judaism of the first century reflects various external influences. Nevertheless, it seems to me

---

[39] The community devoted much of its time to the study of the Torah. According to *The Rule of the Community* (also known as *The Manual of Discipline*), each member of the community had to spend at least one third of the nights in the year reading the Book (1QS 6:7). They ensured that in every group, there should be at least one priest whose duty it was to study the law and to lay its explication before the members of the group. See 1QS 6:3 and *The Damascus Covenant*, CD 13:2ff. See also Ithamar Gruenwald, *Apocalyptic and Merkavah Mysticism* (Leiden: Brill, 1980), 20. In both cases, the groups consisted of ten members. But in 1QS 8:1, a group consisting of twelve laymen and three priests is mentioned, while in CD 10:4–6, six laymen and four priests are mentioned. The age of the officiating priests were to be between thirty and sixty (CD 14:7). For a discussion of the various theories with regard to the history of the community, see J Murphy-O'Connor, 'The Essenes and Their History', *RB* 81 (1974), 215ff.

[40] Gruenwald, *Apocalyptic and Merkavah Mysticism*, 19; H. Braun, *Spätjüdisch–häretischer und frühchristlicher Radikalismus*, vol. 1 (Tübingen: Mohr, 1957); F. F. Bruce, *Biblical Exegesis in the Qumran Texts* (Grand Rapids: Eerdmans, 1959); O. Betz, *Offenbarung und Schriftforschung in der Qumransekte* (Tübingen: Mohr, 1960).

[41] The community believed the word of God had been given in two principle stages of the revelation: before and after the formation of the New Covenant in the 'Desert of Damascus'. See the first four pages of *The Damascus Covenant* (CD). The New Covenant did not mean the giving of new Scriptures, but the revelation of special methods of discovering the inner and true sense of the old ones (e.g., 1QS 8.15–6; 9.12–14.20) and it is juxtaposed to the complementary idea about the various individual degrees in knowledge of Scripture (see particularly, 1QS 5:23; 6:14, 18). See also I. Gruenwald, 'The Jewish Esoteric Literature in the Time of the Mishnah and Talmud', *Immanuel* 4 (1974), 37ff.

that the traditions and assumptions which underpin the rabbinic writings, the Dead Sea scrolls, and the Fourth Gospel are deeply imbedded in Judaism at the core of which is the Jewish Scriptures.[42] For every alleged parallel idea between John and gnosticism or Hellenism, there is a more sensible one in Judaism in its own conceptual context – the Jewish Bible. If there are shared conceptual similarities between John and Qumran, these similarities do not go any further than the same pool into which they both reached for their ideas – Israel's Scriptures.

Asserting influence, dependence and association, solely based on parallels is not warranted if the text is divorced from its natural context. The difficulty in New Testament studies and especially the Fourth Gospel is not a lack of corresponding similarities and parallel ideas. The universal nature of Johannine ideas are conducive to such parallel findings in a wide range of literatures across many cultures.[43] Such concepts as light, darkness, life, death, ascend to and descend from heaven, spirit, word, love, believe, water, bread, birth, and children of God can be found in many religions and cultures if one probes. However, the same idea will have a profoundly different referent and tradition as one moves from religion to religion. Robert Kysar, in an insightful study in his doctoral thesis, *A Comparison of the Exegetical Presuppositions and Methods of C. H. Dodd and R. Bultmann in the Interpretation of the Prologue of the Fourth Gospel*, tried to demonstrate this problem with Johannine ideas. He compared the studies of C. H. Dodd and R. Bultmann on the prologue (Jn. 1:1–18). Kysar paid particular attention to the list of possible parallels each of the two scholars drew up to every conceivable phrase in those verses. Dodd and Bultmann each advance over three hundred parallels, but the overlap in their lists is only 7%.[44] Therefore, the difficulty in the Fourth Gospel is not a lack of parallels. In other contexts, one may find such parallels in a wide spectrum of backgrounds and literatures. Such parallel findings may be interesting, but unhelpful and indeed often exegetically misleading, since entirely different traditions and assumptions may undergird the apparent resemblances and parallels. Therefore, the issue is not

---

[42] See Frank M. Cross, *The Ancient Library of Qumran* (Garden City, NY: Doubleday, 1961), 76–8. See my discussion in chpater six on 'Johannine Conception of Revelation'.

[43] E.g., Hans H. Malmede, *Die Lichtsymbolik im Neuen Testament*, Studies in Oriental Religions, vol. 15 (Wiesbaden: Otto Harrassowitz, 1986).

[44] R. A. Kysar, 'A Comparison of the Exegetical Presuppositions and Methods of C. H. Dodd and R. Bultmann in the Interpretation of the Prologue of the Fourth Gospel' (Diss. Chicago: Northwestern University, 1967), idem, 'The Background of the Fourth Gospel: A Critique of Historical Methods', *Canadian Journal of Theology* 16 (1970), 250–55.

finding parallels, but rather finding the right parallels and finding them in the right place – the actual, original, natural context, which would then shed the right light on our understanding of a given text. In many of the Jewish and rabbinic writings, in Qumran as well as John's Gospel, this natural context is the Jewish milieu at the center of which was the Jewish Bible – its most natural literary formative context.

3.2.4. The Centrality of the Scriptures in Judaism

The conceptual roots of the Fourth Gospel are imbedded in the Old Testament, both in terms of their meaningful explication as well as the Gospel's literary contextual setting. Again, this assertion does not deny the cross-cultural influences upon the Jews. Neither does it deny that there were diversities among the Jews of second-temple Judaism of the Hellenistic period.[45] However, diversity cannot be translated as either transformation, loss of cultural identity or lack of unity. It seems trivial to point out that for most Jews whether they lived in the isolation of Qumran or the heterogeneous environments of metropolitan Jerusalem, Antioch, Ephesus, or Rome, their Scriptures stood as a defining centre and a unifying force. Even amidst such sectarian groupings as the Pharisees, Sadducees, Essenes, and Zealots, the Torah and the prophets – their Scriptures – stood as a central unifying force. The tendency to identify the Torah as the supreme written authority in matters of faith and life is detectable even before the beginning of the exile. However the destruction of the temple in 587 BC and its devastating effect upon priestly functions may have provided the additional impetus to make the Torah the gravitational core. It kept the splinter groups and fragmented sections of Judaism unified and spinning in one orbit. When the priest Ezra determined to give new shape and direction to the community of Jews in restored Jerusalem early in the fourth century BC, he read in a public assembly 'the book of the Torah of Moses', in response to which people wept and committed themselves to what they heard. This 'centre', i.e., the

---

[45] Wilhelm Bousset, *Die Religion des Judentums im späthellenistischen Zeitalter des Großen bis zur Aufklärung* (Berlin: De Gruyter, repr. 1972); Martin Hengel, *Judaism and Hellenism: Studies in Their Encounter in Palestine During the Early Hellenistic Period*, trans. by John Bowden, 2 vols, 2nd edn (Philadelphia: Fortress, 1974); Hans G. Kippenberg, *Religion und Klassenbildung im antiken Judäa*, SUNT 14 (Göttingen: Vandenhoeck & Ruprecht, 1978); Marcel Simon, *Jewish Sects at the Time of Jesus* (Philadelphia: Fortress, 1967); Kurt Schubert, *Die jüdischen Religionsparteien im neutestamentlichen Zeitzlter*, SBS 43 (Stuttgart: Katholisches Bibelwerk, 1970); S. Talmon, ed., *Jewish Civilization in the Hellenistic-Roman Period* (Sheffield: Sheffield Academic Press, 1991).

Scriptures provided second-temple Judaism, and beyond, with an identity and a coherence despite the diversity and cross-cultural interpolations.

3.3. The Fourth Gospel in Its Old Testament Literary Setting

In writing about the use of the Old Testament in the New, Barnabas Lindars used the analogy of a servant in relation to a master:

> The place of the Old Testament in the formation of New Testament theology is that of a servant, ready to run to the aid of the gospel whenever it is required, bolstering up arguments, and filling out meaning through evocative allusions, but never acting as the master or leading the way, nor even guiding the process of thought behind the scenes.[46]

However, Peder Borgen correctly pointed out that for the New Testament writers, the Old Testament was more than a 'servant'. Perhaps a better term would be a 'mentor'. Borgen argued that Lindars makes it sound as if the New Testament authors endowed the Scriptures with whatever meaning they wished. However, he noted, the Scriptures had authority for these writers, and provided the parameters of their christology. Borgen writes, 'Since Moses wrote about Jesus, the Evangelist and Johannine community regarded the Scriptures as valid *sources* to the words and works of Jesus...'[47] Years earlier, Merrill C. Tenney, in an article written examining the literary keys to John's Gospel, captured this relationship better than his other contemporaries. Tenney perceptively wrote,

> Between the revelations of the Old and New Testaments a strong bond of unity exists. Augustine's little couplet, "The new is in the old concealed; the old is by the new revealed," expresses the relationship quite accurately. Apart from the New Testament, the Hebrew canon is a truncated cone, solid but incomplete, its lines pointing to an apex yet unrealized. Without the Old Testament, the new revelation is devoid of an adequate foundation, for its presuppositions are left unexplained and its place in the total purpose of God is undefined.[48]

---

[46] See B. Lindars and P. Borgen, 'The Place of the Old Testament in the Formation of New Testament Theology', *NTS* 23 (1976–77), 59–66, here p. 66.

[47] Ibid., 73.

[48] Merrill C. Tenney, 'The Old Testament and the Fourth Gospel', *BibSac* 120 (1963), 300–8. See further R. Morgan, 'Fulfillment in the Fourth Gospel', *Interpreter* 11 (1957), 155–65; Martin Hengel, 'The Old Testament in the Fourth Gospel', *HBT* 12 (1990), 12–41; Brown, *John*, 1:lix–lxii; C. A. Evans, 'On the Quotation Formulas of the Fourth Gospel', *BZ* 26 (1982), 79–83; C. K. Barrett, 'The Old Testament in the Fourth Gospel', *JTS* 48 (1947), 155–69; Koester, *History, Culture, and Religions*, 110; J. A. Bühner, *Der Gesandte und sein Weg im 4. Evangelium: Die kulture und religionsgeschichtlichen Grundlagen der johanneischen Sendungschristologie sowie ihre traditionsgeschichtliche Entwicklung*, WUNT 2/2 (Tübingen: Mohr-Siebeck, 1977); D. A. Carson, *Divine Sovereignty and Human Responsibility* (Atlanta, GA: John Knox Press, 1981),

Nowhere in the New Testament are these observations truer than in John's Gospel. A careful reading shows the extent to which John depends on the Hebrew Bible for a meaningful explanation of its ideas.[49] The Fourth Gospel in every tenet of its theology presupposes the Old Testament.[50] For

---

132; idem, *The Gospel According to John* (Grand Rapids: Eerdmans, 1991), 59–60; Douglas J. Moo, *The Old Testament in the Gospel Passion Narratives* (Sheffield: Almond Press, 1983), 146–8, 178–82, 233–4; F. W. Young, 'A Study of the Relation of Isaiah to the Fourth Gospel', *ZNW* 46 (1955), 215–33; John Dahms, 'Isaiah 55:11 and the Gospel of John', *EvQ* 53 (1981), 78–88; August H. Franke, *Das Alte Testament bei Johannes: Ein Beitrag zur Erklärung und Beurtheilung der johanneishen Schriften* (Göttingen: Vandenhoeck & Ruprecht, 1885), 64; Wolfgang Roth, 'Scriptural Coding in the Fourth Gospel', *BR* 32 (1987), 6–29; W. C. van Unnik, 'The Purpose of St. John's Gospel', *SE* 1 = TU 73 (1959), 382–411; Schnackenburg, *St. John*, 1:119–52; Stanley E. Porter, 'Can Traditional Exegesis Enlighten Literary Analysis of the Fourth Gospel? An Examination of the Old Testament Fulfilment Motif and the Passover Theme', in *The Gospels and the Scriptures of Israel*, ed. by Craig A. Evans and W. Richard Stegner, JSNTSup 104 (Sheffield: Sheffield Academic Press), 407–11.

[49] For example, the reader is necessarily dependent upon the Old Testament if he or she is to have any understanding of John's historical references. How can one understand, for example, the references to Abraham, Jacob, Moses, Elijah, and Isaiah without a prior knowledge of the Old Testament? See further my discussions in chapters two, five, and six of the present study. Several studies have drawn attention to the Evangelist's precise knowledge of the Palestinian geography. Bruce Schein, *Following the Way: The Setting of John's Gospel* (Minneapolis: Augsburg Publishing House, 1980); J. A. T. Robinson, *The Priority of John* (London: SCM, 1985). It also notes the way in which John appears on occasion to invest his geographical comments with theological significance. Jerusalem and the Temple feature earlier and more prominently in John than in the Synoptic Gospels. Almost 80% of Johannine narrative seems to be located in Jerusalem compared to about 30% in Matthew.

[50] Among the numerous studies in this area, the following are just a sample: Anthony T. Hanson, *The Prophetic Gospel: A Study of John and the Old Testament* (Edinburgh: Clark, 1991); Grundmann, *Der Zeuge der Weisheit*; Wolfgang J. Bittner, *Jesu Zeichen im Johannesevangelium: Die Messias-Erkenntnis im Johannesevangelium vor ihrem jüdischen Hintergrund*, WUNT 2. Reihe, Bd. 26 (Tübingen: Mohr-Siebeck, 1987); Severino Pancaro, *The Law in the Fourth Gospel: The Torah and the Gospel, Moses and Jesus, Judaism and Christianity According to John*, NovTSup 42 (Leiden: Brill, 1975); A. Lacomara, 'Deuteronomy and the Farewell Discourse (Jn. 13:31–16:33)', *CBQ* 36 (1974), 65–84; B. Lindars, 'The Place of the Old Testament in the Formation of New Testament Theology', *NTS* 23 (1976–77), 59–66; W. R. G. Loader, 'The Central Structure of Johannine Christology', *NTS* 30 (1984), 188–216; Otto Moeller, 'Wisdom Motifs and John's Gospel', *BETS* 6 (1963), 93–8; G. Reim, *Johannesevangelium*, SNTSMS, 22 (Cambridge: CUP, 1974); idem, 'Jesus as God in the Fourth Gospel', 158–60; Bruce G. Schuchard, *Scripture within Scripture: The Interrelationship of Form and Function in the Explicit Old Testament Citations in the Gospel of John*, SBLDS 133 (Atlanta, GA: Scholars Press, 1992); A. Mayer, 'Elijah and Elisha in John's Sign Sources', *ExpTim* 99 (1988), 171–3; Max Turner, 'Atonement and the Death of Jesus in John: Some Questions to Bultmann and Forestell', *EvQ* 62 (1990), 99–122; Dieter Zeller, 'Elijah und Elischa im Frühjudentum', *BK* 41 (1986), 154–60; Mark Arrington, 'The Identification of the Anonymous Servant in Isaiah 40–55' (unpublished thesis, Dallas Seminary, 1971); John J. O'Grady, 'Recent Developments in Johannine Studies', *BTB* 12 (1982), 54–8; John J. O'Rourke, 'Explicit Old Testament Citations in the Gospels', *Studia Montis Regii* 7 (1964), 37–60; Anthony Saldarini, *Jesus and Passover* (New York: Paulist, 1984); Bruce H. Grigsby, 'The Cross as an Expiatory Sacrifice in the Fourth Gospel', *JSNT* 15

The extent of the Johannine dependence upon Jewish Scriptures goes beyond ideas. The Scriptures seem to have even influenced John's literary style. These stylistic similarities in conjunction with other factors to which I have already alluded lead me to the conclusion that the *context of thought* out of which the Fourth Gospel emerged was an environment in which the Hebrew Scriptures and the traditions surrounding them were the dominant literary forces. It seems to me, therefore, that the Old Testament is the most natural and sensible conceptual context for John's Gospel. In the following analysis, some of the stylistic similarities will be demonstrated.[51]

(1982), 51–80; G. D. Bampfylde, 'Old Testament Quotations and Imagery in the Gospel According to St. John' (Dissertation; Hull, 1967); Eugene W. Pond, 'Theological Dependencies of John's Gospel on Isaiah' (Thesis, Dallas Seminary, 1985); Phil G. Bowersox, 'The Use of Isaiah 6:10 in John 12:40 and the Theology of Rejection' (Thesis, Dallas Seminary, 1978); James E. Wenger, 'The Use of the Old Testament in the Gospel of John' (Thesis, Dallas Seminary, 1965); D. A. Carson, 'John and the Johannine Epistles', in *It is Written: Scripture Citing Scripture*, ed. by D. A. Carson and H. G. M. Williamson (Cambridge: CUP, 1988), 245–64; Bent Noack, *Zur johanneischen Tradition: Beiträge zur Kritik an der Literarkritischen Analyse des vierten Evangeliums*, Teologiske Skrifter, Bd. 3 (Copenhagen: Rosenkilde og Bagger, 1954); F. Smend, 'Die Behandlung alttestamentlicher Zitate als Ausgangspunkt der Quellenscheidung im 4. Evangelium', *ZNW* 24 (1925), 147–50; W. G. Kümmel, *The Theology of the New Testament* (New York: Abingdon, 1973), 261–321; Herbert Leroy, '"Kein Bein wird ihm gebrochen werden" (Jo 19, 31–37): Zur johanneischen Interpretation des Kreuzes', in *Eschatologie: Bibeltheologische und philosophische Studien zum Verhältnis von Erlösungswelt und Wirklichkeitsbewältigung. Festschrift für Engelbert Neuhäusler zur Emeritierung gewidmet von Kollegen, Freunden und Schülern*, ed. by Rudolf Kilian, Klemens Funk, und Peter Fassl (St. Ottilien: EOS Verlag, 1981), 78–81; Marie-Joseph LaGrange, *L'évangile selon saint Jean*, Ebib, 7th edn (Paris: Gabalda, 1948); Adolf Schlatter, *Der Evangelist Johannes: Wie er spricht, denkt, und glaubt. Ein Kommentar zum vierten Evangelium*, 2nd edn (Stuttgart: Calwer Verlag, 1948); Eduard Schweizer, *Ego Eimi...Die religionsgeschichtliche Herkunft und theologische Bedeutung der johanneischen Bildreden, zugleich ein Beitrag zur Quellenfrage des vierten Evangeliums*, FRLANT, Bd. 56 (Göttingen: Vandenhoeck & Ruprecht, 1939); Kikuo Matsunaga, 'The "Theos" Christology as the Ultimate Confession of the Fourth Gospel', *Annual of the Japanese Biblical Institute* 7 (1981), 124–45; R. A. Holst, 'The Relation of John, Chapter Twelve, to the So-Called Johannine Book of Glory' (Ph.D. diss., Princeton Theological Seminary, 1974); M. de Jonge, 'Jewish Expectations about the "Messiah" according to the Fourth Gospel', *NTS* 19 (1972–73), 246–70; Roger J. Hummann, 'The Function and Form of the Explicit Old Testament Quotations in the Gospel of John', *Lutheran Theological Review* 1 (1988–89), 31–54.

[51] In the past, stylistic comparisons were used in a similar way to make decisions regarding the Aramaism of John or its literary unity or disunity. See Schnackenburg, *Das Johannesevangelium*, 1, Teil, HTKNT (Freiburg: Herder, 1965), 88–94, ET, *Gospel According to St. John*, 1:105–11; W. S. Vorster, 'The Gospel of John as Language', *Neot* 6 (1972), 19–27; Brown, *John*, 1:cxxix–cxxx.

3.3.1. The Semitic Style of the Fourth Gospel

The Jewishness of John's Gospel extends beyond its explicit or implicit references to the Jewish Scriptures. It is evident in the very literary style of the Gospel. By the Jewishness of John, however, I am not proposing an original written Aramaic text. The question of a possible written Aramaic original for John's Gospel has been considered and reconsidered since the turn of the century, going back to A. Schlatter in 1902[52] and his observation that the language of the Fourth Gospel abounds with Semitic idioms. Schlatter was followed by C. J. Ball and his article, 'Had the Fourth Gospel an Aramaic Archetype?'[53] This article apparently planted the seed that later in 1922 blossomed in C. F. Burney's well-known book, *The Aramaic Origin of the Fourth Gospel*.[54] Although Burney insisted on a clear distinction between Aramaism and Hebraism,[55] nonetheless he used Hebraism as an argument for the Aramaic original.[56] In 1923, Montgomery came to a similar conclusion, but his thesis did not require a written Aramaic original.[57] Torrey supported the views held by Burney, but rejected the mistranslations for which Burney had argued.[58] Ten years after publication of Burney's work, Ernest Colwell wrote his doctoral thesis to refute Burney's Aramaic theory.[59] Five years later, E. J. Goodspeed

---

[52] *Die Sprache und Heimat des vierten Evangelisten* (Gütersloh: Bertelsmann, 1902). To argue his thesis, Schlatter paralleled verses in John with material in the New Hebrew of Mechilta, Sifre and rabbinic material such as the Mishna, Targums and Midrashim.

[53] *ExpTim* 21 (1909), 91–3.

[54] (London: OUP, 1922), 2.

[55] Burney, *Aramaic Origin*, 7–10. In his study, Burney makes a distinction between an *Aramaism*, any grammatical or syntactical construction which is ordinary in Aramaic but abnormal in Greek, a *Hebraism*, a construction which is abnormal in Greek but ordinary in Hebrew and a *Semitism*, a construction found in both Hebrew and Aramaic but peculiar to Greek. Burney argued (pp. 17–8) that the Gospel of John contains no Hebraisms, but only Aramaisms and Semitisms. This would exclude the possibility that the style of the Septuagint, which is Semitic, was deliberately imitated. Burney furthermore postulated that the redactor/translator of the Greek of the Gospel mistranslated certain Aramaic originals. For example, the largest source of mistranslations is thought to be the particle δέ. In this way Burney tried to demonstrate that the constructions in the Fourth Gospel were unidiomatic Greek.

[56] Ibid., 96.

[57] J. A. Montgomery, *The Origin of the Gospel According to St. John* (Philadelphia: Fortress, 1923).

[58] C. C. Torrey, 'The Aramaic Origin of the Gospel of John', *Harvard Theological Review* 16 (1923), 305–44, esp. 331.

[59] Ernest C. Colwell, *The Greek of the Fourth Gospel: A Study of Its Aramaisms in the Light of Hellenistic Greek* (Chicago: University of Chicago Press, 1931). It is important to keep in mind that Colwell was a classicist and not a Semitic specialist and thus not very sensitive to the Semitic style and syntax. In his thesis, he argues that certain constructions and translations posed by

followed Colwell, and he not only denied an Aramaic original, but went further and claimed there existed no Aramaic literature in the first century![60] Other scholars such as O. T. Allis, although rejecting Burney's thesis, favoured an oral Aramaic source used by the Evangelist. Allis, in his proposal, argued that John may have composed the Gospel in Greek while mentally translating the Aramaic words, sentences and phrases.[61] In 1933, C. C. Torrey published a monograph in which he actually translated the hypothetical original Aramaic Gospels.[62] In 1946, some fifteen years after Colwell, Matthew Black, in *An Aramaic Approach to the Gospels and Acts*,[63] went on to argue once again for Aramaic influences on the Fourth Gospel and Acts. However, he was much more careful with the formulation of his theory. Black suggested that instead of 'translation', one should speak of 'interpretation'. Nevertheless, he insisted that mistranslations were indeed indicative of an Aramaic original. He also called attention to the fact that assonance, alliteration, and paronomasia in Aramaic frequently can be detected in the discourses of Jesus when these are translated back into the Aramaic.[64] (This idea was later taken up by David Wead: see below.)[65] M. E. Boismard, who had been influenced by Black, presupposed an Aramaic source based on the evidence of textual variants.[66] Similar lines of study

---

Burney are usual Greek usage. He critiqued the Aramaic hypothesis on two counts: first, 'unsound' method and second, doubtful and unconvincing results (pp. 130–1).

[60] E. J. Goodspeed, 'The Original Language of the New Testament', in *New Chapters in New Testament Study* (New York: McMillan, 1937), 127–68.

[61] O. T. Allis, 'The Alleged Aramaic Origin of the Fourth Gospel', *Princeton Theological Review* 26 (1928), 531–82, esp. 531–72.

[62] *The Four Gospels* (New York: Harper, 1933). Torrey concludes that only the last chapter of the Gospel was written in Greek and that syntactical anomalies in the Greek of the Gospel can be explained only by an overly literal translation. This work was followed by another monograph in 1936. In this latter manuscript, Torrey (*Our Translated Gospels*) dates the Four Gospels not later than AD 50 and argues they were written in Palestine. Although these particular conclusions were rejected, yet his theories regarding the Aramaisms in the Fourth Gospel are still considered useful by scholars who contend for an Aramaic source.

[63] (Oxford: Clarendon, 1946).

[64] Black's approach was received favourably especially since his cautious and well-balanced viewpoints were in stark contrast to some of his predecessors. See H. H. Rowley, 'Book Review of M. Black', *Bibliotheca Orientalis* 4 (1947), 35–6, T. Manson, 'Book Review of M. Black', *JTS* 48 (1947), 219–21, and V. Taylor, 'Book Review of M. Black', *ExpTim* 58 (1946–47), 147.

[65] Wead, *The Literary Devices in John's Gospel* (1970).

[66] *L'Evangile de Jean: Études et Problèmes* (Louvain: Desclée de Brouwer, 1958). Boismard's major contribution was his extension of the scope from Greek textual variants to the versions found in the Greek Fathers.

were pursued subsequently. They are mostly refinements of Black's thesis.⁶⁷

If the Aramaic hypothesis has never been fully rejected by the mainstream of Johannine scholars, neither has it been fully accepted. Nevertheless, as Braun has correctly pointed out in the field of textual criticism of John's Gospel, the Aramaic hypothesis frequently comes to our aid and permits a judicious choice among variant readings.⁶⁸ Commentaries such as those of Barrett, Bultmann and Brown readily verify Braun's observation.⁶⁹ D. W. Wead in his thesis *The Literary Devices in John's Gospel*⁷⁰ explored at length the possible linguistic background for John's words with double meaning, arguing for the possible Aramaic origin for many of them. Some scholars have consented to the Aramaic, or Semitic characteristic of the Gospel, without denying its Greek composition.⁷¹

Apart from the Aramaic question, John's explicit and allusive references to the Old Testament in his composition pose another difficult riddle.⁷² There is no consensus as to whether the author used the original

---

⁶⁷ E.g., J. Bonsirven, 'Les Aramaïsmes de S. Jean l'Evangéliste', *Bib* 30 (1949), 405–32 who stressed that Semitic/Aramaic concepts and phrases are embedded in idiomatic Greek, giving evidence that the Evangelist 'meditated' upon the words of Jesus. See also F. Zimmermann, *The Aramaic Origin of the Four Gospels* (New York: Ktav, 1979).

⁶⁸ F. M. Braun, 'Où en est l'étude du quatrième Evangile?', *ETL* 32 (1956), 535–46.

⁶⁹ Also Barrett, *St. John*, 8–11; Schnackenburg, *St John*. 1:105–11; Brown, *John*, cxxix–cxxxv.

⁷⁰ Theologische Dissertationen 4 (Basel: Friedrich Reinhart Kommissionsverlag, 1970).

⁷¹ G. R. Driver, 'The Original Language of the Fourth Gospel', *Jewish Guardian* 5 & 12 (January, 1923), 7–9; W. F. Howard, 'Semitism in the New Testament', in *A Grammar of New Testament Greek*, by J. H. Moulton and W. F. Howard, vol. 2 (Edinburgh: Clark, 1929), 483–4. Barrett, *St. John*, 8–11, gives quite a number of Aramaic characteristics in John's Gospel without denying the Greek composition. G. A. Deissmann, *New Light on the New Testament from Records of the Graeco-Roman Period*, trans. by L. R. M. Strachan (Edinburgh: Clark, 1907), recognizes the colloquial character of the Greek of the Fourth Gospel while also not denying its Aramaism. See also Millar Burrows, 'The Johannine Prologue as Aramaic Verse', *JBL* 45 (1926), 57–69; idem, 'The Original Language of the Gospel of John', *JBL* 49 (1930), 95–139 and Schuyler Brown, 'From Burney to Black: The Fourth Gospel and the Aramaic Question', *CBQ* 26 (1964), 323–39. Cf. Joseph A. Fitzmyer, *A Wandering Aramean: Collected Essays*, SBLMS 25 (Missoula, MT: Scholars Press, 1977).

⁷² Ashton, *Understanding*, 15–35, 45–50, 76–101; Kysar, *Fourth Evangelist*, 102–46, Moisés Silva, 'Semantic Borrowing in the New Testament', *NTS* 22 (1976), 104–10; Klaus Beyer, *Semitische Syntax im Neuen Testament*, vol. 1,1, *Satzlehre*, SUNT 1 (Göttingen: Vandenhoeck & Ruprecht, 1962 and 1968); Voelz, 'Linguistic Milieu of the Early Church', 81–97; Safrai, 'Spoken Languages in the Time of Jesus', 3–8; Tresmontant, *Hebrew Christ*; Martin, *Syntactical Evidence of Semitic Sources in Greek Documents*; Black, 'Biblical Languages', 1:1–11.

Hebrew texts, Greek translations[73] or Aramaic targums,[74] or quoted or alluded from memory. Perhaps his method was a combination of these.[75]

In spite of these uncertainties, anyone familiar with Semitic languages readily recognises the Hebraism of John's composition and literary style. More than a century ago, Lightfoot observed, 'the whole casting of the sentences, the whole colouring of the language, is Hebrew.'[76] This stylistic affinity has been noted by other scholars as well.[77] Beyer, for example,

---

[73] E. D. Freed, in his study, *Old Testament Quotations in the Gospel of John*, NovTSup 11 (Leiden: Brill, 1965) showed that it was generally impossible to decide whether Johannine references to the Old Testament are based on the Hebrew Masoretic text (MT) as it has survived or on the Greek version, the Septuagint (LXX), as it has come down to us. The difficulty in deciding which version is presupposed arises from the fact that, 'In every instance his quoted text appears to be adapted to its immediate context, to his literary style, and to the whole plan of the composition of his Gospel' (p. 129). It is hard to imagine what kind of access to manuscripts the Evangelist may have had.

[74] The problem with targumic and midrashic traditions is somewhat similar to the appeal to the Mandaic materials. There is no objective means of verification. What may seem midrash to one may not seem midrash to another. John may have been familiar with the Pharisaic and early rabbinic exegesis. Twice in the Gospel, there are references to 'searching the Scripture' (5:39; 7:52). The expression 'search' (ἐραυνᾶτε) may reflect the very definition of 'midrash' itself (from דרש, 'to search'; with the noun מדרש, literaly a 'searching'. The verb דרש occurs in a variety of contexts in the Old Testmaent meaning 'to seek', 'to inquire', or 'to investigate' by seeking God's will (2 Chr. 17:4; 22:9; 30:19; Ps. 119:10) and making inquiry of God through prophetic oracles (1 Sam. 9:9; 1 Kgs. 22:8; 2 Kgs. 3:11; Jer. 21:2), or investigating a matter (Deut. 13:14; 19:18; Judg. 6:29; cf. 1QS 6:24; 8:26). In later usage, there is a shift from seeking God's will through prophetic oracle to seeking God's will through the study of Scripture (Ezra 7:10; Ps. 111:2; 119:45, 94, 155; see 1QS 8:15; 4QFlor 1:14; CD 6:7). A principle purpose for searching the Scripture was to find life. This idea is rooted in Scripture itself, for keeping the commandments of the Torah meant life (Lev. 18:5; cf. Bar. 4:1–2). Cf. Peder Borgen, 'Observation on the Midrashic Character of John 6', ZNW 54 (1963), 232–40; idem, *Bread from Heaven: An Exegetical Study of the Concept of Manna in the Gospel of John and the Writings of Philo*, NovTSup 10 (Leiden: Brill, 1965); M. McNamara, *Targum and Testament* (Shannon: Irish University Press; Grand Rapids: Eerdmans, 1972); Anthony Hanson, 'John's Citation of Ps. 82', *NTS* 11 (1964–65), 162; James S. Ackerman, 'The Rabbinic Interpretation of Ps. 82 and the Gospel of John', *HTR* 59 (1966), 186–8.

[75] Freed, *Old Testament Quotations*, is convinced that the Fourth Evangelist knew the Old Testament well, in both Greek and Hebrew forms, and he usually cited the text from memory. Cf. Günter Reim, *Studien zum alttestamentlichen Hintergrund des Johannesevangeliums*, SNTSMS 22 (Cambridge: CUP, 1974), 6. M. P. Miller, 'Targum, Midrash and the Use of the Old Testament. in the New Testament', *Journal for the Study of Judaism* 2 (1971), 61, seems correct in his observation that textual source is of secondary importance when a writer makes allusions to the Old Testament. In the case of the Fourth Gospel, it is almost an impossible task to determine the textual source based on Evangelist's echoes and allusions. On this subject, see further Voelz, 'Linguistic Milieu of the Early Church'; Buth, 'Language Use in the First Century'; Fitzmyer, 'Did Jesus Speak Greek?', 58–63, 76–77; Safrai, 'Spoken Languages in the Time of Jesus', 3–8; Tresmontant, *Hebrew Christ*.

[76] J. B. Lightfoot, *Biblical Essays* (London: Macmillan, 1893), 135.

[77] Nigel Turner, *Style*, vol. 4 of *A Grammar of New Testament Greek*, ed. by James Hope Moulton (Edinburgh: Clark, 1976), 64; Henry C. Vedder, *The Johannine Writings and the*

sixty years after Lightfoot, in a detailed analysis of the conditional clauses in John's Gospel and a comparison of other material drew the same conclusion. He described the Greek of the Gospel as 'stark semitisierende Griechisch'.[78] He also asserts that the Fourth Gospel was written in plain and simple Greek, without solecisms, and used the Greek language for constructing the Gospel from the start. This is the position of the present study as well.

3.3.2. Comparative Stylistic Analysis

The comparative study of style in and of itself is not decisive in determining the influence of one document upon another. Indeed, when style is used as the sole criterion in such comparisons, it may prove misleading. However, style may become one among several other factors which together point in the direction that one document is dependent upon or influenced by another. In the case of the Fourth Gospel and its conceptual and literary milieu, the existence of these other factors[79] together with the stylistic similarities point in the direction of the Jewish and Old Testament setting of this gospel.

Style is a term 'used to name or describe the manner or quality of an expression.'[80] The word comes from the Latin *stilus*, which was an instrument used to write upon waxed tablets. The person who made a clear, sharp impression with the *stilus* was considered a praiseworthy *stilus exercitatus*.[81] Formal study of style goes as far back as Aristotle. In *The Art*

Johannine Problem: An Aid to the Critical Study of the Bible as Literature (Philadelphia: Griffith and Rowland Press, 1917), 17, 64–7, 76; Freed, *Old Testament Quotations*, 6, 95, 130; Oscar Cullmann, *The Johannine Circle* (Philadelphia: Westminster Press, 1975), esp. chapters 4 and 5 on 'Language, Style, and Literary Characteristics'; Margaret Davies, *Rhetoric and Reference in the Fourth Gospel* (Sheffield: JSOT Press, 1992), 68–75.

[78] Beyer, *Semitische Syntax*, 17.

[79] I have already alluded to some of these factors in chapter two. I shall bring out other elements in chapters four, five, and six.

[80] Edward A. Tenny, 'Style', in *Dictionary of World Literature: Criticism, Form-Technique*, ed. by Joseph T. Shipley (New York: Philosophical Library, 1943), 554.

[81] E. Tenny, 'Style', 554; Lane Cooper, *Theories of Style*, Research and Source Works, No. 173 (New York: Burt Franklin, 1968), 11. Many of the contemporary definitions of rhetorical terms rely extensively on Greek and Latin works such as Aristotle's *The Art of Rhetoric*, Book III, trans. by John Henry Freese, LCL (New York: G. P. Putnam's Sons, 1926); *Aristotle: The Poetics; 'Longinus' on the Sublime*, LCL, 2nd edn (Cambridge, MA: Harvard University Press, 1932); Demetrius, *Demetrius On Style*, trans. by W. Hamilton Fyfe and W. Rhys Roberts; Quintilian's *Institutio Oratoria*, Books VIII and IX, trans. by H. E. Butler, *The Institutio Oratoria of Quintitian III, IV*, LCL (New York: G. P. Putnam's Sons, 1926); Cicero, *De Oratore*, Book III, and *De Partitione Oratoria*, and *Rhetorica Ad Herennium*, Book IV. For a survey of rhetoric from the fifth century BC through twentieth-century stylistics, see Edward P. J. Corbett, *Classical*

of *Rhetoric* he wrote, 'It is not sufficient to know what one ought to say, but one must also know how to say it.'[82] Thus although *stylistics* as a subdiscipline of linguistic and literary criticism[83] is a new field, it has extensive roots in ancient rhetoric, grammar, and philology.[84] Interestingly, according to the *Oxford English Dictionary*, the English word *stylistics* first appeared in print in 1882–83 in a biblical study, when Philip Schaff wrote in the *Encyclopaedia of Religious Knowledge* about the need to give 'proper place to New Testament stylistics and rhetoric'.[85]

There are different definitions of style depending on the context in which it is defined. The simplest definition of *style* is the way an author uses words; the manner in which every writer necessarily makes choices in composition.[86] It is in these choices and patterns of 'knitting' words together that different written designs can be distinguished. Every analysis of style is an attempt to find the artistic choices of composition by an author.[87] In the context of biblical literature, these choices are important:

Rhetoric for the Modern Student, 2nd edn (New York: OUP, 1971), 594–630. F. C. Grant surveys early rhetoric and its influence on the New Testament in 'Rhetoric and Oratory', *IDB* 4 (1962), 75–7. George A. Kennedy discusses 'Judeo-Christian Rhetoric' in idem, *Classical Rhetoric and Its Christian and Secular Tradition from Ancient to Modern Times* (Chapel Hill: University of North Carolina Press, 1980), 120–60. Kennedy has a book-length history of Greek rhetoric in *The Art of Persuasion in Greece* (Princeton: Princeton University Press, 1963). For a history of literary criticism beginning with its ancient Greek roots, see René Wellek, 'Criticism, Literary', *The Dictionary of the History of Ideas* (1973), 1:596–607.

[82] *Aristotle: The 'Art' of Rhetoric*, Book III, 3.1.3; 1.3.1, 344–5, 32–3.

[83] Style as a discipline has been made into a subdivision of linguistics and rhetoric as well as literary criticism. Although linguistic and literary studies are considered to be different in scope, aim, and methodology, yet in practice the distinctions are exaggerated. The Austrian linguist/philologist Leo Spitzer was among the earlier scholars who aimed to unify linguistics and literary studies by use of stylistic studies. See René Wellek, *Discriminations: Further Concepts of Criticism* (New Haven: Yale University Press 1970), 187–224.

[84] Oswald Ducrot and Tzvetan Todorov, *Encyclopedic Dictionary of the Sciences of Language*, trans. Catherine Porter (Baltimore: Johns Hopkins University Press, 1979), 75; Stephen Ullmann, *Language, Meaning and Style* (Leeds: University Press, 1981), 130.

[85] See *The Oxford English Dictionary*, 12 Vols (Oxford: Clarendon, 1933), 10:1208 s.v. 'Stylistics'.

[86] Cf. Stephen Ullmann, *Semantics: An Introduction to the Science of Meaning* (Oxford: Blackwell, 1970), 9; Richard A. Lanham, *Style: An Anti-Textbook* (New Haven: Yale University Press, 1974), 13; John Spencer, Nils Erik Enkvist; and Michael Gregory, *Linguistics and Style* (London: OUP, 1964); idem, 'Introduction: Stylistics, Text Linguistics and Composition', *Text* 5 (1985), 251–67. See also T. A. Sebeok, ed., *Style in Language* (Cambridge, MA: MIT, 1960); R. Fowler, *The Languages of Literature: Some Linguistic Contributions to Criticism* (London: Routledge and Kegan Paul, 1971); and *Literature as Social Discourse* (London: Batsford, 1981); G. N. Leech and M. H. Short, *Style in Fiction* (London: Longman, 1981), 19, 74; Luis T. Milic, *Stylists on Style: A Handbook with Selections for Analysis* (New York: Charles Scribner's Sons, 1969); R. M. Eastman, *Style: Writing as the Discovery of Outlook* (New York: OUP, 1970).

[87] G. D. Kilpatrick, 'Two Studies of Style and Text in the Greek New Testament', *JTS* n.s. 41

first, in determining whether, for example, a document is the work of one hand or a multitude of hands, a unified whole or a patchwork, and secondly, based on these principles underlying an author's choice of language, we may be able to decipher the document's literary and conceptual milieu.

Both these factors have played a very significant part in the stylistic studies of the Fourth Gospel. Stylistic analysis has been used both to prove and to disprove the Gospel's compositional unity.[88] Rudolf Bultmann, for example, in his 1941 commentary on John, *Das Evangelium des Johannes*,[89] used stylistic criteria as an important aspect of his argument for the disunity of the Gospel. To distinguish the style of the Evangelist from those of the sources and redactors, Bultmann identified several characteristics of style which he believed to be peculiar to the Evangelist and which separated the work of the Evangelist from that of the sources.[90] Bultmann's reconstruction of John soon was challenged by those who used style-analysis to prove the unity of the Gospel.[91]

(1990), 94–8; S. Chatman, ed., *Literary Style: A Symposium* (Oxford: Blackwell, 1971); Walter Bujard, *Stilanalytische Untersuchungen zum Kolosserbrief als Beitrage zur Methodik von Sprachvergleichen*, SUNT, Band 11 (Göttingen: Vandenhoeck & Ruprecht 1973); Cooper, *Theories of Style*; J. D. Amante, 'Ironic Language: A Structuralist Approach', *Language and Style* 13 (1980), 15–25; Louis T. Milic, *Style and Stylistics: An Analytical Bibliography* (New York: Free Press, 1967); Rene Wellek and Austin Warren, *Theory of Literature* (New York: Harcourt, Brace, 1949), 180; Lanham, *Style*, 13; Eastman, *Style*; Stephen Ullmann, *Semantics: An Introduction to the Science of Meaning* (Oxford: Blackwell, 1970), 9; Sebeok, *Style in Language*. According to Spitzer, the stylistician's goal is to explain as many as possible of the stylistic features in a work and base his conclusions on all the linguistic traits observable in a given author. L. Spitzer, *Linguistics and Literary History: Essays in Stylistics* (Princeton: Princeton University Press, 1948), 19, 91; idem, *A Method of Interpreting Literature* (North Hampton, MA: Smith College, 1949), 64.

[88] Cf. P. H. Menound, *L'Evangile de Jean d'après les recherches récentes*, CTAP 3, 2nd edn (Neuchatel: Delachaux und Niestlé, 1947); J. Jeremias, 'Johanneische Literarkritik', *Theologische Blätter* 20 (1941), 33–46; Schnackenburg, *Das Johannesevangelium*, 94–6; Brown, *John*, cxxxii–cxxxv; Barrett, *St. John*, 10–11; H. N. Ridderbos, 'The Structure and Scope of the Prologue to the Gospel of John', *NovT* 8 (1966), 188–201; E. D. Freed, 'Variations in the Language and Thought of John', *ZNW* 55 (1964), 167–97, here pp. 196–7; M. J. J. Menken, *Numerical Literary Techniques in John: The Fourth Evangelist's Use of Numbers of Words and Syllables*, NovTSup 55 (Leiden: Brill, 1985); J. E. Botha, *Jesus and the Samaritan Woman: A Speech Act Reading of John 4:1–42*, NovTSup 65 (Leiden: Brill, 1991); N. G. Timmins, 'Variation in Style in the Johannine Literature', *JSNT* 53 (1994), 47–64; E. Haenchen, 'Aus der Literatur zum Johannesevangelium', *TRu* 23 (1955), 295–335.

[89] 2. Abt. 15. Aufl. (Göttingen: Vandenhoeck & Ruprecht [KEK, 1941] 1957).

[90] D. M. Smith, *The Composition and Order of the Fourth Gospel: Bultmann's Literary Theory* (New Haven: Yale University, 1965), 9–11, has compiled a useful list of the criteria Bultmann applied – useful in the sense that Bultmann himself never systematically and explicitly discussed these criteria.

[91] E. Käsemann, 'Book Review of Bultmann, R 1941', *Verkündiging und Forschung* 3

In fact, thirty years before Bultmann, Edwin Abbott, in his pioneering works *Johannine Vocabulary*[92] and *Johannine Grammar*,[93] had already paved the way for the study of John's style. But it was E. Schweizer's 1939 monograph, *Ego Eimi: Die religionsgeschichtliche Herkunft und theologische Bedeutung der Johanneischen Bildreden, zugleich ein Beitrag zur Quellenfrage des vierten Evangelium*,[94] which was destined to become one of the most influential works using style-analysis to argue for the compositional unity of the Gospel. Schweizer collected thirty-three characteristic features of Johannine style. These characteristics consist of the identification of certain words, phrases, constructions, grammatical and syntactical idiosyncrasies.[95] Schweizer argued that there are traits which occur 'ausschliesslich oder fast ausschliesslich' in the Gospel. If such a rare usage occurs throughout the document, then it is hardly possible for it to stem from several hands (i.e., several authors). But if such a characteristic only occurs in specific parts, then it is most probable that this represents a source.[96]

Fifteen years after Schweizer, E. Ruckstuhl's important contribution appeared in the form of his thesis, *Die Literarische Einheit des Johannesevangeliums: Der Gegenwärtige Stand der Einschlägigen Forschung*.[97] Ruckstuhl, taking into account certain suggestions by J. Jeremias and P. H. Menoud,[98] expanded Schweizer's thirty-three characteristics to fifty.[99] On the basis of these fifty properties, Ruckstuhl took strong exception to Bultmann and argued for the compositional unity of the Gospel.[100] Some twenty year later in 1977, Ruckstuhl expanded his

---

(1942), 182-201; Jeremias, 'Johanneische Literarkritik', 33-46; Menound, *L'Evangile de Jean*, 17-21.

[92] (London: Adam and Charles Black, 1905).

[93] (London: Adam and Charles Black, 1906).

[94] (Göttingen: Vandenhoeck & Ruprecht, 1939), 82-99.

[95] *Ego Eimi*, 87-8

[96] Ibid., 88. Schweizer writes, '4. Falls dies nicht der Fall ist, ist damit nicht bewizen, dass restlose Einheitlichtkeit vorliegt. Es ist aber hochst wahrscheinlich gemacht, dass mindestens die Einheit am Ende liegt, dass also der endgultige Verfasser entweder alles selbst formuliert oder dann vorliegende Quellen inberarbeitet hat...6. Es ist dabei denkbar, dass dieser endgültige Verfasser (a) seine Vorlage mit dem eigenen Stil durchdringt (b) ihre Eigentumlichkeiten umgekehrt in seinen Stil aufnimmt.'

[97] (Freiburg: Paulus, 1951), 203-5.

[98] Jeremias, 'Johanneische Literarkritik', 33-46; Menound, *L'Evangile de Jean*, 17-21.

[99] Ruckstuhl, *Die Literarische Einheit des Johannesevangeliums*, 197-8. Ruckstuhl also introduced an explicit distinction between style *characteristics* and style *features* which was implicit in Schweizer's approach.

[100] *Die Literarische Einheit des Johannesevangeliums*, 1-19.

previous style list, this time using his analysis to deliver a devastating criticism to Fortna's redaction hypothesis.[101] Then in 1991, Ruckstuhl in collaboration with Peter Dschulnigg, revised and further expanded his statistical comparison.[102]

Although Schweizer and Ruckstuhl were not the first scholars to use stylistic analysis to argue for Johannine literary unity, their works were significant because of their influence and the subsequent reaction they generated. The rationale behind their argument was simple: when two or more specific style characteristics are present in a passage whose literary unity is clear, one may assume that any other passage containing either of these stylistic features would have come from the same author. Ruckstuhl contended: 'if it was possible to imitate any one of the characteristics, it is practically unthinkable that a later hand would have imitated an entire cluster of inconspicuous and unimportant characteristics, especially if there were several alternate ways of expressing oneself'.[103]

Earlier I noted that stylistic analysis also may be used to decipher a document's potential literary and conceptual milieu. Assuming that language is a set of conventions and style a choice within these conventions, more than one text is needed to highlight the variable, 'style'. Thus stylistic analysis inherently is a comparative approach in which texts, authors, genres, as well as languages are collated.[104] When the contrast is among one or more languages, then there is an added cultural component to be considered as well. It is needless to prove that there are stylistic differences among languages which are, to a certain extent, culturally conditioned.[105] Once these differences are categorically known, then it may

---

[101] E. Ruckstuhl, 'Johannine Language and Style: The Question of Their Unity', in *L'Évangile de Jean*, ed. by M. de Jonge (1977), 125–47.

[102] E. Ruckstuhl and P. Dschulnigg, *Stilkritik und Verfasserfrage im Johannesevangelium. Die johanneischen Sprachmerkmale auf dem Hintergrund des Neuen Testaments und des zeitgenössischen hellenistischen Schrifttums*, NTOA 17 (Freiburg: Paulus; Göttingen: Vandenhoek und Ruprecht, 1991).

[103] Ruckstuhl, *Johannine Language and Style*, 127. Freed, in his article, 'Variations in the Language and Thought of John', 196–7, two years earlier had observed, 'I have, of course, assumed the unity of authorship. The variations are so numerous and of so many kinds, and so apparent throughout the Gospel, that they could hardly be due to different sources or to different hands....Is the Gospel, as we now have it, the result of an artistic zeal for variation or the result of mere accident?' See further Ridderbos, 'Structure and Scope', 188–201; Menken, *Numerical Literary Techniques in John*, George Mlakuzhyil, *The Christocentric Literary Structure of the Fourth Gospel*, AnBib 117 (Rome: Pontificio Instituto Biblico, 1987).

[104] Chatman, *Literary Style*.

[105] Angus McIntosh and M. A. K. Halliday, *Patterns of Language: Papers in General, Descriptive, and Applied Linguistics*, Indiana University Studies in the History and Theory of Linguistics (Bloomington: Indiana University Press, 1966), 47, 66; G. D. Kilpatrick, 'Two

be possible to place a document within a particular cultural literary context through a detailed scrutiny of its style. In the Fourth Gospel, this comparative approach, in conjunction with other internal and external indicators, is significant in ascertaining John's literary, conceptual context. Indeed one of the significant by-products of the various style analyses of the Johannine Gospel has been the exposing of John's conceptual context. These style analyses have specially highlighted the Semitic character of the Fourth Gospel which shares many features in its composition which are particularly evident in the compositional style of the Semitic and Old Testament literature.[106]

Beside shared imageries, symbols, motifs, and background ideas, there seems to be evidence that the Evangelist may have structured his narrative after that of Exodus.[107] One reason for this may have been the centrality of the exodus as the focal point in the history of the Jewish people. This structural pattern can be detected not only in the overall skeleton of the narrative, but also in a number of Johannine discourses.[108] Apart from the possible structural strategies, John shares several poetic features common to the literary style of biblical Hebrew literature,[109] for example, the presence of such features as parataxis, that is, short sentences linked by καί, corresponding to the *waw* consecutive.[110] This very prominent stylistic

---

Studies of Style and Text in the Greek New Testament', *JTS* n.s. 41 (1990), 94–8; J. R. Bennett, 'A Stylistics Check List:IV', *Style* 17 (1983), 429–53.

[106] Robert C. Culley, *Studies in the Structure of Hebrew Narrative* (Philadelphia: Fortress; Missoula, MT: Scholars Press, 1976); Brown, *John*, 1:cxxxv–cxxxvi; B. Lindars, *The Gospel of John*, NCB (London: Marshall, Morgan and Scott, 1972), 44–45; Turner, *Style*, 64–79; Haenchen, 'Aus der Literatur zum Johannesevangelium', 295–335; J. P. Louw, 'On Johannine Style', *Neot* 20 (1986), 5–12; Barrett, *St. John*, 5–14; E. Hirsch, 'Stilkritik und Literaranalyse im vierten Evangelium', *ZNW* 43 (1950–51), 128–43; Timmins, 'Variation in Style', 47–64.

[107] Jeffrey Lloyd Staley, *The Print's First Kiss: A Rhetorical Investigation of the Implied Reader in the Fourth Gospel*, SBLDS 82 (Atlanta, GA: Scholars Press, 1988), 74–118; Anthony Hanson, 'John 1:14–18 and Exodus 34', *NTS* 23 (1976), 90; Moises Silva, 'Approaching the Fourth Gospel', *Criswell Theological Review* 3 (1988), 27; Tenney, 'Old Testament and the Fourth Gospel', 300–8.

[108] J. J. Enz, 'The Book of Exodus as Literary Type for the Gospel of John', *JBL* 76 (1957), 208–15; cf. J. P. Fokkelman, 'Exodus', in *The Literary Guide to the Bible*, ed. by Robert Alter and Frank Kermode (Cambridge, MA: Harvard University Press, Belknap Press, 1987), 56–65.

[109] P. Gächter, 'Der Formale Aufbau der Abschiedsrede Jesu', *ZKT* 58 (1934), 155–207; idem, 'Die Form der eucharistischen Rede Jesu (Jn 6:35ff)', *ZKT* 59 (1935), 419–41; Bultmann, 'Johannesevangelium', in K. Galling (Hrsg), *Die Religion in Geschichte und Gegenwart: Handwörterbuch für die Theologie und Religionswissenschaft*, vol. 3 (Tübingen: Mohr, 1959), 840–50; Schnackenburg, *Das Johannesevangelium*, 94–6; Brown, *John*, 1:cxxxii–cxxxv; Barrett, *St. John*, 10–11.

[110] E.g., Jn. 9:6f. For survey of different forms of parataxis, see J. H. Moulton and W. F. Howard, *A Grammar of the New Testament Greek*, vol. 2 (Edinburgh: Clark, 1929), 420–3, 469.

component of Hebrew (Aramaic) narrative structure forms one of the syntactical distinctives of John's Gospel.[111] Other Hebraic elements in the Johannine narrative include the frequency of the 'casus pendens' construction,[112] the numerous asyndetic verses,[113] word order,[114] Greek *aorist* for Semitic *static perfect*,[115] *historic present*, and *periphrastic present* and *imperfect*,[116] the Hebrew *infinitive absolute*,[117] and many other similar shared Semitic syntactical features.[118]

Chiastic patterns in ancient Semitic poetry are well attested in many parts of the Hebrew Bible.[119] By chiasmas is meant 'a series (a, b, c,...) and its inversion (...c, b, a) taken together as a combined unit. In Hebrew poetry, such a unit is generally a parallel couplet, so that the combined

---

[111] Turner, *Style*, 70, 'Biblical Greek will often disguise the parataxis by making one of the verbs a participle, (e.g., answering, said...) but John prefers the co-ordination (answered and said), avoiding some of the redundant participles appearing in Biblical Greek (e.g., coming, rising) and preferring "they came and saw (1:39), he rose and went out (11:31)"'. Kilpatrick, 'Two Studies of Style and Text', 94–8; Lightfoot, *Biblical Essays*, 129–31.

[112] Burney, *Aramaic Origin*, 63–5, counts twenty-seven examples. See also Matthew Black, *An Aramaic Approach to the Gospels and Acts*, 3rd edn (Oxford: Clarendon, 1967), 51f., Moulton and Howard, *Grammar of the New Testament*, 2:424.

[113] In contrast to parataxis, asyndeton is a construction whereby sentences are simply laid side by side without the use of 'καί' (e.g., 1:40, 42, 45, 47; 2:17; 5:12, 15; 9:9; 10:21, 22; 16:19; 19:29, etc).

[114] For details, see Turner, *Style* and his discussion in chapter five. Also see Louw, 'On Johannine Style', 5–12; Vern S. Poythress, 'The Use of the Intersentence Conjunctions DE, OUN, KAI, and Asyndeton in the Gospel of John', *NovT* 26 (1984), 312–40.

[115] E.g., Jn. 11:14, and Black, *Aramaic Approach*, 129.

[116] J. H. Moulton, *A Grammar of the New Testament Greek*, vol. 1 (Edinburgh: Clark, 1908), 120–2, 225–7; Moulton and Howard, *Grammar of the New Testament*, 2:451f., 456f.; Black, *Aramaic Approach*, 130ff.

[117] Moulton and Howard, *Grammar of the New Testament*, 2:443f.

[118] Howard, 'Semitism in the New Testament', in Moulton and Howard, *A Grammar of New Testament Greek*, 2:411–485, passim, as well as Black, *Aramaic Approach*; Burney, *Aramaic Origin*; BDF.

[119] A. R. Ceresko, 'The Chiastic Word Pattern in Hebrew', *CBQ* 38 (1976), 303–11; idem, 'The A:B:B:A Word Pattern in Hebrew and Northwest Semitic, with Special Reference to the Book of Job', *Ugarit Forschungen* 7 (1975), 73–88; and 'The Function of Chiasmus in Hebrew Poetry', *CBQ* 40 (1978), 1–10; J. S. Kselman, 'Semantic-Sonant Chiasmus in Biblical Poetry', *Bib* 58 (1977), 219–23; R. L. Alden, 'Chiastic Psalms (I), A Study in the Mechanics of Semitic Poetry in Psalm 1–50', *JETS* 17 (1974), 11–28; 'Chiastic Psalms (II), A Study in the Mechanics of Semitic Poetry in Psalms 51–100', *JETS* 19 (1976), 191–200; W. H. Shea, 'The Chiastic Structure of the Song of Songs', *ZAW* 92 (1980), 378–96; H. Van Dyke Parunak, 'Some Axioms for Literary Architecture', *Semitics* 8 (1982), 1–16; Yehuda Radday, 'Chiasm in the Torah', *Linguistica Biblica* 19 (1972), 2–23; J. W. Welch, ed., *Chiasmus in Antiquity: Structures, Analyses, Exegesis* (Hildesheim: Gerstenberg, 1981); Nils W. Lund, 'The Presence of Chiasmus in the Old Testament', *AJSL* 46 (1930), 104–26, especially Lund's second work *Chiasmus in the New Testament: A Study in Formgeschichte* (Chapel Hill: University of North Carolina Press, 1942).

(chiastic) unit would be a, b, c//c, b, a.'[120] The Fourth Evangelist, among the New Testament authors, makes abundant use of chiasm in the structural formation of his narrative.[121] Scholars have pointed out the chiastic designs even within the plot development of the Gospel, including the geographical locations.[122] John's use of chiastic and symmetrical patterns throughout the Fourth Gospel is indeed an affirmation of the document's poetic style. Such patterns, beside their mnemonic effect, serve to focus the reader's attention upon the pivotal point of a passage.[123]

Closely associated with chiasm is the use of 'inclusio', a common symmetrical feature in the Old Testament which is evident in the Fourth Gospel as well.[124] 'Inclusio' or inclusion or 'envelope figure' is a pattern in which what is said at the beginning of a piece is repeated at the end.

Other Hebraic features prevalent in both John and the Hebrew Bible

---

[120] Wilfred Watson, *Classical Hebrew Poetry*, JSOTSup 26 (Sheffield: JSOT Press, 1984), 201; S. Bar-Efrat, 'Some Observations on the Analysis of Structure in Biblical Narrative', *VT* 30 (1980), 154-73. See also Robert Alter, 'The Characteristics of Ancient Hebrew Poetry', in *The Literary Guide to the Bible* (Cambridge, MA: Harvard University Press, Belknap Press, 1987), 611.

[121] Peter F. Ellis, *The Genius of John* (Collegeville, MN: Liturgical Press, 1984), 10-18; David Deeks, 'The Structure of the Fourth Gospel', *NTS* 15 (1968-69), 107-28; E. C. Webster, 'Pattern in the Fourth Gospel', in *Art and Meaning: Rhetoric in Biblical Literature*, JSOTSup 19 (Sheffield: JSOT Press, 1982), 230-57; Godfrey Nicholson, *Death as Departure: The Johannine Descent-Ascent Schema*, SBLDS 63 (Chico, CA: Scholars Press, 1983), 26-8; Kilpatrick, 'Two Studies of Style and Text', 94-8; Charles Talbert, 'Artistry and Theology: An Analysis of the Architecture of Jn. 1:19-5:47', *CBQ* 32 (1970), 341-66, X. Léon-Dufour, 'Trois chiasmes johanniques', *NTS* 7 (1960), 249-55; Lund, *Chiasmus in the New Testament*; A. Di Marco, 'Der Chiasmus in der Bibel, 3. Teil (Mat-Jn)', *Linguistica Biblica* 39 (1976), 37-85; Welch, 'Il Chiasmo del Nuovo Testamento', in *Chiasmus in Antiquity: Structures, Analyses, Exegesis*, 211-49; Jeffrey Staley, 'The Structure of John's Prologue: Its Implications for the Gospel's Narrative Structure', *CBQ* 48 (1986), 241-64; E. L. Miller, *Salvation-History in the Prologue of John: The Significance of John 1:3/4*. NovTSup 60 (Leiden: Brill, 1989), 6-12; Mlakuzhyil, *Christocentric Literary Structure*, 125-9.

[122] Staley, *Print's First Kiss*, 58-71; Wayne Meeks, 'Galilee and Judea in the Fourth Gospel', *JBL* 85 (1966), 159-69.

[123] Watson, *Classical Hebrew Poetry*, 205; Talbert, 'Artistry and Theology', 341-66; Staley, 'Structure of John's Prologue', 241-64; Menken, *Numerical Literary Techniques*, in his detailed analysis shows numerous symmetrical patterns throughout the Fourth Gospel. Also see Miller, *Salvation-History*, 6-12; Miakuzhyil, *Christocentric Literary Structure*, 125-29.

[124] Ellis, *Genius of John*, 9-10; Mlakuzhyil, *Christocentric Literary Structure*, 93-7; A. Vanhoye, 'La Composition de Jn. 5:19-30', in *Mélanges Bibliques en Hommage au R. R. Béda Rigaux*, ed. by A. Descamps and A. de Halleux (Gembloux: Duculot, 1970), 259-74; Brown, *John*, 135; Peter Chang, 'Repetitions and Variations in the Gospel of John' (Dissertation, Universite des Sciences Humanines de Strasbourg, 1975), 130-8. A sample of studies in the Old Testament includes: M. Kessler, 'Inclusio in the Hebrew Bible', *Semitics* 6 (1978), 44-49; David Freedman, 'The Structure of Job 3', *Bib* 49 (1958), 503, 508; Jack R. Lundbom, *Jeremiah: A Study in Ancient Hebrew Rhetoric*, SBLDS 18 (Missoula, MT: Scholars Press, 1975), 23-60; Watson, *Classical Hebrew Poetry*, 282-6.

include 'repetition',¹²⁵ 'synonymy',¹²⁶ and the extensive use of various forms of 'parallelism'.¹²⁷ Among these, repetition is an important literary device in the Fourth Gospel and highly prominent in the Old Testament. Throughout the Bible, there are elaborately integrated systems of repetition. Some of these depend on the actual recurrence of individual phonemes, words or short phrases; others are linked instead to actions, images, and ideas that are part of the world of the narrative.¹²⁸ Although repetition is a universal literary phenomenon and is not confined to Semitic literature, it is one of the literary hallmarks of the Hebrew Scriptures. Repetition is a highly effective means if a writer wishes to accentuate a particular theological, moral, or historical point in the narrative. Repetition may be of a single word developed into a thematic key-word (e.g., in John: witness, light, true, life, judge),¹²⁹ or the repetition of a phrase (e.g., 'He who sent me', 5:30, 36; 6:38, 39; 7:16, 28, 29, etc.). Although the use of repetition is not unique to John among the New Testament writings, it is more apparent in the Fourth Gospel than any other New Testament document. Paul Duke goes so far as to assert that repetition is 'a favorite Johannine stylistic feature' which often functions ironically (3:10; 6:42; 7:20, 28, 35–36; 8:22, 58; 11:16; 13:38; 16:17–18, 29–30).¹³⁰ Repetition as a

---

[125] Peter Chang, 'Repetitions and Variations'; I. Eitan, 'La Répétition de la Racine en Hébreu', *The Journal of the Palestine Oriental Society* 1 (1920–1921), 170–86; J. Muilenburg, 'A Study in Hebrew Rhetoric: Repetition and Style', *VTS* 1 (1953), 97–111; David A. Black, 'On the Style and Significance of John 17', *Criswell Theological Review* 3 (1988), 141–59; Robert Alter, *The Art of Biblical Narrative* (New York: Basic Books, 1981), 88–113.

[126] Muilenburg, 'Study in Hebrew Rhetoric', 97–111; Watson, *Classical Hebrew Poetry*, 271–8; D. Black, 'Style and Significance', 149–53; Chang, 'Repetitions and Variations', 24–9.

[127] I. M. Casanowicz, 'Parallelism in Hebrew Poetry', in *The Jewish Encyclopaedia*, vol. 9 (London: 1916), 520–2; A. Berlin, 'Grammatical Aspects of Biblical Parallelism', *HUCA* 50 (1979), 17–43; Watson, *Classical Hebrew Poetry*, 114–59; Robert Lowth, *Lectures on the Sacred Poetry of the Hebrews*, 2 vols (Hildesheim: Georg Olms, 1969). In John, see Chang, 'Repetitions and Variations', 104–15, who believes the occurrences of so many antithetical parallelisms in John is due to Johannine dualism (p. 114, ftnote. 26); D. Black, 'Style and Significance', 151–3; Brown, *John*, 132–3; Mlakuzhyil, *Christocentric Literary Structure*, 122–5; Menken, *Numerical Literary Techniques*; Gächter, 'Der Formale Aufbau der Abschiedsrede Jesu', 155–207, idem, 'Die Form der eucharistischen', 419–41, also 'Strophen im Johannesevangelium', *ZKT* 60 (1936), 99–120; 402–23.

[128] The repeated expression may have acquired in earlier contexts other connotations (e.g., 'the Word' Jn. 1:1). This broadens its field of meaning in its present and future contexts and also adds to the complexity of the problem for the interpreter. The repetition need not be of the word itself but also of the word-root. This is particularly the case with Semitic languages; and the phenomenon abounds in the Old Testament. Cf. Eitan, 'La Répétition', 170–86, Muilenburg, 'Study in Hebrew Rhetoric', 97–111; Alter, *Art of Biblical Narrative*, 88–113.

[129] See chapter two and my discussion under the heading 'cluster concepts', 2.2.1.4.

[130] Duke, *Irony in the Fourth Gospel*, 91.

style characteristic in the Fourth Gospel may be attributed to the emphatic influence of the Old Testament upon this Gospel.

One of the distinguishing hallmarks of Semitic literature in general,[131] and the Hebrew Bible in particular, is word-play.[132] A wide variety of word-plays are used, for example, in the prophetic books of the Old Testament.[133] Scholars have often commented on the pervasive use of punning in Isaiah 1-39.[134] Among the various types of puns employed by Isaiah, one that seems to be prominent is what Glück refers to as the equivocal pun, a pun that normally involves the use of homonyms and results in *double entendre*. He defines it as a device by which 'any one or more of the multiple meanings conveyed or implied by a word in the phrase may suit or change the context and/or create a doubt, shock and/or other sensation in the minds of the listeners or readers, confused, as they are likely to be, by the apparent lack of clarity in the diction.'[135] The prophets utilised word-play as an effective means of criticism of the status quo or the scoffing and mocking of the wicked. But word-play, for the prophets as for the Fourth Evangelist, was also an effective means of accentuating significant theological points.[136]

In the literary context of the Hebrew Bible, word-play encompasses

---

[131] For a discussion on the use of word play in other comparative Semitic literature, start with E. A. Speiser, 'Word Plays on the Creation Epic's Version of the Founding of Babylon', *Orientalia* 25 (1956), 317–23.

[132] Immanuel Casanowicz, *Paranomasia in the Old Testament* (Baltimore: John Hopkins University, 1892); G. Boström, *Paronomasi i den äldre Hebreiska Maschalliteraturen med särskild hänsyn till proverbia* (Lund: Gleerup, 1928); A. Guillaume, 'Paronomasia in the Old Testament', *Journal of Semitic Studies* 9 (1964), 282–90; Walter Herzberg, 'Polysemy in the Hebrew Bible' (Dissertation, New York University, 1979); J. M. Sasson, 'Wordplay in the Old Testament', *IDBSup*, 968–70; G. B. Caird, *The Language and Imagery of the Bible* (London: Duckworth; Philadelphia; Westminster Press, 1980), 109–21; Daniel Grossberg, 'Multiple Meaning: Part of a Compound Literary Device in the Hebrew Bible', *East Asia Journal of Theology* 4 (1986), 77–86; Watson, *Classical Hebrew Poetry*, 237–50; Black, *Aramaic Approach*, 185; W. F. Stinespring, 'Humor', *IDB*, vol. 2 (New York: Abingdon, 1962), 660–2.

[133] Robert Chisholm, 'Word Play in the Eighth-Century Prophets', *BibSac* 143 (1987), 44–52; Caird, *Language and Imagery*, 156–9; J. J. Glück, 'Paronomasia in Biblical Literature', *Semitics* 1 (1970), 50–78.

[134] J. J. M. Roberts, 'Double Entendre in First Isaiah', *CBQ* 54 (1992), 39–48; Luis Alonso Schökel, *Estudios de Poética Hebrea* (Barcelona: J. Flors, 1963), 86–106; Glück, 'Paronomasia', 50–78.

[135] Glück, 'Paronomasia', 53. On the effectivness of 'polysemy' as a literary device, see John Haiman, 'A Study in Polysemy', *Studies in Language* 2 (1978), 1–33.

[136] Some of the Old Testament examples can be found in Micah 1:10–16, 5:1; Amos 5:5; Zephaniah 2:4, 9:3; Proverbs 30:33; Job 15:13; Jeremiah 23:9–12. The poet derives prophetic meaning from the name of the enemy, pagan nation, or from the name of its king. For citation of further examples, see Glück, 'Paronomasia', 50–78.

such features as homonyms, lexical polyvalency, *double entendre*,[137] 'paronomasia',[138] and the like.[139] We have already noted many of these stylistic features in the Fourth Gospel, more so in this Gospel than anywhere else in the New Testament perhaps, with a possible exception of the book of Revelation. The Fourth Gospel abounds with some of these features.[140] The origin of this literary influence, as I have proposed, can be traced back to the Old Testament[141] from which the Evangelist draws heavily and upon which the Gospel depends for the meaningful explication

---

[137] S. Gevirtz, 'Of Patriarchs and Puns', *HUCA* 46 (1975), 33–54; J. Brown, 'Eight Types of Puns', *PMLA* 71 (1956), 14–26; Roberts, 'Double Entendre in First Isaiah', 39–48; Schökel, *Estudios de Poética Hebrea*, 86–106; Watson, *Classical Hebrew Poetry*, 239–44.

[138] The best work in this area remains that of Casanowicz, 'Paronomasia in the Old Testament'. Also see Glück, 'Paronomasia, 50–78; A. Guillaume, 'Paronomasia in the Old Testament', *Journal of Semitic Studies* 9 (1964), 282–90; Chisholm, 'Word Play', 44–52; Grossberg, 'Multiple Meaning', 78; Bar-Efrat, 'Analysis of Structure', 202; Schökel, *Estudios de Poética Hebrea*, 86–106.

[139] Georg Fohrer, 'Two-fold Aspects of Hebrew Words', in *Words and Meanings: Essays Presented to David Winston Thomas*, ed. by P. R. Ackroyd and B. Lindars (Cambridge: CUP, 1968), 95–103; William Holladay, 'Form and Word Play in David's Lament Over Saul and Jonathan', *VT* 20 (April, 1970), 153–89; D. F. Payne, 'Characteristic Word Play in 'Second Isaiah': A Reappraisal', *Journal of Semitic Studies* 12 (1967), 207–29; C. F. Porter, 'Samson's Riddle: Judges 14:14–18', *JTS* n.s. 13 (1962), 106–9; Grossberg, 'Multiple Meaning', 77–86; Herzberg, *Polysemy in the Hebrew Bible*; Harry Torczyner, 'The Riddle in the Bible', *HUCA* 1 (1924), 125–249.

[140] See the second chapter, and further Herbert Leroy, 'Das Johanneische Missverständnis als Literarische Form', *BibLeb* 9 (1968), 196–207; Oscar Cullmann, 'Der johanneische Gebrauch doppeldeutiger Ausdrücke als Schlüssel zum Verständnis des vierten Evangeliums', *TZ* 4 (1948), 360–72; Paul Trudinger, 'Subtle Word-Plays in the Gospel of John and the Problem of Chapter 21', *JRT* 23 (1971), 27–31; F. Manns, 'Les mots à double entente: Antécédents et fonction herméneutique d'un procédé Johannique', *Studii Biblici Franciscani Liber Annuus* 38 (1988), 39–57; E. Richard, 'Expressions of Double Meaning and Their Function in the Gospel of John', *NTS* 31 (1985), 96–112. Paronomasia is not nearly as common in Greek as it is in Hebrew. Paronomasia is slightly different from *amphibologia* in that it is the use of a cognate of a word in different senses, or utilising different words similar in sound as a means of criticism, for irony or to achieve humour. Often this technique in the Old Testament involves the use of the proper name of persons or a place rather than a common noun. The Romans called this literal meaning of a proper name 'nomen omen' meaning the name signifies the destiny. See A. Strus, *Nomen Omen: La stylistique sonore des noms propres dans le pentateuque*, AnBib 80 (Rome: Biblical Institute Press, 1978); idem, 'Interprétation des noms propres dans les oracles contre les nations', in *Congress Volume. Salamanca 1983*, ed. by J. A. Emerton, VTS 36 (Leiden: Brill 1985), 272–85. An example of paronomasia is in John 1:14 where there seems to be a play upon ἐσκήνωσεν and 'shekinah' (שכינה) having the same consonants as the Greek. In John 15:1–3, there may be play on the two verbs αἴρει and καθαίρει. Also in John 9:39, there seems to be a homonemic play on κρίμα and κόσμον, and βλέποντες and βλέπωσιν. Again, various forms of *homonymy* are much more effective in Hebrew than in Greek. They are certainly more prominent in the Hebrew Bible than in the New Testament.

[141] Cf. Manns, 'Les mots à double entente'; Bonsirven, 'Les aramaïsmes', 425–32; Wead, *Literary Devices in John*, 34–9; Black, *Aramaic Approach*; Richard, 'Expressions of Double Meaning', 96–112.

of its ideas and images. Indeed one of the most common features that ties the Fourth Gospel conceptually to the Old Testament Scriptures is shared images (concrete picture words, e.g., metaphor, symbolism). Stephen Ullmann thinks the study of images indicates 'the deepest layer of the stylistic system,' and 'the very heart' of an author's style since the author is free to be creative without regard to linguistic conventions.[142] According to Leaska, 'image' refers to 'that evocative linguistic construct which helps to define the mood, tone, and meaning of the passage in which it occurs.'[143] An image[144] moves the reader beyond the printed page by appealing to his or her original and/or shared sensory impressions.[145] The Fourth Gospel is permeated with Old Testament images, e.g., light, glory, the Lamb, tabernacle, living water, Jacob's well, harvest, Passover, manna, sheep, shepherd, vine, etc.[146] These are reinterpreted from the post-resurrection point of view where Jesus is seen by the Evangelist as the one in whom the Scriptures and their images find their ultimate actualisation. These stylistic features compose the remarkable literary tapestry of John's language, giving the document its poetic character, which some have dismissed as 'pointless'.[147] However, far from 'pointless', these style properties play an

---

[142] *Style in the French Novel* (New York: Barnes and Noble, 1957), 15, 259 respectively.

[143] Mitchell A. Leaska, *Virginia Woolf's Lighthouse: A Study in Critical Method* (New York: Columbia University Press, 1970). See also Ziva Ben-Porat, 'The Poetics of Allusion' (Ph. D. diss., Berkeley: University of California, 1973); Mary McDermott Shideler, *The Theology of Romantic Love: A Study in the Writings of Charles Williams* (Grand Rapids: Eerdmans, 1962), 11–28; William Freedman, 'The Literary Motif: A Definition and Evaluation', *Novel* 4 (1971), 123–31; J. Carter Swain, *Unlocking the Treasures in Biblical Imagery* (New York: Association Press, 1966); Allan Palvio, *Mental Representations: A Dual Coding Approach* (New York: OUP, 1986).

[144] Image, simply put, is a thing that represents something else. Richard A. Lanham, *A Handlist of Rhetorical Terms: A Guide for Students of English Literature* (Berekeley: University of California Press, 1968), 59. It includes figurative expressions such as metaphor, simile, personification and synecdoche.

[145] W. Hamilton Fyfe and W. Rhys Roberts, trans., *Aristotle: The Poetics; 'Longinus': On the Sublime; Demetrius: On Style*, XV. 1. 9; III. 1. 128–29, 170–71, 176–77; also Ullman's explanation of how an 'image' functions, *Language and Style*, 193–201; and W. E. Collinson, 'Comparative Synonymics: Some Principles and Illustrations', *Transactions of the Philological Society* (1939), 54–77.

[146] A prime illustration of such an image is Jesus' remark in 3:14 where he draws a correspondence between his own crucifixion and the incident of Moses lifting up the bronze serpent in the wilderness (cf. 8:28; 12:32, 34). Charles Torrey, 'When I AM Lifted Up from the Earth', *JBL* 51 (1932), 320–22; Rita J. Burns, 'Jesus and the Bronze Serpent', *The Bible Today* 28 (1990), 34–9; A. Jaubert, *Approches de l'Évangile de Jean* (Paris: du Seuil, 1976), 56; F. F. Bruce, *The Gospel of John* (London: Pickering Paperbooks, 1983), 88, 195–6, 266–7; Lindars, *John*, 157–8; also Richard Foulkes, 'Genesis Motifs in Johannine Literature' (Doctoral diss., Strasbourg, 1968).

[147] Turner, *Style*, 76. Blass and Debrunner in BDF §492 confidently state, 'the absence of

important role in consonance with the John's central theological message.[148] These stylistic features also strengthen the hypothesis that the Fourth Gospel should be set within the Old Testament circle of influence.

An author's style in some ways resembles his or her 'verbal fingerprint'. It is unique to each writer. But unlike fingerprints, literary style is influenced both by culture and by a writer's repeated and extensive exposure to a particular strand of literature. Various languages possess stylistic features somewhat unique to themselves in contrast to other languages. In the case of the Fourth Gospel, although written in Greek, the style reveals a Semitic compositional 'fingerprint', and the 'strand of literature' is none other than the Old Testament upon which the Evangelist relied so extensively. Although the stylistic features noted in this chapter in and of themselves do not establish the Semitic milieu of the Fourth Gospel, yet taken together with other factors noted earlier in the second chapter, they seem to show the Semitic influence on John's Gospel and point to the Hebrew Scriptures as the dominant literary environment in which John seems most naturally to fit.

The origin of the Johannine Gospel, which Adolf von Harnack called the greatest riddle presented to us by the earliest history of Christianity, appears to me to be a riddle of our own making, since every page of this Gospel reveals its conceptual origin. The Johannine world of ideas never departs from its Jewish, Old Testament orbit. It is to this context that the Gospel is inseparably fastened for any meaningful explication of its literary milieu, style, imagery, language and theology.

---

rhetorical art in the Johannine discourses is quite clear.' In this study I have tried to demonstrate otherwise.

[148] For the relation between message (content) and means (language, style), see Meir Sternberg, *The Poetics of Biblical Narrative* (Bloomington, IN: Indiana University Press, 1985), especially 365–440.

Chapter 4

The Purpose of the Fourth Gospel

4.1. The Intentions of John

While in the second chapter I defined 'ambiguity' in the Fourth Gospel and delineated its intriguing and complex structure, in the third chapter I proposed that the probable context of thought out of which the ambiguity emerges was an environment in which the Hebrew Scriptures and the traditions surrounding them were the dominant conceptual and literary forces. The second major objective of this research is to examine the function and significance of John's perplexing language. Earlier in chapter one, as part of the overall proposal, I suggested that the essential function of John's language was wedded to his purpose in writing the Gospel. In this chapter I aim to articulate that purpose.

At the present, the majority of scholars believe that John was written for the Johannine community by the Johannine community. Within Johannine scholarship, this assumption is regarded as self-evident. However, in a recent years a few scholars have expressed doubt about this assumption. For example, in a collection of essays edited by Richard Bauckham, serious questions are raised about the current consensus which assumes each of the Gospels, including the Fourth Gospel, was written for specific church groups.[1] Bauckham argues that this consensus has been formed without any substantial argument:

> Nearly all scholars writing about the Gospels now treat it as virtually self-evident that each evangelist addressed the specific context and concerns of his own community, and a large and increasingly sophisticated edifice of scholarly reconstruction has been erected on this basic assumption. It is widely used as the major hermeneutical key for reading the Gospels.[2]

---

[1] Richard Bauckham, 'For Whom Were Gospels Written?', in *The Gospels for All Christians: Rethinking the Gospel Audiences*, ed. by Richard Bauckham (Grand Rapids: Eerdmans, 1998), 9–48.

[2] Bauckham, ed., 'Introduction', in *The Gospels for All Christians*, 1.

Against this Bauckham and his coauthors contend that, with all probability, the Gospels were intended for a much broader circulation among Christian churches. These groups were not scattered, isolated, introverted communities. They were a network[3] in constant, close communication with each other.[4] The Christians, like others in the Roman Empire, were inclined to travel with means readily available in various forms for them to do so.[5] The early Christian movement had a strong sense of being a world-wide movement. What we have learned about the publication and circulation of letters and books in the second century further supports the probable intended wider audience of these documents.[6]

---

[3] See L. M. White, ed., *Semeia* 56: *Social Networks in the Early Christian Environment: Issues and Methods for Social History* (Atlanta: Scholars Press, 1992).

[4] Michael B. Thompson, 'The Holy Internet: Communication Between Churches in the First Christian Generation', in *The Gospels for All Christians*, ed. by R. Bauckham (Grand Rapids: Eerdmans, 1998), 49–70; S. C. Barton, 'The Communal Dimension of the Earliest Christianity', *JTS* n.s. 43 (1992), 399–427.

[5] C. A. J. Skeel, *Travel in the First Century After Christ, with Special Reference to Asia Minor* (Cambridge: CUP, 1901); D. H. French, 'The Roman Road-System of Asia Minor', in *Aufstieg und Niedergang der römischen Welt* II.7.2., ed. by H. Temporini and W. Hasse (Berlin, New York: Walter de Gruyter, 1980), 698–729; N. H. H. Sitwell, *Roman Roads of Europe* (London: Cassell, 1981); W. M. Ramsay, 'Roads and Travel (in NT)', in the supplementary volume of *A Dictionary of the Bible*, ed. by J. Hastings (Edinburgh: Clark, 1904), 375–402; B. M. Rapske, 'Acts, Travel and Shipwreck', in *The Book of Acts in Its Graeco-Roman Setting*, ed. by D. W. J. Gill and C. Gempf (Grand Rapids: Eerdmans, 1994), 1–47; L. Casson, *Travel in the Ancient World* (London: George Allen and Unwin, 1974); idem, *The Ancient Mariners: Seafarers and Sea Fighters of the Mediterranean in Ancient Times*, 2nd edn (Princeton: Princeton University Press, 1991); F. O'Sullivan, *The Egnatian Way* (Harrisburg, PA: David and Charles, 1972); T. Cornell and J. Matthew, *Atlas of the Roman World* (Oxford: Phaidon, 1982), 114; D. A. Dorsey, *The Roads and Highways of Ancient Israel*, American Schools of Oriental Research Library of Biblical and Near Eastern Archaeology (Baltimore: John Hopkins University Press, 1991).

[6] See Bauckham, 'For Whom Were Gospels Written?', 1–48; and S. C. Barton, 'Can We Identify the Gospel Audiences?', in *The Gospels for All Christians*, ed. by R. Bauckham (Grand Rapids: Eerdmans, 1998), 179. See further W. G. Doty, *Letters in Primitive Christianity*, Guides to Biblical Scholarship (Philadelphia: Fortress, 1973); H. Y. Gamble, *Books and Readers in the Early Church* (New Haven: Yale University Press, 1995); G. R. Llewlyn and R. A. Kearsley, 'Letter-Carriers in the Early Church', in *New Documents Illustrating Early Christianity* (Sydney: Ancient History Documentary Research Centre, Macquarie University, 1994), 7:50–57; S. R. Llewelyn, 'Sending Letters in the Ancient World: Paul and the Philippians', *Tyndale Bulletin* 46 (1995), 337–56. On questions related to levels of literacy and oral presentations of such documents, see, for example, P. J. Botha, 'The Verbal Art of the Pauline Letters: Rhetoric, Performance and Presence', in *Rhetoric and the New Testament: Essays from the 1992 Heidelberg Conference*, ed. by S. E. Porter and T. H. Olbricht (Sheffield: JSOT Press, 1993), 412f., R. F. Ward, 'Pauline Voice and Presence as Strategic Communication', in *Semeia* 65: *Orality and Textuality in Early Christian Literature*, ed. by J. Dewey (Atlanta: Scholars Press, 1995), 95–107; W. V. Harris, *Ancient Literacy* (Cambridge, MA: Harvard University Press, 1989); W. Kelber, *The Oral and Written Gospel: The Hermeneutics of Speaking and Writing in the Synoptic Tradition, Mark, Paul and Q* (Philadelphia: Fortress, 1983); J. Halverson, 'Oral and Written Gospel: A Critique of Werner Kelber', *NTS* 40 (1994), 180–95; Loveday Alexander, 'Ancient

In so far as the Fourth Gospel is concerned, I propose that it was written as a theological treatise, in a narrative cast, to establish that Jesus is the Christ according to Israel's Scriptures. In setting forth this proposition, the Fourth Evangelist may have had several objectives in mind, both within his own immediate historical context, and also within a much broader universal context. The Fourth Gospel seems to have a polemic, apologetic[7] and pastoral relevance. John refutes those who deny that Jesus is the Christ, appeals to those who are undecided or do not have the courage to come into the open with their belief, and pastorally strengthens the resolve of the community of faith. He writes to show how Jewish religious authorities rejected their Messiah because of their spiritual dullness and their ignorance of the Scriptures. He appeals to his hearers and/or readers to examine the Scriptures to see their fulfilment in Jesus' life. But then he writes to emphasise that the recognition of Jesus as the Christ and God's self-revelation in him ultimately rests on spiritual illumination grounded in the Spirit-produced regeneration and a lifelong abiding faith. In this situation, the document not only addresses the author's own immediate historical context, but most importantly, it is a lasting product for posterity, for the church. John has this distant audience very much in view (e.g., 1:12–13; 3:18, 36; 10:16; 17:20–21). In this scenario, the Gospel would have been a valuable document irrespective of whoever its readers or hearers. Whether the church, the Jews in the East, the Jews in the Diaspora, proselytes, or all of the above read or heard the Gospel, its central message would not have changed. The message of the Gospel would have been meaningful to both 'insiders' and 'outsiders', both time-bound and timeless.

Book Production', in *The Gospels for All Christians*, ed. by R. Bauckham (Grand Rapids: Eerdmans, 1998), 71–105; R. J. Starr, 'The Circulation of Literary Texts in the Roman World', *Classical Quarterly* 37 (1987), 213–23; Frederick G. Kenyon, *Books and Readers in Ancient Greece and Rome*, 2nd edn (Oxford: Clarendon, 1951); T. C. Skeat, *The Birth of the Codex* (London: British Museum, 1987); Elizabeth Rawson, *Intellectual Life in the Late Roman Republic* (London: Duckworth, 1985); P. E. Easterling and B. M. W. Knox, 'Books and Readers in the Greek World', in *The Cambridge History of Calssical Literature*, vol. 1, part 4: *The Hellenistic Period and the Empire*, ed. by P. E. Easterling and B. M. W. Know (Cambridge: CUP, 1989).

[7] The term 'apologetic' is used here in a sense of a 'reasoned defence' or setting forth and defending a belief, conviction, or a position. See Allison A. Trites, *The New Testament Concept of Witness*, SNTSMS 31 (Cambridge: CUP, 1977), 78–127. C. F. D. Moule, 'The Intention of the Evangelists', 167–179, in *New Testament Essays*, ed. by A. J. B. Higgins (Manchester: University Press, 1959), 168, describes John as a 'skillful apology'.

4.1.1. Clarification of Two Assumptions

Two issues need to be clarified at this juncture. First, although there may be a legitimate difference between the actual intended audience of a given text (i.e., those for whom the text was written) and those who are revealed in the text (implied readers), one must be careful in making this distinction. William Kurz has cautioned us, 'The only evidence for the intended readership of most ancient texts like the Fourth Gospel is the text itself since the text reveals only its implied readers and not its real readers.'[8] Even if adequate data was available and a distinction could be made between Jesus' interlocutors, i.e., implied readers, and the 'real' readers of the Gospel, i.e., intended readers, this might or might not significantly assist us in our understanding the purpose of the Gospel. Such distinctions often confuse the modern reader rather than helping to clarify issues. Secondly, in the case of John's Gospel, there is no compelling reason to make a clear-cut dichotomy between the situation of Jesus and the situation of the disciples. Whether, at the time of John's writing of his Gospel, the Pharisees or the priestly religious party was dominant is not the real issue. The real point is that John singles out these groups as those who brought about the crucifixion of the one whom he believes was the Messiah; and with their indictment, he implicitly charges those groups and the Jewish authorities who continue to reject Jesus as the Christ and to persecute his followers (cf. Rev. 2:9–10). The irony in the text is criticism of those who remain blind to the revelation. The sharp distinction between the pre-AD 70 situation and the post-AD 70 situation in respect of the conflict between the church and 'the Jews' also seems to me to be exaggerated. There is no conclusive evidence that, in so far as the Christians were concerned, there was a dramatic improvement or worsening of the situation for them before or after AD 70. The opposition Jesus faced in the Gospel also seems to have been the experience of many of his followers at the time of the writing of the Gospel.

---

[8] 'The Beloved Disciple and Implied Readers', *BTB* 19 (1989), 100. Culpepper, in *Anatomy of the Fourth Gospel* (Philadelphia: Fortress, 1983), 205–27, was among the first to examine the idea of the implied reader. Although J. L. Staley in *The Print's First Kiss: A Rhetorical Investigation of the Implied Reader in the Fourth Gospel* (Atlanta: Scholars Press, 1988), 13–15, criticised Culpepper for failing to distinguish adequately between 'implied' and 'intended' readers. Cf. Grant Osborne, *The Hermeneutical Spiral: A Comprehensive Introduction to Biblical Interpretation* (Downers Grove: Inter-Varsity Press, 1991), 162f.

4.1.2. The Purpose of the Gospel as Viewed in the Early Church

In the early history of the church, the purpose of the Gospel was seen, not as standing alone, but in relation to the first three Gospels. Clement believed that John was intended to be a spiritual Gospel (πνευματικὸν εὐαγγέλιον) to supplement the Synoptics which concentrated upon bodily facts (τὰ σωματικά). Many expositions of John's purpose developed from this dictum of Clement.[9] Undoubtedly, the mystical language of John was explained in light of this spiritual character. Chrysostom and Origen believed that the author's privileged position in the circle of disciples as the 'Beloved Disciple' gave him intimate insight into the mind of the Master. Chrysostom noted Jesus' special love for John, which earned him the title of 'Beloved Disciple', to be of great importance in providing a clue towards the character and intention of the Evangelist's work. Chrysostom believed that this love was the essential motive of John to write the Gospel.[10] Origen found the most vivid portrayal of this intimacy in the picture of John reclining on the bosom of Jesus at the last supper. Just as the only begotten Son was in 'the bosom of the Father' and that enabled him to reveal God to men, so John's reclining upon the bosom of Jesus symbolises his ability to declare the deepest truth of the Gospel. He argued that the paramount purpose of the Gospel of John is to make absolutely clear the divinity of Jesus.[11] Theodore of Mopsuestia thought the emphasis upon the divinity of the Lord for posterity provided the impetus for the writing.[12] In modern times, the procedure for determining the purpose of the Gospel has followed a complex and highly speculative reconstruction of its original social-historical setting.[13]

---

[9] *Paidagogos und stromateis*, ed. by O. Stählin, GCS (Leipzig: Hinrichs, 1905), 9; Eusebius, *Historia ecclesiastica*, 6.14.7.

[10] John Chrysostom, *Opera*, Patrologia Graeca, curus completus, ed. by J. P. Migne, 2:I. *The Homilies of St. John Chrysostom on the Gospel of St. John*, Parts 1 & 2 (Oxford, 1848).

[11] *The Commentary of Origen on St. John's Gospel*, ed. by A. E. Brooke (Cambridge: University Press, 1896), 32, 20.

[12] Theodore of Mopsuestia, *Corpus Scriptorum Christianorum Orientalium.*: Scriptores Syri, Series 4, Tomus III, interpretatus est, J. M. Vosté (Louvain, 1940), 3:16–4:8, believed that the Christians of Asia recognised that the omission of certain miracles and certain elements of teaching might lead future generations of men to lose sight of Christ's divinity. It was to rule out the possibility of any such misapprehensions in the future that John undertook his task of writing.

[13] But even as late as the 1920s, J. H. Bernard, *A Critical and Exegetical Commentary on the Gospel According to St. John*, ICC, 2 vols (Edinburgh: Clark, 1928), cxxxv, could say, 'The conception of the purpose of John in his Gospel marks a different standpoint between the earlier evangelists and the last. John is anxious to prove the truth of Jesus in the flesh, and at a time when He had been the object of Christian worship for more than half a century. Christian reflection and Christian experience had reached a doctrine of the person of Christ which had not been clearly

4.2. John's Stated Purpose

The statement of John 20:30–31 seems to be the author's own stated purpose for writing:

Πολλὰ μὲν οὖν καὶ ἄλλα σημεῖα ἐποίησεν ὁ Ἰησοῦς ἐνώπιον τῶν μαθητῶν [αὐτοῦ], ἃ οὐκ ἔστιν γεγραμμένα ἐν τῷ βιβλίῳ τούτῳ· 31 ταῦτα δὲ γέγραπται ἵνα πιστεύ[σ]ητε ὅτι Ἰησοῦς ἐστιν ὁ Χριστὸς ὁ υἱὸς τοῦ θεοῦ, καὶ ἵνα πιστεύοντες ζωὴν ἔχητε ἐν τῷ ὀνόματι αὐτοῦ,

Jesus did many other signs in the presence of the disciples, which are not written in this book; v. 31 but these are written that you may believe that Jesus is the Christ, the Son of God, and that believing you may have life in his name.

Several additional statements (e.g., 1:12, 34, 41; 3:16, 36; 5:39; 7:37–38; etc.) further reinforce John 20:30–31. The messianic identity of Jesus is at the forefront of the Gospel beginning with the first chapter where Jesus is declared to be the Messiah (1:41), the One who was foretold by Moses and the prophets (1:45), Son of God, King of Israel (1:49), and the Son of man (1:51). This is in contrast to Mark, for example, where Jesus as the Messiah is not recognised by men until Mark 8:29. The centrality of Jesus as the Christ in John's purpose statement of 20:30–31 is unquestionable. What is not clear, however, is whether the Evangelist's aim is pastoral with a focus on the church or evangelistic with a call to the 'world'. As Gordon D. Fee points out, 'It is of more than passing interest that the one Gospel which has an explicit statement of purpose should also be the Gospel for which there has been such little agreement within scholarship as to its purpose.'[14]

The construction μὲν οὖν, loosely rendered 'therefore', is not given to straight-forward translation. The particle μέν is scarcely translatable. In Luke/Acts, μὲν οὖν is a common resumptive particle, but in John 20:30 μέν in the context of δέ introducing v. 31 seems to frame the thought in verses 30, 31: *On the one hand,* there are doubtless many more signs Jesus did that could have been reported, but on *the other,* these have been recorded so that you may believe (cf. 19:24–25, 32–33).[15] Furthermore μὲν

---

thought out by Christians in the first enthusiasms of devotion to their master. The synoptists draw a picture of Jesus as viewed by his contemporaries; the Fourth Gospel is a profound study of that picture, bringing into full view what may not have been clearly discerned at first.'

[14] G. D. Fee, 'On the Text and Meaning of John 20:30–31', in *The Four Gospels 1992*, ed. by F. van Segbroeck, C. M. Tuckett, et al., vol. 3 (Leuven: Leuven University Press, 1992), 2193.

[15] D. A. Carson, *The Gospel According to John* (Leicester, England: InterVarsity Press, 1991), 661.

οὖν connects John 20:30–31 either to the immediately preceding account – the events of the resurrection – or the whole of the Gospel.[16]

For the early Church, the resurrection is the ultimate proof of the truthfulness of Jesus' words about himself. It renders credible all that he had said and claimed to be. On the other hand, throughout the Gospel, the Evangelist believes Jesus' words and works served the same purpose. Thus there is no compelling reason to decide between the two options. Both reaffirm the same objective and John may have had both in view. The ὅτι clause which follows in 20:31 gives the content to πιστεύητε. The faith of which John writes is not an intellectual 'lip service' or a simple acknowledgement. Chapters 13–21 of the Gospel determine the precise implication of this faith as the laying down of one's own life for others. This faith is supernatural faith brought about through the activities of the Spirit of God within the inner-most being of the one who believes. The fruit of such a faith is the supernatural ability to love as Jesus loved and to live as Jesus lived.

The next question is the tense of the verb in 20:31 and the prolonged debate concerning the present or aorist subjunctive, πιστεύητε or πιστεύσητε.[17] John 20:30–31 is one of only two occasions when the author directly addresses the reader. On the other occasion, 19:35, the address also relates to the purpose of writing, ἵνα καὶ ὑμεῖς πιστεύ[σ]ητε, and there too we encounter the same textual uncertainty about the tense of the verb. In John 20:31, the textual evidence is evenly divided[18] as to whether we should read πιστεύητε, present subjunctive[19] or πιστεύσητε, aorist subjunctive.[20] The former strictly interpreted is taken to mean *in order that you may (continue to) believe*, suggesting that the Gospel was written to deepen faith in those who already have it – Christians – and to encourage them to persevere in the face of opposition. The aorist subjunctive might be taken to mean *in order that you may (come to)*

---

[16] The relationship between the end of John 20 and John 21 is a complex issue. John 20:30–31 clearly has the tone of a conclusion, yet it is followed by another chapter. Those who believe that John incorporated a 'signs source' understand verses 30–31 as the conclusion of that hypothetical document. However, there is no reason why the author could not have written the last chapter as a concluding excursus himself. For a review of this question, see Brown, *John*, 1057–61, 1077–82. See also Minear, 'The Original Functions of John 21', *JBL* 102 (1983), 85–98.

[17] Brown, *John*, 2:1056–61; Bultmann, *John*, 698; Barrett, *St. John*, 575; Lindars, *John*, 617; Schnackenburg, *St. John*, 3:337–9.

[18] B. M. Metzger, *A Textual Commentary on the Greek New Testament* (New York: United Bible Society, 1971), 256.

[19] Supported by P^{66vid}, ℵ*, B, Θ, 0250, 892^{supp}.

[20] Attested by ℵ^c, A, C, D, K, L, W, X, Δ, Π, Ψ, 0100, f^1, f^{13}, 33, 565, and others.

believe, suggesting the purpose of writing was to bring non-Christians to accept Jesus as the Christ, that is, to engender faith in those who do not yet believe.[21] Even though the difficulty seems to revolve around a textual problem, yet the resolution of the textual variant itself is not determinative and cannot be achieved with certainty.[22] The present subjunctive does not necessarily exclude the possibility of the author's wish that those with 'shallow' faith (e.g., 2:23–25) come to genuine belief. On the other hand, the aorist subjunctive, because it is an a-temporal 'tense', by itself may not be sufficient to rule out growth in faith.[23] Elsewhere in his Gospel, John uses *either* tense to refer to both *coming* to faith and *continuing* in the faith.[24] Therefore the solution should be sought in the whole thrust of the Gospel.

4.3. A Record for Posterity

These two interpretive possibilities also reflect the division among Johannine scholars: those who see the primary purpose of the Gospel as pastoral and those who see it as evangelistic. Between the two camps lie numerous other proposals which eventually side with one of the two interpretive possibilities expressed in John 20:31. Before considering these two options, we need clarification regarding the target audience. The purpose statement of John's Gospel contains the word 'you'. Who are the addressees?[25] The extensive reliance of the Fourth Gospel upon the Old Testament presupposes a readership steeped in scriptural knowledge and

---

[21] Although the textual evidence is spread evenly, the majority of recent commentators prefer the present subjunctive. See the influential essay of H. Riesenfeld, 'Zu den johanneische ἵνα-Sätzen', *ST* 19 (1965), 213–20; cf. D. A. Carson's criticism of Riesenfeld in 'The Purpose of the Fourth Gospel: John 20:31 Reconsidered', *JBL* 106 (1987), 641.

[22] W. G. Kümmel, *Einleitung in das Neue Testament*, 17th edn (Heidelberg: Quelle und Meyer, 1973), 194; Barrett, *St John*, 134, 575. Cf. Gordon Fee, 'On the Text and Meaning of John 20:30–31', 2193–205, has taken issue with this conclusion and has argued that the textual question of 20:31 can be resolved with certainty. He argues that πιστεύητε (present subjunctive) is meaningful grammatically for John and he concludes: 'There can be little question that the present subjunctive is the original text in both 19:35 and 20:31.'

[23] Schnackenburg, *St John*, 3:338.

[24] That a distinction exists between the two tenses is amply illustrated by 10:38, γνῶτε καὶ γινώσκητε. But in 6:29, the present subjunctive (πιστεύητε) is used as a composite term to cover both *initial* and *continuing* faith. See Carson, 'Purpose of the Fourth Gospel', 640. There is textual uncertainty in 6:29 also. But the better reading seems to be the present subjunctive.

[25] See H. B. Kosten, *Studies in John* (Leiden: Brill, 1970), 98–110; Robert Kysar, *The Fourth Evangelist and His Gospel: An Examination of Contemporary Scholarship* (Minneapolis: Augsburg Pub. House, 1975), 9–81.

its exegesis, i.e., most naturally a Jewish audience. However, the Evangelist's compulsion to transliterate *Messias* in 1:41, or to explain the rite of purification in 2:6, has become a 'red herring'[26] leading to endless debate about the possible target audience of the Gospel.[27]

4.3.1. The Jewish Readership

The subtle references to minute cultic details, the Old Testament themes, imageries, allusions, and theological assumptions, all in all have led many scholars to conclude that the Fourth Gospel assumes a readership well-grounded in Old Testament knowledge. The most likely audience would have been the Jews since much of the information in the text presupposes a knowledge of the Hebrew Scripture and its theology.[28] Indeed, in spite of

---

[26] Culpepper, *Anatomy*, 221, asks, 'If the readership is Jewish, why are the translations supplied?' But this question may be turned around, 'If the readership is Gentile, why are the Hebrew originals used at all?' Both these questions overlook a heterogeneous audience. Carson, 'Purpose of the Fourth Gospel', 646, commenting on the translation of Semitic words (e.g., 1:38, 41; 4:25; 19:13, 17) and the suggestion that these translations presuppose a non-Jewish readership, believes this conclusion confuses race, religion, and linguistic competence. He argues, 'A Greek-speaking Jew with no knowledge of Hebrew or Aramaic might well appreciate the translations.' However would a Greek-speaking Jew in the Diaspora have been so detached from his own language and culture that he would have needed the translation of the title 'Messiah'? Would he have needed to know about the laws regarding purification (2:6) or needed an explanation about the burial customs of his own people (19:40)? It seems to me the most natural aim of these translations would have been for the benefit of the Gospel's Gentile audience and for the benefit of the future generations of Christians who would read the Gospel.

[27] Carson, 'Purpose of the Fourth Gospel', 644–5, has suggested one method of determining the potential readership is to pose the following questions: Was the Evangelist addressing, 'Who is the Christ?' or was he setting forth 'Who is Jesus?' The response to the first would have been: 'Christ/Messiah is Jesus rather than X or Y.' This, according to Carson, assumes a Jewish readership. But he is unsure about the grammatical correctness of this option. The response to the second question would have been: 'Jesus is the Christ', which assumes a wider audience. Further it is suggested that the latter is both consistent with the tenor of the Gospel and syntactically more in line with its Greek. However, J. V. Brownson, in 'John 20:31 and the Purpose of the Fourth Gospel', *RefRev* 48 (1995), 212–16, has pointed out John's habit of using the definite article with titles in the predicate with εἰμί and has argued that this makes the traditional reading of John 20:31, 'Jesus is the Messiah, the Son of God' more natural than Carson's proposal.

[28] Jesus' self-identification with elements of the Jewish feasts, veiled references to Old Testament events understood as foreshadowings of events in Jesus' life, ministry, death, and resurrection; or the lack of an explanation for terms such as 'the Son of man', 'the Prophet' (1:21, 25; 6:14), the devil (13:2) or Satan (13:27), or when Jesus presents himself as in line with or in fulfilment of such figures as Jacob (1:51) and Moses (3:14; 5:46), all of these assume an audience steeped in Old Testament knowledge. Hartwig Thyen, 'Das Heil Kommt von den Juden', in *Kirche. Festschrift für G. Bornkamm zum 75. Geburtstag*, ed. by D Lühremann and G. Strecker (Tübingen: Mohr-Seibeck, 1980), 174; Stephen S. Smalley, *Thunder and Love: John's Revelation and John's Community* (Milton Keynes, UK: Nelson Word, 1994), 124. But compare H. Thyen, 'Johannes 10 im Kontext des vierten Evangeliums', in *The Shepherd Discourse of John 10 and its Context: Studies by members of the Johannine writings seminar*, ed. by J. Beutler and R. T.

the conflict with the synagogue, the Jews still may have been one of the primary targets of the Johannine mission. Here the Gospel may have had in view the secret Christian Jews (cf. 12:42)[29] or Christian Jews in danger of reverting to Judaism. The epistle to the Hebrews reveals the pressure upon Jewish Christians to return to Judaism. For others, loyalty to their Jewish heritage or theological issues (e.g., strong monotheism) may have been an obstacle.[30] After the fall of Jerusalem in AD 70, Jewish Christians may have faced intense pressure from fellow non-Christian Jews in the dispersion to reject Jesus as the Messiah. John's references to the 'Greeks' and the 'Dispersion among the Greeks' (cf. 7:35) have prompted scholars such as W. C. van Unnik to argue that the Jews in the Diaspora were indeed the target audience of the Gospel. Van Unnik even asserts that 'the other sheep' in John 10:16 is a reference to Jews in the Diaspora[31] rather than a general reference to those who have not yet believed in Jesus or a reference to Gentile mission.[32] Some scholars have even gone so far as to argue that the Gospel was written in Greek for the benefit of the Jews in the Diaspora. However, Greek was the lingua-franca of the time, and many

---

Fortna, SNTSMS 67 (Cambridge: CUP, 1991), 121; Rodney Whitacre, *Johannine Polemic: The Role of Tradition and Theology*, SBLDS 67 (Chico, CA: Scholars Press, 1982), 11; W. D. Davies, *The Gospel and the Land: Early Christianity and Jewish Territorial Doctrine* (Berkeley: University of California Press, 1974), 288–335.

[29] The Nicodemus episode in conjunction with the chastisement in John 12:42 may indicate that hope was still held that the secret Christian Jews would come to a full and open confession of Jesus as the Messiah, just as the preceding passage on John the Baptist may have been an appeal to his disciples. Christianity and its radical claims challenge the entire existing system of Judaism. Therefore the Gospel may have been addressing itself to the confusion of those who would have wondered, 'How can a Jew become a Christian without ceasing to be a Jew?' See S. J. Tanzer, 'Salvation is for the Jews: Secret Christian Jews in the Gospel of John', in *The Future of Early Christianity: Essays in Honor of Helmut Koester*, ed. by B. A. Pearson (Minneapolis: Fortress, 1991), 285–300.

[30] J. A. T. Robinson, 'The Destination and Purpose of St John's Gospel', in *Twelve New Testament Studies* (London: SCM, 1962), 113, argues that a comparison between John and Paul shows that the important contrast for John was not Jews-Gentiles, but Jewish Christians and non-Christian Jews.

[31] W. C. van Unnik, 'The Purpose of St. John's Gospel', SE 1 = TU 73 (1959), 407–8. Robinson, 'Destination', 107–25, points to the Old Testament background (i.e., Ezk. 34:37; Jer. 23:31) to the gathering of the dispersed Jews to support the same position as van Unnik (p. 121). For Robinson, the prophecy of Caiphas (11:52) is of particular importance. He interprets the words 'the whole nation' and 'the scattered children of God' to refer to the Diaspora Jews. The reference to the Greeks in John 12:20f and the careful collection of the pieces of bread into twelve baskets (6:12f) are also seen as symbolically pointing in the same direction. Cf. H. Mulder, 'Ontstaan en Doel van het vierde Evangelie', in *Geref. Theol. Tijdschrift* 69 (1969), 251; Carson, 'Purpose of the Fourth Gospel', 646.

[32] Mulder, 'Ontstaan en Doel', 237.

Palestinian Jews would have been bilingual, if not trilingual.[33] Therefore, such evidence is not conclusive enough to point in any particular direction.

Immediately after chapters two and three and the hesitation of the Jews about Jesus, the Evangelist records the account of the receptivity of the Samaritans. This is seen by some Johannine scholars as an indication that the Samaritans may have been an important audience of the Gospel.[34] This would have not been an unlikely attitude for the early church which believed that the lines of demarcation were removed in Christ. The inclusion of the Samaritan account in the Gospel may have added a further polemical criticism of 'the Jews' in that while the Samaritans were able to recognise Jesus as the promised Messiah, the children of the promise were blind to him (cf. Mt. 4:13-16). It is plausible that the Samaritans as a group were an important element of the Johannine audience.

All things considered, there is not sufficient evidence to warrant narrowing the readership of the Gospel to a particular segment of the Jewish people. What can be asserted with some confidence is that the Gospel does address itself to the Jews in general.[35] They would have been

---

[33] R. Buth, 'Language Use in the First Century: Spoken Hebrew in a Trilingual Society in the Time of Jesus', *Journal of Translation and Textlinguistics* 5 (1992), 298–312; J. W. Voelz, 'The Linguistic Milieu of the Early Church', *Concordia Theological Quarterly* 56 (1992), 81–97; S. Safrai, 'Spoken Languages in the Time of Jesus', *Jerusalem Perspective* 3 (1991), 3–8; C. Tresmontant, *The Hebrew Christ: Language in the Age of the Gospels*, trans. by K. D. Whitehead (Chicago: Franciscan Herald Press, 1989); Matthew Black, 'The Biblical Languages', in *Cambridge History of the Bible* (Cambridge: CUP, 1970), 1:1–11.

[34] James D. Purvis, 'The Fourth Gospel and the Samaritans', *NovT* 17 (1975), 161–98; Teresa Okure, *The Johannine Approach to Mission: A Contextual Study of John 4:1–42*, WUNT 2.31 (Tübingen: Mohr-Siebeck, 1988); Wayne A. Meeks, '"Am I a Jew?" – Johannine Christianity and Judaism', in *Christianity, Judaism and Other Greco-Roman Cults*, ed. by Jacob Neusner, 4 vols, SJLA 12 (Leiden: Brill, 1975), 1:176–8; O. Cullmann, *Der Johanneische Kreis. Sein Platz im Spätjudentum, in der Jüngerschft Jesu und im Urchristentum. Zum Ursprung des Johannesevangeliums* (Tübingen: Mohr-Siebeck, 1975), 39–40, 49–52. There is considerable variation among these positions (and others cited especially by Purvis) regarding the exact extent of Samaritan involvement in the Johannine community and the Fourth Gospel.

[35] This was the view of Karl Bornhäuser, *Das Johannesevangelium: Eine Missionsschrift für Israel*, BFCTh 2/15 (Gütersloch: C. Bertelsmann, 1928). See also Takashi Onuki's dissertation, *Gemeinde und Welt im Johannesevangelium: Ein Beitrag zur Frage nach der theologischen und pragmatischen Funktion des johanneischen 'Dualismus'*, WMANT 56 (Neukirchen-Vluyn: Neukirchener Verlag, 1984). A. Wind, 'Destination and Purpose of the Gospel of John', *NovT* 14 (1972), 43, believes that the expression 'Jesus is the Christ' has its roots in the Christian mission among the Jews as exemplified in Justin's *Dialogue* or the works of Hegesippus and the Christian apologists of the second century; cf. Eusebius, H. E. 2.23.8–10. See also Oscar Holtzmann, *Das Neue Testament nach dem Stuttgarter griechischen Text übersetzt und erklärt II: V Das Evangelium des Johannes* (Giessen: Alfred Töpelmann, 1926), 961. Here Holtzmann argues for a dependence of some sort between John and Justin's *Apology* and compares *Apology* 1.61.4–5 with John 3:4 and *Apology* 1.32.8–18 with John 1:12–14. Like Wind and Holtzmann, Riesenfeld acknowledges that Justin's *Dialogue* serves a missionary purpose ('Zu den johanneischen ἵνα-Sätzen'). See also

an important part of the Gospel's intended audience. The Messianic claims and identity of Jesus is at the heart of the Johannine message. The audience for whom this message would have been of pivotal importance and most meaningful were the Jews. But John also addresses his Gospel to a much wider audience among whom there would have been Gentiles as well.

4.3.2. The Gentile Readership

Because of its numerous references to the Old Testament, John's Gospel would have been most meaningful for the Jews . However, the Gospel would have been as meaningful to a Gentile readership with biblical sophistication. The Old Testament was the Scripture of the early church. Early Christian communities often included Gentile believers who of necessity would have been familiar with the Old Testament. In fact, C. H. Dodd took the view that the Gospel was primarily a missionary work addressed to Gentiles. He noted, 'We are to think of the work as addressed to a wide public consisting primarily of devout and thoughtful persons...in the varied and cosmopolitan society of a great Hellenistic city such as Ephesus under the Roman Empire.'[36]

In contrast to Dodd, Robinson argues that in John the Gentiles do not come into the picture nearly as often as they do in the Synoptics because the Fourth Gospel was not directed towards Gentiles.[37] He proposes that when the Evangelist mentions 'the Greeks', he means the Greek-speaking Diaspora-Jews in their relation to the synagogue.[38] Robinson argues that in John the term 'the Jews' occurs at least 70 times. Nowhere, however, are 'the Gentiles' mentioned *expressis verbis*. He observes that Jesus is the Revelation for Israel (1:31); instead of the Syro-Phoenician woman in the Synoptics, we read about a Samaritan woman who still may say: 'our father Jacob' (Jn. 4:12). Instead of the healing of the son of the Roman centurion, we find the son of the royal officer, perhaps a Jew, a Herodian (Jn. 4:46–54); the only Roman who plays a role is Pilate.[39] However, Mulder

---

P. Winter, 'Z. Verständins d. Joh. ev.', *Vox Theol.* 25 (1955), 149–57; von Unnik, 'Purpose of St. John's Gospel', 382–411; R. M. Grant, 'The Origin of the Fourth Gospel', *JBL* 69 (1950), 305–22; T. C. Smith, *Jesus in the Gospel of John: A Study of the Evangelist's Purpose and Meaning* (Nashville: Broadmans, 1959); E. P. Groenewald, 'The Christological Meaning of John 20:31', *Neot* 2 (1968), 131–40.

[36] C. H. Dodd, *The Interpretation of the Fourth Gospel* (Cambridge: CUP, 1953), 9.

[37] Robinson, 'Destination', 110.

[38] Ibid., 111ff., 116ff.

[39] Ibid., 113f; cf. Mulder, 'Ontstaan en Doel', 237.

attributes this difference between John and the Synoptics to the Jewish war and its decisive impact in causing a negative attitude toward the Gentiles. In this scenario John simply reflects this post-war situation since he wrote after the War and the Synoptics were written before.[40] Although according to Robinson's criteria, *expressis verbis*, it is true that Gentiles rarely come into the picture in the Fourth Gospel, nevertheless, they are very much in the background (10:16; 17:21-23; cf. 1:12a; 3:16; 12:32, 46, etc.).[41] Also Mulder's observation about the Jewish war and the change of attitude towards Gentiles is not the whole truth. The Jews had encountered the heavy hand of the Gentiles, including Rome, long before the war of AD 70. There is no reason to think that Rome's brutal suppression of the Jews in the events of the AD 70 would have intensified their negative attitude toward Gentiles. Furthermore, John's frequent use of the term 'world' on those occasions where it means 'all' (e.g., Jn. 1:19, 29; 3:16f; 12:32), in conjunction with sporadic translations and explanations of Hebrew terminology (e.g., 1:38, 41-42; 4:25; 9:7; 19:13, 17; 20:16, 24), and customs (e.g., 2:9; 4:9; 19:40) or the strained relations that existed between Jews and Samaritans (4:9), is an indication that he anticipated a wider hearing, reading and dispersion of his document. In addition, the overall universal tone and perspective of John's Gospel (e.g., 1:12; 3:16, 17; 12:47; cf. 1:29; 4:42; 7:35; 12:20-22) militates against narrowing its audience only to the Jews.[42]

If Gentiles are indeed one of the target groups of the Fourth Evangelist, what kind of Gentiles might they have been? Naturally, there are many proposals. Some Johannine scholars have suggested that John is addressing an audience who may have had little exposure to Christianity and its Old Testament theological foundations. They would have been preoccupied by the meaning and significance of Jewish Messiahship. Groenewald argues that the appositional 'the Son of God' in 20:31 is for the benefit of these.[43] However, this explanation assumes a Hellenistic background for 'the Son of God' while in fact the richness of the Old Testament background and John's reliance upon the Old Testament

---

[40] Mulder, 'Ontstaan en Doel', 236f.

[41] Raymond E. Brown, '"Other Sheep Not of This Fold": The Johannine Perspective on Christian Diversity in the Late First Century', *JBL* 97 (1978), 5-22.

[42] O. Cullmann, *Der Johanneische Kreis*, 50, and *passim*; Brown, *Community of the Beloved*, 55-8; Barrett, *St. John*, 325, 420-1; Schnackenburg, *St. John*, 2:150; cf. Robinson, 'Destination', 112, 116.

[43] Groenewald, 'Christological Meaning of John 20:31'.

disallows Groenwald's thesis.⁴⁴ This group, as Carson has correctly noted, would seem to be the least likely of all the suggested Johannine target audiences.⁴⁵ Such scepticism does not mean that if someone of such a background read or heard the Gospel, he would not have benefited or even come to believe in Jesus. Neither does it mean that the Evangelist was not concerned to reach this group with the Christian message. It simply means that the immense complexities and subtleties of the Gospel themes would not have engaged this audience since they would have been oblivious to

---

⁴⁴ Major scholarly battles have been fought over the background and meaning of 'Son of God'. In no other New Testament document is the title 'Son of God' as important as in John. This expression first occurs as a confession by Nathanael in John 1:49. The metaphoric use of 'Son of God' in the Old Testament may refer to: the nation (Exod. 4:22–23; Deut. 1:31; 32:6; Jer. 31:9, 20; Hos. 11:1), the Israelite King (2 Sam. 7:14; Ps. 2:7). The 'Son of God' is one who resembles God. The Hebrew language does not have as many adjectives as do some languages. It compensates for the lack by a variety of idiomatic structures including 'Son of God'. Thus 'a wicked man' might be called 'a son of wickedness' (Ps. 89:22); people in trouble are 'sons of affliction' (Prov. 31:5); valorous men are 'sons of valour' (Deut. 3:18). Those deserving execution are 'sons of death' (1 Sam. 26:16); Judas Iscariot can be called the 'son of perdition' (cf. notes on Jn. 17:12). The peacemakers are called 'sons of God' (Mt. 5:9). In later Jewish literature, the 'righteous' are spoken of as God's sons, e.g., *Jubilees* 1:24–25; *Wisdom of Solomon* 2:18; *Ecclesiasticus* 4:10. But the use of 'Son of God' to designate the Messiah ultimately depends on passages such as 1 Sam. 26:17, 21, 25; 2 Sam. 7:14 and Ps. 2:7 (linking sonship and Davidic royalty). The link is retained in Jewish literature (e.g., 1 Enoch 105:2; 4 Ezra 7:28–29; 13:52; 14:9). In 4Q Florilegium (which is pre-Christian) 'Son of God' is another description of the Branch of David (4QFl 1:11–12; 1QSa 2:11ff.). Of the eleven occurrences of 'Son of God' in John, in three passages, the title parallels Messiah or Christ (1:49; 11:27; 20:31), in one, it is connected with the resurrection, a decidedly Jewish notion (5:25), and two relate to the Old Testament Jewish tradition (10:36; 19:7). Even the remaining five are comprehensible within a Jewish framework. The readers of John's Gospel will learn quickly that the categories 'Son' and 'Son of God' are used to depict the unique relation of oneness and intimacy between Jesus and the Father. Jesus' sonship to God, however functionally described, involves a metaphysical, not merely a Messianic, relationship (cf. Jn. 5:16–30; 10:33). Thus the expression 'Son of God' functioned for the Jews, as here, as a rough synonym for 'Christ' or 'Messiah'. See further M. Hengel, *The Son of God* (London: SCM, 1976); R. Bauckham, 'The Sonship of the Historical Jesus in Christology', *JTS* n.s. 31 (1978), 245ff.; John Howton, '"Son of God" in the Fourth Gospel', *NTS* 10 (1963–64), 227–37; F. J. Moloney, 'The Johannine Son of God', *Salesianum* 38 (1976), 71–86; E. Pinto, 'Jesus, Son of God, in the Fourth Gospel', *Bible Today* 21 (1983), 393–8; A. Schilson, 'Jesus Christus – Gottes Sohn', *BK* 34 (1979), 12–17; M. C. Tenney, 'The Concept of Sonship in the Fourth Gospel', in *New Testament Essays in Honor of Ray Summers in His 65th Year*, ed. by H. L. Drumwright and C. Vaughan (Waco: Markhan Press Foundation of Baylor University Press, 1975), 43–54; O. Michel, *TDNT* 2/2 (1971), 1166–75; Barrett, *St. John*, 185–6; J. McPolin, 'The "Name" of the Father and of the Son in the Johannine Writings: An Exegetical Study of the Johannine Texts on Onoma with Reference to the Father and the Son' (Diss. Rome: Pont. Biblical Institute, 1971); Schnackenburg, '"The Son as Jesus" Self-Designation in the Gospel of John', in *St. John*, 2:172–86, 482–5; H. B. Bonsall, *The Son of God and the Word of God in the Setting of John's Gospel* (London: Christian Literature Crusade, 1982 [1972]); E. Pinto, 'Jesus the Son and Giver of Life in the Fourth Gospel' (Diss., Rome: Pont. University Urbaniana, 1981).

⁴⁵ Carson, 'Purpose of the Fourth Gospel', 645–6.

such nuances. Ironically, however, throughout the centuries, John's Gospel has been indeed instrumental in the conversion of such people.

Some scholars have suggested John may have had in view proselytes and God-fearers since they would have had considerable exposure to the Old Testament. For them, the Messianic identity of Jesus would have been of similar importance as for the Jews with whom they had come to share a common faith.[46] The Johannine explanatory remarks where the author defines a Hebrew term or explains a custom may have been specially for the benefit of this group.[47] Others have thought that John is addressing his Gospel to Gentile or even Jewish Christians deeply influenced by docetism.[48] The antidocetic undercurrent in the First Epistle of John is said to support the argument.[49] However, although this issue has been intensely debated, the evidence in the Gospel itself is not conclusive enough to point in this direction. It is quite doubtful whether John's intentions were either to defend or attack a docetic christology.[50]

There are several variations of the proposal in which the purpose of John's Gospel is linked specifically to the Johannine community – a community gathered around the Beloved Disciple.[51] Many of those who hold to this view see the Fourth Gospel as echoing the conflict with the synagogue. If such a community did indeed exist, it is likely that it would

---

[46] Ibid.

[47] Culpepper, *Anatomy*, 219–22; M. C. Tenney, 'The Footnotes of John's Gospel', *BibSac* 117 (1960), 352–4; cf. Tanzer, 'Salvation is for the Jews', 285–300.

[48] For example, we know Nicolatianism in relation to docetism was practised at Pergamum (Rev. 2:6, 15). Ignatius, Bishop of Antioch, writing to the church at Smyrna (not too far from Pergamum) about AD 110 spends much energy in denouncing the docetism which he found there (Ignatius, Smyrna 2–5). Also, according to Ignatius, Judaising tendencies were apparent in Philadelphia (Ignatius, Philad 6).

[49] Cf. Carson, 'Purpose of the Fourth Gospel', 644–5; Ernest Käsemann, *The Testament of Jesus: A Study of the Gospel of John in the Light of Chapter 17* (Philadelphia:Fortress, 1981; London: SCM, 1968). For a refutation of Käsemann's argument, see Martin Hengel, 'The Old Testament in the Fourth Gospel', in *The Gospels and the Scriptures of Israel*, ed. by C. A. Evans and W. R. Stegner, JSNTSup 104 (Sheffield: Sheffield Academic Press, 1994), 384; also Marianne Thompson, *The Incarnate Word: Perspectives on Jesus in the Fourth Gospel* (Peabody, MA: Hendrickson, 1988).

[50] See M. M. Thompson's critique of Käsemann's *Testament of Jesus*, in *The Incarnate Word*; see also Ashton, *Studying John: Approaches to the Fourth Gospel* (Oxford: Clarendon, 1994), 74ff.

[51] We do not seem to have an overwhelming amount of explicit evidence that such a community existed. In Johannine literature, the word 'church' or a well-developed ecclesiology is absent. The term 'ecclesia' does not appear at all in the Fourth Gospel or in 1 and 2 John. It is used three times in 3 John, twice in connection with Diotrephes, whom the writer wishes to discredit. However, this does not prove or disprove that such a community may have existed.

have been a mixed Jewish and Gentile group.[52] Most scholars place the location of the community in Ephesus to which they believe John, the Beloved Disciple, moved with his followers in the AD 50s.[53] Some have suggested that the Gospel was written to address christological confusion in the community – a confusion precipitated in part by the heterogeneous nature of the group.[54] But it is difficult to see how this Gospel with all its complexities could have addressed such a confusion without actually adding to it. Some of the present day theological controversies centred on the christology of the Fourth Gospel illustrate the point all too well.[55]

4.3.3. The Universal Appeal of the Fourth Gospel

The dilemma of determining the readership of the Fourth Gospel with such narrow definitions seems unnecessary because the language of the Gospel is too universal in its appeal and address.[56] For the Evangelist 'the world' (i.e., humanity in its entirety) is God's object of love (3:16) and this 'world' is the sphere of the believing community's mission. The scope of Jesus' own salvific mission is the whole world (1:9, 10a; 16:28). He is the light that shines in the world, enlightening every man by his coming into the world. In John, all those who believe Jesus is the Christ become children of God, *children born not of natural descent, nor of human decision or a husband's will, but born of God* (1:13, cf. 3:6; 12:46). In this new order, 'natural descent' (literally, ἐξ αἱμάτων, 'of bloods', *i.e.*, a blood relationship) is of no significance – which means cultural heritage and race are

---

[52] Klaus Berger's proposal, in *Exegese des Neuen Testaments: Neue Wege vom Text zur Auslegung* (Heidelberg: Quelle und Meyer, 1977), 230f, is perhaps closest to the actual reality and it is in many ways the working of an ancient idea set forth by Clement. Berger suggests that the Fourth Gospel presupposes the Synoptics and tries to initiate the readers into a deeper understanding of what they already know of Jesus. He concludes that John's Gospel had a much wider appeal and served the integration of several groups with different backgrounds.

[53] Sjef van Tilborg, *Reading John in Ephesus*, NovTSup 83 (Leiden: Brill 1996).

[54] Smalley, *Thunder and Love*, 124. Cf. W. F. Howard, *The Fourth Gospel in Recent Criticism and Interpretation*, rev. by C.K. Barrett 4th edn (London: Epworth, 1955 [orig. 1931]), 9.

[55] Compare the formulation of Käsemann, *Testament of Jesus*, in contrast to his teacher Bultmann, *New Testament Theology*, vol. 2 (London: SCM, 1955).

[56] Barrett, *St. John*, 426; Albert Curry Winn, *A Sense of Mission: Guidance from the Gospel of John* (Philadelphia: Westminster Press, 1981), 69–74; José Porfirio Miranda, *Being and the Messiah: The Message of St. John* (Maryknoll, NY: Orbis Books, 1977), 101–2; Onuki, *Gemeinde und Welt im Johannesevangelium;* Käsemann, *Testament of Jesus*, 64; but cf. Klaus Wengst, *Bedrängte Gemeinde und verherrlichter Christus: Der historische Ort des Johannesevangeliums als Schlüssel zu seiner Interpretation*, BTS 5, 2nd edn (Neukirchen-Vluyn: Neukirchener Verlag, 1983), 32–6.

irrelevant to spiritual birth. This inclusive theology would have come as a shock to those Jews who believed that their Jewish heritage and race were central to the salvific promises of God from which the Gentiles were excluded. Therefore in the Fourth Gospel the destined audience of both Jesus and the Evangelist is ultimately 'all flesh' (17:2; cf. 12:32). Nevertheless, such a universal appeal does not deny that the Gospel in its historical setting directly addresses itself to the concerns which would have been of central importance to the Jewish people. Salvation is from the Jews, and the Father seeks [all] those who worship him in spirit and in truth (4:23-24).

There are two issues which are important to recognise in any discussion about an implied and intended audience. First, having a well-defined target audience has become increasingly a requirement imposed in modern times upon writers. But the principle often fails even in the case of contemporary writings, in which case how unjustified is it to impose such a requirement upon a document written two thousand years ago. It is the modern desire for greater precision in every aspect of learning that has imposed the same requirement upon those in the past. An author may wish to write without a well defined pre-determined, intended audience. Or he or she may write to address a wide spectrum of readerships. Secondly, not every element in a given document is necessarily determined by the place, the people, or the occasion. L. T. Johnson has pointed out, 'Reading everything in the Gospel narratives as immediately addressed to a contemporary crisis reduces them to the level of cryptograms, and the evangelists to the level of tractarians.'[57]

Within the context of John's intended audience and his universal outlook, it is also likely that the Evangelist may have written the Gospel with an eye upon future generations of Christians who would not have had any first hand knowledge of what Jesus did, claimed and revealed in his life and work(s). Barrett argues, 'His Gospel must be written: it was no concern of his whether it was also read.'[58] One may modify this statement and say, 'His Gospel must be written. The life-giving message must be

---

[57] L.T. Johnson, 'On Finding the Lukan Community: A Cautious Cautionary Essay', *Society for Biblical Literature 1979 Seminar Paper* (Missoula, Mont.: Scholars, 1979), 1:87–100 (here p. 89); and his recent work, *The Real Jesus: The Misguided Quest for the Historical Jesus and the Truth of the Traditional Gospels* (San Francisco: Harper Collins, 1996). See also J. Riches, 'The Synoptic Evangelists and Their Communities', in *Christian Beginning: Word and Community from Jesus to Post-Apostolic Times*, ed. by J. Becker (Louisville: Westminster/John Knox, 1993), 233–34.

[58] Barrett, *St. John*, 135.

preserved.' In Johannine estimation, this was a record the content of which had to be preserved for posterity which might face the same opposition by the forces of darkness, encounter a similar crisis of faith and unbelief, and be tempted to seek the praise of men rather than the glory that comes from God.[59] It is for this subsequent generation of Christians that he provides his occasional explanations, and again and again directs them back to the Scriptures to verify his record by the witness of the law and the prophets. For this posterity, the witness to Jesus of Nazareth is not in the immediate eye-witness of the Beloved Disciple, or John the Baptist, or the voice from heaven. For these subsequent hearers/readers, the witness to Jesus the Christ is to be found in the pages of the Scriptures of Israel. John wrote a document in one of the most tumultuous periods in the life of the Jewish nation punctuated by a most remarkable event – the birth, death and resurrection of a person whom he believed to be the Messiah. In writing his account, not only is he producing a lasting document, certainly from our point of view, but also in so doing, he summons his immediate readers/hearers as well as readers/hearers of subsequent generations to faith and lasting discipleship in the person whom he believes to be 'the way, the truth, and the life.' The preservation of this message would have been in itself a sufficient motivation for the Evangelist to commit to writing the contents of the Gospel, which would have been nothing more than sheer obedience to the resurrected Lord who instructed his disciples, 'You shall receive power when the Holy Spirit has come upon you; and you shall be my witnesses in Jerusalem and in all Judea and Samaria and to the ends of the earth' (Acts 1:8). The Gospel reflects the 'witness' of John to the risen Lord, a permanent theological record. John wrote the Gospel because he believed he had a life-giving message worthy to be recorded and preserved for future generations of Christians.

4.4. Pastoral Focus But Not Sectarian Perspective

The purpose of John in writing the Gospel seems quite precise (20:31), while application of that purpose, like his intended audience, appears to be broad in scope. Such application generally has been confused with the author's purpose, which in turn has led to an extremely narrow definition of both. While the purpose of the Gospel is to set forth that Jesus is the Christ, the application of this purpose need not be narrowed to either a

---

[59] See my discussion on this topic in chapter six.

pastoral or an evangelistic emphasis because it covers both. Since this purpose and its application is directly linked to John's ambiguous language, further elaboration is necessary.

4.4.1. The Alleged Sectarianism of the Fourth Gospel

A significant movement has emerged since the late 1960s among those arguing for the internal, i.e., pastoral focus of the Gospel. An increasing number of Johannine scholars have argued that the Fourth Gospel is a sectarian document. Various articulations of this hypothesis have in turn strengthened each other and led to the present consensus that the Fourth Gospel has an intensely introverted focus.[60] D. Moody Smith agrees with this commonly held view and writes: 'it can probably be agreed that on any reading of the Gospel and Epistles, there appears a sectarian consciousness, a sense of exclusiveness, a sharp delineation of the community from the world....Comparisons with community consciousness in Qumran, which is likewise related to a fundamental dualism, are entirely apposite and to the point.'[61] David Rensberger maintains,

> Johannine Christianity bears many of the marks of a sect, of a movement that finds light and truth within its own community and falsehood and darkness outside. Precisely this sectarianism sums up the things that seem to render John so intractable for theological interpretation. It emphasises the particularity, and indeed the idiosyncrasy, of this gospel and the community behind it. It points to both the sharp conflicts in which the community was involved and the symbolic universe that apparently distinguished it from much of the rest of early Christianity.[62]

Such conclusions then, in turn, have been read back into the language of John's Gospel as reflecting the language of a sect.

An important component of the sectarian argument is the confidence which some have expressed in the existence of the so-called Johannine community.[63] This somewhat hypothetical community, since the late

---

[60] Ashton, *Studying John*, 71, commenting on Martyn's reconstruction in *The Gospel of John in Christian History* (New York: Ramsey, 1978), acknowledges that Martyn's reading of the Gospel is allegorical, and concludes, 'I shall simply assume it to be broadly correct.'

[61] D. Moody Smith, 'Johannine Christianity: Some Reflections on Its Character and Delineation', *NTS* 21 (1975), 224–48, (here 223–24).

[62] *Overcoming the World: Politics and Community in the Gospel of John* (London: SPCK, 1989), 135–36.

[63] Although Barton, 'Can We Identify the Gospel Audiences?', 174, 176, has questioned the very use of the term *community* as a notoriously ambiguous and ideologically 'loaded' term. See also A. P. Cohen, *The Symbolic Construction of the Community* (Chichester, U.K.: Ellis Horwood, 1985), 11.

1960s, has been one of the most discussed areas of research in the Fourth Gospel.[64] The issue is also related to the question of Johannine redaction as well since each redaction supposedly was destined to meet the needs of a particular audience. We do not have a substantial body of concrete evidence for the existence of such a circle or community. An important problem of method here as elsewhere in Johannine studies (e.g., redactional and sociological reconstructions) seems to be that so much is extrapolated from so very little evidence.[65] The Epistles of John and the Book of Revelation constitute the main sources for possible existence of such a circle. But even based on our knowledge from these sources, we can not assert with certainty that there was such a group because the background, for example, to the Johannine epistles themselves has not been confidently established.[66] Therefore, we may not dogmatically speak of the Johannine community. However, even if there was such a group gathered around the figure of the Beloved Disciple, its existence neither

---

[64] J. L. Martyn, *History and Theology in the Fourth Gospel* (New York: Harper and Row, 1968); Brown, *Community of the Beloved*; R. A. Culpepper, *The Johannine School: An Evaluation of the Johannine-School Hypothesis Based on an Investigation of the Nature of Ancient Schools* (Missoula, MT: Scholars Press, 1975); O. Cullmann, *Der Johanneische Kreis*; ET *The Johannine Circle: Its Place in Judaism, Among the Disciples of Jesus and in Early Christianity – A Study in the Origin of the Gospel of John*, trans. by J. Bowden (London, SCM; Philadelphia: Westminster Press, 1976); J. Becker, *Das Evangelium des Johannes*, Bd. 1, Kapitel 1–10.2. Aufl. Ökumenischer Taschenbuchkommentar zum Neuen Testament, Bd. 4/1 (Gütersloh: Gerd Mohn, 1985), 25–61; Kysar, *Fourth Evangelist*, 83–172; idem, 'Community and Gospel: Vectors in Fourth Gospel Criticism', *Int* 31 (1977), 355–66; A. Yarbro Collins, 'Crisis and Community in John's Gospel', *ThD* 27 (1979), 313–21; J. Bogart, *Orthodox and Heretical Perfectionism in the Johannine Community as Evident in the First Epistle of John*, SBLDS 33 (Missoula, MT: Scholars Press, 1977); Rodney Whitacre, *Johannine Polemic: The Role of Tradition and Theology*, SBLDS 67 (Chico, CA: Scholars Press, 1982); E. S. Fiorenza, 'The Quest for the Johannine School: The Apocalypse and the Fourth Gospel', *NTS* 23 (1976–77), 402–27; Wengst, *Bedrängte Gemeinde;* J. Becker, 'Die Geschichte der johanneischen Gemeinden', *TR* 47 (1982), 305–12. For criticism of the hypothesis, see A. Dauer, 'Schichten im Johannesevangelium als Anzeichen von Entwicklungen in der (den) johanneischen Gemeinde(n) nach G. Richter', in *Die Kraft der Hoffnung*, Festschrift für Alterzbischof D Dr Joseph Schneider zum 80 Geburtstag (Bamberg: St. Otto-Verlag, 1986), 62–83; U. C. von Wahlde, 'Community in Conflict: The History and Social Context of the Johannine Community', *Int* 49 (1995), 379–89; J. S. King, 'Is Johannine Archaelogy Really Necessary?', *EvQ* 56 (1984), 203–11; U. Schnelle, *Antidoketische Christologie im Johannesevangelium* (FRLANT 144, 1987), 11ff., 49ff., 168ff. etc., ET *Antidocetic Christology in the Gospel of John: An Investigation of the Place of the Fourth Gospel in the Johannine School* (Minneapolis: Fortress, 1992); E. Cothenet, 'Les Communautés johanniques', *Esprit et Vie* 107 (1997), 433–40.

[65] Cf. J. W. Pryor, *John, Evangelist of the Covenant People: The Narrative and Themes of the Fourth Gospel* (London: Darton, Longman and Todd, 1992), 7–94.

[66] Brown, 'The Relationship to the Fourth Gospel Shared by the Author of I John and by Opponents', in *Text and Interpretation: Studies in the New Testament Presented to Matthew Black*, ed. by E. Best and R. M. Wilson (Cambridge: CUP, 1979), 57–68.

would have made the Gospel sectarian nor inapplicable to a wider Christian audience or readership. In addition, assuming that there was intense conflict between the synagogue and Christians Jews, there is no evidence to localise this conflict to John nor to assume that such a group would have turned into a sect out of touch with the wider Christian community.

The decade of 1968–1978 saw the publication of several studies which have left a lasting impression upon Johannine research. With these studies, the fate of the Gospel seemed to be sealed as a sectarian writing.[67] Among them, three should be singled out because of their subsequent impact upon the direction that Johannine scholarship has taken in explicating the enigmatic nature of John's language. These three studies are: J. Louis Martyn's 1968 *History and Theology in the Fourth Gospel*;[68] Wayne Meeks's 1972 article, 'The Man From Heaven in Johannine Sectarianism';[69] and Herbert Leroy's 1968 doctoral dissertation, *Rätsel und Missverständnis: Ein Beitrag zur Formgeschichte des Johannesevangeliums*,[70] which was primarily a form-critical examination of Johannine 'misunderstandings' but with important socio-linguistic implications for the Gospel. Both Meeks and Leroy linked John's communal setting to its language as a means for understanding its function.

In these proposals, the Gospel is seen as a document of an introverted community in conflict with Judaism in the post-war AD 70 situation. At first this group was entirely within the Jewish fold. However their Messianic claims about Jesus led to a growing tension with the Jewish religious hierarchy based in Jamnia. This group had come into power in the Jewish community after the first revolt in AD 70. The formation of this power base is relevant in the present study since so many of these

---

[67] However, for an earlier expression of a similar sentiment, see E. Schweizer, 'Der Kirchenbegriff im Evangelium und den Briefen des Johannes', *SE* 1 = TU 73 (1959), 363–81. See also Ernst Käsemann, *Testament of Jesus* (Philadelphia:Fortress, 1981), 38–40, 65–66; D. Moody Smith, 'Johanine Christianity', 1–36, in D. Moody Smith, *Johannine Christianity: Essays on Its Setting, Sources, and Theology* (Columbia, SC: University of South Carolina Press, 1984), 3–4. Originally in *NTS* 21(1976), 222–48; Fernando Segovia, 'The Love and Hatred of Jesus and Johannine Sectarianism', *CBQ* 43 (1981), 258–72.

[68] Ashton, *Understanding the Fourth Gospel* (Oxford: Clarendon, 1991), 107, calls Martyn's work, 'the most important single work on the Gospel since Bultmann's commentary.' See also D. Moody Smith, 'The Contribution of J. Louis Martyn to the Understanding of the Gospel of John', in *The Conversation Continues: Studies in Paul and John*, ed. by R. T. Fortna, et al., J. L. Martyn Festschrift (Nashville: Abingdon, 1990), 293.

[69] *JBL* 91 (1972), 44–72.

[70] BBB 30 (Bonn: Hanstein, 1968).

proposals rely heavily on the post-AD 70 setting of the Gospel and the events at the Council of Jamnia.

Shortly before the destruction of Jerusalem in AD 70, Rabbi Yohanan ben Zakkai went to the Roman camp to obtain permission from the Roman commander to settle in Jamnia and establish a school there. This action was to have an immeasurable lasting consequence for the future of Judaism. During the years which followed the destruction of Jerusalem, the school at Jamnia was to become a highly influential stabilising power base among the Jews who had believed in the invincibility of the Jewish nation (e.g., Sibylline Oracles 3:702–13; 3:755–808).[71] In Pseudo-Philo, it is believed that God would preserve and protect Israel against her enemies, even if she fell into sin.[72] The traumatic events of AD 66–73 would have been a devastating blow to this confidence (cf. II Baruch[73] 14:6–7; 4 Ezra 3:28–36, 6:57). Had the whole covenant purpose of God failed (4 Ezra 7:49; cf. 3:20–27, 4:30, 7:[62]-[72])? This trauma, and indeed the ensuing theological crisis, would have been felt in varying degrees by every Jew who paid the temple tax as an expression of commitment to this symbolic covenant centre of Judaism.[74] It was to this dismal context that Yohanan ben Zakkai and his fellow rabbis endeavoured to apply themselves and reorganise, consolidate, and stabilise Judaism – Judaism which would be dedicated to the cultivation of Torah piety and which could both meet with acceptance from the Romans and ensure the survival of the Jewish people.

In this period, the 'Yavneh academy' attempted to enable the Jewish people to come to terms with the loss of their temple; and they seem to have accomplished it remarkably quickly. One of the means by which they brought about a measure of stability was the introduction of the Eighteen Benedictions into the synagogal liturgy. These Benedictions also contained prayers for the restoration of Jerusalem, the temple, and the house of David. Indeed the rabbinic tradition carefully presented the rules of conduct for the temple against its expected reconstruction. Therefore, underneath, the Messianic hope was not abandoned. The apocalyptic works continued to express vivid anticipation of the Messianic overthrow of Rome (2 *Esdras*

---

[71] Dated by Collins in the period BC 163–145. See *The Old Testament Pseudepigrapha*, ed. by James Charlesworth, 2 vols (London: Darton, Longman and Todd, 1983, 1985), 1:355. All further references to this work will be *OTP*.

[72] Pseudo-Philo 39:4, 6. D. J. Harrington in *OTP*, 2:300.

[73] Syriac Apocalypse of Baruch = II Baruch (Pseudepigrapha).

[74] Michael E. Stone, 'Reactions to the Destruction of the Second Temple: Theology, Perception and Conversion', *JSJ* 12 (1981), 196.

11–13; 2 *Baruch* 39–42; 63; 82).[75] It is significant that 2 *Baruch* looked for the punishment of Rome to be carried out by divine or Messianic action rather than by Jewish military force.

It was also in Jamnia that the long strife between the opposed schools of Shammai and Hillel was brought to an end in favour of the latter. It was in Jamnia that the teachers of the law formed themselves into the great Council of the Bet Din. Gamaliel II, the successor of Johannan ben Zakkai, tried to further consolidate all the Jews into recognising and submitting to the authority of this Council. Gamaliel II, his fellow rabbis, and their immediate disciples (in the period approximately from AD 80 to 140) formed the authorities about which we now speak as 'normative' Judaism.[76] Among the stabilising measures introduced under Gamaliel II were, as I noted earlier, the introduction of the Eighteen Benedictions. Rabbi Shim'on ha-Paqoli is said to have arranged the Eighteen Benedictions, the daily recitation of which Gamaliel made obligatory for every man.[77] The prayer for the extirpation of heretics, the *Birkat ha-Minim*, was formulated by Simeon the Little (Shmu'el ha-Qatan), another disciple of Gamaliel II, and apparently introduced into the Shemoneh Esreh by order of Gamaliel. It seems that *Birkat ha-Minim*, became part of the liturgy of the synagogue around AD 90.[78]

These events, in the context of the reconstruction of the social setting of the Fourth Gospel, are very important for those who think in terms of the post-war situation and the ensuing struggle between Jews and Christian Jews, between the Christian community and synagogue. It is alleged that in this environment and after the introduction of *Birkat ha-Minim*, the Johannine community, composed mostly of Jews, found itself pressed into an ever increasing isolation. It is further alleged that this isolation brought

---

[75] On post-AD 70 messianic hope, see Frederick J. Murphy, '2 *Baruch* and the Romans', *JBL* 104 (1985), 663–9; Emil Schürer, *The History of the Jewish People in the Age of Jesus Christ (175 BC–AD 135)*, rev. edn by Geza Vermes and Fergus Millar (Edinburgh: Clark, 1973), 1:527.

[76] G. F. Moore, *Judaism in the First Centuries of the Christian Era: The Age of the Tannaim*, 3 vols (Cambridge, MA: 1927–30), 1:87–9.

[77] Str-B, 4:208, 237; Moore, *Judaism*, 1:292.

[78] On reconstruction of the post-AD 70 situation, see further J. Neusner, *A Life of Yohanan ben Zakkai ca.1–80 C.E.*, 2nd edn (Leiden: Brill, 1970); Isaiah Gafni, 'The Historical Background', in *Jewish Writings of the Second Temple Period: Apocrypha, Pseudepigrapha, Qumran Sectarian Writings, Philo, Josephus*, ed. M. E. Stone, CRINT (Assen/Philadelphia: Van Gorcum/Fortress, 1984), 27–31. On *Birkat ha-Minim*, see William Horbury, 'The Benediction of the Minim and Early Jewish-Christian Controversy', *JTS* n.s. 33 (1982), 19–61; Reuven Kimelman, 'Birkat Ha-Minim and the Lack of Evidence for an Anti-Christian Jewish Prayer in Late Antiquity', in *Jewish and Christian Self-Definition, 2: Aspects of Judaism in the Graeco-Roman Period*, ed. E. P. Sanders (London: SCM, 1981), 226–44. See also further my discussion in this section.

about a sectarian perception of the world which in turn is reflected in the Gospel's coded enigmatic private language. In this sociological hypothesis, the Johannine language reflects and represents the language of a whole community (very similar to Qumran) rather than the ingenuity, views and expressions of one writer. The purpose of the Gospel, in this scheme, was to strengthen the group and give it self-definition.

Martyn, Leroy and Meeks's studies were received enthusiastically and led many others to espouse this proposed community situation as their essential presupposition in determining John's purpose, the function of its language, and its sectarian character.[79] The momentum has not abated. As late as 1993, Norman Petersen boldly concludes, 'The single most important factor in John's social context is that his people have been rejected by a society of which they had been a part.'[80]

---

[79] Among them: M. de Jonge, *Jesus Stranger from Heaven and Son of God: Jesus Christ and Christians in Johannine Perspective*, ed. and trans. by J. E. Steely, SBLSBS 11 (Missoula, MT: Scholars Press, 1977); Jürgen Becker, 'Aus der Literatur zum Johannesevangelium, 1978-1980', *TRu* 47 (1982), 279-301; Brown, *Community of the Beloved*, 14-17, 40-2, 88-91, Kysar, 'Community and Gospel', 355-66, and *Fourth Evangelist*, 149, 151; Ashton, *Studying John*, 71; idem, *Understanding*, 107-9; Painter, 'Glimpses of the Johannine Community in the Farewell Discourses', *AusBR* 28 (1980), 21-38, and 'The Farewell Discourses and the History of the Johannine Christianity', *NTS* 27 (1981), 525-43; Johannes Beutler, *Martyria: Traditionsgeschichtliche Untersuchungen zum Zeugnisthema bei Johannes* (Frankfurt a.M.: Josef Knecht, 1972), 345; Schnackenburg, 'Zur Herkunft des Johannesevangeliums', *BZ* 14 (1970), 1-23; Lindars, *John*, 37 (but for Lindars the Gospel began and finished before the introduction of the *Birkat ha-Minim*); M. É. Boismard and A. Lamouille, *Synopse des Quatre Evangiles en Francais*. III: *L'Evangile de Jean* (Paris: Cerf, 1977), 59, 207-9; Käsemann, *Testament of Jesus*, 38-40, 65-6; Robin Scroggs, 'The Earliest Christian Communities as a Sectarian Movement', *Studies in Judaism in Late Antiquity. 12: Christianity, Judaism and Other Greco-Roman Cults*, Part Two: Early Christianity, 1-23 (Leiden: Brill, 1975); Béda Rigaux, 'Les destinataires du IVe Évangile à la lumière de Jn 17', *RTL* 1 (1970), 289-319; idem, 'Die Jünger Jesu in Johannes 17', *TQ* 150 (1970), 203-13; W. Wiefel, 'Die Scheidung von Gemeinde und Welt im Johannesevangelium auf dem Hintergrund der Trennung von Kirche und Synagogue', *TZ* 35/4 (1979), 213-27; D. M. Smith, 'Johannine Christianity: Some Reflections on Its Character and Delineation', *NTS* 21 (1974), 222-48; Onuki, *Gemeinde und Welt im Johannesevangelium*; Jerome H. Neyrey, *An Ideology of Revolt: John's Christology in Social-Science Perspective* (Philadelphia: Fortress, 1988); Whitacre, *Johannine Polemic*, 10-11; David Rensberger, *Overcoming the World: Politics and Community in the Gospel of John* (London: SPCK, 1989); H. E. Lona, *Abraham in Johannes 8. Ein Beitrag zur Methodenfrage*, EHS 23/65 (Bern/Frankfurt: Peter Lang, 1979), 391ff.; Bruce D. Woll, *Johannine Christianity in Conflict: Authority, Rank, and Succession in the First Farewell Discourse*, SBLDS 60 (Chico, CA: Scholars Press, 1989); Walter Rebell, *Gemeinde als Gegenwelt: zur soziologischen und didaktischen Funktion des johannesevangeliums*, BBET 20 (Frankfurt: Lang, 1987), 83, 112, 162-3.

[80] *The Gospel of John and the Sociology of Light: Language and Characterization in the Fourth Gospel* (Valley Forge, PA: Trinity Press, 1993), 80.

4.4.2. Analysis and Criticism of Martyn, Leroy, and Meeks

The following is a very brief, critical examination of the sociological proposals of Martyn, Leroy and Meeks with the intention of revealing their inadequacy as an explanation of John's elusive language. This examination is important since the function of John's special language pattern leading to ambiguity must be determined in the context of the general thrust of the Gospel. If, as the present consensus argues, the Fourth Gospel echoes the traumatic experience of an ostracised community which in reaction turns into an isolationist group, then the document's peculiar language needs to be explained in relation to such a paradigm. On the other hand, if the sectarian model proves unsatisfactory, as I believe it does, then various explanations for the Gospel's perplexing language within the sectarian model must also prove unsustainable, which I believe they are. In this light, my study is an endeavour to provide an alternate hypothesis to the preceding dominant consensus.

4.4.2.1. Martyn's Reconstruction

Martyn proposed that the present Gospel was written to console a traumatised community after its ejection from the synagogue.[81] In this hypothesis, the determinative milieu of the community was its conflict with the synagogue where Jews were subjected to persecution if suspected of becoming converts to Christianity.[82] This brought the Johannine community into growing conflict with the Jewish religious hierarchy, dominated by the Pharisees who apparently had come through the war intact.[83] For the Johannine group, the result was an eventual expulsion

---

[81] Although Martyn is credited with this hypothesis, see years earlier A. Loisy, *Le Quatrième Évangile* (Paris: E. Nourry, 1903), 75–94; O. Cullmann, *Early Christian Worship* (London: SCM, 1953: first published in French in 1951).

[82] *History and Theology*, 9.

[83] Although Neusner has argued that the situation was much more complex: the diversity which characterised Judaism in the pre-AD 70 period may have continued after the War. He suggests that in the period AD 70–135, the force of the Pharisees was negligible, and it was not until after the Bar Kokhba revolt that 'rabbinic orthodoxy' became established as the dominant and authentic voice of Judaism. J. Neusner, 'Judaism after the Destruction of the Temple: An Overview', in *Formative Judaism: Religious, Historical and Literary Studies, Third Series: Torah, Pharisees, and Rabbis*, BJS 46 (Chico, CA: Scholars Press, 1983), 93, idem, *From Politics to Piety: The Emergence of Pharisaic Judaism* (Engelwood Cliffs, NJ: Prentice-Hall, 1973), 143–54. Morton Smith, 'Palestinian Judaism in the First Century', in *Israel: Its Role in Civilization*, ed. by Moshe Davis (New York: Jewish Theological Seminary of America, 1956), 74–77, questions Josephus' account of the Pharisees in the *Antiquities* as designed to commend them to the Romans as the one party commanding the popular allegiance to maintain stability in Palestine. In John, in contrast to the Synoptics, we do not find any mention of such groups as the Herodians, Sadducees, etc. We

from the synagogue.⁸⁴ Other factors precipitating the rupture, beside the nature of Johannine christological confessions, may have been the presence of 'heterodox' Jewish elements or the group's relation to Samaritans and Gentiles. According to Martyn, the mechanism employed for the expulsion was the twelfth article of the Eighteen Benedictions of the synagogue's liturgy, the 'Benediction against Heretics' (*Birkat ha-Minim*).⁸⁵ The twelfth article was being used in such a way that Jewish Christians had to either expose their faith in Jesus or invoke a curse on themselves during the synagogue prayers.⁸⁶ The result was a breach in the congregation and a form of expulsion or exclusion of the Christians from the synagogue. In his thesis, Martyn relies heavily on the three occurrences in the Gospel of the term ἀποσυνάγωγος (9:22; 12:42; 16:2) in conjunction with external evidence of the *Birkat ha-Minim*. In such an environment, some Christian Jews may have reverted to secrecy in order to maintain their standing within the Jewish community. Open confession would have meant being cut off from much that had given identity and structure to their lives, social and family ostracism, even economic dislocation.⁸⁷ But those daring to take an open stand increasingly developed a sectarian tendency whereby they would focus upon their own Jewish-Christian traditions and beliefs, fellowship, and exegesis of the Scriptures.⁸⁸

This situation of conflict, crisis, and alienation is believed to be in the background of the composition of the Fourth Gospel. Such experience would have deeply coloured the community's traditions about Jesus in terms of self-definition and identification. The Fourth Gospel, in this

---

only read of the Pharisees who present a fanatical opposition to Jesus. It is believed that the reason John only mentions the Pharisees is because they were the sole group to survive the war intact. See H. Mulder, 'Ontstaan en Doel', 241–5, 58; Feliks Gryglewicz, 'Die Pharisäer und die Johanneskirche', in *Probleme der Forschung*, ed. A. Fuchs, SNTU A.3 (Vienna and Munich: Herold Verlag, 1978), 156f; S. Pancaro, *The Law in the Fourth Gospel*, NovTSup 42 (Leiden: Brill, 1975), 492–534; Wengst, *Bedrängte Gemeinde*, 40–4, 57, 62; W. Meeks, 'Equal to God', in *The Conversation Continues: Studies in Paul and John in Honor of J. Louis Martyn*, ed. by R. T. Fortna and B. T. Gaventa (Nashville: Abingdon, 1990), 309–22.

⁸⁴ Also Wengst, *Bedrängte Gemeinde*, 57, 62, 48–60.

⁸⁵ Martyn, *History and Theology*, 18–41; idem, 'Glimpses into the History of the Johannine Community: From Its Origin through the Period of Its Life in which the Fourth Gospel was Written', in *L'Évangile de Jean*, ed. by M. de Jonge (1977), 147–75, also reprinted in *The Gospel of John in Christian History* (New York: Paulist Press, 1978), 107–21.

⁸⁶ Ibid., 37–62. Cf. W. D. Davies, *The Setting of the Sermon on the Mount* (Cambridge: CUP, 1963), 275f.; Mulder, 'Ontstaan en Doel', 241–5; C. K. Barrett, *The New Testament Background: Selected Documents*, rev. edn (London: SPCK, 1987), 204ff.

⁸⁷ Wengst, *Bedrängte Gemeinde*, 58–9.

⁸⁸ Rensberger, *Overcoming the World*, 27.

scenario, captures and portrays the history of the community as the history of Jesus, thus identifying or mirroring the community's experience in terms of Jesus' experience. The Gospel account would have been recast against this milieu. In Martyn's reconstruction, the Gospel presents a 'two-level drama', in which the events of Jesus' life are, in fact, a reflection of actual events experienced by the Johannine church.[89] Thus the actors in John's drama are seen as representative figures in the immediate environment of the Gospel.

In this reconstruction, the war of AD 66–73 leading to the trauma of the destruction of the temple is pivotal. Just as for J. A. T. Robinson everything in John point to a pre-war south-Judaean situation,[90] for both Martyn and those who further developed his thesis, all things in John's Gospel point to a post-war situation.[91] Such trauma, beside physical suffering and displacement, for many Jews would have called into question Israel's status as the chosen and protected people of God and provoked a profound and far-reaching theological crisis for the Jewish people.[92] The Jerusalem temple provided a focal point and resulted in cohesion and unity for the many diverse groups in Judaism. Its destruction would have precipitated a social crisis.[93] It is in the context of such national catastrophe and the subsequent soul-searching[94] that the Fourth Evangelist, it is

---

[89] Martyn, *History and Theology*, 230.

[90] *Redating the New Testament* (London: SCM, 1976), 254–311; idem, 'The Destination and Purpose of St. John's Gospel', in *Twelve New Testament Studies* (London: SCM, 1962), 116ff.

[91] E.g., Mulder, 'Ontstaan en Doel', 245–250.

[92] The profundity of the crisis may be gauged from the confidence in the invincibility of Jerusalem before the disaster in comparison with the doubts afterward. See footnotes no. 72–73 above. J. Neusner, 'The Formation of Rabbinic Judaism: Methodological Issues and Substantive Theses', in *Formative Judaism*, 1:122.

[93] Martyn, *History and Theology*, 52; Stone, 'Reactions to the Destruction of the Second Temple', 196; Shaye J. D. Cohen, 'Yavneh Revisited: Pharisees, Rabbis, and the End of Jewish Sectarianism', *SBLSP* 21 (Chico, CA: Scholars Press, 1982), 57.

[94] For example, was the catastrophe the result of chastisement for sin? This was the dominant explanation of the disaster. J. Neusner, *Life of Yohanan ben Zakkai*, 212. For some Jews, the sin was associated with the Temple (e.g., in *Apoc. Abr.*, chapter 25; *Sib. Or.* 4; *2 Apoc. Bar.* 10:18; Josephus, *War* 5:402, 412; *Test. Mos.* 2:8f, 5:3f, 6:1). The violations of the Temple by Antiochus and Pompeii were explained as the result of Israel's sin (2 Macc. 5:17–20 and *Pss. Sol.* 2:1–3, 16). R. Yohanan ben Torta, a contemporary of Akiba, comments on the cause in *T. Menah* 13:22, quoted in E. E. Urbach, *The Sages: Their Concepts and Beliefs* (Jerusalem: Magnes Press, 1979/82), 675. For others, it was the result of the factionalism in Jerusalem (e.g., Josephus and his speech before the walls of Jerusalem in *War* 5.376ff.; cf. *4 Baruch* 1:1, 8; 4:7f.). Some Jews thought perhaps the righteous were not as righteous as they appeared (*2 Apoc. Bar.* 14:7). Some attributed the disaster to the work of the Devil: *Yetzer* (*Jub.* 1:20f, 11:4–6; *T. Jud.* 25:3; *T. Zeb.* 9:8; *T. Gad.* 4:7; *T. Ash.* 1:8–9; etc.; also 1QS 3:21–24; CD 12:2–3; *Apoc. Abr.* in *Testament of 12 Patr. Mart. Isa.* 4:1; *Sib. Or.* 3:63–74). Cf. Foerster, *TDNT* 7:156. Others explained the

believed, articulated in the Jewish-Christian response to the event in which Jesus stood for all that Israel had lost.

Irrespective of the correctness or incorrectness of Martyn's reconstruction, the Gospel of John in the context of the events of AD 70 would have been relevant, at least from the point of view of the Jewish Christians. It would have been scarcely avoidable for the Christian community to fail to explain the death and devastation experienced by Israel in the catastrophe of AD 70 in terms of Israel's rejection of Jesus' words. Certainly later Christians did not hesitate to interpret the destruction of the temple as a judgment upon the Jews for their unbelief in Christ (Justin, *Dial.* 108:1–3; cf. *Dial.* 16:2–3, interpreting the Bar Kochba defeat in the same way). Many non-Christian Jews themselves had already concluded that the devastation of Jerusalem and their temple at the hands of the Romans was the result of the judgment of God.[95] Legends even developed about Yohanan ben Zakkai who had seen a sign of coming destruction (*b. Yoma* 39b) in a vision.[96] The catastrophe of the destruction of the temple and all the upheaval associated with it, from the Johannine perspective, were the means by which God awakened Israel to her spiritual blindness just as he had done centuries earlier (cf. Merkabah Mysticism in relation to the destruction of the temple in Ezekiel).[97] For John, the rejection of Jesus by the Jews may have signalled a repetition of the same episodes of the days of Ezekiel. He may have seen the One who came and once again 'tabernacled' amongst them (1:14) departing and removing his glory from the Jerusalem temple and placing it within his new temple, the church.

As already indicated, Martyn's allegorical reading of the Gospel, especially the narrative portions, enables scholars to fill in the gaps in their knowledge regarding the circumstances surrounding its composition.

---

catastrophe within the plan and the will of God (*2 Baruch* 13:9–10, 15:7–8; cf. *4 Ezra*). See Bruce Longenecker, *Eschatology and the Covenant: A Comparison of 4 Ezra and Romans 1–11*, JSNTSup 57 (Sheffield: JSOT Press, 1991), 49–57, and *4 Baruch* 1:6–8, 3:4, 4:1–3; *2 Baruch* 14:5–7, 77:8–10, 78:5, 79:1–4.

[95] Cf. Josephus, *War* 5:412, 6:288, 297–300; *2 Apoc. Bar.* 8:1–5; Tacitus, *Histories* 5:13. See also W. D. Davies, *The Gospel and the Land: Early Christianity and Jewish Territorial Doctrine* (Berkeley: University of California Press, 1974), 295; O. Cullmann, 'L'Evangile Johannique at L'Histoire du Saltut', *NTS* 11 (1965), 111–22.

[96] Neusner, *Life of Rabban Yohanan*, 64f.

[97] For Ezekiel, the departure of the chariot signals the departure of God's glory and the subsequent destruction of the Jerusalem temple. For the post-AD 70 rabbis, the destruction of the temple by the Romans may have indicated a similar interest in the chariot now located in heaven. See Neusner, *Life of Yohanan ben Zakkai*, 145.

Nevertheless, the belief that the Gospel reflects the circumstances of the time of writing is neither new nor original to Martyn. Oscar Cullmann, for instance, had argued years earlier for this two-level drama where he laid great emphasis on the interaction between the two 'levels': that of the time of writing and that of the ministry of Jesus.[98] Similarly Bultmann commenting on the two episodes most often quoted by those who argue for a 'two-level' drama in the Fourth Gospel, wrote,

> Manifestly the two stories in chapters 5 and 9 must be understood against the same historical background. Both reflect the relation of early Christianity to the surrounding hostile (in the first place Jewish) world; in a peculiar way they reflect, too, the methods of its opponents, who directed their attacks against men who did not yet belong to the Christian community, but who had come into contact with it and experienced the power of the miraculous forces at work in it.[99]

The newness of Martyn's proposal consists in the *particularity* of the situation he constructs and in the vigour with which he carries through what amounts to an allegorisation of the narratives. In addition, Martyn's reconstruction proves attractive because it seems to resolve one of the most puzzling features of the Gospel, namely, why John is so Jewish and yet so anti-Jewish.[100]

Martyn's reconstruction of the social setting of the Gospel and the Johannine community may be criticised on several points. First, the accuracy of his historical reconstruction can be questioned. Cohen believes, on the basis of the available rabbinic sources relating to the Jamnia era, that Martyn's theory is historically unfounded.[101] It can be questioned whether Jamnia brought about the break between the Christian community and the synagogue. Indeed the actuality of such a catastrophic break between the Christian and Jewish communities in the period in which the Fourth Gospel was composed may also be questioned. To be

---

[98] Cullmann, *Early Christian Worship*.

[99] Bultmann, *John*, 239, quoted by Barrett, *St. John*, 250. Similarly Richard Bauckham, 'For Whom Were Gospels Written?', 19, points out that Martyn's proposal was related to similar works done by other scholars such as Weeden and his work on Mark, even though Martyn never mentions them.

[100] Thyen, 'Das Heil Kommt von den Juden', 163; Ashton, *Understanding*, 109.

[101] Cohen, *Yavneh Revisited*, 45–61. See also Douglas R. A. Hare, *The Theme of Jewish Persecution of Christians in the Gospel According to Matthew*, SNTSMS 6 (Cambridge: CUP, 1967), 48–56; D. Wenham, 'The Enigma of the Fourth Gospel: Another Look', *TynBull* 48 (1997), 149–78; John Muddiman, 'The Resurrection of Jesus as the Coming of the Kingdom – the Basis of Hope for the Transformation of the World', in *The Kingdom of God and Human Society*, ed. by R. S. Barbour (Edinburgh: Clark, 1993), 212–3; Robinson, *Redating the New Testament*, 272–5; Kümmel, *Einleitung in das Neue Testament*, 197.

sure, there were on-going controversies and conflict, but the evidence for a 'parting of the ways' in a definitive fashion is inconclusive.[102] Philip Alexander correctly observes, 'It is simplistic to look for a decisive *moment* in the parting of the ways, a crucial doctrine or event that caused the final rupture. There was no sudden break between Christianity and Judaism, but rather an ever-widening rift.'[103]

In particular, the decisive importance of *Birkat ha-Minim* in the Jewish–Christian relationship has been questioned.[104] While there is emerging a consensus that the Yavnean sages did introduce a curse on the *minim* towards the end of the first century, yet it is not clear who were the intended *minim*. Neither do we seem to know the precise wording. The twelfth Benediction, in its oldest Palestinian form, reads: 'For apostates may there be no hope, and may the Nazarenes (הנצרים) and the Minim (המינים) perish.'[105] The Nazarenes appear to be Christians, but a number of scholars have argued that the word did not belong to the original 'blessing'.[106] In this case, the question regarding whom the Benediction refers to hinges

---

[102] Cf. William Horbury, *Jews and Christians in Contact and Controversy* (Edinburgh: Clark, 1998), 67–110; Samuel Krauss and William Horbury, *The Jewish-Christian Controversy from the earliest time to 1789*, ed. and rev. by W. Horbury, vol. 1, *History* (Tübingen: Mohr-Siebeck, 1996); M. S. Taylor, *Anti-Judaism and Early Christian Identity: A Critique of the Consensus* (Leiden: Brill, 1995); Steven T. Katz, 'Issues in the Separation of Judaism and Christianity after 70 C.E.: A Reconsideration', *JBL* 103 (1984), 43–76; P. S. Alexander, '"The Parting of the Ways" from the Perspective of Rabbinic Judaism', in *Jews and Christians: The Parting of the Ways AD 70 to 135*, ed. by J. D. G. Dunn, WUNT 66 (Tübingen: Mohr-Siebeck, 1993), 1–25; Archie L. Nations, 'Jewish Persecution of Christians in the Gospel of John' (A paper read at the Society of Biblical Literature annual meeting, Atlanta, GA, Nov. 23, 1986).

[103] Alexander, 'The Parting of the Ways', 3.

[104] William Horbury, 'The Benediction of the Minim and Early Jewish-Christian Controversy', *JTS* n.s. 33 (1982), 19–61, demonstrates the textual development of the 12th Benediction, showing the weak textual foundation of the older view. See further Samuel Krauss, 'Imprecation Against the Minim in the Synagogue', *JQR* 9 (1897), 515–17; W. Nicol, *The Semeia in the Fourth Gospel: Tradition and Redaction*, NovTSup (Leiden: Brill, 1975), 144–5; Pancaro, *Law*, 247; Peter Schäfer, 'Die sogenannte Synode von Jabne: Zur Trennung von Juden und Christen im ersten/zweiten Jh. n. Chr.', *Judaica* 31 (1975), 54–64, 116–24; Neusner, 'Formation of Rabbinic Judaism', 133; R. Bauckham, 'The *Apocalypse of Peter*: A Jewish Christian Apocalypse from the Time of Bar Kokhba', *Apocrypha* 5 (1994), 87–90; Graham Stanton, *A Gospel for a New People: Studies in Matthew* (Edinburgh: Clark, 1992), 142; T. C. G. Thornton, 'Christian Understandings of the *Birkat Ha-Minim* in the Eastern Roman Empire', *JTS* n.s. 38 (1987), 419–31.

[105] Str-B 4:212–13; Moore, *Judaism*, 1:292 with n. 8; cf. 3:97 n. 68. See also S. Schechter, 'Geniza Specimens', *JQR* 10 (1896), 656f; J. Mann, 'Genizah Fragments of the Palestinian Order of Service', *HUCA* 2 (1925), 269ff. It is suggested that the 12th Bendendiction, over a period of time, changed its wording to adapt to the changed situation. K. L. Carroll, 'The Fourth Gospel and the Exclusion of Christians from the Synagogues', *BJRL* 40 (1957-58), 19–32.

[106] J. Jocz, *The Jewish People and Jesus Christ: A Study in the Controversy between Church and Synagogue* (London: SPCK, 1962), 56–7.

upon the term 'Minim'. Philip Alexander has noted the variety of terms which the Rabbis had at their disposal to describe those whom they considered as standing outside of the Jewish community: *minim* ('heretics'), *mesummadim* ('apostates'), *Kutiyyim* ('Samaritans'), and *'Ovedei Kokhavim* ('heathens': lit. 'star-worshippers').[107] In this instance ('the twelfth Benediction'), does 'Minim' (המינים) refer to Christians or Jewish Gnostics? If they are Christians, are they Jewish Christians, Gentile Christians, or all Christians? There is no clear consensus.

As a result of a research project at McMaster University on 'Jewish and Christian Self-Definition', Schiffman and Kimelman argued respectively (1981) that post-AD 70 Judaism did not close ranks against Jewish Christians, and that there is no evidence that the twelfth Benediction was directed at them particularly.[108] Some scholars hold that in the oldest rabbinical texts, the term 'Minim' designates heretical *Jews* and it is only later (from AD 180–200 onwards) that it became a designation for the followers of other 'creeds', especially the Christians.[109] In fairness to Martyn's theory, on the other hand, it appears that the curse was used in reference to Christians much earlier than AD 180. Takashi Onuki and Klaus Wengst postulate that the curse on *minim* was initially part of a policy of expansion by the Yavneh sages, as they sought to consolidate their authority and reinforce Torah 'orthodoxy' against various fringe groups.[110] But within the space of just a few years in the early 80s, this consensus collapsed, at which point the *Birkat ha-Minim* came to be used as a means for expulsion of Christians from the synagogue and the beginning of a fairly systematic persecution of them.[111] Lindars comes to a similar conclusion. He believes that by AD 90 confession of faith in Christ meant perpetual exclusion from the synagogue.[112] Horbury points out that before the outbreak of war in AD 66, there were existing curses on 'separatists' or 'the wicked' and these curses were probably already used

---

[107] Alexander, 'The Parting of the Ways', 6.

[108] Lawrence H. Schiffman, 'At the Crossroads: Tannaitic Perspectives on the Jewish-Christian Schism', in *Jewish and Christian Self-Definition*, 2: *Aspects of Judaism in the Graeco-Roman Period*, ed. by E. P. Sanders (London: SCM, 1981), 2:115–56; R. Kimelman, 'Birkat Ha-Minim and the Lack of Evidence', in *Jewish and Christian Self-Definition*, ed. by E. P. Sanders, 2:226–44; see also Cohen, *Yavneh Revisited*, 59.

[109] Pancaro, *The Law*, 246; H. Hirschberg, 'Once Again – The Minim', *JBL* 67 (1948), 305–18.

[110] Alexander, 'The Parting of the Ways', 9, believes the purpose for introducing the *Birkat ha-Minim* was 'to establish Rabbinism as orthodoxy within the synagogue.'

[111] Onuki, *Gemeinde und Welt im Johannesevangelium*, 29–34; Wengst, *Bedrängte Gemeinde*.

[112] Lindars, *John*, 37, 340.

with special reference to the sect of the Nazarenes (Acts 24:5).[113] Indeed by the time of Justin Martyr, it appears that the Christians were also included in the curse.[114]

Nevertheless, the introduction of the curse into the liturgy of the synagogue makes sense only if those against whom it was aimed still took part in the liturgy. It would have worked by self-exclusion rather than by active expulsion, that is to say, it would have only barred from the synagogue those who recognised themselves as 'minim' (i.e., Nazarenes). In this sense it may have functioned more as exhortation to Jews generally than as a specific means of social exclusion.[115]

Whatever the outcome of the debate concerning the scope and the effects of the curse on the *minim*, the evidence for a widespread movement to break off all contact with Christians in the late first century remains inconclusive. In this context, it is possible that the particular Johannine reinterpretation of the Scriptures may have functioned as an *address to Jews* (rather than as a means of bolstering a beleaguered Christian group). Scholars like Günter Reim, Frédéric Manns, J. C. Thomas, S. Pancaro, and J. D. M. Derrett have even sought to show that John's argument interlocks with specific rabbinic arguments and traditions, so that knowledge of the latter is essential for a clear understanding of the former.[116] Such an engagement is indicative of a relationship and dialogue rather than a schism. John Muddiman has argued that the Johannine community may have tried longer than other Christian communities to maintain wider links within Judaism.[117] For most scholars, this *engagement* with Judaism is understood to mean 'conflict' with it. However, Johannine themes and imageries place the milieu of the Fourth Gospel within first-century

---

[113] Horbury, *Jews and Christians*, 9.

[114] See Justin's *Dialogue*, xvi, xciii, xcvi, cviii, cxxiii, cxxxiii, cf. xxxv, xlvii; A. Lukyn Williams, *Justin Martyr: The Dialogue with Trypho. Translation, Introduction and Notes* (London, 1930); also William Horbury, 'Jewish-Christian Relations in Barnabas and Justin Martyr', in *Jews and Christians: The Parting of the Ways AD 70 to 135*, ed. by J. D. G. Dunn, WUNT 66 (Tübingen: Mohr-Siebeck, 1993), 315–45; J. T. Sanders, *Schismatics, Sectarians, Dissidents, Deviants: The First One Hundred Years of Jewish-Christian Relations* (London: SCM, 1993), 53; S. G. Wilson, *Related Strangers: Jews and Christians 70–170 C.E.* (Minneapolis: Fortress, 1995), 179–83.

[115] This seems to fit with the insight that the Yavnean sages were more concerned to heal breaches than to reinforce them. When 2 *Baruch* considers the *minim*, he instinctively does not curse them, but puzzles about them.

[116] See chapters two and five in the present study. See also the bibliography where I have included some of their works.

[117] 'Resurrection of Jesus', 212–13.

Judaism. The Fourth Evangelist seems to stand as a prophetic figure within Judaism rather than outside of it.[118]

The second point at which Martyn's reconstruction is open to criticism has to do with a methodological problem. One cannot presume, as Martyn does by his two-level drama, that the setting of the Gospel is a mirror of the Gospel narrative. Edwin Judge detects the logical incongruity and writes,

> There is no reason why the [Johannine] community is one that is being kicked out of the synagogue at all. The fact that the Gospel deals with Jesus' conflicts with the Jews may arise because that is what [actually] happened to Jesus. You may well be using that to instruct people who are having some other kind of conflict problem.[119]

The Evangelist's record of Jesus' conflict with 'the Jews' may have a wider purpose than merely to speak to a parallel conflict in the experience of his community. It is quite possible that John may be writing of the opposition to Jesus and his followers because he believed such an opposition marked the lives of many Christians in his own time and perhaps will characterise the environment of some future generations of Christians.

Thirdly, the sharp distinction between pre-AD 70 and post-AD 70 seems to be exaggerated since there is adequate evidence to support the contention that Jewish Christian conflict and a rift on a broad scale[120] was already in progress before the destruction of the Jerusalem temple (e.g., Mt. 10:17–25; Mk. 13:9–13; Lk. 12:11, 21:12–19; cf. Acts 8:1–3; 9:1–2),[121] going as far back as a few months and years after the crucifixion of our Lord.[122] Indeed Martyn's argument in this respect is self defeating. Assuming that the introduction of the *Birkat ha-Minim* into the synagogue liturgy was a

---

[118] See my discussion in chapter five.

[119] Edwin Judge, 'Response to Bruce Malina', in *Protocol of the 48th Colloquy of the Center for Hermeneutical Studies in Hellenistic and Modern Culture*, ed. by H. C. Waetjen (Berkeley, CA: Graduate Theological Union and University of California-Berkeley, 1985), 24–9, bracketed words are my emphasis. The response is to Malina's work, 'The Gospel of John in Sociolinguistic Perspective', in *Protocol of the 48th Colloquy*, ed. by Waetjen, 1–23.

[120] According to Josephus, the period preceding the destruction of Jerusalem was marked by intense and atrocious strife within the Jewish community itself (*B.J.*, 4.3.2–4.7.2), the very thing which seems to have been the chief cause for the Roman intervention (*B.J.*, 4.6.2–3; 4.7.3.).

[121] Barnabas Lindars, 'The Persecution of Christians in John 15:18–16:4a', in *Suffering and Martyrdom in the New Testament Studies*, ed. by G. M. Styler, W. Horbury and B. McNeil (Cambridge: CUP, 1981), 48–69. Luke, in Acts, uses the term 'the Jews' in a similar way to express opposition against Jesus and the Christians (cf. Acts 9:23; 12:3). Thus it may be that the term 'Jews' is used more especially in contradistinction from 'Christians', rather than from 'Gentiles' in the same sense in which it occurs in Revelation 3:9. Paul, too, used the term in this sense (cf. 1 Cor. 10:32). See also my discussion in chapter five.

[122] R. Riesner, *Die Frühzeit des Apostels Paulus*, WUNT 71 (Tübingen: Mohr-Siebeck, 1994), 55–6.

significant dynamic behind the Johannine account (e.g., ch. 9), the effect would have been farther reaching than the Johannine community. If an expulsion of Christians from the synagogues did occur, it would not have been confined to one community. It would have occurred in the Jewish communities and synagogues across the Diaspora cities. The scenario which Martyn has reconstructed would have been true of most Christian communities in the late first century and may not be confined only to the Johannine community.

4.4.2.2. Leroy's Form-Critical Analysis

With the introduction of 'insiders' versus 'outsiders', Herbert Leroy applied sectarian sociology to the language of the Fourth Gospel.[123] What Martyn had proposed in terms of historical dynamics, Leroy described in terms of socio-linguistic. Both arrived at the same conclusion – the Fourth Gospel reflects a sectarian disposition. Leroy proposed that the language of the Fourth Gospel with its 'riddle-like' quality was designed to set apart the 'initiated insider group' from uninitiated 'outsiders'.

Based upon a wide-ranging survey of 'riddle' in folklore and literature, Leroy argued that the Johannine 'dialogue-with-misunderstandings' belongs to a special class of 'riddle' or 'verborgenes Rätsel'.[124] Leroy emphasised that John's language had a social function, expressing and reinforcing the distinction between the 'in-group' which grasped the heavenly, spiritual meaning of Jesus' words and the 'outsiders' (i.e., those outside the Johannine community) for whom such words appeared as riddles and unintelligible. For the 'insiders', those engaged in the community's instruction, catechism, rituals, and the hearing of its preaching, the riddles had a special meaning.[125]

Leroy thus offered a full form-critical examination of the misunderstandings, in which he argued first that 'riddle' was a literary device of a distinct type, and secondly, and more importantly, that this 'form' played a definite role in the life of John's church. He noted that the 'Sondersprache' of the Johannine community was particularly noticeable in the eleven

---

[123] Leroy, *Rätsel und Missverständnis: Ein Beitrag zur Formgeschichte des Johannesevangeliums*, BBB 30 (Bonn: Hanstein, 1968).

[124] Leroy, *Rätsel*, 13–45.

[125] A summary of Leroy's thesis may be found in his article, 'Das Johanneische Missverständis als aliterarische Form', *BibLeb* 9 (1968), 196–207.

selected 'riddles' in chapters two through eight of the Gospel.[126] Leroy devoted almost half of his monograph to a detailed analysis of these passages while he sought, with elaborate effort, to reconstruct the Johannine community and its beliefs. According to Leroy, Johannine 'riddles' involved the investing of the ordinary language with a special, technical meaning knowable only within the circle of the initiated, such as Jesus' talk about 'departing' (ὑπάγειν). This coded language served to reinforce the social distinctness of the Johannine community over against the synagogue, because 'the Jews' failed completely to hear the deeper meaning, and thus were 'thoroughly defamed and made to appear as "the idiots".'[127] The Johannine believer, on the other hand, in discovering the true meaning also realised 'his own superiority over the Jews', because he saw the meaning they had missed.[128] Later development of this thesis, by scholars such as H. E. Lona and B. Malina would go further and claim that in the Fourth Gospel there was a complete breakdown of the linguistic 'code' between Jesus and 'the Jews'.[129].

There are appealing elements in Leroy's thesis. First, his emphasis on the believing community as the privileged illuminated community, the recipient of the divine revelation, coincides with both Johannine and New Testament emphases. It is, as Kermode points out, 'the matter of the circumcised ear'.[130] Secondly, Leroy also correctly accentuates the importance of the activity of the Holy Spirit in the community of faith. It is the Spirit of God who enables its members to understand the revelation.[131] The members of this sanctified community have the presence of the Holy Spirit to guide, lead, and enable them to understand the words of our Lord. Thirdly, Leroy rightly recognises the significance of teachers and preachers in the community who further enable the members to understand 'the riddles', while indeed the whole of the community serves this purpose perpetually.[132] Finally, Leroy's sharp distinction between the 'outsiders'

---

[126] These eleven passages (four of them in 8:31–59) encompass: Jn 2:19–22; 3:3–5; 4:10–15, 31–35, 41–42; 6:51–53; 7:33–36; 8:21–22, 31–33, 51–53, and 56–58.

[127] Leroy, *Rätsel und Missverständnis*, 62.

[128] Ibid.

[129] H. E. Lona, *Abraham in Johannes und Ein Beitrag zur Methodenfrage*, EHS 23/65 (Bern/Frankfurt: Peter Lang, 1979), 393; Malina, 'The Gospel of John in Sociolinguistic Perspective', 1–23; also Rebell, *Gemeinde als Gegenwelt*, 163, cf. 83, 112, 162.

[130] Frank Kermode, *The Genesis of Secrecy: On the Interpretation of Narrative* (Cambridge, MA: Harvard Univ. Press, 1979), 16.

[131] Leroy, 'Johanneische Missverständnis', 196–207.

[132] Ibid., *Rätsel und Missverständnis*, 14–75.

versus the 'insiders' is warranted by the Johannine emphasis (Jn. 10:1–18, 27–29; 13:35; 15:16–20; 17:6–26; cf. Mt. 13:11–17; Mk. 4:11). Such a distinction between the community of God's chosen people and those outside it is seen elsewhere in the Scriptures.[133]

Leroy's hypothesis has been widely received as an explication of the enigmatic character of the Gospel's language, and others have built upon it.[134] However, Leroy's form-critical analysis, his equating of Johannine 'misunderstandings' with 'riddles', seems implausible. Form criticism alone does not explain the enigmatic quality of John's language. Neither is it the most helpful and effective method of approaching the problem. As Carson points out, the theme of misunderstanding is so pervasive in the Fourth Gospel that to endeavour to decipher what is traditional and what is redactional does not prove useful.[135] Hartwig Thyen's comment about the 'subliminal allusions' in the Gospel also weakens Leroy's thesis. Thyen observes how the Gospel is full of subtle allusions to 'specifically Jewish traditions, and of motifs adapted from the Targums and midrash, all of which would be comprehensible only to "insiders"'.[136] This, he argues, 'makes me think, only a group of Christian Jews could possibly have been the first recipients and bearers of the Gospel.'[137] However, once the Jewishness of the readers, rather than their *Christianity*, is acknowledged as the reason why the Gospel is comprehensible to them, then the 'Sondersprache' view of the Johannine language loses its rationale. One must seriously reckon with the possibility that the 'insiders' whom such language addresses are simply 'Jews' and not specifically 'Christian Jews'.[138] Leroy's attempt to infer the social situation of the Johannine community from one small feature of the text is also a doubtful generalisation. He seems to see the misunderstandings as a means of not

---

[133] For example, in the Old Testament, this distinction is made between Israel as God's chosen people and the nations (e.g., Exod. 5:1; 6:6–7; 19:6; 33:13; 34:23; Lev. 18:24; Deut. 2:25; 4:20; 7:6; 14:2; 18:9; 26:18; Ps. 106:5; 135:4; Isa. 43:20, 21). In the New Testament, the distinction is applied to the church and 'the world' (e.g., Jn. 10:14–17, 27–29; 15:16–19; 17:7–26; Phil. 2:15; 1 Pet. 2:9; Tit. 2:14; 1 Jn. 3:1; 4:4–6).

[134] Ashton, *Understanding*, 189–92, 394–404. But see Raymond Brown, 'Review of H. Leroy (Rätsel)', *Biblica* 51 (1970), 152–54; Carson, 'Understanding Misunderstandings in the Fourth Gospel', *Tyndale Bulletin* 33 (1982), 59–89; Okure, *Johannine Approach*, 185–6.

[135] Carson, 'Understanding Misunderstandings', 74, 78.

[136] Thyen, 'Das Heil Kommt von den Juden', 174.

[137] Ibid.

[138] Thyen, 'Johannes 10 im Kontext des vierten Evangeliums', 121, 168.

giving away special knowledge.[139] This special knowledge is the real meaning of Jesus' words which is only revealed to the 'initiated'. In this scenario, John's 'cryptic' language becomes a fence by which the 'outsiders' are kept from access to the revelation. Teresa Okure objects that such an understanding of John implies a lack of interest in the audience, rendering mutual exchange between Jesus and his audience practically null and void.[140]

4.4.2.3. Meeks's Sociological Application

Wayne A. Meeks's seminal article on 'The Man From Heaven in Johannine Sectarianism'[141] has been characterised by J. Z. Smith as 'the result of a happy combination of exegetical and sociological sophistication'.[142] Robin Scroggs considered Meeks's article to be an illustration of the 'immense possibilities' of the most important approach within the field of sociology, viz., the sociology of knowledge.[143] But there were also less enthusiastic responses too.[144] Nevertheless, the way was opened for numerous sociological studies of John's Gospel which have since appeared.[145] Crediting Meeks's study as the innovative breakthrough

---

[139] Rebell, *Gemeinde als Gegenwelt*, 163, cf. 83, 112, 162; Carson, 'Understanding Misunderstandings', 82, 87. Cf. Ashton, *Understanding*, 190.

[140] *Johannine Approach*, 185–6. It seems to me that the Evangelist's explanatory asides further weaken Leroy's thesis. If the point of John's language is to conceal by means of riddle, then there is no need for clarifying the misunderstandings (e.g., 2:21–22; 6:64; 8:27; 10:6; 11:51, 52; 12:16, 37–41; 13:11, 28–30; 18:9, 32; 19:35, 36; 20:9).

[141] *JBL* 91 (1972), 44–72, see also his later works: 'Breaking Away: Three New Testament Pictures of Christianity's Separation From the Jewish Communities', in *To See Ourselves as Others See Us: Christians, Jews, 'Others' in Late Antiquity*, ed. by J. Neusner and E. S. Frerichs (Chico, CA: Scholars Press, 1985), 93–115, here 103 n. 27; 'The Divine Agent and His Counterfeit in Philo and the Fourth Gospel', in *Aspects of Religious Propaganda in Judaism and Early Christianity*, ed. by E. Fiorenza (Notre Dame: University of Notre Dame, 1976); *The Moral World of the First Christians* (Philadelphia: Westminster Press, 1986); 'Social Functions of Apocalyptic Language in Pauline Christianity', in *Apocalypticism in the Mediterranean World*, ed. by David Hellholm (Tübingen: Mohr-Siebeck, 1983), 687–705. See also other works by Professor Meeks in the bibliography.

[142] 'The Social Description of Early Christianity', *RelSR* 1 (1975), 19–25.

[143] 'The Sociological Interpretation of the New Testament: The Present State of Research', *NTS* 26 (1980), 176.

[144] John G. Gager, 'Shall We Marry Our Enemies? Sociology and the New Testament', *Int* 36 (1982), 256–65; C. Duling, 'Insights from Sociology for New Testament Christology: A Test Case', *SBL 1985 Seminar Papers*, SBLSP 24 (1985), 351–68; Thomas F. Best, 'The Sociological Study of the New Testament: Promise and Peril of a New Discipline', *SJT* 36 (1983), 181–94.

[145] E.g., F. F. Segovia, *Love Relationships in the Johannine Tradition* (Chico, CA: Scholars Press, 1982); Carolyn Osiek, *What Are They Saying about the Social Setting of the New Testament?*, expanded and rev. edn (New York and Mahwah, NJ: Paulist Press, 1992); J. P.

was not wholly justified in view of Leroy's detailed and extensive study four years earlier and sociological studies dating even earlier than Leroy, especially by German scholarship.[146] Building upon Martyn's thesis and the sociologists Peter Berger and Thomas Luckmann,[147] Meeks connected Johannine language to its community life. Meeks explored the role which the 'ascent-descent' language of John played for a community experiencing alienation and hostility. He, following Martyn, postulated that

---

Louw, ed., *Sociolinguistics and Communication* (London: United Bible Societies, 1986); Howard Clark Kee, *Chrisitan Origins in Sociological Perspective* (Philadelphia: Westminster Press, 1980); Takashi Onuki, 'Zur literatursoziologischen Analyse des Johannes evangeliums: auf dem Wege zur Methodenintegration', *AJBI* 8 (1982), 162–216; Kenelm O. L. Burridge, *New Heaven, New Earth: A Study of Millennarian Activities* (Oxford, OUP, 1969); Meredith B. McGuire, *Religion: The Social Context*, 4th edn (London: Wadsworth, 1997); Christopher Rowland, 'Reading the New Testament Sociologically: An Introduction', *Theology* 88 (1985), 358–64; Shailer Matthews, *The Social Teaching of Jesus: An Essay in Christian Sociology* (New York: Macmillan, 1897).

[146] Shirley Jackson Case, *The Evolution of the Early Christianity* (Chicago: University of Chicago Press, 1914); idem, *The Social Origins of Christianity* (Chicago: University of Chicago Press, 1923); Edwin A. Judge, *The Social Pattern of the Christian Groups in the First Century* (London: Tyndale Press, 1960); idem, 'The Early Christians as a Scholastic Community', *JRH* 1 (1960), 4–15, 125–37. German scholars had utilised sociological insights since the 1900s as part of the form-critical approach to the Bible. Gerd Theissen, 'Zur forschungsgeschichtlichen Einordnung der soziologischen Fragestellung', in *Studien zur Soziologie des Urchristentums*, 2nd edn (Tübingen: Mohr, 1983 [orig. 1979]), 3–34, believes this new approach was an offshoot of the sociology of literature which postulated that 'types of literature' or genres (*Gattungen*) are bound to and shaped by specific types of social life-settings (*Sitz im Leben*). In fact, the expression 'Sitz im Leben' is a sociological conception. Rudolf Bultmann characterised these two notions as sociological concepts, from the first edition of his 'Geschichte der synoptischen Tradition' in 1921. See further studies by A. Deissmann, *Das Urchristentum und die unteren Schichten*, 2nd edn (Göttingen: Vandenhoeck & Ruprecht, 1908); Adolf von Harnack, *Die Mission und Ausbreitung des Christentums in den ersten drei Jahrhunderten*, 2 vols (Leipzig: J. C. Hinrichs, 1902); Gerd Theissen, 'Soziale Schichtung in der korinthischen Gemeinde', *ZNW* 65 (1974), 232–73; and *Urchristliche Wundergeschichten: Ein Beitrag zur formgeschichtlichen Erforschung der synoptischen Evangelien*, SNT 8 (Gütersloh: Gütersloher Verlagshaus Gerd Mohn, 1974, ET 1983); idem. *Authoritätskonflikte in den johanneischen Gemeinden* (Thessalonika, 1988); Dietfried Gewalt, 'Neutestamentliche Exegese und Soziologie', *EvT* 31 (1971), 87–99; Peter Lampe, *Die standtrömischen Christen in den ersten beiden Jahrhunderten: Untersuchungen zur Sozialgeschichte*, 2nd edn (Tübingen: Mohr-Seibeck, 1988); Klaus Berger, 'Wissenssoziologie und Exegese des Neuen Testaments', *Kairos* 19 (1977), 124–33. For a history of the development of the sociology of religion, see Roland Robertson, *Sociological Interpretation of Religion* (Oxford: Blackwell, 1972), 7–33; John Gager, *Kingdom and Community: The Social World of Early Christianity* (Englewood Cliffs, NJ: Prentice-Hall, 1975); Daniel Harrington, 'Sociological Concepts and the Early Church: A Decade of Research', *TS* 41 (1980), 181–90; B. Malina, *The New Testament World: Insights from Cultural Anthropology* (Atlanta: John Knox Press, 1981); Cyril Rodd, 'On Applying a Sociological Theory to Biblical Studies', *JSOT* 19 (1981), 95–106; D. Kyrtatas, *The Social Structure of the Early Christian Communities* (New York: Vero; London: Methuen, 1987); Richard A. Horsley, *Sociology and the Jesus Movement* (New York: Continuum, 1994).

[147] Peter Berger and Thomas Luckmann, *The Social Construction of Reality: A Treatise in the Sociology of Knowlege* (Harmondsworth: Penguin, 1967).

the story of Jesus in John's Gospel in effect is also the story of the Johannine group in a progressive alienation from the Jewish community.[148] He sums up his argument as follows:

> In telling the story of the Son of Man who came down from heaven and then reascended after choosing a few of his own out of the world, the book defines and vindicates the existence of the community that evidently sees itself as unique, alien from its world, under attack, misunderstood, but living in unity with Christ and through him with God. It could hardly be regarded as a missionary tract, for we may imagine that only a very rare outsider would get past the barrier of its closed metaphorical system. It is a book for insiders.[149]

Meeks envisages a continuing dialectic between the group's historical experience and their symbolic world. He believes that the community's christological claims led to their alienation from other Jews in the synagogue and finally brought about their expulsion. This experience was then projected onto the story of Jesus, who was increasingly depicted as the stranger, never accepted by his own ('the Jews') and totally incomprehensible to them. According to Meeks, these extreme christological motifs, and the accompanying totalistic and exclusive claims, drove the Johannine group into further sectarian isolation.[150] This social situation of the community was mirrored in its depiction of Jesus as opposed to his unbelieving people. Therefore, an important function of the book and its language is to provide and reinforce the community's social identity.[151] In his study, Meeks gives prominent attention to the Nicodemus dialogue which he believes is a virtual parody of a revelation discourse. 'What is "revealed" is that Jesus is *incomprehensible*, even to "the teacher of Israel"...within the context of Jewish piety...The reader without special prior information would be as puzzled as Nicodemus.'[152] For Meeks, the cryptic language of John is a window into the symbolic universe[153] of the group. Why did the community engage in the creation of such a coded

---

[148] Meeks, 'Man From Heaven', 69.

[149] Meeks, 'The Son of Man in Johannine Sectarianism', in *The Interpretation of John*, ed. by J. Ashton (Philadelphia: Fortress; London: SPCK, 1986), 162-63.

[150] Meeks, 'Man From Heaven', 69; cf. 'Breaking Away', 103.

[151] Ibid., 68-72, cf. idem, 'Breaking Away', 93-115.

[152] Meeks, 'Man From Heaven', 57 (author's emphasis). Cf. J. M. Bassler, 'Mixed Signals: Nicodemus in the Fourth Gospel', *JBL* 108 (1989), 635-46; R. Bauckham, 'Nicodemus and the Gurion Family', *JTS* n.s. 47 (1996), 1-37.

[153] This terminology (i.e., symbolic universe) is borrowed from Peter L. Berger and Thomas Luckmann's sociology of knowledge and this probably constitutes the first use of these perspectives in New Testament studies. Peter L. Berger, 'The Sociological Study of Sectarianism', *Social Research* 21 (1954), 467-85.

language? In Meeks's sociological paradigm, the answer is clear – conflict with the synagogue. He writes, 'There can be no question, as Louis Martyn has shown, that the actual trauma of the Johannine community's separation from the synagogue and its continuing hostile relationships with the synagogue come clearly to expression here'.[154] And what can be inferred from the relation between the language and this conflict? According to Meeks, the way in which Jesus relates to 'the Jews' follows a pattern in which he counters rejection with a private language which they could not understand.[155] This coded cryptic language gives the Johannine community a religious legitimacy, a theodicy, in their actual isolation from the larger society.[156] Meeks sees the whole Gospel as a closed system of metaphors, which must be accepted totally or it will be entirely misunderstood.[157]

One can clearly detect in Meeks's proposal echoes of Martyn and Leroy. Meeks's solution is subject to much the same criticism of method in that the text is read in the light of a particular sociological model and the same picture emerges each time – the Johannine community was a sect and its document (i.e. the Gospel) reflects the private language of a sect. However, as I shall endeavour to show later in this chapter, this picture is incompatible with the message and the theology of John's Gospel.

There have been many other sociological studies of the Fourth Gospel built upon Martyn and Meeks's proposals. The vast majority of these studies have articulated in different ways the same central thesis. The conclusions are almost always the same – a sectarian document produced by a rejected and isolated group of Christians to maintain and enforce the social cohesiveness of the sect. These positions are often set forth with such enthusiasm, conviction and an authoritative voice that they leave an impression of factual certainty, when in fact what we have is a hypothetical possibility.

In the context of these sociological models, the language of the Fourth Gospel has been characterised increasingly by such descriptions as a 'private language', 'anti-language', 'sectarian language' or similar depictions[158] by such scholars as Walter Rebell, Jerome Neyrey, Bruce Woll,

---

[154] By 'here', he means in the story of the hostility between Jesus and the Jews in the Gospel. 'Man From Heaven', 69.

[155] Ibid., 68–9.

[156] Ibid., 70.

[157] Ibid., 68.

[158] John E. Hurtgen, *Anti-Language in the Apocalypse of John* (Lewiston, NY: Mellon Press, 1993), 51, describes 'anti-language' as the language of social resistance. It is a language like any

Gerd Theissen, Takashi Onuki, F. F. Segovia, David Rensberger, Klaus Wengst, M. de Jonge, Jürgen Becker, R. Brown, R. Kysar, Johannes Beutler, and D. Moody Smith among others.[159] In these works, once again, the Gospel is set in the context of the conflict between the synagogue and the Johannine community, leading to a traumatic expulsion, subsequent religious dislocation, and isolation and even alienation from the larger Jewish society. Rensberger goes so far as to conclude that the Johannine community would have had sectarian tendencies not only in relation to Judaism but also other Christians.[160]

4.4.3. Further Criticism of the Sectarian Model

The characterisation of Johannine Christianity as sectarian and its language as a language of a 'sect', for the most part, has escaped rigorous critical scrutiny. My general objections to, and overall criticisms of, these models may be summarised as follows. First, these hypotheses essentially depend on the post-AD 70 date of the Gospel. However, there is little explicit internal evidence in the Gospel itself to definitively support its post-AD 70 date. Some scholars in recent years have begun to favour an earlier date for the composition of the Gospel. Klaus Berger, for example, in his 1997 monograph, *Im Anfang war Johannes: Datierung und Theologie des vierten Evangeliums*, has proposed that John's Gospel was composed before AD 70 about the time of the composition of Mark.[161] Some twenty years earlier, J. A. T. Robinson dated the Fourth Gospel to ca. AD 65 and the Epistles to AD 60–65. He contended that unless one *begins* with a late date, there is no more reason for reading the events of AD 85–90 into the Gospel (e.g., Jn. 9:22) than for seeing a reference to the Bar Kochba revolt (AD 135) in 5:45.[162] Leon Morris seven years earlier had examined the

---

other language. Its function is to express and maintain the social structure. Cf. Malina, 'The Gospel of John', 11–12; M. A. K. Halliday in his *Language as Social Semiotic: The Social Interpretation of Language and Meaning* (London: Edward Arnold, 1978); Mary Douglas, *Nature Symbols: Explorations in Cosmology* (New York: Vintage, 1973), 77–92.

159 The works of these scholars have already been cited throughout this chapter. See my earlier footnotes.

160 Rensberger, *Overcoming the World*, 75. Cf. Brown, *Community of the Beloved*, 71–88; Martyn, 'Glimpses', 107–21.

161 (Stuttgart: Quell, 1997).

162 Robinson, *Redating the New Testament*, 254–311. Also see the papers given at the symposium which met to discuss Robinson's thesis on 'Redating of the New Testament': *Die Datierung der Evangelien: Symposion des Instituts für Wissenschaftstheoretische Grundlagenforschung vom 20–23 mai 1982 in Paderborn*, ed. by R. Wegner; Tonbandnachschrift (Paderborn: Deutsches Institut für Bildung und Wissen, 1982); esp. Robinson's own paper (pp.

reasons offered for the late dating of the Gospel and concluded that nothing demanded a date later than AD 70 and expressed his scepticism 'whether we can go much beyond that'.[163] Similar doubts about the late dating of the Gospel has been expressed both in the past and in recent years.[164] Often, for example, the late date of the Gospel is deduced from John's high christology. However, the New Testament evidence offers strong indications that a high christology existed quite early outside the Johannine corpus even if this christology was not always expressed as clearly and explicitly as in John's Gospel.[165]

Second, characterising the Johannine Christianity as 'sectarian' in distinction from other Christian communities in the first century is dubious. As I noted earlier, assuming that under the pretext of the curse on the *minim*, excommunication or exclusion was taking place, this would not have been unique to the Johannine community. It would have been the experience of many New Testament Christians.[166] Robin Scroggs has used the sociological criteria applied to John to show that by the same standards,[167] the Christianity of the Synoptic traditions may also be characterised as a 'sect'.[168] However, once this social category is used indiscriminately and with such broad applications, then it is no longer a meaningful description since one can then categorise various social groups as simply sects. To say that the Fourth Gospel is a sectarian writing assumes too much, and to infer that conflict with Judaism led to isolationism lacks justification. Matthew and Mark also recount a bitter conflict with Judaism (e.g., Mt. 11; 12:24–45; 23:13–36; Mk. 3:22–30; 7:1–

231–3). On the revolt of Bar Kokhba, see B. Isaac and A. Oppenheimer, 'The Revolt of Bar Kokhba, Scholarship and Ideology', *JJS* 36 (1985), 33–60.

[163] *Studies in the Fourth Gospel* (Grand Rapids: Eerdmans, 1969), 283–92.

[164] D. Wallace, 'John 5:2 and the Date of the Fourth Gospel', *Bib* 71 (1990), 177–205; F. L. Gribbs, 'A Reassessment of the Date of Origin and the Destination of the Gospel of John',*JBL* 89 (1970), 38–55; C. H. Dodd, *Historical Tradition in the Fourth Gospel* (Cambridge: CUP, 1963), 213–5; B. F. Westcott, *The Epistle to the Hebrews* (Reprint, Grand Rapids: Eerdmans, 1955), xxxix. Cf. Kysar's survey in *Fourth Evangelist*, 166–72.

[165] Cf. Phil. 2:6–11; Gal. 4:4; 2 Cor. 8:9; Col. 1:15–21; Heb. 1.

[166] See M. Hengel, *The Charismatic Leader and his Followers* (New York: Crossroad, 1981); cf. G. Theissen, *The First Followers of Jesus: A Sociological Analysis of Early Christianity* (London: SCM, 1978); H. C. Kee, *Community of the New Age: Studies in Mark's Gospel* (London: SCM, 1977); J. H. Elliott, *A Home for the Homeless: A Sociological Exegesis of 1 Peter, its Situation and Strategy* (London: SCM, 1982).

[167] E.g., the rejection of the establishment's view of reality; the creation of a new reality with different assumptions; the vitality of the love and mutual acceptance within the group; the voluntary nature of the group; and the demand of total commitment to the group's new reality.

[168] Scroggs, 'Earliest Christian Communities', Part 2:1–23.

13), yet they are not thought of as sectarian. Indeed, much of the New Testament reveals the tension between the Christian community and Judaism. The break between the two was not unique to John. The Fourth Gospel's graphic expressions of such conflict do not necessitate sectarianism.

Third, the theological thrust of the Gospel of John disallows the depiction of it as a sectarian writing. As Teresa Okure in her thesis, *The Johannine Approach to Mission*,[169] has shown, the idea of mission to the world is one of the most important themes of the Fourth Gospel. The sending of the apostles (20:21; 4:38, 17:18) as well as Christ (3:17; 4:34; 5:24; 6:40; etc.)[170] is 'into the world'. Jesus' accomplished mission for the world remains as a permanent offer of salvation to this world despite its rejection (14:23; cf. 1:5; 16:33). To this end, the disciples and the Spirit remain in the world (17:15, 18–23; 16:8–11; 13:35). The social picture that emerges from the Gospel is that of a community intensely interested in the spread of the Christian message, engaged with the world, including the world of 'the Jews'.[171] The picture is not of a Christian community either alienated or seeking isolation, wishing to have nothing to do with the world: 'καθὼς ἀπέσταλκέν με ὁ πατήρ, κἀγὼ πέμπω ὑμᾶς', '...as my Father has sent me, even so I send you' (Jn. 20:21). Such expressions seem to portray a different image of Johannine Christianity than the one offered, for example, by Bryan Wilson who classifies the community as an 'introversionist sect' which 'sees the world as irredeemably evil' and in renouncing it, seeks to establish a separate community.[172] This caricature is precisely what I mean by reading into the Gospel a preconceived social model and then interpreting the document in the light of it. Such models ignore or even suppress other aspects of the text. Wilson's description, for example, is contrary to the theological thrust of the Gospel where the intentions of Jesus and his followers seem to be that of saving the world

---

[169] (Tübingen: Mohr-Siebeck, 1988).

[170] Cf. Mark 1:38 interpreted by Luke 4:18, 43; Mark 9:37; and Matthew 15:24.

[171] Especially Muddiman, 'Resurrection of Jesus', 212–3. Cf. Kysar, *Fourth Evangelist*, 219; Jürgen Becker, 'Beobachtungen zum Dualismus im Johannesevangelium', *ZNW* 65 (1974), 71–87; Onuki, *Gemeinde und Welt*, 42–51; Jeffrey A. Trumbower, *Born from Above: The Anthropology of the Gospel of John* (Tübingen: Mohr-Siebeck 1992), 114; Rensberger, *Overcoming the World*, 146; Luise Schottroff, *Der Glaubende und die feindliche Welt*, WMANT 37 (Neukirchen-Vluyn: Neukirchener Verlag, 1970), 229–33; Bultmann, *John*, 54–5; Barrett, *St John*, 161–2; Schnackenburg, *St. John*, 1:255–6.

[172] Bryan R. Wilson, *Magic and the Millennium: A Sociological Study of Religious Movements of Protest Among Tribal and Third-World Peoples* (New York: Harper and Row, 1973), 18–30; idem, 'Patterns of Sectarianism', *Journal for the Scientific Study of Religion* 8 (1969), 202–3.

rather than abandoning it (cf. Jn. 3:16–18; 4:42; 7:37–38; 10:10; 12:46–47). In the Fourth Gospel, the Evangelist never counsels his audience to nourish an 'everlasting hatred' of those outside the believing community, as one may see in Qumran (1QS 9:21; 3:13–4:25; 1QM).[173] The believers are alerted to the world's hatred towards them, but they are never prompted or permitted to respond in kind. Indeed to the contrary, they are to be characterised by a genuine love and servanthood. If God 'so loved the world that He sent his Son into the world', then the followers of the Son may not do anything less than follow in the steps of their master. In addition, the universal, open invitation of the Gospel (e.g., 3:15, 16, 36; 4:14; 5:24; 6:35, 37, 47, 51, 54; 7:37–38; 8:12; 10:9; 11:25–26; 12:35–36, 46) disallows Wilson's representation.

Fourth, the characterisation of John's language as some form of 'private language', 'anti-language', or 'riddle' is also unwarranted. The language of the Fourth Gospel is incomprehensible to those who refuse to believe its tenets, but this is not because John utilises a private language. In fact, Meeks himself in his contribution to a collection of articles on Judaism in 1975, argued that John turns Jewish arguments against the Jews. He noted, 'the Fourth Gospel is most anti-Jewish just at the point it is most Jewish', an aphorism quoted by many.[174] This could not be the case if the language utilised was a private language. Indeed Meeks's statement may be taken a step further in that the Fourth Gospel is most Jewish also where it is most *Christian*. The Fourth Evangelist, in his defence of the faith, is fully engaged with the Torah, the prophets, wisdom, apocalyptic texts and themes. In addition, the positive presentation of the Messiah beginning from the Prologue onward is decisively informed by the Jewish Scriptures whose language was the language of Judaism.[175] It is granted that language plays a significant role in the identity, cohesiveness and bonding of a social group. However, this in itself does not support the inference that any group with a particular community language and a special community 'hermeneutic' (e.g., messianic hermeneutic) of a nationally shared corpus of literature (e.g., the Hebrew Bible in this case) and tradition may be described as a sect. On this criterion, the whole of early Christianity may

---

[173] Geza Vermes, *The Dead Sea Scrolls in English* (London: Hammondsworth, 1968), 88. Cf. the Qumran War Scroll (1QM) and the struggle of the 'sons of Light' (the members of the Qumran sect) against 'the sons of Darkness', particularly the Kittim (the Gentiles).

[174] Meeks, 'Am I a Jew?', 1:172.

[175] See Klaus Berger's criticism of Meeks in *Exegese des Neuen Testaments*, 230f.

be depicted as a sectarian movement, as indeed some have contended.[176] In fact, the entire first century could be labelled the 'century of the sects'.[177]

Fifth, a far more serious and basic criticism of some sociological studies of New Testament has to do with method. It is not difficult to imagine a community situation and read this imaginary social setting into a given document, just as simply as one can postulate the existence of the community itself. Characteristically, such a method is partial at both poles: certain features of the text are chosen to serve as a key in the inferential process, and then certain features of the background material are chosen to match and confirm the rightness of the theory.[178] Or a particular model or hypothesis is constructed or formulated concerning the social function of the text, based on narrowly defined and selective internal evidence (e.g., John 9); from that point, particular external evidence is sought for its confirmation. Finally, the hypothesis or the model is refined and elaborated in the light of a proposed 'fit' between internal and external evidence. The weakness of this increasingly prevalent method is the so-called 'mirror-reading' or inferring of the situation of a text from its data. The assumption here is that a literary text necessarily provides a clear window into the social world hidden behind the text. However, years ago, René Wellek and Austin Warren cautioned us that a literary work may provide only an outline of social history, and that an author is under no obligation to describe his social world in 'official terms'. Rather, he interacts with that world in a dialogic fashion, both playing upon and transforming its basic traits.[179]

---

[176] Christopher Rowland calls early Christianity a Jewish messianic sect. See *Christian Origins: An Account of the Setting and Character of the Most Important Messianic Sect of Judaism* (London: SPCK, 1985), xvii, 195, 263. Or Bengt Holmberg, *Sociology and the New Testament: An Appraisal* (Minneapolis: Fortress, 1990), 99, writes, 'Belief in a Messiah and in the claim that the Scriptures had actually been fulfilled was simply more or less sectarian, just like other movements on the Jewish scene before AD 70. Pauline Christianity was more open than Johannine Christianity, but can nonetheless be characterized as a sect.' Cf. Meeks, *The Moral World of the First Christians* (Philadelphia: Westminster Press, 1986), 98–104.

[177] Meeks, *Moral World*; Rowland, *Christian Origins*, 65; Holmberg, *Sociology*, 99. See Bryan Wilson, 'An Analysis of Sect Development', *American Sociological Review* 24 (1959), 3–15.

[178] See Martyn's introductory remarks in *History and Theology*, xii.

[179] R. Wellek and Austin Warren, *Theory of Literature*, 3rd edn (New York: Penguin, 1980 [orig. New York: Harcourt, Brace, 1948]). Cf. René Wellek and Thomas Luckmann, *The Social Construction of Reality* (New York: Harcourt, Brace, and Jovanovich, 1956); René Wellek, *Discriminations: Further Concepts of Criticism* (New Haven: Yale University Press, 1970); Norman Petersen, *Literary Criticism for New Testament Critics* (Philadelphia: Fortress, 1978), 24; Meir Sternberg, *Poetics of Biblical Narrative* (Bloomington: Indiana University Press, 1985), 1–7; Culpepper, *Anatomy*, 3; Holmberg, *Sociology and the New Testament*, 127; William Riley,

This approach whereby the literary texts are seen as a window into their social setting is transported to arts and humanities from social sciences and specifically finds its justification in the so-called sociology of knowledge and the sociology of literature. In both these fields there is an assumption that there exists an axiomatic correlation between the form and the content of the text in relation to the shape of a given community. For example, as Barton points out, the emphasis on the rigorous observance of the law in Matthew implies a community in competition with the Pharisees and at risk from Gentile antinomians; the so-called 'messianic secret' in Mark mirrors the interests of an early Christian eschatological sect; the opposition to wealth and the exaltation of the poor in Luke reveals a heterogeneous community made up of those on the margins of society; and the vilification of 'the Jews' in the Fourth Gospel betokens the hostility of the synagogue to the members of the Johannine community.[180]

Needless to say, such a method is fraught with the possibilities of error resulting from *undue selectivity*[181] or *over-interpretation* (making too much of perhaps quite innocent texts). Ernest Baasland criticises Meeks on similar grounds. He argues that Meeks elucidates one unknown (the Johannine group) with another (the social situation presupposed by their Gospel). This, Baasland believes, is circular reasoning in which the reconstruction of a specific, yet hypothetical, social situation (about which nothing else is known) out of a religious, mainly theological or hortatory text, is turned around and the meaning of the text is interpreted with the help of the situation that one now 'knows'.[182] It is also noteworthy that, as Christopher

---

'Situating Biblical Narrative: Poetics and the Transmission of Community Values', *Proceedings of Irish Biblical Association* 9 (1985), 38–52.

[180] Barton, 'Can We Identify the Gospel Audiences?', 176–177. For further elaboration and examples see P. F. Esler, *Community and Gospel in Luke-Acts* (Cambridge: CUP, 1987), 16–23; John M. G. Barclay, 'Mirror-Reading a Polemical Letter: Galatians as Test Case', *JSNT* 31 (1987), 73–93. J. Riches, 'The Synoptic Evangelists and Their Communities', in *Christian Beginning: Word and Community from Jesus to Post-Apostolic Times*, ed. by J. Becker (Louisville: Westminster/John Knox, 1993), 213–41; George Lyons, *Pauline Authobiography: Towards a New Understanding*, SBLDS 73 (Atlanta: Scholars Press, 1985), 75ff, esp. 96–105; Gager, *Kingdom and community*, 9–14. Cf. B. Wilson, *Magic and the Millennium*, 18–30; idem, 'Patterns of Sectarianism'; Berger, 'Sociological Study of Sectarianism', 479.

[181] I.e., fastening upon features of the text which actually support one's case but give a false impression of relating to a particular background. For example, S. Smalley, 'John's Revelation and John's Community', *BJRL* 69 (1986), 549–71; or Bruce Woll, *Johanine Christianity in Conflict*, 91, wherein he conceived a group of charismatic leaders in the Johannine community who considered themselves on equal footing with Jesus or even superior to him and competed with each other. Woll looks for his external evidence in the pneumatic Corinthian Christianity. Martyn, on the other hand, built his case primarily on the episode of John 9.

[182] Ernst Baasland, 'Urkristendommen i sosiologiens lys', *Tidskrift for Teologi og Kirke* 54

Tuckett contends, these reconstructions often do not say anything besides retelling in new terminology what is already known.[183] For example, in the case of Meeks, the sociological component of his article does not seem to add anything to his interpretation of the Gospel, but merely reinforces the interpretation he had already chosen. The mere fact that a social model can be made to fit the data in a given document does not prove its validity.

A further difficulty with these methods revolves around an uncontrolled use of 'allegory'. Here, there are two closely related dynamics in which allegory is used in two senses: 'allegory' as a so-called genre classification, and 'allegory' as a way of interpreting a text (i.e., 'allegorisation'). In the former, allegory as a genre classification,[184] details of the Gospel are seen as none-historical incidents from the community's reconstructed history.[185] The latter describes some critics' handling of the Gospel narratives as depicting a current situation under the guise of a situation or event in the life of the community (i.e., the story is seen as no more historical than that of, for example, the parable of the sower in Mt. 13:1-23). Brown's *Community of the Beloved Disciple* takes the allegorisation process further than Martyn, by treating the chronology of the narrative itself as an allegory, so that the Gospel actually gives a stage-by-stage history of the Johannine community, from the earliest converts among the followers of John the Baptist (chs. 1-3), through the entry of some anti-temple

---

(1984), 45–57 (57 n. 29). A similar circular reasoning may be evident in the work of Professor Gerd Theissen, especially his article, 'Die soziologische Auswertung religiöser Überlieferungen: Ihre methodologischen probleme am Beispiel des Urchristentums', *Kairos* 17 (1975), 284–99. See Peter Lampe's criticism of Theissen in *Die stadtrömischen Christen in den ersten beiden Jahrhunderten: Untersuchungen zur Sozialgeschichte*, WUNT 2.18 (Tübingen: Mohr-Siebeck, 1989 [1987]), 252; and also Werner George Kümmel, 'Das Urchristentum II. Arbeiten zur Spezialproblemen. b. Zur Sozialgeschichte und Soziologie der Urkirche', *TRu* 50 (1985), 327–63.

[183] Christopher Tuckett, *Reading the New Testament: Methods of Interpretation* (London: SPCK, 1987), 145ff.

[184] Allegory is an important interpretive component within *Redaktionsgeschichte* (conventionally translated as 'redaction criticism') the aims of which, according to Francis Watson, 'Toward a Literal Reading of the Gospels', 195–217, in *The Gospels for All Christians*, ed. by Richard Bauckham (Grand Rapids: Eerdmans, 1998), 198–99, would be 'to study the achievement of the evangelist as a creative theologian responding to the particular concerns of his own community.' For example, see W. Marxsen's study, *Mark the Evangelist: Studies on the Redaction History of the Gospel* (Nashville: Abingdon, 1969).

[185] See Bengt Holmberg's criticism of G. Theissen's reading of the Gospels in *Sociology and the New Testament*, 124–5, 127, 139. G. Theissen, *The First Followers of Jesus: A Sociological Analysis of the Earliest Christianity* (London: SCM, 1978). See also further Mark Stibbe, *John as Storyteller: Narrative Criticism and the Fourth Gospel*, SNTSMS 73 (Cambridge: University Press, 1992), 50–66; Culpepper, *Anatomy*, 3; Petersen, *Literary Criticism*, 24.

Samaritans (ch. 4), to the development of a 'high' christology (ch. 5) with the inevitable ensuing conflict with Judaism (chs. 7-10).

Finally, at an even more basic level, my objection to these approaches pertains to an indiscriminate application of social scientific methods to the works of literature in general and the Bible in particular, and here I have specifically in view the Gospel of John.[186] The social sciences began to play a major role in biblical studies with the work of Herman Gunkel (1862-1932), whose form-critical approach was developed under the influence of nineteenth century folklore studies.[187] Gunkel maintained that every literary genre in the Old Testament had an original setting in Israel's national life (*Sitz im Volkesleben*). In order to understand a genre, it was necessary to know the setting from which it came. An inherent danger in Gunkel's proposed method was the fallacy of over-generalisation which is an inherent problem in social studies including sociology. When sociology is used indiscriminately in the study of history to make historical inferences, it inevitably leads to over-generalisation. Sociology is often presented with claims to scientific objectivity and value-neutrality. However, sociology, like most disciplines, is laden with presuppositions and should not be applied indiscriminately with the hope that the end result will be factual, unbiased data. There is a methodical tendency in sociology, historically, and one may add, inherently, to be deterministic and reductionistic[188] in its treatment of supernatural and spiritual phenomena.

---

[186] See a critique by Frederik Wisse, 'Historical Method and the Johannine Community', *Arc* 20 (1992), 35-42. On the method and the application of social scientific approach see Bert F. Hoselitz, ed., *A Reader's Guide to the Social Sciences*, rev. edn (New York: Free Press, 1970), 1; John H. Elliott, *What is Social-Scientific Criticism?* (Minneapolis: Fortress, 1993); Robert R. Wilson, *Sociological Approaches to the Old Testament* (Philadelphia: Fortress, 1984); Emile Durkheim, *The Rules of Sociological Method*, 8th edn (New York: Free Press, 1966); Alex Inkeles, *What Is Sociology? A Methodological Enquiry* (London and Oxford: Alden and Mowbray, 1975); Ervin Laszlo, *The Systems View of the World: The Natural Philosophy of the New Developments in the Sciences* (New York: George Braziller, 1972); Jacques Richardson, ed., *Models of Reality: Shaping Thought and Action* (Mount Airy, MD: Lomond Publications, 1984); Robert Segal, *Religion and the Social Sciences* (Atlanta: Scholars Press, 1989); Max Weber, *Economy and Society: An Outline of Interpretive Sociology*, ed. by Guenther Roth and Claus Wittich, 2 vols (Berkeley and Los Angeles: University of California Press, 1978).

[187] Gunkel, 'Die Israelitische Literatur', in *Die kultur der Gegenwart;* ed. by Paul Hinneberg (Berlin: B. G. Teubner, 1960), I, 7:51-102.

[188] Reductionism refers to the procedure of subsuming one model into another when both of the models are at the same level of abstraction (e.g., to explain biology as simply one form of physics, economy as one form of psychology, etc.). The idea of 'subsuming' is the same as claiming that one's own conceptual system (model, theory) has a higher ontological status than others, which can be sufficiently explained within one's own superior system. Cf. Bruce J. Malina, 'The Social Sciences and Biblical Interpretation', in *Bible and Liberation: Political and Social Hermeneutics*, ed. by Gottwald (New York: Mary Knoll, 1983), 19; Peter L. Berger and Hansfried Kellner,

Thus it often distorts an emphatically theological understanding of the Bible.[189]

Stanley Stowers has pointed out the general tendency in sociological models to 'explain away' religious assumptions. He noted this even in regard to the work of Wayne Meeks. He criticised Meeks's attempt to explain the correlation between belief and social situations as the result of latent factors and not of explicit, conscious thinking and planning.[190] W. G. Kümmel, in his criticism of Gerd Theissen, observed a similar reluctance to let cognitive factors or theological assumptions play a structuring role in the reconstruction of the social life of early Christianity.[191]

In the early 1970s amid ever-increasing applications of literary criticism and sociological methods to the Bible, James Barr, in what he perceived to be the encroaching dangers of reading the Bible for something other than its intended design and purpose, insisted that 'the Bible must be read in a theological mode,' which means, he maintained, 'as a source of true knowledge about the objects described in the Bible – about God, about creation of the world, about his redemption of mankind, about sin and salvation, about the possibility of a future life.'[192] He singled out the decades between 1930 and 1960 as a time marked by revival of biblical influence and authority within Christian theology. This revival, he argued, was due to the fact that biblical scholars held the view that the Bible had authority because it testified to the great truths of God and his work in history for the salvation of mankind. He insisted that it would

---

Sociology Reinterpreted: An Essay on Method and Vocation (Harmondsworth: Penguin, 1982), 76, 90, 142; Robin Gill, *The Social Context of Theology: A Methodological Enquiry* (London and Oxford: Alden and Mowbray, 1975), 26–39, see especially chapter three, 'Explanation in Sociology and Theology'.

[189] Harrington, 'Sociological Concepts and the Early Church', 182f., expresses his reservation candidly, 'The New Testament writings are religious documents, and sociology has no satisfactory method for dealing with the divine or nonrational element that is so important in religious experience.' Note especially Holmberg's cautionary note in *Sociology and the New Testament*, 146. Cf. Norman Gottwald, *The Tribes Of Yahweh: A Sociology of the Religion of Liberated Israel 1250–1050 B.C.E.* (New York: Mary Knoll, 1979), 8–11.

[190] See especially S. K. Stowers, 'The Social Sciences and the Study of Early Christianity', in *Approaches to Ancient Judaism*, ed. by W. S. Green (Missoula, MT: Scholars, 1985), 5:149–81.

[191] Kümmel, 'Das Urchristentum II', 327–63, esp. 347–9, 361, criticises Theissen for neglecting the content of the belief of early Jewish Christian as a decisive factor in their life together and for a one-sided preoccupation with their social situation. See further Robert A. Segal, 'The Social Sciences and the Truth of Religious Belief', *Journal of American Academy of Religion* 48 (1980), 404; Best, 'Sociological Study', 127.

[192] James Barr, 'Reading the Bible as Literature', *BJRL* 56 (1973), 13, 10–33; idem, 'The Bible as Literature', in *The Bible in the Modern World* (New York: Harper and Row, 1973), 53–74.

'indeed be a thin and no doubt a useless reading' of the Scriptures which did not recognise their profoundly religious and theological character.[193] In a different field during the same period, E. D. Hirsch wrote his classic work, *Validity in Interpretation*,[194] with significant implications both for secular as well as sacred literature. Like Barr, he insisted that in the interpretive task there were natural modes for reading and interpreting texts in different fields. Once one steps out of this natural interpretive context and begins to read a text in an interpretive environment which is not natural to it, the result is often misinterpretation or invalid interpretations. Hirsch pointed out that

> Hermeneutic theory has always recognised that there may be different kinds of textual interpretation corresponding to different kinds of texts. The most venerable distinction has been that between *hermeneutica sacra* and *hermeneutica profana*, which is, of course, the distinction that Schleiermacher worked so energetically to overcome, though without success, as may be inferred from the continuing tradition of sacred hermeneutics.[195]

Later he continued:

> The most inclusive programmatic idea put forward in the admirable theoretical compendium by Wellek and Warren is the idea that literary interpretation must be intrinsic. They insist that the study of literature ought to be literary, just as the study and interpretation of philosophical texts ought to be philosophical. Behind this programmatic idea is a notion of validity: the literary study of literature is not simply an appropriate mode of interpretation; it is the only valid mode. To treat a literary text as though it were a document in history or biography is to misrepresent its nature.... All valid interpretation is thus intrinsic interpretation: whatever one may do with a literary text *after* it has been understood on its own terms achieves validity only because that preliminary task has been performed.[196]

In so far as the Scriptures are concerned, we recognise that the biblical texts are theological and religious documents. They are written with an underlying theological aim in view. Therefore, to follow Hirsch's analogy, theology 'is not simply an appropriate mode of interpretation; it is the only valid mode.'[197] To treat a sacred document in any other way is to misrepre-

---

[193] Ibid.

[194] E. D. Hirsch Jr., *Validity in Interpretation* (New Haven: Yale University Press, 1967). See also his later work *The Aims of Interpretation* (Chicago and London: University of Chicago Press, 1976).

[195] Hirsch, *Validity*, 112.

[196] Ibid. 113. For his reference to Wellek and Warren, see their work, *Theory of Literature* (cited earlier).

[197] Ibid.

sent its nature, and such a misrepresentation constitutes a perversion of its meaning. Therefore, not only is theology the most natural mode of the study of biblical documents, but also theology should be the *controlling* factor in their analysis when non-theological methods and disciplines are applied. This is not to say that social scientific methods, sociology or literary criticism are void of any value in biblical studies. Far from it. What it does mean is that in the application of such disciplines as sociology, one must be aware of the limitations and the latent assumptions. It further means, in John's case, that the theological tenets of a Gospel text should not be disregarded at the expense of imposing a reformulated paradigm; that, indeed, the theological purpose of the text and its meaning in God's plan of salvation should be the controlling factor which determines and shapes any conclusion about the biblical text and not the reverse.

Therefore, the sectarian picture of Johannine Christianity, I believe, is unjustifiably read out of the Gospel, and is an unsatisfactory explanation of John's perplexing language. I see the Fourth Gospel resulting from the post-resurrection theological conviction of the author that Jesus was indeed the promised Messiah whose mission had ushered in and established a new order in which Jews, Samaritans, and even Gentiles became one in Christ. Such a community with its commitment to Jesus, and by its belief that God in Jesus lives in and through it (cf. chs. 13–17), may have shown separatist tendencies but not in the sense of alienation from the world (cf. Mt. 5:11, 44; Lk. 6:22, 27).

John tells us of a 'world' which is alienated from God. Persecution may have intensified separatist sentiments and may have strengthened the community's commitment to Jesus (16:1–4; 17:14; 1 Jn. 3:13–14; cf. Acts 4:23–37) and ensured its witness of allegiance to him; however persecution would not necessarily have been the dynamic to shape its identity. The eschatological tradition of the Gospels, for example, as articulated in Matthew (24), Mark (13) and Luke (21) seems to indicate that the events of AD 66–70 themselves, rather than the Jamnian Council, were seen by Christians as making the decisive break with Judaism.

The Pauline epistles are filled with exhortations to separate from the world (e.g., Rom. 12:2; Eph. 2:2; Phil. 1:29; Gal. 1:4; Tit. 2:12; 1 Cor. 2:6–8, 7:31–34; cf. 1 Cor. 1:18–30; 11:32; Rom. 11:7–10; 2 Cor. 4:4; Gal. 4:3; 6:14), though utilising a different type of terminology (life according to the Spirit and life according to the flesh, Gal. 5:16–25); there is no evidence, for example, that the Corinthian community addressed by Paul was subject to persecution.

In the case of the Fourth Gospel, the community would have seen its position in the world as an agent of change and moral preservation (Jn. 1:5; 3:21; 11:36; 15:19; 17:14–16; 1 Jn. 1:5–7; 2:9–10, 16; 4:17). It is also important to remember that the idea of religious fellowship lived out socially (characterised as so-called 'sectarianism') was not a unique concept to the Johannine and New Testament Christians. Indeed it was practised with equal intensity by other contemporary religious groups.[198] Therefore, it seems to me, the primary impetus behind Johannine Christianity, its creation and the determining factor in the shaping of its identity, is its allegiance to Jesus and his new order of reality (18:26; cf. 3:18–21; 12:31; 16:11), rather than social and religious alienation.

4.4.4. The Non-Sectarian Emphasis of the Gospel

An important dimension in the Fourth Gospel which militates against characterising it as an introverted sectarian writing is the evangelistic-apologetic emphasis.[199] This evangelistic-apologetic emphasis does not negate the pastoral intention of the Fourth Evangelist in his Gospel. Indeed, in view of my earlier proposal, this distinction is unnecessary. In so far as the Gospel has an apologetic emphasis, like most apologetic writings, it

---

[198] E.g., Qumran, the Pharisees, Sadducees, and others. See Göran Forkman, *The Limits of the Religious Community: Expulsion from the Religious Community within the Qumran Sect, within Rabbinic Judaism, and within primitive Christianity* (Lund, Sweden: CWK Gleerup, 1972); Gryglewicz, 'Die Pharisäer und die Johanneskirche'; Neusner, 'Judaism after the Destruction of the Temple'; idem, *From Politics to Piety;* Smith, 'Palestinian Judaism in the First Century'; James D. Purvis, *The Samaritan Pentateuch and the Origin of the Samaritans Sect* (Cambridge, MA: Harvard University Press, 1968); A. Dupont-Sommer, *The Jewish Sect of Qumran and the Essenes* (London: Vallentine, Mitchell, 1954); Moshe Weinfeld, *The Organizational Pattern and the Penal Code of the Qumran Sect* (Göttingen: Vandenhoeck & Ruprecht 1986).

[199] Bornhäuser, *Das Johannesevangelium*, 158, 172; C. F. D. Moule, 'The Intention of the Evangelists', in *The Phenomenon of the New Testament* (London: SCM, 1967; reprinted from *New Testament Essays*, 1959), 103f; Anton Fridrichsen, 'La pensée missionaire dans le quatrième évangile', *Arbeiten und Mitteilungen aus dem neutestamentichen Seminar zu Uppsala*, VI, ed. by A. Fridrichsen (Uppsala, 1937), 39–45; W. Oehler, *Das Johannesevangelium eine Missionsschrift für die Welt* (Bertelsmann, 1936); idem, *Zum Missionscharackter des Johannesevangeliums* (Bertelsmann, 1941); Dodd, *Interpretation of the Fourth Gospel,* 9; Van Unnik, 'Purpose of St. John's Gospel', 382–411; E. D. Freed, 'Did John Write His Gospel to Win Samaritan Converts?', *NovT* 12 (1970), 241–56; Carson, *Gospel According to John*, 87–95; L. Morris, *The Gospel According to John* (Grand Rapids: Eerdmans, 1971), 855–7; Trites, *New Testament Concept of Witness,* 78; G. Reim, *Studien zum alttestamentlichen Hintergrund des Johannesevangeliums* (Cambridge: CUP, 1974), ch. 9. For the apologetic emphasis, see Moule, *The Phenomenon of the New Testament,* 101–14; idem, *The Birth of the New Testament*, 3rd edn (London: Adam and Charles Black, 1982), 136–37; H. Y. Gamble, *Books and Readers in the Early Church* (New Haven: Yale University Press, 1995), 103.

intends to persuade the sceptics as much as aiming to strengthen the resolve of the believing community.[200]

The Gospel would have been a document of value for all those who would have come in contact with it, either through hearing it or reading it themselves. By providing an avalanche of scriptural evidence, the Gospel reassured the Christians, perhaps beset by counterclaims, that indeed, Jesus is the Christ, while at the same time the same evidence targeted a divided Judaism in its response to Jesus. On the one hand, it was a critical, scolding appraisal of their unbelief. But on the other hand, it was also a persuasive appeal to them to believe that Jesus is the Christ, the Son God.

However, the seemingly anti-Jewish polemic (e.g., 8:31–59) in John has led some to deny any evangelistic intent.[201] In fact, for some scholars, the Johannine polemic is not just against the Jews. They contend a polemic tone permeates the whole of the Fourth Gospel.[202] This polemic

---

[200] Similarly Hans Windisch, 'Der johanneische Erzählungsstil', *EYXAPIΣTHPION: Studien zur Religion und Literatur des Alten und Neuen Testaments. Fs. Hermann Gunkel zum 60. Geburtstag* (Göttingen: Vandenhoeck & Ruprecht, 1923), 174–213, argued that John was utilising the technique of 'convincing preaching' or of 'pastoral (*seelsorgerliche*) pedagogy' which is seen as part of John's persuasive purpose. He was the first in this century to praise the pastoral and pedagogical techniques of the Evangelist. Schnackenburg, *Das Johannesevangelium*, 1:456, on the other hand, maintains against Windisch that 'Dem Evangelisten geht es nicht um eine pädagogischseelsorgerische Einwirkung Jesu auf die stufenweise Selbstoffenbarung Jesu.' Cf. Brown, *John*, 1:I–XII. For relevant disscusions, see R. F. Collins, 'Representative Figures of the Fourth Gospel'; Xavier Léon Dufour, 'Towards a Symbolic Reading of the Fourth Gospel', *NTS* 27 (1981), 439–56, esp. p. 444; E. Kraft, 'Die Personen des Johannesevangeliums', *EvT* 16 (1956), 18–32; Felix Porsch, *Pneuma und Wort* (Frankfurt: Peter Lang, 1974), 2; Birger Olsson, *Structure and Meaning in the Fourth Gospel: A Text-Linguistic Analysis of John 2:1-11 and 4:1-42*, Coniectanea Biblica, NTS 6 (Lund, Sweden: CWK Gleerup, 1974), 249–50.

[201] The anti-Jewish polemic in John was made popular by Erich Grässer, 'Die antijüdische Polemic im Johannesevangelium', *NTS* 10 (1964–1965), 74–90; George Richter, 'Die Gefangennahme Jesu nach Johannesevangelium', *BibLeb* 10 (1969), 26–39. Cf. J. Painter, *The Quest for the Messiah: The History, Literature and Theology of the Johannine Community* (Edinburgh: Clark,1991), 102f; J. Blank, *Krisis: Untersuchungen zur johanneischen Christologie und Eschatologie* (Freiburg: Lambertus, 1964), 210f.

[202] Apart from the Jews, John's polemic is seen to be focused on heresies, such as docetism or Gnosticism (Irenaeus, *Adv. Haer. III*, 14:1). This was the view also held by such scholars as R. H. Strachan, *The Fourth Gospel: Its Significance and Environment*, 3rd edn (London: SCM, 1941), 44f; the 'anti-docetic polemic' view held by Wilhelm Wilkens, *Zeichen und Werke: Ein Beitrag zur Theologie des 4. Evangeliums in Erzähungs – und Redestoff*, ATANT 55 (Zurich: Zwingli, 1969), 167–8; see the review of his book by J. M. Robinson, 'Recent Research in the Fourth Gospel', *JBL* 78 (1959), 242ff. For the 'anti-Gnostic polemic' view, see R. Bultmann, *John*, 9, who speaks of 'a pointed anti-Gnostic theology' of the Gospel. See also Bultmann's 'Die Bedeutung der neuerschlössenen mandäischen und manichäischen Quellen für das Verständnis des Johannesevangeliums', *ZNW* 24 (1925), 100–46; also Siegried Schulz, *Das Evangelium nach Johannes* (Göttingen: Vandenhoeck & Ruprecht, 1972); idem, *Komposition und Herkunft der johanneischen Reden*, BWANT 81 (Stuttgart: Kohlhammer, 1960), 28–187; P. Borgen, *Bread from Heaven: An Exegetical Study of Manna in the Gospel of John and in the Writings of Philo*,

content, for many scholars, constitutes the single most important reason why John's Gospel cannot be viewed as having a missionary or evangelistic focus, whether for the Jews or the world.[203] Therefore, from their viewpoint, the Gospel can only have an internal pastoral emphasis.[204] Meinertz, for example, is quite adamant that the polemic against the Jews so pervades the Gospel that there is no way that it can be considered 'als eine Missionsschrift für Israel'.[205] However John's polemic stance is not against all 'the Jews' but against the Jewish authorities.[206] His polemic stance may be viewed positively as a persuasive, not alienating, force. John's numerous appeals to the Hebrew Scriptures support the concept, at least to some extent, that he may have had an apologetic agenda focused on the undecided Jews.[207] Or he may have intended to drive a wedge

---

NovTSup 10 (Leiden: Brill, 1965), 148. See the critique by D. Guthrie, *New Testament Introduction: Gospels and Acts* (London: Tyndale Press, 1965), 251; W. F. Howard, *The Interpreters Bible*, vol. 8 (New York: Abingdon, 1952), 437–63, also Fritz Neugebauer, *Die Entstehung des Johannesevangeliums* (Arbeiten zur Theologie, 1/36; Stuttgart: Calwer Verlag, 1968), 28–39. A few have argued that the Evangelist's polemic was in part directed against the disciples of John the Baptist (cf. Acts 19:1ff) who may have claimed the Baptist, rather than Jesus, was the Messiah. This thesis was first advanced by J. D. Michaelis, *Einleitung in das Neue Testament* II (4/1788), 1140 – cited in Kümmel, *Einleitung in das Neue Testament* (Heidelberg: Quelle und Meyer, 17th print., 1973), 185 n. 105; K. G. Bretschneider and W. Baldensperger, cited by Wind, 'Destination and Purpose', 32. Other potential targets of John's polemic have included 1) an anti-Moses polemic: W. Meeks, *The Prophet-King: Moses Traditions and the Johannine Christology*, NovTSup 14 (Leiden: Brill, 1967), 318–9, 297–301; 2) anti-Great Church polemic: Käsemann, *Jesu Letzer Wille nach Johannes 17*, 3rd edn (Tübingen: Mohr-Siebeck, 1971), 65–117, which reveals itself in its 'anti-Sacramental' character. For Brown, *Community of the Beloved*, esp. 81–8, the polemic lies in the reaction to the 'low christology' of 'the Great Church'. There is even a proposed polemic against some of the members of the Johannine community itself: see Meeks, *Prophet-King*, 318–9; Wilkens, *Zeichen und Werke*, 167–8; Schulz, *Das Evangelium nach Johannes*, and *Komposition und Herkunft der johanneischen Reden*, 28–187. B. D. Woll, 'The Departure of "The Way": The First Farewell Discourse in the Gospel of John', *JBL* 99 (1980), 225–39; idem, *Johannine Christianity in Conflict*, 128, 176, n.79, believes that the polemic was directed against Christian prophets who claimed to be Christ (cf. Mk 13:5–6); also Käsemann, *Jesu Letzer Wille nach Johannes 17*, 65–117.

[203] Hans Conzelmann, *Grundriss der Theologie des Neuen Testaments* (Munich: Chr. Kaiser, 1967), 362. Nicol, *Semeia in the Fourth Gospel*, 143, suggests that the Evangelist 'lived in a town where the Synagogue was too hostile for missionary work.'

[204] F. Hahn, *Das Problem der Mission in der sonstigen nach paulinischen Tradition und den johanneischen Schriften: Das Verständnis der Mission im Neuen Testament*, WMANT 13 (Neuchirchener-Vluyn: Neukirchener Verlag, 1963), 123 n. 2; Heinrich Weinel, *Grundriss der theologischen Wissenschaften: Biblische Theologie des Neuen Testaments* (Tübingen: Mohr-Siebeck, 1928), 411; Mulder, 'Ontstaan en Doel', 233–58; Ashton, *Understanding*, 105; Painter, *Quest for the Messiah*, 103; Fortna, *Gospel of Signs*, 224, 229–31; Meeks, 'The Divine Agent', 43–67, esp. 44; N. L. Geisler, 'Johannine Apologetics', *BibSac* 554 (1979), 333–43.

[205] *Theologie des Neuen Testaments II* (Bonn: Peter Hanstein, 1950), 268, 313.

[206] See chapter five.

[207] John's apologetic objectives in part may have been intended to serve as a warning to others.

between the Jewish leadership and the ordinary Jews who may have had an open mind on the Christian message but feared the religious authorities.

Some point to the farewell-speeches in chapters 14–17 of the Gospel, where Jesus stresses the 'holding', 'keeping', or 'remaining' in the faith, as evidence that the Gospel does not have an external (i.e., evangelistic) objective.[208] Some have objected that Johannine irony requires a Christian audience/readership, which weakens its evangelistic intent. F. Vouga argues irony in the Gospel functions by engaging the reader's sympathies for one side or the other of a debate in which the pretensions and misunderstandings of one side are exposed. In the case of John, the *a priori* sympathies of the audience must be on Jesus' side, or else *Jesus* would be shown up as the object of ridicule. Therefore the Gospel is aimed at Christians, who are invited to enjoy a sense of superior insight over against 'the Jews'.[209] However Johannine irony itself, in the post-Easter context, could have functioned as an effective evangelistic tool in beckoning the reader not to follow the path of disbelief but to read deeper, and as such, it would draw the reader into the experience of revelation.[210]

Others who object to any form of evangelistic intent in the Fourth Gospel do so by questioning the logistics. The Book of Acts gives us a glimpse as to how such missionary endeavours were carried out. Clearly the first recipients of the Gospel would have been the Christians. And they would have been the mechanism to disseminate the content of the Gospel. But to say that the Gospel was sieved through the Christian community does not negate its evangelistic emphasis.

What particularly strengthens the outward 'missionary' perspective of the Fourth Evangelist is his emphasis on the theme of 'mission'. As Teresa Okure demonstrates, 'precise meaning, nature and scope of mission in John's Gospel are subjects of perennial debate, but that mission itself is a leitmotif or "foundation theme" of the Gospel is hardly a matter for dispute.'[211] Throughout the Scriptures, and emphatically in the Fourth

---

So Wilhelm Oehler, *Das Johannesevangelium: Ein Missionsschrift für die Welt, der Gemeinde ausgelegt* (Gütersloh: Bertelsmann, 1936), 29; Kümmel, *Einleitung in das Neue Testament*, 197.

[208] Wind, 'Destination and Purpose', 49, cites Feine, Behm, and Kümmel among these.

[209] Francois Vouga, *Le Cadre Historique et l'Intention Thevologique de Jean* (Paris: Beauchesne, 1977), 34f; cf. Rebell, *Gemeinde als Gegenwelt*, 129; Wengst, *Bedrängte Gemeinde*, 34–6.

[210] Gail O'Day, *Revelation in the Fourth Gospel: Narrative Mode and Theological Claim* (Philadelphia: Fortress, 1986), 93–6.

[211] *Johannine Approach to Mission*, 1; as well as Bultmann, 'Die Bedeutung der neuerschlossenen mandäischen und manichäischen Quellen für das Verständnis des Johannesevangeliums', *ZNW* 24 (1925), 100–46 the 'centrale Anschauung' or 'Grundkonzeption'

Gospel, the missionary vision of the people of God receives its impetus from God's own impulse to reach humanity with the light of his self-manifestation. Consistently he is the sending and commissioning agent. He sends the prophets. He sends John the Baptist, the 'Word', the Holy Spirit and the disciples.[212] Indeed the history of salvation may be viewed as one persistent divine missionary endeavour. The Fourth Evangelist seems almost to review this history in his many allusions to the Old Testament.[213] Not only does he review it, he also captures the climax of this divine missionary undertaking for the world (1:14),[214] and highlights it when Jesus characteristically designates his Father as ὁ πέμψας με πατήρ ('the Father who sent me').

This insistently repeated phrase occurs in different forms forty times in the Gospel.[215] John is unequivocal that the work belongs to the Father, αὐτοῦ τὸ ἔργον (4:34; cf. 3:16; 5:17). He has commissioned the Son for its execution, and in this 'work', the Father and the Son are in unison.[216] Jesus

---

of the Gospel is that Jesus is 'der Gesandte Gottes...der Offenbarung bringt durch Worte und Taten' (p. 102); McPolin, 'Mission in the Fourth Gospel', *Irish Theological Quarterly* 36 (1969), 113–22, esp. 114; idem, *John*, NT Message 6 (Wilmington, DE: M. Glazier; Dublin: Veritas, 1979), 75, 97; Ernst Haenchen, 'der Vater der mich gesandt hat', *NTS* 9 (1963), 208–16; Werner Bieder, *Gottes Sendung und der missionarische Auftrag nach Matthäus, Lukas, Paulus und Johannes*, Theologische Studien 82 (Zurich: EVZ-Verlag, 1965), 40; Joseph Kuhl, *Die Sendung Jesu und der Kirche nach dem Johannesevangelium*, Studia Instituti Missiologica Societatis Verbi Domini (St. Augustin: Styler, 1967), 1 also notes that the 'Sendungsidee' constitutes an essential aspect of Johannine theology. See also Rudolf Schnackenburg, 'Die Messiasfrage im Johannesevangelium', *Neutestamentliche Aufsatze. Festschrift für Joseph Schmid zum 70. Geburtstag*, ed. by J. Blinzler, O. Kuss, and F. Mussner (Regensburg: Friedrich Pustet, 1963), 240–64, and *Johannesevangelium*, 1:136–7; R. E. Brown, 'The Kerygma of the Gospel According to John: The Johannine View of Jesus in Modern Studies', *Interpretation* 21 (1967), 387–440, esp. 389–92.

[212] J. Radermakers, Mission et apostolate dans l'évangile johannique', *SE* 2 = TU 87 (1964), 100–21; Martin Hengel, 'Die Ursprünge der christlichen Mission', *NTS* 18 (1971), 35–7; Bultmann, 'Die Theologie des Johannesevangeliums: Die Sendung des Sohnes', in *Theologie des Neuen Testaments*, 3. Aufl. (Tübingen: Mohr, 1958), 385–422; J. P. Miranda, *Der Vater der mich gesandt hat*, EHS 23/7 (Frankfurt a/M.: Herbert and Peter Lang, 1972); Paul Feine, *Theologie des Neuen Testaments*, 21st edn (Berlin: Evangelische Verlagsanstalt, 1953), 313; Conzelmann, *Grundriss der Theologie*, 372; Haenchen, 'Der Vater der mich gesandt hat', 211; McPolin, 'Mission', 114; and Kuhl, *Die Sendung Jesu*, 3–52.

[213] For example, see the allusions in 1:1, 14, 17–23, 25–29, 35, 46–48, 51; 2:1–11, 17, 22, 29; 3:14; 4:6, 25, 37–38; 5:17, 43–47; 6:31–33, 45–46, 58; 8:44, 56, 58, etc.

[214] Zahn, *Grundriss der neutestamentliche theologie* (Leipzig: D. Werner Scholl, 1920), 27; Bultmann, 'Die Theologie des Johannes', 412–26; F. M. Braun, *Jean le théologien: Les grandes traditions d'Israël et l'accord des écritures selon le quatrième évangile*, Ebib, 3 vols (Paris: Gabalda, 1956–1972), 3:71.

[215] Twenty-five times with the verb πέμπειν and nineteen times with ἀποστέλλειν. See Kuhl, *Die Sendung Jesu*, 53-7, 130-33; Miranda, *Der Vater*, 39-43.

[216] The possessive adjectives in 4:34 ('my', 'his') are emphatic, and this emphasis underlines

invariably describes his own work as finishing the Father's work (4:34; 17:4), seeking the Father's will (5:30; 6:38), testifying by his own words and deeds to the things he has seen and heard from the Father (3:11, 32; 5:19; 8:26, 28b, 38, 40) and climactically bringing to fruition and conclusion the enduring saving activity of God (3:17). Jesus has come into the world in the Father's name (5:43; 12:46; 16:28; 18:37; cf. 7:28; 8:42) and for the benefit of humanity.[217] At the centre of the activity of the Son is his self-revelation which, in the Johannine theological formula, is nothing less than the revelation of the Father (1:18).[218]

This revelation is salvific in its aim and universal in its outlook (3:15–16, 36; 5:24; 6:40; etc.).[219] Yet the theme is much broader than is conveyed simply by the verbs πέμπειν, ἀποστέλλειν, and ἔρχεσθαι, καταβαίνειν, which focus exclusively on the 'sending/coming' of Jesus.[220] The theme can be expanded to include the purpose and manner of the mission and the desired response:

(1) *from the perspective of the Father:* the terms διδόναι (3:16), ζητεῖν (4:23c), ἑλκύειν (6:44), ἐργάζεσθαι (5:17), ζωοποιεῖν (5:21), δοξάζειν (12:28), ἔργον (4:34) and γεωργός (15:1, 2);

(2) *from the perspective of the Son:* καταβαίνειν (3:13), λαλεῖν (3:11, 34), κοπιᾶν (4:6, 38), κρίσις (3:19; 5:27), κρίμα (9:39), ἀκούειν (5:30), ζωοποιεῖν (5:21), τιμᾶν (8:49) and ποιεῖν / τελεῖν (4:34; 5:36; 17:4); and

(3) *from the standpoint of the audience:* πιστεύειν (3:16, 17; 20:31), ἀκούειν (5:24), ἔρχεσθαι (5:40, 43), τιμᾶν (5:23), λαμβάνειν (1:11; 5:43) and θερίζειν (4:38).[221]

Further support for the evangelistic persuasive emphasis of the Gospel comes from the marked concentration of the 'mission' terminology in the so-called 'polemic' section of the Gospel (chs. 3–12). This indicates that

---

the perfect correspondence which exists between the Father's will concerning the work and Jesus' intense desire to accomplish it (e.g., 4:34; 5:19-23; 26–27, 30; 6:27, 38; 8:16, 26; 10:18, etc).

[217] Even Jesus' self-designations – 'the Son of Man' (3:13, 14 ; 5:27), 'the Son' (3:16; 6:40; 8:36) and 'the Son of God' (10:36) may have in view his salvific mission. See, for example, 3:13–19 where all three titles are developed in connection either with the 'sending' (3:17), 'giving' (3:16), or 'coming' (3:19) of Jesus into the world. Cf. Okure, *Johannine Approach*, 2; Beutler, *Martyria*, 360 where he emphasises the uniqueness of the Son as the salvific agent. See also Strathmann in *TDNT* 4:4474–508.

[218] Specifically in the ἐγώ εἰμί statements. See chapter six in the present study.

[219] Edeltraud Leidig, *Jesu Gespräch mit der Samaritanerin und weitere Gespräche im Johannesevangelium*, TDiss 15 (Basel: Friedrich Reinhardt, 1979), 152.

[220] C. F. D. Moule, *Essays in New Testament Interpretation* (Cambridge: CUP, 1982), 105–9; Radermakers, 'Mission et apostolate', 100–21; H. Rengstorf in *TDNT* 1 (1964), 398–447.

[221] Miranda, *Der Vater*, 129–307.

Johannine polemic has a positive purpose rather than a negative one.[222] This congregation of terminology encompasses not only the verbs of sending and coming, but also the whole discussion on Jesus' works. Chapters 13–17 which also have a concentration of 'sending and coming' terminology simply recapitulate the earlier section and further underline a continuity between the sending of the Son and the Holy Spirit by the Father and their subsequent missionary outreach through the disciples.[223]

If salvation history can be viewed as a persistent missionary endeavour fuelled by the redemptive aims of God himself, then it may be said that all missionary efforts of the people of God find their impetus in him. Just as Jesus in the Gospel is the One sent by the Father, so are the disciples whose mission derives its meaning and significance from the salvific mission of the Son.[224] The focal point and the unifying theme of the apostolic witness is God's climactic self-revelation in the person of his Son (cf. Acts 2:14–40; 3:12–26; 5:32).[225] It is not surprising, therefore, that the same theme dominates the Fourth Gospel (cf. Jn. 20:31; 1:41; 4:25).[226] It is difficult to imagine a document in which the mission of the Father, the Son and the disciples in the world is seen to be a 'foundation theme', but which is also the product of an 'introversionist sect' that does not wish to have anything to do with the world. This emphatic missionary theology in the Fourth Gospel diametrically opposes the opinion of those who depict John's Gospel as a simply sectarian writing.[227]

---

[222] Also Oehler, *Das Johannesevangelium*, 29; Kümmel, *Einleitung in das Neue Testament*, 197; E. Grässer, 'Die antijüdische Polemik', 74–90.

[223] Cf. John 4:34; 5:20, 26, 30; 7:3, 21; 10:25, 32–33, 37–38, 14:10, 11; 15:22; 17:4. However, the use of mission related terminology is only one aspect of mission in the Gospel. McPolin, 'Mission in the Fourth Gospel', 113–22.

[224] Barrett, *St. John*, 229; J. A. Bailey, *The Traditions Common to the Gospel of Luke and John*, NovTSup 7 (Leiden: Brill, 1963), 105; E. Haenchen, *Johannesevangelium: ein Kommentar* (Tübingen: Mohr, 1980), 247–8; Dodd, *Tradition*, 341–400; Leon Morris, *Studies in the Fourth Gospel* (Exeter: Paternoster Press, 1969), 280; in reference to the Samaritan connection, Cullmann, *The Early Church*, 192; Julius Wellhausen, *Das Evangelium Johannis* (Berlin: Reimer, 1908), 22, argues, 'Jesu selber gilt also hier als der definitive Gründer der samarischen Christengemeinde'.

[225] N. B. Stonehouse, *Origins of the Synoptic Gospels: Some Basic Questions* (London: Tyndale Press, 1964), 129; T. F. Glasson, 'The Speeches in Acts and Thucydides', *ExpTim* 76 (1965), 165; Onuki, *Gemeinde und Welt im Johannesevangelium*, 85–93.

[226] Van Unnik, 'Purpose of St. John's Gospel', 382–411; Wind, 'Destination and Purpose', 66; R. H. Mounce, *The Essential Nature of New Testament Preaching* (Grand Rapids: Eerdmans, 1960), 147; D. R. Carnegie, 'Kerygma in the Fourth Gospel', *Vox Evangelica* (1971), 52–3.

[227] Okure, *Johannine Approach*, 6; cf. de Jonge, *Jesus, Stranger from Heaven*, 118–9; Brown, 'Kerygma of the Gospel', 387–400; Kümmel, *Einleitung in das Neue Testament*, 194–200; Bornhäuser, *Das Johannesevangelium*, 158, 172; Oehler, *Das Johannesevangelium*, 11, 30–31.

An important integral part of this missionary theology is the theme of 'witness'. Although this theme is not confined to John's Gospel, its major occurrence in the New Testament is in Johannine literature, particularly the Gospel.[228] Both the verb μαρτυρεῖν and the noun μαρτυρία occur more frequently in the Fourth Gospel than in any other New Testament writing, and, if the Johannine Epistles are included, more frequently than in all the other New Testament writings put together.

The verb μαρτυρεῖν occurs in the Gospel thirty-three times and in the Johannine Epistles ten times. The noun in the Gospel is used fourteen times and seven times in the Epistles.[229] The 'witness' terminology occurs in a wide range of contexts and is attached to some of the principal Johannine themes. The word 'witness' is either translated to mean 'confess', in a sense of 'belief' and 'allegiance', or it is translated to mean 'testify' in a juridical (forensic) sense of giving evidence. E. Cothenet has rightly argued that in order to understand the religious sense of the word, it is important to recognise its juridical background.[230] The theme of being witnesses to Jesus further strengthens an evangelistic-apologetic emphasis in the Gospel. In the Fourth Gospel, the Father bears witness to the Son (5:36-37; 8:18) as well as the Holy Spirit who is both a witness and advocate (15:26; 16:8-15);[231] the Spirit also bears witness through the disciples (cf. Jn. 15:18-16:4),[232] and above all, there is the witness of

---

[228] E.g., John 1:7, 8, 15; 3:11, 26, 28; 5:31-33, 36-37; 8:18; 10:25; 15:27; 18:23, 26, cf. 1 John 1:1-5. M. R. Wilson, 'Witness as a Theme in the Fourth Gospel' (Ph.D. diss., New Orleans Baptist Theological Seminary, 1992); Trites, *New Testament Concept of Witness*, 78-127, 154-74; Beutler, *Martyria*; idem. 'Glaube und Zeugnis im Johannesevangelium', *Bijdragen* 34 (1973), 60-8; M. C. Tenney, 'Topics from the Gospel of John. Part III: The Meaning of "Witness" in John', *BibSac* 132 (1975), 229-41; J. M. Boice, 'The Idea of Witness in the Gospel of John' (diss. Basel, 1966); C. Burchard, 'Kerygma and Martyria in the New Testament', in *Christian Witness and the Jewish People*, ed. by A. Sovik (Geneva: Lutheran World Federation, 1976), 10-25; J. C. Hindley, 'Witness in the Fourth Gospel', *SJT* 18 (1965), 319-37; L. Kochilletonil, 'The Biblical Idea of Μαρτυρία', *Documenta Missionalia* 5 (1972), 55-64; B. W. Anderson and W. Harrelson, eds, *Israel's Prophetic Heritage* (New York and London: SCM, 1962); L. Morris, *The Apostolic Preaching of the Cross*, 3rd edn (London: Tyndale Press, 1965); D. T. Niles, *Whereof We Are Witnesses* (London: Epworth Press, 1965); L. G. Cox, 'John's Witness to the Historical Jesus', *BETS* 9 (1966), 173-8.

[229] Strathmann, *TDNT* 4 (1967), 474-514.

[230] 'Le témoignage selon saint Jean', *Esprit et Vie* 101 (1991), 401-7.

[231] Trites, *New Testament Concept of Witness*, 117f.; Moule, *Phenomenon of the New Testament*, 91

[232] This witness seems to be against a background of persecution. Cf. Acts 4:18-21, 29-31; 7:54-60; 20:22-24; 26:16-18; Hindley, 'Witness in the Fourth Gospel', 319-37; Trites, *New Testament Concept of Witness*, 79.

Scriptures (5:39).²³³ But there is also the witness of the works of Christ (5:32, 37; 8:37; cf. 3:11), John the Baptist (1:7–8, 15, 19, 32–34; 3:26, 32–33; 5:32, 36), the Samaritan woman (4:39), the Samaritans (4:42), the disciples (1:45, 49; 6:68), especially the Beloved Disciple (20:31; 21:24), and even some of the Jews themselves (7:31; 9:16; 10:21). In the context of Johannine irony, even Pilate becomes an unwitting witness to the truth in his repeated effort to set Jesus free, in his recognition that Jesus is innocent of the charge against him (18:38; 19:4, 6), and in his attempt to have him released (18:39–40; 19:12, 14). Later Pilate once again unknowingly is a witness to the truth by his refusal to change the superscription, 'King of the Jews' (19:19–22).²³⁴

One of the distinct marks of a genuine disciple in the Johannine estimation is being a true witness to Jesus. The 'Beloved Disciple' embodies such a true witness.²³⁵ He appears at the pivotal points in the narrative (Jn. 13:23–25; 19:26–27, 35; 20:2–10; 21:7, 20–24). At the last supper, he is the disciple leaning on the bosom of Jesus (Jn. 13:23–26). He is also the disciple standing near the cross while the other disciples scatter (Jn. 19:25–27). In the dramatic race to the tomb, he is the first to arrive (Jn. 20:2–10). This disciple also is one who abides in the truth, and thus he is a witness to the truth and his witness is true (21:24).

Judas, on the other hand, stands at the opposite end of the pole from the Beloved Disciple. He embodies a figure who is deceitful, disloyal, a traitor (6:64, cf. 21:20). He neither abides in the truth nor follows to the end. At the most intimate moment in the narrative, he leaves the fold (13:30).²³⁶ He is full of vice and belongs to the bosom of his father, the devil, who also did not abide in the truth. Therefore, when he speaks, his witness is a lie. In short, Judas personifies all that a disciple should not be – a false witness to the truth.²³⁷

A contrast of slightly different emphasis is drawn between Nicodemus and the Samaritan woman. Nicodemus, in spite of his exalted social stature, is seen in the Johannine record as an unacceptable model of a disciple and a witness. In contrast to Judas, he is not a false witness. He simply has no

---

²³³ Cf. 2:22; 7:38, 42; 10:35; 13:18; 17:12; 19:24, 28, 36–37; 20:9.

²³⁴ E. Jensen, 'The First Century Controversy over Jesus as a Revolutionary Figure', *JBL* 60 (1941), 271.

²³⁵ Raymond F. Collins, *These Things Have Been Written: Studies on the Fourth Gospel* (Grand Rapids: Eerdmans, 1990), 42–5.

²³⁶ J. S. Billings, 'Judas Iscariot in the Fourth Gospel', *ExpTim* 51 (1939), 40.

²³⁷ R. M. Brown, 'True and False Witness: Architecture and the Church', *TT* 23 (1967), 521–37; Collins, *These Things*, 30.

witness. His is among those who John believes did not confess their faith because they loved the praise of men (Jn. 12:42–43). This fear of the loss of social recognition results in bearing no witness to the truth because he keeps quiet when he should have spoken up (7:50–52). On the other end of the scale is a Samaritan who is also a woman. Her social stature is non-existent. But in contrast to Nicodemus, she not only believes, but brings the entire village to meet the Christ. And her witness is clear: Is not this the Christ (4:29)? The public confession of Jesus as the Christ is of fundamental importance for John, i.e., to bear witness openly.

There are other similar examples throughout the Gospel. These contrasts accentuate a very important element in John – true disciples are also true witnesses to Jesus as the Christ. The one who abides in the truth is also one who bears witness to the truth by public acknowledgement that Jesus is the Christ. As we shall see later in the sixth chapter, such public confession is not a simple intellectual assent nor a religious ritual. To confess that Jesus is the Christ requires a radical reorientation in every dimension of the confessor's life. However, what is pertinent to the present discussion is that such a demand for public confession of Jesus further contradicts the sectarian thesis. An introverted community which has abandoned the world and collapsed into its own sphere hardly would require its members to be witnesses to the truth. For the Fourth Evangelist, such a witness can only be truly legitimate when it is borne outside the community, openly, in the face of opposition and ostracism. And this requires active engagement with the world.

It is hard to imagine that a writer who is so conscious of the mission of the Father and the Son in the world, and who so clearly articulates this theology, would have no interest in 'mission' or would represent a sectarian group. It is highly questionable that a document in which there is so much emphasis upon the outreach of God in the world could be legitimately characterised as the writing of a sect. It seems that if there would have been any tendency in the Christian community toward isolationism, the Gospel itself would have been the greatest safeguard against this because of the emphatic missionary outlook accented in its theology. In the Fourth Gospel, Christians are encouraged to follow in the steps of their Lord in sacrificial self-giving in spite of opposition.[238] However, even if we were to accept a sectarian disposition in Johannine Christianity, this

---

[238] 3:16–17; 15:19–27; 17:15, 18, 20; cf. Käsemann, *The Testament of Jesus*, 59–60, who dismisses Jn. 3:16–17 as uncharacteristic of the Gospel, and Wengst, *Bedrängte Gemeinde*, 125–8, who emphasises it.

in itself does not necessarily negate its evangelistic persuasive focus, nor does it entail disengagement with the world. Admittedly, this solution brings about a tension between exclusivity – not of the world – and inclusivity – in the world. But there is no inconsistency between this separatism, on the one hand, and universalism on the other. The people of God throughout the ages have been expected to be separated from the world morally and yet actively engaged with it for its salvation.[239] Hence Rensberger rightly argues,

No religion that sees itself as the backbone of a society, as the glue that holds a society together, can easily lay down a challenge to that society's wrongs. A cultural religion is all too readily told to mind its own business, because it *has* a business, a well-known role in maintaining society's fabric unmolested.[240]

It is only a morally separated, nonconformist (i.e., to the world's value system) religion that can fundamentally challenge the world's immoral manners and oppressive ways (1 Jn. 2:6, 15–17; cf. Rom. 12:2) without being accused of hypocrisy. It is only such a community that can call others out of human self-absorption and selfishness, which is in opposition to God. Because such an entity is allied with none other than the Almighty, it can expose the deception in the world. It can question its 'unquestionable assumptions' and without fear 'state what it sees, that the emperor is naked after all.'[241] The community of faith, in its engagement within human society, must be able to offer an alternative to the world's ways and value structure. Somehow this community must be unique and distinguishable from 'the world' or else its call to righteousness will be seen as hypocritical, and indeed, its sense of mission to the world would lose its meaning and purpose.

It is in this context that the Fourth Evangelist calls for a choice between the world and God without any intermediate moral ground between the two.[242] However, the emphasis on love in both the First Epistle of John and the Gospel is significant here. Belief must manifest itself concretely in the commitment of one's entire life to walk as Jesus did (Jn. 13:12–17; 1 Jn. 2:6), and love as Jesus loved (Jn. 13:1; 15:13–15; 1 Jn. 3:16), even unto death (Jn 13:34–35; 15:13; 1 Jn 3:16; 4:11–12). François Vouga

---

[239] Cf. Rensberger, *Overcoming the World*, 144; Wilson, *Magic and the Millennium*, 23–4, 45; George MacRae, 'The Fourth Gospel and *Religionsgeschichte*', *CBQ* 32 (1970), 13–24; Onuki, *Gemeinde und Welt im Johannesevangelium*, 19–28.

[240] Rensberger, *Overcoming the World*, 142.

[241] Ibid., 142.

[242] Ibid., 143.

notes that John's purpose in writing is 'to make believers become Christians'.²⁴³ This emphasis on love tempers John's polemical tone. The community's 'fellowship of love' (13:35) in itself serves an evangelistic purpose (17:20–23).²⁴⁴ Therefore, if one assumes a sectarian disposition in Johannine Christianity, which I have argued does not exist, one can still turn the sectarian argument on its head; and the result is a model in which the very exclusivity and peculiarity of the community serves an evangelistic purpose.

It has been said that the Fourth Gospel resembles a perfect cube – whichever side is held up, that side seems to become dominant. However, the difficult and correct approach would be to see the complementary element in all sides.²⁴⁵ The debate on whether the Fourth Gospel was written to deepen faith in those who already had it (Christians) or engender faith in those who did not yet believe is unnecessary in so far as the Gospel seems to cover both aims.²⁴⁶ The two are not mutually exclusive. John's emphasis on love and the person of Jesus Christ has both an internal and external focus. In so far as the sectarian thesis is concerned, I have demonstrated that neither Johannine Christianity, nor its gospel, nor the language of the Gospel, can be in any meaningful way characterised as sectarian since the theological tenets of the Gospel negate the validity of the sectarian hypothesis. However, even if we were to accept the thesis that there are separatist themes in the Fourth Gospel, nevertheless, separation in Johannine theology does not mean disengagement from the world in a sectarian sense. Indeed the community's separatist tendencies (if such tendencies did exist) may have served its ultimate end to call others to join its fold.

---

243 *Le Cadre Historique et l'Intention Thevologique de Jean* (Paris: Beauchesne, 1977), 35.

244 Wilhelm Lütgert, *Die Liebe im Neuen Testament. Ein Beitrag zur Geschichte des Urchristenums* (Leipzig: A. Deichert, 1905), 137–67; W. Bieder, *Gottes Sendung und der missionarische Auftrag nach Matthäus, Lukas, Paulus und Johannes*, Theologische Studien 82 (Zurich: EVZ-Verlag, 1965), 41–3; F. Neugebauer, *Die Entstehung des Johannesevangeliums*, Arbeiten zur Theologie 1/36 (Stuttgart: Calwer, 1968), 12; Conzelmann, *Grundriss der Theologie*, 387, cf. 362.

245 Wind, 'Destination and Purpose', 65.

246 This position is known as the dual purpose and such scholars as Rebell, *Gemeinde als Gegenwelt*; and William Domeris, 'Christology and Community: A Study of the Social Matrix of the Fourth Gospel', *JTSA* 64 (1988), 49–56, have subscribed to it.

4.5. The Centrality of the Messianic Identity of Jesus in the Purpose of the Gospel

It was William Wrede who, at the beginning of the twentieth century, simply and rightly noted that when the evangelists set out to write the Gospels, they wrote with one purpose in mind – Jesus the Nazarene was the promised Messiah and his life full of Messianic manifestations. They, according to Wrede, concerned themselves with those evidences that proved this point.[247]

Whatever one may conclude about the various proposed aims of the Fourth Evangelist in writing the Gospel, what seems quite clear is the significance of the Messianic identity of Jesus which is at the heart of the Gospel's purpose.[248] John is so concerned to present Jesus as the Messiah that he uses the title more frequently than any of the Synoptics. He uses the title Christ (Messiah) twenty-one times as opposed to seventeen times in Matthew, seven or eight times in Mark, and twelve to fourteen times in Luke.[249] In the Gospel, John the Baptist denies that he is the Christ (1:20; 3:28). Everyone – the ordinary Jew (7:25–31, 40–3; 12:34), the Jewish authorities (1:19, 24–5), and the Samaritans (4:25, 29) – discuss messiahship; and the first disciples confess: 'We have found the Messiah' (1:41). Then there are the references to the Lamb of God (1:29), the king of Israel (1:49), and the Holy One of God (6:69), all bearing Messianic connotations.[250] It is also noteworthy that a comparison with Christian writers in the second century (e.g., Hegesippus, cf. Eusebius, *H.E.* II. 23. 8–10), especially Justin's *Dialogue* with the Jew Trypho, proves that this theme (i.e., 'Jesus as the Christ') was the decisive point in the discussions between the church and the synagogue.[251]

---

[247] William Wrede, *The Messianic Secret*, trans. by F. C. C. Greig from the 1901 edn, *Das Messiasgeheimnis in den Evangelien* (Cambridge and London: James Clarke, 1971), 126. In support of Wrede's position, see the recorded apostolic preaching in the book of Acts (e.g., Acts 2:16, 23–28, 33; 36; 3:18–20; 13:23). Cf. Carnegie, 'Kerygma in the Fourth Gospel', 52–3; J. P. M. Sweet, 'Second Thoughts: VIII. The Kerygma', *ExpTim* 76 (1965), 147.

[248] But see N. A. Dahl, 'The Johannine Church and History', in *Jesus in the Memory of the Early Church. Essays by Nile Alstrup Dahl* (Minneapolis: Augsburg, 1976), 130, cf. Wengst, *Bedrängte Gemeinde*, 101; Mounce, *Essential Nature of New Testament Preaching*, 147; Carnegie, 'Kerygma in the Fourth Gospel', 52–3.

[249] On the title 'Messiah', see W. Grundmann, *TDNT* 9 (1974), 527–80.

[250] Brown, *John*, 1:lxx; Barrett, *St. John*, 185–86, 278, 549; Okure, *Johannine Approach*, 259. Bultmann, *Theology of the New Testament*, vol. 2, §45, 37, believes all these titles present Jesus as the eschatological salvation-bringer, and *his coming is the eschatological event*.

[251] Justin Martyr, *Dialogi cum Tryphone Judaeo*, Patrologia Graeca 6, 470–799; also *Apolgia I & II pro Christianis*, Patrologia Graeca 6, ed. by J. P. Migne, 326–472; H. Chadwick, 'Justin

The central issue in John's Messianic emphasis is not the humanity of Jesus, but his claim to divinity. His humanity was acknowledged by all (1:45; 2:1, 3, 5, 12; 6:42; 7:12, 15, 27). There are several factors which seem to indicate that in the Fourth Gospel the deity and not the humanity of Jesus is in focus. John includes no account of the birth, baptism, or temptations of Jesus. Of the seven key miracles in the life of Jesus, five are unknown outside of the Fourth Gospel. It is Jesus' claim to oneness with the Father and an outright claim to deity which is consistently a source of agitation to the Jews (8:58; 10:30-35). Therefore, John's central task is to show that this man who 'dwelt among us' is the Messiah, the eternal Word, and therefore the sole source of revelation and life. To accept the claim, one must accept both that this Jesus who is human (flesh) has come from God (1:14) and that he gives his life (flesh) for the life of the world. Both of these propositions were equally offensive to the Jews.

John 1:14 epitomises this theme of the Gospel regarding the combined divine and human identity of Jesus. Some commentators argue that John seems to affirm a view of Christ which is incompatible with other Messianic views prevalent at the time.[252] However, this does not appear to be the case. Throughout the Gospel, John does not define or distinguish his Messianic idea as opposed to other notions which were prevalent in the first century, even though we know that a considerable variety of Messianic patterns arose within the eschatological traditions in second temple Judaism.[253] While John, in his presentation of Jesus, does not share the

---

Martyr's Defence of Christianity', *BJRL* 47 (1965), 275-97; A Harnack, *Judentum und Judenchristentum in Justins Dialog mit Trypho,* TU 39 (Leipzig, 1913), Barnabas Lindars, *New Testament Apologetic* (London: SCM, 1961); Dahl, *Crucified Messiah.* But van Unnik, 'Purpose of St. John's Gospel', *Sparsa Collecta* 1 (1973), 397, believes the focus of this identity question would have been a missionary, not an apologetic, setting. However, different from Justin, quoting Old Testament citations, in John it is by his works (signs) that Jesus proves to be the legitimate Anointed One sent by God (pp. 398-403).

[252] Cf. Kysar, 'Christology and Controversy', *CurTM* 5 (1978), 355; E. Hoskyns, *The Fourth Gospel,* ed. by F. N. Davey (London: Faber and Faber, 1940), 136; D. Moody Smith, 'The Presentation of Jesus in the Fourth Gospel', *Int* 31 (1977), 288. H. Ridderbos, 'The Prologue to the Gospel of John', *NovT* 8 (1966), 191.

[253] For an extended discussion and treatment, see William Horbury, *Jewish Messianism and the Cult of Christ* (London: SCM, 1998). See also Richard A. Horsley, 'Popular Messianic Movements around the Times of Jesus', *CBQ* 46 (1984), 471-95; M. Smith, 'What is Implied by the Variety of Messianic Figures?', *JBL* 78 (1959), 66-72; M. de Jonge, 'The Use of the Word "Anointed" in the Time of Jesus', *NovT* 8 (1966), 132-48; A. E. Harvey, *Jesus and the Constraints of History* (Philadelphia: Westminster Press, 1982), 78-82; R. A. Horsley and J. S. Hanson, *Bandits, Prophets and Messiahs. Popular Movements in the Time of Jesus* (Minneapolis: Fortress, 1985); Gershom Scholem, *The Messianic Idea in Judaism: and Other Essays on Jewish Spirituality* (New York: Schocken Books, 1971); S. Sharot, *Messianism, Mysticism and Magic: A Sociological Analysis of Jewish Religious Movements* (Chapel Hill: University of North Carolina

Jewish nationalistic messianism, nevertheless he stands very much in the tradition of Jewish Messianic belief. John records two strains of Messianic expectations in the first century. According to the 'normal' view, the Messiah would be known because he would make his appearance at Bethlehem (Jn. 7:42; Mt. 2:5). But according to the apocalyptic strains of Messianic expectation, Messiah's presence on earth would be hidden until suddenly he is revealed to his people (7:27; Mk. 8:27–30; cf. also 4 Ezra 13:52; Pseudo-Jonathan on Micah 4:8; and Justin *Dialogue with Trypho* 8:4; 90:1; 110:1).[254]

It must be said, however, that in spite of diverse Messianic views, it is unusual to find any Jewish Messianic idea which does not take its departure point from God's promises to Israel in the law and the prophets and is not a function of these promises. In the Fourth Gospel, whenever the author introduces the subject of Messiah or Christ, the Scriptures are in the background. Messiah is a concept deeply rooted in Israel's Scriptures.[255] Clearly there are common biblical themes[256] which provide far greater unity to the concept than some scholars are willing to allow.[257] Indeed, the

---

Press, 1982); the collection of essays edited by Jacob Neusner, W. S. Green, and E. Frerichs; *Judaisms and Their Messiahs at the Turn of the Christian Era* (Cambridge: CUP, 1987); Neusner's earlier work, 'Varieties of Judaism in the Formative Age', 59–89; John Barton, 'The Messiah in the Old Testament Theology', in *King and Messiah in Israel and the Ancient Near East*, ed. by John Day, JSOTSup 270 (Sheffield: Sheffield Academic Press, 1998), 365–79, in the same collection of essays, David J. Reim, 'Old Testament Christology', 380–400, and see also other relevant articles in part III, 'The Messiah in Postbiblical Judaism and the New Testament', 402–96; James H. Charlesworth, 'From Messianology to Christology: Problems and Prospects', in *The Messiah: Developments in Earliest Judaism and Christianity*, ed. by James Charelsworth (Minneapolis: Fortress, 1992).

[254] Cf. further Str-B 2:339–340; 3:315; 4:766; S. Mowinckel, *He That Cometh: The Messiah Concept in the Old Testament and Later Judaism*, trans. by G. W. Anderson (Oxford: Blackwell; Nashville: Abingdon, 1956), 304–8; Braun, *Jean le théologien*, 103–15.

[255] Walter C. Kaiser, Jr., *The Messiah in the Old Testament* (Carlisle, England: Paternoster Press, 1995), 13–34 and 136–220.

[256] For example, Messiah is an eschatological figure; he is a person, he is a male figure, he is a Jew, a king from the 'root' or 'seed' of David; Scriptures speak of him; he is an anointed Conqueror; he will triumphantly deliver the people of God from their enemies; etc. See Kaiser's elaborations in *The Messiah in the Old Testament*, 111–231.

[257] Against e.g. Charlesworth, 'From Messianology to Christology', 3. See further Horbury, *Jewish Messianism;* E. Nodet, *Essai sur les Origines du Judïsme* (Paris: Les Éditions de Cerf, 1992); E. P. Sanders, *Judaism: Practice and Belief, 63 BCE–66 CE* (London: SCM, 1992); idem, *Paul and Palestinian Judaism*; Mowinckel, *He That Cometh;* Joseph Klausner, *The Messianic Idea in Israel: From its Beginning to the Completion of the Mishnah*, trans. W. F. Stinespring (New York: Macmillan, 1955); Gerhard Von Rad, *Old Testament Theology*, vol. 2, *The Theology of Israel's Prophetic Traditions*, trans. D. M. G. Stalker (New York: Harper and Row, 1965); James S. Preus, *From Shadow to Promise: Old Testament Interpretation From Augustine to the Young Luther* (Cambridge: MA: Belknap Press of Harvard University Press, 1969); W. Kaiser, *Messiah in the Old Testament*, 145–231.

first level at which the New Testament Christians themselves understood the identity and mission of Jesus is in terms of his fulfilment of these Old Testament promises (Jn. 1:41; Lk. 4:16–30, 24:27; Acts 2:14–36, 13:13–41). Knowledge of Jesus' divine ontological sonship does not seem to have fully dawned on the disciples until after the resurrection, which is certainly not to deny that this knowledge could have been received in some form other than from the historical Jesus himself. Jesus' uniqueness as God's agent lies squarely in that he is both Son and God (1:1, 18; 5:18; 10:33, 36; 19:7). Since most, if not all, contemporary Jewish ideas concerning the Messiah or other divine messengers came from the Scriptures, the Johannine judgment in 5:39 would have had biting force. John seems to assume a common scriptural ground, a shared understanding of fundamental Messianic expectations rooted in the Old Testament about which most Jews would have been in agreement. John, like other New Testament writers, in order to show that Jesus was the Messiah, appealed directly to Israel's Scriptures. What the Rabbis or various sectarian groups within the Jewish nation may have believed or expected[258] is of less importance to John than what the prophets of Israel had said about the Messiah.

Contrary to this view, Joachim Becker has proposed, 'There was not even such a thing as a Messianic expectation until the last two centuries B.C.'[259] Of course, Becker later would admit,

Such a conclusion would contradict one of the most central concerns of the New Testament, which insists with unprecedented frequency, intensity, and unanimity that Christ was proclaimed in advance in the Old Testament. Historical-critical scholarship can never set aside this assertion of the New Testament.[260]

Indeed, J. Alec Motyer has organised the expansive Isaianic description of the Messiah under three basic portraits: Messiah as King (Isa. 7:10–15; 9:1–7; 11:1–16; 14:28–32; 24:21–25; 32:1–8; 33:17–24), Messiah as Servant (Isa. 42:1–4; 49:1–6; 50:4–9; 52:13–53:12) and Messiah as Anointed Conqueror (55:3–5; 61:1–6; 63:1–6). Other passages about the Messiah in the prophets identify him as Son of God, Son of Man, Son of David, King of Israel, Teacher, and Prophet (cf. Jer. 33:14–26; Ezk. 17:22–24; 21:25–27; 37:15–

---

[258] Neusner, *Judaism and Their Messiahs;* E. Schürer, *The History of the Jewish People in the Age of Jesus Christ* II, ed. by G. Vermes, F. Millar and M. Black (Edinburgh: Clark, 1979), § 29 'Messianism', 488–549.

[259] *Messianic Expectation in the Old Testament,* ET David E. Green (Philadelphia: Fortress, 1980), 93.

[260] Ibid.

28; Dan. 7:13–14; 9:24–27; Hag. 2:6–9, 21–23; Zech. 3:8–10; 6:9–15; 12:10; Mal. 4:2).[261]

There are systematic references throughout the Gospel to most, if not all, these Messianic elements singled out by Motyer.[262] The emphasis of the Fourth Gospel is upon the use of the term Messiah.[263] In the Synoptics, Jesus accepts the designation from Peter, although reinterpreting it in terms of the suffering Son of Man (Mt. 16:13–20; Mk. 8:27–30; Lk. 9:24). John preserves the Aramaic form (Messias) along with its Greek equivalent (Jn. 1:41; 4:25).[264] An important element in the Messianic concept is the royal motif of 'the anointed of the Lord'. In the Old Testament, this denotes the King of Israel (1 Sam. 16:6; 2 Sam. 1:14), the high priest (e.g., Lev. 4:3), and, in one passage, the patriarchs, 'my anointed ones' (Ps. 105:15), probably in their role as prophets. Quite apart from occurrences of the verbal adjective, the act of anointing was instrumental in the 'consecration', the setting apart, of Aaron the priest (Exod. 29:7), David the King (1 Sam. 16:1–13), and Elisha the prophet (1 Kgs. 19:16), to mention only a few. Much of the early Christian preaching stressed this *royal* motif, presenting Jesus as the Messianic (i.e., 'anointed') king of Israel. Van Unnik points out the word 'Christ' is not a proper name, but a title in the full etymological sense: the Anointed One, the Messiah promised in the Old Testament.[265] John, as well

---

[261] J. Alec Motyer, *The Prophecy of Isaiah: An Introduction and Commentary* (Downers Grove, IL: Inter-Varsity Press, 1993), 3–16.

[262] In chapters 18 and following, the title 'The King of the Jews' is used several times. Jesus never gives his assent to it, just as he does not permit the Jews to make him a king (6:15). He is also represented as the King of Israel at 1:49 and again in 12:13. Nathanael in his confession accepts the assertion of 1:45, and adds the further titles 'Son of God' and 'king of Israel'. For Messiah as Son of God, see, 2 Sam. 7:14; Ps. 2:7; 1 Enoch 105:2; 4 Ezra 7:28f.; 13:52; 14:9; Mk. 1:11; Rom. 1:3f. For Messianic associations of the 'Son of Man', see William Horbury, 'The Messianic Associations of "the Son of Man"', *JTS* n.s. 34 (1985), 34–55; Bruce Vawter, 'Ezekiel and John', *CBQ* 26 (1964), 450–8. 'Son of David' is prominent in the Synoptics, but not in the Fourth Gospel (7:42). By the time of the composition of the New Testament, the royal term, 'Son of David' and 'Messiah' had become virtually synonymous (cf. 7:40–42). See further E. Lohse, 'huios David', *TDNT* 8:478ff.; W. Wrede, 'Jesus als Davidssöhn', in *Vorträge und Studien* (Tübingen: Mohr-Siebeck, 1907), 147ff. On 'king of Israel', see H. A. Cauthron, Jr., 'The Meaning of Kingship in Johannine Christology: A Structuralist Exegesis of John 18:1–20' (Ph.D. diss., Vanderbilt University, 1984); F. J. Botha, 'King of Israel (in the Gospel of John)', *Theologia Evangelica* 1 (1968), 19–20; M. de Jonge, 'Jesus as Prophet-King in John', *ATR* 51 (1969), 35–7; M. É. Boismard, 'La royauté universelle du Christ', *Assemblées du Seigneur* 88 (1966), 33–45.

[263] G. B. Caird, completed by L. D. Hurst, *New Testament Theology* (Oxford: Clarendon, 1994), 306; T. W. Manson, *The Teaching of Jesus* (Camridge: CUP, 1945), idem, *The Servant Messiah* (New York, 1953); idem, *Jesus the Messiah* (London, 1943).

[264] The confession that Jesus is the Christ is certainly important to Paul as well (Rom. 10:9).

[265] 'The Purpose of St. John's Gospel', *SE* 1 = TU 73 (1959), 390f.

as other New Testament writers, presents Jesus as the Messiah, i.e., the Anointed One, *par excellence* – the anointed prophet, priest and king.[266]

Therefore, while it is helpful to point out the diversity of Messianic views among the Jews, yet it is crucial not to lose sight of the fundamental common themes which unify these views. It is also important to make a distinction between some of the aberrant Messianic ideas which 'floated about' among the Jews and those 'mainstream' ideas which were rooted in Israel's Scriptures.[267] From today's perspective, it may be possible to compare and delineate the Johannine Messianic understanding in the context of first century Judaism. From the point of view of the Evangelist, however, he was entirely in line with Scripture (5:39–40, 46). On the one hand, he was rightly harnessing Messianic expectations, and on the other hand, rightly providing the identity of the true Messiah as opposed to the teachers of Israel who did not understand the Scriptures. Even so, apart from translating the title Messiah into Greek, the Fourth Evangelist uses the title as if there was a common agreement among the interlocutors of Jesus (and his own audience) about the figure to whom he referred as the Messiah. What is in dispute, both in the prologue and the rest of the Gospel, is not Messianism itself but whether Jesus is to be accorded this title,[268] and whether Jesus the man has fulfilled those Messianic aspirations and is justified in his claim to be 'the Anointed of the Lord'. Perhaps from the perspective of Jewish eschatological traditions in the first century, Jesus had not performed the type of spectacular activities which the Jews expected the Messiah to perform such as the cataclysmic overthrow of Gentile powers and setting up a visible kingdom in Zion.

What 'the Jews' particularly found offensive about Jesus may not necessarily have been that God's Word became flesh, but the assertion that the one who was flesh, who lived among them, claimed to be the living Word of God (6:60), Christ, the Son of God.[269] It was the claim by this

---

[266] Robinson, 'Destination', 114.

[267] E. von Hengstenberg, *Christology of the Old Testament and a Commentary on the Messianic Predictions* (Grand Rapids: Kregel, 1970, reprint from ET of 1836–39); David Baron, *Rays of Messiah's Glory: Christ in the Old Testament* (n.p., 1886); Charles A. Briggs, *Messianic Prophecy* (New York: Scribner's, 1889); Kaiser, Jr. *Messiah in the Old Testament;* James E. Smith, *What the Bible Teaches About the Promised Messiah* (Nashville: Thomas Nelson, 1993).

[268] E.g., 7:26f, 31, 41f; 9:22; 10:24; 12:34; cf. 1:20; cf. I Jn. 2:22; 5:1; 11:27; 20:31. Bultmann, *Theology of the New Testament*, vol. 2, §45, 36–37; Sherman E. Johnson, 'The Davidic-Royal Motif in the Gospels', *JBL* 87 (1968), 136–50.

[269] The stress on this theme is further evident by the confession formulae in the Gospel, all of which have or imply the double predicate 'Christ, Son of God' (cf. 1:49; 9:38; 11:27; 20:28, 31; cf. 6:68–69) which should be read within the context of the whole discussion in Jn. 6 of Christ's

apparently mere mortal man that God had given him 'authority over all flesh' (17:2), to judge and give life (5:21-22, 26-27), which incensed the Jews. This they found blasphemous and outrageous (6:61). After Jesus claims to be the bread coming down from heaven, the Jews murmur, 'Is not this Jesus, the son of Joseph, whose father and mother we know? How does he now say, I have come down from heaven?' (6:42; cf. 7:41, 52; 9:29). Therefore, what seems to be disputed in the Gospel is not Jesus' humanity, but his deity. And it is this aspect of the person of Messiah which the Fourth Evangelist accentuates throughout the Gospel. It is also this emphasis upon Jesus' divine origin which appears 'docetic' when seen out of its original context and purpose.[270] However, the Jews systematically refuted and denied the claim that Jesus was the Christ.

A similar thematic focus is present in the First Epistle of John where some deny the reality of the incarnation (1 Jn. 4:2; 2 Jn. 7), the divinity of Jesus (1 Jn. 2:22-23) and his Messianic identity (1 Jn. 2:22, 5:1).[271] In the Gospel, the denial is not simply verbal (5:18; 6:42, 52, 60; 7:25-27, 40-43, 45-52); it entails physical attacks (6:66; 7:30, 32; 8:59; 10:31). In the Epistles, the refutation is accompanied by active campaigns to dissuade others from believing (1 Jn. 2:26; 4:1; 2 Jn. 7-8, 10-11); this activity strongly echoes John 9:22 wherein the point at issue is precisely the Messiahship of Jesus and its significance (cf. 7:13; 19:38). The denial is further met on Jesus' part by a reassertion of the claim (cf. 5:19-30; 6:61-62; 7:33-34, 37-39; 8:24, 28; 9:5, 39-41; 10:25-29, 32, 34-38; 12:44-50), and on the part of the favourable audience by belief and by the confessions σὺ εἶ (1:49; 6:69; 11:27; cf. 9:38; 20:28) and οὗτός ἐστιν (4:29, 42; 1:34; cf. 3:27-30; 20:31; 1 Jn. 4:3, 14-15; 5:1, 5). In the first Epistle, this thematic focus is accentuated by the claim of the antichrists that 'Jesus is not the Christ, the Son of God, come in flesh.'[272] In the Fourth Gospel, the denial

---

divine origin. In the debates with the leaders in Jerusalem (chs. 5, 7-10, 12), the issue centers on Jesus' Messiahship and divine Sonship, where the claim to divine Sonship clearly constitutes the chief stumbling block (5:18; 8:35, 56-59; 10:30-39; cf. 19:7).

[270] Wengst, *Bedrängte Gemeinde*, 100-1; Howard, *Fourth Gospel*, 9; Käsemann, *Testament of Jesus*, 23-6, and *passim*. In his second chapter, Käsemann argues that John is 'naive docetism' focusing on the glory of Christ to the neglect of his true humanity.

[271] Boismard and Lamouille, *Synopse des Quatre; III: L'Evangile de Jean*, 59, 242-4, claim that the opponents may have even challenged John that his portrait of Jesus was different from Jesus' own presentation of himself.

[272] The theme is further reinforced by the very etymological designation of the opponents as the *antichrists*, and by the counter-confession of the author and his exhortation to his readers to continue to believe and live out their faith in Jesus as 'the Christ, the Son of God'. Indeed the denial of messianic claims by the antichrists shows that the claims had indeed been made for Jesus.

by the 'antichrists' is met by an even stronger reassertion: Jesus is the Christ. In the Gospel, this claim is defended by Jesus himself who cites in support of the claim the witness of the Baptist, the Father, the Scriptures, Moses, his own words and works, and his indisputably sinless life (5:31–47; 8:46). The claim is also indirectly defended by the believing audience: the Samaritan woman and the Samaritans (4:29, 42), Nathanael (1:49), Peter (6:68–69), Martha (11:27), the man born blind (9:38), and even the once doubting Thomas (20:28). Above all, it is defended by the Beloved Disciple whose witness is the entire Gospel (21:24). Given this crowd of witnesses, the truthfulness of the claim cannot be easily refuted (cf. 7:17), unless, of course, one chooses to 'remain blind' (9:40–41) to this preponderance of evidence (cf. 10:32; 12:37; 15:22, 24).

Christology is at the core of the Gospel and the first Epistle,[273] and it affects the community and personal belief set within the overall context of Jesus' mission from the Father and its meaning for the world. As to the question of the priority of the Gospel or the Epistle, it seems more sensible to suppose that the Johannine Epistles followed the Gospel since they complement the Gospel theologically. The Fourth Gospel makes no reference to any work outside of itself (20:31) with the exception of the Hebrew Scriptures. However, the author of 1 John speaks of the epistle as 'a repeat' of a former work, one which is concerned with the same issues and rests on the same presuppositions as the previous work (2:7–8, 12–14). The author insists that this present work (i.e., 1 Jn.) contains nothing new, only what the audience knows already (1 Jn. 2:7, 21, 24; 3:11; cf. 2 Jn. 5, cf. 2:25, 27). The purpose of the previous work (1 Jn. 2:26; 5:13) was both to warn against deceivers (2:26; cf. 3:7; 4:6c; 2 Jn. 7) and to exhort Christians to 'remain in' or continue in the teaching which they initially received (2:24). This teaching is that Jesus is the Christ, the Son of God; and eternal life is found only in him (5:13). The thematic similarity of purpose described in 1 John seems to indicate tentatively, at least, that the work in question is the Gospel, not 2 or 3 John. However, there is no consensus as to whether both documents share the same *Sitz im Leben* and confront the same situations.[274] It is believed that the First Epistle was written to combat

---

[273] For a proposal on possible sources of Johannine christology, see Ashton, *Studying John*, 75ff.

[274] Robinson, *Redating the New Testament*, 288. Boismard and Lamouille, *Synopse, III: L'Evangile de Jean*, 59, 242–4, argue there is no docetic refutation in the Gospel. They propose, on a redactional basis, that 1 John in particular is the work of John II-B, the author who wrote the bulk of the final Gospel. He wrote both works towards the end of the first century when he moved from Palestine to Ephesus. See also Howard, *Fourth Gospel*, 9, 11. The alleged heretics the

some form of christological error, possibly docetism.[275] But there is very little agreement whether there is any docetic refutation in the Gospel. The two writings share similar theological themes. There is the same positive assertion of (i.e., 'Jesus is the Christ'), a denial or refutation of the claim (i.e., 'He is not the Christ') and the reassertion of the claim in both documents. There are similar concerns about unity among the disciples in both writings. But these similarities are not indicative of the same *Sitz im Leben*. They simply reveal, first of all, the centrality of christology in both documents. And secondly, they show a particular type of theological crisis confronted by the early church – denial of Jesus as the Christ by Judaism and non-Jewish heretical teachers, and the potentially demoralising effects of these denials as creating confusion and disharmony within the Christian community. While the documents attack the activity of the antichrists, they also urge the Christian community to continue in the faith and to temper their behaviour with love (20:30–31; 1 Jn. 2:26; 5:13). Therefore, while we may debate the life situation of the Gospel and the Epistles of John and their relations, what remains indisputably clear is a steadfast focus on the person and work of Jesus Christ throughout the entire Johannine body of literature.[276]

I began this chapter by suggesting that John's Gospel is a document whose message is both time-bound and timeless. I proposed that the Fourth Evangelist in composing his Gospel not only addressed his own immediate historical situation but also was consciously producing a lasting document and documentation for posterity. At the heart of the Johannine message is the person and work of Jesus the Messiah and the critical implications of accepting or rejecting this message. The articulation of Jesus' Messianic identity is at the centre of John's purpose irrespective of whether his motive for writing would have been pastoral, polemic, or evangelistic. The Fourth Evangelist refutes those who deny that Jesus is the

---

author encounters at Ephesus and the attacks in both the Gospel and the Epistles are from certain Jewish-Christians whose false teachings (2 Jn. 7–11) cause divisions within the community (3 Jn. 9–10). They deny the reality of incarnation (1 Jn. 4:2; 2 Jn. 7), the divinity of Jesus (1 Jn. 2:22–23) and his Messianic identity (1 Jn. 2:22, 5:1). They may have even challenged John that his portrait of Jesus does not coincide with that of Jesus of himself. Boismard and Lamouille do not regard the Johannine adversaries as Judaizers, but Jewish Christians who become disenchanted with their belief in Jesus and return to Judaism (pp. 213–4). They believe John II-B projected his life situation into the Jesus depicted in the Gospel.

[275] Ignatius of Antioch (AD 110), *Trall.* 9–10; *Smyr.* 2; *Eph.* 7 (cf. Polycarp, *Phil.* 2); Irenaeus, *Adv. Haer.* I.26.1; Epiphanius, *Haer.* 28.1.

[276] Peter Stuhlmacher, *Jesus von Nazareth-Christus des Glaubens* (Stuttgart: Glawer Verlag, 1988), 7ff.

Christ, appeals to those who are undecided or do not have the courage to come into the open with their belief, and pastorally strengthens the resolve of the community of faith. He writes to show how the Jews did not recognise their Messiah because of their ignorance of the Scriptures. Thus he appeals to his audience to examine and ponder his record about the person and work of Jesus in the light of the Scriptures. In this respect, the Gospel not only addresses the author's own immediate historical context, but most importantly it is a lasting product for posterity, for the church. The steadfast purpose of John in writing his Gospel was to set forth his reasons why he believed Jesus is the Christ. In this scenario, the Gospel would have been a document of value whoever heard or read it. The message of the Gospel would have been meaningful to both 'insiders' and 'outsiders', both time-bound and timeless.

In the Fourth Gospel, from the perspective of the Fourth Evangelist, while the witness of the disciples may be rejected, it is the witness of Israel's Scripture to the person and work of Jesus as the Christ which remains irrefutable. In John's Gospel, the claim that Jesus is the Christ is systematically defended by the author's appeal to the Scriptures. Indeed when the Evangelist appeals to the witness of the Father, the ground of his appeal is essentially nothing more than the witness of God's revelation in the history of Israel recorded in Israel's Scriptures. The witness of John the Baptist echoes the witness of the Scriptures (1:23, 29). Jesus himself appeals to the Scriptures (5:31–47). The witness of his signs echo the Scriptures as a witness to his identity. And finally, there is the witness of the Beloved Disciple. His witness is that of relentless allusions to the Scriptures which he believes show that Jesus is the Anointed of the Lord. As I shall delineate in the following chapter, it is the validation of this claim and the stylistic manner which the Evangelist utilises that gives the Gospel its enigmatic quality. John has saturated the language of his Gospel with echoes of the Scriptures which support his claim that they testify that Jesus is the One he claimed to be. The following chapter will set forth the function of John's subtle language in the light of what has been delineated as his purpose for writing the Gospel.

Chapter 5

Israel's Scriptures and the Language of John's Gospel

'Of him, Moses wrote in the law and also the prophets'

5.1. The Primary Key to the Function of John's Perplexing Language

In chapter two, I suggested that John's perplexing language, with all its intricacies, in one way or another, seems to be related to his allusions to the Scriptures of Israel. Later, in chapter four, I noted that the identity of Jesus as the Christ is the cornerstone of the Evangelist's purpose in writing his Gospel. For the author of the Fourth Gospel, this 'cornerstone' is solidly grounded in the Scriptures of Israel. In the present chapter, I propose to set forth that the essential function of John's language is wedded to his purpose – a steadfast conviction that Jesus is the embodiment of the saving self-revelation of God according to the witness of Israel's Scriptures. For John, above all else, Jesus is the Promised One because the Scriptures anticipate him, speak of him, witness to him and find their supreme realisation in him.

By this proposal, I do not mean that every occurrence of an ambiguous expression in the Fourth Gospel is directly linked to the Evangelist's allusions to the Old Testament. However, what I do wish to emphasise is that it is these subtle and yet systematic and purposeful echoes, thematic undercurrents and allusions to the Old Testament which seem to give John's language its particular quality whereby it is seen as 'mystical', 'elusive' and 'enigmatic'.

The engagement of the Christian community with the Jewish community, particularly the religious authorities, was one in which, in some respects, the survival of the Jewish religious system was at stake. The Christian claims seriously challenged the viability of Judaism (in its various expressions).[1] Christians, like the Fourth Evangelist, believed that Jesus had fulfilled the law and the prophets and indeed that they were the spiritual and true heirs of Abraham.[2] This is not to say that Johannine Christianity saw itself outside of the Jewish context. The Evangelist saw Christianity in both continuity and discontinuity with Judaism. The battle that ensued between Christians and the Jews at the intellectual level was fought upon holy ground – the revelation of God to Moses and the prophets, Israel's Scriptures. The Fourth Evangelist anchored in the Scriptures his response to those whom he called 'the Jews' – those who denied Jesus' Messianic claims and brought about his crucifixion and continued to deny that Jesus was the Messiah at the time he wrote the Gospel. These were primarily Jewish authorities who used the Scriptures in order to reject the Christian claim that Jesus was the Messiah (7:52). John utilised the Scriptures to demonstrate that indeed Jesus' life and career fulfilled the scriptural portrait of the promised Messiah.

In John's estimation, the religious teachers of Israel stood convicted for their blindness to the fulfilment of the Scriptures. He took the battle into their publicly acclaimed 'domain' (i.e., the Scriptures) in order to show how they were oblivious to the book they prized as the source of life (5:39, 46). One function of such systematic allusive references to the Scriptures may have been to reveal the author's own competence in Scripture and to establish authoritative credibility. The ability to detect deeper levels of meaning in the Scriptures and to harmonise them with the life and career of Jesus would not have been foreign to rabbinic hermeneutics. The Gospel plausibly would have been addressed to the Christian community who may then have disseminated it to address various needs and various groups.

This approach of arguing from Scripture is not unique to John. Other New Testament authors also go to the Scriptures to prove that Jesus is the promised Messiah.[3] However, the subtle manner in which John appeals to

---

[1] Cf. Jacob Neusner, 'Varieties of Judaism in the Formative Age', in *Formative Judaism*, 2nd series, BJS 41 (Chico, CA: Scholars Press, 1983), 59–89; E. P. Sanders, *Paul and Palestinian Judaism: A Comparison of Patterns of Religion* (London: SCM, 1977). Although the diversity within Judaism is acknowledged, one must not lose sight of the common elements around which Judaism was united (e.g., above all else their Scriptures which were sacred to all Jews).

[2] P. J. Hartin, 'A Community in Crisis: The Christology of the Johannine Community as the Point at Issue', *Neot* 19 (1985), 40.

[3] E.g., Acts 1:16; 8:32, 35; 17:2, 11; 18:24, 28; cf. Rom. 1:2; 1 Cor. 15:3, 4; Mt. 21:42; 22:29; 26:54, 56.

the Scriptures to set forth the case is unique to him and the primary source of the 'otherworldly' quality of his language.

5.2. Addressees of the Johannine Polemic: The Identity of 'the Jews'

The theme of conflict is all-pervasive in the Fourth Gospel: between light and darkness, truth and falsehood, believers and the 'world.' The first twelve chapters of the Gospel depict a growing strife between Jesus and his opponents who are simply called 'the Jews' (e.g., 5:16, 18; 7:1; 8:48, 52; 9:22; 10:31, 33; 11:8; 19:7). There is something of an interlude during the Farewell Discourse in chapters 13–17. However, even here, there is an awareness that the conflict that Jesus experienced will also be experienced by his disciples (15:18–16:4). In chapters 18 and 19, the theme resumes and comes to a head as the opponents finally succeed in bringing about Jesus' crucifixion. Even after this climax, the conflict continues. Already in the story of the resurrection, the persecution predicted in the Farewell Discourse begins to take place (20:19).[4]

Nevertheless, while the author often characterises the opponents of Jesus and his followers as οἱ Ἰουδαῖοι ('the Jews'),[5] he never seems fully

---

[4] The prediction of Peter's martyrdom (21:18–19) already presupposes a conflict, though the author draws no connection between Peter's martyrdom and the Jewish opposition described in the rest of the Gospel. Rodney Whitacre, *Johannine Polemic: The Role of Tradition and Theology*, SBLDS 67 (Chico, CA: Scholars Press, 1982), 5–6.

[5] The uses of the designation οἱ Ἰουδαῖοι in John and Acts comprise seventy-five percent of all the New Testament usage. The statistic is as follows: five in Matthew; six in Mark, five in Luke, seventy-one occurrences in John, seventy-nine in Acts; and twenty-six references in Paul: eleven in Romans; eight in 1 Corinthians and seven in the other Epistles, a total of one hundred ninety-two occurrences in the New Testament. Twelve of the sixteen references in the Synoptic Gospels are parallel occurrences of the phrase 'King of the Jews', i.e., Jesus. Of the seventy-one occurrences of the designation in the Fourth Gospel, sixty-eight are in the plural referring to 'the Jews' as a group. On the topic of 'the Jews' in the Fourth Gospel see the following studies: U. von Wahlde, 'The Johannine "Jews": A Critical Survey', *NTS* 28 (1982), 33–60; Malcolm Lowe, 'Who Were the Ἰουδαῖοι?' *NovT* 18 (1976), 101–30; idem, "Ἰουδαῖοι of the Apocrypha', *NovT* 23 (1981), 56–90; John Ashton, 'The Identity and Function of the Ἰουδαῖοι in the Fourth Gospel', *NovT* 27 (1985), 40–75; C. J. Cuming, 'The Jews in the Fourth Gospel', *ExpTim* 60 (1948–49), 290–2; Raymond E. Brown, *The Gospel According to John*, The Anchor Bible Series, 2 vols (Garden City, NY: Doubleday, 1966), 1:lxii; idem, 'The Passion According to John: Chapter 18 and 19', *The Way* 49 (1975), 131; John T. Townsend, 'The Gospel of John and the Jews: The Story of A Religious Divorce', in *Anti-Semitism and the Foundations of Christianity*, ed. by Alan T. Davies (New York: Paulist, 1979), 72–97; Wayne Meeks, 'Galilee and Judea in the Fourth Gospel', *JBL* 85 (1966), 159–69; idem, 'The Man From Heaven in Johannine Sectarianism', *JBL* 91 (1972), 44–72; idem, 'Am I a Jew? Johannine Christianity and Judaism', in *Christianity, Judaism, and Other Greco-Roman Cults*, Part I: New Testament, ed. by J. Neusner

to clarify the objects of his designation.[6] This ambiguity in John's seemingly blanket designation[7] of Jesus' opponents as 'the Jews' (e.g., 5:16, 18; 7:1, 13; 8:48–52)[8] has led some to conclude that one of the most Jewish of all the New Testament writings[9] is 'anti-Semitic', both in intent and in effect.[10] Rosemary Ruether charges that anti-Semitism is endemic to Christianity, that the very confession that Jesus is the Christ implies anti-Semitism.[11] Robert Wilken goes further. He believes that 'Christian anti-Semitism grew out of the Christian Bible, that is the New Testament... Christians have been anti-Semitic because they have been Christians.'[12]

The question of anti-Semitism in the New Testament has been

(Leiden: Brill, 1975), 163–86; John Koenig, 'John: A Painful Break with Judaism', in *Jews and Christians in Dialogue: New Testament Foundations* (Philadelphia: Westminster Press, 1979), 122–36; Reginald H. Fuller, '"Jews" in the Fourth Gospel', *Dialog* 16 (1977), 31–7; Mary Ann Getty, 'The Jews and John's Passion Narrative', *Liturgy* 22 (1977), 6–10; E. Rivkin, *The Shaping of Jewish History* (New York: Scribner's, 1971); Gale A. Yee, *Jewish Feasts and the Gospel of John* (Wilmington, DE: Michael Glazier, 1989), 11–16.

[6] Jesus' opponents appear as if are lumped together and referred to as 'the Jews' (e.g., 5:16, 18; 7:1; 8:48, 52; 9:22; 10:31, 33; 11:8; 19:7).

[7] Such blanket characterisation is more evident in Acts where the opponents of Paul during his missionary journeys are often referred to by Luke as 'the Jews' (9:23; 13:45, 50; 17:5; 18:12, 14; 20:3; 21:12), and Paul himself designates his own harassers as 'the Jews' (20:19; 25:10; 26:2, 21; 28:19).

[8] von Wahlde, 'The Johannine Jews', 33–60, claims to have counted in John's Gospel about 40 instances of a hostile designation 'the Jews'. However, he later concludes that 'there is little or no reason for seeing the Johannine Jews as common people except for the case of 6:41, 52'. See Fuller's explanation in 'The Jews', 31–7; cf. R. Culpepper, 'The Gospel of John and the Jews', *RevExp* 84 (1987), 273–88.

[9] J. B. Lightfoot, *Biblical Essays* (London: Macmillan, 1893), 133.

[10] Rosemary Ruether, *Faith and Fratricide: The Theological Roots of Anti-Semitism* (New York: Seabury, 1974), 111–6. See also Eldon Jay Epp, 'Anti-Semitism and the Popularity of the Fourth Gospel in Christianity', *Central Conference of American Rabbis Journal* 22 (1975), 35–57; N. A. Beck, *Mature Christianty: The Recognition and Repudiation of the Anti-Jewish Polemic of the New Testament* (London/Toronto: Associated University Presses, 1985); Janis E. Leibig, 'John and "the Jews": Theological Anti-Semitism in the Fourth Gospel', *Journal of Ecumenical Studies* 20 (1983), 209–34; C. J. A. Hickling, 'Attitudes to Judaism in the Fourth Gospel', in *L'Évangile de Jean: Sources, rédaction, theologie*, ed by M. de Jonge, BETL 44 (Leuven: Leuven University Press, 1977), 347–54; M. Simon, *Verus Israel*, ET (Oxford: OUP 1986 [1964]), 216–9; S. Freyne, 'Vilifying the Other and Defining the Self: Matthew's and John's Anti-Jewish Polemic in Focus', in *To See Ourselves as Others See Us: Christians, Jews, Others in Late Antiquity*, ed. by J. Neusner and E. Frerichs (Chico, CA: Scholars Press, 1985), 117–43; Hannah Arendt, *Antisemitism: The Origins of Totalitarianism* (New York: Harcourt, Brace, 1966); Samuel Sandmel, *Anti-Semitism in the New Testament* (Philadelphia: Fortress, 1978), 5, 168; Gregory Baum, *Is the New Testament Anti-Semitic?* (New York: Paulist, 1965); M. Casey, *Is John's Gospel True?* (London: Routledge, 1996).

[11] Ruether, *Faith and Fratricide*, 246.

[12] R. L. Wilken, *The Myth of Christian Beginnings* (New York/London: Doubleday/SCM, 1979), 197.

discussed extensively,[13] and further elaboration of the issue is unnecessary and lies beyond the scope of this study. Suffice it to say that, if there have been tragic episodes of anti-Semitism in some segments of the church, many of them have been rooted in ignorance of the New Testament teachings or prompted by an endemic and pervasive anti-Christian polemic in Judaism itself going back to the time of the birth of Christianity. While many critics of the Fourth Gospel single out John 8:44 as a prime example of Johannine anti-Semitism, they fail to note that three verses earlier in 8:41, the religious leaders accuse Jesus of being born from πορνεία ('prostitution', 'fornication'). He is charged with being a Samaritan, demon possessed (8:48), and performing miracles by the power of Beelzebub, 'the prince of demons' (Mk. 3:22–29; Mt. 10:25; 12:24, 27), which Jesus regards as blasphemy against the Holy Spirit. These and similar allegations have been found in Jewish sources throughout the centuries.[14]

---

[13] W. Klassen, 'Anti-Judaism in Early Christianity: The State of the Question', in *Anti-Judaism*, vol. 1, (n. 16), 1–19; J. G. Gager, *The Origins of Antisemitism: Attitudes Toward Judaism in Pagan and Christian Antiquity* (New York, Oxford: OUP, 1985); Lillian C. Freudman, *Antisemitism in the New Testament* (New York: University Press of America, 1994); James D. G. Dunn, 'The Question of Anti-Semitism in the New Testament Writings of the Period', in *Jews and Christians: Parting of the Ways AD 70–135*, ed. by J. D. G. Dunn, WUNT 66 (Tübingen: Mohr-Siebeck, 1992), 177–211; idem, *The Parting of the Ways Between Christianity and Judaism and their Significance for the Character of Christianity* (London: SCM, 1991); R. Kysar, 'Anti-Semitism and the Gospel of John', in *Anti-Semitism*, ed. by Evans and Hagner, 125; F. Mussner, *Tractate on the Jews: The Significance of Judaism for Christian Faith* (London: SPCK, 1984); P. von der Osten-Sacken, *Christian-Jewish Dialogue: Theological Foundations* (Philadelphia: Fortress, 1986); *Anti-Judaism in Early Christianity*, vol. 1: *Paul and the Gospels*, ed. by P. Richardson; vol. 2: *Separation and Polemic*, ed. by S. G. Wilson (Waterloo, Ontario: Wilfrid Laurier University, 1986); *Antisemitism and the Foundations of Christianity*, ed. by A. T. Davies (New York: Paulist, 1979); M. R. Wilson, *Our Father Abraham: Jewish Roots of the Christian Faith* (Grand Rapids: Eerdmans, 1989); E. Haenchen, 'The Book of Acts as Source Material for History of Early Christianity', in *Studies in Luke-Acts,*, ed. by L. E. Keck and J. L. Martyn (Philadelphia: Fortress; London: SPCK, 1966), 258–78; J. Parkes, *The Conflict of the Church and the Synagogue: A Study in the Origins of anti-Semitism*, 3rd edn (New York: Atheneum, 1969 [orig. 1934]); A. R. Eckardt, *Elder and Younger Brothers: The Encounters of Jews and Christians* (New York: Schocken, 1973); J. Neusner, *Jews and Christians: The Myth of a Common Tradition* (London: SCM, 1991); G. F. Moore, 'Christian Writers on Judaism', *HTR* 14 (1921), 197–254; Edward H. Flanner, 'Anti-Judaism and Anti-Semitism: A Necessary Distinction', *Journal of Ecumenical Studies* 10 (1973), 582–3.

[14] For example, *Yebamoth* 4:13: R. Simeon b. Azzai (c. AD 110). See further R. Travers Herford, *Christianity in Talmud and Midrash* (London: William and Norgate, 1903), 35–50; Samuel Krauss, *Das Leben Jesu nach jüdischen Quellen* (Berlin: n. pub., 1902), 55; S. Krauss, and W. Horbury, *The Jewish-Christian Controversy from the Earliest Times to 1789*, I. *History* (Tübingen: Mohr-Siebeck, 1996); W. Horbury, *Jews and Christians in Contact and Controversy* (Edinburgh: Clark, 1998); idem, 'A Critical Examination of the Toledoth Jeshu' (Diss., University of Cambridge, 1970); J. M. Lieu, *Medieval Polemics Between Christians and Jews* (Tübingen: Mohr-Siebeck, 1996); James Parkes, *The Conflict of the Church and the Synagogue* (London: n. pub., 1934); Mariam S. Taylor, *Anti-Judaism and Early Christian Identity: A Critique of the*

In defence of the New Testament Scriptures, it should be said that only a particular perspective in conjunction with a highly selective choice of texts could conclude that these writings are anti-Jewish.[15] After all, most of those who wrote them were Jews themselves. Was it not Paul, a converted Pharisee, who wrote to the church in Rome, 'For I could wish that I myself were accursed and cut off from Christ for the sake of my brethren, my kinsmen by race' (Rom. 9:3)?[16] The central figure of the Fourth Gospel is a Jew who called the Jerusalem temple 'my Father's house' (Jn. 2:15) and whom John records as having said, 'salvation is of the Jews' (Jn. 4:22). James sends his Epistle 'to the twelve tribes scattered among the nations' (James 1:1).[17] Many similar observations may be made throughout the New Testament. All of these writings show a positive orientation towards the Jewish people, even though they ultimately dispute the viability of 'Judaism' because 'Christ is the end of the law' (Rom. 10:4a).

Henry Chadwick began his book on *The Early Church* with this observation, 'The first Christians were Jews differentiated from their fellow countrymen by their faith that in Jesus of Nazareth the Messiah of the nation's expectation had now come.'[18] Most Christians throughout the world can only react in dismay and horror when atrocities are committed against other members of the human race, whether against the Jews in the tragedy of the Holocaust, or Muslims in the genocide of the Balkans, or other racial or religiously motivated hate crimes against human beings throughout the world. The abuse of religious documents including the canonical Christian writings, indeed the whole of the Scriptures, to justify evil-doing has a long precedence in human history.[19] Sacred writings,

---

Consensus (Leiden: Brill, 1995); Hanne Trautner-Kromann, *Shield and Sword: Jewish Polemics against Christianity and the Christians in France and Spain 1100–1500* (ET, Tübingen: Mohr-Siebeck, 1993); R. Bauckham, 'The Parting of the Ways: What Happened and Why', *ST* 47 (1993), 135–51; D. Berger, *The Jewish-Christian Debate in the High Middle Ages: a Critical Edition of the Nizzahon Vetus, with an introduction, translation and commentary* (Philadelphia: Fortress, 1979), idem, 'Mission to the Jews and Jewish-Christian Contrasts in the Polemical Literature of the High Middle Ages', *American Historical Review* 91 (1986), 576–91; H. Chadwick, 'Justin Martyr's Defence of Christianity', *BJRL* 47 (1965), 275–97.

[15] Cf. M. Hengel, *Schriftauslegung im antiken Judentum und im Urchristentum*, M. Hengel und Hermut Löhr, WUNT 73 (Tübingen: Mohr-Siebeck, 1994), 261–2.

[16] J. Issac, *L'Antisémitisme a-t-il des racines chrétiennes?* (Paris: Fasquelle, 1960), 21, idem, *Jesus et Israel*, ET (New York: Holt, 1971 [1959]).

[17] Probably the Jewish Christians in Diaspora.

[18] H. Chadwick, *The Early Church* (London: Harmondsworth, 1967), 1.

[19] Cf. Günter Reim, 'John 8:44 – Gotteskinder/Teufelskinder: wie antijudaistisch ist "Die wohl antijudaistischste Äusserung des NT"?', *NTS* 30 (1984), 619; Richard Lowry, 'The Rejected-Suitor Syndrome: Human Sources of the New Testament "Antisemitism"', *JES* 14 (1977), 229.

because of the divine authority attached to them, have often been abused by those who have needed justification to commit crimes against their fellow humans, or to bring about social and political upheavals in the name of God or human ideologies. In these instances, it is expected, at least from the learned community, to be able to differentiate the guilt that lies inherently in a document, and the guilt that lies at the feet of those who pervert the meaning of a document for their own purposes. A historical abuse of New Testament Scriptures does not make the New Testament writers accomplices in a historic crime. The charge that the New Testament is either anti-Semitic or promotes anti-Semitism is a misrepresentation of these sacred writings.

In so far as the Fourth Evangelist is concerned, he is no more anti-Semitic[20] than one of the most monumental Hebrew prophets, Isaiah, when he graphically denounces the unfaithfulness and unbelief within Judah: 'Alas, sinful nation, people weighed down with iniquity, offspring of evildoers' (Isaiah 1:4); 'Hear the word of the Lord, you rulers of Sodom; Give ear to the instruction of our God, you people of Gomorrah' (Isa. 1:10; cf. 1:21, 23; 3:1-26; 5:1-9; 6:9-12; etc.). And not only Isaiah, but many of the Hebrew prophets scorned the Jewish leaders for their apathy towards truth and their indifference towards the revelation of God in their history (e.g., Jer. 3:2-5; 13:23-24; Ezk. 16:1-63; 23:1-48; Hos. 5:1-15; 9:1-17; Amos 9:1-10; etc.). Such self-criticism within Judaism was characteristic of the Old Testament prophets who stood within the Abrahamic covenant and called Israel to be faithful to her God.[21] Many reformist and separatist movements within Judaism, such as the Essene community at Qumran, may have understood themselves within this prophetic tradition. It is

---

Clark Williamson and Ronald Allen, *Interpreting Difficult Texts: Anti-Judaism and Christian Preaching* (London: SCM, 1989), 92; cf. G. A. F. Knight, 'Antisemitism in the Fourth Gospel', *Reformed Theological Review* 27 (1968), 86; Baum, *Is the New Testament Anti-Semitic?*, 69-74; and the essays in Howard Clark Kee and Irvin J. Borowsky, eds, *Removing the Anti-Judaism from the New Testament* (Philadelphia: American Interfaith Institute/World Alliance, 1998).

[20] Reinhold Leistner, *Antijudaismus im Johannesevangelium? Darstellung des Problems in der neueren Auslegungsgeschichte und Untersuchung der Leidensgeschichte* (Bern/Frankfurt: Herbert Lang, 1974), 143-5; E. H. Flanner, 'Anti-Semitism: A Necessary Distinction', *Journal of Ecumenical Studies* 10 (1973), 582-3; Philip S. Kaufman, *The Beloved Disciple: Witness Against Anti-Semitism* (Collegeville, MN: The Liturgical Press, 1991), 50-63; W. Pratscher, 'Die Juden im Johannesevangelium', *Bibel und Liturgie* 59 (1986), 177-85; F. Vouga, 'Antijudaismus im Johannesevangelium?' *Theologie und Glaube* 83 (1993), 81-9; Walter Rebell, *Gemeinde als Gegenwelt* (Frankfurt: Lang, 1987), 100f.

[21] See Mary C. Callaway, 'A Hammer That Breaks Rocks in Pieces: Prophetic Critique in the Hebrew Bible', in *Anti-Semitism and Early Christianity: Issues of Polemic and Faith*, ed. by Evans and Hagner (Minneapolis: Fortress Press, 1993), 21-38.

certainly not surprising for John the Baptist (Jn. 1:21; cf. Mk. 11:32; Mt. 21:26), Jesus (Jn. 4:44; 6:14; 7:40; 9:17; cf. Mt. 21:11), and his disciples (cf. Mt. 23:34) to see and 'define' themselves within such a prophetic heritage.[22] It is important to recognise the same prophetic voice in the Fourth Gospel, the aim of which is to call Israel to come to terms with its unbelief and rejection of the Messiah. Here the Evangelist appears as the figure of a prophet speaking to the nation, very much in the tradition of the prophets of Israel, proclaiming God's Word as Israel's prophets and sages had always done; his message reactivated past revelation under new conditions. The Evangelist writes with similar prophetic authority.[23]

In the Fourth Gospel, it is crucial to distinguish a theological judgment from an ontological one. A necessary distinction must be maintained between rejection of a race of people and rejection of a religious system.[24] John rejects Judaism on theological, not ontological, grounds. One cannot speak of Johannine anti-Semitism any more than one can speak of Qumran anti-Semitism. John's Gospel reflects the theological confrontation between the developing church and the Jewish religious hierarchy.[25] Nevertheless, many of those who believe in Jesus are the Jews (e.g., 7:31; 10:42; 11:45; 12:11), among them even some of the religious authorities (12:42). Jesus is specifically designated as 'a Jew' (4:9).[26] Israel for John is an indispensable part of the promised single flock (cf. 10:16).[27] The Evangelist's orientation

---

[22] B. Chilton, 'Jesus and the Question of Anti-Semitism', in *Anti-Semitism and Early Christianity*, ed. by Evans and Hagner, 39–52.

[23] J. Barton, *The Oracles of God: Perceptions of Ancient Prophecy in Israel After the Exile* (London: Darton, Longman and Todd, 1986), 126. Cf. Richard B. Hays, *Echoes of Scripture in the Letters of Paul* (New Haven: Yale University Press, 1989), 14, and his similar characterisation of Paul.

[24] J. T. Sanders, *The Jews in Luke-Acts* (Philadelphia: Fortress Press, 1987), muddles this distinction. Following Gager's definition of anti-Semitism as 'a fundamental and systematic hostility towards Jews', Sanders describes Acts as 'anti-Semitic' (pp. xvi–xvii). See the discussion by D. R. A. Hare, *The Theme of Jewish Persecution of Christians in the Gospel According to St. Matthew*, SNTSMS 6 (Cambridge: CUP, 1967); idem, 'Review of Three Recent Works on Anti-Semitism', *RelSRev* 2.3 (1976), 15–21.

[25] The Gospel lacks the racist and political-social elements that characterise anti-Semitism. Vouga, 'Antijudaismus?', 81–9; A. Kusvmirek, 'Zydzi w ewangelii Jana (Die Juden im Johannesevangelium)', *Studia Theologica Varsaviensia* (Warsaw) 30 (1992), 121–35.

[26] See particularly H. Thyen, 'Das Heil Kommt von den Juden', *Kirche: Festschrift für G. Bornkamm*, hrsg. D. Lührmann and G. Strecker (Tübingen: Mohr-Siebeck, 1980), 185–204. Cf. Rudolf Bultmann, *The Gospel of John: A Commentary*, trans. by G. R. Beasley-Murray (Philadelphia: Westminster, 1971), 86; Hengel, *Schriftauslegung*, 261–2.

[27] Thyen, 'Heil', 177; cf. 185–204; F. Vouga, *Le cadre historique et l'intention théologique de Jean*, Beauchesne Religions (Paris: Beauchesne, 1977), 70f.; Walter Rebell, *Gemeinde als Gegenwelt: zur soziologischen und didaktischen Funktion des Johannesevangeliums*, BBET 20 (Frankfurt: Lang, 1987), 100f.; T. Onuki, 'Zur literatursoziologischen Analyse des

to the Jewish festivals, institutions (e.g., 7:10, 37–38; 19:36) and even the law (as in 1:17, 45; 5:45–47; 7:19, 51; 15:25) is not one of hostility.[28] Studious attention to the law will reveal the one in whom the grace and truth of God is embodied (5:46–47). The Torah itself is a witness to Jesus.

5.2.1. Who Then Are the Johannine Jews?

As trivial as the question about the identity of the Johannine Jews may at first appear, there are major disagreements as to how one defines 'the Jews' and the scope of this designation at the time of the composition of the New Testament and in the Fourth Gospel. Apart from the absence of consensus among modern scholars, the problem is further compounded by the disagreement among the Jews themselves in ancient times (not to mention modern times) as to who was 'a true Jew'.[29] In the New Testament, the designation 'Jews' may denote a group identified by a particular ethnic origin and religious practice. 'The Jews' may refer to the entire Jewish people, the residents of Jerusalem, residents of Judea, the religious authorities in Jerusalem, or simply those who are hostile to Jesus.

In the most traditional sense, the category 'Jews' refers to the people belonging to Judea.[30] This seems to be how John uses the name in 7:1 and

---

Johannesevangelium – auf dem Wege zur Methodenintegration', *AJBI* 8 (1982), 162–216, here 190; John Painter, *The Quest for the Messiah: The History, Literature and Theology of the Johannine Community* (Edinburgh: Clark, 1991), 101; Culpepper, 'John and Jews', 280; Klaus Wengst, *Bedrängte Gemeinde und verherrlichter Christus: Der historische Ort des Johannesevangeliums als Schlüssel zu seiner Interpretation*, Biblisch-Theologische Studien 5, 2nd edn (Neukirchen-Vluyn: Neukirchener Verlag, 1983), 45–7; Townsend, 'John and the Jews', 79–81; Hengel, *Schriftauslegung*, 261–2; W. Wiefel, 'Die Scheidung von Gemeinde und Welt im Johannesevangelium auf dem Hintergrund der Trennung von Kirche und Synagogue', *TZ* 35 (1979), 213–27, here 220–4.

[28] John Ashton, *Understanding the Fourth Gospel* (Oxford: Clarendon, 1991), 131, rejects Thyen's 'love-hate' characterisation of John's attitute towards the Jews, and maintains, 'in fact, there is no love and little sympathy, only hostility tinged with fear.' But see John McHugh, 'In Him was Life', in *Jews and Christians*, ed. by Dunn, 157–8.

[29] S. J. D. Cohen, 'Crossing the Boundary and Becoming a Jew', *HTR* 82 (1989), 13–33; M. Goodman, 'Nerva, the *Fiscus Judaicus* and Jewish Identity', *JRS* 79 (1989), 40–44; idem, 'Identity and Authority in Ancient Judaism', *Judaism* 39 (1990), 192–201; idem, 'Proselytising in Rabbinic Judaism', *JJS* 40 (1989), 175–85; Ashton, 'Identity', 40–75; M. Lowe, 'the Ἰουδαῖοι?', 101–30; Ross S. Kraemer, 'On the Meaning of the Term "Jew" in Greco-Roman Inscriptions', *HTR* 82 (1989), 35–53; L. H. Schiffman, *Who Was a Jew? Rabbinic and Halakhic: Perspective on the Jewish-Christian Schism* (Hoboken, NJ: KTAV, 1985).

[30] Thyen, 'Das Heil', 163–84; Lindars, *The Gospel of John*, 102; Philip S. Alexander, '"The Parting of the Ways" from the Perspective of Rabbinic Judaism', in *Jews and Christians*, ed. by Dunn, 4ff. However, Ashton, 'Identity', 51–2, 73, points to two cases where Josephus argues the designation refers to those who had been taken captive to Babylon and did not remain in Judea. The 'true' Jews are those who endured the Babylonian exile.

11:7. Some scholars have argued that the Johannine designation almost always is to be translated as 'the Judeans' rather than 'the Jews'.[31] Malcolm Lowe believes that the same parallel that exists between Galilee and Galileans must be maintained between Judea and Judeans.[32] Yet by the Hellenistic period, the designation ’Ιουδαῖος had taken on a strong religious connotation as it referred to those who were devoted to the Torah, the traditional Jewish customs and the temple in Jerusalem, irrespective of whether they lived in Judea or not.[33] This religious connotation is evident in some of the Johannine references to 'the Jews'.[34]

In the post-biblical ('intertestamental') period, ’Ιουδαῖος does not seem to have been the customary name by which the Jews identified themselves.[35] Rather, ’Ισραήλ appears to have been the preferred Jewish self-identification (cf. e.g., Sir. 17:17; Jub. 33:20; Pss. Sol. 14:5). While ’Ιουδαῖος was the name by which Jews were distinguished from other ethnic and religious groups, 'Israel/Israelite' denoted their self-understanding in terms of election and covenant promise.[36]

In the Old Testament יהודה always seems to retain its original meaning for the tribe of Judah; ישראל is from the beginning a national designation encompassing all Jews. As such, ישראל can include Judah in the pre-exilic literature. Only after 932 BC did ישראל become a designation for the Northern Kingdom, indicating that it was considered the true Israel and Judah the seceding party.

With the deportation of 722 BC, ישראל once again becomes the name

---

[31] R. T. Fortna, 'Theological Use of Locale in the Fourth Gospel', *ATR Suppl. ser.* 3 (1974), 58–95; W. Meeks, 'Breaking Away: Three New Testament Pictures of Christianity's Separation from the Jewish Communities', in *To See Ourselves*, ed. by Neusner, et al., 96; cf. Meeks, 'Am I a Jew?', 182.

[32] Lowe, 'The ’Ιουδαῖοι?', 101–30; idem, 'The Apocrypha', 56–90.

[33] This appears to have been a development which followed the expansion of Judea's political authority under the Hasmoneans and the increased experience of the Diaspora. See 2 Macc. 2:21; 8:1; 14:38. Cf. Robert Murray, '"Disaffected Judaism" and Early Christianity: Some Predisposing Factors', in *To See Ourselves*, ed. by Neusner, et al., 265; Meeks, 'Galilee and Judea', 159–69; idem, 'Am I a Jew?', 1:182; W. Gutbrod, "’Ιουδαῖος", *TDNT* 3 (1965), 375–83; Ashton, 'Identity', 40–75; Kraemer, 'Jew in Greco-Roman Inscriptions', 35–53; Dunn, *Parting of the Ways*, 143–6; J. Plescia, 'On the Persecution of the Christians in the Roman Empire', *Latomus* 30 (1971), 120–32.

[34] 2:6, 13; 3:25; 4:22; 5:1; 6:4; 7:2; 11:55; 18:31; 19:7, 31, 40, 42.

[35] J. Painter, 'Christ and the Church in John 1:45–51', in *L'Evangile de Jean*, ed. by M. de Jonge (1977), 359–62; Ashton, *Understanding*, 153.

[36] ’Ιουδαῖος appears to have had something of an outsider's perspective (hence the regularity of its use by Philo, in *Flacc.* and *Legat* and by Josephus); where as 'Israel(ite)' seems to have been much more an *intra muros* designation. Gutbrod, "’Ισραήλ", *TDNT* 3:383–88; cf. 2 Macc. 1:1, 7, 10.

of the 'people of God', which is no longer used in a political or territorial sense. It is purely the 'name' of God's people, always stressing that the Jews are the theocratic people.[37] Palestinian Judaism would have used ישראל or Ἰσραήλ when speaking of itself. However, when Gentiles referred to Jews in diplomatic correspondence or official records, then they were referred to as οἱ Ἰουδαῖοι. And indeed it is only in the writings of Hellenistic Judaism that Jews, influenced by Gentile usage, begin to refer to themselves as 'Jews'.[38] When the name Ἰσραήλ was used by Hellenistic Judaism, the 'religious' overtones of the word were much more pronounced than in the writings of Palestinian Judaism.[39]

The Fourth Evangelist would have been aware of the differences and various nuances associated with the names Ἰσραηλίτης and Ἰουδαῖος. Rabbis generally referred to their people as Ἰσραήλ and considered themselves Ἰσραηλῖται and Ἰουδαῖοι.[40] He would have been well aware that the rabbis had appropriated to themselves the spiritual legacy of Moses. They considered only those who accepted the tenets of their teachings as members of the 'people of God'. Jewish-Christians were disbarred from the privilege for they had betrayed the religious-national heritage of the 'chosen people' – the Torah of which the rabbis considered themselves to be the experts. It is possible that John may have conceded the use of the designation 'Jews' within the context of the broad spectrum of late second-temple Judaism,[41] while clinging to the title 'Israel(ite)' for those who recognised Jesus as the Christ, the 'King of Israel' (Jn. 1:47–49).[42] In the Fourth Gospel, to the 'outsiders', Jesus is 'King of the Jews' (Jn. 18:33, 39; 19:3, 19, 21); but to those who believe, he is 'King of Israel' (1:47–49; cf. 12:12–19).

The designation Ἰουδαῖος was also used by the Jews to make a distinction among themselves. It was a means of claiming to be 'the true Jews' over against other claimants to the same epithet who were perceived to be outside of the Jewish community.[43] While the emergence of post-

---

[37] G. von Rad, "Ἰσραήλ", *TWNT* 3:357–58; Gutbrod, "Ἰσραήλ", 383–88.

[38] K. G. Kuhn, "Ἰσραήλ", *TWNT.* 3:361–66 (*TDNT* 3:375ff.).

[39] Kuhn, "Ἰσραήλ", 364 *ll.* 39ff; 366 *ll.* 6ff. (German pagination).

[40] Ibid., 363 *ll.* 13–28.

[41] Morna D. Hooker's proposal in *Continuity and Discontinuity: Early Christianity in Its Jewish Setting* (London: Epworth Press, 1986), 27.

[42] Cf. H. Conzelmann, *The Theology of St. Luke*, trans. by G. Buswell (London: SCM, 1982), 145; German orig., *Die Mitte der Zeit* (Tübingen: Mohr, 1953).

[43] For example, 'minim', those who were considered 'apostate Jews', such as Samaritans. Dunn, 'Question of Anti-semitism in New Testament Writings', 185; Ashton, 'Identity', 51–2, 73.

exilic Judaism and the Maccabean revolt may have provided two significant challenges for the Jewish identity, the destruction of the temple in AD 70 would have been by far the most serious single crisis of the second-temple period and would have even further fuelled the conflict as to who were 'the true Jews' and who were false. The Fourth Evangelist may have been aware of such claims and counter-claims wherein a particular leading group among the ethnic Jews (e.g., Pharisees, or οἱ ἄρχοντες) may have sought to establish itself as the authoritative representative of Judaism, 'the Jews'. Indeed, if one accepts the suggestion that the Pharisees were primary players behind the expulsion of Jewish Christians from synagogues, then one can see the Johannine antipathy towards this group.[44] According to John's record, the most sustained opposition to Jesus and his followers came from the religious aristocracy based in Jerusalem[45] at the centre of which were the Pharisees. In the Fourth Gospel, the term οἱ Φαρισαῖοι occurs nineteen times (excluding its occurrence in the pericope of the woman taken in adultery).[46] They are presented as the most vitriolic opponents of Jesus (7:32, 47–48; 8:13, 22, 31, 48, 52, 57; 9:13–40; 11:47, 57; 12:19, 42; 18:3).[47] The author often juxtaposes his references to the Pharisees and to 'the Jews', almost as if using the designations synonymously. This can be seen in the following instances.

In John 1:19, 'the Jews' send priests and Levites to question Jesus. But in 1:24, the author clarifies his reference with the aside, 'Now they had been sent from the Pharisees.'[48] In chapter 7, there is an apparent distinction between 'the Jews' who are Jews, 'the multitudes' who are also Jews (7:11–13; cf. 9:22), and later 'some of the people' (7:25, 31) who

---

[44] See Wengst, *Gemeinde*, 48–60; and on the role of the Pharisees pp. 40–44.

[45] These may have included the Sanhedrin and its minions, the party of high priests, the Sadduccean nobility, and of course, on the forefront of them the Pharisees. By his demonstrative act of cleansing the temple, Jesus especially provoked this latter group who considered the temple as their self-designated 'territory'. An exception is Luke 7:3, which is understandable in view of the fact that Luke was a Gentile. See von Wahlde, 'The Johannine Jews', 33–60; also Hare, 'Three Recent Works', 19.

[46] John 1:24; 3:1; 4:1; 7:32 [twice], 45, 48; 8:13; 9:13, 15, 16, 40; 11:46, 47, 57; 12:19, 42; 18:3.

[47] Roland Deines, *Die Pharisäer: Ihr Verständnis im Spiegel der christlichen und jüdischen Forschung seit Wellhausen und Graetz*, WUNT 101 (Tübingen: Mohr-Siebeck, 1997); Alan Watson, *Jesus and the Jews: The Pharisaic Tradition in John* (Athens, GA: University of Georgia Press, 1995).

[48] Lindars, *John*, 105, believes here the identification of priests and Levites with the Pharisees arises from the fact that they belonged to the Pharisaic party, because of their concern for strict observance of the Jewish Law.

appear as well to be Jews.[49] This distinction between 'the Jews' (vv. 11, 13) and the 'multitudes' (vv. 12, 25, 31) is curious, since it entails that even Jews fear 'the Jews' (7:13).[50] In chapter 8, the Pharisees challenge Jesus on his claim to be the light of the world (8:12-13); but as the narrative unfolds, the reference to the Pharisees rotates back to 'the Jews', even though the interlocutors of Jesus have remained the same (Jn. 8:22, 31 [cf. 12:42], 48, 52, 57). In chapter 9, at the beginning of the account, a similar episode occurs where the Pharisees are mentioned as the primary opponents of the Lord (9:13, 15, 16). Later there is a division among them (9:16) as to whether Jesus is sent by God. However the reference once again changes in 9:18 to 'the Jews'. In this instance, the designation seems to encompass only those members of the Pharisaic party who have rejected Jesus (9:22). 'The Jews' in 10:19, 24, 31, and 33 again refers to the Pharisees in their hostility to Jesus.

In the pivotal point of hostility to Jesus, in chapters 8 and 9, it is quite clear that the primary opponents singled out as 'the Jews' are none other than the Pharisees who also seem to dominate the ruling religious authorities: οἱ ἄρχοντες.[51] In the Fourth Gospel οἱ ἄρχοντες either synonymously refers to 'the chief priests' (7:32; 11:47, 57) or comprises the religious senate, a 'politburo' of some sort,[52] in which the supreme

---

[49] Maybe residents of Jerusalem, or more likely, Jews who are in Jerusalem on the occasion of the Feast of Tabernacles (7:2).

[50] Cf. 9:22; 18:12, 14; 19:38; 20:19; cf. 2:18, 20; 5:10, 15-16, 18; 8:13, 22, 31, 48, 52, 57; 12:42.

[51] Or οἱ ἄρχότες ('the rulers') occur four times (3:1; 7:26, 48; 12:42; and cf. 9:18, 22; 10:19, 24, 31, 33; cf. 9:13, 15, 16, 22; 18:12, 14, 31, 36, 38; 19:7, 12, 14, 21; 20:19) excluding those instances where it is used in the phrase 'ruler of this world'. See C. H. Dodd, *Historical Tradition in the Fourth Gospel* (Cambridge: CUP, 1963), 242 n. 2; also Brown, *The Community of the Beloved*, 41; idem, *John;* M. D. Crossan, 'Anti-Semitism and the Gospel', *TS* 26 (1975), 199; von Wahlde, 'Johannine Jews', 54; John Bowman, *Fourth Gospel and the Jews: A Study in R. Akiba, Esther and the Gospel of John*, Pittsburgh Theological Monograph Series 8 (Pittsburgh, PA: The Pickwick Press, 1975), 100; Baumbach, 'Gemeinde und Welt im Johannesevangelium', *Kairos* 14 (1972), 124; Leistner, *Antijudaismus im Johannesevangelium?*, 143.

[52] The view that the term 'the Jews' may be a reference to some sort of religious group or authorities in Judea was first proposed in modern times by Wilhelm Lütgert, 'Die Juden im Johannesevangelium', in *Neutestamentliche Studien fur George Heinrici zu seinem 70. Geburtstag* UNT 6 (Leipzig: J. C. Hinrichs, 1914), and this view was confirmed by Karl Bornhäuser, *Das Johannesevangelium: Eine Missionsschrift für Israel*, BFCT 2:15 (Gütersloh: Bertelsmann, 1928), and later by Jacob Jocz, 'Die Juden im Johannesevangelium', *Judaica* 9 (1953), 139. See also Dodd, *Historical Tradition*, 242 n. 2. The combination 'Pharisees and chief priests' is somewhat awkward from a historical point of view. However, the combination is attested both in the New Testament (e.g., Mt. 21:45) and elsewhere (e.g., Josephus, *Life*, 21). J. L. Martyn, *History and Theology in the Fourth Gospel* (New York: Harper and Row, 1968), 71-73.

religious authorities are called 'chief priests'.⁵³ Within this group, the Pharisees seem to be dominant (e.g., 11:47, 57; 18:3), if not in numbers, certainly in intimidation and power.⁵⁴ In 7:51, they even rebuke one of their own (i.e., Nicodemus) for questioning their conduct. In chapter 9, they are the ones who examine the blind man; and once again they are the main antagonists to Jesus (9:13, 15, 16, 40; cf. 4:1). In 11:46, the report of Jesus' miracle goes back to the Pharisees in response to which they convene a council to destroy him (11:47–57).

Whatever we make of their position in the party of ruling authorities, according to John's account, the Pharisees indisputably possess enormous power and pose as the primary opponents to Jesus and his followers (12:42). John 1:19 indicates that the priests and the Levites were sent by the Pharisees. These priests and Levites also may have been part of the group which John designates as οἱ ἄρχοντες. Nicodemus is a Pharisee, but also a member of this ruling party, 'a ruler of the Jews' (3:1).⁵⁵ In 7:32, the Pharisees with the chief priests send officers to arrest Jesus, and in 7:48, the Pharisees are the ones who chastise the officers for having failed to arrest him. Here once again the Pharisees are grouped with οἱ ἄρχοντες (7:48; cf. v. 26).

The statement in John 12:42 is quite revealing about the extent of the Pharisaic power within the ruling party: 'Nevertheless, however, many even of the rulers (τῶν ἀρχόντων) believed in him, but for the fear of the Pharisees (διὰ τοὺς Φαρισαίους) they did not confess it (οὐχ ὡμολόγουν), lest they should be put out of the synagogue.'⁵⁶ In chapter 18, the

---

⁵³ John 1:19 indicates that the priests and the Levites were sent by the Pharisees. With all likelihood, this is the group associated with the Sanhedrin or the group designated as οἱ ἄρχοντες. This group after AD 70 would have reformed itself in the form of the Jamnian Council. These οἱ ἄρχοντες collectively may have been considered by the Jews as the supremely religious, those whom Bornhäuser calls the 'Torafanatiker'; Blank, 'die Jerusalemer Kultgemeinde'; and Morton Smith, the 'Yahweh-alone party'. Some have argued the difference in these designations reflects different sources. See G. Baum, *The Jews and the Gospel: A Re-examination of the New Testament* (Westminster, MD: Newman, 1961), 102; Feliks Gryglewicz, 'Die Pharisäer und die Johanneskirche', in *Probleme der Forschung*, ed. by A. Fuchs, SNTU A.3 (Vienna and Munich: Herold Verlag, 1978), 148. In contrast, see E. Bammel, '"John did no miracle": John 10:41', in *Miracles: Cambridge Studies in their Philosophy and History*, ed. by C. F. D. Moule (London: Mowbray, 1965), 197–8; and U. C. von Wahlde, 'The Terms for Religious Authorities in the Fourth Gospel: A Key to Literary Strata?', *JBL* 98 (1979), 231–53.

⁵⁴ Bornhäuser, *Das Johannesevangelium*, 141.

⁵⁵ See Martyn's distinction in *History and Theology*, 87–8.

⁵⁶ Martyn, *History and Theology*, 86–9, seeks to explain the contrast between 'rulers' and the Pharisees by identifying the 'rulers' as those within the local council who were sympathetic, while the Pharisees represent the 'Jamnia loyalists' (cf. 7:48). The abrupt explanation in John 12:42, 'because of the Pharisees', and the absolute use of 'confess' each require elucidation, while the

references to 'the Jews' point to those who are intent on putting Jesus to death. But once again, it is clear that the author has only either the Pharisees or all the ruling authorities (18:12, 14) in view. This notion that the designation 'the Jews' may be a reference to some kind of ruling religious group in Judea was first proposed in modern times by Wilhelm Lütgert,[57] and then confirmed by Karl Bornhäuser in *Das Johannesevangelium: Eine Missionsschrift für Israel*,[58] and later by Jacob Jocz,[59] who maintained that the view was the position of a majority of Jewish scholars at that time. In 1964, Joseph Blank, *Krisis: Untersuchungen zur johanneischen Christologie und Eschatologie*,[60] once again supported this thesis.[61]

Some scholars have attributed the Johannine hostility towards the Pharisees as a reflection of the post-war situation after AD 70 and the strengthened position of the Pharisees.[62] However, the Pharisees irreconcilable attitude towards the Christian community is not confined to the Fourth Gospel and John in his aversion towards the Pharisees is not alone. Already in the Synoptics, the Pharisees are presented as the primary opponents of Jesus and his followers (Mt. 23:34, 35; 27:62; cf. Mk. 3:6; Lk. 11:48-51; 16:14), and indeed with quite descriptive language the harshest criticism is reserved for the Pharisees (Mt. 3:7; 9:34; 12:14, 24, 31, 38, 39; 15:3, 14; 16:6; 21:45; 22:15; 23:13-35; 27:62. Cf. Lk. 11:39-53).

In comparison to Matthew, for example, John is far more understated in his criticism of the Pharisees. And yet his criticism is not any less damning of them. Nicodemus, for example, is a Pharisee, addressed as the teacher of Israel, yet is incapable of understanding even earthly matters,

---

whole verse only makes sense in the light of the explanation given in John 9:22 or the experience anticipated by 16:2.

[57] 'Die Juden im Johannesevangelium', 1914.

[58] BFCT 2:15 (Gütersloh: Bertelsmann, 1928).

[59] 'Die Juden im Johannesevangelium', *Judaica* 9 (1953), 139.

[60] Freiburg im Breisgau: Lambertus-Verlag, 1964.

[61] A slightly varied form of the same view is proposed by G. Reim, *Studien zum alttestamentlichen Hintergrund des Johannesevangeliums*, SNTSMS 22 (Cambridge: CUP, 1974), 142f. See also Meeks, 'Am I a Jew?', 1:163-86 (esp. p. 182); Freyne, 'Vilifying the Other', 123. Morton Smith, *Palestinian Parties and Politics That Shaped the Old Testament* (New York/London; Columbia University Press, 1971), 82-98, suggests a distinction between an exclusivist Yahwehcult, based in Jerusalem, and a syncretistic Yahweh-cult, found in many forms in the Diaspora, typified the whole period from the Assyrian deportation of the northern kingdom in the 8th century BC to the establishment of rabbinic Judaism in post-New Testament times.

[62] H. Mulder, 'ontstaan en Doel van het vierde Evangelie', *Geref. Theol. Tijdschrift* 69 (1969), 241-245. Thus the Herodians and Sadducees are no longer mentioned.

much less heavenly mysteries (3:7–12).⁶³ In Matthew the Pharisees are called by Jesus and John the Baptist a 'brood of vipers' (Mt. 3:7; 23:33). They are accused of blasphemy against the Holy Spirit and thus of committing the unpardonable sin (Mt. 12:30, cf. 24). They are also charged as those who transgress the commandment of God for the sake of their tradition (15:3; Mk. 7:9, 13; cf. Lk. 11:39). They are characterised as blind guides of the blind (Mt. 15:14, cf. Jn. 3:10–12). Repeatedly they are accused of blindness (Mt. 23:16–18, 26). They are accused of neglecting the essential elements of the law and of being fixated on trivial matters (Mt. 23:23; cf. Mk. 7:6–13; Lk. 11:42). They are categorically condemned in the strongest terms for their religious duplicity as those who shut the door of the kingdom of God to the people (23:13). Seven times in Matthew 23:13–29 (cf. Mk. 7:6; Lk. 11:44), they are condemned as hypocrites. They are charged as being thieves of the basest kind – robbing widows and orphans (23:14). This accusation is particularly grievous in light of the special protective injunctions for the widows and the orphans as given in the Torah and the prophets (e.g., Exod. 22:22; Deut. 10:18; 14:29; 16:11, 14; Isa. 1:17, 23; and Jer. 7:6, 22:3; cf. Ps. 10:18; 68:5; 82:3). Indeed, contrary to their reputation as 'the teachers of the law', they are condemned by Jesus for their lawlessness (Mt. 23:28). They are accused of being sons of murderers of the prophets (Mt. 23:30) and condemned and characterised as sons of hell (Mt. 23:15).

In the light of Matthew's presentation, John's characterisation of the Pharisees as children of the devil is not surprising. Indeed, when Jesus says to them, 'you are of your father the devil' (8:44), his interlocutors are Pharisees and not all 'the Jews'. It seems that the author often either begins an episode by introducing the opponents of Jesus as the 'Pharisees' and later refers to them as 'the Jews', or begins a sequence by mentioning 'the Jews' and later clarifies his reference by introducing the 'Pharisees' or religious authorities.

But why this ambivalence and interchange? This ambiguity and vagueness could be an element within Johannine irony whereby this Pharisaic group and the religious authorities become the epitome of Judaism; they are the Jews *par excellence*. If the religious authorities and particularly the Pharisees claimed to be the authoritative representatives of Judaism, 'the Jews', then John's aim is one of ironic scorn. One only needs to remember that the founder of the school at Jamnia, Rabbi Yohanan ben Zakkai, was a Pharisee who had energetically opposed the Sadducees'

---

⁶³ See Wengst, *Bedrängte Gemeinde*, 42–4, 49–50.

party. Yohanan's successors and their disciples were likewise all Pharisees. Already before the year AD 70, Judaism under the influence of the Pharisees had moved decidedly towards what we would call a 'religion of observance' – as distinguished from 'cultic-ritual' piety. Assuming that the writing of the Gospel coincided with the period in which the Yavnean council began the process of unifying and defining Judaism over against other claimants to the Jewish heritage (including Christianity),[64] then it may be that John's use of 'the Jews' bears some irony in the context of the claims being made by these later authorities to be the only legitimate heirs to pre-AD 70 Judaism, to be in fact 'the Jews'.[65]

In particular, some writers believe that the *sages of Yavneh* and their followers in the period after AD 70 simply dropped the title 'Pharisees' but sought to reinforce the same Pharisaic piety as the authentic form of Judaism now deprived of the temple cult.[66] These Pharisaically-minded teachers of the law eventually gained power in the Jewish community.[67] If

---

[64] However, Christianity may have been perceived as a significant threat to that Yavnehian council. Cf. Wengst, *Bedrängte Gemeinde*, 57, 62; K. L. Carroll, 'The Fourth Gospel and the Exclusion of Christians from the Synagogues', *BJRL* 40 (1957), 20; J. D. G. Dunn, 'Let John be John: A Gospel for its Time', in *Das Evangelium und die Evangelien*, ed. by P. Stuhlmacher, WUNT 28 (Tübingen: Mohr-Siebeck, 1983), 309–39. See also C. K. Barrett, *The Gospel of John and Judaism* (London: SPCK, 1978), 68–9; W. Horbury, 'The Benediction of the *Minim* and Early Jewish-Christian Controversy', *JTS* n.s. 33 (1982), 19–61.

[65] See P. Schäfer, 'Die sogenannte Synode von Jabne: Zur Trennung von Juden und Christen im ersten/zweiten Jh.n.Chr.', in *Studien zur Geschichte und Theologie des rabbinischen Judentums* (Leiden: Brill, 1978), 45–64; J. Neusner, 'The Formation of Rabbinic Judaism: Yavneh (Jamnia) from AD 70 to 100', *ANRW* II.19.2 (1979), 3–42; G. Alon, *The Jews in their Land in the Talmudic Age*, vol. 1 (Jerusalem: Magnes, 1980); Freyne, 'Vilifying the Other', 125; Hickling, 'Attitudes to Judaism', 347; D. M. Smith, 'The Contribution of J. Louis Martyn to the Understanding of the Gospel of John', in *The Conversation Continues: Studies in Paul and John, in Honor of J. L. Martyn*, ed. by R. T. Fortna and B. R. Gaventa (Nashville: Abingdon, 1990), 275–94.

[66] 'Judaism after the Destruction of the Temple: An Overview', in *Formative Judaism: Religious, Historical and Literary Studies, Third Series: Torah, Pharisees, and Rabbis*, BJS 46 (Chico, CA: Scholars Press, 1983), 89–93; Isaiah Gafni, 'The Historical Background', in *Jewish Writings of the Second Temple Period: Apocrypha, Pseudepigrapha, Qumran Sectarian Writings, Philo, Josephus*, ed. by M. E. Stone (Assen: Van Gorcum; Philadelphia: Fortress, 1984), 27–31; J. Neusner, *A Life of Yohanan ben Zakkai ca. 1–80 C.E.*, 2nd edn (Leiden: Brill, 1970), 166–73.

[67] So Mulder, 'Ontstaan en Doel', 58; Gryglewicz, 'Die Pharisäer und die Johanneskirche', 156f; Severino Pancaro, *The Law in the Fourth Gospel: The Torah and the Gospel, Moses and Jesus, Judaism and Christianity According to John*, NovTSup 42 (Leiden: Brill, 1975), 492–534; M. H. Shepherd, 'The "Jews" in the Gospel of John: Another Level of Meaning', *ATR Supplement* (1974), 104. But see Neusner, 'Judaism After the Destruction of the Temple', 93; idem, *From Politics to Piety: The Emergence of Pharisaic Judaism* (Engelwood Cliffs, NJ: Prentice-Hall, 1973), 143–54. Cf. Morton Smith, 'Palestinian Judaism in the First Century', in *Israel: Its Role in Civilization*, ed. by Moshe Davis (New York: Jewish Theological Seminary of America, 1956), 74–77.

this is granted, then the Johannine reference to 'the Pharisees' or 'the Jews', in light of the scornful posture towards the original Pharisees in the Gospel, may be a further sarcastic characterisation of the contemporary leadership which was heir to the Pharisaic tradition. These later 'Pharisaic' leaders, along with other religious authorities, collectively epitomise the opposition to Jesus and his followers. John therefore could have understood them as having identified themselves to a dangerous extent with the earlier Jewish leadership to whom he assigns responsibility for Jesus' crucifixion (18:35; 19:6, 15, 21). While this is speculative, it is safe to say that the apparent conflict between the churches of John's time and the contemporary Jewish authorities who had descended from the Pharisees need not be a fresh result of the post-AD 70 situation; it could very well have extended from the time of Jesus himself.[68] Yet it needs to be stressed that John's focus seems to be upon a limited group of Jewish leaders, not upon the Jewish people as such.

5.2.2. 'The Jews' at the Level of Johannine Theology

It is important in the Gospel of John to maintain a bi-focal perspective between history and theology, between sense and reference, between connotation and denotation, without emphasising one at the expense of the other.[69] At the level of history, the Johannine 'Jews' are the dominant religious authorities, particularly the Pharisees, who are the focus of John's scornful irony.[70] They consistently misunderstand Jesus (6:52; 7:35; 8:22). They persecute and seek to kill him (5:16–18; 7:1; 8:59; 10:31). They are the source of hostility and stubborn failure to believe in 'the Light'. In their cry, 'We have no king but Caesar', uttered just as the observance of Passover begins, they renounce Israel's profession to have no king but God, as stated in their Passover hymn *Nishmat kol hay*.[71] 'No king but

---

[68] See my discussion in chapter four. See also Ashton, 'Identity', 67; cf. Dunn, 'Question', 199, no. 89.

[69] Ashton has argued that in the search for 'the meaning', scholars have failed to distinguish between the *sense* of the phrase and its *reference*. J. Ashton, *Studying John: Approaches to the Fourth Gospel* (Oxford: Clarendon, 1994), 52, 63f., idem, 'Identity', 57–9.

[70] See Gryglewicz, 'Die Pharisäer und die Johanneskirche', 148; cf. Bammel, '"John did no miracle"', 197–98; U. C. von Wahlde, 'The Terms for Religious Authorities in the Fourth Gospel: A Key to Literary Strata?', *JBL* 98 (1979), 231–53; Bowman, *Fourth Gospel and Jews*, 41; Lütgert, 'Die Juden im Johannesevangelium', 149, Bornhäuser, *Das Johannesevangelium*, 23, 140f; Pancaro, *Law in the Fourth Gospel*, 293.

[71] Wayne A. Meeks, *The Prophet-King* (Leiden: Brill, 1967), 76–8; Ignace de la Potterie, 'Jésus roi et juge d'après Jn 19,13', *Bib* 41 (1960), 244.

God' was also the Zealots' profession in their struggle against Caesar.[72] With this cry, the religious leaders of Israel rejected more than the kingship of Jesus. They explicitly rejected the kingship of God. In its place, they accepted the kingship of this world, and with it, Caesar's blasphemous claim to divinity. Thus, the Johannine irony emerges again, for while the leaders demand Jesus' death on the grounds of his claim to divinity (19:7), they openly accept Caesar's claim to divinity (19:15).

In bringing these various nuances together, the Evangelist pierces through the religious hypocritical veneer of the 'elders of Israel' to show their spiritual bankruptcy. But the implication of their open acceptance of the kingship of a blasphemous Gentile king was more than a spiritual debacle. In their cry, 'We have no King but Caesar', they abandoned Israel's role as the covenant people.[73] By rejecting their eschatological king, the elders of Israel abandoned the relationship of the nation as God's special people, the subjects of his special protection, care, and covenantal love, and became instead merely one of Caesar's subject *ethne*.[74] Therefore, from John's point of view, it is 'the Jews' (i.e., the religious authorities) who are the true blasphemers. C. K. Barrett maintains,

> John's treatment of the bulk of Israel was historically justified by the events recorded in the Synoptic Gospels, and sharpened no doubt by the continued antagonism between church and synagogue. Theologically it conveys the truth which the whole gospel teaches; the historic Israel was unable to move forward on its own level and so enter the kingdom of God (3:3-5). It had to be regenerated through the Word of God and the Spirit; and this regeneration it refused. Hence, the Old Israel came to stand under the judgment of God (cf. 9:41).[75]

At the level of Johannine theology, 'the Jews' in their rejection and hostility towards Jesus represent[76] the world in its unbelief and rejection of light (e.g., 1:10; 3:19; 7:7; 8:23, 26; 12:31; 14:17, 30; 15:18–19; 16:8, 20, 33; 17:14).[77] 'The Jews' are the living symbol of human insolence, spiritual

---

[72] Josephus, *Antiquities*, 18.1.6 §23; *Jewish War*, 2.8.1 §118; 7.10.1 §410, 418.

[73] Bultmann, *John*, 665; Brown, *John*, 2:894–5.

[74] Meeks, *Prophet-King*, 76; C. F. Evans, 'The Passion of John', in C. F. Evans, *Explorations in Theology*, vol. 2 (London: SCM, 1977), 50–66.

[75] C. K. Barrett, *St. John*, 431.

[76] By representation, I do not mean Jesus' interlocutors are simply 'foils'. They are real historical 'prototypes'. But see Ashton, *Studying John*, 36–70; Felix Porsch, *Pneuma und Wort* (Frankfurt: Peter Lang, 1974), 82–3; M. Michel, 'Nicodème ou le non-lieu de la vérité', *RevSR* 55 (1981), 227–36; also Martyn, *History and Theology*, 110; Myers, 'Irony and Humor in the Gospel of John', 7–8; van den Bussche, *Jean: Commentaire de l'Evangile Spirituel*, BVC (Brugis: Desclée de Brouwer, 1967), 178, prefers to see them as types.

[77] So Bultmann, *John*, 86; N. A. Dahl, 'The Johannine Church and History', in *Current Issues*

blindness and incomprehension when confronted with God's self-revelation in his creation, in human history and in his word. In such situations, those who practice evil naturally shun the penetrating light of revelation (3:20). This connotation begins in 1:10–11 and is further developed in 3:16–21, where a universal generalisation is made out of the foregoing Nicodemus dialogue focusing, as elsewhere, upon οἱ ἄνθρωποι – humanity in general (3:19).[78] In the farewell discourse, it appears that 'the world' has taken the place of 'the Jews'.[79]

Also at the level of Johannine theology, there is a subtle but consistent distinction that the Evangelist makes between σπέρμα and τέκνα – children born of God, seeds coming from the groin of Abraham.[80] The Evangelist's chief polemic is aimed against those who reject Jesus as the Messiah, thereby also rejecting their opportunity of becoming true children of Abraham and, ultimately, true children of God (1:12–13; 8:39–42). Jesus recognises that his opponents are 'descendants' (σπέρμα) of Abraham, but he rejects their claim to be 'children' (τέκνα) of Abraham because they do not do his works (8:37–41).

Throughout Johannine literature there is a recurring insistence that one's relation to God is revealed by what one does. Abraham was a man of steadfast faith in God. It was this unwavering belief in God and his promises which dictated his conduct and brought forth works of righteousness in his life. It was the absence of that Abrahamic faith in the opponents of Jesus which led to their unbelief and rejection of Jesus, and in turn, Jesus' rejection of their claim to be children of Abraham.[81] Such an

---

in *New Testament Interpretation*, ed. by W. Klassen and G. F. Snyder (New York: Harper and Row, 1962), 129, 133–5, 139; A. Grässer, 'Die antijüdische Polemik im Johannesevangelium', *NTS* 11 (1964–65), 74–90; Pratscher, 'Die Juden im Johannesevangelium', 177–85; David Granskou, 'Anti-Judaism in the Passion Accounts of the Fourth Gospel', in *Anti-Judaism in Early Christianty*, ed. by P. Richardson and D. Granskau (Ontario: Wilfrid Laurier University Press, 1986), 1:201–16, here 209; Jouette Bassler, 'Mixed Signals: Nicodemus in the Fourth Gospel', *JBL* 108 (1989), 635–46; Townsend, 'Gospel of John and the Jews', 72–97.

[78] J. N. Suggit, 'Nicodemus – the True Jew', *Neot* 14 (1981), 90–110.

[79] Takashi Onuki, *Gemeinde und Welt im Johannesevangelium: Ein Beitrag zur Frage nach der theologischen und pragmatischen Funktion des johanneischen 'Dualismus'*, WMANT 56 (Neukirchen-Vluyn: Neukirchener Verlag, 1982), 34–7.

[80] M. Vellanickal, *The Divine Sonship of Christians in the Johannine Writings* (Rome: Pontifical Biblical Institute, 1977).

[81] For further elaboration, see Brown, *John*, 357; Barrett, *St. John*, 347; Whitacre, *Johannine Polemic*, 68–89; *APOT* 2:709 (ed. Charles). Against his adversaries, Jesus calls Abraham himself as witness (8:56). The reference to seeing the 'day' of Jesus (8:56) may be presupposes a knowledge of the Jewish tradition of Abraham's future vision, according to Gen. 15:2–20, as it appears in the *Apocalypse of Abraham* and the rabbinic texts: the day of Christ becomes thereby identical with the Day of YHWH, God's eschatological epiphany, and Abraham is a believing

assertion would have been an affront to Judaism and the Jews who saw themselves as the heirs to God's promises and as his children (Jn. 8:31–59).

This brings Johannine theology into focus: Is there any salvific value inherent in being a Jew? While the Fourth Gospel does not address God's specific covenantal promises to the physical seeds of Abraham, his spiritual emphasis, however, is unequivocal: children of God are those who are 'born of God' and 'not of human blood-lines (αἱμάτων), nor of the will of the flesh, nor of the will of man' (Jn. 1:13). For John, in the new dispensation, what is of decisive importance, salvifically, is not ethnicity, heritage, religious tradition, and culture. Rather, it is one's response to Jesus which is determinative (Jn. 1:12–13; 3:18, 36; 6:27–29, 47; 4:20–24; 8:39–47; cf. Lk. 3:8) – thus a distinction is made between true and false Jew (e.g., Rev. 2:9; 3:9; Jn. 4:20–24; 8:39–44; cf. Rom. 2:28–29; Gal. 3:28), Israelites (1:47), vine (15:1), and shepherd (10:1–18).[82] One may be a physical descendent of Abraham but a spiritual child of the devil (8:37–47). Therefore, the Jewish religious hierarchy in its rejection of the revelation of God in Jesus Christ not only represents the world in its hostility to God, but worse yet, it represents the devil in his hostility to life and truth.[83] Whatever value physical descent from Abraham may have in other respects, there is no salvific significance in being the 'seed' of Abraham without producing the Abrahamic works (6:27–29; 8:39). This view is strongly reinforced in John when he places such a positive emphasis upon despised and discarded elements in Jewish society (e.g., the Samaritans). The Johannine outlook, as I have suggested earlier, is very much universal. This does not make the Fourth Gospel anti-Semitic. Neither is it anti-Gentile. Rather, this Gospel takes the side of all those who believe, Jews

---

witness to the revelation of salvation in the Son. See H. E. Lona, *Abraham in Johannes 8. Ein Beitrag zur Methodenfrage*, Europäische Hochschulschriften, Reihe 23: Theologie 65 (Bern: Lang, 1976); G. L. Bartholomew, 'An Early Christian Sermon-Drama: John 8:31–59' (Ph.D. Thesis, Union Theological Seminary, 1974); H. Odeberg, *The Fourth Gospel Interpreted in Its Relation to Contemporaneous Religious Currents in Palestine and the Hellenistic-Oriental World* (Chicago: Argonaut, 1968), 296–7; Schnackenburg, *Das Johannesevangelium*, 2:284.

[82] This contrast between that which is true and that which is false is seen in other ways as well; for example, in water and wine, the temple and the body of Christ, water from Jacob's well and the living water of Christ. In the Samaritan discourse, the water of Jacob is not a living water and does not lead to eternal life, but the water that Jesus gives through the indwelling Holy Spirit springs forth to eternal life. The significance of the contrast between Jacob and Jesus is evident in the deeper meaning of 'living water'. The author identifies the 'living water' with the Holy Spirit (7:38–39). In this contrast the Evangelist intimates in Jesus there is a revelation greater than the old covenant, for Jesus not only brings the revelation of God but gives the Spirit by which this revelation is internalized in believers. See specially J. MacDonald, *Memar Marqah: The Teaching of Marqah*, 2 vols, BZAW 84 (Berlin: Töpelmann, 1963), 2:222.

[83] John 8:44; cf. 19:7.

and Gentiles alike (cf. Rom. 3:29). It is important to hear the text in its own right within the historical context and in relation to its theological message.[84] Long before John, Israel's prophets had already noted God's profound care for all nations, the works of his hands.[85]

5.3. John's Appeal to Israel's Scriptures and Its Implications for His Language

The Old Testament plays the most decisive role in John's argument when formulating a response to those who denied that Jesus is the Christ. The author, in his allusive references to the Scriptures, highlights how he sees them fulfilled in the life of Jesus of Nazareth, whom he believes to be the Messiah according to the witness of Israel's Scriptures.[86] If 'the Jews' justified their refusal to accept Jesus' Messianic claims by appealing to the Scriptures, the Fourth Evangelist uses the self-same Scriptures to show that Jesus is the Messiah. In order to set forth his case that Jesus is the Messiah, John must explain scripturally the rejection of Jesus by the religious teachers of Israel.[87] While the religious authorities believed they could judge Jesus and his claim because they possessed the Torah,[88] John shows that even the Torah witnessed to him. The Scriptures, for the Evangelist, contain the divine blueprint for the life of Jesus – his special redemptive-revelatory role (1:51; 6:31, 45; 10:16), especially his Passion (12:15, 40; 13:18; 15:25; 19:28, 36, 37). The Evangelist's appeal to the Old Testament conveys his conviction that the Scriptures not only testify of Jesus (5:39,

---

[84] Pratscher, 'Die Juden im Johannesevangelium', 177–85.

[85] Cf. Judith M. Lieu, 'Biblical Theology and the Johannine Literature', in *New Directions in Biblical Theology*, ed. by Sigfred Pedersen (Leiden: Brill, 1994), 103; Hengel, *Schriftauslegung*, 263.

[86] A. García-Moreno, 'En torno al derásh en el IV Evangelio', *Scripta Theologica* 25 (93), 33–48. Cf. S. Amsler, *L'ancien testament dans l'église: Essai d'herméneutique chrétienne* (Neuchatel: Delachaux and Niestlé, 1960), 44; Bruce G. Schuchard, *Scripture within Scripture: The Interrelationship of Form and Function in the Explicit Old Testament Citations in the Gospel of John*, SBLDS (Atlanta: Scholars Press, 1992), 155; C. K. Barrett, 'The Old Testament in the Fourth Gospel', *JTS* 48 (1947), 155–69.

[87] For examples, compare Justin Martyr, *Dialogue with Trypho*, 89:1 and 90:1; also Origen, *Contra Celsum*, 2:9, 35, 68; 6:10, 34, 36. Also see M. Hengel, *Crucifixion in the Ancient World and the Folly of the Message of the Cross* (Philadelphia: Fortress Press, 1977), 1–10; J. H. Charlesworth, ed., *The Messiah: Developments in Earliest Judaism and Christianity* (Minneapolis: Fortress Press, 1992).

[88] On the judgment of such Messianic claims, see *Sanhedrin* 93b, the judgment of Bar Koziba (Bar Kochba).

45–46), but even more significantly, the intelligibility of the Scriptures depends on the revelation of God in Jesus Christ.[89] However, as it was noted in the previous chapter, the Johannine appeal to the Scriptures of Israel is not simply just an apologetic response to those who denied Jesus as the Christ. His Gospel primarily is a document for the church in which he sets forth the grounds upon which the Christians believed that Jesus of Nazareth was the Jewish Messiah (1:41, 45), Saviour of the world (4:42) whose birth, death, and resurrection was in precise fulfilment of the Scriptures.

The Fourth Gospel has been called 'the most *alttestamentlich* of New Testament books.'[90] Without some recognition of this dependence, it will be difficult to appreciate the intricacies of its language. The Evangelist draws his organisation, imageries, and fundamental theological concepts from the Old Testament.[91] In contrast, it is puzzling when one reads such curious comments as E. F. Scott's assertion that 'It is doubtful if the evangelist had any first-hand or complete acquaintance with the Old Testament.'[92] Indeed, it is astonishing to read R. T. Fortna's assertion that in the Fourth Gospel, 'There is no deliberate use of the Old Testament such as one finds either in the Gentile gospels of Mark and Luke or in Matthew's elaborately Jewish proof-texting',[93] or Käsemann's remark, 'He

---

[89] Cf. Merrill C. Tenney, 'Literary Keys to the Fourth Gospel: The Old Testament and the Fourth Gospel', *BibSac* 120 (1963), 300–8; D. Moody Smith, *The Theology of the Gospel of John* (Cambridge: CUP, 1995), 76–7.

[90] D. M. Smith, 'The Use of the Old Testament in the New', in *The Use of the Old Testament in the New and Other Essays: Studies in Honor of William Franklin Stinespring*, ed. by J. M. Efird (Durham, NC: Duke University, 1972), 57; Howard Clark Kee, *Jesus in History: An Approach to the Study of the Gospels*, 2nd edn (New York: Harcourt Brace Jovanovich, 1977), 237.

[91] E.g., 'serpent', 'manna', 'tabernacle', 'water', 'light', 'lamb', 'shepherd', 'vine', etc. See Brown, *John*, 32–4, 61–3, 669; T. Francis Glasson, *Moses in the Fourth Gospel* (London: SCM, 1963), 48–59, 65–73, 95–8; E. C. Hoskyns, *The Fourth Gospel*, ed. by Francis Noel Davey (London: Faber and Faber, 1947), 367–8; Brown, *John*, 322; R. Morgan, 'Fulfillment in the Fourth Gospel: The Old Testament Foundations', *Int* 11 (1957), 161–2; Meeks, *Prophet-King*, 307–13; J. G. S. Thomson, 'The Shepherd-Ruler Concept in the Old Testament and Its Application in the New Testament', *SJT* 8 (1955), 406–18; Schnackenburg, *Das Johannesevangelium*, 2:371–2; R. A. Henderson, *The Gospel of Fulfilment: A Study of St. John's Gospel* (London: SPCK, 1936), 101; D. A. Carson, 'John and the Johannine Epistles', in *It is Written: Scripture Citing Scripture*, ed. by D. A.Carson and H. G. M. Williamson (Cambridge: CUP, 1988), 245–64; J. Luzarraga, 'Presentación de Jesús a la luz del A. T. en el Evangelio de Juan', *Estudios Eclesiásticos* 51 (1976), 520.

[92] *The Fourth Gospel: Its Purpose and Theology*, 2nd edn (Edinburgh: Clark, 1908), 197.

[93] *The Gospel of Signs: A Reconstruction of the Narrative Source Underlying the Fourth Gospel*, SNTSMS 11 (Cambridge: CUP, 1970), 12, 223. See similar sentiments by Ashton, *Understanding*, 531–45; A. C. Sundberg, 'On Testamonies', *NovT* 3 (1959), 268–81.

[John] did not despise the use of the Old Testament even though he can get along without it in large sections and he always puts it in the shadow of his tradition about Jesus.'[94] Needless to say, as I have endeavoured to show, the Old Testament makes up the very warp and woof of John's language and theology. Its very diction is affected by the Scriptures.[95]

5.3.1. The Distinctions in Johannine Citations of Scripture

The Johannine references to the Old Testament can be divided into two categories: direct citations and indirect allusions. However, John's indirect references are so thoroughly pervasive, and at the same time, so consistently allusive in character that no single author has yet been able to do justice to the subject. The editors of the 26th–27th edition of the Nestle-Aland Greek New Testament count about two hundred allusions and parallels to

---

[94] E. Käsemann, *The Testament of Jesus* (Philadelphia: Fortress Press, 1968), 37. See on the other hand, C. H. Dodd, *According to the Scriptures: The Substructure of New Testament Theology* (London: Nisbet, 1952); A. T. Hanson, *The Prophetic Gospel* (Edinburgh: Clark, 1991), 253–4; Peter Stuhlmacher, *Jesus von Nazareth-Christus des Glaubens* (Stuttgart:Glawer Verlag, 1988), 7ff; W. G. Kümmel, *The Theology of the New Testament* (New York: Abingdon, 1973), 261–321.

[95] See my discussion in chapter two. See also A. H. Franke, *Das alte Testament bei Johannes. Ein Beitrag zur Erklärung und Beurtheilung der johanneischen Schriften* (Göttingen: Vandenhoeck and Ruprecht, 1885); G. Ziener, 'Weisheitsbuch und Johannesevangelium', *Bib* 38 (1957), 396–418; (1958), 37–60; Moises Silva, 'Approaching the Fourth Gospel', *Criswell Theological Review* 3 (1988), 27; B. Lindars, *New Testament Apologetic: The Doctrinal Significance of the Old Testament Quotations* (London: SCM, 1961), 15–17, 266–70; Schuchard, *Scripture within Scripture*, xi–xii; E. Cothenet, 'Témoinage de l'Esprit et interprétation de l'écriture dans la corpus johannique', in *La vie de la parole: De l'Ancien au Nouveau Testament*, P. Grelot Festschrift (Paris: Desclée de Brouwer, 1987), 367–77; James E. Wenger, 'The Use of the Old Testament in the Gospel of John' (Thesis, Dallas Seminary, 1965); Crawford H. Toy, *Quotations in the New Testament* (New York: Scribners, 1884), xxxv; Meredith Kline, 'The Old Testament Origins of the Gospel Genre', *The Westminster Theological Journal* 38 (1975), 1–27; E. D. Freed, *Old Testament Quotations in the Gospel of John* (Leiden: Brill, 1965); R. E. Nixon, *The Exodus in the New Testament* (London: Tyndale, 1963); Jeffrey Lloyd Staley, *The Print's First Kiss: A Rhetorical Investigation of the Implied Reader in the Fourth Gospel*, SBLDS 82 (Atlanta, GA: Scholars Press, 1988), 74–118; G. B. Caird, *The Language and Imagery of the Bible* (Philadelphia: Westminster Press, 1980), *passim*; J. J. Enz, 'The Book of Exodus as Literary Type for the Gospel of John', *JBL* 76 (1957), 208–15; compare also J. P. Fokkelman, 'Exodus', in *The Literary Guide to the Bible*, ed. by Robert Alter and Frank Kermode (Cambridge, MA: Harvard University Press, Belknap Press, 1987), 56–65; C. A. Evans, 'On the Quotation Formulas in the Fourth Gospel', *BZ* 26 (1982), 79–83; Douglas J. Moo, *The Old Testament in the Gospel Passion Narratives* (Sheffield: Almond Press, 1983), 146–48, 178–82, 233–4; Robert C. Culley, *Studies in the Structure of Hebrew Narrative* (Philadelphia: Fortress Press; Missoula, MT: Scholars Press, 1976); Henry Mowvley, 'John 1:14–18 in the Light of Exodus 33:7–34:35', *ExpTim* 95 (1984), 135–37; J. H. Roberts, 'The Lamb of God', *Neot* 2 (1968), 41–56; Jerome H. Neyrey, 'John III – A Debate Over Johannine Epistemology and Christology', *NovT* 23 (1981), 115–27; Tenney, 'Literary Keys: Old Testament and the Fourth Gospel', 302–4.

the Old Testament in the Fourth Gospel. The allusions are of particular interest to the present study since they are the dominant element which gives the language of John its particular sublime and 'out-of-reach' ethos. These indirect references function very much in unison with the direct citations in the Gospel.

Quotations of the Old Testament in the Fourth Gospel differ from those of the Synoptics. There are far fewer direct citations in John, in contrast, for example, to Matthew which has eighty-seven citations.[96] Isaiah is the only book mentioned by name by the Fourth Evangelist (1:23; 12:38, 39, 41),[97] although the law (1:45; 10:34; 15:25) and the prophets (6:45) are mentioned collectively (1:45; 10:34; 15:25). Appeal is also made to the Scripture, ἡ γραφή, in general (7:38, 42; 13:18; 17:12; 19:24, 28, 37).

The precise number of direct references to the Old Testament by the Fourth Evangelist is disputed since several of John's citations appear to be periphrastic. There are at least seventeen uses of Scripture quotation[98] where some variation of the fulfilment formula, ἵνα πληρωθῇ (12:38; 13:18; 15:25; 17:12; 19:24, 36) is used. There is one direct quotation (by the crowd) without a quotation formula (12:13), and 19:37 does not use a fulfilment formula, but its predictive nature, using the future tense (ὄψονται) from Zechariah, makes clear that it comes under the fulfilment formula of 19:36. Of these, three quotations cannot definitively be identified with a known scriptural passage (7:38-39; 17:12; 19:28)[99] and one saying is a general appeal to Scripture without being an actual quotation (7:42).

In the Fourth Gospel, the ordering of the citations does not appear to

---

[96] A. Loisy, *Le Quatrième Evangile* (Paris: Picard, 1903), 80; M. Hengel, 'The Old Testament in the Fourth Gospel', *Horizons in Biblical Theology* 12 (1990), 31-2; Brown, *John*, lix-lxii.

[97] In John 12:38, 40 (41), it is the Evangelist who quotes Isaiah 53:1 and 6:10. In 1:23, John the Baptist quotes Isaiah 40:3.

[98] 1:23; 2:17; 6:31, 45; 7:38, 42; 10:34; 12:14-15, 38, 39-41; 13:18; 15:25; 17:12; 19:24, 28, 36, 37. Nestle-Aland (26th edition) count nineteen citations, seventeen of them with the introductory formulas, but further about two hundred marginally noted allusions and parallels. However, some see at least twenty-five Old Testament quotations in John; six of which are quoted in such a way as to make clear that a claim of fulfilment is being made. Fourteen begin with a formula such as 'Scripture is fulfilled', or 'Scripture says'. Five times the phrase 'in order that it might be fulfilled' is used. Schuchard, *Scripture within Scripture*, xiv, argues for only 13 explicit Old Testament citations, each of which is identified by means of a formula (1:23; 2:17; 6:31, 45; 10:34; 12:14-15, 38, 40; 13:18; 15:25; 19:24, 36, 37). He excludes from this reckoning John 7:38, 42; 17:12, and 19:28 since he does not see any specific Old Testament passage cited. Although in 19:28, the author identifies the word of Jesus (Διψῶ) as the fulfillment of the Scripture. Also Schuchard excludes 12:13 since he maintains it is a rendering of a popular Jewish festal greeting derived from Ps. 118:117 and this, he believes, may explain why 12:13 has no introductory formula.

[99] ἵνα τελειωθῇ in 19:28.

be the result of a random or accidental collection of different strata of redaction and tradition.[100] Rather the quotations, both direct and indirect, seem to be part of a well-considered, unified plan. Some of these citations have their origins in disputations with Jewish opponents; others have their *Sitz im Leben* in the Johannine apologetic targeted at a wider audience. However, in both instances the central issue seems to be the Messianic identity of Jesus.

The division between the quotations in the first section of the Gospel (1:23–12:16) focusing on the public ministry of Jesus, and the second section focusing on the Passion (12:38–19:37) is highly methodical. The quotations in the former section (1:23–12:16) generally begin with a formula: 'It is written', or something similar.[101] Here every direct quotation of the Old Testament is introduced by use of the perfect participle of γράφω, γεγραμμένον (2:17; 6:31, 45; 10:34; 12:14).[102] On the other hand, the quotations in the latter section (12:38–19:37) are often introduced with the formula 'in order that [the Scripture or what was spoken] might be fulfilled.'[103] In this section virtually all of the quotations are introduced by formulas using the aorist passive subjunctive of πληρόω, πληρωθῇ (12:38–40; 13:18; 15:25; 17:12; 18:9, 32; 19:24, 28, 36–37).[104] In other words, in John 1:23–12:15, out of nine quotations, seven with introductory formulas, there is not one instance of the verb πληροῦν or its equivalent. Yet in the second half of the Gospel, out of the eleven quotation formulas, three of which introduce previous remarks of Jesus, with one exception (19:28) all use the verb πληροῦν.

This conscious formal division between the first and second halves of the Gospel intends to show that Jesus' life and death happened as

---

[100] As suggested, for example, by A. Faure, 'Die alttestamentichen Zitate im 4. Evangelium und die Quellenscheidungshypothese', *ZNW* 21 (1922), 99–121. But see F. Smend's response in 'Die Behandlung alttestamentlicher Zitate als Ausgangspunkt der Quellenscheidung im 4. Evangelium', *ZNW* 24 (1925), 147–50.

[101] With the exception of 1:23 and 12:13, neither of which are spoken by Jesus, framing the Book of Signs (chs. 2–11). See C. H. Dodd, *The Interpretation of the Fourth Gospel* (Cambridge: CUP, 1953), 176.

[102] The plural form of the participle is used similarly to refer back to a previously cited quotation in 12:16. Other non-perfect forms of γράφω are used in a quotation formula when no specific citation is produced (1:45; 5:46; 7:42; 8:17).

[103] See J. O. Tuniv, 'Personajes veterotestamentarios en el Evangelio de Juan', *Revista Latinoamericana de Teologia* 10 (1993), 279–92; R. J. Hummann, 'The Function and Form of the Explicit Old Testament Quotations in the Gospel of John', *LTR* 1 (1988–89), 50.

[104] 12:39 and 19:37 do not use this verb, but they are not exceptions since they are extensions of the respective formulae in 12:38 and 19:36 (as is also indicated by the presence of the linking word πάλιν).

anticipated by the Scriptures. In the first half of the Gospel, the Evangelist attempts to show that Jesus' public ministry[105] conformed to scriptural expectations and requirements. The second division aims to demonstrate that his Passion[106] was in fulfilment of scriptural prophecies.[107] The second section particularly emphasises that the rejection of Jesus and his death were precisely within divine sovereign calculations, not only in a general sense, but in terms of detailed fulfilment of the Scriptures.[108]

It is also important to note that the initial and final quotations in the second section are double quotations, that is, they cite two Old Testament passages linked together, thus forming an inclusio. Here the function of the double quotations also seems to be deliberate, forming as it were, a bracket on the Passion account. The purpose of such an enclosure is essentially to emphasise that what Judaism considered scandalous (the death of the Messiah), was actually in fulfilment of Scriptures.

With the advent of the Messiah, the Jews had anticipated a violent overthrow of Roman domination in Palestine. Nothing could have been further from their imagination than that the Messiah must suffer crucifixion at the hands of the Romans, tinged with the mockery of the placard that proclaimed him 'King of the Jews' (Jn. 19:19–22). On the surface, this

---

[105] John 1:29–12:36a: 1:23, 45; 2:17; 5:46; 6:31, 45; 7:42; 8:17; 10:34; 12:14, 16.

[106] John 12:36b–19:37: 12:38, 39; 13:18; 15:25; 17:12; 18:9, 32; 19:24, 28, 36, 37.

[107] Hummann, 'Function and Form of the Explicit Old Testament Quotations', 31–54; Faure, 'Die alttestamentlichen Zitate im 4. Evangelium', 99–122; Tuniv, 'Personajes veterotestamentarios', 279–92.

[108] Jesus' agony is put in the context of the servant of God in the Psalms. The first two references to the Scriptures in chapter 19 are also from the Psalms, again putting Jesus' Passion in the context of the experience of the Psalmist (cf. Jn. 19:24; Ps. 21:19). See Hoskyns, *Fourth Gospel*, 497, 632; V. C. Pfitzner, 'The Coronation of the King – Passion Narrative and Passion Theology in the Gospel of St. John', *Lutheran Theological Journal* 10 (1976), 6–7; Lindars, *New Testament Apologetic*, 99–108; idem, *John*, 578; Barrett, *St. John*, 425; A. Dauer, *Die Passionsgeschichte im Johannesevangelium. Eine traditionsgeschichtliche und theologische Untersuchung zu Joh 18,1–19, 30*, StANT 30 (Munich: Kösel-Verlag, 1979 [Diss. Würzburg, 1968–69 dir.: R. Schnackenburg]), 298 writes, 'Was vielleicht als Hohn der Feinde verstanden werden konnte, zumindest aber dem Glauben als anstössig galt, war *gottgewollt*. Schon längst war dieser Zug der Passion Jesu durch das Alte Testament vorausgesagt'. In the second reference in John 19:28–29, the Old Testament text seems to be Psalm 69:21. This is said to have been a favourite Psalm of the early Church in connection with Jesus' Passion. See also Gunter Reim, *Studien zum alttestamentlichen Hintergrund des Johannesevangeliums*, SNTSMS 22 (Cambridge: CUP, 1974), 50; Brown, *John*, 929; J. M. Ford, '"Mingled Blood" From the Side of Christ (John xix. 34)', *NTS* 15 (1969), 338. Even Jesus' betrayal by Judas is explained in terms of fulfilment of Scriptures. Indeed, of the seven remaining quotations beginning with 13:18 which predicts the betrayal of Jesus by Judas, the focus of predictive statements on this event shows how scandalous this was for the Evangelist and his readers (Jn. 6:64, 71; 13:11, 18; 17:12).

could only be seen as ludicrous.[109] But John painstakingly shows it to be, in fact, part of God's foreordained plan – the Messiah must suffer death. Not only his death, but also his resurrection to glory, was ordained by God, and predicted in the Scriptures in direct fulfilment of God's salvific plan for the Jews as well as the world. Ultimately, this evidence was meant to demonstrate the scriptural truth of the Christian message and to summon people, especially the Jews, to faith in God, mediated through the person of Jesus Christ.[110]

5.3.2. The Significance of Direct Citations in Determining the Function of the Indirect Allusions

If one were to describe the Fourth Gospel as a portrait of the Messiah, then the direct quotations of Scripture may be compared to the broad, visible outlines of the image, and the subtle allusions may be compared to many careful strokes of the brush, meticulously relating details, accentuating nuances and shades, which together give definition to the face and impressions of mood of the face of the one depicted. Both the broad visible outline and the complex supporting details, not immediately visible, culminate to make the picture. In the Fourth Gospel, the direct citations and the indirect allusions complement each other in a similar manner.

Here again, in the subtle references, one encounters a well-considered, carefully developed plan which supports the claim of the direct citations. In fact, this is where John's direct quotation of Scripture gives insight into the function of allusive references. They are divided along the same lines as the direct citations. In the first half of the Gospel (1:23–12:16), they support the direct citations and further emphasise that Jesus is the one whom he claimed to be: 'just as it is written', and that his life and career is in conformity to the scriptural portrait of the Messiah. In the second half of the Gospel (12:38–19:37), Jesus' rejection and crucifixion take place *in order that Scripture be fulfilled*. Far from proving that Jesus was not Israel's Messiah (as is implied by such a statement as, 'we have heard from the law that the Messiah remains forever' (12:34), his rejection and death, for the Fourth Evangelist, occur to fulfil the Scriptures and so prove that he was the Promised One. Whereas the direct quotations convey this message on the first hearing, the indirect references progressively yield the same

---

[109] R. A. Horsley and J. S. Hanson, *Bandits, Prophets and Messiahs: Popular Movements at the Time of Jesus* (San Francisco: Harper and Row, 1985), 88–134.

[110] Carson, 'John and the Johannine Epistles', 245–64; M. M. Thompson, 'Signs and Faith in the Fourth Gospel', *BBR* 1 (1991), 89–108.

fruit in an assiduous study. This is also where the function of John's complex and enigmatic language is tied to the author's purpose for writing the Gospel. The allusions are to demonstrate how the Scriptures bear witness to Jesus as the Christ. The following analysis will endeavour to illustrate this proposition further.

5.3.3. Johannine Allusions to Consummation of Jewish Religious Institutions in Christ

The fundamental hermeneutic doctrine for the New Testament writers is that Jesus had fulfilled the law and the prophets (Jn. 1:45; 5:39, 46; cf. Lk. 24:27). John follows the same axiom. He sees the life and work of Jesus in relation to the Scriptures in terms of the apostolic exegetical approach of 'This is That' (cf. Acts 2:16). The essential underlying function of the Johannine subtle references to the Scriptures is to show their actualisation in the person and work of Jesus Christ and vice versa – to show how his life, his words and work(s) confirm and fulfil scriptural prophecy concerning him, thus providing justification that he is the Messiah. Whereas the signs in the first half of the Gospel are meant to prove that Jesus is the Christ, the Old Testament testimonia in the second half are meant to prove more specifically that the disgrace of the crucifixion, a controversial reality in any dialogue with Jews, was Jesus' very purpose and work. Therefore, the great scandal, from the Evangelist's point of view, is not the scandal of Jesus and his followers, rather it is the scandal of the failure of the religious leaders of Israel to recognise in Jesus the realisation and fulfilment of the Scriptures. The Jews exclaimed in effect, 'How can Christ die? *What a scandalous claim!* Is he not supposed to remain forever, as we heard from the law? (Jn. 12:34).' John responded in kind: 'You do not know the law, for if you did, you would have realised that it speaks of him. How can you not know that he must first suffer?' (cf. Jn. 5:38–39; Lk. 24:25–27). The challenge of John's appeal to Scripture lay in his particular claim of its fulfilment. If such a claim was true, it potentially had a devastating effect on the religious institutions (e.g., the sacrificial system) of Judaism. But, in fact, this was precisely what John claimed; Jesus not only had fulfilled the Scriptures; but also in fulfilling the Scriptures, he had rendered the fundamental cultic tenets of the Jewish religion obsolete.[111]

This did not mean a new 'foreign' religion. John endeavoured to

---

[111] H. von Campenhausen, *The Formation of the Christian Bible*, trans. by J. A. Baker (London: Black, 1972), 52.

emphasise that Christianity was in continuity with the past. But in the incarnation, an irreversible 'religious metamorphosis' had taken place. The past had been realised in the present. A new chapter in the history of salvation had been opened, sealing closed the previous one, but all in the same book. A new era had begun in which the old tenets were fulfilled with their accomplishment in Jesus Christ. Judaism could no longer be viable as a cult. Its sacrificial practices, its temple cult, its priesthood, had simply witnessed to that which was now realised in Jesus. While this did not mean that one ceased to be a Jew, neither did being a Jew in itself any longer carry any significance. For the Evangelist, the decisive factor was nothing less than a 'rebirth' from above in which the entire existing system of Judaism was challenged and transcended in Jesus Christ. This theme of Jesus' replacement of Jewish institutions advanced on three fronts as follows:

5.3.3.1. Jesus as Fulfilment of the Law

Many scholars agree with Dodd when he wrote, 'The evangelist holds that the real revelation of God's grace and truth is not in the Torah, but in Jesus Christ.'[112] However, according to John, careful attention to the Torah (i.e., 'the law') reveals the One in whom the grace and truth of God is embodied and revealed (5:46–47). It is in the Torah itself that the law of the light of the 'grace and truth' in Jesus Christ is revealed. Thus the Torah itself is witness to the truth and the grace of God in Jesus Christ. Behind the religious leaders' claim of loyalty to the Torah is their claim to know God. John rejects this claim and asserts that they do not know God, 'His [God's] voice they have never heard, his form they have never seen' (Jn. 5:37b).[113] God has borne witness to the Son (5:37a), not only in the Torah, but also

---

[112] Dodd, *Interpretation*, 82. An extreme articulation of this view is offered by J. E. Carpenter, *The Johannine Writings* (1927), 261–2. He suggests that Jesus brings an entirely new truth from heaven. See also Dahl, 'Johannine Church and History', 107; Dauer, *Passionsgeschichte*, 302–303; Lindeskog, 'Anfänge des jüdisch-christlichen Problems: Ein programmatischer Entwurf', in *Donum Gentilicium: New Testament Essays in Honour of David Daube*, ed. by E. Bammel, C. K. Barrett, and W. D. Davies (Oxford: Clarendon, 1978), 269; J. Painter, *John: Witness and Theologian* (London: SPCK, 1975), 32–3. Cf. K. Haacker, *Die Stiftung des Heils. Untersuchungen zur Struktur der johanneischen Theologie* (Stuttgart: Calwer, 1972); Baum, *Jews and the Gospel*, 114.

[113] Cf. Whitacre, *Johannine Polemic*, 68; Pancaro, *Law in the Fourth Gospel*, 220–4. There were others in the Old Testament who claimed to have seen and or heard God (e.g., Gen. 12:7, 18:1, 32:30; Exod. 6:3; Isa. 6:1; Amos 7:7, 9:1; Ezk. 10:18–19, 11:22–23, 43:4, 7; Job 42:5), but their experience seems to have been different from that of Moses (Num. 12:6–8; Deut. 34:10).

internally within human hearts (5:38; 1 Jn. 5:9-10).[114] But the religious teachers of Israel did not receive this testimony.

The massive work of Severino Pancaro eliminated any doubt about the importance of the law in the Fourth Gospel.[115] Pancaro proposed,

> The confrontation between Jesus and the Jews unfolds itself in John as an impressive juridical trial and, within this dramatic framework, the Law appears as a hermeneutical key to much of what John has to say concerning the person of Jesus and his "work".[116]

Since Pancaro's thesis, some Johannine scholars also have come to recognise that John's interest in the law is not just polemic or merely a means of presenting the real subject, Jesus. Rather, the issue of the legitimacy of the law in relation to Christ is itself a crucial concern for the Gospel. It has been suggested that to speak of the fulfilment of the γραφή (writing, scripture),[117] and of the νόμος (law),[118] is one and the same thing in the Fourth Gospel. A comparison of John 7:23 with 10:35 (cf. also 10:34 with 10:35) and John 7:38 and 7:42 with 12:34 seems to indicate that νόμος and γραφή may be used by John synonymously.[119] Assuming that John indeed is using these terms, at least to some extent,[120] interchangeably, then in a sense by fulfilling the Scriptures, Jesus fulfils the law. Of course, John never explicitly speaks of Jesus fulfilling the law.[121] This does not seem to be due to an 'adverse' antinomian disposition towards νόμος in his Gospel.[122] The Fourth Evangelist distinguishes between his use of νόμος and the Jews' use of it, for whom the law was both written and oral.

---

[114] Pancaro, *Law in the Fourth Gospel*, 217-27. See also George J. Brooke, 'Christ and the Law in John 7-10', in *Law and Religion: Essays on the Place of Law in Israel and Early Christianity*, ed. by B. Lindars (Cambridge: James Clarke, 1988), 102-12; Brown, *John*, 227-8.

[115] *The Law in the Fourth Gospel* (Leiden: Brill, 1975); see also William R.G. Loader, *Jesus' Attitude towards the Law*, WUNT 97 (Tübingen: Mohr-Siebeck, 1997).

[116] Pancaro, *Law in the Fourth Gospel*, 1.

[117] BAGD, 166; G. Schrenk, *TDNT* 1 (1964), 749-55.

[118] H. Kleinknecht, (W. Gutbrod) *TDNT* 4 (1967), 1082-85.

[119] 'The Law' is the 'Law' of Moses (1:17; 7:19, 23); the γραφαί (writings, Scriptures) are also the γραφαί of Moses (1:45; 5:39, 46, 47). Therefore, it is possible that νόμος in the Fourth Gospel stands for Scriptures or at least part of them and John has used the terms synonymously. See Pancaro, *Law in the Fourth Gospel*, 26-29.

[120] In the Fourth Gospel, γραφή, γραφαί and γράμματα are never qualified by either ὑμῶν or αὐτῶν. On the other hand, νόμος frequently bears such a qualification (cf. 7:51, 8:17, 10:34, 15:25, 18:31). In fact γραφή is never qualified in this way in the New Testament. John seems to qualify νόμος in this way in order to emphasise that the verity of Jesus' position may be substantiated from the Jews' own sacred Scriptures.

[121] The verbs πληρόω, οὐ...λύω, and τελειόω never appear with νόμος as either subject or object (cf. Mt. 5:17).

[122] Pancaro, *Law in the Fourth Gospel*, 327-8, 514-34.

In harmony with the apologetic of the early Christian church, John maintains a distinction between the written law (i.e., the Old Testament) and the oral tradition of the Jews, which Jesus rejects as the tradition of men (Mt. 15:3, 6, 9; Mk. 7:3-9). For John, then, Jesus fulfils only one aspect of the 'law' of the Jews, the γραφή or 'written law' – the Scriptures.[123] And it is only in this later respect that he uses νόμος and γραφή synonymously.

The New Testament engagement with the law shows the sensitivity to the subject in the apostolic circle as it endeavoured to justify its position in relation to Judaism. Paul, for example, addresses the law in the context of his mission to the Gentiles. He focuses on those points of the law which would have been most contentious for the Jews in relation to the Gentile conversion, for example, circumcision and its relevance in the New Covenant community. John, on the other hand, in the context of his predominantly Jewish audience focuses on Jewish festivals and their relevance to the Christian community. In the climax of Jesus' conflict with the religious leaders in John 7–10, the Decalogue plays a prominent role: for example, Sabbath (7:23; cf. 5:18); parental honour (8:49; cf. 5:23); murder (7:19; 8:40, 44; cf. 5:18); adultery (8:41),[124] theft (10:1, 8, 10), false witness (8:14, 44), coveting (8:44, only occurrence of ἐπιθυμία). From this list, no fewer than five of the commandments are alluded to in 8:40–49.[125] This seems to have a bearing on the meaning of the challenge in 8:46, 'Which of you convicts me of sin?' Idolatry (and its effects) is the central concern of the law. The primary focus of the Decalogue is the demand for Israel's steadfast worship of the one true God and the prohibition against the worship of the false gods of the nations (Exod. 2–7; Deut. 5:6–11). This is also a decisive theme in the Fourth Gospel. A central question which consistently divides the Jews revolves around whether Jesus is a true prophet who promotes the worship of the true God or is a false prophet who advocates the worship of a false god (i.e., himself).[126] According to Deut. 13:1–11, which forms a pair with the promise of Deut. 18:15–18,[127] a prophet who teaches the worship of false gods is to be stoned. The reaction

---

[123] Schuchard, *Scripture within Scripture*, 154.

[124] Fornication and adultery in the Old Testament prophetic tradition are treated as symbols of idolatry and unfaithfulness to the Lord (e.g., Jer. 3:8–9; 13:26–27; 23:10; Ezk. 16:1–63; 23:1–49; Hosea and the allegory of unfaithfulness of the nation).

[125] Brooke, 'Christ and the Law in John 7–10', 102–12.

[126] 7:15–24; Meeks, *Prophet-King*, 56.

[127] For a helpful discussion on this topic, see T. W. Overhold, The Threat of Falsehood: A Study in the Theology of the Book of Jeremiah, SBT 2/16 (London: SCM, 1970); R. P. Carroll, When Prophecy Failed: Reactions and Responses to Failure in the Old Testament Prophetic Traditions (London: SCM, 1979), esp. 184–98.

of 'the Jews' to Jesus in 8:59 and subsequently in 10:31–33 and their gesture of picking up stones to stone him confirms their obedience to the Deuteronomic command (Deut. 13:5) and the conclusion by some of them that Jesus calls upon them to worship a false god.[128]

The problem voiced in Deuteronomy 18:21 is how can Israel recognise 'when a message has not been spoken by the Lord'? Indeed, a problem which plagued Israel throughout its history is false prophecy. Among the criteria which Moses laid down for the coming prophet and his recognition is that 'the prophet' had to be like unto Moses (Deut. 18:15). To a certain extent, all Israel's prophets are 'like unto Moses' in so far as they all spoke for God. And yet, in another sense, none of them is 'like unto Moses' (cf. Deut. 34:10; Jn. 1:18; 3:13).[129]

In John 6, the Evangelist endeavours to show that Jesus is that expected prophet 'like unto Moses'[130] (i.e., a prophet-king, Saviour, Messiah)[131] and he speaks the word of God because he truly knows God (cf. 1:18). This is reinforced in the pericope both by the signs (as 'works' that point to his divine origin) and by the Exodus symbolism employed here. R. H. Smith argues that John's use of 'signs' is 'evident that the tradition of Moses' signs and wonders lies in the background.' He later arranges John's seven 'signs' as inverted parallels to the seven 'signs' of Moses.[132] In 1987 W. Roth went even further and proposed that the Fourth Gospel is 'a selective and inverted narrative rewriting of "The Law" and "The Prophets" of the Hebrew Bible, climaxed in the portrayal of a new creation through the gift of the Spirit by the risen Jesus.'[133] In John's Gospel, the crowd which was fed in 6:2–12 and saw the miraculous sign

---

[128] J. Bergmann, *Jüdische Apologetik im neutestamentlichen Zeitalter* (Berlin: Reimer, 1908), 81; Martyn, *History and Theology*, 72; W. F. Howard, *Christianity According to St. John* (London: Duckworth, 1943), 71; A. F. Segal, *Two Powers in Heaven: Early Rabbinic Reports about Christianity and Gnosticism*, Studies in Judaism and Late Antiquity 25 (Leiden: Brill, 1977), 215–8; B. E. Schein, 'Our Father Abraham' (Ph.D. diss., Yale University, 1972), 169.

[129] See chapter two (§2.4), and my discussion on Moses and Jesus.

[130] Meeks, *Prophet-King*, 318f.; M. de Jonge, 'Jesus as Prophet and King in the Fourth Gospel' *ETL* 49 (1973), 160–77; Lindars, *John*, 244; S. E. Johnson, 'Notes on the Prophet-King in John', *ATR* 51 (1969), 35–37.

[131] These various designations in the Fourth Gospel, 'the Prophet', 'that Prophet', and 'King of Israel' refer to the same anticipated Messianic figure (cf. 1:45, 49; 12:13). R. Bultmann, *The Theology of the New Testament*, vol. 2, trans. by K. Grobel (London: SCM, 1955), §45, p. 37; Barrett, *St. John*, 185–86; also (e.g., 2 Sam. 7:14; Ps. 2:7; 1 Enoch 105:2; 4 Ezra 7:28f.; 13:52; 14:9; Mk. 1:11; Rom. 1:3f). Nathanael has been declared to be 'true Israelite'; Jesus correspondingly is 'true King' – truly King of the true Israel.

[132] 'Exodus Typology in the Fourth Gospel' *JBL* 81 (1962), 329–42.

[133] 'Spiritual Coding in the Fourth Gospel' *BR* 32 (1987), 6–29, here p. 7.

identifies Jesus in 6:14 as 'that prophet'. In his closing words in 12:48-50, Jesus asserts that the word he has spoken is what the Father has commanded him to say, alluding to Deuteronomy 18:18, 'I will put my words in his mouth'.

Elsewhere in the Gospel in chapters 7-10, there are further affirmations that Jesus indeed is 'the prophet' (7:40; cf. 9:17) who speaks the words of God (7:16; 8:26, 28). The figure is with all likelihood that of 'the prophet like unto Moses', the eschatological figure of a Prophet-King, the Messiah.[134] According to Meeks, there is the highly ironic use of 'gods you have not known' (Deut. 13:2, 6) in 7:28, 8:19 and especially 8:55 in which 'the Jews' attempt to stone Jesus (in 8:59) in obedience to Deuteronomy 13:10. Therefore, in essence, unknowingly they are in ironic *agreement* with his charge that they 'do not know' the God he has proclaimed to them.[135]

The feeding sign in John 6 goes beyond mere repetition of the miracles performed by Moses. It seems to signal a whole new Exodus,[136] far greater than that celebrated at the Passover (Jn. 6:32; cf. Exod. 11-17). God acts to give Israel true bread from heaven as opposed to the manna which was much less than ἀληθινός in comparison with Jesus.[137] Exodus symbolism is present also in 8:12 and 8:31-32 where Jesus claims to lead an 'exodus' from the slavery of sin. This is matched in 11:43f by Lazarus' dramatic freedom from the bondage of *death*. The narrative of Lazarus' emergence from the tomb resonates with Exodus overtones which might be quite subliminal in their effect on the reader or might become more conscious: Jesus has been 'sent' (11:42) to deliver in this way; he overthrows the enemy with a mighty word of prophetic command (11:43); Lazarus 'goes out' and is immediately released from bondage (11:44). The motif 'the Lord, who brought you out of the house of bondage (slavery) with a mighty hand' appears (with variations) nine times in Exodus and Deuteronomy, including twice in the 'false prophet' passage (Deut. 13:5, 10). In this light, Jesus cannot be a false prophet promoting idolatry. He is

---

[134] Meeks, *Prophet-King, passim;* Barrett, *St. John*, 330.

[135] Ibid., 56. Meeks believes here the reader is put on the spot to discern who is right, thus leading to a division among the intended readers.

[136] Martyn, *History and Theology*, 2:125-8.

[137] Cf. Ferdinand Hahn, 'Der Prozeß Jesu nach dem Johannesevangelium', EKKNT *Vorarbeiten Heft* 2 (Zürich: Benziger; Neukirchen: Neukirchener Verlag, 1970), 71 n. 20.

not in violation of the law. Rather he is the fulfilment of the Mosaic hope in the law.[138]

Johannine interaction with the Decalogue in the Fourth Gospel is important in several respects. The religious teachers accuse Jesus of disregarding the law (5:10–18; cf. 6:52, 60). They see themselves as loyal to Moses and the Torah (5:36, 45–47; 9:28–29) and Jesus and his followers as violators of that law. Jesus is charged with breaking the Sabbath (5:10, 16; cf. 7:21–23; 9:16), blasphemy (5:18; 10:33; 19:7),[139] and bearing witness to himself (8:13; Num. 35:30; Deut. 17:6; cf. Deut. 19:15).[140] He is accused of being a deceiver, i.e., a false prophet (7:12, 47),[141] and of subverting the Jewish nation by leading its members to apostasy (Jn. 11:47–52).[142] These accusations are summed up in the words which the Jews utter before Pilate: 'We have a law, and according to that law he must die, because he made himself the Son of God' (Jn. 19:7). To respond to these charges, the Fourth Evangelist also appeals to the law. In so far as Moses was of monumental significance for first century Judaism, the Fourth Evangelist wishes to show that in fact Moses is on the side of Jesus. He uses the law as a positive testimony in support of the claim that Jesus was indeed 'that prophet',

---

[138] The references to Elijah may be of some thematic value here. The Jewish understanding of Elijah, for example, was primarily built, not on the account in 1 Kings 17–19, but on the prophesies of his return at the End of the Age in Malachi 3:1 and 4:5. In (Wisdom of) Sirach 48:1–11, Elijah is extolled as one who was God's agent (cf. Jn. 4:34; 5:23, 24, 30, 36, 38; 6:29, 38–40, 44, 57; 7:16, 18, 28, 29, 33; 8:16, 18, 26, 29, 42; 9:4; 10:36; 11:42; 12:44, 45, 49; 13:20; etc.), who raised the dead (cf. Jn. 11:43, 44; 10:18; 19:38–20:14), who brought kings down to destruction and anointed others 'to exact retribution' (Jn. 20:21–23), and whose coming is expected to turn the heart of Israel to its God. Significantly, Elijah's role is described by Malachi 3:3–4 as reforming the priesthood – that is, 'purifying the sons of Levi' and making their worship acceptable to God.

[139] Pancaro, *Law in the Fourth Gospel*, 53ff.

[140] In the Mishnah the application of the principle is extended (*Rosh Ha-Shanah*, 3:1; *Kethuboth*, 2:9). The repeated references to the attempts to seize or kill Jesus in chs. 7–8 are connected with his teaching which is bearing witness to himself as the one sent by the Father. Pancaro, *Law in the Fourth Gospel*, 81ff.

[141] See application of Deut. 13, e.g., *Sanhedrin*, 43a. See also W. Horbury, 'A Critical Examination of the Toledoth Jeshu' (Ph.D. diss., Cambridge, 1970), 226–7; cf. Martyn, *History and Theology*, 75–81, 158–160; Pancaro, *Law in the Fourth Gospel*, 95–7; J. H. Bernard, *A Critical and Exegetical Commentary on the Gospel According to St. John*, ICC (Edinburgh: Clark, 1928), 271. In contrast, see W. Bauer, *Das Leben Jesu im Zeitalter der neutestamentlichen Apokryphen* (Tübingen: Mohr, 1909), 484–5; Str-B 1:1023–4.

[142] Pancaro, *Law in the Fourth Gospel*, 503, suggests Jesus is seen by the Jews to be the enemy of the Jewish nation in so far as his miracles deceive others into accepting his claims. From the Sanhedrin's point of view, this brings about the danger of general apostasy, which can only lead to the end of the Jewish nation which, by definition, is a religious community gathered around the law.

foretold by Moses.[143] Jesus is not guilty of blasphemy since he was prophetically anticipated in the law (Jn. 10:34–36).[144] His teaching is not false since Moses wrote of him (5:45–47).[145] Even his death fulfils the law. However, in so far as the law testifies to Jesus, and he is its fulfilment, to reject him is to reject the law.[146] John challenges 'the Jews' on their claim to be the representatives of orthopraxy, and in fact endeavours to show they are the violators of the law, not Jesus and his followers. The religious teachers of Israel do not 'do the will of God' because they do not believe on Jesus (7:17) and they do not do 'the work of God' which is to receive the One whom God has sent (6:23f).

Indeed, the teachers of the law have acted contrary to law. In their desire to kill Jesus, they are guilty, not only of murder of innocent blood, but also of rejecting him to whom the law testifies, thus incurring again the indictment of 5:37–47. Their judgment upon Jesus has been purely 'according to the flesh' (7:24; 8:15).[147] They have pronounced judgment upon an innocent man without respecting the very conditions which the law sets down as necessary prerequisites for the pronouncement of a 'just' judgment (Jn. 7:51). The chief priests, in their affirmation and recognition of Caesar as the King over Israel (19:15), grossly violate the teaching of Israel's Scriptures (e.g., Judg. 8:23; 1 Sam. 8:7). By rejecting Jesus, they also reject his interpretation of Sabbath observance and his self-revelation.[148]

John presents the 'work' and person of Jesus in terms which would be intelligible to Judaism. However, he is careful to show that the law, as interpreted by Judaism, is in opposition to the law given by Moses. Judaism maintains that God had revealed himself only in the law and it is only in the law that salvation is possible – the law as interpreted and followed by 'normative' Judaism. The Fourth Evangelist rejects this. The value of the law for John lies in the fact that it was a witness to Christ whose advent had fulfilled it.[149] Therefore, the religious authorities are in

---

[143] Brooke, 'Christ and the Law', 112.

[144] Pancaro, *Law in the Fourth Gospel*, 175ff.

[145] Ibid., 231ff.

[146] Ibid., 508–9.

[147] Ibid., 130ff., 166ff., 272ff., 390ff.

[148] *Mekilta* on Ex. 13:12–17; Str-B 1:623–9; Barrett, *St. John*, 359–62.

[149] With the emphasis on his words being fulfilled (e.g., Jn. 18:9, 32; cf. Deut. 13; 18:22). See Pancaro, *Law in the Fourth Gospel*, 523–25; F. L. Hossfeld and I. Meyer, *Prophet gegen Prophet. Eine Analyse der alttestamentlichen Texte zum Thema: Wahre und falsche Propheten*, Biblische Beiträge 9 (Freiburg: Schweizerisches Katholisches Bibelwerk, 1973); Carroll, *When*

fact in violation of the law. They sit in judgment of others while they are the ones who do not keep the law (7:19, 47–52; cf. Exod. 20:13),[150] and unless they receive the One to whom the law witnesses, it is the law which will condemn them (Jn. 5:45; cf. Acts 23:3).

The witness of the law to Jesus and the fulfilment of the law in Jesus resonates throughout John's engagement with Judaism as claimant to be the sole interpreters and guardians of the law. The challenge not to judge based on 'appearances' but to judge with 'righteous judgment' (δικcία κρίσις) in 7:24 is vital in this connection. Jesus' healing on the Sabbath in essence is 'the accomplishment of the redemptive purpose of God towards which the law had pointed.'[151] The challenge here is to see Jesus' breach of Sabbath *halakah* as insignificant in comparison with a man who is now made 'whole'. This is the real purpose of circumcision, in respect of which the *halakah* permitted the suspension of the Sabbath regulations.[152] 'Right judgment' would have discerned this.[153]

Elsewhere, in John 6, on the face of it Jesus seems to be in clear violation not just of *halakah*, but of the law itself and the prohibition against consuming blood (6:53–58; cf. Lev. 17:10–14). The audience of the Gospel would have detected in Jesus' invitation to drink his blood the Passover associations, especially in light of the Baptist's proclamation in 1:29, 'Behold the Lamb of God'. Also at the beginning of the account in chapter 6, the author alerts his audience, 'Now the Passover was at hand' (6:4). This recognition is expected of the audience even if Jesus' interlocutors missed it.

Jesus' fulfilment of the law is further accentuated in the Gospel when John consciously transfers the three gifts associated with the law, *bread*, *water* and *light*, to Jesus. In Judaism, the Torah was regarded to be like 'bread', 'water', and 'light' and was considered to be the source of 'life'. This is evident in contemporary Jewish literature.[154] The 'light', 'bread'

Prophecy Failed, 184–98; Overhold, *Threat of Falsehood*; J. L. Crenshaw, *Prophetic Conflict: Its Effect Upon Israelite Religion*, BZAW 124 (Berlin: de Gruyter, 1971).

[150] Brown, *John*, 316; Schnackenburg, *Johannes*, 2:187.

[151] Barrett, *St. John*, 320–1.

[152] Therefore the difficult διὰ τοῦτο in 7:22 seems to look forward to the idea of complete health in 23b: by healing the man, Jesus has fulfilled the purpose of his circumcision. See J. C. Thomas, 'The Fourth Gospel and Rabbinic Judaism', *ZNW* 82 (1991), 173f, and *m. Sabb.* 19:1; Barrett, *St. John*, 319.

[153] Dodd, *Historical Tradition*, 333, calls 7:23 'an argument which is barely intelligible outside its Jewish context'.

[154] For example, the image of 'light' for the law is found in: *T. Levi* 14:4, 19:1; also Pseudo-Philo, *Bib. Ant.* 9:8; 11:1; 22:3 (in 11:1 the law is described as 'a light to the world'); frequently in

and 'water' are three important themes central to the Johannine presentation of Jesus.[155] T. Francis Glasson, nearly forty years ago, pointed out the way in which the three 'Exodus gifts' of bread, water and light were developed in John 6, 7, and 8.[156] The three gifts are combined in Nehemiah 9:12-15 and Psalm 105:39-41. In the Fourth Gospel, Jesus is the embodiment of what the three gifts represented. He is now the source of *true* bread (6:32), of *living* water (7:38), and of light *for the world* (8:12). Jesus, in claiming to be the ultimate consummation and realisation of what these gifts represented, develops the claim made in 5:19-30 to speak the κρίσις (judgment) of God. Many commentators note the ironic background to 6:35 in Sirach 24:21, where wisdom (there identified with the law) says, οἱ ἐσθίοντές με ἔτι πεινάσουσιν καὶ οἱ πίνοντές με ἔτι διψήσουσιν – and interestingly in the same passage Wisdom invites people to 'come to me' (Sir. 24:19, cf. Jn. 6:35b) and claims to be more nourishing than 'honey', which was a regular image for manna (Sir. 24:20). A. Feuillet proposes that the background of John six is the idea of the 'Messianic banquet' (Isa. 25:6-8; 49:9-10; 65:13; 55:1-3) and that of the 'banquet of wisdom' (Prov. 9:1-6; Sir. 24:19-22).[157] The presentation of the 'word of God' as 'food' is well attested in the texts of the Wisdom literature (Prov. 9:5; Sir. 15:3; 24:21; Wis. 16:26; cf. Ps. 19:11f; 119:103). The ground for such an association is prepared by Deuteronomy 8:2-3 (cf. Isa. 55:1-3).

In the Old Testament, the 'word of God' (דבר, λόγος) is associated with 'food' ('bread')[158] and the food imagery is also used of the law. For the Fourth Evangelist, Jesus is that food. He gives the bread of life (6:27) and he is the bread he gives (vv. 33, 35).[159] If manna represented the 'revelation of God given through Moses', then the 'bread of life' is the 'revelation of God given in Jesus Christ'. Then the implication of the

---

2 *Apoc. Bar.* 17:4; 18:2; 54:5; 78:15-16. 'Light' is an image for prophetic revelation in *Sib. Or.* 5:238f, Pseudo-Philo *Bib. Ant.* 28:3; 51:4-7; *4 Baruch* 9:3. The image of 'light' may also refer to the Temple (*Gen. Rab.* 3:4, 59:5; *Lives of the Prophets* 12:10-13). The 'water' or 'living water' is an expression found at Qumran, referring to the law. The full phrase 'a spring of living water' (באר מים החיים) appears in CD 19:34, referring to that which has been abandoned by those who have left the community. In CD 6:4 (cf. also CD 3:16) the spring of living water is an image for the law in which it provides nourishment and sustains the life of the community. Cf. Sir. 15:1-3.

155 *TWNT* 4:138-140.

156 *Moses in the Fourth Gospel* (London: SCM, 1963), 62-64; 86-94.

157 'Les thèmes bibliques majeures du discours sur le pain de vie', in *Études johanniques* (Bruges, 1962), 47-129, 65-76.

158 J. L. McKenzie, 'The Word of God in the Old Testament', *TS* 21 (1960), 183-206, here 206 n. 34.

159 Pancaro, *Law in the Fourth Gospel*, 466.

contrast seems to be that the law in and of itself was unable to give life to the fathers (Jn. 6:49, 58; cf. Rom. 3:20; 7:7; 8:3) in so far as it was a witness to the One through whom everlasting life would be made available (Jn. 5:39, 46; Rom. 3:21–25, 4:3, 5). The manna was an anticipation of the bread from heaven; and the law, the teaching of Moses (the Torah), was to prepare one to accept the revelation of God in Jesus Christ. If the Jews refuse to accept God's revelation in Christ and continue to cling to the law in the hope that it will give them life, they will die spiritually just as their fathers died physically. This food, just like that food, is appropriated through faith.[160]

The metaphorical use of 'water' has a significant tradition behind it in the Old Testament, Qumran and the rabbinic literature. In the Old Testament, the gift of the Spirit is anticipated and described in evocative terms such as the pouring out of water (Isa. 44:3 [MT]; Joel 3:1f; Isa. 32:15; Zech. 12:10). In Qumran, the metaphorical use of 'water' is less common than in the Old Testament. 1QS 4:21[161] explicitly refers to the 'Spirit of truth' as 'water'.[162] Water is also a metaphor for 'wisdom', 'teaching', and 'revelation' in the Wisdom literature of the Old Testament (Prov. 13:14; 18:4; 16:22; cf. Sir. 15:1–3; 24:21, 23–33).[163] In the Fourth Gospel, both the 'living water' and the 'living bread' are eschatological gifts given by Jesus. The water Jesus will give (δώσω, 4:13f) quenches thirst forever, and the bread he will give (δώσει, 6:27, 35) satisfies one's hunger forever. The bread of life has its temporal type in manna and the living water has its counterpart in the water of Jacob's well. Manna was given by Moses to the Jews just as the well was given by Jacob to the Samaritans. The disclosures of Jesus to the Samaritan woman and to the Jews both lead to the same misunderstanding and to the same request (4:15; 6:34). While Jesus gives and is the bread of life, he only gives the living water and does not appear to be the living water. However, if the 'gift of God' in 4:10 refers, as some commentators contend, to Jesus himself[164] and if the 'living water' stands

---

[160] Ibid., 464–72. John places the emphasis upon faith in Jesus Christ just as Paul does (Jn. 6:29, 35, Rom. 3:22, 26, 28).

[161] 1QS = *Serekh ha-Yahad* or *Rule of the Community* also known as *Manual of Discipline*.

[162] Str-B, 2:434b. Cf. 1QS 3:6–7; Jn. 14:17.

[163] The strongest attestation for the identification of 'water' with 'revelation', 'teaching' or 'knowledge' comes from the Qumran texts (מי = 1QH 8:7, 16; 1QpHab 11:1; CD 3:16; 19:34; 1:15). In a metaphorical sense, מי is often associated with two other terms which are themselves metaphors for knowledge and teaching (revelation), מקור = 1QS 3:19; 10:12; 11:3; 1QH 2:18; 8:5, 7, 16; 10:31; 18:10, 12; 1QSb 1:3:6; מעין = 1QS 3:19; 10:12; 1QH 5:26; 8:6, 12; באר = CD 3:16; 6:3–4, 9; 19:34.

[164] Bultmann, *John*, 132; Pancaro, *Law in the Fourth Gospel*, 476–77.

for revelation, clearly this revelation is inseparable from his person. If the 'living water' is a reference to the Holy Spirit, the Spirit is also inseparable from the person of Jesus (7:37–39; 16:7).[165] In Fourth Gospel, the gift of the Spirit is the function of the revelation of God in Jesus Christ. The mission of the Spirit is the enhancement of the revelation of God in Jesus Christ (16:13–15). Therefore, the fountain of the living water is Jesus who gives the living water. It is noteworthy that the expectation, already met within the *Tanach*, that in Messianic times, living waters would flow out from the temple in Jerusalem (Ezk. 47:1–12; Joel 3:18) or from Jerusalem itself (Zech. 13:1; 14:8), is realized in Jesus, who is himself the living water and its dispenser: 'Whoever drinks of the water that I will give him will no longer thirst forever, but the water that I will give to him will become in him a spring of water welling up to eternal life' (4:14 [trans. mine]; cf. 7:37, 42 and 6:35c). It is the same with the bread from heaven (Jn. 6:25–59). Jesus already gives to his people the manna which the Jews looked forward to receiving again in the latter day (*2 Apocalypse of Baruch* 29:8; *Sibylline Oracles* Frag. III.49; *Mekilta* on Exodus 16:25; Rev. 2:17).

In John 8:12, Jesus claims to be the 'light of life'. While in the Fourth Gospel, both the 'living water' and the 'bread of life' have counterparts, 'light' has no such counterpart. However, C. H. Dodd observes, 'We can hardly doubt therefore that the evangelist is implicitly contrasting the real light of the world with the Torah, which claims also to be a light for the world.'[166] In the Old Testament, the law is metaphorically compared with light (Ps. 119:105; Prov. 6:23). In rabbinic literature and the Apocrypha, the Torah is frequently represented as light (Wisd. 18:4; Sir. 24:32).[167] In Qumran, 'light' is equivalent to 'truth' and there is no 'truth' outside of the law. Those who accept the law are children of the 'light'. Acceptance or rejection of the law makes one a 'son of light' or a 'son of darkness'. In the Fourth Gospel, belief in the light (i.e., Jesus as the Christ) makes people children of the light (12:36). If the Fourth Evangelist was thinking of the Torah when he presented Jesus as the 'light', then Jesus was that light to which the law merely witnessed.[168]

Therefore, in the Fourth Gospel, the gifts of 'bread', 'water', and 'light'

---

[165] E. Schweizer, *TWNT* 6, art. 'πνεῦμα', 368 *ll.* 13ff; 382–84; Eichrodt, *Theologie des Alten Testaments*, 2 vols, 8th edn (Stuttgart-Göttingen, 1968), 2:32ff. Cf. Jer. 31:31ff; Ezk. 36:26ff.

[166] *Interpretation*, 85.

[167] Str-B, 2:357; 521f.

[168] Pancaro, *Law in the Fourth Gospel*, 485–87.

are found not in the law, but in the 'gift of God' (4:10–15) to whom the law was a witness. In true bread (6:32), living water (7:38), and light for the world (8:12), of course, the imagery and rituals of Passover and Tabernacles are connoted. However, Jesus is not just being presented as the replacement for these festivals, but transcendent of them.

Hence for example the manna was not able to deliver from death. But Jesus now claims to be bread of Life coming down from heaven so that one may eat of it and not die, but live forever (6:35, 48, 49, 50, 51). Readers knew well why 'the fathers' died in the desert, even though they had the manna to sustain them. In fact, John reminds them of the reason in 3:14 – they rebelled against God. Manna could sustain their physical life, but could not deliver them from sin. And now Israel has undergone a parallel experience, in which, at least from the perspective of the Christians, the sin of rejecting the Messiah has led to death (on a massive scale).

Moreover, the inadequacy of the cult to protect the people from their own sinfulness has been clearly demonstrated. In the Johannine perspective, the cult and the Scripture are related closely in that the feasts celebrate the salvific activity of YHWH described in Scripture. For John, the religious ceremonies and the Scriptures witness to Jesus because he is the ultimate revelation of this same gracious God,[169] the graciousness that is vividly manifested in the salvific activity of God in the sacrificial death of the Son. In Ezekiel, in the context of what appears to be a very broad review of the law, God declares, 'The soul who sins, it shall die' (Ezk. 18:4, 20; cf. Rom. 6:23). John the Baptist, at the commencement of Jesus' public ministry, cries out, 'Behold the Lamb of God who takes away (by taking it upon himself [ὁ αἴρων]) the sin of the world' (1:29). The law exposes sin but cannot remove it (cf. Rom. 8:3). Jesus, 'the light of life', not only exposes sin but he also is able to remove it (Jn. 3:16–21). Thus the law (νόμος) is fulfilled in an eminent manner in the death of Jesus.

5.3.3.2. Jesus as the Completion of the Sacrificial System

The authors of the New Testament understood the death of Jesus in sacrificial terms (e.g., Eph. 5:2; Heb. 7:27, 9:26, 28; 10:10, 12). The reference to Jesus in the Johannine writings as 'the lamb of God' and various

---

[169] See R. Morgan, 'Fulfillment in the Fourth Gospel', *Int* 11 (1957), 155–6. Also see J. T. Williams, 'Cultic Elements in the Fourth Gospel', *StudBib* (1980), 339–50; F. Mussner, '"Kultische" Aspeckte im Johanneischen Christusbild', in *Praesentia Salutis. Gesammelte Studien zu Fragen und Themen des Neuen Testament* (Düsseldorf: Patmos, 1967); L. Morris, *The New Testament and the Jewish Lectionaries* (London: Tyndale, 1964), 64–72; Bowman, *Fourth Gospel and the Jews*, 56–8.

references to the *blood of Jesus Christ*[170] underline this emphasis. Paul wrote of the death of Jesus as a 'sin offering' (Rom. 8:3), where the phrase περὶ ἁμαρτίας predicated of Jesus is thus to be translated (see the NRSV margin) in accordance with LXX usage. Old Testament atonement language is also applied to Jesus in Heb. 2:17 (ἱλάσκεσθαι) and in 1 Jn. 2:2 and 4:10 (ἱλασμός). However, the common reference to Jesus as a 'sacrifice of atonement' in modern translations of Rom. 3:25 (e.g., NIV; NRSV) is misleading, since the crucial term ἱλαστήριον never refers to an animal victim in any known source. Here the comparison is made directly between Jesus and the Old Testament 'mercy seat' (כַּפֹּרֶת or ἱλαστήριον), and not between Jesus and one of the sacrificial animals in the temple.[171]

The author of Hebrews writes that Christ 'appeared once for all at the end of the age to do away with sin through the sacrifice of himself' (Heb. 9:26). For the writer of Hebrews, Christ's death was the ultimate sacrifice of which the Old Testament sacrifices were merely an illustration (Heb. 9:9–10; 10:1). The inadequacy of the Old Testament sacrifices is highlighted by the fact that they had to be repeated; they could never make perfect for all time those who offered them (Heb. 10:1). Jesus, however, constitutes the perfect offering. Consequently his sacrificial death is all sufficient. Special attention is drawn to the cleansing associated with Christ's sacrificial blood. Whereas the blood of animals cleansed objects and people who outwardly were ceremonially unclean, the blood of Christ is viewed as superior in that it can cleanse or purify inner, human consciences (Heb. 9:14; cf. Titus 2:14).

The two annual Jewish festivals where lambs and goats were sacrificed were Passover and the Day of Atonement. At the former, lambs were sacrificed. At the latter, a bull and a goat were sacrificed (one for the priests, the other for the people) and their blood was applied to the ἱλαστήριον, the golden top-piece upon the Ark of the Covenant. Another goat, traditionally called the 'scapegoat', had the sins of Israel confessed over its head and, with the sins symbolically transferred to it, was sent away to die in the desert carrying on itself the sins of the people (Lev. 16:15ff). The Fourth Evangelist seems to conflate various aspects of the Jewish sacrificial system into one central concept in which Jesus is seen as culminating in himself

---

[170] 1 Jn. 1:7, 5:6–8; Rev. 1:5, 5:9, 7:14, 12:11, 19:13; cf. Acts 20:28; Rom. 3:25, 5:9; Col. 1:20; Eph. 1:7, 2:13; 1 Pet. 1:2, 19; Heb. 9:11ff., 29; 13:12, 20.

[171] See most recently Daniel P. Bailey, 'Jesus as the Mercy Seat: The Semantics and Theology of Paul's Use of *Hilasterion* in Romans 3:25' (Ph.D. dissertation, University of Cambridge, 1999) or the summary of this work in *TynBul* 51.1 (2000), 155–58.

the ultimate fulfilment of all that the Old Testament sacrifices represented. He is both the Passover sacrifice, and the vicarious atoning sacrifice.

In the Fourth Gospel, the climax of the revelation of God's salvific orientation towards his creation occurs in the death of Jesus which is systematically and deliberately associated with the Passover blended with Yom Kippur into one. John puts the emphasis on Passover since it had come to symbolise the whole redemptive work of God. John refers to the Passover more than any other book of the New Testament.[172] Six major passages indicate this thematic development: (a) 1:29–36; (b) 2:13–25; (c) 6:4–14, 22–71; (d) 11:47–12:8; (e) 13:1 (but see also the extended context 13:1–17:26); and (f) 19:13–42, especially vv. 14, 29, 31, 36–37, 42. Three Passover festivals are noted in the Gospel: 2:13; 6:4 and 13:1. The third Passover coincides with Jesus' crucifixion and death. At the commencement of Jesus' ministry, he is proclaimed the sacrificial lamb of God (1:29), thus introducing a theme which is systematically developed and finally, climactically brought to a conclusion in the death of Christ as the Passover sacrifice *par excellence*. For John, the institution of Passover, like other Jewish institutions, simply witnesses to Jesus in whom the Passover has found its ultimate realisation. In ancient Israel, the sacrificial lamb at the time of the Passover symbolised deliverance from the angel of death as well as redemption from bondage in Egypt, leading to the exodus and, finally, entrance into Canaan. In the Fourth Gospel, several supporting themes interwoven into the Passover theme (e.g., depiction of Jesus as the new Moses, manna, references to the serpent raised by Moses in the desert, etc.) further strengthen the view that the association between Jesus and the Passover sacrifice is methodical.[173]

The first appearance of the theme is in John 1:29–36 where the only two uses of ἀμνός in the Gospel (out of only four in the entire New Testament, cf. Acts 8:32; 1 Pet. 1:19) occur at the commencement of Jesus' ministry. The association of Jesus' death with the Passover as with sacrificial connotations is theologically brought into focus by the use a double-meaning word, αἴρω, which means either that Christ *took* upon himself the sin of the world (1 Pet. 2:24; Isa. 53:5) or that he *removed* or *blotted out* sins.[174] The latter statement depends on the former.[175] The

---

[172] Ten times vs. Luke's seven, Matthew and Mark four each.

[173] The references to Moses, the leader of the people during the course of these events, include 1:17, 45; 3:14; 5:45, 46; 6:32; 7:19, 22, 23; 8:5; 9:28, 29.

[174] BAGD, 24; J. Jeremias, *TDNT* 1 (1964), 185–86.

[175] Cf. John Calvin, *The Gospel According to John*, vol. 1, trans. William Pringle (Grand Rapids: Eerdmans, 1956), 65; Hoskyns, *Fourth Gospel*, 176, 534; R. H. Lightfoot, *St. John's*

removal of guilt is a concept frequently found in the Old Testament (Exod. 28:38; 34:7; Num. 14:18; 1 Sam. 15:25; 2 Kgs. 7:9; Ps. 32:5; 85:3; Mic. 7:18).[176] For the Evangelist, the 'lamb of God' has 'taken away' sin by taking it 'upon himself'.[177] It may be countered that the Paschal lambs had no atoning significance in the Old Testament.[178] However, Exodus 13:11–16 seems to regard the Paschal lamb as a substitute for the first-born of Israel. The first-born are not only redeemed by the Passover offering, they are spared death because of the blood of the Lamb. In later Judaism, the slaughtering of the Paschal lambs appears to have been considered a sacrificial rite.[179] Furthermore, that the sacrificial death of Jesus, commemorated in the earliest celebrations of the Eucharist, was associated with the slaughtering of the Paschal lambs is clear from 1 Corinthians 5:7 and 1 Peter 1:18–19.[180] Finally, as I have already noted, the Fourth Evangelist seems to blend the symbolic significance of the various Old Testament sacrifices into one; they are all summed up in the death of Jesus.

Gospel: A Commentary, ed. by C. F. Evans (Oxford: Clarendon, 1956), 96–8; Lindars, *John*, 109; G. L. Cary, 'The Lamb of God and Atonement Theories', *TynBul* 32 (1981), 101–7; Bultmann, *John*, 95–7; and L. L. Morris, *The Gospel According to John*, NICNT (Grand Rapids: Eerdmans, 1971), 144–7; E. W. Burrows, 'Did John the Baptist Call Jesus "The Lamb of God"?', *ExpTim* 85 (1973–74), 245–7.

[176] In these passages the verb נשא (to lift, raise up, carry away, Dan. 2:35), often followed by עון (iniquity, guilt, or punishment of iniquity). Benjamin Davidson, *The Analytical Hebrew and Chaldee Lexicon* (London: Samuel Bagster, 1978), 563f, 590, respectively.

[177] For an extended discussion on the subject, see S. Williams, *Jesus' Death as Saving Event: The Background and Origin of a Concept*, HDR 2 (Missoula, MT: Scholars Press, 1975); Martin Hengel, *The Atonement: The Origin of the Doctrine in the New Testament*, trans. by John Bowden (Philadelphia: Fortress; London: SCM, 1981); V. Taylor, *Jesus and his Sacrifice: A Study of the Passion-Sayings in the Gospels* (London: Macmillan, 1937), 226–7; Max Wilcox, 'The Promise of the "Seed" in the New Testament and the Targumim', *JSNT* 5 (1979), 2–20; C. K. Barrett, 'The Lamb of God', *NTS* 1 (1955), 210–18, see p. 210; idem, *St. John*, 177; C. H. Dodd, 'The Prophecy of Caiaphas: John 11:47–53', in idem, *More New Testament Studies* (Grand Rapids: Eerdmans, 1968), 58–68; J. Morgenstern, 'The Suffering Servant – A New Solution', *VT* 11 (1961), 406–31; Lindars, *John*, 108–9, 406–7; Hoskyns, *Fourth Gospel*, 176; 534; Lightfoot, *St. John's Gospel*, 96–8; E. Haenchen, *John: A Commentary on the Gospel of John* (Philadelphia: Fortress Press, 1984), 2:75; R. C. H. Lenski, *The Interpretation of St. John's Gospel* (Minneapolis: Augsburg Pub. House, 1961), 826–31; Calvin, *Gospel According to John*, 452–55; Brown, *John*, 440–4; Bultmann, *John*, 410–12; Cary, 'Lamb of God and Atonement Theories', 101–7.

[178] Pancaro, *Law in the Fourth Gospel*, 348; cf. Hoskyns, *Fourth Gospel*, 169ff; J. K. Howard, 'Passover and Eucharist in the Fourth Gospel', *SJT* 20 (1967), 332–3.

[179] Str-B, 3:360.

[180] Other recent treatments of the expiatory death of Jesus in John's Gospel include B. H. Grigsby, 'The Cross as an Expiatory Sacrifice in the Fourth Gospel', *JSNT* 15 (1982), 51–80; F. J. Matera, '"On Behalf of Others", "Cleansing", and "Return": Johannine Images for Jesus' Death', *LS* 13 (1988), 161–78; Max Turner, 'Atonement and the Death of Jesus in John – Some Questions to Bultmann and Forestell', *EvQ* 62 (1990), 99–122.

The cleansing of the temple in 2:13–25, placed by the author at the commencement of Jesus' ministry, is coordinated with the Passover. The Passover theme keynotes the outset (2:13) and the conclusion (2:23) of the account. The inclusio usefully surrounds the intervening events of Jesus' temple cleansing with explicit references to the Passover. In so doing, the action of Jesus is cast against the backdrop of Passover activities. The theme receives added impetus when Jesus drives out the animals designated for sacrifice, and then in his conversation with the religious leaders, substitutes his body for the temple and its sacrificial system. In placing the cleansing of the temple very early in his Gospel, 2:13–25, John signifies the arrival of a New Order.[181]

The Passover theme reappears, once again at the outset, in chapter 6:1–14 and 6:22–71 where the feeding of the five thousand takes place near the time of the Passover (6:4); and in the discourse on manna an allusion is made to the exodus from Egypt.[182]

Later in John 11:47–12:8, the words of the high priest, though unknown to himself, once again signifies Jesus as the sacrificial atoning victim, echoing the cry of the Baptist at the outset of Jesus' public ministry (1:29).

Two further references to the approaching Passover are in 11:55 and 12:1. The first is a general reference to the Passover and the second places the following events six days before the Passover. The effect of these two explicit time markers is to link Caiaphas' words with Jesus' being anointed at Bethany by Mary (12:1–8), and then to link both of these events with Jesus' impending death. The Evangelist scrupulously provides the details to ensure that the reader understands Jesus' impending death against background imagery associated with a Passover victim being prepared for sacrifice (12:7).[183]

The theme continues in 13:1–17:26, and is keynoted once again right at the beginning (13:1) of the account. Whereas the first twelve chapters of

---

[181] W. D. Davies, *The Gospel and the Land: Early Christianity and Jewish Territorial Doctrine* (Berkeley: University of California Press, 1974), 289–90.

[182] There are several Passover contextual elements in the account of chapter six including references to Moses as the leader of the Egyptian exodus and the instigator of the Passover, the allusion to the manna, sacrifical associations in Jesus' references to his own death (vv. 53–58), and the language which reflects the exodus as well as the imagery of the Last Supper (cf. 1 Cor. 10:3–4). See Rudolf Schnackenburg, *The Gospel According to St. John*, trans. by Cecily Hastings, Francis McDonagh, David Smith and Richard Foley, vol. 2 (New York: Seabury Press, A Crossroad Book, 1980), 14; B. F. Westcott, *The Gospel According to St. John*, 2 vols (Grand Rapids: Eerdmans, 1954), 102.

[183] Schnackenburg, *St. John*, 2:366, entirely misses the significance of the temporal reference.

the Gospel cover a time period of about two and half years, chapters 13–19 encompass a time period of approximately twenty-four hours. In the events recorded in this segment of the Gospel, Jesus himself appears to be sharing a Passover meal with his disciples (chs. 13–17). Whether this is an actual Passover meal has been debated extensively. The difficulty lies, in part, in the apparent chronological disharmony between the Synoptic and Johannine accounts of the final days of Jesus' life. Notwithstanding, in the light of the many similarities between the Synoptic and Johannine accounts, the meal depicted in John 13–17 seems to be a Passover meal.[184]

John 19:13–42 brings this thematic association to a climax in the actual depiction of Jesus' death as a Passover sacrifice. This account in effect has the same symbolic significance as the cleansing of the temple, namely, the termination of the Jewish cultus and the uselessness of its further observance.[185] Here, the author maintains that three direct quotations of the Old Testament are fulfilled in the death of Jesus, and the quotations in verses 36–37 form a suitable climactic double quotation as if the Evangelist wishes to ensure that his audience do not miss the Passover associations.[186]

Beyond these references to the fulfilment of Scripture, there are several other indications that the events of the Passion are viewed by John in terms of their Passover significance. When Jesus is on the cross, his time of crucifixion is juxtaposed with the slaughter of the Paschal lambs in the temple courtyard on the day of the preparation for the Passover.[187] John

---

[184] J. Jeremias, *The Eucharistic Words of Jesus* (London: SCM, 1966), 56–82, esp. p. 81; J. Rendel Harris, 'The Early Christian Interpretation of the Passover', *ExpTim* 38 (1926–27), 88–90; R. Brown, 'The Problem of History in John', *CBQ* 24 (1962), 5. On chronology, the strongest advocates for two calendars being utilised in Palestine at the time are: A. Jaubert, *La Date de la cène: Calendrier biblique et liturgie chrétienne*, EBib (Paris: Gabalda, 1957); idem, 'The Calendar of Qumran and the Passion Narrative in John', in *John and the Dead Sea Scrolls*, ed. by J. H.Charlesworth (New York: Crossroad, 1990), 62–75; E. Ruckstuhl, *Chronology of the Last Days of Jesus: A Critical Study*, trans. by V. J. Drapela (New York: Desclée, 1965). But see G. Ogg, 'Review of Mlle Jaubert, La Date de la cène', *NovT* 34 (1959), 149–60. J. K. Howard, 'Passover and Eucharist in the Fourth Gospel', *Theol* 20 (1967), 335; Bernard, *St. John*, 2:478. Cf. Isa. 5:1–7; 27:2–11.

[185] See Bultmann, *John*, 677.

[186] While most commentators agree that John in 19:37 cites Zechariah 12:10, there is little agreement about the possible cited text and its version in 19:3. See Reim, *Stuien zum alttestamentlichen*, 52; Schuchard, *Scripture within Scripture*, 138–40; Mark Stibbe, *John as Storyteller: Narrative Criticism and the Fourth Gospel*, SNTSMS 73 (Cambridge: CUP, 1992), 35.

[187] Later in 19:31 and 42, the Evangelist states that it was the day of preparation (either for Passover or Sabbath, since the two seem to have fallen on the same day, according to John's account). The second clue is that throughout the Passion account, there is a correlation of events regarding Jesus' death with the events surrounding Passover. The mention of specific timing is

18:28 and v. 39 indicate that it was the eve of Passover. The Sabbath is called 'great' (19:31) because it coincides with the first day of the Passover festival. The day of preparation was the day on which the Passover sacrifices were killed.[188] Thus Jesus' death not only occurs on the day of the Passover sacrifice, but is equated with the sacrifice itself by virtue of its contemporaneity.

It is noteworthy that the hour of Jesus' rejection by the Jews coincides with the hour in which preparations began for the feast which commemorated the deliverance from Egypt. Out of that great event in which the slave nation of the Hebrews is delivered out of bondage and led into the exodus, Israel, the chosen people of God, is called into existence. Centuries later, it is now in such an hour that Israel calls a blasphemous Gentile king, Caesar, its own king and forfeits its right to be called the people of God. But in the self-same hour, a new exodus begins and a new Israel is born.[189] Jesus is sentenced to death by Pilate at noon,[190] the hour at which the slaughter of the Passover lambs was to begin (19:14; cf. Exod. 12:6).[191]

Hence in 19:14 and the account of the crucifixion, John's emphasis on the time of Jesus' crucifixion is not a simple aside, particularly when the author notes, 'Now it was the day of preparation of the Passover.' Superimposing the time of Jesus' crucifixion (i.e., offering) and the time when the Passover lambs were slain in the temple keynotes a prophetic fulfilment, recalling the Evangelist's earlier account of John the Baptist's words, 'Behold the Lamb of God who takes away the sin of the world' (1:29); and Jesus' own references that he must be lifted up just as Moses lifted up the serpent in the wilderness (3:12; cf. 8:28; 12:32; Num. 21:9).

For the Fourth Evangelist, when Moses lifted up a bronze serpent upon a pole and Israel had to respond to his action in faith in order to escape death, that event foreshadows the lifting-up of Jesus upon the cross. When

---

important, and the repetition unites the account. John 18:28 and 39 prepare the reader for the specific chronology of the events in chapter 19, and the crucial events surrounding Jesus' death are linked on three occasions with the day of preparation, once at the beginning, once in the middle and once at the end (19:14, 31, 42).

[188] G. B. Gray, *Sacrifice in the Old Testament: Its Theory and Practice* (Oxford: Clarendon, 1925), 388.

[189] See Pancaro, *Law in the Fourth Gospel*, 344ff.

[190] There are some textual disputes regarding the time of Jesus' death, but readings for the third hour are almost certainly designed to bring the Fourth Gospel into harmony with the Synoptic accounts.

[191] Gray, *Sacrifice in the Old Testament*, 388–9; Brown, *John*, 2:833; Barrett, *St. John*, 545; David E. Garland, 'John 18–19: Life Through Jesus' Death', *RE* 85 (1988), 494.

the Son of Man is lifted up in death upon a Gentile cross, his death brings about the death of death in his resurrection and exaltation. And just as it was required of the Israelites in the wilderness to respond in faith in order to avoid a certain death, the same is required of the Jews and Gentiles alike who walk in the shadow of death; they must respond in faith to the lifting-up of the Son of Man. In both instances, only those who believe and respond in faith to a seemingly ludicrous demand are healed. For the Fourth Evangelist, the oblation of Jesus embodies the highest expression of immolation, forever rendering the Jewish sacrificial system obsolete.

In his final explicit Old Testament citation, John offers the editorial observation[192] that the events which follow the death of Jesus represent the fulfilment of a second Old Testament prophecy (cf. 19:36).[193] The actual formula which precedes John's citation is, 'And again another Scripture says' (19:37) which may indicate that the Evangelist is quoting from memory and not an actual text in hand. This is also a formula which does not occur anywhere else in the New Testament in precisely the same form.[194] This segment of the Gospel shows how narrative chronology and narrative christology are inseparable in John.[195] Preceding these citations are the breaking of the legs of the two men crucified with Jesus, the spear thrust in the Lord's side, and the testimony of the eyewitness: 'He who saw it has borne witness – his testimony is true, and he knows that he tells the truth – that you also may believe'(19:35). The author goes on to note, 'For these things [the events described in vv. 32–34] took place that the Scripture might be fulfilled, "Not a bone of him shall be broken"' (v. 36). This account puts the death of Jesus on the evening of the fourteenth of Nisan and in this John is alone among the Gospel writers.[196]

---

[192] Cf. John 12:14–15, 38, 39–40; 19:24, 28[?], 36.

[193] John 19:36–37 is John's last citation of the Old Testament in his account of the suffering and death of Jesus. It is also the second of the two juxtaposed citations (cf. 12:13–15, 38–40).

[194] Cf. however, Mt. 4:7; Acts 13:35; Rom. 15:9–12; 1 Cor. 3:20; Heb. 1:5–13; 2:13; 4:5; 5:6; 10:30; also 2 *Clem.* 2:4 and similar examples in the rabbinic literature. See Str-B, 2:583; Reim, *Stuien zum alttestamentlichen*, 52; Schuchard, *Scripture within Scripture*, 138–41. If Jesus is the Paschal Lamb, scholars argue, then John cites the Pentateuch; if not, then John is citing the Psalms. But formal considerations have already strongly suggested that John's citation recalls the Pentateuch (Jn. 18:28, 19:14, 31. See also 19:42; cf. Mt. 27:62; Mk. 15:42; Lk. 23:54).

[195] Stibbe, *Storyteller*, 195–6.

[196] It is not exactly clear what system of time reckoning John uses. Westcott, *St. John*, 282, believed, unlike the Synoptics, John was using Roman time which started at midnight. But in 4:6 and 19:42, the Evangelist seems to be using the Jewish reckoning, which began at 6 a.m. The Roman reckoning was used only by authorities as legal time (contracts, official documents, etc.) otherwise, the Romans too appear to have reckoned time from 6 a.m. (Roman sundials are marked VI, not XII, for noon).

While the Baptist is Jesus' witness at the beginning, the Beloved Disciple is his witness at the end. As with the double citation in 12:38-40, the second part is introduced by πάλιν, 'and again another Scripture says, "They shall look upon him whom they have pierced"'. This citation from Zechariah 12:10 follows the Hebrew text, and it appears again in Revelation 1:7. There, and in Justin as well, the ὄψονται refers to the *parousia*.[197] This future perspective is already present in the Fourth Gospel. The Zechariah citation means the concrete fulfilment of a christological prophecy as well as a future pronouncement of judgment (cf. 8:28; 4:36). Within the Johannine theological structure, the Old Testament is used to substantiate the claims that Jesus does the will of God. For John, Jesus' death epitomises his obedience to the will of the Father. The Scripture expresses God's will, and Jesus is submissive to God's will, thus his activity fulfils the Scripture.

The reference to the Scripture in the depiction of Jesus' death is striking in its wording:

After this, Jesus knowing that all was now finished (τετέλεσται) said to fulfil the Scripture (ἵνα τελειωθῇ ἡ γραφή), 'I thirst.' A bowl full of vinegar stood there, so they put a sponge full of the vinegar on hyssop and held it to his mouth. When Jesus had received the vinegar, he said, 'It is finished' (τετέλεσται); and he bowed his head and gave up his spirit.   (John 19:28-30)

Only here in the entire Gospel does the Evangelist speak of a τελειοῦν of the Scripture, an enhancement over the previous formulaic πληροῦν, which expresses the 'ultimate fulfilment' of the christological prophecies in the Scriptures, in view of what the death and resurrection of Jesus accomplishes. The Evangelist consciously places this ἵνα τελειωθῇ ἡ γραφή between the twice occurring τετέλεσται – Jesus' knowledge that the end had come in verse 28 and his death cry in verse 30.

The amalgamation of several incidents recorded by the Evangelist leaves no doubt that he is associating the death of Jesus with the completion of the Passover and what the Feast symbolised. First, both in Exodus 12:22 and John 19:29, the hyssop branch is mentioned. At this point in the narrative, John departs from the Synoptic use of κάλαμος (Mk. 15:33; Mt. 27:49) and makes direct reference to hyssop (ὕσσωπος) as a correlation with the use of the hyssop branch at Passover (Lev. 14:6-7, 49,

---

[197] Schnackenburg, *Johannes*, 3:344, offers a number of observations concerning the significance of ὄψονται which suggests, 'scheint bei den "Aufschauenden" doch zuerst an die Glaubenden gedacht zu sein. Die Juden sind davon nicht ausgenommen, wenn auch nicht allein gemeint.'

51; Num. 19:6; and Ps. 51[50]:7; cf. Heb. 9:19–22). The allusion to Psalm 69:22, 'for my thirst, they gave me vinegar to drink' should not be missed.[198] Hyssop was associated with the paschal liturgy as means of sprinkling the blood of the Passover lamb on the doorposts. Many scholars (e.g., Hoskyns, Brown, Barrett, W. Bauer, Loisy) see in the hyssop of John 19:29 yet another trait introduced by the Evangelist to signify that Christ is the Paschal lamb.

Secondly, in John 19:34, the flow of water and blood from the side of Jesus after he is stabbed reflects several rabbinic passages in which the proper sacrifice is described in terms of the flow of blood and water or fluid. The idea appears to be that the blood was supposed to flow like water (the καί may be epexegetic, 'blood even water' [fluid]) to prevent congealing.[199] Thirdly, Jesus' body is not allowed to stay on the cross until the next morning (19:31, 38), just as the remains of the Passover meal were not to be left until the next day but burned (Exod. 12:19).

In John 17, Jesus prays, 'I have finished the work (ἔργον) that you gave me to do (ποιεῖν).' In Genesis 2:2, it is written 'and on the sixth day God finished his works (ἔργα) which he had done (ἐποίησεν).' In the details of the development of the Passover theme, John seems to indicate that Jesus' death had a sacrificial significance. He sees the Passover feast with various symbolic elements in its liturgy as a mere picture, a witness, to that eschatological reality of which the death of Christ is the consummation. Thus, his death once for all has accomplished what the institution of the Jewish Passover represented. Jesus has finished the disrupted work of creation by providing the ultimate provision for sin.[200] By making this thematic association between Jesus and the Passover, the Evangelist has several objectives. First he shows how the intricate details of Jesus' death fulfilled the Scriptures, i.e., surely all these details cannot be coincidental. If so, far from disproving Jesus' claims, they actually confirm them. Therefore, these are written so that you may believe [Jesus is the Christ] (19:35). Secondly, by making such associative connections, he shows how the

---

[198] See Brown, *John*, 2:930.

[199] See J. M. Ford, '"Mingled Blood" From the Side of Christ (John xix. 34)', *NTS* 15 (1969), 337–8.

[200] A widespread Jewish haggada records that the first human couple was created on the sixth day, and at the tenth hour – about the time of Jesus' death – sinned. If this tradition is in the background, it means that the Son 'finished' the work of God's creation. See Franz Rosenzweig's idea of 'Death as the Consummation of Creation' (*Der Tod als Vollendung der Schöpfung*) referred to by Martin Hengel, 'The Old Testament in the Fourth Gospel', *HBT* 12 (1990), 31–2. Cf. W. F. Hambly, 'Creation and Gospel: A Brief Comparison of Genesis 1:1–2, 4 and John 1:1–2, 12', *SE* 5 = TU 103 (1968), 69–74.

Scriptures indeed testified of Jesus and how the religious institutions of Israel found their ultimate realisation in Jesus' life and works including his Passion. In turn, these relate back to John's purpose: Jesus is the One whom he claimed to be – the Christ.

5.3.3.3. Jesus as the Locus of God's Presence – The True Temple

It was Israel's expectation that at the dawn of the kingdom of God 'the mountain of the Lord's house shall be established as the chief of the mountains'. Zion was predicted to become the place to which nations would flow like a stream, and out of Zion was to go forth the knowledge of the Holy One of Israel (Isa. 2:1–5; Mic. 4:1ff). Many early Jewish texts referred to the glory of the temple in that eschatological time.[201] For the Fourth Evangelist, that eschatological time was now at hand. The incarnation had brought the presence of God to the midst of his people in a most unprecedented fashion (Jn. 1:14).

The term ἐσκήνωσεν in 1:14, where the Word 'became flesh and dwelt (or tabernacled) among us', is significant in its implication where John presents Jesus as the true temple of God. The word σκηνόω means 'live, dwell'. But the expression conceptually is reminiscent of the 'pitched tent, tabernacle'. In the context of John 1:14 and the apparent consonantal play on σκηνή, 'tent' and 'shekinah' (שכינה), it seems to press home the idea that Jesus embodies the divine presence once again among his people. It echoes the glory of the God of Israel when he dwelt (שכינה, 'that which dwells') in the tabernacle[202] and appeared in the cloud and fire in the wilderness by the Red Sea and on Mount Sinai.[203]

In Isaiah 6, glory is ascribed to the Lord God of Hosts. In John, it is attributed to Jesus (12:41). In saying that Jesus reveals the glory of God (13:31), the Evangelist asserts that the presence of God is in the presence of Jesus, and thus Jesus is the revealer of God (1:18). Later in 1:14, the Old Testament tabernacle/temple motif is further confirmed with the introduction of the word 'glory'.[204] The word may be, if taken literally, the

---

[201] E. P. Sanders, *Jesus and Judaism* (London: SCM, 1985), 77–90, cites and critically discusses the relevant references.

[202] Cf. Exod. 40:35; 25:8; 29:49; Num. 9:15, 16; Zech. 2:14.

[203] Exod. 16:10; 24:16; 33:7–11; 40:34–38; Deut. 5:24. See H. Mowvley, 'John 1:14–18 in the light of Exodus 33:7–34:35', *ExpTim* 95 (1983–84), 135–37.

[204] G. B. Caird, 'The Glory of God in the Fourth Gospel: An Exercise in Biblical Semantics', *NTS* 15 (1968–69), 265–77; M. Pamment, 'The Meaning of Doxa in the Fourth Gospel', *ZNW* 74 (1973), 12–6; J. C. Meagher, 'John 1:14 and the New Temple', *JBL* 88 (1969), 57–68; Lightfoot, *John's Gospel*, 90; A. Hanson, 'John 1:14–18 and Exodus 34', *NTS* 23 (1976), 90.

reflection of the apostle upon the experience of the transfiguration. However, it is more probable that in view of 2:11, 'the manifestation of his glory' may be an allusion to 'the signs' (e.g., 2:1–11; 4:36–54; 5:2–16), particularly his resurrection.[205] Just as the tabernacle represented the locus of God's self-revelation, now in a much more profound sense, Jesus as the living Word of God is the locus of God's self-revelation. Therefore, Jesus can say, he who has seen him has seen the Father (Jn. 14:9; cf. 2:19–21). The tabernacle, and later the temple, were places where the oracles of God were given. The words spoken by Jesus, the incarnate 'Word', are the very words of life (Jn. 6:63). It is in him that the revelatory Word of God for humanity is personally given. Jesus himself is the very locus of divine revelation.[206]

This idea is developed throughout the document in which Jesus is seen as the locus of God's presence (e.g., John 2:19–21, with reference to the ναόν). The perplexing statement of Jesus in 1:51, once observed in the context of 1:14; 2:19, 21; 4:21–24, further supports the Johannine intention that Jesus is the locus of God's presence on earth and his revelation. In 1:51, Jesus alludes to Jacob's vision at Bethel (Gen. 12:8; 13:3–4).[207] It was at Bethel, the site of ancient theophany and divine revelation, that Israel consulted the LORD (Judg. 20:18, 26; 21:2–5; 1 Sam. 10:3). For John, Jesus epitomises the supreme 'Bethel', the house of God *par excellence*. In him, in its truest sense, is the place to behold the divine glory (1:18) and above all, he is the living Word, the Logos, the divine wisdom who reveals the mind of God, and it is in him that the worship of the Father takes place in Spirit and in truth (Jn. 4:21–24). In Jesus, one is enabled to see the Father (Jn. 14:9) and perceive his glory (Jn. 1:14; 2:11; 5:41, etc.). The functions which had primitively accrued to Bethel have finally been fulfilled in Jesus.

In the episode of John 7:1–9 and the Feast of Tabernacles, the theme of Jesus as replacement of the temple is further developed. In this pericope, Jesus' refusal to go to Jerusalem to participate in the Feast of Tabernacles and present himself before the Lord (Deut. 16:16; Lev. 23:33ff) may seem to

---

[205] John 12:23, 31; 3:14; 8:28; 12:34; cf. Exod. 15:2; Isa. 33:10; 52:13, etc.

[206] See BDB, 1014; BAGD, 755; W. Michaelis, *TDNT* 7 (1971), 385–86; Raymond Collins, *These Things Have Been Written: Studies on the Fourth Gospel* (Grand Rapids: Eerdmans, 1990), 205; 199–206; Homer A. Kent, *Light in the Darkness: Studies in the Gospel of John* (Grand Rapids: Baker Book House, 1974), 34; Brown, *John*, 39–40, A. M. Hunter, *The Gospel According to John*, The Cambridge Bible Commentary on the New English Bible (Cambridge: CUP, 1965), 19.

[207] Barrett, *St. John*, 155–6; Bultmann, *John*, 105; R. H. Strachan, *The Fourth Gospel: Its Significance and Environment*, 3rd edn (London: SCM, 1943), 120–2.

place him in breach of the law. The Johannine explanatory footnote in 7:10 and his distinction between φανερῶς and ἐν κρυπτῷ makes this evident, especially since Tabernacles was a public occasion. However, John will soon make it clear that the old tabernacle is replaced and realised in the new tabernacle where the water of the daily ritual is replaced by the Holy Spirit (7:37–39), and the temple lamps are replaced by Jesus himself who brings spiritual illumination not only for Israel but for the whole world (8:12; 9:5). In this episode, Jesus' lack of public participation in the feast and his apparent vacillation is a vivid means both of distancing himself from the Jerusalem celebration and of remaining in contact with it in order to proclaim its fulfilment (and therefore replacement).

In the Fourth Gospel in the context of John's allusions to the tabernacle, the Exodus associations are intentional and part of the theme of the revelation and redemption in the incarnate Word as fulfilling the hope of a second Exodus. In fact, the six main Exodus institutions, i.e., Passover, the Festival of Unleavened Bread, the offering of firstlings, theophany, covenant, and law, which were the central means whereby Israel lived out its community life under God in the annual cycle of worship, are also present in John as fulfilled in Jesus.

For example, the theophany – the self-disclosure of God – as a central theme of Exodus is also the central theme in John's Gospel, particularly in light of the revelatory 'I Am' statements. Jesus' role as the temple-replacement forms the vital background to the strongly sacrificial language in 6:51–58. The basis of the earlier statements that Jesus has life in himself (5:26) and can bestow that life on others (4:50; 5:21) is here revealed. He offers this life through his death, which deals with sin and releases his life for others. The destruction of this temple, therefore – that of Jesus' body – becomes a means of life far greater than anything available through the old temple. John hereby highlights the present reality of the final age.[208]

The actions of Jesus in the temple are far more than a mere critique.[209] Jesus' actions are, instead, indicative not only of a present eschatological reality but also of its consummation. In terminating the activity of the

---

[208] Jack Dean Kingsbury, 'The Gospel in Four Editions', *Int* 33 (1979), 374.

[209] Malachi 3:1–5; Ezekiel 8:1–10:20; 40:1–43:27. C. Hassell Bullock, 'Ezekiel: Bridge Between the Testaments', *JETS* 25 (1982), 2930. On the eschatological significance of the action, see Lynn Losie, 'The Cleansing of the Temple: A History of a Gospel Tradition in Light of Its Background in the Old Testament and in Early Judasim' (Ph.D. diss., Fuller Theological Seminary, 1984); P. Pokorny, *Genesis of Christology: Foundations for a Theology of the New Testament.* ET (Edinburgh: Clark, 1987), 47–8; see also Bultmann, *John*, 128–9; Stuhlmacher, *Jesus of Nazareth – Christ of Faith*, 30.

merchants within the temple, Jesus symbolically performs an activity which is in harmony with his eschatological identity as both Saviour and Judge (Isa. 52:7-12). It is noteworthy that in chapter 2, although the merchants only appear in verses 14-16 and the Jews only in verses 18-20, John's narrative portrays the activity of the merchants as an extension of the activity of 'the Jews'. Actively or passively, the presence of the merchants in the temple has been authorised by the Jewish religious authorities. They challenge Jesus' authority: 'What sign have you to show us for doing this?' (2:18). Jesus' response is not what they expect: 'Destroy this temple, and in three days I will raise it up' (2:19; cf. 5:21; 6:39-40). Jesus does not threaten to destroy. He suggests, instead, that they already have been doing this and they will destroy again.[210] Rather than giving into their thirst for the miraculous and their inability to perceive its function, their demand for a sign that will validate his authority is refused. Since they do not seem to understand his immediate actions nor the true function of his signs, Jesus points to that which both anticipate. He verbalises that which his signs non-verbally signify.[211] Those Jews who truly desire to know who Jesus is, what authority he has, and what his 'cryptic' actions and words mean, must begin by seeing in his death and resurrection after 'three days' the final testimony to his eschatological identity.[212] Jesus' assertion suggests that his purification of the temple (the centre of the sacrificial cultus) in the context of a Passover feast is to be understood as

---

[210] The construction is neither a concessive clause (cf. BDF, 195 §387.2) nor a condition (cf. Dodd, *Interpretation*, 302 n. 1). It seems, instead, to be a prophetic imperative which should be accorded full force. Jesus instructs (cf. 13:27) the Jews to do precisely what he would have them do. See L. Gaston, *No Stone on Another: Studies in the Significance of the All of Jerusalem in the Synoptic Gospels*, SNT 23 (Leiden: Brill, 1970), 207, who favors the translation, 'You will destroy.' See also Nereparampil, *Destroy This Temple*, 84.

[211] Cf. Wolfgang J. Bittner, *Jesu Zeichen im Johannesevangelium: Die Messias-Erkenntnis im Johannesevangelium vor ihrem jüdischen Hintergrund*, WUNT 2. Reihe, Bd. 26 (Tübingen: Mohr-Siebeck, 1987), 28, cf. D. K. Clark, 'Signs and Wisdom in John', *CBQ* 45 (1983), 201-9.

[212] See the observations by M. Rissi, 'Die Hochzeit in Kana (Jo 2, 1-11)', in *Oikonomia. Heilsgeschichte als Thema der Theologie. Oscar Cullmann zum 65. Geburtstag gewidmet*, ed. by I. F. Christ (Hamburg-Bergstedt: H. Reich Verlag, 1967), 90, who writes: 'Hier liegt der Grund, warum der Evangelist Tod und Auferstehung selbst nicht "Zeichen" nennen kann. Die Wunder und der Hingang zum Vater verhalten sich zueinander wie Zeichen und Wirklichkeit.' This 'Wirklichkeit' constitutes God's final fulfilment of his promises for which the resurrection offers a threefold 'witness' to its significance. Other threefold testimonies in the Fourth Gospel include the following: (1) the Baptist's threefold testimony (1:19-21; his testimony also spans a period of three days [cf. vv. 19-28, 29-34, 35-36; cf. Jesus' testimony in 29-34, 35-42, 43-51]); (2) Peter's threefold denial (cf. 13:38; 18:17, 25-27 [contrast his threefold confession, 21:15-19]); (3) Jesus' threefold testimony on the cross (19:26-27, 28, 30). This is enough to demonstrate a pattern based upon the idea contained in Deut. 19:15 (cf. 17:6). Cf. Jn. 8:17; 1 Jn. 5:7-8. See also Mt. 18:15-20; 2 Cor. 13:1; Heb. 10:28.

the inauguration of that which will culminate in the perfect sacrifice of the final eschatological Passover – himself.

The destruction of Jerusalem may have been seen by some Jewish Christians as the punishment inflicted upon the nation for having rejected the Messiah.[213] What remains conspicuous is an absence of a clear apologetic interest in the *function* of this story in the post-AD 70 situation, when 'destroy this temple' would have been a horrific reality.[214] In fact, so poignant and powerful would have been this story for those who faced the traumatic events of AD 70, that this apparent absence of a clear apologetic interest in the function of this story, in itself, is an argument against setting the Gospel in that situation (i.e., post-AD 70). However, it is possible that the prominence given to this story, and then to the festivals, may be John's way of addressing the trauma.[215]

In any case, there is no direct reference to the actual event of the destruction of the temple anywhere in the Fourth Gospel. Even in chapter 2, John quickly clarifies that Jesus spoke of the temple of his own body which in the end may be used with equal force to argue for a pre-AD 70 date of the Gospel. But there is a combination of tragic irony and hope in 4:21. The irony of 'neither on this mountain nor in Jerusalem' becomes painfully evident in the context of the post-AD 70 setting. The fate that befell the schismatic Samaritan temple at the hands of John Hyrcanus[216] has now befallen Jerusalem at the hands of Titus. 'You will not worship on that mountain' had been the Jewish charge against the Samaritans for centuries. Jesus quotes the charge, and augments it with its horrifying complement – 'nor in Jerusalem!' – and then transforms it into a positive statement involving the purpose of God and what he seeks (4:23).

The Johannine Jesus has superseded Israel's most ancient sanctuary, Bethel; he has replaced the tabernacle and the temple. He is the authentic 'dwelling place of God'. Bethel, the tabernacle, and the Jerusalem temple were shadows of which Jesus is the reality. Jesus' advent in the temple envisions his going to prepare a place (14:2),[217] and his death as the true

---

[213] H. J. Schoeps, *Aus frühchristlicher Zeit. Religionsgeschichtliche Untersuchungen* (Tübingen: Mohr, 1950).

[214] Even though this is the period in which many date the Gospel. E.g., Schnackenburg, *St. John*, 1:100–4.

[215] Leroy, *Rätsel und Missverständnis*, 145–7, suggests that this passage (i.e., 2:17–20) is programmatic for the rest of the Gospel and that it lays the foundation for the two levels on which the Gospel operates.

[216] Josephus, *Ant.* 13.9.1 §§254–258.

[217] James McCaffrey, *The House with Many Rooms: The Temple Theme of Jn. 14:2–3*, AnBib, vol. 114 (Rome: Editrice Pontificio Istituto Biblico, 1988).

Lamb of God means the passing away of the sacrificial cultus and the beginning of Jesus' eschatological reign as God's true temple, where God and humanity meet.

5.4. The Witness of the Scriptures to Jesus and the Johannine Hermeneutic

While John's allusions to the Scriptures are distinctive, his interpretive approach to the Scriptures is not. He is very much in line with the apostolic hermeneutical tradition and the rest of the New Testament writers for whom Jesus had fulfilled the law and the prophets (Jn. 1:45; 5:39, 46; cf. Lk. 24:27; Acts 2:16). John's hermeneutical structure is firmly grounded in the post-resurrection conviction that Jesus was indeed who he claimed to be and thus the evidence to support this certainty about Jesus was sought from the Scriptures. But do John or other New Testament writers have any justification for interpreting the Scriptures in the manner they did? Within the context of second temple Judaism of the Hellenistic period there are significant interpretive diversities.[218] Whether the author of the Fourth Gospel is following an already established exegetical school within this diversity remains a subject open to further exploration. John as well as other New Testament writers may have been acquainted with the methods

---

[218] For example, see Michael Fishbane, *Biblical Interpretation in Ancient Israel* (Oxford: Clarendon, 1985); F. F. Bruce, *Biblical Exegesis in the Qumran Texts* (Grand Rapids: Eerdmans, 1959); George J. Brooke, *Exegesis at Qumran: 4 QFlorilegium in Its Jewish Context*, JSOTSup. vol. 29 (Sheffield: JSOT Press, 1985); D. Patte, *Early Jewish Hermeneutic in Palestine* (Missoula, MT: Scholars Press, 1975); Asher Finkel, 'The Pesher of Dreams and Scriptures', *Revue de Qumran* 4 (1963–64), 357–70; M. P. Horgan, *Pesharim: Qumran Interpretation of Biblical Books* (Washington: Catholic Biblical Association, 1979); Craig A. Evans, 'The Function of the Old Testament in the New', in *Introducing New Testament Interpretation*, ed. by Scot McKnight (Grand Rapids: Baker Book House, 1989), 163–93; and J. L. Kugel, *Early Biblical Interpretation* (Philadelphia: Westminster Press, 1986), 38–46; D. C. Braine, 'The Inner Jewishness of St. John's Gospel as the Clue to the Inner Jewishness of Jesus', *Studien zum Neuen Testament und Seiner Umwelt* 13 (1988), 101–55; M. Gertner, 'Midrashim in the New Testament', *JSS* 7 (1952), 267–92; M. P. Miller, 'Targum, Midrash and the Use of the Old Testament in the New Testament', *JSJ* 2 (1971), 29–82; Peder Borgen, *Logos Was the True Light: And Other Essays on the Gospel of John* (Trondheim, Norway: Tapir Publishers, 1983); G. Vermes, 'Bible and Midrash: Early O.T. Exegesis', in *The Cambridge History of the Bible: From the Beginning to Jerome*, ed. by P. R. Ackroyd and C. F. Evans (Cambridge: CUP, 1970), 1:199–231; R. T. France and D. Wenham, eds, *Studies in Midrash and Historiography* (Sheffield: JSOT Press, 1983); Gary G. Porton, 'Defining Midrash', in *Study of Ancient Judaism*, ed. by J. Neusner (New York: KTAV, 1981), 55–94. See also the following studies by Neusner: *Understanding Rabbinic Midrash* (Hoboken, NJ: KTAV, 1985); *What is Midrash?* (Philadelphia: Fortress Press, 1987); *Midrash in Context: Exegesis in Formative Judaism* (Philadelphia: Fortress, 1983).

of Jewish exegesis of Scripture and may have used them in some instances. It may be argued that, after all, New Testament writers had no other starting place when they set out to interpret the Scriptures christologically. However, Jesus' life, teaching, and above all death and resurrection would have provided the first Christians with a revolutionary hermeneutical starting point. As with Paul, so with John, there may have been tensions created by the disjunction between one's Jewish heritage and the post-Easter perspective and convictions. Nevertheless, John consistently seeks to show that his proclamation of the Gospel is grounded in the witness of Israel's Scriptures.

There are several Jewish interpretive techniques with which the Fourth Gospel has been linked. Some scholars have used *Targumim* and *Targumising* to describe John's interpretive approach to the Scriptures.[219] However, the difficulty with such a category lies in its imprecision. It seems as if it has explained something, when, in fact, it has not.[220] Others believe they can detect the principle of midrashim followed by the Fourth Evangelist. It has been claimed that there are extended 'midrashisms' in the Fourth Gospel.[221] Midrash, as a principal vehicle for interpreting the Torah, had gained wide popularity during the Hellenistic period.[222] The Greek word, ἐραυνᾶτε, 'search', 'examine', 'investigate' (5:39; 7:52) in all probability reflects the very definition of 'midrash' deriving from דרש, 'search', with the cognate noun מדרש literally meaning a 'searching'.[223]

---

[219] M. Black, *An Aramaic Approach to the Gospels and Acts*, 3rd edn (Oxford: Clarendon, 1967 [orig. 1946]), 151. See also B. Olsson, *Structure and Meaning in the Fourth Gospel: A Textual-Linguistic Analysis of John 2:1–11 and 4:1–42*, ConBNT 6 (Lund: Gleerup, 1974), 282; B. Lindars, 'Traditions Behind the Fourth Gospel', in *L'Évangile de Jean*, ed. by M. de Jonge (1977), 109–24; A. T. Hanson, 'John's Use of Scripture', in *The Gospels and the Scriptures of Israel*, ed. by Craig A. Evans and W. Richard Stegner, JSNTSup 104 (Sheffield: Academic Press, 1994), 359.

[220] B. D. Chilton, *Targumic Approaches to the Gospels*, Studies in Judaism (Lanham, MD and New York: University Press of America, 1986), 125.

[221] Peder Borgen, 'Observation on the Midrashic Character of John 6', *ZNW* 54 (1963), 232–40; idem, *Bread from Heaven: An Exegetical Study of the Concept of Manna in the Gospel of John and the Writings of Philo*, NovTSup 10 (Leiden: Brill, 1965); Hanson, *New Testament Interpretation*, 97–109; G. Reim, 'Jesus as God in the Fourth Gospel: The Old Testament Background', *NTS* 30 (1980), 158–160; 'John 9 – Tradition und Zeitgenossische messianische Diskussion', *BZ* 22 (1978), 245–53, esp. 250; idem, 'Johannesevangelium und Synagogengottesdienst – eine Beobachtung', *BZ* 27 (1983), 101.

[222] James Sanders, *Torah and Canon* (Philadelphia: Fortress Press, 1972), 1–3.

[223] Davidson, *Analytical Hebrew*, 155; Porton, *Understanding Rabbinic Midrash*. Cf. Renée Bloch, 'Midrash', in *Supplément au Dictionnaire de la Bible*, DBSup 5, cols. 1263–81; ET 'Midrash', in *Approaches to Ancient Judaism I*, ed. by W. S. Green, BJS 1 (Missoula, MT: Scholars Press, 1978), 29–50.

The verb דרש occurs in a variety of contexts in the Old Testament meaning 'to seek', 'to inquire', or 'to investigate'.[224]

The principle purpose of this quest was to find life (cf. John 5:39), which is rooted in Scripture itself, for keeping the commandments of the Torah meant life (Lev. 18:5; cf. Bar. 4:1–2). Midrash, which was tied to the biblical text, existed in two forms: (1) *Halakah*, which was primarily concerned with the legal texts of the Bible and their application,[225] and (2) *Haggadah*, which was concerned with matters of doctrine and of historical tradition. Haggadah often amounted to a rewriting of the biblical text itself.[226] While Roger Le Déaut has contended that midrash had not developed into a literary genre by New Testament times,[227] Renée Bloch emphatically has maintained that midrash as a literary genre existed before New Testament times.[228] B. Olsson has gone so far as to propose that the

---

[224] For example, seeking God's will (2 Chr. 17:4; 22:9; 30:19; Ps. 119:10), making inquiry of the Lord through prophetic oracle (1 Sam. 9:9; 1 Kgs. 22:8; 2Kgs. 3:11; Jer. 21:2), or investigating a matter (Deut. 13:14; 19:18; Judg. 6:29; cf. 1QS 6:24; 8:26). In later usage, there is a shift from seeking God's will through prophetic oracle to seeking God's will through the study of Scripture (Ezra 7:10; Ps. 111:2; 119:45, 94, 155. See 1QS 8:15; 4QFlor 1:14; CD 6:7).

[225] *Halakhah*, from הלך, perhaps here meaning 'to walk'. Halakhic midrash often went beyond the exposition of Torah, and reported as law, customs considered authoritative because of their existence or antiquity. Halakhah was both cumulative and open-ended, that is, it continued to transmit from one generation to the next the teachings of rabbis of the past, and it did so in the knowledge that its task was never completed. In constructing the halakhic midrash, the rabbis of the Hellenistic and Roman periods were fulfilling their function as the 'lawyers' of the people of God. The weakness of the halakhah is that, in their zeal for the Torah, the rabbis sometimes pushed too far their ability to codify morality.

[226] Haggadah, from הגד, perhaps meaning 'meditation' or 'narration', is the term applied to the other type of midrash. See Bloch in 'Midrash', in *Supplément au Dictionnaire de la Bible*, 5, cols. 1263–81; ET 'Midrash', in *Approaches to Ancient Judaism I*, 34. '*Midrash haggada*' seeks 'to define the meaning of the stories and events of history'. For instance, the Book of Chronicles is believed to be an example of a haggadic midrash upon the books of Samuel and Kings. This is a category of the *historical haggadah*, and like many other features of Judaism of the Hellenistic and Roman periods, seems to have its roots in the time immediately following the Babylonian exile. The author of Chronicles apparently had a copy of Samuel-Kings as a reference, reproducing certain texts almost verbatim, yet rewriting others. With the passage of time, *historical haggadah* became ever more fanciful, displaying alternative versions of biblical text which could not possibly have been based upon new 'information' but only represented the views of the authors. Two examples from the second century BC, which illustrate this tendency is *Jubilees* and the *Genesis Apocryphon*, the latter being one of the documents discovered at Qumran. Both documents were expansions of the Book of Genesis. *Doctrinal haggadah* is frequently found alongside historical haggadah, but is different in that its main concern is not historical 'data', but the nature of belief and of pious devotion to God.

[227] Roger Le Déaut, 'Apropos a Definition of Midrash', *Int* 25 (1971), 259–82.

[228] Bloch, 'Midrash', in *Supplément au Dictionnaire de la Bible*, 34, writes, 'Nothing could be more wrong than the idea that midrash is a late creation of rabbinic Judaism'. She has no hesitation in putting large sections of the Gospel into the category of midrash. Also see ET 'Midrash', in *Approaches to Ancient Judaism I*, 37.

Fourth Gospel is a midrash on the Gospel tradition.²²⁹ However, the so-called 'Gospel tradition' was not one written document, as the Hebrew Bible was to Jewish exegetes. Certainly John was not writing a midrash on any one of the Synoptic Gospels, or all of them taken together, whatever view we take of his relation to the Synoptics. John seems to attribute his interpretation directly to Jesus himself.

Midrash as a principle of interpretation and its application in the New Testament is subjected to devastating criticism by Richard Hays who objects to its careless use by some biblical scholars. Although Hays's focus is confined to the Pauline epistles, yet the basic tenets of his criticism are widely applicable, including to the Fourth Gospel.²³⁰ Hays argues that when some scholars claim this or that portion of the New Testament is an instance of midrashic interpretation, it is not at all clear what such affirmations are supposed to mean. If it means that a biblical author has interpreted Scripture in such a manner as to make it applicable to his own time and circumstances, 'surely everyone would have to assent: the claim is true but trivial. In that sense, all readings of Scripture by Jews and Christians always and everywhere are instances of midrash.'²³¹ The difficulty with the label 'midrash' lies in its

> simultaneous imprecision and authoritative mysteriousness: the label *midrash* tends to bring the interpretive process to a halt, as though it had explained something, when in fact we should keep pressing for clarity: what poetic linkages of sound or imagery make this sort of imaginative leap possible, what effects are produced in the argument by it, and what sort of response does it invite from the sympathetic reader's imagination?²³²

Midrash as a 'descriptive category' is so vague that it can be applied to considerable portions of the Old and New Testaments. Almost any free use of Scripture can be called midrash.²³³ To use the name 'midrash' to explain unusual exegeses or free interpretations is highly questionable and unconvincing.²³⁴ Hays highlights other methodical problems with midrash as a

---

²²⁹ Olsson, *Structure and Meaning*, 284–85; cf. Hanson, 'John's Use of Scripture', 361.

²³⁰ Hays, *Echoes of Scripture*, 10–14.

²³¹ Ibid., 197 n. 32.

²³² Ibid., 14.

²³³ For Hays, *Echoes*, 11, midrash does not even offer a proper *historical* background against which one may understand the New Testament writings because of the complexity of various problems, such as the late date of rabbinic sources.

²³⁴ Hays, *Echoes*, 14, believes this is precisely the sense in which midrash has caught the fancy of deconstructionists and some of the modern literary theorists who have found in rabbinic midrash a historical precedent and analogue for their own interpretive practices. His examples of such deconstructionists are: Susan A. Handelman, *The Slayers of Moses: The Emergence of Rabbinic Interpretation in Modern Literary Theory* (Albany: State University of New York Press, 1982);

descriptive category. These include using midrash as a form-critical 'map' when it is not,[235] or speaking of midrash as a hermeneutical method as if the rabbis addressed their hermeneutical task through a series of specific and clearly defined interpretive rules,[236] when such an assumption is destined for disappointment.[237] Therefore, it seems unlikely that midrash is a proper hermeneutical framework within which John's distinct interpretive approach to the Scriptures may be explicated.

Some scholars have suggested John's interpretive method needs to be understood in the context of *Pesharim* which was a prevalent approach in the Qumran community. *Pesher* is given by divine illumination, an interpretation beyond the power of natural wisdom. *Pesher* is the revelation of a mystery.[238] In the Qumran texts, this kind of mystery is denoted by the term רז (*raz*),[239] an expression traceable to the Book of Daniel. For the Essenes at Qumran, the divine purpose cannot be properly understood until the *pesher* has been revealed. Such secrets or mysteries (רז) were communicated by God to the prophets. Nevertheless, the meaning of that communication remains sealed until its *pesher* is made known by God to his chosen interpreter. The chosen interpreter in Qumran was the Teacher of Righteousness, the founder of the Qumran community (1QpHab 2:8–9; cf. 1QpHab 8:1–3). Thus, in this scenario, the revelation comes in two parts, the initial revelation and then its interpretation. The meaning of revelation is not made plain until the two parts are brought together. In addition, the nature of revelation appears to have been predominantly eschatological – the time of the end, the last generation – and the fact that the Teacher of Righteousness had now been raised up to interpret the words of the prophets was a token that the time of the end was imminent.

Pesharim do not seem to have entailed too drastic changes or additions to the biblical text. They are the product of a community which believed itself to be living at the threshold of the eschaton and viewed the events of their time as the fulfilment of Scripture.[240] Much of what is found in *Pesharim* is in the form of what was later called *Midrash*. But in contradistinction to the material found in the rabbinical midrashic

---

William Scott Green, 'Romancing the Tome: Rabbinic Hermeneutics and the Theory of Literature', *Semeia* 40 (1987), 147–68.

[235] Hays, *Echoes*, 12.

[236] Ibid., rules such as the seven *middot* of Hillel and the thirteen *middot* of Rabbi Ishmael.

[237] See Alexander, 'Rabbinic Judaism', 242–44; Hays, *Echoes*, 12.

[238] Bruce, *Biblical Exegesis*, 8–9.

[239] Ibid.

[240] Ithamar Gruenwald, *Apocalyptic and Merkavah Mysticism* (Leiden: Brill, 1980), 23.

literature, many of the Qumran *Pesharim* are presented as the exclusive revelations of secrets. Here, for the first time, one hears that Scripture cannot, and should not, be read only for its external meaning. This awareness of the existence of an inner truth was complemented by the revelation of that very truth.[241] Added to this was the pseudepigraphic way of writing, which was sometimes interpreted as the result of the desire to enhance the element of secrecy. '"Esotericism" thus is taken to mean a special attitude towards Scripture and the explication of its content.'[242]

In view of these various elements, it is easy to characterise *Pesher* as a sectarian hermeneutic because of its claim to exclusive revelation of the true meaning of Scriptures.[243] There are obvious similarities between John's interpretation of Scriptures and *Pesher*. Whether John knew of Qumran, or was in touch with the community, or was influenced by their hermeneutic, is a topic in its own right. However, these similarities are more of an appearance than reality.

The Qumran commentators did not claim, for example, that the Teacher of Righteousness was the one to whom all prophetic Scripture pointed, although his career was foretold there. He was simply the interpreter of mysteries. Qumran scribes believed that all prophetic Scripture was concerned with the fulfilment of God's purpose in the end-time, and that the key to the understanding of this purpose had been granted to their Teacher. But John presented Jesus as the very embodiment and fulfilment of God's purpose, the One in whom all the promises of God found their 'yes' (2 Cor. 1:20); and the Scriptures spoke of him (Jn. 1:45; 5:39–47; cf. Lk. 24:44; Acts 10:43). Furthermore neither John nor other New Testament writers laid claim to an exclusive revelation of the meaning of Scriptures as was the case in Qumran.[244] These writers believed the revelation was clear; the prophetic promise of the Messianic day was realised in their time: 'Blessed are the eyes that see what you see...for many prophets and kings wished to see what you see, and saw it not' (Lk.

---

[241] To see in the Scriptures multiple layers of inner truth apart from the obvious external meaning is the essence of the esoteric approach to Scripture. Apocalypticism was often described as being esoteric in nature, mainly because it pertained to an exclusive revelation of secrets. See D. S. Russell, *The Method and Message of Jewish Apocalyptic* (London: SCM, 1964), 107ff.; A. Böhlig, *Mysterion und Wahrheit* (Leiden: Brill, 1968), 3–40.

[242] Gruenwald, *Apocalyptic and Merkavah Mysticism*, 22.

[243] G. Scholem, *Zur Kabbala und Symbolik* (Zürich: Rhein-Verlag, 1960), 49–116, 159–207, believes it was only natural for Jewish groups who propagated dissident views to base their views and ideas on Scripture. This was generally done by claiming an exclusive revelation of the true meaning of Scripture.

[244] Ibid.

10:23-24; cf. Lk. 16:16; Mk. 1:14-15 [Dan. 2:44; 7:22]; Acts 2:14-17; 2 Cor. 6:2; 1 Cor. 10:11; Heb. 1:2; 9:26; 1 Peter 1:5, 9, 10-12).[245] Thus in contrast to Qumran *Pesherim* which saw the eschatological events yet in the future, in the Fourth Gospel, the dawn of the time of salvation was already a present event. The early Christians looked back on the coming of the Messiah as the surety of salvation.[246]

It is likely that John was familiar with some of the prevalent Jewish interpretive practices at the time of composing his Gospel. But this possible awareness does not mean the adoption or assimilation of these methods. The assumption that an author necessarily has to follow in the steps of some antecedent tradition and cannot be creative is dubious. At the root of every tradition lies an originator.

There were two compelling reasons why the New Testament writers were positively disposed to such creative thinking in the interpretation of the Scriptures. First, they stood at the threshold of what they perceived to be the climactic point of salvation history.[247] The cross and resurrection had changed how the evangelists read and understood the Scriptures. Secondly, and equally as important, it was Jesus himself, according to the evangelists, who had taught his disciples that Scriptures spoke of him (Jn. 5:39-47; cf. Lk. 24:25-27, 44; Mk. 4:11f). Thus, if there is to be any antecedent exegetical 'tradition', then that tradition must be traced back to Jesus himself. He had put into their hands the interpretive key which enabled them to unlock the Scripture and understand how all that was written came true in him (Jn. 1:45; Lk. 24:44; Acts 10:43). However, to say that the New Testament writers, including John, had a privileged position in salvation history which profoundly affected their interpretation of the Scriptures is not to say that there was a total disjunction with their past. Jesus' followers located themselves in the Jewish tradition. They saw themselves as 'true Israel'.[248] It was in the context of the Jewish tradition, and specifically Jewish Messianic tradition, that they addressed the Jews when the made claims 'according to the Scriptures'; and it was the language of Scripture which they used when they spoke about the

---

[245] Dodd, *According to the Scriptures*, 67ff.

[246] See Paul's citation from Isaiah 49 in 2 Cor. 6:2. This 'day of salvation' has now come!

[247] By salvation history, I mean the belief that God's dealings with his people, from the call of Abraham until the coming of the Messiah, should be regarded as a history of salvation. In this context, one may expect a certain pattern in God's dealing with his people which will be reflected in what happens in the Messianic age.

[248] M. F. Wiles, 'The Old Testament in Controversy with the Jews', *SJT* 8 (1955), 113-26.

'gospel'.[249] Those who proclaimed Jesus as Israel's Messiah were faced with a formidable interpretive agenda. Quite naturally, they turned to Israel's Scriptures to support the claim that the crucified Jesus of Nazareth was the risen Saviour, the Messiah of Israel.[250]

John, like Paul, is convinced that the real meaning of the Scriptures was concealed until the time of their realisation which now had come in Jesus Christ, although unlike Paul in 2 Cor. 3:12–18, he does not make any direct statement to this effect.[251] Rather, it seems as if he applies Paul's statement in 2 Cor. 3:14 in minute detail to show that Jesus is the 'meaning' of the Scriptures – the 'revelation of revelation'. This is carried out intricately in John's systematic appeal to the Scriptures. Revelation in the Torah must now be understood in light of the revelation in Christ who reveals the significance of what was given in the Torah. Christ appears to be, for John, the foundational equivalent of the wisdom of God (Jn. 1:1–18; cf. 1 Cor. 1:24, 30; 2:6f.; 8:6; cf. Col. 1:15–18; 2:3); and thus Christ becomes the key for understanding the revelation, whether in the Gospel, in Scripture, or in creation. He is the exegesis of that revelation (Jn. 1:18). The christological interpretation of Scripture is not confined to John. Most, if not all, New Testament writers read their Scriptures in view of the conviction that he is the promised Messiah of Israel.[252]

John's interpretation of the Old Testament is not only christological but also eschatological. In fact, Johannine eschatology is only meaningful in the context of its christology. The two are inseparably interwoven in the Fourth Gospel. G. B. Caird contends:

In the Fourth Gospel there is nothing that could be construed as imminent Parousia, since the End is so totally identified with Christ that eschatology is transposed into Christology (Jn. 11:25). One by one John takes the terms which were traditionally associated with the Last Day, and shows how they have found their total fulfilment in the incarnate life of Jesus.[253]

---

[249] Donald Juel, *Messianic Exegesis* (Philadelphia: Fortress, 1988), 14.

[250] See Nils A. Dahl, *Jesus the Christ: The Historical Origins of Christological Doctrine* (Minneapolis: Fortress Press, 1991); idem, 'The Crucified Messiah and the Endangered Promises', *Word and World* 3 (1983), 251–62; Scholem, *Messianic Idea in Judaism*, 1; W. Foerster and G. Fohrer, 'σωτήρ' and 'σωτηρία' in *TWNT* 7 (1964), 1004–22; 966–1004, = *TDNT* 7 (1971), 1003–21, 965–1033; D. Greeves, 'The Recognized Saviour', *ExpTim* 93 (1981–82), 84–6; Lindars, *New Testament Apologetic*, 75–137, 251–86.

[251] The closest to a direct statement may be in 5:39, 46.

[252] E.g., Paul in 1 Cor. 1:24, 30, 2:6f., 8:6, 9:10, 10:11; 2 Cor. 1:20, 3:12–18; Col. 1:15–18, 2:3; Rom. 4:23f., 15:4; cf. Lk. 24:25–27, 44.

[253] G. B. Caird, *New Testament Theology*, completed and ed. by L. D. Hurst (Oxford: Clarendon, 1994), 263; Dodd, *According to the Scriptures*, 67ff.

John's approach to the Scriptures implicitly follows the principle of 'this is that' spoken by the prophets and witnessed to by the Scriptures (Jn. 1:45; cf. Acts 2:14-17; 10:43). John himself does not express his understanding in these words, but the assumption is always in the background. This interpretive approach should not be confused with typological reading of the Old Testament.[254] John's reading of the Old Testament cannot legitimately be called typological in the sense of typology proper.[255] In the Fourth Gospel, Scriptures bear witness to Jesus and this is more than an analogical correspondence. In typology, the past is read into the present in such that 'this' (present) is similar to or resembles 'that' (past).[256] John does not claim similarities. He does not use the Old Testament to say that certain events and ideas *correspond* to the actions, events, and meaning of Jesus' life in a typological or allegorical way.[257] He seems to be saying much more than that. His contention is far more radical, whereby in effect he claims in Jesus Christ 'this' (present) is the realisation or consummation of 'that' (past). The giving of manna, or sacrifice of the Paschal lamb, is not simply an illustration of Jesus. Rather they are 'shadows' or 'sketches' of the reality of which Jesus is the genuine embodiment, realisation, or consummation. He has put an end to transgression, atoned for iniquity, and brought in everlasting righteousness sealed in his own blood. Therefore, he is vindicated in his right to be hailed as 'the Lord's Anointed', the Holy One of God. It is in this light that the New Testament writers can interpret 'in all the Scriptures the things concerning himself' (Lk. 24:27), and John can say that 'the Scriptures are they which bear witness to him' (Jn. 5:39).

For some modern exegetes, John's hermeneutical approach may seem

---

[254] As with R. N. Longenecker, *Biblical Exegesis in the Apostolic Period* (Grand Rapids: Eerdmans, 1975), 152-57; J. W. Drane, 'Typology', *EvQ* 50 (1978), 195-210; L. Goppelt, *Typos: The Typological Interpretation of the Old Testament in the New* (Grand Rapids: Eerdmans, 1982); R. H. Smith, 'Exodus Typology in the Fourth Gospel', *JBL* 81 (1962), 329-42.

[255] Reim, *Studien zum alttestamentlichen*, 265.

[256] Thus R. P. C. Hanson, *Allegory and Event* (London: SCM, 1959), 56f, defines typology as 'interpreting an event of the present or recent past as the fulfilment of a similar situation recorded or prophesied in Scripture'. Cf. G. W. H. Lampe and K. J. Woolcombe, *Essays in Typology* (London: SCM, 1957); Elizabeth Harris, *Prologue and Gospel: The Theology of the Fourth Evangelist*, JSNTSup, (Sheffield: Academic Press, 1994), 140. However, if typology is defined as M. Knowles, *Jeremiah in Matthew's Gospel: The Rejected Prophet Motif in Matthaean Redaction*, JSNTSup 68 (Sheffield: JSOT Press, 1993), 223, defines it, 'the perception of significant correspondences between the characters and circumstances of two different historical individuals...so that each is understood either as an anticipation or as a fulfilment of the other', then in this sense perhaps Johannine approach may be characterised as typological.

[257] The difference between *typology* and *allegory* is that in typology there seems to be an intrinsic connection between the type and the fulfillment, whereas in allegory the connection is purely arbitrary. Hanson, *Allegory and Event*, 56f.

Chapter 5: Israel's Scriptures and the Language of John's Gospel

fanciful, or perhaps, by modern critical standards, somewhat unsound. For present-day scholars of Judaism who come fresh from artful rabbinic exegesis, the Johannine approach to the Scripture may appear intriguing but not dramatically unusual. Those who are familiar, for example, with Philo, Qumran or Jewish mysticism will feel very much at home with the Fourth Gospel. Nevertheless, whatever our views might be about John's interpretive approach by modern critical standards,[258] including the question of whether John's hermeneutic had an interpretive antecedent, these concerns are inconsequential to our primary exegetical task.

For all we know, it was Jesus himself who 'licensed' his disciples and indeed gave them a mandate to read Israel's Scriptures christologically, i.e., in the light of what they knew about his life, works, and work (Lk. 24:25–27; Jn. 5:39, 45), and of course, for the disciples, the resurrection would have been a hermeneutical watershed. What we can establish with certainty, however, is that John's interpretation of Scripture is not atomistic. He does not take Scriptures out of context. Rather, his hermeneutic is very much governed by his awareness of God's redemptive activity among the Jews throughout the Israelite history as recorded in their Scriptures. Scripture, for John, was being fulfilled in the person and work of Jesus Christ against the background of the saving events of the past. However, whether one can trace a progressive exegesis of Scripture involving particular schemes of salvation history running through the Gospel is a topic in its own right.[259]

We have already noted such redemptive-historical themes in the context of the Passover and John's interaction with the law. Similar themes can be traced in reference to the Johannine 'Word of God'. 'The Word', who appeared to the Patriarchs and to Moses at Sinai, now appears in the person of Jesus Christ (1:14–18).[260] The theophanic revelations of God in

---

[258] But see *The Jerome Biblical Commentary*, ed. by R. E. Brown, et al. (London: Geoffrey Chapman, 1968), 2:611; B. Lindars and P. Borgen, 'The Place of the Old Testament in the Formation of New Testament Theology', *NTS* 23 (1976), 59–66.

[259] A. Guilding, *The Fourth Gospel and Jewish Worship* (Oxford: OUP, 1960), argues for such a systematic exegetical scheme.

[260] God has never been seen or heard except by means of the *Word*. John 1:35–51 goes even further back to the revelation of the Word to Jacob at Bethel (Gen. 28:10–22). The theme is resumed at 5:37, where not only are the theophanies under the old dispensation attributed to the *Word*, but also the occasions on which Moses or the Israelites were reported as hearing God's voice. It seems probable that one of the passages lying behind Jesus' mysterious utterance in 7:38 is the story of the riven rock in the wilderness (Exod. 17:6; Num. 20:8). If this is the case, then the rock is a type of Christ. On the other hand, John may be thinking in a similar vein as Paul in 1 Cor. 10:4 where he regards the *Word* as having been the author of the life-giving water from the rock. In 8:35, there are echoes of Isaac who prefigures Jesus Christ in Genesis 22. Although Issac

the past history of Israel, for the Evangelist, are the culmination of revelation of God in and through 'the Word' which now has been manifested in the climax of redemptive history in the incarnation of 'the Word'. Against this background, the subtle and systematic allusions to the Old Testament express the Evangelist's conviction that in Jesus Christ the consummation of divine redemptive work has been realised.[261] This salvation-historical perspective runs through the document like a thread, from the first chapter to the end. John's Gospel rivets with a sense of events moving towards the consummation of a salvific work of God in human history. The revelation of God in this context entered its climactic dispensation when 'the Word' became flesh. For the Evangelist, Jesus has fulfilled the Scriptures. John shows that what happened to and through Jesus was the result of the outworking of God's purpose. This understanding, in turn, governs John's interpretive approach to the Scriptures.

Salvation history provides the essential framework within which John is able to formulate his christological interpretation of the Scriptures. A significant implication of this salvation-historical perspective is John's view about the viability of Judaism. From the Evangelist's point of view, Judaism as a religious system is obsolete.[262] Its tenets are fulfilled in the person, life, and work of Jesus the Christ. The incarnation, cross and resurrection have sealed the fate of Judaism and closed it as a chapter in God's book of the history of redemption. Judaism, in its sacrificial rituals, its temple cult, and even the law is a shadow of the reality of 'the Word' made flesh. Having

---

is never mentioned by name in John, some commentators find an allusion in 3:16 and 19:17. Brown, *John*, 147, 917; F. M. Braun, *Jean le théologien: Les grandes traditions d'Israël et l'accord des écritures selon le quatrième évangile*, EBib (Paris: Gabalda, 1964), 179–80. In John 8:39–59, there are allusions to the visit of the three angels in Genesis 18, one of whom may be identified with the pre-existent Word. Perhaps it is in view of this that Jesus can claim for Abraham to have seen him. This is particularly striking because Jesus actually recalls an event that happened over a millennium before his birth, something quite incompatible with the actual historical Jesus. In 10:35–36, there seems to be another allusion to the *Word* addressing Israel just after the revelation on Sinai, as narrated in Psalm 82. Then in 12:37–41, in Isaiah's vision in the Temple, it was the *Word*, according to John, whose glory Isaiah had seen and with whom the prophet had conversed. Once more, the *Word* is seen as the visible revelation of God. In 13:18a, there is an echo of the rebellion of the Korahites narrated in Numbers 16. If so, the Evangelist projects back into the wilderness period again, for Jesus uses the words that God is recorded as using then. In looking at 14:8–9, there seems to be a general reference to the theophanies under the old dispensation from Genesis 32 onwards. In all these instances, the Father is revealed through the visible manifestation of the Word, the eternal mode of God's self revelation.

[261] See Hengel, *Schriftauslegung*, 263.

[262] Cf. H. Seebass, 'Moses', *NIDNTT* 2:641 and the even stronger statement by von Campenhausen, *Formation of the Christian Bible*, 52.

demonstrated from the Scriptures that Jesus is the Messiah, in whom the Scriptures find their ultimate fulfilment, and having argued that Jesus' death was neither a fabrication nor an accident but was in absolute conformity to the Scriptures, the Evangelist then shows that the response of Judaism in itself is not surprising, but was foretold in the Scriptures.

5.5. The Prophecy of Isaiah and an Explanation of the Opponents' Incomprehension

An important question which may have faced the Christian community would have been Why was unbelief the response of 'the Jews' to the many signs performed by Jesus? If John could see such a scriptural fulfilment in the life and career of Jesus, why do the Jewish religious elders miss it? Chapter 12 of John plays a prominent part in John's explanation as to why the elders of Israel did not recognise Jesus as the Christ, leading to his rejection and subsequent crucifixion.[263] In this chapter, the Evangelist endeavours to explain the rejection of Jesus by the religious elders in terms of their blindness to the very document they venerated as the source of life (5:39).[264] This explanation would have functioned as both a warning and an invitation. It would have been a warning to the secret Christians to come into the open with their faith or stand under the same judgment. It would have also functioned as an evangelistic invitation and an encouragement to the undecided Jews to examine the Scriptures for themselves and see that Jesus had fulfilled them in his life and works. Therefore, he is the One whom he claimed to be. The effect on the Christian community would have been similar. It would have reassured them in their path and encouraged them not to be intimidated by such 'blind guides of the blind.'

5.5.1. Incomprehension and Spiritual Blindness

The Fourth Gospel hinges on the twelfth chapter both structurally and theologically. This chapter looks backward in a reflective summary and forward to the events of the cross and resurrection, while explaining the

---

[263] Any effort designed to convince the Jews that Jesus was the Messiah had to give a satisfactory explanation for Jesus' rejection and humiliating death upon a Roman cross. This need in the Fourth Gospel is met by the inclusion of a Passion account. D. M. Smith,'The Setting and Shape of a Johannine Narrative Source', in *Johannine Christianity: Essays on Its Setting, Sources, and Theology* (Columbia, SC: University of South Carolina Press, 1984), 236–8; Kee, *Jesus in History*, 238.

[264] Cf. Mt. 15:14, 31; 23:16–17, 19, 24, 26; Lk. 4:18; Rom. 2:19; 11:7; 2 Cor. 3:14.

incomprehension of 'the Jews' and their rejection of the Messiah in terms of spiritual blindness and further prophetic fulfilment of the Scriptures. Structurally, the twelfth chapter ties together the 'Book of Signs' (chapters 2–11) and the 'Book of the Passion' (chapters 13–20)[265] and tries to explain why a Messianic claimant who performed so many Messianic signs was rejected and crucified. The distinctive stylistic feature of this segment of the Gospel is the regularity of the ἵνα πληρωθῇ formula which occurs from 12:38 onwards through the Passion. Undoubtedly, just as the earlier quotation formulas and the quotations themselves were to show that various details in the public ministry of Jesus were to be viewed in terms of correspondence to certain Old Testament passages (i.e., 'just as it is written'), so in this segment beginning in 12:38, the details of the Passion are regarded as accomplished in order to fulfil Scripture (i.e., 'in order that it be fulfilled').[266]

Though unbelief of the religious authorities is the underlying cause of the rejection of Jesus and the crucifixion is the ultimate expression of that unbelief (cf. Acts 13:27), yet the unbelief is predicted and is itself in fulfilment of the Scriptures. To explain the tragic response of unbelief by the Jewish religious leaders, John appeals to the most monumental of the Hebrew literary prophets – Isaiah.[267] Why Jewish leaders and not the whole nation? Careful scrutiny of the prophetic literature reveals that Israel's prophets often saw the unfaithfulness and unbelief of the Israelites as a symptom and consequence of the unfaithfulness and unbelief in the elders of the nation. When the leaders of Israel followed the Lord in righteousness, the nation followed suit. On the other hand, whenever the

---

[265] Dodd, *Interpretation*, 289; Smith, 'Setting and Shape', 239, 240; G. MacRae, 'The Fourth Gospel and Religionsgeschiehte', *CBQ* 32 (1970), 20–1.

[266] All nine quotations from John 12:38 onwards are *specifically* presented as the fulfilment of Scriptures. Fulfilment can be claimed in the mere quotation of Scripture without a fulfilment formula, as it is in 12:14–15. That being the case, the cluster of fulfilment formulae from 12:38 on might indicate a special cluster of *testimonia*, such as was suggested by Rendel Harris in *Testimonies*, 2 vols (Cambridge: CUP, 1916–1920), esp. 1:18.

[267] J. M. Lieu, 'Blindness in the Johannine Tradition', *NTS* 34 (1988), 83–95; Craig A. Evans, 'Obduracy and the Lord's Servant: Some Observations on the Use of the Old Testament in the Fourth Gospel', in *Early Jewish and Christian Exegesis: Studies in Memory of William Hugh Brownlee*, ed. by C. A. Evans and W. F. Stinespring (Atlanta: Scholars Press, 1987), 221–36; idem, *To See and Not Perceive: Isaiah 6:9–10 in Early Jewish and Christian Interpretation*, JSNTSup 64 (Sheffield: Sheffield Academic Press, 1989), 133; also R. Brandscheidt, 'Prophetischer Verstockungsauftrag und Christlicher Glaube. Die alttestamentlichen Zitate in Jn. 12, 37–43', *Trierer Theologische Zeitschrift* 102 (93), 64–76; John Painter, 'The Quotation of Scripture and Unbelief in John 12:36B–43', in *The Gospels and the Scriptures of Israel*, ed. by Craig A. Evans and W. Richard Stegner, JSNTSup 104 (Sheffield: Academic Press, 1994), 429–58.

elders and leaders of the nation failed to trust the Lord and walk before God in righteousness, their unfaithfulness and unbelief spread among the people like an epidemic. Thus often Old Testament writers and prophets speak of Israel in a generic way when in fact the leaders of the nation are in focus.[268] This seems to be in the background of Isaiah's indictment in Isa. 6:9-10 as well, which resonates in John centuries later.[269]

In this respect, the situation of Isaiah is important as a paradigm for understanding what was happening in the Evangelist's day. The Evangelist appeals to Isaiah to demonstrate the continuation of a pattern of unbelief (cf. Acts 7:51). For John, Israel's impenitence (12:37) recalls the visionary call of Isaiah (Isa. 6:1-13). The unbelief of the Jews at the time of Jesus and John resembles the unbelief in the days of Isaiah, giving the impression that this was the pervasive response in Jesus' day.[270] Just as the witness of the prophet to the glory of the eternal Word was met with unbelief, so was the witness of the Evangelist to the glory of the incarnate Word. Jesus and his messengers fare no better than the greatest of Israel's writing prophets. Though the unbelief of Israel is grounded in the divine mystery, an illuminating clue is given: 'Isaiah said this because he saw his (i.e., Christ's) glory and spoke of him' (Jn. 12:41). It was not the Father whom Isaiah saw in his visionary call (cf. Jn. 1:18; Exod. 33:20), but the pre-existent Living Word in his heavenly glory. Isaiah, like Abraham (8:56), had a Christ-vision, and through it became a witness to Christ.[271] Bernard goes further. He contends, 'In the vision of Isaiah 6, the prophet contemplates the awful glory of the invisible God; but the evangelist, in affirming that he spoke of the glory of *Christ*, identifies Christ with the Yahweh of Israel'.[272]

R. E. Clements has shown that the theme of spiritual blindness and deafness which is so prominent in the second segment of the Book of Isaiah presupposes and builds upon the initial presentation of the motif in Isaiah 6:9-10a (cf. Isa. 29:18; 35:5; 42; 16:18-19; 43:8; 44:18).[273] But this

---

[268] E.g., 1 Kgs. 22:17; Isa. 3:12; Jer. 23:2; Ezk. 8:6-18; 34:1-10.

[269] Cf. Isa. 1:10, 23; 3:12, 14-15; 7:1-13.

[270] Lieu, 'Biblical Theology', 93-107; idem, 'Blindness', 83-95.

[271] Schnackenburg, *Johannes*, 2:520, 'Er sprach über Jesus und seine Tätigkeit des 'Heilens'. Der Prophet, der die Herrlichkeit Jesu sah und um seine Heilssendung wusste, musste dennoch bezeugen, dass eine Heilung der ungläubig-verstockten Menschen durch Jesus nach dem Willen Gottes ausgeschlossen ist'.

[272] *St. John*, 452.

[273] R. E. Clements, 'The Unity of the Book of Isaiah', *Int* 36 (1982), 117-129; idem, 'Beyond Tradition-History: Deutero-Isaianic Development of First Isaiah's Themes', *JSOT* 31 (1985), 95-113.

theme also appears elsewhere in the Israelite prophetic literature, and it may be the case that its presence in Isaiah simply reflects a motif common to much of the prophetic material where the people's condition is presented as resulting from their own unbelief, unfaithfulness and sinfulness (e.g., Jer. 5:21; Ezk. 3:7). For example, the similarities between Isaiah 6 and the vision of Micaiah ben Imlah in 1 Kings 22:19-22 have long been recognised.[274]

The impact of Isaiah 6:9-10 in the New Testament (Mk. 4:11-12; Mt. 13:15 par.; Acts 13:38-52; 28:23-28; Rom. 10:16; 11:7-10),[275] especially its importance to the argument of the Fourth Gospel as a means of explicating the unresponsiveness of the Jews and their rejection of revelation, is extensive and well attested.[276] Among the canonical Gospels, there is no direct parallel in the Synoptics to John's combination of editorial references to Isaiah in 12:37-41 and his account of Jesus' final attempt to persuade the Jews to believe in him (esp. 12:35-36). The Johannine explanation for unbelief of the Jews in 12:37-41 and its 'terminal' mood has caused unending difficulty for biblical scholars who have had to explain its serious theological implications.[277] The theme of spiritual blindness evident in the Fourth Gospel[278] is deeply imbedded within the Isaianic tradition (e.g., 29:10, 18-19; 42:6-7, 18-20; 43:8-10; 56:10; 59:9-11),[279] but also present in other prophetic and Deuteronomic material (Deut.

---

[274] N. Habel, 'The Form and Significance of the Call Narratives', *ZAW* 77 (1965), 310.

[275] Lindars, *New Testament Apologetic*, 159-61; J. Gnilka, *Die Verstockung Israels* (Munich: Kösel, 1961). The reference to Isaiah 6:10 is also evidenced outside of New Testament. See, for example, the *Apocryphon of John*, NHC II.22:26-28. Even Justin refers to it in an effort to explain why Trypho cannot understand the Old Testament 'proofs' for the Messiah's two advents (*Dial.* 33.1; also 12.2).

[276] John 12:40 is anticipated in John 9:39 where Jesus claims explicitly to effect blindness (cf. 1 John 2:11).

[277] C. A. Evans, 'The Function of Isaiah 6:9-10 in Mark and John', *NovT* 24 (1982), 124-38; idem, 'The Hermeneutics of Mark and John: On the Theology of the Canonical "Gospel"' *Bib* 64 (1983), 153-72, esp. 162-4. See also F. Watson, 'The Social Function of Mark's Secrecy Theme', *JSNT* 24 (1985), 49-69, esp. 62-3.

[278] For a similar theme of 'spiritual blindness' elsewhere in the New Testament, see for example Mt. 15:14, 31; 23:16, 17, 19, 24, 26; Lk. 4:18. Cf. Rom. 2:19; 11:7; 2 Cor. 3:14; Rev. 3:17; also the Qumran scrolls (e.g., 1QS 4:11; CD 1:9).

[279] Freed, *OT Quotations*, 87; Evans, 'Function of Isaiah 6:9-10', 134-35; Menken, 'Joh 12,40', 200; Lieu, 'Blindness', 88; Schuchard, *Scripture within Scripture*, 102. In Isaiah 29:10, it is the Lord who blinds. In Isaiah 43:8, God as redeemer gathers the blind (cf. 29:18; 35:5; 61:1; see also Ps. 146 [145]:8). Isaiah 56:10 may refer to a condition similar to Isaiah 6:9-10 (Isa. 56:10 in the perfect tense as Jn. 12:40). But while John 12:40 uses τυφλόω, Isaiah 56:10 uses ἐκτυφλόω. Isaiah 42:18-20 bears much in common with Isaiah 6:9-10. Isaiah 42:18-20, like Isaiah 6:9-10, laments over those who have turned back (42:17). The Septuagint's καμμύω appears in the New Testament only at Matthew 13:15 and Acts 28:27.

29:4; Jer. 5:21).[280] Throughout the Fourth Gospel, the tragedy of 'seeing' and 'not being able to perceive' is developed into a complex theme woven into the language of 'light/darkness' (9:5; 1:5; 3:17, 20). Long before reaching chapter 12, there are clear echoes in chapter 9 of the question of the crowd, 'Who is this Son of Man?' (12:34; cf. 9:36), in the awareness of the presence of Light as a time soon to be ended (9:4–5; cf. 12:35; 8:12; 11:9–10), and in the verdict of John 9:39 (cf. 9:18 and Isa. 29:10, 18).[281] The verdict of John 9:39 already anticipates Isaiah 6:9 (cf. Mk. 4:12; 8:18; Lk. 8:10; Mt. 13:13). Jesus' explanation in the accounts of Mark 4:11–12 and Matthew 13:13–15 for teaching in parables is in fulfilment of Isaiah 6:9 as well. Luke 8:10 conveys the Markan idea of purpose, but reserves the full quotation, with the same variation from the Septuagint as Matthew, for the end of his whole account in Acts. For Luke, the prophecy of Isaiah explains why Paul in Rome turned from the Jews to the Gentiles (Acts 28:25–28). The quotation thus becomes a judgment on the total pattern of Jewish unbelief in the face of the preaching of the church. Like Luke-Acts, John uses the quotation in hindsight on the course of the ministry of Jesus.[282]

Both the theme and the vocabulary of 'blindness' are also present in the First Epistle of John (1 Jn. 2:11); but in the Epistle, they are applied to the believing community itself. In First John, the mark of spiritual sight is the love of the brethren (1 Jn. 2:8–11).[283] The same vivid images of 'darkness' occur within the Gospel although they are rather more scattered. In John 12:35, 'the one walking in darkness knows not where he is going (ποῦ ὑπάγει)', and the threat is that darkness might 'seize you (ὑμᾶς καταλάβῃ)'. In the Fourth Gospel, there is One who does know where he is going – Jesus himself (8:21; 13:33, 36; 14:4, 5; 16:5) who is the light of the world (8:12; 11:9). Darkness is unable to 'seize' or 'overcome' (καταλαμβάνω) him (1:5).

---

[280] R. Kühschelm, *Verstockung, Gericht und Heil*, BBB 76 (Frankfurt am Main: Lang, 1990), 85–8.

[281] John 9:39 echoes the preceding verse in 9:18 (cf. Isaiah 29:18 where the positive is expressed).

[282] C. K. Barrett, *Essays on John* (London: SPCK, 1982), 107.

[283] G. Klein, 'Das Wahre Licht scheint schon', *ZTK* 68 (1971), 261–326. In First John, the blinding force is 'the darkness'. Cf. the implicit dualistic verbal parallels in later Gnostic writing such as, *Apoc. Peter* (NHC VII.3) 73:12–13; 76:21–23; also *Gospel of Truth* 29:26–30:16; NB 30:15–16, 'And blessed is he who has opened the eyes of the blind', in *The Nag Hammadi Library in English*, ed. by J. Robinson (Leiden: Brill, 1977), 43. Also in Jewish traditions, we find in the QL and the *Testaments of the Twelve Patriarchs*. NB *T. Judah* 18:6, '...because they have blinded his soul and he walks in the day as in the night'.

Within the context of the Johannine quotation of Isaiah, there are also important questions as to what version of the Jewish Scriptures (i.e., Hebrew, Greek, or Aramaic) the Evangelist may have used. It is difficult to know what kind of access to manuscripts the Evangelist may have had. Were the Scriptures learned by heart and cited or alluded to from memory? Some have suggested that John intentionally deviates from a particular textual tradition and modifies his citations in order to adapt them to their eventual literary and theological context.[284] If John's citations are the product of purposeful editorial modifications to suit his own authorial intent, then it will be impossible definitively to determine his textual traditions.[285] If the Evangelist is citing a given text from memory, which would not have been uncommon in his cultural environment,[286] then questioning whether he cites from a specific textual tradition, or from a text not known to us, or whether he is offering his own rendering of an Old Testament passage would also seem to be an 'an exercise in futility.'[287]

---

[284] M. J. J. Menken, 'The Quotation from Isa. 40:3 in John 1:23' *Bib* 66 (1985), 190–205; idem, 'Die Form des Zitates aus 6,10 in Joh 12,40', 189–209; 'The Old Testament Quotation in John 6:45: Source and Redaction', *ETL* 64 (1988), 164–72; 'The Provenance and Meaning of the Old Testament Quotation in John 6:31', *NovT* 30 (1988), 39–56; 'Die Redaktion des Zitates aus Sach 9:9 in Joh 12:15', *ZNW* 25 (1989), 193–209; 'The Translation of Psalm 41:10 in John 13:18', *JSNT* 40 (1990), 61–79. But on the other hand, see George Richter, 'Die alttestamentlichen Zitate in der Rede vom Himmelsbrot Joh 6,25–51a', in *Schriftauslegung: Beiträge zur Hermeneutik des Neuen Testamentes und im Neuen Testament*, hg. Josef Ernst (Müchen: F. Schöningh, 1972), 193–279. There are also those who claim John's deviations from the textual tradition(s) is symptomatic of his 'defective memory'. See for example, Bent Noack, *Zur johanneischen Tradtion: Beiträge zur Kritik an der Literakritischen Analyse des vierten Evangeliums*, Teologiske Skrifter, Bd. 3 (Copenhagen: Rosenkilde og Bagger, 1954:71–89); Charels Goodwin, 'How Did John Treat His Sources?' *JBL* 73 (1954), 61–75.

[285] See Freed, *Old Testament Quotations*, 129. There is some evidence in the Jewish exegetical procedure in the first century for delibrate deviations in biblical citations. These diversions appear to have been the result of the conscious application of established exegetical techniques, for example, connecting analogous passages from Scripture. Two passages are 'analogous' if they share at least a word or phrase, but very often such passages also share a measure of their contents as well. A portion of one passage, then, could be used as a substitute for a portion of the other, or could be appended to it. The utilisation of such a technique in the Qumran exegesis has been argued by G. J. Brooke, *Exegesis at Qumran*, p. 166 on 4QFlor; p. 294 on 1QM 10:1–8; pp. 297–8 on 1QS 2:2–4; pp. 306–8 on CD 7:15–19; p. 319 on 4QTest 9–20. Its employment in the rendering of texts in Isa OG and in 1QIsa^a has been suggested by Jean Koenig, *L' Herméneutique analogique du Judaïsme antique d'après les témoins textuels d'Isaïe*, VTS 33 (Leiden: Brill, 1982), (Isa OG), 1–103; (1QIsa^a), 199–291. For an extended treatment, see Martin Jan Mulder, ed., *Mikra: Text, Translation, Reading and Interpretation of the Hebrew Bible in Ancient Judaism and Early Christianity*, CRINT, section 2, *The Literature of the Jewish People in the Period of the Second Temple and the Talmud*, vol. 1 (Philadelphia: Fortress, 1988).

[286] Especially Paul J. Achtemeier, '*Omne verbum sonat:* The New Testament and the Oral Environment of Late Western Antiquity', *JBL* 109 (1990), 3, 19, 27.

[287] Achtemeier, '*Omne verbum sonat*', 27. But Schuchard, *Scripture within Scripture*, 151–3,

There are instances in which it appears as though John is relying upon the Septuagint.[288] It is very likely that he knew the Scriptures well enough to allude to them from memory. What remains unconvincing, however, is the thesis that the author of one of the most Jewish New Testament documents, who shows such an in-depth and panoramic knowledge of the Scriptures, and whose own writing shows a dominant Hebrew literary style, either did not know Hebrew or could not have cited from the Hebrew text.[289]

Textually the Isaiah 53:1 quotation in John 12:38 is almost identical in wording with the Septuagint which represents the Hebrew with sufficient accuracy except for inserting κύριε at the beginning, probably to clarify that the prophet is addressing God.[290] The quotation of Isaiah 6:10 in John 12:40 is more complex. It does not agree with any known form of Isaiah, differing quite radically from the Hebrew, the Septuagint, the Targums, and the other quotations of this text in the New Testament. For example, in line one of John's version, God is the subject of blinding although in line five (as laid out in the Nestle-Aland text), Jesus is apparently understood as the subject of healing, i.e., He (God) blinded...and I (Jesus) heal them.[291] John follows the Septuagint at least verbally in line five with καὶ ἰάσομαι αὐτούς, 'and I will heal them'.[292] That God is the healer is clear in the Septuagint and is probably implied though not directly stated in the Hebrew.[293] However, John in the verses immediately following the

---

insists that even if Johannine citations are from memory, they represent perceptible recollections of a specific textual tradition which he argues to be the textual tradition of the Septuagint.

[288] Barrett, *St. John*, 11; Schnackenburg, *St. John*, 1:110; M. Cimosa, 'La traduzione greca dei Settanta nel Vangelo di Giovanni', *BibOr* 39 (1997), 41–55.

[289] Cf. Margaret Davies, *Rhetoric and Reference in the Fourth Gospel* (Sheffield: JSOT Press, 1992), 68–75; J. W. Voelz, 'The Linguistic Milieu of the Early Church', *Concordia Theological Quarterly* 56 (1992), 81–97; S. Safrai, 'Education and the Study of the Torah', in *The Jewish People in the First Century: Historical Geography, Political History, Social, Cultural and Religious Life and Institutions*, vol. 2, ed. by S. Safrai, M. Stern, et al. (Amsterdam: Van Gorcum, 1976), 945–70; C. Rabin, 'Hebrew and Aramaic in the First Century', in *Jewish People in the First Century*, vol. 2, 1007–39; J. A. Fitzmyer, 'Did Jesus Speak Greek?', *BAR* 18 (1992), 58–63, 76–77; J. N. Sevenstern, *Do You Know Greek? How Much Greek Could First Jewish Christians Have Known?* (Leiden: Brill, 1968); R. Buth, 'Language Use in the First Century: Spoken Hebrew in a Trilingual Society in the Time of Jesus', *Journal of Translation and Textlinguistics* 5 (1992), 298–312; C. Tresmontant, *The Hebrew Christ: Language in the Age of the Gospels*, trans. by K. D. Whitehead (Chicago: Franciscan Herald Press, 1989); Robert Kysar, *The Fourth Evangelist and His Gospel: An Examination of Contemporary Scholarship* (Minneapolis, MN: Augsburg Pub. House, 1975), 102–46.

[290] See Dodd, *Interpretation*, 39; Lindars, *John*, 436–7; R. T. Fortna, *The Fourth Gospel and Its Predecessor* (Philadelphia: Fortress Press, 1988), 138.

[291] See Schnackenburg's observation in *St. John*, 2:415.

[292] See Mk. 4:12 interpretive rendition, 'and be forgiven'.

[293] Most English versions of Isa. 6:10 interpret וְרָפָא לוֹ as an impersonal construction (see

quotation identifies Jesus rather than God as the one revealed to Isaiah (Jn. 12:41–42), apparently making Jesus the healer as well. John also effectively changes the initial verbs from the Hebrew hiphil imperatives הַשְׁמֵן and הָשַׁע ('make dull' their heart and 'blind' their eyes) addressed by God to Isaiah to a perfect and an aorist predicated of God himself: τετύφλωκεν... ἐπώρωσεν, 'he (sc. God) has blinded their eyes and hardened their heart' (John inverts Isaiah's word order, placing the blinding first). In the Hebrew text of Isa. 6:10, it is not God who blinds, but God who instructs the prophet to be an instrument of 'obduracy'. Finally, for the idea of the hardening of hearts, the Septuagint uses not the transitive verb ἐπώρωσεν but the less direct intransitive passive ἐπαχύνθη ('to grow dull'), which is followed by Matthew 13:13–15 and Acts 28:25–28.

The reading ἐπώρωσεν in John 12:40 is attested in A, B*, L, X, Θ, Ψ, f¹³, 33, 1071, 1230* and 1242*. But there is also a very similar variant reading, ἐπήρωσεν (πηρόω), which requires attention. This occurs in 𝔓⁶⁶,⁷⁵ ℵ K W Π 1079. The orthographic and lexicographic differences between πωρόω ('harden', 'petrify', 'dull', Mk. 6:52; 2 Cor. 3:14; Rom. 11:7; cf. the noun form πώρωσις in Mk. 3:5; Rom. 11:25; Eph. 4:18) and πηρόω ('disable', 'maim', Mk. 8:17) are slight. However, Martinus Menken has endeavoured to show that early Christian literature in general exhibits a distinct preference for the former (together with the corresponding substantive, πώρωσις) rather than the latter.²⁹⁴ By using the perfect of τετύφλωκεν (with perfective force accruing also to the aorist ἐπώρωσεν), the Evangelist sets the inception of 'blinding' and 'hardening' in the past, the time of Isaiah himself, yet with enduring consequences even to the present, the time of the Evangelist.

In John 12:40, in place of the Septuagint's μήποτε, the Evangelist uses ἵνα μή. Menken suggests the reason for this change is that μήποτε, unlike ἵνα μή, is able to function as an interrogative particle.²⁹⁵ However, there may be stylistic reasons as well for this. There is only one instance of μήποτε in John's Gospel, as an interrogative particle (7:26). Apart from

---

GCK §137.3), such that the literal meaning 'lest one heal it (sc. the people)' becomes semantically equivalent to a passive, i.e., 'lest it *be healed*' (presumably by God?). For the grammar see Franz Delitzsch, *Jesaja*, 3rd edn (Leipzig: Dörflin und Franke, 1879; repr. Giessen and Basel: Brunnen, 1984), 103. However, the contruction וְרָפָא לוֹ could also be interpreted as reflexive, as in the Jewish Publication Society version (*Tanach* [1985]), hence: 'lest it (sc. "that people") repent and *save itself*.'

294 'Die Form des Zitates aus Jes. 6.10 in Joh. 12.40. Ein Beitrag zum Schriftgebrauch des vierten Evangelisten' *BZ* 32 (1988), 189–209, here pp. 192–4.

295 'Die Form des Zitates aus Jes. 6.10 in Joh. 12.40', 204.

'blinding' imagery, Isaiah 6:10 uses a further distinctive image, 'make fat the heart' (MT: הַשְׁמֵן and LXX: παχύνω), which does not appear to have any parallel in the Old Testament and may have invited modification.[296] The Johannine choice of πωρόω to express 'hardening' (rather than 'making fat') does not have a clear precedent in the Septuagint, other Jewish literature, or in the Greek writers.[297] Yet the evidence of Mark[298] and also Paul[299] relates the term to Isaiah 6:10 and suggests that the conception is

---

[296] The rare expression for 'blinding' used in the MT of Isaiah 6:10 (שָׁעַע) is replaced in most of the later references in Isaiah by the more common root (צוּר). The Septuagint translators were faithful to this in using καμμύω in Isaiah 6:10 as well as 29:10 and 33:15, but they used τυφλόω and its derivatives in 29:18; 35:5 and other references in Isaiah (cf. 42:7, 16, 18, 19, 43:8; cf. 61:1). In Qumran, 1QS 4:11 offers an 'interpretation' of Isaiah 6:10. כבד is used of 'ears' in Isaiah 6:10 as in 1 QS 4:11. The Septuagint usually translates by βαρύνω, 'weigh down' or 'burden'. The vocabulary of 'heaviness of heart', the root (כבד), is used of hardening of Pharaoh's heart in the so-called (J) tradition in Exod. 7:14; 8:11, 28; 9:7, 34; 10:1; 1 Sam. 6:6 (Israel compared with Pharaoh). Elsewhere 1QS (1:6; 2:14; 3:3; 5:4 etc.) uses a different phrase for 'hardness of heart', adopted from Jeremiah (שְׁרִרוּת) as in Jer. 3:17; 7:24; 9:13; 11:38 etc. The Septuagint translators apparently did not recognise this as an expression for 'hardness' and offered translations of it. The concept is reflected in the usage of πώρωσιν at Eph. 4:18; cf. Mk. 8:17; Rom. 11:7.

[297] Freed, *Old Testament Quotations*, 88 suggests the influence of Wisdom language in John, because of the use of πωρόω in Job 17:7.

[298] In the Gospel of Mark, the disciples are twice described as unable to *understand* (συνίημι as in Isa. 6:10, Septuagint and 6:9, as alluded to by Mark 4:12, 6:52), because of their hardened (πεπωρωμένη) hearts (8:17). On the second occasion, Jesus immediately asks, 'Having eyes do you not see, having ears do you not hear?' (8:18), cf. Jer. 5:21; Ezk. 12:2 (although these themselves seem to develop the theme of Isa. 6:9–10). See W. Zimmerli, *Ezekiel*, I, Hermeneia (Philadelphia: Fortress, 1979), 269–70. Matthew 13:13 parallels Mark 4:12, though it is closer to Mark 8:18. Neither Matthew nor Luke repeat Mark's rebuke to the disciples. Matthew has no parallel to Mark 8:18 and closes the incident by affirming the disciples' understanding (16:12), cf. Jesus' final question in Mark 8:21, 'Do you not yet understand?'; so also Matthew 17:13. While Mark attributes the disciples lack of understanding to their hardened hearts (Mk. 6:52), Matthew records that the disciples confessed Jesus as Son of God. Mark here has the verb πωρόω in a context which brings us back to Isaiah 6:9–10. Mark also uses the noun 'hardness (πώρωσις) of heart' of the Jewish opposition in 3:5. H. B. Swete, *The Gospel According to Mark* (London: Macmillan, 1898), 50. Matthew seems to exclude it, for their eyes do see and their ears do hear (13:16). So too at the end of the parables Matthew alone has the disciples affirm that *they do* understand (13:51). Neither Matthew nor Luke use πωρόω or πώρωσις. Mark's account is also slightly different when it follows Jesus' rebuke of the disciples with the healing of a blind man (8:22–26). Here Mark may have had in view God's act of salvation in the reversal of judgment (42:18–20; 43:8; cf. Mark 7:31–37; Isaiah 35:3–6). See also E. Hoskyns and F. N. Davey, *The Riddle of the New Testament* (London: Faber, 1931), 119–20; E. Best, *Following Jesus*, JSNTSup 4 (Sheffield: JSOT, 1981), 134–9; E. S. Johnson, 'The Blind Man from Bethsaida', *NTS* 25 (1979), 370–83.

[299] The verb πωρόω, 'harden' is twice used by Paul. In Romans 11:7, it is used in the context of Israel's failure. God's promises have been experienced only by the elect, 'the rest were hardened'. This is said to be in fulfilment of Scriptures (Isa. 29:10; Deut. 29:3, both of which stand within the Isa. 6:10 tradition). Later in Romans 11:25 once again Paul speaks of 'the hardening' (πώρωσις) which has come upon part of Israel. See Zimmerli, *Ezekiel*, 269–70; cf. CD

not unique to John. Rather, the Fourth Evangelist is part of a wider tradition of interpreting Isaiah 6:9-10 in terms of *blinding* (τυφλόω) and *hardening* (πωρόω).[300]

The original text of Isaiah moves from heart to ears to eyes and then in reverse from sight to hearing to understanding. John puts seeing first and omits all reference to hearing. This is because sight is the point of interest. Perception precedes understanding. In this, he moves directly from perception to the inner disposition, the heart (cf. Jn. 2:25). In the Gospel, the blinded eyes are in parallel with the hardened hearts, and the failure to see with the eyes is the failure to perceive (ἵνα νοήσωσιν, 12:40) with the heart. Thus John is not far from the notion of the blinding of the minds (νοήματα), though his use of 'heart' rather than 'mind' may be a Semitism.[301]

This emphasis on 'sight' rather than 'hearing' is carried throughout the Gospel (though cf. 5:24-25; 10:3-5). In the Hebrew text, the prophet is instructed to 'shut' the people's eyes, while in the Septuagint the people shut their own eyes. In so doing, the Septuagint translators make an interpretive decision in which they place the responsibility for peoples'

16:2. In 2 Corinthians 3:14, it is the minds (νοήματα) [John 12:40 uses νοέω, where LXX, Matthew and Luke use συνιήμι] of the Jews which were hardened (ἐπωρώθη) at the reading of Scripture like a veil upon their heart 'up to this day' (2 Cor. 3:15). In the following chapter, Paul speaks more universally of the Gospel as veiled for those who are perishing, the unbelievers, whose *minds* (νοήματα) the 'god of this age' has 'blinded' (ἐτύφλωσεν), the only non-Johannine use of this verb in the New Testament (2 Cor. 4:4). The Pauline parallel use of 'harden' and 'blind' (Rom. 11:7; 2 Cor. 4:4) is particularly striking in comparison with John's quotation of Isaiah. For Paul, the hardening of Israel is temporary (Rom. 11:25-26), though 2 Corinthians 4:3-4 offers less hope to 'those who are perishing'. Some commentators see the Pauline language of 'blinding' in 2 Corinthians 4:4 as close to Hellenistic Judaism (rather than biblical language), especially Philo and in the *Testament of the Twelve Patriarchs*. Philo, *Quaest. in Gen. 21* (the eyes of the soul); 40 (the soul is blind to the most holy visions), but also see *T. Judah* 11:1; 18:3; *T. Dan.* 2:4. There it is the mind, heart or soul which may be blinded (τυφλόω) not by God as in the biblical tradition but by hatred (*T. Gad.* 3:3), passions (*T. Judah* 18:6) or, in closer parallel to 2 Corinthians 4:4, 'the ruler of error' (*T. Sim.* 2:7; *T. Judah* 19:4). In the LXX, τυφλόω is used at Tobit 7:7; Wis. 2:21 besides Isaiah 42:29. The resemblance to Hellenistic Judaism presupposes a dualism and sees blindness as ignorance or an inability to perceive or respond to the truth. However, Paul's use of hardening (πωρόω) does not seem to have a similar precedent in Hellenistic Jewish literature, leaving it at least possible that in the parallel Pauline use of the two terms, we should see the influence of the Isaiah 6:10 tradition known also to John. Cf. Lindars, *New Testament Apologetic*, 162-3; J. A. de Waard, *A Comparative Study of the Old Testament Text in the Dead Sea Scrolls and in the New Testament* (Leiden: Brill, 1966), 7-8; J. A. Robinson, *St. Paul's Epistle to the Ephesians* (London: Macmillian, 1928), 264-74.

[300] Cf. Schnackenburg, *Johannes*, 4:149-50; Evans, 'Isa 6:9-10', 68; Lieu, 'Blindness', 86-8; Menken, 'Joh 12,40', 201-203; Freed, *Old Testament Quotations*, 87-8; Dodd, *According to the Scriptures*, 37 n. 2; Blank, *Krisis*, 303-4.

[301] J. Behm, 'νοέω', *TDNT* 4 (1967), 950.

failure to see at their own feet, i.e., their deliberate unwillingness to see (cf. Jn. 3:19–21). In the Fourth Gospel the Evangelist more or less follows the Hebrew text's meaning but not its vocabulary. He substitutes 'blinding' of the people in place of 'shutting' of their eyes. This seemingly innocent change of emphasis carries important implications. In the ancient world, 'blindness' was a devastating condition. Among the human senses, sight has often been a given a prominence. With the stress on 'blindness', John shows the seriousness of the situation for those who reject Jesus.

5.5.2. Isaiah's Message and Rejection of Revelation in John

The accent of both Isaiah 53:1 and John 12:38 falls on the unexplained references by the prophet to a 'report' (ἀκοή)[302] and to a revelation (cf. ἀποκαλύπτω).[303] In the Hebrew text of Isaiah 6:9–10, the prophet is instructed with hiphil imperatives: 'Make fat, or dull' (הַשְׁמֵן) the heart of this people and 'make heavy' (הַכְבֵּד) their ears and 'turn away' (הָשַׁע) their eyes. The instrument of this hardening appears to be the very message of the prophet (cf. Rom. 10:16). In the Fourth Gospel, it is not so much the works of Jesus as it is his words which consistently cause offence. His words are an aversion to his opponents (10:32–33). Jesus' words are so repugnant to them that even his final plea to find in his works sufficient reason to also believe his words is refused (10:37–39a). John therefore writes, 'though he had done so many signs before them, yet they did not believe in him' (12:37). If one were to reconstruct the passage, line one of John 12:40 might be paraphrased as: Jesus' 'report' or words provoked a response from the Jews which led to loss of their presumed sight. The 'revelation' became the source of their blindness because of the hardness of their hearts (12:40; cf. 9:39; 8:43; see also 4:42; 5:24–25; 6:45, 60; 8:47; 10:3–4, 12:47; 16:27). In Isaiah's question in 53:1, John sees a sombre and tragic continuation of the unresponsiveness to the revelation in his own days. 'The Jews', in spite of Jesus' many signs, did not believe in Jesus (12:37) because they were unable to accept the message, the 'report' (12:38).[304]

The Evangelist has already prepared us for such a response in 1:11. From the beginning of the revelation in his signs (2:11) to the display of the

---

[302] BAGD, 30–1; G. Kittel, *TDNT* 1 (1964), 197–209.

[303] BAGD, 92; A. Oepke, *TDNT* 3 (1965), 563–92.

[304] Barrett, *John*, 431, takes 'report' as 'discourses of Jesus'; Brown, *John*, 485, takes 'report' as the whole of Jesus' words while 'arms' are the revelation of signs; F. F. Bruce, *The Gospel of John*: Introduction, Exposition and Notes (London: Pickering Paperbacks, 1983), 270.

glory of God in the raising of Lazarus (11:4, 40), he had revealed the Father in a succession of significant acts, yet he received no general credence by the very people who had been prepared over centuries for the coming of the light. In Isaiah, it is the content of the prophet's proclamation that causes offence and thus 'blinds' those who are apathetic to the message. The very words that are the means of bringing Israel to repentance simultaneously are the means of hardening the hearts of those who reject those words. John 12:48 maintains that in the last day Jesus' very words would become the judge of those who reject him. But in the Johannine eschatological programme, the incarnation has inaugurated the last day. Now is the last day. One's response, now, to the revelation of God in Christ has eternal consequences (3:36). The words of Jesus have become the judge of those who would not believe. Such judgment is not something Jesus either desires (3:17) or personally executes. Instead, it is an inevitable judgment that the light of his revelation provokes. By rejecting spiritual sight, one remains spiritually blind. If revelation means life, rejection of revelation means death. Thus the very words of Jesus have become the judge, not only of 'the Jews', but of the world (12:48). Comprehension or incomprehension of the revelation of God in Christ according to the witness of Scriptures, for John, is indicative as to whether one possesses spiritual life or abides in death.

5.5.3. Revelation of the Arm of YHWH and Rejection of His Servant

It has been argued that the Isaianic quotations in John 12:38–41 are meant not only to explain why Jesus was rejected, but also to identify him with the 'Servant of the Lord' in Isaiah 53. The Church historically has associated 'the Servant of the Lord' passages of Isaiah (42:1–9; 49:1–13; 50:4–9; 52:13–53:12) with Jesus.[305] However, this interpretation was challenged, among others, by C. K. Barrett and later in 1959 by Morna D. Hooker in her influential thesis, *Jesus and the Servant*.[306] In her study,

---

[305] J. Jeremias' contribution in *TDNT* 5:677–717; Oscar Cullmann in his *Christology of the New Testament* (Philadelphia: Westminster, 1959), 51–82 devoted an entire chapter to Jesus as the Servant of the Lord. See also R. T. France, *Jesus and the Old Testament: His Application of Old Testament Passages to Himself and His Mission* (London: Tyndale, 1971), 110–35; Evans, 'Obduracy', 228ff., W. H. Brownlee, 'Whence the Gospel According to John?' in *John and Qumran*, ed. by J. H. Charlesworth (London: Geoffrey Chapman, 1972), 166–94, esp. 177–78. Other scholars favoring this view would include C. F. Burney, M. E. Boismard, I. de la Potterie, and B. Reicke.

[306] Morna D. Hooker, *Jesus and the Servant: The Influence of the Servant Concept of Deutero-Isaiah in the New Testament* (London: SPCK, 1959). See more recently Hooker, 'Did the Use of Isaiah 53 to Interpret His Mission Begin with Jesus?', in *Jesus and the Suffering Servant: Isaiah*

308 *Chapter 5: Israel's Scriptures and the Language of John's Gospel*

Hooker rejected the notion that the New Testament had a Servant christology and that Isaiah's Servant Songs had been influential on the formation of the christology of the early church. Since its publication, scholars have been embroiled in a controversy as to whether Jesus understood himself in the light of Isaiah's servant, or whether it was rather early Christianity which first made this connection.[307] For those such as E. P. Sanders, Barrett and Hooker have settled the issue.[308] But for others such as Christopher Rowland, 'it is hard not to believe that somewhere in the background, Isaiah 53 has influenced the ideas of vicarious suffering found in the Gospels.'[309]

Among her objections, Hooker noted that the Baptist's cry in John 1:29, 36 betrays no association with Isaiah 53. The Servant in Isaiah 53:7 is linked to 'lamb' (anarthrous) and not 'the lamb' (ὁ ἀμνός), as John has it. Following Barrett, Hooker rejects the possible mistranslation of the Aramaic word טליא into ἀμνός, 'lamb' rather than παῖς, 'servant'.[310] Hooker, like Dodd, believes the Baptist's reference to the 'lamb' is the victorious Messianic lamb of the Apocalypse.[311] She further maintains that the conception of ὑψόω, 'lift up', in Isaiah and John is different: 'Whereas in Deutero-Isaiah the Servant is glorified by his restoration, and Yahweh by the return of Israel, in John both the Father and the Son are glorified already at the crucifixion.'[312] Evans, however, suggests that 'what Hooker sees as a contrast between Isaiah's and John's understanding of *hypsoun* may in fact represent a succinct statement of their close theological affinity.'[313] With respect to the quotation of Isaiah 53:1 in John 12:38, Hooker maintains the Old Testament verse does not refer to Jesus' death

---

53 and Christian Origins, ed. by William H. Bellinger and William R. Farmer (Harrisburg, PA: Trinity Press International, 1998), 88–103.

[307] See most recently the collected essays in William H. Bellinger and William R. Farmer, eds, *Jesus and the Suffering Servant: Isaiah 53 and Christian Origins* (1998).

[308] Sanders, *Jesus and Judaism*, 332; see also Moo, *Old Testament in the Gospel*, 356; D. L. Jones, 'The Title "Servant" in Luke-Acts', in *Luke-Acts: New Perspectives from the Society of Biblical Literature Seminar*, ed. by C. H. Talbert (New York: Cross Road, 1984), 148–65, esp. 158.

[309] C. Rowland, *Christian Origins* (London: SPCK, 1985), 176; also France, *Jesus and the Old Testament*, 110–35; Evans, 'Obduracy', 228ff; L. Goppelt, *Typos: The Typological Interpretation of the Old Testament in the New* (Grand Rapids: Eerdmans, 1982), 194.

[310] Hooker, *Jesus and the Servant*, 104; Barrett, *St. John*, 176.

[311] Hooker, *Jesus and the Servant*, 104; Dodd, *Interpretation*, 235–6; also Str-B, in loc. 1:29 and vol. 2; Brown, *John*, 1:61; Barrett, 'Lamb of God', 210–18.

[312] Hooker, *Jesus and the Servant*, 106.

[313] Evans, 'Obduracy', 230. See particularly G. C. Nicholoson's thesis, *Death as Departure: The Johannine Descent-Ascent Schema*, SBLDS 63 (Chico, CA: Scholars Press, 1983).

and resurrection (themes possibly derived from the whole of the Servant Song), but to 'the failure of Jews to believe the signs which had been performed by Jesus.'[314] In this respect, John is simply using Isaiah 53:1 as a proof-text for the incurable obduracy of Israel.

However, it is worth noting that the relationship between the two Isaianic texts quoted by John is far more significant than simply expressing the idea of obduracy.[315] They are important to John's christology: 'These things said Isaiah because[316] (or when)[317] he saw his glory (τὴν δόξαν) and spoke of him' (12:41; cf. 1:14, 18). B. D. Chilton, in a penetrating examination of the Isaiah Targum, finds a pre-Christian interpretation of the Servant as Messiah, making more plausible the notion that the Servant was already a significant figure for first-century Judaism.[318] The Targum of Isaiah 52:13–53:12 is explicitly Messianic (cf. 52:13, 'Behold, my Servant, the Messiah'; cf. 53:10). When John claims that Isaiah 'spoke concerning him' (12:41), this assertion is similar to an earlier claim that Moses wrote of him (5:46). In Isaiah 6:5, the prophet exclaims: 'I have seen the king, the Lord of hosts.'

The Johannine presentation of Jesus as the Messianic King has already been noted in the preceding chapter of the present study (cf. 1:49; 12:13). Evans has gone further and has endeavoured to show that John 12:1–43 is a midrash on Isaiah 52:7–53:12. However, what Evans calls 'midrash', I would rather describe, as I have argued throughout this study, as a deliberate Johannine intertextual echo and allusion to the Old Testament Scriptures in order to show their fulfilment in Jesus Christ. (See my earlier criticism in this chapter of Midrash as a principle of interpretation or a descriptive category.) In the context of this so-called midrash, Mary's anointing of Jesus' feet in John 12:3–7 is seen as an allusion to Isaiah 52:7: 'How beautiful upon the mountains are the feet of him who brings good tidings, who publishes peace, who brings tidings of good, who publishes salvation, who says to Zion, "Your God reigns!"' This verse contains a few

---

[314] Hooker, *Jesus and the Servant*, 106; also Schnackenburg, *St. John*, 2:413–414.

[315] Evans, 'Obduracy', 230–31.

[316] ὅτι: P66.75 ℵ A B L X Θ Ψ f¹ 33 1071 1546.

[317] ὅτε, D K Δ Π f¹³ 565 700 892 1009 1079 1195 1216 1230 1241 1242 1344 1365 1646 2148 2174.

[318] B. Chilton, *The Glory of Israel: The Theology and Provenience of the Isaiah Targum*, JSOTSup 23 (Sheffield: JSOT, 1993), 91–96, believes the portrait of the Servant as a victorious Messiah arose prior to Bar Kochba (AD 132–135); see also S. H. Levey, *The Messiah: An Aramaic Interpretation: The Messianic Exegesis of the Targum*, Monographs of the Hebrew Union College 2 (Cincinnati: Hebrew Union College, 1974), 67, 70.

vocabulary items found in the Fourth Gospel (e.g., 'peace', 'salvation', 'good tidings'). The verb εὐαγγελίσασθαι is found in the eschatologically understood Isaiah 61:1 passage: 'The Spirit of the Lord is upon me, because the Lord has anointed me to bring good tidings...' (vv. 1ff). Among the (Messianic) tasks mentioned in this passage is the giving of the 'oil of gladness' to 'those who mourn in Zion' (Isa. 61:3). The crowd which went out (ἐξῆλθον) of Jerusalem to greet Jesus (Jn. 12:12–13) may fulfil the exhortation in Isaiah 52:11 to go out (ἐξέλθατε) of Jerusalem. In the exhortation of Isaiah 52:11, members of the audience are told to 'touch nothing unclean,' but to 'purify' themselves. This idea is present in the Johannine Passover/crucifixion context: there as well there is a concern for ritual purity (18:28). The jubilant shouting of the people (Jn. 12:13) echoes the fulfilment of Isaiah 52:8–9. The return of the Lord to Zion, as described in Isaiah, could be seen as fulfilled in the return of Jesus to Jerusalem which he has previously visited. When the people see Jesus, they see God (cf. Jn. 12:45).[319]

The case, set forward by those scholars who have rejected the Isaianic vicarious servant associations in the Fourth Gospel, is unconvincing on several fronts. First, in this antithesis, it seems to me, broad and sweeping conclusions are drawn based on hair-splitting and scanty evidence. For example, the (anarthrous) lamb in Isaiah 53:7 in contrast to the (definite) lamb in the Fourth Gospel in itself does not disprove the association.

Secondly, there is no reason to make such a sharp distinction between the vicarious Lamb of John 1:29 and the victorious Lamb of Revelation (Rev. 6:16; 14:1; 17:14). The images refer to the same figure in the Johannine writings. The conquering, victorious eschatological Lamb is the same Lamb who was slain (Rev. 13:8; 5:6–12). It has already been demonstrated in the present study that such a dual perspective is common in John. The same duality of outlook is evident in the prophetic literature and has been noted by most commentators on the prophets.

Thirdly, at a more fundamental level, it is crucial to maintain a distinction between the meaning of a text or collection of texts, and the possible objections to that meaning. If the New Testament writers read passages such as Isaiah 53 christologically then it is not out of the ordinary. It was their teacher, Jesus, who, according to the evangelists, licensed his followers to 'look for him' and 'see him' in the prophetic pages of Scriptures, and interpret those same Scriptures in light of his life and works (Jn. 5:39–47; cf. Lk. 24:25–27, 44; Mk. 4:11f.; cf. Acts 10:43). It would have

---

[319] For the extended proposal, see Evans, 'Obduracy', 231-33.

been natural for the New Testament writers to read the description of the suffering Servant of Isaiah and associate it with the vicarious suffering of Jesus (e.g., Acts 8:30–35; 2 Cor. 5:21; Phil. 2:7; Mt. 8:17; 1 Pet. 2:24–25). If Moses could have written of him in the law (Jn. 5:46), then surely the prophets, including Isaiah could have spoken of him in their prophecies. One concedes the point that such a hermeneutic may be unacceptable by the standard of modern critical exegesis. As valid as this point may be, as I have already noted elsewhere, our hermeneutical preferences are irrelevant to the hermeneutic of the New Testament writers. Our exegetical task requires that we faithfully bring out what the New Testament writers understood and tried to communicate to their audience; our agreement or disagreement with their conclusions is a separate issue.

Fourthly, the interpretation of the contemporary or pre-Christian Jewish writers of certain biblical passages may or may not be pertinent to the way New Testament authors interpreted the same passages. If the Johannine christological interpretation of Isaiah 53 does not coincide with the interpretation of the rabbis or other Jewish writers, this does not invalidate his reading; neither does it provide a ground upon which one can conclude that because the rabbis, or other Jews, supposedly did not read it christologically, therefore John could have not read it christologically. The late Professor G. B. Caird correctly noted in response to those who deny the conceptual associations between John and Isaiah 53,

For centuries Isaiah 53 has been read by Christians as a direct prophecy of the life and suffering of Jesus. Part of the current scepticism, no doubt, results from rehabilitation of the Jewish Scriptures as speaking to their own time and having their own meaning, apart from any Christian fulfilment.[320]

The disciples of Jesus and the subsequent generation of Christians read and interpreted the Scriptures, including Isaiah, christologically because Jesus had set the hermeneutical precedent for them. The resurrection would have left little doubt in their minds about the correctness of their hermeneutic, regardless of how non-Christians may have interpreted those passages. The decisive influence of Isaiah upon Johannine christology has long been established.[321] The theology of the Fourth Evangelist confirms

---

[320] Caird, *New Testament Theology*, 311ff.

[321] F. W. Young, 'A Study of the Relation of Isaiah to the Fourth Gospel', *ZNW* 46 (1955), 215–33; John V. Dahms, 'Isaiah 55:11 and the Gospel of John', *EvQ* 53 (1981), 78–88; Dahl, *Jesus the Christ*; idem, 'The Crucified Messiah', 251–62; Mark Arrington, 'The Identification of the Anonymous Servant in Isaiah 40–55' (Thesis, Dallas Seminary, 1971); Phil G. Bowersox, 'The Use of Isaiah 6:10 in John 12:40 and the Theology of Rejection' (Thesis, Dallas Seminary, 1978); W. Warren Liu, 'The Use of Isaiah 40–66 in the Gospel of John' (Thesis, Dallas

the church's historic christological interpretation of the Isaianic passages.³²²

5.5.4. Incomprehension and the Question of Divine Determination

The various quotations of Isaiah 6:8–10 in the New Testament have been at the heart of the age-old problem of the sovereignty of God and human responsibility. In the context of John 12:37–41, this problem has given endless difficulty to exegetes who have endeavoured to explain its implications.³²³ In Isaiah 6, the prophet is told to achieve by his ministry the reverse of his expected goal; he is to 'make the heart of this people fat, their ears heavy and their eyes shut, lest they...turn'. The Septuagint (followed by Matthew and Luke) bypasses the question of responsibility by replacing the imperative with an intransitive passive – 'their heart grew dull' (ἐπαχύνθη, Isa. 6:10). Mark addresses the question of responsibility by the theme of purpose; and in John, the same result is achieved by introducing the third person 'he has blinded...he has hardened...' (Jn. 12:40). In the introductory formula of John 12:38, if ἵνα is given its full purposive force, we would have one of the strongest predestinarian expressions in the New Testament. It is possible to take this ἵνα as consecutive or ecbatic, i.e., 'the result of their unbelief was the fulfilment of the word,' especially since ἵνα is epexegetical elsewhere in John (e.g., 1:27; 17:3). But the ecbatic use of ἵνα is rare (usually this is expressed by ὥστε plus the infinitive) and Barrett believes this consequential interpretation is blocked by verses 39 and 40. Thus ἵνα has to be given its full purposive force.³²⁴ In 12:39 the Evangelist concludes, 'For this reason/ therefore (διὰ τοῦτο) they could not believe, because (ὅτι) again Isaiah

---

Seminary, 1978); Eugene W. Pond, 'Theological Dependencies of John's Gospel on Isaiah' (Thesis, Dallas Seminary, 1985). See also M. C. Tenney, 'Topics in the Fourth Gospel: Part II: The Meaning of Signs' *BibSac* 132 (1975), 145–60; idem, 'Literary Keys: Old Testament and the Fourth Gospel'; Juel, *Messianic Exegesis*; H. S. Songer, 'Isaiah and the New Testament', *RevExp* 65 (1968), 459–70; J. M. Lieu, 'Biblical Theology and the Johannine Literature', 93–107; idem, 'What Was From the Beginning: Scripture and Tradition in the Johannine Epistles', *NTS* 39 (1993), 458–77; Brandscheidt, 'Prophetischer Verstockungsauftrag und Christlicher Glaube', 64–76; Kümmel, *Theology of the New Testament*, 261–321.

³²² See my discussion in this chapter in 5.3.3., also see Peter W. Ensor's thesis on *Jesus and His Works: The Johannine Sayings in Historical Perspective* (Tübingen: Mohr-Siebeck, 1996); Williams, *Jesus' Death as Saving Event*; Hengel, *Atonement*; Grigsby, 'Cross as an Expiatory Sacrifice', 51–80.

³²³ Schnackenburg, *St. John*, 2:274, may not be too far from the truth when he relegates the problem to the mystery of the divine decree (pp. 259–74).

³²⁴ Barrett, *St. John*, 431, believes it can hardly be questioned that John means here that the hardening of Israel was intended by God. Freed, *Old Testament Quotations*, 84–88, 122.

said....' The διὰ τοῦτο in verse 39 may look back to the quotation of Isaiah 53:1 in verse 38, or it may look ahead to Isaiah 6:10 in verse 40. The former is indicative; the later explanatory. Many commentators understand 'God' to be the author of blindness in John 12:39–40. The perfect action described in verse 40 seems to strengthen this conclusion,[325] although it is possible, in view of 12:41, that Jesus may be the author of the blindness. He has performed the signs (v. 37). He is the One whose glory Isaiah had seen in his temple vision (12:41). And he may be the one addressed as 'Lord' in the quotation of Isaiah 53:1 in 12:38.[326] Above all, there is also Jesus' remark in 9:39 that he has come to render judgment that those who see may become blind.

Jesus of John's Gospel emphatically asserts oneness with the Father including unison in their works (5:17; cf. 4:34; 9:4; 17:4). Therefore, whether he or the Father is the author of obduracy is not too significant. What does seem pertinent is the idea of Divine election which occurs with frequency throughout the Old and New Testaments (Exod. 33:19; cf. Rom. 9:15). The divine predestination is also a theological problem with which the Jewish writers grapple.[327] Sirach warns, 'Say not: "From God is my transgression", for that which He hateth made He not.[328] Say not: "It is He that made me to stumble", for there is no need of evil men' (Sir. 15:11–12).[329] But the writer of *2 Enoch* believes, 'already before, even to each one there is a place prepared for the repose of that soul, and a measure fixed how much it is intended that a man be tried in this world' (*2 Enoch* 49:2). Josephus suggests that the question of free will was a common point of debate among the Jewish groups.[330] Sadducees, he reports, for example, believed in the freedom of choice, while the Essenes considered 'destiny' to stand above everything, but the Pharisees held a moderate position and believed some

---

[325] Cf. *Apc. Jn.*, II.22:26–8 with John 12:40.

[326] Although in 12:41, 'his glory' refers to Jesus; yet Jesus' glory is God's glory, and δόξα is the key to understanding John's use of Isaiah as a witness to Jesus. Δόξα is that which the Son and the Father share in common (17:5). It is used to describe that which Jesus reveals (1:14; 2:11; 11:4, 40). It 'means throughout the Gospel the manifestation of God's or Christ's true nature'. Wengst, *Bedrängte Gemeinde*, 59–60; A. T. Hanson, *Jesus Christ in the Old Testament* (London: SPCK, 1965), 106.

[327] E.g., *Apocalypse of Abraham*, ch. 22–23; *Apocalypse of Ezra*, 2:17.

[328] So the Hebrew text; the Greek renders it, 'that which He hateth thou shalt not do'.

[329] See further on this passage Gerhard Maier, *Mensch und freier Wille nach den jüdischen Religionsparteien zwischen Ben Sira und Paulus*, WUNT 12 (Tübingen: Mohr-Siebeck, 1971), 85–95.

[330] See *Ant.* 18:1; 13:5. See also Ludwig Wächter, 'Die unterschiedliche Haltung der Pharisäer, Sadduzäer und Essener zur Heimarmene nach dem Bericht des Josephus', *Zeitschrift für Religions und Geistesgeschichte* 21 (1969), 97–114.

matters depend on 'fate' and others on free will.[331] In rabbinic theology, everything in the world is predetermined, but to choose either obedience or disobedience to God is man's own choice.[332] The dualistic theology of Qumran is interpreted by many scholars in terms of 'absolute determinism'.[333] In the *War Scroll* (1QM), from the beginning God has divided humanity into two categories (XIII, 7ff). In the *Thanksgiving Hymns* (1QH), predestinarian ideas are found in the context of creation tradition (I: 7–8, 19; cf. XV:17). In the *Community Rule* (1 QS III:13–IV:26), predestination is associated with the spirit of truth and spirit of falsehood. God has divided people on the basis of which spirit they obey. But there is also the struggle of the spirit of light with the spirit of darkness in the heart of children of light.

In New Testament theology, predestination, in contrast to Qumran, is focused on election unto salvation and far less emphasis is placed upon election unto perdition. However, Ethelbert Stauffer, among other scholars, believes Paul teaches a supralapsarian theology.[334] Romans chapters 9–11 are considered to be the *locus classicus de praedestinatione* in the New Testament upon which Augustine and Calvin based their respective doctrines of election.[335] On the other hand, Räisänen maintains that among the New Testament writings, 'strictest predestinarianism is represented by the Gospel of John and the Revelation'.[336] In Mark 4:11–12, Jesus alludes to Isaiah 6:9–10; and it appears as if, with the use of parabolic languages, he wishes to *prevent* the 'non-elect' from understanding his message. This understanding is emphasised in Mark 4:34, 'He did not speak to them without a parable, but privately to his own disciples he explained everything.' Matthew attributes Jesus' speaking in parables to the consequence of the rejection of his message (Mt. 13:13). And elsewhere in Matthew, Jesus declares, 'many are called but few are chosen' (Mt.

---

[331] Wächter, 'Die unterschiedliche', 98–106, 114.

[332] George F. Moore, *Judaism in the First Centuries of the Christian Era: The Age of the Tannaim*, 3 vols, 2nd edn (Cambridge, MA: Harvard University Press, 1950–54), 1:455f.

[333] J. Scmitt, 'Les écrits du Nouveau Testament et les textes de Qumran', *Revue de Science Religieuse* 30 (1956), 60f.; J. Licht, 'The Doctrine of the Thanksgiving Scroll', *Israel Exploration Journal* 6 (1956), 5f; K. G. Kuhn, 'Peirasmos, hamartia, sarx im Neuen Testament und die damit zusammenhängenden Vorstellungen', *ZTK* 49 (1952), 204–6.

[334] Ethelbert Stauffer, *Die Theologie des Neuen Testaments*, 4th edn (Gütersloh, 1948), 162; cf. C. H. Dodd, *The Epistle of Paul to the Romans* (New York/London: Moffatt, 1932).

[335] Heikki Räisänen, *The Idea of the Divine Hardening* (Helsinki: Publications of the Finish Exegetical Society 25, 1976), 79.

[336] Ibid., 95.

22:14).³³⁷ Luke modified Mark 4:10–12 (Lk. 8:10) and gives the extended quotation of Isaiah when he sums up Paul's ministry in Acts 28:26–27 (cf. 28:28; 13:46ff; 18:6).³³⁸

In the Fourth Gospel, the reference to Isaiah 6:9–10 is not spoken by Jesus, but John alludes to it in an editorial comment on the apathetic response to Jesus' many signs. Hoskyns believes the Johannine quotation 'reads like the crudest possible statement of a naked doctrine of predestination'.³³⁹ Even the Jewish response to Jesus is in fulfilment of Scripture: 'They hated me without a cause' (Jn. 15:25). But the Johannine predestinarian emphasis is even more explicit. In 6:44 Jesus claims, 'No one can come to me unless the Father who sent me draws him' (6:44). Jesus 'loses' nothing of all that the Father has given to him (6:39; 10:29; 17:2). Many Johannine scholars have concluded that the Fourth Evangelist presents God as the one who prevents faith in some. Schrage maintains that in the Fourth Gospel, 'God is expressly called the author of hardening.'³⁴⁰ Even the signs are seen to cause blindness so that God would not heal some.³⁴¹ The Evangelist in 12:37 sums up Jesus' public ministry by the bleak conclusion that, 'Though he (Jesus) had done so many signs (σημεῖα) before them (ἔμπροσθεν αὐτῶν) yet they would not believe (οὐκ ἐπίστευον) in him.' Both here and in the conclusion of the Gospel (20:30), the Evangelist underlines the significance of Jesus' 'signs'.³⁴² In the Fourth Gospel, the signs are tangible deeds in and through which Jesus' claim to oneness with the Father is validated. This implies that the signs should have brought those who saw them to faith in Jesus as the Christ. But, as the Gospel makes clear, not all who saw the signs believed. Although some

---

³³⁷ See Krister Stendahl, 'The Called and the Chosen: An Essay on Election', in *The Root of the Vine*, ed. by Anton Fridrichsen (New York: Harper, 1953), 63–80.

³³⁸ Hans Conzelmann, *Die Apostelgeschichte*, HNT 7 (Tübingen: Mohr-Siebeck, 1963), 149, makes a distinction between Luke's view about the Jews and Paul's view (Romans 11). For Luke, the Jews have been conclusively rejected. But their rejection is not necessarily predetermined. The failure lies with Israel.

³³⁹ Hoskyns, *Fourth Gospel*, 429.

³⁴⁰ W. Schrage, *TDNT*, 8:292. See further discussions in K. L. Schmidt and M. A. Schmidt, 'σκληρόω', *TDNT*, 5:1026; Menken, 'Die Form des Zitates aus Jes. 6,10', 198 n. 34; Schnackenburg, *St. John*, 2:270–4; Räisänen, *Divine Hardening*, 45–98; Painter, 'Quotation of Scripture', 435, 451–7.

³⁴¹ Evans, *To See and Not Perceive*, 135, thinks the tradition of Deuteronomy 29:2–4 supports this view: e.g., 'You have seen all that the Lord did before your eyes in the Land of Egypt...the signs (LXX σημεῖα)...but to this day the Lord has not given you a mind to understand, or eyes to see, or ears to hear'.

³⁴² D. Guthrie, 'The Importance of Signs in the Fourth Gospel', *Vox Evangelica* (1967), 72–83.

'saw his glory' (1:14; 2:11), others remained blind (9:41). C. K. Barrett holds, 'Signs do not suffice if God does not give men eyes to see.... It can hardly be questioned that John meant that the hardening of Israel was intended by God'.[343] Schnackenburg puts it more positively and suggests, 'A predestination of those who belong to Jesus and his community of faith is unmistakable'.[344] Elsewhere Barrett writes, 'The Fourth Gospel expresses the conviction that however clearly Jesus may state the truth, those who are not "His sheep" will not hear His voice" (10:26).[345]

Among the scholars who feel the unbelief captured in John 12:39–40 was the result of divine predestination, there are two groups: those who see the unresponsiveness of 'the Jews' as the consequence of divine judgment upon persistent unbelief, and those who see no anterior cause other than the decree of God. In the latter group, some go so far as to maintain that the origins and destinies of individuals in the Johannine theological formulation are fixed (radical double predestinarianism).[346] Passages such as John 1:13; 3:3–11, 20–21; 5:28; 7:7; 8:43–47; 10:26; 17:9; and 18:37 are cited in support of the thesis. God takes the initiative in 'choosing' or 'drawing' those who are his.[347] Here belief is seen as a gift from God in the Pauline sense.[348] The same potential to receive the gift of faith does not exist among all individuals.

Hence for example when Nathanael is described by Jesus as 'an Israelite in whom there is no deceit' (1:47), this is seen in terms of the 'fixed origin' of the Johannine characters (2:23–25; 5:42; 6:64; 11:9–10). While misunderstandings and progression of faith do take place, the personalities and types of response do not change. In 1:48, Jesus' knowledge of Nathanael is tied to Nathanael's question 'whence' (πόθεν),[349] which keynotes a theme with a vital role in the Fourth Gospel.[350] Here, πόθεν is explained by reference to Jesus' having seen Nathanael sitting under the fig tree, but this does not account for the fact that Jesus

---

[343] Barrett, *St. John*, 430.

[344] Schnackenburg, *St. John*, 2:264, also 271.

[345] Barrett, *Essays on John*, 107.

[346] Jeffrey A. Trumbower, *Born from Above: The Anthropology of the Gospel of John* (Tübingen: Mohr-Siebeck, 1992), 118.

[347] E.g., 3:27; 5:21; 6:37, 44, 64–65, 70; 12:39–41; 15:18–19; 17:6.

[348] Eph. 1:4–23; 2:5–8; cf. Jn. 6:37, 39, 44; 10:14–16, 27, 28.

[349] Interogative adverb and may be rendered, 'from where?', 'from what source?', 'how?'; BAGD, 680.

[350] Regarding Jesus himself (4:11, 6:5, 7:27–28, 8:14, 24, 9:29–30, 19:9) and in respect to the believers (3:3, 8; 8:24, 47; 18:37).

knows there is no deceit 'in' Nathanael. The elaboration of this theme comes in 2:23-25, followed by chapters 3 and 4. After Jesus' first major sign (Jn. 2:1-11) and the mention of several other signs (2:23), the Evangelist notes, 'Jesus did not entrust himself to [those who believed because of the signs] because he knew all human beings, and he did not need anyone to testify concerning the human being, for he himself knew what was in the human being' (2:24). K. G. Kuhn, the noted Qumran specialist, argues that John writes, 'Whoever is from Truth hears my voice' (18:37). It does not say, 'He who hears my word and obeys it, he is a man of Truth,' but rather if he is from the Truth, then he cannot help but hear. He who is from below cannot hear at all, cannot believe, but can only be rebellious against the message of God's salvation in Jesus. What a person is and what he does is determined by his 'whence' – either from below or from above.[351] John 12:39-41 is a case of negative election language.[352] John 17:6, in which Jesus' prays, 'I have made your name known to those whom you gave me out of the world', is seen as further exegetical warrant for the doctrine.

There are, of course, both exegetical and theological problems with this view. One of the most obvious dangers is a comprehensive fatalism whereby moral responsibility is undermined. There is also the risk of losing sight of God's redemptive life-giving orientation towards his creation, so central to biblical theology and particularly to the Fourth Gospel. The thesis of 'fixed origin' comes very close to the Gnostic ideology which John refutes in his First Epistle. The passages which seem to teach fixed origin (e.g., 1:47; cf. 2:23-25; 5:42; 6:64; 11:9-10) may also be explicated in terms of Jesus' omniscience. Some of the statements in John which support predestinarianism (e.g., 6:37, 44, 45b; 17:2, 6) can be taken simply as factual propositions without any relevance to the fixed origins and destinies of those who believe or do not believe. Then, there is repeated emphasis on a faith-response in the Fourth Gospel.

Against those passages which support the predestinarian hypothesis

---

[351] K. G. Kuhn, 'Johannesevangelium und Qumrantexte', in *Neotestamentica et Patristica*, NovTSup 6, FS Oscar Cullmann, ed. by W. C. van Unnik (Leiden: Brill, 1962), 113.

[352] In so far as expressions like στραφῶσιν, 'may turn' (12:40) are concerned which may hint the possibility of repentance, this is dismissed simply as a case of simplification and synonymomy consistent with John's preference elsewhere in his Gospel for *verba simplicia* (cf. 1:38; 20:14, 16). Schnackenburg, *St. John*, 2:415 (cf. idem, *Johannes*, 4:150); Menken, 'Joh 12,40', 206, 208 (ἐπιστρέφω appears only in John 21:20). There may also be a connection with wisdom. The verbs στρέφω and ἰάομαι appear together in the Septuagint Prov. 12:7-8, 18; 26:14, 18. Cf. the use of the latter in Septuagint Job 5:18; 12:21; Eccl. 3:3; Sir. 38:9; Wis. 16:11-12 (contrast ἐπιστρέφω in v. 7; βραχίων in v. 16).

are an equal number of passages which emphasise universalism.[353] Yet Ernst Käsemann insists that the universalism of the Gospel does not negate its predestinarianism because the universal proclamation of salvation 'is not directed to the world as such but to the elect scattered throughout the world.'[354]

One of the major tensions in this discussion is focused on cause and effect. What some scholars find unacceptable is that God can be the active cause of blindness and thus unbelief. C. F. D. Moule endeavoured to resolve the problem by suggesting that 'the Semitic mind was notoriously unwilling to draw a sharp dividing-line between purpose and consequence.'[355] For the Jews, if God permitted something to happen (passive permissive), they took it as meaning that God actually had determined it (active permissive). They blurred purpose and result.[356] They also did not make a distinction between primary and secondary causes, but ascribed everything directly to the first cause – God. Moule wished to move the problem out of a theological realm and into the realm of cultural perception and its effects upon language.

In the Fourth Gospel, the origin of unbelief, just as in the days of Isaiah, is not explicitly explained. People refuse the light of revelation because it exposes their 'evil works' (3:19–20). Although there are examples in the Scriptures where God is known to blind or harden individuals (e.g., Exod. 4:21; 9:12; 10:20, 27; 11:10; 14:8, 17),[357] yet this activity within the context of history of salvation is not the norm for the Creator whose orientation towards his creation is first and foremost constructive and not destructive; i.e., life giving rather than life taking.

In the Fourth Gospel, Jesus responds to the Jews, who accuse him of having been born out of fornication (ἐκ πορνείας), that the reason they are

---

[353] E.g. John 1:7 (πάντες), 12 (ὅσοι δὲ ἔλαβον); 3:15, 16 (πᾶς ὁ πιστεύων), 17, 18, 36; 4:14 (ὃς δ' ἂν); 5:24; 6:35, 37, 47; 51, 54; 7:37–38; 8:12; 10:9; 11:25, 26; 12:35–36, 44, 46, 47; etc.

[354] See E. Käsemann, *The Testament of Jesus*, 64; also his reponse to Günther Bornkamm, 'Towards the Interpretation of John's Gospel', in *The Interpretation of John*, ed. by John Ashton, 2nd edn (Edinburgh: Clark, 1997), 117. Even more emphatic than Käsemann is Trumbower, *Born from Above*, 117, who explains away or simply dismisses the passages of the Gospel with a universal colouring.

[355] C. F. D. Moule, *An Idiom Book of New Testament Greek* (Cambridge: CUP, 1953), 142–3, so also Lindars, *John*, 437, commenting on the verse, 'that the word...might be fulfilled' in 12:38 writes, 'Its semitic character is shown by the final clause, in which consequence and purpose are not clearly distinguished'.

[356] Moule, *An Idiom Book*, 142f., points to Mark 4:12 and suggests it is better to take both ἵνα and μήποτε as instances of the Semitic blurring of purpose and result.

[357] Menken, 'Die Form des Zitates aus Jes. 6,10', 198 n. 34.

unable to comprehend his speech (λαλεῖν)³⁵⁸ is because they cannot hear (οὐ δύνασθε ἀκούειν) his words. They cannot hear because they are of their father the devil, and their will is to do their father's desires (8:43). Later he puts his statement in a different light: ὁ ὢν ἐκ τοῦ θεοῦ τὰ ῥήματα τοῦ θεοῦ ἀκούει· διὰ τοῦτο ὑμεῖς οὐκ ἀκούετε, ὅτι ἐκ τοῦ θεοῦ οὐκ ἐστέ, 'He who is of God hears the words of God; therefore, you do not hear because you are not of God' (8:47). In several cases, it is intimated that 'being of the truth' is a prerequisite for receiving the divine revelation (3:21; 4:23, 24; 18:37). In 8:32 truth is that which is able to make people free when it is received. This means that the truth proclaimed by Jesus as revelation itself is saving revelation; and this revelation is embodied in him who is the embodiment of the reality of God. Jesus is the truth (14:6; 1:17) because the Father is completely present in his person. And those who are of truth are those who are of God rather than of the devil (ἐκ τοῦ διαβόλου).

In these passages, it is almost as if Jesus is teaching 'fixed origin' of those who believe and those who do not. However, while it is true that 'those who are of God hear God's words', yet the conclusion that Jesus teaches the fixed origin of unbelievers and believers is false, otherwise, the Johannine emphasis upon 'new birth' would be meaningless. Those who do not hear God's word are those whose inner disposition has not changed. They are what Paul characterises as the 'natural man' (1 Cor. 2:14), the 'carnal man' (Rom. 8:7; 1 Cor. 3:3) or the 'old man' (Rom. 6:6; Eph. 4:22; Col. 3:9). The penetrating light of the divine Word necessarily offends unenlightened humanity. Those who hear God's word are those who are born anew from God (1:12-13; 3:3-8), and those who do not (e.g., Nicodemus) are in their natural unregenerate state.

There is a sense both in John and elsewhere in the New Testament that Satan is the agent of blinding. The verb τυφλόω in the New Testament is used only three times, once in 2 Corinthians 4:4, and twice in the Johannine writings (Jn. 12:40; 1 Jn. 2:11). Paul uses the term in the context of the inability of unbelievers to comprehend the truth: 'the god of this world [has] blinded the minds/thoughts (ἐτύφλωσεν τὰ νοήματα)³⁵⁹ of the

---

358 The expression λαλεῖν occurs some sixty times in the Fourth Gospel. The term is used by John as 'speaking', but also synonymously with 'witnessing' and 'testimony'. The word μαρτυρεῖν in the Fourth Gospel is a term of revelation and is practically synonymous with λαλεῖν (3:11). This is in keeping with the understanding of Jn. 8:14. The self-revelation of Jesus is here viewed as 'testimony'.

359 In 2 Corinthians 4:4, τὰ νοήματα are blinded while in John 12:40, the hardened heart is not able to perceive (νοήσωσιν).

unbelievers, to keep them from seeing the light of the gospel of the glory of Christ, who is the image of God'.

In John, 'the ruler of this world' (ὁ ἄρχων τοῦ κόσμου τούτου) is the power of darkness (Jn. 12:31; 14:30; 16:11; cf. 1 Jn. 2:11) and it is this darkness that blinds eyes. In 12:31, Jesus having declared the defeat of ὁ ἄρχων τοῦ κόσμου τούτου, warns the audience of the blinding effect of walking in darkness (Jn. 12:35–36a; cf. 1 Jn. 2:11). In 12:35–36a, he announces that the light (he himself, 8:12; 9:5) was to be present for but a short time and exhorts his hearers to walk (περιπατεῖτε) in the light while it is with them so that the darkness (σκοτία) should not overtake them, ἵνα μὴ...καταλάβῃ. He himself has not been overtaken by darkness (οὐ κατέλαβεν, 1:5) rather he has overcome (ἐγὼ νενίκηκα) the world (Jn. 16:33). Consequently, he calls on the Jews to believe in the light so that they may become 'sons of light' (12:36a). Following the report by the Evangelist of the failure to believe (12:37–43), Jesus is depicted as again calling for belief (12:44–50) and announcing: 'I have come as light into the world, that whoever believes in me may not remain in darkness' (12:46). Thus immediately on either side (12:35 and 12:46) of the reference to 'He has blinded their eyes', the Evangelist portrays Jesus speaking of himself in terms of the light in conflict with the power of darkness which overcomes those who walk in it, and it is clear that the power of darkness is to be understood in terms of 'the ruler of this world' mentioned in 12:31.

Whether John directly attributes blindness of the Jews to Satan is not explicitly made clear, even though the idea is implied both in the Gospel and elsewhere in the New Testament.[360] In the Johannine scheme, the devil is not a second creator or an equal power with God. Rather he is a 'murderer' (ἀνθρωποκτόνος) and 'a liar' (ψεύστης, 8:44). People who perform his evil desires do not gain eternal life but die in their sin (8:21). Hence, it would be true to say that in John, as elsewhere in the Scriptures, Satan is the cause of death, evil and unbelief, just as God is the cause of life, belief and good works when people become his agents (6:44; 3:21; 17:11, 15). He is the 'ruler' of 'this world' (ὁ ἄρχων τοῦ κόσμου τούτου,

---

[360] Assuming that both God and Satan are in view (cf. Jn. 6:44, 65; 8:39–47), some scholars suggest the dynamic in John might be something similar to the story of Job 1–2 where God uses Satan to carry out his will (cf. 1 Sam. 16:14–23; 18:18; 19:9; 1 Kgs. 22:23). See Painter, 'Quotation of Scripture', 451–7. But Walter Bauer, *Das Johannesevangelium erklärt* (Tübingen: Mohr, 1933), 165 and Bultmann, *John*, 453 n. 2 correctly dismiss this view. See also R. L. Tyle, 'The Source and Function of Isaiah 6:9–10 in John 12:40', in *Johannine Studies: Essays in Honor of Frank Pack*, ed. by J. E. Priest (Malibu, CA: Pepperdine University Press, 1989), 207 n. 4. The Septuagint, Matthew, and Acts avoid the theodicy question by shifting the blame to the obstinate people themselves. John raises the theodicy question but leaves it ambiguous.

i.e., 'the world of humanity') in its otherness from God and in its hostility to his Son (particularly 1:10c; 3:17b; 8:23; 12:31; 14:17, 30; 15:18–19; 16:8, 11, 33; 17:6, 9, 14, 16, 25; 18:36).

The 'Jews' are identified with this world in chapter 8 (even though there is no formal identification of 'Ιουδαῖοι and κόσμος in the Gospel). Yet this may be a persuasive scheme devised to intensify the alternatives and precipitate a decision for or against the Son (3:19–21).[361] A. Grässer has suggested such a persuasive scheme is behind Johannine dualism as well in order to emphasise the scope of God's saving purpose through his Son in the world which is the object of God's love. John's positive references to 'the world' in this vein are striking (1:29; 3:16–17; 4:42; 6:33, 51; 8:12; 9:5; 12:19), and the theme is particularly prominent in the conclusion to the so called Book of Signs (12:46–7). Therefore, it is unlikely that John would have seen an ontological division between humanity, or for that matter the Johannine community, and 'the Jews'.

Humanity in its entirety has fallen short of God's moral standards. Isaiah confessed, 'we are all as an unclean *thing*' (ונהי כטמא, Isa. 64:5 [6]; cf. Ps. 14:1–3; Jn. 2:25; 1 Jn. 1:10; Rom. 3:9–18, 23; 2:12; 5:12). The κόσμος, like 'the Jews', does not appear to be any more receptive to the truth. All humanity is 'from below' 'and of the flesh' (1:13; 3:6; 8:15). However, since Johannine christological claims are directly challenged by the Jews, they take the brunt of the polemic.[362] It is conceivable that apart from its polemical function, the bipolar language of John plays an important role in underlining the Johannine salvation schema in relation to the κρίσις theme, not so much as a polemic against the Jews, rather, as a practical concern and warning to the Christian community itself against conformity to the world.

Decades after his prophetic commission, Isaiah tells the people of Judah: 'YHWH has poured out upon you a spirit of deep sleep and has closed your eyes and covered your heads' (Isa. 29:10). How is such a statement to be understood? First the purpose of Isaiah is to provide a justification for his proclamation that the Jewish nation has been blind to the revelation of God in her history.[363] Israel has heard of God's

---

[361] 'Die antijüdische Polemik im Johannesevangelium', *NTS* 11 (1964–65), 85, 88–90.

[362] Dunn, 'The Question of Anti-semitism', in *Jews and Christians*, 201–2. See also Granskou, 'Anti-Judaism in the Passion Account', 209; J. H. Charlesworth, 'A Critical Comparison of the Dualism in 1QS 3.13–4.26 and the "Dualism" Contained in the Gospel of John', in *John and Qumran*, ed. by J. H. Charlesworth (London: Chapman, 1972), 76–106.

[363] Ernst Jenni, 'Jesajas Berufung in der neueren Forschung', *TZ* 15 (1959), 321–339 (here 328f.).

deliverance and salvation, the people have seen the work of God in their midst, and yet the response is persistence in unbelief and apathy. The task of Isaiah is not to blind, but to declare Israel's blindness to the revelation; it is not to harden hearts, but to confront the people with their hardened hearts. Some scholars regard Isaiah 6:9–10 as a hindsight conclusion, an afterthought, somewhat similar to the Lukan conclusion of Paul's ministry in Acts 28:24–28. In this scenario, Isaiah, in his old age reflecting upon his prophetic career, concludes that the obduracy of his hearers was the actual result of his preaching intended by YHWH from the beginning.[364] However, it is also possible that the prophet, reflecting upon his prophetic career, may have concluded that his hearers continued in their obduracy *in spite* of his preaching and calling Judah to repentance; thus, the statement, 'hear ye indeed, but understand not; see ye indeed but perceive not' is simply a factual observation. Consequently the action of the prophet is not to be understood in the normal predestinarian sense because his preaching has fallen upon deaf ears. Israel is 'a rebellious people' (כי עם מרי), which 'will not hear the instructions of YHWH' (Isa. 30:9; cf. 28:12). Rather they wish for 'pleasant things' (חלקות) and 'illusory prophecies' (מהתלות חזו) instead of the truth from their prophets (Isa. 30:10–11).

When John quotes Isaiah, his point is along similar lines: i.e., Isaiah's prophecy continues to find attestation even to the present time in the ministry of Jesus. The message of Isaiah, overall, is not to cause obduracy. On the contrary, the prophet vigorously appeals to his hearers to effect repentance (1:16–17, 19–20; 7:9).[365] In John the message and mission of Jesus is to bring life: ἐγὼ ἦλθον ἵνα ζωὴν ἔχωσιν καὶ περισσὸν ἔχωσιν, 'I came that they may have life, and have it abundantly' (Jn. 10:10). In John's theological formulation, God exercises his power actively in one direction – bringing life from death (3:15–16; 10:10; 11:25; 14:6; 5:24; 6:51), as the resurrection finally demonstrates. Anyone can destroy, but who can give life again? Creating life and giving life is exclusively the dominion of God. However, refusal of spiritual life means death (Jn. 5:40; 6:50; 8:24; 11:25–26). People must choose whether they prefer to safeguard their earthly life in remaining 'of the world' (7:7; 8:23; 15:19; 12:25a), or to accept the offer of life in Christ (3:15, 16; 4:14; 5:24, 29; 6:27, 40, 51, 54; 8:51; 10:28; 11:26; 14:3; 17:2) at the expense of abandonment by the world (12:25–26), the

---

[364] Franz Hesse, *Das Verstockungsproblem im Alten Testament. Eine frömmigkeitsgeschichtliche Untersuchung*, BZAW 74 (Berlin: de Gruyter, 1955), 84; Sheldon Blank, *Prophetic Faith in Isaiah* (New York: Scribner's, 1958), 4.

[365] Georg Fohrer, 'Jesaja 1 als Zusammenfassung der Verkündigung Jesajas', *ZAW* 74 (1962), 251–68.

withdrawal of its glory, and even the security of life in it (12:42–43; cf. 9:25-35; 15:20; 16:2, 20). 'Blindness', in the ministry of Jesus and his apostles, just as in the ministry of Isaiah, is the inevitable consequence of refusing to come to the light (Jn. 3:17–21). The incomprehension of Jesus' words is evidence of that judgment – they are unable to understand the truth.[366]

God's active prevention of many from believing seems inconsistent with his saving orientation towards humanity, as we see it in the Fourth Gospel (12:46–47).[367] Causing spiritual blindness so that some would be thwarted from believing and continue in their path of moral decay is fundamentally contrary to God's 'work' (ἔργον) which is nothing less than the redemption and salvation of his creation. Any theological system which holds as its foundational dogma the absolute holiness of God cannot simultaneously affirm that God can be the primary active cause of spiritual blindness and unbelief. The two propositions are mutually exclusive. Affirming one denies the other.[368] Surely the message of the Fourth Gospel above all else is God's inherently redemptive posture towards his creation (Jn. 10:10). John tells us that God's purpose in creation is not for eyes to be blind (cf. Jn. 9:2).[369] On the contrary, the aim of God's saving activity,

---

[366] It is likely that John's νοήσωσιν 'understand' in 12:40 recalls yet another analogous passage from Isaiah (44:18). Both Hoskyns, *Fourth Gospel*, 429 and Bergmeier, *Glaube*, 231, refer to Isaiah 44:18 as a parallel passage in their attempts to explicate John 12:40. Menken, 'Joh 12,40', 205-6, 208-9, has asserted that νοέω in John 12:40 has actually come from this analogous context. Isaiah 44:18 is strikingly reminiscent of Isaiah 6:9–10: 'They have no understanding to perceive; for they have been blinded so that they should not see with their eyes, nor perceive with their heart' (cf. Isa. 32:6; 47:7; also Isa. 44:22). Both the Isaiah 44:18 and John 12:40 passages (Septuagint) conspicuously share a construction in which the verb νοέω is paired with καρδία in the dative where the Evangelist may wish to liken the Jews to their idolatrous forebearers (cf. Isa. 44:9–17; contrast Jn. 19:15) who also rejected revelation.

[367] But see also 1:4; 3:15, 16; 4:32-38; 5:22, 24, 27, 40; 6:27, 33, 35, 40, 51, 54; 8:12; 10:10; 11:25; 14:6; 17:3; 20:31. Blank, *Krisis*, 302-3, writes, 'Die Schwierigkeit, die entsteht, wenn man bei Johannes Gott als Subjekt der Verblendung und Verstockung annimmt, besteht weniger darin, dass in der Schrift eine solche Möglichkeit überhaupt undenkbar wäre, als vielmehr darin, dass diese Aussage im Johannesevangelium sich nur ausserordentlich widerstrebend in den Gesamtzusammenhang einfügen würde.' He adds, 'Man frage sich einmal, ob ein solcher Sinn johanneisch denkbar ist?' Blank does, however, seem to concede that, according to John 6:44, one cannot come to Jesus unless the Father draws him. 'Aber dafür, dass Gott selbst das Nicht-Glauben-Können bewirkte, gibt es sonst im vierten Evangelium keinen Beweis'.

[368] See Johannes Hempel, *Gott und Mensch im Alten Testament: Studien zur Geschichte der Frömmigkeit*, BWANT, 3. Folge 2, 2nd edn (Stuttgart: Kohlhammer, 1936), 122ff.; idem, *Das Ethos des Alten Testaments*, BZAW 67, 2nd edn (Berlin: de Gruyter, 1964); Räisänen, *Divine Hardening*, 45–47.

[369] John 9:2; cf. Jn. 1:4; 3:15-16; 4:32-38; 5:22, 24, 27, 40; 6:27, 33, 35, 40, 51, 54; 8:12; 10:10; 11:25; 14:6; 17:3; 20:31.

ἐργάζομαι, 'work' (5:17), is so that the blind eyes may see.[370] However, there is the necessity of response: 'If anyone chooses (θέλῃ) to do His will...' (cf. Jn. 7:17). Where there is not this willingness which comes from one's inner disposition or orientation towards light, incomprehension and obduracy is the inevitable result, the natural consequence of rejecting revelation.[371] It is inherent in revelation to bring salvation and illumination (Jn. 3:16–18; 8:12; 12:35, 46), but refusal of light is to remain in darkness (Jn. 3:19–21), refusal of the cure means remaining ill (Isa. 6:10; Jn. 12:40); refusal of spiritual life means death (Jn. 5:40; 6:50; 8:24; 11:25–26); rejection of spiritual sight is to remain spiritually blind. If revelation means life, rejection of revelation means death. In this sense, God is not the active author of blindness, otherwise John 3:16 or 10:10 would be meaningless. Rather, blindness is the inevitable consequence of refusing to come to the light (Jn. 3:17–21).

5.6. The Witness of the Scriptures to Jesus and the Prophetic 'Lawsuit'

For John, rejection of Jesus is the rejection of the climactic saving self-revelation of God.[372] Isaiah had been forewarned that the unreceptive attitude to God's revelation was not exhausted in the circumstances of his own prophetic ministry. It was experienced by one prophet after another and found its defining fulfilment in the unreceptive hearing given to him of whom the prophets spoke. In spurning this revelation, John has called the Scriptures to bear witness against the hardness and blindness of the 'elders' of Israel. The Scriptures bear witness that Jesus is the Christ[373] whose glory Isaiah had seen, and just as his witness to the glory of the eternal Word was met with unbelief, so is the witness of the Evangelist to the glory of the incarnate Word. The Evangelist calls the Scriptures, the writings of Moses and the prophets, to bear witness to the authenticity of

---

[370] Jn. 9:45; 12:46–47; Isa. 35:4–6; cf. Jn. 1:5, 9; 3:17–19; 8:12; 10:10; 11:25, etc.

[371] See Don Carson, 'Predestination and Responsibility: Elements of Tension-Theology in the Fourth Gospel against Jewish Background' (Diss., Cambridge, 1975, supervised by B. Lindars), published as *Divine Sovereignty and Human Responsibility: Biblical Perspectives in Tension* (Atlanta: Knox, 1981); A. Feuillet, *Le mystère de l'amour divin dans la théologie johannique*, EBib (Paris: Gabalda, 1972), 35–8; Westcott, *St. John*, 2:21–2.

[372] See my discussion in chapter six.

[373] Bultmann, *Theology of the New Testament*, 2:28, 68; Bruce, *John*, 271–2; Brown, *John*, 1:484; Schnackenburg, *St. John*, 2:274; Becker, *Johannes*, 409.

Jesus' claim to be the Christ. Nevertheless the elders of Israel have rejected the witness and the revelation. In this sense, the Fourth Gospel echoes the prophetic lawsuit brought against Israel by her prophets for the nation's faithlessness and indifference.

Such forensic language[374] also is repeatedly observed in Israel's prophetic writings where YHWH sets forth his case against Israel and against the nations.[375] While the modern readers of the Gospel may miss such overtones, a Jew accustomed to hearing the prophets read, would not have missed the parallels. Once again John has brought the Scriptures to validate his conviction that Jesus is the One whom he claimed to be. He calls upon the testimony of Isaiah against the hardness and blindness of his contemporaries, the teachers of Israel. In view of such established grounds of credibility for the claim, the truthfulness of the claim cannot be easily refuted, unless, of course, one chooses to 'remain blind' (9:40–41) to this preponderance of evidence (cf. 10:32; 12:37; 15:22, 24). In his prophetic voice, the Fourth Evangelist has challenged the teachers of Israel who claim to see, but in fact are spiritually blind (9:41). In the Shepherd discourse, Jesus characterises the religious leaders, as in Ezekiel's indictment of the elders of Israel, as 'thieves', 'robbers' and 'hirelings' who are careless about the flock of God (10:1, 2, 7, 8). Their spiritual dullness is betrayed in their inability to understand Jesus' words (3:10). Neither are they cognisant of the true meaning of Scripture (5:46; cf. 7:52; 8:12) or the fulfilment of it in the life of Jesus. They do not even understand earthly truths, much less the heavenly realities pertaining to who God is, how he relates to his creation and what he seeks (3:10–12; 4:24). They are more preoccupied with humanly-bestowed honour or 'glory' than with the glory that comes from God (5:44; 12:43). While they claim to sit in Moses' seat

---

[374] Several scholars have drawn attention to this undercurrent of a forensic process in the Fourth Gospel, among them, A. E. Harvey, *Jesus on Trial: A Study in the Fourth Gospel* (London: SPCK, 1976); A. A. Trites, *The New Testament Concept of Witness*, SNTSMS 31 (Cambridge: CUP, 1977); Jerome H. Neyrey, 'Jesus the Judge: Forensic Process in John 8:21–59', *Bib* 68 (1987), 509; T. Okure, *The Johannine Approach to Mission: A Contextual Study of John 4:1–42* (Tübingen: Mohr-Siebeck, 1988), 256. Compare with Quintilian, *De Institutio Oratoria* 3.vi.10. Trans. by H. E. Butler, LCL, 4 vols (London: Heinemann, 1921–1933).

[375] In Isaiah 1–39, such forensic language is pervasive. A similar style is evident in the 'trial scenes' of Isaiah 41:2, 4, 26; 43:9, 13; 44:7, 8; 45:21; 46:5. Especially, the 'trial scene' in Isaiah 43:8–13 seems important in John 8, with its emphatic use of the ἐγώ εἰμι and of the 'witness' theme to which 8:18 seems specifically to allude. Stibbe, *John*, 138, lists seven such 'parallels' between John 8 and Isaiah 43:8–12. Knight, 'Antisemitism in the Fourth Gospel, 86, cites Isaiah 1:2–4 as a prophetic parallel to 8:44. See particularly Trites, *Concept of Witness*, 78ff; James Limburg, 'The Root ריב and the Prophetic Lawsuit Speeches', *JBL* 88 (1969), 291–304; Harvey, *Jesus on Trial*, 16f.

(the symbolic locus of the authoritative interpretation of the Torah, Mt. 23:2; cf. Jn. 9:28) and to speak with his authority, it will be Moses who condemns them for their spiritual insolence and ignorance. The spiritual teachers of Israel claimed to be the expounders of the Torah, the authoritative voice of Moses and students of his great legacy by their daily preoccupation with the study of his writings,[376] and yet according to John, it is Moses who will condemn them: 'Do not think that I shall accuse you to the Father: there is one that accuses you, even Moses, in whom you trust. For had you believed Moses, you would have believed me: for he wrote of me' (Jn. 5:45–46). So the lawgiver himself, to whom the leaders of the people appeal, becomes the prosecutor.

While John appeals to the witness of John the Baptist, disciples like Lazarus, the Samaritans and the Samaritan woman, the signs of Jesus, and the blind man, yet his final court of appeal is the Scriptures of Israel; it is they that testify that Jesus is the Christ. It is the Father himself who bears witness to the Son in the words of Moses and the prophets. This Word is identical with the 'Scriptures' in which the Jewish leaders seek eternal life, the very goal that eludes them because they will not hear its testimony.

5.7. Implications of the Witness of the Scriptures for the Johannine Audience

In this chapter I have endeavoured to show how in the Fourth Gospel John puts forward the case that Jesus is the Christ in whose person and work the Scriptures are fulfilled and Jewish religious institutions are consummated. Any meaningful explication of John's Gospel and the function of its language must reckon with the author's systematic allusions to the Scriptures. John's appeal to the Scriptures is set against the background of 'Judaism', in which there had been and continued to be questions or denials that Jesus is the Christ. The Scriptures authenticate the belief that Jesus is the Messiah. However, the Fourth Gospel is not simply a response to those who would have denied the Messianic identity of Jesus. The content of the Fourth Gospel also addresses the 'secret believers' and the undecided[377] – those who feared that their confession of Jesus would

---

[376] The Mishnah can even say, 'Greater stringency applies to (the observance of) the words of the Scribes than to (the observance of) the words of the (written) Law' (*Sanh.* 11:3).

[377] See Thyen, 'Heil', 168–74; idem, 'Johannes 10 im Kontext des vierten Evangeliums', in *The Shepherd Discourse of John 10 and its Context: Studies by Members of Johannine Writings Seminar*, ed. by J. Beutler and R. T. Fortna, SNTSMS 67 (Cambridge: CUP, 1991), 121.

socially prove costly. In the indictment of the religious teachers, there is an implicit warning and appeal to this group. John would have aimed to show that revelation requires a proper response of faith; one cannot 'sit on the fence'. To be exposed to the light of revelation requires a certain response and behaviour. Being a 'secret believer' is incompatible with a proper response.

The Nicodemus episode in conjunction with the pronouncement of the author in 12:42-43 seems to underline this emphasis. Nicodemus last appears in John 19:38-42, where he accompanies Joseph of Arimathea in the burial of Jesus.[378] Joseph, like Nicodemus, is a member of the Sanhedrin (Mk. 15:43).[379] John characterises Joseph also as a disciple who concealed his alliance to Jesus for fear of the Jews, thus correcting the favourable picture of him by Mark and Matthew (cf. Mk. 15:43; Mt. 27:57) so as to align him too with the fearful who are the recipients of the devastating criticism of 12:42-43. The distinction made by John in 12:42-43 between the 'rulers' (οἱ ἄρχοντες) and the Pharisees has led one scholar to suggest that by 'rulers' John always refers to secret believers among the Jewish authorities.[380] This is doubtful however. In Nicodemus, the two groups are clearly united (3:1; 7:50c).[381] Both Joseph's and Nicodemus' contribution in John is to bring no less than seventy-five pounds of burial spices (19:38-42), a gesture often seen as an indication of his open devotion, even of confession.[382] But others see the action as too little, too late and a further affirmation of the Johannine rejection of their type of faith. It was Alfred Loisy who contended that Nicodemus and Joseph confess nothing and have nothing to do with Jesus except with his corpse.[383] The First Epistle may shed some light on the Johannine problem

---

Martyn, 'Glimpses into the History', 90–121 and Brown, *Community*, 71–3 describe these as secret Christian Jews or 'crypto-Christians'. Martyn characterises their behaviour as 'dual allegiance' to the Christian faith and the synagogue. Cf. Loisy, *Quatrième évangile*, 305. See further Wengst, *Bedrängte Gemeinde*, 59–60; Meeks, 'Man From Heaven', 69–70.

[378] Schnackenburg, *St John*, 3:295; Lindars, *John*, 592.

[379] The Sanhedrin in New Testament times consisted of chief priests, elders, and the teachers of the law (with all likelihood the Pharisees). Its membership totalled seventy-one including the high priest.

[380] Martyn, *History and Theology*, 87–88.

[381] See my earlier discussion in 5.2.1.

[382] Cf. Brown, *John*, 2:959–60; idem, *Community of the Beloved*, 72 n. 128; Schnackenburg, *St. John*, 3:296–97; and Lindars, *John*, 592.

[383] Loisy, *Quatrième évangile*, 895–6; also see Rensberger, *Overcoming the World*, 40; Meeks, 'Man from Heaven', 55; Marinus de Jonge, 'Nicodemus and Jesus: Some Observations on Misunderstanding and Understanding in the Fourth Gospel', in de Jonge, *Jesus: Stranger from*

with 'secret believers' and the undecided. The author of the First Epistle refers to situations where some of those who initially accepted the Christian claims later abandoned them (1 Jn. 2:19; cf. 1 Jn. 2:18, 22; 4:2, 3; 2 Jn. 7). This may explain, too, why Judas' betrayal is seen as a source of deep affliction for Jesus himself (13:18, 21–30; cf. 6:70–71).[384] In 5:44, Jesus says to the Jews, 'How *can* you believe who receive glory from one another and do not seek the glory which comes from the one God?' If we were to bypass verse 42, we would find the same theme in 12:43: they *could* not believe (thus fulfilling Scripture) because they loved human glory rather than the glory of God (with an implicit reference back to 'his glory' which Isaiah saw, cf. 12:41). It is this desire for human approval (i.e., the world) which for John makes *belief,* and not simply confession, impossible. As in chapter 9, where claiming to see incurs blindness, so in chapter 12 the seeking of human praise or approval prevents one from seeing. In this scenario, Johannine language with its allusions to the law and the prophets not only aims to show the blindness of the teachers of Israel to the Scriptures, but also to serve as a stern warning to the so-called secret believers. In citing God's verdict on unbelief in Isaiah 6:9–10, the Evangelist warns those who desire both the praise of the world and the approval of God; such a double alliance in itself is an indication of unbelief, since characteristically such people vacillate between belief and disbelief.[385] The Gospel would have invited this group to come forth with an open confession of faith and join the Christian community. Apparently some in this group may have hoped to be disciples of Jesus but also to remain within the framework of synagogue Judaism. For the Evangelist, this could only be done by concealing their discipleship from public knowledge and avoiding an open confession in fear of social ostracism. This lack of courage was tantamount to the rejection of Jesus and

---

Heaven and Son of God, SBLSBS 11 (Missoula, MT: Scholars Press, 1977), 33–4; Paul Duke, *Irony in the Fourth Gospel* (Atlanta: John Knox Press, 1985), 110.

[384] Judas, called 'a devil' by Jesus (6:70) and 'a thief' by John (12:6), may have been seen at the time of the Evangelist as the prototype of the departees who were 'never one of us' (1 Jn. 2:19), 'the anti-Christs', 'the liars' and 'the false prophets' (1 Jn. 2:18, 22; 4:2, 3; 2 Jn. 7) who are also typified as the 'thieves and brigands' in Jn. 10:8, 10a. All these 'anti-Christ' figures have one thing in common: they plunder, scatter and lead astray the flock which Jesus gathers into a unity (10:1–18; 1 Jn. 2:26–27; 3:7). In short, they destroy the community and its witness to Jesus. For example, Judas' rebuke of Mary of Bethany for her wasteful annointing of Jesus (12:4–6) is seen as disturbing the peace of the community at the anticipated Paschal meal (13:2, 21–31), while Judas ends by betraying Jesus himself (18:2–6). In the face of such a threat from within, it becomes particularly necessary to focus on the community and to emphasise its missionary and eschatological significance.

[385] See the crowd in 7:31; 8:30; 10:42; 11:45; 12:11, 42; cf. 2:23–25.

categorically unacceptable to John.[386] The last appeal in 12:44–50 addresses these wavering "believers" as well as those who do not believe at all. The evangelistic appeal of the Gospel need not be elaborated. The document, in setting forth the case that Jesus, is the Christ, would have had an evangelistic function by means of the believing community itself.

The Fourth Gospel would have had a double function for the community of faith as well. The severe criticism in 12:43 implicitly serves as a warning to the Christian community itself. Indeed, subsequent chapters address wavering disciples, too, in such symbolic language of the branches which must needs be cut from the vine (15:6). The evidence of faith is abiding in the truth. And if one abides in the truth, he/she cannot remain in darkness. There can be no double alliance. The faith that abides and is authentic must be willing to risk all. It is the faith that is prepared to run through the storm of opposition which association with Jesus will provoke and to walk in his steps (13:16; 15:20; 16:1–4). It is only to these that Jesus will entrust himself – those who truly trust him (14:12–21, 23; 10:14, 15; cf. 2:23–25).

Apart from warning, the document would have had a significant reassuring effect for the Christian community and confirmed them in the faith. Those same detailed allusions to the fulfilment of Scriptures which showed the blindness of the religious authorities would have served the opposite purpose for the believers. They would have aimed to deepen the faith of the believing community.

The fulfilment of the Scriptures in Jesus' life and career including his rejection by the teachers of Israel and his subsequent death on the cross is at the heart of John's systematic appeal to the Scriptures. It is this infusion of his language with so many details from the law and the prophets brought together in such intricate thematic undercurrents, which gives John's language its unique quality. In this Gospel the moment one assumes that the bottom has been reached, the ground caves in to greater depth. The text constantly seems in reach and yet remains out of reach, so simple to grasp and yet unremittingly pointing beyond itself. Tinted with Johannine irony, this enigmatic language challenges both 'the Jews' and the 'world' whom they represent. It calls into question the certainties of unaided, 'natural' human beings, whether Jew or Greek, who insist on

---

[386] Wengst, *Bedrängte Gemeinde*, 59–60; Jürgen Becker, 'Jn 3, 1–21 als Reflex johanneischer Schuldiskussion', in *Das Wort und die Wörter*, 86–88; Meeks, 'Man From Heaven', 69–70. See also Loisy, *Quatrième évangile*, 895–6; de Jonge, 'Nicodemus and Jesus', 34; Brown, *John*, 2:959–60.

living on the superficial, 'fleshly' level – even the certainties of those who occupy venerated positions as teachers of the Jewish law. John shows the human inability at this 'natural' level to see and perceive in Jesus, the Christ according to the Scriptures, namely, the climax of the revelation of God. The aim of the language is not to exclude but to provoke men and women, Jews and Greeks, to reconsider their certainties, to examine and see the fulfilment of the Scriptures in the life, and above all, the death of the Son of God. It shows that those who seek the δόξα or honour of men and hide their faith because of it (12:43) will have the δόξα or self-manifestation of the glorious God (1:14) hidden from them (cf. 12:36), especially that glory which is revealed in the death and the resurrection of the Son of Man. Ultimately, of course, for the Evangelist, the recognition of Jesus as the Christ, his unity with the Father, his claim to be the One whose origin is from 'above' and not from 'below', rests on abiding faith which is grounded in the regenerating work of the Holy Spirit. Indeed, the comprehension of the witness of Scripture to Jesus and its fulfilment in his life and work, as well as understanding the revelation at the level of true perception, belongs to those who have been born of God and have entered into a life-long discipleship. This is the topic of the following chapter.

Chapter 6

Spiritual Perception and the Language of John's Gospel

6.1. The Language of John as a Theological Language

In this study, I have argued that the language of the Fourth Gospel is a theological language. Its function is a theological function and its significance is a theological significance. The purpose of the Gospel is to prove and proclaim that Jesus is the Christ, the embodiment of the saving revelation of God according to Israel's Scriptures. It is in these conscious refrains consisting of echoes and thematic allusions to the Scriptures that we find the function of John's elusive language – to show that Jesus is the Christ of whom the Scriptures spoke and in whom they found their supreme realisation. However, the recognition of this truth lies beyond the capacity of unaided humans. To be sure, neither the Johannine Jesus nor the Evangelist intends to conceal the revelation by this elusive language. Rather, the significance of this feature is to accentuate that the perception of the revelation of God in Jesus Christ and the recognition of the witness of the Scriptures to him is open only to those who are born of God. In Christianity according to John, as in Christianity according to Paul, 'Those who are unspiritual do not receive the gifts of God's Spirit, for they are foolishness to them, and they are unable to understand them because they are spiritually discerned' (1 Cor. 2:14, NRSV). This sentiment is echoed throughout the New Testament. Spiritual perception ultimately rests on spiritual regeneration leading to an abiding faith, both of which are brought about by the life-giving work of the Holy Spirit. This chapter endeavours to articulate this thesis.

The language of the Fourth Gospel is a theological language because the Gospel itself is a profoundly theological document. Yet D. Moody Smith writes, 'John the evangelist obviously did not write a theological treatise, but a Gospel, a narrative of the ministry of Jesus Christ that stands alongside three broadly similar narratives in the New Testament'.[1] It is, of course, true that John's Gospel is a narrative account of Jesus' ministry. But this narrative is assembled on a purposeful theological skeleton, the interpretation of Jesus Christ and his significance for Israel and the world.[2] Whatever may be its strengths as a piece of literature, it pales by comparison to the breadth and sweep of the book's theological insights into the person and work of Jesus Christ in whom, the author vigorously asserts, God's saving character is revealed. As I have noted repeatedly throughout this study, it is in the context of this theological emphasis that the message of the Gospel, including its language, must be understood.

While Bultmann committed half of the second volume of his *Theology of the New Testament* to articulate the Johannine theology, Ignace de la Potterie summarised the thrust of that theology in one sentence: 'John's theology is above all a theology of revelation'.[3] In this theology, in order to know and see the Father, one must see him in the Son (14:9; cf. 1:18; 10:30). The locus of divine revelation is encapsulated in the person and work of Jesus the Christ, the incarnate Word (1:1–18), according to the Scriptures. However, within the Johannine theological formulation recognition of Jesus' identity and of God's salvific work through him (according to the Scriptures) rests on three pillars: being born of God, the ongoing presence of the Holy Spirit within the believer, and abiding faith. In the Fourth Gospel, only those who are possessed by the Spirit of God and have entered into lasting discipleship actually see and perceive the witness of Scripture to Jesus and its supreme fulfilment in him. In this respect, neither John nor Jesus, whose works and words he records, is being ambiguous for the sake of concealing mysteries from the uninitiated. In fact, if the Evangelist had been asked why did he not write a 'plain Gospel', he might have responded as Jesus did to those who asked him in a similar vein, 'How long will you keep us in suspense? If you are the Christ, tell us

---

[1] *The Theology of the Gospel of John* (Cambridge: CUP, 1995), 1. See also R. G. Hall, *Revealed Histories: Techniques for Ancient Jewish and Christian Historiography*, JSPSup 6 (Sheffield: JSOT Press, 1991), 235; Rodney Whitacre, *Johannine Polemic: The Role of Tradition and Theology*, SBLDS 67 (Chico, CA: Scholars Press, 1982), 2, 5; Howard C. Kee, *Jesus in History: An Approach to the Study of the Gospels*, 2nd edn (New York: Harcourt, Brace, Jovanovich, 1977), 217.

[2] However, this theological emphasis should not be misconstrued as though John's Gospel is a historical allegory, where each person or event represents some abstract idea.

[3] Ignace de la Potterie, 'The Truth in Saint John', in *The Interpretation of John*, ed. by John Ashton, 2nd edn (Edinburgh: Clark, 1997), 79; first published in *RivB* 11 (1963), 3–24. See also Gail O'Day, 'Narrative Mode and Theological Claim: A Study in the Fourth Gospel', *JBL* 105 (1986), 657.

plainly' (Jn. 10:24). Jesus answered, 'I told you, and you do not believe' (10:25). Earlier he had explained, ὁ ὢν ἐκ τοῦ θεοῦ τὰ ῥήματα τοῦ θεοῦ ἀκούει· διὰ τοῦτο ὑμεῖς οὐκ ἀκούετε, ὅτι ἐκ τοῦ θεοῦ οὐκ ἐστέ, 'The one who is of God hears the words of God, therefore you do not hear because you are not of God' (8:47, cf. 18:37). In his discourse with Nicodemus, Jesus once again speaks of this inability of spiritually unregenerate people to comprehend revelatory truth (3:12, 29, 31–34; cf. 1 Cor. 2:14) and of the need to be born of God in order to understand this truth (3:5; 1:12–14; cf. Col. 1:27; 1 Jn. 5:10–12).

6.2. The Resurrection and Its Implication for John's Language

For the early church, the event of the resurrection of Jesus marked a decisive watershed.[4] It was the event that above all others validated Jesus' claims, dispelled doubts, and made unmatching pieces to fit. Christians naturally turned to the Scriptures for clues. Every action and word of Jesus was examined, and confirmation was sought in the Scriptures. The result was the christological interpretation of the Scriptures, an example of which is seen in the Fourth Gospel. The incarnation, cross and resurrection were seen as the realisation of all prophetic aspirations. The Scriptures anticipated this moment in history. The Lord, whom Israel had sought, had suddenly come to his temple (cf. Mal. 3:2); and the herald had gone forth through John the Baptist: 'the voice of one crying in the wilderness, "Make straight the way of the Lord"' (Jn. 1:23, cf. Isa. 40:3). According to the Fourth Gospel, this decisive moment in salvation history occurred when 'the Word became flesh', which in turn set in motion the judgment (κρίσις) of the world. The word of judgment which must be spoken at the last day has been spoken, and it is none other than ὁ λόγος σὰρξ ἐγένετο,[5] though it is a judgment which fundamentally aims at life and salvation.[6] In this respect, christology and eschatology are cornerstones of Johannine theology[7] where, in fact, eschatology seems to be a function of christology.[8]

---

[4] C. F. D. Moule, ed., *The Significance of the Message of the Resurrection for Faith in Jesus Christ*, SBT, 2nd ser., 8 (London: SCM, 1968).

[5] Paolo Ricca, *Die Eschatologie des Vierten Evangeliums* (Zürich: Gotthelf-Verlag, 1966), 98; cf. R. Schnackenburg, *The Gospel According to St. John*, ET, vol. 2 (New York: Seabury Press), 437.

[6] E.g., John 1:4, 12, 16, 29; 3:15–21; 4:10, 14, 34–38, 42; 5:8, 17, 19, 21–22, 24–25, 40; 6:35, 40, 47–48, 50–51, 54; 7:37–38; 8:12, 51; 9:4–5; 10:9–11, 28; 11:25–26; 12:36, 46; 14:14; 20:31.

[7] On the recent research on Johannine eschatology, see the published dissertations by J. Frey,

John's language is wedded to this eschatological-christological articulation of the redemptive work of God through the incarnate Word.

The recorded incomprehension of the disciples before the resurrection of Christ and their subsequent illumination (e.g., Luke 24:13–35) shows the significance of the resurrection event.[9] John makes the point in a slightly different way than the Synoptics when he writes that, after Easter, the disciples 'remembered', ἐμνήσθησαν (2:17, 22; 12:16; cf. 8:27; 10:6; 13:28; 20:9) and understood certain points which escaped them when they first were experienced. These remarks about the disciples' memory occur as an explanation of the past incomprehension and the post-Easter illumination.[10] Throughout the Gospel, there are repeated references to the fuller understanding of the meaning of the actions and words of Jesus and the recognition of the fulfilment of the Scriptures in him (2:17; 12:37–40; 13:18; 19:24, 30, 36). The disciples *ought* to have understood before Easter, but the resurrection was a decisive turning point. While Luke records that the disciples are rebuked for being 'foolish (ἀνόητοι) and slow of heart to believe', i.e., to recognise the witness of Scriptures to Jesus (Lk. 24:25),

---

Die johanneische Eschatologie. Band 1, Ihre Probleme im Spiegel der Forschung seit Reimarus, WUNT 96 (Tübingen: Mohr-Siebeck, 1997); and J. Neugebauer, *Die eschatologischen Aussagen in den johanneischen Abschiedsreden. Eine Untersuchung zu Johannes 13–17*, BWANT 140 (Stuttgart-Berlin-Cologne: Kohlhammer, 1995). For recent examinations of various aspects of Johannine christology, see M. E. Boismard, *Moses or Jesus: An Essay in Johannine Christology* (Leuven: Leuven University Press, 1993); P. N. Anderson, *The Christology of the Fourth Gospel. Its Unity and Disunity in the Light of John 6*, WUNT 2.78 (Tübingen: Mohr-Siebeck, 1996); William Loader, *The Christology of the Fourth Gospel: Structure and Issues* (Frankfurt am Main: Verlag Peter Lang, 1989); P. M. Casey, *From Jewish Prophet to Gentile God: The Origins and Development of New Testament Christology* (Cambridge: James Clarke, 1991); J. D. G. Dunn, *Christology in the Making: A New Testament Inquiry into the Origins of the Doctrine of the Incarnation* (London: SCM, 1980); E. E. Ellis, 'Background and Christology of John's Gospel: Selected Motifs', *Southwestern Journal of Theology* 31 (1988), 224–31; T. E. Pollard, *Johannine Christology and the Early Church*, SNTSMS 13 (Cambridge: CUP, 1970).

[8] Also Joseph Blank, *Krisis: Untersuchungen zur johanneischen Christologie und Eschatologie* (Freiburg im Breisgau: Lambertus Verlag, 1964), 38; G. B. Caird, *New Testament Theology* (Oxford: Clarendon, 1994), 263f.

[9] See Myers, 'Irony and Humor in the Gospel of John', 3; Wead, *The Literary Devices in John's Gospel*, 1–11; Gerald L. Borchert, 'The Resurrection Perspective in John', *RevExp* 85 (1988), 501–13; John J. O'Rourke, 'The Historic Present in the Gospel of John', *JBL* 93 (1974), 585–90.

[10] Clearly revealed in John's explanatory asides. See John J. O'Rourke, 'Asides in the Gospel of John', *NovT* 21 (1979), 212; R. Bultmann, *The Gospel of John: A Commentary*, ET (Philadelphia: Westminster Press, 1971), 375; F. Mussner, *The Historical Jesus in the Gospel of John* (New York: Herder and Herder, 1967), 48–54; F. McColl, *Problemata Johannaea* (Rome: 1965), 35–6; Marianne M. Thompson, *The Incarnate Word: Perspectives on the Fourth Gospel* (Peabody, MA: Hendrickson Publishers, 1988), 123–4; E. D. Freed, *Old Testament Quotations in the Gospel of John* (Leiden: Brill, 1965), 115.

John sets out in intricate detail to show how the Scriptures 'spoke' of Jesus and how he fulfilled them. In the Fourth Gospel, the author's point of view or angle of narration[11] is a decidedly post-Easter perspective, which distinguishes the Fourth Gospel from the Synoptics.[12] The Synoptic authors write presupposing the resurrection. In John, events are related after the resurrection from the hindsight and the illumination brought about by the Holy Spirit.[13] This perspective has given the author of the Gospel two understandings of each event: that of a participant in those events, and that of a disciple following the resurrection. Some of the Johannine double-meaning words as well as asides capture this disparity between the pre-resurrection and post-resurrection understandings.

While some scholars, such as W. Meeks, believe that the language of the Fourth Gospel remains as enigmatic for the modern reader as it appears to have been for the interlocutors of Jesus,[14] other scholars, such as D. A.

---

[11] It was Henry James and one of his pupils, Percy Lubbock, who first brought into prominence 'the literary point of view' in the study of literature. Percy Lubbock, *The Craft of Fiction* (London, 1926), 59-91. On 'literary point of view' and its function and importance, see further Boris Uspensky, *A Poetics of Composition: The Structure of the Artistic Text and Typology of a Compositional Form*, trans. by V. Zavarin and S. Wittig (Berkeley: University of California Press, 1973), 6, 83-96; Robert Weimann, *Structure and Society in Literary Theory* (Charlottesville: University of Virginia Press, 1973); Susan S. Lanser, *The Narrative Act: Point of View in Prose Fiction* (Princeton: University Press, 1981); Wayne C. Booth, *The Rhetoric of Fiction* (Chicago: University of Chicago Press, 1961), 20, 149; idem, 'Distance and Point of View: An Essay in Classification', *Essays in Criticism* 11 (1961), 60-79; Gérard Genette, *Narrative Discourse: An Essay in Method*, trans. by Jane E. Lewin (Ithaca, NY: Cornell University Press, 1980), 186; Meir Sternberg, *Expositional Modes and Temporal Ordering in Fiction* (Baltimore: Johns Hopkins University Press, 1978); J. M. Lotman, 'Point of View in a Text', *New Literary History* 6 (1975), 339-52; R. Alan Culpepper, *Anatomy of the Fourth Gospel* (Philadelphia: Fortress, 1983), 15-49.

[12] B. Westcott, *The Gospel According to St. John* (Grand Rapids: Eerdmans, 1954), xxxvi; R. Schnackenburg, *Das Johannesevangelium*, HTKNT (Freiberg: Herder, 1965), 4:367; O. Michel, 'μιμήσκομαι', *TWNT*, 4:681; O'Rourke, 'Historic Present', 585-90. B. Lonergan, *De Verbo Incarnato* (Rome: Pontifical Biblical Institute, 1964), 23, cites what he calls three 'schemata' through which the New Testament writers view the Christ in their writings. There is a 'schema prospectivum' which is that chosen by the Synoptic writers. This is the first-person point of view. Secondly, he describes the 'schema retrospectivum' which views Jesus as the exalted Son of God seated on the right hand of God ruling the present world. This view, he claims, is found only in Paul. The third, 'schema restrospectivum inversum', shows Jesus as a man but does not consider his life as limited to the earthly life. This schema also views the life of Jesus both in its pre-existence and its present glorification and reign. This latter is found in John and occasionally in Paul.

[13] There are several variables in a given angle of narration: physical, spatial, temporal, psychological, and ideological, among perhaps others. See R. Connolly, *Rhetoric Case Book* (New York, 1953), 588.

[14] W. Meeks, 'The Man From Heaven in Johannine Sectarianism', *JBL* 91 (1972), 68-9. See also Walter Rebell, *Gemeinde als Gegenwelt: zur soziologischen und didaktischen Funktion des Johannesevangeliums*, BBET 20 (Frankfurt: Lang, 1987), 83, 112, 162-63.

Carson, argue that the resurrection has demolished the kind of ambiguity and misunderstandings which we see experienced by Jesus' audience. Carson argues that the experience of the disciples is a unique experience in a particular juncture in salvation history. Johannine 'misunderstandings' are historically implausible subsequent to the resurrection.[15] In the context of this debate, there are several different factors which need to be kept distinct: (1) the understanding of the disciples before and after the resurrection, which is effected by their unique experience but especially in view of the activity of the Holy Spirit after Easter; (2) the incomprehension of the opponents of Jesus, which is not effected by the resurrection because of their unbelief; (3) the understanding of the readers of the Gospel (obviously post-resurrection and post-Pentecost), which is effected by their positive or negative response (i.e., belief or unbelief) to the apostolic witness; and (4) the post-resurrection illumination because of the activity of the Holy Spirit within those who believe. In these distinctions, the resurrection is decisive only in the understanding of those who believe.

It is also noteworthy that the Fourth Gospel has been characterised as 'enigmatic' or 'mystical' by its readers. In this case, as I have endeavoured to show, the ambiguity of the Gospel's language may to a large extent be attributed to the compositional complexities of the Gospel, Johannine allusions to the Old Testament, and the Evangelist's own enigmatic style. To his disciples who had difficulty understanding his speaking 'figuratively',[16] Jesus referred to a time yet future when he would no longer speak ἐν παροιμίαις (16:25). Here clearly the cause of incomprehension is the position of the disciples in the progress of revelation. The resurrection had not yet occurred, and the Holy Spirit, who would lead them into all truth, had not yet been given (8:39; 14:26; 16:13–15). Technically speaking, it is only in this temporary situation that one can argue about the implausibility or plausibility of the Johannine misunderstandings.[17]

Nevertheless, the understanding or lack of understanding of later read-

---

[15] D. A. Carson, 'Understanding Misunderstandings in the Fourth Gospel', *Tyndale Bulletin* 33 (1982), 59–89, here 82, 87. See also Oscar Cullmann, 'Der johanneische Gebrauch doppeldeutiger Ausdrücke als Schlüssel zum Verständnis des vierten Evangeliums', *TZ* 4 (1948), 360–72; idem, *Salvation in History* (New York: Harper and Row, 1967); G. Richter, 'Die Gefangennahme Jesu nach dem Johannesevangelium (18:1–12)', in *Studien zum Johannesevangelium*, Biblische Untersuchungen 13 (Regensburg: Pustet, 1977), 74–87, originally in *BibLeb* 10 (1969), 26–39.

[16] John 16:16; cf. 7:32–35; 8:21–22; 13:33, 36–37; 14:18–20, 28; 16:5.

[17] J. Becker, *Das Evangelium des Johannes*, Kapitel 1–10 (Gütersloh: Mohn/Würzburg: Echter-Verlag, 1979), 135–6, makes a significant distinction between the misunderstanding of the disciples and that of 'the Jews'.

ers of this Gospel is also profoundly affected by their response to the light of revelation; this they share with the original interlocutors of Jesus. The resurrection is not decisive for the understanding of the one who rejects the New Testament claims about Jesus, since such a person would deny the resurrection of Jesus as well. Therefore, the resurrection has only made the misunderstanding of later believers implausible. For unbelievers, the Pauline assertion holds characteristically true, 'For the preaching of the cross is to those who are perishing folly (τοῖς ἀπολλυμένοις μωρία ἐστίν)' (1 Cor. 1:18), because as Paul elsewhere argues, 'the natural man (ψυχικὸς ἄνθρωπος) receives not the things of the Spirit of God, for they are folly (μωρία) to him, and he cannot know them (οὐ δύναται γνῶναι), because they are spiritually discerned (πνευματικῶς ἀνακρίνεται)' (1 Cor. 2:14). This is also a point which we see consistently and emphatically made by Jesus and the Evangelist in his Gospel. Decades after the cross and resurrection, the Evangelist appeals to Isaiah to explicate the unbelief not only of the interlocutors of Jesus, but perhaps even more poignantly, of his own contemporaries.[18] The language of John's Gospel is therefore not a barrier to understanding, neither is it the 'cause' of incomprehension. Lack of understanding is simply the outcome of unbelief. This 'cause' and 'effect' relation is very important in determining whether John's language is sectarian.[19] The resurrection and the subsequent giving of the Holy Spirit are decisive only for those who are receptive to revelation. For those who wilfully reject the light, who are deprived from the guiding presence of the Holy Spirit, there is nothing but spiritual darkness and misunderstanding.

6.3. The Work of the Spirit of Truth in Illuminating the Truth

The Holy Spirit in the Fourth Gospel has a paramount role in leading the disciples to the comprehension of the salvific revelation of God in Jesus Christ. In Johannine theology, the perception of the revelatory truth apart from the work of the Holy Spirit in regeneration and illumination (3:3–12; 1:12–13) is impossible: τὸ γεγεννημένον ἐκ τῆς σαρκὸς σάρξ ἐστιν, καὶ τὸ γεγεννημένον ἐκ τοῦ πνεύματος πνεῦμά ἐστιν (3:6).[20] John's steadfast focus upon the ministry of the Holy Spirit in spiritual illumination

---

[18] Jn. 12:37-41; cf. 6:44; 3:3, 5-6, 12; 5:25; 8:43-44, 47; 10:27; 12:37-41.

[19] See my discussion in chapter four (4.4). Also see Stephen C. Barton's criticism of Meeks in 'Can We Identify The Gospel Audiences?', in *The Gospels for All Christians: Rethinking the Gospel Audiences*, ed. by Richard Bauckham (Grand Rapids, MI: Eerdmans, 1998), 190-93.

[20] See further Jn. 1:12-13; 3:3, 5-7, 12, 27, 31-34; cf. 1 Cor. 2:14; Rom. 8:7.

negates any suggestion that people in their natural unregenerate state can comprehend the revelation.[21] The Spirit plays the key role in enabling Jesus' followers to discern the truth (2:17; 7:39; 11:13; 14:26; 16:13). This ministry of the Holy Spirit is not confined to the historical disciples of Jesus, but applies to his universal disciples as well.

According to the witness of the 'disciple whom Jesus loved' (cf. Jn. 13:23; 19:26; 20:2; 21:7, 20), the Fourth Gospel was intended to present the mission and work of Jesus through insight into the truth about his identity granted by the Holy Spirit after the resurrection (cf. Jn. 14:16–17, 26; 15:26; 16:7–14).[22] This may indeed be one of the reasons for the early church to consider the Gospel of John as the true, spiritual gospel whose witness to the truth encompasses that of the other three Gospels. The emphasis upon the activity of the Spirit in illumination would not have been foreign to the Jews of the Evangelist's own time.[23] This is particularly evident from the Dead Sea scrolls. In the *Rule of the Community* or *Manual of Discipline*,[24] for example in 1QS 3:17–4:26, there is the well-known statement about the two spirits active in the human realm: the spirit of truth and the spirit of falsehood.[25] The spirit of falsehood who governs the 'men of perdition' is

---

[21] John 1:13; 3:5, 8, 27; 4:23–24; 6:63; 7:39; 14:16–17; 15:26; 16:13.

[22] See H. Hegstad, 'Den Hellige Ånd Som Veileder til 'den fulle sannhet' (Joh 16, 13) – prinsippteologisk belyst', *Tidsskrift for Teologi og kike* 64 (93), 95–109; T. R. Hatina, 'John 20:22 in its Eschatological Context: Promise or Fulfilment?' *Bib* 74 (1993), 196–219.

[23] See Tosefta Sotah [*t. Sot*] 13.2f; cf. *t. Sot*, 12.5; 13.4 par. [Hillel]; Babylonian Talmud [*b*] *b. Sot* 48b; Jerusalem Talmud [*y*] *y. Sot* 9.14 [24b 23–25]; *b. Yoma* 9b, 21b; *b. Sanhedrin* 11a [Hillel/Sammuel]; *b. BB* 12a; *y. Taanit* 2:1 [65a 60ff.]; *Genesis Rabbah* [R] 37.7; *ExodR* 32.1; *QohR* 12:7 [end]; *CantR* 8.9.3., etc. Also, *NumR* 15.10 [R. levi b. Rabbi], 25 [R. Tanhuma b. Abba A5]; *PesR* 1.2. The conviction also persisted that the spirit would return upon all Israel in the eschaton. Cf. Peter Schäfer, *Die Vorstellung vom Heiligen Geist in der rabbinischen Literatur*, SANT 28 (Munich: Kösel, 1972), 112–15. Also see Ezk. 36:27, Joel 3:1f and Acts 2:16ff, etc.

[24] 1QS is known both as *Rule of the Community*, so G. Vermes, *The Dead Sea Scrolls in English*, 3rd edn (London: Penguin Books, 1987) and as the *Manual of Discipline*, so Millar Burrows, *More Light on the Dead Sea Scrolls* (London: Secker and Warburg, 1958).

[25] See R. E. Brown, 'The Paraclete in the Fourth Gospel', *NTS* 13 (1967), 113–32; idem, 'The Qumran Scrolls and John: A Comparison in Thought and Expression', in *A Companion to John*, ed. by Michael J. Taylor (New York: Alba House, 1977), 69–90; J. Becker, 'Beobachtungen zum Dualismus im Johannesevangelium', *ZWK* 65 (1974), 71–87; James H. Charlesworth, ed. *John and the Dead Sea Scrolls* (New York: Crossroads, 1990); O. Böcher, *Der johanneischen Dualismus im Zusammenhang des nachbiblischen Judentums* (Gütersloh: Mohn 1965); C. K. Barrett, *Essays on John* (London: SPCK, 1982), 98–115. The influence of Qumran on John has been contested. John Breck, *Spirit of Truth: The Holy Spirit in Johannine Tradition*, Vol. 1: *The Origin of Johannine Pneumatology* (Crestwood, NY: St. Vladimir's Seminary, 1991), 3, 53–87, 157–8, who traces the Johannine 'Spirit of Truth' and 'Paraclete' beyond Qumran to Iranian Zoroasterianism which flourished in sixth century BC. See also Frank M. Cross, *The Ancient Library of Qumran and Modern Biblical Study* (London: Duckworth, 1958); K. G. Kuhn, 'Die Sektenschrift und die iranische Religion', *ZTK* 49 (1952), 312; idem, 'Johannesevangelium

also called רוח הסתר, the 'spirit of secrecy' (1QS 9:22). These two spirits continually wage war with each other.[26] However, most relevant for this study is the view of the Essenes about the Holy Spirit or the Spirit of God. There are some questions as to whether the Holy Spirit or Spirit of God in Qumran is to be equated with the 'spirit of truth'.[27] The main function of the Holy Spirit as God's gift to the community seems to be the purification and sanctification of the believer (1QH 3:21, 4:20–22; 14:25–27; 16:10–12, etc.).[28] In several cases, the Spirit is instrumental in dispensing revelation (e.g., 1QH 13:18f., cf. 1QS 4:2–6), including the revelation of mysteries (1QH 12:11f). The collection of *Thanksgiving Hymns* (1QH) has a stronger emphasis on spirit-given revelation which is mediated by virtue of God-given knowledge of the Torah (1QH 4:10; 5:11f).[29] Indeed, the Spirit grants a knowledge of mysteries both to the prophets and to the Qumran community; the latter benefits from the special charisma of the Spirit which the Teacher of Righteousness has received in his exegesis (e.g., 1QpHab 7:1ff.; 1QH).[30]

Among the New Testament writings, one of the most distinctive designations for the Holy Spirit occurs in the Fourth Gospel where the Spirit is

---

und Qumrantexte', in *Neotestamentica et Patristica: Eine Freundesgabe, Herrn Professor Dr. Oscar Cullmann zu seinem 60. Geburtstag überreicht*, ed. by W. C. van Unnik, NovTSup 6 (Leiden: Brill, 1962), 111–22; D. Winston, 'The Iranian Component in the Bible, Apocrypha, and Qumran: A Review of the Evidence', *History of Religions* 5 (1966), 200–1; Lucetta Mowry, 'The Dead Sea Scrolls and the Background for the Gospel of John', *Biblical Archaeologist* 17 (1954), 78–97; H. Ringgren, 'Qumran and Gnosticism', in *Le Origini dello Gnosticismo*, ed. by U. Biachi, NumSup 12 (Leiden: Brill, 1967), 379–84. See also R. C. Zaehner, *The Dawn and Twilight of Zoroasterianism* (London: Weidenfeld and Nicholson, 1975), 50–1; U. Bianchi, *La Doctrine Zathustrienne des Deux Esprits: Selected Essays on Gnosticism, Dualism and Mysteriosophy* (Leiden: Brill, 1978), 361–89; M. Boyce, *A History of Zoroasterianism* (Leiden: Brill, 1982); W. D. Davies and David Daube, eds., *The Background of the New Testament and Its Eschatology* (Cambridge: CUP, 1956), 153–71; T. Hoffman, 'First John and the Qumran Scrolls', *BTB* 8 (1978), 17–25; but see P. Wernberg-Møller and M. Treves, who contested cosmic determinism and Zoroastrian influence; Wernberg-Møller, 'A Reconsideration of the Two Spirits in the Rule of the Community (1QS III.13–IV.26)', *RevQ* 3 (1961), 413ff.; Treves, 'The Two Spirits in the Rule of the Community', *RevQ* 3 (1961), 449ff.

[26] Josef Schreiner, 'Geistbegabung in der Gemeinde von Qumran', *BZ* 9 (1965), 161–180; Peter Schäfer, 'Geist: II. Judentum', *TRE* 12 (1984), 173–8. Cf. *T. Jud.* 20:1ff.; *T. Ash.* 1:3–9.

[27] Otto Betz, *Offenbarung und Schriftforschung in der Qumransekte*, WUNT 6 (Tübingen: Mohr-Siebeck, 1960), 147ff. Betz argues the 'Spirit of truth' does not seem to have a bearing on revelation. The Spirit of truth intervenes in the eschaton.

[28] See Betz, *Offenbarung*, 140; Werner Foerster, 'Der Heilige Geist im Spätjudentum', *NTS* 8 (1962), 117–34 (129f.); Schreiner, 'Geistbegabung in der Gemeinde von Qumran', 161–180, 175ff.

[29] See further Schäfer, 'Geist', 173.

[30] Cf. Schreiner, 'Geistbegabung', 179.

referred to as 'the Spirit of truth', τὸ πνεῦμα τῆς ἀληθείας (Jn. 14:17; 15:26; 16:13; cf. 1 Jn. 4:6). This title is not found elsewhere in the New Testament. Truth describes both the nature and the activity of the Holy Spirit. Truth comprises the essence of God's character. Therefore, the Holy Spirit is called 'the Spirit of Truth'. 'Truth' also specifies the activity of the Spirit as the advocate and witness for Christ (15:26; 16:14). He bears witness to the truth that Jesus is the one in whom humanity may find the redemptive revelation which leads to eternal life.

There are seven texts in John in which 'truth' and the 'Spirit' are linked and where one of the ministries of the Holy Spirit is presented as testifying to the truth. In John 15:26–27, the Holy Spirit appears as the witness of Christ in the context of the world's hatred of him (15:18–25) and the persecution of his disciples (16:1–4). In the Synoptics when the disciples are brought before the courts (Mt. 10:17–26; Lk. 12:11–12; Mt. 24:9–11 and parallels), it is said that the Spirit will speak through them. Only in the Fourth Gospel is this activity of the Spirit characterised as μαρτυρεῖν, 'witness'. John seems to distinguish between the witness which the Spirit bears from the witness of the disciples: 'the Spirit of truth...will bear witness to me; and you also will bear witness' (15:26–27). It has been suggested that the witnessing activity of the Holy Spirit should be understood within the juridical framework of the Gospel.[31] In support of this proposal, it is striking that in John's Gospel, the act of bearing witness is closely linked with that of judgment. In fact, both are spoken of in parallel terms (cf. 8:14a and 8:16a). Similarly the act of judging (5:27, 29–30) is connected by John with μαρτυρία in 5:31–47. The Holy Spirit in the Fourth Gospel is also referred to by the Greek word παράκλητος (14:16), which means a 'legal assistant, advocate',[32] and with this meaning, it was transliterated into Hebrew and Aramaic (e.g., P. Aboth 4:11: He that performs one precept gets for himself one advocate, פרקליט).[33] The word is found in the Dead Sea Scrolls for an interpreter.[34] This meaning, according to Barrett, does not seem to be prominent in John's usage, where the emphasis is upon the forensic aspect of the Spirit's work (16:8–11) as a 'prosecuting' rather than

---

[31] de la Potterie, 'Truth in Saint John', 76.

[32] Cf. 1 Jn. 2:1, where it is also translated 'advocate', meaning that Jesus stands before the Father as *intercessor*. See Brown, 'Paraclete in the Fourth Gospel', 113–32.

[33] LSJ, s.v.; Barrett, *St. John*, 462; Otto Betz, *Der Paraklet: Fürsprecher im häretischen Spätjudentum, im Johannesevangelium, und in neu gefundenen gnostischen Schriften*, AGJU 2 (Leiden: Brill, 1963); B. Lindars, *The Gospel of John*, 478.

[34] G. Johnston, *The Spirit Paraclete in the Gospel of John*, SNTSMS 12 (Cambridge: CUP, 1970), 80–118.

a defending counsel.³⁵ In the New Testament, words cognate to παράκλητος such as παρακαλεῖν and παράκλησις can refer to Christian preaching (Acts 2:40; 1 Cor. 14:3). This corresponds to the normal Greek usage in which the verb παρακαλεῖν means to 'exhort'. The word group may also refer to 'consolation' and in particular to the consolation to be expected in the Messianic age. This usage is common in the Old Testament (e.g., Isa. 40:1), recurs in the New Testament (e.g., Mt. 5:4; Lk 2:25), and is paralleled in the rabbinic נחמה (e.g., Makkoth 5b) and מנחם used as a name of the Messiah.³⁶ In John chapters 14–16 where Paraclete is another designation for the Holy Spirit, the Spirit is said to be the one who witnesses about Christ – takes 'the things of Christ' and declares them (15:26; 16:14).³⁷

In the context of the believing community, the Spirit's work continues the ministry of Christ within the church in leading the believers 'into all the truth', εἰς τὴν ἀλήθειαν πᾶσαν (16:13).³⁸ The witness of the Spirit does not consist in adding to the revelation but in 'unveiling' the significance of the revelation given in Christ, opening the eyes of the disciples to see the testimony of the Old Testament Scriptures to Jesus. Specifically, the Spirit-Paraclete will teach (διδάξει) the disciples all things (14:26), guide (ὁδηγήσει) them (16:13), and announce (ἀναγγελεῖ) to them the things to come (τὰ ἐρχόμενα, 16:13b). The teaching of 'all the truth' by the Spirit of truth will be all-comprehensive³⁹ and exhaustive (πᾶσαν [16:13]).

6.3.1. The Nature of Truth in the Fourth Gospel

In John 16:13, Jesus speaks of the Spirit of truth leading the disciples 'into all the truth', εἰς τὴν ἀλήθειαν πᾶσαν. What is the nature of 'the truth' which is specified? In the passion account, Pilate in response to Jesus who has said, 'Every one who is of the truth hears my voice', asks Jesus, 'What is truth?' (18:38). The Evangelist's audience has already been given the answer, 'I am the truth' (14:6). In the Fourth Gospel, Jesus is both the truth and the revealer of the truth. By contrast, in the devil, the truth has no roots

---

³⁵ Barrett, *St. John*, 462.

³⁶ Ibid.

³⁷ For meaning of this declaration, cf. 2:22; 12:16. See also 14:17; 15:26; 16:13; the τὸ πνεῦμα τῆς ἀληθείας (רוח קודש = רוח אמת, see 1QS 3:18f; 1QS 4:12). John means 'the Spirit who communicates truth'. Barrett, *St. John*, 463.

³⁸ Cf. 7:16–18; 8:31–32, 40–47; Lindars, *John*, 478.

³⁹ See the twice-used πάντα (14:26).

(8:44).⁴⁰ It is in the essence of the devil to speak lies contrary to God and his revelation, particularly contrary to the revelation of God in Christ.

Truth, ἀλήθεια, in the Fourth Gospel, is a complex idea. It refers to the moral character of God, the sphere of divine reality and to the divine revelation. Truth, like Life, is one of the major theological themes of the Gospel.⁴¹ John uses the term 'truth' twenty-five times in the Gospel, over against once in Matthew and three times each in Mark and Luke. The word occurs twenty times in the three small Johannine epistles, in comparison to forty-seven times in the corpus of Pauline works.⁴² Also, only John records the twenty-five double uses of ἀμήν (truly, truly) by Jesus.⁴³ Out of one hundred eighty-one occurrences of ἀλήθεια, ἀληθινός, ἀληθής, ἀληθῶς in the New Testament, seventy-five (about 41 per cent) occur in John. Some scholars believe the word 'truth' is frequently synonymous with 'mystery' and should be understood against the ἀλήθεια of Hellenistic and Gnostic dualism, where it denotes the eternal divine reality revealed to humanity.⁴⁴ Others trace the Johannine conception of truth to the Hebrew אמת, 'faithfulness' or 'justice',⁴⁵ explaining it in the context of apocalyptic and wisdom literature in later Judaism.⁴⁶ The sense of the word 'truth' in this

---

⁴⁰ N. Dahl, 'Der Erstgeborene Satans und der Vater des Teufels', in *Apophoreta*, FS E. Haenchen, BZNW 30 (Berlin: 1964), 78 n. 29; also de la Potterie, *La vérité dans saint Jean* (Rome: Biblical Institute Press, 1977), 919 and 927; W. Kern, 'Der symmetrische Gesamtaufbau von Jo 8:12–58', *ZKT* 78 (1956), 452; Edwyn Clement Hoskyns, *The Fourth Gospel*, ed. by Francis Noel Davey (London: Faber and Faber, 1947), 394; G. Stemberger, *La symbolique du bien et du mal selon saint Jean* (Paris: Seuil, 1970), 95 n. 20; 128 n. 8.

⁴¹ K. Heinrich, 'Wie eine Religion der anderen die Wahrheit wegnimmt. Notizen über das Unbehagen bei der Lektüre des Johannes-Evangeliums', *ZRGG* 49 (1997), 345–63; M. L. Gubler, '"Ich bin der Weg und die Wahrheit und das Leben" (Joh 14,6)', *Diakonia* 24 (1993), 373–82.

⁴² There is a similar display with the adjective ἀληθής, which is used fourteen times in John, once each in Matthew and Mark, and four times in Paul. It does not occur in Luke. The synonym ἀληθινός is used nine times in John and once each in Luke and Paul. It does not appear in Matthew or Mark.

⁴³ An expression which occurs only in Numbers 5:22 and Nehemiah 8:6. John's use of ἀμήν ἀμήν is often followed by λέγω ὑμῖν (σοι). In the Synoptics ἀμήν is never doubled, and it is usually followed by λέγω (except at Mt. 6:13, where there is doubt about the reading, and Mk. 16:20).

⁴⁴ R. Bultmann, 'Untersuchungen zum Johannesevangelium: Alêtheia', *ZNW* 27 (1928), 113–63; C. H. Dodd, *The Interpretation of the Fourth Gospel* (Cambridge: CUP, 1953), 170–78.

⁴⁵ D. R. Lindsay, 'What Is Truth? Ἀλήθεια in the Gospel of John', *ResQ* 35 (1993), 129–45; J. Gilbert, 'Aspects of the Truth in the New Testament', *Concilium* 83 (1973), 35–42; de la Potterie, 'Truth in Saint John', 68; idem, 'De sensu vocis *'emet* in Vetere Testamento', *Verbum Domini* 27 (1949), 336–54; 28 (1950), 29–42.

⁴⁶ F. Nötscher, '"Wahrheit" als theologischer Terminus in den Qumran-Texten', Festschrift W. Christian (Vienna, 1956), 83–92; I. de la Potterie, 'L'arrière-fond du thème johannique de vérité',

apocalyptic tradition is that of *revealed truth* (i.e., 'mystery') concerning the divine plan (cf. Dan. 10:21; 1 Enoch 21:5; 1QH 7:26-7; 1QS 4:6).⁴⁷ In the Fourth Gospel, Jesus embodies the truth, and this truth is grounded in the testimony of the Scriptures to him (14:6, 26).⁴⁸ In addition, the truth is a salvific truth (1:17; 8:32; 17:17, 19). The linking of 'truth' with grace in 1:14, 17, χάριτος καὶ ἀληθείας,⁴⁹ is reminiscent of the Hebrew pair חסד ואמת (Exod. 34:6, cf. 33:22) signifying God's loyal covenantal love for his people. When John associates 'truth' and 'grace' in 1:17 in the context of God's glory, this glory shows God in his 'faithfulness to his own character, and his character revealing itself in mercy'.⁵⁰

In John, there is also an explicit link between 'truth', the 'word' of God, and the 'word' of Jesus. In chapter eight, Jesus tells those who say they have believed in him, 'If you continue (μείνητε) in my word (ἐν τῷ λόγῳ τῷ ἐμῷ), you are truly my disciples, and you will know the truth (τὴν ἀλήθειαν) and the truth will make you free' (8:31, 32; also 17:17).⁵¹ This is the truth which Jesus has heard from the Father and has come to proclaim (8:40). He is in the world to testify to the truth (18:37; cf. 1 Jn. 5:6). In 17:17 he prays, 'sanctify them in the truth (ἐν τῇ ἀληθείᾳ); your word (ὁ λόγος ὁ σός) is truth'. It is implicit in the Gospel that the truth which Jesus reveals is in harmony with and a continuation of the truth which has been revealed to Israel in its history and through the prophets. The truth of which Jesus speaks here is the revelation which comes from the Father and is passed on in the word of Jesus. To become true disciples of Christ, one must not only believe in his words (cf. 8:31a), one must also continue in his word (8:31b); his word must find room in one's heart (8:37). According to de la Potterie, in John, 'there is a close relationship between the revealed truth and the actual person of Jesus.... Jesus is not just a vehicle of

---

in *Studia Evangelica* TU 73, ed. by K. Aland, et al. (Berlin, 1959), 227-94. Cf. K. G. Kuhn, 'Die in Palästina gefundenen hebräischen Texte und das NT', *ZTK* 47 (1950), 192-211.

⁴⁷ de la Potterie, 'Truth in Saint John', 68-69.

⁴⁸ See Schnackenburg, *Johannes*, 2:288; Stemberger, *La symbolique*, 119; J. M. Boice, *Witness and Revelation in the Gospel of John* (Grand Rapids: Zondervan; Exeter: Paternoster Press, 1970), 151-2; S. Pancaro, *The Law in the Fourth Gospel: The Torah and the Gospel, Moses and Jesus, Judaism and Christianity According to John*, NovTSup 42 (Leiden: Brill, 1975), 99-100; Bultmann, 'ἀλήθεια, κτλ.', *TDNT* 1:245-6; and *John*, 321, *et passim*; de la Potterie, *La vérité dans saint Jean*, 925-6 n. 47; J. Beutler, *Martyria: traditionsgeschichtliche Untersuchungen zum Zeugnisthema bei Johannes*, Frankfurter theologische Studien 10 (Frankfurt: Knecht, 1972), 323-4.

⁴⁹ The same pair of words (with articles) occur in 1:17. Χάρις occurs four times only in John, in the prologue (1:14, 16 *twice*, 17).

⁵⁰ Barrett, *St. John*, 167.

⁵¹ λόγος occurs six times in 8:31-55, and ἀλήθεια is found seven times in 8:32-46.

344 Chapter 6: Spiritual Perception and the Language of John's Gospel

revelation like Moses and the other prophets, who remained, so to speak, exterior to their message'.[52] De la Potterie is right on the mark when he suggests that what is revealed in Jesus (14:6) is the revelation of the triune God, the relationship between Father, Son, and the Spirit of truth. Jesus is able to reveal God as no other has ever been able to do (1:18) because he embodies the truth and life because of his oneness with the Father (10:30; 14:7-14). Therefore he can say, 'the word which you hear is not mine but that of the Father who sent me' (14:24; cf. 7:16) and 'he who has seen me has seen the Father' (14:9). The idea of truth is at the heart of Johannine theology. It is not attained by means of intellectual pursuit (as in Hellenism). Rather, it is received by grace through faith and through the work of the Spirit of truth within the innermost being of the believer.[53]

Truth in the Fourth Gospel is wedded inextricably to the revelation of God in Jesus Christ. Truth is revelation and revelation is the manifestation of the reality of God's saving work in the world through the *Word*. Revelation in the biblical tradition may be understood as God's making himself known (Isa. 60:16).[54] In the Old Testament, God makes himself known by his saving activity and manifestation of his glory (Isa. 52:10; 40:5), which is not detached from his saving work. The term 'revelation' as such is rare in the Fourth Gospel. The verbal form ἀποκαλύπτω occurs only in the quotation of Isaiah in 12:38. However, there are a cluster of expressions which underline the idea. These are: ἐξηγέομαι, 'explain', 'report', 'interpret' (1:18),[55] φανερόω, 'manifest' (2:11; 3:21; 7:11),[56] τὸν οὐρανὸν ἀνεῳγότα, 'the heaven having been opened' (1:51), παρρησία, 'openness' (7:4, 26),[57] δείκνυμι, 'show' (14:8, 9),[58] ὁδηγέω, 'lead' (16:13),[59] ἀναγγέλλω, 'disclose' (16:14, 15),[60] ἀπαγγέλλω, 'report' (16:25),[61] ἀκοή,

---

[52] de la Potterie, 'Truth in Saint John', 71.

[53] Ibid., 73.

[54] See H. W. Frei, *The Identity of Jesus Christ* (Philadelphia: Fortress, 1975); idem, 'Theological Reflections on the Accounts of Jesus' Death and Resurrection', in H. W. Frei, *Theology and Narrative: Selected Essays*, ed. by G. Hunsinger, et al. (New York: OUP, 1993), 45-93; R. W. Jenson, *The Triune Identity* (Philadelphia: Fortress, 1982); R. F. Thiemann, *Revelation and Theology: The Gospel as Narrated Promise* (Notre Dame, IN: University of Notre Dame Press, 1985), chs. 6-7.

[55] BAGD, 275; Barrett, *St. John*, 170.

[56] BAGD, 852.

[57] BAGD, 630.

[58] Ibid., 172.

[59] Ibid., 553.

[60] Ibid., 51.

[61] Ibid., 79.

'report' (12:38),[62] γνωρίζω, 'make known' (15:15),[63] μαρτυρία, 'witness, testimony' or its verbal form μαρτυρέω, 'bear witness'(1:7, 15; 3:11; 5:31–33, 36–37; 8:18; 18:37).[64] Apart from these revelatory terms, the Johannine concept is imbedded deeply in the christology of the Fourth Gospel.

6.3.2. Revelation of Truth in the Person and Work of Jesus Christ

In John's Gospel, Jesus is presented as the locus of God's self-disclosure in his redemptive mode. Only Jesus has made God known (ἐξηγήσατο) since no human being has seen God (1:18).[65] He has come from the Father[66] and is going back to him.[67] He is the unique one, the 'only God' (μονογενὴς θεός) and the one 'in the bosom of the Father' (ὁ ὢν εἰς τὸν κόλπον τοῦ

---

[62] Ibid., 31.

[63] Ibid., 163.

[64] Ibid., 493; C. F. D. Moule, 'The Individualism of the Fourth Gospel', *NovT* 5 (1962), 174f.

[65] The negation in 1:18a is comprehensive. It disallows any other claimant. See I. Gruenwald, *Apocalyptic and Merkavah Mysticism* (Leiden: Brill, 1980), 93–7, and his discussion concerning the debate about the possibility of seeing God among the Tannaim. Moses, Abraham, and Isaiah had seen the preincarnate Word. John may have intended to refute competing claims of heavenly visions, ascent into heaven, or journeys of human figures to gain the knowledge of divine mysteries. See, for example, Enoch (vision – 1 Enoch 14:2, 8; journey – 14:8ff; 39:3; chariot ascent – 70:3; 71:11); Levi (vision, journey – T. Levi 2:5ff); Abraham (chariot ascent – T. Abr. 10; cf. 4 Ezra 4:13; 2 Bar. 6; vision – 36:1ff, 53; cf. 46:7, 76; journey – 3 Bar. 2:1ff); Adam (chariot ascent – *Life of Adam and Eve*, 25–29; cf. vision – 2 Bar. 4:3.); Isaiah (Sir. 48:22–25; cf. *Asc. Isa.* 7ff.). Other traditions also attest the practice (Sir. 44:16; 49:8; 4QSU 40:24). The gaining of such knowledge by *Merkavah mysticism* is well recognised in the first-century AD among the circles of R. Yohanan ben Zakkai and R. Akiba. See C. Rowland, *The Open Heaven* (New York: Crossroads, 1982), 271–348, also see parts 1–4; idem, 'Visions of God in Apocalyptic Literature', *JSJ* 10 (1979), 137–54. Also see A. Segal, 'Heavenly Ascent in Hellenistic Judaism, Early Christianity and Their Environment', *ANRW* II.23.2 (1980), 1352–77; idem, 'Ruler of this World: Attitudes about Mediator Figures and the Importance of Sociology for Self-Definition', in *Jewish and Chrisitian Self-Definition*, ed. by E. P. Sanders, et al. (Philadelphia: Fortress, 1981), 2:248–55. Also, similar claims may have been prevalent among the Qumran community to gain the knowledge of the mysteries of God through reading of Scripture but also through visions and participation in the heavenly world. See J. Strugnell, 'Angelic Liturgy at Qumran', in *Congress Volume, Oxford 1959*, VTSup 7 (Leiden: Brill, 1960), 318–45; Rowland, *Open Heaven*, 115–20; 1QM 10:8ff; 1QH 3:20f; 11:10f; 1QS 11:6ff. Specially to be noted in light of the reference to Moses in 1:17 and the negation of 1:18 are traditions which interpret Moses' ascent of Sinai as an ascent to heaven to acquire knowledge of divine mysteries (Philo, *Moses*, 1:158; *QuEx* 2:29, 40, 46; Josephus, *Ant.*, 3:96; 4:8, 49; 2 Bar. 4:1–7, esp. 5–7; 59:3–12; 4 Ezra 14:3–6). See W. Meeks, 'Moses as God and King', in *Religions in Antiquity*, ed. by J. Neusner (Leiden: Brill, 1968), 354–71.

[66] John 3:17, 34; 5:23–24, 36–37; 6:29, 38–39, 44, 57; 7:16, 18, 28–29; 8:16, 26; 12:44–45, 49; 13:16, 20; 14:24; 17:3, 17, 25.

[67] John 13:1, 3; 14:12, 28; 16:5, 10, 17, 28; cf. 20:17.

πατρός), which is to say, the one who is πρὸς τὸν θεόν (1:1).[68] Only in and through the incarnate Word is God encountered. In 1:51, by evoking the imagery associated with Jacob's dream at Bethel (Gen. 28:10–19) and the image of an open heaven (ὄψεσθε τὸν οὐρανὸν ἀνεῳγότα) where angels ascend and descend upon the Son of Man, it is implied that Jesus is the true source of revelation. Bethel was the locus of ancient theophany and divine revelation (Jud. 20:18, 26: 21:2–5; 1 Sam. 10:3). In the Fourth Gospel, functions which had previously accrued to Bethel have now been realised in Jesus. In addition, John's identification of Jesus with the 'Word' (1:1–3) is a highly significant dimension in the author's idea of revelation and its relation to his christology. If revelation means divine communication, then Jesus is the very Word of God, the agent of creation, life and light.

A wide spectrum of possible backgrounds has been suggested for the Johannine 'Word'. However, the 'Word' in John's Gospel as mediator in creation and redemption ultimately, in my view, must be traced back to the Old Testament[69] rather than to parallels in Hellenistic and non-biblical traditions.[70] In the Old Testament, apart from history as revelation,[71] an important medium of God's revelation among the Israelites is the *word*. Scholars such as Mowinckel and Nygren have proposed that the 'Word' in the Old Testament is more than the verbal communication of divine mysteries. It is an 'activity'[72] or 'deed'.[73] The word of God, and thereby

---

[68] Francis J. Moloney, 'John 1:18: "In the Bosom of" or "Turned Towards" the Father?' *AusBR* 31 (1983), 63–71.

[69] W. F. Howard, *Christianity According to St. John* (Philadelphia: Westminster Press, 1946), 32; E. D. Freed, 'Some Old Testament Influences on the Prologue of John', in *A Light Unto My Path: Old Testament Studies*, ed. by Howard Bream and Ralph D. Heim (Philadelphia: Temple University Press, 1974), 145–6. J. V. Dahms, 'Isaiah 55:11 and the Gosepl of John', *EvQ* 53 (1981), 78–88; and H. Lausberg, 'Jesaja 55, 10–11 im Evangelium nach Johannes', in *Miniscula Philologica*, Nachrichten der Akademie der Wissenschaften im Göttingen 7 (Göttingen: Vandehoeck und Ruprecht, 1979), 131–44. See the occurrence of the *word* in the Old Testament in various contexts, Gen. 1:1–2:2; Isa. 40:26; 55:10; Ps. 148:4–5; 33:9; cf. Gen. 15:1; Ezk. 3:16; 6:1; 7:1; 11:14; 12:1; 13:1; 14:2, 12; 15:1; 16:1; Isa. 9:8; 40:8; Hos. 6:5; Ps. 107:20; 147:15. Cf. Jn. 8:27; 12:48; Col. 3:16; 2 Thess. 3:1; 2 Tim. 2:9; Tit. 2:5; 1 Pet. 1:23; Heb. 4:12–13.

[70] Bultmann, *John*, 36, also translates Logos as the 'Word' but then he believes the meaning of it goes back to Gnostic myth. See also Reese, *Hellenistic Influence*; Francois-Marie Braun, *Jean le théologien*, Tome 2, *Les grandes traditions d'Israel et l'accord des Écritures, selon le Quatrième Évangile*, Études bibliques (Paris: Gabalda, 1967), 123–5; Andre Feuillet, *Johannine Studies*, ET, Thomas E. Crane (Staten Island, NY: Alba House, 1965), 89–91; M. Scott, *Sophia and the Johannine Jesus*, JSNTSup 71 (Sheffield: JSOT Press, 1992), 101–4.

[71] S. Mowinckel, *The Old Testament as Word of God*, trans. by Reidar B. Bjornard (Oxford: Basil Blackwell, 1960), 39–45; Markus N. A. Bockmuehl, *Revelation and Mystery in Ancient Judaism and Pauline Christianity* (Tübingen: Mohr-Siebeck, 1990).

[72] A. Nygren, *The Significance of the Bible for the Church*, Biblical Series 1 (Philadelphia: Facet Books, 1963), 1–3; Mowinckel, *Old Testament as Word of God*, 39; also G. S. Hendry,

also the inspired word of the prophets, is a 'dynamically acting power; it is in itself a factor in history'. When the word 'light[s] upon Israel', it works like an explosion (Isa. 9:8). God can say, 'I have slain them by the words of my mouth' (Hos. 6:5), and Jeremiah knows the word of God in his mouth becomes a fire that will consume the people like wood (5:14).[74] Therefore it is through his dynamic *word* that God 'unveils himself'. The *word* expresses the being of God, in out-going activity.[75] It never returns empty (Isa. 55:11). It is efficacious. It brings about that which it is sent to do (Isa. 55:10ff). For these scholars, the word is never simply oral or written communication. It is the creative power of God that creates and upholds the world (Gen. 1; Ps. 33:9; 107:20). This same power also creates religious and moral life in people (Ps. 19; 119). However, the distinction between the *word* as propositional knowledge and the *word* as dynamic activity is unnecessary. The revelation of God as *deed* and *activity* cannot be divorced from or discovered apart from the record of Scripture. It is that written record which puts history in perspective. The 'word' given through the prophets is not derivative of history, it is a medium of divine revelation in itself.[76] The word of God, and thereby also the inspired word of the prophets, is a dynamic power, in itself a factor in history.

The *word* in the Old Testament is particularly associated with 'wisdom'. Some scholars believe that the deutero-canonical Wisdom of Solomon and other Jewish writings of the Hellenistic period are the possible background of the Johannine 'Word'.[77] In this literature, wisdom is pre-existent (Prov. 8:22-23; Sir. 24:9; Wisd. of Sol. 6:22), issues forth from

---

'Reveal, Revelation', in *A Theological Word Book of the Bible*, ed. by A. Richardson (London, 1950), 196f.

[73] Mowinckel, *Old Testament as Word of God*, 39.

[74] Ibid., 42.

[75] Ibid.

[76] J. Baillie, *The Idea of Revelation in Recent Thought* (New York: Columbia University Press, 1956), 62ff. This proposition is that revelation essentially is equated with the dynamics of history. See especially Wolfhart Pannenberg, ed., *Offenbarung als Geschichte*, KuD Beiheft I (Göttingen, 1961; 3 Aufl. 1965) who came under intense criticism by Barr, Zimmerli, and Hesse. See W. Zimmerli, '"Offenbarung" im Alten Testament: Ein Gespräch mit R. Rendtorff', *EvT* 22 (1962), 15ff; F. Hesse, 'Wolfhart Pannenberg und das Alte Testament', *NZST* 7 (1965), 174ff; James Barr, 'Revelation through History in the Old Testament and in Modern Theology', *Int* 17 (1963), 193-205. This model of revelation is also at the root of the *Heilsgeschichte* conception of revelation. See William J. Abraham, 'Revelation Reaffirmed', in *Divine Revelation*, ed. by Paul Avis (London: Darton, Longman and Todd, 1997), 208.

[77] Brown, *John*, 1:33, 521-23; Braun, *Jean le théologien*, 2:137; A. Feuillet, *Le prologue du quatrième évangile* (Paris: Brouwer, 1968), 224-25, 239-42; H. R. Moeller, 'Wisdom Motifs and John's Gospel', *BETS* 6 (1963), 93-98.

the mouth of the Most High (Sirach 24:3), exists intimately with God (Prov. 8:30, 22–23; Sir. 24:8; Wisd. 9:2, 9), is 'a pure emanation of the glory of the Almighty' (Wisd. of Sol. 7:25) and an agent of creation (Prov. 8:23–31; Wisd. of Sol. 8:4–6; 7:22; Sir. 1; cf. 1:1–3).[78] If this conception is in the background of the Johannine 'Word', then the Evangelist by employing it claims that God is revealed and known only in Jesus Christ who is the wisdom of God incarnate (cf. 1 Cor. 1:24; Eph. 3:11; Col. 2:2–3).[79] For Judaism, wisdom came to be associated with the law (i.e., Torah) in which the full revelation of God was to be found.[80] Even though the law originated with God, its pre-existence was asserted (Exod. R. 30:8) and it was given a distinct ontological status.[81] The word in the Old Testament often appears as an independent 'person' or 'hypostasis'[82] beside God with

---

[78] Wisdom lights the paths of humans (Jn. 1:5, 9; cf. Sir. 50:27–29; Wisd. of Sol. 7:10, 29) on earth (Sir. 1:10–12; Wis. 9:10, 17; Prov. 8:31), teaching (Wis. 7:22; 9:16–18; Job 11:6–7), guiding (Wis. 10:11), showing what pleases God (Wis. 9:10), giving life (Sir. 4:11–12) and immortality (Sir. 4:13; Wis. 6:18–20; 8:13). John 1:23 may echo Isaiah 40:3 and the disciple of Wisdom.

[79] This syncretistic picture of Wisdom does not deny diversities in the understanding of wisdom. B. Mack, *Logos und Sophia* (Göttingen: Vandenhoeck and Ruprecht, 1975), 22–32, identifies three strands of the tradition: hidden (Job 28:27; Sir. 1:9), available (Sir. 24), vanished (1 En. 42). On the Johannine association between Logos and wisdom, see further A. Hanson, 'John 1:14–18 and Exodus 34', in *The New Testament Interpretation of Scripture* (London: SPCK, 1980), 106; Brown, *John*, 1:33, 521–3; R. Bultmann, 'Der Religionsgeschichtliche Hintergrund des Prologs zum Johannesevangelium', in *Exegetica: Aufsätze zur Erforschung des Neuen Testaments*, hg. Erich Dinkler (Tübingen: Mohr-Siebeck, 1967), 6–35; Braun, *Jean le théologien*, 2:123–37; J. Ashton, 'The Transformation of Wisdom: A Study of the Prologue of John's Gospel', *NTS* 32 (1986), 161–86; Feuillet, *Le Prologue*, 289–94; idem, *Johannine Studies*, 89–91; R. G. Hamerton-Kelly, *Pre-Existence, Wisdom, and the Son of Man* (Cambridge: CUP, 1973); Moeller, 'Wisdom Motifs', 93–8; Michael E. Willett, 'Wisdom Christology in the Fourth Gospel' (Ph.D. diss., Southern Baptist Theological Seminary, 1985), 63–113; Basil de Pinto, 'Word and Wisdom in St. John', *Scripture* 19 (1967), 19–27; Dodd, *Interpretation*, 274–77; M. Hengel, 'Jesus als messianischer Lehrer der Weisheit und die Anfänge der Christologie', in *Sagesse et Religion: Colloque de Strasbourg, October 1976*, ed. by J. Leclant, et al. (Paris: Bibliothèque des Centres d'Etudes Supérieures Spécialisés, 1979), 147–88; B. Witherington, *The Christology of Jesus* (Minneapolis: Fortress, 1990), 51–53, 221–28; B. L. Mack, 'The Christ and Jewish Wisdom', in *The Messiah: Developments in Earliest Judaism and Christianity*, ed. by Charlesworth (Minneapolis: Fortress, 1992), 425–48; John Painter, 'Christology and the Fourth Gospel. A Study of the Prologue', *AusBR* 31 (1983), 45–62; idem, 'Christology and the History of the Johannine Community in the Prologue of the Fourth Gospel', *NTS* 30 (1984), 460–74; Walter Grundman, *Der Zeuge der Weisheit: Grundzüge der Christologie des Johannesevangeliums*, mit einer Einfuhrung hg. von W. Wiefel (Berlin: Evang. Verlaganstalt, 1985), 16–29; Barrett, *St. John*, 153, 165–6.

[80] E.g., Ps. 119:47–48, 97, 113, 159, 163, 167; Sir. 24:1–23; Bar. 3:36–4:4.

[81] See M. Hengel, *Judaism and Hellensim*, 169–75, 206–9; James M. Reese, *Hellenistic Influence on the Book of Wisdom and Its Consequences* (Rome: Pontifical Biblical Institute, 1970), 45–9.

[82] Ps. 33:6; 107:20; 147:15; Isa. 55:11.

divine characteristics (cf. Isa. 40:8; Ps. 33:4). In this instance, the *word* implies the *whole essence of God*.[83]

The Fourth Evangelist, by using the term 'Word' for Christ, binds all creation to revelation in him. By focusing on 'the Word' as the agency of revelation,[84] John locks his concept of revelation to the past revelation recorded in Israel's Scriptures. In this sense, John 1:3 clearly reflects Genesis 1, where God creates the world by his Word, and the first λόγος uttered by God is 'Let there be light' (Gen. 1:3). Light was the first manifestation of life (cf. Ps. 36:9 and Jn. 1:4).[85] If wisdom is the reality that emerges from the mouth of God by which the heavens and the earth were fashioned, then Jesus is that Word in the flesh. To reject him is to reject wisdom outside of which one cannot have spiritual understanding. If Wisdom is embodied in the Torah, in which the revelation of God is to be found, then for John, Jesus is the one of whom the law spoke and in whom the law was fulfilled. He is the one in whom the full knowledge of God's gracious purpose, the profound disclosure of his truth, is to be found (1:17). Therefore, in the Fourth Gospel, those who reject Jesus reject wisdom, life and light. They do not comprehend the true meaning of the Scriptures (i.e., their fulfilment in Jesus). Because the life inherent in the Word is the light of people, who are spiritually alienated from their creator, the revelation wrought by the Word is a saving revelation which purges away evil (15:3)[86] and gives life to those who will receive it (1:9–12a).

John's Gospel presents Jesus as the locus of God's self-disclosure. Bultmann, however, in his well known thesis asserted that there is no content to the revelation. 'Jesus as the revealer of God reveals nothing but that he is the revealer.'[87] Jesus, Bultmann noted, only gives 'the fact of the revelation' (*das Dass*) without describing its content (*ihr Was*).[88] Jesus does

---

[83] E.g., Jn. 12:48; Col. 3:16; 2 Thess. 3:1; 2 Tim. 2:9; Tit. 2:5; 1 Pet. 1:23; Heb. 4:12–13.

[84] Brown, *John*, 1:24.

[85] Gubler, "'Ich bin der Weg'", 373–82.

[86] Caird, *New Testament Theology*, 138f; cf. U. Schnelle, *Antidocetic Christology in the Gospel of John: An Investigation of the Place of the Fourth Gospel in the Johannine School* (Minneapolis: Fortress, 1992), 217.

[87] Bultmann, *The Theology of the New Testament*, vol. 2 trans by K. Grobel (London: SCM, 1955), 2:66.

[88] Ibid., also see H. Odeberg, *The Fourth Gospel: Interpreted in Relation to Contemporary Religious Currents in Palestine and the Hellenistic-Oriental World* (Amsterdam: B. R. Grüner, 1974. First published Uppsala, 1929), 94ff, who argued that the *exclusive* emphasis on Jesus as revealer (3:13) indicated a contemporary polemic against Jews who believed that apocalyptic revelation was possible apart from 'the Son of Man'. Johannine insistence on the Son of Man as the *sole* revealer of heavenly truths (1:18; 3:13, 31–36; 14:6) seems to be a refutation of such claims. Since Odeberg and Bultmann, others in recent decades also have argued along a similar

not 'communicate anything', but instead calls people to himself and demands a response. Within this existentialist interpretive framework, Bultmann also concluded that the quest for the 'Historical Jesus' was futile and accused those in the pursuit of it of having lost touch with the God who was 'wholly other', unconfined to the human historical life. He argued, 'the subject of theology is *God*, and the chief charge to be brought against liberal theology is that it has dealt not with God but with man'.[89] For Bultmann, the encounter with the divine is an existential encounter in the event of the Word (i.e., Christian preaching).[90] All historical studies dealt with relativities,[91] and even the knowledge such studies offered was relative and liable to change as research proceeded. As such it had no basis whatsoever to give a value judgment about a historical person. After two great wars (1914–1918, 1939–45), the assumption that the meaningfulness of history was guaranteed by God's immanence within it was demolished. On the contrary, history was without meaning. If one was to find meaning, such meaning had to be encountered from outside the sphere of human history. Therefore, no confirmation or guarantee of the truth of the word can be found within history – even the history of the historical Jesus; for God is not immanent even in this history but makes himself present only in

---

line. J. Jocz, 'Die Juden im Johannesevangelium', *Judaica* 9 (1953), 132f, noted that Jewish scholars have long been aware of this feature of John. Nevertheless, see, for example, Meeks' doctoral thesis, *The Prophet-King: Moses Traditions and the Johannine Christology*, NovTSup 14 (Leiden: Brill, 1967), 295–301, where he argues that the contemporary understanding of Moses as one who *journeyed to heaven*, there to receive heavenly revelations, had influenced John's christology, and that a polemic against contemporary claims that such journeys were made is found in 1:18, 3:11–13, and 5:37; also see Meeks, 'Man From Heaven in Johannine Sectarianism', *JBL* 91 (1972), 44–72, esp. 52f. David Aune, *The Cultic Setting of Realised Eschatology in Early Christianity* (Leiden: Brill, 1972), 99–101, following Meeks, has gone so far as to claim that in the context of the Johannine realised eschatology, the heavenly ascents and revelation were open not only to Jesus' immediate disciples, but also the Johannine church enjoyed a 'recurring actualisation of his future Parousia' in the visions and 'heavenly journeys' which were a feature of their worship. This picture of the Johannine church as a charismatic community is also basic to Bruce Woll's interpretation of the first farewell discourse in *Johannine Christianity in Conflict: Authority, Rank, and Succession in the First Farewell Discourse*, SBLDS 60 (Chico, CA: Scholars Press, 1981). More recently J. D. G. Dunn, in his 'Let John Be John: A Gospel for Its Time', in *Das Evangelium und die Evangelien. Vorträge vom Tübinger Symposium 1982*, ed. by P. Stuhlmacher (Tübingen: Mohr-Siebeck, 1983), 322–5, has taken up this approach and emphasises the importance of apocalyptic and 'merkabah' mysticism for the interpretation of John.

[89] R. Bultmann, 'Liberal Theology and the Latest Theological Movement', in idem, *Faith and Understanding* (London: SCM, 1969), 29.

[90] Ibid., 46–52.

[91] Troeltsch, *The Absoluteness of Christianity and the History of Religions* (1911; London: SCM, 1972), 30–32.

the transcendent and vertical form of the word.⁹² The quest for the Jesus of history was nothing more than a human-centred effort to objectify the God who could not be objectified. Indeed for Bultmann, myth was any language that objectified God, God's words, or God's actions. From this perspective, the scriptural text was also insignificant, because, as objective language, 'every fixed form of words' becomes dogma.⁹³ However Käsemann, Bultmann's pupil, responded to his teacher that one cannot separate the fact of revelation from what is being revealed.⁹⁴

In the Fourth Gospel, the revelation in Christ can only be a climax of salvation history if what is revealed is in harmony and continuation with the revelation recorded in the past in Israel's Scriptures.⁹⁵ The experience of the Israelites of the revelation of God was not an ahistorical existential phenomenon. Israel encountered God in his saving revelation first and foremost in its history.⁹⁶ In John's Gospel, revelation is summed up in the events of incarnation, cross, and resurrection (1:14) defined in history, yet

---

⁹² Francis Watson, 'Toward a Literal Reading of the Gospels', in *The Gospels for All Christians: Rethinking the Gospel Audiences*, ed. by Richard Bauckham (Grand Rapids, MI: Eerdmans, 1998), 203–7.

⁹³ See further Bultmann, *John*, 61, 62 n. 4, 63; and *Theology of the New Testament*, 2:42, 73; idem, 'New Testament and Mythology', in *Kerygma and Myth: A Theological Debate*, ed. by Hans Werner Bartsch, trans. by Reginald H. Fuller (London: SPCK, 1941), 1–44.

⁹⁴ E. Käsemann, *Jesu letzter Wille nach Johannes 17*, 3rd edn (Tübingen: Mohr-Siebeck, 1971), 17–54; ET, *The Testament of Jesus: A Study of the Gospel of John in the Light of Chapter 17* (Philadelphia: Fortress), 12–13, 48; idem, 'The Structure and Purpose of the Prologue to John's Gospel', in *New Testament Questions of Today* (Philadelphia: Fortress, 1969), 138–67, from German 'Aufbau und Anliegen des johanneischen Prologs', FS, F. Delekat (1957), 75–99. See a similar division of views between Luise Schottroff, *Der Glaubende und die feindliche Welt: Beobachtungen zum gnostischen Dualismus und seiner Bedeutung für Paulus das Johannesevangelium*, WMANT 37 (Neukirchen-Vluyn: Neukirchener Verlag, 1970), who emphasised Jesus' 'otherness', in contrast to Hartwig Thyen, 'Aus der Literatur zum Johannesevangelium', *TRu* 39 (1974), 1–69, 221–52, 289–330; 42 (1977), 211–70; 43 (1978), 328–59; 44 (1979), 79–134, and his pupil Wolfgang Langbrandtner, *Weltferner Gott oder Gott der Liebe? Der Ketzerstreit in der johanneischen Kirche*, BBET 6 (Frankfurt am Main: Peter Lang, 1977), who pointed to Jesus' this-worldliness. See also W. Baldensperger, *Der Prolog des vierten Evangeliums: Sein polemisch-apologetischer Zweck* (Tübingen: Mohr, 1898), 171; Lindars, *John*, 53–4; Meeks's criticism in 'Man from Heaven', 57; Brown, *John*, 1:32.

⁹⁵ James D.G. Dunn, 'Biblical Concepts of Revelation', in *Divine Revelation*, ed. by Paul Avis (London: Darton, Longman and Todd, 1997), 17ff.

⁹⁶ See S. Mowinckel, 'Den västorientaliska och israelitisk-judiska litteraturen', *Bonniers allmänna litteraturhistoria*, ed. by E. N. Tigerstedt, I (Stockholm: Bonniers, 1959), 40; idem, *The Old Testament*, 39–45; M. Noth, 'Das Geschichtsverständnis der alttestamentlichen Apokalyptik', *Arbeitsgemeinschaft für Forschung des Landes Nordrhein-Westfalen* (Geisteswissenschaften, H. 21, Köln und Opladen, 1954), 5f = *Gesammelte Studien zum Alten Testament*, ThB 6 (Munich, 1957), 249. Noth argues the Old Testament writers emphasised the history of Israel in the context of the neighbouring people because they saw history as divine work. See also T. C. Vriezen, *An Outline of Old Testament Theology* (Oxford: OUP, 1958), 187.

meta-historical in meaning and implication. This revelation is incomprehensible and meaningless, apart from the revelation of God in the past captured in Israel's Scriptures. Bultmann's insistence on 'the fact of revelation' devoid of content cannot be sustained since it does not coincide with the message of the Gospel. As I have been at pains to show throughout this study, John's proclamation of Jesus, his christology, is inextricably rooted in the text of Israel's Scriptures.

In addition, the Fourth Gospel presents far more than a revealer without a revelation. The incarnation, within which the cross and resurrection are subsumed, provides the very essence of revelation. When God in the Word became flesh and dwelt among us, the eternal became mortal, the timeless became locked in time and space. The event of the incarnation, cross and resurrection is the quintessence of revelation and the exposition of the meaning of it is theology *par excellence*. Then, there is also Jesus' teaching during his earthly life, which together with his person and work constitutes the coherent content of what God has revealed in the incarnate Word. No other divine initiative expresses more clearly and profoundly the divine saving attributes than the incarnation.[97] As von Balthasar observes, if revelation means 'un-veiling', then in the incarnation God has unveiled or 'revealed' himself to the eye of humanity.[98] The saving work of the Father through the Son is the content of the revelation. According to the First Epistle of John, the revelation of God's grace is made known through the death of the Son (1 Jn. 3:16; 4:9–10). To confess that Jesus is the Son of God is primarily a statement concerning his relation to God the Father. In the First Epistle of John as well as the Gospel, Jesus as Son is primarily the revealer of the Father. The revelation of the Father by the Son is focused in 1 John on the crucifixion. For it is through the death of Jesus, the Christ, the Son of God, that the Father's love and forgiveness are made known (4:9–10). Similarly, in the Gospel, the cross is the focal point of the revelation of the redemptive orientation of God toward his creation.[99] To deny that Jesus died as the Christ, the Son (of God) is to deny the core of Jesus' revelation.[100] Jesus coming into the world as the Saviour of the

---

[97] On the other hand, few scholars believe that the cross (i.e., the death) of Jesus provides the key to the interpretation of the whole of Scripture. R. H. Fuller, *A Critical Introduction to the New Testament* (London: Duckworth, 1965), 228; H. Anderson, *The Gospel of Mark* (London: Oliphants, 1976), 94f, 216.

[98] Hans Urs von Balthasar, 'Seeing the Form', in *The Glory of the Lord: A Theological Aesthetics*, 3 vols, trans. by E. L. Merikakis (Edinburgh: Clark, 1982), 1:87, 153f.

[99] 3:16; 15:9, 13; 1 Jn. 3:16; 4:9–10; cf. Rom. 5:8.

[100] 1 Jn. 4:2; 5:6 and Irenaeus, *Against Heresies*, 1:26:1; also R. Schnackenburg, *Die*

world reveals God as Saviour.[101] The title 'Christ' speaks of his mission of salvation (cf. 4:25; 7:26–41; 10:24; Isa. 61:1).[102] In John, 'Christ' and 'Son of God' are both intrinsically related. The Son is the only form in which the Father is 'seeable' and 'knowable'; to 'see', 'know', and 'believe' the Son is to 'see', 'know' and believe the Father (12:44, 45, 49). He is the visible image of the invisible God (Jn. 14:9; cf. Col. 1:15; Heb. 1:3). Because of his oneness with the Father, the Son is able to reveal God as he is.[103]

While Bultmann is correct that the Johannine Jesus systematically draws attention to himself as the revealer, yet in so doing, he draws attention to the Father (12:44, 45; 17:3, 6, 8, 21). This is essentially his mission (1:18). When he makes himself known, he is making the Father known. Clement of Alexandria believed Jesus to be 'the face' (τὸ πρόσωπον) of the Father.[104] But before Clement, Paul had already spoken of 'the knowledge of the glory of God in the face of Jesus Christ' (2 Cor. 4:7). Rensberger compares the language of the Gospel to a hall of mirrors

---

Johannesbriefe, HTKNT 13/3, 5th edn (Freiburg: Herder, 1975), 19–20; W. G. Kümmel, *Introduction to the New Testament*, trans. by H. C. Kee, rev. edn (London: SCM, 1975), 441–2; H. S. Songer, 'The Life Situation of the Johannine Epistles', *RevExp* 67 (1970), 404–5; C. Clemen, 'Beiträge zum geschichtlichen Verständnis der Johannesbriefe', 6 (1905), 272; Robinson, *Redating the New Testament* (London: SCM, 1976), 286 n. 154.

[101] 8:24, 28a; 9:39; 15:22–24; 1 Jn. 4:14–15; 5:9–13.

[102] Jesus' role as the Messiah, the anointed end-time Prophet-King promised by God and expected by most Jews (cf. Deut. 15:15–18). The primary reference of this title is to Jesus.

[103] The language is reminiscent of the Old Testament prophets (cf. Num. 24:13; Isa. 6:8; Jer. 1:5, 10; 9:24; Amos 3:7). Dodd, *Interpretation*, 254–5. C. K. Barrett, '"The Father is Greater than I" (Jn. 14:28): Subordinationist Christology in the New Testament', in *Essay on John* (Philadelphia: Westminster, 1982), 19–36; Peder Borgen, 'God's Agent in the Fourth Gospel', in *The Interpretation of John*, ed. by J. Ashton, 2nd edn (Edinburgh: Clark, 1997), 83–95; John Ashton, *Understanding the Fourth Gospel* (Oxford: Clarendon, 1991), 316–7. The word 'God' is used in John about 89 times (including variants), the majority in statements about Jesus. God is 'the one who has sent Jesus' (43 times, 17 with ἀποστέλλω and 26 times with πέμπω, in all but one instance, on Jesus' lips). Most commonly, God is identified as 'Father' (118 times), in virtually all instances, the Father of Jesus. Jesus refers customarily to God as 'my Father' (25 times) or 'the Father' (79 times). Throughout the Gospel, these statements focus on Jesus' unique claims to authority.

[104] *Stromateis* 5.6.34, I. The word that is regularly used in the Septuagint to translate the Hebrew פנים, perhaps from כסה, 'to hide' or 'conceal'. The concept occurs in the Old Testament in relation to the theme of the hiddenness of God. For example, the phrase 'hide the face' (סתר + פנים) is one expression from a large stock of language relating the motif of the hiddenness of God in the Old Testament. See Deut. 31:17; Mic. 3:1–4; Isa. 59:1ff; Ezk. 39:24, cf. Gen. 3:8; P. S. Fiddes, 'The Hiddenness of Wisdom in the Old Testament and Later Judaism' (D.Phil. thesis, Oxford, 1976); Schäfer, *Hidden and Manifest God*; A. S. van der Woude, 'פנים', *THAT*, vol. 2, col. 452; S. Balentine, *Hidden God: The Hiding of the Face of God in the Old Testament* (Oxford: OUP, 1983), 115, 161; Lothar Perlitt, 'Die Verborgenheit Gottes', in *Probleme biblischer Theologie: Gerhard von Rad zum 70. Geburtstag* (Munich: Kaiser, 1971), 367–82.

where, upon every surface, the face of Christ is reflected.[105] And that reflection also comprises the content of the Revealer's revelation. In the person and work of the Saviour is revealed something deeply profound about the character of God and his redemptive work in the human realm.[106] The content of the revelation is embodied in the Revealer. He reveals that he is a revealer of the Father and the one who has seen him has seen the Father (14:9; 10:30; 12:44).

In the Old Testament, God makes himself known to Israel through the revelation of his name (Exod. 6:2–8).[107] In the Fourth Gospel, Jesus has come to manifest the Father's name (17:6, 26, 12:28).[108] Making known the Father's name implies making known his character. Making known the Father's name underlines Jesus' fundamental mission as the one who 'explains' (ἐξηγέομαι) the Father (1:18).[109] In this capacity, one of the most striking aspects of the Johannine Gospel is the 'I am' declarations on the lips of Jesus where he identifies himself with the God of Israel.[110]

---

[105] David Rensberger, *Overcoming the World: Politics and Community in the Gospel of John* (London: SPCK, 1989), 137.

[106] Jesus reveals the salvific work of God (4:34; 5:17, 36; 8:36; 9:3, 4; 10:25; 14:10; 15:24; 17:4); God's character and nature in his disposition toward his creation (3:16–18; 1:16–17, 29, 36; 6:40; 9:39; 10:10b, 11, 14, 28–30; cf. 1 Jn. 4:9–10).

[107] On speculation related to the Tetragrammaton, see Sean M. McDonough, *YHWH at Patmos: Rev. 1:4 in its Hellenistic and Early Jewish Setting*, WUNT 107 (Tübingen: Mohr-Siebeck, 1999); L. Blau, *Das altjüdische Zauberwesen* (Leipzig: E. Pfeiffer, 1898); Samuel Cohen, 'The Names of God: A Study in Rabbinic Theology', *HUCA* 27 (1951), 579–604; C. T. R. Hayward, 'The Holy Name of the God of Moses and the Prologue of St. John's Gospel', *NTS* 25 (1979), 28f; J. Fossum, *The Name of God and the Angel of the Lord: Samaritan and Jewish Concepts of Intermediation and the Origin of Gnosticism*, WUNT 36 (Tübingen: Mohr-Siebeck, 1985), 248, 255f n. 32, argues that both 'name' (the Tetragrammaton) and the 'Logos' are the same in the prologue of John. But for Barrett, *St. John*, 505, they are closely related in 17:6, but not identical.

[108] Jesus has come into the world in the Father's name (5:43; 12:13). He carries out his work in his Father's name (10:25); and his disciples are kept in the care of the Father's name (17:11, 12). Cf. the reference to believing in the Son's name (1:12; 2:23; 3:18), asking in the Son's name (14:13, 14, [26]; 15:16; 16:23, 24, 26; [20:31]). See G. Rouiller, 'Leben in seinem Namen. Der Evangelist Johannes und seine Theologie des Namens', *Internationale Katholische Zeitschrift* 22 (1993), 54–62.

[109] M. M. Thompson, '"God's voice You Have Never Heard, God's Form You Have Never Seen": The Characterization of God in the Gospel of John', *Semeia* 63 (1993), 177–204.

[110] These expressions are characteristic of John's Gospel alone and virtually unknown in the Synoptics (only in Mk. 6:50; Mt. 14:27; Lk. 21:8). B. Hinrichs, *'Ich Bin': Die Konsistenz des Johannes-Evangeliums in der Konszentration auf das Wort Jesus*, Stuttgarter Bibelstudien 133 (Stuttgart: Katholisches Bibelwerk, 1988), 16ff. R. Bultmann, 'Die Bedeutung der neuerschlossenen mandäischen Quellen für das Verständnis des Johannesevangeliums', *ZNW* 24 (1925), 100–46, esp. 115–7, understood the statements against gnostic background. See further David M. Ball, *'I Am' in John's Gospel: Literary Function, Background and Theological Implications* (Sheffield: Sheffield Academic Press, 1996); Catrin H. Williams, *'I am He': The Meaning and Interpretation of 'ANÎ HÛ' in Jewish and Early Christian Literature*, WUNT (Tübingen: Mohr-

Here again we encounter another feature of John's Gospel rooted in the Old Testament Scriptures (e.g., Exod. 3:14–15; Deut. 32:39; Isa. 41:4; 43:10; 46:4).[111] Whether each Johannine usage corresponds to a specific context in a particular book of the Old Testament is a topic in its own right. Suffice it to say, once again as in other instances, John locks this concept to the whole history of the expression in the Old Testament where God has revealed himself progressively and in specific junctures in Israel's life. These self-disclosures anticipate and culminate God's self-revelation in the incarnate Word who is the bread of life (6:35), the light of the world (8:12, 9:5), the good shepherd (10:11), the way to the Father which is the way to life (10:9, 14:6), and the life (11:25, 14:6, 15:5); in brief, he is the essence of

---

Siebeck, 2000); Karl Kundsin, *Charakter und Ursprung der johanneischen Reden*, Acta Universitatis Latviensis, Theologisjas Fakultates Series 1 (Riga, n. p., 1939), 267–8; E. D. Freed, 'Ego Eimi in John 1.20 and 4.25', *CBQ* 41 (1979), 288–91; W. Manson, 'The ΕΓΩ ΕΙΜΙ of the Messianic Presence in the New Testament', *JTS* 48 (1947), 141; Feuillet, *Johannine Studies*, 83–91; Werner Georg Kümmel, *The Theology of the New Testament* (New York: Abingdon Press, 1973), 283–8; Leonard Goppelt, *Theology of the New Testament*, 2 vols, trans. by John E. Alsup; ed. by Jürgen Roloff (Grand Rapids: Eerdmans, 1982), 293–6; D. Daube, 'The "I Am" of the Messianic Presence', in idem, *The New Testament and Rabbinic Judaism* (London: Athlone, 1956), 325–9; Dodd, *Interpretation*, 93–96; H. Zimmermann, 'Das Absolute "Ego Eimi" als die neutestamentliche Offenbarungsformel', *BZ* 4 (1960), 271–2. E. Schweizer, *Ego Eimi: Die religionsgeschichtliche Herkunft und theologische Bedutung der johanneischen Bildreden, zugleich ein Beitrag zur Quellenfrage des vierten Evangeliums*, FRLANT 38, 2nd edn (Göttingen: Vandenhoeck & Ruprecht, 1965), 21–7, counts 212 occurrences of the formula in the Septuagint. If instances where ἐγώ stands alone with a predicate are included, the number increases to 367.

[111] See also chapter two (2.4). In Exodus, theophany, the self-disclosure of God, must be regarded as the central theme where YHWH makes himself known to Israel in the אֲנִי יְהוָה formula. But similar self-disclosures occur earlier in Genesis, elsewhere in the Pentateuch and later in the prophets. S. S. Smalley, *John: Evangelist and Interpreter* (Exeter: Paternoster Press, 1978), 90–1, points to the Psalms. John Painter, *John: Witness and Theologian* (London: SPCK, 1975), 39–41, draws a contrast to the law, and M. Davies, *Rhetoric and Reference in the Fourth Gospel* (Sheffield: JSOT Press, 1992), 82–7, looks to the Wisdom literature (Prov. 8:12-21; Sir. 24:3-31) of the Old Testament as a background for the 'I Am' sayings in John. The Book of Isaiah has proved fruitful for a number of scholars who have focused on the Isaianic influence on the Johannine 'I Am' sayings. See, for example, Zimmermann, 'Das Absolute "Ego Eimi"', where he finds a strong link in the Septuagint translation of Isaiah where the absolute ἐγώ εἰμι becomes the translation of *ani hu*. He then in turn connects this to the formula *Ani YHWH* (אֲנִי יְהוָה) which he regards as the revelation formula of the Old Testament. See also W. Zimmerli, 'Knowledge of God According to the Book of Ezekiel', in *I am Yahweh*, ed. by W. Brueggemann; trans. by D. W. Stott (Atlanta: John Knox Press, 1982), 39–63, and Pancaro, *Law in the Fourth Gospel*, 59, who has built on Zimmermann's results. Also A. Feuillet, 'Les ego eimi christologiques du quatrième evangile: La révélation énigmatique de l'être divine de Jésus dans Jean et les Synoptiques', *RSR* 54 (1966), 11–12; Brown, *John*, vol. 1, Appendix IV, 535–37; J. C. Coetzee, 'Jesus' Revelation in the Ego Eimi Sayings in John 8 and 9', in *A South Africa Perspective on the New Testament*, ed. by J. H. Petzer and P. J. Hartin (Leiden: Brill, 1986), 170–7. P. B. Harner, *The 'I Am' of the Fourth Gospel* (Philadelphia: Fortress, 1970), 17, 26, sees Isaiah as the main influence on the absolute 'I Am' of John, but does not rule out a link with the Tetragrammaton of Exodus 3:14 nor with the interpretation given to the words by rabbinic Judaism.

life, the self-existing one, the 'I Am'. In its all-embracing significance, 'I am' is the sum of all God's statements about himself.[112]

In Exodus, the formula 'to know that I am YHWH' occurs nine times (6:7; 7:5, 17; 8:22; 10:2; 14:4; 16:12; 29:46; 31:13) where each occurrence is tied to a concrete historical event. The knowledge of YHWH's identity is revealed in his acts in human history. In the Fourth Gospel, the act of God in human history is the 'lifting up' of the Son of Man, 'When you have lifted up the Son of Man, then you will know that I am' (8:28; cf. 13:19). It is in Christ's death, resurrection and glorification that God is revealed. And much of the New Testament theology is given to the explication of the content, meaning, significance and implication of that revelation of which Jesus speaks in 8:28. In being 'lifted up', Jesus is identified with the salvation of YHWH. The claim to be the only God, the claim to be the only Saviour of Israel and the claim to be YHWH, all determine the meaning and significance of the 'I am' expressions both in the Old Testament and the Fourth Gospel. In Isaiah, for example, YHWH is presented as the only saviour because he is the only God (Isa. 43:10–13; cf. 42:8; 44:6), which explains why Jesus can say that those who do not 'believe that I am' will die in their sins (8:24). This further sheds light on the Johannine 'Word'. By identifying himself with YHWH, Jesus can claim that he speaks the very words of YHWH (3:34; 14:10, 24; 17:8; cf. Heb. 1:1–2) and that those words can offer life (6:63, 68). For John, the reason the Son can make the Father known is not only because he was in the bosom of the Father, but because he is also the Word who was in the beginning with God.[113] He is described as God (1:1).[114]

To encounter the truth in John's Gospel is to encounter Christ who embodies the truth.[115] But this truth is neither simply general factual heavenly information nor theological insights. Rather, it is emphatically a redemptive truth, a saving revelation. In asserting that Jesus is 'full of grace and truth' (1:14), the Evangelist underlines the salvific nature of the revealed truth.[116] In the revelation of Jesus through the 'I am' sayings, he is identified with three major themes of the Gospel and the Scriptures: light,

---

[112] J. Richter, 'Ani Hu und Ego Eimi' (Diss., University of Erlangen, 1956), 24, 47–58.

[113] O. Hofius, 'Der in des Vaters Schoss ist, Joh 1, 18', *ZNW* 80 (1989), 163–71.

[114] B. A. Mastin, 'A Neglected Feature of the Christology of the Fourth Gospel', *NTS* 22 (1976), 32–51.

[115] Cf. Bultmann, *Theology of the New Testament*, 2:18–19; Pancaro, *Law in the Fourth Gospel*, 81ff; Thompson, 'God's Voice You Have Never Heard', 177–204.

[116] Bultmann, *John*, 73–74, takes 'grace and truth' as a hendiadys. See also Bultmann, *Theology of the New Testament*, 2:18–19.

life and truth. All that humanity vainly seeks in the creation is only to be found in the creator (Deut. 8:3).

6.3.3. The Witness of the Written Word to the Living Word

For the New Testament writers, revelation was already embodied in the Old Testament Scriptures but hidden until the fullness of time in which the mystery was revealed in Jesus Christ.[117] In the Fourth Gospel, that which is disclosed in the incarnate Word is wedded to Israel's Scriptures. Indeed the revelation of God in Jesus Christ would remain an enigma and incomprehensible if detached from the revelation in Scriptures. The Fourth Evangelist does not locate revelation in anything which has independent life outside of the text. One cannot separate the fact of the revelation or the content of revelation from the *mode* of revelation.[118] Here the historical appearance of the human personality of Jesus is not, as such, revelation. It becomes revelation when this historical appearance is held up to the light of the Scriptures. The truth in the Fourth Gospel is not simply an existential encounter in a moment of crisis. Neither is it a mere subjective supernatural experience (cf. 2 Cor. 12:2–4). In the Fourth Gospel Jesus is identified with the God of Israel's Scriptures who is made known as the Father of Jesus Christ.[119] In the Fourth Gospel what may be known about Jesus and the illumination wrought by the Holy Spirit concerning his identity after the resurrection is not independent of the Scriptures. On the contrary, this knowledge is there in the pages of the Old Testament.[120]

Paul, like many of his Jewish contemporaries,[121] believed that the

---

[117] Mark was able to begin his summary of Jesus' preaching with the words, 'The time is fulfilled' (Mk. 1:15). Cf. Lk. 24:27; Jn. 5:39, 46; cf. Mt. 1:1–17, 22, 23; 2:17; 4:15–16; 5:21–48; 12:19–20; 22:44–45; Mk. 1:2; Acts 1:16, 20; 3:13–26; 4:11; 7:1–53; 8:31–35; Rom. 3:1–11:36; 15:4; Gal. 4:4; Eph. 1:10, 23; Heb. 1:1–2; 1 Pet. 1:5–10; 2:6.

[118] See Balthasar, 'Seeing the Form', 1:55; Gail O'Day, *Revelation in the Fourth Gospel: Narrative Mode and Theological Claim* (Philadelphia: Fortress, 1986), 94.

[119] Smith, *Theology*, 76.

[120] 10:30, 35, 36; cf. 1:23; 2:22; 3:14; 5:39; 7:38, 42; 8:17; 13:18; 17:12; 19:24, 28, 36, 37.

[121] See Peter Schäfer, *The Hidden and Manifest God: Some Major Themes in Early Jewish Mysticsm*, trans. by Aubrey Pomerance (Albany: State University of New York, 1992); Bockmuehl, *Revelation and Mystery*, 10ff; J. D. Levenson, 'The Sources of Torah: Psalm 119, and the Modes of Revelation in Second Temple Judaism', in *Ancient Israelite Religion: Essays in Honor of Frank Moore Cross*, edited by Patrick D. Miller, et al. (Philadelphia: Fortress, 1987), 559–64; Michael Fishbane, *Biblical Interpretation in Ancient Israel* (Oxford: Clarendon, 1985); idem, 'Revelation and Tradition: Aspects of Inner-Biblical Exegesis', *JBL* 99 (1980), 343–61; idem, 'Jewish Biblical Exegesis: Presupposition and Principles', in *Scripture in the Jewish Christian Traditions: Authority, Interpretation, Relevance*, ed. by F. R. Greenspan (Nashville:

interpretation of the Scriptures was sealed and concealed until the time of their prophetic realisation which came about in Christ and the Gospel (2 Cor. 3:12–18). Paul appropriates the Bible's own revelatory language to describe the new revelation (i.e., Deut. 30:12–14; e.g., Rom. 10:8) and to present Christ as the fulfilment of the Torah. Elsewhere in Paul's writings, a similar view is expressed which essentially becomes his hermeneutical ground rule (Rom. 4:23f; 15:4, 1 Cor. 9:10; 10:11; 2 Cor. 1:20).[122] Christ appears to be, for Paul, the foundational equivalent of the wisdom of God (1 Cor. 1:24, 30; 2:6–7; 8:6; cf. Col. 1:15–18; 2:3) and the key for the understanding of all revelation, whether in the Gospel, in Scripture, or in creation.

John articulates precisely the same conviction as Paul, but in an entirely different style, i.e., the subtle but systematic allusions to the fulfilment of Scripture in the life and work of Jesus, which is, as I have noted in previous chapters, what gives his language its particular elusive character. Rather than speaking directly of the 'wisdom of God' (1 Cor. 1:24; Col. 1:15–18; 2:3), John speaks of the 'Word'. In the New Testament, it is the Fourth Gospel which emphatically brings out Jesus as the revelation of God.[123] But both in John and in the rest of the New Testament, the revelation embodied in the person of Jesus Christ is only accessible and meaningful in the light of Israel's sacred Scriptures.[124]

6.3.4. Illumination of the Revelation of Truth by the Holy Spirit

According to the farewell speech, it is the Spirit-Paraclete (ἄλλον παράκλητον), who will 'teach' (διδάξει) and 'remind' (ὑπομνήσει) the disciples of Jesus' words (Jn. 14:15–17, 25–26; 15:26–27; 16:4b–15). In his earthly ministry, Jesus repeatedly noted that he did not speak from himself but that he spoke what he heard from the Father (8:26, 40; 14:24; cf. 5:30). After the resurrection, this task is given to the Holy Spirit, who 'will not speak from himself, but whatever he hears (ὅσα ἀκούει), he will speak (λαλήσει)' (Jn. 16:13). This is the only place in the New Testament where the verb λαλεῖν,

---

Abingdon Press, 1982), 92–110; P. Trevor Williams, *Forms and Vitality in the World and in God: A Christian Perspective* (Oxford: Clarendon, 1985).

[122] Joseph Bonsirven, *Exégèse Rabbinique et Exégèse Paulinienne*, Bibliothèque de Théologie historique (Paris: Beauchesne, 1939), 128f.

[123] Though the claim is foreshadowed in Matthew 11:27 and Luke 10:22.

[124] Cf. R. Bultmann, *Kerygma und Mythos*, ed. by H. W. Bartsch (Hamburg: H. Reich Evangelischer Verlag, 1948, repr. 1981), 133–4; F. C. Baur, *Vorlesungen über neutestamentliche Theologie*, ed. by F. F. Baur (Leipzig, 1864; repr. Darmstadt: Wissenschaftliche Buchgesellschaft, 1973), 128.

'to speak', is used to denote the activity of the Holy Spirit. In using this word, John seems to suggest that the ministry of the Holy Spirit is a continuation of Jesus' own work, which is the revelation of God, denoted also by such expressions as λόγος and λαλεῖν.[125] In John 16:25, Jesus announces to the disciples that he will no longer speak in parables, οὐκέτι ἐν παροιμίαις λαλήσω, but will make an open revelation concerning the Father, παρρησίᾳ περὶ τοῦ πατρὸς ἀπαγγελῶ, alluding to the revelation which was to come through the Holy Spirit after the ascension. While the revelation of Jesus has been veiled (ἐν παροιμίαις), the revelation through the Holy Spirit will be open (παρρησίᾳ...ἀπαγγελῶ).

In this context, the Spirit does not bring a new revelation, but makes fully meaningful the self-revelation of God in Christ by guiding the believer εἰς τὴν ἀλήθειαν πᾶσαν, 'into all the truth' (16:13). 'All the truth' is the truth revealed in Jesus and unveiled by the Holy Spirit. He will do so by bringing to their memory all that Jesus had said, ὑπομνήσει ὑμᾶς πάντα ἃ εἶπον ὑμῖν [ἐγώ] (14:26). In other words, he will cause the disciples to understand the true significance of Jesus' life, works and words. In this context of the activity of the Holy Spirit (ὑπομιμνήσκειν), it is noteworthy that in 16:13-15, the expression ἀναγγελεῖ ὑμῖν ('he will declare to you') is used three times. The compound verb ἀναγγεῖλαι does not simply mean 'to announce'. Rather, it means 'to disclose something which had been unknown or secret'.[126] The word occurs frequently in the Septuagint of Isaiah and Jeremiah. It is also found in the apocalyptic literature, where it does not imply proclamation of a new revelation, but the interpretation or clarification of a previous revelation which had been either veiled or obscured. This also seems to be the sense in the Fourth Gospel.[127]

The Holy Spirit will bring about this unveiling of the revelation of God in Jesus by explaining it in the light of the witness of the Scriptures to him.[128] To remember, in the Fourth Gospel, means remembering Jesus'

---

[125] de la Potterie, 'Truth in Saint John', 77

[126] BAGD, 51.

[127] On the relationship between the Fourth Gospel and apocalypticism, see Christopher Rowland, 'The Parting of the Ways: the Evidence of Jewish and Christian Apocalyptic and Mystical Material', in *Jews and Christians*, ed. by J. D. G. Dunn (Tübingen: Mohr-Siebeck, 1992), 226–230, idem, 'John 1.51 and the Targumic Tradition', *NTS* 30 (1984), 496ff. Rowland places the Fourth Gospel within the apocalyptic tradition. Also see W. C. Grese, '"Unless One is Born Again": The Use of a Heavenly Journey in John 3', *JBL* 107 (1989), 677–93; A Segal, *Two Powers in Heaven* (Leiden: Brill, 1978); August Strobel, *Kerygma und Apokalyptik: Ein religionsgeschichtlicher und theologischer Beitrag zur Christusfrage* (Göttingen: Vandenhoeck and Ruprecht, 1967).

[128] H. van den Bussche, *La discours d'adieu de Jésus* (Maredsous, 1959), 126.

teachings and claims in light of the Scriptures. This remembrance specifically pertains to the perception of the deeper meaning in the Scriptures concerning the realisation of God's redemptive work in the person of the incarnate Word. Indeed, one of the central ministries of the Holy Spirit is to guide the disciples to see the witness of Scriptures in Jesus.[129] This is reiterated again at the end of Jesus' final entry into Jerusalem. It is the Spirit of truth who awakens in the disciples the memory of the prophetic word (itself produced by the Spirit), and with that, the meaning of their former actions.[130] John cites Zechariah 9:9 in shortened form: 'Fear not, daughter of Zion; behold your king is coming, sitting on a donkey's colt' (Jn. 12:15). At first, the disciples do not understand the event; but after Jesus is glorified, then they remember that this had been written of him.

Thus, a significant dimension in the remembrance of the disciples is being able to see the profound correlations between Jesus' life, words and works and that which had been spoken in the past by the prophets; mysteries hidden in the pages of the ancient Scriptures where the Father himself bears witness to the Son through his word. The Scriptures illuminate the way of Jesus even to the cross, and clarify this way to the disciples only after Easter by the Holy Spirit. The Spirit, who 'teaches all things' and 'brings to remembrance' the words of Jesus (14:26), also reveals their significance to those who are born of God. The crux of the matter seems to be this: when Jesus asserts that the Spirit leads the disciples into all the truth (16:13), this truth is not independent of Israel's Scriptures but is deposited in its pages. It is the Holy Spirit who opens the disciples' eyes to see the promised Messiah in the ancient text.

The Holy Spirit in the Fourth Gospel has an indispensable role in leading the disciples to the comprehension of the salvific revelation of God in Jesus Christ. In this Gospel, the perception of the revelatory truth apart from the work of the Holy Spirit in regeneration and illumination (3:3–12; 1:12–13) is inconceivable. In the Holy Spirit, the believing community is privileged to have a constant guide to all truth (Jn. 16:13).[131] In the present age, just as it is impossible to worship God truly apart from the indwelling

---

[129] See E. Cothenet, 'Témoinage de l'Esprit et interprétation de l'écriture dans la corpus johannique', in *La vie de la parole: De l'Ancien au Nouveau Testament*, P. Grelot Festschrift (Paris: Desclée de Brouwer, 1987), 367–77.

[130] Cf. 1QS 3:17–4:26; 1QH 3:21; 4:10, 20–22; 5:11f; 13:18f; 14:25–27; 16:10–12; 1QpHab 7:1f. See further Josef Schreiner, 'Geistbegabung in der Gemeinde von Qumran', *BZ* 9 (1965), 161–80; Peter Schäfer, 'Geist: II. Judentum', *TRE* 12 (1984), 173–8; Betz, *Offenbarung*, 140–7ff; Werner Foerster, 'Der Heilige Geist im Spätjudentum', *NTS* 8 (1962), 117–34 (129f).

[131] Concerning the variant in this text, see Barrett, *St. John*, 407.

presence of the Holy Spirit within the worshipper, it is also impossible to comprehend the word of God truly without the aid of the Spirit of God. They both depend upon being born of God.[132]

6.4. Spiritual Birth as a Necessary Condition for Comprehending the Truth

In the Fourth Gospel, spiritual perception, the understanding of the revelation of God in Jesus Christ, belongs only to those who are born of God. The spiritual life leading to eternal life is generated by the Spirit of God. In his portrayal of the imparting of the Spirit, which (unlike Luke's great Pentecost depiction) becomes the climax of the risen Lord's first appearance to the disciples, John in 20:22 makes conscious use of the second creation motif alluded to in Genesis 2:7 in the Septuagint, where 'the Lord God formed man out of the dust of the ground, and breathed into his nostrils the breath of life; and the man became a living being.' This time, however, it is Jesus who is breathing the breath of eternal life from above into his disciples.

After Jesus commissions the disciples, he breathes on them, saying: 'Receive the Holy Spirit' (Jn. 20:21–22; cf. Mt. 28:18; 2 Tim. 2:2; Mk. 16:14–16). The New Testament hapax legomenon ἐνεφύσησεν appears in Genesis 2:7 to translate ויפח at the animation of Adam: God 'breathed into his nostrils the breath of life (ἐνεφύσησεν εἰς τὸ πρόσωπον αὐτοῦ πνοὴν ζωῆς; ויפח באפיו נשמת חיים), and man became a living being.' In recording this enactment by the risen Lord, the author draws attention to the new creation motif and underlines the Spirit's work of renewal, making the disciples into new creatures born from above (3:3, 5).

In the context of the new creation motif and spiritual birth, there may be an allusion to Ezekiel 37:1–14 and the prophecy concerning the resurrection of the dry bones. There, in verse 9, the Son of Man is told to prophesy to the 'wind-breath-Spirit' to come and breathe on the corpses so that they will live again. In verse 14, the Lord promises, 'I will put my Spirit within you, and you will come to life, and I will place you in your own land'. The passage in Ezekiel 37 looks to the regeneration of Israel immediately prior to the establishment of the Messianic kingdom.

---

[132] Otto Betz, '"To Worship God in Spirit and in Truth": Reflections on John 4:20–6', in *Standing Before God*, ed. by A. Finkel and R. Frizzel (New York: Ktav, 1981), 53–72, suggests the phrase 'in Spirit' (4:23) means the same as 'new birth' (3:5).

The Fourth Evangelist may have seen in the action of Jesus in 20:21–22 a beginning of the fulfilment of Ezekiel's prophecy, just as Peter made use of the prophecy of Joel 2:28–32 in his sermon on the day of Pentecost (2:17–21). In John 20:21–22, Jesus breathed into the disciples the breath of eternal life. In 7:38–39, there is the anticipation of the giving of the Holy Spirit after the resurrection. It seems that even on the eve of the crucifixion, the disciples had not yet realised that there would be a resurrection (20:28). The recognition of who Jesus was appears to have come to them only after the resurrection and ultimately when the Spirit was given to enable the disciples to understand the truth concerning God's self-disclosure in the incarnate Word, the risen Lord, and perceive the significance of the testimony of Scriptures concerning him. This scriptural testimony resonates throughout the Gospel almost like a refrain, validating John's claim that Jesus is the one he claimed to be.

The concept of spiritual renewal is an important topic in New Testament theology. Paul refers to spiritual renewal using the figure of a new creation in Christ (2 Cor. 5:17; Eph. 2:10; Gal. 6:15). John speaks of this in terms of 'being born of God' or 'born from above'. In the Fourth Gospel, being born of the Spirit is the same as being born of God (1:13), and being born of God is the same as being 'of God' or 'from God' (8:47).[133]

The opposite of being born of the Spirit is being born of the flesh (Jn. 3:6). In Ephesians 4:22–24, Paul urges his readers to lay aside their sinful pattern of life and put on their 'new self' which has been created in righteousness and holiness after the likeness of God. The analogy used is that of τὸν παλαιὸν ἄνθρωπον, 'the old man', and τὸν καινὸν ἄνθρωπον, 'the new man'. In Colossians 3:10, Paul refers to the new man as possessing new spiritual life in Christ and as being renewed in knowledge according to the image of God who created him. The new creation is based upon the work of Christ on the cross.

Peter also makes use of the figure of new birth. In 1 Peter 1:3, 23 he uses the term ἀναγεγέννημαι, 'to beget or bring forth again' or 'to regenerate'.[134] The rebirth of which Peter speaks is through the resurrection of Christ from the dead and through the living word of God. In 1 Peter 2:2, Peter again alludes to rebirth with the term ἀρτιγέννητος describing those who have recently experienced the new birth.

Similarly James writes of begetting through the λόγῳ ἀληθείας, 'the

---

[133] Barnabas Lindars, 'John and the Synoptic Gospels: A Test Case', *NTS* 27 (1981), 290–1; Brown, *John*, 1:130–1; and Schnackenburg, *St. John* 1:367–8.

[134] BAGD, 51.

word of truth' (James 1:18), utilising the expression ἀποκυέω, 'give birth' or 'bring forth'[135] in the aorist tense, ἀπεκύησεν, stating that his readers have been 'brought forth' (i.e., 'brought into being') by means of the word of truth. These first believers were the guarantee of more to come in the future as a result of the preaching of the Gospel.

Titus 3:3–7 speaks of rebirth as a past event: 'He saved us (ἔσωσεν ἡμᾶς) by the washing of regeneration (διὰ λουτροῦ παλιγγενεσίας) and renewal of the Holy Spirit (ἀνακαινώσεως πνεύματος ἁγίου)' (v. 5). This is a past event for those who already believe.

In John's Gospel, the concept of spiritual birth, or to use the traditional theological term, 'regeneration', occurs early in the narrative, both in the prologue (Jn. 1:12–13) and subsequently in the discourse with Nicodemus. Whereas Paul places his emphasis upon the legal standing of the one justified by God, John emphasises the new relationship with God into which the believer enters. John uses the figure of new birth, 'from above', to denote the concept of spiritual regeneration or new creation. In the Gospel, Nicodemus is instructed by Jesus that no one can see or enter the kingdom of God unless they experience the new birth. In the First Epistle, John argues that the new birth reveals itself in a new and more Christ-like manner of living. The new birth of which John speaks is much more than an attempt on the part of humans morally to reform themselves or to overcome their alienation from the world, self, and their fellow human beings. It is, in fact, a new supernatural life and nature, not the transformation of the old. Just as the effects of the wind are seen, even so the results of the new birth are seen in a changed manner of life (Jn. 1:13; 3:8).

John uses the phrase 'kingdom of God' in these verses only; but in his other references to the kingdom (Jn. 6:15, 28, 29; 18:36, 37), it is evident that it is not of the world system and can only be entered by faith and the new birth. The new birth is spiritual, not only in its nature but in its source (Jn. 3:5, 6). The kingdom of God is of a spiritual nature and the new birth, the means of entrance into the kingdom, must be spiritual as well. The new birth is a spiritual renewal in the sense that the human spirit is separated from the Spirit of God prior to the birth from above. Therefore, the spirit of a person is made alive by the work of the Holy Spirit in an impartation of spiritual life. This internal conversion will then issue in external change. The new birth is spiritual in its source, power, and objectives. It stands in sharp contrast to John's description of human nature as 'flesh'. This truth is

---

[135] See Walter Bauer's comments in BAGD, 94.

further emphasised by the contrast in John 3:6, 'That which is born of the flesh is flesh and that which is born of the Spirit is spirit'.[136]

If the Father initiated the new birth as a result of his love for the world and worked through the mediation of the Son, then it can be said that the Holy Spirit is the agent of the birth from above. To see and perceive the kingdom of God, one must be born from above (3:3), which is also to say 'born of water and Spirit' (3:5).[137] The interpretations of the phrase 'born of water and spirit' have been varied. The 'water' in the context of its Old Testament usage[138] symbolises the Holy Spirit in relation to hopes for an eschatological act of cleansing.[139] In this sense, 'water and spirit' form a kind of hendiadys, referring to the spiritual regeneration available in Jesus Christ. To be 'born from water and spirit' means a total shift of world view, and dislocation from below to above.

'The water and spirit' may also indicate two inseparable aspects of being born of God. These two aspects are cleansing and giving life. In Ezekiel 36:25-27, the Lord declares,

And I will sprinkle clean water upon you, and you shall be clean; from all your filthiness, and from all your idols will I cleanse you. A new heart also will take away the stony heart out of your flesh, and I will give you a heart of flesh. And I will put my spirit within you, and cause you to walk in my statutes, and you shall keep my judgments, and do them.   (Ezekiel 36:25-27)

This prophecy points to the time of Israel's coming restoration, when the nation shall be 'born in a day' (Isa. 66:8). In the next chapter, Ezekiel pictures this great national revival as the bringing of the dead to new life by the word of the Lord, and employs the figure of the wind to picture the life-giving activity of the Spirit of God. Thus, in the first part of the prophecy, the figure of water is employed in connection with the cleansing away of filthiness; and in the latter portion, the figure of the wind is introduced for the giving of new life.

Jesus joins both figures in his single phrase, 'born of water and spirit'. For the nation to experience regeneration, its members must experience quickening. Nicodemus as 'the teacher of Israel' ought to have been aware of this. He is rebuked for ignorance which is attributed to his unregenerate

---

[136] Bultmann defined the Johannine view of flesh (i.e., *sarx*) as the human and worldly sphere, which is transitory, illusory, inauthentic, helpless, futile, and corrupting: 'The nothingness of man's whole existence.' Bultmann, *John*, 62, 141; idem, *Theology of the New Testament*, 2:58, 63.

[137] See Linda Belleville, 'Born of Water and Spirit', *Trinity Journal* 1 (1980), 125-34.

[138] See my discussion in chapter two in relation to 'living water'.

[139] See Zane C. Hodges, 'Water and Spirit – John 3:5', *BibSac* 135 (1978), 206-20.

state. Jesus proceeds to explain that his own death on the cross would be the grounds of the new life appropriated by faith. The picture Jesus utilises of the desperate condition of humanity is that of the Israelites in the grips of death as the poison of the serpents swept through their bodies (Num. 21:4–9). Their only hope for life was unequivocal obedience to God's requirement, to cast a glance of expectant faith at a bronze serpent lifted up on a standard. In so doing they had to believe God's pledged word and obey it. The event recorded in Numbers 21 foreshadows the true picture of cleansing of sin, the death of death in the death of the Son of Man, which is once again appropriated by believing God's word and looking expectantly to the crucified and risen Lord. When one responds in obedient faith to the death of the crucified Lord as the grounds of freedom from death, the Spirit of God confirms to a person's heart the saving power of that death bringing forth eternal life. Spiritual birth originates from God; and it is experienced by people when 'God's revelation is accepted in believing obedience'.[140] But this obedience is a *public* obedience, and Johannine faith demands public attestation (12:42–43). This is the problem with secret believers such as Nicodemus.

The birth from above which the Spirit brings about is different from anything humanity can produce. The necessity of the new birth must be seen in the context of humanity in its lost condition in the grips of death utterly incapable of comprehending the truth. As such, humanity is not able to 'see' or 'enter' the kingdom of God. Flesh cannot give birth to that which is spiritual, and the spirit does not give birth to that which is fleshly. The Fourth Gospel is emphatic that humanity, as flesh, cannot experience or give rise to spiritual birth by its own means. It needs the impartation of the divine spiritual breath. Just as people's natural birth is not of their own doing, so their spiritual birth is not something they can effect, but only receive from God. The production of life is the work of the living God alone – 'born not of blood nor of the will of the flesh nor of the will of man, but of God' (Jn. 1:13). Flesh can produce only flesh and the Spirit only spirit. Since people cannot produce spiritual life apart from the Spirit of God, they cannot comprehend the truth apart from the Spirit of truth, for they have no spiritual faculty. It is only when they have received spiritual life that they are enabled through the active presence of the Spirit of God within them to discern the truth. As Paul emphatically asserts, 'Those who are unspiritual do not receive the gifts of God's Spirit, for they are

---

[140] Eduard Lohse, 'Wort und Sakrament im Johannesevangelium', *NTS* 7 (1960–1961), 110–25, here p. 116.

foolishness to them, and they are unable to understand them because they are spiritually discerned' (1 Cor. 2:14). Similarly, in the Fourth Gospel, the new birth is not an option, but an absolutely necessary precondition to hearing and seeing the truth (3:31–32; 8:47)

6.4.1. Spiritual Perception

To his opponents who demand plain speech in John 10:24, Jesus responds that he has been speaking to them plainly, but they have refused to believe (10:25). In the Fourth Gospel, even though Jesus openly proclaims his identity (e.g., 5:19–47; 8:12–30; 18:20, 30–38), some do not believe. Indeed on each occasion when he identifies himself, his opponents seek to kill him, a consistent pattern of disclosure met by rejection (7:20, 29–30, 33–34, 37–38, 44; 8:12–13, 58). Even on this occasion when he identifies himself (10:30), once again they try to stone him. This inability to see, the unbelief leading to the rejection of Jesus, is attributed by the Evangelist in part to the love of the praise of other people (5:40–44).

Within John 8:12–59, ἐγώ εἰμι occurs on the lips of Jesus five times (vv. 12, 18, 24, 28, 58) and is used in a variety of contexts and forms elsewhere in the Gospel as a trigger for the reader to recall what has already been claimed by Jesus in the words ἐγώ εἰμι. The Feast of Tabernacles (7:2, 10, 14, 28, 37) provides the context of the ἐγώ εἰμι declarations in chapter 8. The debates about the source of Jesus' teaching (7:16–19), his judgment (7:24), his personal origin (7:27–29), his destiny (7:33–36), whether he is the Christ (7:26–31; 40–44) and his claim to offer living water (7:37–39) have all paved the way for the debate of 8:12–59, 'Who is Jesus?' The question 'Who are you?' (8:25; cf. 8:53) is the underlying theme of the chapter and indeed of the Gospel.[141] As Jesus openly speaks about his origin and identity, the words ἐγώ εἰμι appear frequently alongside the themes of witness[142] and judgment (8:13–18), Jesus' origin and destiny (8:18–20), and Jesus' relation to the Father. Significantly, the incident takes place in the temple (8:20), the centre of the

---

[141] W. Kern, 'Die symmetrische Gesamtaufbau von Joh. 8:12–58', *ZKT* 78 (1956), 451–4, suggests that these verses have a chiastic structure, centering around vv. 31–41. 'I Am' forms an inclusio to the section and so confirms that it is to be regarded as a literary unit. Jesus' debate with the Jews begins with an 'I Am' saying in v. 12, and concludes with an 'I Am' saying in v. 58. Unlike the debate in ch. 6, the debate of ch. 8 centres on the authority for Jesus' self-revelation as the Light of the World rather than the meaning of it.

[142] E. Cothenet, 'Le témoignage selon saint Jean', *Esprit et Vie* 101 (1991), 401–7.

presence of God's glory in the Holy of Holies.¹⁴³ What emerges at the end of the passage is that, in spite of Jesus' repeated and open assertion of his identity, 'the Jews' respond by trying to stone him. Their blindness to signs, testimony, and the open explanation of Jesus results in the verdict of 9:39 confirming their blindness. Further clarification does not help, since again in the last recorded encounter with Jesus in 10:24, they demand that he speak to them 'plainly' (εἰπὲ ἡμῖν παρρησίᾳ), which he has done for the entire time (10:25). Jesus explains their incomprehension as being due to their unbelief. Nevertheless, he proceeds to declare once again his unity and identity with the Father (10:30), to which they respond by trying to kill him.

The frequent usage of the verbs ὁράω, θεάομαι, βλέπω, ἐμβλέπω, and cognate words in John¹⁴⁴ shows the importance of the subject of perception – the ability to see and perceive the revelation of God in the incarnate Word.¹⁴⁵ The verb ὁράω is used nearly thirty times in the Gospel and has different connotations, depending upon the tense and the context. For example, it seems to mean 'to know' in the sense of 'learning',¹⁴⁶ or

---

¹⁴³ C. L. B. Plumb, 'ΕΓΩ ΕΙΜΙ sayings in John's Gospel' (M.Phil. thesis, Nottingham, 1990), 114.

¹⁴⁴ Michaelis, *TDNT* 5:340, 345.

¹⁴⁵ The Johannine ὁράω means 'seeing' on two levels: the first level refers to physical sight, particularly of Jesus (cf. 1:33, 39, 46; 4:45; 5:6; 6:22, 24; 7:52; 12:9) and this is also true with seeing signs, which in itself is insufficient for deeper faith or insight (2:23-25; 4:48; 6:14, 30). The second level signifies a 'seeing' at the deeper level of understanding, making relationship possible (1:50f; 3:3; 9:37f; 11:40; 12:21, 41; 20:25, 27-29). The same two-stage process of 'seeing' underlines John's use of θεωρεῖν. But θεωρέω means further 'to behold', implying a rudimentary stage of 'seeing' spiritual truth, or 'to look with concentration', without having a deeper perception. However John himself places θεωρέω in a parallel with γεύομαι (= to taste, experience) in 8:51, 53, and therefore, for him, it carries a much deeper sense than a rudimentary stage of 'seeing'. He seems to use θεωρέω to denote a vision of God in the life and work of Jesus (12:45). At first, θεωρέω denotes 'perceiving' Jesus at a superficial level, through which one may or may not attain an intensive understanding. For instance, the perception (θεωρέω) of Jesus as the prophet at first gradually led the Samaritan woman to see Jesus as the Christ (4:19, 29). Peter could only see (θεωρεῖ) the burial material in Jesus' tomb, but could not appreciate the significance of resurrection (20:6, 9; cf. 20:12, 14). Similarly, seeing signs at the first stage is not helpful to constitute full faith, see Brown, *John*, 1:502; cf. 2:23; 6:2, 29, where θεωρεῖν is used. Secondly, θεωρέω denotes a closer 'fellowship' with Jesus. That is, although Jesus' departure will hinder his fellowship with his disciples, they will 'see' (θεωρεῖτε) him again in the ἄλλος παράκλητος (14:19; 16:19; cf. 16:16, where ὄψεσθε is used). With this kind of intensive seeing goes the eschatological seeing of his glory in heaven (17:24 - θεωρῶσιν). This glory is identical with God's glory (17:5, 22; cf. 1 Jn. 3:2). The eschatological 'seeing' mentioned in 17:24 implies a direct vision of God's glory in Jesus and having communion with him.

¹⁴⁶ ὄψεσθε in 1:39; ἴδε in 1:46, 7:52, 11:34. Cf. 14:9 for the synonymous use of the verbs γινώσκειν and ὁράω. Other meanings include 'to experience', 3:36 ὄψεται; 'to participate in the Messianic age of salvation', 8:56 ἴδῃ; 'to speak to', 12:21 ἰδεῖν.

also 'to have a prophetic vision'.[147] The ὄψῃ of 1:50 and 11:40 indicates 'experiencing' the divine glory disclosed to those who follow as disciples (cf. 1:14; 2:11), while the ὄψεται of 1:51 implies a vision of God's glory and communication with him in Jesus Christ (cf. 9:35–38). The Evangelist uses ὁράω in its aorist, perfect, and future forms, often having either God or Jesus as the object of 'seeing'. He insists that no one has ever seen (ἑώρακεν) God except the only Son, who had been in perfect communion with the Father and could make him known (1:18).[148] Therefore, the possibility of knowing God is inherent in one's abiding fellowship with Jesus, so that the one who has seen Jesus has also seen the Father (14:9). Indeed, fellowship is the opposite of alienation in both divine and human relationships. It implies abiding or remaining in Christ and his word and walking in the light. This is where the element of 'mystery' in John's language appears. While natural eyes see simply a man, the enlightened eyes of faith are able to see in the historical Jesus the Saviour, the λόγος τῆς ζωῆς (e.g., John 9, the blind man versus the religious authorities).[149]

In the prologue, created order is depicted as being in spiritual darkness (1:5) since it has failed to know its creator. Into this world, Jesus has come as light.[150] The true light enlightens everyone, but it is rejected because of what is in everyone (2:24–25). This human alienation from God is stated as a real and universal darkness.[151] For darkness to be overcome within the heart of people, they must come to the light of the world in faith (8:12, 24) to be exposed to the light and cleansed from their evil works. An abiding faith provides the right to intimate communication with none other than God together with eyes which are enabled by the Spirit of God to see and perceive the truth.

---

[147] 12:41, εἶδεν; cf. Isa. 6:1, 5, etc. Schnackenburg, *St. John*, 2:222.

[148] The emphatic position of οὗτος in 6:46 confirms that it is Jesus alone, in his capacity as the one who continuously (ὁ ὤν) and closely (παρὰ τοῦ θεοῦ) exists with the Father, who has perceived God since the invisible God is revealed in a unique way by the μονογενὴς υἱός by virtue of his intimate love and unity with the Father. See Bultmann, *John*, 82f.

[149] F. Mussner, *The Historical Jesus in the Gospel of St. John* (London: Herder; Freiburg: Burns and Oates, 1967), 21–3; Schnackenburg, *St. John*, 1:267; cf. Balthasar, 'Seeing the Form', 1:458.

[150] Dodd, *Interpretation*, 357. John has no interest in cosmological speculation about how the darkness came about as is evident in Gnosticism. W. Beltz, 'Zum Geschichtsbild der Gnosis', *Zeitschrift Für Religions- und Geistesgeschichte* 40 (1988), 362–6; G. G. Stroumsa, 'Mythos und Erinnerung: Jüdische Dimensionen der gnostischen Revolte gegen die Zeit', *Judaica* 44 (1988), 15–30.

[151] The word σκοτία being used in a metaphysical sense.

6.4.2. Circumcised Ears

Apart from the emphasis on sight, John also has an emphasis upon sanctified ears that are able to hear the call of God (cf. Rev. 2:7, 11, 17, 29; 3:6; 13, 22; Mt. 11:15; Mk. 4:9). John 5:25 demonstrates the author's use of 'hear' with two different subjects: all those in the tombs will 'hear' (meaning all humans), but those who 'hear' (i.e., 'with understanding') shall live. The same distinction is seen later in 10:3–5, where all the sheep 'hear' the shepherd's voice, but only Jesus' own sheep 'hear' and follow, since they are of God and those who are of God 'hear' God's words (8:46). The assertion in 5:28–29 seems to be a restatement of the inaugurated eschatology in 5:25, and it should be interpreted in light of 3:20–21.

In John 6, some are offended by Jesus' remarks about eating his flesh and drinking his blood (6:50–60), bringing about another separation and judgment,[152] and the question is asked: 'Who is able to hear (or listen to) this?' (6:60). The answer is given already in the prologue, only 'those born not of blood nor of the will of the flesh nor of the will of man, but of God' (1:12–13), and then later to Nicodemus (3:1–8). The sheep who hear and respond to the divine shepherd's voice are called out by name (Jn. 10:3). They follow him because they know his voice (10:4); they will not follow a stranger, but they will flee from him, because they do not know the voice of strangers (10:5). There is no possibility that they will follow the wrong shepherd or miss the call of their own. In the words of John 10:14–15, 'I know my own and my own know me, *just as* the Father knows me and I know the Father.'

In the account of the Passion, only those who are of the truth (i.e., born of God) are able to hear his voice, 'Every one who is of the truth hears my voice' (18:37b). Only those who are ἐκ τῆς ἀληθείας and have recognised the sovereign kingship of God revealed in the person of his Son can hear and comprehend the truth. Meeks sees a parallel with the shepherd–sheep imagery in 10:3 and believes the allusion is to the prophet like Moses whom the people of Israel should heed (Deut. 18:15). Meeks argues that the kingship of Jesus, the good shepherd, is redefined in the Fourth Gospel in terms of the mission of the prophet. Undoubtedly, 'shepherd' and 'king'

---

[152] In John 6:66 ἀπῆλθον εἰς τὰ ὀπίσω can be taken to mean 'fell away'; the expression is curious (cf. 18:6; 20:14). Barrett, *St. John*, 306, suggests that the Greek may rest upon a Hebrew construction נסוג אחור which means sometimes 'to turn back' (Isa. 50:5), or 'to be turned back', 'to be repulsed' (Isa. 42:17). Although Barrett prefers, in the present passage, the meaning 'fell away' rather than 'were driven back'.

are parallel terms (cf. Ezk. 37:24).[153] When Isaiah saw the Lord in his kingly glory, he heard his voice and obeyed (Isa. 6:8). Similarly, Ezekiel in his chariot vision heard the voice of the one seated on the throne (Ezk. 1:28, 2:2).[154] Pilate, the representative of an earthly kingdom, is unable to hear or perceive the truth even when it stares him in the face (18:38).[155] If Pilate's blindness is excused as that of a pagan Roman authority, the religious authorities of Judaism have no excuse for their ignorance in rejecting their sovereign heavenly king and accepting the kingship of a blasphemous pagan Gentile king.[156]

The recognition of Jesus as the one who has come from above (8:23) is precisely the faith that is able to hear his words, which are none other than the words of God (7:16; 14:10). This sheds light on John 8:47a. Here, the statement that 'the one who is from God hears the words of God' may refer ultimately to Jesus, who alone has direct auditory contact with God. In 8:47b, therefore, 'you do not hear, because you are not of God' would not be understood just as a judgment on the spiritual state of 'the Jews',[157] but also as a comment on their *spiritual capacity*, in line with 5:37b, 'His voice you have never heard, his form you have never seen.'

The imperceptibility of God is an Old Testament commonplace.[158] In 5:47 the imperceptibility of God is related to the Father's witness on behalf of Jesus. He testifies, but how can they hear his testimony when they cannot hear his voice? This brings the testimony of Moses into emphatic relief (5:39ff): *his* voice is audible. But in 8:47, and especially 8:43, the same idea is applied to the audibility of Jesus' teaching. Like the Sinai fathers, whose response to hearing 'the voice' was *fear* and a request that Moses listen on their behalf (Exod. 20:18–19, Deut. 18:16), so in John it is

---

[153] *Prophet-King*, 66–7.

[154] Cf. also Ezk. 3:12; 10:5; 43:6; 1 En. 15:1; Ap. Ab. 18:14; 19:1; Rev. 1:10, 12–16, 19–20.

[155] Cf. 3:8; 7:27–28; 8:14; 9:29–30. Heinrich Schlier, 'Jesus und Pilatus nach dem Johannesevangelium', in *Die Zeit der Kirche*, ed. by Heinrich Schlier, 4th edn (Freiburg: Herder, 1966), 70.

[156] Ignace de la Potterie, 'Jésus roi et juge d'après Jn. 19,13', *Bib* 41 (1960), 244; Meeks, *Prophet-King*, 76–8; See Josephus, *Antiquities*, 18.1.6 §23; *Jewish War* 2.8.1 §118; 7.10.1 §410, 418; H. W. Beyer, *TWNT*, vol. I, art. βλασφημέω, 620–623; esp. 621, 48ff.

[157] I.e., spiritually deaf, under the devil's power and influence rather than God's.

[158] But with some remarkable exceptions: behind 5:37b may be an allusion to Moses in Numbers 12:8 (see *TDNT* 2:374), or Ezekiel's inaugural vision (see B. Vawter, 'Ezekiel and John', *CBQ* 26 [1964], 454), or Israel at Sinai in Deueronomy 4:12. This last seems particularly close, but that which Moses and Ezekiel enjoyed and Israel experienced at Sinai is denied to first-century Jews in John 5:37 and 8:47. See Nils A. Dahl 'The Johannine Church and History', in *Current Issues in New Testament Interpretation: Essays in Honor of Otto A. Piper*, ed. by W. Klassen and G. F. Snyder (New York: Harper, 1962), 123; Meeks, *Prophet-King*, 299f.

said, 'you cannot hear my word' (8:43b). This incapacity is partly ethical (they are 'of the devil', 8:44) and also partly constitutional (they are 'of this world', 8:23). On both grounds, they are unable to 'recognise my speech' (43a) as the words of one who is 'of God'.

We may compare 4 Ezra, where the fundamental dualism of heaven and earth is what makes the ways of God so puzzling and inaccessible, but where also the relationship between mankind and God has been deeply scarred by sin. We find both ideas expressed together in 4 Ezra 4:10–11 (cf. 10:21):

He said to me, 'You cannot understand the things with which you have grown up [sc. *fire, wind and time*], how then can your mind comprehend the way of the Most High? And how can one who is already worn out by the corrupt world understand incorruption?' Those who dwell upon earth can understand only what is on earth, and he who is above the heavens can understand what is above the height of the heavens.

(4 Ezra 4:10–11)

Thus an earth-bound existence and a corrupt human nature conspire to make God inscrutable. Only those who are born of God can overcome this inscrutability.

The contrast between those who 'hear' the truth and obey and those who do not goes back to the Evangelist's distinction between the children of God and the children of the devil, an analogy which is present throughout Johannine literature. Jesus has come to bring the light of life (Jn. 8:12; 1:4). A similar language is seen in the Dead Sea Scrolls and the references to the 'sons of darkness' and 'sons of Belial', which include both the Gentiles and rebellious Israel. Behind the Johannine analogy lies the account of Genesis 3 and 4 whereby the devil brings death to humankind, and Cain, the first murderer, is his son. Cain was 'of the evil one' (ἐκ τοῦ πονηροῦ) and his deeds were evil (πονηρά), while those of his brother Abel were righteous (1 Jn. 3:12; cf. Jn. 13:34; 15:12). Like Cain, then, anyone who hates his brother is a murderer, ἀνθρωποκτόνος (1 Jn. 3:15).[159] In 1 John, Abel, whose deeds were righteous, is the forerunner of

---

[159] H. Windisch, *Die Katholischen Briefe*, 3rd edn (Tübingen: H. Preisker, 1951), 224; Barrett, *St. John*, 349; Schnackenburg, *Johannes*, 2:287. In Genesis 4:7, interpreting the enigmatic 'sin crouching at the door', the Palestinian Targumic tradition introduces the concept of the evil inclination (*yetzer hara*) which Cain controls: 'I have placed in your hand power over the evil inclination (and its desire shall be towards you [*Ps Jon* only]) that you may govern it so as to be just or to sin' (cf. *Sifre Deut* 45). See G. Vermes, 'Targumic Versions of Genesis 4:3–16', in *Post-biblical Jewish Studies* (Leiden: Brill, 1975), 92–126. As elsewhere in the New Testament, behind ἐπιθυμία (desire) may lie the idea of the evil inclination. See also in contemporary Jewish literature (*T.Benj*. 7–8), and in early Christian literature (*1 Clement* 4:1–7); also A. Goldberg, 'Kain: Sohn des Menschen oder Sohn der Schlange?', *Judaica* 25 (1969), 203–21.

the one who does righteousness in 1 Jn. 3:7. By contrast Cain, by failing to love his brother, is implicitly classed among the children of the devil (cf. 1 Jn. 3:10) who, according to 1 Jn. 3:8, sins from the beginning.[160] Those who also reject the truth have put themselves in line with the devil.[161] There is a unity of mind and purpose between those who reject Jesus and the devil.[162] Since the devil was the first to sin, and he led humanity to rebellion and unbelief; he is the primary source of sin in a general sense. Jesus calls him the 'father' of lies in whom truth has no place (Jn. 8:44–45). In 1 John, we find that the lie is associated with the denial that Jesus is the Christ' (1 Jn. 2:22).[163] Unbelievers who actively reject the truth are unable to hear God (Jn. 8:47) because of their alienation from God.[164] Neither are they able to comprehend God's word (Jn. 5:38; cf. 8:37). When they search the Scriptures, their search is in vain because they cannot see that the Scriptures speak of him.[165]

6.5. Comprehension of Truth and the Johannine Conception of Faith

The knowledge of God and Christ gives life (Jn. 17:3), and this knowledge is attained through faith (20:31). In John, as in Paul, the real medium of salvation is faith.[166] Faith, i.e. believing and confessing Jesus as the Christ,

---

[160] Dahl, 'Der Erstgeborene Satans und der Vater des Teufels', 70–84. The silence of the biblical narrative as to the reasons for the divine preference for Abel's offering is filled by both Josephus (*Ant.* I, 2.1; § 53) and Philo (*Quaest.* in Gen. I.59), who speak of Cain, even before the event, as evil or πονηρός, and of Abel as righteous, δίκαιος, or concerned for righteousness. The Targumic tradition elaborates this, and the apparent lacuna in the MT at Gen 4:8 puts in the mouths of the brothers, in different forms, a debate over theodicy – the justice as well as the love of God in the creation and judgment of the world. J. R. Diaz, 'Palestinian Targum and New Testament', *NovT* 6 (1963), 75–84, here p. 69f, argued that Cain was the son of Eve by the devil.

[161] Sir. 15:11–17; Str-B 4:466–83. See further M. Vellanickal, *The Divine Sonship of Christians in the Johannine Writings* (Rome: Pontifical Biblical Institute, 1977), 260; Schnackenburg, *Johannes*, 2:288.

[162] de la Potterie, *La vérité dans saint Jean*, 919 n. 35. Also see L. Walter, *L'incroyance des croyants selon saint Jean*, Lire la Bible 43 (Paris: Cerf, 1976), 94.

[163] G. Schrenk, 'πατήρ, κτλ', *TDNT* 5:1002.

[164] Blank, *Krisis*, 241–2.

[165] See Caird, *New Testament Theology*, 93.

[166] In several passages, the verb πιστεύειν is used almost synonymously with γινώσκειν (e.g., 6:69; and cf. 17:3 with 3:15, and many other passages). The knowledge of God cannot be detached from knowledge of the incarnate Word (cf. 14:7; 20:31). Saving knowledge is rooted in knowledge of the historical person; it is, therefore, objective and at the same time a personal relation. Bultmann, *John*, 35.

the Saviour, constitutes the only means of gaining access to the life-giving knowledge of God which Jesus brings. That is why faith alone constitutes the believer's victory over the world (1 Jn. 5:4; cf. 4:4; Jn. 16:33). This faith sets the Christian community apart from the world, whether or not the world knows it (3:1, 13–14; 4:5–6). In the New Testament, almost half of the occurrences of the verb πιστεύω, 'believe' (approximately 98 out of 239) are in John.[167] The noun form πίστις, 'faith', is not used by the Evangelist. The verb carries a dynamic which the noun lacks.[168] In the Fourth Gospel, belief is in the active voice and is always focused on its object, Jesus the Christ.[169] Faith involves an appropriation of the person and work of the Saviour as the basis for salvation, and this is attested to in the symbolic partaking of his flesh and blood (6:53–56). Faith must include belief in Jesus' divine origin (3:13; 12:42) and in his death as efficacious deliverance from sin and death (Jn. 1:29; 3:14–17; 13:19). As John 13–17 and later the First Epistle show, for John, the faith response demands of the believer the selfless life exemplified by Jesus himself. Revelation brings illumination which requires a change in one's orientation toward God and neighbour. It calls for conformity to the character of the revealer. It means exposing one's evil works to the light and turning from them. All of which people naturally shun. As Bultmann observes, if God's revelation is present in 'a peculiar hiddenness', the paradoxical incarnation of the Word made flesh, then that revelation is scarcely accessible apart from the commitment of faith.[170] Faith cannot demand authenticating evidence and cannot believe without risk.[171] The movement from superficial understanding to spiritual perception ultimately takes place by faith. In the Fourth Gospel, for those whose response is consistent scepticism and disbelief, even if the truth were to be shouted out from the rooftops, the result would be further

---

[167] John uses πιστεύειν with two distinct constructions (with εἰς and the accusative and with the dative) as a means of distinguishing 'full' from 'initial' faith. See BAGD, 228-30; R. Bultmann and A. Weiser, *TWNT* 6 (1959), 174–230 = *TDNT* 6 (1968), 161–66; D. C. Arichea, 'Translating "Believe" in the Gospel of John', *Bib Trans* 30 (1979), 205–9; M. Tenney, 'Topic from the Gospel of John. Part IV: The Growth of Belief', *BibSac* (1975), 343–57.

[168] See Meeks, 'Man From Heaven', 68; E. Jarvis, 'The Key Term "Believe" in the Gospel of John', *Notes on Translation* 2 (1988), 46–51. On faith, see Barrett, *St. John*, 164. Cf. H. J. Holtzmann, *Evangelium, Briefe und Offenbarung des Johannes* (Tübingen: Mohr, 1908), 40–2.

[169] M. D. Hooker, 'The Johannine Prologue and the Messianic Secret', *NTS* 21 (1974), 43.

[170] Bultmann, *John*, 63–64.

[171] Cf. Wrede, *Charakter und Tendenz des Johannesevangeliums* (Tübingen: Fues, 1847), 6, 9, 45; F. C. Baur, *Kritische Untersuchungen über die kanonischen Evangelien, ihr Verhältnis zu einander, ihren charakter und Ursprung* (Tübingen: Mohr, 1847), 183; idem, *Vorlesungen über neutestamentliche Theologie*, 370–72, Käsemann *Letzter Wille*, 51–54, 112–14.

confusion, incomprehension and unbelief.[172] The truth that people must believe in Jesus in order to perceive his identity and his words recurs repeatedly throughout John's Gospel.

6.5.1. Spurious Faith Does Not Lead to Life and Illumination

In the Fourth Gospel, not all expressions of faith lead to life. Hence in spite of the astonishing response of unbelief to the signs of Jesus in 12:37, John goes on to say that many of the rulers did believe in Jesus (12:42), thus qualifying the observations in 12:37, 39. But even this is further qualified when the author goes on to explain these who believed 'did not confess' (οὐχ ὡμολόγουν) their faith publicly because they did not wish to be cast out of the synagogue. This calls into question the validity of their faith.

Among the New Testament writings, the Fourth Gospel is marked by its emphasis on belief that abides (e.g., Jn. 8:31; 15:1–6). Indeed the evidence of one's faith is abiding in the truth. The distinction between authentic faith and unauthentic faith is quite emphatic in the Fourth Gospel. In 2:23–25, John writes,

> Many believed in his name because they saw the signs that he was doing.[173] But Jesus on his part would not entrust himself to them, because he knew all people and needed no one to testify about anyone (lit. περὶ τοῦ ἀνθρώπου); for he himself knew what was in everyone (lit. ἐν τῷ ἀνθρώπῳ). (John 2:23–25, NRSV)

This passage seems to anticipate the summarising statement at the conclusion of Jesus' public ministry in 12:37, where it is said that people did not believe.

Although in 12:42 John does not hesitate to say that many of the rulers believed, in 12:43 their reluctance to confess openly their faith is attributed not only to the fear of the Pharisees (v. 42; cf. Jn. 9:22) but also to their preference for 'the praise of men' (ἠγάπησαν τὴν δόξαν τῶν ἀνθρώπων) over 'the honour that comes from God' (μᾶλλον ἤπερ τὴν δόξαν τοῦ θεοῦ). Thus, the explanation that they preferred 'the praise of men' indicates the basis for their fear.[174] If faith in Jesus Christ, as Bultmann so

---

[172] E.g., 6:60–66; cf. 8:12, 58; 10:22–30; cf. 9:35; 10:31; 12:37–38; 1 Cor. 1:18–24.

[173] The early response of the crowds to Jesus rests on the fact that they 'saw the signs which he did' (2:23; 6:2; cf. 9:16).

[174] See J. Louis Martyn, 'Glimpses into the History of the Johannine Community', in *The Gospel of John in Christian History* (New York: Paulist Press, 1978), 90–121, 109–115; R. E. Brown, *The Community of the Beloved Disciple: The Life, Loves, and Hates of an Individual Church in New Testament Times* (London: Chapman, 1979), 71–3. Cf. A. Loisy, *Le Quatrième Evangile* (Paris: Picard, 1903), 305; Meeks, 'The Man From Heaven', 69–70; Klaus Wengst, *Bedrängte Gemeinde und verherrlichter Christus: Der historische Ort des Johannesevangeliums als*

uniquely speaks of it, is 'desecularization' and 'transition into eschatological existence',[175] then the fear of rejection or the love of the praise of others is an indication of unbelief and worldliness (i.e., remaining of the world). Bultmann writes,

> Faith is not flight from the world nor asceticism, but *desecularization* in the sense of a smashing of all human standards and evaluations. It is in this sense that the world for the believer is no longer his determining origin (§ 43, 2), he no longer belongs to it. That is why the world does not 'recognise' the believers just as it did not recognise him (1 Jn. 3:1); in fact, it hates them as it hated him (15:18–20; 1 Jn. 3:13). As Jesus' way led him to death, so the way of those who are his will lead them to persecution and death (12:24–26; 16:1–4).[176]

Later Bultmann would point out that the 'faith as the act of believing constantly brings about this desecularization. It is true faith only when it has this constancy; i.e. when it "abides", when it is faithful'.[177]

Nicodemus has been a notorious illustration of the expression of faith which is rejected in the Johannine writings as the kind of faith which does not lead to life. With all likelihood, Nicodemus is part of the group criticised in 12:42. The members of this infamous group, though believing that Jesus is 'from God' (3:2), are accused of not believing his testimony (3:11–12).[178] When John introduces Nicodemus into his account, he is carefully linked to the Jewish religious hierarchy and its 'official' attitude toward Jesus. He is presented as a leading figure. Even among the Pharisees, he stands out as 'a ruler of the Jews', a member of the Sanhedrin. He is described as going to Jesus at night (3:2) and as being 'one of them' (εἷς ὢν ἐξ αὐτῶν, 7:50). Nicodemus enters the Gospel account in chapters 3:1–21; 7:45–52; 19:38–39. He is associated with Joseph of Arimathea in chapter 19, who is also a member of the Sanhedrin, and is presented as another member of this group who did not make their faith public (ὢν μαθητὴς τοῦ Ἰησοῦ κεκρυμμένος δὲ διὰ τὸν φόβον τῶν Ἰουδαίων, 19:38), thus skewing the favourable common tradition about him (cf. Mk. 15:43; Mt. 27:57) so as to align him, too, with the fearful believing rulers of 12:42–43.

Nicodemus comes to Jesus by night, a time John associates elsewhere

---

Schlüssel zu seiner Interpretation, Biblisch-Theologische Studien 5, 2nd edn (Neukirchen-Vluyn: Neukirchener Verlag, 1983), 59–60.

[175] Bultmann, *Theology of the New Testament*, 2:78.
[176] Ibid., 76.
[177] Ibid., 86.
[178] Schnackenburg, *St. John*, 1:563f.

with the realm of unbelief and falsehood (9:4; 11:10; 13:30). Bultmann describes Nicodemus as 'man as he is', in need of an entirely new origin for his salvation and yet unable to see the possibility of it.[179] Nicodemus is described by some as representing a *communal* characterisation. According to John 2:23–25, Jesus did not entrust himself to some in Jerusalem who had believed in him when they saw the signs that he did, because 'he knew what was in a man'. In the Greek, the verb is repeated, but with a slightly different meaning. It may be paraphrased as 'the people *trusted* (ἐπίστευσαν) in his name, but he did not *entrust* (οὐκ ἐπίστευεν) himself to them'.[180] Nicodemus is then immediately introduced in 3:2 as 'a man' (completely obscured by the NRSV) who regards Jesus as a teacher come from God because of his signs. He speaks to Jesus in the plural, and Jesus addresses him in the plural. In fact, Jesus applies the plural both to himself and to Nicodemus. Since the conversation is represented as taking place alone at night, these plurals are both surprising and significant. It is possible that John wishes to make a distinction between the community of faith and those who remain outside of the community, including Nicodemus, because of their fear of the Pharisees and their continuous desire not to jeopardise their social status by open confession of Jesus.[181]

Nicodemus next appears on the scene in John 7:45–52. Here the Pharisees' own officers, sent out to arrest Jesus, return awed by him instead. They are rebuked with the rhetorical question whether any one 'of the rulers or of the Pharisees' has believed in Jesus, and those who do believe are vilified as a 'mob that does not know the law', who are 'under a curse' (7:49). But at this point Nicodemus speaks up. For the Evangelist, this would have been an ideal occasion for Nicodemus to prove the other Pharisees wrong and to defend the one they have scorned by confessing his own faith in Jesus. But instead of a bold expression of faith, he asks, 'Does our law condemn a man unless it first hears from him and finds out

---

[179] Bultmann, *John*, 133–44.

[180] Yet by implication, he will *entrust* himself to those who truly trust him (cf. 10:14, 15). Note the partial parallel to 2:25 in the Jewish commentary on Exodus, *Mekhilta Exod.* 15:32: 'Seven things are hidden from man – the day of death, the day of consolation, the depths of judgment, one's reward, the time of restoration of the kingdom of David, the time when the guilty kingdom (i.e., Rome) will be destroyed, and *what is within another.*' Scriptural proof for this final 'unknown' is elsewhere provided in *Genesis Rabbah* 65 viz. Jer 17:10, 'I the Lord search the heart and examine the mind.' Even in this regard, then, Jesus, far from being limited like other human beings, does what God does (5:19, cf. SB 2:412).

[181] These are the untrustworthy believers in 2:23–25. See Loisy, *Le Quatrième Evangile*, 304; Brown, *John*, 1:135; Rensberger, *Overcoming the World*, 38; Barrett, *St. John*, 211. Cf. Bultmann, *John*, 133, and Schnackenburg, *St. John*, 1:365.

what he is doing?' Some find in these words an indirect defence of Jesus and therefore an implicit testimony to Nicodemus' faith.[182] Others see in this remark the would-be 'teacher of Israel' who cannot bring himself to a real confession of faith in Jesus.[183] He seems to match the description of the 'rulers' mentioned in John 12:42–43, who believed in Jesus but would not confess it for fear that the Pharisees would put them out of the synagogue.[184]

Nicodemus last appears in John 19:38–42 with Joseph of Arimathea. Neither of them is heard when the blind man is interrogated and expelled, when the decision is made to put Jesus to death, or when Jesus himself is on trial. They do not declare their choice until it is too late. Nicodemus' contribution at the death of Jesus is to bring no less than seventy-five pounds of burial spices. While this gesture is seen by some scholars as one of true and open devotion, even of confession,[185] others see it as an act of unbelief.[186] As Alfred Loisy has pointed out long ago, Nicodemus and Joseph confess nothing and have nothing to do with Jesus, except with his corpse.[187]

In the Fourth Gospel, a convenient faith which expresses itself only as long as the personal and social costs are minimal is not an authentic faith leading to life and illumination. Against this background, John 3:14–16 functions as much as a warning as it does as a promise. Believers must 'exalt' or 'lift up' the Son of Man, so that their faith in him may issue forth in eternal life. This 'exaltation' is then described in 3:16a.[188] Jesus, rather than being acknowledged as just a 'teacher from God', must be seen as God's μονογενής, given by God to the world. Only such believers will not perish but have eternal life, because only such acknowledgement reveals the kind of faith that is able to see and perceive that Jesus is the one he claims to be, the one of whom the Scriptures testify.

---

[182] Cf. Marinus de Jonge, 'Nicodemus and Jesus: Some Observations on Misunderstanding and Understanding in the Fourth Gospel', in de Jonge, *Jesus: Stranger from Heaven and Son of God*, SBLSBS 11 (Missoula, MT: Scholars Press, 1977), 34–6; Bultmann, *John*, 311; Brown, *John*, 1:330;

[183] Barrett, *St. John*, 332; Culpepper, *Anatomy of the Fourth Gospel*, 134–6.

[184] Wengst, *Bedrängte Gemeinde*, 59–60.

[185] Brown, *John*, 2:959–60; Schnackenburg, *St. John*, 3:295–97; Lindars, *John*, 592.

[186] Rensberger, *Overcoming the World*, 40; Meeks, 'Man from Heaven', 55; M. de Jonge, 'Nicodemus and Jesus', 33–34; Paul D. Duke, *Irony in the Fourth Gospel* (Atlanta, GA: John Knox Press, 1985), 110.

[187] Loisy, *Quatrième évangile*, 895–896.

[188] 3:14f. ὑψωθῆναι in v. 14 should be given the same double meaning as in John 8:28 and 12:32.

A second category of spurious faith in the Fourth Gospel is one which needs to be sustained by miraculous signs. In the account of John 20:24–29, those who have 'not seen and yet believe' are called blessed (v. 29b). Those who saw the resurrected Jesus had a privileged position. However, Jesus explicitly calls those whose faith is not dependent on sight, 'blessed'. Fortna correctly notes that 'the superiority of faith-without-seeing is the point of the story of Thomas'.[189] The later generation of Christians whose faith is grounded on the apostolic witness should not think that their situation is inferior to that of the disciples of Jesus who had seen the Lord and witnessed his signs. On the contrary, their faith is more genuine because it is founded solely on the word of God, not on 'facts' verified by experience.[190] More than any other scholar, Bultmann recognised John's radical emphasis on a faith independent of signs and this led to his uncompromising focus on belief as an existential encounter independent of any possible external sensory verification.[191] For Bultmann, the 'reproach that falls on Thomas [applies] to all other disciples as well', for the 'doubt of Thomas is representative of the common attitude' of all humans. Just as the miracles were concessions to human weakness, so the resurrection appearances were a concession to the weakness of the disciples. What should have moved the disciples to believe ought not to have been the sight of the risen Jesus; his words alone (cf. 2:22) should have been

---

[189] R. T. Fortna, *The Fourth Gospel and Its Predecessor* (Philadelphia: Fortress, 1988), 245-6.

[190] P. J. Judge, 'A Note on Jn 20:29', in *The Four Gospels 1992*, ed. by F. van Segbroeck, C. M. Tuckett, et al., vol. 3 (Leuven: Leuven University Press, 1992), 2186; Schnackenburg, *St. John*, 3:331, 333 (= *Johannesevangelium*, 1975, 3:394, 398); M. de Jonge, 'Signs and Works in the Fourth Gospel', in *Miscellanea Neotestamentica*, ed. by T. Baarda, et al., NTSup 48 (Leiden: Brill, 1978), 2:119; I. de la Potterie, 'Genèse de la foi pascale d'après Jn. 20', *NTS* 30 (1984), 41–42; H. Wenz, 'Sehen und Glauben bei Johannes', *TZ* 17 (1961), 18–20.

[191] Bultmann, *John*, 63, writing concerning human expectation of what the revelation and revealer should be, contends, 'Thus the offence of the gospel is brought out as strongly as possible by "the Word became flesh". For however much man may await and long for the event of the revelation in the human sphere, he also quite clearly expects – and this shows the peculiar self-contradiction of man's existence – that the Revelation will somehow have to give proof of itself, that it will in some way be recognisable. The Revealer must appear in human form as well as also appearing as a shining, mysterious, fascinating figure, as a hero or "God-man", as miracle worker or mystagogue. His humanity must be no more than a disguise; it must be transparent...All such desires are cut short by the statement: the Word became flesh. It is in his sheer humanity that he is the Revealer...If man wishes to see the δόξα, then it is on the σάρξ that he must concentrate his attention, without allowing himself to fall a victim to appearances. The revelation is present in a peculiar hiddenness'. But see the E. Käsemann's antithesis, *The Testament of Jesus* (London: SCM, 1968); trans. from *Jesu letzter Wille nach Johannes 17*, 3rd edn (Tübingen: Mohr-Siebeck, 1971) and then see the synthesis by M. M. Thompson, *The Humanity of Jesus in the Fourth Gospel* (Philadelphia: Fortress, 1988).

sufficient to convince them.[192] True Abrahamic faith is not a faith that follows the risen Lord by sight, but one that follows in obedient trust.[193]

If faith based on the *word* of Jesus alone is commanded, then we may well ask, Why does the Evangelist have such an emphasis upon signs?[194] Various solutions have been offered,[195] and much controversy has surrounded this question. However, there is no inconsistency between passages in which faith dependent on signs is inadequate (e.g., 2:23-25; 4:48) and passages where signs are presented as important (6:26; 11:47; 12:37). The apparent contradiction has to do with our misunderstanding of the function of the signs. In the Fourth Gospel, the primary aim of the signs and John's positive evaluation of them is based on the fact that they are more than miracles. They are *signs* which reveal Jesus' true identity (2:11, 18; 6:26, 30; 7:31; 9:16) and unity with God (5:17-21) as the revealer of God. They provide a clue to the Johannine idea of the revelation of the glory of God manifested in and through Jesus as the one who 'tabernacled among us' (1:14).

Most Johannine discourses revolve around a particular sign which unmistakably points at the identity of Jesus as the one he claims to be. For

---

[192] Bultmann, *John*, 696 (= *Johannes*, 539). This in turn seems to be reminiscent of Calvin: 'Aus der bloßen erfahrungsmäßigen Beobachtung kann freilich kein Glaube entstehen: wahrer Glaube kommt immer aus dem Worte Gottes' (*Johannes*, 524), quoted by H. Kohler, *Kreuz und Menschwerdung im Johannesevangelium*, ATANT 72 (Zürich: Theologischer Verlag, 1987), 183. See also Schottroff, *Der Glaubende und die feindliche Welt*, 252; esp. 277-8 n. 1: 'Glauben und physisches Sehen sind eine Alternative'.

[193] See the discusion by U. Wilckens, *Auferstehung. Das biblische Auferstehungszeugnis historisch untersucht und erklärt*, Themen der Theologie 4 (Berlin: Kreuz-Verlag, 1970), 73; A. Dauer, 'Zur Herkunft der Tomas-Perikope Joh 20,24-29', in *Biblische Randbemerkungen*, FS R. Schnackenburg, ed. by H. Merklein and J. Lange (Würzburg: Echter, 1974), 56-76, esp. 72-73; E. Haenchen, *John: A Commentary on the Gospel of John*, trans. by R. W. Funk and ed. with Ulrich Busse (Philadelphia: Fortress, 1984), 2:211-12 (= *Johannes*, 573-74); R. Cameron, 'Seeing is not Believing: The History of a Beatitude in the Jesus Tradition', *Forum* 4 (1988), 47-57.

[194] The word σημεῖον occurs sixteen times in the first half of the Fourth Gospel or the so-called 'book of signs', i.e., to the end 12:37. It is not used again until 20:30. Of the 27 occurrences of the word ἔργον in the Fourth Gospel, in 17 cases, the word seems to refer to miracle; but in 4:34 and 17:4, it seems to refer to the total life-work of Jesus. In 12:37 (cf. 21:25), we are told that Jesus 'did many signs' which are not recounted. All the Gospels record that Jesus worked miracles. The Synoptic authors refer to these as 'mighty deeds', δυνάμεις (e.g., Mt. 11:20-23; etc.). By contrast, the Fourth Gospel avoids δυνάμεις and uses σημεῖον, 'sign', and ἔργον, 'work'. Fourteen (out of the seventeen) times σημεῖον appears with ποιεῖν, nine times with πιστεύειν, and six times with verbs of seeing.

[195] Jürgen Becker, 'Wunder und Christologie: Zum literarkritischen und christologischen Problem der Wunder im Johannesevangelium', *NTS* 16 (1969-70), 130-48; D. Moody Smith, 'Setting and Shape', 86, 88; cf. John Painter, 'Text and Context in John 5', *AusBR* 35 (1987), 28-34.

those who expected the arrival of the prophet like Moses, the performance of Moses-like signs would have signified that the performer *was* the predicted one. Just like the Old Testament אוֹת, the σημεῖον refers to 'a symbolical anticipation or showing forth of a greater reality',[196] the reality of the identity of Jesus as creator with the creator (1:3).[197] Signs also are intended to show the extent of human obduracy. What John finds astonishing (12:37) is the persistence of unbelief in spite of the signs.[198] In the Fourth Gospel, it is of supreme importance to acknowledge Jesus for who he is and to reach the full christological confession uttered by a once 'doubting' Thomas, 'My Lord and my God' (20:28; cf. 6:69; 4:29, 42; 1:49). This confession is highly important in the Gospel which begins with the eternal Word of God becoming flesh and reaches its climax when Thomas confesses Jesus as Lord and God.[199] In the Fourth Gospel, the faith which leads to eternal life is a faith which is far more than simply intellectual assent[200] or a faith sustained by ever-present miraculous signs.[201] It is a faith that is prepared to run against the storm of opposition (which association with Jesus will provoke) and to walk in his steps (13:16; 15:20). It is a faith that 'hears my word and believes him who sent me' (5:24). Implicit in the faith of 5:24 is a discipleship which is willing to pay the cost (5:17–18). It is this type of faith that will remain in the truth and will understand.

---

[196] Barrett, *St. John*, 76; cf. Brown, *John*, 1:529f.; Dodd, *Interpretation*, 90.

[197] This then links Johannine signs, not with Hermetic literature, the Mandaean writings, or Philo, but rather to the Scriptures of Israel. See particulaly W. J. Bittner, *Jesu Zeichen im Johannesevangelium. Die Messias-Erkenntnis im Johannesevangelium vor ihrem jüdischen Hintergrund*, WUNT 2.26 (Tübingen: Mohr-Siebeck, 1987); cf. K. H. Rengstorf, 'σημεῖον', *TWNT* 7:201–3; R. Formesyn, 'Le Semeion Johannique et le Semeion hellenistique', *ETL* 38 (1962), 856.

[198] Cf. Barrett, *St. John*, 430.

[199] The confession of God as 'Lord and God' also captures an important element of worship and exaltation of the deity in the Old Testament (e.g., 2 Sam. 7:28; 1 Kgs. 18:39; Ps. 30:2; 35:24; 86:15; 88:1; Jer. 38:17; Hos. 2:23).

[200] But see Schnackenburg, *St. John*, 1:562. The nature of this faith becomes clear in the course of the Gospel, most particularly in the farewell discourses, where *union with the Christ* is set at its heart. 'Because I live, you will live also…you in me, I in you' (14:19f). This union with Christ means that his disciples must expect to be treated like him, facing hatred and persecution (especially 15:18–16:4). On the other hand, they are also given the Holy Spirit who will enable them to see and perceive, hear and understand.

[201] This seems to be the problem of the group described in 2:23–25; they believed because they saw his signs. And yet Jesus avoids them because, unlike other religious leaders, he could not be deceived. He, therefore, did not *entrust himself* to these spurious converts. On the relationship between 'signs' and 'belief', see R. T. Hoeferkamp, 'The Relationship between Semeia and Believing in the Fourth Gospel' (Ph.D. diss., St. Louis: The Faculty of Christ Seminary-Seminex, 1978).

6.5.2. Abiding Faith

Throughout the New Testament, in order for one to discern the substance beneath the appearance (Jn. 7:24; 8:15; cf. 2 Cor. 5:16), faith is the required proper response toward revelation. In the Fourth Gospel, Jesus tells those who have believed him, 'If you continue (ἐὰν ὑμεῖς μείνητε) in my word (ἐν τῷ λόγῳ τῷ ἐμῷ), you are truly my disciples' (8:31). Abiding faith is the litmus test of discipleship and the ground upon which spiritual perception stands (8:31). The faith that takes possession of life is one which persists (12:26; 15:1–8). Abiding faith is also the condition for grasping the content of revelation. The correct perception of Jesus' person and work is not available to all, but only to those who tenaciously continue to abide irrespective of the cost (8:31–32; 9:33–34; 15:1–21; 16:1ff). This is one factor indicating the necessity of faith for true discipleship and illumination in Johannine theology. Faith that does not abide is not faith at all. In fact, the crux of the matter for John is not 'understanding' but 'abiding'.[202] It is abiding which progressively moves one to a deeper perception. In the Fourth Gospel, faith and knowledge are inseparably intertwined.[203] The emphasis on the abiding of believers in Christ (15:1–6) highlights the importance of continuing in the faith for illumination.

Christ's words and the past revelation of God in Israel's Scripture which has anticipated him are incomprehensible apart from spiritual union with God. It is the Spirit of God indwelling the believer and the resulting spiritual union which brings about understanding of revealed truth. This union is concerned with the believer's 'being' and 'abiding' in Christ and, through him, in God. Fellowship with God is made possible in and through the event of the incarnation, cross and resurrection. John's chosen metaphor to describe this unity is the imagery of the vine and its branches in chapter 15. The life which flows from the vine sustains and nourishes all the branches, resulting in fruit-bearing. Elsewhere the picture of the necessary unity is eating the flesh and drinking the blood of the Son of God in chapter 6. It is by coming to the Lamb of God, who is the life-giving food, and by believing in him, that one can absorb his life, be united with him, and comprehend his mind through his Spirit. This does not mean an 'absorption into the divine' or 'deification' as in neo-Platonic mysticism.[204] Rather, it denotes the divine life absorbed by the believer. While John

---

[202] μένειν occurs some forty (39) times in John vs. three times in Matthew, twice in Mark, and seven times in Luke.

[203] Balthasar, 'Seeing the Form', 1:134–35.

[204] Such a neo-Platonic influence may be detected in the writings of Philo.

8:30–59 emphasises that belief in Jesus must persist, John 15:1–17 expresses forcefully the claim that the disciple's life is contingent upon connectedness to Jesus, and that this connectedness must be abiding or permanent.

In John 15:1–4, the nature of the believer's association with Jesus is characterised as, 'Abide in me!' Μένειν ἐν is used in John to denote abiding in Christ (15:4–7; 1 Jn. 2:6, 27f.; 3:6), in God (1Jn. 4:13, 15f), in the love of Christ and the love of God (15:9f.; 1 Jn. 4:16), in the word of Christ (8:31), or in the light (1 Jn. 2:10). The unbelievers, on the other hand, do not have the word of God abiding in them (τὸν λόγον αὐτοῦ οὐκ ἔχετε ἐν ὑμῖν μένοντα, 5:38a), which is evident in their unbelief (ὅτι ὃν ἀπέστειλεν ἐκεῖνος, τούτῳ ὑμεῖς οὐ πιστεύετε, 5:38b) and in their total inability to hear and understand the truth so as to see and perceive the revelation (8:43). They remain in darkness (12:46; cf. 15:6), will not see life (οὐκ ὄψεται ζωήν, 3:36b; cf. 1 Jn. 3:14), and are subject to the wrath of God 'abiding upon' them (cf. μένει ἐπ' αὐτόν, 3:36c). In the Gospel, μένειν ἐν, 'abiding in', denotes also the divine relationship to the believer whereby Christ 'abides' in believers (15:4–5; Jn. 13:24) or the Father 'abides' in them (1 Jn. 4:12–13, 15–16). The phrase has a distinct theological meaning to express the 'lasting relation of immanence' between God and Christ or the believer and Christ, emphasising permanence and persistence. Since God abides in Jesus (14:10b), the expression μείνατε ἐν ἐμοί, κἀγὼ ἐν ὑμῖν in 15:4 implies that in the mutual abiding of Jesus and his disciples, they abide in God himself. So, too, it can be said that in believers there 'abides' the 'anointing' (χρῖσμα, 1 Jn. 2:27), God's 'seed' (σπέρμα, 1 Jn. 3:9), 'eternal life' (ζωὴ αἰώνιος, 1 Jn. 3:15), and the 'love of God' (ἡ ἀγάπη τοῦ θεοῦ, 1 Jn. 3:17). The ultimate goal of indwelling is to reveal the glory of the Father, for in the fruit-bearing of the believers, the world will recognise them as Jesus' disciples and glorify the Father (15:8).

In his theological reflection following the account of Jesus' conversation with Nicodemus, the Evangelist speaks also of 'practising the truth' (ποιῶν), which in a sense is the external manifestation of 'abiding' (Jn. 3:21; 1 Jn. 1:6). In John's Gospel, the faith which produces life not only believes the truth; it 'does the truth' (Jn. 3:21). The faith that abides in Christ obeys the truth[205] and does not practise (i.e., abide in) sin. This point is made explicit in the First Epistle of John (1 Jn. 1:6–7; 2:28–29; 3:4–10; 5:18).

---

[205] Obeying the truth is inherent in believing the truth and believing is manifested in drinking (4:14), eating (6:35, 51), or walking (8:12, 31).

Here, obeying the truth means practising the truth, and practising the truth means that those who abide in Christ ought to walk (i.e., live) as he did, ὀφείλει καθὼς ἐκεῖνος περιεπάτησεν καὶ αὐτὸς οὕτως περιπατεῖν (2:6; cf. 3:6). This abiding or continuing is the basis of progressive spiritual understanding, the perception of the deeper meaning of the Scriptures and their witness to Jesus. There is no illumination without obedience. This has been the experience of the Evangelist himself.

Because discipleship is defined as 'abiding in', 'continuing', and 'remaining' (μένειν) faithful to the end as well as 'practising the truth', those who abide and who therefore perceive, hear, and understand the word of God (8:30–59) may discern the meaning of Jesus' life in the light of the Scriptures. Understanding, perception, or illumination belongs only to those who believe in him (7:37–39). It is confined to the believing community (2:17, 19–22; 12:16; 13:7; 20:9), in whose midst the Holy Spirit resides and works.[206] The Holy Spirit is not given to all, but only to those who believe and follow in discipleship. According to 2:11, only Jesus' disciples could perceive the glory manifested through the signs. The multitudes could see only the miracles, not what they signify. This seems to show the esoteric tendency in the Johannine δόξα theme, according to which the 'glory' is both the manifestation and the concealment of God.[207] It also reinforces the link between seeing, perceiving, and faith. To behold the glory of the incarnate Word is to behold something of the character and the nature of God.[208] It is therefore not surprising that δόξα and φῶς are found in parallelism referring to the manifestation of the power of God for the salvation of his people.[209] After the resurrection of Jesus, the glory of God that was visible in the bodily temple of his Son will be visible in those within whom the triune God resides and manifests his light in the world.[210]

For the Evangelist 'convenient faith', which is not willing to risk all, does not lead to life, nor does it lead to understanding. Martin Warner correctly observes that 'not all who "believe" in his name have "life" in

---

[206] M. de Jonge, 'Jewish Expectations about the "Messiah" according to the Fourth Gospel', *NTS* 19 (1973), 263.

[207] P. Schäfer, *Der verborgene und offenbare Gott* (Tübingen: Mohr-Siebeck, 1991).

[208] See G. B. Caird, 'The Glory of God in the Fourth Gospel: An Exercise in Biblical Semantics', *NTS* 15 (1968–69), 265–77; W. R. Cook, 'The "Glory" Motif in the Johannine Corpus', *JETS* 27 (1984), 291–7; M. Pamment, 'The Meaning of Doxa in the Fourth Gospel', *ZNW* 74 (1973), 12–16.

[209] R. H. Lightfoot, *St. John's Gospel: A Commentary*, ed. by C. F. Evans (Oxford: Clarendon, 1956), 90; Hanson, 'John 1:14–18 and Exodus 34', 9.

[210] Cf. 17:10, 11–26; cf. 14:20; 15:8; 21:19; also J. C. Meagher, 'John 1:14 and the New Temple', *JBL* 88 (1969), 57–68.

his name, but there is an internal relation between a certain type of belief and a certain form of "life"'.[211] The belief that leads to life turns away from 'the world' and tenaciously remains in the vine. Ultimately, perception of the self-revelation of God in the incarnate Word occurs in discipleship.

6.6. The Polarising Effect of Light Shining in Darkness

The inevitable effect of the light shining in darkness is division (3:19-21). The self-disclosure of God in Jesus Christ decisively divides between truth and falsehood. In the declaration 'I am the light of the World', Lindars observes that Jesus' identification of himself with the light means that he is both the revealer of God and the revealer of human hearts (3:19-21).[212] The essential aim of revelation is life,[213] and the goal of the Messiah is peace.[214] But there is also the prophecy of radical division and discord (Jn. 15:20; 16:2).[215] He divides humanity by the word (or sword) of his mouth in judgment (12:48; cf. Rev. 2:12, 16; 19:15).[216] As chaos and darkness came before the first creation (Gen. 1:2), so division and strife must come before the second creation: the last things are as the first (cf. Epistle of Barnabas 6:13).[217] The Synoptic Gospels also indicate that the ministry of Jesus

---

[211] 'The Fourth Gospel's Art of Rational Persuasion', in *The Bible As Rhetoric: Studies in Biblical Persuasion and Credibility*, ed. by M. Warner (London: Routledge, 1990), 154.

[212] Lindars, *John*, 314.

[213] John 1:4; 10:10, cf. 3:15-17; 4:10-15; 5:24, 26; 6:27-68; 8:12; 11:25; 14:6, etc. The motif of giving life through revelation is evocative of the Old Testament wisdom traditions (Prov. 8:22-36; Sir. 24:1-29) and the 'Word' as the unfailing accomplisher of God's life-giving purpose (Isa. 55:10-11). The intention of revelation is to set the recipient free (8:32). The ultimate motive of God in sending his Son is to save the world rather than to condemn it (3:16-17). See C. H. Dodd, *Apostolic Preaching and Its Developments: Three Lectures* (Chicago: Willet, Clark, 1937), 121; Josef Kuhl, *Die Sendung Jesu und der Kirche nach dem Johannesevangelium*, Studia Instituti Missiologica Societatis Verbi Domini 11 (St. Augustin: Styler, 1967).

[214] Jn. 14:27; 16:33; 20:19-26. Cf. Lk. 2:14; 19:38; Acts 10:36; Rom. 5:1; Eph. 2:14-18; Heb. 7:2.

[215] Cf. Mt. 10:35-36; Lk. 12:52-53. The appearance of the Lord (Mic. 7:6) divides even the members of one household (Mt. 10:37 = Lk. 14; Mk. 10:29; Mt. 8:21-22 = Lk. 9:59-60; cf. Jub. 23:16, 19; 1 Eno. 56:7; 70:7; 99:5; 100:1-2; 4 Ezra 5:9; 6:24; 2 Apo. of Bar. 70:3, 7).

[216] See Robert Tannehill, *The Sword of His Mouth* (Philadelphia: Fortress, 1975), 55; Hans Windisch, *Der messianische Krieg und Urchristentum* (Tübingen: Mohr, 1909). Talk of the sword within the prophecies of eschatological affliction or of the day of judgment was also widespread. Cf. Isa. 66:16, Sir. 39:30; Wisd. of Sol. 5:20; Jub. 9:15; 1 Enoch 62:12, 63:11, 90:19, 91:11-12; 4QPs DanAa (= 4Q244); Ps. of Sol. 15:8 (7); Siby. Oracles Frag. III, 797-99; IV 174; 2 Apoc. of Bar. 27:6; 40:1; Lk. 21:24; Rev. 6:4.

[217] In Qumran and the apocalyptic literature, the end of the age would witness an unprecedented unleashing of the powers of evil, and at the end of a great final conflict, God's chief opponent,

constitutes the test by which people stand or fall.[218] In the Fourth Gospel, Jesus becomes the great divide; people stand or fall (3:18; 4:24-29; 6:53-57; 8:24-36), see or remain blind (9:41), by the reaction he brings about.

6.6.1. Divisiveness of the Revelation of God in Christ

The life-giving revelation provokes two diametrically opposite responses: one leads to abiding faith, discipleship and illumination; the other to unbelief, rejection, obduracy and remaining in darkness (Jn. 3:17-19; cf. 12:47-48). The data in the Epistles of John is revealing in terms of continuity with the Gospel. In these Epistles, especially the First Epistle, the division centres upon recognition and confession of Jesus as the Christ. There are two diametrically opposed responses to Jesus. On the part of the antichrist, the response is marked by *denial, disbelief* and *refusal to confess*, and on the part of the believer, by *acceptance, belief* and *confession*. Denial of Jesus derives its inspiration from the deceiver (2 Jn. 7), from the world (1 Jn. 4:4-5), or from the antichrist (1 Jn. 4:3; cf. 2 Jn. 7). Confession receives its impetus from God's Spirit (1 Jn. 4:2), who points the believer back to Jesus' teaching (1 Jn. 1:1-3, 5; 2:24-27; 5:9-12; 2 Jn. 9a). The object of the controversy is Jesus, and what is denied or affirmed about him is also set forth antithetically. Hence either 'he is not the Christ' (1 Jn. 2:22) or 'he is the Christ' (1 Jn. 5:1); either 'he is not the Son of God [Jesus Christ] come in flesh' (1 Jn. 4:2; 2 Jn. 7) or 'he is the Son of God come in flesh' (1 Jn. 4:15; 5:5). To say that he is the Son of God 'come in the flesh' means that he has been sent by the Father to give eternal life to those who believe in him (1 Jn. 4:9-10, 14, 16; 5:13; cf. Jn. 17:3).

The world in John's Gospel faces Jesus either as Saviour or as Judge. The Fourth Evangelist leaves no room in between. Jesus is sent by the Father into the world (1:9; 3:17; 10:36; 16:28) to save the world (3:17; 12:47), to be its light (8:12; 12:46). But rejection of the light means being overcome by darkness (3:19; 9:39; 12:31; 16:11; 16:33).[219] The Johannine theme of

---

Satan, would be condemned (cf. 1QS III.13-iv, 26). In the Fourth Gospel, the devil has already met defeat (12:31; 14:30; 16:11). When the Son of Man is lifted up on the cross, the ruler of this world is vanquished. The crucifixion for John means not only the judgment of this world, but likewise, the judgment of the world's ruler, the devil (12:31). See further Wendy E. Sproston, 'Satan in the Fourth Gospel', in *Studia Biblica 1978*, II. *Papers on the Gospels*, JSNTSup 2, ed. by E. A. Livingstone (Sheffield: JSOT Press, 1980), 308-10.

[218] For example: Mk. 8:38; Mt. 11:6, 21-24; Lk. 7:23; 10:13-16. For the same theme in Paul, see Romans 9-11; 1 Cor. 1:18, 23f.; 2 Cor. 2:15.

[219] The ultimate origin of the darkness in John's Gospel is not explicit. Isaiah resolved the theodicy question by attributing the creation of the darkness to YHWH (Isa. 45:7). Other texts where this occurs include the *Poimandres*, C.H.I.4; 1QS 3:13-4:26; the *Tripartite Tractate*, NHC

κρίσις and σχίσμα in its graphic illustration of the divisiveness of revelation shows that the encounter with revelation will lead either to illumination or to blindness and obduracy, which is why Jesus is able to say that he comes both to judge and not to judge.[220] The apparent contradiction clarifies the polysemantic nature of the word used for 'judgment' in the Fourth Gospel. The word κρίνειν means to 'separate', 'select', 'judge', 'decide' (e.g., 9:39), but it also means to 'condemn' (e.g., 12:47).[221] Believers are not 'judged' (i.e., 'condemned', 3:18), and do not come into 'judgment' (i.e., 'condemnation', 5:24). On the other hand, unbelievers have already been judged (i.e., 'condemned', 3:18, cf. 16:11; 12:31). John can also use the word to speak of a final judgment at the last day (5:27–29; 12:48), as well as in reference to the ministry of the Paraclete (16:8, 11). This Johannine judgment is the inevitable result of light shining in darkness; while some expose themselves to the light, others hide in darkness.

Revelation separates those who accept and believe that Jesus is the Christ who has come from above (7:43; 9:16, 22; 10:19–22; 16:2) from those who do not. Only those who believe in the one who has seen the Father (1:18; 6:46) can see God in him (12:45; 14:9). In the Fourth Gospel, the dividing and polarising effect of light is expressed in a number of ways. First, by the use of such expressions as ἐλέγχω in John 3:20[222] or κρίνειν in 3:16–19; 5:22, 27, 30; 9:39. Secondly, by Johannine antithetical expressions, often attributed to dualistic thinking,[223] which further accentuate the divisiveness of revelation. Thirdly, the segregating effect of revelation is vividly captured in the Gospel's account of Jesus' public ministry (ch. 3–

1.51:1–8; and *First Apocalypse of James*, NHC V.34. All of these texts in some way trace the existence of evil and darkness to the original, eternal, and highest principle; none of them understands good and evil to be co-eternal opposites.

[220] Cf. Bultmann, *John*, 341–2; Blank, *Krisis*; Paola Ricca, *Die Eschatologie des viertern Evangeliums* (Zürich: Gotthelf, 1966).

[221] BAGD, 450–1; Büchsel, *TDNT*, 3 (1965), 921–41. See also my discussion in chapter two (2.2.1.1).

[222] Meaning 'expose, bring to light' (e.g., Eph. 5:11, 13), as well as 'convict, reprove' (e.g., Jn. 8:46; 16:8; Lk. 3:19).

[223] E.g., 'Truth' vs. 'falsehood', 'flesh' vs. 'Spirit', 'life' vs. 'death', 'above' vs. 'below', 'light' vs. 'darkness', 'love' vs. 'hate'. In Qumran for similar divisions, see, for example, 1QS 3:20–21; cf. 1QS 4:11ff.; 1QM 1:1ff.; 13:12; for 'sons of light', see 1QS 1:9; 2:16; 3:13, 24f; 1QM *passim*.. See also Schottroff, *Der Glaubende und die Feindliche Welt*, 228–38, idem, 'John 4:5–15 und die Konsequenzen des johanneischen Dualismus', *ZNW* 60 (1969), 199–214; Kuhn, 'Johannesevangelium und Qumrantexte', 113; James H. Charlesworth, 'A Critical Comparison of the Dualism in 1QS 3:13–4:26 and the Dualism Contained in the Gospel of John', in *John and the Dead Sea Scrolls*, ed. by J. H. Charlesworth (New York: Crossroads, 1990), 76–106; Brown, 'Qumran Scrolls and John', 69–90; Böcher, *Der johanneischen Dualismus*, 11ff; Becker, 'Beobachtungen zum Dualismus', 71–87.

12; 1:11–13). The reaction which the truth provokes escalates the process of separation (κρίσις) and division (σχίσμα).[224]

The various expressions of the divisiveness of revelation must be seen in the context of John's inaugurated eschatology. For the Evangelist, the eschatological realities of 'judgment', 'eternal life', 'resurrection', and 'death' are all summed up in the incarnation of the Word.[225] In this sense in John's Gospel, eschatology is an aspect of christology.[226] Perhaps John and the other New Testament authors did not think that they were living at the time designated as the 'tribulation' which immediately precedes the 'end of the world' in the apocalyptic sense.[227] However, there are sufficient exegetical grounds to assert that they did indeed believe the coming of

---

[224] Most of the references to 'the Jews' link to this theme of κρίσις (3:19; 5:22, 24, 27, 29, 30; 7:24; 8:16; 12:31) and σχίσμα (7:43; 9:16; 10:19). See the division between 'the Jews' (e.g., 7:11, 15, 35), and 'the Jews' (e.g., 7:12, 20, 31–32, 40, 43) where some believe (7:31; 8:31; 10:41–42), while others do not (7:35; 8:48; 10:31–39) with the resulting division (7:43; 9:16; 10:19–21; 11:45–46).

[225] On the subject of 'judgment', see Schnackenburg, *St. John*, 1:398–407, 2:255; Barrett, *St. John*, 181–2, 308; Bultmann, *John*, 154–6, 203–84, 307; Hoskyns, *Fourth Gospel*, 324–6; Lightfoot, *St. John's Gospel*, 203; Westcott, *St. John*, 55–6; Lindars, *John*, 159–60; Dodd, *Interpretation*, 208–12; on 'life', see J. C. Davis, 'The Johannine Concept of Eternal Life as a Present Possession', *Restoration Quarterly* 27 (1984), 161–69; C. H. Dodd, 'Eternal Life', *Harvard Divinity School Bulletin* 48 (1951), 5–15; U. E. Simon, 'Eternal Life in the Fourth Gospel', in *Studies in the Fourth Gospel*, ed. by F. L. Cross (London: Mowbray, 1957), 97–109; C. F. D. Moule, 'The Meaning of 'Life' in the Gospel and Epistles of St. John', *Theology* 78 (1975), 114–25.

[226] Blank, *Krisis*, 38–9, 64–5, 109–10, 119, 122, 124–6, 135–7, 346, 352–3; Hans Pribnow, *Die johanneische Anschauung vom 'Leben'* (Greifswald: Universitätsverlag, 1934), 102–42; Stählin, 'Zum Problem'; Ethelbert Stauffer, 'Agnostos Christos': Joh. ii.24 und die Eschatologie des vierten Evangeliums', *The Background of the New Testament and Its Eschatology* (Cambridge: CUP, 1964), 298–9; Paul W. Meyer, 'The Eschatology of the Fourth Gospel: A Study in Early Christian Reinterpretation' (Th. D. diss., New York: Union Theological Seminary, 1955); Käsemann, *Testament of Jesus*, 16, 20.

[227] The following studies are quite useful in providing the context of thought of this 'apocalyptic sense'. See D. S. Russell, *The Method and Message of Jewish Apocalyptic 200 BC–AD 100*, Old Testament Library (Philadelphia: Westminster Press; London: SCM, 1964); S. Mowinckel, *He that Cometh* (Oxford: Blackwell, 1956), 304ff; P. Volz, *Die Eschatologie der jüdischen Gemeinde im neutestamentlichen Zeitalter* (Tübingen: Mohr, 1934); J. P. Baldensperger, *Die messianisch-apokalyptischen Hoffnungen des Judentums*, 3rd edn (Straussburg, 1903), 176, 188; W. Bousset, *Die jüdische Apokalyptik, ihre religionsgeschichtliche Herkunft und ihre Bedeutung für das Neue Testament* (Berlin, 1903); P. D. Hanson, *The Dawn of Apocalyptic* (Philadelphia: Fortress, 1975); John J. Collins, 'Cosmos and Salvation: Jewish Wisdom and Apocalyptic in the Hellenistic Age', *History of Religions* 17 (1977), 121–42; idem, 'Jewish Apocalyptic Against Its Ancient Near Eastern Environment', *Bulletin of the American Schools of Oriental Research* 220 (1975), 27–36; H. H. Rowley, *The Relevance of Apocalyptic* (New York: Association Press, 1964), 57–64; P. R. Davies, 'The Social World of the Apocalyptic Writings', in *The World of Ancient Israel*, ed. by R. E. Clements (Cambridge: CUP, 1989), 251–71.

Christ had set in motion the beginning of the end.[228] In the Fourth Gospel, the incarnation has decisively inaugurated the 'last days' (4:23; 5:25; 16:32). John 17:1 states, 'the hour has come',[229] and 12:27 refers twice to 'this hour' (cf. 12:23; 13:1; Mk. 14:41).[230] The 'end of time' has already begun, so it is 'now'; but since not all aspects of it are yet consummated, it is also 'future' (6:39, 40, 44, 54; 7:37; 11:24; 12:48).[231] Cullmann characterised it as 'already fulfilled' and 'not yet completed'.[232] That is, not all aspects of it are fully realised, even though Jesus' work is final and requires no completion.[233]

Inaugurated eschatology also refers to the in-breaking of the kingdom

---

[228] E.g., Mt. 3:2; 4:17, 23; 9:35; 10:7; 12:28; 13:11–52; Mk. 1:15; 9:1; Lk. 4:43; 9:2; 11:20; 17:21; Acts 2:17; 2 Tim. 3:1–10; Heb. 1:2; 1 Pet. 1:5, 20; 2 Pet. 3:3; 1 Jn. 2:18.

[229] See J. Seynaeve, 'Le thème de "l'heure" dans le quatrième évangile', *Revue Africaine de Théologie* 7 (1983), 29–50.

[230] This eschatological tension between present and future has been attributed, unconvincingly, one may add, to a complex compositional history of the Gospel. See, for example, R. Bultmann, 'The Eschatology of the Gospel of John', in *Faith and Understanding*, vol. 1 (New York: Harper and Row, 1969), 165–83; idem, *John*, 155–7, 164–7, 219–20, 236, 256–62, 402–3; cf. Robert Kysar, 'The Eschatology of the Fourth Gospel: A Correction of Bultmann's Redactional Hypothesis', *Perspective* 13 (1972), 23–33; Schnackenburg, *St. John*, 2:426–37, 532–4; Käsemann, *Testament of Jesus*, 13–14; Brown, *John*, 1:cxx–cxxi. But see Dodd, *Interpretation*, 147, 209, 395–6, 405–6; David Holwerda, *The Holy Spirit and Eschatology in the Gospel of John* (Kampen: Kok. 1959), 78, 84–5. For the full discussion of various issues related to Johannine eschatology, see G. Stählin, 'Zum Problem der johanneischen Eschatologie', *ZNW* 33 (1934), 225–59; M. Pamment, 'Eschatology and the Fourth Gospel', *JSNT* 15 (1982), 81–5; J. D. Thompson, 'An Analysis of Present and Future in the Eschatology of the Fourth Gospel, and an Examination of the Theological Relationship Between the Two' (Ph.D. diss., Atlanta: Emory University, 1967); S. Pancaro, 'A Statistical Approach to the Concept of Time and Eschatology in the Fourth Gospel', *Bib* 50 (1969), 511–24; John T. Carroll, 'Present and Future in the Fourth Gospel "Eschatology"', *BTB* 19 (1989), 63–69; Robert Kysar, *The Fourth Evangelist and His Gospel: An Examination of Contemporary Scholarship* (Minneapolis: Augsburg Publishing House, 1975), 207–14; Meyer, 'Eschatology of the Fourth Gospel'; G. H. O. Madsen, 'The Theological Significance of 'Nun/Arti' in the Fourth Gospel' (Ph.D. diss., Princeton Theological Seminary, 1972); Moule, 'Individualism of the Fourth Gospel', 171–90; A. Schweitzer, *The Quest of the Historical Jesus: A Critical Study of Its Progress from Reimarus to Wrede* (London: SCM, repr. 1981), 356; Joachim Jeremias, *The Parables of the Jesus*, rev. edn (New York: Scribner, 1961), 82–84; J. M. Robinson, 'The Formal Structure of Jesus' Message', in *Current Issues in New Testament Interpretation.*, Essays in honour of O. A. Piper (New York: Harper and Bros., 1962), 91–110; J. Watts, 'Eschatology in the Johannine Community: A Study in Diversity' (Ph.D. diss., Edinburgh: Faculty of Divinity, 1980).

[231] This was described by Dodd as 'realised' eschatology. He apparently coined the phrase. However, in Dodd's proposal, the 'future' seems to be excluded, which seems to be why he coined the phrase as 'realised'. However, since then, many who use the term do not exclude the future. See Dodd, *Apostolic Preaching;* idem, *The Parables of the Kingdom*, rev. edn (New York: Scribner, 1961), 82–4; see A. A. Hoekema's criticism of 'realised eschatology', in *The Bible and the Future* (Grand Rapids: Eerdmans, 1979), 17–18.

[232] Oscar Cullmann, *Salvation in History* (New York: Harper and Row, 1967), 202.

[233] Blank, *Krisis*, 346; see Bultmann, *John*, 164.

of God in the human realm.[234] Bruce Chilton has argued that in the first century, particularly in the school of Yohanan ben Zakkai, the kingdom of God was conceived as the revelation of God himself.[235] In this context, the phrase 'kingdom of God' meant that God is active among us.[236] John 3:3, 5 presupposes this aspect of the present reality of the kingdom of God. John 18:36 clarifies the spiritual rather than material character of this kingdom.[237] The Synoptics also echo John by noting the spiritual character of the kingdom in the present dispensation[238] without denying its future aspect (e.g., Mt. 6:10; 13:47-50; 16:28; 20:21; 26:29; Lk. 13:29). Mark 1:15 and 9:1 speak of the kingdom as imminent, 'at the door'.[239] When the Gospel writers speak of the kingdom of God in its present form, the emphasis is not upon the territorial rule of God, but upon the universal *saving activity* of God.[240] It is often noted that where the Synoptic Gospels speak

---

[234] In his interrogation by Pilate and the question, 'What is the truth?', the kingship of Jesus is on the forefront of the accusation against him and yet Jesus says: 'For this cause I was born'. But his kingship is not of this world (18:36), and the kingship of this world which is offered to him must be renounced (Mt. 4:8; Lk. 4:5). The title 'king' is used sixteen times in John, mostly in the trial narrative. 'King of Israel' was used by Palestinian Jews for the Messiah. See H. A. Cauthron, Jr., 'The Meaning of Kingship in Johannine Christology: A Structuralist Exegesis of John 18:1-20' (Ph.D. diss., Vanderbilt University, 1984); K. L. Schmidt, βασιλεία, *TWNT* 1 (1933), 579-592 = *TDNT* 1 (1964), 579-90; G. M. Lee, 'The Inscription on the Cross', *PEQ* 100 (1968), 144; F. J. Botha, 'King of Israel (in the Gospel of John)', *Theologia Evangelica* 1 (1968), 19-20; M. de Jonge, 'Jesus as Prophet-King in John', *ATR* 51 (1969), 35-7; J. M. Reese, 'The Non-Political King', *Bible Today* 61 (1972), 823-5; M. É. Boismard, 'La royauté universelle du Christ', *Assemblées du Seigneur* 88 (1966), 33-45. For the political dimension of the term, see C. H. Dodd, *Historical Tradition in the Fourth Gospel* (Cambridge: CUP, 1963), 112; Barrett, *St. John*, 278, 536ff; Ernst Haenchen, 'Jesus vor Pilatus (Joh. 18, 28-29, 15)', in *Gott und Mensch* (Tübingen: Mohr-Siebeck, 1965), 149, 152; Meeks, *Prophet-King*, 64, 76, 81; Schlier, 'Jesus und Pilatus', 56-74; idem, 'The State According to New Testament', in *The Relevance of the New Testament*, ed. by Heinrich Schlier (Freiburg and New York: Herder and Herder, 1968), 215-25.

[235] B. D. Chilton, 'Regnum Dei Deus Est', in *Targumic Approaches to the Gospels: Essays in the Mutual Definition of Judaism and Christianity* (New York/London: Lanham, 1986), 99-107, esp. 101-5.

[236] Ibid., 101, 105.

[237] In the Fourth Gospel, the actual Synoptic expression 'kingdom of God' is absent although the present spiritual reality of the kingdom pervades the Gospel. See A. S. Geyser, 'Israel in the Fourth Gospel', *Neot* 20 (1986), 13-20; Dodd, *Historical Tradition*, 112.

[238] E.g., Mt. 3:2; 4:17; 5:3, 10, 19; 6:33; 9:35; 10:7; 11:12; 12:28; 13:11-52; 18:23; 21:31; 23:13; 25:1; Mk. 1:15; 10:14; Lk. 4:43; 6:20; 9:20; 10:9, 11; 16:16; 17:20, 21; 18:17.

[239] See George E. Ladd, *A Theology of the New Testament* (Grand Rapids: Eerdmans, 1978), 299-308; Brown, *John*, 1:119; Cullmann, *Salvation in History*, 202; Schweitzer, *Quest of the Historical Jesus*, 384.

[240] On this topic, see Norman Perrin, *Jesus and the Language of the Kingdom: Symbol and Metaphor in N.T. Interpretation* (Philadelphia: Fortress, 1976), 40; idem, *Rediscovering the Teaching of Jesus* (London: SCM, 1967), 54f; B. T. Viviano, *The Kingdom of God in History* (Wilmington, DE: M. Glazier, 1988); John Dominic Crossan, *In Parables: The Challenge of the Historical Jesus* (New York: Harper and Row, 1973), 23. Valuable studies of Jewish and New

of the kingdom, the Fourth Gospel speaks instead about the present reality of life characteristic of the kingdom. Nevertheless, as Heinrich Schlier observes, Jesus' kingship, though rooted in the coming world, already exerts its peculiar authority over this one.[241] Jesus' kingship consists in his mission of testifying to the truth (18:37)[242] about God, about humanity, and how the chasm between the two is bridged. It is in this eternal reality that both 'the Jews' and 'the world' face the incarnate one, either for salvation or for judgment.[243]

The imagery of the eschatological harvest in John 4:31–38 further accentuates the present reality of the end time. When the Word became flesh, the definitive separation began and took effect in humanity's response to his mission and claims (9:41; 15:22; cf. Mt. 13:24–30; 25:31–46). John 4:31–38 hinges upon Jesus' finishing 'the work'[244] of the Father which ushers in the eschatological harvest. The arrival of this end time carries with it certain non-negotiable imperatives (δεῖ) for Jesus (3:14, 30a; 4:4; 9:4; 10:16; 12:34; 20:9), for his audience (3:7; 4:24), and for his precursor (3:30b). Its impact is experienced as 'life' by believers and as 'judgment' by unbelievers (3:18–21, 36; 5:29).

The 'work' (ἔργον) of which Jesus speaks designates the totality of the work of salvation carried out conjointly and exclusively by Jesus and the Father.[245] This work inaugurates and establishes definitively a new order in humanity's relationship with God, one which is marked by grace and truth (1:17b; 3:16; 4:10, 24). The time until the resurrection has been the preparation of the field and the sowing phase of God's saving work. God has

---

Testament source material are to be found in M. Hengel and A. M. Schwemer, eds, *Königsherrschaft Gottes und himmlischer Kult*, WUNT 55 (Tübingen: Mohr-Siebeck, 1991).

[241] Schlier, 'Jesus und Pilatus', 56–74; Robert F. Berkey, 'ΕΓΓΙΖΕΙΝ, ΦΘΑΝΕΙΝ, and Realized Eschatology', *JBL* 82 (1963), 177–87; Jürgen Becker, *Das Heil Gottes: Heils und Sündenbegriffe in den Qumrantexten und im Neuen Testament*, SUNT 3 (Göttingen: Vandenhoeck & Ruprecht, 1964), 206.

[242] Barrett, *St. John*, 537; Dodd, *Interpretation*, 176.

[243] Cf. 3:31–36; 8:14, 16, where μαρτυρία and κρίσις are paralleled.

[244] There are nineteen occurrences of the term τελέω (verb form) and τέλος (noun form) 'finish' in its various grammatical forms in the Fourth Gospel (cf. two occurrences in the Synoptics). Often 'finish' is used in context of Jesus doing the wishes of the Father and completing his work.

[245] In the Fourth Gospel, a distinction must be maintained between the 'work' of Jesus (singular) and 'works' of Jesus (plural). The work of Jesus speaks of the totality of his saving activity; the whole purpose for which he had come into the world (Jn. 17:4; 19:30). On the other hand, the 'works' of Jesus refer to the miraculous signs he performed to authenticate his Messianic claim. On the topic of 'works', see P. W. Ensor, *Jesus and His 'Works': The Johannine Sayings in Historical Perspective*, WUNT 2.85 (Tübingen: Mohr-Siebeck, 1996).

done the 'tedious labour' (κόπος),²⁴⁶ irrefutably demonstrated in the death of the Son upon the cross for the sin of the world. The double meaning of the verb κοπιᾶν (4:6, 38) accentuates the tedious nature of the work.²⁴⁷ The noun form κόπος (4:38c) describes the exhausting, hard nature of the work of planting, while the verb form κοπιάω (vv 6, 38a, b) underlines the resulting tiredness experienced by the one who engages in this difficult labour.

The question of whether salvation is accomplished by the incarnation or the Passion/resurrection is not entertained by the Evangelist. The Johannine ἔργον is a single unbroken movement from beginning to end (4:34; 17:4). The work of salvation is accomplished by the Son's uninterrupted journey from the Father into the world and back to the Father (16:28; 13:1). Thus, salvation is accomplished by his incarnation, life, death and resurrection: the sum total of his life on earth.

On the other hand, from the point of view of the disciples, they are at the receiving end of the result of this 'hard work' (κοπιᾶν, 4:6, 38). Here, the post-resurrection phase of God's work of salvation is in view. In contrast to the tedious work of God, the task of harvesting assigned to the disciples is characterised as 'receiving' (λαμβάνειν) of reward, not of one's own work (i.e., sowing). Their work of 'fruit-gathering' is nothing more than enjoying the labour of God. Their work is its own reward (μισθὸν λαμβάνειν). The word μισθός means both 'wages for work' and 'reward' in 4:36.

Theologically, the harvesting phase of the work is inaugurated definitively after the resurrection by Jesus' glorification (3:14; 8:28; 12:28, 34; 17:4–5; 19:30). This is the phase during which the Holy Spirit, the indispensable agent of the new life (6:63; 16:7), is given to believers (20:22) to enable them to become the children of God (1:12–13; 3:3–8, 21), to receive the promised gift of eternal life (4:14; 7:37–38), to perform worship in the spirit and in truth (4:21–24), to grasp fully Jesus' teaching (14:25–26; 16:12–15) and to participate actively in Jesus' work of 'gathering into fellowship' and reconciliation (15:26–27; 4:35–38; 20:21, 23; 21). This, in short, is the phase when the fruit of God's accomplished work of salvation is actually reaped by all those who believe. In its pre-Easter phase, this eschatological era is described as both 'the hour' which 'now is' (4:21, 23; 5:25) and which 'is coming'. The former statement is proclamatory in nature: it draws attention to the fact that the Messianic era has indeed

---

[246] BAGD, 443.
[247] Cf. 4:6 is picked up at 19:14; and 4:7 at 19:28.

dawned with Jesus' coming into the world (4:25–26). For John, the hour of which the prophets spoke and in which the climactic self-revelation of God[248] occurs has come in Jesus.

The coming of the Son of Man from the Father and his return to the Father has set in motion the 'last days' where the eschatological harvest is at last ready to be gathered; and the readiness of the harvest has a sense of urgency associated with it (Mt. 9:37–38; 10:1; Lk. 10:2, 3). This urgency of the situation is registered in 4:35 by the aorist imperatives 'behold' (ἰδού), 'lift up' your eyes (ἐπάρατε), and 'see' (θεάσασθε), and by the emphatic position of 'already' (ἤδη) placed last in 4:35b (though many interpreters take this with the next verse). Such a call to attention would be meaningless if the disciples, the harvesters (4:38), were already engaged in the harvest and receiving wages.

The harvest in 4:35a and 4:35b functions on two completely different levels of meaning. The juxtaposition of verse 35a and 35b underlines the new order. Just as the Samaritan woman earlier is alerted to what constitutes the true worship and worshipper (vv. 20–24), the disciples are now alerted to the nature of God's work. The disciples, like the woman, operate within the natural order. The woman is expecting the Messiah when he is already there speaking with her; the disciples think of an earthly agricultural harvest when, in fact, a more significant harvest, i.e., the eschatological harvest, has already arrived.

In the Old Testament, the imagery of the 'harvest' symbolises the dawn of the end-time.[249] However, in contrast to these passages where the emphasis is upon separation and judgment, in John the emphasis is life (12:47; 10:10) and unification (4:36b). The proverbial curse (4:37), reminiscent of the covenantal curse under the old dispensation,[250] has been reversed in Christ. In the present time of harvest, both sower and reaper can enjoy the fruit of their labour and rejoice together. Both Isaiah and Amos saw the 'end of the age' to be a period when the curse of Deuteronomy 28:30 and Leviticus 26:16 will be reversed (Isa. 62:8–9; 65:21–23; Amos 9:14b). In the past the curse was due to lack of fellowship (Deut. 28:30; Lev. 26:16; Mic. 6:15; Job 31:8–18) and the transitory nature of human life when the sower died before he could enjoy the fruit of his harvest (Deut. 20:6–7). In the Fourth Gospel, both obstacles are overcome in the incarnate Word:

---

[248] Isa. 2:2–3; 11:1–5, 10–12; 40:3–5, 9–11; Joel 2:28–32; Zech. 9:9–11; Mal. 3:1–3.

[249] See, for example, Isa. 9:3; 16:8–10; 17:11; Joel 1:11; 3:13; Mt. 13:30–39; Mk. 9:29; Rev. 14:15.

[250] See, for example, Deut. 28:30c: cf. Lev. 26:16; Mic. 6:15.

instead of enmity and punishment, there is lasting fellowship, and the most vicious enemy of all, death, is overcome through a life-giving faith in Jesus Christ (3:16; 6:40; 10:10; 20:30–31).

The time of the eschatological harvest is the time specifically associated with judgment and separation of the righteous and the unrighteous. In the Fourth Gospel, the righteous are those who believe. In John's Gospel, it is the inherent function of the revelatory light to divide between those who believe and those who do not believe. The light that shines upon everyone (1:9, 1 Cor. 4:5; 2 Tim. 1:10) is for judgment in order to reveal each human disposition toward the light and thus to separate or sift humanity (cf. Mt. 13:1–58).[251] And as Barrett points out, 'It is not true that all men have a natural affinity with the light'.[252] The coming of the light into the world entails κρίσις. It exposes the evil deeds of those who live in darkness and wish to remain in it lest their unrighteous works be exposed (3:20). In the context of this divisive judgment, the Fourth Evangelist has masterfully developed a thematic twist in which any judgment upon the judge is judgment upon oneself. In Jesus' confrontation with the religious authorities in chapters 8, 9, 10 and later in chapter 18, those who judge Jesus favourably as Christ render a positive judgment upon themselves, and those who reject Jesus condemn themselves.[253] In the Fourth Gospel, as

---

[251] Cf. Isa. 30:18; Amos 3:14; 5:18; Zeph. 1:7f; Joel 3:11f, etc. See Gerhard von Rad, *Old Testament Theology*, trans. by D. M. G. Stalker (New York: Harper and Row, 1965), 2:119–25. John emphasises the soteriological function of the Light and points to the present realisation of this κρίσις or judgment which Jesus as light provoked. Blank, *Krisis*, 281–94. Light speaks of the sphere of salvation (Isa. 9:1; 60:1–3, 19f.; Zech. 14:7; Dan. 12:3, etc.), for its use in Judaism, see Str-B 2:428. Light also describes the divine sphere. God is said to be clothed in light (Ps. 104:2; Isa. 60:19f.; cp. Eth. Enoch 14:15ff.; 1 Tim. 6:16); and beside him, sun and moon themselves appear black as the Moors (Apc. Mos. 35f.) Heavenly figures are numinously bright (2 Macc. 15:13; Mk. 9:3; 16:5; Lk. 24:4, etc.), while the devil is associated with the realm of darkness (2 Cor. 6:14).

[252] Barrett, *St. John*, 161.

[253] Ashton, *Understanding*, 226–29. The account of 10:22–39 seems to be Jesus' final encounter with the religious leaders prior to his arrest. There is no direct parallel in the Synoptics, although the verses bear resemblance to the Synoptic accounts of Jesus' trial at the hands of his opponents (Mt. 26:57–75; Mk. 14:53–72; Lk. 22:54, 63–71). In the episode recorded in 10:22–39, the Jews judge Jesus as a blasphemer (10:33; cf. 5:18; Lev. 24:16) for claiming to be one with God (10:30). Jesus' response to this charge in 10:34 sets him in the context of Israel's prophet-judges, especially the eschatological prophet like unto Moses (cf. Deut. 1:7; 19:17; Exod. 21:6; 22:9). As the 'Jews' surround Jesus, ἐκύκλωσαν (surrounded) in 10:24 may be an allusion to Psalm 118 (117). Moses was the premier judge of Israel and the first and only Old Testament individual said to be 'like God' (Exod. 4:16; 7:1). However, Jesus' identity exceeds that of Moses. He is the pre-existent Word become flesh (Jn. 1:1, 14), and speaks what he has seen and heard from God (Jn. 3:31–32; 8:38; 16:27–28) as one who uniquely reposes in the bosom of the Father (Jn. 1:18). O. Hofius, 'Der in des Vaters Schoss ist, Joh 1, 18', *ZNW* 80 (1989), 163–71. The citation of Psalm 82:1–8 in response to the Jews seems to be an ironic reversal of the

elsewhere in the Scriptures, the purpose of judgment is not annihilation but life, not destruction but restoration, not separation and rejection but redemption and reconciliation. For the Evangelist, both the Jews and the world are subjects of God's redemptive love. The world, the 'cosmos', is God's creation and the focus of his salvific love, and the Jews, or Israel, are those who have enjoyed a privileged position in salvation history. In John 10:34-36 at the climax of the conflict where Jesus is accused of making himself to be God, there is a reminder that God's word in the past had come to Israel. The revelation of God has come to Israel once again, but they as the representatives of the world have not received him (Jn. 1:11).

The frequency of such judicial words as κρίσις (eleven times), κρίνειν (nineteen times), κρίμα (9:39), κατηγορία (18:29), κατηγορεῖν (5:45, twice), ἀποκρίνεσθαι (5:17, 19), ἀπόκρισις (1:22; 19:9), βῆμα (19:13), ἐλέγχειν (3:20; 8:46; 16:8), ὁμολογεῖν (1:20, twice; 9:22; 12:42), ἀρνεῖσθαι (1:20; 13:38; 18:25, 27), αἰτία (18:38; 19:4, 6), and μαρτυρεῖν (1:7, 8, 15; 3:11; 5:31, 32-37; 8:18; etc.) suggests that the work of Jesus in John's Gospel is set against a juridical background. After the resurrection, it is the Holy Spirit who carries out the work of judgment and separation (cf. κρίσις, σχίσμα) when he 'reproves the world' (ἐλέγξει τὸν κόσμον) 'concerning sin' (περὶ ἁμαρτίας), 'concerning righteousness' (περὶ δικαιοσύνης), and 'concerning judgment' (περὶ κρίσεως). The three subjects are intricately conected to revelatory truth. Just as the world faces Jesus either as saviour or as judge, the world faces the Spirit of truth either as comforter or as convictor. Truth embodied in Christ constitutes the instrument of this task which brings about the opposite result for those who believe and those who do not.

This juridical emphasis of the Spirit's work is implied in the term παράκλητος (14:16, 26; 15:26; 16:7; cf. 1 Jn. 2:1), and the Spirit's activity is

---

circumstances by Jesus. While religious leaders offer their final judgment on Jesus, their judgment is in fact judgment upon themselves by rejecting the light (12:36, 48). Jesus reveals himself as one standing 'in the midst' of Israel, chastising them for their inability to judge justly. While they desire to kill him, it is in fact their own lives which are being compromised (8:21, 24). While they judge, it is Jesus who has come 'for judgment' (9:39; cf. 5:22, 27-30; 8:16, 26; 12:31; 16:11). Yet Jesus' desire is not to condemn them. Rather, he exhorts them, on the last occasion before his arrest to believe in the light (cf. 3:17; 8:15; 12:47). Jesus' response in 10:34-35 has occasioned numerous conflicting interpretations. The most difficult problem in the passage has to do with who the Evangelist understands the addressees (i.e., gods) of the Psalm to be. The traditional interpretation, and a plausible one as well, understands the addressees of the Psalm as Israel's judges. See the discussion by Jerome H. Neyrey, '"I Said: You are Gods" Psalm 82:6 and John 10', *JBL* 108 (1989), 647-63.

in keeping with such a designation.²⁵⁴ After the resurrection, the Spirit-Paraclete continues to confront the 'world' with Jesus' claim and therefore with his judgment (16:7-15; 14:16-17, 25-26). The references to future judgment are shown to be a ratification of the 'judgment' already effected by Jesus in the present. The work of the Holy Spirit in the believing community is regenerating activity and leading believers into all truth (14:17, 26). In this respect, the Holy Spirit belongs to the community of faith (14:17) and not the world. He teaches them 'all things' (14:26; 16:13), brings to their memory the words of the risen Lord (14:26; 15:26), and speaks of what is yet to come (16:13). The Spirit's revelatory witness belongs to those who are of God (6:37-45).

The hermeneutical implication is that the correct interpretation of the significance of Jesus' life, death, and resurrection, bound together with a correct interpretation of the Scripture, is available only within the community of faith. Therefore, it is only the disciples who are not offended by Jesus' origins (1:45; 6:42; 7:31, 41-52), by his flesh (1:14; 6:51-69), and by his death (6:51-59). Likewise, it is only the disciples who see his glory (1:14; 2:11). To these, the revelation of God is made plain (14:26; 16:13-15). In this context, true worship also takes place in the community of faith. The Fourth Evangelist boldly asserts that it is no longer the Jerusalem temple, but the church, which is the sphere of true worship (Jn. 4:23-24).

6.6.2. The Johannine 'World' and the Function of the Believing Community within It

When light is shunned, darkness is the inevitable choice (cf. 8:24). It is the judgment that the world renders on itself by its reaction to the light (3:19).²⁵⁵ In the Fourth Gospel, a function of the community of faith in the world is to bring about precisely this κρίσις and σχίσμα, the reaction to light, a critical point of decision in which people have either to come to the light and be exposed or to remain in darkness and conceal their evil works. The former is an act of submission to the divine verdict which results in life; the latter is an act of unbelief and rejection of the creator's verdict (cf. 1 Jn. 2:10); this brings death. However, in this judgment of separation

---

²⁵⁴ Brown, 'Paraclete in the Fourth Gospel', 116-7; Johnston, *The Spirit-Paraclete* (Cambridge: CUP, 1970), 80-118.

²⁵⁵ However, Jeffrey A. Trumbower, *Born from Above: The Anthropology of the Gospel of John* (Tübingen: Mohr-Siebeck, 1992), 115, rejects any element of choice and attributes the reaction to light due to the predetermined origin of those who are from 'above' and those who are from 'below'.

provoked by the light of revelation in the world, there is also an implicit warning to the Christian community itself against conformity to the world (i.e., worldliness).[256] Apathy towards the truth is a persistent danger for the community of faith and such a presumption carries with it the divine indictment. The strong emphasis upon moral and behavioural separation from the world throughout the Johannine writings leaves little room for doubt. If the disciples, as sons of light (12:36), are left in the world to be channels of God's light, then they must not conform to the world, otherwise they will lose their prophetic voice needed to confront the world. This is precisely the Evangelist's own position in his world.

In John's Gospel, the 'world' (κόσμος)[257] is the sphere of God's universal saving activity. Though historically Jesus carried out his mission in Palestine, the scope of this mission is the whole world (1:9, 10a; 3:16–17; 16:28), and its destined audience 'all flesh' (17:2; cf. 12:32). As Jesus' immediate audiences in Galilee (1:29–2:12; 4:44–54; 6:1–7:9; 21), Jerusalem (2:13–3:21; 5; 7:10–10:39; 11:55–57; 12:12–20:31), Judea (3:22–36; 11:1–54; 12:1–11) and Samaria (4:4–42) were challenged to respond to the self-revelation of God in the incarnate Word, so are all peoples of the world. Whether personally proclaimed by Jesus or reported later by his disciples (17:20; 20:30–31; 21:24–25; 1 Jn. 1:1–3), Jesus' self-revealing, which is the revelation of the Father (1:18; 17:6), constitutes the only redemptive possibility for the world. The 'world' in John is a complex notion. The κόσμος refers to the whole organised state of human society which 'is not the totality of creation[258] but the world of men and human affairs'.[259] The 'world' is specifically the dominion of God's saving work,[260] yet consistently it stands in opposition to Christ, the Spirit (14:17, 22–24) and the followers of Jesus.[261] The world is also the realm of both those who are born from God and those who remain of the earth, from below, or from the devil. In this

---

[256] So E. Grässer, 'Die antijüdische Polemik im Johannesevangelium', *NTS* 11 (1964–65), 85, 88–90.

[257] The word occurs some seventy-nine times in John in comparison to only fifteen times in the Synoptics.

[258] John 11:9; 17:5, 24; 21:5 are exceptions.

[259] Barrett, *St. John*, 161, 426.

[260] John 3:16, 17; 12:47; cf. 1:29; 4:42; 1 Jn. 2:2; 4:9, 14.

[261] John 15:18–19, 22–23; 17:14a; 1 Jn. 3:1, 13. See Albert Curry Winn, *A Sense of Mission: Guidance from the Gospel of John* (Philadelphia: Westminster Press, 1981), 69–74; Rensberger, *Overcoming the World*, 146; José Porfirio Miranda, *Being and the Messiah: The Message of St. John* (Maryknoll, NY: Orbis Books, 1977), 101–2. In the Pauline Epistles, as Bultmann, *Theology of the New Testament.*, 1:255f, has shown, the term 'kosmos' often contains a definite theological judgment. It is the antithesis to the sphere of God.

sense, the 'world' seems to be equivalent to the αὐλή ('fold') of John 10, which contains both Jesus' sheep and all the others. This is the 'world' into which the Father has sent his Son because of his love for it in order to bestow eternal life on those who believe. This is the 'world' for which Jesus is saviour, light and life.

Just how does Jesus save this 'world'? He saves it by 'casting out the ruler of this world' (12:31) and by 'overcoming the world' (16:33). The disciples can be secure in their knowledge that the forces which hate Jesus and his disciples have been vanquished. Thus, the gathering of the children of God who are scattered abroad (11:52) is precisely how God manifests his love for the world and how the world is 'saved' through Jesus.

Alternatively, the author can speak of the 'world' in its wholly negative sense, as the realm which is opposed to the Saviour and his disciples (7:7, 14:17, 16:20, 17:9, 18:37). Both Onuki and Schottroff have shown that in the Fourth Gospel the 'world' in the negative sense exists only in its negative response to God's revelatory initiative.[262] This is the world for which Jesus does not pray (17:9), because of its very resistance to the truth and the Spirit of truth (14:17, 22-24). This is the world from which Jesus disassociates himself and his followers (1 Jn. 2:15).[263] Nevertheless, the finished saving work of Jesus seems to remain a permanent offer of salvation to those in this very world (14:23; cf. 1:5; 16:33), and to this end, the disciples and the Spirit remain in the world (17:15, 18-23; 16:8-11; 13:35),[264] though Jesus himself no longer remains there visibly (14:33; 17:11). The disciples are in the world but separated from it (15:19; 17:6, 14-16, 18, 21, 23), and they are not to become part of it again.[265] God loves the world because he created it and because it contains those who are 'doing the truth' and who will come to the light (3:20-21). The world loves its own (15:19), even as

---

[262] Takashi Onuki, *Gemeinde und Welt im Johannesevangelium: Ein Beitrag zur Frage nach der theologischen und pragmatischen Funktion des johanneischen 'Dualismus'*, WMANT 56 (Neukirchen-Vluyn: Neukirchener Verlag, 1984), 41-5; Schottroff, *Der Glaubende und die feindliche Welt*, 229-33.

[263] However, the Evangelist never counsels his audience to nourish 'everlasting hatred' of those outside the community, as does Qumran (1QS 9:21). Cf. Vermes, *The Dead Sea Scrolls in English*, 88. See further Bultmann, *John*, 54-5; Barrett, *St. John*, 161-2; Schnackenburg, *St. John*, 1:255-6.

[264] Trumbower, *Born from Above*, 116-7

[265] 1 Jn. 2:15-16; cf. 1QS 3:13-4:25; 9:21.

Jesus loves his own (10:11, 15, 17–18; 13:1; 15:14).[266] One's allegiance is revealed by whom one knows and loves (3:19–20; 8:42; 12:42; 13:35).[267]

In the First Epistle of John, as in the Gospel of John, the 'world' is saved through the instrumentality of the believing community. Their presence in the world is the means by which God 'loves' the world. God's love for the world in John is not analogous to the disciples' love for one another (John 13:34, 15:9, 15:17). Their love, in John, is directed inward, in contrast to the Synoptic commands to love even one's enemies because God sends rain on both the just and the unjust (Mt. 5:44–45; Lk. 6:35; cf. Rom. 12:14).[268] In the Fourth Gospel, it is through their mutual love and abiding faith that God 'overcomes' the world and thus saves it.

6.6.3. Unbelief and 'Evil Works'

When the Spirit convicts the world of sin, he convicts it of unbelief. Humanity, with its rationality affected by sin, is entrapped in its self-absorption. It is this self-centredness which consistently brings about the destruction of human society and its members (Jn. 12:25; cf. Mt. 10:39; 16:25; Mk. 8:35; Lk. 17:33).[269] In this respect, in John's Gospel, evil does not lie in creation, but in the human response to creation and the creator.[270] John does not specify the roots of evil.[271] The reality of its existence is acknowledged when God's revelation is met with human rejection because of people's evil works (3:19). What is designated in the Gospel as ἔργα πονηρά, 'evil works' (3:19–20; 7:7),[272] is closely associated with human selfishness, which results in craving the praise of other people (3:20; 5:42, 44; 7:18; 8:50; 12:43). The obsession with praise from other people is identified by the Evangelist as a cause of unbelief. This human disposition toward selfishness is tantamount to idolatry and the cause of 'evil works' in

---

[266] Trumbower, *Born from Above*, attributes this to the language of fixed origin.

[267] The disciples reveal their love for Jesus concretely (1 Jn. 4:20) in their love for one another, received and carried out as a command (13:34; 15:12, 17; 1 Jn. 3:11, 23; 4:21; 5:1–2).

[268] Trumbower, *Born from Above*, 116–17.

[269] See also Onuki, *Gemeinde und Welt*, 41–5; and Schottroff, *Der Glaubende und die feindliche Welt*, 229–33. Cf. Bultmann, *John*, 54–5; Barrett, *St. John*, 161–2; Schnackenburg, *St. John*, 1:255–6.

[270] So Rensberger, *Overcoming the World*, 146.

[271] But such specification is given in Gnosticism. W. Beltz, 'Zum Geschichtsbild der Gnosis', *Zeitschrift Für Religions- und Geistesgeschichte* 40 (1988), 362–6; G. G. Stroumsa, 'Mythos und Erinnerung: Jüdische Dimensionen der gnostischen Revolte gegen die Zeit', *Judaica* 44 (1988), 15–30.

[272] Cf. Mk. 7:21–22 or 1 Cor. 6:9–10.

the world. Unless it is reversed, as history has again and again recorded, the eventual result invariably is mayhem. John 11:49–50, in the context of the AD 70 devastation of Judah, is a graphic illustration.

Human history is littered with the carnage of human actions, the source of which may well be attributed to 'evil works' of people who seek 'glory' from other people rather than the honour that comes from God. In the Fourth Gospel, those who seek their own δόξα, 'honour', and receive δόξα, 'praise', from one another can never see God's δόξα, 'glory' (5:44; 12:43).[273] Neither can they glorify God's name. The inability of 'the Jews' to see the fulfilment of Scriptures in Jesus is credited to this preference for the honour (δόξα) bestowed by other people (cf. 5:40, 44, and 46–47). The unwillingness of the 'secret believers' to make public confession of their faith is also relegated to the love of the praise of other people (12:42–43) rather than the glory of God. Later in the First Epistle, the Christian community is warned against such a love affair with the world.[274] It is precisely because Jesus exposes the world's works as πονηρά that the world hated and rejected him (7:7)[275] and will reject his light-bearers (Jn. 15:20; Mt. 5:14).

In contrast to the 'evil works' of people stands God's own work, which is a life-giving, redemptive work. The history recorded in the Fourth Gospel is the history of God's saving work among his covenant people and recorded in their Scriptures. The saying of Jesus in John 5:17, 'My Father is working (ἐργάζεται) until now, and I also am working (ἐργάζομαι)', is regarded by some commentators as the key emphasis of the Gospel. The pronouncement represents Jesus' defence against the charge of Sabbath-breaking. The 'working until now' could be taken as God's unceasing care of the universe which is not interrupted by Sabbath. If God is not bound to rest on the Sabbath, the same liberty belongs to the Son.[276] In addition, as Lagrange argued, Jesus' intentional infringement of rabbinical regulations was designed not to invalidate the Sabbath, but 'to distinguish between that

---

[273] See Pancaro, *Law in the Fourth Gospel*, 234–47. The use of δόξα in John involves another case of ambiguity. In 5:41 the meaning is 'honour', 'praise', 'recognition' that one seeks from other human beings, for this is the only δόξα men can give. But the δόξα which comes from God is not of the same nature. For example, the same ambiguity faces us at 7:18. On the surface, we are dealing with human 'respect', 'recognition', and 'honour'. Yet the reader knows that Jesus is sent by the Father. The δόξα ascribed to the Father is not mere human praise or honour. The same distinction is to be maintained in 12:43.

[274] 1 Jn. 2:15–17; cf. Jn. 15:19; 17:6, 14–16, 18, 21, 23.

[275] Cf. Bultmann, *John*, 293–4, on John 7:7.

[276] This view was held by Justin, *Dialogue with Trypho* 29, ANF 1:209; Clement of Alexandria, *Stromateis*, 6:16; Philo, *Legum Allegoriae*, 1:5–6; also *De Cherubim*, 87.

400   *Chapter 6: Spiritual Perception and the Language of John's Gospel*

which was contrary and that which was in harmony with the spirit of the Sabbath law'.[277] In the context of John 5, it is likely that the 'work' of the Father and the Son refers to the saving work of God from which he has not ceased since the beginning of creation.[278] In John 6:29, the purpose of the 'work of God' is spelled out: 'that you believe in him whom he has sent'. For those who wish to turn from their 'evil works' and to do the 'work of God', the 'work' of God is to believe in the Son. In 10:37–38, Jesus not only claims to be 'doing the works of [his] Father' but also urges his listeners to 'believe the works' (cf. 14:11, 15:24).

Sin, ἁμαρτία, which in the Fourth Gospel occurs predominantly in the singular,[279] shows itself in unbelief and rejection of Jesus as the rejection of light.[280] Jesus warns the Jews in 8:21 and 24, 'If you do not believe in me you will die in your sins'. After the resurrection, the Spirit-Paraclete convicts the world concerning sin, which is once again the sin of unbelief and the rejection of God's self-manifestation in the incarnate Word (16:8–9). The fact that unbelief is sin is reiterated again in 15:22, 'If I had not come and spoken to them, they would not have sin' (see also 9:41). Sin in the Fourth Gospel is that state of being which characterises those who have rejected the one who embodies life-giving revelation. This unbelief is sin *par excellence*, the fruit of which is permanent alienation from God, unfaithfulness to the truth and incomprehension of it.

6.7. Concealment of the Word

The focus of the incarnation is the world.[281] The aim of the incarnation is redemption, not destruction (10:10; 12:46, 47); revelation, not concealment. However, the self-disclosure of God demands a certain response. 'I tell my mysteries to those who are worthy of my mysteries' (Gospel of Thomas, *log.* 62). In his teaching on the Sermon on the Mount, Jesus underlines the principle, 'Do not give dogs what is holy, and do not throw your pearls

---

[277] M. J. Lagrange, *Évangile selon Saint Jean*, 2nd edn (Paris, 1925), 141.

[278] Hoskyns, *Fourth Gospel*, 267; O. Cullmann, *Early Christian Worship* (Philadelpha: Westminster Press, 1953), 89–90.

[279] See, for example, 1:29; 8:34, 46; 9:41; 15:22, 24; 16:8, 9; 19:11. The Evangelist does not give an inventory of the evil works (cf. Mk. 7:21–22 or 1 Cor. 6:9–10). He simply characterises the works as evil.

[280] There is no concept of sin, in the sense of rejection of Christ, before his coming into the world, but the Evangelist does speak of those who practise evil (Jn. 3:20, 5:29) and commit sins (Jn. 5:14, 8:34); these are persons on whom the wrath of God rests (Jn. 3:36).

[281] John 3:16, 17; 12:47; cf. 1:29; 4:42; 1 Jn. 2:2; 4:9, 14.

before swine, lest they trample them underfoot and turn to attack you' (Mt. 7:6). The rejection of revelation results in the concealment of revelation, even though the aim of revealing is the opposite of concealing.[282] When the Spirit of truth exposes the sin of the world (16:8f), this sin consists in the world's unbelief and rejection of the saving revelation of God in the incarnate Word. Wilful rejection of the truth of God is tantamount to blasphemy,[283] and the result is the concealment of revelation from those who hate the light (cf. 15:22–24; 16:3; 1 Jn. 2:22–24; 2 Jn. 9) and wish to remain in darkness. The idea that God conceals the truth from those who reject the light is not peculiar to John. The concept is prevalent in the Old Testament.[284] The phrase 'hide the face' (סתר + פנים) is a common expression among a significant stock of language relating to the motif of the hiddenness of God in the Old Testament.[285] God's self-concealment is rooted in God's holiness (Exod. 33:17–34:8). Although not all expressions of the hiddenness of God are to be understood as a manifestation of divine judgment in response to human sinfulness and disobedience,[286] yet in a vast majority of those instances in the Old Testament where God conceals himself from his people, unbelief and unfaithfulness is the primary cause (Jer. 33:7; Isa. 8:17). Even in passages where sin is not explicitly singled out as the cause of the self-concealment of God, it is implied in the context (e.g., Ps. 13:1; Isa. 45:15). God turns his face away, as it were, in response to unbelief, disobedience and unfaithfulness to the revelation on the part of his people and their leaders.[287]

Throughout the Scriptures, there are two emphases: one is God's desire to make himself known; the other is his inaccessibility, his hiddenness from comprehension because of his 'wholly other' nature and moral character. In the Fourth Gospel, this second element is overcome by the incarnation and the coming of the Holy Spirit. God has made himself

---

[282] E.g., Mic. 3:1–4; Isa. 59:1ff; Ezk. 39:24, cf. Gen. 3:8. On the subject of concealment of revelation, see Fiddes, 'Hiddenness of Wisdom"; Schäfer, *Hidden and Manifest God;* van der Woude, 'פנים', *THAT*, vol. 2, col. 452; Balentine, *Hidden God,* 115–61; Perlitt, 'Die Verborgenheit Gottes', 367–82.

[283] The Synoptic Gospels speak of blasphemy against the Holy Spirit as sin (see Mk. 3:28–30; Jn. 8:21; 9:41). Cf. Barrett, *Holy Spirit and the Gospel Tradition,* 2nd edn (London: SPCK, 1966 [orig. 1947]), 103–7.

[284] See Fiddes, 'Hiddenness of Wisdom'; Schäfer, *Hidden and Manifest God;* van der Woude, 'פנים', *THAT* 2:452.

[285] Balentine, *Hidden God,* 115.

[286] Ibid., 76–9.

[287] E.g., Deut. 31:17; Mic. 3:1–4; Isa. 59:1ff; Ezk. 39:24, cf. Gen. 3:8. See also Perlitt, 'Die Verborgenheit Gottes', 367–82; Balentine, *Hidden God,* 161.

accessible in his Son. However, while God has made himself known in the incarnation, yet this revelation is open only to those who receive it, and he continues to be hidden from those who reject him. This element of the concealment of revelation is present in the Synoptics as well in the form of Jesus' parabolic speech (e.g., Mk. 4:10–12).[288] However, even in the Synoptic parables, the concealment of revelation is not arbitrary; it follows rejection (Mk. 2:6–7; 3:5–6, 22–30) of open revelation (Mk. 1:14–15, 21–25, 34, 38–39; 2:1–12, 27–28). This is a point to which we must return.

In 12:31–36 at the close of his public ministry which has been characterised by the rejection and unbelief of 'the Jews', Jesus, having announced that the judgment of the world is at hand in view of the cross (12:32–33), once again invites 'the Jews' to walk and believe in the light: περιπατεῖτε ὡς τὸ φῶς ἔχετε...ὡς τὸ φῶς ἔχετε, πιστεύετε εἰς τὸ φῶς (12:35–36, cf. vv. 45, 46). But then the Evangelist writes, 'After Jesus had said these things, he departed and hid (ἀπελθὼν ἐκρύβη) from them' (12:36). The expression κρύπτω here is another example of Johannine conceptual double meaning. It seems to imply both the literal and figurative sense. Literally, it means 'hide', but figuratively it means 'withdraw from sight or knowledge'.[289] Its occurrence at this juncture, in the context of 12:37–38, and the use elsewhere of another double-meaning word, ὑπάγειν, 'to depart', 'to go away' (e.g. 14:4),[290] is significant in the broader context of the concealment motif when revelation is met with stubborn refusal to believe.[291] It also echoes the scriptural theme of God 'hiding his face' from the sin of rejection of his self-disclosure and disregard for the truth.[292] With this remark, the Fourth Evangelist brings to a close Jesus'

---

[288] But see Vincent Taylor, *The Gospel According to St. Mark* (London: Macmillan, 1952), 257; T. W. Manson, *The Teaching of Jesus* (Cambridge: CUP, 1931), 76; idem, 'The Purpose of the Parables: A Re-examination of St. Mark iv. 10–12', *ExpTim* 68 (1956–57), 133; Frederick C. Grant, *The Gospel According to St. Mark*, The Interpreter's Bible (Nashville: Abingdon Press, 1951), 7:700. Cf. Adolf Jülicher, *Die Gleichnisreden Jesu* (Tübingen: Mohr, 1910), 1:117.

[289] BAGD, 454. Note the ἐκρύβη in 12:36c is in 3rd pers. sing. 2 aor. pass. ind. The passive here has intransitive or reflexive force, hence 'he hid [himself] from them' rather than 'he *was* hidden from them.' The antonym of κρύπτω is φανερόω (7:10; cf. 7:4, 10; 8:59; 10:6).

[290] The verb ὑπάγω is often employed in contexts which elicit more than one meaning. On three occasions, it is used with the verb ζητέω ('seek') thereby introducing misunderstanding in each case. This is typical in the Fourth Gospel where the author uses ambiguous or double meaning words in contexts where a specific, technical or unambiguous expression could have been used.

[291] In 15:22–24, Jesus states that if he had not come and spoken to them or done signs among them (cf. 12:37), the works which none other did (cf. 9:32–33), they would have no sin (ἁμαρτίαν ἔχειν, 9:41; ἁμαρτίαν ἔχειν comes only at John 9:41; 15:22, 24; 19:11; 1 John 1:8), but in view of the words and the works (cf. 9:41), they have no excuse.

[292] E.g., Ps. 13:1; 55:1; 88:14; 89:46; Isa. 1:15; 8:17; 59:2; 64:7; cf. Ezekiel's account of departure of the Shekinah from the temple, 2:1–11:23.

public ministry and with it his open self-disclosure. This conclusion echoes Daniel 12: 'for the words are closed up and sealed till the time of the end. Many shall be purified, and made white, and tried; but the wicked shall do wickedly: and none of the wicked shall understand; but the wise shall understand' (Dan. 12:9–10, KJV).[293] In a similar sense, in John's record, the curtain of open revelation is drawn closed to the wicked who refuse to depart from their evil works and in their unbelief reject the saving revelation of God in his Son. Any further illumination comes only to those who are born from above.

The theme of the concealment of revelation in John's Gospel is not the same thing as the so-called Messianic secret in Mark[294] first proposed by William Wrede in 1901.[295] Scholars who suggest that the evangelists are concerned with the presentation of the 'hidden Messiah' find this idea attested in rabbinic writings[296] and especially in the Pseudepigrapha.[297] It is, however, doubtful whether the concealment motif in the Fourth Gospel and the Markan injunctions to secrecy,[298] which Wrede calls 'cryptic speech',[299] refer to the same phenomenon, in spite of the apparent similarities. Even the existence of such a Messianic secrecy motif in Mark is doubtful.[300] In John, to those who demand plain speech (10:24), Jesus

---

[293] See also Dan. 12:4, 8; cf. Zech. 13:9; Hos. 14:9; Jn. 8:47.

[294] For details of the hypothesis, see the collection of essays edited by Christopher Tuckett, *The Messianic Secret* (London: SPCK, 1983).

[295] *Das Messiasgeheimnis in den Evangelien*, ET: *The Messianic Secret*, Trans. by F. C. C. Greig (Cambridge: James Clarke, 1971), 145, 215ff.

[296] J. C. O'Neill, 'The Silence of Jesus', *NTS* (1969), 153–67.

[297] E.g., 2 Bar. 29:3; 39:7; 73:1; 4 Ezra 7:28; 12:32; 13:26, 32, 52; 14:9; 1 Enoch 48:6–7; 62:7). See *The Old Testament Pseudepigrapha*, ed. by Charlesworth. See also Charlesworth, 'The Concept of the Messiah in the Pseudepigrapha', *ANRW* II.19.1, 188–218; Schäfer, *Hidden and Manifest God*. See also those scholars who see similarities between certain themes in the Fourth Gospel (e.g., 'misunderstandings') and the Messianic secrecy motif in Mark. See D. A. Carson, *The Gospel According to John* (Grand Rapids: Eerdmans, 1991), 52; Brown, *John*, 1:313; Dodd, *Interpretation*, 89; Lindars, *John*, 293; Haenchen, *John*, 2:15–6; M. Hooker, 'The Johannine Prologue and the Messianic Secret', *NTS* 21 (1979), 43; Wrede, *Messianic Secret*, 182–207.

[298] J. Coutts, 'The Messianic Secret in St. John's Gospel', *SE* 3 = TU 88 (1964), 49 (43–57); cf. Georg Strecker, 'The Theory of the Messianic Secret in Mark's Gospel', in *The Messianic Secret*, ed. by Christopher Tuckett, 49–64.

[299] For examples of this cryptic speech, see Mk. 1:29–35, 43f; 3:12; 5:40, 43; 7:17, 36; 8:26, 30; 9:9; 10:10; cf. Lk. 4:31–37, 41; 5:12–16; 8:49–56; 9:18–22; Mt. 8:1–4; 12:15–21; 16:13–20; 17:9–13.

[300] See the criticism of Wrede's thesis by William Sanday, *The Life of Christ in Recent Research* (New York: OUP, 1908), 74. See also H. A. A. Kennedy, 'Book Review of *Das Messiasgeheimnis in den Evangelien*, by William Wrede', *The Critical Review of Theological and Philosophical Literature* 12 (1902), 339–44; A. C. Zenos, 'Book review of *Das Messiasgeheimnis in den Evangelien*, by William Wrede', *The American Journal of Theology* 6 (1902), 575–6; also

responds that he has been speaking plainly, but they have refused to believe (10:25). In the Fourth Gospel, from the beginning, the title Messiah and the Messianic identity of Jesus is a *public* subject of discussion.[301] The kingship of Jesus and his claim to be God are central points in his trial. Jesus openly proclaims his identity to his opponents (e.g., 5:19–47; 8:12–30; 18:20, 30–38). He consistently tries to draw attention to the fact that he is the promised anointed of the Lord. The concealment occurs when his claims are rejected. On each occasion of open revelation, that revelation is matched by equally vigorous denial and an effort to kill the revealer.[302] Even in Mark, Jesus' self-concealment is not arbitrary, as we have already seen. Jesus begins to speak in parables when his open self-disclosure (Mk. 1:14–15, 21–25, 34, 38–39; 2:1–12, 27–28) is met by rejection (2:6–7; 3:5–6, 22–30) and in the wake of the religious authorities' determination to destroy him.[303]

In the Fourth Gospel, however gifted and informed people may be, in their natural state confronted by revelation, they are unable to comprehend spiritual truth. Humans in their natural state cannot obey, understand or please God.[304] One must be born from God to understand the mind of God. The new birth is not a reformation of the old nature, but a creative act of the Spirit of God.[305] In the new birth from God, the believer becomes a partaker of the divine nature, the life of Christ,[306] and the Spirit of God, who makes meaningful the truth about God revealed in the Son. The perception of truth is denied to those who reject the truth. Unless one dies to oneself and is born from above, one cannot comprehend the revelation of God in Jesus or the Scriptures that speak of him. To be able to see and perceive the revelation, a decision must be made between safeguarding one's own earthly life by remaining 'of the world' (7:7; 8:23; 15:19; 12:25a) and accepting the offer of life in Christ (3:15, 16; 4:14; 5:24, etc.) at the expense

---

see J. D. Dunn, 'The Messianic Secret in Mark', in *The Messianic Secret*, ed. by C. Tuckett, 117–29. For a detailed survey of the theory see James L. Blevins, *The Messianic Secret in Markan Research 1901–1976* (Washington: University Press of America, 1981).

[301] See, for example, Jn. 1:20, 3:28; 4:25, 29; 7:25ff; 31ff; 40ff; 9:22; 10:24; 12:34.

[302] Jn. 10:30; 8:58; also 7:20, 29–30, 33–34, 37–38, 44; 8:12–13.

[303] See Robert H. Stein, *An Introduction to the Parables of Jesus* (Philadelphia: Westminster Press, 1981), 33–4; cf. Mk. 14:55–59.

[304] Jn. 3:3, 5, 6; cf. Ps. 51:5; Jer. 17:9; Mk. 7:21–23; 1 Cor. 2:14; Rom. 8:7, 8; Eph. 2:3; Mt. 6:33.

[305] Jn. 3:5; 1:12, 13; 2 Cor. 5:17; Eph. 2:10; 4:24.

[306] Cf. Gal. 2:20; Eph. 2:10; 4:24; Col. 1:27; 1 Pet. 1:23–25; 2 Pet. 1:4; 1 Jn. 5:10–12.

of abandonment by the world and the loss of the glory and security it offers (12:42–43; cf. 9:25–35; 15:18–20; 16:2).

The mission of Jesus is unique in that, due to his oneness with the Father, God becomes visible and accessible in him. To reject him is to reject the climactic self-revelation of God made available to humanity. The primary evidence for the authenticity of Jesus' mission as received from the Father is that he ultimately brings glory to the one who sent him (7:18) by revealing his name, i.e., the Father's person and work. Jesus in his 'exegesis' of God (1:18) is as truthful as God is, and God is described as ἀληθής (3:33; 8:26). Yet the comprehension of this truth is itself conditioned upon abiding faith rooted in the regenerating work of the Holy Spirit. This language is not comprehensible to the natural, unaided person, much less to those who actively reject it in unbelief. Only those who give up the offer of the praise of this world and take up their cross in quest of an honour greater than the world can ever offer will see God. In the Fourth Gospel, in order to grasp the true meaning of the climactic revelation of God in Jesus Christ and experience illumination – particularly the kind the Evangelist himself has experienced (and quite masterfully reflects in his own language) – the fundamental criterion is an abiding faith which coincides with a spiritual birth from above.[307] Such spiritual illumination, as revealed by the author in his own language, involves being able to see the witness and fulfilment of the Scriptures in Jesus' person and work. Those who deny that Jesus is the Christ do not comprehend the revelation because of their unbelief.

But what about those who believe and still find the language of the Johannine Jesus unclear? The language of the Fourth Gospel functions in two ways. For the Evangelist's Christian audience, the enigmatic language of the Gospel beckons them to delve deeper into the Scriptures, to examine them and see their witness to the Messiah and their fulfilment in him. For those who reject John's message, ambiguity serves as an indicator, if to no one else but the author himself, that those who do not understand are not of God. Thus Johannine language emphasises the need for revelation on the one hand, while on the other, it underlines that the understanding of revelation rests on spiritual regeneration leading to an abiding faith.

Readers of the Gospel on its own terms, in the first century or the twenty-first, when confronted with the question posed to Philip, 'From

---

[307] Cf. Jn. 1:12, 13; 3:3–6, 12; 7:24; 8:23, 27, 30–32, 43–47; 12:35–40; 14:6. See the emphasis elsewhere in the New Testament: 1 Cor. 2:14; Rom. 8:7–8; Eph. 2:3, 10; 4:24; Gal. 2:20; Col. 1:27; 1 Pet. 1:23–25; 2 Pet. 1:4; 1 Jn. 5:10–12.

that will feed these people?' (cf. 6:5) must respond with the only correct answer, 'the bread of life comes from heaven; Jesus *is* the true bread that comes down from heaven and gives real, sustaining life' (cf. 6:32–33). John confronts his timeless audience with the same question posed to the blind man, 'Do you believe in the Son of Man?' (9:35). The reaction and the nature of the response will determine whether the true light which shines upon everyone (1:9) has provoked enlightenment or incomprehension, revelation or concealment of Christ.

Chapter 7

Conclusion: The Enigmatic Language of the 'Spiritual Gospel'

> For the words are closed up
> and sealed till the time of the end.
> Many shall be purified, and made white, and tried;
> but the wicked shall do wickedly: and none of the wicked
> shall understand; but the wise shall understand. (Dan 12:9–10)

> While ye have light,
> believe in the light, that
> ye may be the children of light.
> These things spake Jesus, and departed,
> and did hide himself from them. (Jn. 12:36)

In this study I set out to explain the structure, function and significance of the enigmatic quality of the language of the Fourth Gospel within a theological framework. The elusive character of John's language has intrigued biblical scholars throughout the history of Johannine studies. Even today, when one reads the Gospel, while on the surface its language appears to be so familiar and its message so simple to grasp, upon careful examination its complexities gradually become evident.

In the process of setting forth my proposal, I have questioned a number of assumptions which undergird highly imaginative, theoretical explanations for the enigmatic quality of the language of the Fourth Gospel. Some have concluded that this stylistic feature is part of the symbolic world of John and have then proceeded with an allegorical interpretation of the Gospel. Others have thought that behind John's ambiguous expressions may lie Aramaisms of the hypothetical original document. This has never been definitely verified. Form-critically, the enigmatic character of this language has been explained in terms of 'parable' or 'riddle', even though this feature of Johannine language comprises a highly complex structure which cannot be defined adequately in such 'straight-jacket' form-critical categories. It is as much a literary matter as it is conceptual. The level of complexity escapes form-critical contours, and this Johannine feature is not compatible, form-critically, with either 'parable' or any of its derivatives such as 'riddle'. Literary critics have sought to explain John's language in terms of its reader-response or aesthetic effect. Sociologists and socio-linguists have attributed the enigmatic style of Johannine language to its being the private language of a sectarian community. Sociologists came under special criticism in this study since it seemed to me that they often either read their ideas into the text or simply allegorise the texts to fit their ideas.

I proposed to approach John's language from a theological angle. The justification for my method was based on the conviction that every category of literature has its own 'natural mode' of interpretation. To proceed otherwise endangers the integrity of the writings by inadvertently misrepresenting them, and such misrepresentation constitutes a perversion of their meaning. For the Bible, that 'natural interpretive mode' is theology (*hermeneutica sacra*). The Bible is a collection of religious and theological texts. They were written with an underlying theological objective. Therefore, theology is not simply one approach among many; rather, it seems to me, it is the only valid approach to these writings. And it must always remain the controlling factor when other methods and disciplines are utilised in their interpretation.

In so far as the Fourth Gospel is concerned, I further proposed to examine its language in the context of John's stated objective for writing the Gospel, namely, to set forth that Jesus is the Christ according to Israel's Scriptures. It was therefore important to establish the probable *context of thought* from which the text emerged. This conceptual context was deemed to have been within a Palestinian, Jewish setting, in an environment in which the Hebrew Scriptures were the dominant conceptual and literary force. It is to this context that the Gospel is inseparably fastened for any meaningful explication of its literary milieu, style, imagery and theology. In the analysis, I have endeavoured to show the extent to which the Fourth Gospel depends upon the Old Testament for the meaningful explication of its theological message. It is this complex linguistic-literary structure so thoroughly dependent upon the Scriptures which gives John's language its unique elusive quality. The various elements in the fabric of the Johannine allusions point beyond themselves to the themes and images within the Old Testament Scriptures. This is one reason why the language seems both familiar and unfamiliar – familiar because we recognise the echoes; unfamiliar because the Evangelist conflates various strands of these scriptural

Chapter 7: The Enigmatic Language of the 'Spiritual Gospel'

themes, ideas and motifs and recasts them in the light of his post-resurrection insight into Jesus as the Christ.

The primary aim of this feature is neither literary artistry, which of course is quite evident in the Gospel, nor the aesthetic impression upon the readers, which is beyond question. Rather, this phenomenon is wedded to John's purpose and steadfast focus on one issue: to set forth the basis upon which he believes that Jesus is the Christ – the one in whom God has climactically revealed himself; the one of whom the Scriptures speak, to whom the Scriptures point, and in whom the Scriptures find their realisation. Jesus of Nazareth, for the author of the Gospel, is the Jewish Messiah (1:41, 45), the Saviour of the world (4:42), whose birth, death, and resurrection are in precise fulfilment of the Scriptures (20:31). This proposition is systematically defended by John's appeal to the Scriptures. It is in these echoes and thematic allusions to the Scriptures, which John sees as realised in Jesus' life, that the primary answer to the function of John's allusive and elusive language lies.

The significance of this unique composition, on the other hand, is that for the Evangelist, the claim 'Jesus is the Christ' means that he is the embodiment of the self-manifestation of God and the climax of revelation. To see him is to see the face of God. But, this reality is ultimately beyond the limits of human language to capture and beyond the capacity of un-spiritual people to comprehend. The recognition of the self-disclosure of God in the Son of Man at the level of true perception belongs to those who are born of God and are inseparably grafted into 'the vine'. It is the Spirit of God who makes meaningful the revelation of God both in his written word (the Scriptures) and the living Word (the incarnate Son). He is the one who internally brings about illumination by his supernatural work within the believer-disciple.

In the historical context of the Gospel, where the claim that Jesus is the Christ would have been disputed or denied by some within the world of Judaism, any effort to respond apologetically would have had to rest on Israel's Scriptures. Jesus is the Christ, not because philosophically it can be proven according to Greek reasoning, nor necessarily because of his miraculous works, nor even because of the eye-witness testimony of those who had seen him. For John, above all else, Jesus is the Christ because Israel's Scriptures testify of him, point to him and find their supreme realisation in him. It is here that John's language is knitted to his christological purpose rooted in the Old Testament Scriptures. Saturated as it is with echoes and allusions to the Old Testament, John's Gospel consistently either seems unfamiliar even though we understand the words and relate to the images, or appears to point beyond itself. Until we have tuned in to the Evangelist's method and are on the same wavelength with him hermeneutically, making similar associations and seeing similar subtleties, his language is bound to remain strange to us.

But readers cannot share this hermeneutical horizon with John until they have met his fundamental prerequisite for illumination: only those 'who are of God hear God's words' (8:47; 18:37). For the Evangelist, true perception rests upon spiritual birth from God or regeneration (1:12–13), an unwavering resolute faith and a lifelong discipleship, something similar to his own experience. This regenerating work is part of the comprehensive activity of the Holy Spirit in the life of Jesus' followers in leading them into all truth.

Today's readers may disagree with John's method, question his creative exegesis, and even contest the validity and persuasiveness of his arguments in the light of current knowledge of first-century Judaism or other fields. However, cogent as such objections may be, they are of limited relevance once it is assumed that the obligation and responsibility of biblical scholars is to 'rightly divide the word of truth', that is, accurately to bring out John's method and message and meaning, not those of the current theological scene. According to this view, modern exegetes should faithfully reconstruct John's views from the document that lies before them and demonstrate that this reconstruction is faithful to the text and in harmony with its meaning. The text must be allowed to speak for itself; the meaning must emerge from the text rather than be read into it.

If this study has made any contribution in this respect, it has done so by anchoring John's Gospel and its intriguing language to the world of ideas rooted in Israel's Scriptures. Gnostic analogies and Hellenistic parallels do not do justice to the Fourth Evangelist. His Gospel and concepts are knitted to the ideas and images of the Old Testament world. If we are to interpret the Fourth Gospel correctly, John's absolute dependence upon the Old Testament must be one of our fundamental exegetical assumptions. Hence this study focuses attention upon John's use of the Old Testament as a means of understanding and explaining his ideas, and thus seeks to contribute both to Johannine exegesis and Johannine theology.

Bibliography

Aalen, S. 'Truth: A Key Word in St. John's Gospel', in *SE* 2 = TU 87 ed. by F. L. Cross (Berlin: Akademie-Verlag, 1964), 3–24.

Abbott, Edwin A. *Johannine Vocabulary* (London: Adam and Charles Black, 1905).

———. *Johannine Grammar* (London: Adam and Charles Black, 1906).

Abbott, Lyman, et al., eds. *The Bible as Literature* (New York: Thomas Y. Crowell, 1896).

Abbott-Smith, G. *A Manual Greek Lexicon of the New Testament*, 3rd edn (Edinburgh: Clark, 3rd edn, 1963).

Abegg, Martin C. 'The Messiah at Qumran: Are We Still Seeing Double?' *Dead Sea Discoveries* 2 (1995), 125–144.

Abraham, William J. 'Revelation Reaffirmed', pp. 201–215 in Paul Avis, ed., *Divine Revelation* (London: Darton, Longman and Todd, 1997).

Abrahams, I. *Studies in Pharisaism and the Gospels*, 2 vols (Cambridge: CUP, 1917; reprinted 1924).

———. *The Glory of God, Three Lectures* (Oxford: OUP, 1925).

Abrams, M. H. *A Glossary of Literary Terms*, 3rd edn (New York: Holt, Rinehart, and Winston, 1970).

Achtemeier, Paul J. 'Essays on Bible and Theology', *Interpretation* 42 (1988), 226–280.

———. '*Omne verbum sonat:* The New Testament and the Oral Environment of Late Western Antiquity', *JBL* 109 (1990), 3–27.

Ackerman, James S. 'The Rabbinic Interpretation of Ps. 82 and the Gospel of John', *HTR* 59 (1966), 186–88.

Ackroyd, Peter R. *The Second Book of Samuel* (Cambridge: CUP, 1977).

———. *Israel under Babylon and Persia* (London: OUP, 1970).

Adamo, D. T. 'Sin in John's Gospel', *Evangelical Review of Theology* 13 (1989), 216–227.

Aland, Barbara, ed. *Gnosis: Festschrift für Hans Jonas* (Göttingen: Vandenhoeck und Ruprecht, 1978).

Aland, K. 'Eine Untersuchung zu Joh I.3, 4: Über die Bedeutung eines Punktes', *ZNW* 59 (1968), 174–209.

Albrecht, E. *Zeugnis durch Wort und Verhalten. Untersucht an ausgewählten Texten des Neuen Testaments* (Basel: F. Reinhardt, 1977).

Albrektson, Bertil. *History and the Gods: An Essay on the Idea of Historical Events as Divine Manifestations in the Ancient Near East and in Israel* (Lund, Sweden: CWK Gleerup 1967).

Alexander, Philip S. '"The Parting of the Ways" from the Perspective of Rabbinic Judaism', pp. 1–25 in J. D. G. Dunn, ed., *Jews and Christians: The Parting of the Ways AD 70 to 135*, WUNT 66 (Tübingen: Mohr-Siebeck, 1993).

———. 'Rabbinic Judaism and the New Testament', *ZNW* 74 (1983), 237–246.

Allegro, J. M. 'Further Messianic References in Qumran Literature', *JBL* 75 (1956), 174–187.

Allenbach, J. *Biblia Patristica: Index des citations et allusions bibliques dans la littérature patristique* (Paris: Editions du Centre National de la Recherche Scientifique, 1975).

Allis, O. T. 'The Alleged Aramaic Origin of the Fourth Gospel', *Princeton Theological Review* 26 (1928), 531–582.

Alon, G. *The Jews in their Land in the Talmudic Age* (Jerusalem: Magnes, 1980).

Alston, William. *Philosophy of Language* (Englewood Cliffs, NJ: Prentice Hall, 1964).

Alter, Robert. *The Art of Biblical Narrative* (London: George Allen and Unwin, 1981).

Amante, J. D. 'Ironic Language: A Structuralist Approach', *Language and Style* 13 (1980), 15–25.

Amsler, S. *L'ancien testament dans l'église: Essai d'herméneutique chrétienne* (Neuchatel: Delachaux and Niestlé, 1960).

Anderson, B. W. and W. Harrelson, eds, *Israel's Prophetic Heritage* (London: SCM, 1962).

Anderson, H. *The Gospel of Mark* (London: Oliphants, 1976).

Anderson, Paul N. *The Christology of the Fourth Gospel: Its Unity and Disunity in the Light of John 6*, WUNT 2.78 (Tübingen: Mohr-Siebeck, 1996).

Appold, M. L. *The Oneness Motif in the Fourth Gospel: Motif Analysis and Exegetical Probe into the Theology of John*, WUNT 2.1 (Tübingen: Mohr-Siebeck, 1976).

Apresjan, J. D. 'Regular Polysemy', *Linguistics* 142 (1974), 5–32.

Argyle, A. W. 'Fruitfulness through Death (John 12:24)', *ExpTim* 89 (1977–78), 149.

Arichea, D. D., Jr. 'Translating "Believe" in the Gospel of John', *Bible Translator* 30 (1979), 205–209.

Aristotle. *The 'Art' of Rhetoric*, ET by J. H. Freese, Loeb Classical Library 193 (London: Heinemann, 1926).

———. *The Poetics*, ET by W. H. Fyfe, LCL 199 (London: Heinemann, 1927).

Arrington, Mark. 'The Identification of the Anonymous Servant in Isaiah 40–55' (Thesis, Dallas: Dallas Seminary, 1971).

Ashton, John. 'The Identity and Function of the Ἰουδαῖοι in the Fourth Gospel', *NovT* 27 (1985), 40–75.

———. *The Interpretation of John* (Philadelphia: Fortress Press, 1986).

———. 'The Transformation of Wisdom: A Study of the Prologue of John's Gospel', *NTS* 32 (1986), 161–186.

———. *Understanding the Fourth Gospel* (Oxford: Clarendon Press, 1991).

———. *Studying John: Approaches to the Fourth Gospel* (Oxford: Clarendon Press, 1994).

Atkins, I. W. H. *Literary Criticism in Antiquity*, 2 vols (Cambridge: CUP, 1934).

Attridge, Harold W. 'Thematic Development and Source Elaboration in John 7:1–36', *CBQ* 42 (1980), 160–170.

Augenstein, Jörg. *Das Liebesgebot im Johannesevangelium und in Den Johannesbriefen* (Stuttgart: Kohlhammer, 1993).

Aune, D. E. *The Cultic Setting of Realized Eschatology in Early Christianity* (Leiden: Brill, 1972).

Ayala, M. 'El Evangelio de San Juan: su forma literaria', *RevEcl* 24 (1920, 2), 288-291; 331-335.

Baasland, Ernst. 'Urkristendommen i sosiologiens lys', *Tidskrift for Teologi og Kirke* 54 (1984), 45-57.

Bacon, Benjamin Wisner. *The Gospel of the Hellenists* (New York: Holt, 1933).

———. *The Fourth Gospel in Research and Debate* (New Haven, CT: Yale University Press, 1918).

———. 'The Sacrament of Foot Washing', *ExpTim* 43 (1931-32), 218-221.

Bailey, Daniel P. 'Jesus as the Mercy Seat: The Semantics and Theology of Paul's Use of *Hilasterion* in Romans 3:25' (Ph.D. Dissertation, University of Cambridge, 1999).

———. 'Jesus as the Mercy Seat: The Semantics and Theology of Paul's Use of *Hilasterion* in Romans 3:25' [dissertation abstract], *TynBul* 51.1 (2000), 155-158.

Bailey, J. A. *The Traditions Common to the Gospel of Luke and John*, NovTSup 7 (Leiden: Brill, 1963).

Baillie, John. *The Idea of Revelation in Recent Thought* (New York: Columbia University Press, 1956).

Baker, A. E. 'The Parables and the Johannine Problem', *Exp* 48 v. 8 s. 24 (1922, 2), 305-315.

Bal, Mieke. 'The Bible as Literature: A Critical Escape', *Diacritics* 16 (1976), 71-79.

Baldensperger, W. *Der Prolog des vierten Evangeliums: Sein polemisch-apologetischer Zweck* (Tübingen: Mohr, 1898).

Balentine, Samuel E. *The Hidden God: The Hiding of the Face of God in the Old Testament* (Oxford: OUP, 1983).

Ball, David M. *'I Am' in John's Gospel: Literary Function, Background and Theological Implications* (Sheffield: Sheffield Academic Press, 1996).

von Balthasar, Hans Urs. *The Glory of the Lord: A Theological Aesthetic*, 3 vols, ET by E. L. Merikakis, *Seeing the Form*, vol. 1 (Edinburgh: Clark, 1982).

Baltz, F. W. *Lazarus and the Fourth Gospel Community* (Lewiston, NY: Mellen, 1996).

Balz, H. R. *Methodische Probleme der neutestamentlichen Christologie*, WMANT 25 (Neukirchen-Vluyn: Neukirchener Verlag, 1967).

Bammel, E. '"John did no miracle": John 10:41', pp. 179-202 in C. F. D. Moule, ed., *Miracles. Cambridge Studies in Their Philosophy and History* (London: Mowbray, 1965).

———. 'Christian Origins in Jewish Tradition', *NTS* 13 (1967), 317-335.

———, ed. *The Trial of Jesus. Cambridge Studies in Honour of C. F. D. Moule*, Studies in Biblical Theology II. 13 (London: SCM, 1970).

———. 'Joh. 7:35 in Manis Lebensbeschreibung', *NovT* 15 (1973), 191-192.

Bampfylde, G. D. 'Old Testament Quotations and Imagery in the Gospel According to St. John' (Ph.D. diss., Hull University, 1967).

Banks, R. J., ed. *Reconciliation and Hope: New Testament Essays on Atonement and Eschatology* (Grand Rapids: Eerdmans, 1974).

Barber, Cyril J. 'Theology of the Resurrection in John's Gospel' (Thesis, Dallas Seminary, 1967).

―――. 'Some Observations on the Analysis of Structure in Biblical Narrative', *VT* 30 (1980), 154–173.

Bar-Efrat, Shimon. *Narrative Art in the Bible* (Sheffield, England: Almond Press, 1989).

Barclay, John M. G. 'Mirror-Reading a Polemical Letter: Galatians as Test Case', *JSNT* 31 (1987), 73–93.

Barfield, Owen. *Saving the Appearances: A Study in Idolatry* (London: Faber and Faber, 1957).

―――. 'The Meaning of the Word "Literal"', pp. 48–63 in L. C. Knights and Basil Cottle, eds, *Metaphor and Symbol* (London: Butterworths Scientific Publications, 1960).

Barlow, J. R. '"Truth" in John's Gospel' (Thesis, Dallas Seminary, 1971).

Baron, David. *Rays of Messiah's Glory: Christ in the Old Testament* (n.p., 1886).

Barr, James. *The Semantics of Biblical Language* (Oxford: OUP, 1961).

―――. 'Revelation Through History in the Old Testament and in Modern Theology', *Interpretation* 17 (1963), 193–205.

―――. 'Messiah', pp. 646–655 in F. C. Grant and H. H. Rowley, eds, *Hastings' Dictionary of the Bible* (Edinburgh: Clark, 1963).

―――. *Comparative Philology and the Text of the Old Testament* (Oxford: Clarendon Press, 1968).

―――. *The Bible in the Modern World* (London: SCM/ New York: Harper and Row, 1973).

―――. 'Reading the Bible as Literature', *BJRL* 56 (1973), 10–33.

―――. 'Language and Meaning: Studies in Hebrew Language and Biblical Exegesis', *Oudtestamentisch Studien* 19 (Papers read at the Joint British-Dutch Old Testament Conference: London, 1973).

Barrett, C. K. 'The Old Testament in the Fourth Gospel', *JTS* 48 (1947), 155–169.

―――. *Holy Spirit and the Gospel Tradition* (London: SPCK, 1947, 2nd edn, 1966)

―――. 'The Lamb of God', *NTS* 1 (1954–55), 210–218.

―――. *The New Testament Background: Selected Documents* (London: SPCK, 1961).

―――. 'The Interpretation of the Old Testament in the New', pp. 377–411 in P. R. Ackroyd and C. F. Evans, eds, *The Cambridge History of the Bible: From the Beginning to Jerome*, vol. 1 (Cambridge: CUP, 1970).

―――. *Das Johannesevangelium und das Judentum*, Franz Delitzsch-Vorlesungen 1967 (Stuttgart, Berlin: W. Kohlhammer, 1970). ET by D. M. Smith, *The Gospel of John and Judaism: The Franz Delitzsch Lectures, University of Münster, 1967* (London: SPCK, 1975).

―――. Review of Fortna, *Gospel of Signs*, *JTS* n.s. 22 (1971), 571–574.

―――. 'The Dialectical Theology of St. John', pp. 49–69 in idem, *New Testament Essays* (London: SPCK, 1975).

―――. 'John and Synoptic Gospels', *ExpTim* 85 (1973–74), 228–233.

―――. *The Gospel according to St. John: An Introduction with Commentary and Notes on the Greek Text*, 2nd edn (London: SPCK, 1976; Philadelphia: Westminster, 1978 [1955]).

―――. *The Gospel of John and Judaism* (London: SPCK, 1978).

―――. *Essays on John* (London: SPCK, 1982; Philadelphia: Westminster, 1982).

——. '"The Father is Greater than I" (Jn. 14:28) Subordinationist Christology in the New Testament', pp. 19-36 in idem, *Essays on John*.

Barrosse, Thomas. 'The Seven Days of the New Creation in St. John's Gospel', *CBQ* 21 (1958), 507-516.

——. 'The Relationship of Love to Faith in St. John', *TS* 18 (1957), 538-559.

Barth, M. *Die Taufe, ein Sakrament? Ein exegetischer Beitrag zum Gespräch über die Kirchliche Taufe* (Zürich: Theologischer Verlag, 1951).

Barthes, Roland. 'Theory of the Text', pp. 31-47 in R. Young, ed., *Untying the Text: A Post-Structuralist Reader* (Boston: Routledge and Kegan Paul, 1981).

——. 'The Death of the Author', pp. 142-148 in idem, *Image, Music, Text*, ET by S. Heath (New York: Hill and Wang, 1977).

Bartholomew, G. L. 'An Early Christian Sermon-Drama: John 8:31-59' (Ph.D. diss., Union Theological Seminary, 1974).

——. 'Feed my Lambs: John 21:15-19 as Oral Gospel', *Semeia* 39 (1987), 69-96.

Barton, John. *The Oracles of God: Perceptions of Ancient Prophecy in Israel After the Exile* (London: Darton, Longman and Todd, 1986).

——. 'The Messiah in the Old Testament Theology', pp. 365-379 in John Day, ed., *King and Messiah in Israel and the Ancient Near East*, JSOTSup 270 (Sheffield: Sheffield Academic Press, 1998).

Barton, M. *Character Portrayal in the Novel: An Analysis of Flat Characterization* (Ann Arbor: Univ. Microfilms, 1975).

Barton, Stephen C. 'Can We Identify the Gospel Audiences?' pp. 173-194 in Richard Bauckham, ed., *The Gospels for All Christians: Rethinking the Gospel Audiences* (Grand Rapids, MI: Eerdmans, 1998).

——. 'The Communal Dimension of the Earliest Christianity', *JTS* n.s. 43 (1992), 399-427.

Bassler, J. M. 'Mixed Signals: Nicodemus in the Fourth Gospel', *JBL* 108 (1989), 635-646.

Batey, R. A. *New Testament Nuptial Imagery* (Leiden: Brill, 1972).

Bathke, Warren E. *The Titles of Christ in the Gospel of John* (Thesis, Dallas Seminary, 1957).

Bauckham, R. 'The Beloved Disciple as Ideal Author', *JNST* 49 (1993), 21-44.

——. 'The *Apocalypse of Peter*: A Jewish Christian Apocalypse from the Time of Bar Kokhba', *Apocrypha* 5 (1994), 87-90.

——. 'Papias and Polycrates on the Origin of the Fourth Gospel', *JTS* n.s. 44 (1993), 24-69.

——. 'For Whom Were Gospels Written?', pp. 9-48 in Richard Bauckham, ed., *The Gospels for All Christians: Rethinking the Gospel Audiences* (Grand Rapids: Eerdmans, 1998).

Bauer, B. 'Die messianischen Erwartungen der Juden zur Zeit Jesu', pp. 491-516 in B. Bauer, ed., *Kritik der evangelischen Geschichte der Synoptiker* I (Leipzig: Hinrichs, 1841).

Bauer, Walter. *Das Leben Jesu im Zeitalter der neutestamentlichen Apokryphen* (Tübingen: Mohr-Siebeck, 1909).

——. 'Johannesevangelium und Johannesbriefe', *TRu* 1 (1929), 135-160.

———. *Das Johannesevangelium erklärt*, HNT 6 (Tübingen: Mohr-Siebeck, 1912, 3rd edn, 1933).

———. *A Greek-English Lexicon of the New Testament and Other Early Christian Literature*, rev. and augmented by F. Wilbur Gingrich and Frederick W. Danker (Chicago: University of Chicago Press, 1979).

Baur, F. C. *Kritische Untersuchungen über die Kanonischen Evangelien, ihr Verhältnis zu einander, ihren Charakter und Ursprung* (Tübingen: Fues, 1847).

———. *Vorlesungen über neutestamentliche Theologie*, ed. by F. F. Baur (Darmstadt: Wissenschaftliche Buchgesellschaft, 1973, Leipzig, 1864).

Baum, Gregory. *Is the New Testament Anti-Semitic?* (New York: Paulist, 1965).

Baumbach, G. 'Gemeinde und Welt im Johannesevangelium', *Kairos* 14 (1972), 121–136.

Beardslee, William. *Literary Criticism of the New Testament* (Philadelphia: Fortress Press, 1970).

———. 'Amos Niven Wilder: Poet and Scholar', *Semeia* 12 (1978), 8–9.

Beardsley, Monroe. 'The Metaphorical Twist', *Philosophy and Phenomenological Research* 22 (1962), 293–307.

———. *Aesthetics: Problems in the Philosophy of Criticism* (New York: Harcourt, Brace, 1958).

Beasley-Murray, George R. *John*, WBC, vol. 36 (Waco, TX: Word Publisher, 1987).

Beauvery, R. 'Le Fils de Joseph! Manne Descendue du Ciel?' *Assemblés du Seigneur* 50 (1974), 43–49.

Beck, D. R. *The Discipleship Paradigm: Readers and Anonymous Characters in the Fourth Gospel* (Leiden: Brill, 1997).

Becker, H. *Der Kosmische Rhythmus der Sternenschrift im Markus-Ev. u. im Johannes-Evangelium* (Basel: Geering, 1930).

———. *Der Kosmische Rhythmus*. Vol. 2. *Das Sternengeheimnis und das Erdengeheimnis im Johannes-Evangelium* (Basel: Geering, 1930).

Becker, Joachim. *Messiaserwartung im Alten Testament*, ET by David E. Green, *Messianic Expectation in the Old Testament*. (Philadelphia: Fortress Press, 1980).

Becker, Jürgen. *Das Heil Gottes: Heils und Sündenbegriffe in den Qumrantexten und im Neuen Testament*, SUNT 3 (Göttingen: Vandenhoeck & Ruprecht, 1964).

———. 'Aufbau, Schichtung und theologiegeschichtliche Stellung des Gebetes in Johannes 17', *ZNW* 60 (1969), 56–82.

———. 'Wunder und Christologie: Zum literarkritischen und christologischen Problem der Wunder im Johannesevangelium', *NTS* 16 (1969–70), 130–148.

———. 'Die Abschiedsreden Jesu im Johannesevangelium', *ZNW* 61 (1970), 215–246.

———. 'Beobachtungen zum Dualismus im Johannesevangelium', *ZNW* 65 (1974), 71–87.

———. 'Aus der Literatur zum Johannesevangelium (1978–1980)', *ThR* 47 (1982), 279–301, 305–347.

———. 'Die Geschichte der johanneischen Gemeinden', *ThRund* 47 (1982), 305–12.

———. 'Jn 3, 1–21 als Reflex johanneischer Schuldiskussion', pp. 85–95 in H. Balz and S. Schulz, eds., *Das Wort und die Wörter: FS für Gerhard Friedrich zum 65 Geburtstag* (Stuttgart: W. Kohlhammer, 1983).

———. 'Ich bin die Auferstehung und das Leben', *TZ* 39 (1983), 136–151.
———. *Das Evangelium des Johannes*. Bd. 1, Kapitel 1–10. 2. Aufl. Ökumenischer Taschenbuchkommentar zum Neuen Testament, Bd. 4/1 (Gütersloh: Gerd Mohn, 1985, 1979), Bd. 2, Kapitel 11–21. 2. Aufl. Ökumenischer Taschenbuchkommentar zum Neuen Testament, Bd. 4/2 (Gütersloh: Gerd Mohn, 1984, 1981).
———. 'Das Johannesevangelium im Streit der Methoden (1980–1984)', *ThR* 51 (1986), 1–78.
———. *Jesus von Nazaret* (Berlin and New York: de Gruyter, 1996).
Becker, U. *Jesus und die Ehebrecherin: Untersuchungen zur Text- und Überlieferungsgeschichte von Jon 7:53–8:11*, BZNW 28 (Berlin: Töpelmann, 1963).
Beekman, J. and J. Callow. *Translating the Word of God* (Grand Rapids: Zondervan, 1974).
Behler, G. M. *Les Paroles d'Adieux du Seigneur* (Paris: Cerf, 1960).
Behm, J. 'νοέω', *TDNT* 4 (1967), 950.
Bell, H. I. 'Search the Scriptures (Joh 5,39)', *ZNW* 37 (1938), 10–13.
van Belle, Gilbert. *Les parenthèses dans l'évangile de Jean. Aperçu historique et classification: Texte grec de Jean*, Studiorum Novi Testamenti Auxilia 11 (Leuven: Leuven University Press, 1985).
———. *Johannine Bibliography 1966–1985* (Leuven: Leuven University Press, 1988).
———. *The Sign Source in the Fourth Gospel: Historical Survey and Critical Evaluation of the Semeia Hypothesis* (Leuven: Leuven University Press, 1994).
Belleville, Linda. 'Born of Water and Spirit', *Trinity Journal* 1 (1980), 125–34.
Belser, J. E. *Das Evangelium des Heiligen Johannes* (Freiburg: Herder, 1905).
Beltz, W. 'Zum Geschichtsbild der Gnosis', *ZRGG* 40 (1988), 362–366.
Ben-Porat, Ziva. 'The Poetics of Allusion' (Ph.D. diss., Berkeley: University of California, 1973).
———. 'The Poetics of Literary Allusion', *PTL: A Journal for Descriptive Poetics and Theory of Literature* 1 (1976), 105–128.
Bennett, J. R. 'A Stylistics Check List: IV', *Style* 17 (1983), 429–453.
Berger, D. *The Jewish-Christian Debate in the High Middle Ages: a Critical Edition of the Nizzahon Vetus, with an introduction, translation and commentary* (Philadelphia: Fortress, 1979).
———. 'Mission to the Jews and Jewish-Christian Contrasts in the Polemical Literature of the High Middle Ages', *American Historical Review* 91 (1986), 576–91.
Berger, Klaus. *Exegese des Neuen Testaments: Neue Wege vom Text zur Auslegun* (Heidelberg: Quelle and Meyer, 1977).
———. 'Wissenssoziologie und Exegese des Neuen Testaments', *Kairos* 19 (1977), 124–133.
———. *Im Anfang war Johannes. Datierung und Theologie des vierten Evangeliums* (Stuttgart: Quell, 1997).
Berger, Peter L. 'The Sociological Study of Sectarianism', *Social Research* 21 (1954), 467–485.
——— and Thomas Luckmann. *The Social Construction of Reality: A Treatise in the Sociology of Knowledge* (Harmondsworth: Penguin, 1967).

—— and Hansfried Kellner. *Sociology Reinterpreted: An Essay on Method and Vocation* (Harmondsworth: Penguin, 1982).

Bergmann, J. *Jüdische Apologetik im neutestamentlichen Zeitalter* (Berlin: Reimer, 1908).

Bergmeier, Roland. *Glaube als Gabe nach Johannes* (Stuttgart: Kohlhammer, 1980).

Berkey, Robert F. 'ΕΓΓΙΖΕΙΝ, ΦΘΑΝΕΙΝ, and Realized Eschatology', *JBL* 82 (1963), 177-187.

Berkhof, Louis. *Principles of Biblical Interpretation* (Grand Rapids: Baker Book House, 1950).

Berlin, A. 'Grammatical Aspects of Biblical Parallelism', *HUCA* 50 (1979), 17-43.

Bernabé, C. 'Transfondo derásico de Jn 20', *Estudios Bíblicos* 49 (1991), 209-228.

Bernard, J. 'Témoinage pour Jésus-Christ: Jean 5.31-47', *Mélanges de Science Religieuse* 36 (1979), 3-55.

Bernard, J. H. *A Critical and Exegetical Commentary on the Gospel According to St. John*, ICC, 2 vols (Edinburgh: Clark, 1928).

Berquist, J. L. *Judaism in Persia's Shadow* (Minneapolis: Fortress Press, 1995).

Bertram, G. 'ὕψος, κτλ.', *TDNT* 8 (1972), 602-620.

Best, E. *Following Jesus*, JSNTSup 4 (Sheffield: JSOT, 1981).

Best, Thomas F. 'The Sociological Study of New Testament: Promise and Peril of a New Discipline', *SJT* 36 (1983), 181-194.

Betz, H. D. 'Zum problem des religionsgeschichtlichen Verständnisses der Apokalyptik', *ZTK* 63 (1966), 391-409.

Betz, Otto. *Offenbarung und Schriftforschung in der Qumransekte* (Tübingen: Mohr-Siebeck, 1960).

——. *Der Paraklet: Fürsprecher im häretischen Spätjudentum, im Johannesevangelium und in neu gefundenen gnostischen Schriften*, AGJU 2 (Leiden: Brill, 1963).

——. '"Kann denn aus Nazareth etwas Gutes kommen?" (Zur Verwendung von Jesaja Kap. 11 in Johannes Kap. 1)', pp. 9-16 in H. Gese and H. P. Rüger, eds, *Wort und Geschichte: Festschrift für Karl Elliger zum 70. Geburtstag*, AOAT 18 (Kever: Butzon und Bercker; Neukirchen-Vluyn: Neukirchner Verlag, 1973).

——. '"To Worship God in Spirit and in Truth": Reflections on John 4:20-26', pp. 53-72 in A. Finkel and R. Frizzel, eds, *Standing Before God*, ET of German (New York: Ktav, 1981).

——. *Jesus: der Messias Israel: Aufsätze zur biblischen Theologie*, WUNT 42 (Tübingen: Mohr-Siebeck, 1987).

——. 'Zum Geschichtsbild der Gnosis', *ZRGG* 40 (1988), 362-366.

Beutler, J. *Martyria: Traditionsgeschichtliche Untersuchungen zum Zeugnisthema bei Johannes*, FTS 10 (Frankfurt: Joseph Knecht, 1972).

——. 'Glaube und Zeugnis im Johannesevangelium', *Bijdragen* 34 (1973), 60-68.

——. *Literarische Gattungen im Johannesevangelium. Ein Forschungsbericht 1919-1980*. ANRW II, 25/3 (1985), 2506-2568.

—— and R. T. Fortna, eds. *The Shepherd Discourse of John 10 and its Context: Studies by Members of Johannine Writings Seminar*, SNTSMS 67 (Cambridge: CUP, 1991).

Beyer, Klaus. *Semitische Syntax im Neuen Testament*, vol. 1,1: *Satzlehre*, SUNT 1 (Göttingen: Vandenhoeck und Ruprecht, 1962 and 1968).

Bianchi, Ugo. *La Doctrine Zarathustrienne des Deux Esprits: Selected Essays on Gnosticism, Dualism and Mysteriosophy* (Leiden: Brill, 1978).

Bieder, Werner. *Gottes Sendung und der missionarische Auftrag nach Matthäus, Lukas, Paulus und Johannes*, Theologische Studien 82 (Zürich: EVZ-Verlag, 1965).

Billings, J. S. 'Judas Iscariot in the Fourth Gospel', *ExpTim* 51 (1939), 40.

Bittner, Wolfgang J. *Jesus Zeichen im Johannesevangelium: Die Messias-Erkenntnis im Johannesevangelium vor ihrem jüdischen Hintergrund*, WUNT 2.26 (Tübingen: Mohr-Siebeck, 1987).

Black, D. A. 'The Text of John 3:13', *Grace Theological Journal* 6 (1985), 49–66.

——. 'On the Style and Significance of John 17', *Criswell Theological Review* 3 (1988), 141–59.

Black, Matthew. 'The Parables as Allegory', *BJRL* 42 (1959–60), 273–287.

——. *An Aramaic Approach to the Gospels and Acts* (Oxford: Clarendon Press, 3rd edn, 1967).

——. 'The Christological Use of the Old Testament in the New Testament', *NTS* 18 (1971), 1–14.

——. 'The Theological Appropriation of the Old Testament by the New Testament', *SJT* 39 (1986), 1–17.

——. and William Smalley, eds, *On Language, Culture and Religion: In honor of Eugene A. Nida* (The Hague, Paris: Mouton, 1974).

——. 'The Biblical Languages', in *Cambridge History of the Bible* (Cambridge: CUP, 1970), 1:1–11.

Black, Max. 'More about Metaphor', pp. 19–43 in Andrew Ortony, ed., *Metaphor and Thought* (Cambridge: CUP, 1979).

——. *Models and Metaphors* (Ithaca, NY: Cornell University Press, 1962).

Blackwelder, Boyce W. *Light From the Greek New Testament* (Anderson, IN: Warner Press, 1958).

Blanc, Cecile. *Origène: Commentaire au Saint Jean*, 5 vols (Paris: Éditions du Cerf, 1970).

Blank, Joseph. *Krisis: Untersuchungen zur Johanneischen Christologie und Eschatologie* (Freiburg: Lambertus, 1964).

——. *Das Evangelium nach Johannes*, Geistliche Schriftlesung, 4 vols (Düsseldorf: Patmos, 1977–81).

Blank, Sheldon. *Prophetic Faith in Isaiah* (New York: Scribner's, 1958).

——. 'Irony by Way of Attributions', *Semitics* 1 (1970), 1–6.

Blass, F. and Debrunner, A. *A Greek Grammar of the New Testament and Other Early Christian Literature*, trans. and rev. by Robert W. Funk (Chicago: University of Chicago Press, 1967).

Blau, L. *Das altjüdische Zauberwesen* (Leipzig: E. Pfeiffer, 1898).

Blenkinsopp, J. 'John 7:37–39: Another Note on a Notorious Crux', *NTS* 6 (1959), 95–99.

Blevins, James L. *The Messianic Secret in Markan Research 1901–1976* (Washington: University Press of America, 1981).

Bligh, John. 'Four Studies in St. John: I, the Man Born Blind', *HeyJ* 7 (1966), 129–144.

Bloch, Renée. 'Midrash', vol. 5, cols 1263–1281 in l. Pirot, A. Robert, and H. Cazelles, eds., *Supplément au Dictionnaire de la Bible* (DBSup). ET 'Midrash', pp. 29–50 in W. S. Green, ed., *Approaches to Ancient Judaism I*, BJS 1 (Missoula, MT: Scholars Press, 1978).

Bloom, Harold. *The Anxiety of Influence: A Theory of Poetry* (New York: OUP, 1973).

——. '"Before Moses was, I Am": The Original and Belated Testaments', *Notebooks in Cultural Analysis: An Annual Review* 1 (1984), 3–14.

——. 'Literature as the Bible', *New York Reviews of Books* 35 (1988), 23–25.

Bloomfield, Leonard. *Language* (New York: Henry Holt, 1933; London: George Allen and Unwin, 1935).

Blumenthal, M. 'Die Eigenart des johann. Erzählungsstiles', *TSK* 106 (1934–1935), 204–212.

Böcher, Otto. *Der Johanneische Dualismus in Zusammenhang des nachbiblischen Judentums* (Gütersloh: Mohn, 1965).

Bockmuehl, Markus N. A. *Revelation and Mystery in Ancient Judaism and Pauline Christianity* (Tübingen: Mohr-Siebeck, 1990).

de Boer, Martinus C., ed. *From Jesus to John: Essays on Jesus and New Testament Christology in Honour of Marinus de Jonge*, JSNTS 84 (Sheffield: Sheffield Academic Press, 1993).

——. *Johannine Perspectives on the Death of Jesus* (The Netherlands: Kok Pharos, 1996).

Boers, Hendrikus. 'Discourse Structure and Macro-Structure in the Interpretation of Texts: Jn. 4:1–42 as an Example', pp. 159–182 in Paul J. Achtemeier, ed., *Society of Biblical Literature 1980 Seminar Papers*, SBLSP 19 (Chico, CA: Scholars Press, 1980).

——. *Neither on this Mountain nor in Jerusalem: A Study of John 4*, SBLMS 35 (Atlanta, GA: Scholars Press, 1981, 1988).

Bogart, J. *Orthodox and Heretical Perfectionism in the Johannine Community as Evident in the First Epistle of John*, SBLDS 33 (Missoula, MT: Scholars Press, 1977).

Böhlig, Alexander. *Mysterion und Wahrheit* (Leiden: Brill, 1968).

——. *Gnosis und Synkretismus*, WUNT 47 und 48, Teil 1 und 2 (Tübingen: Mohr-Siebeck, 1989).

——. 'Zum Selbstverständnis Des Manichäismus', pp. 317–38 in W. Sundermann, et al., eds, *A Green Leaf: Papers in Honour of Professor Jes P. Asmussen*, Acta Iranica 28, vol. 12 (Leiden: Brill, 1988).

Boice, James M. *The Idea of Witness in the Gospel of John* (Ph.D. diss. Basel, 1966).

Boismard, M. É. *L'Evangile de Jean: Études et Problèmes* (Louvain: Descleé de Brouwer, 1958).

——. 'L'Evolution du thème eschatologique dans les traditions johanniques', *RB* 68 (1961), 507–524.

——. 'La royauté universelle du Christ', *Assemblées du Seigneur* 88 (1966), 33–45.

—— and A. Lamouille. *Synopse des Quatre Évangiles en francais III. L' Évangile de Jean* (Paris: Éditions de Cerf, 1977).

——. *Moïse ou Jésus: Essai de christologie johannique*, BETL 84 (Leuven: Leuven University and Peeters, 1988). ET by B. T. Viviano. *Moses or Jesus: An Essay in Johannine Christology* (Leuven: Leuven University Press, 1993).

Bonneau, Normand R. 'The Woman at the Well: John 4 and Gen. 24', *The Bible Today* 67 (1973), 1252–59.

Bonsall, H. B. *The Son of God and the Word of God in the Setting of John's Gospel* (London: Christian Literature Crusade, 1982 [1972]).

Bonsirven, Joseph. *Le Judaisme Palestinien au temps de Jésus-Christ*, 2 vols, Bibliothèque de Théologie historique (Paris: G. Beauchesne, 1934–35).

——. *Exégèse Rabbinique et Exégèse Paulinienne*, Bibliothèque de Théologie historique (Paris: G. Beauchesne, 1939).

——. 'Les Aramaïsmes de S. Jean l'Evangéliste', *Bib* 30 (1949), 405–432.

Booth, Wayne C. 'Distance and Point of View: An Essay in Classification', *Essays in Criticism* 11 (1961), 60–79.

——. *A Rhetoric of Irony* (Chicago: University of Chicago Press, 1974).

Borchert, Gerald L. 'The Resurrection Perspective in John', *RevExp* 85 (1988), 501–513.

Borgen, Peder. *Logos Was the True Light: And Other Essays on the Gospel of John* (Trondheim, Norway: Tapir Publishers, 1983).

——. 'God's Agent in the Fourth Gospel', pp. 83–95 in J. Ashton, ed., *The Interpretation of John* (Edinburgh: Clark, 2nd print, 1997).

Borig, R. *Das Wahre Weinstock: Untersuchungen zu Joh 15, 1–10*, SUNT 16 (Munich: Kösel, 1967).

Boring, M. E. 'The Influence of Christian Prophecy on the Johannine Portrayal of the Paraclete and Jesus', *NTS* 25 (1978–79), 113–123.

Born, J. B. 'The Literary Features in the Gospel of John: An Analysis of Jn. 3:1–21', *Direction* 17 (1988), 3–17.

Bornhäuser, K. *Das Johannesevangelium: Eine Missionsschrift für Israel*, BFCT 2/15 (Gütersloh: C. Bertelsmann, 1928).

Bornkamm, Günther. 'Die eucharistische Rede im Johannes-Evangelium', *ZNW* 47 (1956), 161–169.

——. 'Towards the Interpretation of John's Gospel: A discussion of *The Testament of Jesus* by Ernst Käsemann', pp. 97–119 in John Ashton, ed., *The Interpretation of John* (Edinburgh: Clark, 1997[2]).

Bostock, D. G. 'Jesus as the New Elisha', *ExpTim* 92 (1980–81), 39–41.

Boström, G. *Paronomasi i den äldre Hebreiska Maschalliteraturen med särskild hänsyn till proverbia* (Lund: Gleerup, 1928).

Botha, F. J. 'King of Israel (in the Gospel of John)', *TE* 1 (1968), 19–20.

——. 'The Jews in the Fourth Gospel', *TE* 2 (1969), 40–45.

Botha, J. E. 'The Case of Johannine Irony Reopened: I and II', *Neot* 25 (1991–92), 209–220, 221–232.

——. *Jesus and the Samaritan Woman: A Speech-Act Reading of John 4:1–42* (Leiden: Brill, 1991).

——. 'Style in the New Testament: The Need for Serious Reconsideration', *JSNT* 43 (1991), 71–87.
Botha, P. J. 'The Verbal Art of the Pauline Letters: Rhetoric, Performance and Presence', pp. 409–428 in S. E. Porter and T. H. Olbricht, eds, *Rhetoric and the New Testament: Essays from the 1992 Heidelberg Conference* (Sheffield: JSOT Press, 1993).
Boucher, Madeleina. *The Mysterious Parable: A Literary Study* (Washington, DC: Catholic Biblical Association of America, 1977).
Bousset, Wilhelm. *Die jüdische Apokalyptik, ihre religionsgeschichtliche Herkunft und ihre Bedeutung für das neue Testament* (Berlin: n. p., 1903).
——. *A History of Belief in Christ From the Beginning of Christianity to Irenaeus*, ET by J. Steely, 1913 Gr. *Kyrios Christos* (Nashville: Abingdon Press, 1970).
——. *Die Religion des Judentum im späthellenistischen Zeitalter des Großen bis zur Aufklärung* (Berlin: de Gruyter, 1972).
Bowan, John. 'The Fourth Gospel and the Samaritans', *BJRL* 40 (1958), 298–315.
Bowen, C. R. 'Love in the Fourth Gospel', *JR* 13 (1933), 39–49.
——. 'The Fourth Gospel as Dramatic Material', *JBL* 49 (1930), 292–305.
Bowersox, Phil. G. 'The Use of Isaiah 6:10 in John 12:40 and the Theology of Rejection' (Thesis, Dallas Seminary, 1978).
Bowker, J. W. 'The Origin and Purpose of St. John's Gospel', *NTS* 11 (1964–5), 396–408.
——. *Jesus and the Pharisees* (Cambridge: CUP, 1973).
Bowman, John. 'The Fourth Gospel and the Samaritans', *BJRL* 40 (1958), 298–315.
——. *The Fourth Gospel and the Jews* (Pittsburg, PA: Pickwick Press, 1975).
——. 'Metaphorically Eating and Drinking the Body and Blood', *Abr-Nahrain* 22 (1983–84), 1–6.
Boyce, M. *A History of Zoroastrianism* (Leiden: Brill, 1982).
Boyd, D. G. 'The Sources Used by John and Their Relation to the Synoptic Gospels' (Ph.D. diss., McGill University, Canada, 1972).
Boyd, W. J. P. 'The Ascension According to St. John', *SE* 6 = TU 112, ed. E. A. Livingstone (1973), 20–27.
Braine, D. D. C. 'The Inner Jewishness of St. John's Gospel as the Clue to the Inner Jewishness of Jesus', *SNT* 13 (1988), 101–155.
Brandscheidt, R. 'Prophetischer Verstockungsauftrag und christlicher Glaube. Die alttestamentlichen Zitate in Joh. 12, 37–43', *TTZ* 102 (1993), 64–76.
Braude, W. G., ed. *Pesikta Rabbati*, 2 vols, YJS 18 (New Haven and London: Yale University Press, 1968).
Braun, Francois-Marie. *Jean le théologien: Les grandes traditions d'Israël et l'accord des écritures selon le quatrième évangile*, Ebib, 3 vols (Paris: Gabalda, 1956–1972).
——. 'La réduction du Pluriel au Singulier dans l'Evangile et la Première Lettre de Jean', *NTS* 24 (1977), 40–67.
Braun, H. 'Où en est l'étude du quatrième Evangile?' *ETL* 32 (1956), 535–546.
——. *Spätjüdisch-häretischer und frühchristlicher Radikalismus*, vol. 1 (Tübingen: Mohr-Siebeck, 1957).

―――. *Qumran und das Neue Testament*, 2 vols (Tübingen: Mohr-Siebeck, 1966).
Brawley, Robert L. 'An Absent Complement and Intertextuality in John 19:28-29', *JBL* 112 (1993), 427-443.
Breck, John. *Spirit of Truth: The Holy Spirit in Johannine Tradition*, Vol 1: *The Origins of Johannine Pneumatology* (Crestwood, NY: St. Vladimir's Seminary Press, 1991).
Bridges, L. M. 'Gems of Illumination: Jesus' Aphorisms in the Gospel of John', *Westar Magazine* 1 (1987), 10-13.
Briggs, Charles A. *Messianic Prophecy* (New York: Scribner's, 1889).
Brock, Sebastian. 'The Mysteries Hidden in the Side of Christ', *Sobornost* 7 (1977-78), 462-472.
Brodie, T. L. 'Jesus as the New Elisha: Cracking the Code', *ExpTim* 93 (1981-82), 39-42.
―――. *The Quest for the Origin of John's Gospel: A Source-Oriented Approach* (Oxford: OUP, 1993).
―――. *The Gospel According to John* (Oxford: OUP, 1993).
Brooke, A. E., ed.*The Commentary of Origen on St. John's Gospel*, 2 vols (Cambridge: CUP, 1896).
Brooke, George J. *Exegesis at Qumran: 4Q Florilegium in Its Jewish Context* JSOTSup, vol. 29 (Sheffield: JSOT Press, 1985).
―――. 'Christ and the Law in John 7-10', pp. 102-112 in B. Lindars, ed., *Law and Religion: Essays on the Place of Law in Israel and Early Christianity* (Cambridge: James Clarke, 1988).
Brooke-Rose, Christine. *A Grammar of Metaphor* (London: Secker and Warburg, 1958).
Broome, Edwin C. 'The Sources of the Fourth Gospel', *JBL* 63 (1944), 107-121.
Brower, Reuben. *The Fields of Light: An Experiment in Critical Reading* (New York: OUP, 1951).
Brown, C. R. 'The Fourth Gospel as Dramatic Material', *JBL* 49 (1930), 292-305.
Brown, Francis; S. R. Driver, and Charles A. Briggs. *The New Brown-Driver-Briggs Gesenius Hebrew and English Lexicon* (repr. Peabody, MA: Hendrickson Publishers, 1979 [orig. 1906]).
Brown, G. and G. Yule. *Discourse Analysis* (Cambridge: CUP, 1983).
Brown, J. 'Eight Types of Puns', *Proceedings of the Modern Language Association of America* 71 (1956), 14-26.
Brown, J. P. 'The Son of Man: "This Fellow"', *Bib* 58 (1977), 361-387.
Brown R. 'The Problem of History in John', *CBQ* 24 (1962), 1-14.
Brown, Raymond E. 'The Sensus Plenior of Sacred Scripture' (Ph. D. diss., Baltimore: St. Mary's University, 1955).
―――. 'The Qumran Scrolls and the Johannine Gospel and Epistles', *CBQ* 17 (1955), 403-419, 559-574.
―――. *The Gospel According to John*, AB, 2 vols (Garden City, NY: Doubleday, 1966).
―――. 'The Paraclete in the Fourth Gospel', *NTS* 13 (1967), 113-132.
―――. 'The Kerygma of the Gospel According to John: The Johannine View of Jesus in Modern Studies', *Interpretation* 21 (1967), 387-440.
―――. 'Jesus and Elisha', *Perspective* 12 (1971), 85-104.

—. 'The Qumran Scrolls and John: A Comparison in Thought and Expression', pp. 60-90 in Michael J. Taylor, ed., *A Companion to John: Readings in Johannine Theology* (New York: Alba House, 1977).

—. 'The Ego Eimi ("I AM") Passages in the Fourth Gospel', pp. 117-126 in Michael J. Taylor, ed., *A Companion to John: Readings in Johannine Theology* (New York: Alba House, 1977).

—. '"Other Sheep Not of This Fold": The Johannine Perspective on Christian Diversity in the Late First Century', *JBL* 97 (1978), 5-22.

—. *The Community of the Beloved Disciple: The Life, Loves, and Hates of an Individual Church in New Testament Times* (London: G. Chapman, 1979).

—. 'The Relationship to the Fourth Gospel Shared by the Author of I John and by Opponents', pp. 57-68, in *Text and Interpretation: Studies in the New Testament Presented to Matthew Black*, eds. E. Best and R. M. Wilson (Cambridge: CUP, 1979).

—. *The Death of the Messiah: From Gethsemane to the Grave—A Commentary on the Passion Narratives in the Four Gospels*, vol. 1 (London: Geoffrey Chapman, 1994).

—. Review of H. Leroy, *Rätsel*, in *Biblica* 51 (1970), 152-54.

Brown, Raymond E., et al., eds. *The Jerome Biblical Commentary* (London: Geoffrey Chapman, 1968),

Brown, R. M. 'True and False Witness: Architecture and the Church', *Theology Today* 23 (1967), 521-537.

Brown, Schuyler. 'From Burney to Black: The Fourth Gospel and the Aramaic Question', *CBQ* 26 (1964), 323-339.

Brown, S. 'Religious Imagination – Then and Now', *Bible Today* 29 (1991), 237-41.

Brownlee, W. H. 'Whence the Gospel According to John?', pp. 166-94 in J. H. Charlesworth, ed., *John and the Dead Sea Scrolls* (New York: Crossroads, 1990).

—. 'Messianic Motifs of Qumran and the New Testament', *NTS* 3 (1956-57), 12-30, 195-210.

—. *The Meaning of the Qumran Scrolls for the Bible, with Special Attention to the Book of Isaiah* (New York: OUP, 1964).

Brownson, J. V. 'John 20:31 and the Purpose of the Fourth Gospel', *Reformed Review* 48 (1995), 212-216.

Bruce, Alexander B. *The Parabolic Teaching of Christ* (London: Hodder and Stoughton, 1882).

Bruce, F. F. *Biblical Exegesis in the Qumran Texts* (Grand Rapids: Eerdmans, 1959).

—. 'History of New Testament Studies', pp. 21-59 in I. Howard Marshall, ed., *New Testament Interpretation* (Grand Rapids: Eerdmans, 1977).

—. *The Defense of the Gospel in the New Testament*, rev. edn (Grand Rapids: Eerdmans, 1977).

—. *This is That: The New Testament Development of Some Old Testament Themes* (Exeter: Paternoster Press, 1978).

—. *The Gospel of John: Introduction, Exposition and Notes* (London: Pickering Paperbacks, 1983).

Bruns, J. Edgar. *The Art and Thought of John* (New York: Herder and Herder, 1969).

Buchanan, George W. *Typology and the Gospel* (Lanham, MD: University Press of America, 1987).

Büchsel, F. 'ἐλέγχω', *TDNT* 2 (1964), 473–475.

Bühner, Jan A. *Der Gesandte und sein Weg im 4. Evangelium: Die Kulture und religonsgeschichtlichen Grundlagen der johanneischen Sendungschristologie sowie ihre traditionsgeschichtliche Entwicklung*, WUNT 2.2 (Tübingen: Mohr-Siebeck, 1977).

Bujard, Walter. *Stilanalytische Untersuchungen zum Kolosserbrief als Beiträge zur Methodik von Sprachvergleichen*, SUNT Band 11 (Göttingen: Vandenhoeck und Ruprecht, 1973).

Bullinger, E. W. *Figures of Speech Used in the Bible* (Grand Rapids: Baker Book House, 1968).

Bullock, C. Hassell. 'Ezekiel: Bridge Between the Testaments', *JETS* 25 (1982), 2930.

Bultmann, Rudolf. *Der Stil der paulinischen Predigt und die kynisch-stoische Diatribe* (Göttingen: Vandenhoeck und Ruprecht, 1910).

——. 'Der religionsgeschichtliche Hintergrund des Prologs zum Johannesevangelium', pp. 3–26 in H. Schmidt, ed., *ΕΥΧΑΡΙΣΤΗΡΙΟΝ: Studien zur Religion und Literatur des Alten und Neuen Testaments*, vol. 2 (Göttingen: Vandenhoeck und Ruprecht, 1923). Reprinted in *Exegetica: Aufsätze zur Erforschung des Neuen Testaments*, hg. Erich Dinkler (Tübingen: Mohr-Siebeck, 1967).

——. 'Die Bedeutung der neuerschlossenen Mandäischen und Manichäischen Quellen für das Verständnis des Johannesevangeliums', *ZTK* 24 (1925), 100–146.

——. 'Untersuchungen zum Johannesevangelium: Alêtheia', *ZNW* 27 (1928), 113–163.

——. 'Johanneische Schriften und Gnosis', *Orientalische Literaturzeitung* 43 (1940), 150–175.

——. *Das Evangelium des Johannes*, KEK 2/20 (Göttingen: Vandenhoeck und Ruprecht, 1941).

——. *The Theology of the New Testament*, ET by K. Grobel, vol. 2 (London: SCM; 1952, 1955).

——. *Primitive Christianity in Its Contemporary Setting* (London: Thames and Hudson; New York: Meridian, 1955).

——. 'Die Theologie des Johannesevangeliums: Die Sendung des Sohnes', pp. 385–422 in *Theologie des Neuen Testaments*, 3. Aufl. (Tübingen: Mohr-Siebeck, 1958).

——. *Jesus and the Word* (New York: Scribners, 1958).

——. 'γινώσκω, κτλ.', *TDNT* 1 (1964), 689–719.

——. *History of the Synoptic Tradition* (Oxford: Blackwell, 1968).

——. *Faith and Understanding*, ET (London: SCM, 1969).

——. 'Liberal Theology and the Latest Theological Movement', pp. 28–52 in idem, *Faith and Understanding* (London: SCM, 1969).

——. *The Gospel of John: A Commentary*, ed. by R. W. N. Hoare and J. K. Riches, ET by G. R. Beasley-Murray (Oxford: Blackwell and Philadelphia: Westminster Press, 1971).

——. *Die drei Johannesbriefe*, KEK 14 (Göttingen: Vandenhoeck und Ruprecht, 2nd print, 1967). ET by R. Philip O'Hara with Lane C. McGaughy and Robert W. Funk, *The Johannine Epistles*, Hermeneia (Philadelphia: Fortress Press, 1973).

Burchard, C. 'Kerygma and Martyria in the New Testament', pp. 10–25 in A. Sovik, ed., *Christian Witness and the Jewish People* (Geneva: Lutheran World Federation, 1976).

Burchfield, R. W., ed. *A Supplement to the Oxford English Dictionary* (Oxford: Clarendon, 1972), 1:850, s.v. 'double entente'.

Burge, Gary M. *The Anointed Community: The Holy Spirit in the Johannine Tradition* (Grand Rapids: Eerdmans, 1987).

Burkett, Delbert. *The Son of Man in the Gospel of John*, JSNTSup 56 (Sheffield: JSOT Press, 1991).

Burkitt, F. C. 'The Mandaeans', *JTS* 29 (1928), 225–237.

Burney, C. F. *The Aramaic Origin of the Fourth Gospel* (Oxford: Clarendon Press, 1922).

——. *The Poetry of Our Lord* (Oxford: Clarendon Press, 1925).

Burns, J. Edgar. 'The Use of Time in the Fourth Gospel', *NTS* 13 (1966–67), 285–290.

——. *The Art and Thought of John* (New York: Herder and Herder, 1969).

Burridge, K. O. L. *New Heaven, New Earth: A Study of Millenarian Activities* (Oxford: OUP, 1969).

Burrows, E. W. 'Did John the Baptist Call Jesus "The Lamb of God"?' *ExpTim* 85 (1973–74), 245–247.

Burrows, Millar. 'Thy Kingdom Come', *JBL* 74 (1955), 1–8.

——. 'The Original Language of the Gospel of John', *JBL* 49 (1930), 95–139.

——. 'The Johannine Prologue as Aramaic Verse', *JBL* 45 (1926), 57–69.

——. *More Light on the Dead Sea Scrolls* (London: Secker and Warburg, 1958).

Busse, Ulrich. 'Offene Fragen zu Joh 10', *NTS* 33 (1987), 516–531.

Buth, R. 'Language Use in the First Century: Spoken Hebrew in a Trilingual Society in the Time of Jesus', *Journal of Translation and Textlinguistics* 5 (1992), 298–312.

Cadman, W. H. *The Open Heaven: The Revelation of God in the Johannine Sayings of Jesus*, ed. by G. B. Caird (Oxford: Blackwell; New York: Herder, 1969).

Cahill, Peter. 'The Johannine Logos as Center', *CBQ* 38 (1976), 54–72.

Caird, G. B. *Jesus and the Jewish Nation* (London: Athlone Press, 1965).

——. 'The Will of God in the Fourth Gospel', *ExpTim* 72 (1960–61), 115–117.

——. 'The Glory of God in the Fourth Gospel: An Exercise in Biblical Semantics', *NTS* 15 (1968–69), 265–277.

——. *The Language and Imagery of the Bible* (Philadelphia: Westminster Press; London: Duckworth, 1980).

——. *New Testament Theology*. Completed and edited by L. D. Hurst (Oxford: Clarendon Press, 1994).

Callaway, Mary C. 'A Hammer that Breaks Rocks in Pieces: Prophetic Critique in Hebrew Bible', pp. 21–38 in *Anti-Semitism and Early Christianity: Issues of Polemic and Faith*, Evans and Hagner, eds (Minneapolis: Fortress Press, 1993).

Calvin, John. *Commentary on the Gospel According to John*, 2 vols, ET by William Pringle (Grand Rapids: Eerdmans, 1956).

Cameron, R. 'Seeing is not Believing: The History of a Beatitude in the Jesus Tradition', *Forum* 4 (1988), 47–57.

Camery-Hoggatt, Jerry. *Irony in Mark's Gospel*, SNTSMS 72 (Cambridge: CUP, 1992).

Campbell, A. Glenn. 'The Greek Terminology for the Deity of Christ' (Thesis, Dallas Seminary, 1948).

Campbell, R. J. 'The Concept of Truth in Johannine Writings Related to Modern Critical Tensions' (Ph.D. diss., Strasbourg, 1970).

Campenhausen, H. von. *The Formation of the Christian Bible*, trans. by J. A. Baker (London: Black, 1972).

Caragounis, Chrys C. *The Son of Man*, WUNT 38 (Tübingen: Mohr-Siebeck, 1986).

Cardwell, K. 'The Fish on the Fire: Jn. 21:9', *ExpTim* 102 (1990), 12–14.

Cargal, Timothy. 'His Blood Be Upon Us and Upon Our Children: A Matthean Double-Entendre?' *NTS* 37 (1991), 101–112.

Carmichael, Calum M. 'Marriage and the Samaritan Woman', *NTS* 26 (1979–80), 332–346.

——. 'Present and Future in the "Eschatology" of the Fourth Gospel', Abstracted in *AAR/SBL Abstracts*, K. H. Richards and J. B. Wiggins, eds (Atlanta, GA: Scholars Press, 1987).

——. *The Story of Creation: Its Origin and Its Interpretation in Philo and the Fourth Gospel* (London: Ithaca, 1996).

Carmignac, J. 'Un Qumranien converti au Christianisme: l'auteur des Odes de Salomon', pp. 75–108 in H. Bardtke, ed., *Qumran-Probleme* (Berlin: Akademie Verlag, 1963).

Carnegie, D. R. 'Kerygma in the Fourth Gospel', *Vox Evangelica* 7 (1971), 39–74.

Carpenter, J. E. *The Johannine Writings: a study of the Apocalypse and the fourth gospel* (London: Constable 1927).

Carroll, John T. 'Present and Future in the Fourth Gospel "Eschatology"', *BTB* 19 (1989), 63–69.

Carroll, K. L. 'The Fourth Gospel and the Exclusion of Christians from the Synagogues', *BJRL* 40 (1957–58), 19–32.

Carroll, Robert P. *When Prophecy Failed: Reactions and responses to failure in the Old Testament prophetic traditions* (London: SCM, 1979).

——. 'Poets Not Prophets', *JSOT* 27 (1983), 25–31.

Carson, D. A. 'Predestination and Responsibility: Elements of Tension-Theology in the Fourth Gospel Against Jewish Background' (Ph.D. diss. Cambridge, 1975).

——. 'Current Source Criticism of the Fourth Gospel: Some Methodological Questions', *JBL* 97 (1978), 411–429.

——. *The Farewell Discourse and Final Prayer of Jesus: An Exposition of John 14–17* (Grand Rapids: Baker Book House, 1980).

——. *Divine Sovereignty and Human Responsibility* (Atlanta, GA: John Knox Press, 1981).

——. 'Understanding Misunderstandings in the Fourth Gospel', *TynBul* 33 (1982), 59–89.

——. 'Purpose of the Fourth Gospel: John 20:31 reconsidered', *JBL* 106 (1987), 639–651.

———. 'John and the Johannine Epistles', pp. 245-264 in D. A.Carson and H. G. M. Williamson, eds, *It is Written: Scripture Citing Scripture* (Cambridge: CUP, 1988).

———. *The Gospel According to John* (Grand Rapids: Eerdmans, 1991).

Carson, Julie Ann. 'The Linguist and Literature: A Critical Examination of Contemporary Theories of Stylistics in America' (Ph.D. diss., Indiana University, 1972).

Carter, Warren. 'The Prologue and John's Gospel: Function, Symbol and the Definitive Word', *JSNT* 39 (1990), 35-58.

Cartlidge, David R. and David L. Dungan, eds, *Documents for the Study of the Gospels* (Cleveland: Collins, 1980).

Cary, G. L. 'The Lamb of God and Atonement Theories', *TynBul* 32 (1981), 101-107.

Casanowicz, Immanuel M. *Paronomasia in the Old Testament* (Baltimore: John Hopkins University, 1892).

Case, Shirley Jackson. *The Evolution of Early Christianity* (Chicago: University of Chicago Press, 1914).

———. *The Social Origins of Christianity* (Chicago: University of Chicago Press, 1923).

Casey, Maurice. *From Jewish Prophet to Gentile God: The Origins and Development of New Testament Christology* (Cambridge: James Clarke, 1991).

———. *Is John's Gospel True?* (London: Routledge, 1996).

Casey, R. P. 'Gnosis, Gnosticism and the New Testament', pp. 52-80 in W. D. Davies and D. Daube, eds, *The Background of the New Testament and its Eschatology* (Cambridge: CUP, 1956).

Cassen, N. H. 'A Grammatical and Contextual Inventory of the Use of Kosmos in the Johannine Corpus with Some Implications for a Johannine Cosmic Theology', *NTS* 19 (1972-73), 81-91.

Casson, L. *Travel in the Ancient World* (London: George Allen and Unwin, 1974).

———. *The Ancient Mariners: Seafarers and Sea Fighters of the Mediterranean in Ancient Times*, 2nd edn (Princeton: Princeton University Press, 1991).

Catchpole, David. 'The Beloved Disciple and Nathanael', pp. 69-92 in Christoper Rowland, et al., eds, *Understanding, Studying, Reading: New Testament Essays in Honour of John Ashton* (Sheffield: Sheffield Academic Press, 1988).

Cauthron, H. A. 'The Meaning of Kingship in Johannine Christology: A Structuralist Exegesis of John 18:1-20' (Ph.D. diss., Vanderbilt University, 1984).

Ceresko, A. R. 'The A:B:B:A Word Pattern in Hebrew and Northwest Semitic with Special Reference to the Book of Job', *Ugarit Forschungen* 7 (1975), 73-88.

———. 'The Chiastic Word Pattern in Hebrew', *CBQ* 38 (1976), 303-311.

———. 'The Function of Chiasmas in Hebrew Poetry', *CBQ* 40 (1978), 1-10.

Cerfaux, L. 'Le thème littéraire parabolique dans l'Évangile de S. Jean', *ConNT* 11 (1947), 15-25.

Ceroke, Christian P. 'Problem of Ambiguity in John 2:4', *CBQ* 21 (1959), 316-340.

Chadwick, Henry. 'Justin Martyr's Defence of Christianity', *BJRL* 47 (1965), 275-297.

———. *Early Christian Thought and the Classical Tradition: Studies in Justin, Clement and Origen* (Oxford: OUP, 1966).

———. *The Early Church* (London: Harmondsworth, 1967).

Chafe, W. L. *Meaning and the Structure of Language* (Chicago: University of Chicago Press, 1970).

Chamberlain, W. D. 'The Need of Man: The Atonement in the Fourth Gospel', *Interpretation* 10 (1956), 157–166.

Chang, Peter. 'Repetitions and Variations in the Gospel of John' (Diss., Université des Sciences Humaines de Strasbourg, 1975).

Charles, R. H. *The Apocrypha and Pseudepigrapha of the Old Testament*, 2 vols (Oxford: Clarendon Press, 1913).

Charlesworth, James H. 'A Critical Comparison of the Dualism in 1QS 3:14–4:26 and the "Dualism" Contained in the Gospel of John', *NTS* 15 (1968–69), 389–418.

——. 'The Odes of Solomon – Not Gnostic', pp. 357–69 in M. Testuz, ed., *Papyrus Bodmer VII–IX* (Cologne and Geneva: Bibliothèque Bodmer, 1959).

——. 'Paronomasia and Assonance in the Syriac Text of the Odes of Solomon', *Semitics* 1 (1970), 12–26.

——. *John and Qumran* (London: Geoffrey Chapman Publishers, 1972).

——. *The Old Testament Pseudepigrapha*, 2 vols (New York: Doubleday, 1983, 1985).

——, ed. *John and the Dead Sea Scrolls* (New York: Crossroads, 1990).

——, ed. *The Messiah: Developments in Earliest Judaism and Christianity* (Minneapolis: Fortress Press, 1992).

——. 'From Messianology to Christology: Problems and Prospects', pp. 3–35 in James H. Charlesworth, ed., *The Messiah: Developments in Earliest Judaism and Christianity* (Minneapolis: Fortress Press, 1992).

——. *The Beloved Disciple: Whose Witness Validates the Gospel of John?* (Valley Forge, PA: Trinity Press International, 1995).

Chatman, S. and S. R. Levin, eds. *Essays on the Language of Literature* (Boston: Houghton Mifflin, 1967).

Chenderlin, F. 'Distributed Observance of the Passover: A Hypothesis', *Bib* 56 (1975), 369–393.

Chernus, I. *Mysticism in Rabbinic Judaism*, Studia Judaica 11 (Berlin: de Gruyter, 1982).

Chevalier, Haakon. *The Ironic Temper: Anatole France and His Time* (New York: OUP, 1932).

Childs, Brevard S. 'The Exegetical Significance of Canon for the Study of the Old Testament', pp. 66–80 in *Congress Volume: Göttingen 1977*, VTSup 29 (Leiden: Brill, 1978).

——. *Introduction to the Old Testament as Scripture* (Philadelphia: Fortress Press, 1979).

——. 'Critical Reflections on James Barr's Understanding of the Literal and the Allegorical', *JSOT* 46 (1990), 3–9.

Chilton, B. D. *A Galilean Rabbi and his Bible* (London: SPCK, 1984).

——. *Targumic Approaches to the Gospels: Essays in the Mutual Definition of Judaism and Christianity*, Studies in Judaism (Lanham, MD and New York: University Press of America, 1986).

——. 'Jesus and the Question of Anti-Semitism', pp. 39–52 in Evans and Hagner, eds, *Anti-Semitism and Early Christianity: Issues of Polemic and Faith* (Minneapolis: Fortress Press, 1993).

—. *The Glory of Israel: The Theology and Provenience of the Isaiah Targum*, JSOTSup 2 (Sheffield: JSOT, 1993).
Chisholm, Robert, Jr. 'Word Play in the Eighth-Century Prophets', *BibSac* 144 (1987), 44–52.
Chomsky, Noam. *Syntactic Structures* (The Hague: Mouton, 1966).
Chrysostom, St. John. *Homilies on the Gospel of St. John and the Epistle to the Hebrews*, ed. by P. Schaff, Nicene and Post-Nicene Fathers of the Christian Church 1/14 (Grand Rapids: Eerdmans, n.d.).
Cimosa, M. 'La traduzione greca dei Settanta nel Vangelo di Giovanni', *BeO* 39 (1997), 41–55.
Clark, D. K. 'Signs in Wisdom and John', *CBQ* 45 (1983), 201–209.
Clark, F. 'Tension and Tide in St. John's Gospel', *ITQ* 24 (1957), 154–165.
Clarke, E. G. 'Jacob's Dream at Bethel as Interpreted in the Targums and the New Testament', *Studies in Religion* 4 (1975), 367–377.
Clarke, T. E. 'The Son of the Living God', *The Way* 8 (1968), 97–105.
Clavier, H. 'La méthode ironique dans l'enseignement de Jésus', *ETR* 4 (1929), 224–241, 323–344.
—. 'La méthode ironique dans l'enseignement de Jésus', *ETR* 5 (1930), 58–99.
—. 'Autour de Jean 5:17', *RHPR* 34 (1944), 82–90.
—. 'Le problème du rite et du mythe dans le quatrième évangile', *Revue d'histoire et de philosophie religieuses* 31 (1951), 275–292.
—. 'La structure du quatrième évangile', *Revue d'histoire et de philosophie religieuses* 35 (1955), 174–195.
—. 'L'ironie dans l'enseignement de Jésus', *NovT* 1 (1956), 3–20.
—. 'Les sens multiples dans le nouveau testament', *NovT* 2 (1957), 185–198.
—. 'L'ironie dans le quatrième évangile', *SE* 1 = TU 73, ed. K. Aland et al. (1959), 261–276.
Clemen, C. 'Beiträge zum geschichtlichen Verständnis der Johannesbriefe', *ZNW* 6 (1905), 271–281.
Clements, R. E. 'The Unity of the Book of Isaiah', *Interpretation* 36 (1982), 117–129.
—. 'Beyond Tradition-History: Deutero-Isaianic Development of First Isaiah's Themes', *JSOT* 31 (1985), 95–113.
—. 'The Messianic Hope in the Old Testament', *JSOT* 43 (1989), 3–19.
—. *The World of Ancient Israel* (Cambridge: CUP, 1989).
Clifford, R. J. and G. W. MacRae, eds. *The Word in the World* (Cambridge: Weston, 1973).
Coetzee, J. C. 'Christ and the Prince of This World in the Gospel and the Epistles of St. John', *Neot* 2 (1968), 104–121.
—. 'Life (Eternal Life) in John's Writings and the Qumran Scrolls', *Neot* 6 (1972), 48–66.
—. 'Jesus' Revelation in the Ego Eimi Sayings in John 8 and 9', pp. 170–177 in J. H. Petzer and P. J. Hartin, eds, *A South Africa Perspective on the New Testament* (Leiden: Brill, 1986).
Coggins, R., A. Phillips and M. Knibb, eds. *Israel's Prophetic Tradition: Essays in Honour of Peter R. Ackroyd* (Cambridge: CUP, 1982).

Cohen, A. P. *The Symbolic Construction of the Community* (Chichester, U.K.: Ellis Horwood, 1985).

Cohen, Samuel. 'The Names of God: A Study in Rabbinic Theology', *HUCA* 27 (1951), 579–604.

Cohen, Shaye J. D. 'Yavneh Revisited: Pharisees, Rabbis, and the End of Jewish Sectarianism', *SBLSP* 21 (1982), 45–61.

——. 'Crossing the Boundary and Becoming a Jew', *HTR* 82 (1989), 13–33.

——, ed. *Studies in the Cult of Yahweh*, 2 vols (Leiden: Brill, 1996).

Cohen, Ted. 'Metaphor and the Cultivation of Intimacy', *Critical Inquiry* 5 (1978), 3–12.

Collins, A. Yarbro. 'Crisis and Community in John's Gospel', *TD* 27 (1979), 313–321.

Collins, John J. 'Jewish Apocalyptic Against Its Ancient Near Eastern Environment', *Bulletin of the American Schools of Oriental Research* 220 (1975), 27–36.

——. 'Cosmos and Salvation: Jewish Wisdom and Apocalyptic in the Hellenistic Age', *History of Religions* 17 (1977), 121–142.

——. 'The Son of God Text From Qumran', pp. 65–82 in M. C. de Boer, ed., *From Jesus to John: Essays on Jesus and New Testament Christology in honour of Marinus de Jonge* (Sheffield: JSOT Press, 1993).

Collins, Raymond F. 'Representative Figures of the Fourth Gospel', *DRev* 94 (1976), 26–46, 118–132.

——. 'Jesus' Conversation with Nicodemus', *Bible Today* 93 (1977), 1409–1419.

——. 'Cana (Jn. 2:1–12), The First of His Signs or the Key to His Signs?' *ITQ* 47 (1980), 79–95.

——. 'Discipleship in John's Gospel', *Emmanuel* 9 (1985), 248–255.

——. *These Things Have Been Written: Studies on the Fourth Gospel* (Grand Rapids: Eerdmans, 1990).

Collinson, W. E. 'Comparative Synonymics: Some Principles and Illustrations', *Transactions of the Philological Society* (1939), 54–77.

Colpe, Carsten. *Die religionsgeschichtliche Schule: Darstellung und Kritik ihres Bildes vom gnostischen Erlösermythus*, FRLANT 60 (Göttingen: Vandenhoeck und Ruprecht, 1961).

——. 'New Testament and Gnostic Christology', pp. 227–243 in J. Neusner, ed., *Religions in Antiquity*, NovTSup 14 (Leiden: Brill, 1968).

——. 'Heidnische, jüdische und christliche Überlieferung in den Schriften aus Nag Hammadi, III', *Jahrbuch für Antike und Christentum* 17 (1974), 109–125.

Colson, J. *L'Énigme du disciple que Jésus aimait*, Théologie historique 10 (Paris: Beauchesne et ses fils, 1968).

Colwell, E. C. *The Greek of the Fourth Gospel: A Study of Its Aramaisms in the Light of Hellenistic Greek* (Chicago: University of Chicago Press, 1931).

——. *John Defends the Gospel* (Chicago: Willett and Clark, 1936).

Combrink, H. J. B. 'Multiple Meaning and/or Multiple Interpretation of a Text', *Neot* 18 (1984), 26–37.

Combs, William W. 'Nag Hammadi, Gnosticism, and the New Testament Interpretation', *Grace Theological Journal* 8 (1987), 195–212.

Connick, C. M. 'The Dramatic Character of the Fourth Gospel', *JBL* 67 (1948), 291–297.

Connolly, R. *Rhetoric Case Book* (New York, 1953).

Conzelmann, Hans. *Die Apostelgeschichte,* HNT 7 (Tübingen: Mohr-Siebeck, 1963).

———. *Grundriss der Theologie des Neuen Testaments* (Munich: Kaiser, 1967).

Cook, W. R. 'The "Glory" Motif in the Johannine Corpus', *JETS* 27 (1984), 291–97.

Cooper, K. T. 'The Best Wine: John 2:1–11', *Westminster Theological Journal* 21 (1978–79), 364–380.

Cooper, Lane. *Theories of Style,* Research and Source work, no.173 (New York: Burt Franklin, 1968).

Corell, Alf. *Consummatum Est: Eschatology and Church in the Gospel of St. John* (New York: Macmillan, 1958).

Cornell, T. and J. Matthew, *Atlas of the Roman World* (Oxford: Phaidon, 1982).

Cosgrove, C. H. 'The Place Where Jesus Is: Allusions to Baptism and the Eucharist in the Fourth Gospel', *NTS* 35 (1989), 522–539.

Cothenet, E. 'Témoinage de l'Esprit et interprétation de l'écriture dans la corpus johannique', pp. 367–377 in Département des études Bibliques de l'institute catholique de Paris, ed., *La vie de la parole: De l'Ancien au Nouveau Testament, Mélanges P. Grelot* (Paris: Desclée de Brouwer, 1987).

———. 'Le témoignage selon saint Jean', *Esprit et Vie* 101 (1991), 401–407.

Coutts, J. 'The Messianic Secret in St. John's Gospel', *SE* 3 = TU 88 (1964), 43–57.

Cox, L. G. 'John's Witness to the Historical Jesus', *BETS* 9 (1966), 173–178.

Crane, T. E. *The Message of St. John: The Spiritual Teaching of the Beloved Disciple* (New York: Alba, 1980).

Cranfield, C. E. B. 'John 1:14 – "Became"', *ExpTim* 93 (1981–82), 215.

Creech, R. R. 'Christology and Conflict: A Comparative Study of Two Central Themes in Johannine Literature and the Apocalypse' (Ph.D. diss., Dallas: Baylor University, 1984).

Crehan, J. *The Theology of St. John* (London: Longman, Todd, 1965).

Crenshaw, J. L. *Prophetic Conflict: Its Effect Upon Israelite Religion,* BZAW 124 (Berlin: de Gruyter, 1971).

de la Croix, Paul Marie. *L'Évangile de Jean et son témoignage spirituel* (Paris: Desclée De Brouwer, 1959). ET, *The Biblical Spirituality of St. John* (New York: Alba House, 1966).

Cross, Frank M. *The Ancient Library of Qumran and Modern Biblical Study* (London: Duckworth, 1958).

Crossan, John Dominic. *In Parables: The Challenge of the Historical Jesus* (New York: Harper and Row, 1973).

———. '"Ruth Amid the Alien Corn": Perspectives and Methods in Contemporary Biblical Criticism', pp. 199–210 in R. Polzin and E. Rothman, eds, *The Biblical Mosaic* (Philadelphia: Fortress Press, 1982).

Crowther, N. B. 'Water and Wine as Symbols of Inspiration', *Mnemosyne* 32 (1979), 1–11.

Cruse, D. A. *Lexical Semantics* (Cambridge: CUP, 1986).

Cuddon, J. A. *A Dictionary of Literary Terms,* rev. edn (New York: Penguin, 1980).

Culler, Jonathan. 'Presupposition and Intertextuality', *MLN* 91 (1976), 1380–1396.
——. *The Pursuit of Signs: Semiotics, Literature, Deconstruction* (London: Routledge, 1981).
——. *On Deconstruction: Theory and Criticism after Structuralism* (London: Routledge, 1983).
Culley, Robert C. *Studies in the Structure of Hebrew Narrative* (Philadelphia: Fortress Press, 1976).
Cullmann, Oscar. 'Der johanneische Gebrauch doppeldeutiger Ausdrücke als Schlüssel zum Verständnis des vierten Evangeliums', *TZ* 4 (1948), 360–372.
——. *Early Christian Worship* (Philadelphia: Westminster Press, 1953).
——. *The Christology of the New Testament*, ET by S. C. Guthrie and C. A. M. Hall (Philadelphia: Westminster Press, 1959).
——. 'L'Evangile Johannique at L'Histoire du Saltut', *NTS* 11 (1965), 111–122.
——. *Salvation in History* (New York: Harper and Row, 1967).
——. *Der Johanneische Kreis. Sein Platz im Spätjudentum, in der jüngerschaft Jesu und im Urchristentum. Zum Ursprung des Johannesevangeliums* (Tübingen: Mohr-Siebeck, 1975). ET by J. Bowden, *The Johannine Circle: Its Place in Judaism, Among the Disciples of Jesus and in Early Christianity* (London: SCM, and Philadelphia: Westminster Press, 1976).
Culpepper, R. Alan. *The Johannine School: An Evaluation of the Johannine-School Hypothesis Based on an Investigation of the Nature of Ancient Schools* (Missoula, MT: Scholars Press, 1975).
——. *Anatomy of the Fourth Gospel: A Study in Literary Design* (Philadelphia: Fortress Press, 1983).
—— and C. C. Black, eds. *Exploring the Gospel of John: in Honor of D. Moody Smith* (Louisville, KY: Westminster John Knox, 1996).
Cuming, C. J. 'The Jews in the Fourth Gospel', *ExpTim* 60 (1948–49), 290–92.
Cumont, Franz. *The Oriental Religions in Roman Paganism* (New York: Dover, 1956).

D'Angelo, M. R. 'A Critical Note: John 10:17 and Apocalypse of Moses 31', *JTS* n.s. 41 (1990), 529–536.
Dahl, Nils A. 'Der Erstgeborene Satans und der Vater des Teufels (Polyk 71 und Joh 813)', pp. 70–84 in W. Eltester, ed., *Apophoreta*, FS E. Haenchen, BZNW 30 (Berlin: Töpelmann, 1964).
——. 'The Crucified Messiah and the Endangered Promises', *Word and World* 3 (1983), 251–262.
——. 'The Johannine Church and History', pp. 122–140 in J. Ashton, ed., *The Interpretation of John* (London: SPCK, 1986). Printed earlier in *Current Issues in New Testament Interpretation*, W. Klassen and G. F. Snyder, eds (New York: Harper and Row, 1962).
——. *Jesus the Christ: The Historical Origins of Christological Doctrine* (Minneapolis: Fortress Press, 1991).
Dahms, J. V. 'Isaiah 55:11 and the Gospel of John', *EvQ* 53 (1981), 78–88.
Dahood, Ebla. 'Genesis and John', *Christian Century* 98 (1981), 418–421.
Dalman, G. *The Words of Jesus*, ET (Edinburgh: Clark, 1902).

——. *Grammatik des Jüdisch-Palästinischen Aramäisch und Aramäische Dialektproben* (Darmstadt: Wissenchaftliche Buchgesellschaft, 1960).
Dart, John. *The Laughing Savior: The Discovery and Significance of the Nag Hammadi Gnostic Library* (New York: Harper, 1976).
Daube, D. 'The New Testament and Rabbinic Judaism: Rabbinic Methods of Interpretation and Hellenistic Rhetoric', *HUCA* 22 (1949), 237-264.
——. 'The "I am" of the Messianic Presence', in idem, *The New Testament and Rabbinic Judaism* (London: Athlone, 1956), 325-329.
Dauer, A. 'Zur Herkunft der Tomas-Perikope Joh 20,24-29', pp. 56-76 in H. Merklein and J. Lange, eds, *Biblische Randbemerkungen, FS R. Schnackenburg* (Würzbur: Echter, 1974).
——. *Die Passionsgeschichte im Johannesevangelium. Eine traditionsgeschichtliche und theologische Untersuchung zu Joh 18,1-19, 30*, SANT 30 (Munich: Kösel-Verlag, 1979. Diss. Würzburg, 1968-69).
——. 'Schichten im Johannesevangelium als Anzeichen von Entwicklungen in der (den) johanneischen Gemeinde(n) nach G. Richter', pp. 62-83 in A. E. Heirold et al., ed., *Die Kraft der Hoffnung,* Festschrift für Alterzbischof D Dr Joseph Schneider zum 80. Geburtstag (Bamberg: St. Otto-Verlag, 1986).
Davidson, B. *The Analytical Hebrew and Chaldee Lexicon* (London: Samuel Bagster, N.D.).
Davidson, Donald. 'What Metaphors Mean', pp. 29-45 in Sheldon Sacks, ed., *On Metaphors* (Chicago: University of Chicago Press, 1979).
Davies, A. T. *Antisemitism and the Christian Mind: The Crisis of Conscience after Auschwitz* (New York: Herder and Herder, 1969).
——, ed. *Antisemitism and the Foundations of Christianity* (New York: Paulist, 1979).
Davies, M. *Rhetoric and Reference in the Fourth Gospel,* JSNTSup 69 (Sheffield: JSOT Press, 1992).
Davies, Paul E. 'Jesus and the Role of the Prophet', *JBL* 64 (1945), 241-254.
Davies, P. R. 'The Social World of the Apocalyptic Writings', pp. 251-271 in R. E. Clements, ed., *The World of Ancient Israel* (Cambridge: CUP, 1989).
Davies, W. D. and David Daube, eds. *The Background of the New Testament and Its Eschatology* (Cambridge: CUP, 1956).
Davies, W. D. *The Gospel and the Land: Early Christianity and Jewish Territorial Doctrine* (Berkeley: University of California Press, 1974).
——. 'The Johannine "Sign" of Jesus', pp. 91-156 in Michael J. Taylor, ed., *A Companion to John: Readings in Johannine Theology* (New York: Alba House, 1977).
——. *The Setting of the Sermon on the Mount* (Cambridge: CUP, 1963).
Davis, J. C. 'The Johannine Concept of Eternal Life as a Present Possession', *ResQ* 27 (1984), 161-169.
Dawsey, James. 'The Lucan Voice: Confusion and Irony', in *The Gospel of Luke* (Macon, GA: Mercer University Press, 1986).
De Pinto, Basil. 'Word and Wisdom in St. John', *Scripture* 19 (1967), 19-27, 107-125.
Deakle, D. W. 'A Study of Literary Pairs in the Fourth Gospel' (Ph.D. diss., New Orleans Baptist Theological Seminary, 1985).
Déaut, Roger Le. 'Apropos a Definition of Midrash', *Interpretation* 25 (1971), 259-82.

Deeks, David. 'The Structure of the Fourth Gospel', *NTS* 15 (1968–69), 107–128.

Deines, Roland. *Jüdische Steingefäße und pharisäische Frömmigkeit*, WUNT 2.52 (Tübingen: Mohr-Siebeck, 1993).

———. *Die Pharisäer: Ihr Verständnis im Spiegel der christlichen und jüdischen Forschung seit Wellhausen und Graetz*, WUNT 2.101 (Tübingen: Mohr-Siebeck, 1997).

Deissmann, A. *Das Urchristentum und die unteren Schichten* (Göttingen: Vandenhoeck und Ruprecht, 1908).

———. *Light From the Ancient East: The New Testament Illustrated by Recently Discovered Texts of the Graeco-Roman World* trans. Lionel R. M. Strachan (London: Hodder and Stoughton, 1910).

Delitzsch, Franz. *Jesaja*, 3rd edn (Leipzig: Dörflin und Franke, 1879; repr. Giessen and Basel: Brunnen, 1984).

Delling, G. *Wort und Werk Jesu im Johannes-Evangelium* (Berlin: Evangelische Verlagsanstalt, 1966).

Demetrius. *On Style*, ET by W. R. Roberts, Loeb Classical Library 199 (London: Heinemann, 1932).

Denis, A. M. 'Jesus Walking On the Waters: A Contribution to the History of the Pericope in the Gospel Tradition', *LS* 1 (1967), 284–297.

Denniston, J. D. *Greek Prose Style* (Oxford: Clarendon Press, 1952).

Derrett, J. D. M. 'Fig Trees in the New Testament', *HeyJ* 14 (1973), 249–265.

———. 'The Zeal of the House and the Cleansing of the Temple', *DRev* 95 (1977), 79–94.

———. 'Fresh Light on the Lost Sheep and the Lost Coin (Jn. 2:13–17)', *NTS* 26 (1979–80), 36–60.

———. 'Why and How Jesus Walked on the Sea', *NovT* 23 (1981), 330–348.

———. 'Binding and Loosing (Matt. 16:19; 18:18; Jn. 20:23)', *JBL* 102 (1983), 112–117.

———. 'The Samaritan Woman's Pitcher', *DRev* 102 (1984), 252–261.

———. *Studies in the New Testament*, 4 vols (Leiden: Brill, 1977–86).

———. 'The Samaritan Woman's Purity (Jn. 4:4–52)', *EvQ* 60 (1988), 291–298.

———. 'Peter's Sword and Biblical Methodology', *Bibliotheca Orientalis* 32 (1990), 180–192.

———. 'The Bronze Serpent', *Estudios Biblicos* 49 (1991), 311–329.

———. 'Impurity and Idolatry: John 13:11; Ezekiel 36:25', *Bibliotheca Orientalis* 34 (1992), 87–92.

———. 'τί ἐργάζῃ (John 6:30): an Unrecognized Allusion to Isa. 45:9', *ZNW* 84 (1993), 142–144.

———. 'John 9:6 Read with Isaiah 6:10; 20:9', *EvQ* 66 (1994), 251–4.

———. 'Lazarus, the Body, and Water (John 11:44; Isaiah 58:11; Numbers 20:9–11)', *Bibliotheca Orientalis* 39 (1997), 169–182.

———. 'Not Seeing and Later Seeing (John 16:16)', *ExpTim* 109 (1998), 208–209.

Derrida, Jacques. 'Living On/Border Lines', pp. 75–176 in H. Bloom, et al., eds, *Deconstruction and Criticism* (New York: Seabury, 1979).

———. *Dissemination*, ET by B. Johnson (Chicago: University of Chicago, 1981).

Detzler, W. *New Testament Words in Today's Language* (Wheaton, IL: Victor Books, 1986).

Deuchesne-Guillemin, Jacques. 'On the Origin of Gnosticism', pp. 349-69 in W. Sundermann, et al., eds, *A Green Leaf: Papers in Honour of Professor Jes P. Asmussen*, Acta Iranica 28, vol. 12 (Leiden: Brill, 1988).

Dewey, Kim. 'Paroimiai in the Gospel of John', *Semeia* 17 (1980), 81-99.

Diaz, J. R. 'Palestinian Targum and New Testament, *NovT* 6 (1963), 75-84.

Dibelius, Martin. *Die Formgeschichte des Evangeliums* (Tübingen: Mohr-Siebeck, 1919, 1933).

Diel, Paul and J. Solotareff. *Symbolism in the Gospel of John*, ET by Nelly Marans (San Francisco: Harper and Row, 1988).

von Dobschütz, E. 'Zum Charakter des 4. Evangeliums', *ZNW* 28 (1929), 161-177.

Dodd, C. H. *The Parables of the Kingdom* (London: Nisbet, 1935).

—. *Apostolic Preaching and Its Developments: Three Lectures* (Chicago: Willet, Clark and Co. 1937).

—. 'The First Epistle of John and the Fourth Gospel', *BJRL* 21 (1937), 129-156.

—. 'Eternal Life', *Harvard Divinity School Bulletin* 48 (1951), 5-15.

—. *According to the Scriptures: The Substructure of New Testament Theology* (London: Nisbet, 1952).

—. *The Old Testament in the New* (London: Athlone, 1952).

—. *The Interpretation of the Fourth Gospel* (Cambridge: CUP, 1953).

—. *Historical Tradition in the Fourth Gospel* (Cambridge: CUP, 1963).

—. 'The Prophecy of Caiaphas: John 11:47-53', pp. 58-68 in C. H. Dodd, ed., *More New Testament Studies* (Grand Rapids: Eerdmans, 1968).

—. 'A Hidden Parable in the Fourth Gospel', pp. 30-40 in C. H. Dodd, ed., *More New Testament Studies* (Grand Rapids: Eerdmans, 1968).

Domeris, W. R. 'The Johannine Drama', *Journal of Theology for Southern Africa* 42 (1983), 29-35.

—. 'The Holy One of God as a Title for Jesus', *Neot* 19 (1985), 9-17.

—. 'Christology and Community: A Study of the Social Matrix of the Fourth Gospel', *JTSA* 64 (1988), 49-56.

Doncoeur, P. 'Des silences de l'Évangile de Saint Jean', *RSR* 24 (1934), 606-609.

Dorman, David. 'The Son of Man in John: A Fresh Approach Through Chapter 6', *Studia Biblica et Theologica* 13 (1983), 121-142.

Dorsey, D. A. *The Roads and Highways of Ancient Israel*, American Schools of Oriental Research Library of Biblical and Near Eastern Archaeology (Baltimore: John Hopkins University Press, 1991).

Doty, W. G. *Letters in Primitive Christianity*, Guides to Biblical Scholarship (Philadelphia: Fortress, 1973).

Douglas, Mary. *Natural Symbols: Explorations in Cosmology* (New York: Vintage, 1973).

Dozeman, Thomas B. '"Sperma Abraam" in John 8 and Related Literature', *CBQ* 42 (1980), 342-358.

Draisma, Sipke, ed. *Intertextuality in Biblical Writings: Essays in Honor of Bas van Iersel* (Kampen: J. H. Kok, 1989).

Drane, J. W. 'Typology', *EvQ* 50 (1978), 195-210.

Driver, G. R. 'The Original Language of the Fourth Gospel: A Criticism of Dr. Burney's Thesis', *Jewish Guardian* (1923), 7-9.
——. 'Problems and Solutions', *VT* 4 (1954), 240-245.
Drum, W. 'Johannine Thought-forms in the Discourses of Jesus', *HPR* 21 (1920-21), 722-732.
——. 'The Words of Jesus and the Meditation of John', *HPR* 21 (1920-121), 813-821.
——. 'Calmes and the Allegorical Interpretation of John', *HPR* 22 (1921-22), 18-24.
——. 'The Symbolism of the Fourth Gospel', *HRP* 22 (1921-22), 162-169.
——. 'A Resume of Johannine Symbolism and Allegory', *HPR* 22 (1921-22), 257-263.
Drummond, James. *An Inquiry into the Character and Authorship of the Fourth Gospel* (London: Williams and Norgate, 1903).
——. *Johannine Thoughts* (London: Lindsey Press, 1909).
——. 'Genesis 1 and John 1:1-14', *ExpTim* 49 (1937-38), 568.
——. 'The Johannine Writings: An Old Man's Speculations', *EvQ* 21 (1949), 219-223.
Ducrot, Oswald and Todorov. T. *Encyclopedic Dictionary of the Sciences of Language*, ET by C. Poter (Baltimore: John Hopkins University Press, 1979).
——. 'Ouvertures johanniques sur la mystique', *Christus* 162 (1994), 180-188.
Duke, Paul D. *Irony in the Fourth Gospel* (Atlanta: John Knox Press, 1985).
Duling, C. 'Insights from Sociology for New Testament Christology: A Test Case', *SBL* 24 (1985), 351-68.
Dumermuth, C. F. 'Number Symbolism in the Gospel of John', *Asia Journal of Theology* 4 (1990), 108-119.
Dungan, D. L. 'John and the Synoptics: The Empty Tomb Stories', *NTS* 30 (1984), 161-187.
Dunn, J. D. G. 'The Washing of the Disciples' Feet in John 13:1-20', *ZNW* 61 (1970), 247-252.
——. *Christology in the Making: A New Testament Inquiry into the Origins of the Doctrine of the Incarnation* (London: SCM, 1980).
——. 'Let John be John: A Gospel for its Time', pp. 309-339 in P. Stuhlmacher, ed., *Das Evangelium und die Evangelien*, WUNT 28 (Tübingen: Mohr-Siebeck, 1983).
——. 'The Messianic Secret in Mark', pp. 117-129 in C. Tuckett, ed., *The Messianic Secret* (London: SPCK, 1983).
——, ed. *Jews and Christians: The Parting of the Ways AD 70 to 135*, WUNT 66 (Tübingen: Mohr-Siebeck, 1992).
——. 'Biblical Concepts of Revelation', pp. 1-22 in Paul Avis, ed., *Divine Revelation* (London: Darton, Longman and Todd, 1997).
Dupont-Sommer, A. *The Jewish Sect of Qumran and the Essenes* (London: Vallentine, Mitchell and Co., 1954).
Du Rand, J. A. 'The Characterization of Jesus as Depicted in the Narrative of the Fourth Gospel', *Neot* 19 (1985), 18-36.
——. 'Repetitions and Variations: Experiencing the Power of the Gospel of John as Literary Symphony', *Neot* 30 (1997), 59-70.
Durkheim, Emile. *The Rules of Sociological Method* (New York: Free Press, 8th print, 1966).
Du Toit, A. B. 'On Incarnate Word: A Study of John 1:14', *Neot* 2 (1968), 9-21.

Easterling, P. E. and B. M. W. Knox, 'Books and Readers in the Greek World', pp. 1–41 in P. E. Easterling and B. M. W. Knox, eds., *The Cambridge History of Classical Literature*, vol. 1 (Cambridge: CUP, 1989).

Eastman, R. M. *Style: Writing as the Discovery of Outlook* (New York: OUP, 1970).

Eckardt, A. R. *Elder and Younger Brothers: The Encounters of Jews and Christians* (New York: Schocken, 1973).

Eco, Umberto. *A Theory of Semiotics* (Bloomington, IN: Indiana University Press, 1976).

———. *Semiotics and the Philosophy of Language* (Bloomington: Indiana University Press, 1984).

Edie, James. 'Ideality and Metaphor: A Phenomenological Theory of Polysemy', *Journal of the British Society for Phenomenology* 6 (1975), 32–41.

Edlow, R. B. 'The Stoics on Ambiguity', *Journal of the History of Philosophy* 13 (1975), 423–435.

Eichrodt, W. *Theologie des Alten Testaments*, 1–3 (Leipzig: J. C. Hinrichs, 1933–39).

Eitan, I. 'La Répétition de la Racine en Hébreu', *The Journal of the Palestine Oriental Society* 1 (1920–1921), 170–186.

Eliot, T. S. *Essays, Ancient and Modern* (London: n. p., 1936).

———. 'Tradition and the Individual Talent', in *Selected Essays, 1917–1932* (New York: Harcourt, Brace, Jovanovich, 1964 [orig. 1919]), 3–11.

Elliott, John H. *A Home for the Homeless* (Philadelphia: Fortress Press, 1975).

———. 'Social-Scientific Criticism of the New Testament: More on Methods and Models', *Semeia* 35 (1986), 1–33.

———. *What is Social-Scientific Criticism?* (Minneapolis: Fortress Press, 1993).

Elliott, Robert C. *The Power of Satire: Magic, Ritual, Art* (Princeton: Princeton University, 1966).

Ellis, E. E. *Prophecy and Hermeneutic in Early Christianity*, WUNT 18 (Tübingen: Mohr-Siebeck, 1978).

———. 'Background and Christology of John's Gospel: Selected Motifs', *Southwestern Journal of Theology* 31 (1988), 224–231.

———. *The Old Testament in Early Christianity*, WUNT 54 (Tübingen: Mohr-Siebeck, 1991).

Ellis, Peter F. *The Genius of John* (Collegeville, MN: The Liturgical Press, 1984).

Emerton, J. A. 'The Hundred and Fifty-three Fishes in John XXI, 11', *JTS* n.s. 9 (1958), 86–89.

———. 'Melchizedek and the Gods: Fresh Evidence for the Jewish Background of John 10:34-36', *JTS* n.s. 17 (1966), 399–401.

———. 'Notes on Some Passages in the Odes of Solomon', *JTS* n.s. 28 (1977), 507–519.

Empson, William. *Seven Types of Ambiguity* (London: Chatto and Windus, 1949).

Enkvist, Nils Erik. 'On Defining Style: An Essay in Applied Linguistics', pp. 1–56 in John Spencer, ed., *Linguistics and Style* (London, 1964).

Ensley, E. C. 'Eternity in Now: A Sermon on John 14:1-11', *Interpretation* 19 (1965), 295–298.

Ensor, Peter W. *Jesus and His Works: The Johannine Sayings in Historical Perspective*, WUNT 85 (Tübingen: Mohr-Siebeck, 1996).

Enz, J. J. 'The Book of Exodus as Literary Type for the Gospel of John', *JBL* 76 (1957), 208–215.

Epp, Eldon Jay. 'Anti-Semitism and the Popularity of the Fourth Gospel in Christianity', *Central Conference of American Rabbis Journal* 22 (1975), 35–57.

Epstein, I., ed. *Hebrew-English Edition of the Babylonian Talmud* (London: Soncino, 1968–88).

Ernst, J. 'Das Johannesevangelium – ein Frühes Beispiel Christlicher Mystik', *Theologie und Glaube* 81 (1991), 323–338.

Esler, P. F. *Community and Gospel in Luke-Acts* (Cambridge: CUP, 1987).

Eslinger, Lyle M. 'Inner-biblical Exegesis and Inner-biblical Allusions: The Question of Category', *VT* 42 (1992):47–58.

Eusebius, *The Ecclesiastical History*, trans. by J. E. L. Oulton and H. J. Lawlor, Leob Classical Library (London: Heinemann, 1942).

Evans, Craig A. 'The Voice From Heaven: A Note on John 12:28', *CBQ* 43 (1981), 405–408.

——. 'On the Quotation Formulas in the Fourth Gospel', *BZ* 26 (1982), 79–83.

——. 'Obduracy and the Lord's Servant: Some Observations on the Use of the Old Testament in the Fourth Gospel', pp. 221–236 in C. A. Evans and W. F. Stinespring, eds, *Early Jewish and Christian Exegesis: Studies in Memory of William Hugh Brownlee*, Homage 10 (Atlanta, GA: Scholars Press, 1987).

——. *To See and Not Perceive: Isaiah 6:9–10 in Early Jewish and Christian Interpretation*, JSNTSup 64 (Sheffield: Sheffield Academic Press, 1989).

——. 'The Function of the Old Testament in the New', pp. 163–193 in Scot McKnight, ed., *Introducing New Testament Interpretation* (Grand Rapids: Baker Book House, 1989).

——. *The Word and Glory: On the Exegetical and Theological Background of John's Prologue* (Sheffield: JSOT Press, 1993).

—— and W. Richard Stegner, eds. *The Gospels and the Scriptures of Israel*, JSNTSup 104 (Sheffield Academic Press, 1994).

Fackre, G. 'Narrative Theology: An Overview', *Interpretation* 37 (1983), 340–352.

Fairbairn, Patrick. *The Typology of Scripture* (Grand Rapids: Zondervan, 1960).

Farmer, William R. *Maccabees, Zealots, and Josephus: An Inquiry into Jewish Nationalism in the Greco-Roman Period* (New York: Columbia University, 1956).

Faulkner, J. 'The World Significance of John', *Biblical Review* 14 (1929), 171–190.

Faure, A. 'Die alttestamentischen Zitate im 4. Evangelium und die Quellenscheidungshypothese', *ZNW* 21 (1922), 99–121.

Fee, G. D. 'The Use of the Definite Article with Personal Names in the Gospel of John', *NTS* 17 (1970–71), 168–183.

——. 'Once More–John 7:37–39' *ExpTim* 89 (1977–78), 116–118.

——. 'On the Text and Meaning of John 20:30–31', pp. 2193–2206 in F Van Segbroeck et al., eds., *The Four Gospels 1992*, FS Frans Neirynck, vol. 3 (Leuven: Leuven University Press, 1992).

Feenstra, Ronald J. 'Hills Flowing With Wine: A Meditation on John 2:1–11', *The Reformed Journal* 38 (1988), 9–10.

Feine, Paul. *Theologie des Neuen Testaments* (Berlin: Evangelische Verlagsanstalt, 21st print, 1953).

Felperin, Howard. *Beyond Deconstruction: The Uses and Abuses of Literary Theory* (Oxford: Clarendon Press, 1985).

Fennema, D. A. 'John 1:18: 'God the Only Son'', *NTS* 31 (1985), 124–135.

Fensham, F. C. 'Love in the Writings of Qumran and John', *Neot* 6 (1972), 67–77.

Fenton, J. C. 'Towards an Understanding of John', *SE* 4 = TU 102, ed. F. L. Cross (1968), 28–37.

——. *The Gospel According to John* (Oxford: Clarendon Press, 1970).

Ferraro, G. 'L "Ora" di Cristo nel Quarto Vangelo' (Ph.D. diss., Rome: Pont. Univ. Gregoriana, 1969).

Festugière, A. J. *La révélation d'Hermès Trismégiste*, 4 vols (Paris: Gabalda, 1950–54).

Feuillet, André. 'The Hours of Jesus and the Sign of Cana', pp. 17–37 in André Feuillet, *Johannine Studies* (Staten Island, NY: Alba House, 1964).

——. *Johannine Studies*, trans. by Thomas E. Crane (Staten Island, NY: Alba House, 1964).

——. *Le Prologue du quatrième évangile: Etude de théologie johannique* (Paris: Desclée de Brouwer, 1968).

——. *Le mystère de l'amour divin dans la théologie johannique* (Paris: Gabalda, 1972).

——. 'Les christophanies pascales du quatrième évangile sont-elles des signes?' *NRT* 97 (1975), 577–592.

Fewell, Danna Nolan, ed. *Reading Between Texts: Intertextuality and the Hebrew Bible* (Louisville, KY: Westminster/John Knox Press, 1992).

Fiddes, P. S. *The Hiddenness of Wisdom in the Old Testament and Later Judaism* (D. Phil. thesis, Oxford, 1976).

Fiebig, P. 'Zur Form des Johannesevangeliums', *Der Geisteskampf der Gegenwart* 64 (1928), 126–132.

Filson, F. V. 'Who was the Beloved Disciple?' *JBL* 68 (1949), 83–88.

Finkel, Asher. 'The Pesher of Dreams and Scriptures', *Revue de Qumran* 4 (1963–64), 357–370.

Firth, J. Raymond. *The Tongues of Men and Speech* (London: OUP, 1964).

——. *Papers in Linguistics* (London: OUP, 1957).

Fischer, Karl-Martin. 'Der johanneische Christus und der gnostische Erlöser', pp. 245–266 in K. Tröger, ed., *Gnosis und Neues Testament: Studien aus Religionswissenschaft und Theologie* (Berlin: Evangelische Verlagsanstalt, 1973).

Fish, Stanley. 'How to Recognize a Poem When You See One', pp. 322–337 in idem, *Is There a Text in This Class? The Authority of Interpretive Communities* (Cambridge, MA: Harvard University Press, 1980).

Fishbane, Michael. *Text and Texture: A Close Reading of Selected Biblical Texts* (New York: Schocken Books, 1979).

——. 'Revelation and Tradition: Aspects of Inner-Biblical Exegesis', *JBL* 99 (1980), 343–361.

———. 'Jewish Biblical Exegesis: Presupposition and Principles', pp. 92–110 in F. R. Greenspan, ed., *Scripture in the Jewish Christian Traditions: Authority, Interpretation, Relevance* (Nashville: Abingdon, 1982).

———. *Biblical Interpretation in Ancient Israel* (Oxford: Clarendon Press, 1985).

———. *Garments of Torah: Essays in Biblical Hermeneutics* (Bloomington: Indiana University, 1989).

Fisher, Eugene J. 'The Divine Comedy: Humor in the Bible', *Religious Education* 72 (1977), 571–579.

Fishman, J. *Sociolinguistics* (Rowley, MA: Newbury House Publishers, 1970).

———. *The Sociology of Language* (Rowley, MA: Newbury House Publishers, 1972).

Fitzmyer, Joseph A. 'The Qumran Scrolls, the Ebionites and Their Literature', *TS* 16 (1955), 335–372.

———. 'The Languages of Palestine in the First Century AD', *CBQ* 32 (1970), 501–531.

———. *A Wandering Aramean: Collected Essays*, SBLMS 25 (Missoula, MT: Scholars Press, 1977).

——— and D. J. Harrington. *A Manual of Palestinian Aramaic Texts*, Bibliotheca Orientalis 34 (Rome: Biblical Institute, 1978).

———. 'Did Jesus Speak Greek?' *BAR* 18 (1992), 58–63, 76–77.

Flanagan, N. 'The Gospel of John as Drama', *BT* 19 (1981), 264–270.

Flanner, Edward H. 'Anti-Judaism and Anti-Semitism: A Necessary Distinction', *JES* 10 (1973), 582–583.

Floor, L. 'The Lord and the Holy Spirit in the Fourth Gospel', *Neot* 2 (1968), 122–130.

Flowers, H. J. 'Interpolations in the Fourth Gospel', *JBL* 40 (1921), 146–158.

Foerster, Werner. 'Der Heilige Geist im Spätjudentum', *NTS* 8 (1962), 117–134.

Foerster, W. and G. Fohrer, 'σωτήρ' and 'σωτηρία' in *TWNT* 7 (1964), 1004–22; 966–1004 = *TDNT* 7 (1971), 1003–21, 965–1033.

Fohrer, G. 'Jesaja 1 als Zusammenfassung der Verkündigung Jesajas', *ZAW* 74 (1962), 251–268.

———. 'Two-fold Aspects of Hebrew Words', pp. 95–103 in P. R. Ackroyd and B. Lindars, eds, *Words and Meanings: Essays Presented to David Winton Thomas* (Cambridge: CUP, 1968).

Fokkelman, J. P. 'Exodus', pp. 56–65 in Robert Alter and Frank Kermode, eds, *The Literary Guide to the Bible* (Cambridge, MA: Harvard University Press, Belknap Press, 1987).

Ford, J. M. '"Mingled Blood" From the Side of Christ (Jn. 19:24)', *NTS* 15 (1968–69), 337–338.

Fordyce, C. J. 'Puns on Names in Greek', *Classical Journal* 28 (1932–33), 44–46.

Forestell, J. T. *The Word of the Cross: Salvation as Revelation in the Fourth Gospel* (Rome: Biblical Institute Press, 1974).

Forkman, Göran. *The Limits of the Religious Community: Expulsion from the Religious Community within the Qumran Sect, within Rabbinic Judaism, and within primitive Christianity* (Lund, Sweden: CWK Gleerup, 1972).

Formesyn, R. 'Le Semeion Johannique et le Semeion hellenistique', *ETL* 38 (1962), 856–894.

Fortna, Robert Tomson. *The Gospel of Signs: A Reconstruction of the Narrative Source Underlying the Fourth Gospel*, SNTSMS 11 (Cambridge: CUP, 1970).

——. 'From Christology to Soteriology: A Redactional-Critical Study of Salvation in the Fourth Gospel', *Interpretation* 27 (1973), 31–47.

——. *The Fourth Gospel and Its Predecessor* (Philadelphia: Fortress Press, 1988).

Fossum, J. *The Name of God and the Angel of the Lord: Samaritan and Jewish Concepts of Intermediation and the Origin of Gnosticism*, WUNT 36 (Tübingen: Mohr-Siebeck, 1985).

Foulkes, Richard. 'Genesis Motifs in Johannine Literature' (Doctoral diss., Strasbourg, 1968).

Fowl, Stephen E. 'The Ethics of Interpretation, or What's Left After the Elimination of Meaning?' pp. 379–398 in D. J. A. Clines et al., eds., *The Bible in Three Dimensions* (Sheffield, England: JSOT Press, 1990).

Fowler, H. W. *A Dictionary of Modern English Usage* (Oxford: OUP, 1926; reprint, 1944).

Fowler, Roger F., ed. *The Languages of Literature: Some Linguistic Contributions to Criticism* (London: Routledge and Kegan Paul, 1971).

——. *Linguistic Criticism* (Oxford: OUP, 1986).

——. *Literature as Social Discourse* (London: Batsford, 1981).

——. *A Dictionary of Modern Critical Terms*, rev. edn (London and New York: Routledge and Kegan Paul, 1987).

Fowler, R. M. 'Who Is "the Reader" in Reader Response Criticism?' *Semeia* 31 (1985), 5–23.

Fox, L. A. 'The Genuineness of St. John's Gospel', *The Lutheran Quarterly* 54 (1924), 323–333.

France, R. T. *Jesus and the Old Testament: His Application of Old Testament Passages to Himself and His Mission* (London: Tyndale, 1971).

—— and D. Wenham, eds. *Studies in Midrash and Historiography* (Sheffield: JSOT Press, 1983).

Frank, E. *Revelation Taught: The Paraclete in the Gospel of John* (Lund: Gleerup, 1985).

Franke, August H. *Das alte Testament bei Johannes. Ein Beitrag zur Erklärung und Beurtheilung der johanneischen Schriften* (Göttingen: Vandenhoeck und Ruprecht, 1885).

Freed, Edwin D. 'Variations in the Language and Thought of John', *ZNW* 55 (1964), 167–197.

——. *Old Testament Quotations in the Gospel of John* (Leiden: Brill, 1965).

——. 'The Son of Man in the Fourth Gospel', *JBL* 86 (1967), 402–409.

——. 'Samaritan Influence in the Gospel of John', *CBQ* 30 (1968), 580–587.

——. 'Did John Write His Gospel Partly to Win Samaritan Converts?' *NovT* 12 (1970), 241–256.

——. 'Some Old Testament Influences on the Prologue of John', pp. 145–161 in Howard Bream and Ralph D. Heim, eds, *A Light Unto My Path: Old Testament Studies* (Philadelphia: Temple Univ. Press, 1974).

——. 'Ego Eimi in John 1:20 and 4:25', *CBQ* 41 (1979), 288–291.

——. 'Theological Prelude to the Prologue of John's Gospel', *SJT* 32 (1979), 257–269.
——. 'Ego Eimi in John 8:24 in Light of Its Context and Jewish Messianic Belief', *JTS* n.s. 33 (1982), 163–167.
Freedman, David N. 'The Structure of Job 3', *Bib* 49 (1968), 503–508.
Freedman, H. and M. Simon, eds. *The Midrash Rabbah*, translated into English, 10 vols (London: Soncino, 1977).
Freedman, William. 'The Literary Motif: A Definition and Evaluation', *Novel* 4 (1971), 123–131.
Frei, Hans W. *The Eclipse of Biblical Narrative* (Hartford: Yale University Press, 1974).
——. *The Identity of Jesus Christ* (Philadelphia: Fortress Press, 1975).
——. 'Theological Reflections on the Accounts of Jesus' Death and Resurrection', pp. 45–93 in H. W. Frei, G. Hunsinger, et al., eds, *Theology and Narrative: Selected Essays* (New York: OUP, 1993).
French, D. H. 'The Roman Road-System of Asia Minor', pp. 698–729 in H. Temporini and W. Hasse, eds, *Aufstieg und Niedergang der römischen Welt*, II.7.2 (Berlin, New York: Walter de Gruyter, 1980).
Freudman, Lillian C. *Antisemitism in the New Testament* (New York: University Press of America, 1994).
Freund, Elizabeth. *The Return of the Reader: Reader-Response Criticism* (New York: Methuen, 1987).
Frey, J. *Die johanneische Eschatologie*, WUNT 1.96 (Tübingen: Mohr-Siebeck, 1997).
Freyne, S. 'The New Testament Concept of Revelation: Some Reflections', pp. 32–48 in W. Harrington, ed., *Witness to the Spirit: Essays on Revelation , Spirit, Redemption* (Dublin: Irish Biblical Association, 1979).
——. 'Vilifying the Other and Defining the Self: Matthew's and John's Anti-Jewish Polemic in Focus', pp. 117–143 in J. Neusner and E. Frerichs, eds, *To See Ourselves as Others See Us: Christians, Jews, Others in Late Antiquity* (Chico, CA: Scholars Press, 1985).
Fridrichsen, Anton. 'La pensée missionaire dans le quatrième évangile', pp. 39–45 in A. Fridrichsen, ed., *Arbeiten und Mitteilungen aus dem neutestamentichen Seminar zu Uppsala*, vol. 6 (Uppsala: Lundequistaska Bokhandeln, 1937).
Friedman, Norman. *Form and Meaning in Fiction*. Athens: University of Georgia Press, 1975.
Friend, H. S. 'Like the Father, Like the Son: A Discussion of the Concept of Agency in Halakah and John', *Ashland Theological Journal* 21 (1990), 18–28.
Frye, Northrop. *Anatomy of Criticism: Four Essays* (Princeton: Princeton University Press, 1957).
——. *The Great Code: The Bible and Literature* (New York: Harcourt, Brace, and Jovanovich, 1982).
Frye, R. N. 'Reitzenstein and Qumran Revisited by an Iranian', *HTR* 55 (1962), 261–268.
Fulco, J. W. *Maranatha: Reflections on the Mystical Theology of John the Evangelist* (New York: Paulist Press, 1971).
Fuller, Reginald H. *A Critical Introduction to the New Testament* (London: Duckworth, 1965).
——. 'The "Jews" in the Fourth Gospel', *Dialog* 16 (1977), 31–37.

Funk, Robert W. *Language, Hermeneutic, and the Word of God: The Problem of Language in the New Testament and Contemporary Theology* (London: Harper and Row, 1966).
—. *History and Hermeneutics* (New York: Harper and Row, 1967).
—. *Parables and Presence: Forms of the New Testament Tradition* (Philadelphia: Fortress Press, 1982).

Gabriel, A. 'Faith and Rebirth in the Fourth Gospel', *Bible Bhashyam* 16 (1990), 205–215.
Gächter, P. 'Der Formale Aufbau der Abschiedsrede Jesu', *ZTK* 58 (1934), 155–207.
—. 'Die Form der eucharistischen Rede Jesu (Jn 6:35ff)', *ZTK* 59 (1935), 419–441.
—. 'Strophen im Johannesevangelium', *ZTK* 60 (1936), 99–120; 402–423.
Gaebelein, A. C. *The Gospel of John: A Complete Analytical Exposition of the Gospel of John* (Wheaton, IL: van Kampen Press, 1936).
Gafni, Isaiah. 'The Historical Background', pp. 27–31 in *Jewish Writings of the Second Temple Period: Apocrypha, Pseudepigrapha, Qumran Sectarian Writings, Philo, Josephus*, ed. M. E. Stone, CRINT (Assen: Van Gorcum; Philadelphia: Fortress, 1984).
Gage, Warren A. *The Gospel of Genesis: Studies in Protology and Eschatology* (Winona Lake, IN: Carpenter Books, 1984).
Gager, John G. *Kingdom and Community: The Social World of Early Christianity* (Englewood Cliffs, NJ: Prentice Hall, 1975).
—. 'Shall We Marry Our Enemies? Sociology and the New Testament', *Interpretation* 36 (1982), 256–265.
Gallagher, Eugene V. *Divine Man or Magician?: Celsus and Origen on Jesus*, SBLDS 64 (Chico, CA: Scholars Press, 1982).
Gamble, H. Y. *Books and Readers in the Early Church* (New Haven: Yale University Press, 1995).
Gammie, John G. 'Spatial and Ethical Dualism in Jewish Wisdom and Apoclyptic Literature', *JBL* 93 (1974), 356–385.
García-Moreno, A. 'En torno al derásh en el IV Evangelio', *Scripta Theologica* 25 (93), 33–48.
Gardner-Smith, P. *Saint John and the Synoptic Gospels* (Cambridge: CUP, 1938).
Garland, David E. 'John 18–19: Life Through Jesus' Death', *R&E* 85 (1988), 485–499.
Gärtner, Bertil E. *The Temple and the Community in Qumran and the New Testament*, SNTSMS 1 (Cambridge: CUP, 1965).
Gaston, L. *No Stone on Another: Studies in the Significance of the Fall of Jerusalem in the Synoptic Gospels*, NovTSup 23 (Leiden: Brill, 1970).
Geertz, C. 'Ethos, Worldview and the Analysis of Sacred Symbols', pp. 126–141 in idem, *The Interpretation of Cultures* (New York: Basic Books, 1973).
Geiger, G. 'Aufruf an Rückkehrende. Zum Sinn des Zitats von Ps. 78, 24b in Joh 6, 31', *Bib* 65 (1984), 449–464.
Geisler, N. L. 'Johannine Apologetics', *BibSac* 554 (1979), 333–343.
Geller, Stephen A. 'Through Windows and Mirrors into the Bible: History, Literature, and Language in the Study of the Text', pp. 3–40 in S. A. Geller et al, eds., *A*

Sense of Text: The Art of Language in the Study of Biblical Literature (Winona Lake, IN: Eisenbrauns, 1983).

Genette, Gérard. *Narrative Discourse: An Essay in Method*, ET by Jane E. Lewin (Ithaca, NY: Cornell Univ. Press, 1980).

Gerhard, J. 'The Literary Unity and the Compositional Methods of the Gospel of John' (Ph.D. diss., Washington: The Catholic University of America, 1975).

Gertner, D. M. 'Midrashim in the New Testament', *Journal of Semitic Studies* 7 (1952), 267-292.

Getty, Mary Ann. 'The Jews and John's Passion Narrative', *Liturgy* 22 (1977), 6-10.

Gevirtz, Stanley. 'Of Patriarchs and Puns', *HUCA* 46 (1975), 33-54.

Gewalt, Dietfried. 'Neutestamentliche Exegese und Soziologie', *EvT* 31 (1971), 87-99.

Geyser, A. S. 'Israel in the Fourth Gospel', *Neot* 20 (1986), 13-20.

Giblin, C. H. 'The Miraculous Crossing of the Sea (John 6:6-21)', *NTS* 29 (1983), 96-103.

——. 'The Tripartite Narrative Structure of John's Gospel', *Bib* 71 (1990), 449-468.

Gilbert, J. 'Aspects of the Truth in the New Testament', *Concilium* 83 (1973), 35-42.

Giles, B. *Jesus the High Priest in the Epistle to the Hebrews and the Fourth Gospel* (Ph.D. diss. Manchester, dir.: F. F. Bruce, 1974).

Gill, Jerry. 'Jesus, Irony and the "New Quest"', *Interpretation* 41 (1980), 139-151.

Gill, Robin. *The Social Context of Theology: A Methodological Enquiry* (London and Oxford: Alden and Mowbray, 1975).

Gilltus, I. S. 'The Tree of Life and the Tree of Death: A Study of Gnostic Symbols', *Religion* 17 (1987), 337-353.

Gingrich, F. W. 'Ambiguity of Word Meanings in John's Gospel', *Classical Weekly* 37 (1943-44), 77.

Glasson, T. Francis. 'John 1:9 and Rabbinic Tradition', *ZNW* 49 (1958), 288-290.

——. 'Exodus Typology in the Fourth Gospel', *JBL* 81 (1962), 329-342.

——. *Moses in the Fourth Gospel* (London: SCM, 1963).

Glasswell, M. E. 'The Relationship Between John and Mark', *JSNT* 23 (1985), 99-115.

Glück, J. J. 'Paronomasia in Biblical Literature', *Semitics* 1 (1970), 50-78.

Gnilka, J. *Johannesevangelium*, Neue Echter Bibel (Würzburg: Echter, 1983).

Godet, Frederick Louis. *Commentary on John's Gospel* (Grand Rapids: Kregel Publications, 1978, reprinted, 1980).

de Goedt, M. 'Un schème de révélation dans le quatrième évangile', *NTS* 8 (1961-62), 142-150.

Goguel, M. *Introduction au Nouveau Testament*, vol II : *Le Quatrième Évangile* (Paris: Leroux, 1923).

Goldberg, A. 'Kain: Sohn des Menschen oder Sohn der Schlange?' *Judaica* 25 (1969), 203-221.

Goldman, E. 'Who Raises Up the Fallen', *Hebrew Studies* 20-21 (1979-80), 54-59.

Good, Edwin. *Irony in the Old Testament* (Philadelphia: Westminster Press, 1965).

——. 'Ezekiel's Ship: Some Extended Metaphors in the Old Testament', *Semitics* 1 (1970), 70-80.

Goodenough, E. R. *By Light, Light: The Mystical Gospel of Hellenistic Judaism* (New Haven: Yale University Press, 1935).

Goodman, Martin. 'Nerva, the *fiscus Judaicus* and Jewish Identity', *JJS* 9 (1989), 40–44.

——. 'Proselytising in Rabbinic Judaism', *JJS* 40 (1989), 175–185.

——. 'Identity and Authority in Ancient Judaism', *Judaism* 39 (1990), 192–201.

Goodwin, Charles. 'How Did John Treat His Sources?' *JBL* 73 (1954), 61–75.

Goodspeed, J. 'The Original Language of the New Testament', pp. 127–168 in *New Chapters in New Testament Study* (New York: Macmillan, 1937).

Goppelt, Leonard. *Theology of the New Testament*, 2 vols, ET by John E. Alsup and ed. by Jürgen Roloff (Grand Rapids: Eerdmans, 1982).

——. *Typos: The Typological Interpretation of the Old Testament in the New* (Grand Rapids: Eerdmans, 1982).

Gottwald, Norman. *The Tribes Of Yahweh: A Sociology of the Religion of Liberated Israel 1250–1050 B.C.E.* (New York: Mary Knoll, 1979).

Granskou, David. 'Anti-Judaism in the Passion Accounts of the Fourth Gospel', pp. 201–216 in P. Richardson and D. Granskau, eds, in *Anti-Judaism in Early Christianty*, vol. 1 (Ontario: Wilfrid Laurier University Press, 1986).

Grant, Frederick C. *The Gospel According to St. Mark*, The Interpreter's Bible (New York: Abingdon Press, 1951).

——. 'Rhetoric and Oratory', *IDB* 4 (1962), 75–77.

Grant, R. M. 'One Hundred and Fifty-Three Large Fish (Jn. 21, 11)', *HTR* 42 (1949), 273–275.

——. *Gnosticism and Early Christianity* (New York: Columbia University Press, 1959).

——. *Gnosticism: A Sourcebook of Heretical Writings from the Early Christian Period* (New York: Harper and Brothers, 1961).

——. 'The Coming of the Kingdom', *JBL* 67 (1948), 297–303.

——. *The Letter and the Spirit* (London: SPCK, 1957).

——. 'The Origin of the Fourth Gospel', *JBL* 69 (1950), 305–22.

Grässer, Erich. 'Die antijüdische Polemic im Johannesevangelium', *NTS* 10 (1964–1965), 74–90.

Grassi, J. A. 'The Wedding at Cana (John 2:1-11): A Pentecostal Meditation?' *NovT* 14 (1972), 131–136.

——. 'Eating Jesus' Flesh and Drinking His Blood: The Centrality and Meaning of John 6:51-58', *BTB* 17 (1987), 24–30.

——. *The Secret Identity of the Beloved Disciple* (New York: Paulist Press, 1992).

Gray, G. B. *Sacrifice in the Old Testament: Its Theory and Practice* (Oxford: Clarendon Press, 1925).

Grayston, Kenneth. *The Gospel of John* (Philadelphia: Trinity Press, 1990).

——. 'The Meaning of "Parakletos"', *JSNT* 13 (1981), 67–82.

Green, Henry A. 'Gnosis and Gnosticism: A Study in Methodology', *Numen* 24 (1977), 95–134.

Green, William Scott. 'Romancing the Tome: Rabbinic Hermeneutics and the Theory of Literature', *Semeia* 40 (1987), 147–168.

Green-Armytage, A. H. N. *John Who Saw: A Layman's Essay on the Authorship of the Fourth Gospel* (London: Faber and Faber, 1952).

Greenbaum, S., G. Leech and J. Svartvik, eds, *Studies in English Linguistics for Randolph Quirk* (London: Longman, 1979).

Greeves, D. 'The Recognized Saviour', *ExpTim* 93 (1981–82), 84–86.

Gregory, J. 'Some Aspects of Seeing in Euripides' Bacchae', *Greece and Rome* 32 (1985), 23–31.

Grese, W. C. *Corpus Hermeticum XIII and Early Christian Literature*, SCHNT 5 (Leiden: Brill, 1979).

——. '"Unless One is Born Again": The Use of a Heavenly Journey in John 3', *JBL* 107 (1989), 677–693.

Gressmann, H. 'The Sources of Israel's Messianic Hope', *AJT* 17 (1913), 173–194.

Gribbs, F. L. 'A Reassessment of the Date of Origin and the Destination of the Gospel of John', *JBL* 89 (1970), 38–55.

Griffiths, D. R. 'Deutero-Isaiah and the Fourth Gospel: Some Points of Comparison', *ExpTim* 65 (1954), 355–360.

Grigsby, Bruce H. 'The Source and Purpose of the Light versus Darkness Motif in the Fourth Gospel' (Th.M. thesis, Dallas Seminary, 1976).

——. 'The Cross as an Expiatory Sacrifice in the Fourth Gospel', *JSNT* 15 (1982), 51–80.

——. 'Gematria and John 21, 11: Another Look at Ezekiel 47, 10', *ExpTim* 95 (1983–84), 177–178.

——. 'Washing in the Pool of Siloam: Thematic Anticipation of the Johannine Cross (John 9:7)', *NovT* 27 (1985), 227–235.

——. '"If Any Man Thirsts": Observations on Rabbinic Background of John 7:37–39', *Bib* 67 (1986), 100–108.

Grill, J. *Untersuchungen über die Entstehung des 4. Evangeliums. 2. Teil: Das Mysterienevangelium des hellenisierten kleinasiatischen Christentums* (Tübingen: Mohr-Siebeck, 1923).

Groenewald, E. P. 'The Christological Meaning of John 20:31', *Neot* 2 (1968), 131–140.

Grossberg, Daniel. 'Multiple Meaning: Part of a Compound Literary Device in the Hebrew Bible', *East Asia Journal of Theology* 4 (1986), 77–86.

Grossouw, W. *Revelation and Redemption: A Sketch of the Theology of St. John* (Westminster: Newman, 1955).

Gruenler, R. G. *The Trinity in the Gospel of John: A Thematic Commentary on the Fourth Gospel* (Grand Rapids: Baker Book House, 1986).

Gruenwald, Ithamar. *Apocalyptic and Merkavah Mysticism* (Leiden: Brill, 1980).

Grundmann, Walter. *Der Zeuge der Wahrheit: Grundzüge der Christologie des Johannesevangeliums* (Berlin: Evangelische Verlagsanstalt, 1985).

Gryglewicz, Feliks. 'Die Pharisäer und die Johanneskirche', pp. 144–158 in A. Fuchs, ed., *Probleme der Forschung*, SNTU A/3 (Vienna and Munich: Herold Verlag, 1978).

Gubler, M. L. '"Ich bin der Weg und die Wahrheit und das Leben" (Joh 14.6)', *Diakonia* 24 (1993), 373–382.

Guilding, Aileen. *The Fourth Gospel and Jewish Worship* (Oxford: Clarendon Press, 1960).

Guillaume, A. 'Paronomasia in the Old Testament', *JSS* 9 (1964), 282–290.

Gunkel, H. 'Die Oden Salomos', *ZNW* 11 (1910), 291–328.

——. 'Die Israelitische Literatur', pp. 51–102 in Paul Hinneberg, ed., *Die Kultur der Gegenwart*, I/7 (Berlin: B. G. Teubner, 1960).

Gunn, David M. 'The Anatomy of Divine Comedy: On Reading the Bible as Comedy and Tragedy', *Semeia* 32 (1984), 115–129.

Gutbrod, W. "Ἰουδαῖος", *TDNT* 3 (1965), 375–83.

Guthrie, D. 'The Importance of Signs in the Fourth Gospel', *Vox Evangelica* (1967), 72–83.

Haacker, K. *Die Stiftung des Heils: Untersuchungen zur Struktur der johanneischen Theologie* (Stuttgart: Calwer, 1972).

Habel, N. 'The Form and Significance of the Call Narratives', *ZAW* 77 (1965), 297–323.

Haenchen, Ernst. 'Gab es eine vorchristliche Gnosis?' *ZTK* 49 (1952), 316–349.

——. 'Aus der Literatur zum Johannesevangelium', *TRu* 23 (1955), 295–335.

——. 'Der Vater der mich gesandt hat', *NTS* 9 (1963), 208–216.

——. *Gott und Mensch* (Tübingen: Mohr-Siebeck, 1965).

——. 'The Book of Acts as Source Material for the History of Early Christianity', pp. 258–278 in L. E. Keck and J. L. Martyn, eds, *Studies in Luke-Acts* (London: SPCK, 1966).

——. *Johannesevangelium: Ein Kommentar* (Tübingen: Mohr-Siebeck, 1980).

——. *John: A Commentary on the Gospel of John*, Hermeneia Series. Translated by Robert W. Funk and edited with Ulrich Busse, vol. 1 (Philadelphia: Fortress Press, 1984).

Hagenbuchle, R. 'The Concept of Ambiguity in Linguistics and Literary Criticism', pp. 213–221 in R. Watts, et al., eds, *Modes of Interpretation: Essays Presented to Ernst Leisi* (Tübingen: Gunter Narr Verlag, 1984).

Hahn, Ferdinand. *Das Problem der Mission in der sonstigen nach paulinischen Tradition und den johanneischen Schriften: Das Verständnis der Mission im Neuen Testament*, WMANT 13 (Neuchirchener-Vluyn: Neukirchener Verlag, 1963).

——. 'Der Prozeß Jesu nach dem Johannesevangelium', *EKKNT Vorarbeiten Heft* 2 (Zürich Benziger; Neukirchen: Neukirchener Verlag, 1970).

——. 'Die Jüngerberufung Joh. 1:35–51', pp. 187–189 in J. Gnilka, ed., *Neues Testament und Kirche: Für Rudolf Schnackenburg* (Freiburg: Herder, 1974).

Haiman, John. 'A Study in Polysemy', *Studies in Language* 2 (1978), 1–33.

Hall, R. G. *Revealed Histories: Techniques for Ancient Jewish and Christian Historiography* (Sheffield: JSOT Press, 1991).

Halladay, W. L. 'Style, Irony and Authenticity in Jeremiah', *JBL* 81 (1962), 44–54.

Halliday, M. A. K. *Language as Social Semiotic: The Social Interpretation of Language and Meaning* (London: Edward Arnold, 1978).

van Halsema, J. H. 'Het raadsel als literaire vorm in Marcus en Johannes', *Gereformeerd Theologisch Tijdschrift* 83 (1983), 1–17.

Halverson, J. 'Oral and Written Gospel: A Critique of Werner Kelber', *NTS* 40 (1994), 180–95.

Hambly, W. F. 'Creation and Gospel: A Brief Comparison of Genesis 1:1–2, 4 and John 1:1–2, 12', *SE* 5 = TU 103, ed. F. L. Cross (1968), 69–74.

Hamerton-Kelly, R. G. *Pre-Existence, Wisdom, and the Son of Man* (Cambridge: CUP, 1973).

Hamerton-Kelly, R. and R. Scroggs, eds. *Jews, Greeks, and Christians* (Leiden: Brill, 1976).

Hamilton, Neil Q. 'Temple Cleansing and Temple Bank', *JBL* 83 (1964), 365–372.

Hampel, V. *Menschensohn und historischer Jesus: Ein Rätselwort als Schlüssel zum messianischen Selbstverständnis Jesu* (Neukirchen-Vluyn: Neukirchener, 1990).

Handelman, Susan A. *The Slayers of Moses: The Emergence of Rabbinic Interpretation in Modern Literary Theory* (Albany: State University of New York Press, 1982).

Hanson, A. T. *Jesus Christ in the Old Testament* (London: SPCK, 1965).

———. 'John's Citation of Psalm 82: John 10.33–36', *NTS* 11 (1964–65), 158–162.

———. 'The Old Testament Background to the Raising of Lazarus', *SE* 6 = TU 112, ed. E. A. Livingstone (1973), 252–255.

———. 'John 1:14–18 and Exodus 34', *NTS* 23 (1976), 90–101. Repr. pp. 97–109, 197–199 in *The New Testament Interpretation of Scripture* (London: SPCK, 1980).

———. *The New Testament Interpretation of Scripture* (London: SPCK, 1980).

———. *The Living Utterances of God: The New Testament Exegesis of the Old* (London: Darton, Longman and Todd, 1983).

———. *The Prophetic Gospel: A Study of John and the Old Testament* (Edinburgh, Clark, 1991).

———. 'John's Use of Scripture', pp. 358–379 in Craig A. Evans and W. Richard Stegner, eds, *The Gospels and the Scriptures of Israel*, JSNTSup 104 (Sheffield: Sheffield Academic Press, 1994).

Hanson, P. D. *The Dawn of Apocalyptic* (Philadelphia: Fortress Press, 1975).

Hanson, R. P. C. *Allegory and Event* (London: SCM, 1959).

Harari, J. V. ed., *Textual Strategies: Perspectives in Post-structuralist Criticism* (London: Methuen, 1979).

Hare, Douglas R. A. *The Theme of Jewish Persecution of Christians in the Gospel According to Matthew*, SNTSMS 6 (Cambridge: CUP, 1967).

———. 'Review of Three Recent Works on Anti-Semitism', *RelSRev* 2.3 (1976), 15–21.

von Harnack, Adolf. *Die Mission und Ausbreitung des Christentums in den ersten drei Jahrhunderten*, 2 vols (Leipzig: Hinrichs, 1902).

———. *Judentum und Judenchristentum in Justins Dialog mit Trypho*, TU 39 (Leipzig: Hinrichs, 1913).

———. *Das Wir in den Johanneischen Schriften*. Sitzungsberichte der Preussischen Akademie der Wissenschaften (Berlin: Verlag der Akademie der Wiss., 1923).

———. *Lehrbuch der Dogmengeschichte* (Freiburg: Herder, 1931).

Harner, Philip B. *The 'I AM' of the Fourth Gospel: A Study in Johannine Usage and Thought* (Philadelphia: Fortress Press, 1946).

Harnisch, W. 'Die Ironie als Stilmittel in Gleichnissen Jesu', *EvT* 32 (1972), 421–436.

Harrington, Daniel. 'Sociological Concepts and the Early Church: A Decade of Research', *TS* 41 (1980), 181-190.

Harris, Elizabeth. *Prologue and Gospel: The Theology of the Fourth Evangelist* (Sheffield: Sheffield Academic Press, 1994).

Harris, J. Rendel. *The Origin of the Prologue of John's Gospel* (Cambridge: CUP, 1917).

——. 'The Early Christian Interpretation of the Passover', *ExpTim* 38 (1926-27), 88-90.

——. *Testimonies*, 2 vols, with the assistance of Vacher Burch (Cambridge: Cambridge University Press, 1916-1920).

Harris, W. V. *Ancient Literacy* (Cambridge, MA: Harvard University Press, 1989).

Harris, Z. *Methods in Structural Linguistics* (Chicago: University of Chicago Press, 1951).

Hartin, P. J. 'A Community in Crisis: The Christology of the Johannine Community as the Point at Issue', *Neot* 19 (1985), 37-49.

Hartman, L. 'He Spoke of the Temple of His Body (Jn. 2:13-22)', *Svensk exegetisk årsbok* 54 (1989), 70-79.

——. 'Aspects of Johannine Literature', *Literature and Theology* 1 (1987), 184-190.

Harvey, A. E. *Jesus on Trial: A Study of the Fourth Gospel* (London: SPCK, 1976).

——. *Jesus and the Constraints of History* (Philadelphia: Westminster Press, 1982).

Hatch, E., H. A. Redpath, et al. *A Concordance to the Septuagint and the Other Greek Versions of the Old Testament (including the Apocryphal Books)* (Oxford: Clarendon Press, 1897).

Hatina, T. R. 'John 20:22 in its Eschatological Context: Promise or Fulfilment?' *Bib* 74 (1993), 196-219.

Hatzfeld, Helmut, 'Methods of Stylistic Investigation', pp. 44-51 in S. C. Aston et al., eds., *Literature and Science: Proceedings of the Sixth Triennial Congress, Oxford 1954*, International Federation for Modern Languages and Literatures (Oxford: Blackwell, 1955).

Hawkes, T. *Metaphor* (London: Methuen, 1972).

Hawthorne, G. F. 'The Concept of Faith in the Fourth Gospel', *BibSac* 116 (1959), 117-126.

Hayes, Curtis W. 'Linguistics and Literature: Prose and Poetry', pp. 173-187 in Archibald A. Hill, ed., *Linguistics Today* (New York: Basic Books, 1969).

Hays, Richard B. *Echoes of Scripture in the Letters of Paul* (New Haven: Yale University Press, 1989).

Hayward, C. T. R. 'The Holy Name of the God of Moses and the Prologue of St. John's Gospel', *NTS* 25 (1979), 16-32.

Hebel, J. Udo. *Intertextuality, Allusion, and Quotation: An International Bibliography of Critical Studies* (New York: Greenwood, 1989).

Heekerens, H. P. *Die Zeichen-Quelle der johanneischen Redaktion: Ein Beitrag zur Entstehungsgeschichte des vierten Evangeliums* (Stuttgart: Verlag Katholisches Bibelwerk, 1984).

Hegstad, H. 'Den Hellige Ånd Som Veileder til "den fulle sannhet" (Joh 16, 13)—prinsippteologisk belyst', *Tidsskrift for Teologi og kirke* 64 (1993), 95-109.

Heil, J. *Jesus Walking on the Sea*, AnBib 87 (Rome: Biblical Institute Press, 1981).

Hein, K. 'Judas Iscariot: Key to the Last Supper Narratives?' *NTS* 17 (1970–71), 227–232.
Heine, Ronald. Origen's *Commentary on the Gospel According to John,* Books 13–32, trans. by R. Heine (Washington, D.C.: Catholic University Press of America, 1993).
Heinrich, K. 'Wie eine Religion der anderen die Wahrheit wegnimmt: Notizen über das Unbehagen bei der Lektüre des Johannes-Evangeliums', *ZRGG* 49 (1997), 345–363.
Heise, Jürgen. *Bleiben: Menein in den Johanneischen Schriften,* Hermeneutische untersuchungen zur Theologie, 8 (Tübingen: Mohr-Siebeck, 1967).
Hellholm, David, ed. *Apocalypticism in the Mediterranean World and the Near East* (Tübingen: Mohr-Siebeck, 1983).
Helmbold, Andrew K. *The Nag Hammadi Gnostic Texts and the Bible* (Grand Rapids: Baker Books, 1967).
Hélou, C. *Symbole et langage dans les écrits johanniques: Lumière–ténèbres* (Paris: Mame, 1980).
Hempel, Johannes. *Gott und Mensch im Alten Testaments: Studien zur Geschichte der Frömmigkeit,* BWANT, 3. Folge 2 (Stuttgart: Kohlhammer, 1936).
——. *Das Ethos des Alten Testaments,* BZAW 67 (Berlin: de Gruyter, 2nd print, 1964).
Henderson, M. W. 'The Priestly Ministry of Jesus in the Gospel of John and the Epistle to the Hebrews' (Ph.D. diss., Southern Baptist Theological Seminary, Louisville, KY, 1966).
Henderson, R. A. *The Gospel of Fulfilment. A Study of St. John's Gospel* (London: SPCK, 1936).
Henderson, W. G. 'The Ethical Idea of the World in John's Gospel' (Ph.D. diss., Louisville: Southern Baptist Theological Seminary, 1945).
Hendry, G. S. 'Reveal, Revelation', pp. 195–200 in A. Richardson, ed., *A Theological Word Book of the Bible* (London: SCM Press, 1950).
Hengel, Martin. *Judaism and Hellenism: Studies in Their Encounter in Palestine During the Early Hellenistic Period,* ET by John Bowden, 2 vols (Philadelphia: Fortress Press, reprint, 1974).
——. *The Son of God* (London: SCM, 1976).
——. *Crucifixion in the Ancient World and the Folly of the Message of the Cross* (Philadelphia: Fortress Press; London: SCM, 1977).
——. 'Jesus als messianischer Lehrer der Weisheit und die Anfänge der Christologie', pp. 147–188 in J. Leclant, et al., eds, *Sagesse et Religion: Colloque de Strasbourg, October 1976* (Paris: Bibliothèque des Centres d'Etudes Supérieures Spécialisés, 1979).
——. *The Atonement: The Origin of the Doctrine in the New Testament,* ET by John Bowden (London: SCM; Philadelphia: Fortress, 1981).
——. 'The Interpretation of the Wine Miracle at Cana: John 2:1–11', pp. 84–112 in L. D. Hurst and N. T. Wright, eds, *The Glory of Christ in the New Testament* (Oxford: OUP, 1987).
——. *The Johannine Question,* ET by John Bowden (London: SCM, 1989).
——. 'The Old Testament in the Fourth Gospel', *Horizons in Biblical Theology* 12 (January 1990), 19–41.

—— and A. M. Schwemer, eds. *Königsherrschaft Gottes und himmlischer Kult*, WUNT 55 (Tübingen: Mohr-Siebeck, 1991).

——. 'Reich Christi, Reich Gottes und Weltreich im Johannesevangelium', pp. 163–184 in M. Hengel und A. M. Schwemer, eds, *Königsherrschaft Gottes und himmlischer Kult im Judentum, Urchristentum und in der hellenischen Welt* (Tübingen: Mohr-Siebeck, 1991).

——. *Die johanneische Frage*, WUNT 67 (Tübingen: Mohr-Siebeck, 1993).

—— and Hermut Löhr. *Schriftauslegung im antiken Judentum und im Urchristentum*, WUNT 73 (Tübingen: Mohr-Siebeck, 1994).

von Hengstenberg, E. *Christology of the Old Testament and a Commentary on the Messianic Predictions* (Grand Rapids: Kregel, 1970; reprint from ET of 1836–39).

Henle, P. 'Metaphor', pp. 173–195 in idem, ed., *Language, Thought, and Culture* (Ann Arbor: University of Michigan Press, 1965).

Henn, Thomas Rice. *The Bible as Literature* (London: Lutterworth, 1970).

Herdan, Gustav. *Quantitative Linguistics* (Washington: Butterworths, 1964).

Herford, Travers R. *Christianity in Talmud and Midrash* (London: William and Norgate, 1903).

Herzberg, Walter. 'Polysemy in the Hebrew Bible' (Ph.D. diss., New York University, 1979).

Hesse, Franz. *Das Verstockungsproblem im Alten Testament: Eine frömmigkeitsgeschichtliche Untersuchung*, BZAW 74 (Berlin: de Gruyter, 1955).

——. 'Wolfhart Pannenberg und das Alte Testament', *NZSTh* 7 (1965), 174–199.

Hickling, J. A. 'Attitudes to Judaism in the Fourth Gospel', pp. 347–354 in M. de Jonge, ed., *L'Évangile de Jean: sources, rédaction, théologie*, BETL 44 (Leuven: Leuven University Press, 1977).

Hiers, Richard. 'Purification of the Temple: Preparation for the Kingdom of God', *JBL* 90 (1971), 82–90.

Higgins, A. J. B. *The Historicity of the Fourth Gospel* (London: Lutterworth Press, 1960).

——. 'The Words of Jesus According to St. John', *BJRL* 49 (1966–67), 363–386.

Hilgenfeld, A. *Judentum und Judenchristentum: Eine Nachlese zu der Ketzergeschichte des Urchristentums, zur ältesten Kirchengeschichte* (Leipzig: Fues-Reisland, 1886).

Hill, Archibald. 'An Analysis of the Windhover: An Experiment in Structural Method', *Publication of the Modern Language Association* 70 (1955), 968–978.

Hill, D. 'The Request of Zebedee's Sons and the Johannine δόξα-Theme', *NTS* 13 (1966–67), 281–285.

——. *Greek Words and Hebrew Meanings* (Cambridge: CUP, 1967).

Hill, E. *The Concept of Meaning* (London: George Allen and Unwin, 1974).

Hindley, J. C. 'Witness in the Fourth Gospel', *SJT* 18 (1965), 319–337.

Hinrichs, B. *'Ich Bin' Die Konsistenz des Johannes-Evangeliums in der Konszentration auf das Wort Jesus*, Stuttgarter Bibelstudien 133 (Stuttgart: Katholisches Bibelwerk, 1988).

Hirsch, Emanuel. *Das vierte Evangelium in seiner ursprünglichen Gestalt verdeutscht und erklärt* (Tübingen: Mohr-Siebeck, 1936).

——. 'Stilkritik und Literaturanalyse im vierten Evangelium', *ZNW* 43 (1950–51), 128–143.
Hirsch, E. D. *Validity in Interpretation* (New Haven, CT: Yale University Press, 1967).
——. *The Aims of Interpretation* (Chicago and London: University of Chicago Press, 1976).
Hirschberg, H. 'Once Again – The Minim', *JBL* 67 (1948), 305–18.
Hitchcock, F. R. M. 'The Dramatic Development of the Fourth Gospel', *Exp* 7 (1907), 266–279.
——. 'Is the Fourth Gospel a Drama?' *Theology* 7 (1923), 307–317.
Hock, Ronald F. *The Social Context of Paul's Ministry, Tent-Making and Apostleship* (Philadelphia: Fortress Press, 1980).
Hodges, Zane C. 'Grace after Grace – John 1:16. Part 1 of Problem Passages in the Gospel of John', *BibSac* 135 (1978), 34–45.
——. 'Water and Spirit—John 3:5', *BibSac* 135 (1978), 206–220.
Hoeferkamp, Robert T. 'The Relationship Between *Semeia* and Believing in the Fourth Gospel' (Th.D. diss., St. Louis: Christ Seminary-Seminex, 1978).
Hoekema, A. A. *The Bible and the Future* (Grand Rapids: Eerdmans, 1979).
Hoffman, T. 'First John and the Qumran Scrolls', *BTB* 8 (1978), 17–25.
Hofius, O. 'Der in des Vaters Schoss ist, John 1:18', *ZNW* 80 (1989), 163–171.
Hogg, J. E. 'Living Water—Water of Life', *American Journal of Semitic Languages and Literature* 42 (1925–26), 131–133.
Holladay, William. 'Form and Word Play in David's Lament Over Saul and Jonathan', *VT* 20 (April, 1970), 153–89.
Hollander, J. *The Figure of Echo: A Mode of Allusion in Milton and After* (Berkeley: University of California, 1981).
Hollis, H. 'The Root of the Johannine Pun', *NTS* 35 (1989), 475–478.
Holman, C. Hugh and William Harmon, based on the original ed. by William Flint Thralland Addison Hibbard, *A Handbook to Literature*, 5th edn (New York: Macmillan Publishing, 1986).
Holmberg, Bengt. *Paul and Power: The Structure of Authority in the Primitive Church as Reflected in the Pauline Epistles* (Philadelphia: Fortress Press, 1980).
——. *Sociology and the New Testament: An Appraisal* (Minneapolis: Fortress Press, 1990).
Holst, R. A. 'The Relation of John, Chapter Twelve, to the So-Called Johannine Book of Glory' (Ph.D. diss., Princeton Seminary, 1974).
Holtzmann, H. J. *Evangelium, Briefe und Offenbarung des Johannes* (Tübingen: Mohr-Siebeck, 1908).
Holtzmann, Oscar. *Das Neue Testament nach dem Stuttgarter griechischen Text übersetzt and erklärt II: V Das Evangelium des Johannes* (Giessen: Alfred Töpelmann, 1926).
Holwerda, David. *The Holy Spirit and Eschatology in the Gospel of John* (Kampen: Kok, 1959).
Hooker, Morna D. *Jesus and the Servant: The Influence of the Servant Concept of Deutero-Isaiah in the New Testament* (London: SPCK, 1959).
——. 'John the Baptist and the Johannine Prologue', *NTS* 16 (1970), 354–358.

——. 'Christology and Methodology', *NTS* 17 (1971), 480–487.

——. 'The Johannine Prologue and the Messianic Secret', *NTS* 21 (1974), 40–58.

——. *Continuity and Discontinuity: Early Christianity in its Jewish Setting* (London: Epworth Press, 1986).

——. 'Did the Use of Isaiah 53 to Interpret His Mission Begin with Jesus?', pp. 88–103 in William H. Bellinger and William R. Farmer, eds, *Jesus and the Suffering Servant: Isaiah 53 and Christian Origins* (Harrisburg, PA: Trinity Press International, 1998).

Horbury, William. *A Critical Examination of the Toledoth Jeshu* (Ph.D., diss., Cambridge, 1970).

—— and B. McNeil, eds. *Suffering and Martyrdom in the New Testament: Studies Presented to G. M. Styler* (Cambridge: CUP, 1981).

——. 'The Benediction of the *Minim* and Early Jewish-Christian Controversy', *JTS* n.s. 33 (1982), 19–61.

——. 'The Messianic Associations of "the Son of Man"', *JTS* n.s. 34 (1985), 34–55.

——. 'Messianism among Jews and Christians in the Second Century', *Augustinianum* 28 (1988), 71–88.

——. 'Jewish-Christian Relations in Barnabas and Justin Martyr', pp. 315–345 in J. D. G. Dunn, ed., *Jews and Christians: The Parting of the Ways AD 70 to 135*, WUNT 66 (Tübingen: Mohr-Siebeck, 1993).

——. 'Antichrist among Jews and Gentiles', pp. 113–133 in Martin Goodman, ed., *Jews in the Graeco-Roman World* (Oxford: OUP, 1998).

——. *Jewish Messianism and the Cult of Christ* (London: SCM, 1998).

——. *Jews and Christians in Contact and Controversy* (Edinburgh: Clark, 1998).

Horgan, M. P. *Pesharim: Qumran Interpretation of Biblical Books* (Washington: Catholic Biblical Association, 1979).

Horsley, Richard A. 'Popular Messianic Movements Around the Times of Jesus', *CBQ* 46 (1984), 471–495.

—— and J. S. Hanson, *Bandits, Prophets and Messiahs: Popular Movements in the Time of Jesus* (Minneapolis: Fortress Press, 1985).

——. *Sociology and the Jesus Movement* (New York: Continuum, 1994).

van der Horst, P. W. 'A Word Play in John 4:12?' *ZNW* 63 (1972), 280–282.

Hoselitz, Bert F. ed., *A Reader's Guide to the Social Sciences*, rev. edn (New York: Free Press, 1970).

Hoskyns, Edwyn Clement. 'Genesis 1–3 and St. John's Gospel', *JTS* 21 (1920), 210–218.

—— and N. Davey. *The Riddle of the New Testament* (London: Faber and Faber, 1931).

——. *The Fourth Gospel*, ed. by Francis Noel Davey, 2 vols, 2nd edn (London: Faber and Faber, 1947 [also used: 1st edn, 1940]).

——. *Crucifixion-Resurrection: The Pattern of Theology and the Ethics of the New Testament* (London: SPCK, 1981).

Hossfeld, F. L. and I. Meyer, *Prophet gegen Prophet. Eine Analyse der alttestamentlichen Texte zum Thema: Wahre und falsche Propheten*, Biblische Beiträge 9 (Freiburg: Schweizerisches Katholisches Bibelwerk, 1973).

Howard, W. F. 'Semitism in the New Testament', pp. 411–485 in J. H. Moulton and W. F. Howard, eds, *A Grammar of New Testament Greek*, vol. 2 (Edinburgh: Clark, 1929).

———. *Christianity According to St. John* (London: Duckworth, 1943; Philadelphia: Westminster Press, 1946).

———. 'The Common Authorship of the Johannine Gospel and Epistles', *JTS* 48 (1947), 12–25.

———. *The Fourth Gospel in Recent Criticism and Interpretation*, rev. by C. K. Barrett, 4th edn (London: Epworth, 1955 [orig. 1931]).

Howton, J. '"Son of God" in the Fourth Gospel', *NTS* 10 (1964), 227–237.

Hoy, David C. 'Must We Say What We Mean? The Grammatological Critique of Hermeneutics', pp. 397–415 in B. R. Watchterhauser, ed., *Hermeneutics and Modern Philosophy* (New York: SUNY, 1986).

Hügel, B. F. von. 'John, Gospel of St.', *Encyclopaedia Britannica*, 11th edn (Cambridge: CUP, 1911), 15:455.

Hulen, A. B. 'The Call of the Four Disciples in John 1', *JBL* 67 (1948), 153–158.

Hultgren, Arnold J. 'The Johannine Foot Washing (Jn. 13:1–11) As a Symbol of Eschatological Hospitality', *NTS* 28 (1982), 539–546.

Hummann, Roger J. 'The Function and Form of the Explicit Old Testament Quotations in the Gospel of John', *Lutheran Theological Review* 1 (1988–89), 31–54.

Hunter, A. M. *The Gospel According to John* (Cambridge: CUP, 1965; London: SCM, 1968).

Hurst, L. D. 'The Neglected Role of Semantics in the Search for the Aramaic Words of Jesus', *JNTS* 28 (1986), 63–80.

Hurtado, L. *One God, One Lord: Early Christian Devotion and Ancient Jewish Monotheism* (Philadelphia: Fortress Press, 1988).

Hurtgen, John E. *Anti-Language in The Apocalypse of John* (Lewiston, NY: Edwin Mellen Press, 1990).

Hutcheon, Linda. 'Postmodern Paratextuality and History', *Texte* 5/6 (1986/87), 301–312.

Hutten, Ulrich von. *Gesammelte Schriften VII* (Leipzig, 1860, xliv; 2nd edn, 1877).

Iacopino, G. 'Iesus Incomprehensus: Gesu Frainteso nell' Evangelo di Giovanni', *RivB* 36 (1988), 165–197.

van Iersel, Bas and Anton Weiler, eds. *Exodus: A Lasting Paradigm* (Edinburgh: Clark, 1987).

Inch, M. 'Apologetic Use of "Sign" in the Fourth Gospel', *EvQ* 42 (1970), 35–43.

Infante, S. R. 'L'Agnello nel Quarto Vangelo', *RivB* 43 (1995), 331–361.

Inkeles, Alex. *What Is Sociology? A Methodological Enquiry* (London: Alden and Mowbray, 1975).

Irenaeus, *Against Heresies*, ET by A. Roberts and W. H. Rambaut, Ante-Nicene Christian Library 5/1 (Edinburgh: Clark, 1868).

Isaac, B. and A. Oppenheimer, 'The Revolt of Bar Kokhba, Scholarship and Ideology', *JJS* 36 (1985), 33–60.

Issac, J. *L'Antisémitisme a-t-il des racines chrétiennes?* (Paris: Fasquelle, 1960).

Isaacs, Marie E. *The Concept of Spirit: A Study of Pneuma in Hellenistic Judaism and its Bearing on the New Testament*, Heythrop Monographs 1 (Huddersfield, England: H. Charlesworth, 1976).

Iser, Wolfgang. *The Act of Reading: A Theory of Aesthetic Response* (Baltimore: John Hopkins University Press, 1978).

——. 'The Reading Process: A Phenomenological Approach', pp. 50–69 in J. Tompkins, ed., *Reader Response Criticism* (Baltimore: John Hopkins University Press, 1980).

Janowski, Bernd. '"Ich will in eurer Mitte wohnen". Struktur und Genese der exilischen *Schekina*-Theologie', *JBTh* 2 (1987), 165–193; reprinted in idem, *Gottes Gegenwart in Israel. Beiträge zur Theologie des Alten Testaments* (Neukirchen-Vluyn: Neukirchener Verlag, 1993), 119–147.

Jastrow, Marcus. *A Dictionary of the Targumim, The Talmud Babli and Yerushalmi, and the Midrashic Literature*, 2 vols. in 1 (New York and Berlin: Verlag Choreb; London: Shapiro, Valentine, 1926).

Jameson, Fredric. *The Political Unconscious: Narrative as a Socially Symbolic Act* (Ithaca: Cornell University Press, 1981).

Jarvis, E. 'The Key Term "Believe" in the Gospel of John', *Notes on Translation* 2 (1988), 46–51.

Jaubert, A. *La Date de la cène: Calendrier biblique et liturgie chrétienne* (Paris: Gabalda, 1957).

——. *Approches de l'évangile de Jean* (Paris: du Seuil, 1976).

——. 'The Calendar of Qumran and the Passion Narrative in John', pp. 62–75 in J. H. Charlesworth, ed., *John and the Dead Sea Scrolls* (New York: Crossroads, 1990).

Jemielity, Thomas. *Satire and the Hebrew Prophets* (Louisville, KY: Westminster/John Knox Press, 1992).

Jenni, Ernst. 'Jesajas Berufung in der neueren Forschung', *TZ* 15 (1959), 321–339.

Jensen, E. E. 'The First Century Controversy over Jesus as a Revolutionary Figure', *JBL* 60 (1941), 261–272.

Jensen, James. 'The Construction of Seven Types of Ambiguity', *Modern Language Quarterly* 27 (1966), 243–259.

Jenson, R. W. *The Triune Identity* (Philadelphia: Fortress Press, 1982).

Jeremias, Joachim. 'Die Berufng des Nathanel', *Angelos* 3 (1928), 2–5.

——. 'Johanneische Literarkritik', *Theologische Blätter* 20 (1941), 33–46.

——. Review of Bultmann, *Johannes* 1941, *DLZ* 64 (1943), 414–420.

——. *The Central Message of the New Testament* (London: SCM/ Philadelphia: Fortress Press, 1965).

——. *The Eucharistic Words of Jesus* (London: SCM, 1966).

——. *Abba: Studien zur Neutestamentlichen Theologie und Zeitgeschichte* (Göttingen: Vandenhoeck und Ruprecht, 1966).

——. *New Testament Theology*, ET (London: SCM, 1971).

Jeremias, Johann. 'Die vier Stimmen im vierten Evangelium', *Nieuwe Theologische Studien* 17 (1934), 37–46.

——. *Die vier Stimmen im 4. Evangelium in den ursprünglichen Stilformen verdeutscht* (Hermhut: Gustav Winter, 1934).

——. 'Die vier Stimmen im vierten Evangelium', *Theologisches Literaturblatt* 56 (1934), 81–87.

Jocz, J. *The Jewish People and Jesus Christ* (London: SPCK, 1949).

——. 'Die Juden im Johannesevangelium', *Judaica* 9 (1953), 129–142.

Johnson, E. E. 'What I Mean by Historical-Grammatical Interpretation and How that Differs from Spiritual Interpretation', *Grace Theological Journal* 11 (1990), 157–69.

——. 'Why I Am Not a Literalist', *Grace Theological Journal* 11 (1990), 137–49.

Johnson, E. S. 'The Blind Man from Bethsaida', *NTS* 25 (1979), 370–383.

Johnson, P. B. 'Jesus as Judge in the Gospel of John' (Ph.D. diss., New Orleans Baptist Theological Seminary, 1966).

Johnson, L. T. 'On Finding the Lukan Community: A Cautious Cautionary Essay', pp. 87–100 in Achtemeier, Paul J., ed., *Society for Biblical Literature 1979 Seminar Papers*, vol. 1 (Missoula, MT: Scholars Press, 1979).

——. *The Real Jesus: The Misguided Quest for the Historical Jesus and the Truth of the Traditional Gospels* (San Francisco: Harper Collins, 1996).

Johnson, Sherman. E. 'The Davidic-Royal Motif in the Gospels', *JBL* 87 (1968), 136–150.

——. 'Notes on the Prophet-King in John', *ATR* 51 (1969), 35–37.

Johnston, George. *The Spirit-Paraclete in the Gospel of John*, SNTSMS 12 (Cambridge: CUP, 1970).

——. 'Ecce Homo! Irony in the Christology of the Fourth Evangelist', pp. 125–138 in L. Hurst and N. T. Wright, eds, *The Glory of Christ in the New Testament: Studies in Christology in Memory of George Bradford Caird* (Oxford: Clarendon Press, 1987).

Jonas, Hans. *Gnosis und spätantiker Geist*, vol. 1: *Die mythologische Gnosis*, FRLANT 51(Göttingen: Vandenhoeck und Ruprecht, 1934, 1964), vol. 2: *Von der Mythologie zur mystischen philosophie*, FRLANT 63 (Göttingen: Vandenhoeck und Ruprecht, 1954, 1966).

——. *The Gnostic Religion: The Message of the Alien God and the Beginnings of Christianity* (Boston: Beacon, 2nd rev. edn, 1963).

Jones, D. L. 'The Title "Servant" in Luke-Acts', pp. 148–165 in C. H. Talbert, ed., *Luke-Acts: New Perspectives from the Society of Biblical Literature Seminar* (New York: Crossroads, 1984).

de Jonge, M. 'The Use of the Word "Anointed" in the Time of Jesus', *NovT* 8 (1966), 132–148.

——. 'Jesus as Prophet-King in John', *ATR* 51 (1969), 35–37.

——. 'Nicodemus and Jesus: Some Observations on Misunderstanding and Understanding in the Fourth Gospel', *BJRL* 53 (1970–71), 337–359.

——. 'Jesus as Prophet and King in the Fourth Gospel', *ETL* 49 (1973), 160–177.

——, ed. *L'Évangile de Jean: sources, rédaction, théologie*, BETL 44 (Leuven: Leuven University Press, 1977).

——. 'Jesus: Stranger From Heaven and the Son of God: Jesus Christ and the Christians in Johannine Perspective', ed. and trans. by J. E. Steely, *SBL Sources for Biblical Study* 11 (Missoula, MT: Scholars Press, 1977).

——. 'Signs and Works in the Fourth Gospel', pp. 107-125 in T. Baarda, et al., eds, *Miscellanea Neotestamentica*, vol. 2, NovTSup 48 (Leiden: Brill, 1978).
Jónsson, Jakob. *Humour and Irony in the New Testament* (Leiden: Brill, 1985).
Joos, Martin. 'Semantic Axiom Number One', *Language* 48 (1972), 257-65.
Josephus, F. *The Jewish Wars*, trans. by G. A. Williamson (Harmondsworth: Penguin, 1959).
——. *Antiquities of the Jews and Wars of the Jews*, trans. by W. Whiston (London: Thomas Nelson, 1862).
——. *The Works of Flavius Josephus* (London: Milner & Sowerby, 1870).
Joubert, H. L. N. 'The Holy One of God (Jn. 6:69)', *Neot* 2 (1968), 57-69.
Judge, Edwin A. *The Social Pattern of the Christian Groups in the First Century* (London: Tyndale Press, 1960).
——. 'The Early Christians as a Scholastic Community', *Journal of Religious History* 1 (1960), 4-15.
——. *Rank and Status in the World of the Caesars and St. Paul* (Canterbury: University of Canterbury, 1984).
Juel, Donald. *Messianic Exegesis: Christological Interpretation of the Old Testament in Early Christianity* (Philadelphia: Fortress Press, 1988).
Jülicher, Adolf. *An Introduction to the New Testament* (New York: Putnam's Sons, 1904).
——. *Die Gleichnisreden Jesu* (Tübingen: Mohr-Siebeck, 1910).
Justin Martyr. *Dialogi cum Tryphone Judaeo, Patrologia Graeca* 6, 470-799A. ET in ANF vol. 1.
——. *Justin Martyr: The Dialogue with Trypho. Translation, Introduction and Notes*, trans. by A. Lukyn Williams (London: Heinemann, 1930).
——. *Apology. Apolgia I & II pro Christianis, Patrologia Graeca* 6, ed. by J. P. Migne, 326-472.

Kaiser, Jr., Walter C. 'The Single Intent of Scripture', pp. 123-141 in K. Kantzer ed., *Evangelical Roots. A Tribute to Wilbur Smith* (Nashville: Nelson, 1978).
——. *The Messiah in the Old Testament* (Carlisle, England: Paternoster Press, 1995).
Kanagaraj, Jey J. 'Mysticism in the Gospel of John: An Inquiry into the Background of John in Jewish Mysticism' (Ph.D. diss., England, University of Durham, 1995).
——. *'Mysticism' in the Gospel of John: An Inquiry into Its Background*, JSNTSup 158 (Sheffield: Sheffield Academic Press, 1998).
Kaplan, A. and E. Kris, 'Aesthetic Ambiguity', *Philosophical and Phenomenological Research* (1948), 415-35.
Käsemann, Ernest. 'Ketzer und Zeuge: Zum johanneischen Verfasserproblem', *ZTK* 48 (1951), 292-311.
——. *Essays on New Testament Themes*, ET (London: SCM, 1964).
——. 'The Structure and Purpose of the Prologue to John's Gospel', pp. 138-157 in *New Testament Questions of Today*, ET (Philadelphia: Fortress Press, 1969).
——. *Jesu letzter Wille nach Johannes 17* (Tübingen: Mohr-Siebeck, 1971, 966, 1967). ET by Gerhard Krodel, *The Testament of Jesus: A Study of the Gospel of*

John in the Light of Chapter 17 (Philadelphia: Fortress Press, 1981; London: SCM, 1968).

Katz, J. J. and J. A. Fodor. 'The Structure of a Semantic Theory', *Language* 39 (1963), 170–210. Repr. pp. 479–518 in idem, eds., *The Structure of Language: Readings in the Philosophy of Language* (New Jersey: Prentice-Hall, 1964).

—— and J. A. Fodor, eds. *The Structure of Language: Readings in the Philosophy of Language* (New Jersey: Prentice-Hall, 1964).

Katz, Steven T. 'Issues in the Separation of Judaism and Christianity after 70 C.E.: A Reconsideration', *JBL* 103 (1984), 43–76.

Kaufman, Philip S. *The Beloved Disciple: Witness Against Anti-Semitism* (Collegeville, MN: Liturgical Press, 1991).

Keck, L. E. 'The Spirit and the Dove', *NTS* 17 (1970–71), 41–67.

Kee, Howard Clark. *The Origins of Christianity: Sources and Documents* (Englewood Cliffs, NJ: Prentice Hall, 1973).

——. *Jesus in History: An Approach to the Study of the Gospels* (New York: Harcourt, Brace, Jovanovich, 1977).

——. *Community of the New Age: Studies in Mark's Gospel* (London: SCM, 1977).

——. *Christian Origins in Sociological Perspective* (Philadelphia: Westminster Press, 1980).

——. *Miracle in the Early Christian World: A Study in Sociohistorical Method* (New Haven: Yale University Press, 1983).

—— and Irvin J. Borowsky, eds. *Removing Anti-Judaism from the New Testament* (Philadelphia: American Interfaith Institute/World Alliance, 1998).

Kelber, W. *The Oral and Written Gospel: The Hermeneutics of Speaking and Writing in the Synoptic Tradition, Mark, Paul and Q* (Philadelphia: Fortress, 1983).

Kempson, Ruth M. *Semantic Theory*, Cambridge Textbooks on Linguistics (Cambridge: CUP, 1977).

——. 'Ambiguity and Word Meaning', pp. 7–16 in S. Greenbaum, G. Leech and J. Svartvik, eds, *Studies in English Linguistics for Randolph Quirk* (London: Longman, 1979).

Kennedy, G. A. 'Judeo-Christian Rhetoric', pp. 120–60 in *Classical Rhetoric and Its Christian and Secular Tradition from Ancient to Modern Times* (Chapel Hill: University of North Carolina Press, 1980), .

——. *The Art of Persuasion in Greece* (Princeton: Princeton University Press, 1963).

Kennedy, H. A. A. 'Book review of *Das Messiasgeheimnis in den Evangelien* by William Wrede', *The Critical Review of Theological and Philosophical Literature* 12 (1902), 339–344.

——. *Philo's Contribution to Religion* (London: Hodder and Stoughton, 1919).

Kennedy, J. 'The Abuse of Power', *ExpTim* 85 (1973–74), 172–173.

Kent, Jr., Homer A. *Light in the Darkness: Studies in the Gospel of John* (Grand Rapids: Baker Book House, 1974).

Kenyon, Frederick G. *Books and Readers in Ancient Greece and Rome*, 2nd edn (Oxford: Clarendon, 1951).

Kermode, Frank. *The Genesis of Secrecy: On the Interpretation of Narrative* (Cambridge, MA: Harvard University Press, 1979).

—. 'Figures in the Carpet: On Recent Theories of Narrative Discourse', pp. 291-301 in Elinor S. Shaffer, ed., *Comparative Criticism: A Yearbook*, vol. 2 (Cambridge: CUP, 1980).
—. 'St. John as Poet', *JSNT* 28 (1986), 3-16.
—. 'John', pp. 440-466 in Robert Alter and Frank Kermode, eds., *Literary Guide to the Bible* (Cambridge, MA: Harvard University Press, Belknap Press, 1987).
Kern, W. 'Die symmetrische Gesamtaufbau von Joh. 8:12-58', *ZKT* 78 (1956), 451-454.
Kertelge, Karl, ed. *Metaphorik und Mythos im Neuen Testament*, Quaestiones Disputatae 126 (Freiburg: Herder, 1990).
Kessler, M. 'Inclusio in the Hebrew Bible', *Semitics* 6 (1978), 44-49.
Kieffer, René. 'Different Levels in Johannine Imagery', pp. 74-84 in Lars Hartman and Birger Olsson, eds, *Aspects on the Johannine Literature*, ConBNTS 18 (Uppsala: Almqvist and Wiksell, 1986).
—. 'Det gåtfulla Johannesevangeliet', *Svensk Theologisk Kvartalskrift* 67 (1991), 109-112.
Kilpatrick, G. D. 'Two Studies of Style and Text in the Greek New Testament', *JTS* n.s. 41 (1990), 94-98.
Kim, Seyoon. *The 'Son of Man' as the Son of God*, WUNT 2.30 (Tübingen: Mohr-Siebeck, 1983).
Kimelman, Reuven. 'Birkat Ha-Minim and the Lack of Evidence for an Anti-Christian Jewish Prayer in Late Antiquity', pp. 226-44 in *Jewish and Christian Self-Definition, 2: Aspects of Judaism in the Graeco-Roman Period*, ed. E. P. Sanders (London: SCM, 1981).
King, J. S. 'Sychar and Calvary: A Neglected Theory in the Interpretation of the Fourth Gospel', *Theology* 77 (1974), 417-422.
Kingsbury, Jack Dean. 'The Gospel in Four Editions', *Interpretation* 33 (1979), 374.
Kippenberg, Hans G. *Religion und Klassenbildung im antiken Judäa*, SUNT 14 (Göttingen: Vandenhoeck und Ruprecht, 1978).
Kirk, K. E. *The Vision of God* (London: Longman, Green, 1932).
Kittay, Eva F. *Metaphor: Its Cognitive Force and Linguistic Structure* (Oxford: Clarendon Press, 1987).
Kittel, G. 'εἶδος',*TDNT* 2 (1964), 373-5.
Kittlaus, L. R. 'The Fourth Gospel and Mark: John's use of Markan Redaction and Composition' (Ph.D. diss., University of Chicago, 1978).
Kjargaard, M. S. *Metaphor and Parable* (Leiden: Brill, 1986).
Klassen, W. 'Anti-Judaism in Early Christianity: The State of the Question', pp. 1-19 in P. Richardson and D. Granskau, eds, *Anti-Judaism in Early Christianty*, vol. 1 (Ontario: Wilfrid Laurier University Press, 1986).
Klausner, Joseph. *The Messianic Idea in Israel: From its Beginning to the Completion of the Mishnah*, ET by W. F. Stinespring (New York: Macmillan, 1955).
Klein, G. 'Das Wahre Licht scheint schon', *ZTK* 68 (1971), 261-326.
Kleinknecht, H. and W. Gutbrod, 'νόμος', *TDNT* 4 (1967), 1082-85.
Klijn, A. F. J. and G. J. Reinink. *Patristic Evidence for Jewish-Christian Sects*, NovTSup 36 (Leiden: Brill, 1973).

Klimkeit, Hans-Joachim. 'Das Tor Als Symbol im Manichäismus', pp. 365-81 in W. Sundermann, et al., eds, *A Green Leaf: Papers in Honour of Professor Jes P. Asmussen*, Acta Iranica 28, vol. 12 (Leiden: Brill, 1988).

Kline, Meredith G. 'Old Testament Origins of the Gospel Genre', *The Westminster Theological Journal* 38 (Fall 1975), 1-27.

Knight, G. A. F. 'Ego Eimi', *New Zealand Theological Review* 1 (1966), 219-224.

———. 'Antisemitism in the Fourth Gospel', *Reformed Theological Review* 27 (1968), 81-88.

Knights, L. C. and B. Cottle, eds. *Metaphor and Symbol*, Colston Papers 12 (London: Colston Research Society, 1947).

Knox, Norman. *The Word Irony and Its Context, 1500-1799* (Durham, NC: Duke University Press, 1961).

Kochilletonil, L. 'The Biblical Idea of Μαρτυρία', *Documenta Missionalia* 5 (1972), 55-64.

Koenig, Jean. *L'Herméneutique analogique du Judaïsme antique d'après les témoins textuels d'Isaïe*, VTSup 33 (Leiden: Brill, 1982).

Koenig, John. 'John: A Painful Break with Judaism', pp. 122-136 in *Jews and Christians in Dialogue: New Testament Foundations* (Philadelphia: Westminster Press, 1979).

Koester, C. R. 'Hearing, Seeing, and Believing in the Gospel of John', *Bib* 70 (1989), 327-348.

———. *The Dwelling of God: The Tabernacle in the Old Testament, Intertestamental Jewish Literature and the New Testament*, CBQMS 22 (Washington: Catholic Biblical Association, 1989).

———. 'The Savior of the World: Jn. 4:42', *JBL* 109 (1990), 665-680.

———. 'Messianic Exegesis and the Call of Nathanael (Jn. 1:45-51)', *JSNT* 39 (1990), 23-34.

Koester, Helmut. 'Geschichte und Kultus im Johannesevangelium und bei Ignatius von Antiochien', *ZTK* 54 (1957), 63-64.

———. *An Introduction to the New Testament*, vol. 1: *History, Culture, and Religion of the Hellenistic Age* (Philadelphia: Fortress Press, 1982).

———. *An Introduction to the New Testament*, vol. 2: *History and Literature of Early Christianity* (Philadelphia: Fortress Press, 1982).

Koetschau, P. *Origen – works: Die Schrift vom Martyrum*, Buch 1, ed. by P. Koetschau (Leipzig: Hinrichs, 1899).

Kohler, H. *Kreuz und Menschwerdung im Johannesevangelium*, ATANT 72 (Zürich: Theologischer Verlag, 1987).

Kooij, J. G. *Ambiguity in Natural Language* (Amsterdam: North-Holland, 1971).

Kosten, H. B. *Studies in John* (Leiden: Brill, 1970).

Kotze, P. P. A. 'John and Reader's Response', *Neot* 19 (1987), 50-63.

Kraemer, R. S. 'On the Meaning of the Term "Jew" in Greco-Roman Inscriptions', *HTR* 82 (1989), 35-53.

Kraft, E. 'Die Personen des Johannesevangeliums', *EvT* 16 (1956), 18-32.

Krauss, Samuel. 'Imprecation against the Minim in the Synagogue', *JQR* 9 (1897), 515-517.

—— and William Horbury. *The Jewish-Christian Controversy from the Earliest Time to 1789*, rev. ed. by W. Horbury, vol. 1: *History* (Tübingen: Mohr-Siebeck, 1996).

Krentz, Edgar. *The Historical-Critical Method* (Philadelphia: Fortress Press, 1975).

Kristeva, J. *Desire in Language: A Semiotic Approach to Literature and Art*, ET by L. S. Roudiez, et al., eds (New York: Columbia University Press, 1980, French edn 1969).

——. *Revolution in Poetic Language*, ET by M. Waller (New York: Columbia University Press, 1984).

——. 'Semiotics: A Critical Science and/or a Critique of Science', pp. 74–88 in T. Moi, ed., *Kristeva Reader* (New York: Columbia University Press, 1986).

Krodel, G. 'John 6:63', *Interpretation* 37 (1983), 283–288.

de Kruijf, T. C. '"Hold the Faith" or "Come to Belief"? A Note on John 20:31', *Bijdragen* 36 (1975), 439–449.

Kselman, S. 'Semantic-Sonant Chiasmus in Biblical Poetry', *Bib* 58 (1977), 219–223.

Kugel, J. L. *Early Biblical Interpretation* (Philadelphia: Westminster Press, 1986).

Kuhl, Josef. *Die Sendung Jesu und der Kirche nach dem Johannesevangelium*, Studia Instituti Missiologica Societatis Verbi Domini 11 (St. Augustin: Styler, 1967).

Kuhn, K. G. 'Die in Palästina gefundenen hebräischen Texte und das NT', *ZTK* 47 (1950), 192–211.

——. 'Die Sektenschrift und die iranische Religion', *ZTK* 49 (1952).

——. 'Johannesevangelium und Qumrantexte', pp. 111–122 in W. C. van Unnik, ed., *Neotestamentica et Patristica:* Eine Freundesgabe, Herrn Professor Dr. Oscar Cullmann zu seinem 60. Geburtstag überreicht, NovTSup 6 (Leiden: Brill, 1962).

Kühschelm, R. *Verstockung, Gericht und Heil*, BBB 76 (Frankfurt am Main: Peter Lang, 1990).

Kümmel, W. G. *Promise and Fulfilment: The Eschatological Message of Jesus*, ET (London: SCM, 1957).

——. *Einleitung in das Neue Testament* (Heidelberg: Quelle und Meyer, 17th print, 1973).

——. *The Theology of the New Testament*, ET (New York: Abingdon Press, 1973; London: SCM, 1974).

——. *Introduction to the New Testament*, ET rev. edn (New York: Abingdon Press, 1973; London: SCM, 1975).

Kundsin, Karl. *Charakter und Ursprung der Johanneischen Reden*, Acta Universitatis Latviensis, Theologisjas Fakultates Series 1 (Riga: n. p., 1939).

Kunjumnen, Faju D. 'The Single Intent of Scripture: Critical Examination of a Theological Construction', *Grace Theological Journal* 7 (1986), 81–110.

Kurfess, A. 'ἐκάθισεν ἐπὶ βήματος (Jo 19,13)', *Bib* 34 (1953), 271.

Kurz, W. S. 'The Beloved Disciple and Implied Reader', *BTB* 19 (1989), 100–107.

Kusvmirek, A. 'Zydzi w ewangelii Jana (Die Juden im Johannesevangelium)', *Studia Theologica Varsaviensia* (Warsaw) 30 (1992), 121–35.

Kuyper, L. J. 'Grace and Truth: An Old Testament Description of God and Its Use in the Johannine Gospel', *Interpretation* 18 (1964), 3–19.

Kyrtatas, D. *The Social Structure of the Early Christian Communities* (New York: Vero; London: Methuen, 1987).

Kysar, Robert. *A Comparison of the Exegetical Presuppositions and Methods of C. H. Dodd and R. Bultmann in the Interpretation of the Prologue of the Fourth Gospel* (Unpub. Ph.D. Diss. Chicago: Northwestern University, 1967).

——. 'The Background of the Fourth Gospel. A Critique of Historical Methods', *Canadian Journal of Theology* 16 (1970), 250–255.

——. 'The Eschatology of the Fourth Gospel: A Correction of Bultmann's Redactional Hypothesis', *Perspective* 13 (1972), 23–33.

——. *The Fourth Evangelist and His Gospel: An Examination of Contemporary Scholarship* (Minneapolis, MN: Augsburg Publishing House, 1975).

——. *John, the Maverick Gospel* (Atlanta, GA: John Knox Press, 1976).

——. 'Community and Gospel: Vectors in Fourth Gospel Criticism', *Interpretation* 31 (1977), 355–366.

——. 'The Gospel of John in Current Research', *Religious Studies Review* 9 (1983), 314–323.

——. 'The Fourth Gospel: A Report on Recent Research', pp. 2389–2480 in H. Temporini and W. Haase, eds, *Aufstieg und Niedergang der römischen Welt*, II.25.3 (Berlin and New York: de Gruyter, 1985).

——. *John*, Augsburg Commentary on the New Testament (Minneapolis: Augsburg Publishing House, 1986).

——. 'Johannine Metaphor—Meaning and Function: A Literary Case Study of John 10:1-18', *Semeia* 53 (1991), 81–112.

Lacomara, A. 'Deuteronomy and the Farewell Discourse (John 13:31–16:33)', *CBQ* 36 (1974), 65–84.

Ladd, George E. *The Pattern of New Testament Truth* (Grand Rapids: Eerdmans, 1968).

——. *A Theology of the New Testament* (Grand Rapids: Eerdmans, 1978).

Lagrange, Marie-Joseph. *L'évangile selon saint Jean*, Études bibliques (Paris: Gabalda, 7th print, 1948).

Lakoff, George and Mark Johnson. *Metaphors We Live By* (Chicago: University of Chicago Press, 1980).

Lamarche, Paul. 'The Prologue of John', pp. 36–52 in John Ashton, ed., *The Interpretation of John* (London: SPCK, 1986).

Lampe, G. W. H. and K. J. Woolcombe. *Essays in Typology* (London: SCM, 1957).

Lampe, Peter. *Die stadtrömischen Christen in den ersten beiden Jahrhunderten: Untersuchungen zur Sozialgeschichte*, WUNT 2.18, 2nd edn (Tübingen: Mohr-Siebeck, 1988 [1987]).

Langbrandtner, Wolfgang. *Weltferner Gott oder Gott der Liebe. Der Ketzerstreit in der johanneischen Kirche. Eine exegetisch-religionsgeschichtliche Untersuchung mit Berücksichtigung der koptisch-gnostischen Texte aus Nag-Hammadi*, BBET 6 (Frankfurt am Main: Peter Lang, 1977).

Lanham, Richard A. *A Handlist of Rhetorical Terms: A Guide for Students of English Literature* (Berkeley: University of California Press, 1968).

——. *Style: An Anti-Textbook* (New Haven: Yale University Press, 1974).

Lanser, Susan S. *The Narrative Act: Point of View in Prose Fiction* (Princeton: University Press, 1981).

Lasen, I. 'Walking in the Light: A Comment on John 11:9-10', *BT* 37 (1986), 432-436.
LaSor, W. S. *The Dead Sea Scrolls and the New Testament* (Grand Rapids: Eerdmans, 1972).
Laszlo, Ervin. *The Systems View of the World: The Natural Philosophy of the New Developments in the Sciences* (New York: George Braziller, 1972).
Lategan, B. C. 'The Truth That Sets Man Free: John 8:31-36', *Neot* 2 (1968), 70-80.
Lattey, C. 'The Semitisms of the Fourth Gospel', *JTS* 20 (1918-19), 330-336.
Laursen, Gerald A. 'A Study of Johannine Terminology Relative to the Holiness of God' (Th.D. diss., Dallas Seminary, 1976).
Lausberg, H. *Miniscula Philologica V: Jesaja 55, 10-11 im Evangelium nach Johannes*, Nachrichten der Akademie der Wissenschaften im Göttingen aus dem Jahre 1979, Nr. 7 (Göttingen: Vandehoeck und Ruprecht, 1979).
Lauterbach, J. Z. 'Jesus in Talmud', pp. 473-570 in idem, *Rabbinic Essays* (Cincinnati: Hebrew Union College, 1951).
Lavergne, C. *Les silences de S. Jean* (Paris: Desclée, 1940).
Law, R. *The Tests of Life: A Study of the First Epistle of St. John* (Edinburgh: Clark, 1909).
Layton, Bentley, ed. *The Rediscovery of Gnosticism: Proceedings of the International Conference on Gnosticism at Yale, New Haven, Connecticut, March 28-31, 1978*, 2 vols, Studies in the History of Religions, Supplements to Numen 41-42 (Leiden: Brill, 1980-81).
Leaney, A. R. C. 'The Gospels as Evidence for First-Century Judaism', pp. 28-45 in *Historicity and Chronology in the New Testament* (London: SPCK, 1965).
——. 'The Historical Background and Theological Meaning of the Paraclete', *Duke Divinity School Review* 37 (1972), 146-159.
Leaska, Mitchell A. *Virginia Woolf's Lighthouse: A Study in Critical Method* (New York: Columbia University Press, 1970).
Lee, Francis N. *The Central Significance of Culture* (Philadelphia: Presbyterian and Reformed Publishing, 1976).
Leech, Geoffrey. *Linguistic Guide to English Poetry* (London: Longman, 1969).
——. *Semantics* (Baltimore: Penguin, 1974).
——. 'Being Precise about Lexical Vagueness', *York Papers in Linguistics* 6 (1976), 149-165.
Leech, G. N. and M. H. Short. *Style in Fiction* (London: Longman, 1981).
Lehrer, A. 'Homonymy and Polysemy: Meaning Similarity of Meaning', *Language Sciences* 3 (1974), 33-39.
Leibig, Janis E. 'John and "the Jews": Theological Anti-Semitism in the Fourth Gospel', *JES* 20 (1983), 209-234.
Leidig, Edeltraud. *Jesu Gespräch mit der Samaritanerin und weitere Gespräche im Johannesevangelium*, Theologischen Dissertationen 15 (Basel: Friedrich Reinhardt, 1979).
Leistner, Reinhold. *Antijudaismus im Johannesevangelium? Darstellung des Problems in der neueren Auslegungsgeschichte und Untersuchung der Leidensgeschichte* (Bern/Frankfurt: Herbert Lang, 1974).

Leitch, V. B. *Deconstructive Criticism: An Advanced Introduction* (New York: Columbia University Press, 1983).
Lenski, R. C. H. *The Interpretation of St. John's Gospel* (Minneapolis, MN: Augsburg Publishing House, 1961).
Léon-Dufour, Xavier. 'Towards a Symbolic Reading of the Fourth Gospel', *NTS* 27 (1981), 439–456.
Lepschy, G. C. *A Survey of Structural Linguistics* (London: André Deutsche, 1982; reprint, 1970).
Leroy, Herbert. *Rätsel und Missverständnis: Ein Beitrag zur Formgeschichte des Johannesevangeliums*, BBB 30 (Bonn: Peter Hanstein, 1968).
———. 'Das Johanneische Missverständnis als Literarische Form', *BibLeb* 9 (1968), 196–207.
Letis, T. P. 'The Gnostic Influences on the Text of the Fourth Gospel', *BIRBS* 1 (1989), 4–7.
Levenson, J. D. 'The Sources of Torah: Psalm 119, and the Modes of Revelation in Second Temple Judaism', pp. 559–574 in Patrick D. Miller, et al., eds, *Ancient Israelite Religion: Essays in Honor of Frank Moore Cross* (Philadelphia: Fortress Press, 1987).
Levey, S. H. *The Messiah: An Aramaic Interpretation: The Messianic Exegesis of the Targum*, Monographs of the Hebrew Union College 2 (Cincinnati: Hebrew Union College, 1974).
Levin, R. Samuel. *The Semantics of Metaphor* (Baltimore: John Hopkins University Press, 1977).
Levinson, S. *Pragmatics* (Cambridge: CUP, 1983).
Lewis, C. S. *Miracles: A Preliminary Study* (New York: Macmillan, 1947).
———. *Reflections on the Psalms* (Glasgow: Collins, 1961).
Lewis, Jack P. 'The Semitic Background of the Gospel of John', pp. 97–110 in James E. Priest, ed., *Johannine Studies: Essays in Honor of Frank Pack* (Malibu, CA: Pepperdine University Press, 1989).
Licht, J. 'The Doctrine of the Thanksgiving Scroll', *Israel Exploration Journal* 6 (1956), 1–13, 89–101.
Liddell, H. G., R. Scott, and H. S. Jones. *A Greek-English Lexicon* (Oxford: Clarendon Press, 9th edn, 1953).
Lidzbarski, M. *Das Johannesbuch der Mandäer*, 2 vols (Repr.; Giessen: Töpelmann, 1966 [1905–15]); ET of portions in G. Meade, *The Gnostic John the Baptizer* (London: Watkins, 1924).
Lieberman, Saul. *Hellenism in Jewish Palestine: Studies in the Literary Transmission, Beliefs, and Manners of Palestine in the I Century B.C.E.–IV Century CE*, TSJTSA 18 (New York: The Jewish Theological Seminary of America, 2nd print, 1962).
Lieberson, Stanley, ed. *Explorations in Sociolinguistics* (Bloomington, IN: Indiana University Press, 1973).
Liebert, Elisabeth. 'That You May Believe: Fourth Gospel and Structural Developmental Theory', *BTB* 14 (4/1984), 67–73.
Lietzmann, H. 'Ein Beitrag zur Mandäerfrage', *Sitzungsberichte der Preussischen Akademie der Wissenschaft: Phil. Hist. Klasse* 17 (1930), 595–608.

Lieu, Judith M. 'Blindness in the Johannine Tradition', *NTS* 34 (1988), 83–95.

———. 'What Was From the Beginning: Scripture and Tradition in the Johannine Epistles', *NTS* 39 (1993), 458–477.

———. 'Biblical Theology and the Johannine Literature', pp. 93–107 in Sigfred Pedersen, ed., *New Directions in Biblical Theology* (Leiden: Brill, 1994).

———. *Medieval Polemics Between Christians and Jews* (Tübingen: Mohr-Siebeck, 1996).

Lieu, Samuel N. C. 'Sources on the Diffusion of Manichaeism in the Roman Empire', pp. 384–99 in W. Sundermann, et al., eds, *A Green Leaf: Papers in Honour of Professor Jes P. Asmussen*, Acta Iranica 28, vol. 12 (Leiden: Brill, 1988).

Lightfoot, J. B. and J. R. Harmer. *The Apostolic Fathers*, 2nd edn rev. and ed. by Michael W. Holmes (Leicester: Apollos, 1989).

Lightfoot, J. B. *Biblical Essays* (London: Macmillan, 1893).

Lightfoot, R. H. *St. John's Gospel: A Commentary*, ed. by C. F. Evans (Oxford: Clarendon Press, 1956).

Limburg, James. 'The Root ריב and the Prophetic Lawsuit Speeches', *JBL* 88 (1969), 291–304.

Lindars, Barnabas. 'The Composition of John 20', *NTS* 30 (1960–61), 142–147.

———. *New Testament Apologetic: The Doctrinal Significance of Old Testament Quotations* (London: SCM, 1961).

———. 'Two Parables in John (Jn. 2:10, 3:29)', *NTS* 16 (1969–70), 318–329.

———. *Behind the Fourth Gospel* (London: SPCK, 1971).

———. *The Gospel of John*, NCB (London: Marshall, Morgan and Scott, 1972).

———. 'The Son of Man in Johannine Christology', pp. 43–60 in B. Lindars and S. S. Smalley, eds, *Christ and Spirit in the New Testament: Essays in honour of C. F. D. Moule* (Cambridge: CUP, 1973).

——— and P. Borgen. 'The Place of the Old Testament in the Formation of New Testament Theology', *NTS* 23 (1976–77), 59–66.

———. 'Traditions Behind the Fourth Gospel', pp. 109–124 in M. de Jonge, ed., *L'Évangile de Jean: Sources, rédaction, théologie*, BETL 44 (Leuven: Leuven University Press, 1977).

———. 'The Persecution of Christians in John 15:18–16:4a', pp. 48–69 in W. Horbury and B. McNeil, eds, *Suffering and Martyrdom in the New Testament: Studies Presented to G. M. Styler* (Cambridge: CUP, 1981).

———. *Jesus: Son of Man* (London: SPCK, 1983).

———. 'Some Recent Trends in the Study of John', *Way* 30 (1990), 329–338.

———. 'John Ashton's Understanding the Fourth Gospel', *SJT* 45 (1992), 245–251.

Lindbeck, George A. *The Nature of Doctrine: Religion and Theology in a Postliberal Age* (Philadelphia: Westminster, 1984).

Lindeskog, G. 'Anfänge des jüdisch-christlichen Problems: Ein programmatischer Entwurf', pp. 255–275. in E. Bammel, C. K. Barrett, and W. D. Davies, ed., *Donum Gentilicium: New Testament Essays in Honour of David Daube* (Oxford: Clarendon, 1978).

Lindsay, D. R. 'What Is Truth? Ἀλήθεια in the Gospel of John', *Restoration Quarterly* 35 (1993), 129–145.

Liu, W. Warren. 'The Use of Isaiah 40–66 in the Gospel of John' (Thesis, Dallas Seminary, 1978).

Llewelyn, G. R. and R. A. Kearsley, 'Letter-Carriers in the Early Church', in *New Documents Illustrating Early Christianity* (Sydney: Ancient History Documentary Research Centre, Macquarie University, 1994), 7:50–57.

Llewelyn, S. R. 'Sending Letters in the Ancient World: Paul and the Philippians', *TynBul* 46 (1995), 337–56.

Loader, William R. G. 'The Central Structure of Johannine Christology', *NTS* 30 (1984), 188–216.

——. *The Christology of the Fourth Gospel: Structure and Issues* (Frankfurt am Main: Verlag Peter Lang, 1989).

——. *Jesus' Attitude towards the Law*, WUNT 97 (Tübingen: Mohr-Siebeck, 1997).

von Loewenich, W. *Johanneisches Denken: Ein Beitrag zur Kenntnis der Johanneischen Eigenart* (Leipzig: Hinrichs, 1936).

Lofthouse, W. F. *The Father and the Son: A Study in Johannine Thought* (London: SCM, 1934).

Logan, A. H. B. 'John and the Gnostics: The Significance of Apocryphon of John for the Debate about the Origins of the Johannine Literature', *JSNT* 43 (1991), 41–69.

Lohmeyer, E. 'Die Fusswaschung', *ZNW* 38 (1939), 74–94.

Lohse, Eduard. 'Wort und Sakrament im Johannesevangelium', *NTS* 7 (1960–1961), 110–125.

Loisy, A. *Le Quatrième Évangile. Les Épitres dites de Jean* (Paris: E. Nourry, 1903, 1921).

Lombard, H. A. 'Prolegomena to a Johannine Theology: Sources, method and status of a narratological model', *Neot* 29 (1995), 253–272.

Lona, E. *Abraham in Johannes: Ein Beitrag zur Methodenfrage*, EHS, Reihe 23: Theologie 65 (Bern: Peter Lang, 1976).

Lonergan, B. *De Verbo Incarnato* (Rome: Pontifical Biblical Institute, 1964).

Longenecker, Bruce. *Eschatology and the Covenant: A Comparison of 4 Ezra and Romans 1–11*, JSNTSup 57 (Sheffield: JSOT Press, 1991).

——. 'The Unbroken Messiah: A Johannine Feature and its Social Functions', *NTS* 41 (1995), 428–441.

Longenecker, R. N. *Biblical Exegesis in the Apostolic Period* (Grand Rapids: Eerdmans, 1975).

Longman III, Tremper. 'The Literary Approach to the Study of the Old Testament: Pitfalls and Promise', *JETS* 28(1985), 385–398.

López, F. M. Melús. 'Características del Evangelio de San Juan', *CB* 12 (1955), 288–95.

Losie, Lynn A. 'The Cleansing of the Temple: A History of a Gospel Tradition in Light of Its Background in the Old Testament and in Early Judaism' (Ph.D. diss., Fuller Theological Seminary, 1984).

Lotman, J. M. 'Point of View in a Text', *New Literary History* 6 (1975), 339–52.

Louw, J. P. 'Narrator of the Father – ΕΞΗΓΕΙΣΘΑΙ and Related Terms in Johannine Christology', *Neot* 2 (1968), 32–40.

——. *Semantics of New Testament Greek* (Philadelphia: Fortress Press, 1982).

——. 'Primary and Secondary Reading of a Text', *Neot* 18 (1984), 18–24.

——. 'On Johannine Style', *Neot* 20 (1986), 5–12.

——, ed. *Sociolinguistics and Communication* (London: United Bible Societies, 1986).

——. 'How Do Words Mean—If They Do?' *Filología Neotestamentaria* 4 (1991), 125–142.

Louw, J. P., and E. A. Nida, *Greek-English Lexicon of the New Testament Based on Semantic Domains*, 2 vols (New York: United Bible Societies, 1988).

Lowe, Malcolm. 'Who Were the Ἰουδαῖοι?' *NovT* 18 (1976), 101–130.

——. 'Ἰουδαῖοι of the Apocrypha', *NovT* 23 (1981), 56–90.

Lowry, Richard. 'The Rejected-Suitor Syndrome: Human Sources of the New Testament "Antisemitism"', *JES* 14 (1977), 219–232.

Lowth, Robert. *Lectures on the Sacred Poetry of the Hebrews*, 2 vols (Hildesheim: Georg Olms, 1969).

Lubbock, Percy. *The Craft of Fiction* (London: Cape, 1926).

Lund, Nils W. *Chiasmus in the New Testament: A Study in Formgeschichte* (Chapel Hill: University of North Carolina Press, 1942).

——. 'The Presence of Chiasmus in the Old Testament', *American Journal of Semitic Languages and Literature* 46 (1930), 104–126.

Lundbom, Jack R. *Jeremiah: A Study in Ancient Hebrew Rhetoric*, SBLDS 18 (Missoula, MT: Scholars Press, 1975).

Lütgert, Wilhelm. *Die Liebe im Neuen Testament: Ein Beitrag zur Geschichte des Urchristenums* (Leipzig: A. Deichert, 1905).

——. 'Die Juden im Johannesevangelium', pp. 147–154 in H. Windisch, ed., *Neutestamentliche Studien George Heinrici zu seinem 70. Geburtstag (14. März 1914) dargebracht von Fachgenossen, Freunden und Schülern*, Untersuchungen zum Neuen Testament 6 (Leipzig: Hinrichs, 1914).

Luzarraga, J. 'Presentación de Jesús a la luz del A. T. en el Evangelio de Juan', *Estudios Eclesiásticos* 51 (1976), 497–520.

Lyman, M. E. 'Hermetic Religion and the Religion of the Fourth Gospel', *JBL* 49 (1930), 265–276.

Lyons, E. *Jesus: Self-portrait by God* (New York: Paulist, 1995).

Lyons, George. *Pauline Authobiography: Towards a New Understanding*, SBLDS 73 (Atlanta: Scholars Press, 1985).

Lyons, John. *Introduction to Theoretical Linguistics* (Cambridge: CUP, 1968).

——. *Semantics*, 2 vols (Cambridge: CUP, 1977).

——. *Structural Semantics: An Analysis of Part of the Vocabulary of Plato* (Oxford: Blackwell, 1963).

Maccoby, H. Z. 'Jesus and Barabbas', *NTS* 16 (1969), 55–60.

MacCormac, Earl R. *Metaphor and Myth in Science and Religion* (Durham: Duke University Press, 1976).

MacDonald, J. *Memar Marqah: The Teaching of Marqah*, 2 vols, BZAW 84 (Berlin: Töpelmann, 1963).

MacGregor, G. H. C. *History or Didactic Drama? The Gospel of John* (New York: Kepler, 1928).

———. *The Gospel of John*, Moffatt New Testament Commentary (London: Hodder and Stoughton, 1928).

Mack, B. *Logos und Sophia*(Göttingen: Vandenhoeck und Ruprecht, 1975).

Mackay, D. G. 'To End Ambiguous Sentences', *Perception and Psychophysics* 1 (1966), 426–36.

Macky, Peter W. *The Centrality of Metaphors to Biblical Thought* (Lewiston, NY: Edwin Mellen Press, 1990).

MacRae, George W. 'The Jewish Background of the Gnostic Sophia Myth', *NovT* 12 (1970), 86–101.

———. 'The Ego-Proclamation in Gnostic Sources', pp. 122–134 in E. Bammel, ed., *The Trial of Jesus: Cambridge Studies in honour of C. F. D. Moule*. SBT 13 (London: SCM, 1970).

———. 'Theology and Irony in the Fourth Gospel', pp. 83–96 in Richard J. Clifford and George W. MacRae, eds, *The Word in the World* (Cambridge, MA: Weston College Press, 1973).

Maddox, R. 'The Function of the Son of Man in the Gospel of John', pp. 186–204 in R. J. Banks, ed., *Reconciliation and Hope* (Exeter: Paternoster Press, 1974).

Madsen, G. H. O. 'The Theological Significance of 'Nun/Arti' in the Fourth Gospel' (Ph. D. diss., Princeton Seminary, 1972).

Maggioni, B. 'La Mystica Di Giovanni Evangelista', pp. 223–250 in E. Ancilli and M. Paparozzi, eds, *La Mistica: Fenemenologia e Riflessione Teologica*, vol. 1 (Rome: Citta Nuova, 1984).

Mahood, M. M. *Shakespeare's Wordplay* (London: n. p. 1957).

Maier, Gerhard. *Mensch und freier Wille nach den jüdischen Religionsparteien zwischen Ben Sira und Paulus*, WUNT 12 (Tübingen: Mohr-Siebeck, 1971).

———. *Johannes-Evangelium* (Neuhausen-Stuttgart: Hänssler, 1984).

Malatesta, Edward. *St. John's Gospel 1920–65* (Rome: Pontifical Biblical Institute, 1967).

———. 'The Literary Structure of John 17', *Bib* 52 (1971), 190–214.

———. 'The Mystery of Faith', *The Way* 11 (1971), 219–225.

———. 'The Spirit or Paraclete in the Fourth Gospel', *Bib* 54 (1973), 539–550.

———. *Interiority and Covenant* (Rome: Biblical Institute Press, 1978).

———. 'The Love the Father Has Given Us', *The Way* 22 (1982), 155–163.

Malina, B. *The New Testament World: Insights from Cultural Anthropology* (Atlanta: John Knox Press, 1981).

———. 'The Social Sciences and Biblical Interpretation', *Interpretation* 36 (1982), 229–242, repr. pp. 11–25 in Norman Gottwald, ed., *Bible and Liberation: Political and Social Hermeneutics* (New York: Mary Knoll, 1983).

Malmede, Hans H. *Die Lichtsymbolik im Neuen Testament*, Studies in Oriental Religions, vol. 15 (Wiesbaden: Otto Harrassowitz, 1986).

Mann, J. 'Genizah Fragments of the Palestinian Order of Service', *HUCA* 2 (1925), 269–338.

Manns, F. 'Exégèse rabbinique et exégèse johannique', *RB* (1985), 525–538.

———. 'Les mots à double entente: Antécédents et fonction herméneutique d'un procédé johannique', *Studii Biblici Franciscani Liber Annuus* 38 (1988), 39–57.

Manson, T. W. *Jesus the Messiah* (London: SCM, 1943).

———. *The Teaching of Jesus* (Cambridge: CUP, 1945).

———. 'The ΕΓΩ ΕΙΜΙ of the Messianic Presence in the New Testament', *JTS* 48 (1947), 137-145.

———. 'The Son of Man in Daniel, Enoch, and the Gospels', *BJRL* 32 (1950), 171-193.

———. 'The Old Testament in the Teaching of Jesus', *BJRL* 34 (1952), 312-332.

———. *The Servant Messiah* (New York: Scribner's, 1953).

———. 'The Purpose of the Parables: A Re-examination of St. Mark iv. 10–12', *ExpTim* 68 (1956–57).

———. *On Paul and John: Some Selected Theological Themes*, ed. by Matthew Black (London: SCM, 1963).

di Marco, A. 'Der Chiasmus in der Bibel, 3. Teil (Mat-Jn)', *Linguistica Biblica* 39 (1976), 37-85.

Marsh, J. *Saint John* (London: SCM, 1968).

Marshall, I. H. *The Origin of New Testament Christology* (Leicester: Intervarsity Press, 1976).

———. *Jesus the Saviour: Studies in New Testament Theology* (London: SPCK, 1990).

Martin, R. A. *Syntax Criticism of Johannine Literature, the Catholic and the Gospel Passion Accounts* (Lewiston: Lampeter; Queenstown: E. Mellen, 1989).

Martin, Raymond A. *Syntactical Evidence of Semitic Sources in Greek Documents*, SBLSCS 3 (Missoula, MT: Scholars Press, 1979).

Marty, William H. 'The New Moses' (Th.D. diss., Dallas Seminary, 1984).

Martyn, J. Louis. 'The Salvation-History Perspective in the Fourth Gospel' (Ph.D. diss., Yale University, 1957).

———. 'Source Criticism and Religionsgeschichte in the Fourth Gospel', pp. 247-273 in David G. Buttrick, ed., *Jesus and Man's Hope*, vol. 1 (Pittsburgh: Pittsburgh Theological Seminary, 1970).

———. *The Gospel of John in Christian History: Essays for Interpreters* (New York: Paulist Press, 1978).

———. 'Persecution and Martyrdom: A Dark and Difficult Chapter in the History of Johannine Christianity', pp. 55-89 in *The Gospel of John in Christian History* (New York: Paulist Press, 1978).

———. 'Glimpses into the History of the Johannine Community', pp. 90-121 in *The Gospel of John in Christian History* (New York: Paulist Press, 1978).

———. *History and Theology in the Fourth Gospel* (New York: Harper and Row, 1968; 2nd rev. and enl. edn, Nashville: Abingdon, 1979).

Marxsen, W. *Mark the Evangelist: Studies on the Redaction History of the Gospel* (Nashville: Abingdon, 1969).

Mastin, B. A. 'Neglected Features of the Christology of the Fourth Gospel', *NTS* 22 (1975–76), 32-51.

Matera, F. J. '"On Behalf of Others", "Cleansing", and "Return": Johannine Images for Jesus' Death', *LS* 13 (1988), 161-178.

Matsunaga, Kikuo. 'Powers in Conflict: A New Clue to the Interpretation of the Fourth Gospel' (Ph.D. diss., McGill University, 1970).

———. 'The "Theos" Christology as the Ultimate Confession of the Fourth Gospel', *Annual of the Japanese Biblical Institute* 7 (1981), 124–145.

Matthews, Shailer. *The Social Teaching of Jesus: An Essay in Christian Sociology* (New York: Macmillan, 1987).

Mawson. C. O. Sylvester. *Dictionary of Foreign Terms*, 2nd edn (New York: revised by Charles Thomas and Crowell, 1934, 1975).

Maxwell-Mahon, W. D. 'Jacob's Ladder: A Structural Analysis of Scripture', *Semitics* 7 (1980), 118–130.

Mayer, A. 'Elijah and Elisha in John's Sign Sources', *ExpTim* 99 (1988), 171–173.

Maynard, H. 'The Function of Apparent Synonyms and Ambiguous Words in the Fourth Gospel' (Ph.D. diss., University of Southern California, 1950).

McCaffrey, James. *The House with Many Rooms: The Temple Theme of Jn. 14:2-3*. AnBib 114 (Rome: Editrice Pontificio Istituto Biblico, 1988).

McCartney, E. S. 'Puns and Plays on Proper Names', *Classical Journal* 14 (1919), 343–358.

McColl, F. *Problemata Johannaea* (Rome, 1965).

McDonald, William E. 'The Literary Criticism of Amos Wilder', *Soundings* 52 (1969), 99.

McDonnell, R. M. A. 'The Interdependence of Luke-Acts and the Fourth Gospel Considered against the Background of a Common School' (Ph.D. diss., Boston University, 1977).

McDonough, Sean M. *YHWH at Patmos: Rev. 1:4 in its Hellenistic and Early Jewish Setting*, WUNT 2.107 (Tübingen: Mohr-Siebeck, 1999).

McEleney, N. J. '153 Great Fishes (John 21:11), Gematriacal Atbash', *Bib* 58 (1977), 411–417.

McFague, Sallie. *Metaphorical Theology: Models of God in Religious Language* (Philadelphia: Fortress Press, 1982).

McGuire, Meredith B. *Religion: The Social Context*, 4th edn (Belmont, CA, and London: Wadsworth, 1997).

McHugh, John, 'In Him was Life', pp. 123–158 in J. D. G. Dunn, ed., *Jews and Christians: The Parting of the Ways AD 70 to 135* (Tübingen: Mohr-Siebeck, 1992).

McIntosh, Angus and M. A. K. Halliday. *Patterns of Language: Papers in General, Descriptive, and Applied Linguistics*, Indiana University Studies in the History and Theory of Linguistics (Bloomington: Indiana University Press, 1966).

McKay, K. L. 'Style and Significance in the Language of John 21:15–17', *NovT* 27 (1985), 319–333.

McKenzie, J. L. 'The Word of God in the Old Testament', *TS* 21 (1960), 183–206.

McKnight, Edgar. *Postmodern Use of the Bible: The Emergence of Reader-Oriented Criticism* (Nashville: Abingdon, 1988).

McLean, B. H. *Citations and Allusions to Jewish Scripture in Early Christian and Jewish Writings through 180 C.E.* (Lewiston, NY: Edwin Mellen Press, 1992).

McNamara, Martin. 'The Ascension and the Exaltation of Christ in the Fourth Gospel', *Scripture* 47 (1967), 65–73.

———. 'Logos of the Fourth Gospel and Memra of the Palestinian Targum (Exo. 12:42)', *ExpTim* 79 (1967–68), 115–117.

―――. *Targum and Testament* (Shannon: Irish University Press; Grand Rapids: Eerdmans, 1972).

McNeil, B. 'The Raising of Lazarus', *DRev* 92 (1974), 269–275.

McNeile, A. H., ed. *A Critical and Exegetical Commentary on the Gospel According to St. John*, 2 vols (New York: Scribner's, 1929).

McPolin, J. 'Johannine Mysticism', *The Way* 18 (1978), 25.

―――. 'The "Name" of the Father and of the Son in the Johannine Writings: An Exegetical Study of the Johannine Texts on *Onoma* with Reference to the Father and the Son' (Diss. Rome: Pont. Biblical Institute, 1971).

Meade, G. *The Gnostic John the Baptizer* (London: Watkins, 1924).

Meadors, E. P. *Jesus the Messianic Herald of Salvation*, WUNT 2.72 (Tübingen: Mohr-Siebeck, 1995).

Meagher, John C. 'John 1:14 and the New Temple', *JBL* 88 (1969), 57–68.

―――. *The Way of the Word: The Beginning and the Establishing of Christian Understanding* (New York: Seabury, 1975).

Mealand, David. 'The Language of Mystical Union in the Johannine Writings', *DRev* 95 (1977), 19–34.

Meeks, Wayne A. 'Galilee and Judea in the Fourth Gospel', *JBL* 85 (1966), 159–169.

―――. *The Prophet-King: Moses Traditions and the Johannine Christology*, NovTSup 14 (Leiden: Brill, 1967).

―――. '"Am I a Jew?"—Johannine Christianity and Judaism', pp. 163–186 in J. Neusner, ed., *Christianity, Judaism, and Other Greco-Roman Cults*, Part One: New Testament (Leiden: Brill, 1975).

―――. 'Breaking Away: Three New Testament Pictures of Christianity's Separation From the Jewish Communities', pp. 93–115 in J. Neusner and E. S. Frerichs, eds, *To See Ourselves as Others See Us: Christians, Jews, Others in Late Antiquity* (Chico, CA: Scholars Press, 1985).

―――. 'The Man from Heaven in Johannine Sectarianism', *JBL* 91 (1972), 44–72. Reprinted pp. 169–205 in J. Ashton, ed., *The Interpretation of John* (London: SPCK, 1986).

―――. *The Moral World of the First Christians* (Philadelphia: Westminster Press, 1986; London: SPCK, 1987).

Meier, J. P. *A Marginal Jew: Rethinking the Historical Jesus*, ABRL (Garden City, NY: Doubleday, 1991).

Meinertz, M. *Theologie des Neuen Testaments II* (Bonn: Peter Hanstein, 1950).

Menken, Martinus J. J. 'The Quotation from Isaiah 40:3 in John 1:23', *Bib* 66 (1985), 190–205.

―――. *Numerical Literary Techniques in John* (Leiden: Brill, 1985).

―――. 'The Old Testament Quotation in John 6:45: Source and Redaction', *ETL* 64 (1988), 164–172.

―――. 'The Provenance and Meaning of the Old Testament Quotation in John 6:31', *NovT* 30 (1988), 39–56.

―――. 'Die Form des Zitates aus Jes. 6.10 in Joh. 12.40: Ein Beitrag zum Schriftgebrauch des vierten Evangelisten', *BZ* 32 (1988), 189–209.

―――. 'Die Redaktion des Zitates aus Sach 9:9 in Joh 12:15', *ZNW* 25 (1989), 193–209.

—. 'The Translation of Psalm 41.10 in John 13.18', *JSNT* 40 (1990), 61–79.

Mennicke, V. 'Bible Interpretation', in *The Abiding Word*, ed. T. Laetsch, 2 vols (St. Louis, MO: Concordia, 1947).

Menoud, P. H. *L'Évangile de Jean d'après les recherches récentes*, CTAP 3 (Neuchatel: Delachaux et Niestlé, 1947).

Metzger, B. M. *Index to the Periodical Literature on Christ and the Gospels* (Leiden: Brill, 1966).

—. *A Textual Commentary on the Greek New Testament* (London and New York: United Bible Societies, 1971).

Meyer, B. F. 'How Jesus Charged Language With Meaning: A Study in Rhetoric', *Canadian Society of Biblical Studies Bulletin* 49 (1989), 5–20.

Meyer, Paul W. 'The Eschatology of the Fourth Gospel: A Study in Early Christian Reinterpretation' (Th.D. Diss. New York: Union Theological Seminary, 1955).

—. 'A Note On John 10:1–18', *JBL* 75 (1956), 232–235.

Michaelis, W. 'Joh. 1:51 – Gen. 28:12 und das Menschensohn-problem', *TLZ* 86 (1960), 561–578.

Michaels, J. R. 'Nathanael Under the Fig Tree', *ExpTim* 78 (1966–67), 182–183.

Michel, M. 'Nicodème ou le non-lieu de la vérité', *RevSR* 55 (1981), 227–236.

Milic, Louis T. *Stylists on Style: A Handbook with Selections for Analysis* (New York: Charles Scribner's Sons, 1969).

Miller, D. M. *The Net of Hephaestus: A Study of Modern Criticism and Metaphysical Metaphor* (The Hague: Mouton, 1974).

Miller, E. L. 'The Christology of John 8:25', *TZ* 36 (1980), 257–265.

—. *Salvation-History in the Prologue of John: The Significance of John 1:3/4*, NovTSup 60 (Leiden: Brill, 1989).

Miller, G. 'The Nature and Purpose of the Signs in the Fourth Gospel' (Ph.D. Diss. Duke University, 1968).

Miller, J. H. 'The Figure in the Carpet', *Poetics Today* 1 (1980), 112.

Miller, M. P. 'Targum, Midrash and the Use of the Old Testament in the New Testament', *JSJ* 2 (1971), 29–82.

Miller, Owen. 'Intertextual Identity', pp. 19–40 in M. J. Valdes and O. Miller, eds, *Identity of the Literary Text* (Toronto: University of Toronto, 1985).

Milligan, W. M. 'Double Pictures in the Fourth Gospel and the Apocalypse', *Exp* 4 (1882), 264–278, 430–447.

Mills, W. E. *The Gospel of John*, Bibliographies for Biblical Research, New Testament Series 4. (Lewiston, NY and Lampeter, UK: Mellen Biblical Press, 1995).

Minear, P. S. 'The Audience of the Fourth Gospel', *Interpretation* 31 (1977), 339–354.

—. 'The Original Functions of John 21', *JBL* 102 (1983), 85–98.

Minor, Mark. *Literary-Critical Approaches to the Bible: An Annotated Bibliography* (West Cornwall, CT: Locust Hill Press, 1992).

Miranda, José Porfirio. *Being and the Messiah: The Message of St. John*, ET by J. Eagleson (Maryknoll, NY: Orbis Books, 1977).

—. *Der Vater der mich gesandt hat*, EHS, Reihe 23: Theologie 7 (Frankfurt am Main: Herbert and Peter Lang, 1972).

Miscall, Peter D. 'Isaiah: New Heavens, New Earth, New Book', pp. 41-56 in D. Fewell, ed., *Reading Between Texts* (Louisville, Kentucky: Westminster/John Knox Press, 1992).

Mitchell, D. R. 'The Person of Christ in John's Gospel and Epistles' (Th.D. diss., Dallas Seminary, 1982).

Mlakuzhyil, George. *The Christocentric Literary Structure of the Fourth Gospel* (Rome: Editrice Pontificio Instituto Biblico, 1987).

Moeller, Otto. 'Wisdom Motifs and John's Gospel', *BETS* 6 (1963), 93-98.

Mol, H. J. *Identity and the Sacred: A Sketch for a New Social-Scientific Theory of Religion* (New York: Free Press, 1977).

Moloney, Francis J. 'The Fourth Gospel's Presentation of Jesus as the Christ and J. A. T. Robinson's Redating', *DRev* 95 (1975), 239-253.

——. *The Johannine Son of Man*, Bibliotech di Scienze Religiose 14 (Rome: Libreria Ateneo Salesiano, 1976).

——. 'From Cana to Cana (Jn. 2:1-4:54) and the Fourth Evangelist's Concept of Correct (and incorrect) Faith', *Salesianum* 40 (1978), 817-843.

——. 'John 1:18: "In the Bosom of" or "Turned Towards" the Father?' *Australian Biblical Review* 31 (1983), 63-71.

Montgomery, J. A. *The Origin of the Gospel According to St. John* (Philadelphia: Fortress Press, 1923).

Moo, Douglas J. *The Old Testament in the Gospel Passion Narrative* (Sheffield, England: Almond Press, 1983).

Moore, F. J. 'Eating the Flesh and Drinking the Blood: A Reconsideration', *ATR* 48 (1966), 70-75.

Moore, G. F. 'Christian Writers on Judaism', *HTR* 14 (1921), 197-254.

——. *Judaism in the First Centuries of the Christian Era: The Age of the Tannaim*, 3 vols (Cambridge, MA: Harvard University Press, 1927-30).

Moore, Stephen D. 'Rifts in (a Reading of) the Fourth Gospel, or: Does Johannine Irony Still Collapse in a Reading that Draws Attention to Itself?' *Neot* 23 (1989), 5-17.

——. *Literary Criticism and the Gospels* (New Haven: Yale University Press, 1989).

van Moorsel, G. *The Mysteries of Hermes Trismegistus*, STRT 1 ((Utrecht: Kemink en zoon, 1955).

Mörchen, R. '"Weggehen": Beobachtungen zu John 12:36b', *BZ* 28 (1984), 240-242.

Moreton, M. J. 'Feast, Sign and Discourse in John 5', *SE* 4 = TU 102, ed. F. L. Cross (1968), 209-213.

Morgan, J., ed. 'Church Divinity, 1984: National Student Essay Competition in Divinity', *Church Divinity Monograph Series* (Bristol: Wyndham Hall Press, 1984).

Morgan, R. 'Fulfillment in the Fourth Gospel: The Old Testament Foundations' *Interpretation* 11 (1957), 155-65.

Morgan, Thaïs E. 'Is There an Intertext in This Text? Literary and Interdisciplinary Approaches to Intertextuality', *American Journal of Semiotics* 34 (1985), 1-40.

——. 'The Space of Intertextuality', pp. 259-279 in P. O'Donnell and R. C. Davis, eds, *Intertextuality and Contemporary American Fiction* (Baltimore: John Hopkins, 1989).

Morgenstern, J. 'The Suffering Servant—A New Solution', *VT* 11 (1961), 406-31.

Morgan-Wynne, J. E. 'The Cross and The Revelation of Jesus as Ego Eimi in the Fourth Gospel (John 8:28)', pp. 219-316 in E. A. Livingstone, ed. *Studia Biblica 1978, II: Papers on the Gospels* (Sheffield: JSOT Press, 1980).

Morris, Leon. *The New Testament and the Jewish Lectionaries* (London: Tyndale, 1964).

——. *The Apostolic Preaching of the Cross* (London: Tyndale Press, reprint, 1965).

——. *Studies in the Fourth Gospel* (Exeter: Paternoster, 1969).

——. *The Gospel According to John* (Grand Rapids: Eerdmans, 1971).

——. *Jesus is the Christ: Studies in the Theology of John* (Grand Rapids: Eerdmans, 1989).

Motyer, J. Alec. *The Prophecy of Isaiah: An Introduction and Commentary* (Downers Grove, IL: InterVarsity Press, 1993).

Motyer, S. 'Method in Fourth Gospel Studies: A Way Out of the Impasse?' *JSNT* 66 (1997), 27-44.

Moule, C. F. D. 'A Note on 'Under the Fig Tree' in John 1:48, 50', *JTS* n.s. 5 (1954), 210-211.

——. 'The Influence of Circumstances on the Use of Christological Terms', *JTS* n.s. 10 (1959), 258.

——. 'The Individualism of the Fourth Gospel', *NovT* 5 (1962), 171-190.

——. *The Sacrifice of Christ: Atonement* (Philadelphia: Fortress Press, 1964).

——. *The Phenomenon of the New Testament* (London: SCM, 1967).

——. 'The Intention of the Evangelists', pp. 165-179 in A. J. B. Higgins, ed., *New Testament Essays: Studies in Memory of T. W. Manson* (Manchester: University Press, 1959). Repr. pp. 100-114 in C. F. D. Moule, *The Phenomenon of the New Testament* (London: SCM, 1967).

——. ed. *The Significance of the Message of the Resurrection for Faith in Jesus Christ*, Studies in Biblical Theology, 2nd Ser., 8 (London: SCM, 1968).

——. *An Idiom Book of the New TestamentGreek* (Cambridge: CUP, 1971, 1953).

——. 'The Meaning of "Life" in the Gospel and Epistles of St. John: A Study in the Story of Lazarus, John 11:1-44', *Theology* 78 (1975), 114-125.

——. *The Origin of Christology* (Cambridge: CUP, 1977).

——. *Essays in New Testament Interpretation* (Cambridge: CUP, 1982).

——. *The Birth of the New Testament*, 3rd edn (London: Adam and Charles Black: 1982).

Moulton, James Hope. *A Grammar of New Testament Greek*, 3 vols (Edinburgh: Clark, 1919, 1920, 1929).

——. and W. F. Howard, *A Grammar of New Testament Greek*, vol. 2. (Edinburgh: Clark, 1929).

Moulton and Milligan, *The Vocabulary of the Greek Testament: Illustrated from the Papyri and Other Non-Literary Sources* (London: Hodder and Stoughton, 1930).

Moulton, Richard G. *The Literary Study of the Bible*, rev. edn (Boston: D. C. Heath, 1899).

Mounce, R. H. *The Essential Nature of New Testament Preaching* (Grand Rapids: Eerdmans, 1960).

Mowinckel, Sigmund. *He That Cometh: The Messiah Concept in the Old Testament and Later Judaism*, ET by G. W. Anderson (Nashville: Abingdon Press, 1956).

———. 'Den västorientaliska och israelitisk-judiska litteraturen', *Bonniers allmänna litteraturhistoria*, ed. by E. N. Tigerstedt, I (Stockholm: Bonniers, 1959).

———. *The Old Testament as Word of God*, ET by Reidar B. Bjornard (Oxford: Blackwell, 1960).

Mowry, Lucetta. 'The Dead Sea Scrolls and the Background for the Gospel of John', *BA* 17 (1954), 78–97.

Mowvley, Henry. 'John 1:14-18 in the Light of Exodus 33:7-34:35', *ExpTim* 95 (1983-84), 135-137.

Muddiman, John. 'The Resurrection of Jesus as the Coming of the Kingdom – the Basis of Hope for the Transformation of the World', pp. 208-223 in R. S. Barbour, ed., *The Kingdom of God and Human Society* (Edinburgh: Clark, 1993).

Muecke, D. C. *The Compass of Irony* (London: Methuen, 1969).

———. *Irony: The Critical Idiom* (London: Methuen, 1970).

Muilenburg, J. 'Literary Form in the Fourth Gospel', *JBL* 51 (1932), 40-53.

———. 'A Study in Hebrew Rhetoric: Repetition and Style', *VT* 1 (1953), 97–111.

———. 'Form Criticism and Beyond', *JBL* 88 (1969), 1-18.

Mulder, H. 'Ontstaan en Doel van het vierde Evangelie', *Gereformeerd Theologisch Tijdschrift* 69 (1969), 233-258.

Mulder, Martin Jan, ed. *Mikra: Text, Translation, Reading and Interpretation of the Hebrew Bible in Ancient Judaism and Early Christianity*. CRINT, section 2, *The Literature of the Jewish People in the Period of the Second Temple and the Talmud*, vol. 1 (Philadelphia: Fortress, 1988).

Müller, Mogens. 'Have You Faith in the Son of Man?' *NTS* 37 (1991), 290-294.

Murphy, Frederick J. '2 *Baruch* and the Romans', *JBL* 104 (1985), 663-669.

Murphy-O'Connor, J. 'The Essenes and their History', *RB* 81 (1974), 215-244

Murray, Robert. '"Disaffected Judaism" and Early Christianity: Some Predisposing Factors', pp. 263-281 in J. Neusner and E. Frerichs, eds. *To See Ourselves as Others See Us: Christians, Jews, Others in Late Antiquity* (Chico, CA: Scholars Press, 1985).

Mussner, F. *The Historical Jesus in the Gospel of St. John* (London: Herder; Freiburg: Burns and Oates, 1967).

———. '"Kultische" Aspeckte im johanneischen Christusbild', pp. 133-145 in *Praesentia Salutis: Gesammelte Studien zu Fragen und Themen des Neuen Testamentes*, Kommentare und Beiträge zum Alten und Neuen Testament (Düsseldorf: Patmos, 1967).

———. *Tractate on the Jews: The Significance of Judaism for Christian Faith* (London: SPCK, 1984).

Myers, Doris. 'Irony and Humor in the Gospel of John', *OPTAT* 2 (1988), 1-13.

Nations, Archie L. 'Jewish Persecution of Christians in the Gospel of John', A paper read at the Society of Biblical Literature annual meeting (Atlanta, 23 Nov., 1986).

Naumann, P. S. 'The Presence of Love in John's Gospel', *Worship* 39 (1965), 363-371.

Navone, John. 'A Theology of Darkness, Terror, and Dread', *Theology* 80 (1977), 348–53.

Neill, S. T. *The Interpretation of the New Testament* 1861-1961 (London: OUP, 1966).

Neirynck, F. *De Semeia-bron in het vierde evangelie: Kritiek van een hypothese*. ET: 'The Signs Source in the Fourth Gospel: A Critique of the Hypothesis', *Evangelica* II (1991), 651–679.

Nereparampil, L. *Destroy This Temple. An Exegetico-Theological Study on the Meaning of Jesus' Temple-Logion in Jn 2:19*, Dharmaram Studies (Bangalore: Dharmaram College, 1978).

Neugebauer, Fritz. *Die Entstehung des Johannesevangeliums*, Arbeiten zur Theologie 1/36 (Stuttgart: Calwer Verlag, 1968).

Neugebauer, J. *Die eschatologischen Aussagen in den johanneischen Abschiedsreden. Eine Untersuchung zu Johannes 13-17*, BWANT 140 (Stuttgart-Berlin-Cologne: Kohlhammer, 1995).

Neusner, J. *Life of Yohanan ben Zakkai ca.1–80 C.E.*, 2nd edn (Leiden: Brill, 1970 and Nashville: Abingdon, 1975).

———. 'Judaism in a Time of Crisis: Four Responses to the Destruction of the Second Temple', *Judaism* 21 (1972), 313–327.

———. *From Politics to Piety: The Emergence of Pharisaic Judaism* (Engelwood Cliffs, NJ: Prentice-Hall, 1973).

———, ed. *Christianity, Judaism, and other Greco-Roman Cults*: Studies for Morton Smith at Sixty (Leiden: Brill, 1975).

———. *The Tosefta: Translated from the Hebrew*, 6 vols (Hoboken, NJ: Ktav, 1977–86).

———. 'The Formation of Rabbinic Judaism: Yavneh (Jamnia) from AD 70 to 100', *ANRW* II.19.2 (1979).

———. 'Varieties of Judaism in the Formative Age', pp. 59–89 in *Formative Judaism*, BJS 41 (Chico, CA: Scholars Press, 1983).

———. 'Judaism after the Destruction of the Temple: An Overview', pp. 83–98 in Formative Judaism: *Religious, Historical and Literary Studies. 3rd Series: Torah, Pharisees, and Rabbis*, BJS 46 (Chico, CA: Scholars Press, 1983).

———. 'The Formation of Rabbinic Judaism: Methodological Issues and Substantive Theses', pp. 99–144 in *Formative Judaism: Religious, Historical and Literary Studies. 3rd Series: Torah, Pharisees, and Rabbis*, BJS 46 (Chico, CA: Scholars Press 1983).

———. *Midrash in Context: Exegesis in Formative Judaism* (Philadelphia: Fortress Press, 1983).

———. *Messiah in Context* (Philadelphia: Fortress Press, 1984).

——— and E. Frerichs, eds. *To See Ourselves as Others See Us: Christians, Jews, Others in Late Antiquity* (Chico, CA: Scholars Press, 1985).

———. *Understanding Rabbinic Midrash* (Hoboken, NJ: Ktav, 1985).

———. *What is Midrash?* (Philadelphia: Fortress Press, 1987).

———, W. S. Green, and E. Frerichs. *Judaisms and Their Messiahs at the Turn of the Christian Era* (Cambridge: CUP, 1987).

———. *Jews and Christians: The Myth of a Common Tradition* (London: SCM, 1991).

Newman, Jr. Barclay M. 'Some Observations Regarding the Argument, Structure, and Literary Characteristics of John', *TBT* 26 (1975), 234–239.

Newman, Jr. Barclay M. and Eugene A. Nida. *A Translator's Handbook on the Gospel of John* (New York: United Bible Societies, 1980).

Newton-DeMolina, David, ed. *On Literary Intention* (Edinburgh: University Press, 1976).

Neyrey, Jerome H. 'Jacob Traditions and the Interpretation of John 4:10-26', *CBQ* 41 (1979), 419-437.

——. 'John III—A Debate Over Johannine Epistemology and Christology', *NovT* 23 (1981), 115-127.

——. 'The Jacob Allusions in John 1:51', *CBQ* 44 (1982), 586-605.

——. *An Ideology of Revolt: John's Christology in Social-Science Perspective* (Philadelphia:Fortress Press, 1988).

——. '"I Said, You are Gods": Psalm 82:6 and John 10', *JBL* 108 (1989), 647-663.

——. 'The Trials (Forensic) and Tribulations (Honor Challenges) of Jesus: John 7 in Social Science Perspective', *BTB* 26 (1996), 107-124.

Nicholson, Godfrey. *Death as Departure: The Johannine Descent-Ascent Schema*, SBLDS 63 (Chico, CA: Scholars Press, 1983).

Nicol, G. G. 'Jesus' Washing the Feet of the Disciples: A Model for Johannine Christology?' *ExpTim* 91 (1979), 20-21.

Nicole, W. *The Semeia in the Fourth Gospel: Tradition and Redaction* (Leiden: Brill, 1972).

——. 'Essays on the Jewish Background of the Fourth Gospel: 8th Meeting Die Nuew-Testamentiese Werkgemeenskap Van Suid Afrika, Pretoria, Univ. of S. Africa', *Neot* 6 (1972), 8-17.

Niedenthal, M. J. 'The Irony and the Grammar of the Gospel', *Princeton Seminary Bulletin* 64 (1971), 22-29.

Niles, D. T. *Whereof We Are Witnesses* (London: Epworth Press, 1965).

Nils, John S., Erik Enkvist, and Michael Gregory. *Linguistics and Style: Language and Language Learning* (London: OUP, 1964).

Nilsson, Martin P. *Geschichte der griechischen Religion, vol. 2: Die hellenistische und römische Zeit*, HAW 5.2.2 (Munich: Beck, reprint, 1974).

Nixon, R. E. *The Exodus in the New Testament* (London: Tyndale, 1963).

Noack, Bent. *Zur johanneischen Tradition: Beiträge zur Kritik an der literarkritischen Analyse des vierten Evangeliums*, Teologiske Skrifter, Bd. 3 (Copenhagen: Rosenkilde og Bagger, 1954).

Nock, Arthur Darby and A. J. Festugière. *Corpus Hermeticum*, 4 vols (Paris: Les Belles Letters, 1945-54).

Nock, Arthur Darby. *Essays on Religion and the Ancient World*, 2 vols (Cambridge, MA: Harvard University, 1972).

Nodet, E. *Essai sur les Origines du Judaïsme* (Paris: Les Éditions de Cerf, 1992).

Noetzel, H. *Christus und Dionysos: Bemerkungen zum religionsgeschichtlichen hintergrund von Johannes 2.1-11* (Stuttgart: Calwer Verlag, 1959).

Norrman, R. *Techniques of Ambiguity in the Fiction of Henry James* (Abo, Finland: Acta Academiae Aboensis, 1977).

Nortjé, J. 'Lamb of God (John 1:29): An Explanation from Ancient Christian Art', *Neot* 30 (1996), 141-150.

Norton, David. *A History of the Bible as Literature*, 2vols (Cambridge: CUP, 1993).
Noth, M. 'Das Geschichtsverständnis der alttestamentlichen Apokalyptik', pp. 4–25 in Arbeitsgemeinschaft für Forschung des Landes Nordrhein-Westfalen, Geisteswissenschaften, H. 21 (Köln und Opladen: Westdeutscher Verlag, 1954). Repr. pp. 248–273 in idem, *Gesammelte Studien zum Alten Testament*, TB 6 (Munich: Chr. Kaiser Verlag, 1966).
Nötscher, F. '"Wahrheit" als theologischer Terminus in den Qumran-Texten', pp. 83–92 in *Festschrift für Prof. Dr. Viktor Christian. Vorderasiatische Studien* (Vienna, 1956).
Nowottny, W. *The Language Poets Use* (London: Athlone Press, 1962).
Nuthall, A. D. *Overheard by God: Fiction and Prayer in Herbert, Milton, Dante and St. John* (New York: Metthuen, 1980).
Nygren, A. *The Significance of the Bible for the Church*, Biblical Series 1 (Philadelphia: Facet Books, 1963).

O'Day, Gail R. *Revelation in the Fourth Gospel: Narrative Mode and Theological Claim* (Philadelphia: Fortress Press, 1986).
——. 'Narrative Mode and Theological Claim: Fourth Gospel', *JBL* 105 (1986), 657–668.
——. *The Word Disclosed* (St. Louis: CBP Press, 1987).
——. 'Toward a Narrative-Critical Study of John', *Interpretation* 49 (1995), 341–346.
Odeberg, Hugo. *The Fourth Gospel Interpreted in Its Relation to Contemporaneous Religious Currents in Palestine and the Hellenistic-Oriental World* (Amsterdam: Grüner, 1929; repr. Chicago: Argonaut, 1968).
Oehler, Wilhelm. *Das Johannesevangelium: Ein Missionsschrift für die Welt, der Gemeinde ausgelegt* (Gütersloh: Bertelsmann, 1936).
——. *Zum Missionscharackter des Johannesevangeliums* (Gütersloh: Bertelsmann, 1941).
Oesterley, W. O. E. *The Jews and Judaism During the Greek Period: The Background of Christianity* (London: SPCK and New York: Macmillan, 1941).
Ogden, C. K. and I. A. Richards. *The Meaning of Meaning* (London: Routledge and Kegan Paul, 1923).
Ogg, G. Review of Mlle Jaubert, *La Date de la Cène*, *NovT* 34 (1959), 149–60.
O'Grady, John F. *Individual and Community in John* (Rome: Pontifical Biblical Institute, 1978).
——. 'Recent Developments in Johannine Studies', *BTB* 12 (1982), 54–58.
——. 'Jesus, the Revelation of God in the Fourth Gospel', *BTB* 25 (1995), 161–165.
Okure, Teresa. *The Johannine Approach to Mission* (Tübingen: Mohr-Siebeck, 1988).
Olsson, Birger. *Structure and Meaning in the Fourth Gospel: A Text-Linguistic Analysis of John 2:1–11 and 4:1–42*, trans. by Jean Gray, ConBNTS 6 (Lund, Sweden: Gleerup, 1974).
Onuki, Takashi. 'Zur literatursoziologischen Analyse des Johannesevangelium—auf dem Wege zur Methodenintegration', *AJBI* 8 (1982), 162–216.

―――. *Gemeinde und Welt im Johannesevangelium: Ein Beitrag zur Frage nach der theologischen und pragmatischen Funktion des johanneischen 'Dualismus'*, WMANT 56 (Neukirchen-Vluyn: Neukirchener Verlag, 1984).

O'Rourke, John. 'Explicit Old Testament Citations in the Gospels', *Studia Montis Regii* 7 (1964), 37–60.

―――. 'The Historic Present in the Gospel of John', *JBL* 93 (1974), 585–590.

―――. 'Asides in the Gospel of John', *NovT* 21 (1979), 210–219.

Osborne, B. 'A Folded Napkin in an Empty Tomb: John 11:44 and 20:7 Again', *HeyJ* 14 (1973), 437–440.

Osborne, Grant. *The Hermeneutical Spiral: A Comprehensive Introduction to Biblical Interpretation* (Downers Grove: Inter-Varsity Press, 1991).

Osgood, Charles and Oliver C. S. Tzeng, eds, *Language, Meaning, and Culture: The selected papers of C. E. Osgood* (New York: Praeger, 1990).

Osiek, Carolyn. *What Are They Saying about the Social Setting of the New Testament?* expanded and rev. edn (New York and Mahwah, NJ: Paulist Press, 1992).

Osten-Sacken, P. von der. *Christian-Jewish Dialogue: Theological Foundations* (Philadelphia: Fortress, 1986).

O'Sullivan, F. *The Egnatian Way* (Harrisburg, PA: David and Charles, 1972).

Overhold, T. W. *The Threat of Falsehood: A Study in the Theology of the Book of Jeremiah*, SBT 2/16 (London: SCM, 1970).

The Oxford English Dictionary. 12 Vols (Oxford: Clarendon, 1933). See vol. 10:1208 s.v. 'Stylistics'.

Page, R. *Ambiguity and the Presence of God* (London: SCM, 1985).

Pagels, Elaine H. *The Johannine Gospel in Gnostic Exegesis: Heracleon's Commentary on John*, SBLMS 17 (Nashville: Abingdon Press, 1973).

Pahk, S. S. 'Structural Analysis of John 6:1–58: Meaning of the Symbol of "Bread of Life"' (Ph.D. diss., Vanderbilt University, 1984).

Painter, John. *John: Witness and Theologian* (London: SPCK, 1975).

―――. 'Christ and the Church in John 1:45–51', pp. 359–362 in M. de Jonge, ed., *L'Évangile de Jean: sources, rédaction, théologie*, BETL 44 (Leuven: Leuven University Press, 1977).

―――. 'The Church and Israel in the Gospel of John: A Response', *NTS* 25 (1978–79), 103–112.

―――. 'Johannine Symbols: A Case Study in Epistemology', *Journal of Theology for Southern Africa* 27 (1979), 26–41.

―――. 'Christology and the Fourth Gospel: A Study of the Prologue', *AusBR* 31 (1983), 45–62.

―――. 'Christology and the History of the Johannine Community in the Prologue of the Fourth Gosepl', *NTS* 30 (1984), 460–474.

―――. 'John 9 and the Interpretation of the Fourth Gospel', *JSNT* 28 (1986), 53–54.

―――. *The Quest for the Messiah: The History, Literature and Theology of the Johannine Community* (Edinburgh: Clark, 1991).

——. 'The Quotation of Scripture and Unbelief in John 12:36b–43', pp. 429–458 in Craig A. Evans and W. Richard Stegner, eds, *The Gospels and the Scriptures of Israel*, JSNTSup 104 (Sheffield: Sheffield Academic Press, 1994).

Palmer, Earl F. *The Intimate Gospel: Studies in John* (Waco, TX: Word Books, 1978).

Palmer, F. R. *Semantics: A New Outline* (Cambridge: CUP, 1981, 1976).

Palvio, Allan. *Mental Representations: A Dual Coding Approach* (New York: OUP, 1986).

Pamment, Margaret. 'The Meaning of *Doxa* in the Fourth Gospel', *ZNW* 74 (1973), 12–16.

——. 'Eschatology and the Fourth Gospel', *JSNT* 15 (1982), 81–85.

——. 'The Son of Man in the Fourth Gospel', *JTS* n.s. 36 (1985), 56–66.

——. 'Path and Residence Metaphors in the Fourth Gospel', *Theology* 88 (1985), 118–124.

Panackel, C. *ΙΔΟΥ Ο ΑΝΘΡΩΠΟΣ (Jn 19,5b): An Exegetico-Theological Study of the Text in the Light of the Use of the Term ΑΝΘΡΩΠΟΣ Designating Jesus in the Fourth Gospel*, Analecta Gregoriana 251 (Rome: Pontificia Università Gregoriana, 1988).

Pancaro, S. 'A Statistical Approach to the Concept of Time and Eschatology in the Fourth Gospel', *Bib* 50 (1969), 511–524.

——. '"People of God" in St. John's Gospel (Jn. 11:50–52)', *NTS* 16 (1969–70), 114–129.

——. 'The Metamorphosis of a Legal Principle in the Fourth Gospel: A Closer Look at John 7:51', *Bib* 53 (1972), 340–361.

——. *The Law in the Fourth Gospel: The Torah and The Gospel, Moses and Jesus, Judaism and Christianity According to John*, NovTSup 42 (Leiden: Brill, 1975).

Pannenberg, Wolfhart, ed. *Offenbarung als Geschichte* (Göttingen: Vandenhoeck und Ruprecht, 1965, 1961).

Parker, P. 'Bethany Beyond Jordan', *JBL* 74 (1955), 257–261.

——. 'John and John Mark', *JBL* 79 (1960), 97–110.

——. 'John, Son of Zebedee and the Fourth Gospel', *JBL* 81 (1962), 35–43.

Parkes, J. *The Conflict of the Church and the Synagogue: A Study in the Origins of anti-Semitism*, 3rd edn (New York: Atheneum, 1969 [orig. 1934]).

Parson, S. *We Have Been Born Anew* (Diss. Rome: Angelicum, 1978).

Parunak, H. Van Dyke. 'Some Axioms for Literary Architecture', *Semitics* 8 (1982), 1–16.

Paschal, Jr., R. W. 'Sacramental Symbolism and Physical Imagery in the Gospel of John', *TynBul* 32 (1981), 151–176.

Patte, Daniel. *Early Jewish Hermeneutic in Palestine* (Missoula, MT: Scholars Press, 1975).

Payne, D. F. 'Characteristic Word Play in "Second Isaiah": A Reappraisal', *JSS* 12 (1967), 207–229.

Perkins, Pheme. 'John's Gospel and Gnostic Christologies,' *Anglican Theological Review Supplement* 11 (1990), 68–76.

——. 'New Testament Christologies in Gnostic Transformation', pp. 433–441 in B. A. Pearson, ed., *The Future of Early Christianity* (Minneapolis: Fortress Press, 1991).

Perlitt, Lothar. 'Die Verborgenheit Gottes', pp. 367–381 in H. Wolff, ed., *Probleme biblischer Theologie: Gerhard von Rad zum 70. Geburtstag* (Munich: Kaiser, 1971).

Perrin, Norman. *Rediscovering the Teaching of Jesus* (London: SCM, 1967).

——. *What is Redaction Criticism?* (London: SPCK, 1970).

——. *Jesus and the Language of the Kingdom: Symbol and Metaphor in N.T. Interpretation* (Philadelphia: Fortress Press, 1976).

Perry, A. M. 'Is John an Alexandrian Gospel?' *JBL* 63 (1944), 99–106.

Perry, Menakhem and Meir Sternberg, 'The King Through Ironic Eyes: The Narrator's Devices in the Biblical Story of David and Bathsheba and Two Excurses on the Theory of the Narrative Text' (Hebrew), *HA-Sifrut* 1 (1968), 263–92, with English summary, 449–452.

Peters, F. E. *The Harvest of Hellenism: A History of the Near East from Alexander the Great to the Triumph of Christianity* (New York: Simon and Schuster, 1970).

Petersen, Norman R. *Literary Criticism for New Testament Critics* (Philadelphia: Fortress Press, 1978).

——. *The Gospel of John and the Sociology of Light: Language and Characterization in the Fourth Gospel* (Valley Forge, PA: Trinity Press International,1993).

Pfitzner, V. C. 'The Coronation of the King: Passion Narrative and Passion Theology in the Gospel of St. John', *Lutheran Theological Journal* 10 (1976), 6–7.

Pierce, E. L. 'The Fourth Gospel as Drama', *Religion in Life* 29 (1960), 453–455.

Pinto, C. S. 'Advocate: Christ's Name for the Holy Spirit', *Bible Today* 30 (1967), 2078–2081.

Pinto, E. 'Jesus the Son and Giver of Life in the Fourth Gospel' (Diss., Rome: Pont. University Urbaniana, 1981).

——. 'Jesus, Son of God, in the Fourth Gospel', *Bible Today* 21 (1983), 393–98.

Pitta, A. 'Ichthys ed opsarion in Gv 21, 1–14: semplice variazione lessicale o differenza con valore simbolico?' *Bib* 71 (1990), 348–364.

Plescia, J. 'On the Persecution of the Christians in the Roman Empire', *Latomus* 30 (1971), 120–132.

Plumb, C. L. B. 'ΕΓΩ ΕΙΜΙ sayings in John's Gospel' (M. Phil. thesis, Nottingham, 1990).

Plummer, A. *The Gospel According to St. John* (Grand Rapids: Baker Book House, 1981, reprint, 1882).

Poffet, J. M., et al. *Jésus et la Samaritaine (Jean 4, 1–42)*, Suppléments aux Cahiers Évangile (Paris: Cerf, 1995).

Pokorny, P. *Genesis of Christology: Foundations for a Theology of the New Testament*, ET (Edinburgh: Clark, 1987).

Poland, Lynn. 'The Bible and Rhetorical Sublime', pp. 29–50 in M. Warner, ed., *The Bible as Rhetoric: Studies in Biblical Persuasion and Credibility* (London: Routledge, 1990).

Pollard, T. E. *Johannine Christology and the Early Church*, SNTSMS 13 (Cambridge: CUP, 1970).

Pond, Eugene W. 'Theological Dependencies of John's Gospel on Isaiah' (Thesis, Dallas Seminary, 1985).

Porsch, Felix. *Pneuma und Wort* (Frankfurt: Peter Lang, 1974).

——. *Johannes-Evangelium*, Stuttgarter Kleiner Kommentar—NT 4 (Stuttgart: Katholisches Bibelwerk, 1988).

Porter, C. F. 'Samson's Riddle: Judges 14:14-18', *JTS* n.s. 13 (1962), 106-109.

Porter, Calvin L. 'John 9:38, 39a: A Liturgical Addition to the Text', *NTS* 13 (1967), 387-94.

Porter, Stanley. 'Can Traditional Exegesis Enlighten Literary Analysis of the Fourth Gospel? An Examination of the Old Testament Fulfilment Motif and the Passover Theme', pp. 396-428 in Craig A. Evans and W. Richard Stegner, eds, *The Gospels and the Scriptures of Israel*, JSNTSup 104 (Sheffield: Sheffield Academic Press, 1994).

Porton, Gary G. 'Defining Midrash', pp. 55-94 in J. Neusner, ed., *Study of Ancient Judaism* (New York: Ktav, 1981).

de la Potterie, Ignace. 'L'arrière-fond du thème johannique de vérité', *SE* 1 = TU 73, ed. K. Aland et al. (1959), 227-294.

——. 'Jesus: King and Judge According to John 19:13', *Scripture* 13 (1961), 97-111.

——. '"Naître de l'eau et naître de l'esprit": Le texte baptismal de Jn 3:5', *Sciences ecclésiastiques* 14 (1962), 417-443.

——. 'I Am the Way, The Truth, and the Life', *Theology Digest* 16 (1968), 59-64.

——. *La vérité dans saint Jean* (Rome: Biblical Institutte Press, 1977).

——. 'Genèse de la foi pascale d'après Jn. 20', *NTS* 30 (1984), 41-42.

——. 'The Truth in Saint John', pp. 67-81 in John Ashton, ed., *The Interpretation of John* (London: SPCK, 1986).

——. '"C'est lui qui a ouvert la voie." La finale du prologue johannique', *Bib* 69 (1988), 340-370.

——. *The Hour of Jesus: The Passion and the Resurrection of Jesus According to John—Text and Spirit* (Slough, England: St. Paul Publications, 1989).

——. 'L'emploi du verbe "demeurer" dans la mystique johannique', *NRT* 117 (1995), 843-859.

Powell, Mark Allan. 'The Bible and Modern Literary Criticism', *American Theological Library Association: Summary of Proceedings*, 43 (1989), 78-84.

——. *What is Narrative Criticism?* (Minneapolis: Fortress Press, 1990).

Poythress, Vern S. 'The Use of the Intersentence Conjunctions 'de, oun, kai' and Asyndeton in the Gospel of John', *NovT* 26 (1984), 312-340.

Pratscher, W. 'Die Juden im Johannesevangelium', *Bibel und Liturgie* 59 (1986), 177-185.

Preisker, H. 'Zum Charakter des Johannesevangeliums', pp. 379-393 in F. W. Schmidt, et al., eds, *Luther, Kant, Schleiermacher in ihrer Bedeutung für den Protestantismus: Forschungen und Abhandlungen George Wobbermin zum 70. Geburtstag* (Berlin: Collignon, 1939).

Preus, James S. *From Shadow to Promise: Old Testament Interpretation From Augustine to the Young Luther* (Cambridge: MA: Belknap Press of Harvard University Press, 1969).

Preuschen, Erwin. *Origenes Werke: Der Johanneskommentar* (Leipzig: Hinrichs, 1903).
Pribnow, Hans. *Die johanneische Anschauung vom 'Leben'* (Greifswald: Universitätsverlag, 1934).
Pritchard, John Paul. *A Literary Approach to the New Testament* (Norman: University of Oklahoma Press, 1972).
Probst, A. 'Jésus et Yahvé', *Revue Réformée* 41 (1990), 44–45.
Pryor, J. W. *John, Evangelist of the Covenant People: The Narrative and Themes of the Fourth Gospel* (London: Darton, Longman and Todd, 1992).
Purvis, James D. 'The Fourth Gospel and the Samaritans', *NovT* 17 (1975), 161–98.

Quast, Kevin. *Peter and the Beloved Disciple: Figures for a Community in Crisis*, JSNTSup 32 (Sheffield: Sheffield Academic Press, 1989).
Quinn, Arthur. 'Rhetoric and the Integrity of Scripture', *Communio* 13 (1986), 326–341.
Quintilian, *De Institutio Oratoria*, trans. by H. E. Butler, LCL, 4 vols (London: Heinemann, 1921–1933).

Rabin, C. 'Hebrew and Aramaic in the First Century', in *Jewish People in the First Century: Historical Geography, Political History, Social, Cultural and Religious Life and Institutions*, 2 vols; S. Safrai, M. Stern, et al. (Amsterdam: Van Gorcum, 1976) 2:1007–39.
von Rad, Gerhard. *Old Testament Theology*, ET by D. M. G. Stalker, 2 vols (New York: Harper and Row, 1965).
——. *Wisdom in Israel* (Nashville: Abingdon, 1972).
Radday, Yehuda. 'Chiasm in the Torah', *Linguistica Biblica* 19 (1972), 2–23.
Radermakers, J. 'Mission et apostolat dans l'évangile johannique', *SE* 2 = TU 87, ed. F. L. Cross (1964), 100–121.
Rainey, F. E. *Semeion in the Gospel of John: A Clue to the Interpretation of the Gospel* (Ph.D. diss., Southwestern Baptist Theological Seminary, 1968).
Räisänen, Heikki. *The Idea of the Divine Hardening* (Helsinki: Publications of the Finish Exegetical Society 25, 1976).
Raja, R. J. 'Notion of Light in St. John', *Bible Bhashyam* 1 (1975), 126–34.
du Rand, J. A. 'Repetitions and variations: experiencing the power of the Gospel of John as literary symphony', *Neot* 30 (1997), 59–70.
Ramos, F. F. 'Simbolismo en el Cuarto Evangelio', *Studium Legionense* 3 (1962), 41–114.
——. 'Simbolismo del Templo en el Cuarto Evangelio', *Studium Legionense* 4 (1963), 11–99.
——. 'Simbolismo del Templo en el Cuarto Evangelio', *Studium Legionense* 5 (1964), 77–144.
Ramsey, A. M. *The Glory of God and the Transfiguration of Christ* (London: Longmans, Green, 1949).
Ramsey, Ian T. *Religious Language* (London: SCM, 1993 [1st edn, 1957]).
Ramsay, W. M. 'Roads and Travel (in NT)', pp. 375–402 in J. Hastings, ed., supplementary volume of *A Dictionary of the Bible* (Edinburgh: Clark, 1904).

Rapske, B. M. 'Acts, Travel and Shipwreck', pp. 1-47 in D. W. J. Gill and C. Gempf, eds, *The Book of Acts in Its Graeco-Roman Setting* (Grand Rapids: Eerdmans, 1994).

Rawson, Elizabeth. *Intellectual Life in the Late Roman Republic* (London: Duckworth, 1985).

Read, D. H. C. 'Inside John's Gospel: Introducing Jesus', *ExpTim* 88 (1976), 46-47.

Rebell, Walter. *Gemeinde als Gegenwelt: zur soziologischen und didaktischen Funktion des Johannesevangeliums*, BBET 20 (Frankfurt: Lang, 1987).

Reed, Walter. 'A Poetics of the Bible: Problems and Possibilities', *Literature and Theology* 1 (1987), 154-166.

Reese, J. M. 'Literary Structure of John 13:31-14:31; 16:5-6, 16-33', *CBQ* 34 (1972), 321-331.

Reim, Günter. *Studien zum alttestamentlichen Hintergrund des Johannesevangeliums*, SNTSMS 22 (Cambridge: CUP, 1974).

——. 'John 9—Tradition und Zeitgenossische messianische Diskussion', *BZ* 22 (1978), 245-253.

——. 'Jesus as God in the Fourth Gospel: The Old Testament Background', *NTS* 30 (1984), 158-160.

Reinhartz, Adele. 'Jesus as Prophet: Predictive Prolepses in the Fourth Gospel', *JSNT* 36 (1989), 3-16.

Reiser, W. 'Truth and Life', *The Way* 19 (1979), 251-260.

Reitzenstein, Richard. *Poimandres: Studien zur griechisch-ägyptischen und frühchristlichen Literatur* (Leipzig: Teubner, 1904; reprint; Darmstadt: Wissenschaftliche Buchgesellschaft, 1966).

——. *Das iranische Erlösungsmysterium* (Bonn: Marcus und Weber, 1921).

——. and H. H. Schaeder, *Studien zum antiken Synkretismus aus Iran und Griechenland* (Darmstadt: Wissenschaftliche Buchgesellschaft, reprint, 1965 [1926]).

Reker B. 'Perspective universelle du salut selon le quatrième Évangile' (Diss. Roma: Pontificia Universitas Gregoriana, 1964).

Rena, J. 'Women in the Gospel of John', *Église et Théologie* 17 (1986), 131-147.

Rengstorf, H. 'ἀποστέλλω', *TDNT* 1 (1964), 398-447.

Rensberger, David. 'The Politics of John: The Trial of Jesus in the Fourth Gospel', *JBL* 103 (1984), 395-411.

——. *Overcoming the World: Politics and Community in the Gospel of John* (London: SPCK, 1989).

Renza, Louis A. 'Influence', pp. 186-202 in F. Lentricchia and T. McLaughlin, eds, *Critical Terms for Literary Study* (Chicago: University of Chicago Press, 1990).

Rese, M. 'Das Selbstzeugnis des Johannesevangeliums über seinen Verfasser', *ETL* 72 (1996), 75-111.

Rhea, Robert. *The Johannine Son of Man*, ATANT 76 (Zürich: Theologischer Verlag, 1990).

Ricca, Paola. *Die Eschatologie des Vierten Evangeliums* (Zürich: Gotthelf, 1966).

Rich, W. G. 'The Understanding of "Kosmos" in the Fourth Gospel' (Ph.D. dissertation, Emory University, 1972).

Richard, Earle. 'Expressions of Double Meaning and Their Function in the Gospel of John', *NTS* 31 (1985), 96–112.

Richard, Ramesh. 'Levels of Biblical Meaning', *BibSac* 143 (1986), 123–133.

Richards, Ivor A. *The Philosophy of Rhetoric* (Oxford: OUP, 1936).

——. *Principles of Literary Criticism* (London: Routledge and Kegan Paul, 1926, repr. 1952).

Richardson, Jacques, ed. *Models of Reality: Shaping Thought and Action* (Mount Airy, MD: Lomond Publications, 1984).

Riches, J. 'The Synoptic Evangelists and Their Communities', pp. 213–41 in J. Becker, ed., *Christian Beginnings: Word and Community from Jesus to Post-Apostolic Times* (Louisville: Westminster/John Knox, 1993).

Richter, George. '"Bist du Elias?" (Joh. 1,21)', *BZ* 6 (1962), 79–92, 238–256; and 7 (1963), 63–80.

——. 'Die alttestamentlichen Zitate in der Rede vom Himmelsbrot Joh 6,25–51a', pp. 193–279 in Josef Ernst, ed., *Schriftauslegung: Beiträge zur Hermeneutik des Neuen Testamentes und im Neuen Testament* (Munich: F. Schöningh, 1972).

——. 'Die Fleischwerdung des Logos im Johannesevangelium', *NovT* 13 (1971), 81–126; 14 (1972), 257–276.

——. 'Die Logosliede im Prolog des vierten Evangeliums', *TZ* 31 (1975), 321–336.

——. 'Präsentische und futurische Eschatologie im 4. Evangelium', pp. 117–52 in P. Fiedler and D. Zeller, eds, *Gegenwart und Kommendes Reich. Schülergabe Anton Vögtle zum 65. Geburtstag* (Stuttgart: Katholisches Bibelwerk, 1975).

Ricoeur, P. *Interpretation Theory, Discourse and the Surplus of Meaning* (Fort Worth, TX: Christian University Press, 1976).

Ridderbos, H. N. 'The Structure and Scope of the Prologue to the Gospel of John', *NovT* 8 (1966), 188–201.

Riedl, J. *Das Heilswerk Jesu nach Johannes* (Freiburg: Basel; Wien: Herder, 1973).

Riesenfeld, H. *The Gospel Tradition and its Beginnings. A Study in the Limits of 'Formgeschichte'* (London: Mowbray, 1957).

Riesner, R. *Jesus als Lehrer: Eine Untersuchung zum Ursprung der Evangelien-Überlieferung* (Tübingen: Mohr-Siebeck, 3rd print, 1988).

——. *Die Frühzeit des Apostels Paulus*, WUNT 71 (Tübingen: Mohr-Siebeck, 1994).

Riffaterre, Michael. 'Intertextual Representation: On Mimesis as Interpretive Discourse', *CI* 11 (1984), 141–62.

Rigaux, Béda. 'Les destinataires du IVe évangile à la lumière de Jn 17', *RTL* 1 (1970), 289–319.

——. 'Die Jünger Jesu in Johannes 17', *TQ* 150 (1970), 203–213.

Riggs, J. R. 'The Fuller Meaning of Scripture', *Grace Theological Journal* 7 (1986), 213–227.

Riley, William. 'Situating Biblical Narrative: Poetics and the Transmission of Community Values', *Proceedings of Irish Biblical Association* 9 (1985), 38–52.

Rimmon, S. *The Concept of Ambiguity – The Example of James* (Chicago: University of Chicago Press, 1977).

Ringgren, H. 'Qumran and Gnosticism' in U. Bianchi, ed. *Le Origini dello Gnosticismo* (Leiden: Brill, 1967).

Rissi, Mathias. 'Die Hochzeit in Kana (Jo 2, 1–11)', pp. 76–92 in I. F. Christ, ed., *Oikonomia. Heilsgeschichte als Thema der Theologie. Oscar Cullmann zum 65. Geburtstag gewidmet* (Hamburg-Bergstedt: H. Reich Verlag, 1967).

——. 'Voll grosser Fische, hundertdreiundfünfzig, Joh 21, 1–14', *TZ* 35 (1979), 73–89.

——. 'Der Aufbau des vierten Evangeliums', *NTS* 29 (1983), 48–54.

Rivkin, E. *The Shaping of Jewish History* (New York: Scribner's, 1971).

——. *A Hidden Revelation: The Pharisees' Search for the Kingdom Within* (Nashville: Abingdon, 1978).

Robert, R. 'Pilate a-t-il fait de Jésus un juge? ἐκάθισεν ἐπὶ βήματος (Jean, xix, 13)', *RThom* 83 (1983), 275–287.

——. 'La double intention du mot final de prologue Johannique', *RThom* 87 (1987), 435–441.

——. 'Le mot final du prologue Johannique: A propos d'un article récent', *RThom* 89 (1989), 279–288.

——. 'Un précédent platonicien à l' équivoque de Jean 1:18', *RThom* 90 (1990), 634–639.

Roberts, A. and J. Donaldson, eds. *Ante-Nicene Christian Library: Translations of the Writings of the Fathers down to AD 325*, 24 vols (Edinburgh: Clark, 1867–72).

Roberts, J. H. 'The Lamb of God', *Neot* 2 (1968), 41–56.

Roberts, J. J. M. '*Double Entendre* in First Isaiah', *CBQ* 54 (1992), 39–48.

Roberts, R. L. 'The Rendering "Only Begotten" in John 3:16', *ResQ* 16 (1973), 2–22.

Robertson, A. T. *A Grammar of the Greek New Testament in Light of Historical Research* (Nashville: Broadman Press, 1934).

——. *The Divinity of Christ in the Gospel of John* (Grand Rapids: Baker Book House, 1976).

Robertson, Roland. *Sociological Interpretation of Religion* (Oxford: Blackwell, 1972).

Robinson, B. P. 'Christ as a Northern Prophet in St. John', *Scripture* 17 (1965), 104–108.

——. 'The Meaning and Significance of the "Seventh Hour" in John 4:42', *Studia Biblica* 2 (1980), 255–262.

Robinson, J. A. *St. Paul's Epistle to the Ephesians* (London: Macmillian, 1928).

Robinson, J. A. T. *Jesus and His Coming* (New York: Abingdon, 1957).

——. 'Elijah, John and Jesus: an Essay in Detection', *NTS* 4 (1958), 263–281

——. 'The Destination and Purpose of St John's Gospel', *NTS* 6 (1959–1960), 117–131; = ID, *Twelve New Testament Studies*, 107–125 (London: SCM, 1962).

——. 'The New Look on the Fourth Gospel', pp. 94–106 in idem, *Twelve New Testament Studies* (London: SCM, 1962).

——. 'The Baptism of John and the Qumran Community', pp. 11–27 in idem, *Twelve New Testament Studies* (London: SCM, 1962).

——. 'The Significance of the Footwashing', pp. 144–147 in W. C. van Unnik, ed., *Neotestamentica et Patristica: Eine Freundesgabe, Hern Professor Dr. Oscar Cullmann zu seinem 60. Geburtstag überreicht*, NovTSup 6 (Leiden: Brill, 1962).

——. 'The Relation of the Prologue to the Gospel of St. John', *NTS* 9 (1963), 120–129.

——. *Redating the New Testament* (London: SCM, 1975).

——. *The Priority of John* (London: SCM, 1985).

Robinson, J. M. 'Recent Research in the Fourth Gospel', *JBL* 78 (1959), 242–252.

———. 'The Formal Structure of Jesus' Message', in *Current Issues in New Testament Interpretation*, Essays in honour of O. A. Piper (New York: Harper and Bros., 1962), 91–110.

———. *The Nag Hammadi Library in English*, rev. edn (San Francisco: Harper and Row, 1988 [orig. Leiden: Brill, 1977])

Rodd, Cyril S. 'Spirit or Finger', *ExpTim* 72 (1961), 157–158.

———. 'On Applying a Sociological Theory to Biblical Studies', *JSOT* 19 (1981), 95–106.

Rogers, Paul C. 'Manna as a Motif' (Thesis, Dallas Seminary, 1983).

Roloff, J. 'Der johanneische "Lieblingsjünger" und der Lehrer der Gerechtigkeit', *NTS* 15 (1968–9), 129–151.

Romeo, J. A. 'Gematria and John 21:11—The Children of God', *JBL* 97 (1978), 263–264.

Rosscup, J. E. *Abiding in Christ: Studies in John 15* (Grand Rapids: Zondervan, 1973).

Roth, W. 'Scriptural Coding in the Fourth Gospel', *BR* 32 (1987), 6–29.

Rouiller, G. 'Leben in seinem Namen: Der Evangelist Johannes und Seine Theologie des Namens', *Internationale Katholische Zeitschrift* 22 (1993), 54–62.

Rowe, T. T. 'Science, Statistics and Style', *London Quarterly and Holborn Review* 33 (1964), 231–5.

Rowland, Christopher. 'Visions of God in Apocalyptic Literature', *JSJ* 10 (1979), 137–154.

———. *The Open Heaven* (New York: Crossroads, 1982).

———. 'John 1.51 and the Targumic Tradition', *NTS* 30 (1984), 498–507.

———. 'Reading the New Testament Sociologically: An Introduction', *Theology* 88 (1985), 358–364.

———. *Christian Origins: An Account of the Setting and Character of the Most Important Messianic Sect of Judaism* (London: SPCK, 1985).

———. 'Parting of the Ways: The Evidence of Jewish and Christian Apocalyptic and Mystical Material', pp. 213–237 in J. D. G. Dunn, ed., *Jews and Christians: The Parting of the Ways AD 70 to 135* (Tübingen: Mohr-Siebeck, 1992).

Rowley, H. H. *The Relevance of Apocalyptic* (New York: Association Press, 1964).

Ruckstuhl, E. *Die Literarische Einheit des Johannesevangeliums: Der Gegenwärtige Stand der Einschlägigen Forschung* (Freiburg in der Schweiz: Paulusverlag, 1951).

———. *Chronology of the Last Days of Jesus: A Critical Study*, ET by V. J. Drapela (New York: Desclée, 1965).

———. 'Und das Wort wurde Fleisch', *BibLeb* 13 (1972), 235–238.

———. 'Johannine Language and Style: The question of their unity', pp. 125–147 in M. de Jonge, ed., *L'Évangile de Jean: sources, rédaction, théologie*, BETL 44 (Leuven: Leuven University Press, 1977).

——— and P. Dschulnigg. *Stilkritik und Verfasserfrage im Johannesevangelium: Die johanneischen Sprachmerkmale auf dem Hintergrund des Neuen Testaments und des zeitgenössischen hellenistischen Schrifttums*, NTOA 17 (Freiburg: Paulus; Göttingen: Vandenhoeck und Ruprecht, 1991).

Ruddick, Jr., C. T. 'Feeding and Sacrifice: The Old Testament Background of the Fourth Gospel', *ExpTim* 79 (1967–68), 340–341.
Rudel, P. 'Das Missverständnis im Johannesevangelium', *NKZ* 3 (1921), 351–361.
Rudolf, Kurt. *Die Gnosis: Wesen und Geschichte einer spätantiken Religion* (Göttingen: Vandenhoeck und Ruprecht, 1978).
Rudolph, T. K. *Die Mandäer*, 2 vols, FRLANT 56–57 (Göttingen: Vandenhoeck & Ruprecht, 1960–61).
Rudskoger, Arne. *'Fair, Foul, Nice, Proper': A Contribution to the Study of Polysemy* Gothenburg Studies in English, I (Stockholm, 1952).
Ruether, Rosemary. *Faith and Fratricide: The Theological Roots of Anti-Semitism* (New York: Seabury, 1974).
Rusch, F. A. 'The Signs and the Discourse: The Rich Theology of John 6', *Currents in Theology and Missions* 5 (1978), 386–390.
Rusinko, Elaine. 'Intertextuality: The Soviet Approach to Subtext', *Dispositio* 4 (1979), 213–235.
Russell, D. S. *The Method and Message of Jewish Apocalyptic 200 BC–AD 100* (London: SCM, 1964).
Russell, E. 'Possible Influence of the Mysteries on the Form and Interrelation of the Johannine Writings', *JBL* 51 (1932), 336–351.
Russell, J. B. *The Devil: Perceptions of Evil from Antiquity to Primitive Christianity* (Ithica, NY: Cornell, 1977).

Sacks, Sheldon, ed. *On Metaphor* (Chicago: University of Chicago Press, 1979).
Safrai, S. 'Education and the Study of the Torah', pp. 945–970 in S. Safrai, M. Stern, et al., *Jewish People in the First Century: Historical Geography, Political History, Social, Cultural and Religious Life and Institutions*, vol. 2, CRINT 1 (Assen: Van Gorcum, 1976).
———. 'Spoken Languages in the Time of Jesus', *Jerusalem Perspective* 3 (1991), 3–8.
Sahlin, Harald. *Zur Typologie des Johannesevangeliums*, Uppsala Universitets Årsskrift 4 (Uppsala: Lundequistaska Bokhandeln, 1950).
Saldarini, Anthony. *Jesus and Passover* (New York: Paulist, 1984).
Salmon, George. *A Historical Introduction to the Study of the Books of the New Testament* (London: John Murray, 1885).
Salom, A. P. 'Some Aspects of the Grammatical Style of 1 John', *JBL* 74 (1955), 96–102.
Sand, A. '"Wie geschrieben steht..." Zur Auslegung der jüdischen Schriften in den urchristlichen Gemeinden', pp. 331–357 in J. Ernst, ed., *Schriftauslegung: Beiträge zur Hermeneutik des Neuen Testamentes und im Neuen Testament* (Munich: Schöningh, 1972).
Sanday, William. *The Life of Christ in Recent Research* (New York: OUP, 1908).
Sanders, E. P., A. I. Baumgarten and A. Mendelson, eds. *Jewish and Christian Self-Definition*, vol. 2: *Aspects of Judaism in the Graeco-Roman Period* (London: SCM, 1981).
Sanders, E. P. *Paul and Palestinian Judaism: A Comparison of Patterns of Religion* (London: SCM, 1977).
———. *Jesus and Judaism* (London: SCM, 1985).

——. *Judaism: Practice and Belief, 63 BCE–66 CE* (London: SCM, 1992).
Sanders, James A. *Torah and Canon* (Philadelphia: Fortress Press, 1972).
——. 'Hermeneutics of True and False Prophecy', pp. 21–41 in G. W. Coats and B. O. Long, eds, *Canon and Authority: Essays in Old Testament Religion and Theology* (Philadelphia: Fortress Press, 1977).
——. 'Text and Canon: Concepts and Method', *JBL* 98 (1979), 5–29.
Sanders, J. N. *The Fourth Gospel in the Early Church: Its Origin and Influence on Christian Theology up to Irenaeus* (Cambridge: CUP, 1943).
——. *A Commentary on the Gospel According to St. John*, B. A. Mastin, ed. (New York: Harper and Row, 1968).
Sanders, J. T. *Schismatics, Sectarians, Dissidents, Deviants: The First One Hundred Years of Jewish-Christian Relations* (London: SCM, 1993).
——. *The Jews in Luke-Acts* (Philadelphia: Fortress Press, 1987).
Sandmel, Samuel. 'Parallelomania', *JBL* 81 (1962), 1–13.
——. *Judaism and Christian Beginnings* (New York: OUP, 1978).
——. *Anti-Semitism in the New Testament* (Philadelphia: Fortress Press, 1978).
Sappan, Raphael. 'Simple and Metaphorical Meaning in "Double Entendre" in Biblical Poetry', *Beth Mikra* 102 (1985), 406–412.
de Saussure, Ferdinand. *Course de linguistique générale* (Paris: Payot, 1916).
Sayce, R.A. *Style in French Prose: A Method of Analysis* (Oxford: Clarendon, 1953).
Schaar, C. 'Old Texts and Ambiguity', *English Studies* 46 (1965), 157–165.
Schäfer, Peter. *Die Vorstellung vom Heiligen Geist in der Rabbinischen Literatur*, SANT 28 (Munich: Kösel, 1972).
——. 'Die sogenannte Synode von Jabne: Zur Trennung von Juden und Christen im ersten/zweiten Jh. n. Chr.', *Judaica* 31 (1975), 54–64, 116–124.
——. *Studien zur Geschichte und Theologie des rabbinischen Judentums* (Leiden: Brill, 1978).
——. *Synopse zur Hekhalot-Literatur*, vols 2 and 3, TSAJ 17, 22 (Tübingen: Mohr-Siebeck, 1981).
——. 'Geist: II. Judentum', *TRE* 12 (1984), 173–178.
——. *Der verborgene und offenbare Gott* (Tübingen: Mohr-Siebeck, 1991).
——. *The Hidden and Manifest God: Some Major Themes in Early Jewish Mysticism*, ET by Aubrey Pomerance (Albany: State University of New York, 1992).
Schechter, S. 'Geniza Specimens', *JQR* 10 (1898), 654–659.
Scheffler, Israel. *Beyond the Letter: A Philosophical Inquiry into Ambiguity, Vagueness and Metaphor in Language* (London: Routledge and Kegan Paul, 1979).
Schein, B. E. *Our Father Abraham* (Ph.D. diss., Yale University, 1972).
——. *Following the Way: The Setting of John's Gospel* (Minneapolis: Augsburg Publishing House, 1980).
Schenke, H. M. 'Die zweite Schrift des Codex Jung und die Oden Salomos', pp. 26–29 in *Die Herkunft des sogenannten Evangelium Veritatis* (Göttingen: Vandenhoeck & Ruprecht, 1959).
Schiffman, L. H. *Who Was a Jew? Rabbinic and Halakhic Perspective on the Jewish-Christian Schism* (Hoboken, NJ: Ktav, 1985).

Schilson, A. 'Jesus Christus – Gottes Sohn', *BK* 34 (1979), 12–17.

Schimanowski, G. *Weisheit und Messias: Die jüdischen Voraussetzung der urchristlichen Präexistenzchristologie*, WUNT 2.17 (Tübingen: Mohr-Siebeck, 1985).

Schlatter, Adolf. *Die Sprache und Heimat des vierten Evangelisten* (Gütersloh: G. Bertlsmann, 1902).

——. *Der Evangelist Johannes: Wie er spricht, denkt, und glaubt. Ein Kommentar zum vierten Evangelium* (Stuttgart: Calwer Verlag, 2nd print., 1948).

——. *Der Evangelist Johannes* (Stuttgart: Calwer Verlag, 4th print, 1975).

Schlier, Heinrich. 'Jesus und Pilatus nach dem Johannesevangelium', pp. 56–74 in idem, *Die Zeit der Kirche*, 4th edn (Freiburg: Herder, 1966).

——. *Essais sur le Nouveau Testament* (Paris: Les Éditions du Cerf, 1968).

——. 'The State According to New Testament', pp. 215–225 in idem, *The Relevance of the New Testament* (Freiburg and New York: Herder and Herder, 1968).

Schmidt, K. L. and M. A. Schmidt. 'σκληρόω', *TDNT* 5:1026.

Schmidt, W. *Der strophische Aufbau des Gesamttextes der vier Evangelien* (Sonderabdruck aus: Anzeiger d. Phil. Hist. Klasse d. Akademie der Wissenschaft in Wien 1921, Nr. IX).

Schmithals, W. *Johannesevangelium und Johnnesbriefe: Forschungsgeschichte und Analyse*, BZNW 64 (Berlin and New York: de Gruyter, 1992).

Schmitt, J. 'Les écrits du Nouveau Testament et les textes de Qumran', *Revue de Science Religieuse* 29 (1955), 381–401 and 30 (1956), 55–74, 261–282.

Schnackenburg, Rudolf. 'Die Messiasfrage im Johannesevangelium', pp. 240–264 in J. Blinzler, O. Kuss, and F. Mussner, eds, *Neutestamentliche Aufsätze: Festschrift für Joseph Schmid zum 70. Geburtstag* (Regensburg: Friedrich Pustet, 1963).

——. *Das Johannesevangelium*, HTKNT 4/1–4, 4 vols. I Teil: *Kommentar zu Kap. 1–4*; II Teil: *Kommentar zu Kap. 5–12*; III Teil: *Kommentar zu Kap. 13–21*; IV Teil: *Ergänzende Auslegungen und Exkurse* (Freiburg: Herder, 1965, 1971, 1975, 1984).

——. *The Gospel According to St. John*, 3 vols (London: Burns and Oates; New York: Seabury Press, A Crossroads Book, 1968, 1980, 1982); vol. 1: *Introduction and Commentary on Chapters 1–4*, ET by K. Smyth; vol. 2: *Commentary on Chpaters 5–12*, ET by C. Hastings, F. McDonagh, D. Smith, F. Foley; vol. 3: *Commentary on Chapters 13–21*, ET by D. Smith, G. A. Kon.

——. 'Zur Herkunft des Johannesevangeliums', *BZ* 14 (1970), 1–23.

——. 'On the Origin of the Fourth Gospel', pp. 223–246 in D. G. Buttrick, ed., *Jesus and Man's Hope*, vol. 1 (Pittsburgh: Pittsbugh Theological Seminary, 1970).

——. 'Zur johanneischen Forschung', *BZ* 18 (1974), 272–278.

——. 'Entwicklung und Stand der johanneischen Forschung seit 1955' in M. de Jonge, ed., *L'Évangile de Jean: sources, rédaction, théologie*, BETL 44 (Leuven: Leuven University Press, 1977).

Schneider, H. 'The Word Was Made Flesh: An Analysis of the Theology of Revelation in the Fourth Gospel', *CBQ* 31 (1969), 344–356.

Schneider, J. *Das Evangelium nach Johannes*, NTD 4 (Göttingen: Vandenhoeck und Ruprecht, 1972).

Schneiders, Sandra M. 'The Johannine Resurrection Narrative: An Exegetical and Theological Study of John 20 as a Synthesis of Johannine Spirituality' (Ph.D. diss., Rome: Pontificia Universitas Gregoriana, 1975).

——. 'History and Symbolism in the Fourth Gospel', pp. 371-376 in M. de Jonge, ed., *L'Évangile de Jean: sources, rédaction, théologie*, BETL 44 (Leuven: Leuven University Press, 1977).

——. 'Symbolism and the Sacramental Principle in the Fourth Gospel' in Pius-Ramon Tragan, ed., *Segrie Sacramenti nel Vangelo di Giovanni*, Studia Anselmiana 66 (Rome: Editrice Anselmiana, 1977).

——. 'The Foot Washing (John 13:1-20): An Experiment in Hermeneutics', *CBQ* 43 (1981), 76-92.

Schnelle, U. *Antidoketische Christologie im Johannesevangelium: Eine Untersuchung zur Stellung des vierten Evangelium in der johanneischen Schule*, FRLANT 144 (Göttingen: Vandenhoeck und Ruprecht, 1987).

——. ET, *Antidocetic Christology in the Gospel of John: An Investigation of the Place of the Fourth Gospel in the Johannine School* (Minneapolis: Fortress Press, 1992).

Schoeps, H. J. *Aus frühchristlicher Zeit. Religionsgeschichtliche Untersuchungen* (Tübingen: Mohr-Siebeck, 1950)

Schökel, Luis Alonso. *Estudios de Poética Hebrea* (Barcelona: J. Flors, 1963).

Scholem, Gershom. *Jewish Gnosticism, Merkabah Mysticism, and Talmudic Tradition* (New York: Jewish Theological Seminary of America, 2nd print, 1965).

——. *The Messianic Idea in Judaism and Other Essays on Jewish Spirituality* (New York: Schocken Books, 1971).

Scholer, David M. *Nag Hammadi Bibliography 1948–69* (Leiden: Brill, 1971).

——. *Nag Hammadi Bibliography 1970–1994* (Leiden: Brill, 1997).

Scholes, R., and R. Kellogg. *The Nature of Narrative* (New York: OUP, 1966).

Schottroff, Luise. 'Johannes 4:5-15 und die Konsequenzen des johanneischen Dualismus', *ZNW* 60 (1969), 199-214.

——. *Der Glaubende und die feindliche Welt: Beobachtungen zum gnostischen Dualismus und seiner Bedeutung für Paulus und das Johannesevangelium*, WMANT 37 (Neukirchen-Vluyn: Neukirchener Verlag, 1970).

Schrage, W. 'τυφλόω', *TDNT* 8:292.

Schreiner, Josef. 'Geistbegabung in der Gemeinde von Qumran', *BZ* 9 (1965), 161-180.

Schrenk, G. 'γραφή', *TDNT* 1 (1964), 749-55.

Schubert, Kurt. *Die Gemeinde vom Toten Meer: Ihre Entstehung und ihre Lehren* (Munich: Reinhardt, 1958).

——. *Die jüdischen Religionsparteien im neutestamentlichen Zeitalter*, SBS 43 (Stuttgart: Katholisches Bibelwerk, 1970).

Schuchard, Bruce G. *Scripture Within Scripture: The Interrelation of Form and Function in the Explicit Old Testament Citations in the Gospel of John*, SBLDS 133 (Atlanta: Scholars Press, 1992).

Schulz, Siegfried. *Untersuchungen zur Menschensohnchristologie im Johannesevangelium: Zugleich ein Beitrag zur Methodengeschichte der Auslegung des 4 Evangeliums* (Göttingen: Vandenhoeck und Ruprecht, 1957).

——. *Komposition und Herkunft der Johanneischen Reden* (Stuttgart: W. Kohlhammer Verlag, 1960).

——. *Das Evangelium nach Johannes* (Göttingen: Vandenhoeck und Ruprecht, 1972).

Schürer, Emil. *The Literature of the Jewish People in the Time of Jesus*, Sophia Taylor, ed., ET by Peter Christie (New York: Schocken, 1972).

——. *The History of the Jewish People in the Age of Jesus Christ (175 B.C. - A.D. 135)*, rev. and ed. by G. Vermes, F. Millar, and M. Black, 3 vols (Edinburgh: Clark, 1973-87).

Schüssler-Fiorenza, Elisabeth, ed. *Aspects of Religious Propaganda in Judaism and Early Christianity* (Notre Dame: University of Notre Dame, 1976).

——. 'The Quest for the Johannine School: The Apocalypse and the Fourth Gospel', *NTS* 23 (1976-77), 402-427.

Schwankl, Otto. 'Die Metaphorik von Licht und Finsternis im johanneischen Schrifttum', pp. 135-167 in Karl Kertelge, ed., *Metaphorik und Mythos im Neuen Testament*, QD 126 (Freiburg: Herder, 1990).

Schwartz, Daniel R. *Studies in the Jewish Background of Christianity*, WUNT 60 (Tübingen: Mohr-Siebeck, 1992).

Schwarz, G. 'Genesis 1:1; 2:2 und John 1:1a, 3a Ein Vergleich', *ZNW* 73 (1982), 136-137.

——. '"Der Wind weht, wo er will"?' *Biblische Notizen* 63 (1992), 47-48.

Schweitzer, Albert. *The Quest of the Historical Jesus: A Critical Study of Its Progress from Reimarus to Wrede*, ET by W. Montgomery (London: reprint, SCM, 1954).

Schweitzer, Alex. *Das Evangelium Johannes nach seinem innern Werthe und seiner Bedeutung für das Leben Jesu kritisch untersucht* (Leipzig: Hinrichs, 1841).

Schweizer, Eduard. 'Der Kirchenbegriff im Evangelium und den Briefen des Johannes', *SE* 1 = TU 73, ed. K. Aland et al. (1959), 363-381.

——. *Ego Eimi: Die religionsgeschichtliche Herkunft und theologische Bedeutung der Johanneischen Bildreden, zugleich ein Beitrag zur Quellenfrage des vierten Evangeliums*, FRLANT 38/56 (Göttingen: Vandenhoeck und Ruprecht, reprint, 1965).

Scobie, C. H. H. 'New Directions in the Study of the Fourth Gospel', *Studies in Religion* 6 (1977), 185-193.

Scott, E. F. *The Apologetic of the New Testament* (London: Williams and Norgate, 1907).

——. *The Fourth Gospel: Its Purpose and Theology* (Edinburgh: Clark, 1908).

——. *The Spirit in the New Testament* (London: Hodder and Stoughton, 1923).

Scott, J. A. 'The Words for "Love" in Jn. 21:15-17', *Classical Weekly* 39 (1945-46), 71-72.

Scott, M. *Sophia and the Johannine Jesus*, JSNTSup 71 (Sheffield: JSOT Press, 1992).

Scroggs, Robin. 'The Earliest Christian Communities as Sectarian Movement', pp. 1-23 in Jacob Neusner, ed.,*Christianity, Judaism and Other Greco-Roman Cults, II: Early Christianity*, SJLA 12 (Leiden: Brill, 1975).

Sebeok, T. A. ed., *Style in Language* (Cambridge: Massachusetts Institute of Technology, 1960).

Sedgewick, G. G. *Of Irony, Especially in Drama* (Toronto: Univ. of Toronto Press, 1948).

Seebass, H. 'Moses', *NIDNTT* 2:641.

Segal, A. F. *Two Powers in Heaven: Early Rabbinic Reports about Christianity and Gnosticism*, SJLA 25 (Leiden: Brill, 1977).

——. 'Heavenly Ascent in Hellenistic Judaism, Early Christianity and their Environment', *ANRW* 23:2 (Berlin: de Gruyter, 1980), 1352–1377.

——. 'Ruler of this World: Attitudes about Mediator Figures and the Importance of Sociology for Self-Definition', pp. 245–268 in E. P. Sanders, et al., eds, *Jewish and Chrisitian Self-Definition* (Philadelphia: Fortress Press, 1981).

Segbroeck, F. van, C. M. Tuckett, et al., eds. *The Four Gospels 1992: Festschrift Frans Neirynck*, 3 vols, BETL 100 (Leuven: Leuven University Press, 1992).

Segovia, Fernando F., ed. *'What is John?' Readers and Readings of the Fourth Gospel* (Atlanta: Scholars Press, 1966).

——. 'John 13:1-20: The Foot Washing in the Johannine Tradition', *ZNW* 73 (1982), 31–51.

——, ed. *Discipleship in the New Testament* (Philadelphia: Fortress Press, 1985).

——. *The Farewell of the Word: The Johannine Call to Abide* (Minneapolis: Fortress Press, 1991).

Sell, J. 'A Note on a Striking Johannine Motif Found at C[optic] G[nostic] VI, 6,19', *NovT* 20 (1978), 232–240.

Selwyn, E. G. 'The Mind of St. John', *Theology* 2 (1921), 243–251.

Sevenster, J. N. *Do You Know Greek? How Much Greek Could the First Jewish Christians Have Known?* (Leiden: Brill, 1968).

Sevrin, J. M. 'Le quatrième évangile et le gnosticisme: questions de méthode', pp. 251–268 in J. D. Kaestli, et al., eds, *La communauté johannique et son histoire: La trajectoire de l'évangile de Jean aux deux premiers siècles* (Geneva: Labor and Fides, 1990).

Seynaeve, J. 'Le thème de 'l'heure 'dans le quatrième évangile', *Revue Africaine de Théologie* 7 (1983), 29–50.

Sharot, S. *Messianism, Mysticism and Magic: A Sociological Analysis of Jewish Religious Movements* (Chapel Hill: University of North Carolina Press, 1982).

Shaw, Harry. *Dictionary of Literary Terms* (New York: McGraw-Hill, 1972).

Shea, W. H. 'The Chiastic Structure of the Song of Songs', *ZAW* 92 (1980), 378–396.

Shedd, Russell. 'Multiple Meanings in the Gospel of John', pp. 247–258 in Gerald F. Hawthorne, ed., *Current Issues in Biblical and Patristic Interpretation* (Grand Rapids: Eerdmans, 1975).

Shepherd, M. H. 'The "Jews" in the Gospel of John: Another Level of Meaning', *ATRS* 3 (1974), 95–112.

Shideler, Mary McDermott. *The Theology of Romantic Love: A Study in the Writings of Charles Williams* (Grand Rapids: Eerdmans, 1962).

Shipley, Joseph T. *Dictionary of World Literature, Criticism, Forms, Technique* (New York: Philosophical Library, 1943).

Sidebottom, E. M. *The Christ of the Fourth Gospel in the Light of the First-Century Thought* (London: SPCK, 1961).

Silva, Moises. *Biblical Words and Their Meaning* (Grand Rapids: Zondervan, 1983).

——. 'Approaching the Fourth Gospel', *Criswell Theological Review* 3 (1988), 17–29.

Simon, Lutz. *Petrus und Der Lieblingsjünger im Johannesevangelium: Amt und Autorität* (New York: Peter Lang, 1996).

Simon, Marcel. *Jewish Sects at the Time of Jesus* (Philadelphia: Fortress Press, 1967).

——. *Verus Israel*, ET (Oxford: OUP 1986 [French 1948]).

Simon, U. E. 'Eternal Life in the Fourth Gospel', pp. 97–109 in F. L. Cross, ed., *Studies in the Fourth Gospel* (London: Mowbray, 1957).

Simmons, B. E. 'A Christology of the "I AM" Sayings in the Gospel of John', *Theological Education* 38 (1988), 94–103.

Sitwell, N. H. H. *Roman Roads of Europe* (London: Cassell, 1981).

Skarsaune, O. *The Proof from Prophecy, A Study in Justin Martyr's Proof-Text Tradition: Text-Type, Provenance, Theological Profile*, NovTSup 56 (Leiden: Brill, 1987).

Skeat, T. C. *The Birth of the Codex* (London: British Museum, 1987).

Skeel, C. A. J. *Travel in the First Century after Christ, with Special Reference to Asia Minor* (Cambridge: CUP, 1901).

Smalley, Stephen S. 'The Johannine Son of Man Sayings', *NTS* 15 (1968), 278–301.

——. *John: Evangelist and Interpreter* (Exeter: Paternoster, 1978).

Smend, F. 'Die Behandlung alttestamentlicher Zitate als Ausgangspunkt der Quellenscheidung im 4. Evangelium', *ZNW* 24 (1925), 147–150.

Smith, D. Moody. 'The Sources of the Gospel of John: An Assessment of the Present State of the Problem', *NTS* 10 (1963–64), 336–351.

——. *The Composition and Order of the Fourth Gospel: Bultmann's Literary Theory* (New Haven: Yale University, 1965).

——. 'The Use of the Old Testament in the New', pp. 3–65 in J. M. Efird, ed., *The Use of the Old Testament in the New and Other Essays: Studies in Honor of William Franklin Stinespring* (Durham, NC: Duke University, 1972).

——. 'The Presentation of Jesus in the Fourth Gospel', *Interpretation* 31 (1977), 367–378.

——. 'The Contribution of J. Louis Martyn to the Understanding of the Gospel of John', pp. 275–294 in R. T. Fortna and B. R. Gaventa, eds, *The Conversation Continues: Studies in Paul and John, in Honor of J. L. Martyn* (Nashville: Abingdon, 1990).

——. 'John and Synoptics: Some Dimensions of the Problem', *NTS* 26 (1979–80), 425–444.

——. 'Johannine Christianity: Some Reflections on Its Character and Delineation', *NTS* 21 (1974/75), 222–48.

——. 'The Setting and Shape of a Johannine Narrative Source', pp. 80–93 in *Johannine Christianity: Essays on Its Setting, Sources, and Theology* (Columbia: University of South Carolina Press, 1984).

——. *John Among the Gospels: The Relationship in Twentieth-Century Research* (Minneapolis: Fortress Press, 1992).

——. *The Theology of the Gospel of John* (Cambridge: CUP, 1995).

——. 'John and the Synoptics: And the Question of Gospel Genre', pp. 1783–1797 in F. van Segbroeck and C. M. Tuckett, et al., eds, *The Four Gospels 1992: Festschrift Frans Neirynck*, BETL 100, 3 vols (Leuven: Leuven University Press, 1992).

———. 'The Milieu of the Johannine Miracle Source', pp. 62–79 in idem, *Johannine Christianity: Essays on Its Setting, Sources, and Theology* (Columbia, SC: University of South Carolina Press, 1984). Originally in *Jews, Greeks, and Christians*, ed. by Robert Hamerton-Kelly and Robin Scroggs (Leiden: Brill, 1976).

———. 'The Setting and Shape of a Johannine Narrative Source', pp. 80–93 in idem, *Johannine Christianity: Essays on Its Setting, Sources, and Theology* (Columbia, SC: University of South Carolina Press, 1984). Originally in *Jews, Greeks, and Christians*, ed. by Robert Hamerton-Kelly and Robin Scroggs (Leiden: Brill, 1976).

Smith, James E. *What the Bible Teaches about the Promised Messiah* (Nashville: Thomas Nelson, 1993).

Smith, Jonathan Z. 'The Social Description of Early Christianity', *Religious Studies Review* 1 (1975), 19–25.

Smith, Morton. 'What is Implied by the Variety of Messianic Figures?' *JBL* 78 (1959), 66–72.

Smith, Morton. *Palestinian Parties and Politics That Shaped the Old Testament* (New York: Columbia University Press, 1971).

———. 'Palestinian Judaism in the First Century', pp. 74–77 in Moshe Davis, ed., *Israel: Its Role in Civilization* (New York: Jewish Theological Seminary of America, 1956).

Smith, R. H. 'Exodus Typology in the Fourth Gospel', *JBL* 81 (1962), 329–342.

Smith, T. C. *Jesus in the Gospel of John: A Study of the Evangelist's Purpose and Meaning* (Nashville: Broadmans, 1959).

Soeding, Thomas. 'Wiedergeburt aus Wasser und Geist: Anmerkungen zur Symbolsprache des Johannesevangeliums am Beispiel des Nikodemusgesprächs (John 3:1–21)', pp. 168–179 in Karl Kertelge, ed., *Metaphorik und Mythos im Neuen Testament*, QD 126 (Freiburg: Herder, 1990).

de Solages, M. *Jean et les synoptiques* (Leiden: Brill, 1979).

Songer, H. S. 'Isaiah and the New Testament', *RevExp* 65 (1968), 459–470.

———. 'The Life Situation of the Johannine Epistles', *RevExp* 67 (1970), 404–405.

Soskice, Janet Martin. *Metaphor and Religious Language* (Oxford: Clarendon Press, 1985).

Soueif, Ahdaf. 'A Linguistic Analysis of Metaphor with Reference to its Historical Development in English Poetry from 1500 to 1950' (Ph.D. thesis, University of Lancaster, 1977).

Sparks, H. F. D. *The Apocryphal Old Testament* (Oxford: OUP, 1984).

Speiser, E. A. 'Word Plays on the Creation Epic's Version of the Founding of Babylon', *Orientalia* 25 (1956), 317–323.

Spencer, Aida Besancon. 'The Wise Fool and the Foolish Wise: A Study of Irony in Paul', *NovT* 23 (1981), 349–360.

Spencer, John, Nils Erik Enkvist, and Michael Gregory. *Linguistics and Style: Language and Language Learning* (London: OUP, 1964).

Sperber, D. and D. Wilson. *Relevance: Communication and Cognition* (Oxford: Blackwell, 1986).

Spero, Shubert. 'Multiplicity of Meaning as a Device in Biblical Narrative', *Judaism* 34 (1985), 462–473.

Spicq, Ceslaus. 'Le Siracide et la structure littéraire du prologue de saint Jean', pp. 183–195 in *Memorial Lagrange: Cinquantenaire de l'école biblique et archéologique française de Jérusalem*, 15 Novembre 1890 – 15 Novembre 1940 (Paris: Gabalda, 1940).

Spitzer, Leo. *Linguistics and Literary History: Essays in Stylistics* (Princeton: Princeton University Press, 1948).

——. *A Method of Interpreting Literature* (Northhamton, MA: Smith College, 1949).

Sproston, W. E. 'Satan in the Fourth Gospel', *Studia Biblica* 11 (1978–80), 307–311.

Stählin, G. 'Zum Problem der Johanneischen Eschatologie', *ZNW* 33 (1934), 225–259.

Staley, Jeffrey Lloyd. 'The Structure of John's Prologue: Its Implications for the Gospel's Narrative Structure', *CBQ* 48 (1986), 241–264.

——. *The Print's First Kiss: A Rhetorical Investigation of the Implied Reader in the Fourth Gospel* (Atlanta: Scholars Press, 1988).

——. *Reading with a Passion: Rhetoric, Autobiography and the American West in the Gospel of John* (New York: Continuum, 1995).

Stanford, W. B. *Greek Metaphor: Studies in Theory and Practice* (Oxford: OUP, 1936).

Stanley, D. M. 'The Johannine Literature', *TS* 17 (1956), 516–531.

Stanton, Graham. *A Gospel for a New People: Studies in Matthew* (Edinburgh: Clark, 1992).

Starr, R. J. 'The Circulation of Literary Texts in the Roman World', *Classical Quarterly* 37 (1987), 213–23.

Stauffer, Ethelbert. *Die Theologie des Neuen Testaments* (Gütersloh: Bertelsmann, 4th print, 1948).

Stein, Robert H. *An Introduction to the Parables of Jesus* (Philadelphia: Westminster Press, 1981).

Stek, John. 'The Stylistics of Hebrew Poetry', *Calvin Theological Journal* 9 (1974), 15–30.

Stemberger, G. *Untersuchungen zur johanneischen Symbolik von Gut und Böse* (Diss. Innsbruck, 1967).

——. *La simbolica del bene e del male in S. Giovanni*. Traduzione di A. Candelaresi e G. Adani (Milano: Edizione Paoline, 1970).

——. *La symbolique du bien et du mal selon saint Jean* (Paris: Seuil, 1970).

Stendahl, Krister. 'The Called and the Chosen: An Essay on Election', pp. 63–80 in Anton Fridrichsen, ed., *The Root of the Vine* (New York: Harper, 1953).

——. 'The Bible as a Classic and the Bible as Holy Scripture', *JBL* 103 (1984), 3–10.

Sternberg, Meir. *Expositional Modes and Temporal Ordering in Fiction* (Baltimore: Johns Hopkins University Press, 1978).

——. *The Poetics of Biblical Narrative* (Bloomington, IN: Indiana University Press, 1985).

Stevens, G. B. *The Johannine Theology: A Study of the Doctrinal Contents of the Gospel and Epistles of the Apostle John* (London: Dickinson, 1894).

Stibbe, Mark W. G. *John as Storyteller: Narrative Criticism and the Fourth Gospel*, SNTSMS 73 (Cambridge: CUP, 1992).

Stimpfle, A. 'Das "sinnlose γάρ" in Joh 4, 44. Beobachtungen zur Doppeldeutigkeit im Johannesevangelium', *Biblische Notizen* 65 (1992), 86–96.

Stinespring, W. F. 'Humor', *IDB*, vol. 2 (New York: Abingdon, 1962), 660–2.

Stone, M. E. 'Lists of Revealed Things in Apocalyptic Literature', pp. 414–452 in F. M. Cross, et al., eds, *Magnalia Dei* (Garden City, NY: Doubleday, 1976).

———. 'Reactions to the Destruction of the Second Temple: Theology, Perception and Conversion', *JSJ* 12 (1982), 195–204.

———, ed. *Jewish Writings of the Second Temple Period: Apocrypha, Pseudepigrapha, Qumran Sectarian Writings, Philo, Josephus* (Assen: Van Gorcum; Philadelphia: Fortress, 1984).

Stonehouse, N. B. *Origins of the Synoptic Gospels: Some Basic Questions* (London: Tyndale Press, 1964).

Story, Cullen I. K. 'The Bearing of Old Testament Terminology on the Johannine Chronology of the Final Passover of Jesus', *NovT* 31 (1989), 316–324.

Stowers, S. K. 'The Social Sciences and the Study of Early Christianity', pp. 149–181 in W. S. Green, ed., *Approaches to Ancient Judaism*, vol. 5 (Missoula, MT: Scholars, 1985).

Strachan, R. H. *The Fourth Evangelist: Dramatist or Historian?* (London: Hodder and Stoughton, 1926).

———. *The Fourth Gospel: Its Significance and Environment* (London: SCM, 3rd print, 1941).

Strack, H. L. *Jesus die Häretiker und die Christen nach den ältesten jüdischen Angaben: Texte, Übersetzung und Erläuterungen* (Leipzig: Hinrichs, 1910).

Strack, H. L. and P. Billerbeck. *Kommentar zum Neuen Testament aus Talmud und Midrasch* (Munich: O. Beck, 1922–8; 3rd print, 1961–65).

Strathmann, H. *Das Evangelium nach Johannes* (Göttingen: Vandenhoeck und Ruprecht, 1968).

Strecker, G. 'The Theory of the Messianic Secret in Mark's Gospel', *SE* 3 = TU 88, ed. F. L. Cross (1964), 87–104. Reprinted pp. 49–64 in Christopher Tuckett, ed., *The Messianic Secret* (London: SPCK 1983).

Strobel, August. *Kerygma und Apokalyptik: Ein religionsgeschichtlicher und theologischer Beitrag zur Christusfrage* (Göttingen: Vandenhoeck und Ruprecht, 1967).

Stroumsa, G. G. 'Mythos und Erinnerung: Jüdische Dimensionen der gnostischen Revolte gegen die Zeit', *Judaica* 44 (1988), 15–30.

Strugnell, J. 'Angelic Liturgy at Qumran', pp. 318–345 in Anderson, G. W. et al, ed., *Congress Volume, Oxford 1959*, VTSup 7 (Leiden: Brill, 1960).

Struthers, Elizabeth Melbon. 'The Theory and Practice of Structural Exegesis: A Review Article', *Perspective in Religious Studies* 11 (1984), 273–282.

Strus, A. *Nomen Omen: La stylistique sonore des noms propres dans le pentateuque* (Rome: Biblical Institute Press, 1978).

———. 'Interprétation des noms propres dans les oracles contre les nations', pp. 272–285 in J. A. Emerton, ed., *Congress Volume: Salamanca, 1983*, VTSup 36 (Leiden: Brill, 1985).

Stuhlmacher, Peter, ed. *Das Evangelium und die Evangelien: Vorträge vom Tübinger Symposium 1982* (Tübingen: Mohr-Siebeck, 1983).

———. *Jesus von Nazareth – Christus des Glaubens* (Stuttgart: Glawer Verlag, 1988).
Stutterheim, C. F. P. *Het Begrip Metaphoor: Een taalkundig en wijsgering onderzoek* (Amsterdam, 1941).
Su, Soon Peng. *Lexical Ambiguity in Poetry* (London: Longman, 1994).
Suggit, J. N. 'Nicodemus—the True Jew', *Neot* 14 (1981), 90–110.
Summers, Ray. *Behold the Lamb: An Exposition of the Theological Themes in the Gospel of John* (Nashville: Broadman, 1979).
Sundberg, A. C. 'On Testamonies', *NovT* 3 (1959), 268–81.
Suriano, T. M. 'Who Then Is This? ... Jesus Masters the Sea', *Bible Today* 79 (1975), 449–56.
Suter, D. 'The Drama of Christian Theology in the Gospel of John', *JR* 49 (1969), 275–280.
Swaim, J. Carter. *Unlocking the Treasures in Biblical Imagery* (New York: Association Press, 1966).
Sweet, J. P. M. and J. Barclay, eds. *Early Christian Thought in its Jewish Context* (Cambridge: CUP, 1996).
Swete, B. *An Introduction to the Old Testament in Greek* (Cambridge: CUP, 1902).
———. *The Gospel According to Mark* (London: Macmillan, 1898).
Swinburne, Richard. *Revelation: From Metaphor to Analogy* (Oxford: Clarendon Press, 1992).

Talbert, C. H. 'Artistry and Theology: An Analysis of the Architecture of John 1:19–5:47', *CBQ* 32 (1970), 341–366.
Talmon, S., ed. *Jewish Civilization in the Hellenistic-Roman Period* (Sheffield: Sheffield Academic Press, 1991).
Tannehill, Robert. *The Sword of His Mouth* (Philadelphia: Fortress Press, 1975).
Tanzer, S. J. 'Salvation is for the Jews: Secret Christian Jews in the Gospel of John', pp. 285–300 in B. A. Pearson, ed., *The Future of Early Christianity: Essays in Honor of Helmut Koester* (Minneapolis: Augsburg/Fortress, 1991).
Tarrelli, C. C. 'Johannine Synonyms', *JTS* 47 (1946), 175–177.
Tasker, R. V. G. *The Old Testament in the New Testament* (Grand Rapids: Eerdmans, 1954).
———. *The Gospel According to St. John*, Tyndale New Testament Commentaries (Grand Rapids: Eerdmans, 1960, repr., 1988).
Taylor, Edward. *Upon the Types of the Old Testament*, edited by Charles W. Mignon (Lincoln: University of Nebraska Press, 1989).
Taylor, M. J., ed. *A Companion to John: Readings in Johannine Theology: John's Gospel and Epistles* (Staten Island, NY: Alba House, 1977).
Taylor, M. S. *Anti-Judaism and Early Christian Identity: A Critique of the Consensus* (Leiden: Brill, 1995).
Taylor, V. *Jesus and his Sacrifice: A Study of the Passion-Sayings in the Gospels* (London: Macmillan, 1937).
———. Book Review of M. Black, *ExpTim* 58 (1946–47), 147.
———. *The Gospel According to St. Mark* (London: Macmillan, 1952).
Teeple, Howard M. 'Qumran and the Origin of the Fourth Gospel', *NovT* 4 (1960), 6–25.

——. 'Methodology in Source Criticism of the Fourth Gospel', *JBL* 81 (1962), 279–286.
——. *The Literary Origin of the Gospel of John* (Evanston, IL: Religion and Ethics Institute, 1974).
Telford, W. R. *The Barren Temple and the Withered Tree* (Sheffield: JSOT Press, 1980).
Temple, S. 'A Key to the Composition of the Fourth Gospel', *JBL* 80 (1961), 220–232.
Tenney, Merrill C. *John: The Gospel of Belief* (Grand Rapids: Eerdmans, 1948).
——. 'The Footnotes of John's Gospel', *BibSac* 117 (1960), 350–364.
——. 'Literary Keys to the Fourth Gospel: The Old Testament and the Fourth Gospel', *BibSac* 120 (1963), 300–308.
——. 'Literary Keys to the Fourth Gospel: The Imagery of John', *BibSac* 121 (1964), 13–21.
——. 'Topics from the Gospel of John. Part III: The Meaning of "Witness" in John', *BibSac* 132 (1975), 229–241.
——. 'Topics in the Fourth Gospel: Part II: The Meaning of Signs', *BibSac* 132 (1975), 145–160.
Thackeray, H. St. J. *A Grammar of the Old Testament in Greek according to the Septuagint*, vol. 1 (Cambridge: CUP, 1909).
Theissen, Gerd. *Urchristliche Wundergeschichten: Ein Beitrag zur formgeschichtlichen Erforschung der synoptischen Evangelien*, SNT 8 (Gütersloh: Gütersloher Verlagshaus Gerd Mohn, 1974).
——. 'Soziale Schichtung in der korinthischen Gemeinde', *ZNW* 65 (1974), 232–273.
——. 'Die soziologische Auswertung religiöser Überlieferungen: Ihre methodologischen probleme am Beispiel des Urchristentums', *Kairos* 17 (1975), 284–299.
——. *The First Followers of Jesus: A Sociological Analysis of Early Christianity* (London: SCM, 1978).
——. *Studien zur Soziologie des Urchristentums*, WUNT 2.19 (Tübingen: Mohr, 1979, 1983, 1989).
——. 'Zur forschungsgeschichtlichen Einordnung der soziologischen Fragestellung', pp. 3–34 in idem, *Studien zur Soziologie des Urchristentums* (Tübingen: Mohr, 1979, 2nd edn, 1983).
——. *Authoritätskonflikte in den johanneischen Gemeinden* (Thessalonika: n.p., 1988).
Theodore of Mopsuestia, *Corpus Scriptorum Christianorum Orientalium*, Scriptores Syri, Series 4, Tomus III, interpretatus est, J. M. Vosté (Louvain, 1940).
Thielman, Frank. 'The Style of the Fourth Gospel and Ancient Literary Critical Concepts of Religious Discourse', pp. 169–183 in Duane Watson, ed., *Persuasive Artistry*, JSOTSup 50 (Sheffield: JSOT Press, 1991).
Thiemann, R. F. *Revelation and Theology: The Gospel as Narrated Promise* (Notre Dame: University of Notre Dame Press, 1985).
Thiselton, Anthony C. 'Semantics and New Testament Interpretation', pp. 75–104 in I. Howard Marshall, ed., *New Testament Interpretation* (Grand Rapids: Eerdmans, 1977).
——. *The Two Horizons: New Testament Hermeneutics and Philosophical Description* (Grand Rapids: Eerdmans, 1980).
Thomas, John Christopher. *Foot Washing in John 13 and the Johannine Community* (Sheffield: Sheffield Academic Press, 1990).

———. 'The Fourth Gospel and Rabbinic Judaism', *ZNW* 82 (1991), 159–182.
Thomas, R. W. 'The Meaning of the Terms "Life" and "Death" in the Fourth Gospel and in Paul', *SJT* 21 (1968), 199–212.
Thompson, J. D. 'An Analysis of Present and Future in the Eschatology of the Fourth Gospel and an Examination of the Theological Relationship Between the Two' (Doctoral diss., Atlanta: Emory University, 1967).
Thompson, Leonard L. *Introducing Biblical Literature: A More Fantastic Country* (Englewood Cliffs, NJ: Prentice-Hall, 1978).
Thompson, Marianne M. *The Humanity of Jesus in the Fourth Gospel* (Philadelphia: Fortress Press, 1988).
———. 'Signs and Faith in the Fourth Gospel', *BBR* 1 (1991), 89–108.
———. '"God's Voice You Have Never Heard, God's Form You Have Never Seen": The Characterization of God in the Gospel of John', *Semeia* 63 (1993), 177–204.
———. *The Incarnate Word: Perspectives on Jesus in the Fourth Gospel* (Peabody, MA: Hendrickson, 1988).
Thompson, Michael B. 'The Holy Internet: Communication Between Churches in the First Christian Generation', pp. 49–70 in R. Bauckham, ed., *The Gospels for All Christians* (Grand Rapids: Eerdmans, 1998).
Thomson, J. A. K. *Irony: An Historical Introduction* (Cambridge, MA: Harvard University Press, 1927).
Thomson, J. G. S. 'The Shepherd-Ruler Concept in the Old Testament and Its Application in the New Testament', *SJT* 8 (1955), 406–418.
Thornton, T. C. G. 'Christian Understandings of the *Birkat Ha-Minim* in the Eastern Roman Empire', *JTS* n.s. 38 (1987), 419–431.
Thrall, W. F., A. Hibbard, and C. Hugh, *A Handbook to Literature* (New York: Odyssey Press, 1936; revised by H. Holman, 1960).
Thrall, William Flint, and Addison Hibbard, *A Handbook to Literature*, 5th edn (New York: Macmillan Publishing, 1986).
Thüsing, Wilhelm. *Die Erhöhung und Verherrlichung Jesu im Johannesevangelium* (Münster: Verlag Aschendorff, 1970).
———. *Studien zur neutestamentlichen Theologie*, ed. by Thomas Söding, WUNT 82 (Tübingen: Mohr-Siebeck, 1995).
Thyen, H. 'Die Einheit der johanneischen Sprache als methodologisches Problem', *TRu* 39 (1974), 48–52.
———. 'Aus der Literatur zum Johannesevangelium', *TRu* 39 (1975), 22–52, 269–330.
———. 'Aus der Literatur zum Johannesevangelium', *TRu* 42 (1977), 211–270.
———. 'Aus der Literatur zum Johannesevangelium', *TRu* 43 (1978), 325–359.
———. 'Aus der Literatur zum Johannesevangelium', *TRu* 44 (1979), 97–134.
———. *Das Heil Kommt von den Juden: Kirche: Festschrift für G. Bornkamm*, hrsg. D. Lührmann and G. Strecker (Tübingen: Mohr-Siebeck, 1980).
———. 'Johannes 10 im Kontext des vierten Evangeliums', pp. 116–134 in J. Beutler and R. T. Fortna, eds, *The Shepherd Discourse of John 10 and its Context: Studies by Members of the Johannine Writings Seminar*, SNTSMS 67 (Cambridge: CUP, 1991).
van Tilborg, Sjef. *Imaginative Love in John* (Leiden: Brill, 1993).

———. *Reading John in Ephesus*, NovTSup 83 (Leiden: Brill, 1996).

Tillmann, F. *Das Johannesevangelium* (Bonn: Hanstein, 1931).

Timmins, N. G. 'Variation in Style in the Johannine Literature', *JSNT* 53 (1994), 47–64.

Tobin, T. H. 'The Prologue of John and Hellenistic Jewish Speculation', *CBQ* 52 (1990), 252–269.

Todorov, Tzvetan. *The Poetic of Prose*, ET by Richard Howard (Ithaca: Cornell University Press, 1977).

Tomkins, Jane, ed. *Reader-Response Criticism: From Formalism to Post-Structuralism* (Baltimore: John Hopkins University Press, 1980).

Torczyner, Harry. 'The Riddle in the Bible', *HUCA* 1 (1924), 125–249.

Torrey, D. Charles. 'When I AM Lifted Up From the Earth: John 12:32', *JBL* 51 (1932), 320–322.

Torrey, C. C. 'The Aramaic Origin of the Gospel of John', *HTR* 16 (1923), 305–344.

———. *The Four Gospels* (New York: Harper, 1933).

———. *Our Translated Gospels: Some of the Evidence* (London: Hodder and Stoughton, 1936).

Tournay, R. J. *Word of God, Song of Love: A Commentary on the Song of Songs* (New York: Paulist, 1988).

Toussaint, Stanley D. 'The Significance of the First Sign in John's Gospel', *BibSac* 134 (1977), 45–51.

Townsend, John T. 'The Gospel of John and the Jews: The Story of A Religious Divorce', pp. 72–97 in Alan T. Davies, ed., *Anti-Semitism and the Foundations of Christianity* (New York: Paulist, 1979).

Toy, Crawford H. *Quotations in the New Testament* (New York: Scribners, 1884).

Tracy, D. *Plurality and Ambiguity* (San Francisco: Harper and Row, 1987).

Trautner-Kromann, Hanne. *Shield and Sword: Jewish Polemic against Christianity and the Christians in France and Spain from 1100–1500*, ET (Tübingen: Mohr-Siebeck, 1993).

Trench, Richard. *Notes on the Miracles of Our Lord* (Grand Rapids: Baker Book House, 1949).

Trepat, J. 'L'evangelista Sant Joan: Idees característiques', *AnSTar* 3 (1927), 405–22.

Tresmontant, C. *The Hebrew Christ: Language in the Age of the Gospels* (Chicago: Franciscan Herald Press, 1989).

Treves, M. 'The Two Spirits in the Rule of the Community', *RevQ* 3 (1961), 449–452

Trigg, Joseph W. *Origen: The Bible and Philosophy in the Third-Century Church* (London: SCM, 1985).

Trites, A. A. *The New Testament Concept of Witness*, SNTSMS 31 (Cambridge: CUP, 1977).

Troeltsch, Ernst. *The Absoluteness of Christianity and the History of Religions* (1911; London: SCM, 1972).

Tröger, Karl-Wolfgang, ed., *Altes Testament – Frühjudentum – Gnosis: Neue Studien zu Gnosis und Bibel* (Berlin: Evangelische Verlagsanstalt, 1980).

Trudgill, Peter. *Sociolinguistics: An Introduction to Language and Society* (London: Penguin Books, 1983).

———. *Introduction to Language and Society* (London: Penguin, 1992).

Trudinger, Paul. 'Subtle Word-Plays in the Gospel of John and the Problem of Chapter 21', *JRT* 23 (1971), 27-31.

———. 'The Seven Days of the New Creation in St. John's Gospel: Some Further Reflections', *EvQ* 44 (1972), 154-158.

———. 'Concerning Sins, Mortal and Otherwise: A Note on 1 John 5:16-17', *Bib* 52 (1972), 541-542.

———. 'The Raising of Lazarus—A Brief Response', *DRev* 94 (1976), 287-290.

———. 'The Meaning of "Life" in St. John: Some Further Reflections', *BTB* 6 (1976), 258-263.

———. 'An Israelite in Whom There Is No Guile: An Interpretative Note on Jn. 1:45-51', *EvQ* 54 (1982), 117-120.

———. 'A "Hot" Apology for the "Cool" Gospel', *DRev* 103 (1985), 66-75.

———. 'The 153 Fishes: a Response and a Further Suggestion', *ExpTim* 102 (1990), 11-12.

Trueblood, Elton. *The Humour of Christ* (NY: Harper and Row, 1964).

Trumbower, Jeffrey A. *Born from Above: The Anthropology of the Gospel of John* (Tübingen: Mohr-Siebeck, 1992).

Tuckett, Christopher, ed. *The Messianic Secret* (London: SPCK, 1983).

———. *Reading the New Testament: Methods of Interpretation* (London: SPCK, 1987).

Tuniv, J. O. 'Personajes veterotestamentarios en el Evangelio de Juan', *Revista Latinoamericana de Teologia* 10 (1993), 279-292.

Turner, Max. 'Atonement and the Death of Jesus in John: Some Questions to Bultmann and Forestell', *EvQ* 62 (1990), 99-122.

Turner, Nigel. *Grammatical Insights into the New Testament* (Edinburgh: Clark, 1965).

———. *Style*. Vol. 4 in James H. Moulton, ed., *A Grammar of New Testament Greek* (Edinburgh: Clark, 1976).

Tyle, R. L. 'The Source and Function of Isaiah 6:9-10 in John 12:40', pp. 205-220 in J. E. Priest, ed., *Johannine Studies: Essays in Honor of Frank Pack* (Malibu, CA: Pepperdine University Press, 1989).

Ullmann, Stephen. *Semantics: An Introduction to the Science of Meaning* (Oxford: Blackwell; New York: Barnes and Noble, 1962).

Underhill, E. *Mystic Way* (London: J. M. Dent and Sons, 1914).

van Unnik, W. C. 'The Purpose of St. John's Gospel', *SE* 1 = TU 73, ed. K. Aland et al. (1959), 382-411. Repr. pp. 167-196 in *The Gospels Reconsidered: Selected papers read at the International Congress on The Four Gospels in 1957* (Oxford: Blackwell, 1960).

———. 'The Quotation from the Old Testament in John 12:34', *NovT* 3 (1959), 174-179.

Urbach, E. E. *The Sages: Their Concepts and Beliefs*, 2 vols, trans. by I. Abrahams (Jerusalem: Magnes Press, 1979).

Urban, W. M. *Language and Reality: the Philosophy of Language and the Principles of Symbolism* (London, 1939).

Uspensky, Boris. *A Poetics of Composition: The Structure of the Artistic Text and Typology of a Compositional Form*, ET by V. Zavarin and S. Wittig (Berkeley: University of California Press, 1973).

Vanderkam, James C. *Enoch and the Growth of an Apocalyptic Tradition* (Washington: Catholic Biblical Association of America, 1984).

Vanderlip, D. G. *Christianity According to John* (Philadelphia: Westminster, 1975).

Vanhoye, A. 'La Composition de Jn. 5:19–30', pp. 259–274 in A. Descamps and A. de Halleux, eds, *Mélanges Bibliques: En hommage au R. P. Béda Rigaux* (Gembloux: Duculot, 1970).

Vassilyev, L. M. 'The Theory of Semantic Field: A Survey', *Linguistics* 187 (1974), 79–93.

Vawter, Bruce. 'What Came to Be in Him was Life (Jn 1:3b–4a)', *CBQ* 25 (1963), 401–406.

——. 'Ezekiel and John', *CBQ* 26 (1964), 450–458.

——. 'Are the Gospels Anti-Semitic?' *JES* 5 (1968), 473–487.

——. 'Some Recent Developments in Johannine Theology', *BTB* 1 (1971), 30–58.

——. 'John's Doctrine of the Spirit: A Summary of His Eschatology', pp. 177–185 in Michael J. Taylor, ed., *A Companion to John: Readings in Johannine Theology* (New York: Alba House, 1977).

Vedder, Henry C. *The Johannine Writings and the Johannine Problem* (Philadelphia: Griffith and Rowland Press, 1917).

Vellanickal, M. *The Divine Sonship of Christians in the Johannine Writings* (Rome: Pontifical Biblical Institute, 1977).

Verhelst, F. 'Sur quelques caractères distinctifs du IV Évangile', *Collectanea Mechliniensia* 2 (1928), 189–195.

Vermes, Geza. *Scripture and Tradition in Judaism* (Leiden: Brill, 1961).

——. 'Bible and Midrash: Early O.T. Exegesis', pp. 199–231 in P. R. Ackroyd and C. F. Evans, eds, *The Cambridge History of the Bible: From the Beginning to Jerome*, vol. 1 (Cambridge: CUP, 1970).

——. *Jesus the Jew: A Historian's Reading of the Gospels* (London: Collins, 1973).

——. *The Dead Sea Scrolls* (London: Penguin, 3rd print, 1987).

Via, Jr., D. O. 'Darkness, Christ, and the Church in the Fourth Gospel', *SJT* 14 (1961), 172–193.

Vielhauer, P. *Geschichte der urchristlichen Literatur: Einleitung in das Neue Testament, die Apokryphen und die Apostolischen Väter* (Berlin: de Gruyter, 1975).

de Viliers, J. L. 'The Shepherd and His Flock', *Neot* 2 (1968), 89–103.

Virgulin, S. 'Caratteristiche del quarto Evangelo', *Bibbia e oriente* 2 (1960), 152–156.

Viviano, B T. *The Kingdom of God in History* (Wilmington, DE: M. Glazier, 1988).

Voeltzel, René. *Le Rire de Seigneur* (Strassburg: Oberlin, 1955).

Voelz, J. W. 'The Linguistic Milieu of the Early Church', *Concordia Theological Quarterly* 56 (1992), 81–97.

Volz, P. *Die Eschatologie der jüdischen Gemeinde im neutestamentlichen Zeitalter* (Tübingen: Mohr-Siebeck, 1934).

Vorster, W. S. 'The Gospel of St. John as Language', *Neot* 6 (1972), 19–27.

Vouga, François. *Le cadre historique et l'intention théologique de Jean*, Beauchesne Religions (Paris: Beauchesne, 1977).

——. 'The Johannine School: A Gnostic Tradition in Primitive Christianity?' *Bib* 69 (1988), 371-385.
——. 'Antijudaismus im Johannesevangelium?' *Theologie und Glaube* 83 (1993), 81-89.
Vriezen, T. C. *An Outline of Old Testament Theology* (Oxford: OUP, 1958).

van der Waal, C. 'The Gospel According to John and the Old Testament', *Neot* 6 (1972), 28-47.
de Waard, J. A. *A Comparative Study of the Old Testament Text in the Dead Sea Scrolls and in the New Testament* (Leiden: Brill, 1966).
Wächter, Ludwig. 'Die unterschiedliche Haltung der Pharisäer, Sadduzäer und Essener zur Heimarmene nach dem Bericht des Josephus', *ZRGG* 21 (1969), 97-114.
von Wahlde, U. C. 'The Terms for Religious Authorities in the Fourth Gospel: A Key to Literary Strata?' *JBL* 98 (1979), 231-253.
——. 'Faith and Works in John 6:28-29: Exegesis or Eisegesis?' *NovT* 22 (1980), 304-315.
——. 'The Witness to Jesus in John 5:31-40 and Belief in the Fourth Gospel', *CBQ* 43 (1981), 385-404.
——. 'The Johannine "Jews": A Critical Survey', *NTS* 28 (1982), 33-60.
——. 'Literary Structure and Theological Argument in Three Discourses with the Jews in the Fourth Gospel', *JBL* 103 (1984), 575-584.
——. *The Earliest Version of John's Gospel* (Wilmington: Michael Glazier, 1989).
——. *The Johannine Commandments: 1 John and the Struggle for the Johannine Tradition* (New York: Paulist Press, 1990).
Waldron, R. A. *Sense and Sense Development* (London: André Deutsch, 1967).
Walker, Norman. 'The Reckoning of Hours in the Fourth Gospel', *NovT* 4 (1960), 69-73.
Walker, Jr., W. O. 'The Origin of the Son of Man Concept as Applied to Jesus', *JBL* 91 (1972), 482-490.
Wallace, Daniel. 'John 5:2 and the Date of the Fourth Gospel', *Bib* 71 (1990), 177-205.
Walter, L. *L'incroyance des croyants selon saint Jean*, Lire la Bible 43 (Paris: Cerf, 1976).
Ward, R. F. 'Pauline Voice and Presence as Strategic Communication', pp. 95-107 in J. Dewey, ed., *Semeia* 65: *Orality and Textuality in Early Christian Literature* (Atlanta: Scholars Press, 1995).
Watson, Alan. *Jesus and the Jews: The Pharisaic Tradition in John* (Athens: University of Georgia Press, 1995).
Watson, Duane Francis. 'The Social Function of Mark's Secrecy Theme', *JSNT* 24 (1985), 49-69.
—— and Alan J. Hauser. *Rhetorical Criticism of the Bible: A Comprehensive Bibliography with Notes on History and Method* (Leiden: Brill, 1993).
——. 'Toward a Literal Reading of the Gospels', pp. 195-217 in Richard Bauckham, ed., *The Gospels for All Christians: Rethinking the Gospel Audiences* (Grand Rapids, MI: Eerdmans, 1998).
Watson, Wilfred. *Classical Hebrew Poetry: A Guide* (Sheffield: JSOT Press, 1984).

Watts, D. J. 'Eschatology in the Johannine Community: A Study of Diversity' (Doctoral diss., University of Edinburgh, 1980).
Watty, W. W. 'The Significance of Anonymity in the Fourth Gospel', *ExpTim* 90 (1978–79), 209–212.
Wead, David. 'We Have a Law', *NovT* 11 (1969), 185–189.
———. *The Literary Devices in John's Gospel* (Basel: Friedreich Rinehardt, 1970).
———. 'Johannine Irony as a Key to the Author, Audience Relationship in John's Gospel', *Biblical Literature* (1974), 33–44.
Weber, Max. *Economy and Society: An Outline of Interpretive Sociology*, Guenther Roth and Claus Wittich, eds, 2 vols (Berkeley: University of California Press, 1978).
Webster, E. C. 'Pattern in the Fourth Gospel', pp. 230–257 in David J. A. Clines, David M. Gunn, and Alan J. Hauser, eds, *Art and Meaning: Rhetoric in Biblical Literature*, JSOTSup 19 (Sheffield: JSOT Press, 1982).
Weimann, Robert. *Structure and Society in Literary Theory* (Charlottesville: University of Virginia Press, 1973).
Weinel, Heinrich. *Grundriss der theologischen Wissenschaften: Biblische Theologie des Neuen Testaments* (Tübingen: Mohr-Siebeck, 1928).
Weinfeld, Moshe. *The Organizational Pattern and the Penal Code of the Qumran Sect* (Göttingen: Vandenhoeck und Ruprecht 1986).
Weisengoff, J. P. 'Light and Its Relation to Life in St. John', *CBQ* 8 (1946), 448–451.
Weiss, H. 'Foot Washing in the Johannine Community', *NovT* 21 (1979), 298–325.
Weiss, Johannes. 'Beiträge zur paulinischen Rhetorik', pp. 165–247 in C. R. Gregory, et al., *Theologische Studien Herrn Wirkl. Oberkonsistorialrath Professor D. Bernhard Weiss zu seinem 70. Geburtstage dargebracht* (Göttingen: Vandenhoek und Ruprecht, 1897).
———. *Earliest Christianity: A History of the Period AD30–150*, 2 vols, ET (New York: Harper and Brothers, 1959).
Weiss, Meir. *The Bible from Within: The Method of Total Interpretation* (Jerusalem: Magnes, 1984).
———. 'Die Methode der "Total-Interpretation": Von der Notwendigkeit der Struktur-Analyse für das Verständis der Biblischen Dichtung', pp. 93–95 in G. W. Anderson, et al., eds, *Congress Volume: Uppsala, 1971*, VTSup 22 (1972).
Welch, J. W., ed. *Chiasmus in Antiquity: Structures, Analyses, Exegesis* (Hildesheim: Gerstenberg, 1981).
Wellek, René and Austin Warren. *Theory of Literature* (New York: Penguin, 1980, 1948).
Wellek, René. *Discriminations: Further Concepts of Criticism* (New Haven: Yale University Press, 1970).
Wellhausen, Julius. *Das Evangelium Johannis* (Berlin: Reimer, 1908).
Wendland, Ernst R. 'What Is Truth? Semantic Density and the Language of the Johannine Epistles with Special Reference to 2 John', *Notes on Translation* 5 (1991), 36.
Wendt, H. H. *The Gospel According to St. John: An Inquiry into Its Genesis and Historical Value*, ET (Edinburgh: Clark, 1902).

Wenger, James E. 'The Use of the Old Testament in the Gospel of John' (Thesis, Dallas Seminary, 1965).

Wengst, Klaus. *Häresie und Orthodoxie im Spiegel des ersten Johannesbriefes* (Gütersloh: Mohn, 1976).

———. *Der erste, zweite und dritte Brief des Johannes*, Ökumenischer Taschenbuchkommentar zum Neuen Testament 16 (Gütersloh: Mohn, 1978).

———. *Bedrängte Gemeinde und verherrlichter Christus: Der historische Ort des Johannesevangeliums als Schlüssel zu seiner Interpretation*, Biblisch-Theologische Studien 5 (Neukirchen-Vluyn: Neukirchener Verlag, 2nd print, 1983).

Wenham, D. 'The Enigma of the Fourth Gospel: Another Look', *TynBul* 48 (1997), 149–78.

Wenz, H. 'Sehen und Glauben bei Johannes', *TZ* 17 (1961), 18–20.

Wernberg-Møller, P. 'A Reconsideration of the Two Spirits in the Rule of the Community (1QS III.13–IV.26)', *RevQ* 3 (1961), 413–441.

Werth, P. *Focus, Coherence and Emphasis* (London: Croom Helm, 1984).

Westcott, B. F. *The Revelation of the Father: Short Lectures on the Titles of the Lord in the Gospel of St. John* (London: Murray, 1884).

———. *The Gospel According to St. John: The Greek Text with Introduction and Notes*, 2 vols (London: Murray, 1908; repr. Grand Rapids: Eerdmans, 1954).

Westerholm, S. *Jesus and Scribal Authority* (Lund: CWK Gleerup, 1978).

Wetter, G. P. '"Ich bin es": Eine Johanneische Formel', *Theologische Studien und Kritiken* 88 (1915), 224–238.

Wheelwright, Philip. *Metaphor and Reality* (Bloomington, IN: Indiana University Press, 1962).

———. *The Burning Foundation*, rev. edn (Bloomington: Indiana University Press, 1968).

Whitacre, Rodney A. *Johannine Polemic: The Role of the Tradition and Theology*, SBLDS 67 (Chico, CA: Scholars Press, 1982).

White, L. M., ed. *Semeia 56: Social Networks in the Early Christian Environment: Issues and Methods for Social History* (Atlanta, GA: Scholars Press, 1992).

White, M. C. 'The Identity and Function of the Jews and Related Terms in the Fourth Gospel' (Ph.D. diss., Emory University, 1972).

Whitehead, Alfred North. *Symbolism: Its Meaning and Effects* (Cambridge: CUP, 1928).

Wiefel, W. 'Die Scheidung von Gemeinde und Welt im Johannesevangelium auf dem Hintergrund der Trennung von Kirche und Synagogue', *TZ* 35 (1979), 213–227.

Wikenhauser, A. *Das Evangelium nach Johannes* (Regensburg: Pustet, 1961).

Wilckens, U. *Auferstehung. Das biblische Auferstehungszeugnis historisch untersucht und erklärt*, Themen der Theologie 4 (Berlin: Kreuz-Verlag, 1970).

Wilcox, Max. 'The Promise of the "Seed" in the New Testament and the Targumim', *JSNT* 5 (1979), 2–20.

Wilder, Amos Niven. *Early Christian Rhetoric: The Language of the Gospel* (Cambridge: Harvard University Press, 1964).

Wiles, M. F. 'The Old Testament in Controversy with the Jews', *SJT* 8 (1955), 113–126.

———. *The Spiritual Gospel: The Interpretation of the Fourth Gospel in the Early Church* (Cambridge: CUP, 1960).

Wilken, R. L. *The Myth of Christian Beginnings* (New York: Doubleday; London: SCM, 1979).

Wilkens, Wilhelm. *Die Entstehungsgeschichte des vierten Evangeliums* (Zollikon: Evangelischer Verlag, 1958).

——. *Zeichen und Werke: Ein Beitrag zur Theologie des 4. Evangeliums in Erzählungs- und Redestoff*, ATANT 55 (Zürich: Zwingli Verlag, 1969).

Willeford, D. D. 'A Study of Religious Feasts as Background for the Organization and Message of the Gospel of John' (Ph.D. diss., Southwestern Baptist Theological Seminary, 1981).

Willett, Michael E. 'Wisdom Christology in the Fourth Gospel' (Ph.D. diss., Southern Baptist Theological Seminary, 1985).

Williams, Catrin H. *'I am He': The Meaning and Interpretation of 'ANÎ HÛ' in Jewish and Early Christian Literature*, WUNT 2.113 (Tübingen: Mohr-Siebeck, 2000).

Williams, James G. '"You Have Not Spoken Truth of Me": Mystery and Irony in Job', *ZAW* 83 (1971), 231-255.

——. 'Irony and Lament: Clues to Prophetic Consciousness', *Semeia* 8 (1977), 51-75.

Williams, J. T. 'Cultic Elements in the Fourth Gospel', pp. 339-350 in E. A. Livingstone, ed., *Studia Biblica II 1978: Papers on the Gospels* (1980).

Williams, P. Trevor. *Forms and Vitality in the World and in God: A Christian Perspective* (Oxford: Clarendon Press, 1985).

Williams, S. *Jesus' Death as Saving Event: The Background and Origin of a Concept*, HDR 2 (Missoula, MT: Scholars Press, 1975).

Williamson, H. G. M. and D. A. Carson, eds. *It Is Written: Scripture Citing Scripture. Essays in Honour of Barnabas Lindars* (Cambridge: CUP, 1988).

Wilson, B. 'An Analysis of Sect Development', *American Sociological Review* 24 (1959), 3-15.

——. *Religion in Sociological Perspective* (Oxford: OUP, 1982).

Wilson, B. R. *Magic and the Millennium: A Sociological Study of Religious Movements of Protest Among Tribal and Third-World Peoples* (New York: Harper and Row, 1973).

Wilson, J. 'The Integrity of John, 3:32-36', *JSNT* 10 (1981), 34-41.

Wilson, M. R. 'Witness as a Theme in the Fourth Gospel' (Ph.D. diss., New Orleans Baptist Theological Seminary, 1992).

——. *Our Father Abraham: Jewish Roots of the Christian Faith* (Grand Rapids: Eerdmans, 1989).

Wilson, R. 'The Fourth Gospel and Hellenistic Thought', *NovT* 1 (1956), 225-227.

Wilson, R. R. *Sociological Approaches to the Old Testament* (Philadelphia: Fortress Press, 1984).

Wilson, S. G. *Related Strangers: Jews and Christians 70-170 C.E.* (Minneapolis: Fortress Press, 1995).

Wimsatt, W. K. *The Verbal Icon: Studies in the Meaning of Poetry* (New York, 1966 [paperback reprint of 1954 edn]).

Wind, A. 'Destination and Purpose of the Gospel of John', *NovT* 14 (1972), 26-69.

Windisch, Hans. *Der messianische Krieg und Urchristentum* (Tübingen: Mohr, 1909).

——. 'Der johanneische Erzählungsstil', pp. 174–213 in Hans Schmidt, ed., *ΕΥΧΑΡΙΣΤΗΡΙΟΝ. Studien zur Religion und Literatur des Alten und Neuen Testaments, Hermann Gunkel zum 60. Geburtstage* (Göttingen: Vandenhoeck und Ruprecht, 1923).

Winn, Albert Curry. *A Sense of Mission: Guidance from the Gospel of John* (Philadelphia: Westminster Press, 1981).

Winston, D. 'The Iranian Component in the Bible, Apocrypha, and Qumran: A Review of the Evidence', *History of Religions* 5 (1966), 200–201.

Winter, Werner. 'Styles as Dialects', pp. 324–330 in Horace G. Lunt, ed., *Proceedings of the Ninth International Congress of Linguists, Cambridge, MA, August 27-31, 1962*, Janua Linguarum Series Marior XII (The Hague: Mouton, 1964).

Wisse, Fredrick. 'The Sethians and the Nag Hammadi Library', pp. 601–607 in Lane C. McGaughy, ed., *SBL 1972 Proceedings*, vol. 2 (n.p.: Society of Biblical Literature, 1972).

Witherington, B. *The Christology of Jesus* (Minneapolis: Fortress Press, 1990).

Witte, J. J. De. *De Betekeniswereld van het lichaam* (Nijmegen, 1948).

Wittig, Susan. 'A Theory of Multiple Meanings', *Semeia* 9 (1977), 75–103.

Wolbert, W. '"Besser, dass ein Mensch für das volk stirbt, als dass das ganze volk zugrunde geht" (Joh 11, 50): Überlegungen zur Devise des Kajaphas', *Theologie und Glaube* 80 (1990), 478–494.

Wolff, M. D. de. 'Irony and Lexical Meaning', pp. 225–234 in H. Bennis and F. Benkema, eds, *Linguistics in the Netherlands* (Dordrecht: Foris, 1985).

Woll, Bruce D. 'The Departure of "The Way": The First Farewell Discourse in the Gospel of John', *JBL* 99 (1980), 225–239.

——. *Johannine Christianity in Conflict: Authority, Rank, and Succession in the First Farewell Discourse*, SBLDS 60 (Chico, CA: Scholars Press, 1981).

Wood, A. Skevington. *The Principles of Biblical Interpretation as Enunciated by Irenaeus, Origen, Augustine, Luther and Calvin* (Grand Rapids: Zondervan, 1967).

Wood, J. E. 'Isaac Typology in the New Testament', *NTS* 14 (1967–68), 583–589.

Woude, A. S. van der. 'פנים', *THAT*, vol. 2, col. 452.

Wrede, William. 'Jesus als Davidssohn', pp. 147–177 in idem, *Vorträge und Studien* (Tübingen: Mohr-Siebeck, 1907).

——. *Charakter und Tendenz des Johannesevangeliums* (Tübingen: Mohr-Siebeck, 1933).

——. *Das Messiasgeheimnis in den Evangelien* [1901]. ET, *The Messianic Secret*, trans. F. C. C. Greig (Cambridge and London: James Clarke, 1971).

Wright, C. J. *The Meaning and Message of the Fourth Gospel* (London: Hodder and Stoughton, 1933).

——. *Jesus, the Revelation of God: His Mission and Message According to St. John* (London: Hodder and Stoughton, 1949).

Wyatt, Nicolas. 'Supposing Him to Be the Gardener (John 20:15): A Study of the Paradise Motif in John', *ZNW* 81 (1990), 21–38.

Wyller, E. A. 'In Solomon's Porch: A Henological Analysis of the Architectonic of the Fourth Gospel', *Studia Theologia* 42 (1988), 151–167.

Yamauchi, E. M. 'Some Alleged Evidences for Pre-Christian Gnosticism', pp. 46–70 in Richard N. Longenecker and Merrill C. Tenney, eds, *New Dimensions in New Testament Study* (Grand Rapids: Zondervan, 1974).

——. *Pre-Christian Gnosticism: A Survey of the Proposed Evidences* (Grand Rapids: Baker, 2nd edn, 1983).

Yee, Gale A. *Jewish Feasts and the Gospel of John* (Wilmington, DE: Michael Glazier, 1989).

Young, F. W. 'A Study of the Relation of Isaiah to the Fourth Gospel', *ZNW* 46 (1955), 215-233.

Zaehner, R. C. *The Dawn and Twilight of Zoroastrianism* (London: Weidenfeld and Nicholson, 1975).

Zahn, Theodor. *Grundriss der neutestamentlichen Theologie* (Leipzig: D. Werner Scholl, 1920).

——. *Das Evangelium des Johannes ausgelegt* (Leipzig: Deichert, 1921).

——. *Introduction to the New Testament*, 3 vols, ET (Grand Rapids: Kregel, 1953, from 3rd German edn, 1909).

Zeller, Dieter. 'Elijah und Elischa im Frühjudentum', *BK* 41 (1986), 154-160.

Zenos, A. C. Review of *Das Messiasgeheimnis in den Evangelien* by William Wrede, *AJT* 6 (1902), 575-576.

Zickendraht, K. 'EGO EIMI', *TSK* 94 (1922), 162-168.

Ziener, G. 'Weisheitsbuch und Johannesevangelium', *Bib* 38 (1957), 396–418.

——. 'Weisheitsbuch und Johannesevangelium', *Bib* 39 (1958), 37-60.

Zimmerli, W. *Ezekiel*, I, Hermeneia (Philadelphia: Fortress Press, 1979).

——. *I am Yahweh*, ed. by W. Brueggemann, ET by D. W. Stott (Atlanta: John Knox Press, 1982).

Zimmermann, F. *The Aramaic Origin of the Four Gospels* (New York: Ktav, 1979).

Zimmermann, H. 'Das Absolute "Ego Eimi" als die neutestamentliche Offenbarungsformel', *BZ* 4 (1960), 54–69, 266-76.

——. 'Meister, Wo Wohnst Du? (Jn. 1:38)', *Lebendiges Zeugnis* 1 (1962), 49-57.

Zumstein, J. 'Chronique Johannique', *Études théologiques et religieuses* 59 (1984), 547-556.

Index of References

Contents: 1. Old Testament; 2. LXX Apocrypha; 3. New Testament; 4. OT Pseudepigrapha; 5. Qumran; 6. Philo; 7. Josephus; 8. Targumim; 9. Mishnah; 10. Tosephta; 11. Babylonian Talmud; 12. Jerusalem Talmud; 13. Midrash Rabbah; 14. Other Rabbinic Works; 15. Greek or Roman Authors; 16. Apostolic Fathers; 17. Nag Hammadi Texts (NHC); 18. Patristic Literature

1. Old Testament

Genesis
1	347
1:1	59, 119
1:1–2:2	95, 346
1:2	384
1:3	349
2	120
2:2	120, 279
2:6	79
2:7	79, 361
2:9	120
2:19	79
3	371
3:3	106
3:8	353, 401
3:14	79
3:17	79
3:19	79
3:22	106
3:24	107
4	371
4:11	79
12:7	259
12:8	101, 281
13:3–4	101, 281
15	99
15:1	346
15:2–20	249
18	295
18:1	259
22	294
22:6	118
24:10–19	102
26:19	73
27:35	98
28:10–19	54, 346
28:10–22	294
29:1–14	102
32	295
32:28	98
32:30	259
40:13	84
40:19	84
49:10	100, 102
50:20	83

Exodus
1:15	109
2–7	261
2:14	110
2:15–21	102
3:14	72, 105, 355
3:14–15	355
4:1–9	111
4:16	393
4:21	318
4:22–23	170
5:1	192
6:2–8	354
6:3	259
6:6–7	192
7:1	393
7:14	304
8:11	304
8:28	304
9:7	304
9:12	318
9:34	304
10:1	304
10:20	318
10:27	318
11–17	263

Genesis (continued)

11:10	318
12:6	276
12:10	97
12:19	279
12:22	278
12:46	97
13:11–16	273
14:8	318
14:17	318
15:2	96, 281
16	110
16:2	110
16:10	280
17:1–7	58
17:6	98, 294
19:6	192
20:13	266
20:18–19	370
21:6	393
22:9	393
22:22	245
24:16	280
25:8	96, 280
25:10	72
25:17–22	72
28:38	273
29:7	224
29:46	356
29:49	96, 280
31:13	356
32–34	111
33:7–11	96, 280
33:13	192
33:17–34:8	401
33:19	313
33:20	298
33:22	343
34:6	343
34:7	273
34:23	192
40:34	112
40:34–38	96, 280
40:35	280

Leviticus

4:3	224
14:5	73
14:6–7	278
14:49	278
14:51	279
16:15ff	271
17:10–14	266
18:5	143, 287
18:24	192
23:33ff	281
24:16	393
26:16	392

Numbers

5:22	342
9:7–10	82
9:12	97
9:15	96, 280
9:16	96
12:6–8	259
12:8	370
14:18	273
16	295
19:6	279
20:1–18	58
20:8	294
20:8ff	98
20:11	58
21:4–9	365
21:9	276
24:13	353
27:17	115
35:30	264

Deuteronomy

1:7	393
1:31	170
2:14	104
2:25	192
3:18	170
4:12	370
4:20	192
5:6–11	261
5:24	280
7:6	192
8:2–3	267
8:3	357
10:18	245
13	264
13:1–3	109
13:1–11	261
13:2	263
13:5	262, 263
13:6	263
13:10	263
13:14	143, 287
14:2	192
14:29	245
15:15–18	353
16:11	245
16:14	245
16:16	281

Deuteronomy (continued)
17:6	264, 283
18:9	192
18:15	108, 109, 262, 369
18:15–22	109
18:15–18	261
18:16	370
18:18	263
18:21	262
18:22	109
19:15	264, 283
19:17	393
19:18	143, 287
20:6–7	392
26:18	192
28:30	392
29:2–4	315
29:3	304
29:4	300
29:29	73
30:12–14	358
31:17	353, 401
32:6	170
32:39	72, 355
34:10	109, 259, 262

Judges
6:29	143, 287
8:23	265
20:18	101, 281, 346
20:26	101, 281, 346
21:2–5	101, 281, 346

Ruth
3:3	117

1 Samuel
6:6	304
8:7	265
9:9	143, 287
10:3	101, 281, 346
15:25	273
16:1–13	224
16:6	224
16:14–23	320
18:18	320
19:9	320
26:16	170
26:17	170
26:21	170
26:25	170

2 Samuel
1:14	224

7:10–14	100
7:14	101, 170, 224, 262
7:28	380

1 Kings
4:25	99, 100
5:5 [MT]	101
16:29	104
17–19	264
18:39	380
19:12	83
19:16	224
22:8	143, 287
22:17	298
22:19–22	299
22:23	320

2 Kings
1:2	79
3:11	143, 287
7:9	273
15:8	104

2 Chronicles
17:4	143, 287
22:9	143, 287
30:19	143, 287

Ezra
7:10	143, 287

Nehemiah
8:6	342
9:12–15	267

Job
1–2	320
5:18	317
9:8b	105
11:6–7	348
12:21	317
15:13	153
17:7	304
28:27	348
31:8–18	392
42:5	259

Psalms
2:2	101
2:4	79
2:7	101, 170, 224, 262
2:9	116
10:18	245
13:1	401, 402

Psalms (continued)

14:1–3	321
19	347
19:11f	267
21:19	256
23	115
30:2	380
32 (LXX 31): 2	99
32:5	273
33:4	349
33:6	348
33:9	95, 346, 347
34 [LXX 33]: 21	97
35:24	380
36:9	349
45:2–3	117
45:6–7	117
45:8	117
45:11	117
45:12b–14	117
51:5	404
51[50]:7	279
55:1	402
68:5	245
69:10	69, 112
69:21 (MT 22)	58, 256
69:22	119, 279
78	110
80:8–19	74, 105
82	295
82:1–8	393
82:3	245
85:3	273
86:15	380
88:1	380
88:14	402
89:20 [MT 21]	101
89:22	170
89:26–27 [MT 27–28]	101
89:46	402
104:2	393
105:15	224
105:39–41	267
106:5	192
106:25 [LXX 105]	110
107:20	346, 347, 348
111:2	143, 287
118 [117]	254, 393
118:25–26	100, 117
119	347
119:10	143, 287
119:45	143, 287
119:47–48	348
119:94	143, 287
119:97	348
119:103	267
119:105	269
119:113	348
119:155	143, 287
119:159	348
119:163	348
119:167	348
126:5	102
135:4	192
146 [145]:8	299
147:15	346, 348
148:4–5	95, 346

Proverbs

1:26	104
6:23	269
8:12–21	355
8:17	104
8:22–23	347, 348
8:22–36	384
8:23–31	348
8:30	348
8:31	348
9:1–6	267
9:5	267
12:7–8	317
12:18	317
13:14	268
26:14	317
26:18	317
30:33	153
31:5	170

Ecclesiastes

3:3	317

Song of Solomon

4:15	112

Isaiah

1–39	153, 325
1:2–4	325
1:4	236
1:10	236, 298
1:15	402
1:16–17	322
1:17	245
1:21	236
1:23	236, 245, 298
2:1–5	280
2:2–3	392
3:1–26	236
3:12	298

Isaiah (continued)

5:1–7	74
5:1–9	236
6	96, 280, 298, 299
6:1	259, 368
6:1–13	298
6:5	309, 368
6:8	353, 370
6:8–10	312
6:9	300, 304
6:9–10	57, 111, 298, 299, 304, 305, 306, 314, 315, 322, 323, 328
6:9–12	236
6:10	254, 299, 302, 303, 304, 312, 313, 324
7:10–15	223
8:17	401
9:1	393
9:1–7	223
9:2 [MT 9:1]	102
9:3	392
9:8	346, 347
11:1	100, 101
11:1–5	392
11:1–16	223
11:10–12	392
14:28–32	223
16:8–10	392
16:18–19	298
17:11	392
24:21–25	223
25:6	70, 106
25:6–8	267
28:12	322
28:24	102
29:10	299, 300, 304, 321
29:17	70, 106
29:18	298, 299, 300, 304
29:18–19	299
30:10–11	322
30:18	393
30:9	322
32:1–8	223
32:6	323
32:15	268
33:10	96, 281
33:15	304
35:3–6	304
35:4	100
35:4–6	324
35:5	298, 299, 304
35:42	298
40:1	341
40:3	254, 333, 348
40:3–5	392
40:5	344
40:8	346, 349
40:9	100
40:9–11	392
40:26	95, 346
41	105
41:2	325
41:4	72, 325, 355
41:26	325
42:1–4	223
42:1–9	307
42:6–7	299
42:7	304
42:8	356
42:16	304
42:17	299, 369
42:18	304
42:18–20	299, 304
42:19	304
42:29	305
43	105
43:8	298, 299, 304
43:8–10	299
43:8–12	325
43:8–13	325
43:9	325
43:10	72, 355
43:10–13	356
43:13	325
43:20–21	192
44:1–5	99
44:3 [MT]	268
44:6	356
44:7	325
44:8	325
44:9–17	323
44:18	298, 323
44:22	323
45:15	401
45:21	325
46:4	72, 355
46:5	325
47:7	323
49	291
49:1–6	223
49:1–13	307
49:9–10	267
49:10	110
50:4–9	223, 307
50:5	369
50:6	118
52:7	116, 309

Isaiah (continued)

52:7–12	283
52:7–53:12	309
52:8–9	117, 310
52:10	117, 344
52:11	117, 310
52:13	96, 281, 309
52:13–14	116
52:13–53:12	223, 307
53	307, 308, 310, 311
53:1	254, 302, 306, 308, 309, 313
53:5	49, 272
53:6–7	74
53:7	308, 310
53:10	116, 309
53:12	120
55:1–3	267
55:3–5	223
55:6	104
55:10	95, 346
55:10ff	347
55:10–11	384
55:11	347, 348
56:10	299
59:1ff	353, 401
59:2	402
59:9–11	299
60:1–3	393
60:16	344
60:19–20	393
61:1	117, 299, 304, 310, 353
61:1–6	223
61:3	117, 310
61:10	70, 106
62:5	70, 106
62:8–9	102, 392
63:1–6	223
64:5 [6]	321
64:7	402
65:13	267
65:21–23	102, 392
66:8	364
66:14	96
66:16	384

Jeremiah

1:5	353
2:13	73, 112
2:21	74, 105
3:2–5	236
3:8–9	261
3:17	304
5:21	299, 300, 304
7:6	245
7:24	304
9:13	304
11:38	304
13:23–24	236
13:26–27	261
17:9	404
17:10	376
21:2	143, 287
22:3	245
23:2	298
23:5	101
23:9–12	153
23:10	261
23:31	166
31:5	70, 106
31:9	170
31:12	106
31:20	170
31:27	102
33:7	401
33:14–26	223
33:15	101
38:17	380

Ezekiel

1:28	370
2:2	370
3:7	299
3:12	370
3:16	346
6:1	346
7:1	346
8:1–10:20	282
8:4	112
8:6–18	298
10	113
10:5	370
10:18–19	259
11:14	346
11:22–23	259
12:1	346
12:2	304
13:1	346
14:2	346
15:1	346
15:1–8	74, 105
16:1	346
16:1–63	236, 261
17:5–10	74
17:22–24	223
18:4	270
18:20	270

Ezekiel (continued)

19:10–14	74
21:25–27	223
23:1–48	236
23:1–49	261
34	115
34:1–10	298
34:2–10	115
34:15	115
34:17	115
34:37	166
36:25–27	364
36:27	338
37:1–14	361
37:9	361
37:14	361
37:15–28	223
37:24	370
39:24	353, 401
43:4	259
43:6	370
43:7	259
47	112
47:1–12	112, 269

Daniel

2:35	273
2:44	291
7:13–14	224
7:22	291
9:24–27	224
10:21	343
12:3	393
12:4	403
12:8	403
12:9–10	403, 406

Hosea

2:23	380
2:24	70, 106
4:12	79
5:1–15	236
5:6	104
6:5	346, 347
6:11	102
8:7	102
9:1–17	236
9:3	102
9:10	99
11:1	170
14:7	106
14:9	403
18:5	102

Joel

1:11	102, 392
2:28–32	362, 392
3:1f	268, 338
3:11–12	393
3:13	102, 392
3:18	269
4:18	70, 106

Amos

3:7	353
3:14	393
4:7	102
5:5	153
5:18	393
7:7	259
9:1	259
9:1–10	236
9:13	70, 106
9:14b	102, 392

Micah

1:10–16	153
3:1–4	353, 401
4:1ff	280
4:4	99, 100
5:1	153
6:15	102, 392
7:6	384
7:18	273

Zephaniah

1:7–8	393
2:4	153
9:3	153

Haggai

1:6	102
2:6–9	224
2:21–23	224

Zechariah

2:14	96, 280
3:8	100, 101
3:8–10	100, 224
3:10	99, 100
3:15	100
3:18–10	100
6:9–15	224
9:9	100, 117, 360
9:9–11	392
12:10	224, 268, 275, 278
12:15	100
13:1	269

Zechariah (continued)
13:7	116
13:9	403
14:7	393
14:8	112, 269
19:37	100

Malachi
3:1	264
3:1–3	392
3:1–5	282
3:2	333
3:3–4	264
4:2	224
4:5	264

2. LXX Apocrypha

Tobit
7:7	305

Wisdom of Solomon
2:18	170
2:21	305
5:20	384
6:18–20	348
6:22	347
7:10	348
7:22	348
7:25	348
7:29	348
8:4–6	348
8:13	348
9:2	348
9:9	348
9:10	348
9:16–18	348
10:11	348
16:7	317
16:11–12	317
16:26	267
18:4	269

Sirach (Ecclesiasticus)
1	348
1:9	348
1:10–12	348
4:10	170
4:11–12	348
4:13	348
15:1–3	267, 268
15:3	267
15:11–12	313
15:11–17	372
17:17	239
24	133, 348
24:1–23	348
24:1–29	384
24:3	348
24:3–31	355
24:8	348
24:9	347
24:19	267
24:19-21	347
24:19–22	267
24:20	267
24:21	267, 268
24:23–33	268
24:32	269
38:9	317
39:30	384
44:16	345
48:1–11	264
46	133
48	133
48:22–25	345
49:8	345
50:27–29	348

Baruch
3:36–4:4	348
4:1–2	143, 287

1 Maccabees
14:12	99

2 Maccabees
1:1–10	239
2:21	239
5:17–20	183
8:1	239
14:38	239
15:13	393

3. New Testament

Matthew
1:1	109
1:1–17	357
1:22	357
1:23	357
2:5	222
2:16	109
2:17	357
3:2	388, 389
3:7	244, 245

Matthew (continued)		13:1-23	203
4:7	277	13:1-58	393
4:8	389	13:10-12	90
4:15-16	357	13:11-17	192
4:17	388, 389	13:11-52	388, 389
4:23	388	13:13	300, 304, 314
5:3	389	13:13-15	300, 303
5:4	341	13:15	299
5:9	170	13:16	304
5:10	389	13:24-30	390
5:11	207	13:30-39	392
5:17	260	13:47-50	389
5:19	389	13:51	304
5:21-48	357	14:27	354
5:44	207	15:3	244, 245, 261
5:44-45	398	15:6	261
6:10	389	15:9	261
6:13	342	15:14	244, 245, 296, 299
6:16-18	117	15:24	199
6:33	389, 404	15:31	296, 299
7:6	401	16:6	244
8:1-4	403	16:12	304
8:11	106	16:13-20	224, 403
8:17	311	16:28	389
8:21-22	384	17:1-13	96
9:34	244	17:13	304
9:35	388, 389	17:9-13	403
9:37-38	392	18:12-14	116
10:7	388, 389	18:15-20	283
10:17-25	189	18:23	389
10:17-26	340	20:21	389
10:25	234	21:11	237
10:35-36	384	21:26	237
10:37	384	21:31	389
10:38	56	21:42	231
10:39	398	21:45	242, 244
11	198	22:1-14	106
11:6	385	22:14	315
11:12	389	22:15	244
11:15	369	22:29	231
11:20-23	379	22:44-45	357
11:21-24	385	23:2	326
11:27	358	23:13	245, 389
12:14	244	23:13-29	245
12:15-21	403	23:13-35	244
12:19-20	357	23:13-36	198
12:24	234, 244, 245	23:14	245
12:24-45	198	23:15	245
12:27	234	23:16	299
12:28	388, 389	23:16-17	296
12:30	245	23:16-18	245
12:31	244	23:17	299
12:38	244	23:19	296, 299
12:39	244	23:23	245

Matthew (continued)

23:24	296, 299
23:26	245, 296, 299
23:28	245
23:30	245
23:33	245
23:34	237, 244
23:35	244
24	207
24:9–11	340
25:1	389
25:31–46	390
26:24	56
26:29	389
26:54	231
26:56	231
26:57–75	393
27:11–12	82
27:46	58, 119
27:48	59, 119
27:49	278
27:57	327, 375
27:62	244, 277
28:18	361

Mark

1:2	357
1:11	224, 262
1:14–15	291, 402, 404
1:15	357, 388, 389
1:21–25	402, 404
1:29–35	403
1:34	402
1:34	404
1:38	199
1:38–39	402, 404
1:43–44	403
2:1–12	402, 404
2:6–7	402, 404
2:27–28	402, 404
3:12	403
3:22–29	234
3:22–30	198, 404
3:28–30	401
3:5	303, 304
3:5–6	404
3:6	244
4:9	369
4:10	90
4:10–12	315, 402
4:11	192
4:11–12	291, 299, 300, 310, 314
4:12	300, 302, 304, 318
4:34	314
5:40	403
5:43	403
6:50	354
6:52	303, 304
7:3–9	261
7:6	245
7:6–13	245
7:9	245
7:13	245
7:17	403
7:21–22	398, 400
7:21–23	404
7:31–37	304
7:36	403
8:6	57
8:17	303, 304
8:18	300, 304
8:21	304
8:26	403
8:27–30	222, 224
8:29	162
8:30	403
8:35	398
8:38	385
9:1	388, 389
9:1–13	96
9:3	393
9:9	403
9:29	392
9:37	199
10:10	403
10:14	389
10:29	384
11:32	237
13	207
13:9–13	189
13:13	55
14:21	56
14:41	388
14:53–72	393
14:55–59	404
15:2–3	82
15:21	118
15:33	278
15:34	58, 119
15:36	59, 119
15:42	277
15:43	327, 375
16:5	393
16:14–16	361
16:20	342

Luke

2:14	384
2:25	341
3:8	250
3:19	50, 386
4:5	389
4:16–30	115, 223
4:18	199, 296
4:31–37	403
4:41	403
4:43	199, 388, 389
5:12–16	403
6:20	389
6:22	207
6:27	207
6:35	398
7:3	241
7:23	385
8:10	300, 315
8:49–56	403
9:2	388
9:18–22	403
9:20	389
9:24	224
9:28–36	96
9:59–60	384
10:2	392
10:11	389
10:22	358
10:3	392
10:9	389
10:23–24	291
11:20	388
11:39	245
11:39–53	244
11:42	245
11:44	245
11:48–51	244
12:11	189
12:11–12	340
12:50	59
12:52–53	384
13:29	106, 389
14	384
14:15–24	106
15:3–7	116
16:14	244
16:16	291, 389
17:20	389
17:21	388, 389
17:33	398
18:17	389
21	207
21:8	354
21:12–19	189
21:24	384
22:54	393
22:63–71	393
23:1–2	82
23:46	58, 119
23:54	277
24:13–35	334
24:25	334
24:25–27	258, 291, 292, 294, 310
24:4	393
24:27	115, 121, 124 223, 258, 285, 293, 357
24:44	290, 291, 292, 310
24:44–46	121

John

1	107
1–3	203
1:1	59, 95, 111, 115, 119, 212, 223, 346, 356, 393
1:3	349, 380
1:4	61, 323, 333, 349, 371, 384
1:4–5	102
1:5	43, 49, 61, 69, 111, 130, 199, 208, 300, 320, 324, 348, 368, 397
1:7	59, 215, 318, 345, 394
1:7–8	216
1:8	61, 215, 394
1:9	44, 61, 82, 102, 172, 324, 348, 385, 393, 396, 406
1:9–10	62
1:9–12a	349
1:10	248, 353
1:10a	172, 396
1:10c	321
1:10–11	249
1:1–14	58
1:1–18	135, 292, 332
1:1–21:25	25
1:1–3	346, 348
1:11	53, 110, 213, 306, 394
1:11–13	387
1:12	162, 169, 318, 333, 354, 404, 405
1:12a	169

John (continued)

1:12–13	48, 122, 159, 249, 250, 319, 337, 360, 363, 369, 391, 409		321, 333, 354, 373, 396, 400
1:12–14	167, 333	1:29–2:12	396
1:13	5, 48, 58, 172, 250, 316, 321, 338, 362, 363, 365, 404, 405	1:29–34	283
		1:29–36	272
		1:30	292
		1:31	168
1:14	54, 55, 62, 63, 95, 96, 97, 101, 112, 130, 154, 184, 212, 221, 280, 281, 309, 316, 330, 343, 351, 356, 368, 379, 393, 395	1:32	69
		1:32–34	216
		1:33	367
		1:34	162, 226
		1:35	212
		1:35–36	283
		1:35–42	283
1:14a	95	1:35–51	294
1:14b	96	1:36	74, 97, 308, 354
1:14–18	111, 294	1:37	56
1:15	215, 216, 345, 394	1:38	56, 59, 62, 104, 131, 165, 169, 317
1:16	333, 343		
1:16–17	354	1:39	59, 150, 367
1:17	238, 260, 272, 319, 343, 345, 349	1:40	56, 150
		1:41	101, 104, 115, 122, 131, 162, 165, 214, 220, 223, 224, 252, 408
1:17b	390		
1:17–23	212		
1:18	59, 63, 89, 96, 101, 109, 111, 112, 114, 115, 213, 223, 262, 280, 281, 292, 297, 298, 309, 332, 344, 345, 349, 350, 353, 354, 368, 386, 393, 396, 405	1:41–42	169
		1:42	131, 150
		1:43	56
		1:43–51	283
		1:45	91, 100, 101, 104, 122, 124, 134, 150, 162, 216, 221, 224, 238, 252, 254, 255, 256, 258, 260, 262, 272, 285, 290, 291, 293, 395, 408
1:19	169, 216, 220, 241, 243		
1:19–20	322		
1:19–21	283		
1:19–28	283	1:45–49	103
1:20	220, 225, 394, 404	1:46	59, 367
1:21	108, 165, 237	1:46–48	212
1:22	394	1:47	98, 99, 150, 250, 316, 317
1:23	91, 229, 254, 255, 256, 333, 348, 357		
		1:47–49	240
1:23–12:15	255	1:47–51	99
1:23–12:16	255, 257	1:48	69, 99, 100, 101, 316
1:24	241	1:49	107, 162, 170, 216, 220, 224, 225, 226, 227, 262, 309, 380
1:24–5	220		
1:25	165		
1:25–29	212	1:50	368
1:26	91	1:50–51	62, 89, 367
1:27	312	1:51	54, 89, 101, 113, 162, 165, 212, 251, 281, 344, 346, 368
1:29	48, 58, 59, 74, 97, 118, 119, 169, 220, 229, 266, 270, 272, 274, 276, 308, 310,		
		2–11	255, 297
		2:1	105, 221

Index of References

John (continued)

2:1–10	69
2:1–11	96, 106, 212, 281, 317
2:1–11:23	403
2:3	221, 292
2:5	221
2:6	105, 165, 239, 383
2:9	169
2:9–10	75, 76
2:10	405
2:11	101, 281, 306, 316, 344, 368, 379, 383, 395
2:12	221
2:13	239, 272, 274
2:13–25	272, 274
2:13–3:21	396
2:14–16	283
2:15	235
2:17	150, 212, 254, 255, 256, 334, 338, 383
2:17–20	284
2:17–21	362
2:18	69, 70, 113, 242, 283, 379
2:18–20	283
2:19	43, 54, 55, 70, 97, 281, 283, 299
2:19–21	112, 281
2:19–22	54, 69, 86, 191, 383
2:20	131, 242
2:21	97, 112, 281, 284
2:21–22	70, 193
2:22	78, 212, 216, 334, 341, 357, 378
2:23	274, 317, 354, 367, 374
2:23–25	164, 316, 317, 328, 329, 367, 374, 376, 379, 380
2:24	59, 317
2:24–25	368
2:25	59, 305, 321, 376
2:28–29	382
2:29	212
3	317
3–12	213, 387
3:1	241, 242, 243, 327, 373
3:1–8	369
3:1–21	375
3:2	58, 69, 375, 376
3:3	5, 25, 57, 58, 69, 316, 337, 361, 364, 367, 389, 404
3:3–5	191, 248
3:3–6	405
3:3–8	48, 319, 391
3:3–11	316
3:3–12	90, 337, 360
3:4	167
3:4–10	382
3:5	43, 57, 69, 333, 338, 361, 363, 364, 389, 404
3:5–6	337, 402
3:5–7	337
3:6	5, 57, 172, 321, 337, 362, 363, 364, 383, 404
3:7	48, 390
3:7–12	245
3:8	51, 316, 338, 363, 370
3:10	152, 325
3:10–12	245, 325
3:11	62, 213, 215, 216, 227, 319, 345, 394
3:11–12	375
3:11–13	350
3:12	57, 89, 276, 298, 333, 337, 405
3:12–13	5
3:12–15	89
3:12–26	214
3:13	58, 89, 109, 213, 262, 349, 373
3:13–14	373
3:13–19	213
3:14	54, 69, 84, 96, 113, 121, 165, 212, 213, 270, 272, 281, 357, 390, 391
3:14–15	298, 377
3:14–16	377
3:14–17	373
3:14–21	43
3:15	200, 318, 322, 323, 372, 404
3:15–16	213, 322, 323
3:15–17	384
3:15–21	333

John (continued)

Ref	Pages
3:16	44, 49, 51, 62, 79, 162, 169, 172, 200, 212, 213, 295, 318, 322, 323, 324, 352, 377, 390, 393, 396, 400, 404
3:16–17	169, 217, 321, 384, 396
3:16–18	200, 324, 354
3:16–19	49, 50, 386
3:16–21	249, 270
3:17	111, 169, 199, 213, 300, 307, 318, 321, 345, 385, 394, 396, 400
3:17–19	324, 385
3:17–21	323, 324
3:18	50, 159, 250, 318, 354, 385, 386
3:18–21	208, 390
3:19	45, 58, 61, 69, 213, 248, 249, 385, 387, 395, 398
3:19–20	83, 318, 398
3:19–21	61, 306, 321, 324, 384
3:20	50, 83, 249, 300, 386, 393, 394, 398, 400
3:20–21	316, 369, 397
3:21	59, 208, 319, 320, 344, 382, 391
3:22–23	131
3:22–30	402
3:22–36	396
3:25	239
3:26	215, 216
3:27	60, 316, 337, 338
3:27–30	49, 226
3:28	215, 220, 404
3:29	91, 333
3:30	60
3:30–34	89
3:30a	390
3:30b	390
3:31	48, 58, 60, 89
3:31–32	366, 393
3:31–34	333, 337
3:31–36	349, 390
3:32	62, 63, 213
3:32–33	216
3:33	405
3:34	213, 345, 356
3:36	50, 159, 162, 200, 213, 250, 307, 318, 367, 390, 400
3:36b	382
3:36c	382
4	58, 111, 119, 204, 317
4:1	241, 243
4:2	328
4:3	328
4:4	60, 103, 373, 390
4:4–42	396
4:5	268
4:5–6	131, 373
4:6	49, 69, 212, 213, 277, 391
4:7	391
4:9	109, 131, 169, 237
4:10	73, 268, 333, 390
4:10a	49
4:10–15	191, 270, 384
4:11	73, 316
4:12	75, 76, 80, 168
4:13f	268
4:13–16	167
4:14	69, 130, 200, 269, 318, 322, 333, 382, 391, 396, 404
4:15	60, 268
4:15–26	6
4:18	62
4:19	57, 367
4:20–24	131, 250, 392
4:21	80, 284, 391, 398
4:21–23	112
4:21–24	281, 391
4:21–3	54
4:22	235, 239
4:23	55, 80, 284, 319, 388, 391
4:23c	213
4:23–24	63, 103, 173, 338, 395
4:24	4, 319, 325, 390
4:24–29	385
4:25	131, 165, 169, 212, 214, 220, 224, 353, 404
4:25–26	392
4:29	103, 217, 220, 226, 227, 367, 380, 404
4:31–35	191
4:31–38	390
4:32–38	323

Index of References

John (continued)

Reference	Pages
4:34	25, 59, 111, 119, 199, 212, 213, 214, 264, 313, 354, 379, 391
4:34–38	333
4:35	25, 392
4:35a	392
4:35b	56, 392
4:35–38	102, 391
4:36	49, 278, 391
4:36b	392
4:36–54	96, 281
4:37	25, 392
4:37–38	212
4:38	49, 199, 213, 391, 392
4:38a	391
4:38b	391
4:38c	391
4:39	216
4:39–42	103
4:41–42	191
4:42	102, 122, 169, 200, 216, 226, 227, 252, 306, 321, 333, 380, 396, 400, 408
4:43–45	44
4:44	44, 57, 108, 237
4:44–54	396
4:45	367
4:46–54	168
4:48	367, 379
4:50	282
5	58, 104, 185, 204, 396
5–10	63
5–12	24
5:1	225, 239
5:1–2	398
5:2	131
5:6	367
5:8	333
5:9–13	353
5:10	242, 264
5:10–18	264
5:11	60
5:12	150
5:13	386
5:14	60, 347, 399, 400
5:15	150
5:15–16	242
5:16	232, 233, 264
5:16–18	247
5:16–30	170
5:17	58, 212, 213, 313, 324, 333, 354, 394, 399
5:17–18	380
5:17–21	379
5:18	115, 223, 226, 232, 233, 242, 261, 264, 382, 393
5:19-23	213
5:19	62, 213, 333, 376, 394
5:19–30	226, 267
5:19–47	366, 404
5:20	214
5:2–16	96, 281
5:21	213, 282, 283, 316
5:21–22	226, 333
5:22	49, 323, 386, 387, 394
5:23	213, 261, 264
5:23–24	345
5:24	111, 199, 200, 213, 264, 318, 322, 323, 380, 384, 386, 387, 404
5:24–25	305, 306, 333
5:24–26	63
5:25	60, 89, 170, 337, 369, 388, 391
5:26	214, 282, 384
5:26–27	213, 226
5:27	50, 113, 213, 323, 340, 386, 387
5:27–29	386
5:27–30	394
5:28	60, 89, 316
5:28–29	369
5:28–30	90
5:29	322, 387, 390, 400
5:29–30	340
5:30	50, 63, 111, 152, 213, 214, 264, 358, 386, 387
5:31	394
5:31–32	63
5:31–33	215, 345
5:31–47	227, 229, 340
5:32	214, 216
5:32–37	394
5:33	130
5:36	49, 59, 152, 213, 216, 264, 354
5:36–37	215, 345

Index of References

John (continued)

5:37	63, 111, 216, 294, 350, 370
5:37a	259
5:37b	259, 370
5:37–47	265
5:38	260, 264, 372
5:38a	382
5:38b	382
5:38–39	258
5:39	43, 115, 121, 122, 124, 134, 143, 162, 216, 223, 231, 251, 258, 260, 268, 285, 286, 287, 292, 293, 294, 357
5:39ff	370
5:39–40	225
5:39–47	290, 291, 310
5:40	58, 83, 213, 322, 323, 324, 333, 399
5:40–44	366
5:41	101, 281, 399
5:42	316, 317, 398
5:43	213, 354
5:43–47	212
5:44	325, 328, 398, 399
5:45	197, 266, 272, 294, 326, 394
5:45–46	252
5:45–47	238, 264, 265
5:46	115, 124, 134, 165, 225, 231, 255, 256, 258, 260, 268, 272, 285, 292, 309, 311, 325, 326, 357
5:46–47	99, 238, 259, 399
5:47	260, 370
6	70, 71, 86, 107, 267
6–7	24
6:1–14	274
6:1–71	110
6:1–7:9	396
6:2	367, 374
6:4	239, 266, 272, 274
6:4–14	272
6:5	316, 406
6:7	356
6:9	105
6:11	57
6:12	44
6:12f	166
6:13	105
6:14	108, 165, 237, 263, 367
6:15	108, 224, 363
6:17	49
6:18	134
6:19–21	105
6:20	105
6:2–12	262
6:22	367
6:22–71	272, 274
6:23	57
6:23f	265
6:24	367
6:25–59	269
6:26	379
6:27	44, 113, 213, 267, 268, 322, 323
6:27ff	69
6:27–29	250
6:27–68	384
6:28	363
6:29	111, 164, 264, 345, 363, 367, 400
6:30	367, 379
6:31	251, 254, 255, 256
6:31–33	212
6:32	263, 267, 270, 272
6:32–33	406
6:33	43, 69, 267, 321, 323
6:33–58	58
6:34	268
6:35	72, 200, 267, 268, 270, 318, 323, 333, 382
6:35b	267
6:35c	269
6:37	107, 200, 316, 317, 318
6:37–45	395
6:38	111, 152, 213
6:38–39	345
6:38–40	264
6:39	44, 152, 315, 316, 388
6:39–40	283
6:40	63, 199, 213, 322, 323, 333, 354, 388, 393
6:41	72, 110, 233
6:42	109, 152, 221, 226, 395

Index of References 527

John (continued)		7:1	60, 232, 233, 238, 247
6:44	213, 264, 315, 316, 317, 320, 323, 337, 345, 388	7:1–9	281
		7:1–13	298
6:45	63, 251, 254, 255, 256, 306	7:2	131, 239, 242, 366
		7:3	214
6:45b	317	7:4	85, 344, 402
6:45–46	212	7:5	356
6:46	368, 386	7:7	62, 248, 316, 322, 397, 398, 399, 404
6:47	200, 250, 318		
6:47–48	333	7:8	56
6:48	72, 270	7:9	322
6:49	268, 270	7:10	238, 282, 366, 402
6:50	270, 322, 324	7:10–10:39	396
6:50–51	333	7:11	242, 344, 387
6:50–60	369	7:11–13	241
6:51	110, 200, 270, 318, 321, 322, 323, 382	7:12	221, 242, 264, 387
		7:13	51, 85, 226, 233, 242
6:51–53	191		
6:51–58	90, 282	7:14	131, 366
6:51–59	395	7:15	221, 387
6:51–69	395	7:15–24	261
6:52	226, 233, 247, 264	7:16	152, 263, 264, 344, 345, 370
6:53	113		
6:53–57	385	7:16–18	341
6:53–56	373	7:16–19	366
6:53–58	266, 274	7:17	227, 265, 324, 356
6:54	200, 318, 322, 323, 333, 388	7:18	264, 345, 398, 399, 405
6:55	63	7:19	238, 260, 261, 266, 272
6:57	264, 345		
6:58	106, 212, 268	7:20	152, 366, 387, 404
6:60	63, 90, 225, 226, 264, 306, 369	7:21	214
		7:21–23	264
6:60–66	374	7:22	266, 272
6:61	226	7:23	260, 261, 266, 272
6:61–62	226	7:24	265, 266, 366, 381, 387, 405
6:62	114		
6:63	4, 281, 338, 356, 391	7:25	241, 242
		7:25ff	404
6:64	193, 216, 256, 316, 317	7:25–27	226
		7:25–31	220
6:64–65	316	7:26	51, 85, 242, 243, 303, 344
6:65	320		
6:66	44, 90, 226, 369	7:26f	225
6:68	216, 356	7:26–31	366
6:68–69	225, 227	7:26–41	353
6:69	114, 220, 226, 372, 380	7:27	75, 76, 221, 222
		7:27–28	316, 370
6:70	87, 316, 328	7:27–29	366
6:70–71	328	7:28	152, 213, 263, 264, 366
7	58, 119, 267		
7–9	58	7:28–29	345
7–10	204, 263	7:29	152, 264

John (continued)

7:29–30	366, 404	7:52	75, 76, 143, 226, 231, 286, 325, 367
7:30	226	7:52b	81, 108
7:31	216, 225, 237, 241, 242, 328, 379, 387, 395	7:71	256
		8	242, 267, 321, 393
		8:5	272
7:31ff	404	8:12	55, 61, 69, 72, 102, 103, 130, 200, 263, 267, 269, 270, 282, 300, 318, 320, 321, 323, 324, 325, 333, 355, 366, 368, 371, 374, 382, 384, 385
7:31–32	387		
7:32	226, 241, 242, 243		
7:32–35	85, 336		
7:33	55, 86, 264		
7:33–34	75, 76, 226, 366, 404		
7:33–36	191, 366	8:12–13	242, 366, 404
7:34	104	8:12–30	366, 404
7:34–35	87	8:12–59	24, 366
7:35	86, 166, 169, 247, 387	8:13	241, 242, 264
		8:13–18	366
7:35–36	152	8:14	261, 316, 319, 370, 390
7:37	269, 366, 388		
7:37–38	112, 131, 162, 200, 238, 318, 333, 366, 391, 404	8:14a	340
		8:14–21	103
		8:15	265, 321, 381, 394
7:37–39	226, 269, 282, 366, 383	8:16	213, 264, 345, 387, 390, 394
7:38	216, 254, 260, 267, 270, 294, 357	8:16a	340
		8:17	255, 256, 260, 283, 357, 402
7:38–39	250, 254, 362	8:18	215, 264, 325, 345, 366, 394
7:39	73, 338		
7:40	108, 237, 263, 387	8:18–20	366
7:40ff	404	8:19	263
7:40–43	229, 226	8:20	366
7:40–44	366	8:21	86, 104, 300, 320, 394, 400, 401
7:41	226		
7:41f	225	8:21–22	75, 76, 85, 87, 191, 336
7:41–52	395		
7:42	75, 76, 216, 222, 254, 255, 256, 260, 269, 357	8:22	86, 152, 241, 242, 247, 356
7:43	71, 386, 387	8:22–26	304
7:44	366, 404	8:23	5, 58, 62, 248, 321, 322, 370, 371, 404, 405
7:45	241		
7:45–52	226, 375, 376		
7:47	264	8:24	58, 226, 316, 322, 324, 353, 356, 366, 368, 394, 395, 400
7:47–48	241		
7:47–52	266		
7:48	241, 242, 243	8:24–36	385
7:49	376	8:25	366
7:50	81, 375	8:26	63, 213, 248, 263, 264, 345, 358, 394, 405
7:50c	327		
7:50–52	80, 217		
7:51	50, 81, 238, 243, 260, 265	8:27	193, 334, 346, 405

Index of References

John (continued)		8:47b	370
8:28	54, 84, 96, 114, 226, 263, 276, 278, 281, 353, 356, 366, 391	8:48	131, 232, 233, 234, 241, 242, 387
		8:48–52	233
8:28b	213	8:49	213, 261
8:29	264	8:50	398
8:30	328	8:51	322, 333, 367
8:30–32	405	8:51–53	191
8:30–59	382, 383	8:52	232, 233, 241, 242
8:31	241, 242, 343, 374, 381, 382, 387	8:53	80, 366, 367
		8:53–56	99
8:31a	343	8:55	263
8:31b	343	8:56	212, 249, 298, 367
8:31–32	263, 341, 381	8:56–58	191
8:31–33	191	8:56–59	226
8:31–55	343	8:57	241, 242
8:31–59	191, 209, 250	8:58	103, 152, 212, 221, 366, 374, 404
8:32	63, 319, 343, 384		
8:32–46	343	8:58–59	72
8:34	400	8:59	113, 226, 247, 262, 263, 402
8:35	90, 226, 294		
8:36	213, 354	9	58, 185, 190, 201, 242, 328, 368, 393
8:37	51, 216, 343, 372		
8:37–41	249	9:1	103
8:37–47	250	9:1–4	69
8:38	43, 213, 393	9:2	323
8:39	43, 250, 336	9:3	354
8:39–42	249	9:4	61, 264, 313, 354, 376, 390
8:39–44	250		
8:39–47	250, 320	9:4–5	300, 333
8:39–59	295	9:5	61, 102, 111, 226, 282, 300, 320, 321, 355
8:40	213, 261, 343, 358		
8:40–43	63		
8:40–47	341	9:6	103
8:40–49	261	9:6–7	149
8:41	43, 234, 261	9:7	111, 112, 131, 169
8:41–44	43	9:9	150
8:42	58, 213, 264, 398	9:13	241, 242, 243
8:43	306, 319, 370, 382	9:13–40	241
8:43a	371	9:15	241, 242, 243
8:43b	371	9:16	57, 71, 216, 241, 242, 243, 264, 280, 374, 379, 386, 387
8:43–44	337		
8:43–47	316, 405		
8:44	60, 61, 87, 212, 234, 245, 250, 261, 320, 325, 342	9:17	108, 237, 263, 348
		9:18	242, 300
		9:22	182, 197, 225, 226, 232, 233, 241, 242, 244, 374, 386, 394, 404
8:44–45	372		
8:45–47	63		
8:46	50, 227, 261, 369, 386, 394, 400		
		9:24	353
8:47	58, 90, 306, 316, 319, 333, 337, 362, 370, 372, 403, 409	9:25–35	323, 405
		9:28	272, 326
		9:28–29	264
8:47a	370	9:29	226, 272

John (continued)

9:29–30	316, 370	10:17–18	87, 398
9:32–33	402	10:18	63, 120, 213, 264
9:33	57	10:19	71, 242, 387
9:33–34	381	10:19–21	387
9:34	103	10:19–22	386
9:35	103, 374, 406	10:21	150, 216
9:35–38	368	10:22	150
9:35–39	114	10:22–23	131
9:36	300	10:22–30	88, 374
9:37f	367	10:22–39	393
9:38	103, 225, 226, 227	10:24	51, 62, 85, 225, 242, 333, 353, 366, 367, 393, 403, 404
9:39	50, 63, 103, 154, 213, 299, 300, 306, 313, 353, 354, 367, 385, 386, 394	10:25	214, 215, 333, 354, 366, 367, 404
		10:25–29	226
9:39–41	50, 82, 226	10:26–27	63
9:40	88, 241, 243	10:26	88, 316
9:40–41	227, 325	10:27	316, 337
9:41	248, 316, 325, 385, 390, 400, 401, 402	10:27–29	192
		10:28	44, 316, 322, 333
9:45	324	10:29	315
10	115, 393	10:30	72, 106, 332, 344, 354, 357, 366, 367, 393, 404
10:1	261, 325, 392		
10:1–5	88		
10:1–18	192, 250, 328	10:30–35	221
10:1–21	88	10:30–39	226
10:2	325, 356	10:31	226, 232, 233, 242, 247, 374
10:3	63, 116, 369		
10:3–4	306	10:31–33	262
10:3–5	305, 369	10:31–39	387
10:4	369	10:32	226, 227, 325
10:5	369	10:32–33	214, 306
10:6	85, 88, 193, 334, 402	10:33	115, 170, 223, 232, 233, 242, 264, 393
10:7	68, 72, 325	10:34	254, 255, 256, 260, 393
10:8	115, 261, 325, 328		
10:8–30	354	10:34–35	394
10:9	72, 200, 318, 355	10:34–36	265, 394
10:9–11	333	10:34–38	226
10:10	200, 261, 322, 323, 324, 328, 354, 384, 392, 393, 400	10:35	216, 260, 357
		10:35–36	295
		10:36	113, 115, 170, 213, 223, 264, 357, 385
10:11	354, 355, 398		
10:11ff	110	10:37–38	214, 400
10:12	270	10:37–39a	306
10:13–16	385	10:38	164
10:14	329, 354, 376	10:41–42	387
10:14–15	369	10:42	237, 328
10:14–16	316	11:1–44	69
10:14–17	192	11:1–54	396
10:15	329, 376, 398	11:4	307
10:16	159, 166, 169, 237, 251, 390, 397	11:7	239
		11:8	232, 233

John (continued)		12:1–43	309
11:9	55, 300, 396	12:3–7	309
11:9–10	300, 316, 317	12:4–6	328
11:10	61, 376	12:6	51, 328
11:11	88	12:7	274
11:11–14	88	12:9	367
11:12	88	12:11	237, 328
11:12–24	68	12:12	117
11:13	88, 338	12:12–13	117, 310
11:14	51, 85, 150	12:12–19	240
11:16	75, 76, 152	12:12–20:31	396
11:18	131	12:13	100, 114, 117, 224, 254, 255, 262, 309, 310, 354
11:19	61		
11:23	57		
11:23ff	69	12:13–15	277
11:24	388	12:14	117, 255, 256
11:25	292, 318, 322, 323, 324, 355, 384	12:14–15	254, 277, 297
		12:15	251, 360
11:25–26	88, 200, 322, 324, 333	12:16	193, 255, 256, 334, 341, 383
11:26	318, 322	12:19	75, 76, 241, 321
11:27	170, 225, 226, 227	12:20–21	117
11:31	150	12:20–22	169
11:34	367	12:21	367
11:36	75, 76, 208	12:23	96, 281, 388
11:40	307, 367, 368	12:24–25	90
11:42	263, 264	12:24–26	375
11:43	263, 264	12:25	44, 398
11:43f	263	12:25a	322, 404
11:44	263, 264	12:25–26	322
11:45	237, 328	12:26	104, 381
11:45–46	387	12:27	388
11:46	241	12:28	213, 354, 391
11:47	241, 242, 243, 379	12:31	96, 208, 248, 281, 320, 321, 385, 386, 387, 394, 397
11:47–12:8	272, 274		
11:47–52	264		
11:47–57	243	12:31–36	402
11:48	80	12:32	54, 83, 84, 169, 173, 276, 396
11:49	79		
11:49–50	399	12:32–33	402
11:49–52	43, 79, 83	12:33	84
11:50	44	12:34	54, 96, 114, 220, 225, 257, 258, 260, 281, 300, 390, 391, 404
11:51	80		
11:51–52	81, 193		
11:52	60, 80, 166, 397		
11:54	51, 60, 85	12:35	49, 61, 130, 300, 320, 324
11:55	239, 274		
11:55–57	396	12:35–36	200, 299, 318, 402
11:57	241	12:35–36a	320
11:57	241, 242, 243	12:35–40	405
12	328	12:36	60, 61, 113, 269, 330, 333, 394, 396, 402, 406
12:1	274		
12:1–8	116, 274		
12:1–11	396	12:36a	320

John (continued)

12:37	227, 298, 306, 313, 315, 325, 374, 379, 380, 402	13–17	207, 214, 232, 272, 274, 275, 373
		13–19	275
		13–20	297
12:37–38	374, 402	13–21	163
12:37–40	334	13:1	55, 59, 119, 218, 272, 274, 345, 388, 391, 398
12:37–41	193, 295, 299, 312, 337		
12:37–43	320	13:2	87, 165, 328
12:38	254, 255, 256, 277, 297, 302, 306, 308, 313, 318, 344, 345	13:3	345
		13:5–10	69
		13:7	383
12:38–19:37	255, 257	13:11	193, 256
12:38–40	255, 277, 278	13:12–17	218
12:38–41	307	13:16	329, 345, 380
12:39	254, 255, 256, 312, 313, 374	13:18	58, 216, 251, 254, 255, 256, 295, 328, 334, 357
12:39–40	277, 313, 316		
12:39–41	254, 316, 317	13:19	72, 356, 373
12:40	83, 251, 254, 299, 302, 303, 305, 306, 312, 313, 317, 319, 323, 324	13:20	264, 345
		13:21–30	328
		13:21–31	328
		13:23	338
12:40–41	254	13:23–25	216
12:41	254, 280, 298, 309, 313, 328, 367, 368	13:23–26	216
		13:24	382
12:41–42	303	13:26	70
12:42	166, 182, 237, 241, 242, 243, 328, 373, 374, 375, 394, 398	13:27	87, 165, 283
		13:28	334
		13:28–30	193
12:42–43	217, 323, 327, 365, 375, 377, 399, 405	13:30	55, 69, 216, 376
		13:31	280
12:43	45, 325, 328, 329, 330, 374, 398, 399	13:33	55, 85, 86, 87, 300, 336
12:44	264, 318, 353, 354	13:34	371, 398
12:44–45	345	13:34–35	218
12:44–50	226, 320, 329	13:35	192, 199, 219, 397, 398
12:45	61, 117, 264, 310, 353, 367, 386, 402		
		13:36	56, 57, 300
12:45–47	63	13:36–37	85, 86, 336
12:46	61, 169, 172, 200, 213, 318, 320, 324, 333, 382, 385, 400, 402	13:37	75, 76
		13:38	152, 283, 394
		14–17	211
		14:1	43
12:46–47	200, 321, 323, 324	14:1–3	87
12:47	169, 306, 318, 385, 386, 392, 394, 396, 400	14:1–10	87
		14:2	284
		14:3	104, 322
12:47–48	385	14:4	87, 300, 356, 402
12:48	307, 346, 349, 384, 386, 388, 394	14:5	86, 300
		14:6	58, 63, 69, 82, 83, 87, 319, 322, 323, 341, 343, 344, 349, 355, 384, 405
12:48–50	263		
12:49	264, 345, 353		

John (continued)

14:7	63, 372
14:7–14	344
14:8	344
14:8–9	295
14:9	63, 101, 281, 332, 344, 353, 354, 367, 368, 386
14:10	214, 354, 356, 370
14:10b	382
14:11	214, 400
14:12	345, 346
14:12–21	329
14:13	354
14:14	333, 354
14:15–17	358
14:16	340, 394
14:16–17	338, 395
14:17	63, 130, 248, 321, 340, 341, 395, 396, 397
14:18–20	85, 336
14:19	367
14:19f	380
14:20	383
14:22–24	396, 397
14:23	199, 329, 397
14:24	344, 345, 356, 358
14:25	78
14:25–26	358, 391, 395
14:26	336, 338, 341, 343, 354, 359, 360, 394, 395
14:27	116, 384
14:28	85, 336, 345
14:30	248, 320, 321, 385
14:33	397
15	105, 381
15:1	63, 250
15:1–2	213
15:1–3	154
15:1–4	382
15:1–6	374, 381
15:1–8	381
15:1–12	51, 73
15:1–17	382
15:1–21	381
15:2	51, 74
15:3	349
15:4	358
15:4–5	382
15:4–7	382
15:5	355
15:6	329, 382
15:8	382, 383
15:9	352, 398
15:9–10	382
15:12	371, 398
15:13	218, 352
15:13–15	218
15:14	398
15:15	63, 345
15:16	354
15:16–19	192
15:16–20	192
15:17	398
15:18	43
15:18–19	248, 316, 321, 396
15:18–20	375, 405
15:18–25	340
15:18–16:4	215, 232, 380
15:19	5, 208, 322, 397, 399, 404
15:19–20	56
15:19–27	217
15:20	323, 329, 380, 384, 399
15:22	50, 214, 227, 325, 390, 400, 402
15:22–23	396
15:22–24	353, 401, 402
15:24	227, 325, 354, 400, 402
15:25	238, 251, 254, 255, 256, 260, 315
15:26	130, 215, 338, 340, 341, 394, 395
15:26–27	340, 358, 391
15:27	215
16	88
16:1ff	381
16:1–4	207, 329, 340, 375
16:2	56, 182, 244, 323, 384, 386, 405
16:3	401
16:4b–15	85, 358
16:5	85, 300, 336, 345
16:7	269, 391, 394
16:7–14	338
16:7–15	395
16:8	50, 248, 321, 386, 394, 400
16:8–9	400, 401
16:8–11	199, 340, 397
16:8–15	215
16:9	400
16:10	345

John (continued)

16:11	320, 321, 385, 386, 394	17:11	55, 72, 231, 320, 354, 397
16:12	356	17:11–26	383
16:12–15	391	17:12	44, 58, 170, 216, 254, 255, 256, 354, 357
16:13	56, 130, 338, 340, 341, 344, 358, 359, 360, 395	17:13	112
16:13b	341	17:14	5, 207, 248, 321, 396
16:13–15	49, 269, 336, 359, 395	17:14–16	208, 397, 399
		17:15	199, 217, 320, 397
16:14	340, 341, 344	17:16	5, 321
16:15	344	17:17	343, 345
16:16	85, 317, 336, 367	17:18	5, 199, 217, 397, 399
16:17	345		
16:17–18	86, 152	17:18–23	199, 397
16:19	150, 367	17:19	55, 343
16:19–24	86	17:20	217, 396
16:20	248, 323, 397	17:20–21	159
16:21–22	90	17:20–23	55, 219
16:22	96, 268	17:21	353, 397, 399
16:23	354	17:21–23	55, 169
16:24	354	17:22	55, 72, 367
16:25	51, 85, 86, 336, 344, 359, 398	17:23	397, 399
		17:24	55, 63, 104, 367, 396
16:26	354		
16:27–28	393	17:25	55, 321, 345
16:28	5, 86, 172, 213, 345, 385, 391, 396	17:26	55, 354
		18	232, 393
16:29	51, 85, 86	18–19	118
16:29–30	152	18:2–6	328
16:30	86	18:3	82, 241, 243
16:32	388	18:4	268
16:33	199, 248, 320, 321, 373, 384, 385, 397	18:5	83
		18:6	369
17	55, 56, 107	18:8	72
17:1	55, 388	18:9	193, 255, 256, 265
17:2	173, 315, 317, 322, 396	18:12	242, 244
		18:14	242, 244
17:3	312, 323, 345, 353, 372, 385	18:17	283
		18:20	51, 85, 366, 404
17:4	49, 55, 59, 119, 213, 214, 279, 313, 354, 379, 390, 391	18:23	215
		18:24	231
		18:25	394
17:4–5	391	18:25–27	283
17:5	55, 367, 396	18:26	208, 215
17:6	55, 316, 317, 321, 353, 354, 396, 397, 399	18:27	394
		18:28	82, 117, 231, 276, 277, 310
17:6–26	192	18:28–19:15	81
17:7–26	192	18:29	394
17:8	353, 356	18:30–38	366, 404
17:9	316, 321, 397	18:31	75, 76, 239, 242, 260
17:10	55, 383		

John (continued)			277, 278, 283, 357, 391
18:32	84, 193, 255, 256		
18:33	240	19:28–29	256
18:35	247	19:28–30	278
18:35–36	87	19:29	150, 272, 278, 279
18:36	242, 321, 363, 389	19:30	59, 119, 278, 283, 334, 390, 391
18:36–37	5		
18:37	63, 130, 213, 316, 317, 319, 333, 343, 345, 363, 390, 397, 409	19:31	57, 239, 272, 275, 276, 277, 279
		19:32–33	162
		19:32–34	277
18:37b	369	19:34	70, 98, 279
18:37–38	57	19:35	163, 164, 193, 216, 277, 279
18:38	82, 216, 242, 341, 370, 394		
		19:35–37	63
18:39	240, 276	19:36	58, 97, 98, 193, 238, 251, 254, 255, 256, 277, 334, 357
18:39–40	216		
19	232		
19:1	118	19:36–37	216, 255, 272, 275, 277
19:3	240, 275		
19:4	216, 394	19:37	251, 254, 255, 256, 275, 277, 357
19:5	75, 76		
19:6	57, 216, 247, 394	19:38	226, 242, 279, 375, 384
19:7	115, 170, 223, 226, 232, 233, 239, 242, 248, 250, 264		
		19:38–20:14	264
		19:38–39	375
19:9	316, 394	19:38–42	327, 377
19:10–14	105	19:40	165, 169, 239
19:11	48, 86, 400, 402	19:41	120
19:12	45, 216, 242	19:42	239, 272, 275, 276, 277
19:13	45, 81, 131, 165, 169, 394		
		20:2	338
19:13–42	272, 275	20:2–10	216
19:14	75, 76, 118, 216, 242, 272, 276, 277, 391	20:3	233
		20:6	367
		20:8	63
19:15	99, 110, 247, 248, 265, 323, 384	20:9	193, 216, 334, 367, 383, 390
19:17	118, 131, 165, 169, 295	20:11–12	71
		20:12	367
19:19	109, 240	20:14	317, 367, 369
19:19ff	75, 76	20:15	120
19:19–22	216, 256	20:16	131, 169, 317
19:20	82	20:17	345
19:21	240, 242, 247	20:19	232, 242
19:24	58, 216, 254, 255, 256, 277, 334, 357	20:19–26	384
		20:21	199, 391
19:24–25	162	20:21–22	361, 362
19:25–27	71, 216	20:21–23	264
19:26	338	20:22	52, 361, 391
19:26–27	216, 283	20:23	391
19:28	58, 59, 118, 119, 216, 251, 254, 255, 256,	20:24	169
		20:24–29	378
		20:25	63, 367

John (continued)		7:54–60	215
20:27–29	367	8:1–3	189
20:28	225, 226, 227, 362, 380	8:30–35	311
		8:31–35	357
20:29	63	8:32	74, 231, 272
20:29b	378	8:35	231
20:30	162, 315, 379	9:1–2	189
20:30–31	63, 94, 161, 162, 163, 228, 393, 396	9:23	233
		10:36	384
20:31	21, 45, 101, 111, 122, 162, 163, 164, 169, 170, 174, 213, 214, 216, 225, 226, 227, 323, 333, 354, 372, 408	10:43	290, 291, 293, 310
		13:13–41	115, 223
		13:27	297
		13:35	277
		13:38–52	299
		13:45	233
21	391, 396	13:46ff	315
21:1–14	71, 105	13:50	233
21:5	396	17:2	231
21:7	216, 338	17:5	233
21:11	71, 105	18:6	315
21:12	233	18:12	233
21:15	45	18:14	233
21:15–19	283	19:1ff	210
21:18–19	232	20:19	233
21:19	383	20:22–24	215
21:20	216, 317, 338	20:28	271
21:20–22	56	23:3	266
21:20–24	216	25:10	233
21:22	44	25:25	49
21:23	44	26:2	233
21:24	216, 227	26:16–18	215
21:24–25	396	26:21	233
21:25	379	28:19	233
		28:23–28	299
Acts		28:24–28	322
1:8	174	28:25–28	300, 303
1:16	231, 357	28:26–27	315
1:20	357	28:27	299
2:14–17	291, 293	28:28	315
2:14–36	115, 223		
2:14–40	214	Romans	
2:16	258, 285	1:2	231
2:16ff	338	1:3f	224, 262
2:17	388	2:12	321
2:33	84	2:19	296
2:40	341	2:28–29	250
3:13–26	357	3:1–11:36	357
4:11	357	3:9–18	321
4:18–21	215	3:20	268
4:23–37	207	3:21–25	268
4:29–31	215	3:23	321
5:30	84	3:25	271
7:1–53	357	3:29	251
7:51	298	4:3	268

Romans (continued)

4:23f	292, 358
5:1	384
5:8	352
5:9	271
5:12	321
6:6	319
6:23	270
7:7	268
8:3	268, 270, 271
8:7	319, 337, 404
8:7–8	405
8:8	404
9–11	314, 385
9:3	235
9:15	313
10:4a	235
10:8	358
10:9	224
10:16	299, 306
11:7	296, 299, 303, 304, 305
11:7–10	207, 299
11:25	303, 304
11:25–26	305
12:2	207, 218
12:14	398
13:1–2	87
15:4	292, 357
15:9–12	277

1 Corinthians

1:1–3	385, 396
1:1–5	215
1:5	385
1:5–7	208
1:6	382
1:6–7	382
1:7	271
1:8	402
1:10	321
1:18	337, 385
1:18–24	374
1:18–30	207
1:23–24	385
1:24	292, 348, 358
1:30	292, 358
2:1	340, 394
2:2	271, 396, 400
2:6	218, 382
2:6–7	292, 358
2:6–8	207
2:7	227
2:7–8	227
2:8	130
2:8–11	300
2:9–10	208
2:10	382, 395
2:11	299, 300, 319, 320
2:12–14	227
2:14	319, 331, 333, 337, 366, 404, 405
2:15	397
2:15–16	397
2:15–17	218, 399
2:16	208
2:18	328, 388
2:19	328
2:21	227
2:22	225, 226, 228, 328, 372, 385
2:22–23	226, 228
2:22–24	401
2:24	227
2:24–27	385
2:25	227
2:26	226, 227, 228
2:26–27	328
2:27	227, 382
2:27–28	382
3:1	192, 375, 396
3:2	367
3:3	319
3:6	382
3:7	227, 328, 372
3:8	372
3:9	382
3:10	372
3:11	398
3:12	371
3:13	375, 396
3:13–14	207
3:14	382
3:15	371, 382
3:16	218
3:16	218, 352
3:17	382
3:20	277
3:23	398
4:1	226
4:2	226, 228, 328, 352, 385
4:3	226, 328, 385
4:4–5	385
4:4–6	192
4:5	393
4:6	63, 130, 340
4:6c	227

1 Corinthians (continued)

Ref	Pages
4:9	396, 400
4:9–10	352, 354, 385
4:10	271
4:11–12	218
4:12–13	382
4:13	382
4:14	385
4:14–15	226, 353
4:15	385
4:15–16	382
4:16	382, 385
4:17	208
4:20	398
5:1	226, 228, 385
5:4	373
5:5	226, 385
5:6	343, 352
5:6–8	271
5:7	74, 273
5:7–8	283
5:9–10	260
5:9–12	385
5:10–12	333, 404, 405
5:13	227, 228, 385
6:9–10	398, 400
7:31–34	207
8:6	292, 358
9:10	292, 358
9:24	49
10:3–4	274
10:4	98, 294
10:11	291, 292, 358
10:32	189
11:32	207
14:3	341
15:3	231
15:4	231

2 Corinthians

Ref	Pages
1:20	290, 292, 358
3:12–18	292, 358
3:14	292, 296, 299, 303, 305
3:15	305
4:3–4	305
4:4	207, 305, 319
4:7	353
5:16	381
5:17	362, 404
5:21	49, 119, 311
6:2	291
6:14	393
8:9	198
12:2–4	357
13:1	283

Galatians

Ref	Pages
1:4	207
2:20	404, 405
3:28	250
4:3	207
4:4	198, 357
5:16–25	207
6:14	207
6:15	362

Ephesians

Ref	Pages
1:4–23	316
1:7	271
1:10	357
1:23	357
2:2	207
2:3	404, 405
2:5–8	316
2:10	362, 404
2:13	271
2:14–18	384
3:11	348
3:18	49
4:18	303, 304
4:22	319
4:22–24	362
4:24	404, 405
5:2	270
5:11	50, 386
5:13	50

Philippians

Ref	Pages
1:29	207
2:6–11	198
2:7	311
2:9	84
2:15	192
3:12a	49

Colossians

Ref	Pages
1:15	353
1:15–18	292, 358
1:15–21	198
1:20	271
1:27	333, 404, 405
2:2–3	348
2:3	292, 358
3:9	319
3:10	362
3:16	346, 349

1 Thessalonians
2:16	55
5:4	49

2 Thessalonians
3:1	346, 349

1 Timothy
6:16	393

2 Timothy
1:10	393
2:2	361
2:9	346, 349
3:1–10	388

Titus
2:5	346, 349
2:12	207
2:14	192, 271
3:3–7	363
3:5	363

Hebrews
1	198
1:1–2	356, 357
1:2	291, 388
1:3	353
1:5–13	277
1:18–9	117
2:13	277
2:17	271
4:5	277
4:12–13	346, 349
5:6	277
7:2	384
7:27	270
9:9–10	271
9:11ff	271
9:14	271
9:19–22	279
9:26	270, 271, 291
9:28	270
9:29	271
10:1	271
10:10	270
10:28	283
10:30	277
13:12	271
13:20	116, 271

James
1:1	235
1:18	363

1 Peter
1:2	271
1:3	362
1:5	291, 388
1:5–10	357
1:9	74, 291
1:10–12	291
1:18–19	273
1:19	271, 272
1:20	388
1:23	346, 349, 362
1:23–25	404, 405
2:2	362
2:6	357
2:9	192
2:24	48, 272
2:24–25	311
2:25	116
5:4	116

2 Peter
1:4	404, 405
3:3	388

1 John
1:1–3	385, 396
1:1–5	215
1:5	385
1:5–7	208
1:6	382
1:6–7	382
1:7	271
1:8	402
1:10	321
2:1	340, 394
2:2	271, 396, 400
2:6	218, 382
2:7	227
2:7–8	227
2:8	130
2:8–11	300
2:9–10	208
2:10	382, 395
2:11	299, 300, 319, 320
2:12–14	227
2:15	397
2:15–16	397
2:15–17	218, 399
2:16	208
2:18	328, 388
2:19	328
2:21	227
2:22	225, 226, 228, 328, 372, 385

1 John (continued)

2:22–23	226, 228
2:22–24	401
2:24	227
2:24–27	385
2:25	227
2:26	226, 227, 228
2:26–27	328
2:27	227, 382
2:27–28	382
3:1	192, 375, 396
3:2	367
3:6	382
3:7	227, 328, 372
3:8	372
3:9	382
3:10	372
3:11	398
3:12	371
3:13	375, 396
3:13–14	207
3:14	382
3:15	371, 382
3:16	218
3:16	218, 352
3:17	382
3:23	398
4:1	226
4:2	226, 228, 328, 352, 385
4:3	226, 328, 385
4:4–5	385
4:4–6	192
4:6	63, 130, 340
4:6c	227
4:9	396, 400
4:9–10	352, 354, 385
4:10	271
4:11–12	218
4:12–13	382
4:13	382
4:14	385
4:14–15	226, 353
4:15	385
4:15–16	382
4:16	382, 385
4:17	208
4:20	398
5:1	226, 228, 385
5:4	373
5:5	226, 385
5:6	343, 352
5:6–8	271
5:7–8	283
5:9–10	260
5:9–12	385
5:10–12	333, 404, 405
5:13	227, 228, 385

2 John

3	63
5	227
7	226, 227, 228, 328, 385
7–8	226
7–11	228
9	401
9a	385
10–11	226

3 John

9–10	228

Revelation

1:5	271
1:7	278
1:10	370
1:12–16	370
1:19–20	370
2:6	171
2:7	369
2:9	250
2:9–10	160
2:11	369
2:12	384
2:15	171
2:16	384
2:17	269, 369
2:29	369
3:6	369
3:9	189, 250
3:13	369
3:17	299
3:22	369
5:6–12	310
5:9	271
6:4	384
6:16	310
7:14	271
12:11	271
13:8	310
14:1	310
14:15	392
16	110
17:14	310
19:7–9	106
19:13	271

4. OT Pseudepigrapha

Apocalypse of Abraham
1–32	249
18:14	370
19:1	370
22–23	313
25	183

Apocalypse of Ezra
2:17	313

Apocalypse of Moses
35–36	393

Ascension of Isaiah
7ff	345

2 Baruch
4:1–7	345
4:3	345
6	345
8:1–5	113, 184
10:18	183
13:9–10	184
14:5–7	184
14:6–7	178
14:7	183
15:7–8	184
17:4	267
18:2	267
27:6	384
29:3	403
29:8	269
36:1ff	345
36:53	345
39–42	179
39:7	403
40:1	384
46:7	345
46:76	345
53	345
54:5	267
59:3–12	345
63	179
70:3	384
70:7	384
73:1	403
76	345
77:8–10	184
78:5	184
78:15–16	267
79:1–4	184
82	179

3 Baruch
2:1ff	345

4 Baruch
1:1	183
1:6–8	184
1:8	183
3:4	184
4:1–3	184
4:7–8	183
9:3	267

1 Enoch
14:2	345
14:8ff	345
14:15ff	393
15:1	370
21:5	343
39:3	345
42	348
48:6–7	403
49:2	313
49:3	345
56:7	384
62:7	403
62:12	384
63:11	384
70:3	345
70:7	384
71:11	345
89:12–90:41	116
90:19	384
91:11–12	384
99:5	384
100:1–2	384
105:2	170, 224, 262

2 Enoch
49:2	313

4 Ezra (2 Esdras)
3:20–27	178
3:28–36	178
4:10–11	371
4:13	345
4:30	178
5:9	384
6:24	384
6:57	178
7:28	403
7:28–29	170, 224, 262
7:49	178
7:[62]–[72]	178
10:21	371

4 Ezra (continued)		*Testament of Abraham*	
11–13	179	10	345
12:32	403		
13:26	403	*Testament of Moses*	
13:32	403	2:8–9	183
13:52	170, 222, 224, 262, 403	5:3–4	183
		6:1	183
14:3–6	345		
14:9	170, 224, 262, 403	*Testaments of the 12 Patriarchs*	
Jubilees		T. Simeon	
1:20–21	183	2:7	305
1:24–25	170		
9:15	384	T. Levi	
11:4–6	183	2:5ff	345
23:16	384	14:4	266
23:19	384	16:3–5	113
33:20	239	19:1	266
Life of Adam and Eve		T. Judah	
25–29	345	11:1	305
35–36	393	18:3	305
		18:6	300, 305
Lives of the Prophets		19:4	305
12:10-13	267	25:3	183
Martyrdom of Isaiah		T. Zebulon	
4:1	183	9:8	183
Psalms of Solomon		T. Dan	
2:1–3	183	2:4	305
2:16	183		
14:5	239	T. Gad	
15:8 (7)	384	3:3	305
		4:7	183
Pseudo-Philo, Biblical Antiquities			
9:8	266	T. Asher	
11:1	266	1:8–9	183
22:3	266		
28:3	267	T. Benjamin	
39:4–6	178	7–8	371
51:4–7	267		

5. Qumran and Related Literature

Sibylline Oracles		*Thanksgiving Hymns (1QH)*	
3:49	269	1:7–8	314
3:63–74	183	1:19	314
3:702–13	178	3:20f	345
3:755–808	178	3:21	339, 360
3:797–99	384	4:10	360
4	183	4:10	339
4:174	384	4:20–22	339, 360
5:238f	267		

Index of References

Thanksgiving Hymns (continued)
5:11f	339, 360
7:26–7	343
11:10f	345
12:11f	339
13:18f	339, 360
14:25–27	339, 360
15:17	314
16:10–12	339, 360

Pesher Habakkuk (1QpHab)
2:8–9	289
7:1ff	339, 360
8:1–3	289

War Scroll (1QM)
all cols.	200
1:1ff	386
7:7ff	314
10:1–8	301
10:8ff	345
13:12	386

Community Rule (1QS)
1:6	304
1:9	386
2:2–4	301
2:14	304
2:16	386
3:3	304
3:7	130
3:13	130, 386
3:13–4:25	200, 397
3:13–4:26	130, 314, 385
3:17–4:26	338, 360
3:18	131
3:18–19	130, 341
3:20–21	386
3:21	130
3:21–24	183
3:24	130
3:24f	386
3:25	130
4:2–6	339
4:4	130
4:5	130
4:6	343
4:11	130, 299, 304
4:11ff	386
4:12	341
4:21	130, 131, 268
4:23	130, 131
5:4	304
5:23	134
6:3	134
6:7	134
6:14	134
6:24	143, 287
8:1	134
8:6	130
8:15	143, 287
8:15–6	134
8:26	143, 287
9:12–14:20	134
9:21	200, 397
9:22	339
11:6ff	345

Community Rule, Appendix A (1QSa = 1Q28a)
2:11ff	170

Isaiah Scroll (1QIsa^a)
all cols.	301

Damascus Document (CD)
1–4	134
1:9	299
3:16	267
6:4	267
6:7	143, 287
7:15–19	301
10:4–6	134
12:2–3	183
13:2ff	134
14:7	134
16:2	305
19:33–34	130
19:34	267

Blessing of Jacob (4QPBless = CommGen A = 4Q252)
all cols.	100

Florilegium (4QFlor = 4Q174)
all cols.	100, 301
1:11–12	170
1:14	143, 287

Pesher Isaiah (4QpIsa = 4Q161–165)
8–10	100

Mysteries (4QMyst^a = 4Q299)
6	130

Testimonia (4QTest = 4Q175)
9–20	301

4QpsDan^b ar (= 4Q244)
all cols. 384

4QSU
40:24 345

6. Philo

De Abrahamo
171 118

De cherubim
87 399

In Flaccum
239

Legatio ad Gaium
239

Legum allegoriae
1.5–6 399
3.226 33
3.231 33

De vita Mosis
1.158 345

Quaestiones in Genesin
1.21 305
1.40 305
1.59 372

Quaestiones in Exodum
2.29 345
2.40 345
2.46 345

De somniis
2.3–4 33
2.64 74

De specialibus legibus
1.200 33

7. Josephus

Jewish War
2.8.1 §118 248, 370
4.3.2 §128 to
  4.7.2 §458 189
4.6.2–3
  §398–418 189
4.7.3 §459–475 189
5.8.4 §376ff 183
5.8.4 §402 183
5.8.4 §412 113, 183, 184
6.5.3 §288ff 113, 184
6.5.3 §297–300 113, 184
7.10.1 §410–418 248, 370

Antiquities
1.2.1 §53 372
3.4.7 §96 345
4 §8 345
4 §49 345
13.5.9 §171–173 313
13.9.1 §254–258 284
18.1.2–6 §11–25 313
18.1.6 §23–25 248, 370

Life
5 §21 242

8. Targumim

Tg. Pseudo-Jonathan

Genesis
4:7 371
4:8 372

Isaiah
52:13–53:12 116, 309

Micah
4:8 222

Tg. Hagiagrapha

Songs of Songs
4:15 112

9. Mishnah

Aboth
4:11 340

Kethuboth
2:9 264

Rosh Ha-Shanah
3:1 264

Sanhedrin		13. Midrash Rabbah	
11:3	326		
		Genesis	
Shabbath		3:4	267
19:1	266	37:7	338
		56:4	118
Yebamoth		59:5	267
4:13	234	65	376

		Exodus	
10. Tosephta		30:8	348
		32:1	338
Sotah			
12:5	338	*Numbers*	
13:2–4	338	15:10	338
		15:25	338
Menah			
13:22	183	*Qohelet*	
		5:11	99
		12:7 [end]	338

11. Babylonian Talmud		*Song of Songs*	
		8:9:3	338
Baba Bathra			
12a	338		

14. Other Rabbinic or Jewish Works

Makkoth			
5b	341	*Eighteen Benedictions*	
		12	182, 186-188
Sanhedrin			
11a	338	*Mekhilta on Exodus*	
39b	113, 184	13:12–17	265
43a	264	15:32	376
93b	251	16:25	269

Sotah		*Pesiqta Rabbati*	
48b	338	1:2	338

Yoma		*Sifre Deuteronomy*	
9b	338	45	371
21b	338		
39b	113, 184		

15. Greek or Roman Authors

12. Jerusalem Talmud			
		Aristotle	
Sotah		*Art of Rhetoric*	
9:14 [24b 23-25]	338	3.1.3.1	145
		3.1.3.32–33	145
Taanith		3.1.3.344–45	145
2:1 [65a 60ff]	338	3.3.1.3	145

De Sophisticis Elenchis
165ff   38

Cornutus
De Natura Rerum
28.1	33
32.14	33
62.11	33
76.4–5	33

Corpus Hermeticum
Poimandres
1.4	385

Demetrius
On Style
3.1.128–129	155
3.1.170–171	155
3.1.176–177	155
15.1.9	155

Homer
Iliad
16.228	74

Maximus of Tyre
Diss.
4.5a	33

Plato
Phaedo
114c	74

Plutarch
Pyth.
407b	33

Porphyry
De Styge ap. Stab. Ecl.
2.1.19	33

Quintilian
De Institutio Oratoria
3.4.10	325

Tacitus
Histories
5.13	113, 184

Trypho
Rhetores Graeci
3.193.14	33–34

Xenophon
Oeconomicus
18.6	74
20.11	74

16. Apostolic Fathers

Barnabas
6.13	384
7.3	118

1 Clement
4.1–7	371

2 Clement
2.4	277

Hermas, *Visions*
5.1.3ff	116

Ignatius
Ephesians
7	228

Philadelphians
6	171

Smyrnaeans
2	228
2–5	171

Trallians
9–10	228

Polycarp, *Philippians*
2	228

17. Nag Hammadi Texts (NHC)

Apocalypse of James
V. 34	386

Apocalypse of Peter
II. 73.12–13	300
II. 76.21–23	300

Apocryphon of John
II. 22.26–28	299, 313

Gospel of Thomas
62	400
107	116

Gospel of Truth
I. 29.26–30.16	300
I. 31.35–32.30	116

Tripartite Tractate
   I. 51.1–8   386

18. Patristic Literature

Chrysostom
in Joh. Hom.
   85.1   118
   88.2   161

Clement of Alexandria
Stromateis
   5.6.34   353
   6.16   399

Epiphanius
Adversus Haereses
   28.1   228
   33.3.6   126

Eusebius
Historia Ecclesiastica
   2.23.8–10   167, 220
   3.36–39   23
   5.20.5–6   23
   6.14.7   1, 23, 161

Irenaeus
Adversus Haereses
   1.8.5   126
   1.26.1   228, 352
   3.14.1   209

Justin Martyr
Apology
   1.32.8–18   167
   1.61.4–5   167

Dialogue with Trypho
   8.4   222
   12.2   299
   16   188
   16.2–3   113, 184
   29   399
   33.1   299
   35   188
   47   188
   89.1   251
   90.1   222, 251
   93   188
   96   188
   108   188

   108.1–3   113, 184
   110.1   222
   123   188
   133   188

Origen
Contra Celsum
   2.9   251
   2.35   251
   2.68   251
   6.10   251
   6.34   251
   6.36   251
   6.42   33

Comm. Joh.
   32.20   161

Theodore of Mopsuestia
Comm. Joh.
   3.16–4.8   161

Index of Authors

Figures in *italics* indicate that the author is cited only in the *notes* on that page.

Aalen, S.	*61*	Aune, D. E.	*350*
Abbott, E. A.	2, *44*, 147	Ayala, M.	2
Abbott, L.	*12*		
Abraham, W. J.	*347*	Baasland, E.	202
Abrams, M. H.	*37*, *76*, *91*	Bacon, B. W.	70, *125*
Achtemeier, P. J.	*301*	Bailey, D. P.	271
Ackerman, J. S.	*143*	Bailey, J. A.	214
Ackroyd, P. R.	71, *123*, *124*	Baillie, J.	*347*
Adcock, F. E.	*123*	Baker, A. E.	6
Aland, B.	*127*	Bal, M.	*14*
Albright, W. F.	*131*, *132*	Baldensperger, W.	*351*, *387*
Alden, R. L.	*150*	Balentine, S. E.	*353*, *401*
Alexander, P. S.	132–33, *158*, 186, 187, *238*, 289	Ball, C. J.	140
		Ball, D. M.	*354*
Allegro, J. M.	*100*	Balthasar, H. U. von	*352*, *357*, *368*, *381*
Allen, R.	236	Baltz, F. W.	23
Allis, O. T.	141	Bammel, E.	243, 247
Alon, G.	246	Bampfylde, G. D.	*139*
Alston, W.	67	Bar-Efrat, S.	46, 77, 79, 83, *151*, 154
Alter, R.	8, 26, 73, 75, 91, 102, *151*, *152*		
		Barclay, J. M. G.	202
Amante, J. D.	*146*	Barlow, J. R.	*61*
Amsler, S.	*251*	Baron, D.	225
Anderson, B. W.	215	Barr, J.	14, 39, 205, *347*
Anderson, H.	*352*	Barrett, C. K.	2, 6, 7, 8, 9, *13*, 22, 23, 24, 42, 44, 45, 46, 48, 50, 51, 52, 55, 56, 57, 59, 63, 69, 71, 74, 75, 80, 81, 82, 84, 87, 100, 101, 105, 107, 108, 114, 118, 120, 125, 132, 137, 142, *146*, 149, 163, 164, 169, 172, 173, *182*, 185, 199, 214, 220, 246, 248, 249, 251, 256, 262, 265, 266, 273,
Anderson, P. N.	334		
Apresjan, J. D.	47		
Arendt, H.	233		
Arichea, D. D.	373		
Arrington, M.	138, *311*		
Ashton, J.	11, 12, 13, 14, 24, 27, 28, 45, 50, 81, 93, *125*, 131, 142, 171, 175, 177, 180, 185, 192, 193, 210, 232, 238, 239, 240, 247, 248, 252, *348*, *353*, *393*		

	276, 279, 281, *300*, *302*, *306*, 307–8, 312, 316, *338*, 340, *341*, *343*, *344*, *348*, 354, *360*, *369*, *371*, *373*, *376*, *377*, *380*, *387*, *389*, *390*, 393, *396*, *397*, *398*, *401*	Berkhof, L.	*31*
		Berlin, A.	*152*
		Bernabé, C.	71
		Bernard, J. H.	6, *45*, *50*, *51*, *59*, 74, *81*, *84*, *99*, *100*, *121*, *161*, *264*, 275, 298
Barrosse, T.	62	Bertram, G.	*84*
Barth, M.	69	Best, E.	*304*
Barthes, R.	*92*	Best, T. F.	*15*, *193*, *205*
Bartholomew, G. L.	*250*	Betz, O.	*100*, 102, *131*, *134*, *339*, *340*, *360*, *361*
Barton, J.	222, *237*		
Barton, S. C.	*158*, *175*, 202, *337*	Beutler, J.	5, *180*, 197, *213*, *215*, *343*
Bassler, J. M.	*195*, *249*		
Bathke, W. E.	*114*	Beyer, K.	*142*, *143*–44, *370*
Bauckham, R.	22, *157*–58, *170*, *185*, *186*, *195*, *235*	Bianchi, U.	*127*, *339*
		Bieder, W.	*212*, *219*
Bauer, W.	*50*, *127*, *264*, 279, 320, *363*	Billings, J. S.	*13*, *216*
		Bittner, W. J.	*138*, *283*, *380*
Baum, G.	*233*, *236*, *243*, *259*	Black, D. A.	*152*
Baumbach, G.	242	Black, Matthew	*124*, *141*, *142*, *150*, *153*, *154*, *167*, *286*
Baur, F. C.	*358*, *373*		
Beardslee, W.	*11*	Black, Max	66
Beardsley, M.	66	Blanc, C.	*1*
Beasley-Murray, G.	*50*, *52*, *59*, *73*, *74*, *75*, *80*, *84*, *96*, *105*, *115*, *120*	Blank, J.	*209*, *244*, *305*, *323*, *334*, *372*, *386*, *387*, *388*, *393*
Beauvery, R.	*110*	Blank, S.	*322*
Beck, D. R.	70, *233*	Blass, F.	*155*
Becker, H.	*126*	Blau, L.	*354*
Becker, J.	*13*, *17*, *20*, *27*, *63*, *131*, *176*, *180*, 197, *199*, 223, *324*, *329*, *336*, *338*, *379*, *386*, *390*	Blenkinsopp, J.	69, 73, *113*
		Blevins, J. L.	*404*
		Bligh, J.	*112*
		Bloch, R.	286, 287
		Bloom, H.	*14*, *92*
Beekman, J.	*37*	Bloomfield, L.	*36*
Behm, J.	*305*	Blumenthal, M.	2, 6
Belle, G. van	8, *17*, 24, 25, 26, 53	Böcher, O.	*13*, *63*, *131*, *338*, *386*
Belleville, L.	*364*		
Beltz, W.	*368*, *398*	Bockmuehl, M.	*346*
Ben-Porat, Z.	*91*, *155*	Boers, H.	*14*
Bennett, J. R.	*149*	Bogart, J.	*176*
Berger, D.	*235*	Böhlig, A.	*127*, *290*
Berger, K.	*172*, *194*, 197, *200*	Boice, J. M.	*215*, *343*
Berger, P. L.	16, *194*, *195*, *202*, *204*	Boismard, M. E.	24, 26, *141*, *180*, *224*, *226*, *227*, *307*, *334*, *389*
Bergmann, J.	*262*	Bonneau, N. R.	*102*
Bergmeier, R.	*323*	Bonsall, H. B.	*170*
Berkey, R. F.	*390*	Bonsirven, J.	*82*, *142*, *358*

Booth, W. C.	76, 78, 81, 335		256, 260, 266, 273,
Borchert, G. L.	334		275, 276, 279, 281,
Borgen, P.	22, 137, *143*, 209,		295, 306, 308, 324,
	285, 286, 294, 353		327, 329, 338, 340,
Born, J. B.	13, 64		347, 348, 349, 351,
Bornhäuser, K.	167, 208, 214, 242,		355, 362, 367, 374,
	243, 244, 247		376, 377, 380, 386,
Bornkamm, G.	318		388, 389, 395, 403
Borowsky, I. J.	236	Brown, R. M.	216
Boström, G.	153	Brown, S.	127, 142
Botha, F. J.	224, 389	Brownlee, W. H.	116, *131*, 307
Botha, J. E.	12, 24, 76, 146	Brownson, J. V.	165
Botha, P. J.	158	Bruce, F. F.	26, 29–30, 50, *51*,
Boucher, M.	52, 77		69, 74, 80, 96, *100*,
Bousset, W.	136, 387		105, 113, 134, 155,
Bowan, J	126		285, 289, 306, 324
Bowen, C. R.	13, 62	Bruns, J. E.	12, 114
Bowersox, P. G.	*139*, 311	Buchanan, G. W.	13, 126
Bowman, J.	114, 242, 247, 270	Büchsel, F.	50, 51, 386
Boyce, M.	339	Bühner, J. A.	137
Boyd, D. G.	22	Bujard, W.	146
Braine, D. D. C.	96, 285	Bullinger, E. W.	46, 77, 78
Brandscheidt, R.	297, 312	Bullock, C. H.	282
Braun, F.-M.	2, *125*, 142, 212,	Bultmann, R.	7, 9, 22, 25, 45, 46,
	222, 295, 346, 347,		47, 50, 51, 52, 53,
	348		56, 59, 61, 62, 64,
Braun, H.	131, 134		69, 73, 74, 75, 80,
Breck, J.	132, 338		81, 83, 87, *100*,
Briggs, C. A.	225		106, 112, 113, 116,
Brodie, T. L.	24, 94		120, 125, 126, 127,
Brooke, A. E.	1, 161		135, 142, 146, 147,
Brooke, G. J.	260, 261, 265, 285,		149, 163, 185, *194*,
	301		199, 209, 211, 212,
Brooke-Rose, C.	65		220, 225, 237, 248,
Brown, J. P.	114		262, 268, 273, 275,
Brown, G.	40, 41		281, 282, 320, 324,
Brown, J.	154		332, 334, 342, 343,
Brown, R. E.	2, 5, 9, *15*, 26, 28,		346, 348, 349–53,
	30, 45, 46, 48, 50,		354, 356, 358, 364,
	51, 52, 56, 57, 59,		368, 372, 373–76,
	63, 72, 74, 80, 84,		377, 378–79, *386*,
	87, 94, 95, 96, *100*,		387, 388, 396, 397,
	105, 108, 112, 120,		398, 399
	121, 125, 131, 137,	Burchard, C.	215
	139, 142, *146*, 149,	Burchfield, R. W.	47
	151, 152, *163*, 169,	Burkett, D.	133
	176, 180, 192, 197,	Burkitt, F. C.	129
	203, 209, 210, 212,	Burney, C. F.	2, 140, *150*, 307
	214, 220, 232, 242,	Burns, J. E.	85, 155
	248, 249, 252, 254,	Burridge, K. O. L.	15, 27, *194*

Burrows, E. W.	273	Chadwick, H.	1, 220, 235
Burrows, M.	69, 95, 113, 142, 338	Chafe, W. L.	39
		Chang, P.	13, 151, 152
Bussche, H. van den	248, 359	Charlesworth, J. H.	23, 128, 129, 132, 222, 251, 321, 338, 386, 403
Buth, R.	124, 143, 167, 302		
Cadman, W. H.	54, 69, 96, 100	Chatman, S.	146, 148
Cahill, P.	14	Chevalier, H.	77
Caird, G. B.	34, 35, 47, 63, 66, 81, 153, 224, 253, 280, 292, 311, 334, 349, 372, 383	Childs, B. S.	27, 30
		Chilton, B. D.	116, 237, 286, 309, 389
		Chisholm, R.	153, 154
Callaway, M. C.	236	Chomsky, N.	36
Callow, J.	37	Cimosa, M.	302
Calvin, J.	48–49, 51, 73, 74, 80, 120, 272, 273	Clark, D. K.	283
		Clavier, H.	7, 12, 75, 76, 84, 87, 121
Cameron, R.	379		
Camery-Hoggatt, J.	77	Clemen, C.	353
Campenhausen, H. v.	258, 295	Clements, R. E.	298
Cardwell, K.	71	Clifford, R. J.	2, 9
Cargel, T.	82	Coetzee, J. C.	355
Carmichael, C. M.	120	Cohen, A. P.	175, 185
Carmignac, J.	129	Cohen, S.	354
Carnegie, D. R.	214, 220	Cohen, S. J. D.	183, 185, 187, 238
Carpenter, J. E.	259	Collins, A. Y.	176
Carroll, J. T.	388	Collins, J. J.	100, 387
Carroll, K. L.	186, 246	Collins, R. F.	13, 70, 96, 106, 209, 216, 281
Carroll R. P.	261, 265		
Carson, D. A.	4, 12, 23, 25, 26, 48, 49, 50, 51, 52, 53, 75, 80, 81, 96, 100, 115, 137, 162, 164, 165, 166, 170, 171, 192, 193, 208, 252, 257, 324, 336, 403	Collins, R. F.	216
		Collinson, W. E.	155
		Colpe, C.	129, 130
		Colson, J.	3, 23
		Colwell, E. C.	140
		Combrink, H. J. B.	30, 41
		Combs, W. W.	129
		Connick, C. M.	13, 79
Carson, J. A.	35	Connolly, R.	335
Carter, W.	65, 71	Conzelmann, H.	47, 210, 212, 219, 240, 315
Cartlidge, D. R.	123		
Cary, G. L.	273	Cook, S. A.	123
Casanowicz, I. M.	152, 153, 154	Cook, W. R.	96, 383
Case, S. J.	194	Cooper, L.	144, 146
Casey, M.	233, 334	Corbett, E. P. J.	144
Casey, R. P.	129	Corell, A.	59, 106, 120
Casson, L.	158	Cornell, T.	158
Catchpole, D.	22	Cosgrove, C. H.	11
Cauthron, H. A.	224, 389	Cothenet, E.	176, 215, 253, 360, 366
Ceresko, A. R.	150		
Cerfaux, L.	2, 3	Cottle, B.	65
Ceroke, C. P.	106	Coutts, J.	403

Cox, L. G.	215	Delling, G.	49, 59
Crenshaw, J. L.	266	Denis, A. M.	106
Cross, F. M.	135, 338	Derrett, J. D. M.	9, 10, 65, 69, 94, 100, 106, 121, 188
Crossan, J. D.	12, 242, 389		
Cruse, D. A.	34	Derrida, J.	15, 92
Cuddon, J. A.	77	Detzler, W.	63
Culler, J.	65, 91, 92	Deuchesne-Guillemin, J.	127
Culley, R. C.	149, 253		
Cullmann, O.	7, 15, 29, 47, 48, 51, 52, 56, 57, 72, 74, 84, 107, 113, 114, 144, 154, 167, 169, 176, 181, 184, 185, 214, 307, 336, 388, 389, 400	Diaz, J. R.	372
		Dibelius, M.	25
		Diel, P.	13, 65
		Dobschütz, E. von	2, 6
		Dodd, C. H.	8, 22, 26, 29, 48, 50, 61, 65, 73, 74, 75, 80, 95, 96, 100, 105, 107, 114, 125, 129, 131, 135, 168, 198, 208, 214, 242, 253, 255, 259, 266, 269, 273, 283, 291, 292, 297, 302, 305, 308, 314, 342, 348, 353, 355, 368, 380, 384, 387, 388, 389, 390, 403
Culpepper, R. A.	12, 13, 14, 26, 64, 76, 82–83, 125, 128, 160, 165, 171, 176, 201, 203, 233, 238, 335, 377		
Cuming, C. J.	232		
Cumont, F.	124		
D'Angelo, M. R.	121		
Dahl, N. A.	220, 221, 248, 259, 292, 311, 342, 370, 372		
		Domeris, W. R.	13, 114, 125, 219
		Doncoeur, P.	6
Dahms, J. V.	94, 138, 311, 346	Dorman, D.	114
Dahood, E.	94	Dorsey, D. A.	158
Dart, J.	128	Doty, W. G.	158
Daube, D.	64, 73, 339, 355	Douglas, M.	16, 197
Dauer, A.	176, 256, 259, 379	Draisma, S.	91
Davey F. N.	41, 221, 304	Drane, J. W.	293
Davidson, B.	273	Drinkard, J. F.	124
Davidson, D.	65	Driver, G. R.	142
Davies, M.	67, 74, 144, 302, 355	Drum, W.	2, 3, 13
		Drummond, J.	2, 13, 94
Davies, P. E.	107	Dschulnigg, P.	148
Davies, P. R.	387	Ducrot, O.	145
Davies, W. D.	54, 69, 113, 166, 182, 184, 274, 339	Duke, P. D.	12, 76, 77, 78, 82–83, 125, 152, 328, 377
Davis, J. C.	61, 387		
Dawsey, J.	75	Duling, C.	193
Deakle, D. W.	14	Dumermuth, C. F.	65
Déaut, R. le	287	Dungan, D. L.	22, 123
Debrunner, A.	155	Dunn, J. D. G.	70, 133, 234, 239, 240, 246, 247, 321, 334, 350, 351, 404
Deeks, D.	151		
Deines, R.	241		
Deissmann, A.	142, 194	Dupont-Sommer, A.	208
Delitzsch, F.	303	Du Rand, J. A.	12, 85

Index of Authors

Durkheim, E.	204	Fishbane, M.	27, 285, 357
Du Toit, A. B.	95	Fitzmyer, J. A.	124, 142, 143, 302
		Flanagan, N.	13
Easterling, P. E.	159	Flanner, E. H.	234, 236
Eastman, R. M.	145, 146	Flowers, H. J.	2
Eckardt, A. R.	234	Fodor, J. A.	36, 37, 40
Eco, U.	38	Foerster, W.	183, 292, 360
Edie, J.	66	Fohrer, G.	154, 292, 322
Edlow, R. B.	33, 36, 38	Fokkelman, J. P.	149, 253
Eichrodt, W.	269	Ford, J. M.	256, 279
Eitan, I.	152	Fordyce, C. J.	46
Eliot, T. S.	14, 92	Forkman, G.	208
Elliott, J. H.	15, 198, 204	Formesyn, R.	380
Elliott, R. C.	79	Fortna, R. T.	8, 24, 26, 148, 210,
Ellis, E. E.	334		239, 252, 302, 378
Ellis, P. F.	80, 120, 151	Fossum, J.	354
Emerton, J. A.	27, 71, 129	Foulkes, R.	155
Empson, W.	34, 38, 39	Fowl, S. E.	93
Enkvist, N. E.	35, 145	Fowler, H. W.	79
Ensor, P. W.	63, 312, 390	Fowler, R. F.	38, 39, 145
Enz, J. J.	149, 253	Fowler, R. M.	93
Epp, E. J.	233	France, R. T.	307, 285, 308
Ernst, J.	3	Franke, A. H.	138, 253
Esler, P. F.	202	Freed, E. D.	5, 10, 94, 95, 110,
Eslinger, L. M.	91		114, 126, 133, 143,
Evans, C. A.	129, 137, 248, 253,		144, 146, 148, 208,
	285, 297, 299, 305,		253, 299, 301, 304,
	307, 308-9, 310,		305, 312, 334, 346,
	315		355
		Freedman, D.	151
Fackre, G.	85	Freedman, W.	91, 155
Farmer, W. R.	124	Frei, H. W.	14, 27, 344
Faure, A.	255, 256	French, D. H.	158
Fee, G. D.	5, 24, 162, 164	Frerichs, E.	222
Feine, P.	212	Freudman, L. C.	234
Felperin, H.	93	Freund, E. C.	15, 92
Fensham, F. C.	62	Frey, J.	333
Fenton, J. C.	8, 9, 48, 52, 53, 73,	Freyne, S.	233, 244, 246
	76, 87	Fridrichsen, A.	208
Ferraro, G.	62	Friedman, N.	66
Festugière, A. J.	126, 128	Frye, N.	14, 27, 34, 125
Feuillet, A.	24, 73, 125, 324,	Frye, R. N.	129
	346, 347, 348, 355,	Fulco, J. W.	3
	267	Fuller, R. H.	233, 352
Fewell, D. N.	15, 92, 94	Funk, R. W.	30
Fiddes, P. S.	353, 401		
Finkel, A.	285	Gächter, P.	149, 152
Firth, J. R.	40	Gafni, I.	179, 246
Fischer, K.-M.	116, 130	Gager, J. G.	15, 193, 194, 202,
Fish, S.	13		234

Gallagher, E. V.	*1*	Green, W. S.	222, 289
Gamble, H. Y.	*158, 208*	Green–Armytage, A.	23
García-Moreno, A.	*251*	Greeves, D.	292
Gardner-Smith, P.	*21*	Gregory, J.	103
Garland, D. E.	*118, 276*	Gregory, M.	*35, 145*
Gärtner, B. E.	*69, 113*	Grese, W. C.	*126, 128, 359*
Gaston, L.	*283*	Gribbs, F. L.	198
Geertz, C.	*65, 71*	Grigsby, B. H.	10, *71, 112, 138,*
Geiger, G.	*110*		*273, 312*
Geisler, N. L.	*210*	Grill, J.	6
Geller, S. A.	11, *14*	Groenewald, E. P.	*168,* 169–70
Genette, G,	*335*	Grossberg, D.	*153, 154*
Gerhard, J.	*23*	Gruenwald, I.	*134, 289, 290, 345*
Gertner, D. M.	*285*	Grundmann, W.	*125, 138, 220, 348*
Getty, M. A.	*233*	Gryglewicz, F.	*182, 208, 243, 247*
Gevirtz, S.	*154*	Gubler, M. L.	*342, 349*
Geyser, A. S.	*389*	Guilding, A.	54, *69, 112, 294*
Giblin, C. H.	12, *106*	Guillaume, A.	*153, 154*
Gilbert, J.	*342*	Gunkel, H.	*128,* 204
Giles, B.	*107*	Gutbrod, W.	*239, 240*
Gill, J.	*75*	Guthrie, D.	*210, 315*
Gill, R.	*205*		
Gilltus, I. S.	*127*	Haacker, K.	259
Gingrich, F. W.	6, *48*	Habel, N.	299
Glasson, T.	74, *94, 106, 110,*	Haenchen, E.	5, 9, *17, 46, 59, 73,*
	214, 252, 267		*80, 81, 107, 126,*
Glasswell, M. E.	22		*127, 146, 149, 212,*
Glück, J. J.	*153, 154*		*214, 234, 273, 379,*
Gnilka, J,	*299*		*389, 403*
Godet, F. L.	*50*	Hagenbuchle, R.	36
Goedt, M. de	*98*	Hahn, F.	*100, 210, 263*
Goguel, M.	*42*	Haiman, J.	*153*
Goldberg, A.	*371*	Hall, R. G.	*332*
Good, E.	*66, 75, 76*	Halladay, W. L.	75
Goodenough, E. R.	3	Halliday, M. A. K	16, *148, 197*
Goodman, M.	*238*	Halsema, J. H. van	5, 11
Goodspeed, J.	140–41	Halverson, J.	*158*
Goodwin, J.	*301*	Hambly, W. F.	94, *120, 279*
Goppelt, L.	72, *95, 114, 293,*	Hamerton-Kelly, R.	*26, 95, 348*
	308, 355	Hamilton, N. Q.	*69, 113*
Görg, M.	*96*	Hampel, V.	*114*
Gottwald, N.	*205*	Handelman, S. A.	288
Granskou, d.	*249, 321*	Hanson, A. T.	70, *94, 96, 138,*
Grant, F. C.	*145, 402*		*143, 149, 253, 280,*
Grant, R. M.	34, *69, 71, 113,*		*286, 288, 313, 348,*
	129, 168		*383*
Grässer, E.	*209, 214, 249, 396*	Hanson, J. S.	*221, 257*
Grassi, J. A.	*23*	Hanson, P. D.	*387*
Gray, G. B.	*276*	Hanson, R. P. C.	*293*
Green, H. A.	*129*	Harari, J. V.	*34*

Hare, D.	*185, 237*	Hickling, C. J. A.	*132, 233*
Harmon, W.	*47*	Hiers, R.	*69, 113*
Harnack, A. von	*2*, 123, 156, *194, 221*	Hill, A.	*35*
		Hill, D.	*63*
Harner, P. B.	*72, 355*	Hill, E.	*40*
Harnisch, W.	*75*	Hindley, J. C.	*215*
Harrelson, W.	*215*	Hinrichs, B.	*354*
Harrington, D.	*178, 194, 205*	Hirsch, E.	*2, 5, 149*
Harris, E.	*67, 293*	Hirsch, E. D.	*14, 30*, 40, *93*, 206
Harris, J. R.	*133, 275, 297*	Hirschberg, H.	*187*
Harris, W. V.	*158*	Hitchcock, F. R. M.	*13*
Hartin, P. J.	*231*	Hock, R. F.	*15*
Hartman, L.	*2*	Hodges, Z. C.	*50, 111, 364*
Harvey, A. E.	*45, 81, 221, 325*	Hoeferkamp, R. T.	*106, 380*
Hatina, T. R.	*338*	Hoekema, A. A.	*388*
Hatzfeld, H.	*35*	Hoffman, T.	*339*
Hauser, A. J.	*11*	Hofius, O.	*89, 101, 356, 393*
Hawkes, T.	*67*	Holladay, W.	*154*
Hayes, C. W.	*35*	Hollander, J.	*93*
Hays, R. B.	*93, 237, 288, 289*	Hollis, H.	*10, 84*
Hayward, C. T. R.	*354*	Holman, C. H.	*37, 47*
Hebel, J. U.	*91*	Holman, H.	*37*
Heekerens, H. P.	*26*	Holmberg, B.	*15, 201, 203, 205*
Hegstad, H.	*338*	Holst, R. A.	*139*
Heil, J.	*106*	Holtzmann, H. J.	*373*
Hein, K.	*70*	Holtzmann, O.	*167*
Heine, R.	*1*	Holwerda, D.	*388*
Heinrich, K.	*342*	Hooker, M. D.	*240*, 307–8, *309, 373, 403*
Hellholm, D.	*193*		
Helmbold, A. K.	*128*	Horbury, W.	*114, 179, 186*, 187, *188, 221, 224, 234, 246, 264*
Hélou, C.	*3*		
Hempel, J.	*323*		
Henderson, M. W.	*107*	Horgan, M. P.	*285*
Henderson, R. A.	*252*	Horsley, R. A.	*194, 221, 257*
Henderson, W. G.	*62*	Horst, P. W. van der	*73, 102*
Hendry, G. S.	*346*	Hoselitz, B. F.	*204*
Hengel, M.	*3, 8, 23, 24, 25, 94, 120, 130, 131, 136, 137, 170, 171, 198, 212, 235, 237, 251, 254, 273, 279, 295, 312, 348, 390*	Hoskyns, E.	*8, 9, 21, 41, 46, 48, 49, 50, 51, 52, 53, 59, 69, 73, 74, 80, 81, 87, 100, 105, 113, 120, 121, 129,* *221, 252, 256, 272, 273, 279, 304, 315, 323, 342, 387, 400*
Hengstenberg, E. v.	*225*		
Henle, P.	*65*		
Henn, T. R.	*11*	Hossfeld, F. L.	*265*
Herdan, G.	*36*	Howard, W. F.	*2, 6, 21, 24, 142, 149, 150, 172, 210, 226, 227, 262, 273, 275, 346*
Herford, T. R.	*234*		
Herzberg, W.	*153, 154*		
Hesse, F.	*322, 347*		
Hibbard, A.	*37, 47*	Howton, J.	*170*

Hoy, D. C.	92	Joubert, H. L. N.	*114*
Hügel, B. F. von	*3*	Judge, E. A.	15, 189, *194*, *378*
Hultgren, A. J.	10, *70*	Juel, D.	*100*, 292, *312*
Hummann, R. J.	*139*, 255, 256	Jülicher, A.	13, *402*
Hunter, A. M.	72, *105*, *281*		
Hurtado, L.	*125*	Kaiser, W. C.	30, 222, 225
Hurtgen, J. E.	*196*	Kanagaraj, J. J.	*3*
Hutcheon, L.	92	Kaplan, A.	39
Hutten, U. von	24	Käsemann, E.	127, *146*, *171*, 172, 177, *180*, 210, 217, 226, 252, 253, 318, 351, *373*, *378*, *388*
Iersel, B. van	*110*		
Inch, M.	*106*		
Infante, S. R.	*75*	Katz, J. J.	36, 37, 40
Inkeles, A.	*204*	Katz, S. T.	*186*
Isaac, B.	*198*	Kaufman, P. S.	*236*
Isaacs, M. E.	*51*	Kearsley, R. A.	*158*
Iser, W.	15, 92	Kee, H. C.	15, 26, *123*, *194*, *198*, *236*, 252, 296, *332*
Issac, J.	*235*		
		Kelber, W.	*158*
Jameson, F.	92	Kellner, H.	*204*
Jarvis, E.	*373*	Kellogg, R.	*76*
Jastrow, M.	*96*	Kempson, R. M.	36
Jaubert, A.	*51*, *65*, *84*, *155*, *275*	Kennedy, G. A.	*145*
Jemielity, T.	*79*	Kennedy, H. A. A.	2, 5, 6, *403*
Jenni, E.	*321*	Kennedy, J.	*80*
Jensen, E. E.	*216*	Kent, H. A.	*96*, *281*
Jensen, J.	39	Kenyon, F. G.	*159*
Jenson, R. W.	*344*	Kermode, F.	2, 3, *11*, *12*, *13*, *14*, 191
Jeremias, Joachim	6, *48*, *99*, *133*, *146*, *147*, *272*, *275*, *307*, *388*	Kern, W.	*342*, *366*
Jeremias, Johann	6	Kessler, M.	*151*
Jocz, J.	*186*, *242*, *244*, *350*	Kieffer, R.	*3*, *63*
Johnson, E. E.	30	Kilpatrick, G. D.	*145*, *148*, *150*, *151*
Johnson, E. S.	*304*	Kimelman, R.	*179*, 187
Johnson, L. T.	173	King, J. S.	*176*
Johnson, M.	*65*, *66*	Kingsbury, J. D.	*282*
Johnson, S. E.	*108*, 225, 262	Kippenberg, H. G.	*136*
Johnston, G.	*12*, 72, *76*, *83*, *340*, *395*	Kittay, E. F.	*67*
		Kittel, G.	*62*, *306*
Jonas, H.	*127*	Kittlaus, L. R.	22
Jones, D. L.	*308*	Kjargaard, M. S.	*65*, *67*
Jonge, M. de	25, 26, 27, *48*, *108*, *139*, 180, 197, *214*, 221, 224, 262, *327*, 329, *377*, *378*, *383*, *389*	Klassen, W.	*234*
		Klausner, J.	222
		Klein, G.	*300*
		Kleinknecht, H.	*260*
		Klimkeit, A. F. J.	*127*
		Kline, M. G.	*253*
Jónsson, J.	*3*, *75*, *76*	Knight, G. A. F.	*236*
Joos, M.	*29*	Knights, L. C.	*65*

Index of Authors

Knowles, M.	293	Lamouille, A.	*180*, 226, 227
Knox, N.	76	Lampe, G. W. H.	293
Knox, B. M. W.	*159*	Lampe, P.	*194*, 203
Kochilletonil, L.	*215*	Langbrandtner, W.	*127*, *351*
Koenig, Jean	*301*	Lanham, R. A.	36, 47, *145*, *146*, *155*
Koenig, John	*233*		
Koester, C. R.	10, *95*, *100*	Lanser, S. S.	*335*
Koester, H.	69, *123*, *124*, *127*, *129*, *137*	LaSor, W. S.	*131*
		Laszlo, E.	204
Kohler, H.	*379*	Laursen, G. A.	*61*
Kooij, J. G.	36, 40	Lausberg, H.	*346*
Kosten, H. B.	*164*	Lavergne, C.	6
Kotze, P. P. A.	76	Layton, B.	*127*
Kraemer, R. S.	*238*, *239*	Leaney, A. R. C.	*131*
Kraft, E.	*209*	Leaska, M. A.	155
Krauss, S.	*186*, *234*	Lee, F. N.	*124*, *389*
Krentz, E.	*11*, *26*	Leech, G.	31, 35, 36, 37, 40, 46, 67, 68, 78, 79, *145*
Kris, E.	*39*		
Kristeva, J.	*15*, *91*, *92*		
Krodel, G.	*106*	Lehrer, A.	*37*
Kruijf, T. C. de	*45*	Leibig, J. E.	*233*
Kselman, S.	*150*	Leidig, E.	*213*
Kugel, J. L.	*285*	Leistner, R.	*236*, *242*
Kuhl, J.	*212*, *384*	Leitch, V. B.	*92*
Kuhn, K. G.	*132*, *240*, *314*, *317*, *338*, *343*, *386*	Lenski, R. C. H.	*50*, *273*
		Léon-Dufour, X.	3, *13*, *65*, 69, 71, *151*, *209*
Kühschelm, R.	*300*		
Kümmel, W. G.	*72*, *139*, *164*, *185*, *203*, *205*, *210*, *211*, *214*, *253*, *312*, *353*, *355*	Leroy, H.	3, 8, *16*, 46, 47, 87, *139*, *154*, *177*, *180–81*, *190–93*, *196*, *284*
Kundsin, K.	*72*, *355*	Letis, T. P.	*126*
Kunjumnen, F. D.	*30*	Levenson, J. D.	*357*
Kurfess, A.	*45*	Levey, S. H.	*116*, *309*
Kurz, W.	160	Levin, R. S.	*65*
Kusvmirek, A.	*237*	Levinson, S.	*34*
Kuyper, L. J.	*133*	Lewis, C. S.	*14*, 66
Kyrtatas, D.	*194*	Lewis, J. P.	*132*
Kysar, R.	8, *13*, *17*, *21*, *26*, *57*, *65*, *72*, *81*, *85*, *99*, *106*, *123*, *135*, *142*, *164*, *176*, *180*, *197*, *198*, *199*, *221*, *234*, *302*, *388*	Licht, J.	*314*
		Lidzbarski, M.	*126*, *127*
		Lieberman, S.	*123*
		Lietzmann, H.	*129*
		Lieu, J. M.	*234*, *251*, *297*, *298*, *299*, *305*, *312*
		Lieu, S. N. C.	*127*
Lacomara, A.	*138*	Lightfoot, J. B.	*143*, *150*, *233*
Ladd, G. E.	*389*	Lightfoot, R. H.	46, 49, 50, 56, 74, 81, 84, *105*, *106*, *272*, *273*, *280*, *383*, *387*
Lagrange, M.-J.	*100*, *139*, *399–400*		
Lakoff, G.	*65*, 66		
Lamarche, P.	*95*		

Limburg, J.	325	Lyons, J.	36, 37, 38, 40, 46
Lindars, B.	5, 9, 24, 26, 44, 45, 48, 50, 51, 56, 59, 61, 69, 71, 73, 74, 75, 76, 80, 81, 87, 100, 102, 104, 108, 113, 114, 133, 137, 138, 149, 155, 163, 180, 187, 189, 221, 241, 253, 256, 262, 273, 286, 292, 294, 299, 305, 318, 327, 340, 341, 351, 362, 377, 384, 387, 403	MacCormac, E. R.	67
		MacDonald, J.	250
		MacGregor, G. H. C.	65
		Mack, B.	348
		Mackay, D. G.	36
		Macky, P. W.	66, 68
		MacRae, G. W.	2, 9, 72, 76, 79, 83, 128, 132, 218, 297
		Maddox, R.	114
		Madsen, G. H. O.	388
		Maggioni, B.	3
		Mahood, M. M.	37
Lindbeck, G. A.	93	Maier, G.	313
Lindeskog, G.	259	Malatesta, E.	17
Lindsay, D. R.	342	Malina, B.	3, 16, 189, 191, 194, 197, 204
Liu, W. W.	311		
Llewelyn, G. R.	158	Malmede, H. H.	135
Loader, W. R. G.	59, 85, 95, 96, 138, 260, 334	Mann, J.	186
		Manns, F.	11, 47, 132, 154, 188
Loewenich, W.	2		
Logan, A. H. B.	127	Manson, T. W.	73, 107, 114, 141, 224, 355, 402
Lohmeyer, E.	70		
Lohse, E.	224, 365	Marco, A.	151
Loisy, A.	94, 181, 254, 279, 327, 329, 374, 376, 377	Marsh, J.	87
		Marshall, I. H.	114
		Martin, R.	124, 142
Lombard, H. A.	19, 122	Marty, W. H.	13, 70, 106
Lona, E.	180, 191, 250	Martyn, J. L.	8, 15, 16, 26, 84, 175, 176, 177, 180, 181–90, 194, 196, 197, 201, 203, 242, 243, 248, 262, 263, 264, 327, 374
Lonergan, B.	335		
Longenecker, B.	98, 184		
Longenecker, R. N.	293		
Longman III, T.	15		
López, F. M. M.	5		
Losie, L. A.	132, 282	Marxsen, W.	203
Lotman, J. M.	335	Mastin, B. A.	356
Louw, J. P.	30, 46, 63, 64, 115, 149, 150, 194	Matera, F. J.	273
		Matsunaga, K.	139
Lowe, M.	232, 239	Matthew, J.	158
Lowry, R.	235	Matthews, S.	194
Lowth, R.	152	Mawson, C. O. S.	47
Lubbock, P.	335	Mayer, A.	107, 138
Luckmann, T.	16, 194, 201	McCaffrey, J.	284
Lund, N. W.	150, 151	McCartney, E. S.	46
Lundbom, J. R.	151	McColl, F.	334
Lütgert, W.	219, 242, 244, 247	McDonald, W. E.	11
Luzarraga, J.	252	McDonnell, R. M. A.	22
Lyman, M. E.	126	McDonough, S. M.	354
Lyons, G.	202	McEleney, N. J.	71

McFague, S.	65	Minor, M.	11
McGuire, M. B.	127, 194	Miranda, J. P.	172, 212, 213, 396
McHugh, J.	238	Miscall, P. D.	94
McIntosh, A.	148	Mlakuzhyil, G.	12, 24, 148, 151, 152
McKenzie, J. L.	267		
McKnight, E.	15, 92	Moeller, O.	125, 138, 347, 348
McNamara, M.	143	Moloney, F. J.	69, 85, 114, 170, 346
McNeile, A. H.	6		
McPolin, J.	3, 170, 212, 214	Montgomery, J. A.	140
Meade, G.	126	Moo, D. J.	75, 138, 253, 308
Meagher, J. C.	97, 280, 383	Moore, G. F.	179, 186, 234, 314
Mealand, D.	3	Moore, S. D.	26
Meeks, W. A.	3, 13, 15, 16, 23, 26, 29, 45, 48, 65, 66, 69, 81, 87, 89, 98, 108, 110, 111, 126, 132, 151, 167, 177, 180, 181, 182, 193-96, 200, 201, 202, 203, 205, 210, 232, 239, 244, 247, 248, 252, 261, 262, 263, 327, 329, 335, 345, 350, 351, 370, 373, 374, 377, 389	Moorsel, G. van	128
		Mörchen, R.	44
		Morgan, R.	137, 252, 270
		Morgan, T. E.	15, 92
		Morgenstern, J.	273
		Morris, L.	23, 50, 52, 72, 73, 74, 80, 87, 197-98, 208, 214, 215, 270, 273
		Motyer, J. A.	223-24
		Motyer, S.	20
		Moule, C. F. D.	61, 63, 100, 114, 159, 208, 213, 215, 318, 333, 345, 387, 388
Meier, J. P.	128		
Meinertz, M.	210		
Menken, M. J. J.	12, 146, 148, 151, 152, 299, 301, 303, 305, 315, 317, 318, 323	Moulton, J. H.	5, 55, 149, 150
		Moulton, R. G.	12
		Mounce, R. H.	214, 220
		Mowinckel, S.	222, 346, 347, 351, 387
Mennicke, V.	29		
Menound, P. H.	146, 147	Mowry, L.	132, 339
Metzger, B. M.	17, 163	Mowvley, H.	94, 253, 280
Meyer, I.	265	Muddiman, J.	185, 188, 199
Meyer, P. W.	387, 388	Muecke, D. C.	76, 78
Michaelis, W.	101, 210, 281, 367	Muilenburg, J.	2, 11, 13, 152
Michaels, J. R.	69, 99, 100	Mulder, H.	166, 168-69, 182, 183, 210, 244, 246
Michel, M.	170, 248, 335		
Milic, L. T.	145, 146	Mulder, M. J.	301
Miller, D. M.	39	Müller, M.	114
Miller, E. L.	61, 151	Murphy, F. J.	179
Miller, G.	62	Murphy-O'Connor, J.	134
Miller, J. H.	39, 77	Murray, R.	239
Miller, M. P.	143, 285	Mussner, F.	5, 234, 270, 334, 368
Miller, O.	92		
Milligan, W. M.	2	Myers, D.	12, 76, 82, 248, 334
Milligan, G.	55		
Mills, W. E.	17		
Minear, P. S.	163		

Nations, A. L.	186	Okure, T.	56, 70, 73, *167*, *192*, 193, 199, 211, 213, 214, 220, 325
Naumann, P. S.	62		
Navone, J.	*61*		
Neill, S. T.	*131*	Olsson, B.	17–18, *106*, *209*, 286, 287–88
Neirynck, F.	22		
Nereparampil, L.	*283*	O'Neill,	69, *113*, *403*
Neugebauer, F.	*210*, *219*	Onuki, T.	16, 22, *167*, *172*, *180*, 187, *194*, 197, 199, 214, 218, 237, 249, 397, *398*
Neugebauer, J.	*334*		
Neusner, J.	113, *179*, *181*, *183*, *184*, *186*, 208, 222, 223, 231, 234, 246, 285		
		Oppenheimer, A.	*198*
		O'Rourke,	14, 53, *138*, *334*, *335*
Newman, B. M.	69, 99		
Newton-DeMolina, D.	*30*	Osborne, G.	*160*
Neyrey, J. H.	3, *15*, 16, 80, *101*, *180*, 196, 253, *325*, *394*	Osgood, C.	*124*
		Osiek, C.	*193*
		Osten-Sacken, P.	*234*
Nicholson, G.	25, 85, *151*, *308*	O'Sullivan, F.	*158*
Nicol, G. G.	24, 25, 26, 70, *186*, *210*	Overhold, T. W.	*261*, *266*
Nicole, W.	*17*	Page, R.	38, 42
Nida, E. A.	46, 47, 63, 69, 99	Pagels, E. H.	*1*, *126*
Niedenthal, M. J.	*76*	Painter, J.	72, 96, *100*, *112*, *125*, *180*, *209*, *210*, 238, 239, 297, *315*, *320*, *348*, *355*, *379*
Niles, D. T.	*215*		
Nilsson, M. P.	*123*		
Nims, J. F.	*78*		
Nixon, R. E.	*253*	Palmer, F. R.	38, 40
Noack, B.	*139*, *301*	Palvio, A.	*91*, *155*
Nock, A. D.	*123*, *126*, *128*	Pamment, M.	65, 96, *114*, 280, *383*, *388*
Nodet, E.	*222*		
Noetzel, H.	*125*, *126*	Pancaro, S.	12, 57–58, 94, *138*, *182*, *186*, *187*, 188, 246, *247*, 259, 260, 264, 265, 267, 268, 269, 273, 276, *343*, 355, 356, *388*, *399*
Norrman, R.	33, 38		
Nortjé, J.	*75*		
Norton, D.	*11*		
Noth, M.	*351*		
Nötscher, F.	*342*		
Nowottny, W.	40, 66	Pannenberg, W.	*347*
Nygren, A.	*346*	Parkes, J.	*234*
		Parunak, H. v. Dyke	*150*
O'Day, G. R.	12, 19, 48, 76, 83, *211*, *332*, *357*	Patte, D.	*285*
		Payne, D. F.	*154*
Odeberg, H.	*133*, *250*, *349*	Perkins, P.	*127*, *130*
Oehler, W.	208, *211*, *214*	Perlitt, L.	*353*, *401*
Oepke,	*81*, *306*	Perrin, N.	*389*
Oesterley, W. E. O.	*124*	Perry, M.	*75*
Ogden, C. K.	37, 38, 66	Peters, F. E.	*123*
Ogg, G.	*275*	Petersen, N. R.	2, 5, *14*, 16, 26, *132*, *180*, *201*, *203*
O'Grady, J. F.	*138*		
		Pfitzner, V. C.	*256*
		Pierce, E. L.	*13*

Pinto, B.	95, 125, 348	Reese, J. M.	346, 348, 389
Pinto, E.	170	Reim, G.	94, 95, 96, 97, 101, 106, 114, 138, 143, 188, 208, 222, 235, 244, 256, 275, 277, 286, 293
Pitta, A.	71		
Plescia, J.	239		
Plumb, C. L. B.	367		
Poffet, J. M.	102		
Pokorny, P.	282	Reinhartz, A.	107
Poland, L.	92	Reiser, W.	61
Pollard, T. E.	133, 334	Reitzenstein, R.	128
Pond, E. W.	139, 312	Rena, J.	70
Porsch, F.	209, 248	Rengstorf, H.	213, 380
Porter, C. F.	154	Rensberger, D.	3, 4, 17, 175, 180, 182, 197, 199, 218, 327, 353, 354, 376, 377, 396, 398
Porter, C. L.	112		
Porter, S. E.	14, 138		
Porton, G. G.	286		
Potterie, I. de la	3, 45, 61, 69, 81, 115, 247, 307, 332, 340, 342, 343–44, 359, 370, 372, 378	Renza, L. A.	92
		Rese, M.	23
		Rhea, R.	114
		Ricca, P.	333
Powell, M. A.	11, 14, 26	Richard, E.	11, 47, 81, 87, 114, 154
Poythress, V. S.	5, 23, 150		
Pratscher, W.	236, 249, 251	Richards, I. A.	35, 37, 38, 66, 67
Preisker, H.	2, 49	Richardson, J.	204
Preus, J. S.	222	Riches, J.	173, 202
Preuschen, E.	1	Richter, G.	26, 70, 107, 127, 209, 301, 336, 356
Pribnow, H.	387		
Probst, A.	106	Ricoeur, P.	34, 68
Pryor, J. W.	176	Ridderbos, H. N.	24, 146, 148, 221
Purvis, J. D.	167, 208	Riesenfeld, H.	164, 167
		Riesner, R.	189
Quast, K.	23	Riffaterre, M.	92
Quinn, A.	14, 26	Rigaux, B.	180
		Riggs, J. R.	30
Rabin, C.	302	Riley, W.	201
Rad, G. von	222, 240, 393	Rimmon, S.	34, 39, 42
Radday, Y.	150	Ringgren, H.	339
Radermakers, J.	212, 213	Rissi, M.	71, 283
Rainey, F. E.	62, 106	Rivkin, E.	233
Räisänen, H.	314, 315, 323	Robert, R.	45, 115
Raja, R. J.	61	Roberts, J. H.	75, 253
Ramos, F. F.	13	Roberts, J. J. M.	153, 154
Ramsay, W. M.	158	Robertson, A. T.	107
Ramsey, I. T.	3, 4	Robertson, R.	194
Rapske, B. M.	158	Robinson, J. A.	305
Rawson, E.	159	Robinson J. A. T.	23, 131, 132, 138, 166, 168, 169, 183, 185, 197, 225, 227, 353
Read, D. H. C.	96		
Rebell, W.	17, 180, 191, 193, 196, 211, 219, 236, 237, 335		
		Robinson, J. M.	127, 209, 300, 388
Reed, W.	14	Rodd, C. S.	194

Rogers, P. C.	73	Schmidt, K. L.	13, 315, 389
Romeo, J. A.	71	Schmidt, M. A.	315
Rosenzweig, F.	279	Schnackenburg, R.	2, 5, 9, 17, 45, 50,
Roth, W.	138, 262		53, 57, 61, 69, 73,
Rouiller, G.	354		74, 80, 81, 87, 96,
Rowe, T. T.	5		106, 112, 113, 120,
Rowland, C.	15, 194, 201, 308,		125, 138, 139, 142,
	345, 359		146, 149, 163, 164,
Rowley, H. H.	132, 141, 387		169, 170, 180, 199,
Ruckstuhl, E.	5, 23, 24, 25, 26,		209, 212, 252, 266,
	147–48, 275		274, 278, 284, 298,
Rudel, P.	2, 6		302, 305, 309, 312,
Rudolf, K.	127		315, 316, 317, 324,
Rudolph, T. K.	129		327, 333, 335, 343,
Rudskoger, A.	37		352, 362, 368, 371,
Ruether, R.	233		375, 376, 377, 378,
Rusinko, E.	92		380, 387, 388, 397,
Russell, D. S.	290, 387		398
Russell, E.	126	Schneider, H.	83
		Schneiders, S. M.	13, 65, 70, 71
Sacks, S.	66	Schnelle, U.	22, 126, 176
Safrai, S.	124, 142, 143, 167,	Schoeps, H. J.	284
	302	Schökel, L. A.	153, 154
Sahlin, H.	107	Scholem, G.	127, 221, 290, 292
Saldarini, A.	138	Scholer, D. M.	128
Salmon, G.	75	Scholes, R.	76
Sanday, W.	403	Schottroff, L.	65, 127, 199, 351,
Sanders, E. P.	222, 231, 280, 308,		379, 386, 397, 398
	345	Schrage, W.	315
Sanders, J. A.	27, 286	Schreiner, J.	339
Sanders, J. N.	59, 74, 105	Schrenk, G.	260, 372
Sanders, J. T.	188, 237	Schubert, K.	131, 136
Sandmel, S.	132, 133, 233	Schuchard, B. G.	138, 251, 253, 254,
Sasson, J. M.	153		261, 275, 277, 299,
Saussure, F. de	8, 36		301
Sayce, R. A.	67	Schulz, S.	20, 209, 210
Schaar, C.	33	Schürer, E.	123, 179, 223
Schaeder, H. H.	128	Schüssler-Fiorenza, E.	176
Schäfer, P.	186, 246, 338, 339,	Schwankel, O.	13, 73
	353, 357, 360, 383,	Schwarz, G.	51
	401, 403	Schweitzer, Albert	388, 389
Schechter, S.	186	Schweizer, E.	23, 28, 52, 126,
Scheffler, I.	66		139, 147–48, 177,
Schein, B. E.	138, 262		269, 355
Schenke, H. M.	128	Schwemer, A. M.	390
Schiffman, L. H.	187, 238	Scmitt, J.	314
Schilson, A.	170	Scobie, C. H. H.	17
Schimanowski, G.	133	Scott, E. F.	11, 252
Schlatter, A.	139, 140	Scott, J. A.	62
Schlier, H.	108, 370, 389, 390	Scott, M.	346

Scroggs, R.	26, 180, 198	Spencer, A. B.	75
Sebeok, T. A.	145, 146	Spencer, J.	35, 145
Sedgewick, G. G.	76	Sperber, D.	40
Seebass, H.	295	Spicq, C.	125
Segal, A. F.	82, 125, 204, 205, 262, 345, 359	Spitzer, L.	35, 146
		Sproston, W. E.	385
Segbroeck, F. van	22, 378	Stählin, G.	161, 388
Segovia, F. F.	70, 177, 193, 197	Staley, J. L.	12, 13, 73, 102, 103, 106, 149, 151, 160, 253
Sell, J.	125, 126		
Sevenstern, J. N.	302		
Sevrin, J. M.	126, 129	Stanford, W. B.	34, 66
Seynaeve, J.	388	Stanton, G.	186
Sharot, S.	221	Starr, R. J.	159
Shaw, H.	47, 86	Stauffer, E.	314, 387
Shea, W. H.	150	Stein, R. H.	404
Shedd, R.	9, 53	Stemberger, G.	69, 342
Shepherd, M. H.	246	Stendahl, K.	14, 131, 315
Shideler, M. M.	155	Sternberg, M.	75, 156, 201, 335
Shipley, J. T.	77	Stibbe, M. W. G.	2, 3, 12, 125, 203, 275, 277, 325
Short, M. H.	145		
Silva, M.	29, 34, 142, 149, 253	Stimpfle, A.	44
		Stinespring, W. F.	153
Simon, L.	23	Stone, M. E.	178
Simon, M.	136, 233	Stonehouse, N. B.	214
Simon, U. E.	387	Story, C. I. K.	84
Sitwell, N. H. H.	158	Stowers, S. K.	205
Skeat, T. C.	159	Strachan, R. H.	13, 61, 101, 209, 281
Skeel, C. A. J.	158		
Smalley, S. S.	17, 114, 165, 172, 202, 355	Strack & Billerbeck	64, 186, 222, 264, 265, 269, 273, 277, 308, 372, 393
Smalley, W.	124		
Smend, F.	139, 255	Strathmann, H.	213, 215
Smith, D. M.	15, 22, 26, 28, 85, 124, 146, 175, 177, 180, 197, 221, 246, 252, 296, 297, 331-32, 357, 379	Strauss, D. F.	24
		Strecker, G.	403
		Strobel, A.	359
		Stroumsa, G. G.	368, 398
		Strugnell, J.	345
Smith, J. E.	225	Strus, A.	154
Smith, J. Z.	193	Stuhlmacher, P.	228, 253, 282
Smith, M.	181, 208, 221, 244, 246	Stutterheim, C. F. P.	67
		Su, S. P.	36, 41
Smith, R. H.	262, 293	Suggit, J. N.	249
Smith, T. C.	168	Summers, R.	74
Soeding, T.	13	Sundberg, A. C.	252
Solages, M. de	22	Suriano, T. M.	106
Solotareff, J.	65	Swain, J. C.	91, 155
Songer, H. S.	312, 353	Sweet, J. P. M.	220
Soskice, J. M.	66	Swete, B.	304
Soueif, A.	67		
Speiser, E. A.	153		

Talbert, C. H.	13, 14, 130, 151	Trigg, J.	1
Talmon, S.	136	Trites, A. A.	159, 208, 215, 325
Tannehill, R.	384	Troeltsch, E.	350
Tanzer, S. J.	166, 171	Trudinger, P.	10, 13, 71, 100, 154
Tasker, R. V. G.	48, 51, 59, 74, 105, 106	Trueblood, E.	75
		Trumbower, J. A.	199, 316, 318, 395, 397, 398
Taylor, M. S.	186, 234		
Taylor, V.	141, 273, 402	Tuckett, C.	22, 128, 203, 378, 403
Teeple, H. M.	26, 131, 132		
Telford, W. R.	100	Tuniv, J. O.	255, 256
Tenney, M. C.	53, 61, 74, 105, 106, 114, 120, 137, 149, 170, 171, 215, 252, 253, 312, 373	Turner, M.	138, 273
		Turner, N.	5, 143, 149, 150, 155
		Tyle, R. L.	320
Tenny, E. A.	144	Tzeng, C. S.	124
Theissen, G.	194, 197, 198, 203, 205		
		Ullmann, S.	34, 35, 36, 37, 42, 46, 53, 65, 66, 67, 81, 94, 145, 146, 155
Thiemann, F.	344		
Thiselton, A. C.	34, 47, 92		
Thomas, J. C.	132, 188, 266		
Thompson, J. D.	388	Underhill, E.	3
Thompson, L. L.	30	Unnik, W. C. van	123, 138, 166, 168, 208, 214, 221, 224
Thompson, M. M.	171, 257, 334, 354, 356, 378		
		Urbach, E. E.	183
Thompson, M. B.	158	Urban, W. M.	42, 52
Thomson, J. A. K.	76	Uspensky, B.	77, 335
Thomson, J. G. S.	252		
Thornton, T. C. G.	186	Vanhoye, A.	151
Thrall, W. F.	37, 47, 86	Vassilyev, L. M.	39, 47
Thyen, H.	2, 3, 17, 26, 165, 185, 192, 237, 238, 326, 351	Vawter, B.	17, 114, 224, 370
		Vedder, H. C.	2, 13, 143
		Vellanickal, M.	249, 372
Tilborg, S. van	12, 62, 172	Verhelst, F.	2, 3
Timmins, N. G.	146, 149	Vermes, G.	118, 200, 285, 338, 371, 397
Tobin, T. H.	125		
Todorov, T.	28, 145	Via, D. O.	61
Tomkins, J.	15, 92	Virgulin, S.	2, 5
Torczyner, H.	154	Viviano, B. T.	389
Torrey, C. C.	6, 140–41	Voeltzel, R.	83, 84
Torrey, D. C.	84, 155	Voelz, J. W.	124, 142, 143, 167, 302
Tournay, R. J.	104		
Toussaint, S. D.	106	Volz, P.	387
Townsend, J. T.	232, 249	Vorster, W. S.	2, 5, 139
Toy, C. H.	253	Vouga, F.	8, 211, 218–19, 236, 237
Tracy, D.	92		
Trautner-Kromann, H.	235	Vriezen, T. C.	351
Trench, R.	106		
Trepat, J.	2	Waard, J. A. de	305
Tresmontant, C.	124, 143, 167, 302	Wächter, L.	313, 314
Treves, M.	339		

Wahlde, U. C. von	8, 14, 24, 176, 232, 233, 241, 242, 243, 247	Whitacre, R. A.	25, 166, 176, 180, 232, 249, 259, 332
Waldron, R. A.	37, 38	White, L. M.	158
Walker, W. O.	114	Whitehead, A. N.	84
Wallace, D.	198	Wiefel, W.	180, 238
Walter, L.	372	Wilckens, U.	379
Ward, R. F.	158	Wilcox, M.	273
Warner, M.	383–84	Wilder, A. N.	11, 12
Warren, A.	14, 36, 146, 201, 206	Wiles, M. F.	3, 126, 291
		Wilken, R. L.	233
Watson, A.	241	Wilkens, W.	209, 210
Watson, D. F.	11, 203, 299, 351	Willett, M. E.	125, 348
Watson, W.	46, 47, 77, 91, 151, 152, 153, 154	Williams, A. L.	188
		Williams, C. H.	354
Watts, D. J.	388	Williams, J. G.	75
Wead, D.	2, 5, 12, 47, 51, 75, 76, 81, 141–42, 154, 334	Williams, J. T.	270
		Williams, P. T.	358
		Williams, S.	273, 312
		Williamson, C.	236
Weber, M.	204	Wilson, B.	15, 201, 214
Webster, E. C.	151	Wilson, B. R.	199–200, 202, 218
Weiler, A.	110	Wilson, D.	40
Weimann, R.	335	Wilson, J.	50
Weinel, H.	210	Wilson, M. R.	215, 234
Weinfeld, M.	208	Wilson, R.	125, 126
Weisengoff, J. P.	61	Wilson, R. R.	204
Weiser, A.	373	Wilson, S. G.	188
Weiss, H.	70	Wimsatt, W. K.	66
Weiss, J.	63	Wind, A.	167, 210, 211, 214, 219
Weiss, M.	11, 27		
Welch, J. W.	150, 151	Windisch, H.	209, 371, 384
Wellek, R.	14, 35, 36, 145, 146, 201, 206	Winn, A. C.	172, 396
		Winston, D.	132, 339
Wellhausen, J.	214	Winter, W.	35, 168
Wendland, E. R.	42, 63	Wisse, F.	129, 204
Wenger, J. E.	139, 253	Witherington, B.	348
Wengst, K.	25, 172, 176, 182, 187, 197, 211, 217, 220, 226, 241, 245, 246, 313, 327, 329, 374, 377	Witte, J. J. De	67
		Wittings, S.	30
		Wolbert, W.	80
		Wolff, M. D. de	77
		Woll, B. D.	16, 180, 202, 210, 196, 350
Wenham, D.	185, 285		
Wenz, H.	378	Wood, A. S.	1
Wernberg-Møller, P.	339	Woolcombe, K. J.	293
Werth, P.	41	Woude, A. S.	353, 401
Westcott, B. F.	23, 45, 50, 51, 59, 74, 81, 84, 115, 198, 274, 277, 324, 335, 387	Wrede, W.	2, 220, 224, 373, 401, 403
		Wyatt, N.	120, 121
Wheelwright, P.	39, 66, 68, 84		

Yamauchi, E. M.	*129, 130*
Yee, G. A.	*233*
Young, F. W.	*138, 311*
Yule, G.	*40, 41*
Zaehner, R. C.	*339*
Zahn, T.	*23, 212*
Zeller, D.	*107, 138*
Zenos, A. C.	*403*
Ziener, G.	*253*
Zimmerli, W.	*304, 347, 355*
Zimmermann, F.	*142*
Zimmermann, H.	*72, 355*
Zumstein, J.	*17*

Index of Subjects

Apocalypticism 134, 178, 222, 342, 343, 359, 387
Authorship 23, 24, 27, 180

Bar Kokhba 184, 197
Belief 368, 373–375, 378, 381, 383, 385
Beloved Disciple 23, 44, 161, 171, 174, 176, 216, 227, 229, 278
Birkat ha-Minim 179, 182, 186, 187, 189
Blasphemy, 87, 234, 245, 248, 264, 265
Blind Man 57, 102, 103, 111, 112, 227, 243, 326, 406

Caesar 99, 110, 247, 248, 265, 276,
Caiaphas 79, 80, 83, 274
Categories of Faith
—true faith 163, 218, 249, 329, 368, 370, 377, 379, 380, 382, 384
—sensational faith 378, 380
—inauthentic faith 327, 374–377, 383
Children of the Devil 371, 372
Children of God 172, 249, 250, 371
Christian Conduct 216, 218, 219, 363, 373, 382, 396
Church 159, 173, 174, 220, 229, 252, 395
Clement of Alexandria 1, 161, 353
Conceptual Milieu
—Gnosticism 126–130
—Hellenism 125, 132, 134, 169
—Judaism 21, 108, 132, 133, 136, 169, 200, 348, 408
—Old Testament 124, 135–139, 144, 154–156, 222, 252, 253, 346
—Qumran 130, 131, 133, 134
Context 39–41, 123, 135, 139, 206
Creation 59, 95, 119, 120, 279, 323, 325, 346–349, 360, 361, 363, 384, 398, 400

Date of the Gospel 197, 198
Deconstruction 30, 92
Discipleship 56, 104, 174, 216, 380, 382–384
Docetism 171, 228
Double Meaning
—conceptual 52–60, 70, 79, 84, 87, 104, 105, 111, 402
—discussion of 6–8, 11, 37, 47, 49, 51, 52, 81
—lexical 34, 41, 46–51, 74, 88, 154
—grammatical 43, 44, 45, 46, 81, 163, 164
Dualism 131, 314, 321, 342, 371, 386

Eusebius 1, 220
Evil
—its nature as unbelief 250, 318, 320, 371, 398
—its manifestation as works 249, 265, 368, 395, 398, 399, 400
Exegesis
—John and rabbinic 112, 116, 120, 266, 286–290, 294, 309
—John's own 94, 101, 121, 285, 286, 288–291, 293, 294, 311, 333

Gnosticism 1, 127

Hermeneutics 5, 6, 29–31, 40, 42, 52, 55, 77, 206, 207, 326, 350, 410
Holy Spirit
—advent of 75, 174, 401

—ministry 191, 215, 269, 336, 337, 339, 358, 359
—regeneration and illumination 5, 48, 122, 159, 335, 337, 338, 344, 360, 361, 363–365, 395
—titles 340, 341, 386

Insiders vs. Outsiders 16, 190–192
Intertextuality 91–94
Irony, 7, 9, 75–85, 88, 160, 211, 216, 247, 267

Jamnia 177–179, 185
Jewish Councils
—Sanhedrin 80, 327, 375
—Yavneh Academy 178, 186, 87, 207, 245, 246
Jewish Feasts
—Day of Atonement 270, 272
—Passover 70, 97, 117, 118, 247, 263, 270, 283
—Tabernacles 281, 282, 366
Jewish Groups
—Essenes of Qumran 134, 236, 313, 338, 339
—Pharisees 32, 57, 81, 88, 103, 136 160, 181,202, 241–247, 313, 327, 374–376
—Sadducees 136, 313
—Zealots 136, 248
Jewish Revolt (AD 66–73) 169, 183, 187
Johannine Addresses 27, 157, 158, 160, 164–174
Johannine Apologetic 159, 208, 210, 255
Johannine Asides 84, 85, 97, 282
Johannine Community 157, 171, 172, 175, 176, 179, 181–183, 188, 190, 191, 195–198, 202, 203
Johannine Polemic 54, 83, 159, 167, 208, 210, 214, 249
John the Baptist 48, 49, 69, 91, 108, 174, 203, 212, 237, 245, 276, 278, 326, 333

John and Isaiah 74, 84, 102, 104, 117, 118, 236, 254, 297–306, 308–312, 315, 322
John and Jews 31, 32, 54, 83, 165–168, 173, 210, 211, 232–238, 240–250
John and the Scripture
—direct references 254–257, 278
—echoes and allusions 10, 54, 58, 69, 73, 80, 91, 94, 95, 97–107,110, 111, 115–120, 122, 212, 230, 257, 268, 279, 309, 361, 369
—fulfilment of 58, 69, 91, 101, 115, 119, 231, 251, 252,258, 259, 261, 277, 278, 280, 358, 362, 403, 409
John and the Synoptics 4, 22, 42, 49, 58, 71, 118, 162, 168, 169, 198, 220, 224, 244, 254, 278, 288, 300, 334, 335, 342, 389, 403
John's Language
—alleged sectarianism 16, 175, 177, 180, 190, 337
—ambiguity 7, 8, 33–36, 38, 39, 41–44, 74, 86, 87, 116, 332, 336
—compound fabric 64, 95, 121
—denotation vs. connotation 37, 38, 41, 247
—description of 2–5, 16, 24, 196
—elusive quality 3–5, 7, 11, 329, 405
—figurative vs. plain 50, 51, 67, 85, 86, 88–90, 332, 336, 367
—homonymy 37, 154
—linguistics analysis of 34–38, 40, 42,
—literary analysis of 12–14, 38, 39, 87
—research into 5–12, 14, 16–18
—riddle 190–192, 200
—sense and significance 31, 38, 247
—social function of 15–18, 182, 190, 191, 194–196
Judah 102, 174, 236, 238, 239, 321, 322, 399
Judas 51, 70, 82, 216, 328

Kingdom of God 69, 106, 113, 280 363–365, 387–389

Lazarus 88, 263, 307, 326
Law 99, 111, 260–262, 264–266, 268, 348, 349

Mary (the Mother) 71, 83
Mary (Magdalene) 116, 120, 274, 309
Messiah/Christ 83, 101, 104, 107, 110, 114, 122, 159, 162, 167, 168, 171, 172, 174, 207, 209, 220, 221, 223–228, 231, 249, 251, 252, 256, 257, 284, 292, 309, 326, 341, 353, 360, 372, 385, 404
Messianic Motifs 99, 106, 112, 116, 117, 222, 224, 225, 269, 310
Messianic Secrecy 202, 403
Messianism
—Jewish 115, 169, 178, 179, 221, 222, 225, 291, 403
—Johannine 101, 174, 177, 220, 223, 225, 309, 404
Metaphor 65–69, 72, 74, 75
Method
—form criticism 177, 180, 190, 192, 204, 407
—literary criticism 12–14, 408
—sociology 15–18, 176, 184, 185, 189, 193, 194, 201, 202, 203–205, 408
—source and redaction 25–28, 146–148, 176, 192
—theological 19, 21, 205–207, 332, 408
Mission 49, 172, 199, 210–215, 217, 218, 353, 354, 405
Mount Zion 54, 280

Nathanael 89, 98, 99, 101, 134, 227, 316, 317
New Testament Theology 198, 314, 356, 362
Nicodemus 48, 80, 81, 86, 88, 90, 103, 195, 216, 217, 243, 244, 249, 327, 333, 363, 364, 375–377, 382

Old Testament Imagery
—eschatological harvest 102, 390, 392, 393
—fig tree 69, 99–101
—light 102, 111, 266, 267
—messianic banquet 70, 106
—shekinah 96, 113, 280
—water 58, 73, 98, 111, 112, 266–269, 364
Old Testament Images for Jesus
—Bethel 54, 101, 281, 284, 346
—branch 100, 266
—bread 73, 107, 110, 263, 266–270
—bronze serpent 69, 272, 276, 365
—Lamb of God 49, 59, 70, 74, 220, 270, 273, 310
—manna 110, 267, 270
—Passover 82, 97, 98, 110, 118, 266, 272, 274, 275, 279
—tabernacle 95, 97, 280–282
—Temple 54, 55, 112, 113, 280, 282, 283
Old Testament Offices for Christ
—king 59, 81, 82, 107, 108, 162, 220, 223–225, 240, 309, 390
—priest 107, 108, 225
—prophet 107, 108, 114, 223, 225, 262, 263, 369
Old Testament Personalities in John
—Abraham 80, 98, 99, 102, 231, 249
—Elijah 107, 108
—Isaac 118
—Jacob 80, 98, 168, 346
—Moses 69, 89, 91, 97, 102, 106–112, 134, 162, 231, 240, 262–265, 267, 268, 272, 276, 294, 309, 326, 344, 369, 370, 380
Origen 126, 161

Paul 93, 102, 122, 207, 235, 261, 286, 292, 300, 304, 314, 315, 319, 322, 331, 337, 353, 357, 358, 362, 363, 372

Perception 5, 20, 90, 122, 159, 300, 318, 319, 324, 325, 327, 328, 330, 331, 332, 336, 337, 349, 360, 364–367, 370, 372–374, 377, 381, 383, 384, 395, 404, 405, 409, 410
Persecution (of Christians) 160, 174, 187, 189, 207, 232, 340, 375
Peter 44, 45, 86, 224, 227, 362
Philip 101, 134, 405
Pilate 45, 57, 82, 83, 118, 216, 264, 276, 341, 370
Post–Easter Perspective 54, 78, 84, 101, 155, 285, 334–337
Prophets 91, 153, 162, 212, 222, 223, 231, 236, 254, 262, 322, 325, 339, 343, 344, 347, 360, 392
Purpose of the Gospel 157, 161, 164, 168, 172, 174, 210, 211, 219, 220, 227, 228, 230, 258, 329, 331, 409

Resurrection 54, 78, 81, 84, 90, 163, 281, 291, 311, 322, 333, 334, 336, 337, 362, 390
Revelation
—concealment of 78, 193, 358, 401–404
—content of 351, 352, 354, 356, 357
—Jesus as 61, 83, 96, 97, 101, 111, 168, 213, 214, 221, 252, 267, 268, 281, 292, 332, 344, 345, 349, 359, 379, 396
—language of 20, 21, 72, 73, 82, 84, 103, 115, 344, 346, 350, 351, 355
—of God 105, 281, 282, 319, 324, 347, 348, 351, 389, 392, 402, 405
—rejection of 103–104, 265, 296, 324
—saving nature of 337, 340, 349, 356

Sabbath 58, 261, 264–266, 399
Salvation History 214, 259, 291, 295, 333, 336, 351
Samaritan Woman 58, 102, 103, 168, 216, 217, 227, 268, 326, 392

Satan/Devil 70, 250, 319, 320, 341, 342, 371, 372, 385, 396
Saviour 102, 252, 283, 292, 352–354, 356, 373, 385, 397
Secret Believers 326–328, 399
Seed of Abraham 98, 231, 249, 250
Shepherd 88, 110, 115, 116, 250, 325, 369
Sign(s) 70, 105, 111, 258, 283, 306, 315, 316, 326, 378, 379
Simile 68, 69
Sin 178, 270, 271, 321, 365, 371, 372, 400, 401
Sociology
—application to John 15–17, 177
—criticism of 185, 188, 189, 201–204, 217
—private language 16, 180, 191, 192, 195, 196, 200
—sectarian thesis 175, 177, 179–183, 193–196
Spiritual Gospel 1, 27, 161, 338
Style
—Aramaism 140–142, 150, 224
—chaismus 150, 151
—coherence 22–27, 146–148
—inclusio 151, 256
—parallelism 152
—paronomasia 74
—poetic quality 64, 149, 151, 155
—repetition 152
—semitism 140, 142–144, 149, 156, 305
—study of 145, 146, 148
—style and milieu 144, 148, 156
—synonymy 49, 152, 342
—word–play 102, 153, 280
Symbolism 65, 68, 70, 71, 75, 99, 278
Synagogue
—conflict and separation 166, 171, 177, 181, 185, 186, 188–190, 195–198
—AD 70 (significance of) 160, 166, 240, 244, 246, 247, 284, 399

Theology of Irony 9, 46, 56, 76, 78, 80–85, 248, 284
Theology of John
—atonement 48, 59, 107, 118, 119, 271, 272, 311
—Christology 52, 72, 73, 198, 221, 227, 228, 292, 295, 308, 311, 321, 333, 345, 346, 352, 387
—death of Christ 58, 83, 84, 118, 120, 256, 257, 265, 271–273, 275, 277–279, 284, 352, 365
—eschatology 112, 117, 280, 282, 285, 291, 292, 307, 333, 387, 388, 391, 392
—predestination 83, 312, 315–319, 322,
—salvation 49, 58, 59, 74, 82, 110, 119, 173, 213, 214, 270, 272, 295, 321, 323, 352–354, 391, 397
Theological Themes
—abide/remain 227, 330, 368, 374, 381–383
—above vs. below 321, 330
—cross 84, 120, 291, 352, 360, 402
—darkness 82, 83, 300, 320, 368, 384, 401
—death 365, 371
—death of death 120, 277
—division 384–386, 390, 393, 395
—fellowship 208, 219, 368, 381
—flesh vs. spirit 4, 5, 362, 364, 365
—glory 184, 280, 281, 325, 343, 344, 379, 383, 399
—grace 259, 343
—hear 369, 370, 372
—hour 55, 388, 391, 392
—incarnation 259, 307, 352, 388, 400, 401, 402
—incomprehension 336, 367, 372
—judgement 50, 81, 113, 184, 266, 267, 307, 313, 316, 333, 340, 366, 386, 390, 392, 393–395, 402
—life 61 266, 322, 342, 365, 382, 383, 390, 392

—lifted up 83, 84, 121, 276, 356
—light 44 55, 61, 82, 83, 172, 247, 300, 320, 349, 386
—living water 47, 73, 110–112
—origin of Jesus 58, 81–83, 262
—sending of the Son 111, 199, 212, 214
—sight 111, 305, 306
—spiritual birth 48, 69, 122, 250, 259, 319, 332, 333, 361–366, 404
—spiritual blindness 50, 57, 103, 104, 111, 159, 184, 248, 296–300, 306, 313, 323, 337, 367, 368
—spiritual death 58, 263, 320, 322, 400
—thirst 58, 110, 119, 268, 279
—truth 61–63, 317, 329, 338, 340–344, 356, 359, 370, 382, 383, 394
—unity of Father and Son 72, 106, 221, 313, 353, 354, 379
—wash 111, 112
—work(s) 119, 120, 172, 212, 213, 265, 279, 323, 324, 344, 345, 352, 354, 359, 365, 388, 390, 392, 394, 397, 399, 400
Theological Vocabulary 44, 48–50, 56–62, 84, 212, 213, 215, 310, 342, 344, 345, 349, 354, 386
Thomas 86, 378, 380
Torah 136, 240, 251, 259, 264, 266, 267, 269, 287, 292, 326, 339, 349, 358
Typology 109, 110, 118, 293

Unbelief 248, 296–298, 300, 306, 320, 328, 336, 337, 366, 372, 374, 375, 380, 382, 385, 400–402

Wisdom 267, 348, 349, 358
Witness 138, 174, 215–217, 229, 251, 265, 267, 279, 324, 326, 340, 345, 357, 366
Word 97, 221, 281, 294, 295, 332, 334, 344, 346–350, 355, 356, 358, 383

Word of God 95, 107, 225, 267, 281, 294, 347
World 53, 169, 173, 199, 207, 218, 248, 298, 321, 375, 384, 385, 394–398

Yohanan ben Zakkai 113, 178, 179, 184, 245, 389

Index of Greek Words

αἴρω 48, 59, 270
ἀκολουθέω 56, 59
ἀλήθεια 263, 340, 341, 343, 369, 405
ἀμνός 272, 308
ἀναβαίνω 56, 89
ἄνωθεν 48
ἀποστέλλω 213
βασιλεύς 81, 117
βαστάζω 51, 120
γινώσκω 43, 345
γογγύζω 90, 110
γραφή 254, 260, 261
δόξα 96, 120, 213, 309, 330, 383, 399
διψῶ (διψάω) 58, 119
ἐγώ εἰμι 72, 366
ἐξηγέομαι 115, 344, 345, 354
ἔργον 119, 120, 212, 213, 279, 323, 390, 391, 398, 399
ζητέω 87, 213
ἴδιος/ἴδιοι 53, 85
ἱλάσκομαι 271
ἱλασμός 271
ἱλαστήριον 271
καθαίρω 51, 74
καταλαμβάνω 49, 300
κόσμος 321, 394, 396
κρίνω 49, 50, 386, 394
κρίσις 213, 266, 321, 333, 386, 387, 393–395

λόγος 267, 333, 343, 349, 359, 368
μαρτυρία 215, 345
μαρτυρέω 215, 340, 345, 394
μένω 343, 382, 383
μισθός 49, 391
νόμος 260, 261
ὁράω 367, 368
παράκλητος 340, 341, 394
παρρησία 50, 85, 86, 88, 89, 344, 359, 367
πέμπω 212, 213
περὶ ἁμαρτίας 271
πιστεύω 43, 45, 163, 213, 315, 373, 376
πνεῦμα 51, 340
ποιέω 120, 213, 279, 382
πονηρός 371, 398, 399
σημεῖα 57, 70, 315, 380
σκηνόω 95, 96, 280
σπέρμα 249, 382
σχίσμα 71, 386, 387, 394, 395
τέλος/τελέω 55, 59, 213, 278
τέκνα 249
τετέλεσται 59, 119, 278
τυφλοί/τυφλόω 57, 111, 303, 305, 319
ὑπάγω 86, 87, 191, 300, 402
ὑψωθῆναι 84, 120, 308

Wissenschaftliche Untersuchungen zum Neuen Testament
Alphabetical Index of the First and Second Series

Adna, Jostein: Jesu Stellung zum Tempel. 2000. *Volume II.119.*
Anderson, Paul N.: The Christology of the Fourth Gospel. 1996. *Volume II/78.*
Appold, Mark L.: The Oneness Motif in the Fourth Gospel. 1976. *Volume II/1.*
Arnold, Clinton E.: The Colossian Syncretism. 1995. *Volume II/77.*
Avemarie, Friedrich und *Hermann Lichtenberger* (Ed.): Bund und Tora. 1996. *Volume 92.*
Bachmann, Michael: Sünder oder Übertreter. 1992. *Volume 59.*
Baker, William R.: Personal Speech-Ethics in the Epistle of James. 1995. *Volume II/68.*
Balla, Peter: Challenges to New Testament Theology. 1997. *Volume II/95.*
Bammel, Ernst: Judaica. Volume I 1986. *Volume 37* – Volume II 1997. *Volume 91.*
Bash, Anthony: Ambassadors for Christ. 1997. *Volume II/92.*
Bauernfeind, Otto: Kommentar und Studien zur Apostelgeschichte. 1980. *Volume 22.*
Bayer, Hans Friedrich: Jesus' Predictions of Vindication and Resurrection. 1986. *Volume II/20.*
Bell, Richard H.: Provoked to Jealousy. 1994. *Volume II/63.*
– No One Seeks for God. 1998. *Volume 106.*
Bergman, Jan: see *Kieffer, René*
Bergmeier, Roland: Das Gesetz im Römerbrief und andere Studien zum Neuen Testament. 2000. *Volume 121.*
Betz, Otto: Jesus, der Messias Israels. 1987. *Volume 42.*
– Jesus, der Herr der Kirche. 1990. *Volume 52.*
Beyschlag, Karlmann: Simon Magus und die christliche Gnosis. 1974. *Volume 16.*
Bittner, Wolfgang J.: Jesu Zeichen im Johannesevangelium. 1987. *Volume II/26.*
Bjerkelund, Carl J.: Tauta Egeneto. 1987. *Volume 40.*
Blackburn, Barry Lee: Theios Anēr and the Markan Miracle Traditions. 1991. *Volume II/40.*
Bock, Darrell L.: Blasphemy and Exaltation in Judaism and the Final Examination of Jesus. 1998. *Volume II/106.*
Bockmuehl, Markus N.A.: Revelation and Mystery in Ancient Judaism and Pauline Christianity. 1990. *Volume II/36.*
Böhlig, Alexander: Gnosis und Synkretismus. Teil 1 1989. *Volume 47* –Teil 2 1989. *Volume 48.*

Böhm, Martina: Samarien und die Samaritai bei Lukas. 1999. *Volume II/111.*
Böttrich, Christfried: Weltweisheit – Menschheitsethik – Urkult. 1992. *Volume II/50.*
Bolyki, János: Jesu Tischgemeinschaften. 1997. *Volume II/96.*
Büchli, Jörg: Der Poimandres – ein paganisiertes Evangelium. 1987. *Volume II/27.*
Bühner, Jan A.: Der Gesandte und sein Weg im 4. Evangelium. 1977. *Volume II/2.*
Burchard, Christoph: Untersuchungen zu Joseph und Aseneth. 1965. *Volume 8.*
– Studien zur Theologie, Sprache und Umwelt des Neuen Testaments. Ed. by D. Sänger. 1998. *Volume 107.*
Byrskog, Samuel: Story as History – History as Story. 2000. *Volume 123.*
Cancik, Hubert (Ed.): Markus-Philologie. 1984. *Volume 33.*
Capes, David B.: Old Testament Yaweh Texts in Paul's Christology. 1992. *Volume II/47.*
Caragounis, Chrys C.: The Son of Man. 1986. *Volume 38.*
– see *Fridrichsen, Anton.*
Carleton Paget, James: The Epistle of Barnabas. 1994. *Volume II/64.*
Ciampa, Roy E.: The Presence and Function of Scripture in Galatians 1 and 2. 1998. *Volume II/102.*
Crump, David: Jesus the Intercessor. 1992. *Volume II/49.*
Deines, Roland: Jüdische Steingefäße und pharisäische Frömmigkeit. 1993. *Volume II/52.*
– Die Pharisäer. 1997. *Volume 101.*
Dietzfelbinger, Christian: Der Abschied des Kommenden. 1997. *Volume 95.*
Dobbeler, Axel von: Glaube als Teilhabe. 1987. *Volume II/22.*
Du Toit, David S.: Theios Anthropos. 1997. *Volume II/91.*
Dunn , James D.G. (Ed.): Jews and Christians. 1992. *Volume 66.*
– Paul and the Mosaic Law. 1996. *Volume 89.*
Ebertz, Michael N.: Das Charisma des Gekreuzigten. 1987. *Volume 45.*
Eckstein, Hans-Joachim: Der Begriff Syneidesis bei Paulus. 1983. *Volume II/10.*
– Verheißung und Gesetz. 1996. *Volume 86.*
Ego, Beate: Im Himmel wie auf Erden. 1989. *Volume II/34.*

Ego, Beate und *Lange, Armin* sowie *Pilhofer, Peter(Ed.):* Gemeinde ohne Tempel - Community without Temple. 1999. *Volume 118.*
Eisen, Ute E.: see *Paulsen, Henning.*
Ellis, E. Earle: Prophecy and Hermeneutic in Early Christianity. 1978. *Volume 18.*
- The Old Testament in Early Christianity. 1991. *Volume 54.*
Ennulat, Andreas: Die 'Minor Agreements'. 1994. *Volume II/62.*
Ensor, Peter W.: Jesus and His 'Works'. 1996. *Volume II/85.*
Eskola, Timo: Theodicy and Predestination in Pauline Soteriology. 1998. *Volume II/100.*
Feldmeier, Reinhard: Die Krisis des Gottessohnes. 1987. *Volume II/21.*
- Die Christen als Fremde. 1992. *Volume 64.*
Feldmeier, Reinhard und *Ulrich Heckel* (Ed.): Die Heiden. 1994. *Volume 70.*
Fletcher-Louis, Crispin H.T.: Luke-Acts: Angels, Christology and Soteriology. 1997. *Volume II/94.*
Förster, Niclas: Marcus Magus. 1999. *Volume 114.*
Forbes, Christopher Brian: Prophecy and Inspired Speech in Early Christianity and its Hellenistic Environment. 1995. *Volume II/75.*
Fornberg, Tord: see *Fridrichsen, Anton.*
Fossum, Jarl E.: The Name of God and the Angel of the Lord. 1985. *Volume 36.*
Frenschkowski, Marco: Offenbarung und Epiphanie. Volume 1 1995. *Volume II/79* - Volume 2 1997. *Volume II/80.*
Frey, Jörg: Eugen Drewermann und die biblische Exegese. 1995. *Volume II/71.*
- Die johanneische Eschatologie. Band I. 1997. *Volume 96.* - Band II. 1998. *Volume 110.* - Band III. 2000. *Volume 117.*
Freyne, Sean: Galilee and Gospel. 2000. *Volume 125.*
Fridrichsen, Anton: Exegetical Writings. Ed. von C.C. Caragounis und T. Fornberg. 1994. *Volume 76.*
Garlington, Don B.: 'The Obedience of Faith'. 1991. *Volume II/38.*
- Faith, Obedience, and Perseverance. 1994. *Volume 79.*
Garnet, Paul: Salvation and Atonement in the Qumran Scrolls. 1977. *Volume II/3.*
Gese, Michael: Das Vermächtnis des Apostels. 1997. *Volume II/99.*
Gräßer, Erich: Der Alte Bund im Neuen. 1985. *Volume 35.*
Green, Joel B.: The Death of Jesus. 1988. *Volume II/33.*

Gundry Volf, Judith M.: Paul and Perseverance. 1990. *Volume II/37.*
Hafemann, Scott J.: Suffering and the Spirit. 1986. *Volume II/19.*
- Paul, Moses, and the History of Israel. 1995. *Volume 81.*
Hamid-Khani, Saeed: Revelation and Concealment of Christ. 2000. *Volume II/120.*
Hannah, Darrel D.: Michael and Christ. 1999. *Volume II/109.*
Hartman, Lars: Text-Centered New Testament Studies. Ed. by D. Hellholm. 1997. *Volume 102.*
Heckel, Theo K.: Der Innere Mensch. 1993. *Volume II/53.*
- Vom Evangelium des Markus zum viergestaltigen Evangelium. 1999. *Volume 120.*
Heckel, Ulrich: Kraft in Schwachheit. 1993. *Volume II/56.*
- see *Feldmeier, Reinhard.*
- see *Hengel, Martin.*
Heiligenthal, Roman: Werke als Zeichen. 1983. *Volume II/9.*
Hellholm, D.: see *Hartman, Lars.*
Hemer, Colin J.: The Book of Acts in the Setting of Hellenistic History. 1989. *Volume 49.*
Hengel, Martin: Judentum und Hellenismus. 1969, ³1988. *Volume 10.*
- Die johanneische Frage. 1993. *Volume 67.*
- Judaica et Hellenistica. Band 1. 1996. *Volume 90.* - Band 2. 1999. *Volume 109.*
Hengel, Martin and *Ulrich Heckel* (Ed.): Paulus und das antike Judentum. 1991. *Volume 58.*
Hengel, Martin und *Hermut Löhr* (Ed.): Schriftauslegung im antiken Judentum und im Urchristentum. 1994. *Volume 73.*
Hengel, Martin and *Anna Maria Schwemer:* Paulus zwischen Damaskus und Antiochien. 1998. *Volume 108.*
Hengel, Martin and *Anna Maria Schwemer* (Ed.): Königsherrschaft Gottes und himmlischer Kult. 1991. *Volume 55.*
- Die Septuaginta. 1994. *Volume 72.*
Herrenbrück, Fritz: Jesus und die Zöllner. 1990. *Volume II/41.*
Herzer, Jens: Paulus oder Petrus? 1998. *Volume 103.*
Hoegen-Rohls, Christina: Der nachösterliche Johannes. 1996. *Volume II/84.*
Hofius, Otfried: Katapausis. 1970. *Volume 11.*
- Der Vorhang vor dem Thron Gottes. 1972. *Volume 14.*
- Der Christushymnus Philipper 2,6-11. 1976, ²1991. *Volume 17.*
- Paulusstudien. 1989, ²1994. *Volume 51.*

Hofius, Otfried und *Hans-Christian Kammler:* Johannesstudien. 1996. *Volume 88.*
Holtz, Traugott: Geschichte und Theologie des Urchristentums. 1991. *Volume 57.*
Hommel, Hildebrecht: Sebasmata. Band 1 1983. *Volume 31* - Band 2 1984. *Volume 32.*
Hvalvik, Reidar: The Struggle for Scripture and Covenant. 1996. *Volume II/82.*
Kähler, Christoph: Jesu Gleichnisse als Poesie und Therapie. 1995. *Volume 78.*
Kammler, Hans-Christian: Christologie und Eschatologie. 2000. *Volume 126.*
- see *Hofius, Otfried.*
Kamlah, Ehrhard: Die Form der katalogischen Paränese im Neuen Testament. 1964. *Volume 7.*
Kelhoffer, James A.: Miracle and Mission. 1999. *Volume II/112.*
Kieffer, René and *Jan Bergman (Ed.)*: La Main de Dieu / Die Hand Gottes. 1997. *Volume 94.*
Kim, Seyoon: The Origin of Paul's Gospel. 1981, ²1984. *Volume II/4.*
- „The 'Son of Man'" as the Son of God. 1983. *Volume 30.*
Kleinknecht, Karl Th.: Der leidende Gerechtfertigte. 1984, ²1988. *Volume II/13.*
Klinghardt, Matthias: Gesetz und Volk Gottes. 1988. *Volume II/32.*
Köhler, Wolf-Dietrich: Rezeption des Matthäusevangeliums in der Zeit vor Irenäus. 1987. *Volume II/24.*
Korn, Manfred: Die Geschichte Jesu in veränderter Zeit. 1993. *Volume II/51.*
Koskenniemi, Erkki: Apollonios von Tyana in der neutestamentlichen Exegese. 1994. *Volume II/61.*
Kraus, Wolfgang: Das Volk Gottes. 1996. *Volume 85.*
- see *Walter, Nikolaus.*
Kuhn, Karl G.: Achtzehngebet und Vaterunser und der Reim. 1950. *Volume 1.*
Laansma, Jon: I Will Give You Rest. 1997. *Volume II/98.*
Labahn, Michael: Offenbarung in Zeichen und Wort. 2000. *Volume II/117.*
Lange, Armin: see *Ego, Beate.*
Lampe, Peter: Die stadtrömischen Christen in den ersten beiden Jahrhunderten. 1987, ²1989. *Volume II/18.*
Landmesser, Christof: Wahrheit als Grundbegriff neutestamentlicher Wissenschaft. 1999. *Volume 113.*
Lau, Andrew: Manifest in Flesh. 1996. *Volume II/86.*
Lichtenberger, Hermann: see *Avemarie, Friedrich.*
Lieu, Samuel N.C.: Manichaeism in the Later Roman Empire and Medieval China. ²1992. *Volume 63.*

Loader, William R.G.: Jesus' Attitude Towards the Law. 1997. *Volume II/97.*
Löhr, Gebhard: Verherrlichung Gottes durch Philosophie. 1997. *Volume 97.*
Löhr, Hermut: see *Hengel, Martin.*
Löhr, Winrich Alfried: Basilides und seine Schule. 1995. *Volume 83.*
Luomanen, Petri: Entering the Kingdom of Heaven. 1998. *Volume II/101.*
Maier, Gerhard: Mensch und freier Wille. 1971. *Volume 12.*
- Die Johannesoffenbarung und die Kirche. 1981. *Volume 25.*
Markschies, Christoph: Valentinus Gnosticus? 1992. *Volume 65.*
Marshall, Peter: Enmity in Corinth: Social Conventions in Paul's Relations with the Corinthians. 1987. *Volume II/23.*
McDonough, Sean M.: YHWH at Patmos: Rev. 1:4 in its Hellenistic and Early Jewish Setting. 1999. *Volume II/107.*
Meade, David G.: Pseudonymity and Canon. 1986. *Volume 39.*
Meadors, Edward P.: Jesus the Messianic Herald of Salvation. 1995. *Volume II/72.*
Meißner, Stefan: Die Heimholung des Ketzers. 1996. *Volume II/87.*
Mell, Ulrich: Die „anderen" Winzer. 1994. *Volume 77.*
Mengel, Berthold: Studien zum Philipperbrief. 1982. *Volume II/8.*
Merkel, Helmut: Die Widersprüche zwischen den Evangelien. 1971. *Volume 13.*
Merklein, Helmut: Studien zu Jesus und Paulus. Volume 1 1987. *Volume 43.* – Volume 2 1998. *Volume 105.*
Metzler, Karin: Der griechische Begriff des Verzeihens. 1991. *Volume II/44.*
Metzner, Rainer: Die Rezeption des Matthäusevangeliums im 1. Petrusbrief. 1995. *Volume II/74.*
- Das Verständnis der Sünde im Johannesevangelium. 2000. *Volume 122.*
Mittmann-Richert, Ulrike: Magnifikat und Benediktus. 1996. *Volume II/90.*
Mußner, Franz: Jesus von Nazareth im Umfeld Israels und der Urkirche. Ed. by M. Theobald. 1998. *Volume 111.*
Niebuhr, Karl-Wilhelm: Gesetz und Paränese. 1987. *Volume II/28.*
- Heidenapostel aus Israel. 1992. *Volume 62.*
Nissen, Andreas: Gott und der Nächste im antiken Judentum. 1974. *Volume 15.*
Noack, Christian: Gottesbewußtsein. 2000. *Volume II/116.*
Noormann, Rolf: Irenäus als Paulusinterpret. 1994. *Volume II/66.*
Obermann, Andreas: Die christologische Erfüllung der Schrift im Johannesevangelium. 1996. *Volume II/83.*

Okure, Teresa: The Johannine Approach to Mission. 1988. *Volume II/31.*
Oropeza, Bristo J.: Paul and Apostasy. 2000. *Volume II/115.*
Ostmeyer, Karl-Heinrich: Taufe und Typos. 2000. *Volume II/118.*
Paulsen, Henning: Studien zur Literatur und Geschichte des frühen Christentums. Ed. von Ute E. Eisen. 1997. *Volume 99.*
Park, Eung Chun: The Mission Discourse in Matthew's Interpretation. 1995. *Volume II/81.*
Philonenko, Marc (Ed.): Le Trône de Dieu. 1993. *Volume 69.*
Pilhofer, Peter: Presbyteron Kreitton. 1990. *Volume II/39.*
– Philippi. Volume 1 1995. *Volume 87.*
– see Ego, Beate.
Pöhlmann, Wolfgang: Der Verlorene Sohn und das Haus. 1993. *Volume 68.*
Pokorný, Petr und Josef B. Souček: Bibelauslegung als Theologie. 1997. *Volume 100.*
Porter, Stanley E.: The Paul of Acts. 1999. *Volume 115.*
Prieur, Alexander: Die Verkündigung der Gottesherrschaft. 1996. *Volume II/89.*
Probst, Hermann: Paulus und der Brief. 1991. *Volume II/45.*
Räisänen, Heikki: Paul and the Law. 1983, ²1987. *Volume 29.*
Rehkopf, Friedrich: Die lukanische Sonderquelle. 1959. *Volume 5.*
Rein, Matthias: Die Heilung des Blindgeborenen (Joh 9). 1995. *Volume II/73.*
Reinmuth, Eckart: Pseudo-Philo und Lukas. 1994. *Volume 74.*
Reiser, Marius: Syntax und Stil des Markusevangeliums. 1984. *Volume II/11.*
Richards, E. Randolph: The Secretary in the Letters of Paul. 1991. *Volume II/42.*
Riesner, Rainer: Jesus als Lehrer. 1981, ³1988. *Volume II/7.*
– Die Frühzeit des Apostels Paulus. 1994. *Volume 71.*
Rissi, Mathias: Die Theologie des Hebräerbriefs. 1987. *Volume 41.*
Röhser, Günter: Metaphorik und Personifikation der Sünde. 1987. *Volume II/25.*
Rose, Christian: Die Wolke der Zeugen. 1994. *Volume II/60.*
Rüger, Hans Peter: Die Weisheitsschrift aus der Kairoer Geniza. 1991. *Volume 53.*
Sänger, Dieter: Antikes Judentum und die Mysterien. 1980. *Volume II/5.*
– Die Verkündigung des Gekreuzigten und Israel. 1994. *Volume 75.*
– see Burchard, Chr.
Salzmann, Jorg Christian: Lehren und Ermahnen. 1994. *Volume II/59.*

Sandnes, Karl Olav: Paul – One of the Prophets? 1991. *Volume II/43.*
Sato, Migaku: Q und Prophetie. 1988. *Volume II/29.*
Schaper, Joachim: Eschatology in the Greek Psalter. 1995. *Volume II/76.*
Schimanowski, Gottfried: Weisheit und Messias. 1985. *Volume II/17.*
Schlichting, Günter: Ein jüdisches Leben Jesu. 1982. *Volume 24.*
Schnabel, Eckhard J.: Law and Wisdom from Ben Sira to Paul. 1985. *Volume II/16.*
Schutter, William L.: Hermeneutic and Composition in I Peter. 1989. *Volume II/30.*
Schwartz, Daniel R.: Studies in the Jewish Background of Christianity. 1992. *Volume 60.*
Schwemer, Anna Maria: see Hengel, Martin
Scott, James M.: Adoption as Sons of God. 1992. *Volume II/48.*
– Paul and the Nations. 1995. *Volume 84.*
Siegert, Folker: Drei hellenistisch-jüdische Predigten. Teil I 1980. *Volume 20 –* Teil II 1992. *Volume 61.*
– Nag-Hammadi-Register. 1982. *Volume 26.*
– Argumentation bei Paulus. 1985. *Volume 34.*
– Philon von Alexandrien. 1988. *Volume 46.*
Simon, Marcel: Le christianisme antique et son contexte religieux I/II. 1981. *Volume 23.*
Snodgrass, Klyne: The Parable of the Wicked Tenants. 1983. *Volume 27.*
Söding, Thomas: Das Wort vom Kreuz. 1997. *Volume 93.*
– see Thüsing, Wilhelm.
Sommer, Urs: Die Passionsgeschichte des Markusevangeliums. 1993. *Volume II/58.*
Souček, Josef B.: see Pokorný, Petr.
Spangenberg, Volker: Herrlichkeit des Neuen Bundes. 1993. *Volume II/55.*
Spanje, T.E. van: Inconsistency in Paul?. 1999. *Volume II/110.*
Speyer, Wolfgang: Frühes Christentum im antiken Strahlungsfeld. Band I: 1989. *Volume 50. –* Band II: 1999. *Volume 116.*
Stadelmann, Helge: Ben Sira als Schriftgelehrter. 1980. *Volume II/6.*
Stenschke, Christoph W.: Luke's Portrait of Gentiles Prior to Their Coming to Faith. *Volume II/108.*
Stettler, Hanna: Die Christologie der Pastoralbriefe. 1998. *Volume II/105.*
Strobel, August: Die Stunde der Wahrheit. 1980. *Volume 21.*
Stroumsa, Guy G.: Barbarian Philosophy. 1999. *Volume 112.*

Stuckenbruck, Loren T.: Angel Veneration and Christology. 1995. *Volume II/70.*
Stuhlmacher, Peter (Ed.): Das Evangelium und die Evangelien. 1983. *Volume 28.*
Sung, Chong-Hyon: Vergebung der Sünden. 1993. *Volume II/57.*
Tajra, Harry W.: The Trial of St. Paul. 1989. *Volume II/35.*
– The Martyrdom of St. Paul. 1994. *Volume II/67.*
Theißen, Gerd: Studien zur Soziologie des Urchristentums. 1979, ³1989. *Volume 19.*
Theobald, Michael: see *Mußner, Franz.*
Thornton, Claus-Jürgen: Der Zeuge des Zeugen. 1991. *Volume 56.*
Thüsing, Wilhelm: Studien zur neutestamentlichen Theologie. Ed. von Thomas Söding. 1995. *Volume 82.*
Thurén, Lauri: Derhetorizing Paul. 2000. *Volume 124.*
Treloar, Geoffrey R.: Lightfoot the Historian. 1998. *Volume II/103.*
Tsuji, Manabu: Glaube zwischen Vollkommenheit und Verweltlichung. 1997. *Volume II/93.*
Twelftree, Graham H.: Jesus the Exorcist. 1993. *Volume II/54.*

Visotzky, Burton L.: Fathers of the World. 1995. *Volume 80.*
Wagener, Ulrike: Die Ordnung des „Hauses Gottes". 1994. *Volume II/65.*
Walter, Nikolaus: Praeparatio Evangelica. Ed. by Wolfgang Kraus und Florian Wilk. 1997. *Volume 98.*
Wander, Bernd: Gottesfürchtige und Sympathisanten. 1998. *Volume 104.*
Watts, Rikki: Isaiah's New Exodus and Mark. 1997. *Volume II/88.*
Wedderburn, A.J.M.: Baptism and Resurrection. 1987. *Volume 44.*
Wegner, Uwe: Der Hauptmann von Kafarnaum. 1985. *Volume II/14.*
Welck, Christian: Erzählte 'Zeichen'. 1994. *Volume II/69.*
Wilk, Florian: see *Walter, Nikolaus.*
Williams, Catrin H.: I am He. 2000. *Volume II/113.*
Wilson, Walter T.: Love without Pretense. 1991. *Volume II/46.*
Zimmermann, Alfred E.: Die urchristlichen Lehrer. 1984, ²1988. *Volume II/12.*
Zimmermann, Johannes: Messianische Texte aus Qumran. 1998. *Volume II/104.*

www.ingramcontent.com/pod-product-compliance
Lightning Source LLC
Chambersburg PA
CBHW052042290426
44111CB00011B/1590